THE
COLUMBIA
HISTORY
OF THE
BRITISH
NOVEL

THE COLUMBIA HISTORY OF THE BRITISH NOVEL

JOHN RICHETTI
EDITOR

JOHN BENDER, DEIRDRE DAVID, MICHAEL SEIDEL
ASSOCIATE EDITORS

Columbia University Press
New York

Columbiµa University Press
New York   Chichester, West Sussex
Copyright © 1994 Columbia University Press
All rights reserved

Library of Congress Cataloging-in-Publication Data

The Columbia history of the British novel / John J. Richetti,
    general editor : associate editors, John Bender, Deirdre David, Michael Seidel.
    p. cm
Includes index.
ISBN 0–231–07858–7
1. English fiction—History and criticism.   I. Richetti, John J.
PR821.C65   1994
823.009—dc20   92–35749
                                                                              CIP

Casebound editions of Columbia University Press Books are Smyth-sewn and printed on
permanent and durable acid-free paper.

Printed in the United States of America

c 10 9 8 7 6 5 4 3 2 1

Contents

Introduction
    John Richetti   *ix*

Licensing Pleasure: Literary History and the Novel in Early
Modern Britain
    William Warner   *1*

Defoe and Early Narrative
    Richard Kroll   *23*

Sex, Lies, and Invisibility: Amatory Fiction from the
Restoration to Mid-Century
    Toni O'Shaughnessy Bowers   *50*

Richardson and His Circle
    James Grantham Turner   *73*

Fielding and the Novel at Mid-Century
    Jill Campbell   *102*

From Swift to Smollett: The Satirical Tradition in Prose Narrative
    G. S. Rousseau   *127*

Sterne: Comedian and Experimental Novelist
    John Allen Stevenson   *154*

Sentimental Novels of the Later Eighteenth Century
    G. A. Starr   *181*

Frances Burney and the Rise of the Woman Novelist
    Kristina Straub   *199*

The Gothic Novel, 1764–1824
    George E. Haggerty   *220*

Novels of the 1790s: Action and Impasse
    Patricia Meyer Spacks   *247*

Jane Austen
    James Thompson   *275*

Walter Scott: Narrative, History, Synthesis
    Judith Wilt   *300*

A Novel of Their Own: Romantic Women's Fiction,
1790–1830
    Anne K. Mellor   *327*

"Speak what we think": The Brontës and
Women Writers
    Barry V. Qualls   *352*

Dickens
    John Kucich   *381*

Thackeray and the Ideology of the Gentleman
    Ina Ferris   *407*

George Eliot and the Novel of Ideas
    Gillian Beer   *429*

Trollope
    N. John Hall   *456*

Wilkie Collins and the Sensation Novel
    Ronald R. Thomas   *479*

Disraeli, Gaskell, and the Condition of England
Mary Poovey   508

Shaping Hardy's Art: Vision, Class, and Sex
George Levine   533

The Nineteenth-Century Novel and Empire
Patrick Brantlinger   560

Lewis Carroll and the Child in Victorian Fiction
Robert M. Polhemus   579

The Avoidance of Naturalism: Gissing, Moore, Grand,
Bennett, and Others
David Trotter   608

Rudyard Kipling to Salman Rushdie: Imperialism
to Postcolonialism
Michael Gorra   631

Bennett, Wells, and the Persistence of Realism
Robert Squillace   658

Joseph Conrad
Daniel R. Schwarz   685

D. H. Lawrence
Vincent P. Pecora   715

Isherwood, Huxley, and the Thirties
Michael Rosenthal   740

James Joyce
Michael Seidel   765

Virginia Woolf
Vicki Mahaffey   789

Forster, Ford, and the New Novel of Manners
David Galef   819

Samuel Beckett's Postmodern Fictions
    Brian Finney   842

Satire between the Wars: Evelyn Waugh and Others
    George McCartney   867

The Reaction against Modernism: Amis, Snow, Wilson
    Rubin Rabinovitz   895

Sleeping with the Enemy: Doris Lessing in the Century
of Destruction
    Lynne Hanley   918

Drabble to Carter: Fiction by Women, 1962–1992
    Carol McGuirk   939

The Contemporary Novel
    Michael Wood   961

Biographies of British Novelists   989

Notes on Contributors   1019

Index   1023

Introduction

IN a memorable and ringing affirmation, D. H. Lawrence called the novel "the one bright book of life." For Lawrence the novel was much more than a literary genre; it was a means to intensely vital knowledge, far superior to science or philosophy or religion. In place of their abstract and partial views of life, the novel offered the "changing rainbow of our living relationships." But at about the same time that Lawrence was celebrating the power of the novel to give its readers the full and authentic feel of human experience, the Hungarian literary critic Georg Lukács more somberly traced its degenerative descent from classical epic. Describing the novel in gloomy and decidedly melodramatic terms as the epic of a world "abandoned by God" and as a record of modern humanity's homelessness in *The Theory of the Novel: A Historico-Philosophical Essay on the Forms of Great Epic Literature* (1920), Lukács looked back to the immediacy and communal integrity of ancient epic and saw the novel as the expression of what he called a dissonance in modern life whereby individuals are estranged from the external world. The novel records, he said, a profound irony at the heart of modern experience "within which things appear as isolated and yet connected, as full of value and yet totally devoid of it, as abstract fragments and as concrete autonomous life, as flowering and as decaying, as the infliction of suffering and as suffering itself." During the 1920s Lawrence saw the novel as the unique record of concrete and living experience, whereas for Lukács, writing in Central Europe during the bitter aftermath of World War

I, it was symptomatic of the ironic and contradictory confusion peculiar to modern life in the West.

Whether taken as a rapturous affirmation of the possibility of individual fulfillment or as a depressing rendition of modern emptiness and alienation, the novel has invariably been understood by critics and novelists alike as the distinctively modern literary form, a response to uniquely modern conditions. Lawrence and Lukács agreed that modern life was deeply unsatisfactory, but they had opposite notions of what the novel could do to ameliorate it. For Lawrence the novel could transfigure and vivify life; for Lukács the novel eloquently but helplessly recorded its despair and emptiness. A third and to my mind more relevant attitude regarding the purpose of the novel, and one that takes a broader historical and literary perspective, has since emerged for modern criticism. For M. M. Bakhtin, a Russian critic whose neglected writings from the Stalinist period were rediscovered by Western readers in the 1970s, the novel was not only the unique marker of European modernity but a literary mode that expressed, in its essential and defining formal qualities, revolutionary and, potentially, utterly liberating linguistic energies.

According to Bakhtin, the novel represented an absolute and thus exhilarating breakthrough from older literary forms and from the hierarchical and repressive view of life he felt they embodied. In one of his essays Bakhtin distinguished the novel as being radically distinct from other literary genres in its rendering of a new "multi-languaged consciousness," which made contact as literature never had before with "the present (with contemporary reality) in all its openendedness." The epic offers the world as a finished and frozen entity, an event from the distant past evoked in a special, specifically literary language appropriate to its inspiring grandeur and remoteness. But the novel, in Bakhtin's most influential formulation of his thesis, is defined by its rendering of the dynamic present, not in a separate and unitary literary language, but in the competing and often comic discord of actual and multiple voices—what he termed polyglossia or heteroglossia—whereby language is used in ways that communicate a "relativizing of linguistic consciousness." Speech in the novel, whether that of characters or narrators or authors, is thus always for Bakhtin "dialogical," representing the process of shifting and contested signification peculiar to language itself, or at least to modern notions of the way language works. The novel is dialogical in Bakhtin's special sense because it renders the incessant shaping of reality as perceived by human beings through rival forms of language, which itself is not a static or ahistorical entity but rather finds dynamic and diverse embodiment in the competing dialects of particular social groups that struggle for dominance. In its evocation of the novel's subversion of static and hierarchical notions of language and reality, Bakhtin's version of the novel's positive and liberating function in the modern world seems to me more convincing, or at least more useful, than Lawrence's utopian intensity or Lukács's post–Great War gloom. Bakhtin's theory shifts the critical emphasis from the novel's subject matter, the nature of modern life and consciousness, to its form, the expressive relativizing of language. For readers of *The Columbia History of the British Novel*, it is interesting that Bakhtin singles out the British comic novelists, notably Fielding, Smollett, Sterne, and Dickens, for their instinctive grasp of the dialogical principle. When they described the purpose of the novel, Lukács and Lawrence were thinking primarily of the late nineteenth- and early twentieth-century novel of personal development, the bildungsroman, but Bakhtin took an inclusive historical view that looked back as far as François Rabelais's *Gargantua and Pantagruel* (1532–1552) and traced the novel's evolution through the late seventeenth and eighteenth centuries and into the modern period. In thus broadening the novel's scope and historical reference in order to explain its peculiar power, Bakhtin saved readers from modern self-pity and enabled critics and literary historians to look beyond the modern predicament as the novel's only subject.

Nonetheless, the issue of the value and meaning of the novel from our present situation remains unresolved for many readers and critics. Clearly, the novel has become in the last three hundred years many different things for many readers as well as for novelists themselves. But for all that, the term itself remains both simple and elusive. So various and so multiple, the novel can be described but never, it seems, adequately defined. A minimalist description of the novel might say that it is an extended (too long to read at one sitting) narrative in prose about imaginary but vividly particularized or historically specific individuals. But however one describes it, the novel has been from its beginnings (themselves a subject of much dispute) for its writers and readers an aggressively and self-consciously new literary category. For many twentieth-century critics and historians of the novel, it is the narrative form that uniquely expresses the condition of Western culture and consciousness since the emergence of what everyone recognizes as the modern age—an age in which we still live and that lacks clear definition or any sense of single or simple self-consciousness but that nonetheless situates itself, like the novel, as somehow separate and distinct from all that has preceded it.

Crucial to the culture of the modern age is individualism, an understanding of the world that the Western European tradition takes for granted as part of the natural order of things but that in fact represents the fairly recent historical development of a consciousness or sense of self that remains strange and even incomprehensible to people outside that tradition. Novels both promote and mimic the values intrinsic to this individualism. In most novels that come to mind, particular persons in their individualized immediacy are presented as being more important or more immediate than communities or cultures with their long traditions and accumulated ways, and the novel is most often about the clash between such individuals and the larger social units that necessarily produce them. The novel presupposes that clash, even if it often records an eventual reconciliation or reintegration of the individual with the surrounding society. The novel thus implies, as the literary and cultural critic Edward Said has remarked, a universe that is necessarily unresolved or incomplete, a universe in a process of development, evolving or progressing toward a more nearly complete or more complex form of consciousness as it records the multiplicity and infinite diversity of individuals. Such a view is distinctively Western or Judeo-Christian, since, as Said points out, there are no novels in Islamic culture until it comes into contact with the literary culture of the modern West. For Islam, the world is complete, created by God as a plenum, full of every conceivable entity such a world could have. But for the Judeo-Christian tradition, the fallen and sinful world (along with the individuals who compose it) is radically incomplete and yearning, in a religious sense, for individual salvation and for the transfiguring judgment day when human history shall end. In the thoroughly secular and psychologized context of the novel, this world is viewed rather more optimistically and is conceived as a process of progressive human development, reaching for higher or more complex forms of development for individuals and for their communities, for personal fulfillment and social utopia. In other words, the novel articulates the central, self-defining characteristics of Western religious and secular culture. If approached analytically and critically, say its defenders, it provides an unparalleled opportunity for self-knowledge for those within that tradition. For those outside that tradition or on the margins of Western culture and its privileged classes, members of colonized non-Western societies or members of minority groups or culturally deprived social classes within them, the novel in its three-hundred-year sweep just might provide access to a liberating understanding of the cultural forms that oppress them. Whatever else it may be, the novel is a vividly informative record of Western consciousness during the last three hundred years.

That Western individualism is the recurring subject matter of the novel is not in dispute, but just about everything else about the novel is. Where did it come from? How and why did it take form? How does the novel differ from the long prose fictions that preceded it from classical antiquity onward? How exactly is it distinct from long narratives in verse, from classical epic and medieval romance? At its best in the works of acknowledged masters like the great nineteenth-century realists such as Austen, Balzac, Dickens, Flaubert, Tolstoy, Stendhal, George Eliot, James, Manzoni, Galdós, and Dostoevsky, does the novel communicate a truth about modern European humanity that is otherwise unavailable? Is the novel, in the hands of such masters of the form, an unsurpassed instrument of moral and historical knowledge? Or is it, as some academic critics have increasingly come to claim, actually a subtle means for the repression and regulation of individuals that only masquerades as an impartial rendering of the way things are? Is the novel really, as much modern criticism would have it, the imposition of an ideological view of the world, forcing upon its readers notions of linear development and of a stable external reality that are at best fairly recent cultural constructions? Does novelistic realism represent the naturalizing of a view of the world and of personal identity peculiar to post-Enlightenment European thought and especially to white males with cultural power and economic privilege?

These are cogent and disturbing accusations that many of the chapters in this volume will present and even endorse in one way or another. But a traditional and alternative "humanist" view at least in part survives, even among the most politically sensitive critics. Should we hold fast, many wonder, to an older and much more hopeful view that the novel somehow records a struggle against imposed ideological and cultural limitations and points the way to personal liberation and self-fulfillment? Is the novel both a record of authentic individual consciousness separating itself from history and communal ideologies (insofar as that is possible) and an impetus for its readers to achieve a similar liberation? Is the novelist an artistic visionary whose imagination, intelligence, and craft can render social and historical relations with a fullness that allows readers to understand the world they live in?

For a history of the British novel, this last is the most important critical question these days, especially since the emergence of feminist criticism during the past quarter-century. A number of the chapters in this volume will argue that the British novel begins as a profoundly female form in several senses of the term. Even though the most familiar examples (the "canonical" works, as critics say nowadays) of British eighteenth-century fiction were written by men, the bulk of fiction produced throughout the eighteenth century was written by women. Although we cannot be certain that the audience for this fiction was predominantly female, women seem to have been perceived as the core audience for much British fiction. Moreover, the early British novel, whether written by a man or by a woman, presents domestic life as its recurring central subject and, with its focus on the interior and private lives of characters, moves dramatically away from the traditional concerns of literature with public life and masculine heroism in love, war, and politics. Indeed, some feminist critics have extended this argument, finding in the emerging British novel the establishment of a new modern self that is, they argue, gendered female. For such critics, the novel articulates a consciousness whose sensitivity and interior self-awareness were, and to some extent still are, recognized as feminine rather than masculine personality traits. The individual that the eighteenth- century novel imagines and bequeaths to subsequent British fiction as the ideal moral and social personality is characteristically feminized, since (so goes the argument) its male heroes define themselves as such by acquiring certain feminine qualities that include a self-effacing sensitivity and an empathic understanding of others in place of the dominance, self-possession, and control that typify conventional masculine heroism.

Certainly, the British novel in its eighteenth-century phase tends to deal mostly with domestic and private experience rather than public or political life, and marriage and courtship provide its crucial focus. Another strain of fiction, however, initiated in 1719 by Defoe's *Robinson Crusoe*, offers masculine adventure in exotic places; its subject is the exploration and conquest of the non-European world by male European adventurers. Although it is sometimes the vehicle for serious and complex imagining, such adventure fiction has tended, since Defoe's novel appeared, to be restricted to children's stories. As some critics have suggested, this relegation to the nursery of life in the external world of action and military conquest may point to European culture's deep uneasiness with its own recent history. By these lights, the novel's emphasis on domestic intensities and private or personal quests may be the culture's instinctive masking of the patriarchal domination of women's lives and of the economic domination and even imperialistic exploitation of the rest of the world—forces that lie at the heart of the modern Western history in which we still live.

The early British novel is not only for the most part domestic in its settings; it is also intensely parochial, attentive to the complex local networks of social and linguistic stratifications that to this day characterize British life. In trying to do justice to the diversity of local manners and dialects among the people of their island nation, British novelists, it can be argued, have helped to create something like a national personality by promoting an image of eccentric distinctiveness as the peculiar sign of the inhabitants of Great Britain. From Defoe's vividly individual rogues and whores to Fielding's and Smollett's portrait galleries of memorable country squires, innkeepers, servants, aristocrats, and petty criminals to Sterne's zany and self-obsessed narrators, there is a clear progression to the memorable quirkiness of many of the inhabitants of the British nineteenth-century novel—to Dickens's and Trollope's characters, for example, many of whom have come to represent for the rest of the world (for better or worse) the essence of Britishness in their comically mannered self-enclosure. But there is a more significant aspect to the eighteenth-century British novel's focus on quirky individuality. Perhaps more so than its French and German and Spanish counterparts, British fiction is in this representation of eccentricity notably alert to a modernity of personal expressiveness that emerges within new and more efficient systems of social organization.

That is to say, in its attention to radical particularity the early British novel records the characteristic stresses and strains of the momentous transition from traditional hierarchical modes of life to those rationalized and regularized forms of social organization that characterize the modern nation-state. As it develops in the early eighteenth century in Britain, realistic narrative comes to involve the ventriloquizing of particular individuals who by definition do not fit neatly into didactic or general categories. The difference between John Bunyan's *Pilgrim's*

Progress (1678) and Defoe's *Robinson Crusoe* (1719) lies precisely in Crusoe's historically and psychologically particularized identity that is never wholly contained by moral allegory as that of Bunyan's hero is. Committed, usually, to didactic intentions for their fictions, novelists like Defoe, Richardson, and Fielding modify or even subvert those intentions by imagining characters who, as their stories progress, tend to move beyond the general and the typical into identities quite their own. Such eccentric individuality is obviously a kind of resistance to old moral and psychological categories, but it also entails precisely the isolation of identity into discrete units that allows for a new, more abstract and efficient ordering of individuals apart from their complex positioning in communal history and moral tradition.

As the most advanced country in eighteenth-century Europe, Great Britain was widely admired at the time as the nation with the most flexible and stable political and economic institutions (for example, the most efficient tax-gathering apparatus of any European state) and the largest, most prosperous middle class. From its beginnings in the work of Defoe and Richardson, as many of the chapters that follow will show, the British novel focuses intensely upon the blurring of lines between those traditional status divisions whereby society had been organized for centuries. More than other European fiction, eighteenth-century British novels depict and dramatize the emergence of recognizably modern kinds of individuality wherein persons acquire worth, status, or power either by luck, by redefined and expanded economic opportunity, or by the exercise of extraordinary moral virtue. To some extent, the nineteenth-century British novel retains this singular, perhaps insular, focus on particularized characters, with their local surroundings and peculiar institutional circumstances, but it also acquires a more complex sense of history and society. After Sir Walter Scott more or less invented the historical novel at the beginning of the nineteenth century, novelists were necessarily more acutely aware of a broader, encompassing world of time and space. In the novels of George Eliot or Dickens or Thackeray, for example, individual destiny plays itself out in provincial British places that are thrown into relief against the backdrop of the larger world. More and more, the Victorian novelist embodies an overseeing or supervising intelligence that places individuals within those immense, controlling forces that we attempt to understand by labeling them history and society. The British novel opens up to include more of the historically changing and expanding world and is itself subject to foreign influences, becoming part of a world literature written in English in America and other new English-speaking countries as well as in Great Britain. And the influence also works in the other direction. With the exercise of cultural and political hegemony first by the British Empire in the nineteenth century and then by the United States in the mid-twentieth century, English has become a world language whose literature occupies a dominant position in an emerging global culture that parallels the global economy we hear so much of these days.

But whatever the British novel's origins or its ideological role since the eighteenth century in forming or reflecting an important corner of Western consciousness, the pivotal place of the novel in modern contemporary literary culture in Great Britain and in America is indisputable. Since the early twentieth century, the novel along with other literary kinds has tended to split more dramatically than ever into self-consciously artistic and popular forms, as mass commercial culture has become a vast industry and as literary modernism and so-called postmodernism have fostered a separate realm of writing read by a tiny minority and kept alive by academic attention. But in spite of the gulf between the tradition established by writers like James Joyce and Virginia Woolf and the books that make up the vigorous trade in popular best-sellers, the novel in numerous guises continues to flourish. Librarians and best-seller lists testify to the novel's centrality by dividing the world of writing into fiction and nonfiction. With glossy and colorful covers, in categories ranging from reprints of the classics to lurid best-sellers and sensational thrillers, from science fiction to romances, westerns, and gothics, novels in the broad sense of the word crowd the bookshelves of supermarkets, drugstores, airport souvenir shops, chain bookstores in shopping malls, and gas stations and truck stops on interstate highways. And yet for all its popular vigor, the novel still carries a stigma of frivolity and artistic inferiority, partly because it is, after all, merely a false story, a set of imaginary happenings that is by its very nature inferior in the eyes of many readers to, say, history or biography.

Perhaps the British novel has always been sustained by its perennial battle with its detractors, who have tended to view it with suspicion as a popular form and as something of a waste of time for readers who could be more profitably employed with true and useful things. In *Northanger Abbey* (1818), Jane Austen imagines a young lady apologizing for her reading by saying it is "only a novel," and then Austen herself supplies a defense of fiction quite as impassioned as Lawrence's, calling it "only some work in which the greatest powers of the mind are displayed, in which the most thorough knowledge of human nature, the happiest delineation of its varieties, the liveliest effusions of wit and humour are conveyed to the world in the best chosen language." For the coyly ironic Austen, this is an extraordinary statement, one that the English critic Frank Kermode recently quoted as he reviewed some contemporary novels in the *London Review of Books*. Kermode is moved in his review to defend what he sees as an embattled literary institution: "And yet it can be argued that even in the present state of things the novel may be the best available instrument of ethical inquiry; that its own extraordinary variety of means equips it as our best recorder of human variety, even at a time when biography is challenging that position; and that its capacity for wit and humour and poetry continues to exist and even to expand."

Kermode's eloquent defense of the novel seems to be a perennial necessity, and "Is the novel dead?" is a predictable theme when panels of novelists are convened to discuss the state of modern culture. Always in crisis and seemingly aware of its own fragility and moral and cultural ambiguity, the novel has been since its beginnings more of an occasion for modern narration to question its own purposes than a stable narrative institution. Paradoxically, that instability seems to be the essence of the novel's strength and endurance, and the collaborative history of the British novel that this volume attempts to provide will highlight for readers just that fruitful instability. Modern literary history is a stern and unforgiving taskmaster, in many cases nowadays interrogating the past (as critics like to say) to reveal its hidden complicity with power and privilege. Some of the chapters in this history of the British novel, collectively written by many contributors, will trace the roots of the novel's insecurity by pointing to the hidden—or at least obscured—cultural or ideological agendas of novels and novelists; other chapters will seek to contextualize novelistic production as inseparable from the demands of the literary marketplace or in some cases from the psychosexual pathologies of particular authors. But whatever the scandalous charge, ideological or personal, most novels can take it, since at their best they themselves are about their own shortcomings. The novel dramatizes the very failures critics attribute to it. Novelists deliver deep meditations on human complicity in social injustice; they point by their own lack of final answers and their tendency toward multifarious explorations of the moral world around us, to the biggest social and moral questions. By shaping imaginary lives, the novel may thus illuminate what a culture most desires or fears. In reading a novel we can hear, as Bakhtin would say, the dialogue among competing versions of truth that is the novel's uniquely dynamic version of the truth itself.

John Richetti

THE
COLUMBIA
HISTORY
OF THE
BRITISH
NOVEL

Licensing Pleasure: Literary History and the Novel in Early Modern Britain

The Scandal of Novel Reading

NOVELS have been a respectable component of culture for so long that it is difficult for twentieth-century observers to grasp the unease produced by novel reading in the eighteenth century. Long before it became an issue for debate in literary studies, a quantum leap in the number, variety, and popularity of novels provoked cultural alarm in England during the decades following 1700. The flood of novels on the market, and the pleasures they incited, led many to see novels as a catastrophe for book-centered culture. While the novel was not clearly defined or conceptualized, the targets of the anti-novel campaign were quite precise: seventeenth-century romances, novellas of Continental origin, and those "novels" and "secret histories" written by Behn, Manley, and Haywood in the decades following 1680. The central themes of this debate may be culled from several texts: Samuel Johnson's 1750 *Rambler No. 4* essay on the new fiction of Richardson, Fielding, and Smollett; Francis Coventry's enthusiastic pamphlet in support of Fielding, "An Essay on the New Species of Writing Founded by Mr. Fielding: With a Word or Two upon the Modern State of Criticism" (1751); and in *The Progress of Romance*, a literary history in dialogue form by Clara Reeve published in 1785.

These texts mobilize criticism and alarm, praise and prescription in an attempt to modulate the comparatively new vogue for novel reading. Francis Coventry mocks the unreflected "emulation" produced in readers by the French romances of an earlier day: "This [vogue] obtain'd a long Time. Every Beau was an *Orondates*, and all the Belles were *Stari-ras*." Though Samuel Johnson could not account for the fashion for romance, his *Rambler No. 4* essay describes the more powerful identification that recent "familiar histories" like *Clarissa* and *Tom Jones* induce in their readers: "If the power of example is so great, as to take possession of the memory by a kind of violence, and produce effects almost without the intervention of the will, care ought to be taken that . . . the best examples only should be exhibited." If novels produce effects "almost without the intervention of the [reader's] will," then readers are at risk of becoming automatons, and the author must assume responsibility for the novel's moral effects.

The power and danger of novels, especially to young women not exposed to classical education, arose from the pleasures they induced. In *The Progress of Romance*, Clara Reeve's leading character, Euphrasia, remembers "my mother and aunts being shut up in the parlour reading *Pamela*, and I took it very hard that I was excluded." Closeted with a novel, some are included, and others excluded, from the circle of pleasure. Coventry remarks upon the tenacity with which readers clung to their pleasures: "For tho' it was a folly, it was a pleasing one: and if sense could not yield the pretty creatures greater pleasure, dear nonsense must be ador'd." Opposing this pleasure "lecture would lose it's force; and ridicule would strive in vain to remove it."

But what is so pernicious about reading novels? *The Progress of Romance* ends with a staged debate between the woman scholar Euphrasia and a high-culture snob named Hortensius. Hortensius develops a wide-ranging indictment of novel reading. First, novels turn the reader's taste against serious reading: "A person used to this kind of reading will be disgusted with every thing serious or solid, as a weakened and depraved stomach rejects plain and wholesome food." Second, novels incite the heart with false emotions: "The seeds of vice and folly are sown in the heart,—the passions are awakened,—false expectations are raised.—A young woman is taught to expect adventures and intrigues. . . . If a plain man addresses her in rational terms and pays her the greatest of compliments,—that of desiring to spend his life with her,—that is not sufficient, her vanity is disappointed, she expects to meet a Hero in Romance." Finally, novels induce a dangerous autonomy from parents and guardians: "From this kind of reading, young people fancy themselves capable of judging of men and manners, and . . . believe themselves wiser than their parents and guardians, whom they

treat with contempt and ridicule." Hortensius indicts novels for transforming the cultural function of reading from providing solid moral
nourishment to catering to exotic tastes; from preparing a woman for
the ordinary rational address of a plain good man to leading her to
expect a proposal from a hero out of romance; and from reinforcing
reliance upon parents and guardians to promoting a belief in the subject's autonomy. Taken together, novels have disfigured the reader's
body: the taste, passions, and judgment of stomach, heart, and mind.
Here, as so often in the polemics that surround novels, the reader is
characterized as a susceptible female whose moral life is at risk. By
strong implication, she is most responsible for transmitting the virus of
novel reading.

From the vantage point of the late twentieth century, and after nearly nine decades of film and five of television, the alarm provoked by
novel reading may seem hyperbolic or even quaint. But a condescendingly modernist "pro-pleasure" position renders the alarm with novel
reading, and its effects on early modern culture, unintelligible. Though
it is difficult to credit the specific object of the alarm of the eighteenth-
century critics of novels—after all, we recommend to students some of
the very novels these early modern critics inveighed against—given our
current anxieties about the cultural effects of slasher films, rap music,
MTV, and soap operas, it seems contradictory to dismiss those who
worried about the effects of novels when they were new. But there are
fundamental obstacles to deciphering the eighteenth century's anxious
discourse on the pleasures of novels. After psychoanalysis, most concede the difficulty of knowing why one experiences pleasure; it is even
more difficult to define the content or cause of the pleasure of eighteenth-century novel readers. However, we can trace certain clear
effects of the campaign against these unlicensed pleasures. First, cultural critics sketched the profile of the culture-destroying pleasure seeker who haunts the modern era: the obsessive, unrestrained, closeted
consumer of fantasy. Then, novelists like Richardson and Fielding,
accepting the cogency of this critique, developed replacement fictions
as a cure for the novel-addicted reader. In doing so, they aimed to
deflect and reform, improve and justify the pleasures of a new species of
elevated novel.

Since Plato's attack on the poets, philosophers and cultural critics had
worried the effects of an audience's absorption in fictional entertainment. During the early eighteenth century the market gave this old cul-

tural issue new urgency. Although there had been a trade in books for centuries, several developments gave the circulation of novels unprecedented cultural force. At a time when state censorship in England was subsiding and technological advances were making all printed matter more affordable, the market in printed books offered a site for the production and consumption of a very broad spectrum of entertainment. Published anonymously, or by parvenu authors supported by no patron of rank, novels appeared as anonymous and irresponsible creations, conceived with only one guiding intention: to pander to any desire that would produce a sale. Novels not only violated the spirit of seriousness expected of readers of books like *The Pilgrim's Progress* or *Paradise Lost*, they made no pretense to making any lasting contribution to culture. Novels were the first "disposable" books, written in anticipation of their own obsolescence and in acceptance of their own transient function as part of a culture of serial entertainments. Although only a small part of print culture in the early decades of the eighteenth century, novels appear to have been the most high-profile, fashionable, and fast-moving segment of the market. The vogue for novels helped to constitute a market culture—in the modern sense of commodities for purchase by the individual. In short, novels desanctified the book. Little wonder that novels were figured as an uncontrollable menace to culture.

Many of the vices attributed to the novel are also characteristics of the market: both breed imitation, gratify desire, and are oblivious to their moral effects. The market appears as a machine evidencing an uncanny automatism. Once they had become "the thing," nothing could stop novels on the market. In critiquing novels, cultural critics deplored the market's powerful, autonomous effect upon culture. Coventry's description of the imitations provoked by the success of Fielding's novels develops a general rule about success and emulation in a market-driven culture: "It is very certain, that whenever any thing new, of what kind soever, is started by one man, and appears with great success in the world, it quickly produces several in the same taste." Producers for the market have become mere factors of the market. Using the by now clichéd terms for describing the Grub Street hacks, Clara Reeve emphasizes how the accelerating multiplicity of novels complicates her own efforts at the classification and criticism of romances and novels. Rampant production also allows bad imitations to proliferate and engenders new institutions to deliver novels indiscriminately into the hands of every reader: "The press groaned under the weight of Novels, which sprung up like mushrooms every year. . . . [Novels] did but now begin to increase upon us, but ten years more multiplied them tenfold. Every work of merit produced a swarm of imitators, till they became a public evil, and the institution of Circulating libraries, conveyed them in the cheapest manner to every bodies hand." An uncontrolled multiplicity threatens to metastasize culture. For the scholar surveying the production of many ages, the market has the effect of blurring the distinctness and expressive readability of culture. Thus in his *History of Fiction* (1814) John Dunlop complains that while earlier epochs developed "only one species of fiction," which could then be read as "characteristic" of the age, more recently "different kinds have sprung up at once; and thus they were no longer expressive of the taste and feelings of the period of their composition." The critical histories of the novel by Reeve and Dunlop aim to restore the character to culture.

If, according to a formula developed in the writings of the French cultural critic Michel Foucault, power operates less by repressing or censoring than by producing new "reality," new "domains of objects and rituals of truth," then the success of novels on the market changed culture by producing a need to read. Clara Reeve describes this newly incited desire: "People must read something, they cannot always be engaged by dry disquisitions, the mind requires some amusement." Between uncritical surrender to novel reading and a wholesale rejection of novels in favor of "serious" reading, Richardson and Fielding traced a third pathway for the novel. In Reeve's words, the strategy was to "write an antidote to the bad effects" of novels "under the disguise" of being novels. This requires a cunning pharmacology. When Lady Echlin, Richardson's most morally exacting correspondent, warns that "the best instruction you can give, blended with love intrigue, will never answer your good intention," Richardson replies with a celebrated reformulation of the old demand that art should both amuse and instruct: "Instruction, Madam, is the Pill; Amusement is the Gilding. Writings that do not touch the Passions of the Light and Airy, will hardly ever reach the heart." Coventry describes the manner in which Fielding, "who sees all the little movements by which human nature is actuated," intervenes in the market for novels. "The disease became epidemical, but there were no hopes of a cure, 'till Mr. Fielding endeavour'd to show the World, that pure Nature could furnish out as agreeable entertainment, as those airy non-entical forms they had long ador'd, and persuaded the ladies to leave this extravagance to their Abigails with their cast cloaths." Thus the "disease" of romance, associated with the craze for new fashions, can be "cured" only by cutting new paths toward pleasure. Then the old novels, with their corrupting pleasures, can be passed on, along with old dresses, to the lady's servant.

It is beyond the scope of this chapter to give a detailed account of how the popularity of the "histories" published by Richardson and Fielding in the 1740s effected an upward revaluation of the novel in Britain. However, the key elements of their successful strategy are implicit in the metaphors of the antidote, the vaccine, and the gilded pill. First, a broad spectrum of earlier writings—romances, novellas, and secret histories written on the Continent and in Britain—are characterized as essentially equivalent. Deemed licentious, fantasy-ridden, and debased, they are decried as a cultural disease. Next, Richardson and Fielding produce substitute fictions to absorb the reader. Although Richardson and Fielding wrote antinovels, they didn't write nonnovels. Just as a vaccine can achieve its antidotal function only by introducing a mild form of a disease into the body of the patient, their novels incorporated many elements of the dangerous old novels of Behn, Manley, and Haywood into this "new species" of fiction. By including improving discourse familiar from conduct books, spiritual autobiography, and the periodical essay, the "histories" of Richardson and Fielding could appear radically "new."

Cervantes' *Don Quixote* (1605/1615) and Lafayette's *Princess de Cleves* (1678) had demonstrated the power of a modern fiction composed on the textual "grounds" of the earlier romance. Those who elevated the novel in England pursued a similar strategy by appropriating elements from the earlier novel—such as the female libertine, or the intricate seduction scheme—and articulating (by connecting together, and thus "speaking") them in a new way, with a new meaning, as part of a new form of novel. Thus, within Richardson's *Clarissa*, the rake Lovelace, by using disguise and manipulation to pursue seduction, upholds the old novel's ethos of amorous intrigue within the plot lines of the new. The bad old obsession with sex and passion is still there, but through Clarissa's resistance and its attendant critical discourse, sex is sublimated to the virtuous sentiments of the new and improving novel. Incorporated into a new species of novel, the old novel gilds the pill from within, helping to insure the popularity of the new novel. To secure the enlightening cultural address of their novels, Richardson and Fielding disavowed rather than assumed their debt to those popular novels whose narrative resources they incorporated and whose cultural space they sought to occupy. They simultaneously absorbed and erased the novels they would supplant.

The new novel reorients rather than banishes spontaneous reader identification; now a morally improving emulation is promoted. When, in *The Progress of Romance*, Hortensius complains that Richardson's epistolary novels "have taught many young girls to wiredraw their language, and to spin always long letters out of nothing," Euphrasia defends the cultural value of studying and imitating Richardson over the "studies" of an earlier generation: "Let the young girls . . . copy Richardson, as often as they please, and it will be owing to the defects of their understandings, or judgments, if they do not improve by him. We could not say as much of the reading Ladies of the last age. . . . No truly, for their studies were the French and Spanish Romances, and the writings of Mrs. Behn, Mrs. Manly, and Mrs. Heywood [*sic*]." In order to serve as an antidotal substitute for the poison of novels, the elevated novels of Richardson and Fielding had to be founded in an antagonistic critique and overwriting of the earlier novels of Behn, Manley, and Haywood. This elevating novel brought a new disposition of pleasure and value to its readers. But the novel's rise is not a spontaneous or organic development. On the contested cultural site of novel reading at mid-century, it is, as the Marxist critic John Frow suggests in a different context, not so much the old that has died, but the new that has killed.

Sublimating the Novel by Telling Its History

The successes of *Pamela* (1740), *Joseph Andrews* (1742), *Clarissa* (1747–1748), and *Tom Jones* (1749), as well as the many imitations they provoked on the market, helped to countersign the elevated novel as a significant new cultural formation. But such validation also depended upon those critics who grasped the possibilities of this new kind of fiction and sought to describe its signal features, cultural virtues, and history. This project often required inventive critical strategies. By rescuing the elevated novel from the general cultural indictment of novels, the early literary critics and historians I have cited—Samuel Johnson, Francis Coventry, Clara Reeve, and John Dunlop—made their texts supplements to the project of elevating the novel.

For Johnson, a critical intervention on behalf of the new novel meant arguing, by way of response to the recent popularity of *Tom Jones* and *Roderick Random*, in favor of the "exemplary" characters of Richardson over the more true-to-life "mixed" characters of Fielding and Smollett. In a pamphlet published anonymously, "An Essay on the New Species of Writing Founded by Mr. Fielding" (1751), Coventry follows the basic procedure Fielding had devised in the many interpolated prefaces to *Joseph Andrews* and *Tom Jones*: he transports critical terms and ideas developed earlier for poetry, epic, and drama to the novel. But Coventry goes farther. Just as Aristotle modeled the "rules" of tragedy upon Sophocles, and early modern French and English critics defined the rules for epic through criticism of Homer, Coventry made Fielding's work the template for the "species" of writing he had "founded." As the "great Example" and "great original" for "future historians of this kind," Fielding's work provides the terms for a new inventory of neoclassical "laws": "As Mr. Fielding first introduc'd this new kind of Biography, he restrain'd it with Laws which should ever after be deem'd sacred by all that attempted his Manner; which I here propose to give a brief account of." In his "word or two on the modern state of criticism," Coventry bewails the decline of criticism from earlier epochs (from Horace to Pope), quotes and corrects the modern scorn for critics, and inveighs against the partisanship discernible in the reception of new plays. Coventry's way of posturing as a critic—he is unctuous, defensive, and yet arrogant—is the very antithesis of the imperious law-givings and definitive pronouncements characteristic of Fielding's narrators. But both styles of address suggest there is as yet no preestablished cultural vantage point or institutionalized discourse for the criticism of novels.

But such an anchor for the articulation of the novel was developing. Written thirty-five years later than Johnson's or Coventry's criticism, Reeve's *Progress of Romance* (1785) composes what seems to be the first scholarly literary history of novels in English. Within the term *romance* Reeve comprehends not only the Greek romance, the medieval romances (in both verse and prose), and the seventeenth-century heroic romance; she also goes backward to the epics of Homer and forward to the "modern novels" of France and England. The inclusion of Homeric epic in the category of romance is a classification dubious enough to have been rejected by virtually every subsequent literary historian of the novel; but it gives Reeve's protagonist, Euphrasia, a way to refute the high-culture bias of her polemical antagonist, Hortensius. In addition, by developing the term *romance* into a global category inclusive of fictional entertainments produced over a vast expanse of "times, countries, and manners," she uses the historicist horizon of her study to develop an indulgence that protects the now unfashionable romances as well as the modern novels under contemporary attack. The literary history and criticism of the English novel that has developed over the two hundred years since Reeve's text—from John Dunlop and Hippolyte Taine to Ian Watt and Michael McKeon—inevitably comes to be implicated in the task Richardson and Fielding seemed to set going in England: that of securing an elevated cultural address for the novel.

We can begin to grasp the broader cultural uses of literary history by attending to the way John Dunlop introduces his ambitious three-volume *History of Fiction: Being a Critical Account of the Most Celebrated Prose Works of Fiction, from the Earliest Greek Romances to the Novels of the Present Age* (1815). In order to articulate the general cultural value of fiction over history Dunlop quotes Lord Bacon:

Fiction gives to mankind what history denies, and, in some measure, satisfies the mind with shadows when it cannot enjoy the substance: . . . Fiction strongly shows that a greater variety of things, a more perfect order, a more beautiful variety, than can any where be found in nature, is pleasing to the mind. And as real history gives us not the success of things according to the deserts of vice and virtue, Fiction corrects it, and presents us with the fates and fortunes of persons rewarded or punished according to merit. And as real history disgusts us with a familiar and constant similitude of things, Fiction relieves us by unexpected turns and changes, and thus not only delights, but inculcates morality and nobleness of soul. It raises the mind by accommodating the images of things to our desires, and not like history and reason, subjecting the mind to things."

By appealing to Bacon on the value of fiction, Dunlop not only invokes the authority of a major British thinker but also neatly hurdles almost two hundred years of wrangling over the morally dubious effects of taking pleasure from fiction. By using the general term *fiction* for his history of romances and novels, Dunlop encompasses the polemical terms of the debate he would nonetheless inflect and recast. Eighteenth-century defenses of the novel (from Congreve and Richardson to Fielding and Reeve) usually engage a set of polar oppositions still familiar to us: the novel is to the romance as the "real" is to the "ideal," as fact is to fantasy, as the probable is to the amazing, as the commonplace is to the exotic, and so on. Fiction is developed by Dunlop as a third term that can at once finesse and reconcile these polar oppositions. Fiction does this by becoming art, delivering "a more perfect order, a more beautiful variety" than "nature."

Through Dunlop's use of Bacon, Renaissance and Romantic aesthetics meet in a justification of fiction that is, finally, psychological. Through fiction, the reader is no longer "subject" to things, nor disgusted with "a familiar and constant similitude of things." Instead, fiction "relieves" and "delights," and "raises the mind by accommodating the images of things to our desires." The cultural efficacy of fiction comes from its successful gratification of the reader's pleasure. Dunlop's translation of Bacon assumes yet reverses the anxiety about the reader's pleasure that had motivated earlier condemnations of the novel. When Dunlop glosses Bacon's emphasis upon "delight," it becomes apparent that the pleasure Dunlop promotes is quite different from the pleasure that novel readers had been accused of indulging. Instead of obsessive, personal, deluded, erotic pleasures, we are called to soft and social ones: "How much are we indebted to [fiction] for pleasure and enjoyment! it sweetens solitude and charms sorrow. . . ." These pleasures improve and uplift the reader, by taking him or her into an elevated social and emotive space: "The rude are refined by an introduction, as it were, to the higher orders of mankind, and even the dissipated and selfish are, in some degree, corrected by those paintings of virtue and simple nature, which must ever be employed by the novelist if he wish to awaken emotion or delight." Having confirmed its beneficial effect, Dunlop can confirm the novel's rise from its earlier disreputable cultural position:

This powerful instrument of virtue and happiness, after having been long despised, on account of the purposes to which it had been made subservient, has gradually become more justly appreciated, and more highly valued. Works of Fiction have been produced, abounding at once with the most interesting details, and the most sagacious reflections, and which differ from treatises of abstract philosophy only by the greater justness of their views, and the higher interest which they excite.

Dunlop's description of his project helps us to apprehend the broader purpose of his literary history: to sublimate the novel so as to produce a new disposition, or arrangement, of the pleasure of novel reading. With his title, which neither exiles all novels from culture in favor of drama, epic, sermons, or conduct books, nor favors the simple, uncritical acceptance of all novels into his narrative of the history of fiction,

Dunlop announces that his history is to be "critical"—that is, it will judge works according to their quality so as to focus upon only "the most celebrated" prose fiction. What results, in both Reeve and Dunlop as well as in every subsequent literary history, is a chronological panorama, a certain spectacular sequential cinematography of culture in which selected cultural practices and productions are narrated as significant and valuable. By this means literary history (selectively) licenses (sublimated) pleasures. Through this literary history, novels produced in the market can be inserted into a (more or less) continuous narrative and turned toward higher cultural purposes: for example, serving as an expression of "the voice of the people" (Taine) or being part of "the Great Tradition" (Leavis).

Dunlop writes as though the culturally elevating role for fiction were already achieved. In fact, his own literary history is designed to promote that end. To argue the centrality of fiction to culture, Dunlop begins his introduction with an elaborate analogy between gardening and fiction making, which quickly implicates his own literary history. The analogy also indexes what we might call the necessary violence of literary history. Just as the "savage" has gathered, and placed around his dwelling, plants that please him, so too have men lived events "which are peculiarly grateful, and of which the narrative at once pleases himself, and excites in the minds of his hearers a kindred emotion." What are gathered are "unlooked-for occurrences, successful enterprise, or great and unexpected deliverance from signal danger and distress." A gardener learns that one must not just collect but also weed out the

useless or noxious, and [those] which weaken or impair the pure delight which he derives from others . . . the rose should no longer be placed beside the thistle, as in the wild, but that it should flourish in a clear, and sheltered, and romantic situation, where its sweets may be undiminished, and where its form can be contemplated without any attending circumstances of uneasiness or disgust. The collector of agreeable facts finds, in like manner, that the sympathy which they excite can be heightened by removing from their detail every thing that is not interesting, or which tends to weaken the principal emotion, which it is his intention to raise. He renders, in this way, the occurrences more unexpected, the enterprises more successful, the deliverance from danger and distress more wonderful.

The same process that describes the "fine arts" of gardening and fiction making—selecting, weeding, and intensifying with an eye toward pleasure—applies also to the literary history Dunlop composes. Dunlop's "critical" history of fiction becomes an improving and enlightening cultivation of fiction for culture. By using the fiction of widely different epochs to survey the variety of cultural achievements, literary history makes novels more than instruments of private (kinky, obsessive) gratification. They are drawn into the larger tableau of cultural accomplishment—which Dunlop calls "the advance of the human mind"—until a certain disinterested moral and aesthetic pleasure appears to be the telos of all fiction making.

But the gardening metaphor insinuates certain assumptions into the project of this literary history. Literary history as cultivation spatializes time, so that the successive conflicts between the often antagonistic types of fiction written in England over the course of a century by, for example, Behn, Richardson, Fielding, and Radcliffe, are arranged to appear as one harmoniously balanced array of species that can be surveyed in one leisurely stroll, as one wanders through a garden. However, it proves as implausible to have a literary history without a literary historian as it is to have a garden without a gardener. It is the valuative role of the literary historian—the critic holding the scales over each text read—that produces the synchronic moment of judgment through which a narrative of the progress or history of romance, novel, and fiction can be grasped and told. Then, the way in which that story is told has a feedback effect: which writers are included and excluded, which are brought into the foreground, cast into the shade, or weeded away, determines what kinds of writing and authorship will come to count as "tradition" that grounds subsequent value judgments. This is the ironic terminus of a hegemonic literary history. Literary history can easily become tautological and self-confirming, a garden wall to protect specimens collected against the very factors it might have interpreted: history, change, difference.

A Vortex Mis-seen as an Origin

Once Dunlop's literary history gets under way, it becomes apparent that civilizing the novel requires a certain calculated violence. In a chapter entitled "Sketch of the Origin and Progress of the English Novel," Dunlop offers a typology of the elevated novel: novels are divided into the "serious" (Richardson, Sheridan, Godwin), the "comic" (Fielding, Smollett), and the "romantic" (Walpole, Reeve, Radcliffe). But before offering this schematic overview of what we would now call the eighteenth-century novel, Dunlop does some weeding by giving cursory negative treatment to the novels of Behn, Manley, and the early Haywood. Behn's novels, we are informed, "have not escaped the moral contagion which infected the literature of that age." Though Dunlop merely alludes to "the objections which may be charged against many" of Behn's novels, he ends the passage describing the "faults in points of morals" of Behn's "imitator," Eliza Haywood, in this fashion: "Her male characters are in the highest degree licentious, and her females are as impassioned as the Saracen princesses in the Spanish romances of chivalry."

By orientalizing these early novels and by characterizing them as inappropriately erotic—too feminine, too European, and too immoral—Dunlop relegates to the margins of *The History of Fiction* some of the most popular novels published in England between 1683 and 1730. How is the eclipse of an influential strain of popular fiction to be understood? Dunlop's dismissal of Behn, Manley, and Haywood from his history confirms a judgment that critics of the early amorous novel had been making since the 1730s. This negative judgment might be attributed to changes in sensibility, taste, or style, or to the idea that a certain formula has exhausted its appeal. But these words merely relabel rather than explain the cultural change we are trying to interpret. It is, no doubt, correct to argue that the novels of amorous intrigue are an integral expression of the culture of the Restoration, with the zeal of Charles II's court for sexual license, its eschewal of the dour asceticism of the Commonwealth, and its enthusiastic translation of French cultural forms. Such a historical placement of the early novel allows one to align its passing with the reaction, after 1688, against the excesses of the Restoration. Pleasures disowned become discomforting, and through embarrassment, a kind of unpleasure.

Some feminist literary historians have attributed the devaluation of Behn, Manley, and Haywood to their gender. However, even before Richardson and Fielding won ascent from the market for their novels of the 1740s, the moral improvement of the novel of amorous intrigue was undertaken by Elizabeth Rowe, Jane Barker, and Penelope Aubin. Explanations based upon taste, political history, and gender fail to come to terms with the particular way in which the novels of Behn, Manley, and Haywood were devalued and overwritten in the 1740s.

The erasure or forgetting of earlier cultural formations is an obscure process. Unlike material objects, cultural ideas and forms do not become used up or out of date. Cultural forms—from letters and love stories to national constitutions—can be rejuvenated by new technology, foreign transplants, and political strife. In other words, recycling seems to be the rule rather than the exception in culture. Thus, for example, the novel of amorous intrigue, developed in the late Restoration by Behn under strong influence from the Continental novella and the aristocratic literature of love, was exploited for politically motivated scandal and satire by Delariviere Manley in the *New Atalantis* (1709). Then, following the spectacular success of *Love in Excess* (1719–1720), this species of novel was turned into repeatable "formula fiction" on the market by Eliza Haywood in the 1720s. To remove elements from culture one must understand "forgetting" as, in Nietzsche's words, "an active and in the strictest sense positive faculty of repression." The incorporation of the novel of amorous intrigue within the elevated novel of the 1740s is one of the means by which old pleasures are disowned and effaced. As I have noted above, novelists like Richardson and Fielding promote this forgetting, first by defacing the novel of amorous intrigue and then by providing their own novels as replacements for the novels they characterize as degraded and immoral. These new novels overwrite—disavow but appropriate, waste but recycle—the novels they spurn.

Reeve and Dunlop do not commit their literary histories to exercising a "good memory." Unlike certain late-twentieth-century counter-hegemonic literary histories—whether feminist, African-American, or gay and lesbian—the works of Reeve and Dunlop do not set out to counteract a biased cultural memory. Instead they are constrained by the protocols of a culturally elevating literary history to be critical and selective, and thus forgetful. In the introduction to *The Progress of Romance*, Reeve tells her readers that she seeks "to assist according to my best judgment, the reader's choice, amidst the almost infinite variety it affords, in a selection of such as are most worthy of a place in the libraries of readers of every class, who seek either for information or entertainment." The effacement of Behn's novels from those literary histories written in the wake of the novel's elevation does not depend upon the good will of the literary historian. Thus, while Reeve is generous with Behn—"let us cast a veil of compassion over her faults"—and Dunlop is severe, both ignore all her novels except *Oroonoko*. By contrast, the novels of Richardson and Fielding are given positions of special priority in both accounts of the novel's rise. The success of the elevated novel in the 1740s—its appearance in culture as the only novel worthy of reading, cultural attention, and detailed literary history— means the early novels of Behn, Manley, and Haywood will be pushed into the margins of literary histories, where they nonetheless never quite disappear but serve—as they do in Richardson and Fielding's texts—as an abject trace or degraded "other" needed to secure the identity of the "real" (i.e., legitimate) novel.

From Reeve forward, scholarly literary history develops a paradoxical relationship to the forgotten texts of the past. It retrieves from the archival memory of culture and reads again what its contemporary culture has almost completely forgotten. This activity pushes Reeve toward a certain regret about the shifts in cultural value that can look quite arbitrary to one who has looked long enough down the "stream of time."

Romances have for many ages past been read and admired, lately it has been the fashion to decry and ridicule them; but to an unprejudiced person, this will prove nothing but the variations of times, manners, and opinions.—Writers of all denominations,—Princes and Priests,—Bishops and Heroes,—have their day, and then are out of date.—Sometimes indeed a work of intrinsic merit will revive, and renew its claim to immortality: but this happiness falls to the lot of few, in comparison of those who roll down the stream of time, and fall into the gulph of oblivion.

This passage naturalizes the process of disappearance and forgetting— by its reference to the wheel of fortune that gives "princes and priests, bishops and heroes . . . their day" and then takes it away, as well as by its metaphorical characterization of the movement of a "work of . . . merit" down "the stream of time" into "the gulph of oblivion." These analogies obscure the particular cultural strife at work within shifts in cultural memory. Thus the differences of gender, politics, and class that separate Behn and Richardson, casting the first down into "oblivion" while the second is raised up into prominence, are conducted through the literary histories that translate them for a later age. Though literary historians attempt to be "unprejudiced" (Reeve) and embrace an ethos of "judgment, candour, and impartiality" (Coventry), and though their histories aspire to secure general moral or universal aesthetic grounds for critical judgment, the actual practice of literary history does not occlude but instead reflects cultural division.

Since one of the meanings of *gulf* is a "whirlpool, or absorbing eddy," I can accommodate my thesis about the novel's rise to Reeve's metaphor. The elevation of the new novel over the old novel of amorous intrigue produces a vortex or whirlpool within the land/seascape of eighteenth-century British culture. Where one kind of reading is thrown up, another is thrown down; where one kind of pleasure is licensed, another is discredited. This turbulent vortex of reciprocal appearance and disappearance is mis-seen as the origin of the novel. But in order for the elevated novel to appear, the novel of amorous intrigue must be made to disappear into a gulf of oblivion. Thus birth requires a burial, but only after the murder of the other novel. While this vortex first appears in the cultural strife of the 1740s, it is also readable in every subsequent literary history devised to tell of the novel's rise.

To apprehend "the rise of the novel" as a vortex of cultural conflict helps to refocus the way gender difference and strife crosscut the expansion of novel reading in early modern culture. In aligning romances with French fashions and insisting that both are distinctly female addictions, Coventry was repeating one of the clichés of his age. The romance was associated with women because of its popularity with women readers. Reeve, by casting *The Progress of Romance* in the form of a series of salon-like lectures and debates between Hortensius and Euphrasia (with Sophronia acting the role of a nonpartisan judge), inscribes the debate about romance and its value within a battle of the sexes. Euphrasia rejects Hortensius's sweeping critique of romances, first by asking how Hortensius can banish all "fiction" of questionable moral standards—for this would mean indicting the classical authors boys study in their youth—and then by rejecting any double standard by which novels might receive sweeping censure because they are the favorite reading of women. By exfoliating her account of the novel's progress in a series of lessons that finally wins the willing conversion of a skeptical male, Reeve's text acquires the shape and feel of a seduction. Hortensius seems to relent in his opposition to romance because of his high regard for Euphrasia. But the resolution of this staged debate does not overcome the deeper resonances of the gendered contest around romances and novels. The pejorative terms applied to romance (*fanciful, wishful, out of touch with reality,* etc.) are also applied to women. The favorable terms applied to novels (*realistic, rational, improving*) are congruent with those that describe the male as a politically responsible member of the public sphere.

Within the context of the debate about novels, it is not surprising that male and female critics offer different pathways toward the novel's elevation. In elevating the novel, Coventry follows Fielding's attempt to splice classical knowledge and criticism into the reading of the novel. Although John Dunlop, like Reeve, applies a modern, historicist, more or less tolerant horizon of scholarship to the novel, his appeal to philosophical grounds for evaluating fiction helps push the novel toward a monumental cultural role. In elevating the novel, Clara Reeve (like Mary Wollstonecraft and Laetitia Barbauld later) turns the novel into a form for transmitting social knowledge. Reeve ends her literary history by offering two lists to parents, guardians, and tutors, "intended chiefly for the female sex": "Books for Children" and "Books for Young Ladies." This two-stage course of reading includes fables, spellers, conduct books, periodical essays, and only one item on the second list we would describe as a novel—"Richardson's Works." Following this curriculum prepares young female minds for an informed and critical reading of the romances and novels Reeve has described in *The Progress of Romance*. Literary history acquires the pedagogical function it still serves in literary studies: it becomes a reading list with its entries contextualized by narrative.

The gendered divide that expresses itself throughout the course of the institutionalization of the novel in England and in the various accounts of its "rise" is only one instance, though perhaps the most pervasive and important one, of the partisanship David Perkins has detected in much literary history. Given the way literary history is used to shape pleasure and define value, how could it be different? Thus the various positions upon what constitutes the first novel, and implicitly, what is the most valuable paradigm of novelistic authorship, work within the earliest literary histories of the elevated novel, and are reflected in the divergent critical valuations of Richardson and Fielding. In this way, the rivalry of Richardson and Fielding on the market during the 1740s was reproduced in the earliest literary criticism and history of the novel. Coventry ignores Richardson in proclaiming Fielding's unheralded achievements, while Johnson's prescription for the novel's cultural role is rigged to favor Richardson's fictional practice. The antagonism of Richardson and Fielding expresses itself through the writings of Hazlitt, Coleridge, Scott, and every subsequent literary historian of their differences. This antagonism shows little sign of dissipating in our own day. It is not just that different values reflect themselves in divergent accounts of our cultural repertoire. There are also always different agendas for the future dispositions of pleasure and value. Thus recent feminist critics have found Richardson most useful in their critical work, but Fielding *not*.

The elevation of the novel and its countersigning by literary history is neither simply right nor wrong, good nor bad. New discursive formations—like the elevated novel—incite new and valuable cultural production. Thus, however unfair or tendentious its judgments about the early novels of Behn, Manley, and Haywood, literary history's sublimation of "the novel" enables the ambitious novelistic projects of the nineteenth and twentieth centuries. One example is the quixotic ambition to write "the Great American Novel." Literary history does not have to be fair, or oriented toward the categories we would now credit, in order for it to bear its effects into culture. Yet its judgments are also always—and interminably—open to revision. The appeals court of culture is always in session. The recent feminist revaluation of the women novelists of the early eighteenth century seems to depend upon a contemporary reinterpretation of what is happening in the novels of Behn, Manley, and Haywood: explicit treatments of gender, sexuality, and power that have critical currency in our own time.

The Rise of Debate about the Rise of the English Novel

This chapter's account of the cultural scandal of novel reading, and of the inventive responses of novelists and literary historians to that scandal, suggests a signal tendency of most literary histories of the novel. Like a museum, literary history turns the strife of history into a repertoire of forms. It does so by taking differences that may have motivated the writing or reading of novels within specific historical contexts—differences of religion, politics, class, social propriety, or ethical design, to name a few—and converts them into differences of kind. Thus, for example, the polemic between Richardson and Fielding about the sorts of narrative and character fiction should possess comes to represent, within literary history, two species of novel: the Richardson novel of psychology and sentiment, and the Fielding novel of social panorama and critique. The novels of amorous intrigue written by Behn and the early Haywood have a bad difference that puts them entirely outside the frame of literary history of the elevated novel.

Notice the reversal of vision that literary history effects. If we interpret the writings of Behn, Richardson, and Fielding as part of the cultural history of Britain, we can find complex patterns of antagonism and detect the conscious and unconscious efforts of each author to distinguish his or her writing from its antecedents. By differentiating his novels from Behn's, Richardson engenders many of the differences evident between their novels. By contrast, literary history "finds," upon the archival table of its investigations, different novels, which it then attempts to distinguish and classify. Differences among novels are no longer effects of history, but the initial data for literary classification. Thus the category "novel" acquires a paradoxical role: pregiven and yet belated in its arrival, "the novel" is made to appear ready at hand, but it is actually that which the literary history of the novel defines. Often presented as the humble, minimal, and preliminary axiom of a literary history, the idea of the novel operates within the literary history of canonical texts as a kind of law. Changes in the idea of the novel during the nineteenth century were a necessary precondition for the belated emergence of the novel's origins as a compelling enigma.

Through the nineteenth and twentieth centuries, the novel keeps rising, and *The Columbia History of the British Novel* is one more symptom of that movement. Space does not permit a full genealogy of the evolution of the question of the novel's origins. But I can offer a brief sketch of those changes whereby the question becomes one of the Gordian knots of literary studies. Over the course of the nineteenth and twentieth centuries, novels are collected, edited, reviewed, and taught in schools and universities. Three basic shifts in the category of "the novel" are concomitants of this modern institutionalization of the novel as an object of knowledge in literary studies. First the novel is nationalized. Novels were once considered the type of writing most likely to move easily across linguistic and national boundaries. The critics and literary historians I have quoted in this chapter found the romances and novels of different nations on the same shelves. Reeve and Dunlop discuss the novels of Cervantes, Marivaux, and Rousseau within the same conceptual coordinates as the novels of Richardson and Fielding. But in the nineteenth century, novels come to be understood as a type of writing particularly suited to representing the character, mores, landscape, and spirit of the nation. At its most significant, a novel is, in the phrase of the French literary historian Hippolyte Taine, an expression of "the voice of the people."

In the wake of this idea, a thesis develops that would never have

occurred to Reeve or Dunlop: that the modern English novel has little
or nothing to do with earlier novellas and romances, and thus it does not
develop out of Italian, Spanish, or French precursors. Instead the novel
is said to derive from distinctly English discourses: the journalism of
Addison and Steele, the party writers of the reign of Queen Anne, the
new Science, religious autobiography like Bunyan's, writers of travel and
adventure, and so on. This position was first clearly enunciated by the
nineteenth-century professor of English at Glasgow, Walter Raleigh, in
his book *The English Novel* (1894). It has been developed much more
fully in recent books by Michael McKeon and J. Paul Hunter. While
Reeve's "progress of romance" and Dunlop's "history of fiction" are
inclusively multinational, extending backward to ancient and medieval
times and across the channel to include Continental romance and novella, national literary histories cut these temporal and spatial links. Traits
of the British culture—empiricism, protestant individualism, moral seriousness, and a fondness for eccentric character—are promoted from secondary characteristics of novels which happened to have been written in
England to primary radicals of the novel's generic identity.

By narrowing the vortex of the novel's formation, a nationalist
British literary history produces a new object of cultural value now
dubbed "the English novel." The English novel becomes the subject
and eponymous protagonist in a series of literary histories written by
Walter Raleigh (1894), George Saintsbury (1913), and Walter Allen
(1954). The phrase appears again in the titles of William Lyon
Phelps's *Advance of the English Novel* (1916), Ernest Baker's *History of
the English Novel* (1924–1936), and Arnold Kettle's *Introduction to the
English Novel* (1951). Within these literary histories, Richardson and
Fielding and Smollett and Sterne become the "dream team" of eighteenth-century fiction, and, in Saintsbury's famous metaphor, they are
the four wheels of that carriage of English fiction that, with its full
modern development into a repeatable "formula" by Austen and Scott,
is "set a-going to travel through the centuries." After Saintsbury,
Defoe is added as a fifth early master of the English novel. With Ian
Watt's *Rise of the Novel* (1957), the modifier "English" is implied but
erased. Now the rise of "the English novel" marks the rise of "the"
novel, that is, *all* novels. A synecdoche wags the dog. In this way a
national literary history overcomes what has always worried the earliest promoters and elevators of the novel in Britain: the belatedness and
indebtedness of English fiction.

The claim for the priority of the English novel made by this group of literary historians involves a shift in the novel's distinct identity: instead of consisting in its moral coherence, the novel's identity comes to derive from its adherence to some sort of realism. Although the kernel of this thesis is at least as old as the distinction between romance and novella defined by Congreve, Reeve, and others, the nineteenth century contributes an arduous and subtle development to the idea of what constitutes realism. With the development of the idea of society as an organic totality, the novel becomes—for Balzac, Dickens, and Eliot—uniquely appropriate for its study and analysis. Novelistic realism is complicated and enriched by those novelists—especially Flaubert and James—who undertake to aestheticize the novel. As art, the novel realizes its equality with poetry, and prepares itself for entrance into the "Great Tradition" (Leavis's 1948 title) of Western literature. The idea of the novel as art means that novel studies, and literary histories of the novel, come to privilege the novel's "form." Claims for the novel's formal coherence are not fatal to the idea of the novel's realistic imitation of social or psychic life. Instead the two ideas work together in literary histories from Ernest Baker's ten-volume *History of the English Novel* to Ian Watt's *Rise of the Novel* (1957). For Ian Watt "formal realism" becomes the distinctive characteristic of the novel and the crucial invention necessary for its "rise" to being the most influential linguistic vehicle of subjective experience.

With the idea of the novel's nationalism, its realism, and its power to express a personal interiority emerge three questions that have preoccupied scholarly study of the early British novel for at least one hundred years. Out of the concept of the novel's Englishness emerges a new question: how, where, and why does the *English* novel begin, originate, arise? This question is framed so as to assure that its answer will come from within the study of British culture. Once the novel is given a modern, relatively scientific epistemological mission—to be realistic in its representation of social and psychological life—one must ask, what constitutes realism? What form of writing should serve as the paradigm for novelistic mimesis? These are not so much questions that can be answered as a terrain for interminable negotiation and invention. Finally, how is the Englishness and realism of the novel implicated in the invention of the modern subject? With Watt, and those many critics and literary historians who have followed in his wake, the notion that the novel is a fully actualized form of a nation's literature, characterized by realism, is brought into alignment with two relatively new ideas about the novel's beginnings: its sudden birth and its distinctive modernity. Recently, new work on the novel's rise, influenced by Marxism, feminism, and poststructuralism, has sought to contest and complicate this classic interpretation of the rise of the novel. Instead of trying to summarize this rich vein of work, I will close with an observation. The themes of the novel's modernity and sudden birth, its realism and aesthetic greatness, its expression of nationhood or moral guidance to the reader—whether formulated early or late in the novel's "progress"—all these themes serve to update the cultural project that unfolded in the eight decades after 1740, and that this essay has explored: the impulse to elevate the novel and to sublimate the pleasures it incites.

William Warner

Selected Bibliography

Baker, Ernest. *The History of the English Novel.* New York: Barnes and Noble, 1924.

Coventry, Francis. "An Essay on the New Species of Writing Founded by Mr. Fielding." London, 1751. Los Angeles: Augustan Reprint No. 95, 1962.

Dunlop, John Colin. *The History of Fiction.* 3 vols. London, 1814.

Frow, John. *Marxism and Literary History.* Cambridge: Harvard University Press, 1986.

Perkins, David. *Is Literary History Possible?* Baltimore: Johns Hopkins University Press, 1992.

Raleigh, Sir Walter. *The English Novel: A Short Sketch of Its History from the Earliest Times to the Appearance of "Waverley."* London: John Murray, 1894.

Reeve, Clara. *The Progress of Romance.* Colchester, 1785.

Saintsbury, George. *The English Novel.* London: Dent, 1913.

Taine, Hippolyte A. *History of English Literature.* 1863. Trans. H. Van Laun. New York: Frederick Ungar, 1965.

Watt, Ian. *The Rise of the Novel.* Berkeley: University of California Press, 1957.

Defoe and Early Narrative

But my poor old island's still
Unrediscovered, unrenameable.
None of the books has ever got it right.
Elizabeth Bishop, "Crusoe in England"

"The school of example, my lord, is the world: and the masters of this school are
history and experience."
Henry St. John, Viscount Bolingbroke, Letters on the Study and Use of History

Defoe and "the Novel"

NO account of the rise or origin of the English novel can neglect the prose narratives of Daniel Defoe. Most critics recognize that Defoe's plots are not often formally coherent or satisfying. But few major accounts of Defoe's narratives have explained their workings by emphasizing the extent to which they defy ordinary novelistic categories. Of Defoe's seven major narratives—*Robinson Crusoe* (1719), *Memoirs of a Cavalier* (1720), *Captain Singleton* (1720), *Moll Flanders* (1722), *A Journal of the Plague Year* (1722), *Colonel Jack* (1722), and *Roxana* (1724)—only *Memoirs of a Cavalier* can be described as formally controlled throughout. Otherwise, Defoe's narratives are marked by an episodic and apparently arbitrary narrative arrangement.

Ian Watt's analysis of Defoe in *The Rise of the Novel*, for example, reflects a preference for what he calls "formal realism" and an appreciation of psychological characterization (Watt recognizes, however, that these critical conventions have been invented since Defoe). Thus by categorizing *Robinson Crusoe* as a romance and *Moll Flanders* as, in effect, a novel, Watt articulates a standard distinction between two texts that are in many ways remarkably alike. By calling Robinson Crusoe an example of possessive individualism at work, Watt also adheres to a formal criterion for what constitutes a novel: the appeal to a certain economic motive explains the coherence of the story and gives it a formal meaning. Other critics have emphasized the extent to which Defoe used certain Puritan conventions, like the spiritual autobiography. Robinson Crusoe, Moll Flanders, and Roxana, all in their various ways, learn to spiritualize their otherwise mundane and secular existence. According to this model, Robinson learns, in the course of his exile on his island, increasingly to ascribe providential meanings to his experiences; Moll, having repented of her life of crime when faced with the gallows in Newgate, rediscovers wealth, her son, and her happiness in Virginia before she returns to England. And although Roxana's tale records the success of a life as mistress and courtesan that earns her substantial material wealth, the threatening reappearance of her long-abandoned daughter toward the end, and the final paragraph of the book, in which Roxana is seen paying for her sins in a life of poverty, can be taken as peculiar inversions of the same master plot.

The conventional critical account of the differences between Bunyan and Defoe calls upon similar assumptions about what constitutes a novel—as opposed to other forms of prose narrative—and shows that Defoe's narratives approach the novel more nearly than Bunyan's *Pilgrim's Progress*. Defoe occupies a place in a story that is already about the novel, so that the critic is already committed to certain criteria of judgment that will cause him or her to perceive either certain elements in Defoe, or certain of Defoe's narratives—usually *Moll Flanders*, *Robinson Crusoe*, and *Roxana*—as clearer harbingers than others of what was to come in the classic novels of, say, Samuel Richardson and Henry Fielding.

Critics have argued recently that structures laid down by Richardson and Fielding have become the standard for judging whether a work of prose is truly novelistic. By using their work as the yardstick, the argument goes, critics agree to suppress the extent to which Richardson and Fielding—as well as other writers—both used and discarded the earlier prose narratives of Aphra Behn, Delariviere Manley, and Eliza Haywood. Behn, Manley, and Haywood, that is, wrote narratives whose techniques Richardson and Fielding gentrified and masculinized, thereby obliterating their predecessors from most subsequent accounts of the early novel in England. In other words, we have been so well trained to have certain expectations of what a novel consists of that we find Behn, Manley, and Haywood somewhat incoherent or formless as writers. At this juncture, these critics suggest, we should discard our prejudices, recognize that Behn, Manley, and Haywood had other sorts of things in mind, and judge them according to their own apparent aims, according to the genres with which they were most directly engaged, and according to the cultural and literary expectations of the early rather than the middle years of the eighteenth century. I find this thesis persuasive on most counts, and I think the same approach should be taken with regard to another important and early writer of prose fiction—Daniel Defoe.

I believe that we cannot understand what Defoe succeeds in doing unless we base our interpretation upon the following premises: (1) we should not seek in any given text evidence of what we expect or want a "novel" to do (especially since Defoe explicitly attacks novels); (2) we should search Defoe's main prose narratives for a common nexus of attitudes about narrative, even though some of his stories are less satisfactory to our taste than others; (3) by attending as far as possible to what those narratives tell us about their own procedures, we should look for the literary "unity" that is presented to us (if any), or alternatively for the coherence Defoe sought in writing his narratives; and (4) we should recognize that Defoe operated out of a literate culture that, in practice if not in theory, recognized only the loosest of boundaries between genres, and tended to experiment with forms and techniques from a wide range of sources in both high and low culture.

Although the Restoration and the eighteenth century are often thought of as a period in which literature was governed by strict rules of decorum, it was in fact an age in which literary forms were continually exploding under constant scrutiny and revision: the looseness of the category *novel* fits an age that celebrates the fluidity of many other literary forms (such as Dryden's *Absalom and Achitophel*, Pope's *Dunciad*, or Swift's *Tale of a Tub*). Moreover, the looseness of generic categories, especially in the early eighteenth century, reflects a series of cultural uncertainties and conflicts which themselves provide topics for Defoe's narratives: the outcome of certain political and cultural controversies was by no means clear to Defoe or his contemporaries. When we examine the characteristic habits of Defoe's presentation, we repeatedly find a number of distinguishing rhetorical features; and yet we find important signs that Defoe was engaged in a debate about the moral and cognitive relationship of prose narrative to the world (both the world it apparently describes and the world encountered by the reader). This debate is part of a wider set of concerns shared by other early eighteenth-century critics and writers, and Defoe's participation in it demonstrates the degree to which he belonged to that milieu, not his uniqueness (except perhaps imaginatively). In particular, it is Defoe's obsession with history as a mode of knowledge, as a mode of writing, and as a setting for character and action that best reveals his ambitions for the nature and function of his narratives.

Defoe and "History"

We should take seriously what Roxana says about the quality of the tale she tells. "My Business," she insists, "is History." Defoe incorporates similar statements about the kind of narratives he is to present in several of his prefaces. The preface to *Moll Flanders* begins, "The World is so taken up of late with Novels and Romances that it will be hard for a private History to be taken for Genuine"; the "Editor" of *Colonel Jack* opines, *"If he has made it a* History *or a* Parable, *it will be equally useful, and capable of doing Good "*; we are told of *Roxana,* that *"the Work is not a Story, but a History"*; Captain Singleton describes himself as following an historical method. In his *Serious Reflections* [on] *Robinson Crusoe* (1720), although Defoe begins by asserting that "the fable is always made for the moral, not the moral for the fable," his energies are directed to claiming that *Robinson Crusoe,* "though allegorical, is also historical," and that all its details, including Robinson's attempts at providential interpretation, "are all histories and real stories" and "are all historical and true in fact." For Defoe as for any neoclassical author, narratives always have moral purpose, but a moral purpose visible only by observing second causes and common actions (or "the ordinary course of life"). The actions of providence are not immediately evident, so that while Defoe speaks of "emblematic history," he also opposes it to "romance," and writes that "Nothing is more frequent than for us to mistake Providence, even in its most visible appearances." Though we can infer the actions of providence, it is not a simple business:

The only objection, and which I can see no method to give a reason for and no answer to, is, why, if it be the work of Providence, those things should be so imperfect, so broken, so irregular, that men may either never be able to pass any right judgement of them, as is sometimes the case, or make a perfect judgement of them, which is often the case, and so the end of the intimation be entirely defeated, without any fault, neglect, or omission of the man.

Some critics see Defoe's claims about history as linking his narratives to the genre of spiritual autobiography, which is indeed a kind of history, but one that does not sufficiently describe the mechanisms that distinguish Defoe's works from, say, *Grace Abounding* or *The Pilgrim's Progress*. Indeed, when the editor of *Colonel Jack* places history and parable before his reader as alternative ways of thinking about the narrative, he reminds his early-eighteenth-century reader of the extent to which history is like parable in that both are supposed, in order to please and instruct, to convey morals or precepts *by means of* the narrative examples they present. But history is also, and crucially, distinguished from parable, in that the narrative vehicle from which we are expected to draw precepts to govern our moral and political conduct is itself the record of randomly occurring events. If we draw from what we read in history books an order or design, or some clear moral, we do so at the cost of simplifying or editing those narrative particulars that escape or inundate the moral they supposedly serve. In parable, of course, the narrative is predetermined by the moral purpose it expresses. What exists before history is written is raw experience, and the patterns or teleology we find in history come as superimpositions upon that experience. Moreover, I think Defoe was aware that some of those patterns are imposed for ideological purposes: to see it any other way amounts to holding that providence directly controls each and every one of our actions—an idea Defoe carefully refutes in his *Serious Reflections*.

Defoe apparently recognized at least two steps in the process of legitimizing a historical record: the first is simply to record the facts; the second is to render those facts morally significant. Both processes involve a crucial editorializing of the raw materials of experience, which of itself is formless. To give any literary shape to his account, the historian must impose some kind of significance or teleology upon the chaos of facts confronting him, but the moralist repeats this process of truncation and reduction even more vigorously in order to convey a moral to an audience temporally and spatially removed from the historical moment in question. This process of reduction is epitomized in the fundamental distinction Locke draws between the two aspects of our entire mental life: we have experience, then we reflect upon it. Locke's radical politics emerges at the point where he makes clear that the activity of reflection—which is primarily marked by the use of language—incorporates a series of reductions that commit a sort of violence upon the raw elements of the world as well as upon our cognitive life: it inevitably simplifies and thereby controls them to facilitate social and political "commerce."

What seems, then, to be almost obsessively at issue in Defoe is the tension between the local details of a particular person's experience, especially as the narrator recalls them, and the meanings that that individual attempts to impose upon the experience, which the reader is asked to confirm. In this sense, Robinson's experiences and his attempts to rationalize them are equally matters of historical record. This may be the effect of a movement toward secularization in English culture since Bunyan, as some critics assert; according to one argument, *The Pilgrim's Progress* forges an extraordinary coherence between the allegorical dimension and the narrative vehicle, approaching in many places the condition of Watt's formal realism (for example, in the Vanity Fair episode, which uncannily presents the atmosphere of a Restoration law court like the one that sentenced Bunyan).

But in Defoe we detect a strain, either within the narrator, within the author, or both, as they struggle to assign meanings to what are evidently violent, chaotic, or random events, often exacerbated by the narrator's criminal or eccentric behavior. Thus there is considerable critical commentary, for example, about the extent to which *Moll Flanders* is an ironic novel. The question is, how can Moll's repentance become the precipitating cause for her reward, when she is actually rewarded for her life of crime rather than for her act of repentance? The explicit providential explanation for the outcome does not fit all the facts of the case. The critics' concern with irony in this context raises crucial questions about the extent to which Defoe was aware of what he was doing as he wrote and whether he consciously strove to endow a completed narrative with a unified moral and formal structure. It is possible to argue that Moll's repentance in Newgate supplies precisely the right ironic commentary upon her earlier experiences, thus bestowing on the novel a coherence its earlier episodic nature lacks.

Such concerns with symmetry do not account sufficiently for Defoe's other narratives, nor do they account for the degree to which Defoe's obsession with history as the chief correlative to his own strategies signals the possibility of another kind of irony altogether. That Defoe is capable of unified plots is evidenced by *Memoirs of a Cavalier*. But unlike modern critics searching for organic form, Defoe is not primarily interested in formal unity or formal irony: the ironies that occur in Defoe's narratives occur more locally and insistently in response to certain crises that the narrator attempts to render significant. Defoe is correspondingly unconcerned about the tidiness of his narrative endings, since formal perfection is not central to his purpose: his endings often feel contrived and hurried, or, as in the case of *Robinson Crusoe*, close the narrative in a rather indeterminate way. Thus, at the beginning of his tale, Colonel Jack writes that "my Life has been such a Checquer Work of Nature"; and the challenge in Colonel Jack's tale, as in all of Defoe's, is for the narrator to coordinate the details of his or her experience with the language, if not the fact, of providence. (Thus Robinson cries out, "How strange a Chequer Work of Providence is the Life of Man!") The tension between the particulars of the narrators' experiences and the language of moral accounting—whether that of religion, conscience, reflection, or providence—is rendered all the more palpable, in virtually every case, by the sheer force and abundance with which the local details of an individual's history are rendered (Defoe's novels are full of lists, letters, journal accounts, and moments of dialogue, many of which are highly reminiscent of Bunyan). And this tension emerges even more explicitly in *Captain Singleton, Colonel Jack, Moll Flanders, Robinson Crusoe,* and *Roxana,* where the means of calibrating from moment to moment the fortunes of the narrator are fiscal or, in a slightly broader sense, economic. The acquisitive energy that many critics celebrate as a feature of Robinson's, Moll's, or Roxana's personalities is also, I think, inseparable from the sheer energy generated by the act of tale-telling itself, an energy that is underscored by the multiple kinds of narratives in any given Defoe story.

Except for Roxana, who becomes progressively richer until the final twist of fortune recorded only in the last paragraph, all the narrators find themselves wealthy at the end; and the reader is left with an uncomfortable sense that the language of reflection, conscience, or providence does not adequately explain the causes or conditions of that wealth. Thus Captain Singleton spends the first half of his career wandering in Africa (here the author finds ample opportunity to incorporate exotic detail beyond the thematic requirements of the story) and the second half as a pirate, accompanied by the canny and pacific Quaker, William. Having become very rich, the narrator is moved by his sojourn in Arabia and by William's presence to reflect on himself, apparently for the first sustained period in his life. He writes to William:

It is not material to record here what a Mass of ill-gotten Wealth we had got together: It will be more to the Purpose to tell you, that I began to be sensible of the Crime of getting of it in such a Manner as I had done, that I had very little Satisfaction in the Possession of it.

William talks to Captain Singleton further, and our narrator declares that

William had struck so deep into my unthinking Temper, with hinting to me, that there was something beyond all this, that the present Time was the Time of Enjoyment, but that the Time of Account approached; that the Work that remain'd was gentler than the Labour past, *viz. Repentance.*

But even so, William proceeds to argue that there is no point in disposing of their wealth, and so, in the final few pages of the book, William and Captain Singleton become even richer by selling their goods, and Captain Singleton, upon returning to England, bestows on William's sister a sum of five thousand pounds and proceeds to marry her. The book's ending thus bestows on Captain Singleton rewards in excess of his act of repentance, which immediately precedes his homecoming. The mere fact of repentance does not determine the kind or quantity of reward that follows it.

The apparent effects of conscience upon Roxana's behavior are virtually nil. Such effects would be difficult to detect in any case, since Defoe's characteristic narrative form makes it hard to tell, as the narrator recounts her story, whether she felt pangs of conscience during the actual experiences or whether the intrusion of conscience is merely a reflection of the repentant and virtuous perspective from which she writes. Thus Roxana writes about the interventions of conscience at an important moment as though they are a series of gaps in her experience—as if she were thinking in formal terms about the condition of her own tale:

There was, and would be, Hours of Intervals, and of dark Reflections which came involuntarily in, and thrust in Sighs in the middle of all my Songs; and there would be, sometimes, a heaviness of Heart, which intermingl'd itself with all my Joy. . . . Conscience will, and does, often break in upon [people] at particular times, let them do what they can do to prevent it.

Both the "repentant" Roxana and the Roxana in the midst of whoring and managing her wealth reflect on the character's experience in similar terms; and her reflection does little to alter the course of her career, which only suddenly and finally experiences a reversal—for completely mysterious reasons.

The arbitrariness of assigning meanings to a sum of separate experiences—and the fact that such assignation reflects distinct cultural assumptions—is highlighted, especially in *Robinson Crusoe* and *A Journal of the Plague Year*, by the narrator's use of the Bible as a means to pin down and summarize his experience. With Robinson, this habit is persistent; he frequently flicks open the pages of the scriptures to reassure himself of the meaning of events that—for him as well as for his reader—might as well be a series of random occurrences. The narrative conditions under which this habit is recorded only heighten the reader's perception that the action is slightly desperate. About a third of the way through his account, Robinson has apparently switched from his direct narrative into a journal mode, but the entry for June 27 records Robinson sick with an ague. He first calls on God, *"Lord look upon me, Lord pity me, Lord have Mercy upon me"*; then he falls asleep and has an apocalyptic dream in which a kind of revenging angel threatens him for having failed to repent; finally he is struck by his impiety and believes God (who is symbolically associated throughout with his father) is punishing him. In the course of his speculations (or "Reflections") Robinson slips out of his journal, as if the fever and fear have marred the internal consistency of his subsequent record. Returning to the journal for June 28, Robinson begins to reconsider his relation to God on a grand scale, and finds himself "struck dumb with these Reflections." He immediately experiments with tobacco, which disturbs his head, and, intoxicated by its fumes, he "open'd the Book casually," to read these words: *"Call on me in the Day of Trouble, and I will deliver, and thou shalt glorify me ."* Rather than interpreting the application of this injunction as adequate to the "Case," as Robinson calls it, we should remain conscious of the arbitrary relation between the biblical motto and what Robinson assumes it glosses, especially considering the cognitive dissonance that Robinson experiences at this juncture. Later, we find Robinson creating even more arbitrary connections between events when he says that it was on the same calendar date that he left his father and later went to sea, or that he was both born and saved from drowning on the thirtieth of September.

The entire plot of *A Journal of the Plague Year* is precipitated by the narrator's ("H. F.") gesture of turning the pages of the Bible, much as Robinson continually does. H. F. is unsure whether he should, like his brother, flee London as the plague mounts. He is most explicitly concerned about protecting his goods, but he then writes:

This lay close to me, and my Mind seemed more and more encouraged to stay than ever, and supported with a secret Satisfaction, that I should be kept: Add to this that turning over the Bible, which lay before me, and while my Thoughts were more than ordinarily serious upon the Question, I cry'd out, WELL, *I know not what to do, Lord direct me!* and the like; and [at] that Juncture, I happen'd to stop turning over the Book at the 91*st Psalm*, and casting my Eye on the second Verse, I read on to the 7th Verse exclusive.

Not only does the Bible supply these somewhat unsatisfactory means of justifying and glossing actions, but—Defoe seems to suggest—it is in the action of some biblical narratives themselves that we find a similar cryptic relationship between human experience, rendered via second causes, and the actions of the divine, which remain inscrutable. The chief figure of this narrative and historical conundrum is of course Job, whose afflictions strike him as disproportionate to divine action in the world as he understands it; and the problem of reconciling divine omniscience with human knowledge is never truly resolved in that book. It is for this reason, I suggest, that *Job* crops up as a kind of master plot for *Robinson Crusoe*: at the end of his story, Robinson writes, "I might well say, now indeed, That the latter End of *Job* was better than the Beginning." Colonel Jack is left at the end of his career in retirement or "Exile," where "I had . . . leisure to reflect, and to repent, to call to mind things pass'd, and with a just Detestation, learn as *Job* says, *to abhor my self in Dust and Ashes*." And Roxana's wanderings in the world begin as her husband leaves her with five children. She is comforted by Amy, an "old Aunt," and another woman, who "sat down like *Job*'s three Comforters, and said not one Word to me for a great while." To align the events of ordinary life unequivocally with the motions of providence is, Defoe seems to say in *A Journal of the Plague Year*, "Turkish predestinarianism." We cannot, H. F. writes, see the plague as arising from anything but "natural causes": though God can choose to work within "the ordinary course of things," our business is to attend to second rather than first causes, which are as obscure to us as the origins and essence of the plague itself.

Whereas the language of providence and of reflection attempts recursively to endow the details of the narrative with a total and harmonizing significance, Defoe's narratives also incorporate a language of anticipation, as if either the narrator—or Defoe—wants to assert control over the storytelling that is to come, which will in the course of time prove to have providential or at least formal significance. Given the general roughness of Defoe's technique—some critics think he might have written *Captain Singleton* in great haste to capitalize on the success of *Robinson Crusoe*—such assurances of control seem more hopeful than otherwise. Further, in highlighting the contradiction between the narrator's predictions and the actual course of events, they are at odds with the sense that the outcome is consistently providential; that is, they seem to intensify rather than settle the problem of narrative control. This foreshadowing of future events is pervasive. "I am hastening to my own story," writes Colonel Jack; Roxana refers to the impending close of her story ("this End of my Story"); Moll says that she is "too near the End of my Story"; characters commonly refer to some "new scene" of their lives that is about to follow (immediately before coming across the footprint for the first time, Robinson writes, "But now I come to a new Scene of my Life").

This internal and repetitive irony has two thematic implications that deserve mention. First, Defoe indulges the typical neoclassical fascination with forensics, which follows naturally from his interest in criminal life. When Moll is finally imprisoned for theft, her "governess," who acts as advisor and fence, tries to tamper with the evidence, but to no avail, since, it transpires, "I was to have three Witnesses of Fact against me, the Master and his two Maids; that is to say, I was as certain to be cast for my Life, as it was certain that I was alive." The point is that, finally, empirical knowledge prevails against the attempt to subvert it—though such attempts are repeatedly made by Defoe's characters who tell several versions of their stories to the reader and to other listeners in the tale. In contrast to Fielding's interpolated narratives, Defoe's tend to obscure or edit rather than confirm the certainty of some preexisting truth: critics have often pointed out that Robinson's journal changes the particulars of what we have hitherto been told. Roxana is hounded by a French Jew who tries to prove that she was not truly married to the man whose jewels she possesses. He is, of course, correct, but a struggle ensues over who is to have legal possession, and Roxana, who deserves the jewels, treats the Jew to considerable abuse. *A Journal of the Plague Year* is centrally about the forensic problem of inferring the causes of the plague, of detecting its signs and its course, and of creating an adequate report of the entire event: H. F. uses the empirical vocabulary of experiment, evidence, and hypothesis throughout. At best, he states, we can develop a method of judging the relative validity of signs and evidence: "Seeing then that we could come at the certainty of things by no method but that of inquiry of the neighbours or of the family, and on that we could not justly depend, it was not possible but that the uncertainty of this matter would remain as above."

The second thematic implication of Defoe's peculiar irony is more directly political. His novels invite an analogy between the narrators' attempts to force patterns on the flux of experience, and the structure of imperialism, where one nation imposes its will, its language, and its institutions upon another. This is most clearly evidenced in *Robinson Crusoe*. The distinct vocabulary that emerges in the course of time to fit Robinson's circumstances and behavior is the dual language of family and sovereignty. Like Gray's *Elegy*, *Robinson Crusoe* is not about solitary experience, but about how solitary experience establishes the conditions for social and political life. (Typically for the period, Defoe was to write in *Serious Reflections* that "Man is a creature so formed for society, that it may not only be said that it is not good for him to be alone, but 't is really impossible that he should be alone.") This view receives support from Novak's argument that Defoe was not a possessive individualist (as Watt assumes), but that he supported an older, mercantilist ideal of trade that was "basically communal rather than individualistic." It takes about a third of the book for Robinson to establish himself on the island after his shipwreck, but from that point forward he begins increasingly to imagine himself as the head of a family (if only a family of animals), and as king or lord of the island. Robinson's tenure almost exactly coincides with the Restoration period (1660– 1688), which saw the collapse of the Stuart monarchy under Charles II and James II; and Defoe's skepticism about the Stuarts, who attempted to rule without the consent of Parliament, is echoed by Robinson's increasingly absolutist vocabulary. Robinson first speaks of himself as "King and Lord of all this Country indefeasibly," and then begins to speak of his "Family." He also becomes a lord of manorial property, but he increasingly assumes the garb of an absolutist monarch: "I had the Lives of all my Subjects at my absolute Command. I could hang, draw, give Liberty, and take it away, and no Rebels among all my Subjects." Later, Robinson celebrates his absolute mastery over Friday and the Spaniard he has rescued from the cannibals, speaking proudly of his tolerance even toward pagans and papists: we have witnessed a process through which the language of sovereignty has increasingly defined experience.

The tension between Robinson's impulses toward political patronage and toward control within a context where the desire for sovereignty wins out, is best dramatized in those moments when Robinson, having discovered that the Indians of the region are indeed cannibals, thinks about exterminating them. There is a virtually seamless movement from Robinson's dream about saving a "Savage" and making him his servant, to his conscious decision to enslave one at the earliest opportunity, and then to his saving and subjugating Friday. But Robinson's attitude toward the cannibals veers drastically between a desire to exterminate them and the recognition that they are only accountable to God, not to himself. Whether Defoe intended it or not, this dramatizes the conflict within the European imperialistic sensibility between a genocidal and primitivistic impulse. After witnessing the remnants of the first cannibal feast, Robinson declares, "I could think of nothing but how I might destroy some of these Monsters," but he repents, realizing that they are "innocent" as far as he knows. Robinson twice repeats this thought process, each time checking himself; but, significantly, he finally expresses his murderous impulses when he sees that an intended victim is a European. The imperial motives of the narrator are also manifest in *Captain Singleton*, where Captain Singleton provokes some Africans to attack him so that he can justify enslaving them according to a "Law of Arms" defined unilaterally by himself. The point comes across clearly in the discrepancy between what we observe and Captain Singleton's language of self-justification.

My major thesis, then, is that history describes the mechanisms of Defoe's novels not because it represents some given literary form but because it constitutes a *mode*, a way of reading or interpreting experience that does not dictate formally perfect endings. Unlike spiritual autobiography, history is open-ended; and even if Defoe owes some debt to spiritual autobiography, Hans Frei suggests that he wrote in an age in which biblical narrative was subject to the same scrutiny as secular history. This is not to repeat the conventional criticism that Defoe is flawed because his plots are too episodic: rather, the episodes serve a cumulative function by revealing how characters become readers within the plots, thus directing Defoe's readers how to read the world. Like the ending of Samuel Johnson's *Rasselas* in which there is no conclusion, the open forms of Defoe's narratives encourage the reader to apply what they learn. As Moll Flanders puts it, "The Moral indeed of all my History is left to be gather'd by the Senses and Judgment of the Reader; I am not Qualified to preach to them, let the Experience of one Creature completely Wicked, and compleatly Miserable be a Storehouse of useful warning to those that read." In brief, history is, for Defoe's narrators and readers equally, an instrument of knowledge.

The two chief metaphors for this activity are the reading of history—situating the self in time—and the narrator's development of topographical or geographical knowledge—situating the self in space. Both metaphors presuppose that useful knowledge is primarily visual, just as reading must be thought of as a visual negotiation with graphic signs: a tract often credited to Defoe, *An Essay upon Literature* (1724), analyzes the development of systems of writing in different cultures, and argues that politically and economically viable cultures are literate, not oral. Thus, the claim in *Colonel Jack*, *Memoirs of a Cavalier*, *Moll Flanders*, *Robinson Crusoe*, and *Roxana* is that the narrator's account has been transcribed and edited from an orally delivered version. This calls to our attention the fact that the book is an artificial and ultimately arbitrary compilation of manuscripts or accounts. And as the editor or publisher of *Moll Flanders* points out, we cannot expect these accounts to be complete, since "no Body can write their own Life to the full End of it."

Moreover, we see Robinson engaged in the activity of editing his own journal, and Roxana editing her story. Roxana also appears partly conscious that her account, like the accounts of others within her tale, is fragmentary. The end of the novel is taken up with Roxana's long-abandoned daughter, Susan, pursuing her mother. Amy acts as a kind of detective shielding Roxana from exposure, and she reports that Susan's discourse "consisted of broken Fragments of Stories, such as the Girl herself had heard so long ago." Other spies and observers populate Defoe's narratives: Robinson constantly uses his spyglass from a lookout; the cavalier records how often he patiently observed Gustavus Adolphus's military councils so that he is able to reveal the fatal discrepancy between that king and Charles I ("And here I experienced the Truth of an old *English* Proverb," he writes, *"That Standers-by see more than the Gamesters."*); Colonel Jack acts like Addison's Mr. Spectator when he returns to London, because since he is believed to be French, he can observe events from an ironic perspective; H. F. becomes a special observer of events in the plague-stricken city because he is made an inspector; Moll spies on the gentleman whom she has met in Bath; Amy spies on Roxana's first husband; Roxana's Quaker friend acts as her spy, and so on.

The two texts in which the topos of historical reading serves most obviously as a catalytic force are *Captain Singleton* and *Colonel Jack*.

Both narrators are educated in the course of time by tutors who teach them literacy and cartography. We can detect a comparable development in Robinson's perspective on his experience when he calculates that his island is located in the mouth of the Orinoco River, and the turn of events during the plague is marked in part by H. F.'s leaving London, traveling to Greenwich, and surveying the Thames from a prospect, as if to provide himself literally and symbolically with a broader perspective on events in the city. Moll writes that, even on her second visit to Virginia, she only had a vague knowledge of the American colonies, and "I, that till I wrote this, did not know what the word Geographical signify'd": the very act of writing here expands the writer's consciousness of space.

Emerging from no background at all, both Captain Singleton and Colonel Jack aspire to become gentlemen, and their growth in literacy is closely related to a redefinition of the gentleman in which they, along with their creator, are engaged. Their tales thus inscribe both cognitive and social ambitions. Colonel Jack raises the issue of how we are to take his story, since he hopes that "my History will find a place in the World." Imbibing the rumor that he is the son of a gentlewoman, he acts as "a kind of Historian"—though an oral historian who gleans his knowledge from "old Soldiers and Tars." His early career as a criminal coincides with his illiteracy: in time, he discovers how valuable it would be to read, not least in order to calculate the interest he makes on a sum he has left in safekeeping with a gentleman. Finally realizing that not knowing how is a handicap even within his doubtful profession, he learns to read in six months, and the narrative immediately propels him from his criminal life into army service and thence to Virginia, which, as it does for Moll, proves to be an environment that makes a new person of him. He learns to rule the slaves on his master's estates by benevolence instead of force, creating a bond of gratitude rather than fear; and he soon succeeds on his own estates by the same principle. (Colonel Jack later becomes a grateful supporter of the Hanoverian succession after he benefits from a general pardon to those involved in the 1715 rebellion: he is thus repaid in kind.)

The middle of the book involves several changes at once: having described his success, the narrator pauses to "Impose a short Digression on the Reader," which provides the first important moment of self-reflection. He suffers a kind of hell, but not one generated by genuine religious feeling "but from meer Reasonings with myself, and from being arriv'd to a Capacity of making a right Judgement of things more than before." This is a Lockean rather than a providential development, one confirmed by a new love of books, especially "*Livy's* Roman History, the History of the *Turks*, the *English* History of *Speed*, and others; the History of the *Low Country* Wars, the History of *Gustavus Adolphus*, King of *Sweden*, and the History of the *Spaniard's* Conquest of *Mexico*." He instantly mentions a new servant whom "Fate" places in his way. This man is "an excellent Schollar" with a "liberal Education," and Colonel Jack learns Latin; the plantation does better than ever during the next twelve years. Colonel Jack is increasingly burdened with a conscience about his state, and causes his "Tutor" to turn from teaching him Latin to instructing him in the scriptures, but biblical instruction is interspersed with "History," stimulating Colonel Jack's desire to see more of the world: this introduces the second half of his tale, which is more episodic than the first, although it finally returns him to Virginia, to a wife, and from there to trade and riches in the West Indies. The reader learns of his wealth through the appropriate journals, books, and lists. As in *Roxana*, the plot ends rather abruptly with Colonel Jack living in retirement, as if to create some physical space between himself and his past and between the reader and the "History" that he has presented. If we are led to repentance, as he hopes, the means of persuasion follows a historical method. The reader must contemplate the distinction between example and precept, between raw experience and some account of its total significance: as it surfaces in the course of the narrative, the language of providence is too wayward to achieve that result on its own.

Like *Colonel Jack*, *Captain Singleton* falls into two parts. At first, Captain Bob, as he is also known, travels extensively in Africa, crossing deserts and lakes, meeting exotic animals, and confronting native peoples; for a change of career, he becomes a pirate, gets very rich, and has a last-minute spasm of conscience about his wealth. Even more patently than *Colonel Jack*, the narrative is more concerned with revealing its historical method than with securing a satisfactorily providential ending: in the first paragraph, Captain Singleton explicitly makes such method his subject. He becomes literate fairly early on in his career, learning a smattering of Latin, writing "a tolerable Hand," and reading "Charts and Books." The meandering style of the accounts of his African journey is explained to some extent by the fact that, since he didn't understand navigation at the time, he kept no journal of his exploits. The journey becomes slightly more purposeful when the gunner acts as a tutor: he is "an excellent Mathematician, a good Scholar, and a compleat Sailor," and teaches Captain Bob "all the Sciences useful for Navigation, and particularly . . . the Geographical Part of Knowledge." This training "laid the Foundation of a general Knowledge of things in my Mind." Eventually, the party meets a European in an African village, a "Gentleman" and scholar, who knows the region and the way to the sea. The European recounts his own "History," and though the party stays to accumulate more gold and ivory, this is the end of the African venture, as if to suggest that cartographic knowledge is really the most valuable plunder Captain Singleton has gained.

William the Quaker becomes Captain Singleton's mentor and guide in the second part. William is always pacific, but at the same time bent on profit. The demise of their joint career as pirates is precipitated by an expedition to Ceylon, where they encounter hostile natives who almost get the better of them. At this juncture, Defoe, having stated that William already knows the tale of Captain Knox's experience there, concludes the episode by reproducing a long passage from Knox's story. Critics often see this as a clumsy device by an author too keen to capitalize on the success of *Robinson Crusoe*. But if this passage is the product of haste, it merely reveals more baldly Defoe's concern with parallel history—we are given comparative stories to judge—and this method of reading is adumbrated within Knox's own tale, since he has as his companions two early-seventeenth-century tracts, Charles Bayly's *Practice of Pietie* (1620), and Richard Rogers's *Seven Treatises Leading and Guiding to True Happiness* (1603). He then miraculously happens on a Bible, and, deciding to escape from Ceylon, finally reaches a Dutch harbor, which causes Knox and his native helper to thank God for his providence. The providential significance of Knox's tale is heavily marked by Knox's engagement with devotional texts; but what is relatively easy for Knox to interpret in his life as divine guidance is less easy for Defoe's reader to see in Captain Singleton's tale. This difference in narrative meaning is highlighted by the juxtaposition of Knox's and Singleton's accounts, whereby the latter cannot so easily ascribe events to providential action.

A less indirect exercise in the parallel reading of history is *Memoirs of a Cavalier*. The book is cleanly divided into two parts to enforce the comparisons Defoe asks his reader to make. Accordingly, we discover that the story is not just about the dangers of civil war. In fact, the cavalier first observes and serves Gustavus Adolphus in his brilliant military exploits on behalf of Protestant Christendom against the French, but we also see Gustavus Adolphus disappear from the scene, and his generals fatally divide their energies after his death. The *Memoirs* are in large part about the value of good counsel; thus in the second part, which describes the course of the English Civil War, Charles I condemns himself by his inability to choose or to take advice. Charles's failure is underscored by Prince Rupert's notorious impetuosity on the battlefield: in both cases action is singular, rash, and unpremeditated. The central issue is one of political and military method: the cavalier measures all strategies against the "Method of the King of Sweden." This establishes a pattern that is matched not among the royalists but, finally, in that model of virtue, the parliamentarian Sir Thomas Fairfax. Defoe's purpose is thus somewhat subversive, since the analogies his history sets up show the values of good republican as well as good Protestant government. He does provide a list of "providences," as he calls them, but the list is drawn up by a Roman Catholic, which means that readers still have to judge the application of these incidents to the cavalier's experience, just as the cavalier reminds us that his private history must be compared with or supplemented by public history. He writes: "The History of the Times will supply the Particulars which I omit, being willing to confine my self to my own Accounts and Observations; I was now no more an Actor, but a melancholly Observator of the Misfortunes of the Times."

Defoe and "Character"

Just as it is a mistake to ask Defoe to present us with conventional novelistic criteria for judging his narratives, so it would be a mistake to think of Defoean character as primarily psychologistic in its nature and growth. This is not to say that a character's individual circumstances cannot create intense emotion: Defoe powerfully conveys Moll's agonies in Newgate and Roxana's terror at being discovered by her daughter. Critics are also prone to celebrate Moll's and Roxana's energetic commitment to a criminal or sinful life and their feverish dedication to the acquisition of wealth. And it is also possible to think of Robinson Crusoe as profoundly egocentric. But nevertheless I think that in Defoe, character as such remains remarkably static, as changing circumstances induce different emotions that—while they often change

Thing your Wife, shall I now give the Lye to all those Arguments, and call myself your Whore, or Mistress, which is the same thing?" But later, she has learned to assume a range of roles to manipulate her circumstances: in her role as a criminal, "generally I took up new Figures, and contriv'd to appear in new Shapes every time I went abroad."

As one critic has phrased it, Defoe characteristically renders the self as "displaced." He tends to depict characters' propensity to discover aspects of themselves in others, or others' tendencies to assume, as if by osmosis, the narrator's qualities. In *Roxana*, Amy shares and manages Roxana's plot to the extent that even their sexual histories are intertwined: in a reversal of the usual anthropological model, female bonding is secured by trading in men. Amy's management of Roxana's reputation by manipulating gossip is also a participation in Roxana's identity since that identity is inseparable (until the end) from her public value. Moll develops a symbiotic relationship with her "governess" or fence; Robinson has Xury at the beginning (whom he sells) and Friday at the end (whom he has effectively enslaved), almost as if they play the fool and Edgar to Robinson's Lear. The episodes in *Robinson Crusoe* conclude with Friday committing daring exploits in the Pyrenees, defeating wolves and a bear. These incidents are curiously at odds with the story as a whole, although we could read Friday's action as Crusoe's projected desire for dramatic activity after years of enforced domesticity on the island. Moll, Roxana, and Captain Singleton also develop relationships with Quakers, who represent a community that itself was tangentially related to English society as a whole. Like the Jews in European intellectual life, these characters have a peculiar perspective on a society in which they participate and yet in some sense resist; and Quaker pacifism (in *Captain Singleton*) and honesty (in *Moll Flanders* and *Roxana*) differentiate these figures from a world in which the narrators would otherwise find only projections of their worse motives.

Roxana is also a name that clothes an identity with a certain reputation, one that both she and Amy are keen to manipulate and censor: the issue is often a question of how Roxana is known or said to be known, so that gossip as a form of social advertising assumes a high value. Significantly, the truth about Roxana's private identity and her past surfaces in the figure of her long-abandoned daughter who tenaciously pursues her; and it is equally significant that only at this point in the plot do we learn that Roxana's true name is the same as her daughter's, Susan. (Roxana reports this as if there were an identity linking her with her daughter: "She *was* my own Name," she writes [my emphasis].) Here, true identity comes as a threat both to the narrator and to the continuity of narrative itself: *Roxana* breaks off soon after the protagonist flees to Holland to escape the potential consequences of discovery. True identity presents an equally significant threat to Moll, since it is by such knowledge that she learns that she has married her own brother: few themes could better threaten social and narrative development than incest. Roxana's real name also threatens her politically, since she has earlier enjoyed the changeability of public and conventional definition, such that even her gender becomes fluid: she tells the merchant who proposes to her, "I wou'd be a *Man-Woman*; for as I was born free, I wou'd die so." (She elaborates elsewhere by writing, "while a Woman was single, she was a Masculine in her politick Capacity.")

I have suggested that the abiding question seems to be how the individual enters both a political and fiscal economy. Defoe's narratives appear to pose it by more than one device: like the individual in Thomas Hobbes's *Leviathan* or John Locke's *Essay Concerning Human Understanding* and *Two Treatises of Government*, the character begins life as a social minimum, a kind of atom that only becomes defined as a character and a social or political agent by virtue of accumulating experience in the public world. The obligations individuals develop are not the most obvious or natural ones, so that, as in Hobbes's contract by which such individuals yield up their powers to the sovereign, we are made conscious of the artifice by which those individuals deal with the world and with others. The emphasis on the artifice necessary for the construction of a viable social economy explains in part why narrators dissimulate even to those they love, and why characters are often obsessed by clothing, since they are conscious of how they are seen and marked from without: in the last part of her story, Roxana becomes increasingly defined by the fact that she has on occasion donned a Turkish costume; and her daughter intuits the truth about her precisely because that costume has become a public and forensic sign of who Roxana is. One symptom of Moll's economic and social confidence at the end of her story is the fact that she dresses her husband James in finery "to make him appear, as he really was, a very fine Gentleman." The preface to *Roxana* appropriately speaks of tale-telling as a form of dressing up: the editor will not dress up *"the Story in worse Cloathes than the* Lady."

In contrast to the Victorian hero or heroine, Defoe's characters become less rather than more essentially themselves. They always have tangential relations to their own family histories—or have none—and often they abandon the family obligations they do develop, as if to render the construction of social bonds as strenuous as possible. Robinson deliberately defies his father; H. F. remains in plague-stricken London while his brother escapes (much as the fickle Restoration court escapes to Oxford). Although the cavalier retains an important tie to his father, it is clear that the paternal role is assumed by Gustavus Adolphus, the ideal king and military commander, virtues the cavalier subsequently imputes to Fairfax. Captain Singleton and Colonel Jack only have pasts and families by hearsay: thus Captain Singleton has a gypsy woman "whom I was taught to call Mother," only after he has been stolen and sold; his life of wandering seems predetermined by this upbringing. Similarly, Colonel Jack wanders in search of gentility partly because "my Nurse told me my Mother was a Gentlewoman." Roxana and Moll both abandon families and children, although Moll rediscovers her son by her brother in Virginia, and Roxana is eventually hounded by one of the children she has abandoned.

In shedding or escaping familial ties, characters seem constantly to be inventing and reinventing themselves. The strain of invention is marked in part by the completeness of Captain Singleton's and Colonel Jack's ignorance of Christian truths (in religious terms, both characters are blank slates who must make themselves); in part by a common obsession to render the self genteel, as if to defy a social category that was conventionally inherited, not made, in the century before Defoe's; and in part by the fact that Defoe invents characters whose relationship to male Protestant English society after 1688—the Whig settlement Defoe recommends—is or becomes quite tangential. Two narrators are women; it transpires that Robinson, Captain Singleton, and Colonel Jack become Catholics; Colonel Jack participates briefly in the 1715 rebellion; though a royalist, the cavalier comes to admire Fairfax as a model commander (and by implication magistrate); and H. F. operates under dire circumstances that render all social relations eccentric and strange: here the plague functions as one of those scenes of erasure that permit us to reimagine how a society could construct itself out of whole cloth. And though Roxana and Crusoe know their family background, they are foreigners: Roxana is the daughter of French Huguenots, and Crusoe the son of a German, Kreutznauer, born in Bremen.

Given Defoe's obsessions with money and commerce, it is also unsurprising that characters come to operate as public counters within a system of exchange, and if they accumulate value in the process of time it is not in psychological but in fiscal terms. Not only do the characters usually make money in the course of things, but they themselves also operate as monetary units that gain value merely by having circulated around the world the way goods were supposed to do in Defoe's mercantilism. Thus Captain Singleton begins badly, but well, by being sold as a baby. Roxana constantly makes money, but also becomes, crucially, a prince's "Idol," by which epithet she realizes how as a sexual creature she is using herself as a commodity. Of the prince, she says, "I had . . . perfectly engrossed him"; and she writes, "Thus far am I a standing Mark of the Weakness of Great Men, in their Vice . . . [for] they raise the Value of the Object which they pretend to pitch upon, by their Fancy." Here the term "Mark" conflates public and narrative signs with the public nature of currency, so that dressing up is an attempt to raise one's value in both economies. Similarly, Moll circulates both at home and in the colonies, which constantly increases her value. As for Colonel Jack and Robinson Crusoe, early investment in the colonies continues to increase their wealth even as their local fortunes fluctuate, and the narrative "end" is signaled by the return on those investments. In a less dramatic way this is also true of Captain Singleton, who places some of his spoils at the disposal of a gentleman who ensures that they earn interest. And because for Defoe London is the hub of commerce, London exercises a pull for all—except the cavalier, whose concerns are exclusively political.

Finally, how do the narratives prove political? We have seen that *Memoirs of a Cavalier* recommends a figure like Sir Thomas Fairfax, and it seems from other texts that Defoe favors a kind of benevolent patriarchy, which he carefully opposes to the tyranny he associates with late Caroline culture. To promote the values of such patriarchy, which would ensure a cooperative society, he also develops not only a language of contract but of gratitude and sentiment that will provide the means for understanding. The importance of contracts is reinforced by Defoe's emphasis on the graphic or writing: for example, Moll negotiates her marriage to her brother (as it transpires) by conducting a dialogue on a windowpane with his diamond ring, then on a sheet of paper. Her jeweler-landlord shows Roxana "a Contract in Writing" to engage her in marriage; and the genuineness of her bond to her last husband, the Dutch merchant, is proven by a mutual exchange of accounts. He brings to her boxes "full of Books, and Papers, and Parchments, *I mean*, Books of Accompts, and Writings"; she in turn produces proofs of her investments in real estate; and he seals his love for her by returning "all my Writings into my own Hands again."

We have already seen, in other narratives, how instrumental literacy is to the self's dealings with the world. If contracts are seen as graphic documents, one problem that emerges is anthropological: what constitutes a contract with nonliterate or preliterate societies? This is obviously of concern to Robinson, but it is of special interest in *Captain Singleton*, where the wanderings in Africa are not only the occasion for depiction of the exotic, but for testing the conditions under which the explorers can feel safe in their dealings with African tribes. Early on, the text reminds us of the Hobbesian postulate about the state of nature: after realizing that not all "Savages" are cannibals, Captain Singleton remarks however that they are "only civil for Fear." Captain Singleton himself becomes the contractual magistrate of his group, just as he remarks that another tribe is "brutish," using a term with an unmistakably Hobbesian ring. There is a fascination henceforth with the signs that either the party or the Africans make to indicate peaceful intentions: thus at one point, "one of our Company remember'd the Signal of Friendship which the Natives made us from the South Part of the Island, *viz.* of setting up a long Pole, and put us in Mind, that perhaps it was the same thing to them as a Flag of Truce was to us." Later, the party wounds and then heals a "royal" African prisoner, who swears an oath of loyalty to Captain Singleton by breaking an arrow in two and setting the point against his breast; and he subsequently becomes known as "the Black Prince." He in turn ensures that the natives voluntarily submit to enslavement by the Europeans, and it also becomes their task to convey the appropriate "Signal of Peace" to those other tribes whose dialects they do not know. In his career as a pirate, the question becomes for Captain Singleton whether he can trust the hoisting of the white flag, and in Ceylon he is betrayed, since "I thought all Nations in the World, even the most savage People, when they held out a Flag of Peace, kept the Offer of Peace made by that Signal, very sacredly." Thus Defoe reminds us of the necessity for some bonding fiction between peoples, but characteristically leaves the answer up in the air.

Defoe's social prescriptions are rendered perhaps more clearly than elsewhere in *A Journal of the Plague Year*, which in some ways is Defoe's most satisfying book. The general strategy is to ask us to imagine a circumstance in which ordinary human life comes to a standstill (a plague, which I think Defoe presents as a metaphor for the South Sea Bubble that had ruined thousands the year before Defoe's book appeared) and thus to reimagine the terms by which we bond to survive. Two features stand out. First, Defoe incorporates a long digression involving three men—John, Thomas, and Richard—who succeed in saving a group of refugees from the plague-stricken city by illegally leading them outside the city confines to Epping. The group does not survive, however, by communal effort alone, for it is forced ultimately to rely on the benevolence of a local magistrate. Defoe's polity is not as republican as it seems at first, but rather prescribes a benign magistrate of the kind Colonel Jack exemplifies by his benevolent treatment of his slaves in Virginia: the carrot substitutes for the stick, Whig for Tory hegemony.

Second, more clearly in this book than elsewhere, Defoe begins to sketch the possibilities for a kind of affective and sentimental means of knowing others. As the plague progresses, the space of the book is filled with gestures and cries, there being some experiences for which mere words are inadequate. And in circumstances that emphasize the special distress of suffering families, Defoe presents the possibility that a gestural and lachrymose rhetoric of the body may transcend language. In a key episode, H. F. visits Robert the Waterman, whose family is locked with the plague inside their house. Robert weeps as H. F. asks why he has abandoned them, to which Robert replies:

"I do not abandon them; I work for them as much as I am able; and blessed be the Lord, I keep them from want"; and with that I observed that he lifted up his eyes to heaven, with a countenance that presently told me I had happened on a man that was no hypocrite, but a serious, religious, good man.

One man struck with grief dies of a broken heart; another man's head literally sinks between his shoulders. This is hardly realism, any more than are similar moments in Smollett and Dickens; but it all amounts to a gestural and sentimental rhetoric that begins to cordon the family off from the larger concerns of the polity and anticipates the private and sentimental worlds of Sterne and *The Man of Feeling*.

Richard Kroll

Selected Bibliography

Backscheider, Paula R. *Daniel Defoe: His Life*. Baltimore: Johns Hopkins University Press, 1989.

Boardman, Michael M. *Defoe and the Uses of Narrative*. New Brunswick, N.J.: Rutgers University Press, 1983.

Brown, Homer O. "The Displaced Self in the Novels of Daniel Defoe." *English Literary History* 38 (1971): 562–90.

Hunter, J. Paul. *The Reluctant Pilgrim: Defoe's Emblematic Method and Quest for Form in "Robinson Crusoe."* Baltimore: Johns Hopkins University Press, 1966.

Kay, Carol. *Political Constructions: Defoe, Richardson, and Sterne in Relation to Hobbes, Hume, and Burke*. Ithaca, N.Y.: Cornell University Press, 1988.

McKillop, Alan Dugald. *Early Masters of English Fiction*. Lawrence: University of Kansas Press, 1956.

Novak, Maximillian E. *Economics and the Fiction of Daniel Defoe*. Berkeley: University of California Press, 1962.

Richetti, John J. *Daniel Defoe*. Boston: Twayne, 1987.

Sill, Geoffrey M. *Defoe and the Idea of Fiction, 1713–1719*. Newark: University of Delaware Press, 1983.

Starr, George A. *Defoe and Spiritual Autobiography*. Princeton, N.J.: Princeton University Press, 1965.

Sutherland, James. *Daniel Defoe: A Critical Study*. Cambridge: Harvard University Press, 1971.

Sex, Lies, and Invisibility: Amatory Fiction from the Restoration to Mid-Century

THE sensational tales of sexual intrigue published by and for English women in the late seventeenth and early eighteenth centuries were among the most widely read texts of their day, rivaling best-sellers like *Gulliver's Travels* and *Robinson Crusoe* in popularity. Today, however, these amatory fictions tend to be virtually invisible in traditional accounts of literary history, briefly noticed as primitive and inconsequential progenitors of "the" novel. While traditional historians may admit that the early realism of Defoe, Richardson, and Fielding shares some features with amatory narratives, they nevertheless consistently define the work of the canonical Augustan novelists according to how essentially different it is from that produced by their female contemporaries, how much of an improvement, how completely path-breaking. The very category "amatory fiction" functions in such schemes as a kind of negative space, insignificant except as it helps to define the privileged category "novel," from which it is always excluded.

Any new consideration of amatory fiction, then, must remain suspicious of that very category, which represents less a discrete species with definitive formal characteristics than a constellation of texts that may have little in common except their exclusion from received gender and genre hierarchies. Still, undertakings like this volume necessarily presuppose some sort of taxonomy, and the inclusion of these texts here is important enough to justify a certain amount of categorizing, so long as it is recognized as such. Moreover, despite formal diversity so considerable as to make their unity as a genre arguable, many amatory fictions do share certain thematic concerns, social functions, and historical positions. It is in terms of these common characteristics that they are discussed here.

The amatory fictions of the early eighteenth century were a mixed breed. Their ancestry goes back to the Italian *novelles*, to Cervantes (particularly his *Exemplary Novels*, translated by Mappe in 1640), and to French romances of the seventeenth century, especially the work of Gauthier de Costes de la Calprenède (1614–1663) and Madeleine de Scudéry (1607–1701). Perhaps the most important single influence was that of the *Portuguese Letters*, first translated into English by Sir Roger L'Estrange as *Five Letters from a Nun to a Cavalier* in 1677. After the prodigious success of this supposedly authentic set of letters from a lovesick nun to the man who has abandoned her, many authors, male and female, tried their hand at scandalous writing of various sorts.

But three women—Aphra Behn (c. 1640–1689), Delariviere Manley (c. 1670–1724) and Eliza Haywood (c. 1693–1756)—held undisputed preeminence during the eighteenth century as authors of scandalous fiction. Indeed, the work of this "fair Triumvirate" (as they were first called in 1732; Janet Todd calls them the "naughty triumvirate") was so well known that it was routinely equated by their contemporaries with subversive and transgressive female creativity itself, and for the rest of the century women writers struggled to live down the infamous trio's licentious personal and literary styles and to make female authorship more respectable. In an effort to understand "amatory fiction," then, we might do worse than to look closely at the works of these three authors, asking why they were so powerful in their time and why their power has been so problematic ever since.

"Love," Eliza Haywood explains in her *Reflections on the Various Effects of Love* (1726), "is . . . dangerous to the softer Sex; they cannot arm themselves too much against it, and for whatever Delights it affords to the Successful few, it pays a double Portion of Wretchedness to the numerous Unfortunate." The comment might be seen as epitomizing the assumptions of amatory fiction, where love almost always brings fleeting pleasure to self-centered, fickle men and lasting misery to the women who trust them. In amatory writing's most typical plot, an innocent young girl is seduced by an experienced, older man who promises her everlasting love but abandons her ruthlessly once his physical desires have been sated. Often the perfidious male is married already; usually he is of aristocratic birth; frequently he is the young woman's relative or guardian, a circumstance that makes his behavior even more shocking, puts her in a most defenseless and victimized position, and allows for titillating suggestions of incest.

That women trust men is, in these stories, both their greatest error and their unavoidable fate, since desirable young women must by definition be entirely naive about sexual matters. Like the culture that produced them, amatory works placed young women in a double bind: without sexual experience, they are the natural prey of more experienced male predators; with sexual experience, they are whores. A young woman in Augustan society, after all, could not actually experiment with the other sex and keep her good reputation, not even so far as to hold a private conversation, receive a letter, or be seen in a public place in the company of a man; she had very little means of discovering mysterious and dangerous male ways. But she could read amatory fiction and learn to avoid the fate of the women it depicted.

Warning the innocent is the stated purpose of many, though not all, writers of amatory fiction. The great exception is Aphra Behn, the first member of the "fair Triumvirate," whose stories are often virtually amoral, distributing rewards and punishments with very little reference to Christian, poetic, or even secular justice. In her *Love Letters Between a Nobleman and His Sister* (1684–1687), for instance, Behn narrates a series of illicit love affairs involving a small group of young people related by marriage or blood. She includes in a subplot the almost obligatory amatory narrative of seduced and abandoned female innocence, but concentrates most of her attention on the sexual exploits of persons of both sexes who are equally devoid of innocence and without moral scruple, characters with whom she clearly expects the reader to identify. Behn's heroine, Sylvia, still appalls undergraduates with her heartless, roaming sexual desire and her incapacity for guilt, faithfulness, or remorse. Predatory and mercenary, Sylvia always manages to get what she wants, and ends the novel as insouciant and sexually adventurous as she began it. Likewise in *The Fair Jilt* (1688), the unrestrained sexuality of the corrupt Miranda brings her love, wealth, title, and safety from the law; she is rewarded for years of criminal behavior and sexual aggression with a quiet life in the country and a doting husband. Behn's editor, Montagu Summers, notes with dismay how "sparingly and little" Miranda's culpable behaviors are punished, and how positively she is portrayed. Behn does include some criticism of Miranda (though, as

Summers notes, not much), but she is more interested in depicting Miranda's power than in warning (or convincing) female readers of their powerlessness.

Behn's eighteenth-century followers, however, found it necessary to appeal directly to an ethic of female instruction, and to ensure that evil characters were punished and correct moral lessons drawn. They worked within an increasingly moralistic culture, and their fictions were closely tied to bourgeois values. In Behn and Manley the ideal and most passionate sexual relationship is the extramarital affair, free from the blighting considerations of property; but in Haywood, chronologically the last of the three great Augustan writers of amatory fiction, monogamous marriages based on love and faithfulness become increasingly important denouements (though the action usually takes place in the period before marriage). It becomes typical for eighteenth-century amatory writing to go to great lengths to insist upon its moral and didactic purposes. Indeed, as in Defoe and Richardson, the action often stops dead while the author pauses to comment sententiously upon it. After narrating a particularly vivid tale of seduction and abandonment, one of Manley's narrators pauses to point out that the life of the unfortunate heroine after her abandonment was "one continu'd Scene of Horror, Sorrow, and Repentance"; she finally died "a true Landmark: to warn all believing Virgins from shipwracking their Honour upon (that dangerous Coast of Rocks) the Vows and pretended Passion of Mankind." Haywood's *The Perplex'd Dutchess; Or, Treachery Rewarded* (1727) portrays a female protagonist much like Miranda in Behn's *Fair Jilt*. But unlike Miranda, Haywood's Duchess is "tormented by guilt and fears" even in the midst of her ill-gotten successes, and ends her life "in the most forlorn, unfriended, and unpitied state; not all her Riches being able to procure her one Moment's ease from the Racks of a guilty Thought," while the virtuous married couple she attempts to defraud goes on to achieve political power and domestic bliss.

But while moralizing increasingly permeates these texts, the sexual exploits that provoke it are always represented with lingering delight. Indeed, the emphasis on sexuality is perhaps the most noticeable feature of amatory fiction. When in Behn's *The Dumb Virgin; Or, The Force of Imagination* (1698) the hero Dangerfield walks beneath the window of the beautiful Maria just as she is leaning out, the description of her *dishabille* is characteristic:

He saw her in all the heightning Circumstances of her Charms. . . . her Night-gown hanging loose, discover'd her charming Bosom . . . her Breasts with an easy Heaving, show'd the Smoothness of her Soul and of her Skin; their Motions were so languishingly soft, that they cou'd not be said to rise and fall, but rather to swell up towards Love, the Heat of which seem'd to melt them down again; some scatter'd jetty Hairs, which hung confus'dly over her Breasts, made her Bosom show like *Venus* caught in *Vulcan's* Net, but 'twas the Spectator, not she, was captivated.

In Haywood's *Love in Excess*, the innocent Melliora begs her guardian Count D'Elmont to leave her bedroom, where he has come uninvited. "What!" he replies, "when I have thee thus! Thus naked in my Arms, Trembling, Defenceless, Yeilding, Panting with equal Wishes?" And Manley's unnamed Duke, guardian to the lovely and innocent Charlot, sneaks into her room while she is "uncovered in a melancholy careless Posture," and proceeds to rape her:

She was going to rise; but he prevented her, by flying to her Arms, where, as we may call it, he nail'd her down to the Bed with Kisses; . . . whilst yet her Surprise made her doubtful of his Designs he took Advantage of her Confusion to accomplish 'em; neither her Prayers, Tears, nor Strugglings, could prevent him.

As these examples suggest, amatory novels are not squeamish about sexual matters, and they routinely connect sexuality to voyeurism, exploitation, and violence. Indeed, most critics of amatory fiction accurately mark its connection to today's so-called soft pornography. As in pornography, the language of lust in amatory fiction follows codes of male arousal: sexual excitement is created visually, and bodies, especially female bodies, are routinely fetishized, as in the description of Behn's Maria (who, significantly, is unable to speak) leaning out of her window. There are many scenes like the one in *Atalantis* between the Duke and Charlot, where predatory men sneak around to gaze on the near-naked bodies of unsuspecting, supine young women. When Haywood's Count D'Elmont gazes on his ward's vulnerable female body, that body is described in the slow detail typical of amatory fiction, detail obviously meant to arouse the reader as it does the desiring Count.

He beheld the Lovely Melliora in her Bed, and fast asleep, her Head was reclin'd on one of her Arms; a Pillow softer and whiter far than that it lean'd on, the other was stretch'd out, and with it's Extention had thrust down the Bed-Cloths so far, that all the Beauties of her Neck and Breast appear'd to view. He took an inexpressible Pleasure, in gazing on her as she lay.

Sometimes this familiar scene is reversed, and female intruders gaze hungrily at scantily clad men whose bodies seem arranged for consumption. Indeed, such representation of female sexual desire is a hallmark of amatory writing and distinguishes it from canonical realist novels.

> The Dutchess softly enter'd that *little Chamber* of *Repose*, the Weather violently hot the *Umbrelloes* were let down from behind the Windows, the Sashes open, and the Jessimine that cover'd 'em blew in with a gentle Fragrancy; ... and to compleat the Scene, the young *Germanicus* in a dress and posture not very decent to describe ... newly risen from the *Bath*, and in a loose Gown ... he had thrown himself upon the Bed, pretending to Sleep, with nothing on but his Shirt and Night-Gown, which he had so indecently dispos'd, that slumbring as he appear'd, his whole Person stood confess'd to the Eyes of the Amorous Dutchess. (Manley, *New Atalantis*.)

But if amatory fiction can be credited with representing female desire, often that desire takes the form of an inversion of masculine appetite as it was constructed by Augustan imaginations. Here the Duchess eyes Germanicus with precisely the sort of appropriating, lascivious gaze that men normally use on women in amatory fiction. But her looking becomes an unconscious parody of the controlling, sexual gaze of male characters rather than a challenge to it. The reader is invited to snicker along with Germanicus, who is not really the unwitting object of the Duchess's gaze at all (as Melliora really is for Count D'Elmont in *Love in Excess*). On the contrary, he is secretly awake throughout the scene, and has staged his own "seduction" in league with his male friend Fortunatus, the Duchess's sated lover, who waits to burst in and accuse the Duchess of infidelity. Furthermore, the Duchess thinks that the man she is gazing on is Fortunatus, with whom she had arranged a rendezvous. At a crucial moment in their lovemaking when she might have clearly seen Germanicus's face, she closes her eyes in ecstasy, and so "her own Desires help'd the Deceit." While on the surface it recognizes the Duchess's desire, the Germanicus episode in fact denies it most emphatically by suggesting that female desire is at best only a somewhat comic, easily manipulated and collusive version of male desire. Male desire remains the primary agent in the scene: men still define and dictate sexuality, and women are still denied authentic, alternative sexual desire. The Duchess de l'Inconstant is a pawn in the familiar game of male sexual control as surely as if she were herself reclining on the bed.

Behn's Miranda, far more in control when she turns her boldly sexual gaze on a handsome young priest, is perhaps a more promising representation of female desire.

She gaz'd upon him, while he bow'd before her, and waited for her Charity, till she perceiv'd the lovely Friar to blush, and cast his Eyes to the Ground. . . . At last she . . . gave him a Pistole; but with so much Deliberation and Leisure, as easily betray'd the Satisfaction she took in looking on him. (*The Fair Jilt*)

But here too, female desire is undercut in the act of being imagined. To show a woman wanting a man, Behn reverses traditional positions and roles, making Miranda the aggressor and the priest the shrinking object of lust, but keeping intact the assumption that desire manifests itself as mastery. After staring the priest down, Miranda goes on to replicate the typical actions of a man bent on sexual conquest: she dreams of the young friar naked in bed, then tricks him into a private interview (in the confessional, no less) where she addresses him in the codified language of the male seducer: she calls him her "cruel Charmer," begs for his "Pity," and holds him by his clothes when he attempts to flee. Angered at the priest's resistance, Miranda even issues the ultimate threat a man could make to a woman in Augustan times: "I will either force you to abandon that dull Dissimulation, or you shall die, to prove your Sanctity real. . . . I will ruin thee, [and] take away your Life and Honour." As the scene lurches toward its parodic climax, Behn reverses every cliché of female and male sexual roles:

The trembling young Man . . . demanded what she would have him do? When she reply'd— . . . Come to my Arms, my trembling, longing Arms. . . . At these Words she rose from his Feet, and snatching him in her Arms, he could not defend himself from receiving a thousand Kisses from the lovely Mouth of the charming Wanton.

"I own your Power," the still-resisting priest gasps. His ordeal ends when Miranda, unable actually to rape him, accuses *him* of rape instead. The other priests, hurrying to rescue her, "found *Miranda* and the good Father very indecently struggling; which they mis-interpreted, as *Miranda* desir'd." The hapless young priest is arrested and spends many years in prison, while Miranda, as we have seen, comes to a comfortable end.

Behn's reversal of genders, though it lends comedy and exposes stereotypes, does little to revise the system of sexual force that amatory fictions continue to uphold, a system that most often worked, in fiction as in practice, to enhance male prerogatives and reinforce women's comparative powerlessness. Undoubtedly, in Miranda's upside-down rape of the priest, Behn is laughing at the expense of the patriarchal love-as-rape scenarios that permeated her culture's art and social relations, scenarios that invariably represented men as lustful brutes and women as sexual prey. But Behn also makes ridiculous her sexually powerful woman—a rapist without a penis who must finally attribute to her intended victim the violent act she threatens, achieving victory only by reassuming the typical posture of cringing female. Of course, Miranda's deliberate assumption of the role of sexual victim is itself a paradoxically powerful move, a strategy that beats patriarchy, as it were, at its own game; and certainly the mere representation of a powerful woman exercising sexual desire is extraordinarily subversive (enough so, perhaps, to contribute to the continued exclusion of *The Fair Jilt* from the canons of eighteenth-century literature). But along with the potentially empowering aspects of amatory fiction's scenes of female lust, there are also disturbing assumptions at work. Amatory fiction's women actively desire, often initiate, and thoroughly enjoy heterosexual sex; but they consistently define and act out their desire according to the force-oriented ethic of the Augustan rake. Within such a framework, representations of female sexuality fail to exemplify a positively or uniquely female form of sexual desire, though they do succeed in creating a space for such representation. Even the most transgressive scenes, then, function in contradictory ways, at once revolutionary and conventional: they show women exercising sexual desire, and at the same time bolster phallocentric patterns of sexual dominance.

The co-optation of female sexuality by established sex-as-force systems points to the pervasive masculinist orientation at work in these texts written by and for women, an orientation also signaled by the repeated use of misogynist truisms. "'Tis the Humour of our Sex," Behn announces in a female voice, "to deny most eagerly those Grants to Lovers, for which most tenderly we sigh."

So contradictory are we to our selves, as if the Deity had made us with a seeming Reluctancy to his own Designs; placing as much Discords in our Minds, as there is Harmony in our Faces. We are a sort of aiery Clouds, whose Lightning flash out one way, and the Thunder another. Our Words and Thoughts can ne'er agree.

Likewise, Manley's female narrator pauses to counsel the Duke when he is wondering whether to "possess" Charlot right away or "permit her time to know and set a value upon what she granted." "*One ought never*," the narrator remarks, "*allow 'em* [women] *time to Think, their vivacity being prodigious, and their forsight exceeding short, and limited; the first hurry of their Passions, if they are but vigorously follow'd, is what is generally most favourable to Lovers.*" Not that giving Charlot a chance to think would much jeopardize the Duke's chances. After all, as we learn later in *Atalantis*, "when once a young Maid pretends to put her self upon the same Foot with a Lover at Argument, she is sure to be cast." And when in *Love in Excess* a man sees his girlfriend flirting with another man, Haywood genders his jealous feelings to the detriment of women: "Envy, and a sort of Womanish Spleen transported him," she informs us. Behn even goes so far as to unite her disparagement of her own sex with denigration of the genre she works in. "Women enjoy'd," she remarks in *The Unfortunate Bride; Or, The Blind Lady a Beauty* (1698), "are like Romances read . . . meer Tricks of the slight of Hand, which, when found out, you only wonder at your selves for wondering so before at them." Like its presentation of female desire as a faint replica of male desire, amatory fiction's repeated—indeed, excessive—reference to misogynist stereotypes signals its fundamental implication in androcentric codes that work to mitigate the threat of female subjectivity and sexuality.

This is not to say that the many representations of women's desire offered in these texts have no subversive power. On the contrary, no appraisal of the sexual force of amatory fiction can afford to leave out its tremendous potential for subversion. Merely by assuming a position as subject (both the central subject of the narrative and the possessor of active sexual subjectivity), even if that position is ironized, amatory fiction's desiring women threaten traditional male prerogatives based on female subjugation and objectification, and provide space for readers to imagine something new. It is important to remember that the facet of eighteenth-century prose fiction that is considered most revolutionary by critics as different as McKeon and Armstrong—its habit of making ordinary women of central importance—originated not in Richardson (as is often taught), but in amatory fiction. Furthermore, the bald statement of misogynist truisms, disturbing as it is, sometimes has a comic ring. Occasionally such stuff is presented in italics (as in the quotation from Manley above); despite the notoriously unsystematic way some

Augustan writers and printers used italic type, it is possible that in some cases this may suggest more self-consciousness and control than critics generally grant these writers—perhaps even a sense of humor. But caution is also required. Insofar as these texts do not themselves succeed in representing a uniquely female sexual desire, their representations of women as desiring subjects may be less an expression of new, boldly female sensibilities than a repackaging for women of the usual male-oriented social and intimate arrangements.

In this sense, Augustan amatory fictions are the direct ancestors of modern supermarket romances with their lurid, fetishistic covers, their sexually demanding men and innocent, desirable, passive women, and their insistence that sexual violence, correctly interpreted, reveals or engenders love. Indeed, without mitigating the immense cultural and historical distance between Augustan England and the contemporary United States, we can trace a distinct line of inheritance from Augustan amatory fiction to today's semipornographic mass-market romances. Recent work on the ideological functions of modern pulp reading, especially the work of Janice Radway, illuminates by implication the cultural work of Augustan England's amatory fictions and demonstrates the continuing power of the past in the present.

A latter-day variant of amatory fiction, Harlequin romances are written especially for female consumption, offering sex and love in arousing, but usually not graphic, packages. They inspire obsessive reading, and are considered by readers and critics alike to be low, throw-away forms of writing, requiring of their audience little sophistication or application. Readers of Harlequin-type romances read in order to replicate predictable sensations and reaffirm cherished assumptions. So these romances seldom challenge dominant ideologies; they work instead to shore up traditional social positions (woman as the object of sexual desire, man as its subject) and expectations (heterosexual monogamy; female devotion to children). Although readers often use these texts as a means of escape and sometimes even of resistance, their participation draws them ever more tightly into the ideological web of male privilege and female subordination. Readers read obsessively because the books manage to promise a space for female protest and desire while never quite providing it; they whet, but never satisfy, both the reader's sexual appetite and her appetite for socially transgressive autonomy. Amatory fictions work the same way; as Richetti observes, they tend more often to "flatter and exploit" than to "challenge or rede-fine" readers' assumptions.

Like the Harlequins and other forms of romance, amatory fictions tend to repeat a limited number of characteristic topoi (obsessively recurrent formulas, assumptions, or ideas). Among the most frequent-ly encountered of these is the idea that love is an irresistible force: lovers are its victims, and escape is impossible. "Almighty Love," intones a fallen woman in Haywood's *British Recluse* (1722), "despises all Con-troul." "You know, Sir," young Felisinda explains to her father in Hay-wood's *Force of Nature*, "that our Passions are not the effect of *Will*, but *Fate*." In Behn's *The Nun; Or, The Perjur'd Beauty* (1697), a young man who finds himself desiring the woman his best friend loves cries out "I could wish I did not love you, *Ardelia*! But that were impossible!" As early as 1709, this topos was so familiar that Manley could attack it head-on:

Are there such violent Desires that Reason cannot suppress? Is Love such an irresistable Tyrant? Will he trample upon all Obstacles? Are the most sacred ties of no obligation in his Sense? O no! for if it were but *true Love*, 'twould seek the good of the Person belov'd.

Also frequently invoked in amatory tales is the notion that men are inherently changeable (either insincere to begin with or honestly inca-pable of keeping their many vows of faithfulness), while women are naturally more trusting and trustworthy. "Without dispute," Behn declares, "Women are by Nature more Constant and Just, than Men, and did not their first Lovers teach them the trick of Change, they would be *Doves*, that would never quit their Mate." Men adore women until women succumb sexually; then men begin to cool off, just as women really fall in love. "The same unaccountable thing that cools the Swain," Manley remarks toward the end of the first volume of *Atalan-tis*, "more warms the Nymph: Enjoyment (the death of Love in all Mankind) gives Birth to new Fondness, and doating Extasies in the Women; they begin later, withheld by Modesty, and by a very ill tim'd Oeconomy, take up their Fondness exactly where their Lover leaves it." Women continue pathetically to love forever, despite male faithfulness and even abuse. Alovisa, for example, in Haywood's *Love in Excess*, resists the importunities of a hopeful lover even though her husband is openly unfaithful and unkind. "I Love my Husband still," she cries, "with an unbated Fondness, doat upon him! faithless and cruel as he is, he still is lovely!"

Always, amatory narrators pause over protracted physical and verbal struggles between desiring men and resisting women. Women resist, but faintly; they are implicated in the force men universally use over them. Moreover, women's struggles to escape male advances actually make them more vulnerable in the intimate combat that will inevitably end in male victory, for female resistance always heightens male desire. In this representative passage from Haywood's *British Recluse*, several of these topoi figure at once:

My Hands were the first Victims of his fiery Pressures, then my Lips, my Neck, my Breast; and perceiving that, quite lost in Ecstasy, I but faintly resisted what he did, far greater Boldnesses ensued—My Soul dissolv'd, its Faculties o'er-power'd—and Reason, Pride, and Shame, and Fear, and every Foe to soft Desire, charm'd to Forgetfulness, my trembling Limbs refus'd to oppose the lovely Tyrant's Will! And, if my faultering Tongue entreated him to desist, or my weak Hands attempted to repulse the encroaching Liberty of his; it serv'd but, as he said, the more to inflame his Wishes.

That this description is placed into the mouth of a woman who will shortly become yet another sexual victim and whose life is blighted by the event, suggests the degree to which the repeated topoi of amatory fiction anesthetized readers to its misogynist assumptions, and implicated them in the patterns of an androcentric universe.

It is a truism of amatory fiction that intelligence ("wit") is antithetical to that all-important female attribute, beauty; the two cannot coexist in one woman. Behn points directly to this convention in *The Dumb Virgin*, where she creates two sisters, one merely beautiful and the other merely witty, who seem to the man who wants them both to be the separate halves of one supremely desirable woman. Love is typically reduced to sexual desire, and sex itself to acts of force often indistinguishable from rape. Indeed, sex that is not violent is worth remarking: the Duke's passion for Charlot in *New Atalantis* is extraordinary because "to heighten it, resistance was not at all necessary." Sexual compulsion always serves to awaken desire in female characters. The central, abiding, and most sacred relationships, except in anomalous works like Haywood's *British Recluse*, are neither heterosexual liaisons nor relationships between women, but friendships between men.

Even such a brief catalog of the recurrent topoi of amatory fiction reveals that this writing is built around assumptions that undermine, to varying extents, the ostensible effort to represent female subjectivity. What function could such negative formulae serve for amatory fiction's readers, most of whom were women, that would keep them endlessly coming back for more? Recent work in history and literary theory, as well as recent critical studies of the works themselves, suggest several explanations for the fascination of Augustan society, and particularly of its women, with amatory fiction. These are proffered here, in highly abbreviated form, to indicate the status of current efforts to understand the function of amatory fiction in Augustan England.

We might begin by considering the double function we have already seen these works performing—both informational and sensual. Behn, Manley, Haywood, and their peers were writing for women increasingly cut off from the world outside the domestic circle. That world was, they knew, full of traps laid especially for them; even the smallest error could result in permanent social alienation. Under these circumstances, amatory fiction provided Augustan women with a sense of involvement in the outside world—which, for all its dangers and disappointments, had great advantages over restrictive domesticity—while allowing them to maintain a safe distance from it. Countless innocent heroines go pathetically to their ruin like so many lambs to the slaughter, without the benefit of amatory fiction to guide them; but readers were invited to take a stance Richetti describes as "sadly wiser but deeply sympathetic," to assume a pleasantly unfamiliar posture of worldly wisdom and experience vis-à-vis characters they could identify with but still feel superior toward. This sense of controlled danger must have combined with the exotic eventfulness of the plots and the representation of sexual thrills that many readers would have been unlikely to experience in marriage to make these works supremely attractive, especially to the ladies and would-be ladies who voraciously consumed them.

Amatory works encouraged the notion that to read them was to engage in a rebellious, scandalous activity parallel to the sexual explorations their heroines (but not their readers) were constantly engaged in. They routinely depict romance reading and novel reading as dangerous for women, inevitably connected to (and sometimes even conflated with) sexual experience. When Manley's Duke prepares to seduce Charlot, he gives her salacious reading material first. "By this dangerous reading, he pretended to shew her, that there were Pleasures her Sex were born for, and which she might consequently long to taste!"

Like Charlot, Augustan women picking up *Love in Excess* or *The New Atalantis* must have felt that they were tasting forbidden fruit.

Another reason for the great popularity of amatory fictions may have been their ability to represent peculiarly female negotiations of shifts occurring in the early eighteenth-century English economy, a man's world becoming newly oriented toward trade, commerce, capital, and profit. Under these conditions, it is perhaps not surprising, as Williamson observes, that amatory fiction's men are predatory and selfish, its women always on the defensive and fearful of abandonment. Furthermore, amatory writing catered to popular interest in the decadent lives of the rich and famous, and presented female heroines as what Beasley calls "the formal representation of an ideal of order, set against . . . power-mongering, lasciviousness, and corruption." In this analysis, amatory fiction served important political functions, building self-consciousness and solidarity among its female readers.

There is yet another argument for the enormous popularity of Augustan amatory fiction, one that also demonstrates the seldom-noted participation of these works in their culture's most pressing public debates. It is neither accidental nor simply predictable that amatory fiction's most common plots are plots of seduction and betrayal, that it so obsessively represents false oaths, failed promises, and broken vows. The compulsiveness with which vows are made and broken in these works demonstrates more than the ostensible lesson that women should not trust men's promises; it goes to the heart of Augustan questions about the status of personal honor and the authority of words in a world where sacred vows to God and king recently had been rendered negotiable and contingent.

The problem of broken vows constituted a significant and prolonged crisis in English culture at the end of the seventeenth century. Before this period, the fact that someone made a statement on oath was understood to guarantee the truth of the statement; the act of taking a vow itself unquestionably guaranteed the fulfillment of a promise. But this understanding of the nature of oaths gave way during the seventeenth century to a new idea satirized in Butler's *Hudibras* (1663): "Oaths are but words, and words but wind, / Too feeble implements to bind." Words were no longer entities with real-life authority and causal functions; oaths and vows, which once had assured performance, were no longer trustworthy. Furthermore, the dissonance between old and new notions concerning the efficacy of oaths could be exploited by those most ready to deploy the new nominalism against the old idealism. "Oaths," as Susan Staves notes, "were regarded as political weapons" at the end of the century.

Shifts in the understanding of the meaning of oaths extended to private relations of trust, including sexual relations and marriage. In the seventeenth century, a promise of marriage was binding, and failure on the part of one of the pair subsequently to marry was grounds for legal action. But amatory fiction depicts a new universe, where a woman who trusts the promises of her suitor does so at her own risk, and earns as much scorn as pity when she finds herself abandoned. Even marriage vows were subject to the new provisionality. It is no coincidence that the first parliamentary divorce was granted in 1698.

The events of the Glorious Revolution constituted what Staves calls "the most dramatic Restoration crisis of conscience over oath-taking," and provided the immediate context of the obsessive concerns of amatory fiction. A short review of those events may be in order. In 1688, England's unpopular Roman Catholic king, James II, the legitimate but controversial heir, fled to France in fear of his life, wrongly believing that his Protestant daughter Mary and her husband William of Orange were advancing with a large army to force him from his throne. By fleeing, James was ousted (or ousted himself) as effectively as if civil war had taken place, and many Englishmen congratulated themselves on the achievement of what came to be known as the "Glorious (because bloodless) Revolution."

Bloodless though the revolution may have been, the very significant changes it wrought did not come about without struggle. William and Mary took immediate measures to ensure that subjects would cooperate with the new regime, whatever their private thoughts about its legitimacy. New oaths of allegiance were drawn up, and penalties for those who balked were severe. Still there was considerable resistance, especially at first, and many English subjects continued well into the eighteenth century to feel the force of their former oaths of allegiance to King James. James's presence on the Continent was a source of anxiety to English governments for decades, and his supporters ("Jacobites") attempted more than once forcibly to restore his heirs to the throne. Eventually, though, the fact of possession, the reluctance of the nation to go to war for a tyrannical Catholic king who had deserted his throne, the increasing military and commercial success of Augustan England (interpreted by some as God's blessing on the revolution), and the simple passage of time all worked together to smooth over the explosive possibilities of 1689. The succession continued to be granted to Protestants, even though James's son and grandsons survived until 1788. Doubt about the legitimacy of the changes effected by the Glorious Revolution or about the positions of subjects who had broken vows for purposes of expediency became something one did not openly express. Yet such doubts persisted, often in somewhat disguised forms.

One place where they surfaced with regularity was in amatory fiction's obsessive representation of broken vows. The usual vow-breaker in amatory fiction is the male seducer; but amatory fiction is also concerned with bigamy (a favorite theme of Manley, who was herself the victim of a bigamous husband), adultery, and lovers who are unfaithful to personal codes of honor (Philander in Behn's *Love Letters*; Mosco in Manley's *New Atalantis*). The representation of broken oaths links amatory fiction to wider crises of cultural conscience and political process in Augustan England.

For instance, Behn's *History of the Nun; Or, The Fair Vow-Breaker* (1689) turns on the problem of broken vows, conflating a familiar amatory fable with a political warning in the immediate context of the Glorious Revolution. In Behn's version of the tale, the intelligent and beautiful young Isabella turns down an offer of marriage from a young man named Villenoys in favor of taking holy orders. She becomes a nun; he goes off to war. While in the monastery, however, Isabella—to her own horror—falls helplessly in love with Henault, her closest friend's brother. She struggles greatly with her passion, mortifying herself in various ways. Henault, meanwhile, is troubled by his irresistible desire for a nun, a desire that he knows amounts to "Sacrilege."

Eventually the two run off together, despite Isabella's vows. But once they leave the monastery, things begin to go badly. They are poor; Isabella becomes pregnant. At last, Henault reluctantly accedes to his father's demands, leaving Isabella behind to campaign with the army. He joins Villenoys's regiment, and they become close friends. The war itself is given characteristically short shrift. "It is not my business to relate the History of the War," the narrator says; we learn only that "they acted very Noble" and that in one battle Henault falls. Isabella grieves extravagantly when she receives official news of his death. Though much courted, she turns down all suitors. But when Villenoys arrives, she has again fallen into poverty. She decides out of "interest" to favor Villenoys's suit after an extended period of mourning.

Five years after what turns out to be a loving and comfortable marriage, Villenoys decides to go away overnight. That night a visitor calls on Isabella. It is, of course, Henault, who did not die after all but has been doing slave labor all these years. Terrified of the charge of adultery (and noticing that Henault is poor) Isabella sneaks into the guest room and smothers him. Only then does she feel love for him again. When Villenoys returns, Isabella is tormented by a sense of guilty innocence: "She fell on her knees, and cry'd, 'Oh! you can never Pardon me, if I should tell you, and yet, alas! I am innocent of Ill!'" She tells Villenoys that Henault died naturally in his sleep. They decide to put the body in a sack and throw it in the river. But while Villenoys is waiting for her to sew the sack closed, Isabella deliberately stitches it to his coat. When he throws the sack into the river, he goes along with it and is drowned. No one suspects Isabella until a traveler who had been a slave with Henault exposes her as "the Murderess of two Husbands (both belov'd) in one Night." While awaiting execution, she spends her time exhorting others "never to break a Vow." Even on the scaffold she makes a speech "of half an Hour long," the burden of which is "a warning to the *Vow-Breakers*."

In Behn's representation, Isabella's decision to break her nun's vows and run off with Henault is to blame for all the macabre events that ensue. Yet Isabella is powerless *not* to break her vows. "She had try'd all that was possible in Human Strength to perform," the narrator informs us when as a young nun Isabella is struggling with her desire for Henault.

She had try'd Fasting long, Praying fervently, rigid Penances and Pains, severe Disciplines, all the Mortification, almost to the destruction of Life it self, to conquer the unruly Flame; but still it burnt and rag'd but the more; so, at last, she was forc'd to permit that to conquer her, she could not conquer, and submitted to her Fate, as a thing destin'd her by Heaven . . . and this being her real Belief, she the more patiently gave way to all the Thoughts that pleas'd her.

Like other resisting-yet-desiring maidens in amatory fiction, Isabella is "forc'd to permit" just what she most wants. Behn is careful not to present Isabella's submission as mere self-delusion, a simple capitulation to her own desires; the point is that she is really being compelled, she honestly resists. Helpless against "Fate," she is nevertheless guilty, too.

Never break a vow, Behn's story warns a vow-breaking society. In 1689, such a moral could not have been more appropriately placed than in a tale where vows are impossible to keep. Henault, like King James, is apparently gone forever; but really the first husband remains alive, and comes back to expose his wife's unintentional perfidy (as well as her continued love). The story represents sympathetically the moral and religious uncertainty many were experiencing in the context of the Glorious Revolution, the sense of being without choice but nevertheless at fault. One critic has called Behn's attention to vow-breaking "a mere excuse for a romantic and improbable tale," thus reinforcing the traditional view of amatory fiction as irrelevant rubbish. But on the contrary, *The History of the Nun* is as political as it is "romantic." As Ann Messenger observes, "although the sexual passion of a French nun may seem far removed from the turmoil of England's government in 1688, the issue of broken loyalty unites them." Behn's conflation of politics and sexual relations gives the lie to traditional distinctions between public and private concerns, male and female experience, amatory and realistic fiction. Without being any less sensational, melodramatic and bizarre, her story is at the same time a political parable of the Glorious Revolution in an anxious contemporary voice.

The obsession with broken vows epitomized in Behn's *History of the Nun* is related to another source of amatory fiction's extraordinary power: its persistent representation of agency (and therefore, responsibility) as complex and shifting, never finally assignable. Like the matter of broken vows, the problem of political agency was enormously troubling at and after the Glorious Revolution. Who, many wondered, was responsible for what had happened? Was it God's will that James lost the throne, or was it the tragic result of the king's own error, or of his subjects' disobedience? Was James's flight an act of abdication, or was his replacement a treasonous usurpation? Amatory fiction places questions of agency in a sexual context, participating in feminized guise in the central political issues of its day, issues that continued to haunt British consciences until at least the 1740s when the last organized Jacobite uprising took place.

As we have seen, sexual relations are most often figured in these texts as relations of force and deceit; rape is the central paradigm for sexual experience. Yet these writers almost always include complicating factors that mitigate the helplessness of victims (i.e., women), making them complicit in their own undoings. When Manley relates a story involving a young woman named Louisa and her bigamous seducer, she is careful to insist that Louisa herself must be held partially responsible for her own downfall: "*Louisa* had no very strong Head; his superficial Reasons might quickly take place, especially when they were seconded by Inclination: Unknown to her self she lov'd him, else all his Attempts would have been insignificant." At the same time, Louisa's responsibility is oddly denied, too. After all, she can't help it that she has "no very strong Head," and her love for her seducer is "unknown'd to her self." Manley's formulation is typically dissonant, but need not be dismissed as merely contradictory or slapdash. Instead, it may indicate how complex a subject seduction was for Augustan writers. Unable to decide whether they had been conquered or liberated in 1689, disturbingly aware that abdication and usurpation had become indistinguishable, Augustan writers expose as interested and false the traditional habit of distinguishing seduction from rape according to definitive assignments of agency.

This complex attitude toward agency is epitomized in Haywood's *Love in Excess*, the eighteenth century's best-selling work of amatory fiction. When Haywood's Melliora finds herself solicited by her guardian, Count D'Elmont, she is disturbed to find that although she feels powerless and afraid, and does all she can to resist his advances (going so far as to plug up the keyholes to her room and eventually entering a monastery to escape), she nevertheless enjoys D'Elmont's attentions and inwardly returns his desire. In this difficult situation, Melliora "carry'd with her a World of troubled Meditations . . . but when she Reflected how dear that Person she had so much cause to fear, was to her, she thought her self, at once the most unfortunate and most Guilty of her Sex." Melliora is the paradigm of the besieged maiden in amatory fiction, a maiden who, for all her innocence, victimization and passivity, is yet a "guilty" party. Even when she is held down on her bed and physically overpowered by D'Elmont, her own desire is cast as partially responsible for the event. For on the fateful night when the count has crept into her room to gaze on her asleep, she is already, unfortunately, dreaming about him. Just as D'Elmont begins to have second thoughts about taking advantage of her, Melliora undoes herself by talking in her sleep.

The resistless posture he beheld her in, rouz'd all that was Honourable in him, he thought it pity even to wake her, but more to wrong such Innocence, and he was sometimes Prompted to return and leave her as he found her. . . . He, stooping to the Bed, and gently laying his Face close to her's, (Possibly Designing no more than to steal a Kiss from her, unperceiv'd) that Action,

Concurring at that Instant, with her Dream, made her throw her Arm (still Slumbering) about his Neck, and in a Soft and Languishing Voice, Cry out, O! D'Elmont Cease, cease to Charm, to such a height—Life cannot bear these Raptures!—And then again, Embracing him yet closer—O! too, too Lovely Count—Extatick Ruiner!

"If he had now left her," the narrator remarks dryly, "some might have applauded an Honour so uncommon; but more wou'd have Condemn'd his Stupidity." The near-rape that follows takes place in this complicated setting. Melliora is desiring, but still innocent (since she is asleep); D'Elmont is aggressive, but responsive as well. Haywood carefully shifts the burden of intention and responsibility for sexual violence, making rape itself less a separate category than an extreme case of (mutual) seduction, and destabilizing the positions of seducer and seduced.

As this example indicates, representations of rape and seduction are often hard to tell apart in amatory fiction; the crucial question of agency is difficult to resolve. By making rape and seduction versions of each other, amatory fiction challenges the agency-based distinction usually drawn between the two, demonstrating that choice and intention are always themselves constrained, overdetermined, and diffuse. But characteristically, the challenge operates to double purpose. By suggesting that all seductions are forms of rape, amatory fiction exposes the patriarchal strategy of making the victim guilty by proving that she was "really" seduced rather than raped; but by suggesting that all rapes are varieties of seduction, amatory fiction abets the familiar process of male exoneration, whereby victims are cast as complicit actors. Like its persistent interest in the guilt of vow-breakers helpless to keep their vows, amatory fiction's complex representations of seduction-as-rape and its refusal definitively to assign positions of aggressor and victim in seduction-rape scenarios constitute significant instances of Augustan society's efforts to interpret its own history.

Despite great popularity and relevance in their day, amatory fictions are now held in contempt. However interesting these texts may be as part of the Augustan cultural landscape, most critics still feel that they are simply not very good literature; their present value seems to be mainly that of rather embarrassing curiosities, "justly neglected" (as John Richetti puts it) except by "the most thorough of specialists or dedicated of graduate students." But there are exceptions to this rule. Most prominent among those who have recently championed amatory fiction as serious literature is Ros Ballaster, who has written the only full-length study of the genre. Ballaster's important book joins a growing body of revisionist studies that suggest new ways to approach the question of value. Rather than denigrate (or praise) amatory fictions wholesale, critics might better ask why we define "good" literature as we do, how our assumptions about literary value still work to valorize some voices and exclude others, and how our capacities for pleasure might be augmented by respectful engagement with works we have been trained to resist or dismiss.

And as I have tried to suggest here, amatory fiction remains largely invisible for reasons other than its supposed poor quality. These texts are difficult to focus on because they seem to mar the picture: they fail to affirm traditionally valued purposes and strategies for reading, and they defy critical paradigms for realism. The brainchildren of sexually infamous and socially marginal women, they insistently represent a world where women's experiences of sexual power are central, and where such experiences conflate unexpectedly with political issues in the public world. They are obsessed with a limited number of recurrent ideas, especially with broken vows and with disturbing sexual relations in which seduction often looks a lot like rape, choice like constraint, and coercion like complicity.

But it may be precisely because of their traditionally defined liabilities that Augustan amatory fictions are in fact crucial to literary history now. Amatory fictions powerfully formulate acute Augustan social dilemmas, and expose assumptions and equivocations that later centuries have continued to hold dear. Behn, Manley, Haywood, and their peers re-present public issues of authority and accountability as issues of gendered power relations, making problematic the assumption that political relations and intimate relations are essentially different. They represent sexual contracts, subject as they are to interpretation and change, not as a special case but as the epitome of contract itself. They make explicit the difficulty of distinguishing complicity and force, whether in political or sexual relations, and so expose myths of definitive agency and accountability.

Positioned as they are at the fringes of respectable discourse and at the beginning of the century that laid the foundations of long-standing political and domestic structures, amatory fictions demonstrate the historical fabrication of authority systems that have come to seem eternal and inevitable. Their challenges are not radical, programmatic, or sustained; they tend to capitulate to existing power arrangements. Yet intimations of resistance remain latent in acts of collusion. Defying codes for literary and moral respectability, amatory fictions invite us to turn a critical eye on our tendency to organize experience according to exclusionary categories. They offer us a chance to imagine alternatives to the rigid roles of victim and oppressor, and to understand history—social or literary—not as a process of competitively "rising" and "falling" groups or genres, but as a narrative of reciprocal pleasures, shared anxieties, and promiscuously mingling bodies and voices.

Toni O'Shaughnessy Bowers

Selected Bibliography

Armstrong, Nancy. *Desire and Domestic Fiction: A Political History of the Novel.* New York: Oxford University Press, 1987.

Ballaster, Ros. *Seductive Forms: Women's Amatory Fiction from 1684 to 1740.* Oxford: Clarendon, 1992.

Beasley, Jerry C. "Politics and Moral Idealism: The Achievement of Some Early Women Novelists." In Mary Anne Schofield and Cecilia Macheski, eds., *Fetter'd or Free? British Women Novelists, 1670–1815.* Athens: Ohio University Press, 1986.

Langbauer, Laurie. *Women and Romance: The Consolations of Gender in the English Novel.* Ithaca, N.Y.: Cornell University Press, 1990.

McKeon, Michael. *The Origins of the English Novel 1600–1740.* Baltimore: Johns Hopkins University Press, 1987.

Messenger, Ann. *His and Hers: Essays in Restoration and Eighteenth-Century Literature.* Lexington: University Press of Kentucky, 1986.

Perry, Ruth. *Women, Letters, and the Novel.* New York: AMS Press, 1980.

Radway, Janice A. *Reading the Romance: Women, Patriarchy, and Popular Literature.* Chapel Hill: University of North Carolina Press, 1984.

Richetti, John J. *Popular Fiction before Richardson: Narrative Patterns 1700–1739.* Oxford: Clarendon, 1969, 1992.

Schofield, Mary Anne. *Masking and Unmasking the Female Mind: Disguising Romances in Feminine Fiction, 1713–1799.* Newark: University of Delaware Press, 1990.

Schofield, Mary Anne. *Quiet Rebellion: The Fictional Heroines of Eliza Fowler Haywood.* Washington, D.C.: University Press of America, 1982.

Spencer, Jane. *The Rise of the Woman Novelist from Aphra Behn to Jane Austen.* New York: Blackwell, 1986.

Spender, Dale. *Mothers of the Novel: 100 Good Women Writers Before Jane Austen*. New York: Pandora, 1986.

Staves, Susan. *Players' Scepters: Fictions of Authority in the Restoration*. Lincoln: University of Nebraska Press, 1979.

Todd, Janet. *The Sign of Angellica: Women, Writing, and Fiction 1660–1800*. London: Virago, 1989.

Williamson, Marilyn L. *Raising Their Voices: British Women Writers, 1650–1750*. Detroit: Wayne State University Press, 1990.

Richardson and His Circle

SAMUEL RICHARDSON (1689–1761), the first literary super-star, sent all Europe into convulsions of enthusiasm, suspense, boredom, grief, revulsion, and adoration. By 1800 his massive novels had been translated into at least eight languages. But critical opinion, then as now, was divided. "I heartily despise him and eagerly read him, nay, sob over his works in a most scandalous manner," Lady Mary Wortley Montagu confessed. Coleridge found Richardson's mind "vile," his novels "day-dreamy" and claustrophobic—an overheated sickroom compared to the breezy, open landscape of Henry Fielding's. Fielding himself jeered at the social-climbing pretensions of Richard-son's first novel in a devastating parody, but dissolved into admiring tears over *Clarissa*. For Samuel Johnson, Fielding merely describes the face of a clock, whereas Richardson explores and explains its inner workings: "There is more knowledge of the heart in one letter of Richardson's, than in all *Tom Jones*." This vision of Richardson as a great moralist and psychologist was shared, surprisingly, by some of the most radical figures of European literature. Though Voltaire hoped he would never be "condemned to reread *Clarissa*," Diderot vowed that, if poverty forced him to sell his books, he would keep only the Bible, Homer, Sophocles, Euripides, and Richardson. Laclos, author of *Les liaisons dangereuses*, declared *Clarissa* "le chef-d'oeuvre des romans," a novel of "utmost genius." The Marquis de Sade agreed.

Diderot's enthusiasm for "the divine Richardson" helps us to grasp just how revolutionary he seemed to his contemporaries. Diderot senses that the novel has been changed so irrevocably that the frivolous term *roman* no longer applies, though no new name has been found. What earlier moralists did with maxims, Richardson does with far more powerful materials—"actions" and "images." We regard his characters as real acquaintances, cry out to them, debate with them. Readers do not remain passive, but interact with the text, and the text in turn transforms its readers, mysteriously strengthening their impulse to do good and shun evil. Oddly enough, the novels of a starchy Puritanical Englishman become a "touchstone" for the Enlightenment philosophe, confirming his love of "Virtue" and his vision of a material universe troubled and energized by the clash of contradictions. What Diderot especially values is Richardson's ability to articulate the secrets of the unconscious, to "bring the torch into the depths of the cavern," to capture the "dissonant tone" of a speaker concealing the truth, to express the struggles and divisions within families and even within a single individual. Especially compelling are his portraits of a wise and intelligent heroine whose every action is wrong (Clarissa) and a male protagonist (Lovelace) who combines every possible extreme of good and evil.

These qualities did not develop early in Richardson, whose conventional petit-bourgeois life has encouraged the view that he must have created his masterpieces by accident. Coleridge speaks for many readers when he admires the novels but recoils from "so very vile a mind, so oozy, so hypocritical, praise-mad, canting, envious, concupiscent!" It is true that Richardson's work is heavily didactic, and includes such jewels as *The Young Man's Pocket Companion* (1734), which dictates strict rules to the apprentice and forbids him to attend any public entertainment except Lillo's *London Merchant*. It is true that Richardson's own life (until he began writing fiction at the age of fifty) seems unpromisingly "middle class"—the son of a joiner, apprenticed to the (semi)respectable trade of printing, married his master's daughter, rose to be a prosperous publisher and printer to the Crown. Worse still, he grew uncommonly fat and conducted himself like Uriah Heep, "a sly sinner, creeping along the very edges of the walks . . . afraid of being seen" (the portrait is Richardson's own, so we should suspect irony). Nevertheless, two episodes in the early life of the Good Apprentice suggest a strong narrative drive and an imagination inspired by secrets. First, he was excited and filled with "strong desire" by the myth of the ring that makes its wearer invisible: "I was a very sheepish boy, and thought I should make a very happy use of it on a multitude of occasions." The invisibility conferred by fiction—all his novels pretend to be real letters, written in the grip of events and only later discovered by their "editor"—would allow him to indulge this "strong desire to be master" and to enjoy the "happy" results of shedding inhibitions and scruples. And second, he recalls that as a bashful thirteen-year-old (with a reputation for storytelling) he was employed to write love letters by "the young Women of Taste and Reading," who "revealed to me their Love Secrets": "I have been directed to chide, and even repulse, . . . at the very time that the Heart of the Chider or Repulser was open before me, overflowing with Esteem and Affection, and the fair Repulser dreading to be taken at her Word." In thus acting as a "Secretary" (in several senses), Richardson learned important lessons in the erotics of intimacy, the contradiction between words and feelings, and the power of writing for others.

The Novels

Richardson's first full-length fiction clearly grows out of his "Secretarial" experience as a boy; *Pamela, or Virtue Rewarded* (1740) takes its cue from a volume of form letters he composed to help the semiliterate write and behave. In one of these *Familiar Letters* (eventually published in 1741), the father of a servant-girl "on hearing of her Master's attempting her Virtue" orders his daughter home immediately, because to stay is to encourage him ("God grant that you have not already yielded to his base desires!"); in the next letter the daughter announces she has already left, intact. The story ends in a mere ten lines. But Richardson's mind obviously dwelt on what might happen if the girl did remain virtuous but did not in fact leave. The result is a lively and spontaneous novel told mostly in her own letters, supplemented by third-person narrative and by the journal she keeps after her abduction. Richardson starts with stock comedy characters (the pert but genteel *fille de chambre*, the lecherous squire) but invests them with an unprecedented moral seriousness, claiming for the lower-class heroine an ethical status hitherto granted in fiction only to the nobility; indeed, her strange name "Pamela" comes directly from the princess in Sir Philip Sidney's aristocratic romance *Arcadia* (1584). *Pamela* brings to life in minute-by-minute descriptions her hesitations and terrors, her rationalizations for not leaving when she could, her struggles with her own heart as well as with Mr. B.'s arrogant if clumsy sexual harassment, her claustrophobia and suicidal impulses under house arrest, her attempts to conceive these "trials" as a God-given spiritual crisis, the dawning of a new respect in Mr. B.'s eyes, his conversion from Don Juan to Prince Charming, his struggles with the social ignominy of marrying a servant-girl, her adjustments to the role of social leader, their wedding, her difficult negotiations with snobbish relatives, and finally her triumphant handling of the discovery that her husband has an illegitimate daughter. The response was a tidal wave of lachrymose praise ("If all the Books in England were to be burnt, this Book, next the Bible, ought to be preserved"), followed by an undertow of mockery from those who found its subject trivial and its emotions overblown. *Pamela* became a modern industrial product, generating new editions with testimonials, murals in Vauxhall Gardens, critiques, parodies, translations, plays (one by Voltaire and two by Goldoni), engravings, six operas, a Heroic Poem, a pictorial fan, two waxworks, and several sequels tracing "Pamela in High Life," including one by Richardson himself (1741).

In *Pamela* Richardson had developed a new kind of domestic fiction from the structure of courtship-comedy, and in the follow-up (sometimes known as *Pamela II*) he attempts another kind of comedy, in which already familiar characters encounter the problems of married life in the fashionable world: the vices of the Town, the principles of education, the pros and cons of breast-feeding, the jealousy of the husband when the first baby arrives, the jealousy (and class insecurity) of the wife when Mr. B. takes up with an Italianate Countess. Many readers find the new improved Pamela—the genteel oracle of social propriety and slavish gratitude to a complacent husband—a poor substitute for the vivid unpolished "sauce-box" of the opening letters. Richardson's ear remains sharp in scenes involving conflict or absurdity, but the long passages of discussion in what he imagines to be the upper-class world manage to sound both mincing and turgid. Nevertheless, the postmarital parts of *Pamela* (the second half of the original volume 2, and the sequel added as volumes 3 and 4) deal seriously with a broad range of social issues, centered on the corruption and reform of the aristocracy and the tension between sexuality and social stability. Toward the end of part 2, for example, Pamela's circle discusses whether "*a Reform'd Rake makes the best Husband*," that is, whether the double standard should be tolerated, whether male sexual predation should be regarded as mere "sowing wild oats" or seasoning while women were held to strict standards of chastity and ferociously punished if they strayed. Pamela denounces this hypocrisy with great fervor, and yet (as her friends immediately cry out) she herself is married to a reformed rake whom she extols as a godlike benefactor and "Master." Her reply, that Mr. B. was a dignified "Gentleman of Sense" and not a common town rake, suggests both the inadequacies of *Pamela* and the genesis of Richardson's tragic masterpiece, *Clarissa*. For although Mr. B. is *supposed* to be a dashing aristocratic sensualist before his conversion, Richardson actually shows him as a confused adolescent, a Squire Booby (the cruel name given him in Fielding's parody *Shamela*). And when Richardson next attempted to create an upper-class libertine, this time successfully, he turned out to be an infinitely more dangerous character, indeed one of the most fascinatingly Satanic in literature: Robert Lovelace, the nemesis of Clarissa Harlowe.

Clarissa, or The History of a Young Lady, published in three cliff-hanging installments between December 1747 and December 1748, vastly magnifies the resources of the epistolary novel. In this million-word collection, both the female victim and the male pursuer write their experiences "to the moment"; each corresponds with strongly drawn confidant(e)s who become major characters in their own right, and with a throng of minor relatives, servants, and accomplices, all distinguished by their own manners of writing. Moreover, the letter itself—the physical object and the unique perspective it embodies—plays an even greater part in the action. Pamela's journal acts as a sexual symbol when she sews it into her underskirts, and as an agent of conversion when Mr. B. finally reads it, awestruck by its pathos and authenticity. But in *Clarissa* the story hinges at each stage on the various meanings of "correspondence." Clarissa dates her own downfall from her secret exchange of letters with Lovelace, when he is banished the house by her apoplectic father after a duel provoked by her equally irascible brother, a former college mate. Lovelace's spy network constantly intercepts and manipulates the letters of others. When Clarissa refuses a clandestine interview by the gate of her father's estate, Lovelace replaces the letter untouched so that she is forced to meet him in person—and she is duly abducted. When her confidante Anna Howe warns Clarissa that the respectable London house where Lovelace lodged her is in fact a brothel, and his friends actually highwaymen and confidence tricksters, the letter never reaches her; Lovelace captures it, edits it (marking each point with marginal index fingers to prod his revenge), and replaces the women's authentic letters with forgeries that serve his own plot. By such manipulations of word and appearance he baffles and torments

Clarissa, putting off the issue of marriage in the hope that she, like "every woman" according to libertine doctrine, will sooner or later give way to her desire and become his whore. This tangle of deceit and "trial" continues up to "the final Outrage," when he tricks her back into the brothel, drugs her, and rapes her unconscious body. Rather than subsiding into rueful acceptance as he hoped, Clarissa disintegrates with a violence equal and opposite to his own; the room is filled with torn fragments of letters, scattered across the page in a typographical equivalent to her frenzy. Hereafter, in the novel's most surprising turn and the most controversial for readers in 1748, Lovelace loses all vestige of control over Clarissa's text, her body, her interpretation of the world. The ground shifts to religious tragedy as she, fully convinced of her "ruin" despite her inviolate will, prepares to waste away and die. In the process she gains a verbal and personal authority that had eluded her before. Lovelace continues his hysterical plotting, longing once again to capture female letters, dreaming that "the Seal would have yielded to the touch of my warm finger . . . and the folds, *as other plications have done*, opened of themselves to oblige my curiosity." But he cannot (or will not) grasp the true situation. When the anorexic heroine feels on the point of death, she sends him one last letter, finally tricking him as he has constantly deceived her: reading of her departure for "her father's house," the secular Lovelace assumes that she has finally lifted the ferocious curse her father laid on her after the abduction/elopement; he cannot recognize the biblical allusion and the massive *pompe funèbre* it ushers in. While the nineteen-year-old Clarissa expires in a halo of saintly rapture, and Mrs. Sinclair the brothel-keeper dies in hideous squalor, the alienated Lovelace slinks off to Europe, only to "expiate" his crime and embrace death in a suicidal duel with Clarissa's mysterious cousin Morden.

Both during and after this outpouring of fictional letters, Richardson himself engaged in an immense correspondence with literati, friends, and anonymous admirers, debating the ethics and the outcome of *Clarissa*. In a sense, this circle of (mostly female) writers and readers helped to generate the text itself, since Richardson made numerous changes in response to their criticisms. Over time the master printer built an extraordinary apparatus around his novel, to counteract what he took to be careless or perverse misinterpretations and to highlight those aspects that his friends found most improving. *Clarissa* was revised, expanded with original letters ("restored" from manuscript and

marked with special symbols), set in large print for the weak-eyed, for-
tified with footnotes explaining the wickedness of Lovelace, and supplemented with hundreds of pages describing the characters, summarizing all 537 letters (with the moral of each in italics), indexing those
morals alphabetically, extracting the Maxims and Sentiments, and
gathering the biblical passages that inspired the heroine's final days.
Modern critics rejoice in Richardson's overanxious attempts to control
the interpretation of his own book, since they suggest a split between
the official morality preached by *Clarissa* and the "real" meaning of the
text—a psychoanalytic truth about repressed sexuality, perhaps, or a
political truth about patriarchy and class hierarchy, or a deconstructive
truth about the inherent instability of all textual meaning. Certainly
some of Richardson's later efforts suggest a panic or cover-up, particularly those highly visible footnotes and plot summaries that drive home
character features that should have been conveyed wholly in the letters
themselves. Having showed, he feels he must also tell. Many of his
additions, however, *did* belong in the original manuscript and *were* suppressed from the first edition too timidly, following readers' criticism
that he later overrode; one particularly demented fantasy (in which
Lovelace plans to rape Anna Howe and her mother on a boating trip)
was struck out on the advice of a young correspondent, but returned triumphantly in the third edition (volume 4, letter 42). And Richardson
held fast to the grim essentials of the plot—the rape and Clarissa's
death—in the face of almost universal protest.

The consultatory mode of authorship contributed most to Richardson's third novel, *Sir Charles Grandison* (1753–1754)—his most popular with contemporary readers including Jane Austen, though few critics now recognize its substance. Richardson appealed widely for materials to incorporate into this pendant to *Clarissa*, the story of a good and
beautiful man. Many scenes are set in Italy, where he had never been,
and among the aristocracy, where he had never belonged (though, as he
was proud to point out, he had never been to a masquerade or a brothel either, and still painted them convincingly from report). The knight-
errant hero, who rescues the brilliant and beautiful Harriet Byron from
a vile seducer on Hounslow Heath, turns out to have lived abroad and
become involved with Lady Clementina della Porretta, a baroque saint
driven insane by the conflict between her love for the Anglican Sir
Charles and her fervent Catholicism. He is thus inhibited from acting
upon his growing love for Harriet, and this impasse, seen largely

through Harriet's own vivid eyes, forms the central core of the narrative. Why is he mysteriously unhappy? Will he marry the magnificent Clementina once he has helped bring her back to health? If not, can Harriet accept a man who frankly loves two women? Around this core grows a mass of subsidiary narratives, ranging in tone from slapstick comedy (as Sir Charles's boisterous sister torments her new husband), through feminist satire (as Harriet rejects alternative lovers), to operatic melodrama, when Clementina runs mad or when Olivia, another Italian noblewoman, pulls a knife on the hero. (Richardson amused himself by dividing the Dramatis Personae into "Men," "Women," and "Italians.") Now that he has left behind the claustrophobic unity of *Clarissa*, he feels free to explore all the "natural passions" that spring up within the Grandison circle—that loose group of orphaned siblings and protégés that replaces the conventional family: Charlotte Grandison's love for her brother, so strong that it makes all other men seem worthless; the fervent embraces of Harriet and Sir Charles's fifteen-year-old ward Emily; the more-than-brotherly love between Sir Charles and Clementina's crippled brother Jeronymo. The narrative mode is equally varied. Richardson experiments with scenes written as drama within letters written to the moment, flashbacks from older letters, direct narrative by an elderly clergyman, even the "minutes" taken by a concealed stenographer. But the letter always remains open and transparent, designed to be read by the whole group,in marked contrast to the deadly secrecy that shrouds almost all communication in *Clarissa*.

If *Pamela* is comedy and *Clarissa* tragedy, then *Grandison* is clearly romance, with its paragon lovers and its meandering episodic plot (Richardson did not know from one volume to the next what he would do with the story, whereas in writing *Clarissa* the terrible conclusion had always been in his view). But it is a thoroughly up-to-date romance, set not in some supernatural realm but in a polite and constitutional society. Wherever possible, tears are shed instead of blood— and in prodigious quantities; even the ex-villain Sir Hargrave manages a small flood, and the good characters seem to have tear ducts as infinite as their nobility. The breadth of *Grandison* allowed Richardson to tackle what he had attempted in *Pamela II*, an encyclopedic range of problems germane to the life of a new community based on sensibility. Sir Charles, in the vanguard of what Richardson hopes is a reforming spirit among the leaders of society, deals intelligently and gracefully with the remnants of feudal barbarism among his own people (dueling, lechery, violence, snobbery), and guides his family and friends through the intricate tangles of choosing their mates—the most painful tangle being his own. Aware that the wickedness of Lovelace generated most of the reader's interest, *Grandison* tries to transfer some of this interest to the Good Man, involving him in "perverse accidents" and making him a "designer" of plots and stratagems, "a Rake in his address, and a Saint in his heart"; those who love him also fear that "had he been a wicked man, he would have been a *very* wicked one." Twentieth-century readers have generally ridiculed this attempt to make goodness intriguing. By modern standards of quotidian realism, the bad characters are too marginal and the good too successful, too idealistic, and too articulate in moments of crisis. But we should still recognize *Grandison*'s affinities with genres we currently value—its high flights resembling opera, and its minute analysis of elite behavior anticipating the roman-fleuves of Henry James and Proust. In terms of its literary progeny, *Grandison* has actually been quite influential; not only Jane Austen but George Eliot praised this panoramic and morally earnest novel centered on an outstanding heroine. Without *Grandison* there may have been no *Middlemarch*.

Virtue Rewarded?

Critics have never quite accepted Richardson's attempt, in *Pamela*, to graft a sharply realistic narrative manner onto a fairy-tale narrative structure. But we should not underestimate that realism. In the first half of the novel, for example, Richardson's impressive social and psychological detail manages to suggest a growing attachment between Pamela and Mr. B. long before love is explicitly declared. She invents reasons not to leave his service, not to encourage other suitors, not to escape from the country house to which he abducts her (as she describes it, the bull in the next field vividly embodies her vision of male sexuality). She feels a stab of concern when an accident threatens B.'s life, and admits she "does not hate him." She lingers over the details of his appearance and behavior even when they intimidate her; he, meanwhile, flips hysterically between rage and tenderness, boisterous lechery and nervous hesitation, apparently in the grip of a strong if unacknowledged internal conflict. When the subject of marriage comes up, even mockingly, Pamela's reactions—sudden blushes, overprompt denials, overly detailed accounts of how she would spend her time as a wife—

suggest that she has dreamed of the possibility and suppressed her yearning. When she does leave captivity, introspection lays bare a divided and "treacherous" heart that calls her back into bondage: "and yet all the time this Heart is *Pamela*." Struggling to understand how she could love a man who treated her so imperiously, she realizes that he has given her consequence: "Cruel as I have thought you, and dangerous your Views to my Honesty, You, Sir, are the only Person living that ever was more than indifferent to me."

Pamela is a social hybrid, of humble, rustic background yet brought up in privileged circumstances as the personal waiting-woman to Mr. B.'s mother. She has acquired sumptuous clothes, soft hands, and such refined accomplishments as embroidery, estate management, and letter writing; she later attributes her novelistic skills to the training she received in administering charity, when she learned to make fine discriminations between the deserving poor and their imitators. In a sense, then, she and Mr. B. are siblings, and their intimacy develops within this domestic web; the first hint of his seductive intentions comes when he offers to share his dead mother's underwear, and the first hint that she likes him comes when she refuses to leave before finishing his embroidered waistcoat. This kind of detail renders plausible, if anything could, the huge shift in character between the squire-and-wench routine at the start and the Exemplary Couple at the close of the novel. Pamela's intriguing mixture of naïveté and sophistication, which troubled the more dismissive readers, thus matches the upper servant's unique position in the household, perceptively rendered by Richardson. Less plausible, however, is her ability to recognize, and be shocked by, sexual innuendo: the adolescent may well be sensitive to the leers of the servants who "seem as if they would look one through" and the master who kisses her "as if he would have eaten me," but how would she know that the corrupt housekeeper Mrs. Jewkes speaks "like a vile *London* Prostitute"?

Before their eyes mist over with sentimental gratitude, Pamela (and her author) convincingly reveal the sociopolitical tensions played out in the amorous maneuvers of squire and servant. Her ability to swallow her fear and answer back when bullied, dismissed by Mr. B. as sexy "sauce" or criminal insubordination, suggests (to the alert reader) not cheek but courage in the face of tyranny, and as her "trials" become grimmer, so does the tone of her defiance: "Oh! what can the abject Poor do against the mighty Rich, when they are determin'd to oppress?"

Pamela's "Virtue" becomes essential because she has no other property in a world where status, identity, and personal value all depend on property; she resists not merely the man's sexual predation, but the landowner's assertion of absolute power over his chattels. "How came I to be his Property?" she asks; "What Right has he in me, but such as a Thief may plead to stolen Goods?" This political acuity (Mr. B.'s bawd and collaborator calls Pamela's observation "downright Rebellion") may support Terry Eagleton's view of Richardson as a revolutionary class warrior—not, of course, for the proletariat, but for the virtuous and hardworking bourgeoisie. Certainly his villains are either flaming aristocrats or hapless servants corrupted by them, though after *Pamela* his sympathetic characters (Clarissa, Sir Charles Grandison, Harriet Byron) likewise stem from the gentry. Militant class hatred certainly sharpens the realism of *Pamela* and wells up at moments throughout Richardson's work. Pamela's failure to escape across the open fields is credible, not just because she feels ambivalent fear and attraction for the rampant male, but because the country was indeed a war zone, patrolled and mined by "the mighty Rich" in league with one another. Mr. B. asserts class power to shut off every avenue for the imprisoned woman, corrupting the postal service and intimidating any local clergy (like the sweet but powerless Williams) who might offer refuge; his peers meanwhile dismiss the affair as an inconsequential frolic: "What is all this, but that the 'Squire our Neighbour has a mind to his Mother's Waiting-maid? . . . He hurts no Family by this." Nevertheless, in *Pamela* (as later in *Grandison*) these towering abuses are cured by a voluntary surrender to middle-class values, not by total war; repeatedly the vicious snob, once touched by the fairy wand of goodness wielded by Pamela (or Sir Charles), converts on the spot to piety, sobriety, and early dining. Except in the case of Lovelace, Richardson's imagination seems reformist rather than revolutionary.

This transition from social drama to wish fulfillment drains much of the novel's artistic vitality. Pamela's sharply phrased class awareness dissolves, except for the occasional flicker of sarcasm, into sugary glorification of her lord and master. Richardson's aristocrats, particularly Mr. B.'s tumultuous sister, Lady Davers, come to life when they unleash their violent prejudice (and stoke the middle-class reader's indignation), but the magic of Pamela transforms them into cardboard figures who mouth statements like "I believe there is something in Virtue, that we had not well considered" or "We People of Fortune . . . are generally educated wrong." Reformist zeal may also blind Richardson to the vulgarity of the values that triumph in this story of "Virtue Rewarded." What kind of reward does Pamela receive for her refusal to submit to a man who thinks her entire being, sex and soul, can be purchased for cash? Why, that same man (to whom she yields her entire being in a vow of marital obedience), and copious quantities of the very cash that would have supported her as a kept mistress (handed over, a hundred guineas at a time, the morning after the wedding night). As her parents, former ditch-diggers, enumerate the splendors of the farm they have been given in Kent, they exult "that all is the Reward of our Child's Virtue!" and Pamela herself reminds us that "the *Kentish* Estate was to be Part of the Purchace of my Infamy." Of course, there is all the difference between skulking in private as an insecure concubine and basking in public recognition as a wife, commanding a large budget for charitable works—though throughout part 2 Pamela still agonizes over her unworthiness, shuns public gatherings, and fears that Mr. B. will turn her away. But Richardson's economic realism, which gives palpable solidity to the "happy" scenes as well as the "trial" scenes, does tend to undermine that difference.

Satirical "anti-Pamelists" were quick to exploit the vein of materialism that runs through Richardson's arriviste fantasy. The best known among them is Henry Fielding, whose *Shamela* (1741) parodies both the epistolary novel itself (Shamela is a Covent Garden whore angling for the innocent Squire Booby after bearing a child by the well-hung Parson Williams) and the rapturous readers' testimonials appended to Richardson's second edition: Parson Tickletext gives new meaning to the cult of sensibility and the technique of "writing to the moment"— "Oh! I feel an Emotion even while I am relating this: Methinks I see *Pamela* at this Instant, with all the Pride of Ornament cast off!"—but Parson Oliver brings him down to earth with a pungent critique of Richardson's subversive, pornographic novel. Oliver then supplies the true letters of Pamela, in which lewd reality alternates with faux-genteel protestations ("so we talked a full Hour and a half about my Vartue"). Fielding continued this taunting in his first full-length novel, *Joseph Andrews* (1742), where Pamela's brother, a truly virtuous and beautiful serving-man, resists the seductions of *his* employee. Richardson-baiting is left behind as Joseph (kicked out from the household rather than locked in) wanders the roads with the quixotic Parson Adams, but the satire returns in the last volume, where marriage and social climbing have turned Pamela into a cold-hearted snob, worse than those she encountered while a servant herself. Other negative tributes include (all from 1741) the anonymous *Pamela Censured*, James Parry's *True Anti-Pamela*, and Eliza Haywood's *Anti-Pamela, or Feign'd Innocence Detected*, the scandalous life of Syrena Tricksy. Soon there appeared a French translation of Haywood's novel (1743) and a separate French *Antipamela, ou Mémoires de M. D.* (1742).

Most notorious of these anti-Pamelas must be John Cleland's *Memoirs of a Woman of Pleasure* (London, 1748–1749), whose low-born heroine Fanny Hill *does* give in without a struggle to the first attractive young gentleman, *does* live the life of a "London prostitute," and yet achieves by rising in her profession exactly what Pamela achieves by abstaining: wealth, family, and respectable married bliss in a higher class. Early in the novel Fanny's friend Esther decides to take the Shamela route ("by preserving their VARTUE, some had taken so with their masters, that they had married them, and kept them coaches, and lived vastly grand"), but Fanny arrives at a similar conclusion without losing her sentimental ideals; she can sacrifice the pleasures of Vice to "the delicate charms of VIRTUE" because she finds married sex with her true love even more intense than illicit copulation with her customers. Other critiques of *Pamela* also focus on sexuality. *Pamela Censured* picks out all the scenes where Mr. B. manhandles or leaps upon his servant, retells them as suggestively as possible, then protests that no young person could read them without being corrupted (girls will masturbate uncontrollably, boys will become intriguers and rapists, boasting that they would have succeeded where Mr. B. faltered). The letters of *Shamela* convert the same scenes into irresistibly lewd travesties, but the Fielding figure, Parson Oliver, adopts a more solemn approach: "There are many lascivious Images" in Richardson's novel, "very improper to be laid before the Youth of either Sex"; "I cannot agree that my Daughter should . . . see the Girl lie on her Back, with one Arm round Mrs. *Jewkes* and the other round the Squire, naked in Bed, with his Hand on her Breasts, &c." Richardson *does* create scenes like this, intensely sexual from the young man's perspective but horrifying from Pamela's; the buckish readers who see only the former, whether they leer or pretend to disapprove, see just half the story.

These frivolous and/or moralistic parodies help us grasp the significance of Richardson's original novel. They are often right about the details, if wrong about what those mean for the integrity of the work. All the anti-Pamelists perceive, quite rightly, that Richardson has presented a divided heroine, torn apart by impulses that run counter to her strict and "Puritanical" morality—but they cannot give him credit for this perception. Seeing only the stock figure of the wily serving-wench, they cannot believe in those involuntary actions (trembling, hesitating, convulsing, fainting) that convince us of Pamela's psychological crisis; they assume that she must be fully conscious and calculating, trained in the "arts of the Town"—the whorish stratagems of Shamela or Syrena Tricksy. The parodists are wrong to dismiss Richardson as a sly pornographer, and yet there *is* something voyeuristic about the desire to share the most intimate moments in an adolescent girl's first crisis, and to experience her feelings, not mediated by time and third-person narrative, but "to the moment," through the peephole. Pornographic mirror images of Pamela's career do remind us of an important truth—that official definitions of female "Virtue" focused obsessively and exclusively on the vagina, on what *Shamela* calls "a poor Girl's little *&c.*"; Richardson merely insists that a poor girl's etc. could be as valuable (for society and for the novel) as a Countess's.

Conservative critics like Fielding were right to find something subversive in Richardson's Cinderella fantasy of social climbing, presented as an authentic social document; the "Instruction" conveyed by *Pamela* to servant-maids, Parson Oliver complains, is "To look out for their Masters as sharp as they can," so that "if the Master is not a Fool, they will be debauched by him, and if he is a Fool, they will marry him." (Fielding should be considered an expert on this catastrophe, since he himself married his servant-woman a few years later.) It is not simply the miscegenation of classes that Fielding finds unthinkable, but the destruction of a whole hierarchy of values: moral seriousness belongs exclusively to the gentry, so the sexuality of a servant-girl cannot be anything but a joke. *Joseph Andrews* puts these wenches in their proper place with the bawdy, lighthearted treatment of Betty at the inn (no romance names for her), who avoids pregnancy by receiving two lovers at once. Joseph's beloved Fanny seems to form an exception to Fielding's farcical treatment of the lower orders; she is at least taken seriously as a love object, though her subjectivity never occupies the reader (she cannot read or write). But Fanny turns out to be Pamela's long-lost sister, just as Joseph (like Tom Jones later) turns out to be a son of the upper classes, mysteriously mislaid when young.

How then did the *Pamela* experience contribute to the creation of *Clarissa*? We have already seen that the shortcomings of Mr. B. prompted Richardson to create a more formidable and expressive libertine, too dangerous to "reform," too violent to be salvaged by the sentimental compromises and conversions that wrap up *Pamela*. This suggests a revolutionary break between the two works. Richardson would later try to present his novels as a smooth, homogenous progression, a steady accumulation of moral truths, by publishing *A Collection of the Moral and Instructive Sentiments, Maxims, Cautions, and Reflexions, Contained in the Histories of Pamela, Clarissa, and Sir Charles Grandison.* (It is just as well that Diderot did not read this attempt by the author to highlight the least impressive aspect of his work.) But when he was actually writing *Clarissa*, and defending his decision to push it to an uncompromisingly tragic conclusion, he understood how deeply he had broken from the earlier novel—a break inspired not by a moralizing program but by powerful artistic ambition. To soften *Clarissa* by reformation and happy ending would be to collude in the atrocities committed by Lovelace, to trivialize the heroine's suffering—and to repeat himself: "What had I done more than I had done in Pamela? . . . What of extraordinary would there be in it?" He now dismisses the *Pamela* solution as "trite" and calls Mr. B. "a lordly and imperious Husband, who hardly deserved her"—a sweeping condemnation that implicates Pamela in the delusion, for praising him so highly in public and in her prayers. When we draw up our list of anti-Pamelas, we must place *Clarissa* at its head.

Clarissa: Fiction, Drama, and Originality

Richardson clearly wanted to be seen as a literary original, an untutored genius closer to Nature than Art—indeed he exaggerated his own ignorance of literature to strengthen the claim that everything came from his own "extraordinary" creativity. (It seems appropriate that the poet-critic Edward Young chose Richardson as the addressee of his groundbreaking *Conjectures on Original Composition*, though Diderot may overstate the case when he equates the English novelist with Homer.) Like all major authors, however, he achieves this originality by transforming the themes, genres, and myths of earlier writing. We have already seen how Richardson borrows the name "Pamela" from Arcadian romance, how he combines the materials of comedy with the seriousness of spiritual autobiography, how he rewrites the Cinderella story as a detailed chronicle of social transformation—and we can still trace this fable in the cruel brother and ugly sister of Clarissa, though the Prince has now become the Big Bad Wolf. We should now examine his use of previous drama and "Novel," even though, paradoxically, these two main influences on his fiction filled him with disgust. In *The Young Man's Pocket Companion* he attacks the theater as a vile corruption, fit only for the idle gentry and hostile to "People of Business and Trade," who appear only as cuckolds and buffoons. The "mere Novel" was even worse, a shallow and trivial form for "Story-Lovers and Amusement-Seekers"; Richardson presents his grand moral System "in the humble guise of a *Novel* only by way of Accommodation to the Manners and Taste of an Age overwhelmed with a Torrent of Luxury, and abandoned to Sound and senselessness." Yet he wrote his best work in what he called "the Novel Kind"—at a length that only the leisured classes could read—and (as we shall see) drew extensively on the theater to create his compulsive and intense protagonists.

Richardson was not the first to narrate a scandalous seduction in letters written in the heat of the moment; Aphra Behn's *Love-Letters Between a Nobleman and His Sister* introduced this kind of novel to England in 1686. He certainly knew other epistolary sources like the (nonfictional) letters of Mme de Sévigné and the (fictional) letters of Ninon de L'Enclos, which he believed genuine. He was not the first to modernize romance by analyzing the emotional crises of the aristocracy at vast length, for the seventeenth-century novels of Mlle de Scudéry had done precisely this. Jane Barker and Elizabeth Rowe, in the early eighteenth century, had already tried to combine popular fiction with a religious and didactic purpose, and Defoe had already filled the novel with minute details taken from ordinary life. Nor was Richardson the first to make a single thwarted and obsessive love affair the center of the narrative; the author of *Clarissa* may not have known Prévost's *Manon Lescaut* (though Prévost himself translated Richardson's novels), but he *had* read a translation of Mme de Lafayette's *Princesse de Clèves*. These French and English predecessors—almost exclusively female, we should note—helped to generate both Lovelace and Clarissa.

Though Lovelace clearly derives from the boisterous rakes of English Restoration comedy, Richardson has given him a layer of French refinement that makes his cruelty all the more appalling. He spent his formative years "at the French Court," and his troubles with women may derive from an early misunderstanding of the French initiation game, in which the young man is "put into the world" by a fashionable seductress like Ninon de L'Enclos, and then left to fend for himself. Lovelace can never overcome his fury at being conquered and abandoned in his teens by a woman of his own class, a "Quality-jilt," and he harps on this episode whenever he tries to explain why he must persecute and ruin Clarissa. Lovelace's situation and behavior resemble those of the Duc de Nemours, the libertine who falls in love with the Princesse de Clèves: like Nemours (and unlike the Rovers and Horners of the English theater) he abandons all other sexual adventures and flings himself obsessively into the chase, disguising himself and haunting the edges of Clarissa's estate in hopes of glimpsing her; like Nemours, he proposes marriage once the obstacles are removed, only to be rejected because of the damage he has already done. But Richardson plays a significant variation on Lafayette's novel, since here the heroine is single and the obstacles that turn potential love into tragedy are created by Lovelace himself. Clarissa, in turn, resembles the Princesse in her awareness that she "does not hate" her dangerous lover (a typical French euphemism for desire), in her refusal to compromise once she fully understands that danger, and in her sensitivity to the implications of small favors and gestures—a delicacy born of danger that some English readers interpreted as prudery. And as a letter writer she resembles another of Richardson's French prototypes, Mme de Sévigné. Pamela's epistolary "voice" went from servant-girl's pertness to homiletic gravity without ever achieving the tone of a real aristocrat, but Clarissa sounds like a grande dame; like Sévigné's, her letters breathe intimacy, wit, and stylishness, casual upper-class colloquialism and vivid sketches of character. She writes "freely" about her oppressive family, with a subtle sarcasm created from the restricted vocabulary of politeness. It is all the more frustrating, then, that her verbal freedom cannot be translated into action, cannot halt the encroachment of the arrogant brother or the unwelcome suitor.

Clarissa also resembles the spirited heroines of Restoration comedy, sexually virtuous but free enough in wit and style to match the rakish hero. Discussing Lovelace with her confidante, she slips into the sparklingly offhand tone of Congreve's Millamant, suggesting not just worldly intelligence but amusement and even conspiratorial pleasure in his addresses: "Bashfulness in Mr. Lovelace, my dear!"; "The man, you know, has very ready knees"; "What will not these men say to obtain belief, and a power over one?"; "What shall I do with this Lovelace?" He is a "contradictory creature," an "impatient creature," an "artful wretch"—all terms that with a tap of the fan could turn from insult to endearment. Her flustered response to a supposed offer of marriage— "Would he have had me catch at his first, at his *very* first word?" (letter 107)—sounds like Millamant during the proviso scene in *The Way of the World*, a parallel all the more poignant since Lovelace is deliberately preventing their confrontation from evolving into a courtship ritual with a happy ending. Even her tragic perplexity is tinged with drawing-room slang: "I am strangely at a loss what to think of this man. He is a perfect Proteus!" The horror of Clarissa's predicament increases, then, when we see her as a worldly heroine in a Restoration comedy situation that has been grotesquely hardened, translated into a realm where the comedic resolution is impossible and where her gracious liberty of style must fight to the death with the predatory violence of libertinism.

The Congrevean comedy-heroine is expected not only to outwit her brutal father and trounce the deadly alternative suitor (as Clarissa does with the repulsive Solmes, her father's choice), but to grill her future mate with merciless wit and penetration,only to soften by the final act and accept his proposal of marriage. (This is precisely what Charlotte Grandison does in Richardson's kinder, gentler fiction.) Lovelace constantly complains about Clarissa's "penetration," which "obliges" him (so he claims) to proceed "by the Sap," by secret military tunnels (letter 99); his rape of her unconscious body may be read as a crude physical counterpart to this quality that he fears in her. Clarissa sees through Lovelace, perceiving, where others find aristocratic confidence, only the nervous arrogance of the upstart, an insecurity that could erupt or implode into violence. In the psychological realm it is she who is the aristocrat and he the parvenu—a precise reversal of the social position of their families. Clarissa's critical yet fascinated vision of Lovelace dominates the start of the novel, since Richardson cleverly withholds the man's own letters for nearly two hundred pages. As he closes in, and his real intentions become agonizingly apparent to the reader (though not to Clarissa), she continues to exercise her suspicious intelligence on the character he presents to her, exposing the "half-menacing strain" of his compliments, the contradiction between his sugared words and the "lines of his own face," his habit of "visibly triumphing . . . in the success of his arts" (letter 98). After her capture they still play the game of scrutiny, like the alert and predatory couples of comedy, "great watchers of each other's eyes; and indeed . . . more than half-afraid of each other" (letter 125). Clarissa continues to play the tragic Millamant, verbally reducing her partner/opponent to "a simpleton, hesitating, and having nothing to say for himself" (letter 107), and Lovelace recognizes her power to "beat me out of my play," to silence his speeches and disrupt the trained seducer's well-oiled sequence of moves. Her tone becomes inevitably darker after her violation, but the dynamics are the same: "Abandoned man!—*Man* did I say? . . . well may'st thou quake; well may'st thou tremble and falter, and hesitate, as thou dost!" (letter 263). Only her resolution to die gives her a more effective role.

Lovelace is himself a dramatist, theatrical in his actions and in his letters (which are thick with quotes from Restoration drama and sometimes written out in play form, with speaking parts and stage directions). But Clarissa is similarly creative, even though her desire to shape the world is thwarted; the letter fragments she scatters after the rape, for example, cite the same heroic plays that Lovelace loves to quote, giving us an eerie sense of the compatibility that underlies their destructive deadlock. They struggle, however, over what *kind* of drama will emerge. Lovelace—who is always contriving plots to rival Horner, dressing up cronies to impersonate respectable characters, and giving episodes theatrical titles like "The Quarrelsome Lovers"—obviously wants to define the whole business as a Restoration sex comedy, with Clarissa as the fallen woman. This genre assumes that issues of sex and power are fundamentally lightweight, that women really *like* to be outwitted or violated by "Men of Spirit," and that the rake, however wicked he has been, can save everything by an offer of marriage in "the last Act" (Lovelace's very words). Clarissa hopes that she might be involved in an eighteenth-century sentimental comedy, where the rake reforms sincerely and intends marriage from the start. Once the rape destroys all vestige of this illusion, however, she improvises a tragedy out of what few resources are left her—quite literally, snatching up scissors or a penknife to impersonate Lucretia, or spending her last few pounds on a coffin decorated with emblems of her own design. Richardson draws attention to this generic shift in his letters to outraged readers; his goals are Pity and Terror, the high emotions of classical tragedy.

Like his predecessors in drama and real life, Lovelace prefers the artifact of seduction to the pleasures of union. Perverted creativity inspires both his original attraction to Clarissa and the cat-and-mouse games he plays thereafter. "I love dearly to exercise my invention," he explains; "I have ever had more pleasure in my Contrivances than in the End of them. I am no sensual man; but a man of spirit"—adding, with gratuitous misogyny, that "One woman is like another." (This passage was restored to the third edition in an attempt to darken Lovelace's character.) He must force Clarissa into sexuality (to prove that "every Woman is the same"), and yet sex is empty and disgusting for him—"a vapour, a bubble!" He craves intimacy with her, and yet cannot imagine sexual love within marriage, since he equates consummation with linguistic and emotional vacuum; like Dom Juan in Molière, he fears that once he has conquered "there is nothing more to be said." Lovelace repeatedly gloats over the "illustrious subject" that Clarissa provides "to exercise [his] pen upon," as if the chief motivation of his pursuit were to stimulate the act of writing. As Clarissa stubbornly refuses to conform to his scenario, writing becomes a compensatory fantasy realm, where "Robert the Great" controls everything according to his "imperial will and pleasure" (letter 99). He tries to think of Clarissa as a fiction, an author's character who must simply be what he dictates: "I might have had her before now, if I would. If I would treat her as flesh and blood, I should find her such" (letter 157.1).

But Lovelace also presents himself as the passive agent or mouthpiece of a "subject" outside himself. At times he blames his "plotting villain of a heart," as if that organ did not belong to him ("I so little its master!" [letter 153]). Sometimes he blames the place, hoping that the move to London will solve all his problems automatically. Then he blames the women in the London brothel, who urge him to carry on with the rape. Most of all, he blames Clarissa, ascribing to her all the "Power" that in reality he has stripped away from her; while she is treated like a Middle Eastern hostage, constantly spied upon and physically barred from approaching the windows and the door, Lovelace wails that "every time I attend her, I find that she is less in *my* power, I more in *hers*" (letter 99). In an extreme version of this conceit, he imagines that Conscience has stolen his pen and written moral reflections into his text; he then proceeds to beat and choke this female Conscience figure to death. In a text stuck on with wax to the main letter, Lovelace admits that he is "afraid of the gang of my cursed contrivances" and "*compelled* to be the wretch my choice has made me!" The paradox of libertine freedom could hardly be taken further. Richardson has created a tormentor who perceives his own futility and yet seems powerless to change it: "I am a machine at last, and no free agent" (letter 246).

Richardson's "extraordinary" libertine does not repent, of course, but flings himself even more deeply into the character that conventional society expects of him: "Am I not a *Rake*, as it is called? And who ever knew a Rake stick at any-thing?"; "Were I now to lose her, how unworthy should I be to be the Prince and Leader of such a Confraternity as ours!—How unable to look up among men!" (letters 127, 104). Lovelace frets about the "figure" he will make in "Rakish Annals," afraid of not matching up to a pre-scripted libertine identity. And for all this, Clarissa must pay: "If I forgive thee, Charmer, for . . . these contempts, I am not the Lovelace I have been reputed to be; and that thy treatment of me shews that thou thinkest I am" (letter 103). When Laclos's Valmont shifts the blame to his victims or to the way of the world, we always read it as a cynical maneuver, but Lovelace seems genuinely indignant and genuinely unaware of the contradiction that sustains his pursuit of Clarissa and reduces it to stalemate: one the one hand, he tries to force her into his own script, to impose a prefabricated character on her (much as her father wants to do with his monstrous arranged marriage); on the other hand, he continually describes himself as passive and "female," casting *her* in the active role of initiator, of definer, of "subject." Even when "Conscience" holds his pen, he presents himself as the victim of a larger circumstance: "What a happy man . . . had I been, had it been given me to *be* only what I wished to *appear* to be!" (letter 246). The fate he wishes on Clarissa—to be a fiction wholly controlled by someone else's will, with no gap between projected appearance and inner essence—he really desires for himself.

"A total revolution of manners"

Though critics treated the magisterial *Clarissa* with far more respect than the upstart *Pamela*, they still worried that the intensity and directness of Richardson's realism—the very quality that made his work so compelling—might undermine his moral intention. No one doubted his power to arouse the most intense emotions, but many readers (even among his friends) thought it was used irresponsibly. The rape arouses "Horror" rather than the nobler Pity and Terror. Endless scenes of attempted seduction have the effect of pornography (the same argument that was used in *Pamela Censured*, which Richardson obviously took to heart). The long-drawn-out treatment of cruelty and death impose a kind of torture on the reader—or else we may be corrupted by a perverse delight in another's suffering. Samuel Johnson famously praised the "Sentiment" of *Clarissa* rather than the story (if you read it for the story you will hang yourself), but "Sentiment" may bring on an unwholesome kind of sympathy that undermines our judgment. Mary Wortley Montagu, for example, found Richardson emotionally irresistible and socially deplorable: she wept like "an old Fool" over *Clarissa* and yet despised his "miserable" style and "low" characters (far from being role models, Anna Howe is "a more vicious character" than the prostitute Sally Martin, Clarissa should be locked up in Bedlam, and Charlotte Grandison should have "her Bum well whipp'd"). Richardson's confusing mélange of "tenderness" and impropriety "will do more general mischief than the Works of Lord Rochester."

Richardson insists relentlessly that Clarissa must be worshiped as a Christian paragon and that Lovelace, if not absolutely evil, is much too vicious to be attractive. Some of Richardson's friends did recognize the powerful critique of patriarchal aggression in Lovelace: Astraea Hill calls for a Protestant nunnery to protect women from "mask'd male Savages" (Lovelaces, Solmeses, *and* Harlowes); Sarah Fielding sees that Lovelace destroys "every thing that is valuable, only because everything that is valuable is in his Power." But most readers found Lovelace more entertaining, Clarissa more culpable, her rape more arbitrarily cruel, and her death more devastating, than Richardson had intended. The heroine was widely criticized for overdelicacy, rashness, excessive delay in accepting Lovelace's offers of marriage, inadequate knowledge of her own heart, and failure to escape once she knows the extent of his villainy—all developments of the portrait of unconscious desire first sketched in *Pamela*. Even the sympathetic Johnson notes that "there is always something which she prefers to truth," though he (like Diderot) praised those complexities and contradictions that other contemporaries paraded as faults.

Richardson asked for such criticisms—quite literally, since he insisted on sharing his manuscripts and provoking a detailed analysis in reply. Readers in his inner circle responded, not with detached technical observations, but with intense emotional outbursts and detailed proposals for alternative scenes and endings. As Diderot put it, the reader plays an interactive "rôle" in the drama of Clarissa. Richardson's correspondents display a sensibility bordering on erotic excitement: Sarah Fielding becomes "all sensation" as she reads; Colley Cibber cruises London in search of girls who look like Clarissa; Lady Bradshaigh (who wrote under a romantic pseudonym) alternately blushes, cajoles, and throbs with pain. *Clarissa* stimulated not only the feeling heart but the fiction writer in the reader. Lady Bradshaigh sketched out, and her sister Lady Echlin actually wrote, an alternative ending for *Clarissa* running to 136 pages, with a critical preface. Sarah Fielding produced *Remarks on Clarissa* as a short story, in which the characters reveal themselves by their obtuse or sympathetic responses to the great book; those who dismiss women's issues as trivial ("Letters wrote between Misses!"), those who cannot endure any narrative longer than an almanac, those who blame Clarissa and exonerate Lovelace, are matched to their obnoxious counterparts in *Clarissa* itself. Fielding's brother Henry, whose fiction-writing career had been launched by the desire to puncture *Pamela*, praised *Clarissa* by sending Richardson a "Narrative" of the emotions that overwhelmed him during the rape and its aftermath: "God forbid that the Man who reads this with dry Eyes should be alone with my Daughter when she hath no Assistance within Call!" Henry Fielding's "Heart" breaks down the barriers between fiction and life, mingling Clarissa and his own daughter for the thrill of imagining virtue in danger.

Lady Echlin's preface and alternative ending encapsulate the problems forced upon the reader of *Clarissa*. The heroine's "conduct is quite inconsistent with her character," since she could not possibly be so credulous as to let herself be recaptured after once escaping from the brothel. Lovelace's belief that every woman can be "subdued" is in fact ratified, not disproved, by the terrible actions that follow. The reader becomes "too much oppresst, or distracted, to admitt a rational sensibility." Nor is justice properly done; the wicked siblings are not punished enough, and Lovelace is removed by the arbitrary and anti-Christian means of a duel. Echlin avoids all this by giving the villains sudden attacks of conscience as they try to recapture Clarissa: her wasted form shocks them so deeply that they convert and repent. This narrative-stopping device brings *Clarissa* into line with *Pamela* and *Grandison*, and throws into greater relief Richardson's "extraordinary" decision to make Lovelace an exception to his general weakness for sentimental conversions. Echlin's desire for a happy ending (or at least a wistfully sad one, since the reconciled Clarissa and Lovelace still die of "consuming Illness") shows how threatening Richardson's tragic vision could seem. Threatening and perhaps misogynistic: significantly, Echlin's version hinges on female agency and "sensibility," since it is Sally

Martin—devilishly unrepentant in the original *Clarissa*—who first breaks down in remorse and destroys the plot.

Richardson's response to these improvements, as to all the calls for a happy ending, seethes with the indignation of the artist defending his integrity and of the moralist exposing upper-class indulgence. Since Lady Echlin's Lovelace stops short of the "capital Crime," he actually did no evil; why then kill him off at all? Why not shower him with rewards, make him "a Governor of one of the American Colonies," where he could shine "as a Man you had reformed"? This echoes his withering criticism of the happy-ending school in the postscript to the 1751 edition: after trampling on Clarissa, murdering other women by forcing them to die in clandestine childbirth, and "glorying in his wickedness" for years, Lovelace has only "as an act of grace and favour to hold out his hand to receive that of the best of women, whenever he pleased, and to have it thought that Marriage would be a sufficient amends for all his enormities to others, as well as to her." Those who would let Lovelace off the hook trivialize women's oppression and turn Clarissa's suffering into entertainment (they would keep the earlier scenes "for the sake of the *sport* her distresses would give to the *tender-hearted* reader"). Richardson's spirited defense raises as many problems as it solves, however. His sarcastic praise of Echlin's "good" characters and "excellent Heart" hints at a scandalous truth, that the needs of a good heart and a good novel might be diametrically opposed. (Richardson tried to heal this rift in *Grandison*, with doubtful success.) His argument for the necessity of rape—as if all Lovelace's coercion and mental cruelty amounted to nothing, and only vaginal penetration were real—resembles the libertine creed more than the Christian. And Richardson shares Lovelace's main assumption, that Clarissa's "trials" are necessary to prove her virtue and so must be escalated ad infinitum. The more scenes of sexual torment the novelist dreams up, the more moral the novel must be, and so on to the logical conclusion: "Clarissa has the greatest of Triumphs . . . *in*, and *after* the Outrage, and *because* of the Outrage." Richardson repeatedly insists that "the Tendency of all I have written is to exalt the Sex," but we must be suspicious of an exaltation that necessarily involves exposing an imaginary heroine to the most protracted sexual abuse.

However dubious his motives, Richardson does at least take rape seriously, as many recent feminist and deconstructionist critics appreciate. As a physical event, a single penetration during a drugged coma might not seem a matter of life and death—so Lovelace insinuates when he compares Clarissa to the suicidal Lucretia: "Is death the *natural* consequence of a Rape?" But Clarissa understands what Lovelace pretends to deny, that rape is primarily a symbolic act, an attempt to shatter the whole edifice of female identity. As Terry Castle puts it, "A kind of demented fatality leads Lovelace from hermeneutic violence against her to actual sexual violence: his very literal infiltration of Clarissa's body is intimately related to that infiltration of sign systems he has already effected in order to control her. . . . Clarissa's celebrated 'long time a-dying' becomes, thus, a methodical self-expulsion from the realm of signification." The entering of her body means total violation, not only because it destroys her technical virginity (barring her forever from conventional marriage), but also because she has been robbed of every other space to call her own, bullied out of her inheritance, imprisoned first in her father's house and then in the brothel contrived by Lovelace. What he calls her "pride" in bodily integrity was the last self-possession left to her, and now only by starving that alienated body to nothing can she regain her "father's house." The psychological association of penetration and death—a natural link, perhaps, for an author whose six sons all died in infancy—recurs throughout the novel: in dreams, Clarissa is stabbed by Lovelace and tumbled into a mass grave; in real life she turns knives on herself or begs Lovelace to "let thy pointed mercy enter!" In her will (read out to the whole family) she forbids any surgical opening of her body and imagines Lovelace "viewing *her dead*, whom he ONCE before saw in a manner dead" (letter 507). Lovelace meanwhile (in yet another instance of the weird compatibility that underlies their conflict) fantasizes about having her corpse opened—sending the bowels to her father and keeping the heart himself "in spirits"—since only he can truly "interpret" and "possess" her.

Richardson's greatest gift, as Diderot rightly perceived, was the uncanny psychological accuracy that allowed him to enter the most private recesses and the most extreme experiences like an invisible magician. But his novelistic imagination sometimes undermines the consistency of the moral system he claims to be presenting. For example, Richardson preaches domesticity, "family values," and absolute submission to patriarchal authority, but he shows the actual family as a Gothic nightmare, worse than anything in *Frankenstein* because it is realistic enough to be typical; well might Diderot hail *Clarissa* as a terrifying new Gospel that hews apart man and wife, daughter and mother, brother and sister. Again, the stomach-churning Swiftian description of Mrs. Sinclair's physical decay is meant to drive home the central moral of the book: that the rake cannot possibly "reform" to make a good husband, that nothing can cleanse this abomination but "a *total revolution* of manners" (letter 499). We admire this militant refusal to compromise, until we remember that these lines are delivered by Belford, Lovelace's fellow rake and confidant. Not only does Belford reform, he receives the highest honors, marries well, inherits Lovelace's fortune, and earns such respect from the dying Clarissa that she appoints him executor of her will (therefore guardian of those papers that survive to constitute the novel); he becomes in effect the authorized narrator for the last three volumes. Richardson thus accommodates precisely the reformist doctrine he attacks most fervently, just as he "accommodates" his moral intention to the corrupt form of the novel. And Lovelace raises another good question about this new hero: since he was privy to all the evil inflicted on Clarissa, why did he not intervene earlier, like a knight rescuing a damsel from the giant's castle?

For better or worse, Richardson aspired not merely to entertain or mirror contemporary life but to transform it; even in *Familiar Letters* he claims to present "rules to think and act by, as well as forms to write after." Yet this didactic, exemplary function does not fit well with the imperatives of narrative art. The means by which a novelist commands "extraordinary" attention frequently subvert the end—instruction in Christian piety and social duty. Capturing the reader requires excitement, arousal, the imposition of will, the intermingling of emotive and creative power. And if all successful novels work a kind of seduction, then *Clarissa*, which compels the reader to witness voluptuous cruelty at astonishing length, seems to draw us into a sadomasochistic bond. In his correspondence Richardson equates himself with Pygmalion, but (as Lady Bradshaigh points out) Pygmalion gave life to his creation, not death. Richardson, like Lovelace, assumes that "my Girl" must be put through a mounting series of trials as an experiment; how does this differ from the urge to "sport" with Clarissa's sufferings, condemned in those who call for a happy ending? It is a kind of torture to read page after page of Lovelace's plots and deceptions, knowing that Clarissa, in the next room, cannot see them. But is the reader a fellow victim or the torturer's accomplice? The power of this author's cruelty is recognized by no less an expert than the Marquis de Sade: "If after twelve or fifteen volumes the immortal Richardson had *virtuously* ended by converting

Lovelace and having him *peacefully* marry Clarissa, would you . . . have shed the delicious tears which [he] won from every feeling reader?" The novelist's supreme goal is to create "interest," de Sade continues, and this is best achieved when "our souls are torn," when "virtue crushes vice."

A psychoanalyst might assume that Richardson really resembled Lovelace and repressed this side of his psyche, but it would be more accurate to say that the agency of the novelist—what the author does to the reader—resembles what Lovelace tries to do to Clarissa. Richardson himself seems to exploit the parallel at times. His correspondence and prefatoria glisten with playful hints that he too is an "Encroacher" or a "Designer." He often defends Lovelace, quotes him as an authority, or confirms his libertine theories of "Women," triumphantly flaunting his female readers' indulgent response to Lovelace as evidence for their corruption—just as Lovelace flaunted his sexual conquests to make the same point. Circulating his manuscript in a female coterie (reminiscent of that group he served at thirteen?) allowed Richardson to run his emotional experiments, provoke an intense reaction, and then ride over the protests, violating the will of lady after lady. Responsive fans like Lady Bradshaigh replied in kind; as each new volume is pressed upon her she cries "Would you have me weep incessantly? . . . I cannot, indeed I cannot!" Richardson "teaches" the male reader to "gain his horrid ends," Bradshaigh complains, and reduces the female reader to a trembling victim: "I am as mad as the poor injured Clarissa, and am afraid I cannot help hating you." "A tender heart" could not possibly draw such "shocking scenes"; he must be one of those "detestable wretches" who "delight in horror," like the artist who had a man tortured so that he could paint a more authentic Crucifixion. After a night of weeping over Clarissa, "what must I say to the Man who has so disappointed and given me so much Pain? Why that I admire him for the Pain he gives, it being an undoubted Proof of his Abilities." After the rape she declares "you now can go no farther"—echoing the very words that Lovelace uses to announce the outrage itself.

Artistic power lies in extremity; so Bradshaigh implies and de Sade later confirms. The imagination must press into the cavern until it can "go no farther." This, according to de Sade, is precisely what Richardson bequeathed to the novel. In *Sir Charles Grandison*, however, Richardson refused to follow this "extraordinary" path. Here damsels are inevitably rescued and libertine giants reduced to dwarves. Erotic tension yields to the faintly prurient display of magnanimity ("Her bosom heaved with the grandeur of her sentiments"). The robust feminism of Harriet and Charlotte lapses into self-deprecation, feminine "delicacy," and compliance. The hero, splendid as a rational manager, does not throb and suffer enough: as Taine put it, "his conscience and his peruque are intact"; we can only canonize him and then "have him stuffed." *Grandison* unfolds in a dreamworld of elective affinities, where real parents have been conveniently killed off. Significantly, when we do learn about Sir Charles's and Clementina's family we encounter episodes of monstrous cruelty, abused authority, and heart-rending suffering—and it was precisely these scenes that pumped the tears from readers like Wortley Montagu, Diderot, and Stendhal. This study of sensibility without obsession, sublimity without abjection, only proves de Sade's disturbing thesis: ever since *Clarissa*, the novelist is bound to explore, not virtue alone, but the uttermost capacities of vice, the deepest "folds" of the human heart.

James Grantham Turner

Selected Bibliography

Barbauld, Laetitia, ed. *The Correspondence of Samuel Richardson, Selected from the Original Manuscripts*. London, 1804.
Books, Douglas, ed. *Joseph Andrews and Shamela*. London: Oxford University Press, 1971.
Castle, Terry. *Clarissa's Cyphers: Meaning and Disruption in Richardson's Clarissa*. Ithaca, N.Y.: Cornell University Press, 1982.
Diderot, Denis. "Éloge de Richardson" (1761), available in all standard editions and in *Oeuvres esthétiques*, ed. Paul Vernière. Paris: Garnier, 1959, 29–48.
Doody, Margaret Anne. *A Natural Passion: A Study of the Novels of Samuel Richardson*. Oxford: Clarendon, 1974.
Doody, Margaret Anne, and Peter Sabor, eds. *Samuel Richardson: Tercentenary Essays*. Cambridge: Cambridge University Press, 1989.
Eagleton, Terry. *The Rape of Clarissa: Writing, Sexuality and Class Struggle in Samuel Richardson*. Oxford: Blackwell; Minneapolis: University of Minnesota Press, 1982.
Eaves, T. C. Duncan, and Ben D. Kimpel. *Samuel Richardson: A Biography*. Oxford: Clarendon, 1971.
Echlin, Lady Elizabeth. *An Alternative Ending to Richardson's Clarissa*. Dimiter Daphinoff, ed. *Swiss Studies in English* 107. Berne: Francke, 1982.

Fielding, Sarah. *Remarks on Clarissa*. London, 1749. Facsimile ed. Peter Sabor. Los Angeles: Clark Library, 1985.

Flynn, Carol Houlihan. *Samuel Richardson, a Man of Letters*. Princeton, N.J.: Princeton University Press, 1982.

Halsband, Robert, ed. Lady Mary Wortley Montagu, *Complete Letters*. Vol. 3. Oxford: Clarendon, 1957.

Haywood, Eliza. *Anti-Pamela, or Feign'd Innocence Detected*. London, 1741.

Pamela Censured, in a Letter to the Editor. London, 1741. Facsimile ed. Charles Batten. Los Angeles: Clark Library, 1976.

Paulson, Ronald, and Thomas Lockwood, eds. *Henry Fielding: The Critical Heritage*. London: Routledge, 1969.

Traugott, John. "*Clarissa*'s Richardson: An Essay to Find the Reader." In Maximillian E. Novak, ed., *English Literature in the Age of Disguise*. Berkeley and Los Angeles: University of California Press, 1977.

Fielding and the Novel at Mid-Century

THIS volume, this "history of the British novel," represents a collective inquiry into the emergence and evolution of one profoundly influential literary form. Here, I will pursue one aspect of that inquiry by focusing on the achievements of an early practitioner of the form, Henry Fielding. In his own varied literary career as poet, journalist, essayist, playwright, and, of course, novelist, Fielding himself frequently took up the subject of the history of literary forms, lamenting the decline of venerable forms, greeting the arrival of new forms with distrust or distaste, commenting on the cause and consequences of literary empires' rise and fall, and engaging in the practice of both old and new forms with a certain shameless abandon.

Sometimes Fielding presents his views of literary history directly, in expository prose; at other times he communicates those views more subtly or more imaginatively, through networks of allusion, through narrative incidents, or through emblematic scenarios. Were Fielding, for example, to address the subject of this essay—"Fielding and the Novel"—he might compose a prose essay under that title, or he might just as easily create a farcical scene in a play in which a character named Fielding encounters a character named The Novel, and the two of them banter, argue, fall in love, duel, or perhaps dance. Much of the humor of such a scene would derive from the incommensurability of the two characters who thus meet up on stage, one a historical personage with human character and agency, the other a mere generic abstraction; and Fielding's treatments of literary history often raise questions, in particular, about how the agency of individual authors interacts with the seemingly inert influence of existing conventions and forms.

In fact, Fielding *did* compose a scene much like the one I have just described. The final act of his 1730 play, *The Author's Farce*, consists of a "puppet show" in which live actors play the parts of puppets named for a variety of current entertainments and literary genres: tragedy, comedy, oratory, pantomime, opera—and, notably, the novel. "Mrs. Novel," as Fielding calls his human/puppet embodiment of the novel form, not only competes within the puppet show for the love of "Signior Opera," but steps outside the puppet show's frame to flirt with a parson who has burst in upon the show to try to close it down. Mrs. Novel thus exchanges words with the representatives of other forms of entertainment in the puppet show, with the author of her play, and with the parson and constable who interrupt it. The confrontations that ensue between different ways of talking—novelistic, tragic, comedic, oratorical, operatic, even (in Monsieur Pantomime's case) nonverbal— as well as between different levels of action (within the play and inside the play-within-the-play) are amusingly absurd.

These confrontations also are suggestive of what I will describe as a characteristic quality of the novels that Fielding began to produce a decade after this play was performed. Although those novels do not present us with personified embodiments of a handful of genres, the way *The Author's Farce* does, their language characteristically incorporates the voices of any number of genres, juxtaposing the verbal mannerisms and formal features of a variety of discourses, playing upon the gaps and dissonances that appear between them, and often locating a phrase, an event, or a character in several contexts or frames of reference simultaneously. Further, the multiple frames of reference that Fielding's novels stubbornly superimpose are often historically as well as formally disjunctive ones. That is, if his novels may be called, in some significant sense, novels of the "mid-century," they define the space they inhabit in the "middle" or midst of history not as a comfortably balanced, central, or intermediate one, but as one that is, jarringly, both early and late.

As a critic has recently observed, the puppet show scene in *The Author's Farce* provides a graphic emblem not only for the distinctive nature of the prose in Fielding's novels, but for novelistic discourse in general, as it is described by *one* side in current theoretical debates. The writings of the Russian theorist Mikhail Bakhtin emphasize the multiplicity of social dialects within any single language—the separate vocabularies and manners of speech that belong to the members of different professions, age groups, economic classes, sexes, and so on. He characterizes the novel as a genre uniquely capable of encompassing the diversity of speech types and voices (the "heteroglossia") that other literary genres exclude. In encompassing this linguistic diversity, the novel admits into its pages the fact of social difference—and, therefore, the possibility of social struggle. Furthermore, according to Bakhtin, the novel characteristically emphasizes the variability within a language over time, as well as the diversity of voices within it at any one time. Dramatizing the way that past, present, and imminently future uses of the language coexist, the novel calls attention to the historical nature of social realities and forms, to the gaps and contradictions between past and present beliefs and institutions, and to the incompleteness of historical change itself, which leaves traces of old social realities amid the new. Bakhtin repeatedly refers to Fielding's novels as paradigmatic examples of novelistic discourse, thus described; the chaotic scene of dialogue between wildly diverse—even ontologically dissimilar—characters on the stage of *The Author's Farce* might seem to him, as to critics influenced by his work, a fitting anticipation of Fielding's later achievements as a novelist.

To other theorists and critics of the novel, however, that scene would not seem to provide an apt representation of novelistic discourse at all—unless, perhaps, the scene were revised to present Mrs. Novel holding forth on the theater's stage alone. In sharp contrast with Bakhtin's description of the novel, some recent accounts have characterized the novel as offering a specialized, insular, and illusorily harmonious discourse—one that carefully excludes some parts of social life from its pages, maintaining the divisions between different "spheres" within society so successfully as to conceal them. In particular, in this view, the genre of the novel functions to maintain the division between private and public spheres of action and experience, taking only the former for its subject matter and disavowing any connection between the realm of the "personal" and that of political or economic life. In doing so, the novel effaces the way that the institutions of personal life, and even ways of talking about personal experience, change over time, emerging from a process of historical struggle between different interest groups.

If Fielding's novels can be invoked as paradigmatic within Bakhtin's theory, they become anomalous in this second account of the nature of the novel. *Tom Jones* in particular not only acknowledges but insists on the connections between matters of personal and of political importance; and all of Fielding's novels call attention to the ongoing power of history to shape the conventions of personal identity as well as of public life. Thus, Fielding's interest in literary history is part of his more general interest in historical process: in the world of his novels, the individual formulates his identity through social conventions that are as transient, perhaps, as some of the literary conventions Fielding ridicules in his plays. Such possible uses of the novel form, emphasized by Bakhtin's account and particularly vividly realized in Fielding's work, appear in the novels of his contemporaries and successors as well.

Though Fielding does not consistently strive to conceal the conventional nature of social life or the influence of historical change, he often expresses a kind of horrified surprise at the extent to which individual personality may be shaped by these contingencies—what he calls in an early essay the "Force of Fashion on the Mind." When Fielding employs the device of the puppet show in *The Author's Farce* to parody popular entertainments, he refers to the crude puppet shows offered in country towns and at fairs, thus implying that the tastes of the town have sunk to a low level; but the device also resonates more broadly with a suggestion that there is something puppetlike about following the dictates of current fashion (whether a rage for the opera, the pantomime, or, for that matter, the novel). A thematics of puppetry, literally staged in the final act of *The Author's Farce*, appears as well in Fielding's other plays, in his essays, and in his novels, often serving to express both the comic and the dark possibilities of the control of individual identity from the outside. Fielding repeatedly comes back to the idea that some people might as well be puppets, their movements manipulated by strings and their bodies and minds made of something less animate than flesh and blood. He returns often as well to the scene of the masquerade, a popular entertainment in his time, and more generally to the idea of people wearing masks, whether literal or figurative ones.

A mask may be donned voluntarily, to please or to deceive a viewer, and Fielding frequently employs images of masking to portray the human proclivity to affectation, which he names as the proper target of ridicule in his preface to *Joseph Andrews*. He also often suggests, however, that masks may come to dominate their wearers, the artificial self they represent overpowering any organic identity that might be presumed to lie beneath. Thus Fielding's thematic interests in puppet life and in masks are closely linked, and they are both linked, perhaps less obviously, to his complicated and evolving exploration of the many meanings of "adoption." An affected identity might be called an adopted rather than an innate or genuine one; new institutions and beliefs, unlike timeless or natural ones, must be adopted by a culture in the course of history; in a more straightforward sense of the word, Tom Jones is an adoptive rather than a biological son of Allworthy, as Joseph Andrews turns out to be the adopted child of those he had thought were his blood relations. Especially in his earlier writings, Fielding tends to attach a pejorative sense to adoption as it appears in my first two examples: at times he links these senses of adoption to the stricter, familial one to suggest that a person who adopts a character or who lives by adopted beliefs is—like a puppet—not really flesh and blood, and so, in some sense, is not related to other people by blood ties.

Even in his early works, however, this opposition between adoptive and natural identities and relations is not strictly maintained. *The Author's Farce* closes with a sequence of increasingly absurd revelations of lost identities and family bonds, including the discovery that one of the puppets on stage is the son of one of the human characters in the play's frame narrative. At times teasingly, at times seriously, Fielding repeatedly suggests that there may be more of a continuum between identity that seems merely artificial, affected, or allegorical (a human being who tries to "name" himself with the affected virtue of piety or wit or generosity; a puppet character named "Mrs. Novel") and what we ordinarily recognize as an individual human self. Though some of the characters in his novels have at least apparently naturalistic names such as Tom Jones, Joseph Andrews, or Abraham Adams, and others, like the puppets in *The Author's Farce*, are named for a quality, an occupation, or an obsession (such as Booby, Allworthy, Thwackum, or Square), these characters interact in the same plane of novelistic reality and may turn out to have closer ties to each other, including blood ones, than might initially appear.

The characters on stage in the final scene of *The Author's Farce* are presented as puppets, I have suggested, because they are so shaped, controlled, and defined by their particular historical moment; yet, significantly, that same historical moment generates a number of different puppets with their own distinctive ways of talking and moving, rather than manipulating them in unison. For Fielding, historical determinism is never singular and monolithic: he is interested in the contradictions, gaps, and disjunctions within a society's system of practices and beliefs at any one time. In *The Author's Farce*, these disjunctions between different ways of talking and acting are trivial ones, and they appear in the spaces *between* the characters we see on stage. In the course of Fielding's career as a novelist, he becomes increasingly interested in locating these disjunctions within the individual, so that character itself becomes the meeting place of disparate genres, multiple discourses, incompatible frames of reference. In the works he wrote before becoming a novelist, and to greater or lesser extents in all of his novels as well, Fielding takes a satirist's view of inconsistencies within human identity, treating them as comical or scandalous secrets to be exposed by the keen observer's pen. However, even in his early novel, *Joseph Andrews*, Fielding begins to express uncertainty or distrust about the satirist's view of identity. In *Tom Jones* and *Amelia*, he bodies forth the possibility that it is in fact the tense and often unstable coexistence of disparate discourses or frames of reference within a single self that preserves the possibility of individual character, keeping it alive and dynamic within the grid of history's dictates.

Fielding himself at mid-century presents us with a vivid example of a culture's past, present, and future in collision within the individual soul. Mid-eighteenth-century England lay uneasily between a long cultural past and that future we now inhabit as our present world. Many recognizably modern institutions developed rapidly in the course of Fielding's lifetime, changing the cultural landscape around him in radical— though frequently preliminary or partial—ways. Often, Fielding joined the chorus of doomsayers who denounced such changes as signaling, if not the end of the world, the end of the social and cultural world as they knew it. Sometimes Fielding showed more pragmatic adaptability, accepting the changes he witnessed or even capitalizing upon them (perhaps with a gesture of knowing irony). Occasionally he even ran forward to carry the banner for new views or institutions, insisting on their promise with real imaginative zeal.

Fielding's relation to Sir Robert Walpole, Prime Minister of England from 1720 to 1742, illustrates the complexity—perhaps the irresolvable ambiguity—of his attitudes toward the political and economic changes of his time. In Walpole's day, the post of Prime Minister was not an officially designated one; it was Walpole's enemies, complaining

of the disproportionate power he wielded at court and in the government, who dubbed him the country's "prime" minister. They saw his
influence as dangerously eroding the traditional authority of the king,
already significantly curtailed by the 1688 Glorious Revolution and the
subsequent Act of Settlement that formalized certain limits on royal
power. And Walpole's critics rightly saw his methods of influence as
forever altering the nature of English national government: Walpole
developed a variety of bureaucratic and administrative means to exert
control of a distinctively modern nature, including an effective system
of bartering government posts at home and an extensive network of
spies or "secret service men" abroad.

At points in his career, Fielding joined such conservative literary figures as the members of the Scriblerus Club (Swift, Pope, Gay, and others) in attacking Walpole, sometimes making him the target of merry
ridicule, sometimes suggesting, more seriously, that Walpole presided
over a far-reaching degradation of England's culture. Fielding even
donned the pseudonym "Scriblerus Secundus" for some of his early
satiric works to indicate his identification with this group. Scholars
have debated, however, whether Fielding adopted a more positive view
of Walpole at other times, and whether he may even have accepted
secret patronage from him. More important for our purposes is the
question of whether Fielding at some moments, or in some respects,
entertained enthusiasm for the wide historical changes with which
Walpole's regime was associated.

Those changes were as much economic as political. The features of
a modern capitalist economy, so familiar to us now, were just being consolidated in England in the first half of the eighteenth century, and they
existed alongside surviving values and institutional arrangements from
an older economic system. The Bank of England and the maintaining
of a substantial national debt, initiated at the end of the seventeenth
century, developed so rapidly and so consequentially in the early eighteenth century as to represent what some have called a financial revolution. Others have described the eighteenth century as the period in
which a true "consumer society" was born in England; an unprecedented emphasis on changing fashions and on the exchange and acquisition
of consumer goods gave commodities a new role in English culture. Yet
these changes were not instantaneous or thoroughgoing. Within
specifically literary culture, a strong strain of nostalgic or reactionary
sentiment persisted alongside newer views: English literary culture at

mid-century had one foot in the Augustan era of the first part of the century, with its neoclassical values and its suspicion of change, and one foot in the "Whig" ethos of the years to come, with its enthusiasm for trade and for the new financial and economic institutions, its acceptance of limitations on royal power, and its support for ministerial means of managing national government. Though some have called Fielding a consistently "good Whig," he, too, seems to have his two feet planted in different historical moments, and his work is characteristically divided in mood about the historical changes that surrounded him.

Suggestively, as a London magistrate in the last years of his life, Fielding himself sponsored two innovations that resonated broadly with Walpole's new order. The more fanciful of these was a commercial agency founded by Fielding and his half brother John, which they called "The Office of Intelligence: or, Universal Register of Persons and Things." The services offered by the Fieldings' registry are familiar to us from the modern institutions of employment agencies, real estate agencies, travel agencies, and consignment shops, although the "universal" aspirations of their registry might strike us as unusual: the agency was to serve as a clearinghouse for services of every kind, matching (for a small fee) vacant jobs with would-be workers, vacant houses with buyers or renters, unwanted goods with new owners, and so on. Fielding put a great deal of effort into promoting or "puffing" this venture in his periodical writing and even in his last novel. Though the "Universal Register" does not seem to have made his fortune, his hope that it might do so, and the faith he expressed that it could perform great services to society, make Fielding, in this venture at least, a voice for the commercial conception of society that was becoming more and more dominant during his lifetime.

More specifically, the basic premise of the "Universal Register"— Fielding's discovery that information gathering is itself a valuable product—parallels in the commercial sphere one of Walpole's great discoveries in the realm of governance: the utility of centralized information as a form of power. Fielding's second scheme or innovation also applied the power of centralized information, and to much more consequential effect for the future of English society. From his position as magistrate at Bow Street in London, Fielding argued passionately the need for a troop of regular, skilled constables to pursue and apprehend criminals; and his lobbying resulted in the establishment of the "Bow Street Runners," the first efficient, professional police force in England. This innovation, now seemingly an inevitable part of civil life, improved law enforcement by providing professionals to "run after" those who had committed a crime; but this improvement, as Fielding emphasized in his proposals, depended on the scheme's first and crucial provision— that of a centralized location for the reporting of crimes.

Critics and theorists of the novel have suggested that there is something about the novel form, with its capacities for centralized or totalizing narration (its inclusion of sweeping perspectives and minute detail, its apparent access into individual consciousnesses, its compelling effects on readers) that makes it appropriate that it emerged as a genre during the same period in which police forces, penitentiaries, and other systems of surveillance, reporting, and control developed as crucial forms of state power. How apt, then, that Fielding the novelist was also Fielding, the founder of the Bow Street Runners. And yet (to return more directly to our subject of Fielding and the Novel), Fielding did not simply or immediately embrace the new genre of the novel, at least not as it was practiced by one of its great popularizers, Samuel Richardson.

Readers from Fielding's day to our own have noted that this great writer was initially catapulted into his career as a novelist, having first gained fame as a playwright and having achieved some minor competence in other forms, by his cranky resistance to Richardson's vastly popular first novel, *Pamela*. Within six months of *Pamela*'s publication in 1740, Fielding had dismissed it handily in a brilliant parody, *Shamela*, poking fun at the moral pretensions of *Pamela*'s heroine and at *Pamela* itself, lowering the mode of the novel's events to broad burlesque, and shrinking the protracted span of its action to a whirlwind thirty or forty pages. Energetic and hilarious as this dismissal had been, Fielding somehow was moved to respond to *Pamela* again the following year; but what begins as another burlesquing of Richardson's novel, *Joseph Andrews*, becomes, as it goes on, Fielding's own first full-length contribution to the emerging genre. The particular story of Fielding's entry into the new novel form bespeaks, then, that same ambivalence we have remarked in his responses to other new institutions and practices. Though both he and Richardson were to engage in the practice of writing novels, they clearly interpreted that practice quite differently, and contended openly for the authority to define the new genre in their own ways, reminding us that any historical innovation may be shaped in alternative directions or put to different, perhaps even opposing, purposes. Even within Fielding's novels, however, the interpretation of the new genre is a complex, self-reflective, and often divided one—one that may be made to look more unitary and self-consistent than it is when defined within a system of contrasts with Richardson's works.

The contrasts that have regularly been drawn between Richardson's and Fielding's novels are at once helpful and potentially misleading. Readers have always noticed that Fielding did not follow Richardson's example in employing the epistolary form of narration used in *Pamela*. Indeed, he vigorously parodied that form in *Shamela*, and then ridiculed it again in *Joseph Andrews*, where he also first offered his own alternative to the form: a narrator who describes events and characters in the third-person past tense, from outside the plane and time frame of the novel's action, speaking in his own distinctive voice. Fielding would develop his use of that narrative voice in *Tom Jones*, where the narrator again holds forth on matters literary and philosophical in the first chapters of each of the novel's books. The use of this omniscient and magisterial narrative voice has been linked by readers to Fielding's treatment of character, which they see as strikingly different from Richardson's. The nature of that difference has often been described as the difference between "internal" and "external" characterization: Richardson's fiction of a text composed by Pamela herself, written as events occurred, allows him to render those events from "inside" her present consciousness, whereas Fielding, it has been observed, generally describes characters as they would be seen and understood from the outside.

Some readers have seen this difference as a sign of the decided inferiority of Fielding's human understanding, as well as of his works. In Richardson and Fielding's own time, Samuel Johnson commented that there was as great a difference between the two novelists "as between a man who knew how a watch was made, and a man who could tell the hour by looking on the dial-plate." Readers more sympathetic to Fielding have argued that his choice of external characterization reflects not the superficiality of his vision, but the profundity of his philosophical recognition that in life itself, other people's characters are always only experienced through external and often misleading evidence. Thus, the insistent theme of misrecognitions, particularly in *Joseph Andrews*, serves to illustrate the verisimilitude of Fielding's narrative technique, and shows the effects—often comic, sometimes tragic—of the opacity

of one person's true character to another. Fielding is not simply philosophical, however, about this opacity: an element of longing for mutual transparency and full access to others' inner selves appears in his novels. This longing contributes to an elegiac strain within them, which
has been too frequently overlooked as critics concentrate on drawing
broad distinctions between Fielding's work and Richardson's.

In drawing such distinctions, critics rightly observe that Richardson's and Fielding's novels have different generic affiliations as well as
different forms of narration and characterization. Fielding called some
of his plays "dramatic satires," and his novels, too, are indebted to satiric traditions in a way Richardson's do not seem to be. This is one way
in which they seem more closely tied to Augustan literary culture than
do Richardson's novels, as satire was a highly developed and valued
form among the Scriblerus Club members and other writers of the early
eighteenth century. However, as I have already briefly noted, Fielding's
own stance toward satire is a complex one, and his view of satire's powers becomes increasingly dark in the course of his novel-and essay-writ-
ing career.

Further, while Richardson's first novel draws on the native English
traditions of spiritual autobiography, model-letter books, and conduct
manuals, Fielding, in his preface to *Joseph Andrews* and elsewhere,
explicitly declares the generic roots of his own novels in the tradition of
classical epic. When Richardson and Fielding adopt these distinct
generic lineages for their novels, they strike quite different stances
toward recent developments in literary history—and in social history as
well. The classical heritage Fielding invokes was made available to him
through the traditional education he received as an upper-class boy;
Richardson was well schooled instead in the growing body of literature,
largely didactic or religious in nature, written in English for the aspiring middle class. More broadly, the classical epics so valued by the
Augustans contain an image of male heroism, located in a world of militaristic values, that many of the newer works of mid-eighteenth-century England, often focused on female virtue and located in a world of
domestic relations, did not honor. The nature of these newer works
bespoke important, if somewhat inchoate, changes within English
social life: a new valuation of "companionate" rather than arranged
marriages, and an increasing idealization of female nature, as of the
roles of wife and mother. With *Pamela, or* [Female] *Virtue Rewarded*,
Richardson places himself at the very center of these social changes;

while Fielding's affirmation of epic models seems to leave him outside them, belatedly harking back to a fading world.

Some critics have been so impressed with the contrasting concentrations of Fielding and Richardson on male and on female ideals that they have summed up the differences between these two early novelists by declaring Fielding a paradigmatically virile and masculine writer, "a man's man," and Richardson "in all seriousness, one of our great women." (We might thus revise the imagined dramatic scene with which we began as a testy encounter between "Mr. Novel" and "Mrs. Novel," with Fielding and Richardson filling these respective puppet roles.) Critics have also remarked, however, that in his final novel, *Amelia*, Fielding explores the subjects of female heroism and domestic relations which Richardson had so momentously made his own, thus changing places with Richardson, who turned to questions of *male* virtue in the last novel he wrote. This crisscrossing of characteristic interests, satisfying in the neatness of its apparent reversals, had in fact been prepared for by elements in Fielding's earlier novels. For, despite his avowed and important debts to epic and the concentration on male character in his first three fictional works (reflected in their titles), Fielding from the first presents conventional notions of male heroism as extremely vexed, and he expresses a complex and ambivalent attitude toward emerging ideals of female character as well.

The availability of other selves for "internal" characterization, the legitimacy of satiric attacks on personal character, the viability of epic models of heroism, the authenticity of female claims to special virtue—all of these questions are posed in complicated and dynamic ways in Fielding's novels. His treatment of them evolves within the course of each of his novels, as well as between them. Fielding knew that the reader's experience of a novel itself has a "history," unfolding over time, and he capitalizes upon the dynamic nature of that experience, raising expectations only to explode them, moving the reader through different views of an event, a character, or a phrase—sometimes in the developing span of an elaborate plot, sometimes in the course of a single sentence. The highly mobile point of view conjured by Fielding's prose allows for the extraordinary effects of tone that critics have described as his characteristic "double irony" or "double reversals."

Fielding's most masterful achievements of style derive from this capacity of his prose to sustain multiple implications simultaneously, or in quick succession. So however, do the clumsiest, seemingly most incompetent or ill-considered aspects of some of his works. To an unsympathetic reader, *Jonathan Wild*, Fielding's first novelistic work, may seem merely inconsistent in its use of an ironic persona; the tone of *Amelia*, his last, has struck some readers as oscillating wildly, bathetically, between earnest feeling and an unintentional atmosphere of burlesque. In these works, however, as in *Shamela*, *Joseph Andrews*, and *Tom Jones*, incoherences—problems of tone, awkward junctures between incommensurate discourses, inconsistencies in narrative strategy—are themselves made to signify: within each work, Fielding thematizes the experience of Babel, calling attention to those gaps within social discourse we have learned to overlook.

Toward the close of *Jonathan Wild*, Mrs. Heartfree has been relating her adventures at some length to a small audience gathered in Heartfree's prison cell, when a "horrid uproar" alarmed the company and "put a stop to her narration at present." The narrator comments, "It is impossible for me to give the reader a better idea of the noise which now arose than by desiring him to imagine I had the hundred tongues the poet once wished for, and was vociferating from them all at once, by hollowing, scolding, crying, swearing, bellowing, and, in short, by every different articulation which is within the scope of the human organ." Fielding does not give voice in *Jonathan Wild* to every different articulation within the scope of the human organ, but he does there unleash a dizzying diversity of forms of expression. The uproar that breaks into Mrs. Heartfree's story dramatizes, within the narrative, a much more constant process of disruption and interruption occurring throughout *Jonathan Wild*, where it is generally another among the narrator's own "hundred tongues" that breaks off the prevailing discourse of the moment. The mode of this early work is primarily ironic and satirical, but the targets of its satire are many, and sometimes apparently incompatible with each other; and the ironic persona who delivers the tale suffers strange transformations, sometimes admitting other points of view into his narration in the form of references to the opinions of "weak men," sometimes temporarily (as if inadvertently) assuming those alternative views himself.

Fielding builds the satirical fable of *Jonathan Wild* around the life story of an infamous criminal of that name, convicted and hanged in London in 1725. Wild was not simply a thief: he presided over a substantial and organized gang of thieves, and, with an audacity that seems

to have impressed as well as offended his contemporaries, he also gar-
nered reward money by helping victims regain what his own gang
members had taken. He exploited the system for capturing thieves as
well, informing on members of his gang who challenged his authority
in some way. Thus, without carrying out a robbery himself, Wild might
profit at several levels from the event. At intervals throughout *Jonathan
Wild*, Fielding links Wild's criminal enterprise to legitimate capitalist
entrepreneurship, implicating capitalism in Wild's amoral greed, by
emphasizing that it is his employing of other hands to labor for his
profit that defines his "greatness" as a man. The insistence with which
Fielding uses the term "greatness" and the phrase "the great man" to
refer to Wild calls attention to a political target for his satire as well as
an economic one: during his long tenure as prime minister, the many
opponents of Sir Robert Walpole sneeringly referred to him as "the
great man." In 1728, in *The Beggar's Opera*, John Gay had already made
this satiric connection, identifying Jonathan Wild and Robert Walpole
as moral if not social equivalents; Fielding deepens the connection,
underlining the way that Wild and Walpole have both made their fortunes by presiding over systems, exploiting institutions, and simply,
impudently, assuming an authority over others that has no particular
source.

These elements of Fielding's satire easily intertwine, as Walpole's
forms of governance and the institutions of a developing capitalism
constitute important and interrelated features of Fielding's newly modern world. (We might note, for that matter, the peculiar similarity of
the service offered by Wild in obtaining information about stolen goods
and matching dispossessed owners with missing property and the kind
of service conceived of by Fielding in his own innovation, the office of
the "Universal Register." In *Jonathan Wild*, a version of that service is
treated as the tellingly criminal epitome of modern enterprise.) Fielding extends his satire of things modern in *Jonathan Wild* into the specifically literary sphere, parodying the popular genres of criminal biography, travel narrative, and epistolary romance at different points in the
tale. However, the main literary tradition with which his satire engages
is not a modern but an ancient one: the world of epic, with its ideas of
honor and glory and its delineation of the character of a hero. Epic references are always near at hand for the narrator of *Jonathan Wild*, who
compares Jonathan Wild to Aeneas and his sidekick to Achates, dwells
at a number of points on the nature of heroic greatness, and offers his

reader rhetorical flourishes adopted from epic, as when he provides a long epic simile about bulls and cows to describe the cacophonous interruption of Mrs. Heartfree's story. Thus, one of the hundred tongues in which Fielding erupts into speech in that episode, as throughout *Jonathan Wild*, is a tongue derived from epic.

Fielding's epic similes in *Jonathan Wild* (as in *Joseph Andrews* and *Tom Jones*) are entertaining because they place such homely references in the high diction and elaborate syntax of epic style, providing a measure of the distance between epic grandeur and the pedestrian modern world. However, Fielding's voicing of epic language in *Jonathan Wild* does not only serve, in the mode of mock-epic, to express the degeneracy of modern times. Instead, when Fielding violently, anachronistically, yokes together references to distinctively modern phenomena and to famous classical figures or events, he works to unsettle accepted "heroic" values in both, prying each loose from its familiar context by means of the other. Over and over again in *Jonathan Wild*, Fielding emphasizes the destructiveness of heroes' actions in history, although, speaking within his ironic persona, he pretends to celebrate that destructiveness, praising military heroes' willingness to massacre whole nations for the sake of their honor. The true worth of heroic character is thus drawn into question in *Jonathan Wild* in two ways: by this appalling praise for the heroic leader's spectacular sacrifice of human lives, and by the equation created between such heroic acts and the ignoble scheming of Jonathan Wild, who, we are told, has modeled himself on the epic and historical heroes he read about in school.

Fielding does not content himself with expressing the bankruptcy of both ancient and modern heroism in *Jonathan Wild*; he also attempts, at points, to advance an alternative set of values that he can affirm, albeit indirectly and perhaps only partially. He refers to the virtues of good nature, friendliness, generosity, and domestic devotion, although he claims to see them as merely "silly" weaknesses; and he embodies these "weaknesses" in the characters of Mr. and Mrs. Heartfree, whose story begins as a subplot of Wild's adventure but eventually becomes an equally weighty center of interest. Although Wild and the Heartfrees interact within the same space of narrative, they inhabit largely separate frames of reference, belonging to different literary genres and moral universes, so that Fielding's treatments of these characters can interrupt each other but cannot be simultaneously engaged. It is an episode involving Wild that literally interrupts Mrs. Heartfree's narration of her adventures; the chorus of dissimilar voices unleashed at this interruption creates a boundary between Wild's and Mrs. Heartfree's incompatible ways of speaking, enacting and expanding upon the irreconcilable discord we might hear between them.

Throughout *Jonathan Wild*, Fielding typically marks such borders rather than erasing them or moving smoothly across them: he calls attention to the breaks or ruptures within our ways of constructing social meaning, including the separation we respect implicitly between public and private life. The Heartfrees' virtues are largely those of private life, whereas the various men satirized in the character of Wild aspire to success in the public spheres of politics or finance. Wild's tale too, however, includes events of a personal nature: Fielding interweaves the story of his courtship and unhappy marriage to Laetitia Snap with that of his commercial and quasi-political exploits. Significantly, the moments of greatest instability in the narrator's tone—the moments of wavering between ironic and earnest expression—tend to occur as he moves between his domestic and his public (political, economic, criminal) plots. (In particular, the narrator equivocates throughout *Jonathan Wild* about whether "greatness"—that is, amoral, insatiable ambition and greed—tends to thrive or tends to provide its own punishment in this world; and he gives different answers to this question for public and for private life.) A few utopian moments in *Jonathan Wild* suggest the possibility of healing this public-private division: the "very grave man" who opposes Wild's authority in Newgate exhorts the debtors to form a true community there, in which public good and private benefit will be identified; and the book's final pages leave us with a vision of an extended Heartfree family living "all together in one house" as one "family of love."

The utopian prospect of unification (of persons and of parts of life) is only glimpsed, however, among the increasing images of fragmentation in the closing chapters of *Jonathan Wild*, from the dialogue between Jonathan and the ordinary at Newgate, with its ellipses indicating lacunae in the text, to the narrator's closing acknowledgment that he must bring together "those several features" of Jonathan's character "which lie scattered up and down in this history." "History" is more than a merely conventional term in this formulation: in its final pages, *The History of the Life of the Late Mr. Jonathan Wild the Great* reminds us that the various languages it has employed (of epic greatness, of modern political parties, of ancient empires, of capitalist ambition, of domestic virtue) all unfold in history and meet confusedly there: Wild shall "stand unrivalled on the pinnacle of GREATNESS" only "*while* greatness consists in power, pride, insolence, and doing mischief to mankind . . . ," the narrator concludes—letting slip his ironic mask, even as he reveals that it has been constructed out of his historical moment.

In *Shamela*, the multiple voices in which Fielding speaks—or, I should say, the multiple pens with which Fielding writes—are formalized as belonging to the several correspondents whose letters make up this brief work. *Pamela* itself includes a few letters from writers other than Pamela, and Richardson would expand the epistolary form in *Clarissa* to encompass letters from a number of correspondents; but the variety of letter writers in *Shamela* works directly and explicitly to challenge the authenticity of any one writer's presentation of events. Before we arrive at the text of Shamela's first letter, we are given a mock dedication and two supposed encomiums to the editor of the volume (parodies of Richardson's elaborate self-flattering apparatus in later editions of *Pamela*), and also a pair of letters between two readers of *Pamela*—Parson Tickletext, who has been taken in by the seductive power of Pamela's appearance in letters, and Parson Oliver, who disabuses Tickletext of his illusions and offers the letters to follow as the eye-opening authentic original of Pamela's tale. These "framing materials" in *Shamela* serve not only to introduce Shamela's letters and the challenge they pose to *Pamela*'s authenticity, but also to establish a multileveled structure of perspectives, like the one set up by the puppet show in *The Author's Farce*, with similarly peculiar interactions between frame and framed, reader (or editor) and character or text.

The specific content of the framing materials also provides a more implicit critique of the false apparent unity of *Pamela*'s world: in these introductory letters, Fielding rather gracelessly cobbles together ridicule of Richardson's literary success with ridicule of two of his favorite political targets, Sir Robert Walpole and Lord Hervey. The incongruity of the effect is itself significant. Encountering the unexpected figures of the Prime Minister and one of his allies on the threshold of Fielding's parody of a novel, we have to wonder how the world of political conflict is or is not relevant to the apparently self-contained domestic world conjured by Richardson's tale. Fielding makes us feel the division that may be quietly maintained between public and private spheres of life by crossing that division—bringing together the separate languages of each without overcoming the dissonance we are likely to hear between them.

Lord Hervey, satirized under the name of "Miss Fanny" in the dedication to *Shamela*, makes a brief appearance in *Joseph Andrews* as well. There, he provides the satiric original for Beau Didapper, the effeminate man who ineffectively threatens Fanny's virtue in Book 4. Fielding and others had frequently satirized Lord Hervey not only for his political allegiances but for his supposed effeminacy and sexual ambiguity, but such a satirical reference seems out of place in the final book of *Joseph Andrews*. Fielding in fact addresses the subject of satire at several points in *Joseph Andrews*, most explicitly in Book 3, chapter 1, where he defends general satire but rejects particular satire—or satire of recognizable individuals—as the equivalent of public executions. Five chapters later, in narrative rather than expository form, he again links verbal satire to physical violence and questions its legitimacy when he describes his main characters' encounter with the Roasting Squire. Intent, we are told, on finding the "ridiculous" in all he meets, the Roasting Squire exploits his social power to abuse and humiliate by any means, indulging in practical jokes that force their victims into ridiculous postures, or that even hurt them physically, rather than serving to expose real hidden weaknesses. The ridiculous is precisely what Fielding named in the preface to *Joseph Andrews* as the source of his own work's comic elements, though he there confidently asserts that the effect of ridiculousness attaches itself to individuals only because they have assumed affectations of some kind. Laughter, in this view, functions morally, to reveal concealed faults and inconsistencies; but in the course of *Joseph Andrews*, Fielding questions whether laughter can be an amoral, merely aggressive force as well.

He conveys this questioning largely through a complicated interplay between disparate genres and literary modes—drama, satire, the novel as defined by Richardson, the epic as defined by Milton—in the rhetoric, images, and narrative events of *Joseph Andrews*. Allusions to *Paradise Lost* especially enrich the texture of the scenes involving the Roasting Squire (in the "natural amphitheatre" where Joseph, Fanny, and Adams picnic, and in the tormenting of Adams with a "devil" or firecracker at the Squire's estate). The verbal and narrative recollections of Milton's poem in these scenes quietly advance epic forms of expression as an alternative to satiric ones. Both epic precedents and satiric ones, however, are invoked by Fielding in *Joseph Andrews* to dislocate Richardson's epistolary novel form—to denaturalize its modes of representation by bringing them up against those of very different literary forms.

The opening gambit in Fielding's response to Richardson in *Joseph Andrews* has always struck readers as self-evidently comical and debunking: Fielding replaces the serving-maid who so fervently defends her chastity in *Pamela* with a male servant, who rejects his mistress's advances with equal fervor. The comedy of the scenes between Lady Booby and Joseph, critics have commented, is like the comedy of cross-dressing; Joseph appears in a garment adopted from his sister's wardrobe of virtues, rather than one natural to himself. Fielding does exploit our different expectations about female and male chastity to play these scenes for broad comic effect. Even in the opening scenes of the novel, however, the implications of this comic reversal of roles are ambiguous. Why does what constitutes a virtue in one sex become ridiculous when asserted by the other? Should virtues be like clothing, to be donned only when they are in fashion, becoming to one wearer but absurd on another? As the novel leaves its burlesque relation to *Pamela* behind, Joseph no longer functions primarily as a figure of absurdity, and even, some have claimed, becomes the hero of the novel. If so, he does so neither by abandoning his initial association with feminine roles nor by proving that all the features of his identity are natural rather than adopted. The description of Joseph's physical appearance, Fielding's comments on his tears at the abduction of Fanny, the story of his replacement of a girl in the cradle as a baby—all continue to link Joseph with feminine postures and roles, but not in ways that Fielding consistently ridicules. One function of this evolving treatment of Joseph's gender identity is to question the value and humanity of the traditional male "hero"—a term Fielding uses to describe the would-be rapist of Fanny, who embodies such unthinking aggression that his head, Fielding tells us, might as well be made of solid bone.

Joseph's identity is, in a number of ways, characterized by borrowing or adoption: he adopts his sister's model of righteous virtue; his own name turns out, unexpectedly, to be an adoptive one; he even has to borrow the clothing he wears from other people at several points in the novel. Through Joseph, however, Fielding dignifies the idea of adopted identity, rather than making it an emblem (as a purely satirical writer might) of the gap between essential and assumed character. Gammar

Andrews tells us that after finding Joseph in the cradle in place of her little girl, she came to love him "all to nothing as if [he] had been my own girl." The plot revelations that come at the close of *Tom Jones* even more emphatically trace a continuum between adoptive and biological relations: the discovery that Tom is in fact Bridget Allworthy's illegitimate son makes good on his long-standing adoptive relation to Allworthy by revealing that Allworthy is his uncle by blood, if not actually his father. Tom's character, like Joseph's, emerges in the course of his novel through a complex interplay between different discourses, but the dynamic tensions within his character might be fruitfully located in competing "texts" from political and social rather than literary history.

The events of political history intrude directly into the plot of *Tom Jones* when Tom encounters soldiers on their way to fight against the Jacobite rebellion. The references to this rebellion set the novel's action in 1745, the year the followers of "Bonnie Prince Charlie," advancing south from Scotland, sought to reclaim the British monarchy for the Stuart line, dethroned in the Glorious Revolution of 1688. Tom expresses Fielding's own sympathies with the existing government of England when he decides to volunteer and join the soldiers in their defense of England's Protestant religion and constitutional liberty. While Fielding made a name for himself writing against the ministry of Robert Walpole early in his career, in the mid-1740s he was one of the staunchest supporters of the new ministry (Henry Pelham's) in print, and published two periodicals and several pamphlets specifically in response to the Jacobite threat. In these polemical writings, he urges his countrymen to join the King's army and take arms against the invading Jacobites; but in *Tom Jones*, his hero never makes it into battle. Instead, the King's soldiers turn out to be an unruly bunch; Tom soon quarrels with one of them, is injured, and gets left behind; and his pursuit of the troops and of their glorious cause is gradually replaced by a pursuit of Sophia and of love. Although the trajectory toward battle with Jacobite forces is thus never carried out, the invocation of this political context, and then the movement of the plot between Tom's patriotic and his romantic aims, traces a connection between the apparently separate matters of national government and of personal identity and desire.

The political writings of Fielding and other propagandists on both sides of the Jacobite debate often made this connection explicitly, with each side in the conflict warning that the victory of the other would spell catastrophe not only for the rule of the nation but for relationships between the sexes and within the family. Critics of *Tom Jones* have noted that the "patriarchalist" arguments made in favor of Jacobitism involved analogies between the government of nations and of families, advocating the absolute authority of kings and husbands and fathers to rule over their respective realms. Thus, Squire Western's support for the Jacobite cause accords neatly with the views he expresses about his own right to control his wife's and daughter's lives. This analogizing between national and domestic rule, important to formulations of patriarchalist political philosophy, does not, however, sum up all the claims made by both Jacobite and anti-Jacobite propaganda about the consequences of their conflict for the realm of personal experience. Whig writing against the rebellion (including Fielding's) insisted that a Jacobite victory would usher in not only a different government but different definitions of male and female identity—definitions associated with the earlier era of Stuart rule, and ones that afforded men much less dignity and control.

Among the central motifs of much Whig propaganda, visual as well as verbal, were certain stereotyped images of the typical Jacobite man and woman. The Whig image of the Jacobite man drew on the existing type of the Restoration Cavalier gentleman, and mixed appealing with negative qualities: he might be witty, dashing, gallant, and successful with the ladies, but also too easily swayed by those ladies, weak-willed, and superstitious. Whig polemics invoke a more thoroughly negative image of the Jacobite woman: she must necessarily be headstrong and dominating, and possibly fierce, cruel, and perverse as well. At best, her courage and spirit make her seem a more lively alternative to the timid, gentle, chaste, and compassionate women conjured in Whig propaganda of this period to prove the humanity of their own cause.

Fielding engages this contemporary discourse about masculine and feminine character when he constructs his male and female protagonists, Tom and Sophia, in *Tom Jones*. He employs the language of this discourse to characterize them, placing them within its insistent oppositions—but, significantly, he invokes terms from the conventional accounts of *both* Whig and Jacobite men and women to describe them, forcing together the opposed categories of character within their single identities. Tom is both a good, modern, moral hero (even volunteering to fight in the Whig cause) and something of a Cavalier figure (occupied in various love affairs, brave to a fault, and irresistibly dashing);

Sophia, we are told at a number of points, is courageous and spirited as well as gentle, compassionate, and, of course, chaste. This has troubled critics of *Tom Jones*, who have variously identified Tom and Sophia with one or the other side of the Whig-Jacobite conflict: some have argued that, within the political allegory of *Tom Jones*, Tom should be identified with Bonnie Prince Charlie himself, others that he represents the Whig opposition to that prince's cause. At several points in the novel, Fielding in fact foregrounds an effect of diverse, even opposed frames of reference meeting within the individual characters of his hero and heroine.

In one such scene, Tom decides (like a good Cavalier hero) to challenge Northerton to a duel, but only because (like a good Christian hero) he thinks it would be wrong to sustain malice or unforgivingness toward him over time. In another, Sophia simultaneously shows courage and gentle love when she runs away from her father's home. Though these do not seem necessarily to be mutually exclusive qualities, Fielding highlights a sense of conflict or dissonance between them; he connects both scenes, in fact, to descriptions of cacophonous outbreaks of multiple, dissonant voices something like the one that interrupts Mrs. Heartfree in *Jonathan Wild*. He also sets both scenes at midnight, as if to suggest that the conflicting discourses or frames of reference that meet within his characters belong to one day—or era—and to the next, and come confusedly into contact at the midpoint between days (as they might, say, at mid-century). "Twelve Times did the iron Register of Time beat on the sonorous Bell-metal," Fielding tells us, when Sophia "softly stole down Stairs, and having barred and unlocked one of the House Doors, sallied forth. . . ."; "The Clock had now struck Twelve . . . when *Jones* softly opening his Door, issued forth. . . ."

Fielding portrays the male protagonist of his last novel, *Amelia*, as *perpetually* poised between two days, or two cultural eras. For Captain Booth, this suspension of his own identity between two eras is so severe that he is nearly paralyzed, rarely able, literally or figuratively, to "sally" or "issue forth." For much of *Amelia*, Booth is confined to his home to avoid arrest for debt; when he is not there, it is because he has failed to avoid arrest and is even more closely confined in prison. Booth's actions, however, are restricted not only by physical confinement but by a nearly constant sense of internal conflict. The conflicts that stymie Booth's will again and again are generated by his double allegiance to older and to emerging ideas of male character. As a gentleman and especially as a soldier, Booth feels it is his duty to accept challenges to duel, but his Christian conscience recoils at the thought of shedding blood; his Cavalier sense of male honor makes him respond to Miss Mathews's advances in prison (as Tom does to Molly's, to Mrs. Waters's, and to Lady Bellaston's), but his devotion to his wife and to the ideal of a loving marriage renders him nearly senseless with guilt about this affair; his assumptions about a gentleman's proper occupation make it inconceivable to him to look for work beneath a military post, but he is unable to find such a post and cannot support the little family he so loves.

The conflicting frames of reference within which Booth attempts to define himself and to act also shape (and misshape) his efforts to interpret the events around him: Booth is always interpreting others' actions in the wrong contexts, wavering in the general assumptions he brings to social relations, and failing to reconcile his disparate views of the same events. The narrator of *Amelia* himself partakes of this kind of interpretive confusion and instability. Rather than projecting a single, sustained, omniscient view of the events and characters he describes, this narrator seems to waver, like Booth, between old and new assumptions (particularly about relations between the sexes and between social classes), offering one explanation and then another, in succession, without ever reconciling his inconsistencies. Only Amelia is able to achieve constancy of identity and point of view in this novel; while Booth hangs suspended between present and past models of male character, she seems to have moved forward vigorously into a crucial new model for female identity, that of the idealized wife and mother. However, ambivalences about this role (in particular, uncertainties about whether it complements and supports or competes with and challenges traditional male authority) shadow Fielding's treatment of Amelia, creating problems of tone and linking Amelia to various "doubles" within the novels—women who echo her dignified and appealing qualities in a satiric or burlesque key.

Some of Fielding's most successful early works capitalized upon the comic possibilities of female claims to heroism. In *Shamela*, he ridiculed Richardson's invention of a new, specifically female kind of heroic behavior; in one of his most popular plays, *Tom Thumb*, he added an extra dimension to the script's hilarity by casting a woman in the part of the play's tiny but histrionic hero. In *Amelia*, he seems to offer a female hero in all earnestness—but many of his original readers were not impressed. Some of them found Fielding's apparent change of heart in this novel unconvincing and ridiculous; many focused specifically on the novel's account of the injury to Amelia's nose, scoffing at Booth's description of her heroic behavior on the occasion and pretending to believe that the accident left Amelia with no nose at all. In revisions of the novel, Fielding emphasized that Amelia's nose was successfully reconstructed by a surgeon, and his treatment of this reconstruction is itself significant: whereas earlier he might have drawn out the satiric possibilities of a facial feature that had been artificially reshaped or assumed, he here treats the reconstructed nose, altered by accident and reclaimed by careful artifice, as at least as humanly dignified and appealing as Amelia's original nose. Thus, in his final novel, Fielding embraces a sense of human character as altered by time and history, its features layered by the perhaps indistinguishable, though sometimes contradictory, contributions of nature, artifice, and circumstance.

The character we encounter in tracing Fielding through his life's works is itself thus layered, often clearly shaped by the accidents of his historical situation, and strikingly contradictory in the multiple impulses he expresses over time. The man who so memorably ridiculed Richardson's tale of a master marrying his maid went on, eventually, to marry his own; the same writer who produced devastating satires of Walpole's ministry was to become a most vocal supporter of the ministerial establishment. The ways that Fielding strikes us as enmeshed in history, and the ways that historical change involves him, frequently, in contradictions, do not seem, however, to silence him, as they often do Booth. Sometimes cacophonously, always energetically, Fielding's voice, at mid-century, issues forth.

Jill Campbell

Selected Bibliography

Bakhtin, Mikhail. *The Dialogic Imagination: Four Essays*. Ed. Michael Holquist. Trans. Caryl Emerson and Michael Holquist. Austin: University of Texas Press, 1981.

Battestin, Martin C., with Ruthe R. Battestin. *Henry Fielding: A Life*. New York: Routledge, 1989.

Bender, John. *Imagining the Penitentiary: Fiction and the Architecture of Mind in Eighteenth-Century England*. Chicago: University of Chicago Press, 1987.

Brown, Homer Obed. "*Tom Jones*: The 'Bastard' of History." *Boundary 2* 7 (1979): 201–33.

Carlton, Peter J. "*Tom Jones* and the '45 Once Again." *Studies in the Novel* 20 (1988): 361–73.

Castle, Terry. *Masquerade and Civilization: The Carnivalesque in Eighteenth-Century English Fiction and Culture*. Stanford: Stanford University Press, 1986.

Hammond, Brean S. "Politics and Cultural Politics: The Case of Henry Fielding." *Eighteenth-Century Life* 16 (1992): 76–93.

Hunter, J. Paul. *Occasional Form: Henry Fielding and the Chains of Circumstance*. Baltimore: Johns Hopkins University Press, 1975.

McKeon, Michael. *The Origins of the English Novel, 1600–1740*. Baltimore: Johns Hopkins University Press, 1987.

Paulson, Ronald. *Satire and the Novel in Eighteenth-Century England*. New Haven, Conn.: Yale University Press, 1967.

Rawson, C. J. *Henry Fielding and the Augustan Ideal under Stress: 'Nature's Dance of Death' and Other Studies*. Boston: Routledge and Kegan Paul, 1972.

From Swift to Smollett: The Satirical Tradition in Prose Narrative

S MOLLETT'S most enduring contribution to the English novel lay in combining diverse strains of satire and picaresque tales into a thoroughly original cast of fiction. Upon these preexisting narrative modes he imposed dozens of characters, 840 in all (excluding the characters in his *Travels*), and fabricated comic scenes that have delighted readers for over two centuries; and while it is wrong to think of him primarily as a "satiric novelist" or as the Georgian realist par excellence who embodied "picaresque satire in prose," it is fitting to acknowledge the prominent place of these features in his fiction. His "brisk, masculine, and nervous style," as he himself called it, possesses a stylistic force rarely found in the sweep of the English novel—indeed he seems to have converted his own rambunctious energy in real life into a kind of fictional *jouissance*. His complex systems of morality and didacticism resulted in his becoming one of the most profound social commentators of his era, and his hawk's eye for vivid detail rendered him the Hogarth of eighteenth-century prose, especially in the "progress pieces" and the depiction of "grotesques." These insignia are as crucial to his accomplishment as any incorporations of satire and the picaresque.

His vision of the world derived from a wide array of literary traditions that embraced the blend of idealism and irony of Cervantes's *Don Quixote*, revenge tragedy, comedy of "humors," the great satires of Swift and Pope, rogue tales, Hogarthian grotesque, and a more local British heritage of sea stories and Scottish lore that he knew firsthand. Scott,

Dickens, Henry James, and many other novelists have commented on his extraordinary originality, as have those of Smollett's twentieth-century literary heirs who knew to what degree he was one of their so-called founding fathers. He was an uneven novelist, capable of miscalculation and unpredictability and often writing too quickly and erratically, and his penchant for experimentation in the novel cost him as much aggravation as it reaped reward and financial benefit; but he remains the only competitor of Sterne in the satirical phase of the English novel at mid-century.

Satire did not, of course, *lead* to the early eighteenth-century novel in any prescriptive or formal sense, but shaped it in so many ways that the overlaps of the two forms—satire and novel—have always been worthy of study, despite the frustrations involved in trying to arrive at neat conclusions about reciprocity or coherent theories about influence. A more secure approach reasons that satiric narrative enriched the early British novel. Even in the domain of readerly expectations, no coherent patterns can be traced through the early novelists from Defoe and Fielding to Sterne and Jane Austen. Satire was an ancient form of literature, already highly developed in its Horatian and Juvenalian poetic incarnations, and by the end of the seventeenth century it had undergone such transformation that it had become impossible to set it off from such competing forms as pastoral and autobiography, let alone to delineate its boundaries from the newly developing novel of the 1720s. The single aspect of satire clearest to its readers of the 1720s was that it assumed moral norms with which readers could agree or disagree. It was these norms, or values, that rendered it such a controversial form.

Satire had been especially suited to broad concerns of chaos and incoherence—the clutter and medley of diurnal life—rather than nobler strains of order, integration, and perfection. By the time the great English poets Dryden, Pope, and Swift laid their imprints upon the form of satire, it had become the accepted vehicle for criticism of confused systems of patronage and social order, as well as human frailties and irrationalities—so much so that some readers perceived its goals as inflexible and unbending, and consequently dubious. Satirists shaped their readers to believe that its norms were the correct ones, its values solid, whether in the sphere of the public realm versus the private or the city versus the country. Set the chronological dials to approximately 1725, in the aftermath of the South Sea Bubble when England's economic climate was turbulent and fraught with anxiety, and it is clear that for good reason madness and bestiality have become two of satire's most fundamental images.

Even so, satire, both in poetic and prose forms, was unable to cope with the demands for realism of the new reading public. The matter is not that satire failed (it hardly failed), or even that it had become worn out and tired, but rather that in some primal way the imagination of its greatest authors (the Popes and Swifts) existed in a realm removed from the pressing needs of the moment. The urgency of the moment was at stake, not form or artistic failure. It was not that satiric narrative was incapable of coping with the concerns of the day—the rampant sense that the world had gone mad or the new cannibalism of life in the cities—but rather that its psychological mechanisms for coping were unsuited to the needs of contemporary readers, especially young readers. In Swift's case, the coping mechanisms were further complicated by his sense that all moral norms had been toppled and replaced with values impossible to consider reasonable; and because of the insidious ways he saw these new values absorbed into the infrastructure of his society, he became incensed with virtually all forms of creation—even literary and novelistic creation. Stated in another key, satire (exposure) and realism (concern for the moment) did not get along. An example of the disparity is found in Swift's *Tale of a Tub*, the story of a hack driven mad in the process of turning out prose paid for by the word. He is a quixotic figure in reverse who has no means of coping with the bestiality of his modern society, and he has neither the desire nor the inclination to belong to, or connect with, his milieu. He lives in a cluttered and filthy urban garret far removed from nature and the land, and harbors no sense of private spaces, either within the house or outside in the garden; a public creature exclusively, he defines himself in the present place and time only, without reference to the past or to his own family's roots. The more the hack churns out words, the worse he writes and the more confused his opinions become. Swift ridicules him as an utterly alienated figure—a dupe among knaves—in a work brilliant for its glittering depiction of the impoverished writer in the brave new world of print technology and new publishing arrangements. Viewed, however, from the perspective of realism—the moment, the present crisis, characters and life as they are today—Swift's prose narrative fails to cope with the social realities of the hack's world and its values. Two generations later, Smollett's Roderick Random, also crude and alienated, will be presented in altogether different ways.

The extent to which satire had been appropriated by the novel is grasped by consulting *Gulliver's Travels* (1726). Here the master-servant and fool-knave relation is as central to Swift's purpose as the author's sense of time (the relative present) and place (exotic places that reflect on England and Ireland). Despite Lemuel's travels to remote islands—Lilliput, Brobdingnag, Laputa, Houyhnhnmland, places inhabited by pygmies and giants, horses and monkeys—he domesticizes these creatures and dresses them up to resemble local, familiar Britons who appear contemporary, at least on the surface. Lemuel's first-person narrative no doubt lent Swift's story contemporaneity, as did the author's description of Lemuel's response to the odd creatures and places he encounters; and Swift's critique of modern learning (projects) and technology (print, publishing, architecture, mathematics) is so specific in Book 3—the Voyage to Laputa—that the reader of 1726 must immediately have understood why the narrator decried the lack of utility in modern science.

Furthermore, the critique of rationality in Book 4—Swift's "excremental vision"—is so directly focused on modern targets that readers could construe it as a commentary on the squalid conditions of their own lives (with respect to sewage, plumbing, hygiene, plague, refrigeration, diet) as well as a philosophical pronouncement about the essence of *human* nature and *natural* nature. But Swift's ending is far from optimistic, as his readers from the 1720s onward have known, and by the end of the story Gulliver appears so very foolish that contemporary readers must have wondered whether Swift had not been satirizing his protagonist all along. Although we today are sympathetic with Lemuel's responses to the strange sounds and smells he experienced, we also want to laugh at him. But no sooner do we do so than we—especially Swift's most attentive readers—grow aware that we are laughing at ourselves, either unaware of the evil Lemuel has witnessed, or so jaded by its modern versions that we have become immune to the phenomenon of evil itself. Swift maneuvers a secure position between these extremes—like a steersman between the rocks of Scylla and Charybdis—by making Lemuel appear merely silly rather than philosophically pained, tragically afflicted, or even chthonically enraged. Swift's book ends as it began: a tightly constructed prose satire permeated with the attributes of the newly developing prose novel.

But social life in England drastically altered in the aftermath of the South Sea Bubble, and coupled to its transformations were diverse new needs for information from a hungry reading public. The old forms of Augustan satire broke down, were no longer adequate; and under the various agendas of the Walpole administration, and—more critically— in the ever-growing English cities, not even Swift's version of satiric realism in *Gulliver's Travels* was sufficient for readers of the 1730s and 1740s who wanted their literature to be entirely up to the moment. The extraordinary element of the up-to-the-moment syndrome is that all sorts of literature we may consider less than au courant from our perspective today passed as remarkably immediate for those readers—for example, the French and Spanish translations that were consumed in great quantities between the publication of *Gulliver's Travels* and *Roderick Random*, especially Cervantes's *Don Quixote* (the most popular foreign work of fiction up to the publication of *Tristram Shandy*) and Le Sage's *Gil Blas*. Even Fielding found *Don Quixote* irresistible as he fictionalized the "don's" adventures in England in 1734. Narratives depicting Christian piety and heroism, such as many epistolary novels by women, and political satire, such as *The Court Secret* (1740), were found on the same shelves as anti-Walpole journalism and oriental travelogues. Even more popular, as many Fielding critics have shown, were works of romance: the form celebrating sentimental love within a wide series of fictive conventions. (Smollett was dubious, as he wrote in the preface of *Roderick Random*, that "romance" could accommodate his novelistic intentions, even if he did make forays into this form during the 1750s and 1760s.) Added to these were dozens of fictions we would call spy novels (often called by this name, as in Giovanni Paolo Marana's *The Turkish Spy*, Thomas Lediard's *The German Spy*, and others), as well as secret histories permeated with racy love and high intrigue. Satire was present in varying degrees in many of these works of the 1720s, 1730s, and 1740s, but not in the form in which it would appear in Smollett's first and perhaps most satiric novel, *Roderick Random*. Strains of satire are evident throughout Mrs. Haywood's novels of the 1720s and 1730s, but they appear in incongruent forms that adhere to another satiric tradition than the one found in Swift's prose works. Satire was even present in works of high didacticism and pious polemics. In short, it was ubiquitous.

During the 1730s the problem was how to satisfy a craving for contemporary realism, especially in its low-life versions, outside the confines of journalism and periodical essays. As John J. Richetti has written, the novel was, especially then, permeated with a "native journalistic instinct for the notorious and the sensational." All sorts of prose writing—secret histories, *chroniques scandaleuses*, romances of many varieties, voyages both real and imaginary, utopian and dystopian prose, rogue and other criminal stories, accounts of spiritual life and salvation, shilling pamphlets—attempted to cope with this demand for contemporary realism, though few fulfilled it with literary mastery. The old masters were no longer writing, the new not yet on the scene. By the 1730s Defoe was dead; Fielding, still a devoted playwright, had not yet written novels; Richardson, the successful printer, was still churning out didactic manuals instructing young women on how to behave; and Smollett, a Scot, was ten years old in 1731, growing up on the banks of rustic Loch Lomond, hundreds of miles north of London and Birmingham, a place remote enough not to be contaminated by the squalor of Glasgow and Edinburgh. No one knows exactly which literature, especially which prose works, Smollett read in these formative years before he entered the University of Edinburgh as a medical student. He must have read widely if his two poetic satires, *Advice* and *Reproof*, are an indication, but he grew up luxuriating on the banks of the lake, close to the land and its rustic values, within an environment as different as can be imagined from the one in London he would never genuinely consider to be home.

Seeking fame and fortune, he migrated to London in 1739 at eighteen, a penny in his pocket and persuaded that he could do other things if medical practice did not pan out, soon to experience the greatest jolt of his life—the chaos and confusion of one of the world's largest cities. Here he found a density of population he had never before imagined, as well as every form of violence and carnality, perversion and panhandling, rendering the people there alienated from each other, veritable accomplices in their daily transgressions. Fielding and Richardson had both been living in London for a long time and were better prepared for its vices, but Smollett was shocked by its aberrations. Like Fielding, he tried to gain entry to the city's literary life through the drama; but his first play, *The Regicide*, fell flat on its nose and he soon turned to the writing of prose narratives such as *Roderick Random*. Fielding had also turned to the writing of prose fiction in the 1740s, though for reasons very different from Smollett's, and if Fielding was temperamentally as attracted to epic, Quixotism, and roguery (as in *Jonathan Wild*), as Richardson was to tragedy and sentiment, Smollett found himself lured by a modified form of picaresque fiction—an old Iberian form dating from the time of Cervantes and Lazarillo de Tormes in the sixteenth century whose essence chronicles the adventures of master and servant on the rogue road of life. But in Smollett, modification occurs as the result of his extraordinary endings, while reconciliations occur between characters and their society in ways no earlier picaresque writer could have imagined.

The advantage of this modified picaresque model for Smollett lay in its realism and the opportunities it presented for eschewing romance at all costs. Its essential mold combining adventure and wanderlust in a world overrun by knaves and fools was, to be sure, one of its main attractions for Smollett, as was the fact, so glaring to him, that it mirrored his own experiences, including his sexual encounters, in dangerous London as well as at sea as a ship surgeon. A loose, rambling form, picaresque sprawled to wherever the hero went; it was anecdotal and episodic, and thrived on a low level of probability, likelihood, and specific setting. The picaresque storyteller imagined his authority as deriving from the simple fact that his male cronies (there was little room for women in this patriarchal picaresque world, except to fulfill the most stereotypic of roles) wanted to listen to his stories recounting exotic adventures. The more the picaro rambled in picaresque, even when in the mode of a Swiftian "progress piece," the more he endeared himself to his listeners.

But picaresque also had disadvantages nowhere evident in satire. Satire existed in a more certain mental landscape, defined its values more clearly, was less self-conscious about its versions of didacticism and morality, and, most importantly, thrived on the vices of the city (as in Samuel Johnson's *London*, a modern imitation of the Third Satire of Juvenal, the Roman poet). Satire, not romance in any version, was the literary form, perhaps even subgenre, best equipped to capture the realism of the modern city and cope with its versions of brutality, even if it could not accommodate Smollett's other imaginative space: his unrelenting search for exotic adventure. Nothing can detract from the hard fact that the London to which Smollett arrived in 1739 was steeped in squalor and assaulted all his senses, forming one of the most lasting and recurring experiences of his life.

London may have been the setting for many romantic liaisons as the young Smollett entered it, but one would never know it from his early satiric novels. When romantic love appears in *Roderick Random* or *Peregrine Pickle*, it is subdued and merely idealized in the most conventional of fictional ways. It is the picaresque hero himself who is romanticized, as several critics have noted, not the innocent women in these novels. Romance in these early novels of Smollett is absorbed, incorporated, diminished, and even inverted, but never made a principle of organization or the shaping block of one of the narratives. The first readers of these novels who had read in the romance tradition could hear the voices of romance as a backdrop—as a curtain behind which the young Scot novelist sometimes stood, as in his depictions of Narcissa—but never as any essential feature, let alone original pillar, of his early novels.

Perhaps it was this ambivalence and anxiety—Smollett's allegiance to satire and picaresque and his fierce recoil from romance—that dominated the substratum of his imagination when he conceived *Roderick Random* (1748). Here his themes are human violence and brutality, more specifically the transgressions and alienation that result from such acts even in unique circumstances; and this may be why he cast the most autobiographical and confessional of his novels in this mold. The vision is so dark and dreary that it borders on the cannibalistic, as each raw experience follows on one still rawer. But every tug toward the picaresque (as in the picaro's thirst for adventure through the encountering of new character types) drew Smollett back to fictive satire, specifically of the type that exposes vice and corruption within urban settings.

Smollett composes here as a sort of Hogarth "drawing pictures in prose" rather than as a Swift who relies on parody of an already established form to lash out at his targets; his book is conceptualized as a series of intricate "pictures" intended to capture the entirety of society in its wide diversity. In *Roderick Random* Smollett uses his quill rather than the pallet (as Hogarth did) to portray the sequence of his hero's dissipations through drink ("Gin Lane" and "Beer Street") and sex ("A Rake's Progress"), all in a first novel of the tough "I was born" variety. His fictional canvas is broad (there are 126 characters in a book less than half the size of *Tom Jones*) and far-flung (Random travels from Scotland to England, Carthagena, Paraguay, Buenos Aires, and back). Fools, knaves, and dupes lurk everywhere: amid the crowds and mobs in the cities he visits, as well as in empty spaces on the rogue road of life and at sea. But there is nothing Swiftian about the strategies of presentation—no parody of an established form (travel literature), no exotic remote landscapes populated by pygmies, giants, and imaginary rational horses against whom the protagonist is constantly being evaluated, all for the purpose of beguiling the innocent reader into believing that the final product—*Gulliver's Travels*—had been something other than what its surfaces revealed.

Instead, the preface of *Roderick Random* hits the satiric nail in the center when it claims that of "all kinds of satire, there is none so entertaining, and universally improving, as that which is introduced, as it were, occasionally, in the course of an interesting story." Here the story derives essentially from the picaresque: an essentially good and morally honest Rory is turned into a criminal manqué as he makes his way through the kingdoms of villainy. Yet Smollett's achievement here entails his blending of "picaresque realism" with diverse strains (not merely poetic varieties) of "satire." To achieve this end he uses the techniques of rogue biography (first person direct narrative suffused with dialogue) and couplet satire, and he also relies on *Gil Blas*, his supposed model.

No one could have read *Roderick Random* in tandem with *Gulliver's Travels* and thought they were similar. Sailors and the high seas dominate both books, as do a diversity of characters; both books are "pictures" in this sense but their tone and feel differ. Lemuel awakens at the end of his travels as a type of Swiftian Frankenstein's monster, alienated from his surroundings and awestruck that he has returned to yahooland, while Rory emerges from his picaresque road of life—a Dickensian nightmare to the finish—as a reclaimed saint who has arrived in heaven through the gates of a rustic paradise. In the end there is no means to reconcile these two satiric traditions in English fiction, although Fielding and Austen perform heroic attempts by invoking the values of the country estate over the moral chaos and mannerly disorder of the city. But a full account of the satiric differences of *Gulliver's Travels* and *Roderick Random* would necessitate further study of this tradition of satiric novel writing in the two decades between 1726 and 1748, a diverse and rich mountain of fiction, even if not distinguished by literary genius.

In *Roderick Random,* realism is achieved primarily through situation and irony rather than character analysis, as we see money won and lost, tricks deployed, stratagems contrived, the ravages of war ironically played out, vices like gambling rampant, heiresses duped, and every kind of innocence and goodness inverted. The grotesques who populate the book—the Bowlings, Straps, Weasels, Banters, Wagtails, Thickets,

Chatters, Quiverwits, Straddles—cut against the grain of realism by virtue of their degree of cunning and knavery. But Smollett recoups what he has lost in grotesquerie from his brilliant blend of situation, satire, irony, and the picaresque threads of his narrative. Geographically, only the sea is made subordinate to modern urban sprawl. Roderick finds himself lonely in both places, suggesting a new type of character realism in the form of what modern sociologists have called "the lonely crowd." A second tier of realistic and contemporary themes also emerges: a world of children and their games, their pranks, and their play; school life and education (anticipating the bildungsroman); the ravages and ironies of war; the relatively new vice of sodomy (especially at sea where its tentacles cannot be escaped); and the perennial lure of foreign places basking under strange moons and exotic suns. The more Roderick and his fellows try to escape the clutches of these stratagems, the more alienated they become in a global world Smollett represents as "urban" as well as consistently violent and brutal. George Steiner has remarked, perhaps with *Roderick Random* in mind, that Smollett's world dwells on the making and losing of money. It is, more minutely, about the versions of despair and brokenness that arise when transactions involving money go awry.

Smollett does everything he can in *Roderick Random* to assert his sense of temporality. His characters are varied and racy, his pace so quick, that readers imagine they are hearing today's news. Time and space are viewed from the perspective of the present, even when the action is occurring outside England. In familiar and local places, London and Bath, the crowds are so large, the mobs so violent, that characters constantly fear for their lives; in South America and Europe the reader gladly forgoes the next twist in the plot to learn about local custom and practice. Love and intrigue (Miss Williams's sad story is but one example) thrive everywhere, as they did in the sprawl of historical London of the late 1740s. There are narrative insets and incorporations of other stories, such as the "history of Melopoyn" (a pathetic poet imprisoned with Roderick in the Marshalsea prison) and "Marmozet" (David Garrick, the actor and playwright, who continues to appear in Smollett's novels), and flashbacks of the novelist's own life, as in the account of Smollett's attempt to produce *The Regicide*. In Smollett's vision the forms of urban dissipation are excessive, as is its crime (we *expect* to find Random in prison), all of which circumstances must have met the reader's expectations just as they satisfied Hogarth's viewers in "The Rake's Progress."

Even the end of the novel courts realism through its combination of fantasy and escape. Here Random's picaresque wanderings through the land of nightmares come to an end and he is happily married—but only by returning to rustic Scotland, the country whose literature always plays an important role in the landscape of Smollett's novels. In brief, Smollett does everything possible to lend to his brand of the novel an aura of realism and the present. Yet in almost every episode or anecdote, every grotesque character or despondent situation, the satirist and ironist in him is evoked. And even the use of first-person narrative, allegedly to permit readers to glimpse the hero intimately, counteracts the energies of novelistic realism by converting it to a prose amalgam of new-style satire and a modified version of the old picaresque. It is a blend that English fiction had never seen before and from which many nineteenth-and twentieth-century novelists would learn. But the continuity of satire is a crucial element in this version: for all his novelistic inventiveness, Smollett, like his satiric predecessors, returns to the themes of the perpetual madness and bestiality of the modern world.

Peregrine Pickle, published four years later in 1751, is *Roderick Random* composed in another key and amplified to almost three times the size. Instead of 126 characters there are 226, twice as many as are found in *Tom Jones*, and at its heart lies an aberrant hero who, like Random, is a particular kind of rogue. The same amalgam of new-style satire and modified picaresque is evident, although the novel is written in the third person and is less autobiographical. The story is of a hot-blooded scalawag, "Perry" Pickle, who sympathizes with the distressed and downtrodden, yet whose own life appears to be strung together only by random episodes and a series of romantic escapades. Here, as in *Roderick Random*, there is an unquenchable thirst for adventure—adventure that ends happily as Perry marries Emilia, inherits a vast fortune, and retires to his country estate. The narrative meanders and races in ways never found in its much tighter predecessor. Smollett tried to organize this huge hulk of material into a tripartite division: the hero's youth, dominated by stories of the sea and his own life in school; the hero on the Grand Tour; and the hero as a fortune hunter in London. But his structure is less evident than Fielding's tripartite division in *Tom Jones*, and Smollett's "plan" (if that is what it is) has neither the mythic nor the Christian elements of Fielding's book, nor its brilliant contrasts between city and country dramatized in the language of Providence and the carnivalesque. In this version of the amalgam of satire and the picaresque, the latter seems to triumph, but the habit of lashing out at specific social institutions and individuals remains Smollett's most salient feature, seen in his attacks on writers who had hindered his writing career and, again, in the spleen directed at Fielding. Smollett's awareness of social confusion and the need for temporality is again evident, as in his brilliant contrasts between the city and country, land and sea, stereotypes of male and female in a milieu where gender is subservient to money; but human transgression and its consequential alienation are treated less analytically than his readers might have liked. Finally, these matters bear heavily on the novel's tone, suggesting that Smollett has cultivated adventure purely for its own sake in this book, without considering its implications for form and substance.

The new feature in *Peregrine Pickle* entails three interpolated narratives, longer and odder inset pieces than those found in any previous English novel and probably deriving from the new taste for lengthy narrative. The longest of these, occupying almost a fifth of the novel and occupying the space of more than fifty thousand words, is the "Memoirs of Lady Vane," the story of Frances Vane, a prominent socialite in love with pleasure. The others recount the distresses of Daniel Mackercher, an ally of James Annesley in the infamous suit brought against the Earl of Anglesey, and Count d'Alvarez, who was sold into slavery and later found in Bohemia. By the late 1740s, readers of novels expected to find such interpolations or self-contained digressions. Fielding had made use of them as early as the inset about "Mr. Wilson" in *Joseph Andrews*, and there are several in *Tom Jones*: the Man of the Hill, the King of the Gypsies, the puppet show, and smaller ones, but Smollett's incorporation was original in a number of other ways that his readers immediately recognized.

Lady Vane's "Memoirs" are penned by a woman, whereas the other voices are male, and more significantly by a woman who, no matter how much she loves pleasure, continues to be viewed sympathetically by the novelist. At the end of her rueful story of escape and wandering, Smollett shows her to have learned through her far-flung experiences, as when she demands a settlement of a thousand pounds from her last lover. Again, transactions involving money in a fundamental way form the core of the Smollettian fantasy in these early novels. But Frances's story is also organically related to the moral realm of *Peregrine Pickle* and is not merely an extraneous island of erotic intrigue. Peregrine, perhaps in the role of Smollett's mouthpiece, accepts her account of her amours at her own valuation and passes no judgment on her, just as the historical Smollett allegedly took her story in dictation and accepted it entirely. Finally, this unusual account of an articulate "courtesan of pleasure," published on the heels of another set of "Memoirs of a Woman of Pleasure" (Cleland's), permitted Smollett to glance at the anti-Pamela tradition and at contemporary female novelists ranging from Eliza Haywood and Penelope Aubin to Sarah Fielding and Charlotte Lennox. He accomplished this by catering to both male and female readers—vicarious experience satisfied both—and by extending his views about money to include female needs, feminist consumption, and female materialism. He further catered to the expectations of female readers by giving the "woman of pleasure" a voice of her own through which she could plead that she was virtuous in ways that merited explanation. These "Memoirs," the size of a novella, amounted to much more than another conventional or interruptive feature, predictable by mid-century in long English novels.

The effect of the three interpolations (the two inset stories pertaining to *male* vicissitude are less original) was to give Smollett's amalgam of satire and the picaresque a peculiarly original flavor, but it did not work as well in this second novel as it had in *Roderick Random*. If the first part of *Peregrine Pickle*—populated with the grotesque figures of Mrs. Grizzle, Tom Pipes, Keypstick, Hatchway, Hawser Trunnion and his memorable comrades at the "garrison"—was entirely original for its novelistic incorporations, parts 2 and 3 were less so. The large themes in part 1—real and surrogate families, the sense of "home" as a spiritual rather than a physical place, life at sea and in school, the new social relations of uncles and nephews, mothers and sons, boys and girls—caused some readers to wonder if Smollett had new philosophical interests he was bringing to bear on the novel, and several modern critics have speculated on the *differences* between *Roderick Random* and *Peregrine Pickle* despite their abundant formal similarities. But these philosophical concerns have never been identified and studied because of the dearth of biographical material about Smollett's intellectual life before he took over the editorship of the *Critical Review* in 1756. Still, there is no doubt that Smollett was beginning to think in a new fashion about the ways in which societies are held hostage to terrorists like Perry the prankster, joker, drinker, exploiter, dissimulator. The only step Perry does not take is the final, anarchic one dissolving rule and order. Viewed from our perspective two hundred years later, it is clear that

Peregrine Pickle has much to offer the cultural historian of child rearing, puberty, and adolescence, as well as of school and student life.

The second part of the novel, "Perry on the Grand Tour," practically sank the novel with its lack of up-to-the-minute temporality. The problem lay not in Smollett's caricature-like simpletons (the tutor Jolter, the valet Tom Pipes, the painter Pallet who hitches up with Perry in Europe) but in their actions and in the reasons for their erratic and immature behavior. Here Smollett reverted to satire, as his hero and his traveling buddies deride foreign customs, alien figures (Pallet and the physician, who cross-dress, attend masquerades, and are jailed), and public institutions (colleges and societies)—all for the purpose of detecting vice and stamping out brutality. Some early readers were amused by these escapades; others thought there was something serious, almost philosophic, about Smollett's new interest in play and prank; but not even the last section of the novel—Peregrine's tour through polite society as a fortune hunter—or the three inset pieces could rescue the book. In the last part, Perry undergoes "a rake's progress" and descends into the hell of poverty and despair, only to be rescued by philanthropists, Emilia's love, and his good luck in being restored to his father's estate and inheritance.

Peregrine Pickle was widely read in England and Europe and brought fame to its author, but was not the best-seller that *Roderick Random* was; nor has it enhanced Smollett's reputation in our time. However, there are signs of a change of tide. The novel's stylistic energy and ebullience in the presentation and development of character is apparent, as is its concession to female and middle-class readers, and there is a fresh sense in our time that Smollett possessed more profound insight into the social order and its confusion when held under stress than he has been given credit for. His novels have been studied for their views of economic wealth and luxury, and as a prose stylist he had much to offer readers seeking to understand how social creatures are transformed for the worse at the moment they become the victims of economic circumstance; but these are ultimately depressing topics for readers in any generation, verging on despair and the pathological.

At the time of its publication in 1751, the critical consensus was that not even *Peregrine Pickle*'s exposure of the secrets of "polite society," or its recurrent amorousness, could redeem its male hero, who is so remarkably "crude" and "brutal" (though not as heinous in his acts as his successor, the archvillain Fathom). Nor was the novel redeemed by its constant ironic attack on targets chosen from every niche of human society. No matter how unusual are the twists of his story in *Peregrine Pickle*, Smollett has revealed himself as a Rabelaisian Panurge or Pantagruel—the quintessence of the satirist—rather than as a sentimental novelist capable of inventing a sympathetic protagonist about whom we care. In the end we care more about Perry's *world* than his own fate, no matter how loud is Emilia's love song or how much money awaits him on his country estate.

The secret of *Peregrine Pickle* is found in the preface of Smollett's next novel, *Ferdinand Count Fathom*, an extraordinary pronouncement because it so strongly contradicts the story that follows while being so genuinely applicable to *Peregrine Pickle*:

A novel is a large diffused picture, comprehending the characters of life, disposed in different groups, and exhibited in various attitudes, for the purposes of an uniform plan, and general occurrence, to which every individual is subservient. But this plan cannot be executed with propriety, probability or success, without a principal personage to attract the attention, unite the incidents, unwind the clue of the labyrinth, and at last close the scene by virtue of his own importance.

Smollett's first two novels, *Roderick Random* and *Peregrine Pickle*, are much finer examples of this aesthetic than his third, as a consequence of the satiric potential of this view of the novel. Yet in *Fathom* something much uglier and potentially more horrifying than satire surfaces: the utter blackness of human existence—a world so bleak in its versions of villainy that the reader wonders how any of us has escaped from slitting his wrists long ago. As one critic has written, "as a picture of unregenerate evil, *Fathom* is Smollett's masterpiece in satirical black comedy." True, but Smollett's contemporaries did not see the book in this light, and even for those who penetrated its "satirical black comedy" this content hardly redeemed it. Whether the culprit was the incoherent form of *Fathom*—a blend of elements—its satirical versions, the inherent villainy of its aberrant hero who remains depressing at best, or something else altogether, this third novel fell flat. Only in our century has *Fathom* regained some of the critical, and in my view experimental, respect it deserves.

But if satire thrives on incongruence and a rhetoric of irony, *Fathom* is satiric in ways few of Smollett's dedicated readers of the 1740s and 1750s could have overlooked. Obsessed with roguery and criminality, the rakish Rory, villainous Perry, and despicable Fathom always think they can beat society at its own game, and in the first two novels they do, perhaps as the result of inherent moral goodness rewarded by Providence. But Fathom exists in another sphere where neither chance nor luck can help him, nor the restoration of lost fathers and forgotten inheritances. Random and Pickle both endure hardship despite a picaresque optimism that always seems to play out in their favor, but Fathom's relation to hardship is that of happiness to the fool: at least the knaves plot their steps carefully (even Random and Pickle in their worst moments). But treacherous fools like Fathom compel their authors to send their readers a message too Swiftian to be missed. "Happiness . . . is a perpetual Possession of being well Deceived . . . The Serene Peaceful State of being a Fool among Knaves." Swift iterated it in one satirical key, now Smollett in another.

Smollett's form in this third novel also baffled his readers, and did not enhance his reputation, no matter what symmetries they detected in the forces of good (Renaldo, Monimia, Farrel) triumphing over evil (Fathom) within a providential order ultimately just. The fairness of Providence sets the tone and shape of the book. A fraction of the length of *Peregrine Pickle*, it possesses a fraction of the number of characters—only seventy-one—and cultivates romantic sensibility rather than the innovative satiric picaresque. Instead of glancing at Apuleius or Petronius, Smollett disengages himself from formal satire and extols fancy and the imagination, fear and the passions. Nor does he incorporate the epistolary tradition or the type of moral allegory Sarah Fielding was then writing. Here the plot centers around the exploits of "the treacherous Fathom," born a renegade in 1708 in the low countries, "a principal character [chosen] from the purlieus of treachery and fraud." This morality play, soaked in black humor as it were, is played out in a sentimental romance, and early readers wondered whether the loosely connected story amounted to anything more than a string of flat characters monolithically good and evil. No middle, or gray, was sensed. Early readers were asking whether the novel possessed an appropriate mimesis or representation and wondered whether sentimental romance was being cultivated for ends they could not fathom. *Fathom* did not seem at all to fit the paradigm of a "satiric Smollettian novel."

Yet, however odd the book may have seemed to general readers then, *Fathom* abounds with new features of great interest to historians of the English novel. The dedication is written by Smollett to himself ("To Dr. S——"), suggesting that an author assumes an autobiographical role whether or not he wishes to. Then, in the dictum about the novel as "a large diffused picture, comprehending the characters of life"—a broad canvas rather than a narrow section—a new completeness axiom is introduced to the English novel that reaches a zenith in Trollope, Thackeray, and Dickens. The range in *Fathom* is more limited than this aesthetic suggests, perhaps as a result of Smollett's fascination with roguery and crime, and in view of his intention to demonstrate, through plot and character analysis, that "fear is the most interesting of the passions." In chapter 21, Smollett introduces a scene of still-warm corpses and murderers in an abandoned farmhouse that is so chilling, the reader wonders what his intention is.

Experiment and inventiveness also abound in his formal plot: the novel begins in middle Europe, shifts to England, returns to the Continent, and ends (as it did in *Roderick Random*) with redemption in rustic retreat in a northern English county. There is nothing comic or lighthearted in this bleak picture of human depravity found in broad daylight as well as in prisons and asylums; villainy and madness dominate *Fathom*'s pages as do fun and pranks in *Peregrine Pickle*, and the book has an altogether different flavor. Furthermore, the reader's expectations of realism are thwarted by twists in the story that are by turns fanciful, romantic, sentimental, Gothic, treacherous, and unpredictable—all registering a threshold of the "merely probable" that troubled Smollett's readers. Even the flat, stereotypic character types drawn from many nationalities and religions function in this "probable" way: Jews and Mohammedans, Europeans and Turks, creatures from social classes high-born and low-born; and no episode in the "love scenes," no instance of the novelist's benevolence displayed toward Fathom, staves off the Gothic sense of impending evil that lurks throughout the novel. Nothing in the imagined world of the great Augustan verse satirists— the Popes and Swifts and their imitators during the 1730s—approximated this extremity of bleakness. The vision is so black that one wonders what Smollett's imagination was if it produced a book like this on the heels of two rollicking novels filled with light and sunshine.

For all of *Pickle*'s formal oddities and digressive incorporations, that novel still resembled "the Smollettian mold" and the Fieldingesque novel through its penchant for incorporations and digressions and its reliance on picaresque satire. But *Fathom* was unrecognizable and fulfilled few, if any, of the reader's novelistic expectations. Smollett, discouraged and having lost favor with some printers after its publication in 1753, then turned to other forms of writing—histories, compilations, journalism, reviews—which informed the content of his last four works of fiction: the themes of prisons and punishment in *Sir Launcelot Greaves* (1762); the newly leisured sightseer in *Travels Through France and Italy* (1766); Japanese culture in *The Adventures of an Atom* (1769); and a new version, and inversion, of the *res in urbis* theme—the country within the city—in *The Expedition of Humphry Clinker* (1771). In certain ways *Sir Launcelot Greaves* is an even odder experiment in fiction than *Fathom*. A "romance" about "English Quixotism" and knight errantry, it is the story of the young, melancholic Sir Launcelot Greaves, heir to a titled Yorkshire estate, who decides to become an "errant knight," and his hunchback peasant squire, Timothy Crabshaw. The book makes clear that Smollett's forays into romance (as in *Count Fathom*) were always made at a price.

Greaves is in love with the lovely Aurelia Darnel, whose father disapproves of their marriage, and Smollett spends much energy separating and uniting them, many times, until their marriage paves the way for the recovery of Greaves's estate. Marriage always saves the day in Smollett's fictions; here it takes a back seat to romantic love and Quixotism, to such a degree that even Gilbert, Greaves's horse, is thoroughly Cervantic. The pace is quick, the characters unfamiliar in the satiric prose tradition from Swift to Smollett, deriving as they do from the quixotic romance tradition. The story cultivates action rather than character (virtually all the characters are monochromatic grotesques named for their chief attributes: Cowslip, Crabshaw, Dawdle, Fang, Ferret, Gobble, etc.), and situation rather than theme. The remaining material satirizes local politics, elections, and various forms of patronage, rather than grand universal themes of life and death, reason and the passions; and the relatively small amount of satire is conveyed through familiar quixotic figures rather than animated norms (Houyhnhnms and Yahoos), as it had been in Swift. Yet the satire is also concrete and specific, as in the old forms of Smollettian villainy and grotesquerie from the 1740s.

It is hard to imagine why Smollett thought this model of the novel could succeed in 1762, even with its illustrations and serialization (*Greaves* is the first novel by a major English writer to employ both techniques). The versions of realism are problematic throughout, as incident after incident requires some deus ex machina to salvage the good guys. And its notion of fictive temporality is constantly placed in jeopardy despite the development of the themes of madness (Smollett quotes profusely from contemporary psychiatric theory), imprisonment (hero and heroine are incarcerated next to each other and the penitentiary lurks as a motif throughout the book), and politics (corruption is rampant among local politicians). Indeed the theme of incarceration extends so far into the novel's fabric that one wonders whether Smollett's Greavian penitentiaries reveal an arrière-pensée.

Smollett must have considered his brand of "English Quixotism" thoroughly original (it anticipated Richard Graves's in *The Spiritual Quixote* by a decade), especially the suggestion that chivalry could revive manners and morals in Georgian England. The "romantic" landscape found in the book was Smollett's antidote to the cannibalistic city—London—he saw developing in the 1750s, and in Greaves's exposure of fools, knaves, and dupes, Smollett indulged the lingering satiric element in his psyche that needed to assert its affinities with Swift in *A Tale of a Tub*. But however integrated a "modern knight" Greaves may be, however dedicated to the cause of uprooting corruption where he finds it (a type of picaro in reverse), his story seemed antiquated to readers of the first volume of *Tristram Shandy*. Also, Smollett's women in *Launcelot Greaves* appear stuffier than they had ten years earlier, his men less subjected to psychological scrutiny (for all Greaves's clinical madness, Smollett does little to establish its nature). Ultimately, the versions of realism and representation in the novel are shellacked with an antique veneer, such that the reader is pulled in the opposite direction of "the contemporary moment"—1762—and of a novelist "writing to the moment."

Launcelot Greaves, like its equally problematic predecessor, *Fathom*, gained little critical acclaim. Appearing when novels of sentiment and sensibility were becoming increasingly popular, it introduced a cast that was derivative and quixotic (though the book was called a "a modern romance"), lending it an atmosphere of the precious and cutting against the grain of the realistic sentimental fiction then coming into vogue. Nor did it treat of manners and morals in the contemporary scene, as women novelists from Lennox to Frances Burney would. It confronted the present by recreating an old, Cervantic world alien to the social needs of the new decade presided over by a new king, and its satirical vignettes were not strong enough in themselves to redeem the book. So, for the second time, Smollett turned away from novel writing to pursue compilations and histories.

Fortune also bandied him about during the 1760s. While Sterne blazed into the spotlight with *Tristram Shandy*, Smollett was recovering from a term in prison, grieving the death of his only child, and witnessing the disintegration of his personal health, both mental and physical. Bitter and broken, he went to the Mediterranean in search of recovery and regeneration, returning to England only one more time. While abroad he wrote the vivid *Travels Through France and Italy* (1766), cast as letters by a splenetic traveler, and the very Swiftian *Adventures of an Atom*, the more intriguing of the two works from the perspective of the historian of the "satiric tradition" of the novel.

The Adventures of an Atom is a throwback to Pope in *The Dunciad* and Swift in *Gulliver's Travels*, necessitating a "key" to unlock its seventy-nine characters (Got-hama-baba is George II, Fika-kaka the Duke of Newcastle, Sti-phi-rum-poo Earl Hardwicke, and so forth) and dense political references (every Japanese figure stands for someone English). This violent and scatological roman à clef is thoroughly "excremental" in its vision, if idiosyncratic in its presentation of Orientalism; and close perusal shows it also to be one of the shrewdest commentaries on contemporary British politics. The challenge of *Atom* lies less in its unities (a fragment, it appears to have no unity) or style (typically energetic and masculine) than in its versions of allegory and scatology; as a result, some of its first readers wondered what kind of fiction it was—this was the source of the debates about its authorship—and fewer could understand the author's purpose. Novel readers accustomed to *Sophia*, *The History of Lady Julia Mandeville*, *The Fool of Quality*, *The Castle of Otranto*, *The Man of Real Sensibility*, *The Vicar of Wakefield*, *The Man of Feeling*, *The Tears of Sensibility*, and, of course, *A Sentimental Journey* and *Tristram Shandy*, were baffled by a prose fragment with isomorphic targets.

The story is of a "talking atom" contained within the body of haberdasher Nathaniel Peacock, but the "atom" inexplicably breaks away after it has undergone several transformations and political reincarnations. The "atom" (whatever it actually is) was part of the Japanese prime minister's anus, afterward having passed through the guts of a duck and the generative organs of a sailor into Peacock's pineal gland. While inside Peacock, the atom narrates events it experienced in Japan (England) from 1754 to 1767, but the reader unfamiliar with these political events is at sea. Few satirical works of the classical period are more interesting for the historian of the prose fragment than *The Atom*. Impossible to construe as a novel, even in the experimental mold of *Random* or *Fathom*, it raises more puzzles than it solves and does not even attempt to be contemporary or temporal in the way Smollett had been in *Launcelot Greaves*. It is Smollett writing in his most satirical and Swiftian mood.

No such puzzlement greeted Smollett's last novel, the magnificently crafted *Humphry Clinker*, completed while the writer was abroad in search of health. Composed in the epistolary mode, but with letters that never resemble Richardson's, this comic "expedition" is built around five correspondences that show a relativity of viewpoints about human experience as it relates to social organization. The book is in every way a "large broad picture" written in accordance with Smollett's earlier aesthetic. The correspondences are by the protagonist Matthew Bramble, a prickly and misanthropic Welsh squire with a heart of gold; Bramble's ward, Jery Melford, an Oxford University spark in search of his own identity; Jery's younger sister Liddy, a romantic boarding-school girl who is actually an inexperienced young noodle; Bramble's sister Tabitha (Tabby), a grasping and prudish spinster who has become man-crazy; and their commonsensical maid Win Jenkins, who writes hilarious misspelled letters yet whose religion permits her to see what the entourage actually is: "a family of love where every sole is so kind and courteous."

The five sets of letters are weighted in the correspondences of Bramble (prickly as his first name is biblically benevolent) and Melford (a realist who comments intelligently on Matt's excesses). Most of the eighty-three letters, spanning over nine months from April Fools Day to Christmas, are written from Matthew to his personal physician, Dr. Lewis, and from Jery to his Oxford tutor, Sir Watkin Phillips. Henry James adjudged this complex point of view to be Smollett's greatest contribution to the development of the English novel, but it is only one of the book's interesting aspects. Smollett's achievement is more complex than any single element and includes the managing of satire, comedy, and romance under the aegis of a new epistolary model, as well as his new vision of the social order linking sex and sensibility, the city and the country, chaos and decay, life and death. He also fulfills certain readerly expectations while thwarting others, as when he operates against all expectations generated by the book's title (Clinker does not appear until the second third of the novel). His form here is a tightly constructed prose vehicle: an epistolary satire "right up to the moment," especially in its exposure of urban decay and confusion, but always with a new twist in the story line; the novel glitters in ways no previous book of Smollett's had.

Humphry Clinker's 233 characters exceed the number in *Peregrine Pickle*, a book more than twice its size, and many of the figures are historical ones (real politicians, statesmen, preachers, scholars, physicians) at whom potshots are taken. Despite this, manners and morals never lie far from the novelist's imagination. The plot is episodic, loosely strung together, perpetually interrupted by accidents, detours, fires, flashbacks, characters who reappear from earlier Smollett novels (such as a repentant Fathom), and interpolations (like Jery's account of Paunceford and Serle, who suffer economic reversal). The five-way correspondences require that everyone's point of view be subjected to interpretation by everyone else. And the autobiographical elements are so strong (Smollett as Bramble) that even while exercising caution, it is impossible for the reader not to recognize that Smollett has refined his earlier satiric thrust into a symbolic myth about the good life, based on health of mind and body, the family, the country, and the pastoral north. But Smollett's epistolary vehicle also mitigates excessive contradictions by reasserting trifling comic values, as when Bramble informs Tabby that she must decide between him and "her lap dog." Smollett's epistolary mode sparkles in the way Pope's couplets had, and as Jane Austen's tight fictions would a generation later. The book's comic and terrifically grotesque flavor is further strengthened by Matt's "goutiness," the most resistant to therapy, if also most "male," of chronic Georgian diseases because few women contracted it while everyone seems to have endured its agonies without incurring serious jeopardy. Smollett's story (*Humphry Clinker*) and Bramble's medical condition (gout) are both inherently comic insofar as no great harm ever comes to either: the story ends happily and the victims of gout always recover. But in Smollett's time women were thought not to contract gout, virtually assuring readers that gout was a male condition. Moreover, there is something genuinely comic in the bloated male bodies populating the pages of *Humphry Clinker*.

Satire is diffused throughout *Humphry Clinker* and developed in relation to the clutter and filth of the British cities the group visits: a constant reminder of the assault on their physical senses, especially the olfactory (jokingly, Sterne nicknamed "Smelfungus Smollett" for his sensitivity to smell). But clutter and chaos extend thematically beyond the city to all social forms, including politics, patronage, preferment, language, and social mobility. Smollett also rewarded the reader's expectation for modernity and temporality by raising "the contemporary city" (London, Edinburgh, Bath) to the level of major theme awaiting the satirist's lash for "London's vile milk." His sharp eye misses nothing in London's economies, traffic between import and export, conspicuous consumption, corruption, inflation, luxury, high living, late nights, and gluttony. All converge to a Swiftian type of decay that no amount of "romance" or "Quixotism" can abrogate.

The characters promote their own hobbyhorses: Matt a patriarchal view of society, which he extends from "the body politic," an old trope, to his own "natural body" in his words "an hospital these fourteen years"; Jery the leveling out of the social classes and systems of patriarchy to such extremity that social "chaos is to me a source of infinite amusement"; Clinker, the ragged postilion and child of Methodist love whose real father is none other than Bramble, a desire to find out who he really is; Win the wish to see the "inner light" of every spirit; and Tabby, the human embodiment of sex over sensibility, the demonic quest to market herself as marriage material. Even lesser characters have their hobbyhorses, for example, the grotesque Lismahago, a Scottish soldier scalped by North American Indians, "a tall meager figure, answering with his horse, the description of Don Quixote mounted on Rozinante," whose imagination dwells on his exotic adventures. Of the five main figures, Jery and Matt play off each other: young and old, sensible and irritable, rational and sentimental. Careful scrutiny of Bramble is needed before his type of sentimentalism is understood, but there are also similarities between the two men when it becomes evident that Bramble's earlier libertinism accompanied an ingrained benevolence. Indeed, this coupling of robust sexuality and human goodness seems to be one of Smollett's main themes, and literally produced the hero for whom the book is named, Humphry Clinker—Matt's real son.

The remarkable twist in character development is that Bramble's satiric proclivity wanes as he recovers the "good life" (as described above). Smollett suggests through his satiric persona that the healthier we grow, the less we carp about the physical and moral decay surrounding us; and he defines "health" as equally partaking of "mind and body." Still, Smollett's materials did not end here. He catered to the reader's need for being "right up to the moment" by inserting diverse subjects then hotly debated in Britain. *Humphry Clinker* is, after all, a novel published in the aftermath of the Seven Years' War and conceptualized during a period (the late 1760s) when the most basic ideas of liberty and freedom, democracy and government, isolation and nationalism, were coming under fire. It is a postwar novel (as is *Roderick Random*, for a different war) as well as something else: a sociological treatise on the quality of life and the dangers encroaching on human happiness. Economics and luxury, pro and con, loom on every page, as does social commentary, and Smollett writes at his best in this last novel when anatomizing present conditions. Here, in a work that is the inverse of *Greaves*, an acquired historical narrative technique (Smollett had written prolific histories of England and Scotland) helped him less than a vivid prose style and energetic sentence structure, dominated by active verbs, adverbs, and pleonasms directed at the five senses.

Three of Smollett's topical subjects in *Humphry Clinker* make the point: the satire on Methodism, the incorporation of materials about the New World, and the philosophical treatment of the concept of regeneration. By 1771, readers of fiction had come to expect hostility to Methodism, with its mad enthusiasm, its professions of "new light," and its sudden "epiphanic moments" (think of Fielding's attacks on such hypocritical Methodists as Blifil). Smollett's tack is different. He suggests that Methodism is an urban religion, the result of new forms of alienation in which city dwellers pay a quid pro quo for their separation from the land. Even Tabby's conversion to "the New Light" implies dislocation from her native heath. In this critique of urban Methodism, Smollett reveals himself as a kind of English physiocrat, claiming that when people become ecologically uprooted and join a culture without "a history," they pay a price. The inclusion of exotic accounts of the New World (Lismahago's life among the Iroquois and Miami and his romantic adventures with Squinkinakoosta) is Smollett's way of addressing readers who are informed about foreign news.

Finally, his theory of regeneration is so intrinsic to the novel's main themes—the city and the country, primitive and civilized societies, the social classes and the professions, human health, leisure, travel, sex, marriage, luxury, simplicity—that it is impossible to imagine *Humphry Clinker* without it. What a different story this would be without the triple sets of weddings at the end, "romantic closure" for all the travelers except Bramble, and—despite his continued celibacy—Bramble's own physical recovery on a rustic, if feudal, country estate in Scotland. The symbolic journey reflects Smollett's profound belief in the country over the city and in provincial integrity over urban decay; and what is regeneration if not the ability to begin anew and survive? But his version of bodily and spiritual rejuvenation is not Fielding's: it is not the country estate, with its moral hierarchies and inscriptions of the providential order, which resuscitates the fallen and depraved, but a plain ethic of rusticity and simplicity; almost the belief that the return to nature and the land has the greatest healing effect on mankind.

With regard to literary history, Smollett was the first of the major eighteenth-century British novelists to descant freely on the dialectic between metropolitan and provincial values, a topic that mushroomed into national debate by the end of the century. For Smollett, regeneration occurred specifically by communion with rusticity, the only solace for one who had been dislocated by the jumble of city life, its violent assault on the physical senses, and the leveling and confusing of the social classes. Smollett had always been attuned to the theme of city versus country, and to the ways the new leisured classes were changing the face of Britain by leaving certain regions uninhabited and occupying others. But his idiosyncratic method in *Humphry Clinker* elevates place and setting and prompts him to include the inset stories of Baynard, Dennison and Lismahago. This, then, is a new version of romantic pastoral featuring the theme of *res in urbis* (the country brought into the city).

One other concern pertaining to Bramble is essential: the loop of "mind and body" that runs throughout the story—a type of exuberant discourse derived from medical lore. Indeed, it may be that Bramble's prickliness and benevolence notwithstanding (the biblical Matthew) the reason his names begins with *M* and *B* is further to enrich the story along the lines of mind and body, just as Swift enriched Lemuel the wanderer by calling him "Gulliver" (gull). Bramble's health is poor at the start, both in "mind and body," but Smollett the physician knew that his semiautobiographical protagonist would not mend until *both* mind and body improved. During the years (1761 to 1768) when Sterne was winning acclaim for *Tristram Shandy*, Smollett proposed a competing theory of the human organism based on a monism of the vital organic self: one in which mind and body were linked through nerve and sense in a perpetual neural feedback system. Bramble's benevolence as well as his irritability stem from precisely this neural physiognomy, as novelist and protagonist make plain that both are anatomical monists rather than latter-day Cartesian dualists.

This view suggests that a valid sense of selfhood occurs only when individuals consult their anatomies in relation to their souls, hence mind and body rather than either in exclusion. In his masterpiece, Sterne had proposed an equally vitalistic model, which centered on an integrated system of animal spirits and nerves, for understanding the workings of the human imagination in relation to "the springs of life." But Smollett's version implies that we can understand Bramble for the princely heart he is—as a modern "man of feeling"—only by consulting the psychoanatomical loop that pours out its impressions in "letters to my doctor." The incorporation of this neural material into epistolary fiction was another of Smollett's inventions, a concession to temporality that provided his readers with a sense that their novelist was working for them all the time in being "right up to the minute."

Smollett's achievement, then, in *Humphry Clinker* is various, brilliant if uneven, and in some fundamental way experimental once again. It is as if he had been searching all along for a new paradigm for the novel while working within competing models to Fielding, Richardson, and, self-consciously in the last years of his life, Sterne. As an acute observer of the social scene, particularly the contemporary "cannibalistic" city, he had no peer: his vision of the balance of power between the city and country is altogether different from that of Richardson, for example, whose plots thrive on socially aggressive and upwardly mobile middle-class families, like the Harlowes, who exploit the poor within the city, and pour money into their country estates (Harlowe Place) to ape the manners of the aristocracy. And even if Sterne, Austen, and others abjured Smollett's version of "the raw and coarse" or failed to acknowledge their indebtedness to his work, it is hard to imagine their own novels without Smollettian predecessors. So much brick and mortar did he give to the temple of the English novel.

All his novels are in some rudimentary sense "satirical"—but satirical in ways that embrace and incorporate realism, comedy, romance, and the picaresque. Moreover, the novels differ from each other, and it would be erroneous to think that *all* his books are constructed as "simple satirical novels"—no better than to believe that *Tristram Shandy* is such. Smollett's loyalties in fiction—to satire, the picaresque, the comic and grotesque—altered from book to book, even changed within one book, and if we cannot appreciate why these divergent allegiances were so consequential for him, this has much more to do with our own sense of plot, character, time, space, and the rest of the Aristotelian unities in the aftermath of Jamesian fiction than with Smollett's sense of the developing novel.

G. S. Rousseau

Selected Bibliography

Beasley, J. C. *Novels of the 1740s.* Athens: University of Georgia Press, 1982.

Beasley, J. C., et al. *The Georgia Edition of the Works of Tobias Smollett.* Athens: University of Georgia Press, 1989.

Becker, G. *Documents of Modern Realism.* Princeton, N.J.: Princeton University Press, 1964.

Byrd, M. *London in the Eighteenth Century.* New Haven, Conn.: Yale University Press, 1982.

Carretta, Vincent. *George III and the Satirists form Hogarth to Byron.* Athens: University of Georgia Press, 1990.

Hunter, J. P. *Before Novels: The Cultural Contexts of Eighteenth-Century English Fiction.* New York: Norton, 1990.

Kernan, A. B. *The Plot of Satire.* New Haven, Conn.: Yale University Press, 1965.

McKeon, Michael. *The Origins of the English Novel, 1600–1740.* Baltimore: Johns Hopkins University Press, 1987.

Moore, R. E. *Hogarth's Literary Relationships.* Minneapolis: University of Minnesota Press, 1948.

Paulson, Ronald. *Satire and the Novel in Eighteenth-Century England.* New Haven and London: Yale University Press, 1967.

Paulson, Ronald. *The Fictions of Satire.* Baltimore: Johns Hopkins University Press, 1967.

Richetti, John J. *Popular Fiction before Richardson: Narrative Patterns 1700–1739.* Oxford: Clarendon, 1969.

Rousseau, G. S. *Tobias Smollett: Essays of Two Decades.* Edinburgh and New York: Seabury Press, 1982.

Rousseau, G. S., and P. G. Boucè, eds. *Tobias Smollett.* New York: Oxford University Press, 1971.

Spacks, Patricia Meyer. *Imagining a Self.* Cambridge, Mass.: Harvard University Press, 1976.

Sterne: Comedian and Experimental Novelist

W HY read Sterne? Such a question arises not only because of our historical distance from him (he died in 1768) but somehow seems inherent in the very nature of his enterprise as a novelist. From the time he burst onto the public consciousness with the appearance of the first two volumes of *Tristram Shandy* in the winter of 1759–60, there have been voices that have said that, because of its oddity and difficulty, Sterne's work couldn't be read, or that, because of its impropriety, it shouldn't be read. Yet he has never lacked powerful defenders, although the defenses have been even more various than the attacks. Sterne's advocates have loved his jeux d'esprit and his pathos; they have praised his originality and his brilliant use of sources; he has been termed the last of the Augustan satirists and the first prophetic voice of modernism; readers have admired him for creating characters of unsurpassed immediacy and for steadfastly refusing to adhere to any convention of novel writing. Perhaps it is his capacity to inspire such varied—indeed, contradictory—responses even among those who defend him that led Goethe to comment several times that Sterne was a "free soul." Certainly, whatever limitations Laurence Sterne the man faced (and he faced many), Sterne the novelist seems remarkably resistant to categorization or description, much less final judgment. It is very hard to pin him down.

Such a variety of response is difficult to map. In the discussion that follows, I have tried to create such a map around three landmarks in the collected commentary on Sterne. These brief remarks, one by Sterne himself and two by his critics, turn up in almost any discussion of him—so regularly, in fact, that they might be called the enduring clichés of Sterne criticism. My intention is not the further circulation of coins rubbed almost smooth by time. Instead, I would like to see if we can, by highlighting these comments, restore their roughness of surface and make them useful again. Between them, they raise virtually all of the central issues we confront in trying to understand Sterne and his career as a novelist.

"I wrote not to be *fed*, but to be *famous*."

So wrote Sterne to a friend in January 1760, with the first installment of *Tristram Shandy* just published and already creating a stir. The statement can be passed over as a relatively innocuous answer to the question Pope asked himself, "Why did I write?" or it can serve, as it generally does, as a prelude to brief remarks about Sterne's contemporary popularity. But much of Sterne's life, and (just as interestingly) a great deal of information about what it meant to be a novelist at the nascence of the genre are compressed into or implied by the remark. What does it mean, in the context of mid-eighteenth-century England, that someone wrote to be famous?

The facts of Sterne's life hardly suggest a candidate for fame, literary or otherwise. When he was born, in Ireland, in November 1713, he entered the world as a gentleman's son, but his hold on the privilege that honorific implied was an uncertain one. Young Laurence might have claimed an Archbishop of York as great-grandfather, and prominent Yorkshire landowners as living relations, but his father was a younger son, mired in an unpromising military career (hence, the Irish birth), and there was little in the future novelist's early childhood to separate him from the kind of life endured by those whose class status was technically much lower. The family was poor, they moved frequently from garrison to garrison, and Sterne's younger siblings died with numbing regularity. But in the matter of class, as in so much else, Sterne is hard to categorize, for if his early years show little gentility, he did ultimately enjoy, with family help, a gentleman's education, and his school years culminated in a Sterne family fellowship to Jesus College, Cambridge. While his parents gave him almost nothing, his more distant family saw to it that this poor relation could enter that almost obligatory path of the shabby but well-educated genteel: the priesthood. In 1735, Sterne was ordained and took up the first of several vicarages he would hold, all in the neighborhood of York. *Tristram Shandy* was still a quarter-century away.

Sterne's life between his ordination and his sudden elevation to literary fame cannot, at least in its externals, have been very different from that of many provincial clergy. In these years, he married (not happily) and had one daughter; he intrigued (with no great distinction) in politics, mostly ecclesiastical; he farmed a bit, hunted, and played the violin; he read a lot; he fought to keep an incipient consumption (which eventually killed him) at bay; over time, he gained more lucrative livings and more prominent church positions. Family connections, both his own and his wife's, helped at times, but it is also clear that Sterne felt considerable resentment about the obligations those connections created; eventually, he quarreled with his uncle, Jaques Sterne, an important figure in the clerical world of York. His career as a clergyman was at best moderately successful, and outside of the small world of Yorkshire church affairs, Sterne was totally obscure. The 1750s were an especially difficult decade: he had become alienated from his powerful uncle, his wife, never a source of much happiness, descended into madness, and a persistent public rumor had it that Sterne had mistreated his widowed mother. Yet some reservoir of confidence and ambition survived, for at the very end of that dark decade, in as he says, "a bye corner of the kingdom, and in a retir'd thatched house," he wrote the opening volumes of *Tristram Shandy*, bravely published them at his own expense, and sent half the copies to London, to all appearances serenely assured that, whatever his past, his future would be glorious.

The Life and Opinions of Tristram Shandy, Gentleman, volumes 1 and 2, appeared on the London market on January 1, 1760. Sterne himself arrived in the capital about three months later. By then, the great city was more than ready to receive its new sensation. One historian of fame has called Sterne "the first English author who can be called a celebrity," a judgment that remains safely this side of hyperbole. Sterne was lionized, petted, and feted by the great and the already famous. A new country dance was named the "Tristram Shandy" (as was a racehorse), and London prostitutes, it is said, approached potential customers for a time by asking them if they wanted their clocks wound up. And while Sterne may have written for fame, not money, he got both, selling his copyrights for a lucrative sum. If it is strictly true that the mild prosperity Sterne enjoyed from his clerical livings meant he didn't need this money to survive, he would undeniably enjoy spending it.

What is striking about this success story is what it reveals about Sterne's ambition to be "*famous.*" *Fama* is a goddess that writers have always worshiped, but, in Sterne's case, the emphasis is different. For the fame he achieved in the early months of 1760 seems to have had little to do with the traditional idea of artistic immortality, the desire that his powerful rhyme should outlive the gilded monuments of princes. The voice that touched Sterne's trembling ear was not that of Phoebus, but of a living, laughing body of admirers, pressing him with invitations to dinner, huddling to warm themselves by his aura. Sterne may well have had traditional notions of writerly fame in mind when he made his remark, but by the time he found himself at the center of London's admiring gaze, he had fervently embraced a more immediate role as that characteristically modern phenomenon, the celebrity: someone whom people want to know (or know about) *now.*

Sterne's celebrity, while it originated in the popularity of his novel and is therefore in part a creation of the marketplace, cannot be explained in terms of sales alone. From a modern point of view, an eighteenth-century writer did not have to sell very many copies in order to enjoy status as a best-seller. Fielding once defined "Nobody" as "All the people in Great Britain, except about 1200," and by that yardstick, Sterne—as well as fellow best-selling authors like Fielding and Richardson—could be said to be read by almost no one. (England's population in 1761 was a little over six million.) The various installments of *Tristram Shandy*—after the initial two volumes in 1760, he brought out further two-volume continuations in 1761, 1762, and 1765, and he brought out the last volume, the ninth, in 1767—had press runs of four thousand, and that figure appears to be close to the final sales for each. Richardson's sales were comparable, and even *Tom Jones*, a blockbuster by the standards of Georgian England, did not exceed ten thousand copies sold. The new kind of writing, the novel, was "popular" only in a special sense; even taking into account the existence of lending libraries, it was entertainment only for a small portion of the populace. The small size of the audience is brought into sharp focus by an extraordinary statement by Arthur Cash, Sterne's most recent biographer: "[Sterne] had probably been introduced personally to about half the people who bought his books, and many had become his personal friends."

If the most popular novelists had comparable—and by our standards, relatively small—sales, what separates Sterne from his contemporaries? Why is he the first literary celebrity in England? Neither Fielding nor Richardson, to take the two most prominent examples, became celebrities in the way Sterne did. Fielding was well known, but as a novelist was never the focus of public attention and curiosity as Sterne was. Richardson was notoriously vain about his work; he is, after all, the one Samuel Johnson summed up so memorably: "That fellow Richardson could not be contented to sail quietly down the stream of reputation, without longing to taste the froth from every stroke of the oar." But Richardson was a shy man, who generally preferred letters to face-to-face encounters. What he wanted—and plenty of it—was praise. Sterne's contemporary fame, what I am calling his celebrity, seems to be a function neither of his sales nor of the public evaluation of his work (the good reviews of the first two volumes of *Tristram Shandy* gave way to generally unkind notices thereafter). What the historical record shows, rather, is a remarkably personal bond between Sterne and his devotees, as Cash's comment above suggests. They wanted not just the book but the man behind the book (one reader said, "I'd ride fifty miles just to smoak a pipe with him"); he desired not just an audience with the money to buy what he wrote and like what they read, but faces, individuals, who wanted to know him.

Bishop Warburton, a lion of letters who liked *Tristram Shandy* on its first appearance and a man who tried hard to make himself Sterne's patron (an overture Sterne rebuffed with little grace), dismissed the novelist at the time of his death in a revealing way. Sterne was, he said, "the idol of the higher mob." Warburton was clearly bitter that Sterne had refused the velvet collar of patronage, but the comment is revealing in other ways, too. It shows one influential but conservative literary figure's incredulity in the face of the new image of the writer that Sterne embodied—impatient with patrons and intoxicated by the spotlight of wider attention. But the intended insult falls flat. Sterne would have embraced Warburton's remark, the essence of it anyway, if not the tone. To be such an "idol" was exactly what he wanted, and it is that desire that separates him from his popular contemporaries. But one important question at the heart of this issue is still hanging: how did *Tristram Shandy*—a novel, words on a page—make all this happen? (*A Sentimental Journey* was not published until very shortly before Sterne's death.) Sterne's vanity and ambition did not make him a celebrity; a book did. How?

The simple answer is that, in *Tristram Shandy*, Sterne was being perfectly honest when he described the work as "a portrait of myself." Sterne wrote about himself, and many of those first readers, such as the man who would ride fifty miles to share a pipe, liked what they read. But the whereabouts of Sterne's self are harder to determine. There is plenty of evidence, on the one hand, to suggest that those first readers freely associated Sterne with Tristram, and even the briefest look at contemporary accounts of the author reveals that he was most often referred to, not as "Laurence Sterne," but as his character. As Johnson reports his one meeting with Sterne: "Tristram Shandy introduced himself; and Tristram Shandy had scarcely sat down," and so forth. Sterne apparently liked being called Tristram, but—to complicate matters—he also encouraged the identification of himself with Yorick, who is, after all, the clergyman in the novel. When Sterne published his sermons in the wake of his initial burst of fame, he titled them *Sermons of Mr. Yorick*, and he went on, at the end of his career, to make Yorick the narrator of *A Sentimental Journey*. Clearly, he promoted the identification of his narrator/characters with himself, but he did so in a complex way.

The situation is further muddied if we try to specify more precisely the nature of the connection between the novelistic lives of Tristram and Yorick and the real one of Sterne. To put it simply, there is almost no connection. Yorick is a clergyman to be sure, and both Yorick and Tristram travel, as Sterne did, on the continent; Sterne seems to have pilloried real people of his acquaintance; the sermon Trim reads in volume 2 of *Tristram Shandy* is one Sterne actually preached. But such autobiographical gleanings are few. Nothing important that happens to Tristram—not the tribulations of his birth and naming, not the constellation of family and servants, not the incidents of either his or Yorick's travels—ever happened to Sterne. Moreover, surprisingly little of *Tristram Shandy* is even about Tristram; it's about Walter or Toby, and much of the action (even the last incident in the book) takes place long before Tristram is born.

Thus, the harder we look, the odder things get. Sterne is not, in the usual manner of autobiographical novels as we have come to know them, writing about himself, fictionalizing however superficially his own experiences. Instead, he has imagined a world, populated it with people, and invented incidents and conversation out of airy nothingness. And yet, stubbornly and undeniably, both of his fictions are projections of Sterne, and not just in the narrow sense that all novels are expressions of a peculiar individual reality. Even Flaubert, after all, the theorist of the artist-god who remains wholly removed from the fiction he creates, admitted in a very Sterne-like way that Madame Bovary was just himself. But that was a deathbed confession; Sterne's readers all knew that Tristram "was" his author, but in what sense?

We will look more closely at the texture of Sterne's fiction in the next section, but for now it will perhaps suffice to say that what Sterne conveys of himself is his *voice*, especially if we take "voice" to be one of our culture's principal metonyms of "personality." *Tristram Shandy* is largely made up of talk, characters telling stories, arguing with each other, passing the time; but, far more than this, it consists of a voice, Tristram's, talking to us. Listen to two passages, chosen more or less at random:

As for the clergy—No—if I say a word against them, I'll be shot.—I have no desire,—and besides, if I had,—I durst not for my soul touch upon the subject,—with such weak nerves and spirits, and in the condition I am in at present, 'twould be as much as my life was worth, to deject and contrist myself with so sad and melancholy an account,—and therefore, 'tis safer to draw a curtain across, and hasten from it, as fast as I can, to the main and principal point I have undertaken to clear up. (Volume 3, chapter 20)

"It is with Love as with Cuckoldom"—the suffering party is at least the *third*, but generally the last in the house who knows any thing about the matter: this comes, as all the world knows, from having half a dozen words for one thing; and so long, as what in this vessel of the human frame, is *Love*—may be *Hatred*, in that—*Sentiment* half a yard higher—and *Nonsense*—no, Madam,— not there—I mean at the part I am now pointing to with my forefinger—how can we help ourselves? (Volume 3, chapter 4)

The voice is urbane, yet vulnerable, apparently spontaneous, amusingly disjointed, running always close to the edge of one scandal or another, ready at all times to embrace innuendo. Above all, it is a performing voice, and what it performs—or, better, creates the illusion of performing—is a personality.

There is no particular reason to assume that such a voice *was*, definitively, Laurence Sterne. We are all now suspicious in a healthy way about identifying anything as essential, especially in matters of the self. This voice, too, is a construction, more artful and self-conscious than most. But it was at least part of Sterne's genius that he recognized in the new form of the novel the opportunity to perform or project a distinctive voice of personality. Fielding had done it already, in *Tom Jones* particularly, but he had kept the voice separate from Tom's story: Fielding's narrator controls the action openly but is not part of it. To a remarkable degree, however, Sterne's voice *is* the story, *is* the action of all of his fiction. But that does not really state the difference strongly enough, for Sterne takes another step beyond Fielding. Not only did he make his voice the center of his novels, he realized—at least after the publication of the first installment of *Tristram Shandy*—that such a voice (however invented) could be the source of this new brand of writerly fame, personal celebrity. The novel—either because of its formal freedom, or because of the kind of audience it attracted, or because the era was increasingly shaped by a mercantile cast of mind, or (most likely) because of the fortuitous combination of all these forces—allowed for what we might call the commodification of personality. The book, with its square shape and hard covers, could become almost literally a package, a package for a voice to be bought and sold. We may regard with some distaste the resulting loss of distinction between a person and a product, but whatever our response, we should not lose sight of the historical importance of what Sterne represents, for it is not a trivial moment in the making of the world that we live in. And perhaps our judgment may be tempered somewhat if we keep in mind that celebrity (however commodified) was something Sterne longed for, something he found, and by every account, something he loved.

But Sterne's celebrity, however determined by history and personality, and however significant as an image of the future world, is not the end of the story. Celebrity ends with death, and then the only form of fame left for the writer is the old-fashioned one, the immortality of reputation. As Tristram says, "Death opens the gates of fame." The fiction of Laurence Sterne has endured, at least until now. And having looked at the author and what his career represents in the history of the novel, it is time to examine more closely his work, for in the end it gained Sterne not only contemporary celebrity but also lasting reputation.

"Nothing odd will do long. *Tristram Shandy* did not last."

Boswell records this among other miscellaneous observations made by Samuel Johnson on a day in March 1776—about eight years after Sterne's death. Johnson must have taken some satisfaction in pronouncing this terse obituary. As noted above, the two men met only once, late in 1761, and the conversation went badly (Sterne may have shown Johnson a pornographic picture). Johnson was wrong, of course, but it is worth analyzing for a moment how he was wrong. Was he mistaken to assume that literary oddity and endurance are incompatible? Or was he in error when he said *Tristram Shandy* was odd? He was undeniably mistaken to imply that Sterne's novel would not last (to give Johnson credit, Sterne was somewhat neglected, as many writers are, in the years immediately following his death), but—as is so often the case with Johnson's critical blunders—the question he raises is central. What is the relationship between endurance and oddity in works of art? Can something genuinely bizarre last? One popular answer, at least in the case of Sterne, has been to deny that he is odd. With marvelous dexterity, this school of thought works to normalize Sterne's fiction. Such an approach, however, finally does confirm Johnson's point about the kind of art that will survive: nothing odd, it turns out, will do for long. In this section, I want to look at some of the most prominent attempts to grapple with Sterne's work, including especially the many discussions that have insisted in one way or another that Johnson was wrong about Sterne, that his work is not odd. If my own discussion is weighted more heavily toward *Tristram Shandy*, and leaves less room for *A Sentimental Journey*, that reflects both the balance of the criticism that now exists and the fact that most readers are likely to approach Sterne through his first novel.

Most any modern reader who casually picks up *Tristram Shandy* will think Johnson's opinion frankly obvious. It begins with the hero's intimate account of his own conception, and then proceeds, digressing at every single opportunity, to recount a very few events from his earliest childhood. While there are plenty of Tristram's opinions, delivered in that distinctive voice we glanced at above, there is in fact very little of his life; most of the events we do see occur not to him but to his father, Walter, and to his Uncle Toby; and many of these take place long before his birth. Along the way, there are interpolated stories, extracts in French and Latin, a missing chapter, chapters out of numerical order, and a host of typographical peculiarities: a blank page, a black page, marbled pages, straight lines, crooked lines, doodles, dashes, and asterisks. Whatever the other oddities of *Tristram Shandy*, it *looks* strange. Lest we fall into the error of thinking this sense of oddity is born of our own ignorance, we must remember that it was a contemporary, Johnson, who called it odd, and he was hardly the first. Everyone thought it was peculiar when it appeared ("a succession of Surprise, surprise, surprise," Hume said) and the argument was not about whether it was strange but whether you liked the strangeness. Horace Walpole, for one, hated it, calling it a "very insipid and tedious performance . . . the great humour of which consists in the whole narrative going backwards." But his friend and correspondent, Horace Mann, confessed, "You will laugh at me, I suppose, when I say that I don't understand Tristram Shandy, because it was probably the intention of the author that nobody should. . . . It diverted me, however, extremely."

The oddity of Sterne bears much further scrutiny, but I think it can best be approached by looking in some detail at arguments on the other side. A great deal of modern criticism has aligned itself against Johnson, though in a bewildering variety of ways. Let us make a first distinction, however, between approaches that are historical and those that are nonhistorical. I will look at the latter first.

The nonhistorical approach is typified by one critic who, in the 1960s, called Sterne "an inexplicable anachronism," and who in support of his point approvingly quoted this remark from several decades before: "To see what Sterne's achievement really was, is, I believe, only in these last few years possible, in a mind made aware by *The Magic Mountain, Ulysses*, and *Remembrance of Things Past*." For this school of thought, Sterne was of course strange to a reader like Johnson, in the same way as any prophet who is ahead of its time is perceived as strange. Sterne understood, virtually at the beginning of its history, that the novel's destiny lay not with the kind of work being done around him, but with at least three hallmarks of the modern novel: difficulty, self-consciousness, and the attempt to render in all its subtlety the manifold subjectivity of the inner life.

Setting aside the question of whether Sterne's contemporaries or his predecessors were really uninterested in these possibilities for the novel, it is undeniably true that his own work manifests all these qualities: he is difficult, he does promote self-consciousness, and he is sensitive to the peculiarities of interior experience. The difficulty of *Tristram Shandy* is undeniable. It is hard to read a book whose story line, such as it is, is hopelessly fragmented and delayed. These frustrations, moreover, have as one of their consequences a kind of alienation effect: as readers, we become self-conscious of our complicity in what Richardson rather peevishly called readers' desire for "Story, story, story"; such a desire for an apparently seamless and progressive unfolding of linked events can falsify our experience of ourselves and the world. Once we have achieved that awareness, we can become more cognizant of the way our experience does unfold—disjointedly, digressively, above all, subjectively. Such is an abstract rendering, at least in part, of the world of Sterne from this modernist point of view, and such a description points up obvious congruences with the world of Joyce or Woolf.

This approach to Sterne, while it has not disappeared, has gradually diminished in importance over the last twenty years, especially in light of the broad return to history that has marked so much recent criticism. Critical trends aside, however, an understanding of Sterne as an "inexplicable anachronism" seems to me to ignore the fact that reading *Tristram Shandy* is not very much like reading *Ulysses* or *To the Lighthouse*. And the difference is not simply a matter of costume, or setting, or language. These writers differ in fundamentals, for the difficulty or self-awareness or stream of consciousness narration of the high modernists is, finally, in the service of realistic presentation and authorial objectivity. Sterne's digressions and moments of self-consciousness may sometimes work to create a realistic effect (more on this below), but Sterne seems at least equally interested in exposing how all attempts at realistic representation are doomed. Before the first volume is half over, Tristram interrupts the action in a by-now familiar way to comment on his problems as a storyteller:

When a man sits down to write a history,—tho' it be but the history of *Jack Hickathrift* or *Tom Thumb*, he knows no more than his heels what lets and confounded hinderances he is to meet with in his way,—or what a dance he may be led by one excursion or another, before all is over. Could a historiographer drive on his history, as a muleteer drives on his mule,—straight forward;—. . . he might venture to foretell you to the hour when he should get to his journey's end;—but the thing is, morally speaking, impossible: For if he is a man of the least spirit, he will have fifty deviations from a straight line to make with this or that party as he goes along, which he can no ways avoid. He will have views and prospects to himself perpetually solliciting his eye, which he can no more help standing still to look at than he can fly; he will moreover have various
Accounts to reconcile:
Anecdotes to pick up:
Inscriptions to make out:
Stories to weave in:
Traditions to sift:
Personages to call upon:

Panegyricks to paste up at this door:
Pasquinades at that:—All which both the man and his mule are quite exempt from. (Volume 1, chapter 14)

The striking thing about this passage is the way that it can be read both as a statement of an aesthetic of realism and as a devastating critique of all fictional attempts to be real. The historian-novelist who wants to be accurate cannot be a muleteer, but our experience of reading the first thirteen chapters of *Tristram Shandy* has already insinuated into our minds the sinking feeling that unless a writer *is* a muleteer, he or she will never finish. We can look at Sterne in two ways: as (at times) a marvelous realist (Ian Watt refers to Sterne's "mastery of realistic presentation") and as perhaps the eighteenth century's most acute critic of fictional realism. He can be both because he seems to be attracted to both roles, and he will inevitably resist all attempts to slow or stabilize his oscillation between them. The reasons for this oscillation will be explored more fully below; for now, it suffices to say that such an attitude toward realism makes any attempt to understand Sterne as a prophet of modernism inherently problematic.

If the effort to make Sterne not "odd" by aligning him with the familiar voices of modernism runs into trouble, what about the many attempts to deny Johnson's comment precisely by putting these novels into an eighteenth-century context? I will first look at those arguments based on the phenomenon of sensibility, and then move on to look at Sterne's relation to Augustan satire and to John Locke.

"Sensibility" in mid-eighteenth-century England was not so much a political or intellectual movement as it was a fashion. It certainly had its roots in both religion and philosophy, as a certain strain of English thought from the late seventeenth century onward turned away from the gloomy images of human nature conjured up by Hobbes and by the sterner spokesmen for Calvinistic Protestantism. Sensibility emphasized the infinite capacity of the human heart for sympathetic feeling. We respond to the plight of others instinctively and powerfully, and our tears become the legible sign of our basic goodness. A taste developed for works of art that provoked or at least represented these tender feelings, and in many ways the novel led all the rest. Among Sterne's immediate predecessors, writers as different as Fielding and Richardson show the effects of this taste: with the long-suffering Clarissa, Richardson proved himself a master of the ability to elicit a sympathetic response;

Fielding, with heroes like Parson Adams or Tom Jones, consistently created characters with a good heart.

Sterne's name has become almost synonymous with sensibility, and little wonder. In the welter of voices that makes up the texture of *Tristram Shandy*, one note sounds with apparent clarity again and again—the feeling heart. We see it especially clearly in Toby and his servant Trim: the former famously and literally refuses to hurt a fly, and rushes generously to the bedside of the dying Le Fever, a perfect stranger; the latter poignantly epitomizes the fragility of human life at the death of Bobby Shandy, and is given to melancholy spells when he thinks of the fate of his brother. But sensibility is not merely something Tristram discusses in others—it is a large part of his portrait of himself. Think of his encounter with the ass of Lyons, or with poor, mad Maria, and so on. In the 1780s, the most commonly reprinted version of Sterne's work was a kind of golden treasury called *The Beauties of Sterne; Including All His Pathetic Tales, and Most Distinguished Observations on Life, Selected for the Heart of Sensibility*, a fact that suggests that for a number of contemporary readers this was the aspect of Sterne that appealed the most. His last work, *A Sentimental Journey Through France and Italy*, takes the note of sensibility that appeared intermittently in *Tristram Shandy* and turns it into the dominant strain, as the traveling Yorick moves from one feeling moment to the next. This latter work includes a panegyric on sensibility that effectively sums up both its meaning and its appeal: "Dear sensibility! sources inexhausted of all that's precious in our joys, or costly in our sorrows! . . . —eternal fountain of our feelings! . . . This is the divinity which stirs within me—. . . that I feel some generous cares beyond myself—all comes from thee, great great SENSORIUM of the world!"

Sensibility, however, was a taste fraught with contradictions. The emphasis was more on the good feelings of the responsive heart than on the heart's responsibility to do anything to relieve the suffering that inspired it. Toby does rush to Le Fever's deathbed and offer help, and he assists Le Fever's son after the child is left orphaned, but our primary focus throughout the episode is on what Toby's feelings tell us about him and his good heart. It is tempting to say that such an emphasis on responses tends to blur the reality of suffering; suffering, in fact, can be seen as a good thing, since we require it—and require it in others!—to know our own generous feelings. In particular, the fact that so much of this pathos was inspired by women and the poor makes many modern readers very uncomfortable, and it is quite possible to perceive at least a tacit complicity between sensibility and oppression of all stripes. The privileged revel in their good hearts, and they relieve suffering only in localized (and perhaps selfish) ways.

Lest we revel too much in the indignation that is our age's sensibility, it is important to examine whether Sterne himself—notwithstanding his status as a high priest in the cult—embraced sensibility in an uncritical way. The panegyric above hints at some ironic distance: Yorick feels divinity within him, and most of Sterne's first readers would have recognized the allusion to the moment in *Paradise Lost* where Adam and Eve eat the forbidden fruit; they, too, feel "Divinity within them breeding wings / Wherewith to scorn the earth." The possibility that sensibility is, if not an absolutely false divinity, then an ambiguous one, is in fact a far more insistent idea in Sterne than for many of his contemporaries.

Look, for instance, at the scene between the wayfaring Tristram and the pathetic mad girl, Maria: she is "beautiful," but "unsettled in her senses" (thwarted love, of course); she sits upon a bank, her goat beside her, and plays her pipes to the Virgin. Tristram is smitten with the full force of "an honest heart-ache," and then:

MARIA made a cadence so melancholy, so tender and querulous, that I sprung out of the chaise to help her, and found myself sitting betwixt her and the goat before I relapsed from my enthusiasm.

MARIA look'd wistfully for some time at me, and then at her goat—and then at me—and then at her goat again, and so on, alternately—

—Well, *Maria*, said I softly—What resemblance do you find?

I do entreat the candid reader to believe me, that it was from the humblest conviction of what a *Beast* man is,—that I ask'd the question; and that I would not have let fall an unseasonable pleasantry in the venerable presence of Misery, to be entitled to all the wit that ever *Rabelais* scatter'd—and yet I own my heart smote me, and that I so smarted at the very idea of it, that I swore I would set up for Wisdom and utter grave sentences the rest of my days—and never—never attempt again to commit mirth with man, woman, or child, the longest day I had to live. (Volume 9, chapter 24)

The idea of the "beauties of Sterne" takes on an entirely appropriate double entendre here, and we must ask, what is Sterne trying to evoke: a tear for Maria? a laugh at his own expense? Both, surely, but also more, for he seems intent as well on exposing for our amused and ironic scrutiny the potentially erotic charge lurking in every "heart-ache" of

sensibility. Sterne admits that his pathos is inevitably tinged with something more than a little goat-footed; Richardson, to take just one point
of contrast, insists that the slow decline of pious Clarissa only works to
throw into higher relief the most important doctrines of Christianity.
His own less noble feelings he projects onto Lovelace, whom he conveniently kills off.

Sterne is never only one thing. The anthologists may have wished
him safely and solely sentimental, but he is better seen as a unique
hybrid, a sentimentalist who is at times perfectly sincere, but one who
also often remembers the potential in sentiment for the pompous or the
narcissistic or the exploitative or the merely futile (one strong undercurrent in the Le Fever tale is the uselessness of Toby's good feelings).
Sterne's sensibility ties him to his era, but the way he weaves it into his
work also sets him apart slightly; he remains capable at all times of a
canny laugh at the spectacle of his own bleeding heart.

The ironies of the Maria episode inevitably raise questions about
Sterne as a satirist, and a number of critics have tried to understand him
in relation to the norms of eighteenth-century satire; some have even
gone so far as to call him the last of the Augustan satirists and these
critics insist that a true historical reading of Sterne must begin with that
context. He is not odd, that is, in the light of Swift and Pope. An anecdote that Sterne himself recounts encourages this point of view. Speaking of an encounter he had in 1760 with a certain elderly gentleman,
Sterne tells us:

> He came up to me, one day, as I was at the Princess of Wales's court. "I want
> to know you, Mr. Sterne; but it is fit you should know, also, who it is that wish-
> es this pleasure. You have heard, continued he, of an old Lord Bathurst, of
> whom your Popes, and Swifts, have sung and spoken so much; I have lived my
> life with geniuses of that cast; but have survived them; and, despairing ever to
> find their equals, it is some years since I have closed my accounts, and shut up
> my books, with thoughts of never opening them again; but you have kindled a
> desire in me of opening them once more before I die; which I now do; so go
> home and dine with me.

We could pause a long time over these remarks, for they are rich with
all kinds of implications (for instance, is the relentlessly mercantile tone
of Bathurst's comments a reflection of what traditional patronage feels
like from the patron's point of view, or is it Sterne's later coloring, an
intriguing revelation about his feelings for a system he regarded with

ambivalence?). We should also note that Bathurst never actually says that Sterne is *like* Swift and Pope, but the story has given license to a number of critics who want to see family resemblances between Sterne and the Augustans. Sterne does share with the Augustans (and with earlier figures, such as Rabelais) a love of elaborate intellectual foolery, the so-called tradition of learned wit we see in works like *A Tale of a Tub* or the *Peri Bathous*. But while it is important to understand Sterne as a satirist, it is not necessarily most accurate to see him as an Augustan satirist, and such an attempt may be as anachronistic as the effort to make him modern. In fact, the problems with assigning Sterne a place as the last Augustan are manifold: his temperament is strikingly different, his politics are all wrong, and his aims as a writer, on balance, seem to be quite different. The world of the Augustans was once memorably summed up by one critic with the phrase, "the gloom of the Tory satirists"; Sterne was not gloomy, he was a staunch Whig, and he lacks the militancy that is at the heart of the kind of Juvenalian satire Pope and Swift most often practiced.

For the contrast in temperament, we can look to Tristram's insistence (which seems very much to be Sterne's) that his book is "if . . . wrote against any thing,—'tis wrote, and please your worships, against the spleen." Swift and Pope often make us laugh, but they seem intent on embracing spleen, and exploiting it as the organ from which their truest work will emerge. Some of that may have been constitutional, but it was certainly reinforced by their politics and their increasingly splenetic horror at what the Whigs wrought. Sterne, however, was neither a Tory nor a politically angry man. We can see both his politics and their tone in the scene where Toby and Trim must regretfully demolish their toy fortifications in order that they may honor the terms of the Tory Peace of Utrecht. The sentiment is Whig orthodoxy, but the spirit could hardly be gentler (and it is amusing to speculate what Bathurst thought of the scene; his own peerage was one of those created by the Tories so that the Peace of Utrecht could be saved).

The largest difficulty with this approach, however, emerges when we ask the question, what, if Sterne was a satirist, was his satire *about*? While the capaciousness of the satiric imagination in Swift and Pope is such that we may often wonder if there is a limit to their range, we can also point to a core of issues that form the heart of their enterprise: the Whigs, especially Walpole; abuses in learning; bad writing; religious differences; the sin of Pride. Sterne may have aligned himself with the

Whigs, but as the destruction of the toy fortifications suggests, there is little political militancy. He does poke fun at Walter Shandy's mad theorizing on child development, but Walter is a character, not merely an attitude, and the response he generates is complex and in part sympathetic. Sterne undoubtedly wrote *A Sentimental Journey* to balance genial travels against Smollett's angry ones, but that was only the most minor of his intentions or effects. Sentiment itself, as we have seen, receives ironic treatment, but that irony is only part of the story; Sterne is also genuinely sentimental, and the anthologists erred more by simplifying than by falsifying the role of sensibility in his writing. The fact is, Sterne frequently wants us to adopt an ironic viewpoint toward something in his work, but that irony is only rarely the sum of his intention. This is a crucial point, and we can see it repeated if we look at the way he uses the thought of John Locke. With Locke, the question of what is to be taken ironically and what is to be taken straight is central, but it is also a question without a final answer.

Locke has been a name to conjure with in much Sterne criticism, and he has a central place in the critical tradition that wants to place Sterne firmly in an eighteenth-century setting. Locke clearly belongs in any comprehensive discussion of Sterne (*Tristram Shandy* is seeded with references, direct and allusive) and several connections between the novelist and the philosopher have been discovered. It has been argued that Locke provided Sterne both with a model of the human mind that we can see at work in his fiction, particularly in the way character unfolds, and that such a model also provided the novelist with a structure for his apparently shapeless work, especially *Tristram Shandy*. Such a conviction led one critic, writing a few decades ago, to insist that "in *Tristram Shandy*, the name and influence of Locke are pervasive." Are they?

Locke's *Essay Concerning Human Understanding* (dated 1690, published 1689) proved in many ways as influential on the philosophy of its time as Newton's physics; indeed, many thought Locke had formulated the laws of thought as reliably as his contemporary had articulated the governing principles of gravity and motion. Locke's aim was to describe how the mind worked, and the mechanics he developed were empirical. At birth, our minds are empty slates, devoid of innate knowledge but nonetheless receptive to new ideas, which come to us and accumulate in our minds through one of two channels: through our experience of outward objects as perceived by our senses, or through the mind's reflection on its own operations. As Locke himself puts it, "In all that great extent wherein the mind wanders, . . . it stirs not one jot beyond those *Ideas*, which *Sense* or *Reflection* have offered for its Contemplation."

To be sure, Sterne is interested in both sensation and reflection. *Tristram Shandy* is a work filled with sensation, most of it—though not all—painful; we can balance the hot chestnut in Phutatorius's breeches with the Beguine's tender treatment of Trim's wound. And Tristram is much given to reflection on his mind's operations. The passage quoted above in which he refuses the role of the muleteer-historian is only one of a number of places where the narrator pauses to consider how his mind works. But lurking behind these twin pillars of the Lockean mind is a necessary principle of combination, a process of association; without that, our ideas would remain discrete quanta of intellectual possibility. It is this quality of association that interests Sterne most of all. As early as the fourth chapter of the first volume, he announces, in explanation and extenuation of his mother's ill-timed query about the clock:

From an unhappy association of ideas which have no connection in nature, it so fell out at length, that my poor mother could never hear the said clock wound up,—but the thoughts of some other things unavoidably popp'd into her head,—*& vice versa*:—which strange combination of ideas, the sagacious *Locke*, who certainly understood the nature of these things better than most men, affirms to have produced more wry actions than all other sorts of prejudice whatsoever. (Volume 1, chapter 4)

Annotators will typically refer readers of this passage to these words of Locke's:

Some of our *Ideas* have a natural Correspondence and Connexion one with another. . . . Besides this there is another Connexion of *Ideas* wholly owing to chance or Custom; *Ideas* that in themselves are not at all of kin, come to be so united in some Mens Minds, that 'tis very hard to separate them, they always keep in company, and this one no sooner at any time comes into the Understanding, but its Associate appears with it.

Locke here is describing, as Sterne is narrating in the passage about his mother, peculiar associations, and Locke is scrupulous throughout the *Essay* to acknowledge the individuality of all minds. But the examination of such peculiarity is not Locke's central aim, and he describes such oddity primarily as a concession to the limitations of his larger effort, which is to describe how all minds work and thus what all "human understanding" has in common. Not so Sterne. His interest in the sagacious philosopher centers on those moments where Locke speaks of human understanding as flawed or ridiculous or, especially, as subjective. And such knowledge intrigues Sterne largely because he finds it so funny. Mrs. Shandy's association of clock winding with conjugal union is "unhappy" only for the Shandy family; for readers, it's meant to be the first good joke in the book. And association will be the source of other jokes, particularly involving Toby, whose mental track of association is worn so smooth that anything—even Walter awkwardly reaching across his body—reminds him of fortifications.

But Sterne (and here we reach the nub of a problem we have seen before), while always a jester, is rarely only a jester. The individuality of association and the resultant peculiarity of mind are undoubtedly sources of humor, but they seem to be more, and to be bound up with both the way he constructs character and the way he builds structure. But how far? If we think of character, what Sterne learned from Locke allowed him to formulate an intellectual basis for the creation of fictional people who look very much like characters in the old "humours" tradition. The one-track mind of Walter or Toby can be explained in a Lockean way, but their provenance in the comic world is ancient. Ben Jonson could create an enthusiast without reference to Locke and so, one suspects, could Sterne. His use of the *Essay* to "explain" such a traditional character type may be less an attempt to be realistic than it is another joke at the expense of learning: Locke's version of the *Principia* only leads Sterne back to the funnymen of the Roman or the Elizabethan stage.

The more important issue is structure, for the form—or lack of it—of Sterne's work has bedeviled many readers and is doubtless one source of Johnson's complaint that *Tristram Shandy* was odd. What we might call the strong Lockean position on this matter is aptly summarized by James Work, one of Sterne's best editors: "The most important structural device [in *Tristram Shandy*] is the principle of the association of ideas upon which the whole progression of the book is based." It is true that mental associations are one principle at work in the book: we have seen Mrs. Shandy's wry connection and Toby's unwavering focus on the science of siegecraft. As far as "progression" goes, Tristram's narration of his life and opinions often seems based on some personal internal logic: recounting his birth makes him think ahead to his baptism, which leads him to remember a French debate on prenatal baptism he has read about, which becomes a bawdy joke. However, to say that these associations are "the most important structural device" or that the "whole progression" of the book is based on them may be a bit grandiose. Certainly, Work's comment (and this viewpoint has been quite influential, at least until recently) seems to reflect the taste of a few decades ago, when critics were loath to appreciate any literary work whose unity they could not demonstrate. Thus, to insist on a Lockean structure in Sterne, for all its apparent historicity, may be another modern imposition.

Again, as with the muleteer-historian, the central question is the extent of Sterne's commitment to realistic representation. To say that he has adopted Locke as *the* source of structure and the engine of progression is to imply a desire on his part to consistently imitate not an action but a consciousness (Tristram's, mostly), and to imitate it on the basis of assumptions borrowed from Locke. The beauty of teleology is that it can almost always be imposed on any sequence we can look at retrospectively (like a plot), and the divagations of Tristram's mind are no exception. But are we actually to assume that, say, Slawkenbergius's Tale is interpolated in precisely the place that it is because Sterne is putting it in the service of an attempt "realistically" to re-create (along Lockean lines) the way a mind like Tristram's would work? Nonsense. Sterne placed it there because it was funny. And yet, that is not quite the end of the matter either. For if the kind of systematic mimetic structure the strong Lockeans have discovered in *Tristram Shandy* is a critical imposition, we should also acknowledge that in some Sternean and very unsystematic way, mimesis does take place. A picture of a consciousness does emerge—forcefully enough, as we have seen, that many of those first readers wanted to meet the man whose consciousness they presumed they had already encountered in the pages of his book. However artificially Sterne has manipulated the idea of Lockean association, his manipulation is not so artificial that all we are left with are the jokes. There is a doubleness at the heart of Sterne, a doubleness that is difficult to accept. As readers, we tend to be like the Widow Wadman: we long to put our fingers on "the place," the place where ambiguity disappears and we can say with certainty, Sterne's aims were mimetic and Locke was his model; or, Sterne's goals were satiric and Locke was his target. It is a harder task to comprehend how he could do both.

We can return now to a question raised above: if Sterne is a satirist, what is his satire about? We have seen the ways in which both sensibility and Lockean psychology are and are not targets in the way that satire traditionally establishes its objects of attack. Lurking behind and between those issues, however, is a more central one, one I have touched on already: representation. For it is with representation that Sterne's doubleness is most apparent. If Sterne has one great satiric target, it is the novel itself, and yet he has embodied that satire in a work that stubbornly—against all odds, I am tempted to say—remains a novel.

Jean-Jacques Mayoux has beautifully articulated this fundamental truth about Sterne; speaking of *Tristram Shandy*, he says, "If every representation is in some degree a parody, is not every parody in danger of becoming in some way representative?" Mayoux's point, of course, is a general one: both parody and mimesis, as selections from and stylizations of reality, exist on a continuum, and the difference between them is a difference of degree and not of kind. Yet the way they shift in Sterne, one into the other and then back again, is central to our experience of reading him. A great deal of *Tristram Shandy* does seem directed at exposing by parody the difficulties of fictional representation: Tristram's ludicrously delayed birth, to take one large example, the narrator's hilarious inability to get Walter and Toby down the stairs, to cite a smaller instance. Defoe's density of detail, Richardson's moment-by-moment rendering of the sensitive consciousness, Fielding's godlike narrator—all this and more falls apart in Tristram's bumbling hands. But even as Tristram's problems expose the fallacies of mimesis and the contradictions of fictional convention, the picture shifts, and the muddle of writing suddenly looks like the muddle of life. A parody of realistic writing becomes, ironically, an effective representation. How very odd.

"Irresponsible (and nasty) trifling"

Thus, in 1948, did F. R. Leavis exclude Sterne from *The Great Tradition*, his influential study of the English novel. The fact that the dismissal was relegated to a footnote—perhaps the most quoted footnote in modern literary criticism—only emphasizes the magisterial contempt it conveys. Leavis hardly commands the deference today that he once did, and in fact, people went on busily reading and writing about Sterne even in the years of his greatest influence. Yet we cannot dismiss Leavis's few, biting words as easily as Leavis dismissed Sterne. Charges that Sterne was somehow improper, and so not fit to be read, dogged him when he first published, and—appropriately transmogrified—they dog him today. To many, his oddity has been less troubling than his wickedness. What, then, have been the attacks, and what defenses have been made?

Bishop Warburton, rumor had it, bestowed a purse upon Sterne at the time of *Tristram Shandy*'s first appearance, but he also had words of advice for the clergyman-novelist. He wrote Sterne during the composition of volumes 3 and 4: "You say you will continue to laugh aloud. In good time. But one . . . would wish to laugh in good company, where priests and virgins may be present." This was not, needless to say, the audience Sterne aimed to please, and the novel that began with a fateful instance of coitus interruptus proceeded in the next installments to recount the tale of Slawkenbergius's extraordinary nose, the sexualization of the word "whiskers" in sixteenth-century Navarre, and the Beguine's masturbatory therapy for Trim. And that is only a small selection.

There were two problems for contemporary readers. The sexual content itself troubled some; beyond that, there was the fact that such content issued from the pen of a clergyman. This double provocation to public morality is summed up by a comment about *Tristram Shandy* made by Lady Bradshaigh in a letter to Richardson, her great friend: "Upon the whole, I think the performance, mean *dirty Wit*. I may add *scandelous* considering the *Man*." (By contrast, after the publication of *Sir Charles Grandison*, Richardson's last novel, she gushed to the author, "Oh, Sir, you ought to have been a Bishop!") The scandal of Sterne's profession, "the shiten shepherd" as Chaucer puts it, was a strictly contemporary issue, but the discomfort inspired by the sexuality of Sterne's fiction has never disappeared. In particular, as Warburton's comment partially foretold, Sterne has consistently presented problems for female readers.

While Sterne's initial readership was not exclusively male, there is evidence that a number of women were uncomfortable with Sterne's bawdy. As the wife of one clergyman said of *Tristram Shandy*: "I have [not] read, or shall read it; . . . as *I cannot presume* to depend on my own strength of mind, I think it safest and best to *avoid* whatever may prejudice it." Such self-censoring tendencies were overcome by Clara Reeve, the author of the early Gothic novel *The Old English Baron*, but she clearly regretted her courageousness: "It is not a woman's book. . . . I have never read this book half through, and yet I have read enough to be ashamed of." A few decades later, Coleridge, while dismissing the possibility that *Tristram Shandy* could do moral harm, insisted that it was, as Reeve implied, a man's book: "Sterne's morals are bad, but I do not think can do much harm to any one whom they would not find bad enough before. Besides, the oddity and erudite grimaces under which much of the dirt is hidden take away the effect for the most part; although, to be sure, the book is scarcely readable by women." It is not clear whether Coleridge thought a woman's reading Sterne would corrupt her—probably not; what he implies, however, is a masculine preserve of humor from which women should be kept.

Troubled reactions to the sexual content of Sterne's fiction have never disappeared, as Leavis's comment indicates; however, the connection between that content and a female readership has again become a serious critical issue. For some readers in the last ten years or so, Sterne has reemerged as a writer who is almost exclusively for men. Worse, he is a spokesman for corrupt attitudes toward women. One very recent critic, echoing Reeve, has called *Tristram Shandy* "a man's book, if ever there was one," and a number of other readers hear, in Tristram's lubricious meanderings, the voice of patriarchal oppression. The new, gender-based, attacks on Sterne are not, obviously, the same as those made two centuries ago, and the differences need to be looked at; at the same time, such continuities as do exist also merit examination.

The most significant difference involves a change in attitudes toward the portrayal of sexuality in all forms. The eighteenth century was franker in many ways than the century or century and a half that followed. Yet if Sterne's contemporaries were not Victorians, a comment like Reeve's suggests that, at least for some, there was a distinction made between materials suitable for men and for women. The recent attacks on Sterne, of course, have nothing to do with an attempt to revive paternalistic restriction of women's reading; no serious reader today invokes the standard of that which brings a blush to the cheek of a young girl as the line of censorship or condemnation. The feminist critique of Sterne (and it is not universal) is based not on the fact that much of the material in his fiction is sexual, but on the way that sexuality is represented. From this point of view, the book's sexual interests and humor are exclusively male, and women appear only as objects of erotic desire or (more commonly) sexual frustration. Moreover, there is the unflattering portrait of "Madam," the imaginary prude in his audience whom Sterne addresses whenever the fog of innuendo becomes especially thick. By reducing women almost exclusively to a sexual function, the argument says, Sterne perpetuates stereotypes; and by relying on the existence of a male preserve of sexual humor, he has reinforced one potent image of oppression.

For anyone interested in the unfolding shape of Sterne criticism over time, it is remarkable to see the way the debate has returned to one of its original roots. In part, this reflects the new didacticism of much criticism generally, a didacticism which, after all, though it claims to be political, has the effect of reintroducing to the evaluation of literature the kind of moral concern that dominated literary criticism for much of its history. But Sterne seems to have a special ability to provoke moral reactions—a clergyman shouldn't write this, innocent women shouldn't read it, these books have no place in a world of transformed gender relations, and so on. We have moved away from the ad hominem tone of much of the early moral reaction, and we have left completely behind the paternalistic censorship that would make Sterne available only to those with a key to the club library. But if we step farther back, we cannot help but be struck by the way moral issues continue to inform the critical discussion. My opening query—why read Sterne?—remains for many a pressing moral question.

It is not easy to defend Sterne from some of the recent feminist opposition to his work. *Tristram Shandy* is relentlessly phallocentric, and reading it we can feel ourselves in a kind of literalized Lacanian universe, where quite nonsymbolic phalluses are indeed a universal ground of signification: everything refers to, because all meaning is generated by, the male genital. Sigurd Burckhardt has shown quite well how the law of gravity in the novel always pulls us down to that very spot. That is the place where fortifications and windows and hot chestnuts fall, where the Widow Wadman longs to put her finger, where even an innocent word like "nose" ends up. What's more, women are largely absent from the stage, and their cameo appearances are usually in the service of some joke at their expense. *Tristram Shandy* creates a world of male talk, and the novel often seems like an extended example—or series of examples—of that peculiar English custom, the segregation of the sexes for after-dinner conversation. Figuratively, we are always sitting with the men over their port.

Despite all this, Sterne has his defenders. The main line of defense is based on the idea that Sterne is not representing male oppression in order to endorse it, but to satirize it. Walter's mechanical lovemaking and his wild theories of child rearing; Toby's infantile retreat to a world of toy soldiers; the man-midwife Slop's "vile instruments"; Tristram's inability to escape the whole catalog of male sexual anxieties (impotence, size, deformity, castration)—all this and more shows that Sterne's intention is to make fun of men. The long section of the narrative that is, at least intermittently, concerned with Tristram's birth gives us plenty of evidence for both sides of this argument. Here, while the important business of Mrs. Shandy's labor proceeds upstairs and out of sight, we have an extended conversation involving Walter, Toby, Trim, and Dr. Slop. Trim reads Yorick's sermon, issues of politics and religion are discussed, pipes are smoked, and so forth. The worlds of men and women do not meet, except for Slop's incompetent and nose-disfiguring intervention at the very end. From one point of view, this scene reinforces the idea that women's labor (not only childbirth, but generally: Mrs. Shandy is surrounded by women working to help her) is not worth our attention. Moreover, women and their work are reduced to purely reproductive roles—their business is birth. On the other hand, however, Sterne makes it clear that the whole crew of men are useless—they idly sit and smoke, their talk is mostly trivial and self-interested, they have nothing to do. Men are narcissists and bores, and they insist on hogging the stage. As is so often the case, however, the overall effect of this part of the narrative is difficult to characterize definitively. It's easy to laugh at this fraternity; but, because they are all we have on which to focus our attention, they consume our interest and we become in some way engaged with them. This is satire, surely, but it is satire in which Sterne seems to concede not only that women are worthy of respect (they, after all, are accomplishing something), but that they are outside his ken, or at least outside the bounds of what he is interested in talking about. It's easy to see how female readers can recognize Sterne's satire on men and still feel themselves without a foothold in the book. The men may very well be making fools of themselves; Sterne may understand quite accurately how the walls that contain them also limit and cripple them; but nonetheless the separation remains. It is perhaps worth remembering that both of the primary female characters in the novel, Mrs. Shandy and the Widow Wadman, are shown in the posture of eavesdropping.

To conclude, there is no single answer to the question, why read Sterne?—just as there is no one reason we should not. Rather than catalog either set of reasons again, however, I will take a small risk and say that, at least today, those who like Sterne enjoy him because they still find him to be funny. Comedy does not travel well, and it rarely keeps. A change of place or the passing of time will spoil many of the best jokes, and Sterne has not survived these perils unscathed. Much of the humor of Sterne's fiction is thus lost to us; and footnotes and annotation and commentary only twist the knife, for what is most fatal to a joke, even worse than time and place, is an explanation. "Oh, now I see," the reader says, and glumly turns the page. And yet, for some, enough jokes do survive that Sterne's stated ambition—to make us laugh—still finds fulfillment.

And many of those who still laugh at *Tristram Shandy* laugh loudest at its fractured form. Sterne may be, as the title of this chapter suggests, both a comedian and an experimental novelist, but his experiments are some of his best comedy. To return to a point made earlier, he does not experiment to revolutionize the novel (though, from our vantage point, it often looks that way), but to have fun with the conventions he saw hardening all around him in the genre's first half-century or so—conventions of progression, of unity of action, of a fourth wall standing between book and author on one side and the audience on the other. The way he exposes those conventions, primarily by refusing to obey them, is the best continuing joke that he has, and because the novel has proven to be such an enduring and popular literary form, the fun Sterne has at the expense of its standard conventions can evoke laughter today. His oddity has never lessened, and his irresponsibility can rankle even after two centuries—but the gift of laughter is the soul of Sterne, and for those who see it, that gift is still enough.

John Allen Stevenson

Selected Bibliography

Brissenden, R. F. "'Trusting to Almighty God': Another Look at the Composition of *Tristram Shandy*." In Arthur H. Cash and John M. Stedmond, *The Winged Skull, Papers from the Laurence Sterne Bicentenary Conference*. London: Methuen, 1971.

Brown, Marshall. "Sterne's Stories." In Marshall Brown, *Preromanticism*. Stanford: Stanford University Press, 1991.

Burckhardt, Sigurd. "*Tristram Shandy*'s Law of Gravity." *English Literary History* 28 (Spring 1961): 70–88.

Cash, Arthur H. *Laurence Sterne*. 2 vols. London: Methuen, 1975 and 1986.

Howes, Alan B., ed. *Laurence Sterne: The Critical Heritage*. London: Routledge, 1974.

Hunter, J. Paul. "Clocks, Calendars, and Names: The Troubles of Tristram and the Aesthetics of Uncertainty." In J. Douglas Canfield and J. Paul Hunter, eds., *Rhetorics of Order/Ordering Rhetorics in English Neoclassical Literature*. Newark: University of Delaware Press, 1989.

Lanham, Richard. *"Tristram Shandy": The Games of Pleasure*. Berkeley and Los Angeles: University of California Press, 1973.

Mayoux, Jean-Jacques. "Laurence Sterne." In John Traugott, ed., *Laurence Sterne: A Collection of Critical Essays*. Englewood Cliffs, N.J.: Prentice-Hall, 1968.

Perry, Ruth. "Words for Sex: The Verbal-Sexual Continuum in *Tristram Shandy*." *Studies in the Novel* 20 (Spring, 1988): 27–42.

Sentimental Novels of the Later Eighteenth Century

T HE form of the sentimental novel is typically that of an anti-bildungsroman: instead of a progress toward maturity, it deals sympathetically with the character who cannot grow up and find an active place in society. Its ideal is stasis or regression, which makes for episodic, cyclical narratives that often go nowhere or back where they began. Owing to different social assumptions about masculinity and femininity, the sentimental heroine can figure in conventional romance plots that end with wedding bells, since her role conforms to the popular sense of what a young woman should be; the sentimental hero poses an implicit challenge to accepted notions of masculinity, and he cannot be assimilated into the world represented in the novels. As a consequence, sentimental novels tend to become satires on "the world," but satires in which the hero himself cannot usually take part because of his naïveté, good nature, and general childlikeness. From one point of view, the cult of sentiment represents a clear challenge to traditional social, economic, and gender hierarchies, which it seeks to replace with bonds of fraternal benevolence embracing all mankind. From another point of view this movement is not egalitarian at all, but rather attempts to create a new aristocracy, possessing spontaneity, warmth, and delicacy of feeling, in place of an existing aristocracy perceived as emotionally artificial, cold, and coarse.

The sentimental novel often deals with adolescence, but in one way or another the onset of adulthood, the goal of the bildungsroman, is obstructed, evaded, or undone. The sentimental novel shows change stopped or reversed—and often time along with it. The bildungsroman treats time respectfully, as not only measuring but fostering the processes it celebrates. In the sentimental novel time becomes a major enemy, the agent of feared or despised changes. Various strategies are devised to arrest or fragment its ongoingness, and to retrieve or redeem moments that seem to stand outside time or otherwise defy it. One such strategy is to break down the linear, causal, sequential flow of narrative into discrete episodes; another is to arrange episodes in nonchronological order (as Sterne does), or to introduce digressions (as Sterne and Mackenzie both do), or to posit gaps (as Mackenzie does with his "lost" chapters), all tending to disrupt temporal continuity. If the sentimental novelist is to free his hero from the ordinary effects of time, drastic tactics are called for, since narrative is always threatening to imply progress simply by unfolding in time. Such tactics as Sterne's and Mackenzie's, sometimes regarded as experimental departures from the realistic conventions of the standard novel, or as attempts to get beyond the "literary" artificiality of inherited narrative modes, are especially appropriate to the sentimental novel because of the significance attached to time. What is most benign about time in the bildungsroman—its efficacy as agent of growth and development—becomes in the sentimental novel its most malign feature: the power of time to transform boys into men and sons into husbands is the very thing that the sentimental novel tries to elude or deny.

We tend to think of the language of sentimentalism as an affected or exaggerated jargon: "tears and flapdoodle," as Mark Twain was to call it. Yet what is most characteristic of sentimentalism is not the set of terms with which it attempts to revivify the language of emotion, for these terms quickly dwindle into clichés, but rather a fundamental skepticism about the adequacy of language itself as a medium of expression or communication. The distinctive sentimental attitude toward language is to be discovered not in the shibboleths of its pioneers but in the conviction of sentimentalists of each generation that language, like the world that uses it, is profoundly debased: better suited to self-disguise than self-revelation, more often employed to exploit than to enlighten, ideally to be avoided but at all events to be used, if used it must be, with mistrust. Sentimental writers have responded to this impasse with two centuries of narratives in which articulateness is associated with villainy, and true heroism is more or less tongue-tied. Sentimental figures tend to be babes linguistically (as in other ways), out of whose mouths comes much odd-sounding sense.

The menaced sentimental hero yearns for silence and the pure expressiveness of preverbal gesture. True, he may seldom reach this state—Mackenzie's Harley comes closer than most—and there may be something inherently paradoxical about the very attempt to represent it in words. All the same, Harley and his brethren prefer childish prattle to adult Babel, and the splash of a single tear is the next best thing to the perfect stillness of womb and tomb. The sentimental hero denies the desirability as well as the necessity of mastering language. Shunning forbidden knowledge—and to him there is really no other kind—he naturally repudiates the word, which is its key. He is disturbed less by the arbitrariness or artificiality of a system of verbal signs, which he finds equally in other social institutions, than by the enormities of adulthood to which language-learning is a kind of forced initiation. Eighteenth-century British fiction contains a number of wise fools, comic characters like Smollett's Win Jenkins, who utter truths greater or other than those they intend. But the sentimental hero belongs rather to a tradition of saintly fools, whose most eloquent testimony to truth is often garbled or mute.

The heroes of most sentimental novels are humorless. The image of the outside world is that found in satire: most people prove to be self-serving, callous, hypocritical, and so on. Moreover, the narrators are capable of considerable irony, as in *The Man of Feeling*. But the senti-mental hero himself is generally lacking in irony and devoid of wit—perhaps owing to the authorial realization that wit is itself a form of control, a way of ordering, judging, and mastering one's world that would run contrary to the passive, victimized posture of most senti-mental heroes.

Some critics have seen sentimentalism as springing from a basic optimism that renders satire unnecessary (men are naturally good, and need to be reminded of their latent goodness rather than their manifest shortcomings); or ineffectual (men's goodness can be elicited better through sympathetic tears than scoffing laughter); or immoral (satire indulges impulses in author and reader just as base as those it purports to chastise). In this view, later eighteenth-century literature exhibits a gradual moderating—some would say a blurring and emasculating—of the rigorous Augustinian or Augustan visions of man and society on which the satire of Swift and Pope had been based. This demanding ethos is supposed to have given way to a bland faith in progress—a con-fidence that though the world is not yet all it might be, philanthropy and forbearance will bring it around, since its defects lie more in reformable institutions than in human nature itself.

Others have seen sentimentalism as the expression of a thoroughgoing pessimism: the belief that one can scarcely hope to improve society, but at most to escape from it. The idea of progress is not only an illusion but a snare, tempting man to linger in a city of destruction that he had better flee, even if flight inward (or backward) is the only route open to him. In this view, too, the individual may be inherently good, but society turns him into a predatory beast, and its customs and institutions are so incurably vile that the good man must be an exile or a victim—never the active, socially engaged hero of traditional epic or comedy.

In practice, the sentimental novel seldom subscribes completely to either of these extreme positions. Often the hero seems to spring from the sunnier conception of human nature, even though nearly everyone else in the same book reflects the more despairing vision. But if the philosophical or theological assumptions about human nature that underlie the sentimental novel are somewhat ambiguous, sentimentalism seems clearly if indirectly indebted to the English religious tradition in another of its functions: namely, as a technique for reviving the role of emotion in human conduct. Stigmatized as "zeal" or "enthusiasm" during the Restoration, the ardor associated with Puritanism had become suspect. Sentimentalism arises in the eighteenth century partly as a reaction against this taboo, and represents a kind of return of the repressed, a reopening of channels through which a broad range of human emotion, from passionate intensity to exquisite delicacy, might once again find expression. As a rehabilitation of enthusiasm, sentimentalism seeks legitimacy by appealing not to tradition or authority but to its truth to nature. The overtly secular character of much eighteenth-century sentimentalism seems, to adapt T. E. Hulme's remark about Romanticism, a matter of spilt religion—of religious instincts or energies reasserting themselves, but adjusting to a world in which their religious pedigree could be a liability rather than an asset. (When sentimental novels do set themselves the task of religious advocacy, as in Chateaubriand's *Atala* at the end of the century, religion itself becomes highly emotionalized and aestheticized).

It is worth observing the spirit in which Sterne introduces religious considerations into a work like *A Sentimental Journey*. Of all the early novelists, Sterne appears to be the adherent of sensibility most remote from Puritanism and most in accord with the affable, undemanding

worldliness of the Anglican establishment. Yet behind the gregariousness of Yorick (and of Sterne himself) lies an individualism that is
always threatening, as in the Puritan past, to dissolve into downright
solipsism. Communal, fraternal, and sexual bonds bring people together only very partially, tentatively, and precariously. The test of behavior
is not its conformity to some divinely imposed, biblically sanctioned
norm, but rather its capacity to amplify, intensify, and elevate one's own
sensations. In this respect Sterne is closer to D. H. Lawrence, and both
are closer to what can be labeled Puritanism, than to the ideals of moderation and social accommodation invoked from many Anglican pulpits
in the eighteenth century. To the pure all things are pure, as Sterne slyly
reminds us, and whether we call this a religion of self-cultivation, a religion of the heart, or a latter-day recrudescence of Antinomianism, it
clearly embraces enthusiasm in place of restraint, and prefers the
redeeming excess to the prudent, Pharisaical mean.

Yorick is intent on confirming his membership in an aristocracy of
the spirit, and on identifying and attaching himself to other chosen ves-
sels. Discriminating between different kinds and degrees of feeling thus
becomes a constant and crucial task; and in its analytical aspect as well,
Yorick's absorption in his own emotional life draws on earlier religious
habits of self-scrutiny. A preoccupation with nuance can lead to subtleties akin to those of the seventeenth-century French romance, with
its elaborately refined *cartes de tendre*, and may owe something to this
tradition. Yet English novelists probe the niceties of sentiment less out
of punctilio than from a conviction that they offer the best and almost
the only gauge of one's true status, social or spiritual. Outside the pages
of Richardson, what is at issue is seldom salvation versus damnation in
any literal sense. But when the question is whether one belongs to
Yorick's elite or to the herd of Smelfunguses and Mundunguses, almost
as much can seem to be at stake. Phrased in this way the problem may
sound trivial, yet Sterne demonstrates that this secular variant of the
central Calvinist worry—am I after all a sheep or a goat?—can be at
once droll and all-important.

The main traits of the sentimental novel can be found as early as
Sarah Fielding's *David Simple* of 1744 and Samuel Richardson's *Sir
Charles Grandison* (1754), and the genre begins to flourish in the 1760s
in such works as Oliver Goldsmith's *Vicar of Wakefield* (1766), Laurence
Sterne's *Sentimental Journey Through France and Italy* (1768), and
Henry Brooke's *Fool of Quality* (1766–1772). But the fullest expression

of the genre is Henry Mackenzie's *Man of Feeling* (1771). As author, Mackenzie puts himself at three or four removes from his hero, Harley. There is first an editor who introduces the book, telling how he got the fragmentary manuscript from a country curate who was using it as gun-wadding on their hunting expeditions. The curate in turn had come upon it among the effects of its presumed author, a "grave, oddish kind of man" who shunned adult company but was "gentle as a lamb" and enjoyed "playing at te-totum with the children." This author figure, finally, is a friend of Harley—but he is also an omniscient narrator, capable of recounting not only Harley's unexpressed thoughts and feelings, but his actions when alone. The supposititious author and editor are not only sympathetic toward Harley but in important respects just like him; at the same time, both are assigned a capacity for urbane irony that Harley does not share.

Like most sentimental novelists and most sentimental readers, Mackenzie takes a somewhat equivocal position toward his subject. In his horror at the brutality and treachery of ordinary adult "civilized" life, and in his sympathy for its victims, he is very close to his hero. But the very qualities that distinguish Harley as a sentimental hero tend to keep him from judging the world harshly or condescendingly: to allow him such attitudes would be to confer on him a power to retaliate that would belie his character as humble, charitable, downtrodden innocent. Mackenzie, however, wants to register not only Harley's helpless dismay, but his own active indignation at the world's villainies, and it is through his editor, his narrator, and other spokesmen who turn up in the course of the story that Mackenzie can pass judgment on them. Moreover, there are some features of his hero with which Mackenzie evidently does not wish to be identified: by making his subordinate narrators speak of Harley from time to time with gentle but wry amusement, the author can prevent our supposing that he is as naive or ineffectual as this "child in the drama of the world." In short, Mackenzie presents himself as a genuine man of feeling but also as something of a man of the world: framing devices permit him this necessary combination of oneness with the hero and distance from him.

This pattern also holds true of the hero's relation to characters within the book, and to the reader. Like other sentimental heroes, Harley exercises generosity and compassion toward those less fortunate than he. The objects of his alms and tears sometimes reciprocate with tales of their own beneficence toward others still lower on the ladder of helplessness and woe. Whether or not one's feelings of pity necessarily imply a sense of superiority to their object, the sentimental novel suggests that for pity to be a pleasurable emotion some such comparison, favorable to oneself, must be drawn. Not that the principle is openly avowed. To declare baldly, as Hume does in his *Treatise on Human Nature*, that "the misery of another gives us a more lively idea of our happiness," and "therefore, produces delight," would be fatal to the entire enterprise. Within the novels, gestures of commiseration are portrayed as uplifting to both parties; that the bestower is in some sense gratified at the expense of the recipient, whom he has a certain interest in not raising to his own level, is unthinkable. At any rate, the thought does not occur to the sentimental hero; nor can the thought occur to the reader without destroying the flattering illusion that his pleasure in witnessing so much distress does credit to the goodness of his heart.

However we choose to regard our benevolence toward a hero like Harley, this response does seem to involve a certain distance between us and him. Another kind of distancing results from the attitude of our culture toward sentimentality itself: we laugh uneasily at so-called heroes who cry so easily and so copiously; we find ludicrous and embarrassing their tendency to exaggerate; we are disturbed yet contemptuous about what we take to be their self-indulgence. This would be enough to account for the condescending tone in most modern criticism of sentimental fiction, even if there were no more legitimate aesthetic grounds for it. Yet distancing is not the whole story. The modern sensibility recoils with amusement from the traits I have just mentioned, yet it hankers on some level for the pastoral world that these qualities serve to create. Here people are still capable of intense emotions; here they still care about each other; here they do not disregard one another's pain and suffering. The outer world Harley encounters is anything but pastoral, and may be more cruel, rapacious, and gross than our familiar one. Yet his sheer responsiveness to it constitutes a kind of pastoral alternative to the cynical, "adult" blunting of response that the world more commonly induces. Thus Harley's spontaneity, naïveté, and innocence make him a pastoral figure with whom a part of us wishes to identify, despite (or perhaps because of) our own compromised, inhibited worldliness.

Moreover, Harley witnesses or is told about instances of such melodramatic wrongdoing that his reaction is one of pure revulsion. Villains and villainy are presented so starkly that he is not perplexed by difficulties of evaluation, nor are we. Instead, we are invited to check the intensity of our response against the example set us by the hero. What matters is not the qualitative accuracy of moral judgment, but the quantitative adequacy of moral feeling—the goodness not of our heads but of our hearts. The focus within the novel is not on actions, which involve choice and responsibility, but on reactions—particularly reactions so abrupt as to preclude deliberation. The very idea of pausing to weigh motives and circumstances is alien to the man of feeling; it smacks of the prudential, calculating, worldly wisdom that the sentimental novel sets out to discredit, and introduces an element of cold-blooded circumspection into a process which (in the sentimental view) ought to be instinctive and instantaneous.

A further source of appeal in books like *The Man of Feeling* should be mentioned. Within the story, Harley is not exactly quiescent, since his feelings are in constant turmoil, yet action is not something he initiates or performs, but something he undergoes and responds to. His life touches him deeply, but he seems powerless to affect its shape or outcome. In all this his role resembles that of a reader more than that of a conventional hero, and the resulting emphasis on passive responsiveness relieves the reader of certain burdens just as it does Harley. We are not challenged to bestir ourselves, to gird up our loins, to sally forth as pilgrims or soldiers in one or another cause, as we are by much other literature. This is seen as a problem by Hugh Murray, author of *The Morality of Fiction* (1806), who remarks that "there is perhaps only one point of view in which the tendency of [Mackenzie's] writings may perhaps be objected to. They seem to contain something peculiarly enervating and unfavourable to active exertion."

Throughout the book the orphan Harley is sentimentally in love with the unattainable Miss Walton. But sex is everywhere associated with betrayal, and is one of the chief sources of evil and misery: the Misanthropist is soured by a trusted friend eloping with his fiancée, the Prostitute is driven to the brink of the grave by the conventional consequences of a conventional seduction, and Signor Respino nearly ruins an entire family out of "criminal passion" for the incorruptible wife. "Passion" of the sexual variety is invariably "criminal"—which puts Harley in an awkward position as a lover. When Miss Walton eventually reveals to him that she is not unattainable but had secretly loved him all along, death is the only way out of his impasse.

Marriage represents the ultimate threat to Harley's innocence; sexual consummation would be a betrayal of his essential childlikeness and

an assumption of all the compromises, grossnesses, and responsibilities
of adulthood in a fallen world. His gentle retreat into death is thus a
more consistent and plausible finale to his brief career than marriage
would be. Death is alluded to throughout the novel, not as the steady
goal of a unified plot, but as an object of wanly pleasurable contemplation for those condemned to a world they long to escape. The book
begins as it ends with the author in a state of pleasing melancholy, discussing graves. Mackenzie repeatedly sets up death as an alternative to
sexual consummation, analogous to it but more desirable—especially if,
as in Harley's case, the hero can be "buried in a certain spot near the
grave of his mother." At the same time, by not actively pursuing death,
Harley remains a purer sentimental hero than someone like Goethe's
Werther; the childlike Harley cannot be so bold or resolute—in short,
so "manly"—as to perform any decisive action, let alone commit suicide.

The bildungsroman attaches such importance to learning processes
that the question of whether man is innately good or depraved is not
crucial to it. The sentimental novel not only introduces actual infants in
idealized roles, but finds in childhood some of the same virtues imputed to the noble savage during the eighteenth century. Sentimentalism
is akin to primitivism insofar as it looks upon social institutions as
thwarting or perverting human dignity. Normal education thus represents a force for evil. In the bildungsroman, satires on education aim at
practical reform, and assume that one can and must learn to live in the
world, whereas the sentimental novel challenges not only the methods
but the goal of conventional education.

Skepticism about formal education is only one expression, however,
of the more general sentimental principle that the path from innocence
to experience is a downhill one. Henry Fielding may attach positive
value to a young man's acquisition of prudence, but for the sentimental
novelist the wisdom of the serpent does not complement but rather
contaminates the innocence of the dove. In the sentimental novel, at
any rate, the hero does not mature or degenerate, largely because those
two processes are regarded as synonymous, and also because process
itself is a sentimental bête noire.

When character change does occur in sentimental fiction, it is reminiscent of the Protestant (and ultimately Pauline) pattern of dramatic
conversion. Such works hold out the possibility of sudden, total transformation that comes about not through reflection, resolution, and

deliberate action but rather through something like an infusion of grace. The notion of conversion explains the perplexing fact of human change by postulating sudden leaps or twitches that mark a basic alteration of course. But the clearest instances of this abrupt movement from darkness to light occur in sentimental works of the following century—for example, in the Scrooge of Dickens's "Christmas Carol." In such novels as *The Man of Feeling*, the action may be as peripatetic as that of *Tom Jones*, and the hero may encounter as socially and morally varied a series of other characters, but the result tends to be a reiterated confirmation of the attitudes he set out with, not a revision or revaluation of them. In Mackenzie's novel, the indictment of the world becomes more comprehensive with each episode, but not more complex or profound. Great stress is laid on openness to experience, but only in the sense that the hero must be prepared to have his susceptibilities set a-jangling in all sorts of odd moments and unlikely places; such openness does not extend to the point of allowing the hero to be transformed by his experience. Affected yet not changed, he may become sadder, but he cannot grow wiser. Far from being embarked on a voyage of discovery, in search of something he doesn't already know or have, he is on a mission of recovery, trying to recapture a sense of fixity amid distressing flux, or to regain a long-lost haven of secure devotion.

Another way of illustrating the incompatibility of the sentimental novel with the bildungsroman, with education, and with process generally is to consider briefly the convention of love at first sight. The sentimental ethos, prizing instantly formed bonds of sympathy between strangers, tends to regard such moments of heightened sensibility as both possible and creditable to the parties involved: what better example could there be of benign directness and spontaneity in human affairs? The adversaries of sentimentalism not only challenge the substance and worth of sudden attachments, but also put forward an alternative conception of love as something gradual and cumulative, to be established only over time. According to this view, one does not fall in love, but learns to love. (Austen's *Sense and Sensibility* embodies both aspects of the latter position: on the one hand, it satirizes the giddy and groundless infatuation that Willoughby inspires in Marianne; on the other hand, it presents Edward Ferrars as an unhandsome hero whose manners require intimacy to make them pleasing). In love as in other matters, the bildungsroman insists on our constantly testing and revising what Austen calls first impressions, and like any educative process, this takes time. Only through a careful monitoring of their unfolding experiences can heroines come to know what others and they themselves are really like, and we are expected to read their stories in the same spirit. The sentimental novel demands something quite different from its heroes and its readers: we are expected to react instantly to good and evil with appropriate degrees of sympathy or abhorrence, but there is little question of our having to learn better how to tell them apart, since there are no gradations between innocence and depravity in the morally melodramatic world of sentimentalism. The kind of ethical workout so edifying to characters and readers alike in the bildungsroman, and so central to the educative pretensions of most eighteenth-century novels, is largely absent from the sentimental novel.

The convention of love at first sight helps to bring out a political aspect of sentimentalism as well. To conservatives, the notion of love at first sight is not merely silly but dangerous: it breaks through the barriers of class, circumvents the testing rituals of courtship, and allows the sexual relationship between individuals to overshadow the social and economic relationship between families that has always been the chief basis for upper- and middle-class marriage. Love at first sight transforms strangers into intimates, as happens repeatedly in *A Sentimental Journey*; and although Sterne balks at carrying this process (or any other) to its ultimate conclusion, others saw and drew out its implications. Love at first sight does for two persons what Christian conversion had done for one: it holds out the possibility of an immediate and total remaking of their essential situation. It thus lends plausibility to the notion that sudden transformation is possible on a more extended, perhaps even universal scale. If all mankind could be brought to undergo the change of heart represented in religious terms by Christian conversion and in more secular terms by love at first sight, the millennium could arrive overnight. A sentimental doctrine such as love at first sight thus appears subversive insofar as it helps discredit the belief that significant social relationships, including those between men and women, have to develop over time and cannot be formed or altered all at once. Sentimental fiction acknowledges that in the world as presently constituted, the distances between classes may be great, but it suggests the arbitrariness of those gaps by showing that they can collapse under the force of a single soulful glance.

The sentimental mode emphasizes the primacy of individual feelings, and this emphasis has sometimes been seen as revolutionary—as tending to subvert the principles and duties that support institutions like the family, the church, and society at large. Customary rules of conduct and belief seem cold, oppressive, and inauthentic in competition with the keen promptings of impulse; in prizing the latter, the sentimental mode seems to place in jeopardy the entire moral and social system. The maintenance of order depends (according to its defenders) on a subordination of individual to social considerations, and of feeling to judgment; by reversing both priorities, sentimentalism seems to level or overturn an established, hierarchical scheme of things.

Some pioneers of sentiment, such as Rousseau, recognize and welcome the political consequences of preferring feeling to thought. Yet most of its early English devotees seem innocent of any leveling intention when they value the heart over the head. They assume that the existing order will remain intact; their highest hope is to find shelter from it and to relieve some of its victims, not to topple its institutions. When four kindred souls achieve a harmonious "little society" at the end of *David Simple*, or when some women establish a more extensive utopian community in Sarah Scott's *Millennium Hall* (1762), the result is an oasis amid a world of distress, to which the new creation poses an appealing alternative but not, as each author is careful to make clear, a real threat.

From the beginning, sensibility encourages patterns of sensation and expression that—although held up as natural—differ from those of the generality of mankind. From Sterne onward there are those who value sensibility for its *not* being widely shared, for its representing a more elevated state of emotional and moral development than most people have attained. But like the signs of grace for which earlier Calvinists had to scrutinize themselves, the tokens of belonging to the sentimental elite have to be watched for and nurtured, as we see Yorick doing so sedulously in *A Sentimental Journey*. This makes for a curious paradox. On the one hand, the surest evidence of possessing sensibility is a capacity for spontaneous stirrings of benevolence toward others, an acute responsiveness to touching scenes and incidents in life as well as art. On the other hand, one's own feelings can displace the ostensible objects of those feelings as one's chief concern. Thus the very egotism that sentimentalism sets out to overcome can taint sentimentalism itself. As Hugh Murray observes in *The Morality of Fiction*, "the votary of sentiment is . . . often found to bestow too great a share of his benevolence on himself. There is a selfish, as well as a social sensibility; and, when this is the case, we cannot wonder that the former should some-times predominate. It is fostered by that minute attention to his own feelings, which forms one of his favorite employments."

In the later eighteenth century, philanthropic movements of all kinds, including efforts to abolish the slave trade, to improve the condition of prisons and madhouses, and to make better provision for orphans, fallen women, and animals, were inspired and sustained by the ethos of sensibility. These struggles for more humane treatment of society's outcasts or victims have been regarded as progressive in spirit, creditable to the minds and hearts of their promoters, and as evidence of egalitarian stirrings. The Wedgwood medallion, from which an enchained African pleads, "Am I not a man and a brother?" has thus seemed an apt emblem of sentiment in the service of liberty and fraternity, if not of equality.

What has been investigated less, even by those hostile to sentimentalism, is its tendency to leave the existing social hierarchy intact or stronger than ever. For one thing, the high degree of stylization and artifice of most of this writing situates it in a cultural context that is unmistakably and unshakably genteel. Like the tradition of pastoralism, with which it has many affinities, sentimental literature allows both author and audience to explore the delights of simpler, more spontaneous, more "natural" life without having to give up the morally equivocal pleasures of power, privilege, and worldly protocol that they enjoy within existing society. A work like Sterne's *Sentimental Journey* may call into question some of the artificial distinctions and stratifications of eighteenth-century culture, yet its very texture as a work of art—all the deft posing, all the playful rococo embellishments, all the self-consciousness and wit and lightness of touch—tends to celebrate, at a much deeper level than any overt social statement, the grace, the polish, and the erotic inexhaustibility of artifice itself. Along the way, in Sterne's book as in others, there may be a dabbling in the pleasures of the primitive; Yorick will temporarily renounce Paris and the children of art for provincial peasants who are children of nature, Werther will read Ossian to Lotte, René will abandon Europe for the wilds of America, and the mothers of Paul and Virginia will retreat to bucolic Mauritius. But short of death, this "going native" never reaches the point of throwing off once and for all a concern for civilized, hierarchical customs and values. The heroine of Bernardin de Saint-Pierre's *Paul and Virginia* (1788) drowns because she insists upon keeping her clothes on, and despite the presence of various egalitarian motifs in the book, Virginia's fully dressed fate is an emblem of the ultimate stability and inescapability of the status quo in sentimental literature. As in the pastoral, the element of pathos here can be regarded as a cathartic reinforcement of the existing scheme of things rather than a challenge to it. In this respect the sentimental novel can be thought of as profoundly conservative, implying as it does that the actions of sentimental heroes and heroines have little impact beyond their own immediate circle.

This sense of inconsequentiality may be acknowledged in a jocular or a melancholy spirit, as the different endings of *Paul and Virginia*, *The Man of Feeling*, and *A Sentimental Journey* demonstrate. Despite their great tonal range, however, these works and most others of their kind do not hold out much hope of changing the ways of the world—or even much prospect that a sensitive soul can come to lasting terms with the world, except through defeat, exile, or death. This is not a conservatism that endorses things as they are, but one that may strengthen the hold of existing conditions by suggesting that they are immutable and inevitable.

In the area of relations between the sexes, sentimental fiction appears, on the face of it, to question hierarchical values in the name of more egalitarian ones. The ethos of sensibility challenges a number of prevailing gender assumptions: that the public, civic realm is more important than the private, familial realm; that dominance is a worthier posture than submission, strength more creditable than weakness, determination better than diffidence; and that ways culturally defined as "manly" must take precedence over the concerns and characteristics thought of as inherently "feminine." Sentimental fiction calls into question this subordination of feminine to masculine values, but not in the interest of equality. Sentimental novels tend to assert that the constellation of feeling and behavior ordinarily regarded as feminine is not merely the equal of the masculine one, but is preferable to it in all essential respects. This position can reflect a genuine concern with women's status and welfare, particularly when it appears in works by women, such as Sarah Fielding's *David Simple*; but male authors like Sterne and Mackenzie seem motivated rather by a wish to challenge the customary conception of what men themselves are and should be. They do so by attaching the highest value to traits ordinarily despised as womanish, such as emotional sensitivity, delicacy, and expressiveness—the prime example being the capacity of the sentimental hero to shed tears, and his pride in doing so.

Sentimental novels often involve a quest for a haven secure from the world, but the very nature of this goal tends to prevent any but fleeting, partial, or symbolic attainments of it short of death. This helps to account for the failure of sentimental novels to achieve much in the way of genuine resolutions, let alone triumphant finales, except when death is the ultimate answer to the problems of hero and author. And sentimental novels usually lack the kind of cumulative development that eventually transforms the hero of a bildungsroman into an adult. But different social assumptions about masculinity and femininity make sentimental novels about young women different in each of these respects from those about young men. In the eighteenth century, the idea of a woman of feeling was much less anomalous and paradoxical than that of a man of feeling, for it tended to reinforce rather than subvert common assumptions about femininity. Proneness to tears is weakness, weakness is effeminacy, and effeminacy is shameful—unless one happens to be a woman, in which case such traits are natural and becoming. The sentimental hero violates gender stereotypes and is praised for doing so, but this calls for a great deal of authorial justification. The creator of a sentimental heroine is spared the necessity for this kind of special pleading, and is released from the need to portray the sentimental figure as misunderstood, despised, and alienated from the bulk of society. Since she shares the dovelike innocence and diffidence of the sentimental hero, the sentimental heroine will be similarly vulnerable to the aggressions and duplicities of worldlings; but since the qualities that make her vulnerable are those that the community values in young women, the fact that she has them may facilitate her integration into adult society. The sentimental hero is called upon by the world to renounce childlike virtues for manly ones, and chooses not to; the sentimental heroine faces no such impasse, since the virtues demanded of her as a woman are the same ones prized in her as a child. The transition from boy to man is seen from the sentimental perspective as a fall from grace, and from the worldly perspective as a necessary and desirable shedding of puerility, but in either view as a drastic change. Between girl and woman, all parties see a fundamental continuity.

Since the sentimental view of woman is not at odds with the view of her held by the world at large, the glorification of sentimental heroines poses no such ideological challenge as the idealization of sentimental heroes. When the main character is female, there need be no incompatibility between the sentimental novel and the bildungsroman.

Although the sentimental heroine (like her male counterpart) is seen as a superior person, there is nothing eccentric in her position, either in relation to the rest of her own sex or to the opposite sex. Such merging of the sentimental novel with the bildungsroman and of the sentimental heroine with her environment can be seen in a work like Burney's *Evelina* (1778), which has as its subtitle *The History of a Young Lady's Entrance into the World*. Many features of this world are perceived as alien and threatening: the rakish aggressiveness of Sir Clement Willoughby, the encroaching vulgarity of the Branghtons and Madame Duval, the heartless boisterousness of Captain Mirvan, the mindless arrogance of Mr. Lovel; but instead of driving Evelina out of "the World," they themselves are gradually pushed to its margins so that Evelina can assume her rightful place at its center. Moreover, this happens without Evelina having to relinquish her feminine passivity. Evelina's worst tormentors, Madame Duval and Lovel, are both brutally scourged by Captain Mirvan, and although critics have been puzzled and disturbed by all the Punch-and-Judy-style violence on the part of the Captain, its evident function in the book is to settle scores with Evelina's persecutors without imputing any vengefulness to the heroine herself.

Evelina is commonly regarded not as a sentimental novel but as a kind of bildungsroman enlivened by social comedy, or as a social comedy given substance and continuity by the "Entrance into the World" plot. In a book about a young woman, however, such features can coexist with sentimental ones in a way hardly possible in books about young men. For Mackenzie's Harley, to marry would mean taking on the assertiveness and authority he is intent on avoiding; for an Evelina, marriage involves not a betrayal but a public validation of her submissiveness and dependence. For this to be so requires playing down any evidence that she is physically attracted to the man, which would jeopardize the innocence indispensable to her character as sentimental heroine. On this matter Burney is very circumspect, not only in her presentation of Evelina herself, but in the antithesis she sets up between the young men in Evelina's life, Sir Clement Willoughby and Lord Orville. Burney's aim and method come out clearly in Evelina's words:

I could not but remark the striking difference of [Sir Clement's] attention, and that of Lord Orville: the latter has such gentleness of manners, such delicacy of conduct, and an air so respectful, that, when he flatters most, he never distresses, and when he most confers honour, appears to receive it! The former obtrudes his attention, and forces mine; it is so pointed, that it always confuses me, and so public, that it attracts general notice.

The imagery of the second sentence suggests that more than mere attention is at issue: Sir Clement's obtrudes, is pointed, and Evelina feels violated and pained by it. However one interprets Evelina's language, it is clear here and elsewhere that Sir Clement is the embodiment of aggressive masculinity, unsettling to the heroine and to society at large. Lord Orville, on the other hand, is desexualized—"so feminine his delicacy," Evelina exclaims at one point—without being altogether emasculated. He can act boldly, responsibly, and decisively among men, as when he flings out of the room the monkey that has attacked Mr. Lovel and terrified everyone else, yet he is all gentleness, modesty, and tact among women, and particularly with Evelina. This combination— the lion among men who is a lamb before women—marks Lord Orville as distinctly the hero of a female sentimental novel, since the hero of a male sentimental novel tends to be more uniformly lamblike.

The sentimental implications of a book like *Evelina* can be summed up as follows. In a novel focusing on a young woman, the sentimental ethos can be reconciled with "Entrance into the World," since the sentimental heroine epitomizes the popular ideal of what a young woman should be; and such a book can culminate in marriage without ceasing to be a sentimental novel, since the traits that go to make up a sentimental daughter or sister are those that society continues to look for in wives and mothers. Where women are concerned, sentimentalism can be a powerful agent of socialization, a process scarcely possible for the hero of a male sentimental novel. In the female sentimental novel, however, the sentimental male himself need no longer be at odds with society. A modicum of conventional masculinity is allowed him, but it is quarantined in clearly designated spheres of male activity, so that he is made amenable to the same kind of socialization and domestication as the heroine herself.

The fact that it could thus be enlisted in the service of social stability helps to explain the enduring popularity of the female sentimental novel, for it holds out to women the gratifying prospect that their psychological and moral ideals will not unfit them for the world, but rather guarantee their admittance to it on the best possible terms. With the male sentimental novel, this has never been the case.

G. A. Starr

Selected Bibliography

Barker, Gerard A. "*David Simple*: The Novel of Sensibility in Embryo." *Modern Language Studies* 12, no. 2 (1982): 69–80.

Barker-Benfield, G. J. *The Culture of Sensibility: Sex and Society in Eighteenth-Century Britain.* Chicago: University of Chicago Press, 1992.

Braudy, Leo. "The Form of the Sentimental Novel." *Novel* 7 (1973): 5–13.

Brissenden, R. F. *Virtue in Distress: Studies in the Novel of Sentiment from Richardson to Sade.* New York: Barnes and Noble, 1974.

Brown, Marshall. *Preromanticism.* Stanford: Stanford University Press, 1991. Chapter 5, "The Economy of Sensibility."

Mullan, John. *Sentiment and Sociability: The Language of Feeling in the Eighteenth Century.* Oxford: Oxford University Press, 1988.

Platzner, Robert L. "Mackenzie's Martyr: The Man of Feeling as Saintly Fool." *Novel* 10 (1976): 59–64.

Rawson, Claude. *Satire and Sentiment, 1660–1830.* Cambridge: Cambridge University Press, 1993.

Spacks, Patricia Meyer. *Desire and Truth: Functions of Plot in Eighteenth-Century English Novels.* Chicago: University of Chicago Press, 1990.

Todd, Janet. *Sensibility: An Introduction.* New York: Methuen, 1986.

Tompkins, J. M. S. "Didacticism and Sensibility." In *The Popular Novel in England.* London: Constable, 1932."

Frances Burney and the Rise of the Woman Novelist

THE novelist, playwright, biographer, and diarist Frances Burney has had considerable political importance in the last ten years of academic thinking about the eighteenth-century novel. Feminist reevaluations of women's literature and history are in large part responsible for this importance. More than any of the hundreds of women who wrote novels during the eighteenth century, Burney is likely to turn up on reading lists for comprehensive examinations and on syllabi outside of women's literature courses. Her name joins that of Jane Austen, who for twenty years or so had been the token woman included in the canon of eighteenth-century British novelists. While Burney may be in danger of slipping into the role of token, twin to Austen, the importance of her presence on these lists and syllabi may take some of its charge from Virginia Woolf's famous recommendation that women writers since the eighteenth century should lay a wreath upon her grave in gratitude for being the first respectable, middle-class woman to earn money by writing. Woolf was not exactly accurate in granting Burney this honor, but her remark associates Burney with something rather more helpful to women than tokenism: Burney's is a name that emblematizes a change in terms of the subject matter available to women writers and in the ideological and artistic possibilities open to them. As Woolf suggests, after Burney, it was imaginable for a woman of her class to trade her traditional role as financial dependent for the equally respectable but more autonomous role of working woman.

However conventional and respectable her family life may have been (and there is reason to doubt the veracity of her image as a traditional daughter, wife, and mother), Burney was also a careerist and, more importantly, she was seen as such by her contemporaries. That is to say that her life was shaped by work, as well as the other way around. The popular image of Jane Austen hiding her manuscripts in progress so as not to contaminate her personal life with her artistic one has, however reductively if not falsely, served to contain the impact of her artistic accomplishments, to keep them from suggesting how a woman's writing might have a direct and liberatory impact on her life.

That Burney was singled out by Woolf for exercising professional autonomy while retaining her status as a respectable, middle-class woman is also significant. In the eighteenth century, retaining such a status while working for money as a writer meant more than simply taking charge of one's life by writing one's own life script. Besides constituting a departure from the norm that a "lady" would not make her living outside the domestic roles prescribed for her by eighteenth-century gender ideology, it meant a careful and responsible reimagining of the lives possible for eighteenth-century, middle-class, white Englishwomen. Burney's writings show a keen, lifelong interest in assessing the culturally determined options for defining female life and identity, in realistically assessing the force of those possibilities, and in exploring what women, particularly women writers like herself, might make of these possibilities through their own exertions. This careful but innovative negotiation of the "life stories" available to women of her class and race is an aspect of her life that is certainly found in her works—particularly her novels. One way of reading Burney's fiction is as imaginative castings into the cultural reservoir of plots available to eighteenth-century middle-class women for creating themselves and their lives. Her novels all implicitly ask the question, What can a woman do with the stories she is given to represent female life? How can she control these stories, make them work for instead of against her? Burney's fiction both embodies and thematizes the labor of reworking the plots available to eighteenth-century middle-class women for imagining the trajectory of their lives and the nature of their identities.

I will focus on these questions as they are asked in Burney's fiction, but I also want to consider the ways in which Burney herself becomes a sort of heroine in a number of stories implicitly or explicitly narrated about her by modern critics of her work and of the eighteenth-century novel in general. One does not usually think of critics or literary historians as storytellers, but in writing about literature, one often finds oneself narrating a kind of story. A book about the eighteenth-century novel, for example, tells us the story of its "rise" from humble beginnings in romance to the exalted status of "high art." Individual writers as well as genres are fitted into plot structures, and Burney has been habitual fodder for narratives that depict rising and falling fortunes. As I will argue later, the dual plot possibilities of rising and falling are inextricably tied to gender and have wide-reaching implications for women's lives and identities in the eighteenth century. How does Burney's gender affect the "stories" that are told of her? The same dualistic structure of rising and falling that dominated the heroines' plots that Burney sought to rework in her fiction tend to determine the ways in which her life and works have been represented and evaluated in academic criticism. It strikes me as ironic that gendered narrative patterns seem to play a major role in shaping the image of a writer who was such a self-conscious (and angry) critic of the stories available to women for imaging their lives. By pointing out this irony, I hope to engage, with Burney as my model and mentor, in my own reworking of feminine plots and possibilities.

Love Stories: The Rise and Fall of the Heroine

Beginning early in the century, as Jane Spencer notes, love was popularly identified as the most "natural" subject for women writers, and love plots are important in eighteenth-century novels written by both men and women. The course of love for heroines follows a paradigmatic trajectory in eighteenth-century novels. Heroines usually either rise or fall. This formulation is, of course, a deliberate oversimplification, but it identifies for us a skeletal structure and gives us a place to begin thinking about the formal conventions that faced writers such as Burney. What, exactly, does it mean to "rise" and to "fall" in the love stories of eighteenth-century fiction? Love plots entail repeated rises, falls, and paradoxical movements—one falls in love in order to rise to perfect happiness—and even a "downward," tragic plot, as in Richardson's *Clarissa* (1748), can entail an ascension of the heroine to perfect (if unearthly) bliss. Heroes share the dual prospect of tumbling down to a bad end or rising in stature and happiness. Tom Jones is either "born to be hanged" or destined to the heights of marriage to the perfect Sophia and inheritance from Squire Allworthy, just as Pamela is either to be seduced and abandoned or ascendant through an "upward" marriage.

Most important for our purposes is what rising and falling signified within eighteenth-century ideologies of femininity and the effect of that significance on the public image of the woman writer. The tendency to conflate the writer with the heroine—to view the former's story as of a piece with the latter's—was particularly evident in popular representations of women who wrote. Hence, the rises and falls of fictional heroines could not always be kept at a distance from the public images of their creators. And the narrative possibilities represented by the rises and falls of women—be they heroines or writer-heroines—are inextricably connected with women's sexuality. For a heroine as well for her female author, to rise meant marriage—not marriage in all its everyday pleasures, pains, interests, and boredoms, but a transcendently happy union with an ideal husband, perhaps accompanied by a radical improvement in class and financial standing, as in a Cinderella story. To fall, on the other hand, meant "ruin" in a specifically sexual sense. This duality is inextricably tied to the reduction of feminine identity to a simplistic "angel-whore" dichotomy. As Penelope Aubin expressed it in her novel *Charlotta Du Pont* (1723), "Youth once vitiated is rarely reformed, and Woman, who whilst virtuous is an Angel, ruined and abandoned by the Man she loves, becomes a Devil."

This is not to say that all eighteenth-century novels with love plots slavishly adhere to one or the other trajectory, sending their heroines either to marital bliss or to sexual ruin. Rising and falling, in the love story, are a pair of extremes that are always in tension with less spectacular possibilities for representing life. In Defoe's *Roxana* (1724), for instance, the tragic fall of the heroine is oddly balanced against the accretive detail of Roxana's story of successful sexual self-management. Clarissa's ascendence to otherworldly virtue lies in tension with Anna Howe's earthbound domestication in marriage to Hickman. In Richardson's *Sir Charles Grandison* (1751), the marriage of the admirable hero with the equally admirable heroine is less a climax than an occasion for painting in bustling, cheerful detail a broad canvas depicting the social and material order in which the couple will live. Indeed, the decisive nature of the heroine's rise or fall is often depicted in novels (and in other eighteenth-century literary forms) as a matter for romance having little to do with the life that is allegedly the stuff of novels. The rise of Belinda's curl at the end of Pope's *Rape of the Lock*

suggests a cynicism about such romantic transcendence that is frequently articulated within a long novelistic tradition of satirizing the
literary extremes of romance, of which Charlotte Lennox's *Female
Quixote* (1752) is perhaps the best-known example. My point, then, is
not that all writers plotted their heroines' lives according to this simplistic pattern of rise or fall; rather, rising and falling are among the
repertoire of romantic tropes that eighteenth-century novels incorporated in a variety of complex ways, from straightforward repetition to
total rebuttal or transformation. As Michael McKeon has argued, eighteenth-century novels both articulate and transform romance elements.
The treatment of the rise and fall of heroines is part of this process of
articulation and transformation.

Having made this qualification I return to the issue of how the rising and falling of heroines in eighteenth-century novels affected the
way women writers of the century were thought of and perceived
themselves. Using two brief examples—one drawn from the fiction of
Jane Barker, one from the diaries of Frances Burney—I want to show
how the heroine's dual possibilities placed certain expectations upon
women writers as they imagined their own stories and, hence, their
own selves. These expectations circumscribed women's thinking about
their work as writers; but they also provided starting points, ideological and formal materials for the work of imagining lives beyond those
limitations.

Jane Barker's fictional character Galesia, in her novels *Bosvil and
Galesia* (1713) and *A Patch-Work Screen for the Ladies* (1723), stands as
the figure of a writer who represents, as Spencer says, the authorial concerns of Barker herself. While it would be difficult to substantiate the
strictly autobiographical nature of the character, it is obvious that Galesia is at the least a vehicle for articulating some of Barker's hopes and
anxieties as a writer. Galesia, with a good deal of ambivalence, gives up
on her personal love story in order to concentrate on literary work, as
she wryly notes: "I, finding my self abandoned by *Bosvil*, and thinking
it impossible ever to love again, resolved to espouse a Book, and spend
my Days in Study." Galesia neither falls into ruin nor ascends to perfect
marital bliss, and in this sense she resists the pull of the romantic
dichotomy. But her representations of her aspirations as a writer almost
obsessively repeat the dual possibilities of rising and falling. In verses
dedicating herself to poetry, Galesia draws on the traditional imagery
of the Muses and poetic "flight" in order to express her desire to follow

the example of the (safely dead) poet Katherine Philips, the "Orinda" of the poem:

> Methinks I hear the Muses sing,
> And see 'em all dance in a ring;
> And call upon me to take Wing.
>
> We will (say they) assist thy Flight,
> Till thou reach fair ORINDA's Height,
> If thou can'st this World's Follies slight.

The "Follies" are specifically sexual; poetry, like the reputation of Orinda, is the chaste opposite, according to Spencer's reading of these lines, of her relationship with the problematic Bosvil: "Then gentle Maid cast off thy Chain, / Which links thee to thy faithless Swain, / And vow a Virgin to remain."

In this same vein, Galesia dreams of climbing a mountain (Parnassus?) associated with literary achievement, and learning from an unidentified higher power that such heights preclude "Hymen."

Rising, for Galesia, would seem, then, to offer a way out of the determining structure of rise versus fall implicit in her sexuality. The price for this escape seems a large one—the renunciation of her sexuality—and Galesia has a hard time avoiding that sexuality in any case, as it tends to emerge at the most inopportune moments of poetic flight. In the second edition of *Bosvil and Galesia*, Bosvil appears in this dream sequence and attempts to cast her down from her mountain. Even more tellingly, in *A Patch-Work Screen* Galesia finds a lofty retreat specifically associated with her intellectual and literary pursuits, but this retreat is violated and denied her by the literal entrance of female sexuality "in ruin." Like an early version of Charlotte Brontë's Jane Eyre, gazing from the leads of Thornfield with its soon-to-emerge sexual secrets, Galesia finds only momentary release from the claustrophobia of middle-class female life:

> Out of this Garret, there was a Door went out to the Leads; on which I us'd to frequently to walk to take the Air. . . . Here I entertain'd my Thoughts, and indulg'd my solitary Fancy. Here I could behold the *Parliament-House*, *Westminster-Hall*, and the *Abbey*, and admir'd the Magnificence of their Structure, and still more, the Greatness of Mind in those who had been their Founders.

Just as Jane's moment of mental expansion is interrupted by the maniacal laughter of "Grace Poole," actually the mad and sexually depraved Bertha

Rochester, Galesia's is broken in on by a character who epitomizes the sexual ruin of a woman. As though she stepped from the pages of an eighteenth-century romance by Eliza Haywood or Aphra Behn, she has been seduced, abandoned, and left pregnant. She knocks on the door of Galesia's refuge while fleeing parish officers across the rooftops of London. Galesia's mother forbids her daughter further use of her garret retreat for fear that she might encounter, even in a passive way, similar or even more "pernicious" "Adventures." Thus even though Galesia herself resists the love plot of marriage or "ruin," her flight from that plot is obstructed by the sexuality that she must deny in order to "rise" as a writer.

This scene hints rather broadly at the personal and professional struggles of many eighteenth-century women writers, and it has a good deal of relevance for women in the late twentieth century who seek to define themselves, in a traditionally masculine way, through their work rather than their sexuality. Barker's fiction suggests that women's sexuality is the force that ultimately gives their lives its shape and meaning. It portrays the reductively and rigidly dichotomous possibilities of marriage versus "ruin" that that sexuality imposes on women's lives. The scene on the leads calls into question Galesia's denials of her sexuality; even more forcefully, however, Barker depicts the way a woman's sexuality hobbles her dreams of shaping her life through work rather than love. In the dream mountain scene, Bosvil threatens to topple Galesia from Parnassian heights. Spencer reads this threat as Galesia's fear of seduction, but her reading also admits the possibility that what Galesia fears is marriage—the "up" side of the coin. Barker's fiction assumes the incompatibility of marriage with a literary career; the romantic "rise" into marital bliss might mean a fall for the woman writer. On the other hand, the young woman who spoils Galesia's garret retreat, her "Cave on the Top of *Parnassus*," obtrudes into her literary and intellectual work space the opposing possibility of women's fall through sexual "ruin." Significantly, Galesia's life is not forced into the mold of either rising or falling in the feminine, sexual sense, but it is impossible for her to get on with her life and work without feeling the limiting effects of that mold.

After the successful publication of *Evelina* in 1778, when she was twenty-six years old, Frances Burney found herself, figuratively, out on the leads with Galesia and Jane Eyre. Like her predecessor and her successor in rooftop ruminations, Burney found the new heights she achieved through intellectual labor heady and exciting. But also like them, she could not escape feeling the threat of a fall:

I am now at the summit of a high hill; my prospects on one side are bright, glowing, and invitingly beautiful; but when I turn around, I perceive, on the other side, sundry caverns, gulphs, pits, and precipices, that, to look at, make my head giddy and my heart sick. I see about me, indeed, many hills of far greater height and sublimity; but I have not the strength to attempt climbing them; if I move, it must be downwards. I have already, I fear, reached the pinnacle of my abilities, and therefore to stand still will be my best policy. (*Diaries and Letters*, volume 1)

Burney's pessimistic conviction that her literary rise must be followed by a fall derived, at least in part, from her conception of the female maturing process and the diminution of happiness and power she supposed it entailed. In sum, Burney's sense of her destiny as a woman writer was, like Barker's, inevitably affected by the plots available to women for imaging female life. These plots overwhelmingly suggested that the only sure escape from "ruin" was marital bliss—if such could be found. But even a happy marriage could be problematic for a woman's literary ambitions, as Galesia's dream suggests. Burney was to be more successful than Galesia could have imagined at combining a happy marriage with a literary career, but, as Doody and others point out, Burney's success in both the literary and domestic realms was earned through tough choices and hard work. The point remains that among the plots available to both Burney and Barker for imagining their lives, none offered much room for a woman's work substantially to shape her life's trajectory. The prospect of rising or falling still haunted both a woman's career and her personal life, since both were presumed to be influenced overwhelmingly by her sexuality.

Burney's fiction thematizes the sexualization of women's labor through the ideological process of defining femininity. Her heroines in *Cecilia* (1782) and *The Wanderer* (1814) both try to take some control over their lives through work. And both discover the ways in which that work is inevitably redefined according to the heroine's sexual destiny. Cecilia turns to books and study when she is bored by the vapidity of London social life, and, like Galesia, throws herself into work—this time philanthropic as well as scholarly—when the hero, Delvile, disappoints her romantic expectations. But Cecilia's love story, however unsatisfactory, will not go away; it repeatedly intrudes upon her Rasselas-like search for a meaningful "course of life" outside the framework of love. Try as she does to get on with her life through books, good deeds, and friendship, the romantic extremes of marital bliss versus "ruin" (the unspoken significance behind her secret marriage to Delvile) continue to undermine her sanity to the point of actual madness. Juliet, in *The Wanderer*, takes up, one by one, a series of the limited number of vocations available to women, only to find that none of them protect her from the physical and emotional abuse to which her gender exposes her. As she sews in a milliner's shop her face and body are on display along with the goods she produces, and she finds herself the target of an opportunistic male's sexual predation. Even working as a paid companion to an irascible old lady puts her at the mercy of the latter's misogynist son. The problem with all of Juliet's lines of work is, quite simply, that none of them give her any power over others and the way in which they treat her. As a result, her work is hopeless: it cannot change any of the "plots" to which those who are more powerful—either by virtue of class, material advantage, or gender—care to subject her.

Acting, music, sewing, commerce, and domestic labor successively fail to bring Juliet more than momentary comfort or safety. She finally achieves both in marriage to her man of choice, but Burney suppresses the redemptive powers of Prince Charmings by giving Juliet a pointedly ineffectual hero to fall in love with. In the novel's conclusion, Burney explicitly attributes Juliet's survival of "the DIFFICULTIES of the WANDERER" to her own "resources," describing the heroine as

a being who had been cast upon herself; a female Robinson Crusoe, as unaided and unprotected, though in the midst of the world, as that imaginary hero in his uninhabited island; and reduced either to sink, through inanition, to nonentity, or to be rescued from famine and death by such resources as she could find, independently, in herself.

If the careers available to women do not afford them control over their own stories, but rather lead to the same predicaments their sexuality brings upon them, what are the "resources" to which Burney refers? I will argue that these resources lie in intelligent, controlled resistance to the plots of rising and falling, to the romantic extremes into which the love story tends to cast women's lives.

Working over the Plot

Burney's heroines cannot, like their author, shape a love story directly through the work they do. Burney literally helped to make possible her marriage to the penniless Alexandre d'Arblay by earning enough money with *Camilla* (1796) to build her family a home, Camilla cottage. But she knew the odds against women of her class gaining significant material rewards from their labor; as *The Wanderer* makes clear, occupations other than writing offered women even less hope of financial power and the concomitant authority to create their own "plots" and identities. (And writing was, as Burney well knew, a tenuous career available to only a few.) Burney's heroines, then, illustrate the limits imposed on female labor as a means of controlling the course of one's life. Alternatively, Burney's novels suggest that women's best resources lie in an intelligent skepticism toward the romantic modes in which the plots of marriage or sexual ruin would place them. Rising and falling are exposed by Burney's fiction as the melodramatic (and destructive) extremes of life to which overly reductive expectations of feminine identity subject women.

Burney's first novel, *Evelina*, demonstrates the utility of such skepticism. A beautiful young woman who lacks a family name that would give her a definite place in the class structure, Evelina finds she is cast in the role of either angel or whore by men like Sir Clement Willoughby. Sir Clement falls in love with Evelina in his own fashion, which means that he either idolizes her as "an angel," as he does upon first seeing her at a ball, or he assumes just the opposite, that she is a "devil." Later, finding her unexpectedly without a protector in a public place, an unthinkable position for a respectable young lady, Sir Clement responds to Evelina's embarrassed inability to explain her situation by assuming the license to make his own "construction." In both instances, Sir Clement's "constructions" follow the drearily bipolar model of ascension or fall, angel or "ruined" woman.

Sir Clement is not the hero of the novel, so his behavior cannot be taken as the best that Burney expected from men. But the best that she does seem to expect is oddly unlike the Prince Charming required in a Cinderella love story. Rather than confirming the romance plot of rising or falling, Burney's heroes function, in different ways, as points of resistance to the female plot of "rising" angel or "fallen" whore. The hero, Lord Orville, is a more cautious interpreter of Evelina than Sir Clement. His response to Sir Clement's effusions over the "angel" Evelina—"a pretty modest-looking girl"—suggests a slightly more subtle if not overly imaginative interpretive framework. Like Harleigh, Juliet's beloved in *The Wanderer*, Orville can value the heroine even when the signals of her social status are mixed: he does not leap to the obvious, extreme conclusions. But this ability depends less on elevating the heroine to angelic heights and more on rather pedestrian forms of lifting. In an important scene just before Evelina marries him, Orville lifts Evelina into a chair to protect her from a monkey that the misogynist prankster, Captain Mirvan, has unleashed on the company. This scene illustrates the extent and importance of the heroine's elevation in Burney's fiction: the most that can be expected from the heroine's "rise" into married bliss is a slightly removed vantage point from which to observe the social violence that is the stuff of Burney's plots.

Lord Orville is usually identified as the most idealized of Burney's heroes. The rest are often described as somewhat flat—disappointing as characters and as romantic figures. The disappointed and sometimes puzzled responses that readers have had to Burney's heroes may result from the ways in which Burney uses male characters to subvert the dichotomous possibilities of the heroine's plot. Burney's heroes expose the overly simplistic extremes of rising or falling, either by positing commonsensical alternatives or by embodying—with a vengeance—a slavish adherence to the dichotomous definition of femininity. *Camilla* is the most explicit of Burney's novels in its exposure of the misogynist tendencies implicit in limiting women to rising or falling. Whereas Sir Clement's reductive interpretations of the heroine in *Evelina* are marginal to the main love story, in *Camilla* the romantic hero, Edgar, is instrumental in instigating and driving a plot of rise or fall that nearly destroys the heroine. Edgar is advised by a blatantly woman-hating mentor to assume that any symptom of moral weakness in Camilla, the girl he wants to marry, automatically disqualifies her to be his wife. As Doody argues with brilliant hilarity, the novel is less about the heroine's failure to deserve her marital reward (who would, on those terms?) than it is about the absurdity and destructiveness of Edgar's expectations. I would add the observation that *Camilla* is a narrative about the gap between a young, middle-class woman's experience and the romance plot that divides women into deserving angels or fallen women. The gap has its comic effects at the expense of the deadly Edgar, but it also nearly destroys the heroine's health and sanity and can only be closed when the hero wakes up to the romanticism of his expectations.

Camilla, like *The Wanderer*, discounts the redemptive powers of Prince Charmings; one of the common themes of the two novels is women's frustrations as they try to control their lives through their own efforts. While *The Wanderer* focuses on the futility of women's labor, *Camilla* treats another, particularly feminine form of labor under capitalism: consumption. Like Juliet's labor, Camilla's consumption only binds the heroine more tightly to the distortions of the romance plot and reinforces Edgar's reductive misinterpretations. Throughout the novel, Camilla incurs expenses that culminate in a climactic act of disastrous feminine consumption. Camilla purchases a new ball dress that she cannot afford because she has bought into a romantic fantasy that Edgar will see her at the ball in all her splendor and fall in love with her once more. The plan backfires horribly, of course, marking Camilla's final attempt to create her own story of romantic success. The dream of the heroine's control over the romantic plot is, in fact, a nightmare. In a dream sequence, Camilla literally confronts her inability to write her own plot. Ill and delirious, she dreams that she is dying and is asked by a supernatural voice (like the one heard by Galesia on her mountaintop) to write her claims to justice with a stern and unforgiving "iron pen." Julia Epstein points out that this scene dramatizes the violence and pain that was associated with writing for Burney, as a woman who found it both central to her sense of self and a cultural no-woman's-land. When Camilla tries to obey the injunction, she cannot write: the pen makes no mark. This writer's nightmare sums up Camilla's futile attempts to control her own story when "writing" to an audience as radically binary in its thinking about heroines as Edgar.

Paradoxically, then, Burney's plots are often about the inadequacy of plotting. Perhaps no Burney character illustrates this inadequacy better than Elinor Joddrell in *The Wanderer*, who, until recent feminist interpretations, has been read as Burney's conservative commentary on the new political ideologies of the French Revolution. Julia Epstein and Margaret Doody give us more subtle readings of the feminist and revolutionary politics of this character, but I want to focus on Elinor to suggest that one of the points she illustrates most forcefully is the folly, for women, of "overwriting" their life plots according to the extremes of rising and falling.

Elinor falls in love with Harleigh, who does not return her passion. Since she cannot "rise" in the plot of romantic love, Elinor decides to fall, dramatically, by killing herself for love. As Doody suggests, Elinor's elaborately staged public suicide evokes the recent suicide attempt of Mary Wollstonecraft in despair over the lost affections of her lover, Gilbert Imlay. While there is no explicitly sexual element in Elinor's "fall," then, it is taken for granted that her "ruin" is possible, if not accomplished. By "falling," Elinor stages the ultimate gamble to win the love of Harleigh, but her scheme, like Camilla's ball dress, yields the opposite result. Elinor "falls" to a self-inflicted knife wound, but Juliet's reactive fall into a faint at the sight of Elinor elicits more concern from Harleigh than Elinor's romantic suicide attempt. Elinor's repeated attempts to be a romantic heroine who gives up her life for love make her seem silly even to herself, as she admits to Juliet while asking her to arrange a final "conference" with Harleigh:

No! the soft moment of indulgence to my feelings is at an end! When I allowed my heart that delicious expansion; when I abandoned it to nature, and permitted it those open effusions of tenderness, I thought my dissolution at hand, and meant but to snatch a few last precious minutes of extacy from everlasting annihilation! but these endless delays, these eternal procrastinations, make me appear so unmeaning an idiot, even to myself, that, for the remnant of my doleful ditty, I must resist every natural wish; and plod on, till I plod off, with the stiff and stupid decorum of a starched old maid of half a century. Procure me, however, this definitive conference. It is upon no point of the old story, I promise you. You cannot be more tired of that than I am ashamed.

Elinor's words reveal the ineffectuality of female plotting in a life more prone to "delays" and "procrastinations" than climactic extremes. Elinor must learn to "plod" rather than "plot" in order to get on with her life. And this lesson entails a certain loss of elevation, as Elinor finally reflects: "'Alas! alas!' she cried, 'must Elinor too,—must even Elinor!—like the element to which, with the common herd, she owes chiefly, her support, find,—with that herd!—her own level?'"

The characterization of Elinor illustrates two themes that are central to Burney's fiction. First, it points to the cultural odds against a woman's control over her own "plot" and the subtlety and strength necessary to counter those odds. Elinor's direct approach to controlling her own plot through dramatic self-display inevitably becomes a ridiculous self-parody. On the other hand, Juliet's methods of self-imposed silence and sparing self-disclosure are not unproblematic options, as the misinterpretations to which she is subjected attest, but they are her best choice in a culture that denies women the direct control over their lives to which Elinor aspires. As Juliet wryly points out to Harleigh, a direct approach to "female difficulties" will only expose her to the reductive interpretations that she seeks to avoid. Telling Harleigh about the marriage into which she has been forced and enlisting his aid to help her escape it would ultimately cast Juliet in the role of conniving "devil." Even men like Harleigh are not to be trusted with all of the information about the experience of feminine victimization. Second, it shows us the silly reductiveness of romantic extremes. Women, Burney's fiction suggests, are both more commonplace and more complex and interesting than the fallen or ascendant heroine. Elinor is more attractive and interesting at the level of self-deprecating "plodding" than in her passionate extremes. Women's lives are simply not like the dramatic ups and downs of romance plotting.

One of the major accomplishments of Burney's fiction lies in its resistance to the tendency of romantic plots to stifle the complexity of feminine identity and experience by reducing them to dichotomous extremes. This resistance lies, as we have seen, in Burney's curiously "disappointing" heroes, the errors her heroines commit through a mistaken trust in romantic conventions, and even in their occasional commonsensical skepticism about romance. Another way in which Burney struggles against the reductive tendencies of female plotting is through the structure of her novels. Like Elinor, Burney tells us that women's experience is more about "delays" and "procrastinations" than rising or falling. This message is conveyed through two features common to Burney's work. One is that Burney's romantic love plots are characterized by the strategy of waiting and delay. The course of true love is circuitous in Burney's novels. The other feature is that Burney's endings tend more toward the whimper than the bang: they emphasize open-endedness, lack of closure, and the "plodding" rather than "plotting" aspect of feminine life and experience.

In a fascinating discussion of Burney's "The Witlings"—an early attempt at writing a comedy for the stage that was repressed by the order of her father, Charles Burney, and her adopted "daddy," Samuel Crisp—Margaret Doody points to the innovative nature of the play's dramatic action. Burney, Doody argues, has written a play that thematizes waiting. By doing so, the play comments on social time-wasting and provides an aesthetic solution to the "stilted quality" of much eighteenth-century drama by incorporating "the real essential *waiting* of late eighteenth-century comedy in the structure of the play." Waiting is also a large and important part of the plot structure of Burney's novels. While things do happen to Burney heroines, even romantic things, the pacing of the plot often serves to undermine climactic structures so that they crumble even as they seem to build. The most striking example of this strategy is the sequence in *Cecilia* in which the unfortunate Harrel commits suicide at the public pleasure grounds of Vauxhall. Doody points out the oddity of this part of the novel, which drags on for a considerable number of pages after the shooting, recounting the anticlimactic actions of characters as they wait, in the aftermath of the tragedy, until they can go home. Less dramatically, perhaps, but just as strikingly, Burney's heroines from Evelina through Juliet spend large portions of their time waiting for their constraining circumstances to change so that they can move on, both physically and psychologically. Evelina must wait for carriages; Cecilia sits through the tedium of social calls; Camilla is, literally, stranded up a tree; Juliet is continually waiting for some character or other to leave the room so that she can escape from embarrassment and emotional pain. While the heroine waits, Burney gives us the often violent, almost always painful satiric scenes that have earned her, rightly or wrongly, her reputation as a novelist of "manners." These scenes should not be read, however—as they sometimes have been—as removed from the love stories of Burney's heroines; they provide a pointed commentary on those love stories by dramatizing what eighteenth-century writers on middle-class women's employments and education well knew— that little of women's time is spent in romantic climax or the depths of ruin, and much of it is spent in the tedium of waiting for someone else, usually male, to make something happen.

Another characteristic feature of Burney's plots is the frustration of the heroine's attempts to direct action. Elinor Joddrell is an extreme example of a woman whose attempts to take charge of her life meet with continual defeat. But Burney's heroines often find themselves frustrated in their attempts to direct events by the sheer randomness of experience. Evelina's letter to Orville miscarries in an early example of how happenstance derails the romance plot, but Burney's later heroines all encounter some character or characters who, like Mr. Dubster in *Camilla*, stall the action of the novel into stretches of comic tedium by their unintended obstructions. The benevolent but absent-minded Giles Arbe in *The Wanderer* is perhaps Burney's most accomplished plot-spoiler: his inability to deliver notes and to remember who should or should not be privy to certain information renders all Juliet's plans useless. While clearly marked as a "good" character, Arbe stands for the randomness of life's events that thwarts the heroine's attempts to control the course of her life.

Waiting and anticlimax are woven into the very experience of reading *The Wanderer*. The name of the heroine is not revealed until well into the novel, and when it is, it proves no great revelation, as it might in an earlier novel by Haywood or Behn. Her story, the tale of her identity as the product of an aristocratic secret marriage, is a carefully guarded secret until very late in the novel, and when it emerges it does so in an oddly offhand way when a friend of the heroine lets it slip to someone she thinks is already in the know. The romantic plot of a concealed true identity so dear to novelists ranging from Behn to Henry Fielding is submerged to the point of unimportance in the snarled plot lines of "female difficulties." William Hazlitt's famous, negative review of *The Wanderer* inadvertently stumbled on this characteristic feature of the Burney novel: "The difficulties in which she involves her heroines are, indeed, 'Female Difficulties';—they are difficulties created out of nothing." What irritates Hazlitt, as Epstein observes, is precisely Burney's point. The story of women's experience that Burney tells is about stalled plots, arbitrary obstacles, and random difficulties.

Hazlitt also had difficulty with Burney's endings, which are another means she uses to resist the constraining plots of the rising or falling heroine. "The whole artifice of her fable," he assesses quite rightly, "consists in coming to no conclusion. Her ladies stand so upon the order of their going, that they do not go at all." Indeed, while Burney's endings are in some ways conventionally romantic (depicting the happy marriage of the heroine), Hazlitt is not alone in finding something oddly inconclusive about her novels. *Cecilia* is the most explicitly antiromantic in its conclusion; while the hero and heroine end up married, Cecilia must give up her fortune to achieve this status, and Burney makes a point of qualifying her heroine's happiness:

> Yet human it [Cecilia's life] was and as such imperfect! she knew that, at times the whole family must murmur at her loss of fortune, and at times she murmured herself to be thus portionless, tho' an HEIRESS. Rationally, however, she surveyed the world at large, and finding that of the few who had any happiness, that there were none without some misery, she checked the rising sigh . . . and . . . bore partial evil with chearfullest resignation.

Burney records her friend Edmund Burke's objection to this ending:

> He wished the conclusion either more happy or more miserable; "for in a work of imagination," said he, "there is no medium."

> I was not easy to answer him, or I have much . . . to say in defence of following life and nature as much in the conclusion as in the progress of a tale; and when is life and nature completely happy or miserable? (*Diaries and Letters*, volume 2)

Further defending *Cecilia*'s conclusion to her mentor Samuel Crisp, Burney speaks against the extremes of "every other book of fiction" and her wish to avoid them:

I think the book, in its present conclusion, somewhat original, for the hero and heroine are neither plunged in the depths of misery, nor exalted to UN*human* happiness. Is not such a middle state more natural, more according to real life, and less resembling every other book of fiction? (*Diaries and Letters*, volume 2)

Even when Burney's novels end more unequivocally in marital happiness than *Cecilia*, the romantic exaltation of the heroine is suppressed, for readers such as Hazlitt (and myself), in relation to the repetitions and circumlocutions of the plot. Even the almost fairy-tale ending of *Evelina*, in which the heroine returns to her native Berry Hill and "the arms of the best of men," calls conclusive endings into question. "The best of men" in Evelina's language identifies either her new husband, Lord Orville, or her adopted father and mentor, Mr. Villars; is Evelina's happy ending exaltation into married bliss or a return to where the novel began, with her adopted father? There is an implied circularity here that introduces ambiguity to even the most "exalted" of endings for Burney's heroines.

In sum, Burney's novels are shot through with skepticism about rising or falling heroines. The "middle state" is more "according to real life," in Burney's view, because it resists the oversimplification of feminine identity and experience according to a dichotomous model of rising or falling, angel or demon. Feminine happiness or misery, Burney knew, could not be represented or interpreted apart from the dichotomizing influence of the prevailing gender ideology, and her fiction represents a lifelong effort to work against reductive representations and interpretations of women's lives. Hence, there is considerable irony in the ways in which that gender ideology has shaped the representations of Burney's career as a novelist for over two hundred years of literary history.

The Rise (and Fall) of Women Novelists

Burney's fiction and her career as a novelist have been persistently read through the lens of her gender. Criticism contemporary with Burney's work and published soon after her death tends to assess her work as that of a "very woman," as Julia Epstein says, either the precious craft of an infantilized author or the tired, overdone product of a decaying coquette's last flash of literary vanity. Since the mid-nineteenth century, critical attention has shifted from her fiction to her published diaries, bringing to the surface the earlier, implicit emphasis on Burney's life as a woman as opposed to her work as a novelist. Despite important dissenting arguments, the overwhelming tendency in Burney criticism has been to characterize her career as an initial, meteoric rise in youth (never mind that she was nearly thirty when she published her first novel) followed by a steady fall through *Cecilia* and *Camilla* that ended with a resounding bump—*The Wanderer.*

Even recent critics such as Spencer retrace this trajectory in discussing Burney's career, albeit from a feminist point of view: "Burney's anxiety for paternal approval and her fear of public exposure led her on a search for correctness of language and sentiment that tended to kill her early vitality." The tenacity of this view of Burney's work and literary reputation should be analyzed in the light of the historical use of the rising and falling metaphor in eighteenth-century fictional representations of women. When applied to the women who wrote the fiction, the metaphor has the same reductive effects. Women's work tends to be sorted according to a dichotomy of falling or rising, and—as Burney's alleged rise-and-fall career suggests—what goes up must come down. In other words, the same gendered logic of rise and fall that shaped eighteenth-century women novelists' plots tends to shape literary and historical accounts of those novelists.

I would suggest that the metaphor of "the rise" that informs so many studies of the eighteenth-century novel (chief among them Ian Watt's *Rise of the Novel*, 1957) is, like many of our richest, most historically burdened metaphors, implicitly gendered. And like many other gendered metaphors, it reduces historical complexities to orderly narratives and taxonomies. Watt, for example, admits the historical reality that the majority of novelists during much of the century were women, but the story he tells of the novel's rise to "formal realism" is the tale of a masculine dynasty. (Austen is the only woman novelist he discusses at any length.) It seems that when there is rising to be done, men will do it, and Watt is neither alone nor especially to blame for perpetuating this cultural "structure of feeling," as Raymond Williams would call it. As Terry Lovell points out, the reputation of novel writing was threatened by its "feminization" through the large number of women who wrote novels during the eighteenth century and enhanced by the emergence of a greater number of male writers during the late eighteenth and early nineteenth centuries. During the period of the novel's "first expansion," Lovell suggests, "writing might have become a feminized occupation, with all the characteristics of such occupations—low pay and low status." It took male novelists to bring this reputation "up."

Watt has often been attacked for eliding the work of eighteenth-century women novelists, and McKeon's and J. Paul Hunter's subsequent books on the beginnings of the novel include a wide range of writers—not all male, not all novelists—in their narrations of the English novel's early history. But their complex and rich histories include women in their stories of the novel's development but do not specifically address how femininity figures in those stories. McKeon's dialectical process complicates Watt's story of the novel's rise in relation to capitalism, and Hunter's sophisticated sense of how literary form develops from broad social and literary contexts similarly complicates Watt's tale of a male dynasty. Women are included in an "equal opportunity" fashion that does not allow for much attention to historical differences between how men and women were represented in eighteenth-century culture and how these differences might, in turn, affect the representation of women novelists. The investigation of gender differences is not, of course, McKeon's or Hunter's project, and my point is not to denigrate their work but to suggest that the inclusion of women writers does not in itself advance our understanding of the complex relationship between eighteenth-century ideologies of gender and the historical trajectory of the novel's form and definition.

Watt's novel rises in relation to an ascending middle class; Hunter's novel reaches higher levels of social and literary respectability; McKeon's follows a path of uneven, dialectical development. None of these "big stories" is helpful in accounting for why women have traditionally been left out of accounts of the novel's rise and why Frances Burney's career has repeatedly been characterized in terms of rise and fall. While they allow the woman novelist to rise just like the men, such stories of the novel's emergence, which accept the metaphor of rising without thinking through its implications for both heroines and women writers, have not been helpful in analyzing the specific phenomena of women's literary careers in the eighteenth century.

A similar reductionism with respect to eighteenth-century women's writing results when feminist literary historians and critics pursue uncritically the project of charting the rise of the woman novelist. Jane

Spencer's *Rise of the Woman Novelist: From Aphra Behn to Jane Austen* argues that women novelists rose to a position of respectability and literary authority in the eighteenth century by means of a feminist fall. That is, women novelists rose to public acceptance by giving up their earlier critiques of masculine authority, particularly as that authority affected women's sexuality. Spencer sees the early fiction of Eliza Haywood as more liberating than her later novel, *Betsey Thoughtless*, for instance, and the novels of Frances Burney are a political falling-off from those of Delariviere Manley and Jane Barker, notwithstanding the gains in public acceptance represented by Burney's respectability and professional success. Spencer writes that this feminist fall from political critique was arrested by the polemical fiction of the 1790s, particularly that of Mary Wollstonecraft and Mary Hays. But this conception that the woman novelist's rise in public acceptance was facilitated by her fall from feminism is belied, in part, by Spencer's interesting and complex discussion of a range of novels that resist such sorting. Resistance to oppressive notions of women and their sexuality occurs, it seems, in "subversive" forms in much of the fiction that fails to meet Spencer's feminist standards. Spencer's book reveals the deficiencies of the very paradigm of rising and falling that it espouses in its title and central thesis. Historical narratives of rising and falling, whether they reflect a feminist outlook or some other political perspective, tend to reinforce a Calvinistic, damned-or-saved taxonomy of texts and writers. Burney's fiction could teach us of the dangers of such a taxonomy, especially for the historically silenced and underrepresented.

This is not to say that feminist politics have no place in women's literary history. In fact, as I said at the outset of this chapter, Burney's importance as a writer is explicitly and profoundly political. What I argue here is that gender identity and gendered experience are encoded not only in the stories told by a culture's fictions, but in the stories we tell about those fictions. Just as Burney knew that she could best tell effective new stories of female identity and experience by careful and knowledgeable reworkings of the old ones, feminist critics and literary historians do some of their best work by knowing and reworking the "plots" of literary history. Otherwise, it is too easy to repeat the oppressions of past narratives in our haste to write new stories. The vast and complex range of narratives in eighteenth-century women's fiction is best understood if we in turn understand the political implications of the historical narratives we write about them.

Much of the enormous amount of exciting, revisionary critical attention received by the work of Frances Burney in the last few years is symptomatic of a healthy trend in women's literary history toward making the big historical narratives of rising and falling literary forms more reflective of the specificity of the writers' texts and lives, rather than the other way around. The feminist reassessment of Burney's fiction does not guarantee the emergence of a literary history that self-consciously questions the political implications of its own rises and falls, of course, but it is a positive signal that tomorrow's students of the novel's history will find room within the historical narratives of the novel's development for serious consideration of the rich array of stories told by eighteenth-century women writers.

Kristina Straub

Selected Bibliography

Doody, Margaret Anne. *Frances Burney: The Life in the Works.* New Brunswick, N.J.: Rutgers University Press, 1988.

Eighteenth-Century Fiction 3, no. 4 (July 1991), special *Evelina* issue.

Epstein, Julia. *The Iron Pen: Frances Burney and the Politics of Women's Writing.* Madison: University of Wisconsin Press, 1989.

Poovey, Mary. *The Proper Lady and the Woman Writer.* Chicago: University of Chicago Press, 1984.

Ross, Deborah. *The Excellence of Falsehood: Romance, Realism, and Women's Contribution to the Novel.* Lexington: University Press of Kentucky, 1991.

Schofield, Mary Anne, and Cecilia Macheski, eds. *Fetter'd or Free? British Women Novelists, 1670–1815.* Athens: Ohio University Press, 1985.

Spencer, Jane. *The Rise of the Woman Novelist: From Aphra Behn to Jane Austen.* Oxford: Blackwell, 1986.

Spender, Dale. *Mothers of the Novel: 100 Good Women Writers Before Jane Austen.* London: Pandora, 1986.

Straub, Kristina. *Divided Fictions: Fanny Burney and Feminine Strategy.* Lexington: University Press of Kentucky, 1987.

Todd, Janet. *Feminist Literary History.* New York: Routledge, 1988.

The Gothic Novel, 1764–1824

T HE first Gothic novelist celebrated his literary inspiration with all the fanfare of a bored aristocrat telling his dreams over breakfast. "I waked one morning . . . from a dream, of which all I could recover was, that I had thought myself in an ancient castle . . . and that on the uppermost bannister of a great staircase I saw a gigantic hand in armour." Because this particular bored aristocrat was Horace Walpole, and because his literary ambitions were a match for his midnight reveries, the Gothic novel was born.

Walpole told his readers in the preface to the second edition of *The Castle of Otranto* (1764) that he had attempted "to blend the two kinds of romance" in the novel. What Walpole called "the two kinds of romance" are what literary critics now call the "romance" and the "novel." Walpole claims that the romance favors "imagination and improbability" while the novel gives preference to copying "nature," with the result that "the great resources of fancy have been dammed up by a strict adherence to common life." *Otranto* uses "the great resources of fancy" as the occasion for an outrageously improbable "political" tale— what I would call the paradigmatic Gothic plot—one of nefarious usurpation and ultimate revenge, set against a vaguely historical (hence "Gothic") backdrop, enlivened by scenes of supernatural agency, brutal sexual aggression, undisguised incestuous longings, sadomasochistic fantasy, and an astonishingly lurid and versatile architectural motif. Although it was almost thirty years before the Gothic novel achieved its greatest popularity, Walpole anticipated its full range of concerns and techniques for handling those concerns in his tour de force.

Of course, as Walpole himself may have understood, there is always more than authorial agency at work in the creation of literary genres. Various literary historians have attempted to pinpoint the origins of the Gothic novel. Antiquarian interest in Gothic architecture, changing popular tastes, frustration with "reason," new concepts of subjectivity and emotional response, including theories of "pleasurable terror" or the "sublime," the politics of individualism, the French Revolution—all these things have been posited, more or less successfully, as explanations for the emergence of the Gothic novel in the later eighteenth century. Walpole's paradigmatic text, however, provides a less circumstantial explanatory resource. *The Castle of Otranto* itself reveals the degree to which Gothic fiction provides the terms for its own analysis.

Otranto tells a story of sex and power linked at so many points and in so many ways that the two can only be understood in terms of one another. Walpole was not alone in imagining the intersections of sexuality and power in the middle of the eighteenth century; the French cultural historian Michel Foucault, for example, has studied the ways in which "sexuality" emerged as a function of ideological control during this period. He argues, for instance, in the first volume of his *History of Sexuality*, that specific relations in modern society—such as those of the family, the school, and the medical profession—institutionalized a relation between sexuality and power. Walpole's novel crystallized a particular vocabulary for documenting this relation and for dramatizing the virulence with which various repressions—"damming-ups," in Walpole's terms—exercise the control inherent to "bourgeois culture."

The Gothic novel, emerging as it does at the moment when the battle lines of cultural reorganization are being formed in the later eighteenth century, shimmers with subversive potential. If the emergence of the novel itself celebrates the codification of middle-class values, as several critics have argued, the Gothic novel records the terror implicit in the increasingly dictatorial reign of those values. Gothic fiction seems particularly, if not aggressively, open to interpretation from various social, political, and sexual points of view. The Gothic novel achieves this potential precisely because it reflects, in perhaps predictable but nonetheless powerful ways, the anxiety that culture itself generates in its members. Gothic fiction thereby challenges the cultural system that both commodifies desire and renders it lurid and pathological.

Manfred, the usurper and sexual aggressor of *The Castle of Otranto*, who turns every relation into a perversion and who finds ways to turn the very passages of the castle into a sexual nightmare for the vulnerable heroine, is the perfect figure to memorialize the anxieties that Walpole is chronicling. Manfred acts out of a personal ambition that gives political ramifications to a desire that is at once ruthless and self-serving. The first victim of this megalomania is his "sickly puny" son Conrad, who early in the novel is "dashed to pieces" by an "enormous helmet" that crashes into the court of the castle on Conrad's wedding day. The story of the indirect murder of a sickly child by a politically important and abusive father who mistreats his wife and indulges his own urges finds an analogy in Walpole's own personal situation. The author was the effeminate son of the "great" Sir Robert Walpole, a statesman of unparalleled power during the first half of the eighteenth century; and he adored his mother as much as he detested his father's mistreatment of her. Because this novel establishes the "dysfunctional family" as a Gothic trope or central metaphorical device, it is tempting to suggest that Walpole's Gothic is a reflection of his own family life. Freud's concept of the Oedipus complex could easily be applied to a case such as Walpole's. Whatever the sources of the Gothic in Walpole's own psyche, however, there are Oedipal tensions enough in culture itself. Jacques Lacan, an influential post-Freudian theorist, sees the "Oedipus complex" as a precondition of cultural awareness, what he calls "cultural subordination": in order to become a member of a culture, what Lacan calls "the Symbolic order," it is necessary to suppress private desire in the ways that Freud's analysis outlines. You cannot kill your father or marry your mother, so you make little compromises that trap you into working against your own "best" interests. Gothic novelists refuse to settle for these compromises. In this sense, what Walpole begins to articulate in *The Castle of Otranto* becomes a complex gesture of cultural defiance. The impulse to connect prince, unauthorized sexuality, and Gothic convention in a single narrative of unmistakable force anticipates the technique of psychoanalysis, but Walpole's is a psychoanalysis that draws out "madnesses" rather than trying to contain them. He provides, in other words, a counterpoint to the narratives of cultural subordination that abounded in the "realistic" fiction he was resisting.

After his son dies, Manfred, in what would have been understood by contemporary readers as an incestuous gesture, courts the dead boy's fiancée, Isabella, throwing over his indulgent wife and insulting his daughter Matilda in the process. When Isabella resists him, she becomes the victim of sexual aggression so violent that it turns the castle itself into a Gothic nightmare. Her flight through the castle is depicted in vivid detail:

> The lower part of the castle was hollowed in to several intricate cloisters; and it was not easy for one under so much anxiety to find the door that opened in to the cavern. An awful silence reigned throughout those subterraneous regions, except now and then some blasts of wind that shook the doors she had passed, and which grating on the rusty hinges were re-echoed through that long labyrinth of darkness.

Here Walpole introduces what becomes the hallmark of Gothic fiction: in a single image he combines the sexual anxiety of a victimized female, the incestuous desire of a libidinous male, the use of the physical features of the castle itself to represent political and sexual entrapment, and an atmosphere deftly rendered to produce terror and gloom. This scene is retold hundreds of times in Gothic fiction; it is absolutely basic to the form. Because he understands that Gothic fiction can represent abject terror and frenzied aggression in ways that other fiction only approximates, Walpole's depiction of this moment, and others like it, takes on a kind of talismanic importance in the history of the form. If he fails at the level of plot or larger structures, here at the moment of Gothic intensity Walpole demonstrates just how and why the Gothic can succeed as it does.

Between the publication of *The Castle of Otranto* in 1764 and the apparent waning of interest in the Gothic novel in the 1820s literally hundreds of Gothic novels were consumed by the British reading public. (A bibliography of over three hundred Gothic titles, organized by year, can be found in Maurice Lévy's comprehensive *Le roman "gothique" anglais*.) Writers inspired by Walpole's experiment developed the Gothic in various directions. In the pages that follow, I will outline what I see as the most interesting of those directions and a few of the works that exemplify them.

"Female Gothic"

Some writers took inspiration from the historical setting of Walpole's work and the narrative possibilities of an inherently threatening past: abandoned rooms may be haunted, locked chests may harbor dreadful secrets, tattered manuscripts may divulge horrifying transgressions.

Although different from one another in countless ways, these writers shared the tendency to use the conventions of Gothic fiction to add excitement to tales that were primarily historical (and sentimental) romances, committed more to the heroine's tears than to her terrors. Often they used a heroine's own suspicions as a way of instructing her as to the foolishness of Gothic imaginings: the ghosts that wander unchecked in *The Castle of Otranto* here turn out to be explainable in physical terms, in obedience to rules of realism—"the limits of credibility," as Clara Reeve calls them. Gothic writers like Clara Reeve and Charlotte Smith were unwilling to violate these limits, and they use Gothic effects simply to heighten the moral lessons of otherwise sentimental tales.

Reeve called *The Old English Baron* (published as *The Champion of Virtue* in 1777) "the literary offspring of the Castle of Otranto," but it is a far cry from Walpole's lurid masterpiece. In it she tells a tale of wrongful usurpation and uses some of the less shocking devices of *Otranto*, such as "incoherent dreams," a "haunted" chamber, even "ghosts" and a skeleton. But her imagination is less engaged by scenes of haunting than by the legal squabbles of a group of petty aristocrats, and her attempts to articulate "sentimental" codes of social interaction seem far more deeply felt and dramatically persuasive.

Smith, in such novels as *Emmeline, the Orphan of the Castle* (1788), *Ethelinde, or, The Recluse of the Lake* (1789), and *The Old Manor House* (1793), brings the use of setting to a new level of Gothic sophistication. As Lévy says, "No one before Radcliffe could better transcribe the secret impulse of terror felt by a young girl given up to an architecture, where the softest sound and the lightest shade are amplified by the resonance and obscurity of the vaults to fit the dimensions of a nightmare" (my translation). In the last of these novels, Smith tells the story of a persecuted heroine, Monimia, and her "lover-mentor" Orlando. Less interested than Walpole in the Gothic dimensions of her plot, she still uses such techniques as seemingly supernatural events and unreasonable persecution of the heroine to heighten the emotional intensity of her tale. In doing so she also insists on female education and the importance of female clear-headedness. She thus anticipates some of the central concerns of later writers and suggests the intersection of Gothic and sentimental fiction more directly than her contemporaries. Her novels also help to demonstrate the degree to which the Gothic became a crucial element in female education, and at the same time they help to explain what may have inspired some of Radcliffe's less satisfying turns, especially in the direction of "explanation."

What both Reeve and Smith contribute to the Gothic novel cannot be summed up, however, in a list of techniques or literary concerns. Literary history, even in a volume of this kind, does not work that way. What they did, independent of their specific accomplishments, was to make the Gothic available for respectable female readers and writers. Their refusal to violate the letter of the law of realism has at times worked against their popularity with critics of the Gothic. But their works are never completely tame and rational. For what such writers achieve in the way of local emotional intensity can never be fully undermined by the stern dismissal of the supernatural with which they bring their works to a close. Moreover they pose challenges to any pat notions of what Gothic novels can accomplish.

Recent feminist rereadings of Gothic fiction have added considerably to the sophistication with which these novels and other examples of "female Gothic" are discussed. The place of female characters within Gothic works has always been problematic, as the description of Isabella's plight in *The Castle of Otranto* might suggest. No Gothic novel is without its suffering heroine, who is both "sexualized" as an object of desire and "victimized" by a powerful aggressor who is also a potential rapist. The first task of feminist criticism was to articulate the problem of the abuse of the female in Gothic fiction and to explore the ways in which female novelists subverted or reinscribed the cultural norms of female sexualization and victimization. Just as feminist theory moved from simple "identity politics" to a more rigorously theoretical stance, which emerged from rereadings of Marx and Freud and, more recently, Lacan, so feminist criticism of the Gothic has moved from descriptions of the role of women in the tales themselves to a more sophisticated analysis of how women could be drawn to Gothic fiction as both writers and readers and what they could discover in it for themselves.

One of the most intriguing of such rereadings of the Gothic, Claire Kahane's "The Gothic Mirror," articulates a position that challenges previous modes of understanding the Gothic. Kahane suggests that the Gothic castle offers the typically motherless heroine a setting in which her own victimization can be confronted and somehow overcome. She does this by "maternalizing" the space that threatens her—the subterranean regions of the castle. These secret spaces, dark and womb-like as they are, come to represent the maternal space that the heroine both desires and fears. Kahane says, "What I see repeatedly locked into the forbidden center of the Gothic which draws me inward is the spectral presence of a dead-undead mother, archaic and all-encompassing, a ghost signifying the problematics of femininity which the heroine must confront."

This kind of interpretation offers a great deal to critics who are attempting to understand the attraction Gothic fiction might have held for the thousands of females who read and wrote them. It is too easy to say that female readers are attracted to the thrill of illicit sexuality or the masochistic enjoyment of their victimization that the Gothic everywhere represents. Kahane's position offers another way to understand what is attractive to women in these works and why the plight of the Gothic heroine has such seemingly universal power.

A key work in this regard is Sophia Lee's Elizabethan romance, *The Recess* (1783). The peculiar space signified by the novel's title comprises a set of subterranean chambers constructed under an abbey, which in the near past of the novel is a retreat in which the sister-heroines of the work, Matilda and Ellinor, spend their childhood. Formerly a convent, the space is cavelike but consists of various rooms, centered on "a vaulted passage" whose light "proceeded from small casements of painted glass so infinitely above our reach that we could never seek a world beyond." This remembered space assumes a suggestive, womb-like quality, and the distinctly charged memories of this childhood world are suffused with the idea of the girls' mother, the majestic but threateningly distant (and doomed) Mary, Queen of Scots. Just as Mary is a mother both inaccessible and dangerous—should the girls be acknowledged publicly, their lives would surely be in danger—the maternal space is the scene of horror (the incestuous relation of their foster parents, their own brutal incarceration and near-rape) as well as love (both between the sisters and between them and their historically important male companions, Leicester and Essex). The tale of unhappiness and loss that besets them—each is doomed to misery in love and to wretchedness in life—returns repeatedly to this exotic space and the ominous happiness that it represents. In the end, however, it can only torment these girls with all they lack. The literally absent mother, glimpsed distantly only once before her execution, hovers over the work with a similarly threatening presence that always seems to promise happiness but in fact brings misery and despair. If later Gothicists create maternal specters to challenge heroines with the limits of their own subjectivity, Lee tries to maternalize history itself as harrowing and fraught with danger in a particularly female way. By doing so she offers Gothic fiction as a medium for female novelists, perhaps most especially for her student Ann Radcliffe.

Ann Radcliffe's evocation of female anxiety in works such as *The Mysteries of Udolpho* (1794) has earned her the title "Mistress of Romance." When Emily St. Aubert first sees the Castle of Udolpho, where she will live with her aunt and her aunt's villainous husband, Montoni, it has an almost animate presence for her:

Emily gazed with melancholy awe upon the castle, which she understood to be Montoni's; for though it was now lighted up by the setting sun, the gothic greatness of its features, and its mouldering walls of dark grey stone, rendered it a gloomy and sublime object. . . . Silent, lonely, and sublime, it seemed to stand the sovereign of the scene, and to frown defiance on all who dared to invade its solitary reign.

Emily's first view of the castle connects it to its owner, and there is every reason to think that the castle itself, "gloomy and sublime," is a constant reminder of the evil Montoni. Such descriptions were inspired by the philosophy of Edmund Burke, whose *Philosophical Enquiry into the Origin of Our Ideas of the Sublime and the Beautiful* (1757) popularized the notion of pleasurable terror and outlined an entire range of techniques for engaging the emotions associated with the Gothic. Radcliffean "sublime" always involves a fascination with what is fearful. This fascination could be equated with desire, but it is not necessarily a desire for the "owner" of the castle. Later, when Emily has suffered enough mental abuse from her stepfather to realize that she is in real danger, she finds the dreary castle itself more terrifying and more attractive than anyone who inhabits it: in seeking her aunt in a distant tower, for instance, she "proceeded through a passage adjoining the vaults, the walls of which were drooping with unwholesome dews, and the vapours, that crept along the ground, made the torch burn so dimly, that Emily expected every moment to see it extinguished." She then looks through "a pair of iron gates" to see "by flashes of uncertain light, the vaults beyond, and near her, heaps of earth, that seemed to surround an open grave." These descriptions are more specific than Walpole's "long labyrinth of darkness," and the details help to draw a picture that makes understandable the critics' desire to connect passages of the castle and passages of memory. Emily seems drawn into these dim, vaporous, and unwholesome spaces; she sees them uncertainly, and she fears for her own safety, even as she insists on penetrating further into the gloom and secrecy of this dark interior. The spectral presence of the castle itself has an alarming "uncanniness," as if Emily, trapped in the passages of repressed memory, recognized in these threatening spaces something about herself that she had always known.

Kahane argues persuasively that when the "secret" of the castle turns out to be the history of the sexually transgressive Madame Laurentini, this threatening maternal figure becomes, in a way, the "meaning" of the work. "As a victimizer victimized by her own desire," Kahane says, "Laurentini is presented as Emily's potential precursor, a mad mother-sister-double who mirrors Emily's own potential for transgression and madness." "Female Gothic," in other words, confronts the heroine with her own desires and thrills her with the possibility of transgression. In Radcliffe's novels the impulse toward transgression is not acted upon but remains only a threat—one that is always contained by the forced conclusions upon which the author insists. Emily as heroine cannot transgress, and readers do not for a moment imagine that she will.

As heroine, however, she can—indeed she must—suffer. Some critics have gone so far as to suggest that the attraction a heroine like Emily comes inexplicably to feel for the inward reaches of the castle is in fact the sign of a repressed masochistic desire for the dark hero himself. Cynthia Griffin Wolff calls this figure the demon-lover: "Despite the fact that the man is darkly attractive, the woman generally shuns him, shrinking as from some invisible contamination. Too often to be insignificant, this aversion is justified when he eventually proves to be a long-lost relation: an uncle, a step-father, sometimes the biological father himself—lusting after the innocent daughter's chastity." In Wolff's analysis, the demon-lover, who "dominat[es] the fiction as its undeniable emotional focus," is secretly attractive to the heroine and becomes the source of a power that releases her from the confines of a sentimental world.

Such a description seems even more appropriate to Radcliffe's earlier *Romance of the Forest* (1791) than it does to *The Mysteries of Udolpho*. Not only is the Marquis de Montalt, the villain of that novel, physically attractive and almost kind to Adeline, the heroine, he is urbane; and his chateau, unlike the usual Gothic setting, is beautifully if oppressively decorated and showy in its luxuriance—"fitted up in the most airy and elegant taste."

It would be tempting to say that this world of negative possibility is in some way deeply attractive to the novelist and her heroine and that Radcliffe gives voice to secret desires in her depiction of this powerful paternal figure. But from another perspective, the world of male prerogative gives rise to Gothic experience throughout the text. The terror invoked is not a thrilling and titillating frisson but real, uncompromising fear. According to this reading, Radcliffe portrays female experience as fraught with actual rather than imagined danger.

Where Adeline does find consolation is in the bosom of a sentimentalized family structure, that of the sympathetic M. La Luc, and more specifically in the person of his ineffectual son, Theodore. Adeline's attraction to Theodore is immediate and compelling. The structure of the novel, however, requires that they be separated for most of it. This is convenient in two ways: first, it allows Adeline to undergo the ordeal of her repeated flight and incarceration on her own and to discover the kind of power that even her attachment to Theodore would deprive her of; second, it allows her to imagine him, as she does at regular intervals throughout the bulk of the novel, in terms like these:

Even when sleep obliterated for a while her memory of the past, his image frequently arose to her fancy, accompanied by all the exaggerations of terror. She saw him in chains, and struggling in the grasp of ruffians, or saw him led, amidst the dreadful preparations for execution, into the field: she saw the agony of his look and heard him repeat her name in frantic accents, till the horrors of the scene overcame her, and she awoke.

Such moments of fearful imagination abound in *The Romance of the Forest*, as they do in each of Radcliffe's novels, and their function is clear. Adeline heightens suspense and her own dread by imagining Theodore in chains, Theodore bleeding, Theodore suffering untold torments. But she also challenges the assumptions of patriarchy by finding this ineffectual and indeed emasculated hero a desirable alternative to the stern and powerful Marquis de Montalt. The "exaggerations of terror," in other words, offer Radcliffe a way of imagining an alternative to the ideology that places women under the power of men. Her "man" is never depicted as powerful, nor does he seem particularly able to extricate himself from the hold that law and society—in the form of the army and the Marquis—have over him. Insofar as the Marquis de Montalt comes to represent the source of power in a phallocentric system, Theodore, pathetic as he is (or as Adeline imagines him), represents a conceivable alternative. In his suffering lies his power, both to capture the heart of Adeline and to undermine the unequivocal power of the Marquis. Theodore's suffering, and Adeline's imagination of his pain, place him in the only relation that will allow her to feel attraction. Theodore plays on Adeline's emotions precisely to the degree that he is restrained, controlled, victimized, and emasculated. To the degree, that is, that Theodore becomes *like a woman*, he is attractive to the heroine of *The Romance of the Forest*.

If Adeline can become a sister-lover to the suffering Theodore, that is not to say that the relation is naturalized in an unerotic way. For Radcliffe the Gothic centered upon discovering the threat of desire in the domestic realm, to which female novelistic characters were increasingly restricted, and then learning how to accommodate that desire to lived experience in the world. The Radcliffean endings, which have been decried for chasing away the ghost in disappointing "explanations," are nevertheless an attempt to bring the fantasy of female power back into a space in which it might have some real meaning. That space for Radcliffe is a maternalized space, just as her novels establish the maternal as the area of Gothic exploration. With this focus Radcliffe looks forward to later female writers, such as Charlotte Brontë and George Eliot, for both of whom the maternal specter holds a particular fascination and whose vision of male subjectivity is complicated in similar ways.

The other Radcliffe, Mary-Ann, whose publications traded on the popularity of her predecessor, can serve to suggest some of the more lurid contours Radcliffean "sublime" can assume. In *Manfroné, or, The One-Handed Monk* (1809), the demon-lover, who appropriately loses his hand in a duel with the heroine's father at the moment of attempting to rape her, soon returns as the mysterious monk who mumbles from behind his obfuscating cowl to "haunt" the heroine, Rosalina, first in the candlelit aisles of the abbey adjoining her father's castle; then in the subterranean passages that elaborately connect the abbey and the castle and contain in assorted dungeons pathetic prisoners variously thought to be murdered or otherwise victimized by Rosalina's hotheaded father; and finally as her father's guest in the castle itself. Rosalina laments the loss of her mother and learns the details of her history, slowly coming to realize that her father is a murderous tyrant who only stops short of killing *her*, in a crucial scene, because he is distracted by the shouts of his soldiers.

The novel is replete with midnight trysts, threatened sexual violence, and mere physical brutality, and it creates a "Gothic" atmosphere of unrelieved gloom. Nowhere are there the shimmering vistas of Ann Radcliffe, the picturesque moments that dispel the darkness with rays of hope. Here the misery and the victimization are total. The hero, Montalto, in this case a strong if ineffectual rival of both the father and Manfroné, manages to fight to save Rosalina from the villain, who has finally decided to stop at nothing to "possess" her. Montalto, like Theodore before him, must suffer symbolic castration before earning the right to rescue the heroine: "Twice was the murderous dagger upraised and twice did it drink the blood of Rosalina's fond lover!— Groaning, he sunk on the pavement, and the shades of death encompassed him." Later, surprisingly, he rises from this symbolic death of his masculinity into a union with the heroine, whom he frees from the father and the villain to join him in a bracing, if muted, conclusion.

Discussions of "female Gothic" have often centered on Mary Shelley's *Frankenstein, or, The Modern Prometheus* (1818). I will discuss that novel in a later section of this chapter, but it will be helpful here to mention some recent feminist readings of *Frankenstein* by such critics as Kate Ferguson Ellis, Sandra M. Gilbert and Susan Gubar, Barbara Johnson, and Mary Poovey. They have suggested that Shelley's tale has as much to do with female as male desire and that Victor Frankenstein's imaginative aspiration and his ungainly creation are by no means a celebration of male creativity. For Ellis, *Frankenstein* is a critique of bourgeois family life and an attempt to show that the "guilt-imposing" home is as nefarious as the public world of male domination. Gilbert and Gubar see the creature as a reflection of the silencing and oppression of the female in patriarchal culture, and they hear the creature's pleas as the entreaties of the author herself from within a marriage that was by no means "liberating." Johnson argues that the novel expresses the anxiety of motherhood and the horror of maternal responsibility that Shelley herself experienced. Finally, Mary Poovey suggests that the novel is about the conflict between the codes of Romantic "originality" and Victorian "female domesticity" and becomes "a troubled, veiled exploration of the price [Shelley] had already begun to fear . . . egotistical self-assertion [as an author] might exact." These are only a few of dozens of feminist readings that the novel has received, but they begin to demonstrate how rewarding such analysis can be.

All these critics seem to suggest that "female Gothic," while it hardly freed women from the limitations placed on them in contemporary culture, at least suggested ways in which their victimization—in the world outside Gothic fiction as well as within it—could be subverted both to turn patriarchal violence against itself and to claim a space for women. As Michelle Massé explains in her excellent chapter on Gothic masochism, many things can be named as sources of conflict in Gothic fiction, "but all point, in the best Gothic tradition, to something more ominous." In her analysis, that "something" is "the refusal of the heroine's existence as subject." That is why the idea of female space is so fraught in these works, both haunted and supported by the spectral mother who challenges patriarchy with the threat of undomesticated female power. Even the more "shocking" of these novels, such as *Manfroné*, insist on a resilient and even at times intrepid heroine. The thrill of survival is complemented, what is more, not by a paternal suitor who will protect but rather by a feminized hero who will join the heroine in her experience of the world and its vicissitudes. Admittedly, this seems little better than the brutally patriarchal closure that seemed inevitable in novels by the 1790s. But even this "little," I believe, begins to explain why "female Gothic" became popular for women in the later eighteenth century and remained so for ensuing generations.

Imps of the Perverse

The simple air of sexual violence in *The Castle of Otranto*—in which, because of Manfred's desire, his son Conrad is "dashed to pieces," his son's fiancée is brutalized, and his daughter is sacrificed to his unbridled lust—is raised to an eloquent expression of sadomasochistic, incestuous, homoerotic, and otherwise perverse transgression in a series of works that take their inspiration from the more sensationalistic imitators of Walpole. Among the first of such imitators is William Beckford, whose *Vathek* (1786), although not strictly a Gothic novel, provided a model for erotic brutality in fiction that became immediately available to Gothic writers. Such writers emphasized the horrific and sensational details of Gothic narrative at the expense of historical or even narrative credibility. As diverse in their specific concerns as any group of writers is likely to be, these authors all took such delight in moments of sexual intrigue, physical abuse, or monstrous psychological torment that any didactic aim of fiction was seemingly lost. What they shared, however, and what still attracts their audiences, was their willingness to confront areas of experience that were traditionally ignored. Inspired perhaps by the convention of the "imp of the perverse" sent from the devil to tempt hero or heroine with pleasures of the flesh and other modes of infernal seduction, these writers explored various forms of "perverse" or transgressive sexual practice: sadomasochism, incest, miscegenation, cannibalism, necrophilia, and homosexuality. They treated these issues as intelligently as they were treated anywhere at the time, including in medical literature or social science.

Vathek (1786) is more an "Oriental" tale than a Gothic novel. Concerned as it is, however, with necromancy and sensual indulgence, it has earned a place for itself in discussions of Gothic works. The title character, "ninth Caliph of the [proverbially pederastic] race of the Abassides," is an Eastern Faust, who has his own Mephistopheles in the form of Giaour, a monstrous emissary of the devil who goads him on to ever more energetic perversion. Various examples of what Beckford's own society would have considered sexually grotesque find praise in the novel. Vathek's appropriately named Palaces of the Five Senses, for instance, seem in themselves blissfully innocent, and it is only when the hero turns from physical satisfaction to intellectual pursuits that his desires begin to seem corrupt. An "insatiable curiosity" for knowledge leads him from the delectable pleasures of the flesh to the frustration of secret knowledge, until he is ready to sacrifice everything for the ability to know.

Vathek's approach to the world of forbidden knowledge is littered with corpses and animated with hatred. Children sent to celebrate his munificence are cast into the maw of his desires, and subjects who try to save him from a fire are consumed by the power of his will. Vathek's destructive self-indulgence and his desire for nefarious satisfaction may seem like an unconscious exposure of the author's own pederastic fascination. His appetites, after all, are a source of positive energy and could even save him from destruction, just as love seems to offer him freedom from the confines of morality. But instead both desire and love cause Vathek to feel that he is already damned, trapping him in a position of concupiscence and shame. This paradox the novel tries not so much to resolve as to bring into vivid relief: when Vathek achieves final damnation, his "burning" heart suggests that his very desire has consumed him.

In the continuation of *Vathek* that Beckford planned but never executed, other damned souls were to share with the caliph in the Halls of Eblis fully developed stories of pederasty, masochism, necrophilia, and incest. They were going to tell, that is, Gothic tales of their own damnation, which would defy the silence that culture imposes on such "perversity." Beckford himself knew the cost of violating that silence: he was hounded out of England on account of a handful of love letters penned to a young nephew. In a sense, *Vathek* is his own history of perversity, his own refusal to settle for the terms that culture offers.

In other novels that involve soul-selling, such as Charlotte Dacre's *Zofloya, or, The Moor* (1806), sexual desire is equally central to the damnation of the individual. In this novel, Dacre tells the story of the proud Victoria, who finds herself attracted to her husband's brother's immense servant Zofloya, who lures her with compliments and flattering asides. In a carefully constructed tale of gradual dissipation, Victoria sacrifices her relations to satisfy her seemingly insatiable desire, only slowly realizing that Zofloya alone can soothe her soul. Even at his first appearance in the novel, she finds herself obsessed with the darkly handsome servant. "Why *he* should be connected with her dreams, who never entered her mind when waking, she could not divine: but certain it was, that his exact resemblance, though as it were of polished and superior appearance, had chiefly figured in her troubled sight." Later, when he has encouraged her to murder her husband, attempt the seduction of her brother-in-law, Henriquez, and imprison and torture his fiancée, her relations with the Moor become more explicit. After Henriquez has killed himself, and Victoria is fleeing the authorities, she meets Zofloya in the mountains. Here she sees the Moor in "his proper sphere":

Dignity, and ineffable grace, were diffused over his whole figure;—for the first time she felt towards him an emotion of tenderness, blended with her admiration, and, strange inconsistency, amidst the gloomy terrors that pressed upon her breast, amidst the sensible misery that oppressed her, she experienced something like pride, in reflecting that a Being so wonderful, so superior, and so beautiful, should thus appear to be interested in her fate.

The implications of creating an "imp of the perverse" who is a seductive "Moor" has vast cultural and psychological implications. Anyone familiar with eighteenth-century literature knows that miscegenation was as frightening a "perversion" as incest or homosexuality to the cultural imagination. In the context of the present discussion, however, it is easy to see how Victoria's "desire" for Zofloya is precisely what leads her to destroy herself as she does. Her desire for the "Moor" falls outside what is socially acceptable and therefore subjects her to the Law that marks her as an aberration. In killing her husband and throwing herself at her husband's brother, Victoria is only playing out what desire itself has already rendered inevitable. External evil, in the form of Zofloya, is really only the evil of desire, insofar as it marks Victoria and places her, or rather displaces her, in a social structure. In an effective display of the ways in which private desire can be projected as ruthless Law, Zofloya himself casts Victoria into oblivion with a "loud demoniac laugh" at the novel's close. This is the "perverse" laugh of the desiring heroine herself as culture represents her.

Matthew G. Lewis's central plot in *The Monk* (1796)—that of the seemingly virtuous Monk Ambrosio, who is seduced by the scheming Matilda, herself disguised as the young novice Rosario—is fraught with uncontrollable sexual desire and motivated by "perverse" sexual transgression throughout. The ambiguous sexuality of Rosario/Matilda provides a backdrop of homoeroticism against which the larger dramas of the plot are played out. When Matilda herself turns out to be an agent of Satan—the catalyst of "perversity"—gender recedes as the determining factor in desire. Ambrosio's "lusts" would in any case be difficult to categorize.

After Ambrosio's desire for Matilda cools, he turns his lascivious attentions on the young Antonia, daughter of the proud Elvira, his confidante. Having employed occult arts to enter Antonia's bedchamber and render her defenseless against his lust, Ambrosio is interrupted by Elvira, who challenges and accuses him. He responds by murdering Elvira in one of the most brutal scenes of Gothic fiction: he grabs her, throws her on the bed, stifles her face with a pillow, kneels on her stomach, and struggles mercilessly as she wraps her arms around him in her final agony, until he realizes that she has become a "Corse, cold, senseless, and disgusting."

More than a hundred pages pass before the reader is informed that this woman with whom Ambrosio is struggling on the bed of his proposed sexual violation is in fact his own mother. The excessive emotion of what turns out to be the only "bed scene" in the novel, a scene between a sexually confused young man and his mother, seems in retrospect the emotional center of the work.

Antonia, who is therefore Ambrosio's sister, is not spared the incestuous obsession of the unfortunate friar. Toward the close of the novel, he discovers her in the underground vault of the Convent of St. Claire:

Naturally addicted to the gratification of the sense, in the full vigour of man-hood, and heat of blood, he had suffered his temperament to acquire such ascendancy, that his lust was become madness. . . . He longed for the posses-sion of [Antonia's] person; and even the gloom of the vault, the surrounding silence, and the resistance which He expected from her, seemed to give a fresh edge to his fierce and unbridled desires.

After Ambrosio accomplishes Antonia's "dishonour" in the "violence of his lustful delirium," he curses her fatal charms and blames her for his fall from grace. He determines further that she must never leave the dungeon. When she tries to escape, he kills her by plunging his dagger twice into her bosom—suggesting at once his incestuous desire and the murderous impulse it harbors.

Such scenes are usually dismissed as merely sensational. It seems to me that however sensationalistic such scenes seem, they are also as political as anything in late-eighteenth-century fiction. It is the nature of patriarchy to make incest, for instance, its most basic prohibition; for unless the terms of familial desire are carefully controlled, according to the logic of patriarchy, the fabric of society will break down. Studies by anthropologists such as Claude Lévi-Strauss and others have demon-strated that the distribution of power depends on the control of intrafa-milial relations by means of an "exchange" of women and that the incest taboo serves as much a political as a sexual function.

When Ambrosio "rapes" and murders his mother Elvira for getting in the way of his desire for Antonia; and when he rapes and murders his sister Antonia because she comes to represent the hideousness of his own desires; he violently transgresses the most basic law of patriarchal culture. After Ambrosio is informed of his incestuous violations, dur-ing the closing pages of the novel, he is horrified. But this horror comes so late that the effect of the incest is at least potentially subversive and that by abusing the relations between himself and his mother and sister he is doing more than giving his villainous character an appallingly misogynist twist. The act of incest is political because it defies the attempt of society to control desire. Cultural critics have suggested that the regulation of marriage ties is a restriction that serves the purposes of the patriarchy; Ambrosio at the very least defies such a restriction in his experiments with "perversion." In raping and murdering the women in his life, moreover, Ambrosio underlines the other, the forbidden desire that Rosario at first represented. At one point in the midst of Ambrosio's decline into wickedness, the narrator tells us that in a moment of reflection "He regretted Rosario, the fond, the gentle, and submissive." If Ambrosio must be forced to fulfill the role of the male in patriarchal culture, he does so violently, with none of the subterfuge at work in the society around him. He turns the romantic fiction inside out in order to show that sexuality is always about power and that power, perhaps more importantly, is always about sexuality.

Michel Foucault, the French historian of sexuality, would argue that this attempt at subversion is not only doomed to failure but is in fact an aspect of the extension of cultural control that he calls "the deployment of sexuality." Foucault claims that sexuality itself becomes a mode of social knowledge and control. "In a society such as ours," he says, "where the family is the most active site of sexuality, and where it is doubtless the exigencies of the latter which maintain and prolong its existence, incest . . . occupies a central place; it is constantly being solicited and refused; it is an object of obsession and attraction, a dreadful secret and an indispensable pivot." But Lewis exposes this "affective intensification of the family space" and ridicules the terms of the Oedipal "fantasy" almost as directly as Foucault does. By turning the Oedipal "fantasy" into vivid and horrifying reality, Lewis exposes the very process of cultural control that Foucault came later to describe. What Foucault calls the pathologization of pleasure has its fictional equivalent in a novel like *The Monk*, in which sexuality becomes a form of public madness that defies the culture that would attempt to control, contain, or even know it.

The characters in Charles Robert Maturin's *Melmoth the Wanderer* (1820) manage not to succumb to the nefarious skill of the infernal Melmoth, the "perverse" emissary who appears in each of the several interpolated tales of the novel to tempt them with "escape" from present difficulties. They do not need to sell their souls to the devil, however, when their bodies have already condemned them to a hell on earth.

In the most famous of the interpolated tales, for instance, "The Tale of the Spaniard," Alonzo de Monçada tells the story of his own incarceration at the hands of the Inquisition. The political abuses of the Inquisition are hideous and disturbing, as are the intrusions of infernal temptation; but Maturin makes the body itself the site of transgression. The body, in other words, traps the subject within an ideology that literally dismembers the body for its own purposes. When Monçada and a guide are pushing their way through an underground passage, which is so constricted it almost to causes suffocation, Monçada says that he "could not help recollecting and *applying*" a story about a group of travelers exploring the vaults of the Egyptian pyramids. "One of them . . . who was advancing as I was, on his hands and knees, stuck in the passage, and, whether from terror, or from the natural consequences of his situation, swelled so that it was impossible for him to retreat, advance, or allow a passage for his companions." When the others realize that this companion threatens their own survival, their guide "proposed, in the selfishness to which the feeling of vital danger reduces all, to cut off the limbs of the wretched being who obstructed their passage." At this suggestion, the companion manages somehow to squeeze himself out of the way. "He was suffocated, however, in the effort, and left behind a corse." What is interesting here is not just the vivid portrayal of the physical effects of fear. Notice that the community of travelers is beset by fear because one individual has "blocked" their passage. They have no trouble planning to free their own way by dismembering the person before them. It could be said that this act, this brutal and self-centered substitute for castration, helps to dramatize the ways in which bourgeois culture handles the individual. Castration, figurative or literal, is all there is for those who stand in the way of what the culture values most, in this case its own survival.

When later in his tale, Monçada hears the tale of illicit heterosexual love in the confines of a monastery, the result is strikingly similar. In this case, his companion tells him the story of a novice and her growing sentimental attachment to a young monk. The narrator, a "parricide," gives the following account:

One evening as the young monk and his darling novice were in the garden, the former plucked a peach, which he immediately offered to his favourite; the latter accepted it with a movement I thought rather awkward—it seemed like what I imagined would be the reverence of a female. The young monk divided the peach with a knife; in doing so, the knife grazed the finger of the novice, and the monk, in agitation inexpressible, tore his habit to bind up the wound. I saw it all—my mind was made up on the business—I went to the Superior that very night. The result may be conceived. They were watched.

After setting a trap for the two, after he is certain that they have arranged to spend the night together, the parricide brings the Superior and other monks to witness the depravity: "we burst into the cell. The wretched husband and wife were locked in each others arms. You may imagine the scene that followed."

The convent's Superior, "who had no more idea of the intercourse between the sexes, than between two beings of different species," is so horrified at this spectacle of "two human beings of different sexes, who dared to love one another," that his own sexual proclivities may be called into question. If they are; if, that is, he represents the "homosexuality" implicit in monastic life, he also helps to explain how what is transgressive in one context becomes the very agent of cultural control in another. The kind of surveillance that comes "naturally" in a convent—religious life builds surveillance into its communal system—here has had the salubrious effect of ferreting out heterosexual desire and extirpating it from the society in question. Such surveillance succeeds by employing those who would otherwise find themselves in violation of the Law they are so desperate to serve.

What does happen is that these lovers are lured, as they try to escape, into the underground passages of the convent and are trapped there by the parricide in a chamber that is nailed shut and from which they can never escape. Before long they turn on one another, and before the narration ceases, the husband sinks his teeth into the wasted flesh of his mate. This cannibalistic conclusion to a tale of sexual transgression is not unique to Maturin, but it is presented here as a deft reminder of the relativity of desire. Love becomes literally an appetite, and desire becomes indistinguishable from murderous aggression. By walling these young lovers up in the subterranean passage and listening to their moans, the parricide acts out the cultural mechanism that the Gothic harbors at its core.

If male homosexuality is one of the secrets of Gothic fiction, as it seems at first to be in the scene just cited, and as it is in *Vathek* and *The Monk* as well as in *Frankenstein* and in *The Private Memoirs and Confessions of a Justified Sinner*, which I shall discuss, it includes the subversive potential of desire that is not subject to the Oedipal fantasy that patriarchy has provided for the control of relations. What has happened in these works is that a particular version of cultural subversion has been codified, with the result that desire itself becomes a cause for the particular forms of cultural hysteria suggested in repeated scenes of mob violence, brutal beatings, and even murderous conflagrations. Eve Kosofsky Sedgwick has argued that identification and desire are inextricable in "homosocial" relations. Where she sees male heterosexual empowerment, however, I think it is also possible to discern the beginnings of an organized "homosexual" protest against the status quo. For it is not just that the relations among men tend to exclude women, but also that the desire that is articulated between men seems only to be expressible in terms of violence and abuse. Gothic fiction is at least partly about "homosexual panic," the fear of acknowledging those forms of desire that threaten society's regulation and control of sexuality. But it is also, in the cases I outline, about the debilitating quality of that control. The force of cultural subordination is itself a Gothic nightmare, and these novelists are as ready as anyone to acknowledge that force and perhaps to defy it.

What is powerful about these works is their ability to articulate this "horror" without flinching at its cultural implications. In Maturin's account especially, the values of the culture, the force of "good," is represented by a man who has murdered his father. The Law of the Father, in other words, is a self-victimizing law, a system that inevitably defeats itself. Gothic fiction looks at how that defeat occurs and posits an anarchy of desire outside of social control. Or at least it tries to posit such desire, for of course in an ideological system such as that flourishing in the later eighteenth and early nineteenth centuries, as in our own, there is no "escape."

Double Vision

The relation between an individual and the cultural constraints that define her or him is most vividly portrayed, both within Gothic fiction and without, in the figure of the evil twin, the alter-ego, the double. Doubles appear often enough in Gothic novels to be thought of as the sine qua non of the genre. This last section discusses the conventions of the double as they are employed in three more works of Gothic fiction.

Sedgwick argues persuasively in *Between Men* that a certain strain of Gothic fiction finds an analogy in Freud's case history of Dr. Schreber, the state judge who published an account of his own bizarre psychological experiences that was later studied by Freud. For Sedgwick it is clear that "paranoia is the psychosis that makes graphic the mechanisms of homophobia." Sedgwick describes a "large subgroup" of classic Gothic novels, "whose plots might be mapped almost point for point onto the case of Dr. Schreber: most saliently each is about one or more males who not only is persecuted by, but considers himself transparent to and often under the compulsion of, another male." In Freud's case history Schreber tells, with shame but without equivocation, of his sense that an ever-watchful God has chosen him for a special communication. In order to receive this communication, which would come in the form of divine rays preferably through his anus, Schreber felt that God insisted on his dressing in woman's underwear in order to create the "voluptuousness" appropriate to the "wife" of God. Freud interprets Schreber's paranoia as an elaborate displacement in which Schreber avoids confronting his own homosexuality.

Ignoring the homophobia that is rife in Freud's own text, I find two things useful for my argument here: first, he has made explicit the connection between paranoia and sexuality, and, second, he shows how, in the Schreber case, the source of patriarchal law becomes the very agent of sexual transgression. Schreber "loves" the very God who is watching and who will punish him. Surveillance and desire, in other words, are inextricably bound in the workings of Schreber's private "nightmare." But Schreber's private nightmare is, in fact, the nightmare of culture itself. God, authority, and Law become the brutal, victimizing "top" in a sadomasochistic configuration of desire.

In *Caleb Williams* (1794), William Godwin portrays such a configuration. The novel tells of the personal obsession of a young man for the elusive secrets of an older, mysterious benefactor. James Thompson suggests that the novel is a story of "surveillance," in which psychology and politics are both at work and in which paranoia becomes a political as well as a psychological condition. "To put this as simply as possible," Thompson says, "surveillance in *Caleb Williams* should be seen not merely in terms of the function of an authoritarian state, the professionalization of the police force, and the development of the penitentiary. . . . As an anarchist, Godwin was vitally interested in the mechanisms by which the state extended its influence of power into the lives of individual subjects." Lacan says that "desire becomes bound up with the desire of the Other, but that in this loop is the desire to know." Desire/Other/Knowledge: this figure emerges repeatedly in Gothic fiction as the figure of haunting. The double stands precisely at the "junction" of desire and knowledge, which, for Lacan, is the "junction . . . out of which revolutions come."

Caleb Williams anticipates this triad in a vivid portrayal of male-male desire. Caleb's obsession with his master, Falkland, and the history of Falkland's relation with his enemy Tyrrel form the dramatic center of the work. The socially fraught relations between these three men are sexualized in various ways: Caleb's interest in Falkland has sexual overtones from early in the novel, and he talks openly, even aggressively, about his "love" for his benefactor; Falkland, who in turn is described as having "polished manners . . . particularly in harmony with feminine delicacy," becomes locked in rivalries with both Caleb and his uncouth neighbor Tyrrel; Tyrrel mocks Falkland "as an animal that was beneath contempt" and clearly displays his jealousy of this ladies' man; Falkland in a fit of rage stabs Tyrrel from behind; and so on. Sexuality itself is understood in terms of power in each of these relations. Desire person- alizes power inequalities in a way that makes the police state an inevitability, as Thompson argues. For the minute that Caleb finds his master interesting enough to "know," Caleb's entire story falls into place. He seeks knowledge and then he is sought by it. When Falkland becomes the hunter, with Law on his side, Caleb is doomed. Once drawn into the ideological structure that is figured in the triad Desire/Other/Knowledge, in other words, he is trapped in the structure of the Law itself, from which there is no escape.

Mary Shelley's *Frankenstein* (1818) tells the tale of a very different young man, but one with similarly "unspeakable" longings: "It was the secrets of heaven and earth that I desired to learn," Victor Frankenstein tells us. In his "fervent longing to penetrate the secrets of nature," Frankenstein articulates a desire that is not a mere physical response to people in the world, but rather an intellectual response to the physical workings of the world itself. It is strange, therefore, that the terms in which his desires are worked out are so strikingly familiar; the challenge to authority and the incestuous terms of his project are established by methods almost identical to those used in other works I have considered.

Victor Frankenstein creates a second self out of the assorted body parts he finds in his assiduous trips to graveyards and charnel houses. When he first encounters his creation, however, he greets it with some- thing less than pleasure:

I started from my sleep with horror; a cold dew covered my forehead, my teeth chattered, and every limb became convulsed: when, by the dim and yellow light of the moon, as it forced its way through the window shutters, I beheld the wretch—the miserable monster whom I had created. He held up the curtain of the bed; and his eyes, if eyes they may be called, were fixed on me. His jaws opened, and he muttered some inarticulate sounds, while a grin wrinkled his cheeks.

This passage centers itself, as all of Gothic fiction does, on the con- frontation with the horror that is oneself, the horror that one's relation to the world is painfully inappropriate and distorting to the privacy of self and that the life that one wants so desperately is really only a death that one can barely escape. Moonlight is used here to create a world between light and darkness and to suffuse the scene with its unsettling glare. Just as the animated corpse seems a figure of death-in-life, so the moonlight is a light that suggests darkness—later it becomes metaphorically associated with the creature. Here, it "forced its way through the window shutters," as a way of suggesting that Frankenstein cannot shut out the light of knowledge he has discovered; nor can he himself hide from the pursuit of his creation, who here peeps into the bed where he has sought refuge. A waking dream? The detail of observation—the eyes, the grin, the hand—all suggest the grotesque reality of this vision. The personal pronoun "I" is the real center of attention, and the creature exists as an object, to be observed, to be feared, and to be rejected. Desire/Other/Knowledge: Victor Frankenstein has worked hard to take control of the forces of this triad. In doing so, he has created the myth that is a part of modern culture, and he has given his name to that myth. Frankenstein and his creature have become one in the popular imagination because culture makes certain that Frankenstein's desire is turned back on himself.

James Hogg's *Private Memoirs and Confessions of a Justified Sinner* (1824) dramatizes the haunted relationship between Robert Wringham and his satanic double Gil Martin. In the first of the novel's two parts, "The Editor's Narrative," the bookish and lonely Robert Wringham forms an emotional attachment to his lively and athletic older stepbrother, George. Gradually Robert, variously described as "devilish-looking," "moody and hellish looking," with "a deep and malignant eye," becomes a kind of "shadow" to George, who tries in vain to avoid the inevitable physical confrontation that leaves Robert a bloodied victim, symbolically castrated and feminized. George begins to see Robert as a "limb of Satan" and starts to feel that he is haunted by "some evil genius in the shape of his brother." Shortly later, George is struck down (from behind) and Robert, after various complications, disappears.

In the second part of the novel, "Private Memoirs and Confessions of a Sinner, written by himself," Robert tells the story of his own haunting by a double. In a narrative that suggests a paranoid relation to the world, he admits seeing the "beauty of women . . . as the greatest snare to which mankind are subjected." Isolated in his particularly virulent misogyny, he becomes "open" to the seduction of the mysterious Gil Martin, who teaches Calvinist "justification" as a creed that legitimates the acting out of suppressed desires, and which leads Robert into a series of self-justifying acts of violence against other men. Not surprisingly, the only relations charged with emotion are those between men: Hogg is exposing the inner workings of a culture that objectifies women and places male relations under strict scrutiny. "I had heart-burnings, longings, and yearnings, that would not be satisfied," Robert Wringham tells his readers: his desire literally consumes him, and his alter-ego has become a function of ego itself.

In her discussion of this novel, Sedgwick says that "As [Robert] pushes blindly, with the absurdly and pathetically few resources he has, toward the male homosocial mastery that alone and delusively seems to promise him a social standing, the psychologized homophobic struggle inside him seems to hollow out an internalized space that too exactly matches the world around him." The double works as an effective fictional representation of this replicated vision. Gil Martin has an intimate knowledge of his "subject" because internal paranoia and cultural conditioning are one and the same. The paranoia Robert Wringham expresses, in other words, is the paranoia that culture breeds in those among its members who are tempted to transgress the narrow limits of the "normal." As a "late" Gothic hero, Robert Wringham recognizes that the guilt he feels, as well as the special justification he claims, are the prices that culture exacts for offering him even his tentative place at its margin. In this novel, then, subjectivity itself is the source of the haunting. "Transgression" and "perversity" have been planted within the individual psyche in order to do the work of culture more effectively. Gothic fiction has dramatized this transition and has decried its effects in various ways, but nowhere more effectively than in these double visions.

Gothic Success/Gothic Failure

In the eighties and early nineties, there has been a resurgence of critical interest in the Gothic, which at the time of this writing shows no sign of waning. Excellent studies, such as those listed in the bibliography, and others by Margaret L. Carter, William Patrick Day, Annie LeBrun, Ellen Moers, David Punter, Joseph Wissenfarth, and Judith Wilt, have moved the Gothic from the margins of literary history and criticism to the center of the debates on cultural, psychological, social, and political criticism. At least one critic, however, argues that Gothic fiction is a failure: Elizabeth Napier claims that "the imprecision and extremes to which the Gothic has been subjected are in part a result of instability and cross-purposes in the form itself." It is important to understand, however, that the instability of Gothic "form" is a function of Gothic content. For if I am right in describing the Gothic as the scene of conflicted emotion, "aberrant" desire, social torment, public transgression, and patriarchal victimization, then no "formal stability" could represent the implicit contradictions, inconsistencies, and subversive impulses that give Gothic its energy of resistance.

In Gothic fiction, writers, readers, and critics are engaged, to some degree in spite of themselves, in an enterprise that breaks fictional codes in order to bring into high relief the inconsistencies of normative culture. That it can be neither systematically described nor legally codified is one of its strengths. For Gothic fiction both reflects and reacts to the increasingly ruthless limitations that "cultural subordination" imposes. Maternal specters, incestuous desire, intrafamilial aggression, sadomasochistic relations, romantic friendship, homosexuality, necromancy, or necrophilia—all signify resistance to the culture's impulse to define and deny "perversity."

In *Gothic Fiction/Gothic Form*, I described the attempt of Gothic writers to find in the "tale" the appropriate affective form for the expression of private obsessions. But in their frenzied brutality and uncensored sexual explicitness, in their broken narratives and strings of "local" effects, Gothic novels refuse to subscribe to the cultural "narratives" that were being written to control and contain private desire. However conventional they are, or however predictable in their horrors they become, Gothic novels resist the mechanisms of repression and work to subvert literary expectations and cultural assumptions. If this is their perversity, it is also their power.

George E. Haggerty

Selected Bibliography

Ellis, Kate Ferguson. *The Contested Castle: Gothic Novels and the Subversion of Domestic Ideology*. Urbana, Ill.: University of Illinois Press, 1989.

Foucault, Michel. *The History of Sexuality*. Vol. 1, *An Introduction*. Trans. Robert Hurley. New York: Vintage-Random House, 1980.

Gilbert, Sandra M., and Susan Gubar. *The Madwoman in the Attic: The Woman Writer and the Nineteenth-Century Literary Imagination.* New Haven, Conn.: Yale University Press, 1979.

Haggerty, George E. *Gothic Fiction/Gothic Form.* University Park: Pennsylvania State University Press, 1989.

Johnson, Barbara. "My Monster/My Self." *Diacritics* 12 (1982): 2–10.

Kahane, Claire. "The Gothic Mirror." In Shirley Nelson Garner, Claire Kahane, and Madelon Springnether, eds., *The (M)other Tongue: Essays in Feminist Psychoanalytic Interpretation.* Ithaca, N.Y.: Cornell University Press, 1985.

Keily, Robert. *The Romantic Novel in England.* Cambridge, Mass.: Harvard University Press, 1972.

Lacan, Jacques. *Écrits: A Selection.* Trans. Alan Sheridan. New York: Norton, 1977.

Lévy, Maurice. *Le roman "gothique" anglais, 1764–1824.* Toulouse: Associations des Publications de la Faculté des Lettres et des Sciences Humaines de Toulouse, 1968.

Massé, Michelle A. *In the Name of Love: Women, Masochism, and the Gothic.* Women Reading Women. Ithaca, N.Y.: Cornell University Press, 1992.

Napier, Elizabeth R. *The Failure of Gothic: Problems of Disjunction in an Eighteenth-Century Literary Form.* Oxford: Clarendon, 1987.

Sedgwick, Eve Kosofsky. *Between Men: English Literature and Male Homosexual Desire.* New York: Columbia University Press, 1985.

Thompson, James. "Surveillance in William Godwin's *Caleb Williams.*" In K. W. Graham, ed., *Gothic Fictions: Prohibition/Transgression*, 173–98. New York: AMS Press, 1989.

Wolff, Cynthia Griffin. "The Radcliffean Gothic Model: A Form for Female Sexuality." *Modern Language Studies* 9 (1979): 98–113.

Novels of the 1790s: Action and Impasse

NOVELISTS of the 1790s articulated new ambitions and claimed new status for their genre, often abandoning the defensive tone that had dominated earlier justifications of the novel. Richardson's elaborate proclamations of moral purpose, for instance, had presupposed the prevailing belief that fiction generated dubious moral effects, encouraging the young to think too much about love and fostering idleness, fantasy, and the substitution of sentimental self-indulgence for benevolent action. Theoretically, imaginative like literal history could teach its readers about life. In practice, the multiplying "histories" of young men and young women faced with such problems as confronting the sexual advances of a titled and lascivious London woman or escaping the horrors of a secluded Italian castle might instead cause their readers to find actual experience unsatisfying. Virtually all eighteenth-century novelists announced their impeccable moral intent, but little evidence suggests that even avid consumers of fiction thought its principal effects uplifting.

Political actualities in the century's final decade altered literary as well as other possibilities. In the aftermath of the French Revolution, British and Continental thinkers alike grappled with freshly articulated questions about individual rights and social responsibility. Although the Terror in France, particularly the execution of the king and queen, aroused horror on the other side of the English Channel, the impetus to imagine a more equitable social order remained powerful. In response to radical insistence on the inadequacies of current social arrangements, Parliament instituted a series of fierce repressive mea-

sures. Printers of "revolutionary" material were prosecuted and imprisoned. Those who attended as well as those who addressed "seditious"
public meetings risked their freedom. Writers took sides. One thinks
most readily of Burke and Paine as symbolic literary antagonists in the
period, but a host of novelists likewise entered the fray, both on the side
of the established order and in support of new political imaginings.

At the eighteenth century's end, novelists made explicit ideological
claims and manifested new kinds of theoretical self-awareness. Their
consciousness of the possibility of changing minds and hearts matters
more to their fictions' effect than do their specific political positions,
which range across a broad spectrum. "Every writer who advances principles, whether true or false, that have a tendency to set the mind in
motion, does good," Mary Hays maintains in her preface to *Memoirs of
Emma Courtney*. Truth matters less than energy. The activity of the
mind, to whatever end, is a self-evident good. The argument that fiction's moral function depends not on the doctrine it advances but on the
action it produces marks the new emphasis of the 1790s. William Godwin, in a preface to Mary Wollstonecraft's fragmentary *Wrongs of
Woman*, suggests that "these sketches," if "filled up in a manner adequate to the writer's conception, would perhaps have given a new
impulse to the manners of a world." He too claims that fiction generates productive action. Late-century novelists implicitly acknowledge
the contested nature of all doctrine as they articulate new social possibilities or defend established custom against perceived threats. They
seek and sometimes find innovative ways "to set the mind in motion."

Novels written well before the 1790s, it goes without saying, had
managed to set their readers' minds in motion. Debate about the characters of Clarissa and Pamela, and consequently about the import of the
novels they inhabited, began with Richardson's earliest readers, continued despite his insistent and explicit asseveration of his novels' moral
meaning, and has only intensified over the centuries. Defoe and Smollett, sentimental novels and Gothic: virtually all more or less "canonical" eighteenth-century fiction has stimulated controversy over its psychological or ideological significance. But the statements of intent by
such writers as Hays, Godwin, and Wollstonecraft establish an
unprecedented context for novelistic endeavor by subordinating the
importance of fixed meaning to that of energizing action.

The postulate that the novel may spur intellectual and ultimately
social action implies not only a new sense of fiction's importance but a

specific set of problems for novels of the 1790s. For instance, novelists faced the challenge of imagining worthy action for characters as well as for readers. If a novel aspired not only to instruct its reader in norms of virtuous and mannerly behavior but to provoke mental activity, must it not reconceive the possibilities of human conduct? Old plots, familiar characters doing familiar things, would not energize the mind, yet new models for action seemed hard to come by. Benevolence, sanctioned by the tradition of the sentimental novel, provided the established way to manifest active virtue. Even Hermsprong, Robert Bage's idealized version of "man as he is not," finds little to do with himself beyond bestowing good on others. He offers verbal defiance to an oppressor, and he stops a runaway horse, saving the heroine's life. But mainly he gives away money to worthy recipients, calms social unrest, and helps the poor and the sick. Like most of the period's protagonists, he also talks a lot, offering the rhetoric of a new vision that seldom manifests itself in radically new forms of action.

Far from acting in powerful, exemplary ways, male protagonists often assume the role of victim. Caleb Williams, the title character in William Godwin's remarkable 1794 novel, gets in trouble by virtue of a quality labeled "curiosity" but subsequently struggles mainly for survival, a goal that leads him to self-defeating revenge and finally to despair. Walsingham Ainsworth, protagonist of Mary Robinson's *Walsingham; or, The Pupil of Nature* (1797), fills four volumes with letters reporting his own helpless misery. His eventual happiness, briefly related, results from no action of his own. Orlando Somerive, the central male figure of Charlotte Smith's *Old Manor House* (1794), declares his right of self-determination in his choice of a bride but exercises no choice in the matter of a career, becoming a soldier because someone gives him a commission. Sent to America to fight in a war he does not understand, he suffers as the victim of incomprehensible social forces. Like Caleb, he seeks to survive.

As for heroines, they too—with the notable exception of Anna St. Ives—often function as victims or as reactors rather than as self-sustaining actors. Matilda, the second-generation heroine of Elizabeth Inchbald's *Simple Story* (1791), in its structure and its implications one of the period's most strikingly original novels, reads and weeps and gazes out the window but performs no willed action more significant than caressing her father's hat. The central female figure in *Hermsprong* vacillates between doing what her father wants and what her lover wants. What she herself wants can only determine her action insofar as it conforms to the will of male authority. The heroine of *The Old Manor House* suffers and suffers. Her noteworthy action, like that of Gothic heroines, consists of escape.

For women in these novels (again, Anna St. Ives constitutes the startling exception), marriage still determines fate. In other words, despite novelists' implicit and explicit claims to help innovate ideological possibility, existing social frameworks impose themselves at the level of assumption. Writers have difficulty imagining around them. Their perplexity about what fictional characters can *do* perhaps suggests why the period's novelists, seeking to effect action in their readers' minds, emphasize in their characters the importance of internal rather than external activity—"energy of mind." Internal vitality alone, late-eighteenth-century fiction suggests, allows new behaviors to be imagined. Even those claiming ideological purpose understand its fulfillment to depend on individual psychology.

The problem of how characters act within the plots of 1790s novels leads to further questions about action, none consistently resolved in the period's fictions and all crucial to subsequent developments. Four of these questions will organize my discussion of the period's fiction. How does the problem of action implicate the imagining of character? What is the relation between feeling and action in the generation of plot? How do "public" and "private" action bear on one another? How does the notion of action affect that of form? To investigate these questions will help to clarify ideological aspirations and insufficiencies in these novels and to define sources of the emotional and intellectual energy manifest in the texts themselves.

Action and Character

Many novelists of the 1790s found gender—to their minds a primary constituent of character—problematic. Conventional eighteenth-century assumptions about gender will even now sound familiar. Women defined their femininity by passivity, concern for others, and "natural" preoccupation with pleasing those around them. The good woman, rigorously chaste, devoted her life to service: to caring for parents, husband, children, to charitable efforts in the community. Emotion dominated her character and often determined her actions; reason belonged especially to men, although the novel of sensibility had established the principle that feeling might also signify male virtue and that women too must cultivate reason. Men were above all *manly*—a word novels obsessively reiterate to imply courage, fortitude, assertiveness, and moral uprightness. Men's superior intellectual powers and superior strength entailed the obligation of leadership. Men decided—"naturally"—what women should do.

None of these truisms remained unchallenged as the century neared its end. A new wave of feminism, stimulated by the French Revolution and its doctrine of equality, affected even conservative writers. Hannah More herself, who held fast to old truths and was unwilling even to read Mary Wollstonecraft's *Vindication of the Rights of Woman* (on the ground that women already had more power than was good for them), believed that women deserved education to bring them closer to parity with men. And far more radical ideas made their way into fiction.

Perhaps the most economical novelistic expression of the challenge to gender categories appears in *Walsingham*. Its protagonist whines interminably about his persecution by his cousin Sidney, who has deprived him of a privileged position with his aunt and uncle and who Walsingham believes has seduced his beloved Isabella. Isabella marries another, announcing that she has always considered Walsingham a brother. The novel's last two pages explain everything: Sidney is a woman. She has lived in male disguise from infancy, the victim of her mother's avarice. (Her father's will provides greater rewards to his widow if she bears a male child.) She loves Walsingham as a prospective husband. Ecstatic, Walsingham writes his confidante of

the heroic virtues of my transcendent Sidney! Indeed, so completely is she changed, so purely gentle, so feminine in manners; while her mind still retains the energy of that richly-treasured dignity of feeling which are [*sic*] the effects of a masculine education, that I do not lament past sorrows, while my heart triumphs, nobly triumphs in the felicity of present moments.

A woman with heroic virtues and feminine manners, with "dignity of feeling" (not sloppy, feminine feeling) and energy of mind, feminine in manners, masculine in education, a woman who transcends the limitations ordinarily attached to her gender—such a woman can compensate a man for any suffering.

The androgynous ideal suggested by Sidney's rather unconvincing transformation invested other newly imagined characters as well. *Anna St. Ives* (1792) and its eponymous heroine exemplify the fresh novelistic possibilities. The fairy-tale plot of low-born lover winning rich and beautiful lady assumes an unfamiliar form, given Thomas Holcroft's innovative conception of female thought and action. The result—a work that retains dramatic excitement despite an abundance of doctrinal lectures by its virtuous characters—demonstrates how assumptions about gender delineate the parameters of novelistic action.

From *Clarissa* and *Pamela* through *Evelina* and *Cecilia* to Wollstonecraft's *Mary*, novels titled with women's names abound in the eighteenth century. In most of them, including even Wollstonecraft's, the heroines react—sometimes ingeniously and courageously—to situations created by men. Anna St. Ives generates situations to which men must react. Initially she allows herself to be courted by Coke Clifton, a man chosen for her by others. Even this acceptance of outside influence, however, stems from her own determination to make Clifton into a man who will contribute greatly to social good. Meanwhile, Frank Henley, son of her father's steward, loves her. She leads him to confess his love, acknowledges hers for him, kisses him (extraordinary behavior for an eighteenth-century heroine), and persuades him to join her in improving Clifton's character. Later, having decided that Clifton does not merit their effort, she announces her intent to marry Frank instead. Clifton arranges to abduct the lovers, confining them in separate impregnable strongholds. Anna escapes, climbing a wall to do so. Frank, also eludes captivity, wounding Clifton in the process. Anna presides over the subsequent arrangements, which promise a ménage à quatre (with Clifton's sister its fourth member) designed to make everyone happier and better, whatever their personal desires.

On what basis, Holcroft's novel inquires, do men and women accept preestablished limits on their opportunities for action? Why can't a woman kiss a man, if a man can kiss a woman? Why can't a woman climb a wall? Why can't a man be instructed by a woman? Why can't a woman initiate moral action? To imagine such possibilities fulfilled surpasses all bounds of "realism"—although aspects of Clifton's response seem almost comically realistic, as he experiences the frustration of dealing with a woman who refuses to act like one. Clifton belongs to the world as it is. Anna, behaving as though no such world exists, provides a blueprint for the future.

Frank and Anna resemble other eighteenth-century protagonists in their marked "sensibility" and in their orthodox insistence on the importance of controlling passion by reason. But they differ from their fictional predecessors in maintaining an equation between pure energy and passion under the control of reason. Both characters, as they repeatedly stipulate, place the good of society before their own. Both test their own conduct by its utility for social improvement. Both see themselves (and each other) as energized by their high social goals. Initially Anna sees Clifton too as a possessor of striking energy, as someone worthy of her effort. As it becomes clear that Clifton believes the fulfillment of his individual desires to be a sufficient reason for his existence, Anna feels increasingly contemptuous toward him. When he confronts her, intending rape, she sounds like Clarissa as she argues that her soul is above him, but she invokes no religious authority, instead claiming androgynous internal power. "Courage has neither sex nor form: it is an energy of mind, of which your base proceedings shew I have infinitely the most." Given that fact, it follows, in her view, that she will triumph, and so she does.

Not only does Anna kiss Frank, she tells Clifton's sister and Clifton himself about it. Her fiancé feels angry, but he dissembles. Anna does not anticipate his anger. Her motives, she considers, are pure, for her highest principle is "truth." Because of her conviction that truth will always prove its power, it does not occur to her that her action, and her proclamation of it, might be misinterpreted. The kiss-and-tell episode may seem to support the charge of psychological implausibility frequently brought against Holcroft, but in fact this novel's enterprise depends on the transposition of psychological terms into moral ones. Although the major characters announce their intense and complicated feelings, those feelings express themselves most persuasively through their convictions. Even Clifton, making atrocious plans for kidnap and rape, invokes hallowed principles of male supremacy to justify his behavior toward Anna and truisms about class hierarchy to explain his detestation of Frank. Frank's avaricious and reprehensible father acts on the basis of self-love, a principle he explicitly endorses. He feels as profoundly justified in embezzling money as Frank and Anna feel in planning their own union in order to improve the state of society.

The text never explicitly suggests that rationalization allows these characters to fulfill their desires. Indeed, the elevated tone in which Frank and Anna declare their high intentions seems to endorse them. Yet meretricious as well as admirable behavior allows for justification by principle. If the central characters' energy derives, as they claim, from their ability to use their passions under the control of reason, the novel's energy stems partly from its capacity to hint at the ways in which passion may direct reason even as reason loudly proclaims its dominance. Frank and Anna, after all, get what they want most: each other. And they take subtle revenge on Clifton, forcing him to exist within their domestic system. They accomplish the aims of passion by dedicating themselves—passionately—to the service of principle. Clifton, with more dubious principles, suffers from conflicting passions. He can't win.

Holcroft does not demonstrate a capacity for delicate psychological analysis. But his imagining of a somewhat androgynous hero and heroine shows his ability to depict the use of abstract concepts to serve personal ends. Anna (like Sidney in *Walsingham*, but more convincingly) has the courage, knowledge, and moral force of a man, with the gentleness, grace, and compassion of a woman. Frank, likewise possessed of courage and integrity, willingly subordinates himself to a woman's leadership. His ambiguous status as the son of a servant, prevented by his father's greed from receiving university education, provides a metaphorical equivalent for his "feminized" aspect, which is signaled most loudly by his unfailing compassion and helpfulness. Both characters embody political ideals. They thus indicate new ways to imagine fictional heroes and heroines.

The woman possessed of male as well as female virtues appears even in novels by writers of politically conservative orientation. About Mary Ann Hanway, Gina Luria observes in the introduction to a modern facsimile edition of *Ellinor*, "nothing is known." Her conservative views, however, emerge clearly in the novel, published in 1798, which consistently celebrates old ways in preference to new. Its heroine proves fairly orthodox in her femininity, although more self-reliant than earlier fictional young women forced to make their way without the sanction of known families. She saves herself by virtue of her "powerful and energetic mind"—a characteristic now no longer assigned only to men. A peripheral character, Lady John, embodies the virtues of the "masculinized" woman. If she makes herself slightly ridiculous by her predilection for riding and hunting, she acts with unostentatious benevolence and with high regard for the freedom of others. Moreover, Lady John employs a rhetoric of deep conviction:

I have, from the time I threw off my frock, stood up a champion for the *rights of women*; have boldly thrown down my gauntlet to support their equality, immunities, and privileges, mental and corporeal, against the incroachments of their masculine tyrants. If this *then* was the rule of my conduct; if I dared to judge and act for myself, at *sixteen*, allowing no guide but rectitude, no monitor but conscience; fearless of the judgment, careless of the opinion of [the] world . . .

If, she continues, she acted thus at sixteen, certainly she will behave in comparable ways at forty. The association between rectitude and "masculine" freedom and assertiveness in a woman demonstrates how thoroughly new ideas had, by the century's end, permeated literary culture. Even through a clumsy novel, fresh breezes blow.

Anna and Lady John, claiming male prerogatives, yet remain sexually conventional. Anna angrily rejects Clifton's proposal of cohabitation; Lady John enters a loveless marriage at her father's behest and lives in chastity after separating from her husband. But other conceptions of the new woman include more daring sexual possibilities. In *Memoirs of Emma Courtney* (1796), Mary Hays's heroine makes high moral claims for herself and for her sex in terms by now familiar ("Shall I, then, sign the unjust decree, that women are incapable of energy and fortitude?") and dares to declare her sexual passion for a man before he reciprocates it. Mary Wollstonecraft, in her unfinished novel *The Wrongs of Woman* (1798), depicts her heroine, Maria, as willingly entering a sexual liaison while married to another man. Maria also passionately offers her own plea in a divorce court, and the novel's tone and substance insist that the reader should not condemn her.

The titles or subtitles of several of the period's novels—*Ellinor; or, The World As It Is*; *Man As He Is*; *Hermsprong; or, Man As He Is Not*; *Caleb Williams; or, Things As They Are* (Godwin's title for the first edition)—emphasize the degree to which writers concerned themselves with social actualities in relation to imagined options. An improved social order, as the foregoing accounts have suggested, depends—so fiction has it—on new kinds of character to create it. *Hermsprong* self-consciously invents the new hero, a young man whose moral force derives from his upbringing among American Indians. If Robert Bage has some difficulty conceiving new things for Hermsprong to do, he vividly imagines new ways for his hero to *be*.

The distinction between "being" and "doing" often attaches itself to gender dichotomies, with "being"—the more passive role—assigned to women. Hermsprong is far from passive. His ideological importance consists partly in his redefinition of *being* in relation to *doing*—and of *manliness*. The word *manly* assumes ever more complex meanings as it recurs in the novel.

In the imaginative and ideological scheme of *Hermsprong*, the antithesis of *man* is not *woman* but *child*—and women and children do not categorically resemble one another. Men and women do, or should. Hermsprong's speeches about his own nature and his lectures on characteristics of women as they should be emphasize comparable attributes. Early in the novel, he describes himself:

I cannot learn to offer incense at the shrines of wealth and power, nor at any shrines but those of probity and virtue. I cannot learn to surrender my opinion from complaisance, or from any principle of adulation. Nor can I learn to suppress the sentiments of a freeborn mind, from any fear, religious or political.

He expects of Caroline, whom he loves, the same kind of noncompliance. She too must respect her own freedom, must defend her opinions, must refuse to surrender. The crucial issue between Hermsprong and Caroline concerns her dutiful deference to her tyrannical father. Hermsprong's insistence that a higher duty commands her to follow "the truth of things" threatens to separate them permanently. (Caroline successfully justifies herself—introducing an unexpected note of relativism into a work largely organized by absolutist statements—by pointing out that she has followed the path that she *thought* right, and that no one can do more.) Women, Hermsprong maintains, waste their energies on trifles. They deserve educations that will enable them to use those energies in ways comparable to men's.

Caroline's father, Lord Grondale, is Hermsprong's chief antagonist. A self-absorbed, self-satisfied, arrogant man who assumes his right to absolute power, Lord Grondale has never before encountered real opposition. Hermsprong's explanation of why even a woman can and should defy such a man (he is speaking to Mrs. Garnet, an elderly and impoverished, hence repudiated relative of Lord Grondale's) summarizes his moral position, and the novel's:

Can you fear a man . . . whose mind is mean—so mean as to incite him to commit acts of injustice, of inhumanity! can he be feared? He, whose life has scarce been marked by one act of energy? who owes the little consequence he possesses to his title and his money? How feeble must be the resentments of a man humiliated by his vices? Oppose him with the manly spirit of conscious rectitude, you will find him a child; a sulky, pouting one indeed; but still a child.

His invocation of "manly spirit" to a woman emphasizes his insistence that both genders can and should share the same moral qualities. Long-standing convention has labeled courageous spirit "manly"; Hermsprong considers it equally appropriate to women. Moral qualities, and the energetic acts they generate, define adulthood. Lacking them, even the most socially powerful human being reveals himself a child.

Hermsprong's "being," dependent on that moral integrity he recommends to others, changes the meaning of his action. Although Hermsprong occupies himself mainly in benevolence (along with his talking and thinking), the significance of such conduct differs from that of comparable behavior in, say, *The Man of Feeling* or *A Sentimental Journey*. When Harley, in *The Man of Feeling*, bestows money on a worthy recipient or weeps over a good woman gone wrong, he declares his difference from, and implicitly his superiority to, the objects of his generosity. The feelings such figures allow him to experience constitute their narrative and moral justification. *Hermsprong* delineates a new version of benevolence. Its hero's acts of charity often occur "offstage," and are only briefly reported. Many of those he helps—Mrs. Garnet and the local curate are important cases in point—attract his attention specifically because of their moral resemblance to him. He wants to learn from Mrs. Garnet, he says; he admires the curate. Hermsprong acts not to indulge his feelings but in the service of justice and of moral equality. Even his more generalized charity—for example, his bestowing of money and help on inhabitants of a storm-ravaged village—rarely emphasizes social or moral difference. Hermsprong considers benevolence more an obligation than an indulgence.

Bage does not imagine Hermsprong in altogether innovative terms: his wealth allows his defiance of Lord Grondale; his high birth facilitates his marriage to Caroline. The novel relies upon even as it deplores class hierarchy. But it presents a protagonist whose moral substance locates his heroism, who insists on and as much as possible enforces the moral equality of women, who needs not fight or pursue adventure to declare himself a man: a representation of considerable consequence.

Feeling and Action

In 1796 William Beckford published a little book called *Modern Novel Writing*, following it a year later with *Azemia*, a parodic merging of Oriental tale and sentimental novel. Both works employ pastiche to criticize the English novel, emphasizing incoherence and sentimentality as principal weaknesses of the genre. Beckford focuses on such characters as Sterne's mad Maria and Richardson's Pamela, from much earlier in the century, as founding figures of sensibility, but he also evokes the divided aims of such a novel of the 1790s as *Ellinor*, with its intricate plot, its intermittent stress on sensibility, and its claim of bold originality. The effort to combine sensibility with originality often led to the kind of narrative muddle that Beckford mocks. It also had more provocative consequences when novelists seriously confronted the problem of how to reconcile a high valuation of personal feeling with a concern for social issues.

Many commentators have discussed Mary Wollstonecraft's difficulties over sensibility. As *Vindication of the Rights of Woman* makes clear, she believed that female sensibility constituted female weakness, an educational and social imposition on women. Yet her novels rely heavily on sensibility to characterize her heroines and the men who attract them. A characteristic passage from *The Wrongs of Woman*:

> Active as love was in the heart of Maria, the story she had just heard made her thoughts take a wider range. The opening buds of hope closed, as if they had put forth too early, and the happiest day of her life was overcast by the most melancholy reflections. Thinking of Jemima's peculiar fate and her own, she was led to consider the oppressed state of women, and to lament that she had given birth to a daughter. Sleep fled from her eyelids, while she dwelt on the wretchedness of unprotected infancy.

Maria, who has just listened to Jemima's narrative of the disasters afflicting an unprotected working-class woman, employs the conventional language of sensibility ("the opening buds of hope," "the most melancholy reflections") to comment not only on her personal situation of requited romantic love but also on social actualities. Her love for her infant merges with her awareness of women's plight; her justifiable worry about her own immediate predicament grows as she ponders Jemima's experience. Wollstonecraft's novel criticizes sensibility but indulges in sentimental flights, as though exquisite sensitivity alone responds adequately to the suffering women endure and witness.

Sensibility rarely impels action. Jemima, hardened by her experience, proves more forceful than Maria in planning and in expediting. Maria, however, acts powerfully—although only verbally—in the courtroom, defending Darnford against the charge of seduction and incidentally defending her own adultery. Her ability to do so depends explicitly on her transcendence of sensibility: "A strong sense of injustice had silenced every emotion, which a mixture of true and false delicacy might otherwise have excited in Maria's bosom." Like "delicacy," the "sense of injustice" constitutes an emotion—but emotion of a kind that promises fresh narrative possibilities. In its inclusiveness—it implies reaction to a whole class of human beings rather than to suffering individuals—and in its implicit invocation of principle as well as sentiment, it differs from the emotional responsiveness that had governed many previous fictional heroes and heroines. Delicacy suggests weakness, a sense of injustice promises strength. Delicacy reacts to minute stimuli, the sense of injustice claims large ones. Maria fails in the courtroom. The judge considers her reasoned, energetic plea irrelevant and relies instead on the ancient principles of male supremacy and male possession. Yet the power of that plea energizes Wollstonecraft's text, dramatizes her argument, and strengthens her fictional character.

Sensibility in the old sense continues to display itself in late-century novels. But these novels also render less familiar sorts of feeling. Mary Hays's Emma Courtney sometimes resembles a much earlier heroine: "[My] tender and faithful heart refuses to change its object—it can never love another." But she does not accept the traditional female fate of passive waiting for male response. Her attachment organizes her life and provides her with energy, not only because of its powerful sexual component but because she uses it as a stimulus to thought. Her thinking leads her to a complex awareness of women's categorical situation as social victims, oppressed by "the barbarous and accursed laws of society." But it also enables her to make compelling claims for herself. Passion, she says, has brought her to reason. She writes to a male correspondent about his admiration of "the destructive courage of an Alexander, . . . the pernicious ambition of an Augustus Caesar, as bespeaking the potent, energetic, mind!" Then she asserts her own comparable potency and energy. Although she bemoans her victimization, she more insistently argues—and the argument is revolutionary—that her self-destructive passion constitutes strength rather than weakness, stimulating intellectual and emotional vitality.

The assumption, exemplified in every novel I have mentioned, that energy in itself embodies value implies consequent valuing of new sorts of emotion. If an admirable character can plausibly admire the energy of destructive courage and pernicious ambition, it follows that even such feelings as resentment and rage may measure worth and incite action. Anna St. Ives, Caleb Williams, Wollstonecraft's Maria, Hermsprong, Emma Courtney—all experience intense anger at manifestations of social injustice. Fictional women, of course, had found anger a source of energy much earlier in the century: Pamela and Clarissa come readily to mind. But such heroines feel angry because of what has happened to them. They do not characteristically generalize their conditions. Protagonists of late-century novels, whose anger pervades and stimulates more action than does that of their fictional predecessors, can usually justify their emotion in social terms.

The novels so far considered in this chapter lack the psychological intricacy and depth that twentieth-century readers expect. For that matter, they lack the psychological intricacy and depth of Richardson's first two novels. In late-century novels, political and moral agendas often supersede psychological ones; notation of emotion substitutes for its exploration. Two novels of the period that have attracted recent readers, however, *Caleb Williams* and *A Simple Story*, provide richly inflected psychological analysis. Elizabeth Inchbald's anything-but-simple story offers new kinds of emotion and new ways of thinking about them.

A Simple Story (1791) tells a two-generation tale of fathers, literal and metaphorical, and daughters. The first-generation protagonist, Miss Milner, falls in love with her guardian, a Catholic priest named Dorriforth. Freed from his vows by a relative's death, through which he inherits an important estate, Dorriforth, now Lord Elmwood, marries his ward, despite the prolonged opposition of another priest, Sandford, and despite Miss Milner's willfully and provocatively bad behavior. When Lord Elmwood has to go abroad and then to stay longer than he had planned, his wife lapses into infidelity. Before his return, she flees. Lord Elmwood sends their small daughter, Matilda, after her, wishing never to see either female again.

After Lady Elmwood's death, Lord Elmwood allows Matilda, now seventeen, to inhabit one of his residences, on condition that he never see her. When they accidentally encounter one another, he banishes her. From the cottage where she takes refuge, she is abducted by a lascivious nobleman. Lord Elmwood rescues her, learns to love her, and marries her to her cousin, now heir to his estate.

The novel's power derives from its capacity to render emotional nuance with remarkable spareness and to suggest links between such nuance and the pressures of social reality. *A Simple Story* ends with an explicit moral: "And Mr. Milner, Matilda's grandfather, had better have given his fortune to a distant branch of his family . . . so he had bestowed upon his daughter A PROPER EDUCATION." The "proper education" here endorsed appears to be Matilda's harrowing education in the school of adversity. Whatever ironies it conceals, the statement clearly insists that Matilda's experience and Miss Milner's carry social as well as personal significance.

Dorriforth and Miss Milner are distinguished from their fictional contemporaries by the rendered intensity of their sexual feeling, conveyed both by direct statement (Lord Elmwood, on hearing that Miss Milner loves him: "For God's sake take care what you are doing—you are destroying my prospects of futurity—you are making this world too dear to me") and by physical gestures such as Miss Milner's changes of color, her fainting, her weeping, her setting down of a coffee cup. But pride, jealousy, envy, and anger also become objects of detailed investigation, not of moral condemnation. Such feelings of course permeate works of fiction from early romance to postmodern narrative (and nonnarrative). Rarely in the eighteenth century, though, are they explored rather than deplored.

After their engagement and before their marriage, Miss Milner and Lord Elmwood struggle for power. Pride controls both antagonists, pride given different forms and different kinds of authority. Miss Milner takes seriously the truism that a woman holds power over a man only before her marriage. She wishes to test her control. Why didn't she keep her lover in suspense longer, she asks herself, so that she could have seen her dominion's extent? Would he love her still if she behaved badly? How badly can she behave and get away with it? Deliberately she disobeys her fiancé. Although she knows that she risks alienating him, she continues to declare (to a confidante) that he loves her too well to reject her. If he fails to forgive her when she does something unforgivable—well, he doesn't love her enough. After she performs the "unforgivable" action and Lord Elmwood announces his plan to go abroad for an indefinite period, breaking the engagement, she refuses to acknowledge openly her grief and despair. Pride makes her follow polite forms and disguise her feelings.

Lord Elmwood's sense of his own dignity forbids him to submit to a young woman's defiance. His ungenerous (though not implausible) interpretation of Miss Milner's behavior as betraying incurable frivolity, and his unwillingness to discuss rather than simply to command her conduct, suggest a rigidity and self-importance confirmed by his subsequent actions. The intersection of this man's and this woman's individual pride promises precisely the kind of disaster that the narrative enacts.

A third person initially dominated by pride is Mr. Sandford, who urges Lord Elmwood to marry a woman characterized by her lack of capacity for intense feeling. Arrogant in his conviction of rightness, Sandford encourages Lord Elmwood to view Miss Milner as immoral. With equal arrogance he suddenly decides—apparently on the basis of the young woman's appearance as she struggles to conceal her emotions—to command the marriage he has previously opposed, suggesting that marriage alone will allow Lord Elmwood dependably to control the flighty young woman he loves.

The novel's second half documents, not as moral triumph but as psychological process, the transformation of pride in the two central characters. (Sandford also relinquishes his pride, but more by authorial fiat than by emotional or moral logic.) Each recognizes the wrong he or she has committed, without acknowledging, as the novel in its totality does, the positive as well as negative value of their pride. The psychological complexity of Inchbald's achievement derives partly from her examination of the range of meanings attached in her historical moment to inclusive moral categories. Pride, *A Simple Story* demonstrates, signifies many kinds of feeling, motivates many kinds of action. If *Anna St. Ives* energizes its narrative by dramatizing individual uses of moral interpretations to control dangerous feeling, Inchbald's novel finds energy in an opposite movement: from moral inclusiveness to emotional discrimination.

The novel narrates only in summary fashion Lady Elmwood's infidelity, remorse, and self-abasement. On her deathbed she announces that she has no will but her husband's. She consequently makes no formal provision for her daughter, although she pleads with Lord Elmwood, in a letter posthumously delivered, to care for their child. Her pride becomes humility because she knows herself to have sinned. What she fails to know—what, indeed, she can no longer afford to know—is that her personal force has depended on just the kind of self-assertion that has led to her misbehavior. Inchbald, however, draws her readers to understand this fact and to recognize the pathos of how much a woman, by virtue of her gender, must yield. Lord Elmwood, with characteristic reticence, neglects to tell his wife about the illness that delayed his return. Believing herself willfully abandoned, she embarks on adultery in a misguided claim of autonomy. The novel does not invite its readers to condone such behavior, but it allows us to understand the action's origins in a pride that signifies not arrogance but striving for independence. Lady Elmwood's betrayal paradoxically testifies to the intensity of her love as she reacts to apparent neglect. The laws of ethics and of society condemn this woman. She rightly condemns herself. But the pride that leads her to break her marriage vows when her husband appears to lose interest stems in part from an admirable rejection of the indignities routinely visited upon women.

Lord Elmwood's pride takes longer to yield, both because society reinforces it due to his gender, rank, and wealth, and because he has not in any such obvious sense as his wife done wrong. After his wife's death, his pride manifests itself in his refusals: he insists that no one mention his wife or daughter, that his nephew never oppose him, that his personal prohibitions carry absolute force. His daughter exists in total emotional deprivation, the consequence of his sadistic arrangement that she live in his house without encountering him. Only her abduction allows Lord Elmwood to obviate his own forbiddings. Rescuing her, he learns—although he never explicitly admits it—his mistake: his daughter's emotional deprivation has entailed his own. He relinquishes pride for paternity.

In the rigidity and inflexibility of his pride, Lord Elmwood appears monstrous: an appropriate mate, in fact, for the young woman Sandford wanted him to marry. But his pride conceals—or perhaps constitutes—an emotional malady that largely results from society's gender arrangements. If Miss Milner painfully conceals her feelings, Lord Elmwood has little capacity to express his. Emotionally inarticulate, he cannot discuss with his fiancée the difficulties between them; he cannot tell her of his physical weakness (the illness that keeps him away); he cannot deal with his own suffering, so he forbids anyone to remind him of it. His cry when his daughter faints in his arms ("Her name did not however come to his recollection—nor any name but this—'Miss Milner—Dear Miss Milner.'") signifies a continuing anguish never verbally acknowledged. To the novel's end he exercises an autocrat's control, yet the discovery of a channel for his emotions has disrupted the action of his pride, a pride that, like Miss Milner's, conceals its own pathos.

Matilda has little pride: her painful "education" has humbled her. Capable of resentment, she remains incapable of defying a father or of self-initiated action. Never deviating from virtue, she receives her reward in a father's love and a young man's devotion. Far more than her mother, she resembles the conventional eighteenth-century heroine of sensibility: a reactor, a weeper, an actual or potential victim, the product of a "PROPER EDUCATION." Inchbald attaches the epithet "proper" to the education that generates sensibility, the education Wollstonecraft deplored. "Proper" meaning appropriate? respectable? conventional? Certainly all three—the novel demonstrates how precisely Matilda's education in submissiveness coincides with the demands of a society organized on the basis of paternal power. On the other hand, it also demonstrates, in a way virtually inconceivable before the 1790s, that paternal power entails a train of emotional problems, for fathers as well as for daughters. Lord and Lady Elmwood, in their emotional complexity, experiencing the incompatibility of fully experienced personal feeling with reason (to use eighteenth-century terms), capture the narrator's interest as well as the reader's. Matilda, less demanding and less provocative, displays only the kind of feeling that "reason" allows: "reason" meaning (a crucial perception, this) the structure of rules ordained by society. Matilda, as a consequence, can only react. Her parents create action.

In novels of the late eighteenth century the relations of feeling to action, like those of character to action, indicated experimental directions for fiction. Like the question of character, that of feeling was now seen to involve matters of social actuality and possibility.

Public and Private Action

That novels might discuss social and political phenomena was hardly a new idea. Fielding had satirized doctors and lawyers and urban immorality; Smollett incorporated diatribes about London and Bath and about government corruption into the fabric of his novels. A sentimental hero encountering a neglected old soldier inevitably reflected on the inadequacies of a government that failed to reward him. Novels of the 1790s often continued a familiar tradition in a familiar way; *Walsingham* and *Ellinor* offer typical examples.

The most important new development in the treatment of politics and society by novels of the 1790s was an emphasis on analogies between private and public experience, for example between the situation of individuals within families and that of citizens within a nation. Like set-piece discussions of social ills, such analogies could find crude or subtle, explicit or implicit statement. Wollstonecraft is explicit. When Maria asks the rhetorical question, "Was not the world a vast prison, and women born slaves?" she establishes the theoretical groundwork for *The Wrongs of Woman*, which simply elaborates the metaphor by following the experience of Maria, the immediate victim of imprisonment, and Jemima, her warder. Maria, already victimized by sensibility before being confined to the madhouse, has made an unfortunate marriage, the result of romantic fantasies that led her to misinterpret her future husband's character. The man turns out to be a libertine, the father of an illegitimate child, an alcoholic gambler, and interested primarily in Maria's money. When he tries to sell her sexual favors to a friend, she flees with their baby girl. England offers her no protection: her husband repeatedly finds her, often through the betrayal of other women. She attempts to flee to the Continent, but his agents waylay her, separate her from her infant, and relegate her to the madhouse. Jemima tells a yet more horrifying story of working-class sexuality, betrayal, deprivation, and suffering.

Both Maria's autobiography (recorded in a memoir for her daughter) and Jemima's (presented in an oral narrative) narrate kinds of events familiar in eighteenth-century novels. The representation of female suffering in Wollstonecraft's fiction, however, exists to stimulate generalization rather than just to titillate. The particular case in all its lurid specificity exemplifies social malaise. Comments by the characters—Jemima herself, Maria and her lover Darnford listening to Jemima's story, Maria as she tells her own tale—and by the narrator insist that individual instances embody social evil. Several novels of the period flirt with the notion of social determinism. Wollstonecraft makes it specific and insistent, demonstrating in detail processes of cause and effect that create the inevitabilities of female lives.

Already a polemicist, Wollstonecraft predictably employed the novel as a vehicle of social commentary. More surprising cases abound. Charlotte Smith, whose first novel, *Emmeline* (1788), a considerable popular success, presents itself as pure romance, in the 1790s used the romance framework politically. *Desmond* (1792) followed three earlier romances. Unlike its predecessors, it offers a male protagonist and an explicit (and explicitly justified) concern with politics. *The Old Manor*

House, written a year later, returns to familiar elements of romance: a poor, oppressed heroine, a gallant soldier-lover, an old house scaring its inhabitants with mysterious noises and happenings. But it also suggests that personal experiences have political meanings.

Monimia, Charlotte Smith's romantically named heroine, exists as an orphaned dependent in a great house, nominally cared for by an aunt who actually exploits and envies her. Pretty and good, she early attracts the attention of Orlando Somerive, son of a neighboring family related to the mistress of the house. He sees her from the beginning as victim of "injustice" and "oppression," but she has no rebellious spirit and no obvious way of rebelling, since she lacks family and money. Orlando, the younger son of a father with limited income whose elder son has squandered the family's assets, holds a marginally more comfortable position. For years he meets Monimia secretly at the manor house. Then the time comes when, for the good of his family and for the sake of his own independence, he must assume a profession and leave Monimia. Having no particular vocational interest, he gladly accepts the offer of a commission from a man who (unbeknownst to Orlando) wishes to seduce his sister, and soon finds himself in the midst of the American Revolution. Hardships follow, for him and for Monimia, but eventually he returns to England, they marry in poverty, and the discovery of a secreted will brings them prosperity.

Little in this plot suggests political awareness or purpose. But an incidental reference to "the politics of Rayland Hall" at the end of a passage describing the servants' reactions to the news of Orlando's plans to become a soldier (the butler expects as a result to seduce the maidservant; the housekeeper hopes to find out what Monimia is up to) indicates the prevailing narrative consciousness that happenings in a house resemble those in the larger world. Most consistently emphasized is the powerlessness of poverty. Monimia has been reared to believe that her poverty in effect constitutes a sin. She reacts with wonder and gratitude to Orlando's revelation that the amount of money a person possesses does not determine the degree of his or her human rights. Orlando says that the tyranny of the privileged, resisted, will fall. Monimia's aunt governs her only by "usurped authority." Such lessons help Monimia to value herself for the first time (the text says so explicitly). Implicitly, they fortify her when, left alone, she must resist the dangers of country and city.

Meanwhile, Orlando acquires further political wisdom as a soldier, realizing that he fights for politicians, not for his country, and that the Americans are fighting for values to which the English pay lip service. He sees that governments endeavor to keep their populations in ignorance, which alone creates unquestioning obedience. When he returns to London, to experience firsthand the chicanery of lawyers and to hear about that of doctors, his fight for his rights is informed by the knowledge that his individual plight resembles that of millions. He differentiates himself by his knowledge, his ability to apply it, and his willingness to act on it.

The plot of threatened powerlessness relieved by unexpected wealth duplicates that of countless earlier works. Orlando's political sentiments sound fairly commonplace, and the political comprehension of the novel as a whole hardly goes beyond them. Nonetheless, the implication that conventional romance problems have a place in larger political structures represents an important development in the history of the novel.

Tyranny and usurped authority constitute central threats within *The Old Manor House* and preoccupy many novelists of the period, as one might expect in the aftermath of the American and French revolutions. *A Simple Story*, for instance, beyond its mild allusions to Catholic politics and to the frivolity and viciousness of fashionable life, manifests little concern with the realm outside the domestic. On the other hand, it concerns itself centrally with issues of authority and power. Instead of the familiar plot of generational conflict over a daughter's marital choice, it converts a lover (an ex-Catholic priest, remember) into a metaphorical father and plays out essentially the same conflict in terms that render it both more ostensibly equal and more intimately painful. Now it becomes clear that the "daughter" can't win: either she destroys her marriage (as Lady Elmwood does) or she submits, in her own view, to becoming a cipher. The second-generation daughter, the *real* daughter, has learned the lesson of cipherhood. In the context of the period's other novels, this becomes a political plot.

Hermsprong makes explicit the political implications of father-daughter relations with the hero's personal defiance of Lord Grondale as tyrant and his insistence that the lord's daughter also resist tyranny on abstract grounds of justice. Hermsprong's antipathy toward him seems to Lord Grondale intensely personal: the nobleman personalizes all resistance. Through Hermsprong's doctrine, the novel insists that such efforts to interpret behavior on the basis of individual feeling themselves amount to political acts. As for the traditional arrangement by which fathers dictate their daughters' marriages, that exemplifies the authoritarianism that threatens the country. The hero passionately articulates his understanding of how personal and political mingle in human experience:

> I cannot, I fear, submit to be fettered and cramped throughout the whole circle of thought and action. You [the English] submit to authority with regard to the first, and to fashion with regard to the last. I cannot get rid of the stubborn notion, that to do what we think is right to do is the only good principle of action. You seem to think the only good principle of action is to do as others do.

Fashion and authority constrict equally. To resist both establishes the only moral basis for action, political or personal—and the action of resistance, the novel suggests, is inevitably political.

William Godwin's *Caleb Williams* (1794) explores more thoroughly than any other novel of the period the painful intersection of political and personal history. Its interest for many modern readers derives primarily from its psychological clarity, subtlety, and intricacy, but such qualities, from Godwin's stated point of view, serve to emphasize the revolutionary social message he wished to impart. As he says in his preface, he wrote in "a high state of excitement," telling himself, "I will write a tale, that shall constitute an epoch in the mind of the reader, that no one, after he has read it, shall ever be exactly the same man that he was before." He wished to make people understand how tyranny works. In England as it actually exists, the novel maintains, justice does not operate for the poor. Caleb, the protagonist, determines to win justice for himself and fails, not only because of the manifest inequities of the social system but because of the ways in which he has internalized its assumptions.

Godwin announces as his novel's central psychological principle the rather old-fashioned theory of the ruling passion. Curiosity fatally governs Caleb; concern for reputation as disastrously controls his employer, Falkland. The novel's action turns on Caleb's discovery of Falkland's secret: the man with a reputation for impeccable virtue has murdered an enemy and allowed two other men to be executed for his crime. Falkland promises his young secretary a terrible penalty for this knowledge. Although Caleb leaves Falkland's house, he cannot evade his power: the power of the upper class to decide the fates of their inferiors. Wherever

Caleb goes, news of his manufactured crime (Falkland accuses him of treacherous theft) follows him, making all communities shun him. When he finally decides to fight back, when he actually appears in a courtroom to testify against Falkland, his persecutor presents himself ravaged by illness and psychic distress. He dies shortly after Caleb's public accusation, and Caleb feels himself a murderer too, destined to desperate unhappiness even after Falkland has expired.

The characteristic that drives Caleb to uncover Falkland's secret manifests itself less as curiosity than as intolerance of ambiguity. After Caleb leaves Falkland's house, curiosity does not reveal itself as a crucial trait, but impatience with ambiguity—a need to clear things up, to make them straightforward—remains. Falkland's compulsion to keep his reputation unstained is, by assertion, rather more consistent than Caleb's curiosity, yet it inadequately elucidates his relentless and ingenious persecution of Caleb.

The effort to interpret that persecution has compelled generations of readers. I argued earlier that new kinds of emotion become the subjects of investigation in novels of the 1790s. The thesis applies to *Caleb Williams* perhaps more aptly than to any other single work. What makes the novel so curiously absorbing is its ambiguous representation of an intense relationship between two men, an indissoluble tie based on a quasi-paternal-filial connection, a link of love assuming the form of hate, an affiliation finally converted into identification. To call the feeling between Caleb and Falkland love masked as hate clumsily hints at the intricacy of an emotional tie never adequately labeled within the text. Caleb must flee and must not escape. Falkland must pursue as retribution but also as protection (for example, he prevents Caleb's imprisonment and even arranges for him to receive a small financial donation). Caleb cannot fathom what is going on. His ultimate reliance on legal process constitutes, among other things, a final, unsatisfactory effort at clarification.

The problem of interpretation exists vividly within the text, presenting a challenge to characters as well as readers. In this respect as in others, *Caleb Williams* resembles other novels of the period. *Walsingham*, for instance, an epistolary novel with a single point of view, narrates the experience of a man who interprets every occurrence as persecution. If the reader gets the impression that the narrator inadequately understands his own experience, the denouement with its gender conversion dramatically confirms the ubiquitousness of misinterpretation in Walsingham's letters. *A Simple Story* raises the interpretive problem in relation to Miss Milner's premarital behavior. Before Dorriforth meets her, he receives two diametrically opposed accounts of her behavior and character. When she embarks with apparent enthusiasm on a life of frivolity, those around her develop radically different explanatory theories. And Dorriforth/Elmwood in fact never adequately grasps his fiancée's or his wife's nature.

Caleb Williams makes the problem of interpretation explicitly political, at least in part. The novel obsessively reiterates the difference between laws—both literal legal sanctions and general social rules—for the rich and for the poor. That difference, in practice, depends on interpretation. The same act performed by a rich man and a poor one is understood as having utterly different meanings. The poor have no rights because the law always assumes that truth inheres in the rich. Such assessment on the basis of class manifestly carries social meaning, but even efforts at personal understanding derive from and register in the social order. Thus Caleb, defying ambiguity and announcing to himself his "freedom" as he leaves Falkland behind, perceives that "every man is fated to be more or less the tyrant or the slave." He decides that he himself will remain "disengaged" from this corrupt system and will "never fill the part either of the oppressor or the sufferer"—this at the moment he sets forth on the path that destines him to face precisely that choice of roles in relation to Falkland. He can suffer at his former employer's hands or he can "oppress" by revealing the older man's crime. He has no other choice, and his efforts to explain the operations of the social system so as to avoid its most sinister effects are necessarily doomed to failure.

Nonetheless, Caleb continues his interpretive struggle, which, like his refusal to be tyrant or slave, most often involves an attempt to declare his individuality, his specialness. In prison, for instance, he develops an elaborate mental life, imaginatively placing himself in every conceivable situation and planning the conduct appropriate to every human difficulty. He believes himself uniquely prepared for all experience, triumphantly self-sufficient. This reading of his situation, like his earlier ones, proves insufficient to the actualities that soon assail him. His self-interpretation cannot survive society's pressures.

The conflict between Falkland and his irrational enemy Tyrrel, which ends in Tyrrel's murder, turns in its early stages on questions of interpretation. Tyrrel, predictably, understands interpretation as a kind of fraud. He takes his own view as simple truth. Falkland's effort to convince Tyrrel of his obligation of charity toward his social inferiors meets a significant negative response: "I always knew you had the wit to make good your own story, and tell a plausible tale. But I will not be come over thus." Despite his brutality and obtuseness, Tyrrel has perceived an important fact. Individual interpretations—the "stories" or "tales" that people tell—indeed belong to the interplay of power that defines human relations. Substituting physical for mental power and using his social position to maximum advantage, Tyrrel exploits the weapons available to him. But so do Falkland and Caleb.

The particular subtleties of the emotional connections between Falkland and Caleb indeed seem "particular," not just the effects of social forces. On the other hand, the structural duplication of the father-son bond in the situation between the two men suggests that the most delicate idiosyncrasies of domestic relations involving inequalities of power inevitably reflect larger social patterns. Dramatizing a prolonged effort at both literal and metaphorical escape, *Caleb Williams* insists at every level on escape's impossibility.

In its unrelieved pessimism, Godwin's novel shows every avenue of hope systematically blocked, enforcing a fiercely negative view of the human prospect. Although like Godwin's they investigate with more or less consistency the connections between the "private" and the "public," the period's other works of fiction characteristically discover a way out of despair in the imagined nature of an energetic individual—a Hermsprong, an Anna St. Ives, even a Sidney. Godwin alone faces the possibility that the idea of individualism is itself a fiction, an interpretation necessary for hope but antithetical to logic.

Action and form

In a preface to the Standard Novels edition of *Caleb Williams*, Godwin emphasized not only the book's political purpose but its formal intensity. He explained how he plotted backward, beginning with the events of the third volume, "a series of adventures of flight and pursuit," then working back to the narrative of secret murder, the second volume's project, and finally telling the story of Falkland's early career, which lends pathos to his later corruption. A rigorous sense of narrative logic governed his planning. In the finished work, the results of that logic help to create both the painful impression of inevitability that governs

Caleb's repeated frustration and bafflement and the more generalized impression that hope constitutes only an illusion.

If Godwin shared Mary Hays's project of putting the mind in motion, he pursued this endeavor partly by blocking accustomed paths of thought and feeling. His narrative of composition suggests his recognition that a fiction's shape helps determine its most profound effects. Judging by their novels' evidence, few of his contemporaries shared that recognition; if they did, few could find narrative patterns that would provoke energetic reaction. It is perhaps for this reason—that the new imagining of the novelistic enterprise did not typically include the imagining of new forms—that novels of the 1790s, despite their large ambitions, have not found a wide audience. Often the period's novelists poured their new wine into old bottles.

Formal conventions, in short, lagged behind ideological innovations in the novels of the 1790s. *Anna St. Ives* and *Walsingham*, both epistolary in form, thus appear to declare themselves old-fashioned, even as they articulate fresh ideas. *Memoirs of Emma Courtney*, also loosely epistolary, tells its story in long letters from Emma to her foster son that incorporate shorter letters from the past. The epistolary mode implicitly announces personal relations as the preeminent subject of the novel. For writers who wished to make their readers think about the social implications of personal experience, reliance on fictional correspondence conveyed a contradictory message by allowing readers to relax into familiar and relatively passive ways of reading.

As for third-person narratives, also employed during the period, they most often preserve the loose one-thing–after–another structure made familiar by the picaresque novel. *Ellinor* and *The Old Manor House* exemplify the type. They do not lack plot, but events often take place on the page mainly for their own sake; the reader is invited to interest herself in the multiplicity of happenings as instances of the infinite possibility of circumstance, not as episodes stimulated by the novelistic pattern of action in itself, however energizing a doctrine the fiction advances.

Only a few 1790s novelists appear to acknowledge a need for fictional form to emphasize ideological meaning. In *Hermsprong* Bage invents a narrator who himself plays a peripheral part in the novel's happenings. Gregory Glen, an illegitimate child with no clearly defined social place, has the potential to provide an outsider's perspective on conventional structures and thus to insist on social meanings even within a romance plot. His view of the world, as a "child of nature" in quite a different sense from Hermsprong, might present a slightly skewed counterpart to the hero's and participate in a rich interplay of attitudes. Hermsprong is wealthy and titled; Gregory is poor and lacks even a real last name. How provocative to pursue the conjunctions and disparities of attitude between them! Bage does not, however, pursue anything of the sort. Only intermittently does he give his narrator a distinctive voice and character. For long stretches, Gregory offers no commentary beyond almost sycophantic approval of Hermsprong. At the outset he suggests his own moral and political position, but that position soon disappears from view. The novel hints at but never fully achieves structural innovation.

Godwin and Inchbald, alone among the writers discussed in this chapter, successfully developed—at least in single novels—expressive structures of novelistic action. Many critics have considered the two-part structure of *A Simple Story* a flaw. It reflects a possible historical disjunction: Inchbald may have written the first section in 1779 and ten years later combined it with a second. Sandford's nature appears to have changed between the two parts, and Catholicism no longer constitutes a plot issue. Yet a profound unity—indeed, the unity of action recommended by Aristotle, who in 1792 had been newly translated and annotated—controls the novel as a whole. In different keys, the two parts tell the same story: of a daughter's longing for and eventual union with a father (or "father"). Part 1 ends, apparently happily, with the unexpected marriage of Lord Elmwood and Miss Milner. Part 2 undoes the marriage and kills the woman, then tells the story of a well-trained girl's achievement of apparent happiness through a career of flawless compliance. The first part appears to reward a spirited female for her spirit. Its sequel reveals that assertiveness, willed autonomy, and desire for power are unacceptable components of female nature. The combination of reiterated action with divergent implication exerts a powerful effect. The revisionary moral weight of the second section bears heavily on the transgressive imaginings of the first, effecting an uneasy reconciliation by means of the stated "moral" about a proper education, which reinforces retroactively the negative interpretation of Miss Milner's premarital behavior. On the other hand, the daring vision of a young woman in love who yet ventures to claim power also affects one's understanding of its more orthodox aftermath. The shadow of a challenging, inventive mother stands behind the sublimely well-behaved and altogether uninventive daughter, implicitly commenting on the high cost, for a woman, of achieving social approval. Here as in the century's conduct books, a proper education instructs a woman in giving up—giving up her hopes, her autonomy, her revealed energy. But Miss Milner's presence in the background provides a graphic reminder of the loss entailed.

The two-part pattern that enables this ironic conjunction reinforces the narrative's impact and dramatizes the harsh alternatives that delimit every female prospect. Like the tight plotting of *Caleb Williams*, the apparently more diffuse structural arrangement of *A Simple Story* precisely suits the fable it contains. When Godwin, in the same preface that reported his mode of plotting, revealed his hope that his novel would constitute an epoch in the reader's mind, he suggested no necessary connection between the plotting and the grand effect of which he dreamed. Yet the relentless logic of his plot contributes to the moral disturbance the novel creates, as does the bipartite division of Inchbald's work. Both novelists demonstrated the possible interplay of form and function in ideological fiction. Inchbald, unlike Godwin, makes no ideological claims for her accomplishment, presenting it as only "a simple story." But her novel, too, arguably constitutes an epoch in the mind: a work that significantly shifts our perception of moral possibility.

Patricia Meyer Spacks

Selected Bibliography

Butler, Marilyn. *Jane Austen and the War of Ideas*. Oxford: Clarendon, 1987.

Butler, Marilyn. *Romantics, Rebels and Reactionaries: English Literature and Its Background, 1760–1830*. Oxford: Oxford University Press, 1981.

Castle, Terry. *Masquerade and Civilization: The Carnivalesque in Eighteenth-Century English Culture and Fiction*. Stanford: Stanford University Press, 1986.

Johnson, Claudia. *Jane Austen: Women, Politics, and the Novel*. Chicago: University of Chicago Press, 1988.

Kelly, Gary. *The English Jacobin Novel*. Oxford: Clarendon, 1976.

Paulson, Ronald. *Representations of Revolution 1789–1820*. New Haven, Conn.: Yale University Press, 1983.

Schofield, Mary Anne, and Cecilia Macheski, eds. *Fetter'd or Free? British Women Novelists, 1670–1815*. Athens: Ohio University Press, 1986.

Spacks, Patricia Meyer. *Desire and Truth: Functions of Plot in Eighteenth-Century English Novels*. Chicago: University of Chicago Press, 1990.

Tompkins, J. M. S. *The Popular Novel in England, 1770–1800*. Lincoln: University of Nebraska Press, 1961.

Jane Austen

J ANE AUSTEN lived from 1775 to 1817 and wrote six novels. They were composed in a slightly different order, but completed and published as follows: *Sense and Sensibility*, 1811; *Pride and Prejudice*, 1813; *Mansfield Park*, 1814; and *Emma*, 1816. Both *Northanger Abbey* and *Persuasion* were published posthumously in 1818, though the former was written long before and only slightly revised for publication. Austen also left in manuscript several volumes of short fiction—juvenilia—brief, highly ironic sketches that satirize various forms of popular fiction, especially sentimental fiction. Also left were several unfinished works, including an early novella, *Lady Susan*, a dark fragment from her middle years, *The Watsons*, and the beginnings of a very different style of novel that she was working on when she died, *Sanditon*. Though she never married, Austen was very close to her elder sister Cassandra, to whom she wrote hundreds of letters, which have been collected and published; what we know about her life comes largely from these letters.

For a number of reasons, Jane Austen's novels occupy a crucial place in literary history. Her writing has remained well loved for a remarkably long time. She has a following inside and outside of academia, as indicated by the many inexpensive paperback editions of her books that are available, the global membership of the Jane Austen Society, and the steady stream of articles and books that continue to appear about her novels, which themselves have remained in print ever since they were first published. If, as Roland Barthes remarked some time ago, literature is what gets taught, Austen's works are among the few that belong on both sides of the fence. Her novels would be read even if they were not taught; like *Jane Eyre*, *Pride and Prejudice* is a novel that many people would read anyway.

To literary historians, Austen's novels occupy an important place in literary history not simply because of the presumption of intrinsic quality but for their innovations in narrative form. As early as 1815, Sir Walter Scott recognized in his review of *Emma* that this novel was distinctively different—a new species of writing about common life. The most influential discussion of Jane Austen's technological innovations in narrative is Ian Watt's *Rise of the Novel*, where he argues, in effect, that after the many fits and starts of eighteenth-century novelistic form—the various experiments in first- and third-person narratives, epistolary novels, and other clumsy devices—with her "technical genius" Austen finally got it right. In his epistolary novels, Richardson mastered a realism of presentation, and so was able to achieve a high degree of verisimilitude in conveying the minutiae of daily life. In his turn, Fielding, with his omniscient and judgmental narrators who see directly into the hearts of characters, achieved a mastery of realism of assessment. Jane Austen, however, was the first novelist capable of conveying both the interior and exterior of human life, in her "reconciliation" or synthesis of Richardson's psychological skills and Fielding's sociological scope. By the use of a nonintrusive but still omniscient narrator, Austen developed the means of representing the totality of human life.

In two pages, Watt brilliantly sums up the conventional literary historical view of Austen's "successful resolution" of the eighteenth-century novel. Austen followed Burney and Richardson "in their minute presentation of daily life," but unlike them, Austen could also stand far enough away to display everyday life objectively and comically because hers were not first-person narratives in which the autobiographer or letter writer was the main actor. Like Fielding's, her third-person narrators were free to judge the action, but hers were more judicious and less interfering. In sum, Austen achieved the best of both worlds:

Her analyses of her characters and their states of mind, and her ironical juxtapositions of motive and situation are as pointed as anything in Fielding, but they do not seem to come from an intrusive author but rather from some august and impersonal spirit of social and psychological understanding. At the same time, Jane Austen varied her narrative point of view sufficiently to give us, not only editorial comment, but much of Defoe's and Richardson's psychological closeness to the subjective world of the characters. In her novels there is usually only one character whose consciousness is tacitly accorded a privileged status, and whose mental life is rendered more completely than that of the other characters. . . . Jane Austen's novels, in short, must be seen as the most successful solution of the two general narrative problems for which Richardson and Fielding had provided only partial answers.

The function that Austen's work serves here, or the problem it is asked to solve, is not merely technical, because almost inevitably in discussions such as this, technical issues or issues of narrative form modulate into moral or ideological questions that turn on the truth of her vision. Watt continues: "She was able to combine into a harmonious unity the advantages both of realism of presentation and realism of assessment, of the internal and of the external approaches to character; her novels have authenticity without diffuseness or trickery, wisdom of social comment without a garrulous essayist, and a sense of the social order which is not achieved at the expense of the individuality and autonomy of the characters." What is at stake here is no longer technical prowess but harmonious authenticity, not the way she conveys life stories but what she conveys, which is another matter entirely.

Austen described her purview in a letter as "pictures of domestic life in country villages," a scale that is condensed even further in another self-deprecating and trivializing description of her own novels, "the little bit (two Inches wide) of Ivory on which I work with so fine a Brush." But despite this small scale, Austen found the means of displaying the inside and the outside of human life, how her characters think and feel, along with how they interact with others. Inaugurating the Great Tradition of the English novel, as F. R. Leavis puts it, Jane Austen "makes possible" George Eliot. In sum, Austen's novels have been valued so highly and she has been accorded such an important place in the history of the novel for formal as well as substantive reasons. Both views, however, turn on assumptions about the value of realism and presuppose that the purpose of the novel is to represent human life stories accurately or truthfully and convincingly; whether for her improvements in the way lives are shown or in what aspects of human life are shown, Austen has long been celebrated as a masterful innovator as well as a brilliant practitioner.

To begin to explore some of these innovations and their connections with truth, let us look at an unremarkable passage that exhibits these formal skills or features. In her earliest novel, *Northanger Abbey*, the very ordinary protagonist, Catherine Moreland, has fallen in love with Henry Tilney, only to be separated from him by his father, the self-important and manipulative General Tilney. At the conclusion, Henry unexpectedly turns up at Catherine's house, and the lovers are reunited in Austen's typically understated manner. After Catherine's abrupt return home from an extended visit to Bath and then to the Tilneys' estate, Catherine's mother finds her daughter's spirits depressed, and sets out to remedy Catherine's repining with an apt moral essay from *The Mirror*:

On entering the room, the first object she beheld was a young man whom she had never seen before. With a look of much respect, he immediately rose, and being introduced to her by her conscious daughter as "Mr. Henry Tilney," with the embarrassment of real sensibility began to apologise for his appearance there, acknowledging that after what had passed he had little right to expect a welcome at Fullerton, and stating his impatience to be assured of Miss Moreland's having reached her home in safety, as the cause of his intrusion.

The physical space in which this scene takes place is given minimal description: we can only figure out by inference that it is downstairs, and that it contains the preoccupied, listless, disappointed Catherine, for whom Mrs. Moreland went in search of the therapeutic essay "about young girls that have been spoilt for home by great acquaintance"—the mother's diagnosis of her daughter's disaffection. All the room contains are the three human figures, with Catherine at "her work," occupied with the perennial needlework of middle-class domestic women. Rather than relying on a multitude of physical or descriptive details, Austen chooses to set the scene with the social relations, sketching the concerned mother and the affectionate but distracted daughter, each more or less occupied by a range of domestic chores that are more gestured toward than they are described. In short, the characters are simply situated "at home." Into this scene Henry Tilney is inserted without any further detail about his appearance, equipage, or dress. Instead he is furnished with an appropriate social explanation for his call: polite and appropriate concern for the well-being of Catherine, a recent guest and friend of his sister's. Austen's focus here is not on physical space but on social relations, on what brings these three together and on what ties them together—the nets of concern, affection, duty, or responsibility. The author sets her stage with emotional explanations. The paragraph continues by recounting Mrs. Moreland's response to Henry's explanation:

He did not address himself to an uncandid judge or a resentful heart. Far from comprehending him or his sister in their father's misconduct, Mrs. Moreland had been always kindly disposed towards each, and instantly, pleased by his appearance, received him with the simple professions of unaffected benevolence; thanking him for such an attention to her daughter, assuring him that the friends of her children were always welcome there, and intreating him to say not another word of the past.

Again what is conveyed here has little to do with the material world of possessions, objects, and appearances but has all to do with a world of social obligations. Mrs. Moreland and Henry Tilney, who have never before met, initiate a social bond that follows the pattern of deference and obligation. What matters is unaffected benevolence, thanks, and assurance. With that assurance, the three figures in this vaguely sketched interior space are tied together in a clearly delineated social relation of both polite and genuinely concerned conduct.

But while this conventional bond is drawn, it is significant that Austen has chosen to narrate this scene from the perspective of the least knowledgeable figure, for Mrs. Moreland is not aware of the affection between Catherine and Henry. Apart from the conventional benevolence, thanks, and assurance, another separate and entirely different relation exists, and that is the one readers are most attuned to—Catherine's romance with Henry. The narrative pattern of this paragraph has a slightly defamiliarizing effect on the reader, shifting our outlook from the customary one that follows or is embodied within Catherine. The narrative apparatus briefly pulls back to occupy the position of conventional maternal authority. And after providing maternal assurances, the next paragraph turns to Henry's awkward subject position:

He was not ill inclined to obey this request, for, though his heart was greatly relieved by such unlooked-for mildness, it was not just at that moment in his power to say any thing to the purpose. Returning in silence to his seat, therefore, he remained for some minutes most civilly answering all Mrs. Moreland's common remarks about the weather and the roads.

This subsequent conversation is the equivalent of white noise, unimportant filler. Twentieth-century readers may have the advantage of familiarity with hundreds of subsequent domestic romances, and therefore we know what Henry has come for, but what we are explicitly given by the narrator is noise about roads and weather. The principal figure in the landscape has disappeared; nothing has been said about her since the "conscious" (i.e., self-conscious) Catherine introduced Henry a page earlier. After a page of this noise that brings the interaction to a standstill—the equivalent of "meanwhile back at the ranch"—the narrative finally returns to its customary center of attention:

> Catherine meanwhile,—the anxious, agitated, happy, feverish Catherine,— said not a word; but her glowing cheek and brightened eye made her mother trust that this good-natured visit would at least set her heart at ease for a time, and gladly therefore did she lay aside the first volume of the Mirror for a future hour.

Here the narrative explicitly acknowledges and exploits the gap between inside and outside, between the internal happy Catherine, that contradictory list of states of feeling, and the external Catherine, her glowing cheek and brightened eye. The highly compressed description of interior state—six words contained within and demarcated by dashes—is quickly superseded by Mrs. Moreland's kind but obtuse view, with some sly mockery of the supposed efficacy of moral essays (which are always recommended by social commentators, while novels are just as regularly denigrated as distracting if not injurious). In short, ever so briefly the narrative probes inside, beneath the skin, to give us a tantalizing glimpse of what Catherine is really feeling. But instantly that view is withdrawn, and we are brought back to the social surface. The narrative displays its capacity to move within, but it does so only to highlight the disparity between interiority and exteriority.

There are several ways to describe this phenomenon. The focus of the whole is not entirely on the gap between inside and outside, for that distinction is largely immaterial to Mrs. Moreland and even to Henry. It could be said that the narrative follows a pattern of increasing interiorization or idealization, starting from firm social relations and moving toward highly individualized happiness. It could also be said that the focus of the narrative circles about this trio until it finally settles briefly on Catherine. All the way through the reader is teased with the contrast between initiated (Catherine and Henry) and uninitiated (Mrs. Moreland). Furthermore, this sequence could be read as a narrative tour de force designed to display technique: the narrator shows off what she can know and what she can tell. This last point implies that the scene involves more than just these three subjects, for it also necessarily contains or implies a narrator and a reader. If the narrator is showing off with a brief flash of what she can do, so too she is staking a sort of claim.

It is Catherine's character and Catherine's decorum or reputation that is safely contained within those dashes: Catherine's feelings are displayed ever so gently and briefly; the anxious, agitated, happy, feverish, Catherine, with glowing cheek and brightened eye ever so delicately suggests a physical body and its pleasures. The narrator exposes an affectionate concern for her creation not at all unlike the maternal affection of Mrs. Moreland (which in turn is not dissimilar from the propriety interest evident in the narrator's phrase "my heroine"). Unlike earlier passages in the novel where Catherine's capacity for heroism is doubted, and the middle sections of the novel where her naïveté and her fondness for the Gothic make Catherine look very foolish, here the narrator does not make fun of Catherine, but rather seems to express her affection for the anxious, agitated, happy, feverish, Catherine, and, in a way, to privilege these emotions, at least in contrast to the mundane thoughts of the remedial essays that construct girls as correctable objects. Catherine's happiness could easily be mocked or minimized as the giddy feeling of a silly girl, but it is not. One might even say that this novel offers a generic choice, rejecting the exaggerations or extravagances of the Gothic in favor of the humble domestic romance. Here at the end of the novel Catherine's happiness is presented as the appropriate end to her conduct, and marriage to Henry as a suitable reward.

After a lengthy paragraph that takes up most of a page, the narrative finally gets Catherine and Henry alone:

His first purpose was to explain himself, and before they reached Mr. Allen's grounds he had done it so well, that Catherine did not think it could ever be repeated too often. She was assured of his affection; and that heart in return was solicited, which, perhaps, they pretty equally knew was already entirely his own; for, though Henry was now sincerely attached to her, though he felt and delighted in all the excellencies of her character and truly loved her society, I must confess that his affection originated in nothing better than gratitude, or, in other words, that a persuasion of her partiality for him had been the only cause of giving her a serious thought. It is a new circumstance in romance, I acknowledge, and dreadfully derogatory of an heroine's dignity; but if it be as new in common life, the credit of a wild imagination will at least be all my own.

Represented apart from Mrs. Moreland, these two reach an understanding that is not rendered in dialogue but only reported after the fact; but no veil has been decorously thrown over the pair, for the narrator is capable of describing both Henry's and Catherine's motivations, which, it is implied, are clearer to the narrator and her readers than to the characters. And thereafter, focus on the lovers is dissolved in a direct address of narrator to reader about matters of invention. The arch or wry voice, so typical of Austen, implies that men's attractions to women are very commonly stimulated by women's partialities; but the whole matter of courtship in general, and Henry and Catherine's in particular, has been replaced by the matter of fiction with the terms *romance*, *heroine*, and *imagination*. As so often happens in *Northanger Abbey*, the narrator insists upon the constructedness of this tale even while she insists that this tale is much more believable and reasonable than the common run of novels, those mere romances that precede it.

With this insistence on fictionality, the scene necessarily comes to be understood as one constructed out of a series of characters situated between the narrator and the reader. And what is understood about character becomes less a matter of realism, depth psychology, and accuracy in portraying life stories, and more a matter of what the novelist can invent and what she chooses to tell. As such, these last few sentences about the heroine's dignity are a fitting end to a passage that has demonstrated the author's magisterial skills at telling. From sentence to sentence it becomes clear that this is less a matter of revealing truth than of the narrator's deciding what she wishes to tell. For the narrative shifts all the way through, from one subject position to another and from one consciousness to another, and finally steps back and sets the three constructed consciousnesses, or subject positions, into a pattern. From a high seat of surveillance, the all-seeing narrator decides what they can know and what we can know. That is, the narrator intrudes into and recedes from interior space at will, at the very same time as she concedes that she is constructing this space.

Little of this swirling, shifting, and variable narration registers with readers because the shifts are rendered so fluid and unmarked through the technique of free indirect discourse. Free indirect discourse is the term used for paraphrase or condensed dialogue, presented indirectly by the narrator without the signal of quotation marks or "he said/she said." Furthermore, free indirect discourse can dispense with "she thought/he thought," so that it is sometimes difficult to distinguish between what is said and what is thought. Consider the following sentence: "Far from comprehending him or his sister in their father's misconduct, Mrs. Moreland had been always kindly disposed towards each, and instantly, pleased by his appearance, received him with the simple professions of unaffected benevolence; thanking him for such an attention to her daughter, assuring him that the friends of her children were always welcome there, and intreating him to say not another word of the past." It is apparent that the first clause represents Mrs. Moreland's thought—she would not speak of "his father's misconduct" to Henry; but the rest of the sentence could be a condensation of her genial remarks of welcome, presented indirectly to the reader. While all of this is clear enough in the reading, the intriguing part comes in the all but invisible transition (here signaled only by a semicolon) from thought to speech. It is this very technique that renders character transparent in narrative, enabling the narrative to move fluidly from exteriority to interiority, showing both the inside and the outside of character, mind and body—in this case, individual judgment in the first half of the sentence and social interaction in the second half. It is this technique that enables the novelist to represent both the nature of character and its position in social space, producing the impression of a totality.

Let us compare this early novel with a later one containing a similar encounter between the protagonists. Here, toward the end of *Emma*, is a paradigmatic moment in Austen's work, as a character carefully analyzes a minute detail of social interaction: Mr. Knightley's acknowledgment of Emma's reparation for her unkindness to Miss Bates at the Box Hill outing. Distressed by Mr. Knightley's condemnation of her thoughtless and cruel sport of Miss Bates, the very next morning a chastened Emma makes a penitent call on the Bateses to make up for her slight. When Mr. Knightley comes to call, her father praises Emma for her attention to the Bateses, praise that both Emma and Mr. Knightley know she does not deserve:

Emma's colour was heightened by this unjust praise; and with a smile, and shake of the head, which spoke much, she looked at Mr. Knightley.—It seemed as if there were an instantaneous impression in her favour, as if his eyes received the truth from her's, and all that had passed of good in her feelings were at once caught and honoured.—He looked at her with a glow of warm regard. She was warmly gratified—and in another moment still more so, by a little movement of more than common friendliness on his part. He took her hand;—whether she had not herself made the first motion, she could not say—she might, perhaps, have rather offered it—but he took her hand, pressed it, and certainly was on the point of carrying it to his lips—when, from some fancy or other, he suddenly let it go.—Why he should feel such a scruple, why he should change his mind when it was all but done, she could not perceive.—He would have judged better, she thought, if he had not stopped.—The intention, however, was indubitable; and whether it was that his manners had in general so little gallantry, or however else it happened, but she thought nothing became him more.—It was with him, of so simple, yet so dignified a nature.—She could not but recall the attempt with great satisfaction. It spoke such perfect amity.—He left them immediately afterwards—gone in a moment. He always moved with the alertness of a mind which could neither be undecided nor dilatory, but now he seemed more sudden than usual in his disappearance.

Unlike the compact and economical encounter in *Northanger Abbey*, this whole paragraph focuses on some very slight gestures. Communication, such as it is here, is perfectly silent, gestural, and physical. Various things seem to be communicated: a message of correction, advice taken and acted upon; a message of approval that the advice was taken. There are also distinct undercurrents of desire and the pleasure of physical touch. Emma's desire for Mr. Knightley has yet to be acknowledged by herself, and he has yet to declare himself—so there are several levels of signification here, the most diffuse of which is that Emma's sense of well-being is more dependent on his good opinion than she has yet realized. These undercurrents complicate Emma's relatively simple attempt to indicate that she is in agreement with Mr. Knightley. And because their interaction is gestural, the narrator emphasizes that it is one-sided; the whole paragraph consists of Emma's interpretation of his gestures, punctuated by a whole series of words like *seemed*, *might*, and *could*. The paragraph then consists of an unusual mixture of assurance and tentativeness. The dashes indicate the rapid flow of thought, as Emma quickly runs through all the possible meanings of his gesture. Like the poetry of surmise in Wordsworth's "Solitary Reaper," where he tries to understand the Gaelic song—"perhaps the numbers flow / For old, unhappy, far-off things"—the meaning can only be imagined, never known. The most significant difference between the representation of this encounter and that in the earlier novel is that here the narrative does not move around from one character to another; in fact, throughout the novel, we see directly into Mr. Knightley's consciousness only once, and even this insight is qualified by the quotation of Cowper's doubting line, "Myself creating what I saw." The present passage is definitely Emma's view of Mr. Knightley, her train of thought. Compared with *Northanger Abbey*, the narrative here is much more single-minded focusing on Emma's interpretation of what Mr. Knightley may have meant by that gesture. One consequence of such a focus is a powerful sense of interiorization, as if the whole paragraph takes place within Emma's consciousness and exteriority has been diminished to the momentary grasp of the hand. Additionally, by concentrating so insistently in the later novels on the interpretation of others' words and gestures, Austen turns penetration or interpretation of character and the corresponding transparency or opacity of character into an overt theme in the narrative; in passages such as this, characters anatomize what one can know of another. This thematization of opacity occurs when the technique is most assertively transparent—seeing directly into the heart of Emma, we are asked to doubt her capacity to know another. In *Emma*, this contradiction is particularly rich because Emma always assumes she knows more than she does. But still, while there are impediments, character is knowable here. This thematization presumes a depth of character, a desire to know, and finally, knowability—seeing into the heart of Emma, we are not encouraged to doubt the depth or consistency of her character. In sum, one can stress the power of the narrator, and her motive of order, or one can stress how little the characters can know of others.

To look at an example in the middle of Austen's career, let us turn to *Pride and Prejudice*. As many have noticed, this narrative seems to shift in the middle from an exterior, comic or satiric form that conveys Elizabeth's pride in her superior judgment to a more introspective, subjective, and reflective narrative in which she contemplates her mistakes. Up to Darcy's first proposal of marriage at the Hunsford Parsonage, the narrative is largely cast in dialogue and is presented by a narrator who is an arch and intrusive social commentator, but the tone of assurance is fractured by Elizabeth's humiliating discovery that she has had overmuch confidence in her judgment. After rudely spurning his proposal of marriage (only to find to her mortification that she has vastly misjudged him), Elizabeth accidentally meets Darcy by touring his home, after she has had plenty of time to reflect on her mistaken judgment of him. The magnificence of Darcy's estate, Pemberley, along with the extravagant praise of his loyal housekeeper, unsettle anew Elizabeth's opinion of him:

They were within twenty yards of each other, and so abrupt was his appearance, that it was impossible to avoid his sight. Their eyes instantly met, and the cheeks of each were overspread with the deepest blush. He absolutely started, and for a moment seemed immoveable from surprise; but shortly recovering himself, advanced towards the party, and spoke to Elizabeth, if not in terms of perfect composure, at least of perfect civility.

She had instinctively turned away; but, stopping on his approach, received his compliments with an embarrassment impossible to be overcome. Had his first appearance, or his resemblance to the picture they had just been examining, been insufficient to assure the other two that they now saw Mr. Darcy, the gardener's expression of surprise, on beholding his master, must immediately have told it. They stood a little aloof while he was talking to their niece, who, astonished and confused, scarcely dared lift her eyes to his face, and knew not what answer she returned to his civil enquiries after her family. Amazed at the alteration in his manner since they last parted, every sentence that he uttered was increasing her embarrassment; and every idea of the impropriety of her being found there, recurring to her mind, the few minutes in which they continued together, were some of the most uncomfortable of her life. Nor did he seem much more at ease; when he spoke, his accent had not of its usual sedateness; and he repeated his enquiries as to the time of her leaving Longbourn, and of her stay in Derbyshire, so often, and in so hurried a way, as plainly spoke of the distraction of his thoughts.

At length, every idea seemed to fail him; and, after standing a few moments without saying a word, he suddenly recollected himself, and took leave.

Despite the concern with Elizabeth's and Darcy's feelings, this scene remains grounded in its surroundings, Darcy's estate, Pemberley. Elizabeth never forgets where she is, as the narrative reminds us of the scenery, and Darcy's social status is never allowed to recede from notice. Up to this point, the narrative could easily function as stage directions for a play, for everything that is supposed to transpire within registers on the face as blush or across the body as start. From here on, however, the narrative turns within, and follows Elizabeth's emotional reaction to Darcy's unexpected appearance:

The others then joined her, and expressed their admiration of his figure; but Elizabeth heard not a word, and, wholly engrossed by her own feelings, followed them in silence. She was overpowered by shame and vexation. Her coming there was the most unfortunate, the most ill-judged, thing in the world! How strange must it appear to him! In what a disgraceful light might it not strike so vain a man! It might seem as if she had purposely thrown herself in his way again! Oh! why did she come? or, why did he thus come a day before he was expected? Had they only been ten minutes sooner, they should have been beyond the reach of his discrimination, for it was plain that he was that moment arrived, that moment alighted from his horse or his carriage. She blushed again and again over the perverseness of the meeting. And his behaviour, so strikingly altered,—what could it mean? That he should even speak to her was amazing!—but to speak with such civility, to enquire after her family! Never in her life has she seen his manners so little dignified, never had he spoken with such gentleness as on this unexpected meeting. What a contrast did it offer to his last address in Rosing's Park, when he put his letter into her hand! She knew not what to think, nor how to account for it.

They had now entered a beautiful walk by the side of the water, and every step was bringing them forward to a nobler fall of ground, or a finer reach of the woods to which they were approaching; but it was some time before Elizabeth was sensible of any of it; and, though she answered mechanically to the repeated appeals of her uncle and aunt, and seemed to direct her eyes to such objects as they pointed out, she distinguished no part of the scene. Her thoughts were all fixed on that one spot of Pemberley House, whichever it might be, where Mr. Darcy then was. She longed to know what at that moment was passing in his mind; in what manner he thought of her, and whether, in defiance of every thing, she was still dear to him. Perhaps he had been civil, only because he felt himself at ease; yet there had been *that* in his voice, which was not like ease. Whether he had felt more of pain or of pleasure in seeing her, she could not tell, but he certainly had not seen her with composure.

In free indirect discourse, the train of her thoughts is recounted in full, grammatical, and neatly constructed sentences; urgency or passion is only marked by the series of exclamation points. And though the scene conveys Elizabeth's agitation, none of it is represented in an agitated style—the narration still conveys order, control, and rationality. Her emotional state is carefully assessed in an abstract, Johnsonian vocabulary of embarrassment, shame, and vexation, vocabulary that negates the particularity and subjectivity of her emotions: anyone meeting her spurned suitor in such circumstance would feel shame and vexation. What most distinguishes this passage from the early example from *Northanger Abbey* is that the narrative does not tell us about Darcy, only Elizabeth; aside from one unusual passage about Elizabeth's "fine eyes," Darcy's consciousness is never represented in *Pride and Prejudice*. And as such, his character remains opaque and inaccessible: "She longed to know what at that moment was passing in his mind" speaks of a desire that can never be fulfilled. But of course, if his subject position is said to be impenetrable, hers is an open book, open for all the readers of *Pride and Prejudice*. In a contradiction that is not so different from the high modernist perspective of, say, Virginia Woolf, *Pride and Prejudice* may assert that complex characters are not easily known, that their riches consist of a hyperinteriority, but such an assertion has the obvious effect of raising the price of interior riches, of the depths of character to be plumbed in an Elizabeth Bennet or a Mrs. Dalloway, both of whom are to be immensely valued over the shallow and easily known Mr. Collinses of the world. Reuben Brower writes, in a typical view, that "what most satisfies us in reading the dialogue in *Pride and Prejudice* is Jane Austen's awareness that it is difficult to know any complex person, that the knowledge of a man like Darcy is an interpretation and a construction, not a simple absolute. . . . A reasoned judgment of character [is] reached through long experience and slow weighing of possibilities."

The most remarkable reunion scene in Austen occurs in her last finished novel, *Persuasion*. Seven years earlier, Anne Elliot and Captain Wentworth were engaged to be married, but because his calling was unsettled, and due to the persuasion of elders, Anne calls off their marriage. At the opening of the novel, Captain Wentworth has returned wealthy, secure, and, though affecting indifference to Anne, still resentful. The first meeting of these former lovers takes place at the home of Anne's sister, Mary. Mary is now married to Charles Musgrove, and Captain Wentworth has come to go shooting with Charles; Wentworth stops to say hello to Mary, where Anne first sees him:

The others appeared; they were in the drawing-room. Her eye half met Captain Wentworth's; a bow, a curtsey passed; she heard his voice—he talked to Mary, said all that was right; said something to the Miss Musgroves, enough to mark an easy footing: the room seemed full—full of persons and voices—but a few minutes ended it. Charles shewed himself at the window, all was ready, their visitor had bowed and was gone; the Miss Musgroves were gone too, suddenly resolving to walk to the end of the village with the sportsmen: the room was cleared, and Anne might finish her breakfast as she could.

"It is over! it is over!" she repeated to herself again, and again, in nervous gratitude. "The worst is over!"

Mary talked, but she could not attend. She had seen him. They had met. They had been once more in the same room!

Soon, however, she began to reason with herself, and try to be feeling less. Eight years, almost eight years has passed, since all had been given up. How absurd to be resuming the agitation which such an interval had banished into distance and indistinction! What might not eight years do? Events of every description, changes, alienations, removals,—all, all must be comprised in it; and oblivion of the past—how natural, how certain too! It included nearly a third part of her own life.

Alas! with all her reasonings, she found, that to retentive feelings eight years may be little more than nothing.

Now, how were his sentiments to be read? Was this like wishing to avoid her? And the next moment she was hating herself for the folly which asked the questions.

In the later novels such as *Emma* or *Persuasion*, when the narrator shows the interior state, she does not summarize it with such conventional terms as *embarrassment* and *vexation*. By conveying her agitation in the style and sentence structure (a whole series of inelegant, short, stubby clauses), the narrator does not have to say that Anne Elliot is uncomfortable, and, as a consequence, we get the most dramatic and immediate use of free indirect discourse to achieve transparency. Here, the external event is minimized, rendered in almost phantasmagorical fashion—"the room seemed full—full of persons and voices"—as the text concentrates only on Anne's response. The dialogue is background noise that the narrative doesn't even bother to repeat. The narration no longer conveys order, control, and rationality, for the event, while ordinary, is painful and irrational—in fact, most of the passage consists in Anne's difficult struggle to impose rationality on it. Like much of *Persuasion*, this passage is Wordsworthian in its focus on memory, the pain of remembering, and how memory separates one individual from another. Austen's most solitary protagonist, Anne Elliot suffers alone. The intensely subjective passage quoted represents an interior sermon in which she cautions herself to expect nothing but changes, alienations, and removals, none of them for the better. A few lines later, Mary relates to Anne Wentworth's comment on their meeting again after all these years: " 'Altered beyond his knowledge!' Anne fully submitted, in silent, deep mortification."

Her mortification is followed by the narrator's summarizing of Wentworth's attitude in indirect discourse:

Frederick Wentworth had used such words, or something like them ['You were so altered he should not have known you again'], but without an idea that they would be carried round to her. He had thought her wretchedly altered, and, in the first moment of appeal, had spoken as he felt. He had not forgiven Anne Elliot. She had used him ill; deserted and disappointed him; and worse, she had shewn a feebleness of character in doing so, which his own decided, confident temper could not endure. She had given him up to oblige others. It had been the effect of over-persuasion. It had been weakness and timidity.

Wentworth's response is given in shorthand as petulance and misunderstanding. His and Anne's responses to the encounter are kept entirely separate. And the responses are gendered: the range of emotions she feels is conveyed, following the path of pain and reaction, but his feelings are summarized, condensed, reported as a state, not conveyed as a process. Their thoughts are both transparent, but they are rendered differently. Their alienation and emotional distance are embodied in the very shape of the narrative: hers painful and slow, his curt, conventional, and clichéd—she had used him ill. The passages discussed so far have all been part of courtship plots within domestic novels of courtship and marriage, and they have all dealt with the relations between the female and male protagonists. There are of course many scenes of large social gatherings, scenes of solitary heroines' meditations, and scenes of female characters interacting. Save for the solitary meditations, none of these other configurations results in the detailed examination of consciousness or reflects the relation between one consciousness and another. The configuration examined here is explicitly gendered because the reflections are not symmetrical; they usually concern the female interpretation of the male ("she longed to know what at that moment was passing in his mind"). Such scenes therefore accept the assumptions of heterosexual monogamy, that marriage between male and female is the goal of social intercourse, that the unmarried state is unstable and seeks the rest or stability of marriage. The gender difference in responses becomes more pronounced as the narration becomes more interiorized, implying that women differ from men more on the inside than on the outside, more in their emotional than in their physical lives.

Austen's most difficult novel is *Mansfield Park*, the only one admirers are regularly willing to admit that they have to work at liking. Its scenes of reunion illuminate Austen's narrative technique and presentation of consciousness. Also, because the moral and historical arguments about aristocracy, responsibility, and the state of England are so explicit in *Mansfield Park*, it is here easiest to see the connection between narrative form, how the protagonist's subject position is constructed, and theme— what that subjectivity signifies. Claiming that *Pride and Prejudice* was too "light, bright and sparkling," with *Mansfield Park* Austen apparently set out to compose a more serious and less comic novel, "on a complete change of subject." Unlike the witty and confident Elizabeth Bennet before her or Emma after her, *Mansfield Park*'s heroine seems humorless and often prudish. Fanny Price is a Cinderella figure, a poor relative subject alternately to abuse and neglect as she is brought up as a dependent among her rich relatives at Mansfield Park. Only her cousin Edmund fully appreciates Fanny's worth, and she has to endure the unwanted attentions of the lively Henry Crawford along with the jealousy aroused by Edmund's attraction to Henry's equally lively sister Mary. Such a plot produces a solitary and unusually silent protagonist with no confidants—only the narrator and the reader are privy to her interior struggles and resentments. As a consequence, both Fanny's consciousness and the narrator's presentation of it assume unusual prominence in the novel, and interpreters struggle to decide if we are asked to take Fanny as the authorial spokesperson; that is, should we believe that she is always right—a moral paragon like Elinor Dashwood in *Sense and Sensibility* or Anne Elliot—or are her judgments often self-interested and partial, fallible like Elizabeth Bennet or Emma Woodhouse? Fanny and Edmund are reunited after her long exile to her parents' house in Portsmouth, during which time a whole series of disasters have been visited on the Bertrams of Mansfield Park: the eldest son is mortally ill, and both daughters have eloped (the eldest daughter, Maria, ran off with Henry Crawford, who was supposed to marry Fanny). Edmund travels to Portsmouth to bring Fanny back to Mansfield Park:

By eight in the morning, Edmund was in the house. The girls heard his entrance from above, and Fanny went down. The idea of immediately seeing him, with the knowledge of what he must be suffering, brought back all her own first feelings. He so near her, and in misery. She was ready to sink, as he entered the parlour. He was alone, and met her instantly; and she found herself pressed to his heart with only these words, just articulate, "My Fanny—my only sister—my only comfort now." She could say nothing; nor for some minutes could he say more.

He turned away to recover himself, and when he spoke again, though his voice still faltered, his manner showed the wish of self-command, and the resolution of avoiding any farther allusion. "Have you breakfasted?—When shall you be ready?—Does Susan go?"—were questions following each other rapidly. His great object was to be off as soon as possible. When Mansfield was considered, time was precious; and the state of his own mind made him find relief only in motion. It was settled that he should order the carriage to the door in half an hour; Fanny answered for their having breakfasted, and being quite ready in half an hour. He had already ate, and declined staying for their meal. He would walk round the ramparts, and join them in the carriage. He was gone again, glad to get away even from Fanny.

He looked very ill; evidently suffering under violent emotions, which he was determined to suppress. She knew it must be so, but it was terrible to her.

This is a curiously mixed passage—of great emotional conflict and suffering, yet seen almost from afar. Very little dialogue is rendered directly, only Edmund's elliptical address to Fanny; the rest is reported indirectly. Fanny appears to say nothing of significance here at all, though as is usual in this novel, it is her response, her feelings that matter. By conveying so clearly the sense of containment of emotion, of that which is too painful to speak, Austen has captured the contradiction of intimacy and distance in the very form of the narrative. Edmund's feelings are physically transparent and yet distant: they can be assumed, conjectured at, even seen, but not told directly.

The whole scene is rendered from Fanny's perspective, though not really from within her, as is common earlier in the novel; here, we are looking through her or with her as she solicitously watches Edmund. With its isolated and vulnerable protagonist, the watcher who sees all of the others' flaws and failures, *Mansfield Park* more than any of Austen's previous novels thematizes the connection between subjectivity and selfishness, the consequences of toying with another's feelings, of thinking too much of oneself and too little of others, of the unwillingness to harmonize one's feelings and desires with others. In these last few chapters there is no longer any room for irony between a knowing narrator and Fanny's adolescent gushes on picturesque nature or the jealousy and resentment of the Crawfords Fanny indulged in earlier. By this point in the novel, Fanny has grown into the role of silent watcher, judge of others' conduct. Upon her return to Mansfield Park from Portsmouth, Fanny becomes a mature, fully developed protagonist, one who is not simply the moral center, the angel of the house, but rather has grown into the position of the narrator; in the last few chapters, Fanny's subject position becomes indistinguishable from the all-wise perspective of the narrator.

Fanny watched him [Edmund] with never-failing solicitude, and sometimes catching his eye, received an affectionate smile, which comforted her; but the first day's journey passed without her hearing a word from him on the subjects that were weighing him down. . . . She looked at him, but he was leaning back, sunk in a deeper gloom than ever, and with eyes closed as if the view of cheerfulness oppressed him [the spring landscape], and the lovely scenes of home must be shut out."

As Fanny's subjectivity assumes the wider purview of the narrator, in turn the narrator's role expands into assertive authorial omniscience and manipulation. In the last two chapters, the narrator sums up and closes by distributing punishment to the vicious and reward to the virtuous. The narrator opens the last chapter with this vast, providential overview:

Let other pens dwell on guilt and misery. I quit such odious subjects as soon as I can, impatient to restore every body, not greatly in fault with themselves, to tolerable comfort, and to have done with all the rest.

My Fanny indeed at this very time, I have the satisfaction of knowing, must have been happy in spite of every thing. She must have been a happy creature in spite of all that she felt or thought she felt, for the distress of those around her. She had sources of delight that must force their way. She was returned to Mansfield Park, she was useful, she was beloved; she was safe from Mr. Crawford, and when Sir Thomas came back she had every proof that could be given in his then melancholy state of spirits, of his perfect approbation and increased regard; and happy as all this must make her, she would still have been happy without any of it, for Edmund was no longer the dupe of Miss Crawford.

Fanny never speaks again in this last chapter, but she does not need to: she has assumed ascendancy in the household and become the domestic guardian of virtue. It is as if the narrator has been grooming Fanny to take over both Mansfield Park and *Mansfield Park*.

At issue in the preceding discussion has been the development of the quintessential novelistic technique for representing subjectivity, the way that Austen uses free indirect speech to convey interiority. Literary historians tracing the development of novelistic technique uniformly conclude that Austen was the first great English novelist to master this technique of narrated monologue. In *Transparent Minds*, Dorrit Cohn writes:

The pattern set by Jane Austen thus unfolds throughout the nineteenth century: precisely those authors who, in their major works, most decisively abandoned first-person narration (Flaubert, Zola, James), instituting instead the norms of the dramatic novel, objective narration, and unobtrusive narrators, were the ones who re-introduced the subjectivity of private experience into the novel: this time not in terms of direct self-narration, but by imperceptibly integrating mental reactions into the neutral-objective report of actions, scenes, and spoken words.

Free indirect discourse is not, however, merely another technique in the progression to develop the best method of rendering character, such that Austen is better at it than Richardson, Fielding, or Burney. Conventional literary history has assumed that the rise of the novel is the rise in formal realism: representing everyday life more accurately, more persuasively, better. But there are historical and ideological issues at stake here as well. Given the nationalist and conservative political climate of the period in which Austen wrote, beginning with the French Revolution and extending through the Napoleonic Wars, unbridled subjectivity or Romantic celebration of the freedom of the individual subject as conveyed in radical Jacobin novels such as Mary Wollstonecraft's or William Godwin's could be construed as coming at the expense of—indeed as an enemy of—social constraint and custom: individualism is necessarily set against preexisting social rules and order. Thus Austen's representation of subjectivity has considerable bearing on whether she is read historically as a conservative or a progressive writer, whether she celebrates or deplores the new Romantic individualism. In depicting in such detail the interior states of her protagonists, does Austen ask us to believe that there is a preexisting, immanent set of rules of conduct that all individuals must come to respect and obey? Or do her protagonists rely on their inner resources to determine for themselves what they should do and desire?

The significance of Austen's use of free indirect discourse and her representation of subjectivity is by no means a dead topic. Just as with Ian Watt's discussion of Austen's innovations in narrative technique, technical analysis soon modulates into moral issues, so that what sets Austen apart is the truth of her characters, and thus the nature of the novel as such—its truth and thus its moral force. It is evident that free indirect discourse has a lot to do with the representation of social order and authority. Literary historians concerned with such matters often connect the novel as a discourse with the issues of discipline as defined by theorist Michel Foucault: the ways in which a social formation orders itself and individual subjects within it by means of its various knowledges, technologies, and disciplines. The novel is one such technology and the authority of novelistic discourse is crucially dependent on its vision—what John Bender calls its transparency: "Transparency is the convention that both author and beholder are absent from a representation, the objects of which are rendered as if their externals were entirely visible and their internality fully accessible." What has been identified as free indirect discourse is but one aspect of "narrative as an authoritative resource": "novelistic conventions of transparency, completeness, and representational reliability (perhaps especially where the perceptions being represented are themselves unreliable) subsume an assent to regularized authority"—i.e., what Theodor Adorno calls the administered life.

The use of Foucault to describe the function of novelistic authority by contemporary critics can be seen as an extension of an insight provided long ago by Jean-Paul Sartre, when he wrote of the nineteenth-century novelistic narrator:

He tells his story with detachment. If it caused him suffering, he has made honey from this suffering. He looks back upon it and considers as it really was, that is, *sub specie aeternitatis*. There was difficulty to be sure, but this difficulty ended long ago; the actors are dead or married or comforted. Thus, the adventure was a brief disturbance which is over with. It is told from the viewpoint of experience and wisdom; it is listened to from the viewpoint of order. Order triumphs; order is everywhere; it contemplates an old disorder as if the still waters of a summer day have preserved the memory of the ripples which have run through it. . . . Behind [even] the inexplicable, the author allows us to suspect a whole causal order which will restore rationality to the universe.

Novelistic narrative derives its authority from its transparency and employs that authority in a regulative or constitutive fashion, representing ordered subjects in an ordered world. This is what Fredric Jameson means by his assertion that "the aesthetic act is itself ideological, and the production of aesthetic or narrative form is to be seen as an ideological act in its own right, with the function of inventing imaginary or formal 'solutions' to unresolvable social contradictions." Behind Jameson is the pioneering work by Georg Lukács from 1920, *The Theory of the Novel*, in which Lukács argues that the novel is fundamentally organized backward, representing the world as backdrop to the fortunes of the individual subject: "the novel is the epic of an age in which the immanence of life is no longer directly given, in which the meaning of life has become a problem, yet which still thinks in terms of totality." That is to say, while focusing so relentlessly on the particular life, the novel still aspires to show the meaning of the whole; the novel is thus both a representation and an interpretation of life, an attempt to show it as it is while implicitly, through the necessary ordering of its form, showing how the world ought to be.

The representation of subjectivity or interiority of character is the crucial step in the novel's ordering. However idiosyncratic a particular character, it is at the same time typical of human behavior. Character is thus a representation of human subjects, but it is also an interpretation of how they behave and how they ought to behave; as Sartre puts it, the novel "is explanatory; it aims at producing a psychological law on the basis of this example." Psychological law presumes that characters are consistent and predictable; that is to say, character is ordered and ultimately rational, however irrational individual acts may be. Social order is thus dependent on the assumptions of individual stability and readability, for without stable and consistent character, no stable and consistent or even meaningful society can be represented. In Bender's words, "the nature and function of novelistic realism lie in its ability to produce meaning by containing its own contradictions and thus to leave the impression that consciousness and subjectivity are stable across time."

To return to the point with which we began, Jane Austen's work is accorded a special place in the history of the novel, for her work functions as a marker of transition, her novels provide a convenient bridge between the eighteenth-century novel and the nineteenth-century novel, from the genre's rise to its triumph (in conventional terms), from a society organized by custom and tradition to one organized around the individual subject's development, from outside to inside. This transitional function cannot in itself explain Austen's appeal, but her position in literary history as great innovator and her position in the canon as great novelist are related; discussions of the former inevitably seem to end up as discussions of the latter. For Watt, because Austen has a foot in the psychological world of Richardson and a foot in the sociological world of Fielding she is uniquely capable of negotiating that most fundamental contradiction of novelistic discourse, between subjectivity and objectivity, between the individual subject position and collectivity. Despite the increasing transparency of her narrative, and its increasingly subjective form, Austen retains an authoritative narrative voice that checks the subjectivity of her protagonists.

The most famous discussion of Austen's narrative virtuosity and its perfect harmony between exteriority and interiority is Wayne Booth's analysis of *Emma*. In *The Rhetoric of Fiction*, Booth emphasizes the ironic distance the narrator has to maintain in order to ensure the reader's sympathy with Emma despite her many faults, and Austen achieves this by using "the heroine herself as a kind of narrator." Seen entirely from the outside, Emma would be distasteful; but seen from the inside she can be comically sympathetic, for we can see through all her self-deception. But despite the sympathy, we long for her reform, because of the reliable narrator who establishes the social norm: "her most important role is to reinforce both aspects of the double vision that operates throughout the book: our inside view of Emma's worth and our objective view of her great faults." In a passage of profound admiration, Booth concludes that Austen's combination of transparency and authority produces human truth and perfection:

When we read this novel, we accept her ["Jane Austen" or the narrator] as representing everything we admire most. . . . She is, in short, a perfect human being, within the concept of perfection established by the book she writes; she even recognizes that human perfection of the kind *she* exemplifies is not quite attainable in real life. . . . The "omniscience" is thus a much more remarkable thing than is ordinarily implied by the term. All good novelists know all about their characters—all that they need to know. And the question of how their narrators are to find out all that *they* need to know, the question of "authority," is a relatively simple one. The real choice is much more profound than this would imply. It is a choice of the moral, not merely the technical, angle of vision from which the story is to be told.

The object of admiration here has come a long way from free indirect discourse, for it is no longer Austen's representation but her interpretation, not her showing of the world but her judgment of it. What is being celebrated is a specific vision of order, authority, and judgment, and what is not fully acknowledged is the historical specificity of that order, authority, and judgment. Austen represents the world as it ought to be, but we have to add that what we mean by this is the way one individual may have wanted it to be in 1816. In equating this one vision with perfection, we negate or occlude the historical tendrils that root a text in its time. These tendrils include assumptions about class, gender, and sexuality—a whole set of assumptions that we may no longer find appropriate in deciding what makes one indvidual better than another.

   Marilyn Butler makes the argument about Austen's connection between character and morality from a historical perspective, seeing Austen as a conservative opponent to Romanticism and the French Revolution: "Where the heroine is fallible, the novel as a whole can be said to enact the conservative case; where the heroine is exemplary, she models it." This is a reasonable argument, but on the level of form it is exactly backward, because whatever the personal politics of the novelist, the novel as such cannot enact the conservative case. Produced by the Enlightenment, novelistic discourse enacts the liberal dilemma: preserving individual freedom—not so much protecting it from the tyranny of a despotic state as preventing it from encroaching on the individual freedoms of others. The essential tension of novelistic discourse—between the individual and the collective—is always resolved by or collapsed into subjectivity because the novel explains the social by way of the individual—as Lukács argues, the world is but a frame to situate the individual: "The novel tells of the adventure of interiority; the content of the novel is the story of the soul that goes to find itself, that seeks adventures in order to be proved and tested by them, and by proving itself, to find its own essence." Austen's novels are no different in this respect, for each assumes the outward form of a biography of a problematic individual—"The development of man is still the thread upon which the whole world of the novel is strung"—but they are among the last to retain an authoritative narrator who assumes the collective voice of judgment with its inevitable irony. Despite their separate and individual protagonists, Austen's novels evoke a powerful nostalgia for a past when collective judgment perhaps seemed possible and desirable. But it is not simply the keenness of judgment that readers find so appealing in Austen's novels; it is rather the sense of balance between the individual and the social. Austen's innovations in narrative technique enable a dialectic between interiority and exteriority, individual and collective; her novels present the illusion of perfect balance, negotiating the fundamental social contradiction of her time, and not coincidentally of the novel itself.

James Thompson

Selected Bibliography

Bender, John. *Imagining the Penitentiary*. Chicago: University of Chicago Press, 1987.
Booth, Wayne. *The Rhetoric of Fiction*. Chicago: University of Chicago Press, 1961.
Butler, Marilyn. *Jane Austen and the War of Ideas*. Oxford: Clarendon, 1975.
Cohn, Dorrit. *Transparent Minds: Narrative Modes for Presenting Consciousness in Fiction*. Princeton, N.J.: Princeton University Press, 1978.
Jameson, Fredric. *Political Unconscious*. Ithaca, N.Y.: Cornell University Press, 1981.

Lukács, Georg. *The Theory of the Novel.* Trans. Anna Bostock. 1971. Reprint. Cambridge, Mass.: MIT Press, 1978.

Sartre, Jean-Paul. *What is Literature? and Other Essays.* Cambridge, Mass.: Harvard University Press, 1988.

Watt, Ian. *The Rise of the Novel.* Stanford: Stanford University Press, 1957.

Walter Scott: Narrative, History, Synthesis

ONE of the great comic moments in eighteenth-century fiction occurs in the early chapters of Samuel Richardson's last novel, *Sir Charles Grandison*. Delivered a wrathful *carte* from the double-dyed villain from whom he rescued a lady in peril, the double-dyed hero responds tranquilly, yes, I'll meet him—for breakfast.

We don't usually think of Sir Charles Grandison as a comedian, far less an ironist. Yet he is in fact quite aware that his disruption of the approved code for settling things, establishing Right by Might Between Men, will stop the breath of all hearers somewhere between laughter and horror. Lest the laughter dismantle his manhood and shake his domestic authority, Sir Charles hastens to add that he will wear his sword to that breakfast—undrawn, loosened, for defense only. He modestly indicates that in the past his sword, when sanctioned by its defensive role only, has bested all comers.

Commenting two generations later on his key predecessor, Walter Scott noted that readers could not identify with Richardson's prudent paragon because the novelist had endowed him with such unvarying firmness of character and perfection of education, rooted in such absolute worldly and familial security, that his revolutionary refusals had no force. In the thousand pages of his existence Sir Charles's major actions are always to waive action, to hang fire—while his rakish and stupid father sets up a mistress, tyrannizes his daughters, and wastes the estate; while the macho young aristocrats of two continents challenge him to duels; while the dark lady and the fair lady who each have his affections await his determining move. History lies sleeping around him, offering no challenges from or invitations to the turmoil of public life, while heredity effaces itself, sending forth no troubling images of a past or a patrimony to be matched, eluded, or redeemed.

It was Scott's own project as a novelist to wake this sleeper, History, to articulate those troubling psychodomestic images, and to integrate them with each other and with Richardson's manly prevaricator, producing in the long-running, multiple "passive hero of the Waverley Novels" the most influential of his culture's essays in modernity, even with the competing accomplishment of Byron. For Byronic modernity explored its visions in registers of irony and fragmentation, its lyrics and dramas reaching after the consolidations and consolations of narrative without real faith in it. Scott's vision, hitting modernity's true notes of loss and limitation, of risky investment in self-creation and blue-chip respect for self-undermining, partakes of narrative faith. So does his culture, even when (especially when) contemplating its contaminated and bulky beginnings and its huddled, obscure conclusions. Complaining about the bulky beginnings and huddled conclusions of each Waverley Novel was a national pastime Scott initiated himself, but as a faithful recorder of his culture's understanding of history he could follow no other form.

Scott often fell short of wholeness and proportion as a plotmaster and as a philosopher of Western history, but he sought such coherence. His commitment was to that "Universal" and "continuous" History, time seen all of a piece, all of a pattern, whose first form he studied in his late novels of Christian chivalry, whose modern form, born out of the Scottish Enlightenment and consolidated in narrative in the Scottish/English Waverley Novels and articulated by Macaulay and Hegel, was liberalism.

This Universal History was dreamed and rationalized in the eighteenth and nineteenth centuries as a linear process, unstable and somewhat arbitrary at its beginning and end but governed by a dynamic middle made up of surges toward "synthesis," a process duplicated as form by nineteenth-century fiction itself. Readers of the Waverley Novels— historians and critics from 1814 to the present—have always recognized that the novels of Scott are a rich moment of exposure of this process and of the discourses of fiction and history which, allied with and contesting each other within the precincts of the republic of letters, aspired to articulate it. The project, the Universal Liberal History of Western Culture, imagined a human communal pattern moving psychologically from the irrational toward the rational, and politically from the sacred to the economic, while the horizon of expectations widened toward the accommodation of moderate change and desire was rechanneled from glory to security, diverted away from war toward the hundreds of new adventures of mind and spirit and body made possible— at least for the middle and upper classes—by security.

As Nietzsche saw, as science-fiction writers from Mary Shelley and H. G. Wells and Olaf Stapledon to Frank Herbert and Arthur Clarke have seen, Universal Liberal History might, so conceived, come to an end, either defeated by an unruly antithesis or immobilized, confounded by its own success. Indeed it was recently argued, in a controversial essay and book by conservative historian Francis Fukuyama, that the History that the Waverley Novels so indelibly and anxiously premised *has* come to an end. In a 1989 essay amplified in a 1991 book, *The End of History and the Last Man*, Fukuyama returned to the question whether there is a universal and directional human history leading toward Liberal Democracy, broadly conceived, and argued that there is, looking not only at contemporary South America and Eastern Europe but at the macropolitics of the last four hundred years, and working from contemporary versions of the definition of "human nature" found in classic philosophical literature.

For Fukuyama, History bears, is bearing out, Liberal Democracy's claim to exercise in wholeness the Platonically conceived threefold nature of man—his Reason, his Desire, and his "Thymos," the latter a complex element of the spirit, which requires that the self stand forth, alone and/or in company with a community or a community's significant values, as *most* valuable, that it stand forth in worth-full identity, be recognized. To know; to do; to be known to do. Recognition, the last of these virtues, is the cause of History, of History's brilliant constructions of "values," of its dark dramas of competing, captured, resisting values. And Liberal Democracy, constructing or tolerating so many forms of recognition, striving to equalize recognition for all, does, according to Hegel and now Fukuyama, formally answer all three of these elements of human nature.

Fukuyama, interestingly, sees two possible alternatives, or as yet unabsorbed possibilities, in this scheme of things, two grits in the wheel of the wagon of Universal History wending west to Liberal Democracy. These are the political and value systems of Islam and of feminism. Walter Scott, in his way, saw the same alternatives. The Saracen's head, debased on pub signs, swings over many a European town in the Waverley Novels: the madwoman laughs and groans at the crossroads. The narrative strives to integrate them into the synthesis, or leave them behind, but the consolidation is never complete, as I shall argue.

The Waverley Novels still await a full-scale treatment of their Orientalist impulse and of the ways in which this enables (and disables) Scott's vision of race in Universal History; though many have touched on the loss-gain equation in the novels' treatment of various British races, the powerful contemporary theorizing of race in culture and its fictions has not quite reached Scott criticism. But the equally powerful contemporary theorizing of gender has. Gone are the days when a critic might complacently note, as Andrew Hook did in the 1972 introduction to the Penguin edition of *Waverley*, that Scott rescued the novel from "the danger of becoming the preserve of the woman writer and the woman reader," offering "a new masculinity," which allowed the novel to become "the most appropriate form for writers' richest and deepest imaginative explorations of human experience." In one of the best of the recent books on Scott, Ina Ferris has linked the anxieties and diffusions of gender within the Waverley Novels to the drama of competing discourses—history, fiction, and criticism—at the turn of the century. Literary criticism, hungering for the adult authority of historiography, which was culturally gendered masculine, faced a new, huge, middle-class reading public already gendered female, already reading "the novel," also culturally gendered feminine. The transformation critics sought made use of a category crucial to evolving Western culture, the "feminine," or "proper" novels of Fanny Burney and Maria Edgeworth. This new kind of novel, replacing the amoral and sensual Gothic, and distinguished by such linear qualities as moral fineness, "accuracy," and "observation," cleared a space for a still newer kind of novel, whose fine and "feminine" observation and accuracy could also accommodate those "richest and deepest" qualities that had been languishing since Shakespeare, or since Fielding, waiting for a masculine vessel, the necessary receptacle for lost "height and depth."

Shakespeare the writer-actor had, of course, taken his work to his public in the flesh; the narrator of *Tom Jones* abominated the "little reptile of a critic" whose discourse had by the eighteenth century aspired to mediate the relationship of artist and public and to "give laws" to govern that new province of writing, the novel. But Walter Scott was a critic before he was a novelist, and a lawyer before that, and a collector of historical artifacts and songs before anything. This was the perfect biography for one aspiring to the masculine space cleared by a new kind of criticism that was gaining authority from the policing, so to speak, of the novel as it moved from "female" romance through "proper feminine" moral acuteness to that "masculine" height and depth which included "history."

Yet even as he acquiesced in this transformation, this usurpation of the feminine novel by the masculine (historical) novel, Scott was ambushed by—and accepted the ambiguity of—gender. In culture, even in history, as in biology, masculinity often seems in its very strenuousness the less stable, the more artificial construct. For one thing, critical reception of the Waverley Novels during the sixty years after their publication provoked a gender migration similar to that which took place for the American classics. First these novels cleared a space for men to write novels; then they became novels for novelists' characters to read and then for readers' children to read, culturally set aside from the topos of (now masculine) *writing*, enmeshed in the (still feminine) topos of *reading*. Second, historiography itself, thus challenged, aspired to organize a narrative of "the highest and deepest," moving from the polemic and controversialist passions of the seventeenth and early eighteenth centuries through the ironic stance of the rationalist and the amateur worship of separated scraps and fragments of the antiquarian, to the sweeping and ultimately mythic narratives of the Universal Historian.

Contemporary psychohistorians of History like Michel Foucault and Hayden White have linked this mythic historiography, this dream of continuity, the flow of all that disappears in fragments into a recomposed unity, with that fascination with androgyny, with the "oceanic," ultimately with the Good Mother, that underlay the nineteenth century's more conscious strivings after masculinity and the disciplines of the Father.

A key element in the construction of the long narrative that makes up the Waverley Novels and accelerated these changes in the genre was anonymity, a sly, spry baiting and baffling of the public that was its own publicity, a spectacle of Thymos which Plato could hardly have dreamed of, and which even yet enchants and irritates. The Walter Scott we recognize was born in 1771 into Georgian Scotland and died in the Reform Bill England of 1832. He followed his father into the Law at age fifteen, his multiplex culture into translation at twenty-two, his ambition into the *Edinburgh Review* and the Sheriffdom of Selkirk at twenty-eight, his antiquarianism into collecting, translating, and publishing *The Minstrelsy of the Scottish Border* at thirty-one, and his aristocratic lineage into poetry at thirty-four with *The Lay of the Last Minstrel*, which embellished an ancient tale of his own ancestors. These are selves Scott could himself recognize, legitimized by all that was open and precious in his history. The author of the Waverley Novels was a being he could not quite recognize himself, and so anonymous publication of *Waverley: or 'Tis Sixty Years Since*, in 1814, became the foundation of a new body of work generated by a new self, the Author of Waverley, a being recognized and lionized from the start as the Great Unknown.

Walter Scott told himself and his friends a number of disarming reasons for this turn to prose anonymity. He had written some chapters of the story in 1809 while working on the poem *The Lady of the Lake*, but mislaid them until they surfaced during a hunt for fishing tackle in 1813. His poetic drama *Rokeby* that same year had not had the huge momentum of his first three poems; both he and his publisher were looking for a novelty to replace the perhaps fading and too-much-known Walter Scott. *The Bridal of Triermain*, an Arthurian quest-romance issued anonymously in the summer of 1813, had given him a taste for this particular jest.

The artist as fisher, as jester, as self-marketer—these are powerful components of an identity, but they don't fully explain Scott's commitment to this identity. No one in public life, and few in the reading public, doubted that the Great Unknown was Walter Scott. Yet for twelve years and thirty-two novels and tales this open secret gave Walter Scott unprecedented control over the drama of recognition by which the novelist and the historical novel itself were formed and (to exaggerate only slightly the influential analysis of Marxist critic Georg Lukács in *The Historical Novel*) simultaneously helped to construct the bourgeois culture of Victorian Britain.

No sooner did this drama of doubleness begin, however, than multiplicity joined anonymity as its hallmark. We can already discern the several voices in the single narrator who tells the stories of *Waverley* (1814) and *Guy Mannering* (1815). In *The Antiquary* (1816) the title character feels the stress of multiple motives, the jostling of several aesthetic personae: he is, like the Author of Waverley, a lover of discrete objects, patterns, and plots found in the papers, attics, and earths of

History, and also a historian, writer, and critic. By this time Scott is conceiving his tales as well as his tellers as multiples. In the now-pro-liferating editorial front and back matter of *The Antiquary* the Author of Waverley himself "takes respectful leave, as one who is not likely again to solicit" readers, while Scott is conceiving a four-story *Tales of My Landlord* to follow, narrated by a new cast of quarreling personae.

Out of the Author of Waverley, that open secret, that hidden publi-cist, he created complaining antiquarians, antagonistic secular and sacred historians, keen-eyed editors and literary philosophers of the Fieldingesque ironic and the Byronic Romantic schools to call atten-tion to all the elements of his composition but one—genius, greatness, originality. In the most comprehensive study to date of this self-multi-plication, Jane Millgate follows the ins and outs of "the anonymity game," as Scott's genuine humility and his respect for Augustan gener-ic form diffuses his will to recognition, enabling him to conceal even from himself the originality of both his fiction and his view of history.

The anonymity game extended its second phase after the first three novels, and its third phase after three series of *Tales of My Landlord* comprising *The Black Dwarf* and *Old Mortality* (1816), *The Heart of Midlothian* (1818), and *The Bride of Lammermoor* and *A Legend of Mon-trose* (1819). *Rob Roy* (1817) intervened in this series. Something mag-ical and compulsive seems to be at work in the writer's imagination here, a leap after or into "three," which perhaps prepares us for the extraordinary blend of the realistic and ironic with the fey that charac-terizes the second half of Scott's career, what we might call, with an eye to subsequent intellectual history, the pre-Raphaelite novels of chival-ry. Scott originally wished to publish the first of these, *Ivanhoe* (1819), in the name of its fictitious narrator, Laurence Templeton, who had been conceived as an English imitator of the Scottish Author of Waver-ley, thus creating a third Unknown, but was talked out of it by a pub-lisher who feared that Scott's much-prized multiplicity was becoming simple confusion. But Scott needed, and created, several new casts of narrating characters to take him where he wanted to go, first to the epic matter of England (*Ivanhoe*, *The Monastery* [1820], *The Abbot* [1820], *Kenilworth* [1821], *The Fortunes of Nigel* [1822], *Woodstock* [1826]) and Britain (*The Pirate* [1821], *Peveril of the Peak* [1823], *St. Ronan's Well* [1823], *Redgauntlet* [1824], *The Fair Maid of Perth* [1828]) and France (*Quentin Durward* [1823]) and Switzerland (*Anne of Geierstein* [1829]), and ultimately to the more general epic of East and West in the *Tales of the Crusaders (The Betrothed* and *The Talisman* [1825]), *Count Robert of Paris* (1831), and the never-published *Siege of Malta.*

This movement among the various locations of Universal History relies also on a Universal Psychology which, however clearly "developing" in the main, continually throws up unabsorbed elements of antique personality and psychological "sports" that continue to anchor modernity in its origins. As Scott claimed the reason for the anonymity and multiplicity of his writing self was humility and not fear or ambition, so he claimed the attraction he felt for chivalry, the historical origin of modernity, came from chivalry's idealization of loyalty and love and its sublimation of violence, and from the curious and elaborate rituals by which these idealizations and sublimations were both licensed and channeled. He saw himself inside a historical synthesis striving to bring an end to war, the absorption of Thymos by economics, as Fukuyama would say. And he came to feel and depict by Tory instinct rather than Marxist critique that qualm many in the West felt and still feel about the probability that war is not sublimated but rather enlarged by commerce, and that loyalty is not rechanneled but erased.

The large body of prefaces, postscripts, and narrative interventions exfoliated in the Waverley Novels (and I don't even count here the additional series of slightly obfuscatory tell-all prefaces written between 1829 and 1831 as part of the best-selling Magnum Opus edition), is part of a long-running fable of composition that began even before the novels, when Scott developed a prose-framing apparatus for his first poem, *The Lay of the Last Minstrel.* The plot of this fable, like the plot of chivalry, is the expression and attempted diffusion of wrath—wrath in this case connected not only with the springs of personal and national history but also with the situation of fictional composition itself in these early decades of modernity.

The personal sources of Walter Scott's subtle wrath are of his gender and of his time: a wife not his first love, a family to support, a lawyer-father to love and subvert, a lost male heroism to "harness" (his favorite description of composition, as it was to be Dickens's) in work, a schizoid national-imperial identity to attack and defend. The sources of the wrath of the composer of fiction are what they always are: a kingdom of fantasy leased, not owned, invented in whorish negotiation with progenitors, competitors, and critics.

Scott's novels have one more aesthetic source, also of his gender and his time. The less than noble satirical squabbling of Richardson and Fielding and the less than serious self-communing of Sterne have given way at the turn of the century to the feminized scene of the "proper novel," whose moral safety is grounded in a serene narrative persona distinguished by "accuracy and observation." At this time too the partisan polemics of antiquarian and apologetic historians has given way to the "stately" narratives of turn-of-the-century History. With serenity and safety and stateliness, dullness threatens. The woman novelist who leavens serenity with the language of narrative color and excess, or the male historian who returns to partisan violence, trespasses gender and genre boundaries hardening into shackles in the early nineteenth century. But in the new historical novel Walter Scott can lay hold of all these values, both these genders, both genres. In the new form, the "excess" of the past is an element licensed to the novelist as "variety" and to the historian as "truth." The cross-disciplinary consequence here is a new variety in what is allowed to constitute history, as well as a new truth standard—Universal History, Universal Psychology—to which fiction must be held by that third discipline, criticism, which was stabilized in the cauldron of the Waverley Novels.

Inside the Synthesis

Still central to the analysis of both history and psychology in Scott's novels is Alexander Welsh's recognition that the hero of the Waverley novels never kills anyone—though men die, and causes and institutions die. The hero carries a sword, and indeed draws it (often, as with *Old Mortality*'s Henry Morton, successively on both sides of the same cause), but the plots of modernity check his swing at the crucial moment. The sword of his fathers hangs minatory or inviting on the castle wall, but the hero always has more than one father, and the pen of the lawyer, the purse of the merchant, the tempered tongue of the diplomat and the latitudinarian have intervened, and beckon too. The old codes of chivalry, for all their apparent allegiance to invisible realities, issued in solidly material consequences; the stakes of personal and communal honor were an eye for an eye, blood for blood, the Right made good body to body. The new codes of modernity, for all their apparent ensnarement by the merely carnal, issue from invisible exchanges of credit and debt, the stakes of personal and communal honor counted in increments of physical restraint and delayed emotional gratification. The times are with the temporizer: the sword is too blunt for its object.

Readers have rightly made much of the first Waverley hero's first act depicted in the opening retrospect: the five-year-old Edward Waverley reaches passionately for his uncle's carriage and coat of arms, emblem of the "idea of personal property." Equally important, though, is the opening moment of the novel's present time: disentangling itself finally, six chapters in, from its retrospect, the narrative opens the library door along with the uncle, where the teenage Edward is practicing swordplay with the ancestral weapon from the wall.

Our young hero is "acting" a romantic battle here, readying himself for the sport of military captaincy that will succeed the sports of shooting, fishing, and reading, which he has in turn picked up and abandoned during a desultory and neglected youth whose main reality has been dreaming about his own and his culture's past. But, interestingly, it is not so much the active deeds of a more vibrant ancestry that mesmerize Edward as he haunts the long avenues and ruined monuments of Waverley Honour. Singled out from the ancestral store, rather, are two keen memories of loss and self-abnegation. One is the moment when Sir Willibert of Waverley, returning at last from the Crusades to see his betrothed give her heart to the man who had protected her at home, "flung down his half-drawn sword, and turned away forever from the house of his ancestor": the other is the moment when the youngest son of the seventeenth-century Waverley, sent out from the Hall by his Royalist mother during the civil war to draw off Commonwealth pursuit of the king, was brought home successful, and dying. Presumably, the older son carried on the line.

Edward Waverley is the son of a younger brother who, because he assumed the older one would marry and carry on the line, the title, the property, turned aside from the house and politics of his Royalist ancestors to build a new domain in the shifting sands of Whig politics. The title and property are held by the infertile older brother. The tale that ensues, *Waverley: or 'Tis Sixty Years Since*, seems at one level the story of a man seeking the dream of the active sword and the fertile bride that are the conditions of holding title, holding ground, entering the synthesis of Universal History. Edward goes north on a Whig captaincy obtained by his politic father and diverts himself from his duties to vacation with his uncle's Scottish Royalist friend Bradwardine; he explores political and erotic outlawry with Bradwardine's Highland rival and ally Fergus MacIvor and his sister and fellow Royalist Flora, and finally joins the army of the Young Pretender in the most serious of the Jacobite uprisings of 1745.

Yet even the dream of chivalry in Scott is only the *half*-drawn sword, its nightmare is the death of the (younger) son at the behest of (mother) country, its still deeper nightmare the death of the father at the hands of the son. These deaths are all accomplished by Edward—by proxy. Scott's language and his plots deal us moment after moment of innuendo and rumor whereby Edward (half) draws his sword, (half) kills with it, (half) dies by it. A Scottish outlaw steals Edward's identifying seal and creates with it a phantom Waverley who induces his troop to mutiny, and the loving Rose Bradwardine hears a rumor that that traitor Waverley was captured and executed. The real Edward does join the rebel army, but hates the life (and death) of the sword. And most necessary of all to Scott's plots, when the time-serving Sir Richard Waverley dies near the end of the revolt, a newspaper falsely prints that his son's reputed activities in the rebel army resulted in death for both the elder Waverleys, and "Good God! Am I a parricide?" cries Edward.

No, he is not. That particular dream, often elaborated in the Gothic novel that was fiction's first grasp at history, brushes by as a rumor and is put to flight by reason. But there is more to these dramas of proxy crime and guilt than the Universal Historian's patterned movement out of war toward law, out of monarchy through pretenders and parties to universal representation. Underneath, as Alexander Welsh argues, is a shifting in Universal Psychology around the bargain of man with death itself.

Once, as Scott sees it, the outrage of mortality was assuaged by "glory," the immortality attached to the name of the warrior. Now a man comes to consciousness, to the "real history of his life," awash in ambiguous and even inglorious names: Edward Waverley bears no fewer than *four* aliases while the plot maneuvers him toward the Scottish manor of his bride-to-be, whose property, in a complicated legal, political, financial, and moral "redemption" at the end, replaces his entailed English property as "home." No glory here, just the modern bargain with death called bodily survival, domesticity, fertility, whose emblem is the half-drawn sword, the passive entry into the killing field where other men do history's killing and suffer its death. The Waverley Novels feature a succession of ingenious endings (many readers feel they are clumsy) in which an alter ego or accidental third party or coincidental fatality disrupts the final duel between the hero and his enemy, saving the protagonist's "credit" while it refashions his "honor" into historical survival. "Honour is a homicide . . . but credit is a decent honest man," says the legal authority (and merchant) in *Rob Roy*. Honor is also a suicide, as Baillie Nicol Jarvie's literary ancestor Falstaff knew.

Scott set at the head of *Waverley*, and thus in some sense as the touchstone for all the Waverley Novels, and perhaps of all the historical novels of the Western tradition, the moment from *Henry IV: Part II* when all authority, legal, national, even personal and moral, wavers, shifts uneasily, then passes to its diffused modern form. The realist and sensualist Falstaff, making merry with "Justices" named Shallow and Silence, sees his friend Pistol arrive, big with tidings, and Justice Shallow importantly steps forward to receive and interpret the news on the grounds that "I am, sir, under the king, in some authority." The swaggering soldier's challenge—"Under which king, Besonian? Speak, or die"—is on the title page of *Waverley*.

As Universal History, the phrase points to the drama of choices, and speeches, by which authority is composed, and recomposed, both under the king and *as* the king, and to the link in that composition between the world historical personage of "the king" and the professional and middle classes who increasingly exercise authority in the West. It points to the change in that composition from the divine right of Richard II through the tainted alliances of the usurping Henry IV to the self-mythicized energies of Henry V and the modern construction of the bureaucratized Tudor state. As Universal Psychology the phrase points to the struggle of the male to enter a personal history situated somewhere between slavish imitation of the legitimate father and slavish rebellion with the illegitimate one, Falstaff; that is, to his struggle to formulate an identity in which the choice of independent personhood is somehow harmonized with the continued possession of the oedipal property that is his destiny.

The maneuvering of the self, and of events, until one's personal choice coincides with one's patriarchal destiny, exposes to the hero—and the reader—of the Waverley Novels the fictiveness both of authority and of identity. Like Shakespeare's Hal the male protagonists move quickly off the paths of their fathers into the domain of the outlaw. For whether the counterpaternal world is the elevated realm of suicidal honor or the earthy precinct of the jester-cynic (and like Shakespeare, Scott usually provides counterfathers at both poles), it still offers the necessary standpoint from which a son can face and assess the inevitable thievery, outlawry, and moral compromise of his domestic and social heritage. As with Hal, Scott's protagonist always makes his way back to the paternal world, hyperconscious of the selves he has put on and put away, of the underlying arbitrariness by which he has designated one experience a "dream" and another an "awakening."

For Shakespearean comedy, of course, the counterpaternal world is most often "the green world" outside history, the greenwood of merriment, sensuality. This holds essentially true too of the English history plays. Only in the classical history plays, a *Troilus and Cressida*, an *Antony and Cleopatra*, does the Shakespearean protagonist awake, like Edward Waverley and many a *Waverley* hero after him, to the nightmare of modern history—to find that he has drawn his sword in the camp of the enemy against the fatherland.

However, some element of Shakespearean pastoral still governs Scott's imagination of the "dream" from which one "awakens" to the real history of one's life, an element to which Scott's building of the medieval house and reforesting of the medieval acres of Abbotsford is testimony. Scott's conflation of the greenwood and the camp of the enemy most often carries a comic and progressive view of Universal History: *Ivanhoe*'s Robin Hood, like *As You Like It*'s Duke Senior, holding alternative court under the greenwood tree. Shakespeare's only Scottish history harbors a more ambiguous and dangerous image of the conflation, a disinherited son reclaiming his father's ground as both the camp of the hereditary English enemy and the greenwood tree, when Birnam Wood comes to Dunsinane. I will return to this image at the end of this chapter with a look at *The Bride of Lammermoor*, Scott's *Macbeth*.

From *Waverley* on, choosing a king shapes both Universal Psychology and Universal History in Scott's novels. If the choice seems at first to be between a pure king-of-honor associated with the timeless values of the greenwood and a king-of-credits contaminated by timely commerce with shifting ideals, turning coats, and mobile markets, it soon grows less simple. The incident that catapults Edward Waverley across the Highland Line into the greenwood is an example of Scott's instinct for the materialist basis of History. His first truly royal figure, the exotic Highland Chief Fergus MacIvor, controls an economy in which the romantic credits of fealty, mystery, and love circulate alongside the real credits of coins, lands, and titles. What looks at first like a Highland thieving of Lowland cattle is really a momentary breakdown in the complex network of "protection" by which the supposedly peaceable Fergus feeds a tenantry too large for a farming community, but large enough for an army. More deeply still, the thieving is actually an exercise in quarrel and reconciliation designed by Fergus to produce emotional capital in old Lowland and Highland cavaliers, capital to be expended in the Jacobite rebellion for the Stuart Pretender.

Edward's journey north through Fergus's land to the camp of the Stuart brings him face to face with that homicidal, suicidal honor from which he instinctively recoils, leaving it to Fergus's opposite number, the Hanoverian Prince's chieftain, Colonel Talbot, to negotiate Edward's return to his king. The credits Talbot employs to buy Edward back his reputation and his estate include a complex transference of land and cash but also, and importantly, the new modern capital of his "vote in the House" of Parliament.

Scott's first novel thus sets up a narrative of historical process. The story begins by referring, through the Shakespearean headnote, to the macro beginning of modernity in the duel between Plantagenet cousins, and dramatizes, by reference to Edward's early fixation on the death of the youngest Waverley son in the service of King Charles II, the acceleration of this process in the seventeenth-century civil war that produced everywhere houses with a Hanoverian brother and a Stuart brother, swords half-drawn upon each other. It ends by enforcing a unity on the warring human houses, transferring the war to the fictive house of political parties. Colonel Talbot's negotiations result in a property transferred from Scottish Jacobite to English Hanoverian ownership.

The allegiance to Hanoverian government by the father, Sir Richard Waverley, was an ignoble matter of a younger son's looking to survive and prosper: the allegiance of the son, Edward, to the same government is now a fealty laid hold on from a rational distance after a thick experience of doubt and dream and contemplation—the authentic, if speckled, fealty of modernity. The Waverleyan drama finds its synthesis in unions; the freely chosen (every reader feels it destined) marriage of English Edward and Scottish Rose grounds, well after the fact, the Scottish-English union of 1707, that confirming icon of Universal History's "desire."

But if between 1814 and 1832 Scott and the enormous reading public of the Waverley Novels accepted and enacted the fact of union as

History's desire, the terms of union were always still up for renegotia-
tion. Walter Scott, sheriff and "writer"—to the court, to the people
under the authority of the British Empire—was yet, as Peter Garside
and others have demonstrated, a Scottish patriot in his own way. And
it is interesting to note that the two elements of Scotland almost erased
in the synthesis of union, which Scott is most famous for (almost)
restoring to some degree of separateness within the synthesis, are the
Royal Scottish Regalia and the Scottish bank note. These are fitting
symbols of the old and new nationhood the Waverley Novels held
unerased within that synthesis, a nationhood degenerated somewhat
into spectacle and game, yet speaking of the price of unity and the
uncertain solubility of elements of that nationhood.

The "Soldan" and the Lady

As postcolonial theorists study the long and devious meditation of
English literature upon English imperialism, the Waverley Novels
might rightfully achieve an unexpected new prominence. The enforced
union of England and Scotland in 1707 marked the formal beginnings
of an English imperialism confirmed in the eighteenth and nineteenth
centuries by an unusually large presence of Scotsmen in the military and
commercial brigades of conquerors/light-bringers. It seems quite likely
that the writer, and especially the readers, of the Waverley Novels
understood, however obscurely, that in the dramas of imperial union on
and among the islands of Great Britain—dramas highlighting the consolidation of various races Celtic, Pictish, and Scandinavian under the
dominance of the Anglo-Saxon—they were together experiencing,
even at some level promoting, the imperial elation that accompanies the
rationalizations of "unity."

The excitement of empire, as the West has known it, is intimately
bound up with the awe of origins, the desire for mingled with fear of
the primitive and even the prehuman, symbolized for the West primarily by the ancient civilizations of the East. As a philosophical channel
for this excitement, Universal History constructs from these materials
a coherent "development" by which all that has been (East) is restored
or rearranged in what is, and is coming to be (West). As Edward Said
formulated it in his influential *Orientalism* (1978), the "discourse" of
Orientalism had its beginnings roughly contemporary with the Waverley Novels. Orientalism used the new disciplines of linguistics and anti-

quarian anthropology and history to manage and domesticate an East whose imaginative parameters were an almost boundaryless sexuality and a sacred origin: both real and fictional journeys to the East were invariably imaginatively cast as *returns*. Yet what the Western imagination saw in the Orient was a series of terms that countered the identity the West had constructed for itself. To the rational certainty, linear progressiveness, and shapeliness of the West is opposed the Oriental world of uncertain, fluid dreams infinitely multiplying themselves past resolution, definition, materiality.

These qualities of "the other," iconically both Eastern and female, make "the lady" and "the Soldan" (or Sultan) close relatives in literary forms of Orientalism. The Western adventurer pilgrim who crosses water to engage with this dyad in its own land meets what Freud would call the oceanic of his own origins, the contradictory elements of his identity whirled asunder. Should he try to master it, or marry it, he may, devolving, *become* it. Scott's imagination of the Crusades, from the brief background references in *Waverley* to the open treatment in *Ivanhoe* and *The Talisman*, is haunted by the figure of the Templar, the Roman Catholic priest-knight whom he sees as devolved because of long residence in the East, fallen—in terms borrowed from Gibbon's *Decline and Fall of the Roman Empire*—from "Roman" rationality and civilization back to the "barbarian" Orientalism from which he came. Within this Orientalism stand the sensual pasha or the Turk or the "Soldan," the "unbelieving dog" the Templar has himself become, and the harem girl who confirms the Templar's reversion. The ancestor of the hero of the Waverley Novels is the Crusader, who has on the contrary neither married nor mastered the Orient; instead he has been humbled, even humiliated, by it.

It is in this light that we should see the romantic triangle of Wilfrid of Ivanhoe, the priest-knight Brian de Bois Gilbert, and the Oriental Rebecca of York. In this light as well we should view the truly astonishing shape-shifting and momentary Orientalizing and feminizing of the Scottish hero of *The Talisman*. Both the Saxon Wilfrid of Ivanhoe and the Celtic David, Prince Royal of Scotland, are depicted as having broken with and been disinherited by their fathers for following the Normans, perhaps the first major imperialist race of the West, into the Orient. In each novel an Oriental redefines the Christian purpose of the Crusades. Isaac the Jew's comment that "the noblest of you will take the staff and sandal in superstitious penance and walk barefoot to visit

the graves of dead men" and the Kurdish Saracen Sheerkohf's marveling at "that insanity which brings you hither to obtain possession of
an empty sepulchre" both point to still another aspect of Orientalist
discourse. This is the Western tendency to regard the East as exhausted, emptied. The breasts of Jerusalem, "*communis mater*—the mother of
all Christians" as *Ivanhoe*'s Prior Aymer calls her, remain flat until reen-
gorged by the violent visitations of faith-bearing Crusader sons. In both
novels the faithless Templar has reverted not to the faith of his Islamic
enemy but to the Eastern brand of folk magic and demonology that the
faith system of Islam sought to contain and reorganize even as the faith
system of early Christianity sought to contain and reorganize the folk
and earth magic of Western pre-Christian culture.

In both novels what Scott calls in *Ivanhoe* the "habits of predomi-
nating over infidel captives and Eastern bondsmen" have transformed
the Crusader governments into Sultans contemptuous (and fearful) of
the complexly chartered and peopled third space of government
between the ruler and the people that is just beginning to be constructed in Western law. "I have caught some attachment to the Eastern form
of government," proclaims the baron of the Crusader kingdom in *The
Talisman*, complaining about the feudal privileges Richard Coeur de
Leon is forced to allow his barons. *The Talisman* begins in fact with a
debate between East and West on "liberty." The Westerner claims the
"Christian freedoms" of modern indulgence in pork and wine that have
replaced the rigidity of the old Semitic law, while the Oriental argues
that the "slavery" of chivalric love and marriage limits a man in the most
precious part of his manhood. Thus are the complex "freedoms"—of
the Western female to give laws to her knight and of Western knights
and barons to win charters from their rulers—contrasted with the Oriental's primitive, lascivious, and tyrannical patriarchal rule over his
harem and his councillors.

This is a species of self-congratulatory Orientalism fundamental
even to the Western liberal construction of gender roles: see for instance
George Meredith's liberal Diana of the Crossways, who complains that
"men may have rounded Seraglio Point: they have not yet doubled Cape
Turk." Less liberal thought, of course, is always backsliding out of the
evolving synthesis of contracted freedoms and toward the life of "the
Turk," a backsliding dramatized not only by Scott in the harem-yearn-
ing, skirt-wearing priest-warriors of the Temple, but also, interestingly, by the Scott of *Redgauntlet* and later the Thackeray of *Henry*

Esmond. Both novels feature Stuart "Pretenders" whose political "cause" fails because they link their rights as rulers to the right to keep a mistress. Writing in the Regency England of George IV, Scott was perfectly aware of the propensity of the Hanoverian kings to keep even more mistresses than the Stuarts: it was simply that as the psychic "sports" and "throwbacks" of Universal History the Catholic Stuart kings had to be not only feminized but Orientalized, like the Templars.

In this Orientalizing light the "dark lady" of Scott's romance plots stands forth not only as the symbolic psychic double of the hero's forbidden desire but specifically as the racial "other," the locus of the return forbidden and prized by Universal History (the Oriental) and Universal Psychology (the mother). We can see this pattern dimly in *Waverley*'s Flora MacIvor, educated in Paris and transported to the Highlands. Her recovery of Celtic tradition and Gaelic language, and her devotion to Stuart and Highland liberties are "purer" than they can be for the brother who seeks entry into the political and commercial synthesis of Great Britain, and her toleration of the English youth Waverley's attraction to her is entirely maternal. We can see this atavism in the witches and "gypsies" of the Scottish novels that followed, all imagined by their "superstitious" countrymen to be chattels of the "black man" of Semitic and Persian myth systems. We can also see it most clearly in *Ivanhoe*, in the witch Ulrica, parricide arsonist, reverted to the pagan chants of Saxon destroyer gods. And of course in Rebecca, whom Ulrica mistakes at their first meeting for a Saracen or an Egyptian. The most memorable of Scott's Oriental/dark women, the Jewess Rebecca, stands for the ultimate blocked return to the *communis mater*. As the Oriental woman she both attracts and repels the chivalrous Wilfrid striving toward the Norman-Saxon synthesis; as the Oriental woman she obsesses the Orientalized Templar, Sir Brian de Bois Gilbert.

When Ivanhoe opens his eyes and ears to the lady who has nursed him after being wounded in the tournament at Ashby de la Zouche, he hears an "unintelligible" language and sees "Eastern" clothing and so begins speaking to her in Arabian. He responds with sexual arousal and "emotion" to her as an Oriental, but turns at once "cold, composed and collected" when she reveals the specific of her race. Something hard, even incestuous, retards the full assimilation of the Jewess into the Orientalist fantasy. "Composed" he might be, this man of the new synthesis, and courteous in the exchange of healings and rescues that marks his relationship with Rebecca during the plot. Yet, as Scott says in a famous ending, "it would be inquiring too curiously to ask" whether this figure of multiple and guilty fantasy did not continue to challenge Ivanhoe's composure and the Western bride Rowena who confirmed it.

If it is part of Universal History to celebrate contemporary Western freedom by locating slavery (of women and workers) in the Oriental past, then we expect to find the black man standing with the Oriental woman at the edge of the synthesis. Brian De Bois Gilbert, himself "burned to almost Negro blackness" by the Palestinian sun, appears attended by two African slaves richly dressed to mark their master's importance and carrying Turkish daggers and Saracen javelins. Orientalized Templar and African slaves speak "Arabian" together, as Reginald Front de Boeuf does with the "sable functionaries" who do his torturing for him. Scott's descriptions emphasize the naked black skin of the slaves, and his footnote disingenuously explains that he uses them both for dramatic visual contrast to the white protagonists and to point up the Orientalization of the Templars: "What can be more natural" than that these corrupted Westerners copy the corrupt Saracens who enslaved the Africans.

For all his tolerant humanism, then, Scott instinctively plotted according to the duplicitous racial dynamic laid down by Universal History. The Westerner, Front de Boeuf, had "perhaps learnt his lesson of cruelty" in the East, while the chivalrous and witty Easterner who meets the Crusader in the opening pages of *The Talisman* had "caught a part of [the Crusaders' Western] manners." Black male and female slavery is a primitive Eastern habit caught by the worst in the West, chivalry a Western achievement imitated by the best in the East.

This exchange is strangely figured in the extraordinary bodily transformations of Kenneth, the protagonist of *The Talisman*, who undergoes both black male slavery and femininity before he reclaims his real Scottish persona. Forbidden by his venal and politically astute father to fight in the East under the banner of the Norman English king, the heir to the Scottish throne masks his royalty (or puts it to sleep) in the frayed silk and unwieldy steel of a poor knight whose half-defaced coat of arms "seems to read," ambiguously enough, "I sleep—wake me not." He falls in love, between battles, with a Plantagenet princess whom Richard of England destines as Saladin's bride: if the jealousy and prudence of his Western allies will not let him win the Orient in battle, the monarch will, if necessary, marry it.

Angry at the presumptuous knight, Richard transfers him as feudal dependent to the Saracen whose talisman cured him: the Saracen paints the knight black and sends him back to Richard as a "Nubian" body slave to guard him from Western-hired Moslem assassins. Richard guesses the deception when he makes to suck the assassin's poison from the wounded (and dyed) skin of his protector, but sends him, thus degraded, to deliver the Soldan's proposal of marriage to Edith, hoping his cousin will be "disgusted" by the black skin of the man standing in for the "Paynim" who wants her for his harem. The scene in which Edith rages at the mute black Sir Kenneth, both for being the enslaved and enslaving Oriental in his black skin and for being in features the white Western man she loves and cannot have, is perhaps the novel's most powerful one. It is a schizoid moment of Orientalist desire and disgust that the subsequent untangling of the plot and reordering of races—the killing of white evildoers, marriage of white protagonists, and brotherhood of Western chivalric monarch with Westernized Eastern monarch—cannot quite reprogram into the synthesis.

And the novel is not yet finished with strange moments of desire/disgust. His body dissolved across racial lines, Sir Kenneth is immediately afterward subjected, symbolically, to another transformation across gender lines in a long ballad sung at Richard's command by his minstrel Blondel, whose hero Sir Kenneth is explicitly called by his king to emulate. In this long ballad a lady requires her knight to fight a tournament dressed only in her nightgown. He does so, and she rewards him by wearing the bloody rags to dinner that evening.

These fantastic visions of racial and gender blurring constitute an excess familiar to readers of Gothic novels and of the Romantic and often Orientalist tales of Byron and Southey. The excess is referrable, in part, to new visions of the role, and necessity, of imagination in Universal Psychology. But it also points to a genuine new consciousness of race and gender in the movement of history, as well as to the limitations of that consciousness.

Magic

For all its engagement with utilitarian politics and the new realism of character, with Universal History and the complex psychology of the modern mind within the patterns of history, the historical novel is fundamentally a descendant of the Gothic novel. The reading public being created through the novel in the late eighteenth century first experienced "history" there as prophecy—a pleasurable consciousness of doom associated with the painful reign and inevitable fall of the proud and the powerful, and with the continuing poignant revelation of the inadequacy of reason. For English Gothic fiction, history was a place where one could explore and experience the disappearing engines of unbridled wrath, pride, and lust. The barons and clerics of Horace Walpole and Ann Radcliffe, Clara Reeve and M. G. Lewis, exercised a prepolitical, ahistorical brand of power drawn in rationalist terms as a kind of madness. The immense dilation of power and ambition, the preternatural humanity, of the great Gothic villains, could be safely walled off in the past, which because it was the prerational time could contain an accompanying preternatural apparatus of omens, tales, and powers prophesying, actually accomplishing, the fall of the preternatural human and the return of the rest of the world to Christian salvation history.

The Gothic historic could present the fall of magnified humanity, trace its "backslidings" through paganized Christian and Islamic forms of belief further back to prehistoric magic and superstition, because it thought it knew, through Universal History, which direction was forward. In the evolving syntheses of Universal History those cultures of the past driven by preternatural humans under supernatural compulsions, prerational cultures of earth and air magic and their descendants, tragic and comic myth, are left behind, or more often aestheticized, and returned to the synthesis as entertainments.

Scott takes a prominent role in this effort, as collector-purveyor of the supernatural tales first of Scotland and then of the wider West and finally the Orientalized East, through his poetry, prose fiction, and nonfiction essays, and through the legendary-artifact-stocked museum-dwelling of Abbotsford itself. He is convinced of this developmental view of magic, even lends it, anachronistically, to some of his favorite heroes. *The Talisman*'s Saladin, for instance, chants a set of verses about Ahriman, the ancient Persian Manichean Lord of Darkness, claims descent from him, and takes the moderate modern view that it is well neither to erase his culture's memory of origin in "Elementary Spirits" nor to organize the heterogeneity of magic too rigidly into the categories of modern psychology and ethics; rather one should "memorialize" them both, let them roam loosely within the synthesis of Islam. One of the things Scott likes best about his medieval novels is that his

Protestant characters of that time can chide the medieval Catholic church for its accommodating preservation of pre-Christian elements in its "worship" of saints and stones and bones and fountains, while the narration itself preserves both Catholic heterogeneity and Protestant morality equally, and almost as equals, in the amber of its tolerant irony.

Although developmental narrative shapes the synthesis of Universal History (and vice versa) and the view of those like Saladin who are the narrative in character-disguise, the view of history most poignantly felt, even pursued, by characters experiencing rather than directing time is quite different, more "Gothic." Not evolutionary but revolutionary (and ceaselessly counterrevolutionary). Reversal, not synthesis, is the form of time: "the world turned upside down," as the outlaw Rob Roy comments, like an hourglass constantly reset by some fatal hand. Primitive magic, sometimes whimsical, sometimes fatally prophetic, is the hallmark of this form.

All the Waverley Novels pay homage to this primitive sense of History. The accommodation to "real history" (that is, narrative synthesis), by which the hero shoulders the reward/burden of marriage, inheritance, continuation, life itself at the end of the narrative, almost always contains some element of that curious quality one sees most vividly in the finally successful lovers of *Old Mortality*, man and woman gamely continuing, but stunned in some vital organ by one too many magic reversals. All the Waverley Novels pay homage too to magic as the origin of religion and philosophy. Tidily packed away in whimsical tales or fatal prophecies, magic is traded, preserved, energized by the lower classes, and pondered and critiqued by the powers of the synthesis, the clerics and lords, the politicians, the narrators. The typical hero, himself a man of reason, will "despise most of the ordinary prejudices about witchcraft, omens, and vaticination, to which his age and country still gave such implicit credit that to express a doubt of them was accounted a crime equal to the unbelief of Jews or Saracens." But it was precisely the point of the Gothic Historic in the Waverley Novels to take readers to the age and country where the older and wilder form of "vaticination," visionary prophecy, contested with the Jew and the Saracen for the position at the origin of the Western Christian synthesis. Staging this contest on the prepared ground of Universal History, the Waverley Novels carry forward, almost by accident, an element of history as unruly as the witches and omens, and linked with them—the politics of class.

The man quoted above striving to "despise" the primitive visionaries closer to him than Jew or Saracen is Edgar, Master of Ravenswood, the protagonist of *The Bride of Lammermoor*, the last novel the Scottish "Author of Waverley" wrote before Walter Scott created the new cast of narrating characters who produced the English *Ivanhoe*. Abundant allusions and analogies would seem to make the novel Scott's *Macbeth*, a historical tragedy of magic. If it is, it is a *Macbeth* without a Malcolm, without the figure who returns to shoulder the inheritance and carry it forward from the timeless oscillation of revenge and reversals to the evolving synthesis of history.

Shakespeare's Malcolm, dispossessed heir, man of reason turned to war, shrewdly associates himself with the Christian magic of English Edward the Confessor, and approaches his usurped patrimony of Dunsinane "screened" not only by the leaves of Birnam Wood but also by the passionate anger of MacDuff, who kills Malcolm's enemy for him in the way many a minor character does for the hero of the Waverley Novels. Edgar of Ravenswood, last son of a Scottish Cavalier family dispossessed by a Whig lawyer married to an ambitious Douglas, seems at first to be placed as the Malcolm of this drama. And in fact, the political history around him is poised to carry this most modern of the antique and choleric Ravenswoods, this reflective, tolerant, and self-critical mind, forward into the synthesis that preserves the best of the aristocratic races if they embody the changes called for by Universal Psychology. For the Scottish Tories are due for a period "on top" in the politics of British union in the novel's time, and had not Edgar, like Macbeth, turned his face from the rational "prospect of belief" urged by the novel's various Banquos toward the "witchcraft, omens and vaticinations" of women in the wild, he would have gone with the tide to virtual restoration of his heritage. Once fixed in the "prospect" of magic, however, Edward's particular combination of virtues and flaws bring him to Macbeth's fate: the best he can do, after manifold struggles, is to plunge directly into the prophecy which organizes his death.

Two interesting modern differences characterize Scott's use of the standard women-in-the-wild stewardship of magic. Lady Macbeth, Shakespeare's human witch, the wife "unsexed" by spirits of the air, becomes in Scott's novel the mother *and the daughter* of Edgar's usurping enemy. Lady Ashton has not brought forth men children only: defending her usurped castle against Edgar, she needs her wrathful son Sholto, her fey teenage son Henry, and especially her romantic daughter Lucy to divert Edgar from the restoration that Universal History has in mind for the Ravenswoods to the destruction that prophecy has in mind. The daughter's love and the mother's hate combine to attract Edgar toward the dueling ground where the drawn swords of both Whig opponents and Cavalier allies call to his own half-drawn one, a killing ground he has repeatedly tried to leave or transform.

Falling in love with the daughter of his enemy promises a transformation, but the wrathful mother in control of the daughter has lost sight of the rational goal of her fight—security for her family and a foot in both camps of the evolving synthesis. For Lady Ashton, history is simply a series of violent reversals, which she means to arrest while she is at the top. Manipulating Lucy into another marriage to block Ravenswood is a small price to pay. The maddened bride's attempted murder of her husband, even the bride's death in fits, is a small price, for it gives the "grieving" family the right at last to the trial by arms that Edgar refused in the early chapters.

When Edgar rides out to meet Sholto Ashton in the last pages of the novel he might, like Macbeth, be thinking of two magical prophecies that attached his death to an apparently impossible condition. One is a verse from Thomas Rhymer claiming that the "last Lord" of Ravenswood will die when he "stables his horse in the Kelpie's [quicksand's] flow" on the way to claim a dead bride. The other is a legendary tale chronicling the fatal love meeting between a sixteenth-century Ravenswood and a supernatural lady at a Gothic fountain on the ancient grounds. At the behest of his Christian counselors, the tale goes, he tested her humanity; she plunged back into the fountain, bloodying the waters, and his death followed. The story and the fountain became the bane of the family.

Scott creates two "witches" of the peasant classes to evoke and deploy this antihistorical prophecy within the sensitive minds of the declining aristocrat, Edgar Ravenswood, and the ascending one, Lucy Ashton. The politics of class are strong on this level of the plot. While the movement of Universal History seeks the alliance of blood and brain—the moderate aristocrat and the lawyer's daughter—in a revitalized and democratized ruling class, the plots of prophecy in Scott most often carry the contravening grievances of the poor, who take the short view, not the historical one, looking at close quarters for revenge and reversal.

The better-educated, blind Alice Gray's scorn is for the newer rulers: when called "witch" by an Ashton she swears she will go willingly to the stake if "the usurer, and the oppressor, and the grinder of the poor man's face, and the . . . subverter of ancient houses" burns at the same stake. The more chilling and fantastic Ailsie Gourlay, one of those who commit real crimes under pretense of magic, is in the pay of Lady Ashton, but scorns all the "great ones": "They wad gie us whinstanes for loaves, if it would serve their ain vanity, and yet they expect us to be gratefu', as they ca' it, as if they served us for true love and liking." Alice wields the plots of prophecy to separate Edgar from Lucy out of genuine fear of the probable bloody renewal of the Ravenswood/Ashton feud. Ailsie taunts Edgar and terrorizes Lucy with them partly for pay but mostly out of a diabolical love of mischief-making and a classic professional interest in death: with her fellow Shakespearean hags Maggie and Annie, Ailsie presides at the washing and winding of the neighborhood's corpses. Prophecy, and its aestheticized sister tragedy, are interested in glorious deaths; Universal History in sometimes inglorious survivals.

Scott's witches and wizards operate the plots of magic either to gain power over the great or out of self-delusion, often both. A fascinated rationalist, a commercial enchanter, Scott can never erect a supernatural structure without a probable rational origin: even the tale of the suicidal nymph of the Ravenswood fountain, the narrator speculates, sounds like the aristocrat's deliberately garbled version of a more sordid occurrence, the Ravenswood baron's murder of a lower-class mistress who crossed him. Ordinarily Scott makes the plots of magic, belief not assimilated to the synthesis of Univeral History, work *with* History, clearing the ground of figures unequipped to stay in the synthesis. Such is the case in *Waverley*, where the ancient superstition of the Bodach Glas, the death-bringer of his clan, seals Fergus MacIvor's resolve to die, leaving Edward Waverley free of his dark glamor. Such is the case in *Ivanhoe*, where Ulrica's invocation to the Saxon demon makes hotter the fire that eliminates the Norman villain Front de Boeuf, and opens the gates of Torquilstone Castle for the invading Saxons.

Only in *The Bride of Lammermoor* do the plots of magic erase and humiliate the plan of History. No Ravenswood, no Ashton, survives to take the inheritance, marry, bear children, enter History. Edgar disappears in the quicksand and Lucy into her grave; the Ashton sons die without heirs; the wounded bridegroom, heir at law, leaves Scotland never to return. We look in vain to the last chapter's summing up for the sign of continuation, of fertility and order, that always is History's mark in the Waverley Novels.

The sign is there in the novel though, in the great feast that precedes the final tragic movement of the novel, a feast that takes place, as it must, in the only thriving place in the community. Not the ancient Ravenswood tower where Edgar lives, its larders and movables cleaned to the walls at novel's opening by the funeral feast for his father. Not the usurped manor of Ravenswood itself, where the Ashtons have been making sterile "improvements," but the small port of Wolf's Hope, once a purely feudal dependency of the Ravenswoods, now learning and consolidating its new commercial and political freedoms under British modernity.

The man who had "headed the insurrection" by which the villagers had taken back control of their property and labor while the Ravenswoods fought the Ashtons over the larger properties is John Girder, the cooper, an artisan whose now well-furnished and plenished house, lovingly described several times in the novel, hosts the Master of Ravenswood and his kinsman the Marquis of A. for the meeting that unites the two Ravenswoods on the path, as they think, to their reinsertion into History. Magic will divert Edgar from that path, and the Marquis of A. will get his trivial time at the top of party politics, says the narrator. But it is the artisan and his "insurrection" that is really marked to enter Universal History. If John Girder's head is "weelnigh dung donnart" with his sudden elevation to Queen's cooper and with the hosting of aristocrats, if he remains a little bit pompous in his good fortune, if his new authority has the dangerous undertow of setting him to "build castles in the air" about his future, nevertheless his "oration" at the end of the feast has the tempered certainty that is the sign of Universal History in the Waverley Novels: "Let the house be redd up, the broken meat set by. Let every man and woman here set about their ain business, as if there was nae sic thing as marquis or master, duke or drake, laird or lord, in this world."

Judith Wilt

Selected Bibliography

Farrell, John P. *The Dilemma of the Moderate from Scott to Arnold.* Ithaca, N.Y.: Cornell University Press, 1980.

Ferris, Ina. *The Achievement of Literary Authority: Gender, History, and the Waverley Novels*. Ithaca, N.Y.: Cornell University Press, 1991.

Fleishman, Avrom. *The English Historical Novel: Walter Scott to Virginia Woolf*. Baltimore: Johns Hopkins University Press, 1971.

Johnson, Edgar. *Sir Walter Scott: The Great Unknown*. New York: Macmillan, 1970.

Millgate, Jane. *Walter Scott: The Making of the Novelist*. Toronto: University of Toronto Press, 1984.

Welsh, Alexander. *The Hero of the Waverley Novels*. New Haven, Conn.: Yale University Press, 1963.

Wilt, Judith. *Secret Leaves: The Novels of Walter Scott*. Chicago: University of Chicago Press, 1985.

A Novel of Their Own: Romantic Women's Fiction, 1790–1830

I N the opening decades of the nineteenth century, women dominated both the production and the consumption of novels. The
success of the circulating or lending libraries, which spread rapidly throughout England during the late eighteenth century, meant that
hitherto prohibitively expensive books were now available to a new and
ever-growing readership, a readership composed in large part of
increasingly literate and leisured upper- and middle-class women who
preferred to read literature, and especially novels, written by women.
The contents of the ten leading circulating libraries in London in 1800,
tabulated by the London Statistical Society (cited in Richard Altick's
*The English Common Reader: A Social History of the Mass Reading Public
1800–1900*, 1957), suggests that the bulk of the writers for and the sub-
scribers to these libraries were female. Three-quarters of the two thousand books in circulation were either "Fashionable Novels, well known"
(439 volumes) or "Novels of the lowest character, being chiefly imitations of Fashionable Novels" (1008 volumes). Two additional categories
also appealed primarily to women readers: "Romances" (76 volumes)
and "Novels by Miss Edgeworth, and Moral and Religious Novels" (49
volumes). A cursory survey of the literary reviews of the period suggests
that by 1830 over two hundred living women writers could claim
authorship of at least one novel, and that by far the most prolific novelist of the period was "A Lady." After surveying both the number of
editions of individual novels and their reception in the leading literary
reviews, Ann H. Jones concludes in *Ideas and Innovations: Best-Sellers of*

Jane Austen's Age that the most popular novelists of the period from 1800 to 1820 were women: Maria Edgeworth, Elizabeth Hamilton, Amelia Opie, Mary Brunton, Jane and Anna Maria Porter, and Sydney Owenson. Only two men are on the list, Walter Scott and Thomas Surr. By 1830, several more women novelists would rival these seven in popularity: Ann Radcliffe, Mary Shelley, Susan Ferrier, Marguerite Gardiner (Countess of Blessington), Elizabeth Le Noir, and Jane West—and, posthumously, Jane Austen.

Historians of the novel, especially those concerned with documenting the "great age of the novel"—the Victorian period—and including feminist literary historians interested in tracing the development of the novel as a female literary tradition, have tended to overlook the significance of this enormous body of female-authored literature. Focusing almost exclusively on Jane Austen, Walter Scott, and a recent addition to the canonical history of the novel, Mary Shelley's *Frankenstein*, historians of the novel have usually identified the Romantic novel either with a nationalistic and bourgeois recuperation of the past (as in Scott's historical fiction), with an equally conservative celebration of a morally reinvigorated gentry class (in Jane Austen's fiction), or with a Gothic evocation and criticism of the excesses of sensibility (in the work of Ann Radcliffe and Mary Shelley). Even perceptive feminist critics of the novel have asserted that the female-authored fiction of the Romantic period registers the triumph of a patriarchal domestic ideology. Basing their conclusions primarily upon conduct books and religious tracts written by men and women, including Addison and Steele's *Spectator*, they have eloquently argued that women writers of the Romantic era were either forced to accommodate themselves to, indirectly subvert, or gain power wholly within a cultural construction of the proper lady as a modest, domesticated woman, one confined to the private sphere, one who did not speak in public.

A closer look at the large number and wide range of women's fiction produced between 1790 and 1830 suggests a rather different story. Despite recent arguments to the contrary, Romantic women novelists did not resign the construction of "feminine discourse" in the novel to men, obediently reproducing the hegemonic ideology of bourgeois capitalism and relocating it in an idealized middle-class patriarchal family. In the Romantic period, women novelists more frequently employed their writing as a vehicle for ideological contestation and subversion, exploiting the novel's capacity for disruptive humor and sustained interrogation of existing social codes, and for what Bakhtin called its "heteroglossia" and "dialogism" (its ability to present and maintain opposing voices and points of view). While the psychological and rhetorical accommodations noted by many critics undoubtedly occurred in writing by women of the Romantic period, I emphasize here the existence of an equally strong Romantic female literary tradition that openly challenged and revised the patriarchal domestic ideology in powerful ways. We can no longer assume that the doctrine of the separate spheres, the sexual division of labor into the public/male and the private/female realms, was universally accepted during the Romantic period.

Although several of these women novelists invoked a modesty topos in introducing their work to the public, the sheer bulk of their publications suggests that they did not succumb to the debilitating female "anxiety of authorship" assigned to them by recent feminist critics. Many were capable of the authorial self-confidence—even arrogance— exemplified by Harriet Lee, who, in her introduction to the Standard Novels edition of her *Canterbury Tales* in 1832, claimed:

I think I may be permitted to observe, that when these volumes first appeared [in 1797], a work bearing distinctly the title of "Tales," professedly adapted to different countries, and either abruptly commencing with, or breaking suddenly into, a sort of dramatic dialogue, was a novelty in the fictions of the day. Innumerable "Tales" of the same stamp, and adapted in the same manner to all classes and all countries, have since appeared; with many of which I presume not to compete in merit, though I think I may fairly claim priority of design and style.

Following Harriet Lee, I suggest that the Romantic woman's novel played a key role in the construction of a new ideology of gender, which I have called "feminine Romanticism" and which I discuss more fully in *Romanticism and Gender* (1992). Repudiating the economic and gender systems promoted in the eighteenth-century novels of Defoe, Fielding, Richardson, Sterne, and Mackenzie, and rejecting the political assumptions of the male Romantic poets, the female novelists of the Romantic era celebrated not the achievements of the imagination or the overflow of powerful feelings, but rather the workings of the rational mind, a mind relocated—in a gesture of revolutionary gender implications— in the female as well as the male body. They thereby insisted upon the fundamental equality of women and men. Typically, they endorsed a commitment to a development of subjectivity based on alterity, and grounded their moral systems on what Carol Gilligan (in *In a Different Voice*, 1982) has taught us to call an "ethic of care," one that insists on the primacy of the family or the community and their attendant practical responsibilities over the rights of the individual. These writers based their notions of community on a cooperative rather than possessive interaction with Nature—imaged as a female friend, mother, or sister—and promoted a politics of gradual rather than violent social change, a transformation that extends the values and practices of the domestic affections into the public realm.

In opposition to the conservative domestic ideology so well described by Leonore Davidoff and Catherine Hall in *Family Fortunes: Men and Women of the English Middle Class, 1780–1850*, many Romantic women novelists used their fiction to promote significantly different social agendas. Some rejected the public sphere altogether as irredeemably brutal, corrupt, and self-destructive, and construed the ideal male as one who in the end is absorbed entirely into the feminine, private sphere. Charlotte Smith, for example, in *The Old Manor House* (1794), offers a wide-ranging critique of masculinity in all its cultural forms. She first condemns the eighteenth-century "new man of feeling" by parodying the lyrics of Gray, Collins, and Cowper. The spontaneous overflow of powerful feeling in a man, expressed in her protagonist Orlando's "Ode to Poverty," functions in her novel as a sign of self-indulgence and social irresponsibility, like Orlando's momentary failure to provide his wife with a home and income. She then calls into question the aristocracy's chivalric code of honor from which Orlando's name is derived, not in the name of the rights of the common man, as William Godwin did that same year in *Caleb Williams*, but rather in the name of gender transformation. In Smith's novel, Orlando gives up both the chivalric and the democratic constructions of masculinity in order to take up the subject position of a woman. He is finally portrayed as feminine, the vulnerable dependent of a wealthy aristocratic woman, delicately featured, refined, loving, loyal, and passive—in short, as a modest heroine. When he goes to America to fight in the war against the colonies, he is immediately captured and—in a subversion of the popular racist and sexist American captivity narratives—cared for by a noble Indian chief. Orlando's femininity embodies a critique not just of the political elitism of feudal aristocracy but also of patrilineal bourgeois capitalism. His revulsion at the brutality of imperialist wars, at primogeniture and the indulgence of the eldest son, and at the greed of modern commerce are all endorsed in Smith's novel.

Other female novelists of the Romantic period contested the political domination of the patriarch—whether benevolent or tyrannical—by presenting all-female families or communities as the only sites of personal fulfillment. In *Adeline Mowbray* (1804), Amelia Opie tracks the damage done to a woman who tries to live out Godwin's radical notion of free love without marriage and his abstract system of political justice. At the conclusion, Opie offers as her radical social alternative (both to free love and to patriarchal domesticity) an all-female family of choice (Mrs. Pemberton, Mrs. Mowbray, and the West Indian Savannah), whose members overcome class and racial differences and collectively take on the responsibility of rearing Adeline's motherless daughter. A similar female family of choice emerges in the second draft for the conclusion of Mary Wollstonecraft's *Maria, or The Wrongs of Woman* (1798), where Maria—abandoned by both her husband and her lover— decides that she will "live for" her daughter, together with the lower-class Jemima.

More powerfully, many Romantic women novelists openly challenged the patriarchal doctrine of the separate spheres—the doctrine that would, in a classic example of antifeminist backlash, triumph as the official ideology of Queen Victoria's reign—by articulating a very different domestic ideology. The feminine Romanticism embodied in women's fiction from 1790 to 1830 constitutes (to use feminist author Rita Felski's term) an alternative "counter-public sphere." Many women novelists of the Romantic era whom I can discuss only briefly in this essay—including Mary Wollstonecraft, Ann Radcliffe, Mary Hays, Helen Maria Williams, Mary Brunton, Jane Austen, Maria Edgeworth, Susan Ferrier, Mary Shelley, and others—explicitly or implicitly advocated the "domestic affections" as a political program that would radically transform the public sphere. Inspired by Mary Wollstonecraft's call, in *Vindication of the Rights of Woman* (1792), for a "REVOLUTION in female manners," they proclaimed the importance of female education, rational love, an ethic of care, and gender equality in a challenge to the domestic ideology that relegated women to the home, and to the laissez-faire capitalist system that placed the rights of the individual, rational choice, and an ethic of justice above the needs of the community as a whole. The values of this "counter-public sphere" have much in common with the socialist call for equitable distribution of public goods and services, and should be recognized as a viable alternative political ideology, one that would give women not just a room (or a novel) but a nation of their own.

In endorsing Wollstonecraft's belief that females were capable of the same rational and moral development as males, in presenting us with heroines who think as well as feel, who act with prudence, avoid the pitfalls of sexual desire, and learn from their mistakes, Romantic women novelists explicitly corrected the tradition of eighteenth-century fiction by women that Jane Spencer has called "the didactic tradition" of "reformed heroines." In these didactic novels the author—or a male mentor—functions as a moral teacher, guiding the development of the heroine from her fallible youth to her mature acceptance of the status quo and the role of dutiful wife. This is the plot of such female bildungsromans as Mary Davy's *Reform'd Coquet* (1724), Eliza Haywood's *History of Miss Betsy Thoughtless* (1751) and Frances Burney's *Evelina* (1778).

Such Romantic women novelists as Ann Radcliffe, Maria Edgeworth, Helen Maria Williams, Mary Hays, Susan Ferrier, and Jane Austen transformed this tradition by putting forth a subtle critique of masculinity, highlighting the flaws in intelligence and moral virtue demonstrated by their male and female characters as well as the dangers of passionate love, sensibility, and the creative imagination for both men and women. By focusing as much on the failures of traditional marriages as on the heroine's acquisition of a meritorious husband, these Romantic novelists resisted the conservative tendencies of a Hannah More—who in *Coelebs in Search of a Wife* (1808) and elsewhere argued that the rational woman, however powerful at home, should uphold the doctrine of the separate spheres and acknowledge the superiority of men in the public realm. In its place they put forth a telling critique of the authority of the father and husband, a defense of egalitarian marriages, and the claim that the domestic affections provide the only viable foundation for all public and private virtues and happiness.

In her compelling novel *Belinda* (1801), Maria Edgeworth paints the portrait of the new woman who will replace Pope's "fairest of mortals" as the envy of her age. Belinda Portman is an attractive young woman of sound sense, wide reading, prudence, personal modesty, and a loving heart who can resist the negative female role models set before her in the self-indulgent, irresponsible aristocrat Lady Delacour and the overly aggressive, masculinized Harriet Freke. In introducing this macho woman as a "freak" or "caprice" of nature, Edgeworth reveals what Patricia Juliana Smith has called her "lesbian panic." At the same time Edgeworth introduces a more balanced feminism, one that does not insist, as Harriet does, on the superiority of women, but would combine the best moral and intellectual qualities associated with each gender. Belinda Portman preserves the sensibility and modesty associated with femininity but unites them with shrewd judgment, a personal sense of honor, sound moral principles based on reasoning and observation, earned self-esteem, and a generous capacity for loyalty and love. She is thus rationally and morally superior to both her lovers, the compulsive gambler Mr. Vincent and the misguided Clarence Hervey (who, taking a page from Rousseau's *Emile* and Richard Edgeworth's friend Thomas Day, has reared an innocent, passive, obedient Sophie to be his wife, but eventually finds her insufferably boring). *Belinda* is a textbook example of the new feminine Romantic ideology. Belinda, the rational woman, achieves a marriage of equality and compatibility with Clarence Hervey, one modeled on the egalitarian marriage of their middle-class friends the Percivals; and the Herveys' goodwill and tactful intervention finally succeed in reconciling the vivacious but tormented Lady Delacour with both her husband and her daughter.

In *The Absentee* (1812), Edgeworth makes clear that such egalitarian marriages are the model for good government. After condemning the irresponsible practices of both Irish and British aristocrats (she likens the tyranny of absentee British landlords in Ireland to that of slaveholders in Jamaica), she supports a "union" between England and Ireland that is dramatized in her novel by the marriage of the Anglo-Irish Lord Coulambre, a young man in whom "English prudence governed but did not extinguish, his Irish enthusiasm," to the Irish Grace Nugent, a young woman of intelligence, passionate loyalty, and "civil courage." Many critics have read Edgeworth as advocating a benevolent paternalism, as being "complicit" in a bourgeois patriarchy. It is true that Edgeworth, like many Romantic women novelists, endorsed Edmund Burke's concept of the family as the paradigm for a successful system of government—but she insisted on the equal rights of the mother and the father to guide and control those children who need to be governed. She finally advocated a family-politic in which a liberal and universal educational reform instituted by enlightened rulers (like her father and herself at Edgeworthstown) would *gradually* improve the social order without the political turmoil or financial and personal costs of a military revolution. Gender equality and racial harmony could be achieved, she believed, by converting the aristocracy, the laboring classes, and even slaves (as in her story "The Grateful Negro") to the values and practices of the professional (and now maternalistic as well as paternalistic) middle classes.

Like *Belinda*, Susan Ferrier's *Marriage* (1810) can be read as a fictional translation of the feminine Romanticism propounded in Wollstonecraft's *Vindication*. Ferrier first details the damage wrought by women's affirmation of passionate love and intense sensibility. The spoiled, willful Juliana rejects the aristocratic marriage arranged by her tyrannical father to elope with Henry Douglas, a handsome but penniless Scots Guardsman. But this marriage, founded only on mutual sexual desire, proves disastrous (as do all such marriages in the novels of feminine Romanticism). Unable to tolerate the rough manners or coarse food of her Scots in-laws, Juliana finally abandons her husband, returning to London to live parasitically upon her brother's shallow goodwill. Juliana replicates Wollstonecraft's portrait in *Vindication* of the selfish, ignorant, neglectful society lady (modeled on Wollstonecraft's employer Lady Kingsborough) who cares more for her pug dog than for her own daughters.

These twin daughters, Adelaide and Mary, function in the novel as exemplars of faulty and successful female education, respectively. Adelaide, living with her mother in London, learns by example to be "heartless and ambitious"; even more cold and selfishly calculating than her mother, she marries the elderly, obstinate Duke of Altamont for his money. She then finds his dogged refusal to satisfy her every whim intolerable and runs off with her cousin Lindore, only to see his sexual ardor rapidly cool into "indifference" and herself condemned to a life of "wretchedness" as a "friendless . . . outcast" in a foreign land.

In contrast, Mary Douglas is raised by her "rational, cheerful, sweet-tempered" aunt, a woman with a "noble and highly gifted mind" who voluntarily gave up her first passionate love when it met with her female guardian's disapproval and instead married a man whom she has found enduringly compatible and sensible. Inspired by her aunt's benevolence, rationality, and devotion to a Christian ethic of care, Mary learns to control her emotions, to respond to the needs of the poor and the sick, and to worship devoutly. Rejecting the marriage arranged by her mother with the wealthy man-of-fashion, Lord Glenallen, Mary—through her devoted care of the blind, lonely Mrs. Lennox—wins the devotion of Charles Lennox, a wise, handsome, loving young Colonel who respects Mary's virtues and shares her capacity for benevolence and lasting love.

While Ferrier's novel overtly endorses the "happy Marriage" of Mary Douglas and Charles Lennox as providing "as much happiness as earth's pilgrims ever possess," it implies a more subversive and revolutionary domestic ideology than that suggested by Mary's insistence that she will "never marry, unless I marry a man on whose judgment I could rely for advice and assistance, and for whom I could feel a certain deference that I consider due from a wife to her husband." Ferrier insistently associates this "happy" marriage with death—Mary and Colonel Lennox plight their troth over the deathbed of his mother, and Sir Sampson dies on their wedding day, leaving them the inheritance they need to live. Moreover, Colonel Lennox is portrayed in such an idealized, bland, stereotypical way that the reader knows he has failed to engage the author's imagination.

The novelist's own sympathies—and the modern reader's—lie not only with Mary but also, and perhaps more strongly, with her cousin Emily Lindore. Raised within the dissipated household of her vain, apathetic father and Aunt Juliana, she has remained "insupportably natural and sincere," becoming at the same time independent and willful, clever and insightful. While she lacks the religious training and consequently the benevolence and sympathy that Mary has learned from her Aunt Douglas, Emily engages us by her wit and by her refusal to submit to her Aunt Juliana's petty tyrannies. Emily has long loved her cousin Edward Douglas despite his faults, which she clearly sees: "he was handsome, brave, good-hearted, and good-humoured, but he was not clever." Their marriage is one of greater equality than is Mary's, for Edward's patriarchal privileges will be more than matched by Emily's superior intelligence. To Mary's belief that a woman must defer to her husband, Emily responds:

Now, I flatter myself, my husband and I shall have a more equitable division: for though a man is a reasonable being, he shall know and own that woman is so too—sometimes. All things that men ought to know better, I shall yield: whatever may belong to either sex, I either seize upon as my prerogative or scrupulously divide. . . .

While Mary is the ostensible heroine of the novel who wins all her arguments with Emily and attains the husband that Emily half desires,

Emily is the voice of shrewd, worldly female intelligence. Her utterances sparkle with the same energy and comic wit that enliven Ferrier's personal letters, suggesting that she is in part a projection of the author. And Emily's choice of a husband whose faults she knows and can tolerate, a husband who remains devoted to her and admires her, suggests that Ferrier endorsed more egalitarian marriages than those described by Hannah More. To find other powerful examples of such egalitarian marriages we have only to look to the fiction of Charlotte Smith (especially the marriage of Lionel Desmond and Geraldine Verney in *Desmond*, 1792), of Elizabeth Le Noir (especially the marriage of Clara and Mr. Forrest in *Clara de Montfier*, 1808), or of Jane Austen (the Crofts, the Gardiners, Elizabeth Bennet and Fitzwilliam Darcy, Emma Woodhouse and Mr. Knightley, and, especially, Anne Elliot and Captain Wentworth).

In the fiction of feminine Romanticism, such egalitarian marriages, and the lasting domestic harmony they can bring, grow out of rational love rather than sexual passion, especially where the women are concerned. Female Romantic novelists almost all endorsed Wollstonecraft's claim in *Vindication of the Rights of Woman* that

one grand truth women have yet to learn, though much it imports them to act accordingly. In the choice of a husband, they should not be led astray by the qualities of a lover—for a lover the husband, even supposing him to be wise and virtuous, cannot long remain.

Were women more rationally educated, could they take a more comprehensive view of things, they would be contented to love but once in their lives; and after marriage calmly let passion subside into friendship—into that tender intimacy, which is the best refuge from care.

Maria Edgeworth opposed passionate erotic love, which she defined as that "liberty" which uneducated girls equate with "escape from habitual restraint to exercise their own will, no matter how," both in her life—she declined her only proposal of marriage (from the Swedish diplomat Edelcrantz, a man with whom she was, according to her sister, "exceedingly in love") to remain with her father and siblings in Ireland—and in her fiction. In her *Letters for Literary Ladies* (1799), she portrays the perils and penalties that befall a girl who, following Rousseau's Julie, defines herself as an ardent advocate of intense romantic love and of sensation for its own sake, and who chooses "the eager genius, the exquisite sensibility of enthusiasm" over "the even temper, the poised judgment, the stoical serenity of philosophy." Preferring the lot of the Mackenzian woman of feeling to that of the rational philosopher, Edgeworth's Julia impulsively marries Lord V——. He is a man who shares none of her tastes for literature but who desires "public admiration, dissipation, and all the pleasures of riches and high rank" and "whose easiness of temper and fondness" for Julia, she thinks, will give her "entire command at home and abroad." Within five years, Julia is thoroughly bored by the fashionable world and separates from her demanding husband. Living alone, she falls easy prey to the advances of her admirers, elopes with one to France, is abandoned, and finally returns to London a year later, penniless and dying, broken in spirit, and filled with remorse.

In contrast, the prudent Caroline achieves Wollstonecraft's and Edgeworth's ideal of a non-eroticized domestic life, defined in a "Letter from a Gentleman" (modeled on Richard Lovell Edgeworth) as

the pleasure which men of science and literature enjoy in an union with women, who can sympathise in all their thoughts and feelings, who can converse with them as equals, and live with them as friends; who can assist them in the important and delightful duty of educating their children; who can make their family their most agreeable society, and their home the attractive centre of happiness.

While Edgeworth's heroines do not work outside the home and are not political leaders, as Wollstonecraft advocated, Edgeworth does share the latter's conviction that men as well as women must commit themselves to the domestic affections and the education of children as the bases of all personal and public happiness.

The dangers of excessive sensibility and of sexual passion for men as well as for women are spelled out in Helen Maria Williams's *Julia* (1790). A woman's answer both to Rousseau's *La nouvelle Héloïse* and to Goethe's *Werther*, this novel tracks the enormous emotional havoc wreaked by a young man who cannot restrain his passion. Williams's Julia is a young woman of refined sensitivity, poetic tastes, modest genius, and affectionate disposition, who prefers the "satisfactions of home" to the frivolous joys of dissipation in London society. She is joined by her closest friend and cousin, Charlotte, a sweet-tempered girl who worships Julia. When Charlotte goes on a tour of Italy with her father, she meets and falls in love with Frederick Seymour, a young diplomat who combines a good understanding with an "enthusiasm . . .

awake to every generous impression" and a "warmth of feeling." Frederick is moved by Charlotte's modest simplicity and good-heartedness—she is so different from the vain and silly society women he has hitherto encountered—and soon proposes to her. She accepts with perfect joy.

But when the engaged lovers return to London, Frederick meets Julia, whose superior beauty attracts his eye and whose intelligence can understand the subtleties of his thought and wit in ways that Charlotte cannot. His passion is aroused; despite his pledge to Charlotte, he is overwhelmed with love for Julia. And even though in other circumstances, Julia might have returned his love, her intense affection for her cousin and her uncle effectively stifles her sexual response; as Williams tells us, her "exquisite sensibility was corrected by the influence of reason." Despite several encounters in which Frederick manifests his love and once even saves her life, Julia maintains her self-control. Frederick, honor-bound, marries Charlotte, but cannot hide his passion for Julia from prying eyes. During her first pregnancy, Charlotte finally discovers Frederick's love for Julia, and in her misery turns away from Julia, who suffers this loss of her earliest and best friend in painful silence. His constitution weakened by his emotional turmoil, Frederick dies of a winter cold on the night of his son's birth, in unrelieved misery caused by his hopeless and uncontrolled desire, which has destroyed not only his happiness but that of his wife and his beloved Julia.

As opposed to Goethe and the masculine Romantic Sturm und Drang school, Williams explores the damage done by a prohibited and irrational passion, the cruelty it wreaks on innocent bystanders, the ways in which it destroys a potentially happy family. When Julia sees a painting of "Charlotte at Werther's Tomb," which anticipates Frederick's death, she comments that *Werther* "is well written, but few will justify its principles." In *Julia*, passion destroys Frederick. But Williams, deploring the gender restrictions in England, insists that such erotic desire is even more dangerous for women since they cannot distract themselves with the routines of business or the dissipations of pleasure as men do, but must bear their sufferings in a silent conflict for which "life is frequently the atonement."

As did Wollstonecraft and Edgeworth, Williams firmly endorsed the enduring domestic affections over unlicensed sexual passion as the basis of true love and benevolence. "Our affections are not constantly active, they are called forth by circumstances; and what can awaken them so forcibly, as the renewal of those domestic endearments which constitute the charm of our existence?" Julia's lifelong affection for her father, uncle, and cousin lead to the numerous acts of charity she eagerly performs for those in need—an old soldier, hungry peasants, a young child—even wounded animals. That attachment is the foundation of the happy family unit she and Charlotte eventually construct after Frederick's death, which includes Charlotte's father and son as well as the two women. Williams clearly implies that heterosexual passion does not contribute to domestic love: she firmly excludes it from her happy family.

From *The Advantages of Education, or, The History of Maria Williams* (1793) by "Prudentia Homespun" (Jane West) through Mary Brunton's *Self-Control* (1810), Jane Austen's *Sense and Sensibility* (1811), Frances Burney's *The Wanderer* (1814), and Lady Blessington's *The Governess* (1839), and countless others, Romantic women novelists advocated rational rather than erotic love. Fully aware of the prevailing sexual double standard, these women writers knew that sexual desire too often left their female friends and heroines seduced, abandoned, and pregnant—with only prostitution—the career of the "fallen woman"—available to them. Several writers directly challenged the injustice of this double standard, none more powerfully than Mary Hays in *A Victim of Prejudice* (1799) or Amelia Opie in her tale "The Father and Daughter" (1801), but all warned young women against trusting their passions over their judgment.

The education of women, rational love, egalitarian marriages, an ethic of care—these are the cornerstones of the feminine Romantic ideology laid out in the leading women's novels of the Romantic era. Jane Porter, for instance, made them the basis of her historical fictions. Although her protagonists, Thaddeus in *Thaddeus of Warsaw* (1803) and William Wallace in *The Scottish Chiefs* (1810), are men, they consistently regard the values of the domestic affections and loyalty to the family and its ideals as their highest commitments. She thus prepared the way for Walter Scott's commitment to domesticity and a feminine Romantic ideology in his historical fiction.

While most of the women novelists of the Romantic period endorsed these values overtly, a few powerful writers focused instead on the horrors of their absence or violation. The leading writers of the female Gothic tradition displayed the violence that results, especially to women, when a society fails to sustain gender equality and an ethic of care. The novels of Ann Radcliffe, Clara Dacre Byrne, Regina Maria

Roche (*The Children of the Abbey*, 1796), and, most powerfully, Mary Shelley expose the dark underside of the doctrine of the separate spheres, of the sexual division of labor, and of patriarchal economic systems, both pre- and postindustrial. The father, whether as patriarch or priest, is here unmasked as the author of violence against women, the perpetrator of sadistic tortures and even incest, and thus as the violator of the very bonds of affection and responsibility that constitute the family-politic. His crimes almost always occur amid Alpine landscapes, the loci of the sublime that Edmund Burke had identified with the terrifying revelation of God's divine power. By moving the exercise of sublime power out of nature and into the household, this female Romantic Gothic tradition domesticates the terror of the sublime as the experience of paternal transgression—represented as father-daughter incest—that is everywhere most monstrous and most ordinary.

The novels of Ann Radcliffe exemplify this paradigm. A devotee of Salvator Rosa, the acknowledged master of sublime landscape painting, she repeatedly invokes his images to create the settings for her novels, employing them to a twofold purpose. On the one hand, Radcliffe uses Rosa's Alpine landscapes of dark nights, mountainous peaks and chasms, raging torrents, and fierce storms to establish an environment in which human cruelty and physical violence can flourish. Her sublime landscapes are characteristically peopled by banditti, fierce gypsies, hired assassins, and pirates. Traveling peacefully at night along the road to Rousillon in *The Mysteries of Udolpho* (1794), Emily St. Aubert and her father must skirt a blazing fire around which a predatory group of gypsies are dancing. Similarly, Count de Villefort and his daughter Blanche, seeking respite from a raging midnight storm among the French Alps, find themselves the prisoners of a gang of thieves, assassins and pirates. And in *The Italian* (1797), Vivaldi and his servant Paulo, looking for Ellena through the mountainous regions of the Puglia, find themselves "among scenes, which seemed abandoned by civilized society to the banditti who haunted their recesses."

Radcliffe's purpose, however, is not to reinscribe Burke's and Rosa's sublime landscapes as settings in which one fears for one's life at the hands of both natural and human forces. Instead, as Kate Ferguson Ellis has suggested, Radcliffe believes that sublime horror originates not in nature but only in men. She calculatedly moves the terror of the sublime from the outside into the home, that theoretical haven of virtue and safety for otherwise "unprotected" women. In *The Mysteries of*

Udolpho, banditti not only rove among the savage Alps but actually inhabit the homes of the female characters.

Montoni, for example, is the husband of Emily St. Aubert's aunt and is Emily's legal guardian, but he is also the leader of a fierce band of *condottieri*, paid mercenaries who function as little more than bandits and murderers. Montoni's status as one of the banditti is established by his willingness to protect Orsini, a confessed assassin, and by the persistent rumor that he has murdered his cousin, Signora Laurentini, in order to inherit the Castle of Udolpho. Within the castle itself, Montoni reenacts the role of the legendary Bluebeard, tormenting his wife, imprisoning her when she is ill, and refusing her medicine and care until he can sneeringly rejoice at her early death. And he regards his niece by marriage as his personal property, to dispose of in marriage as he chooses, or, when she resists, to abandon to the metaphorical wolves, withdrawing his protection so that the rapist Verezzi may pursue her. Radcliffe's point is clear: in her novels, the deepest terror women face lies with the exercise of patriarchal authority *within the home*.

Radcliffe emphasizes this point by showing just how easily such tyrants can gain access to vulnerable young women. Montoni is Emily's legal guardian. Blanche de Villefort's chateau has been penetrated through a secret passageway by cruel pirates, who kidnap her faithful guard Ludovico. More subtly, Radcliffe draws a parallel between Valancourt, the noble and heroic young man with whom Emily St. Aubert has fallen in love, and her captor Montoni. Emily's father first assumes that Valancourt is a highwayman and actually wounds him in the belief that he is a bandit about to attack them. Both Valancourt and Montoni are gamblers who have lost their fortunes in play. Both spend time in prison. Both marry real or putative inheritors of the St. Aubert estates. Although at the end of *The Mysteries of Udolpho*, Valancourt is redeemed by his enduring love for Emily, his remorse, his generosity, and his innocence of the added crimes of whoremongering and blackmail, it is actually Emily, as Ellis has argued, who has been responsible for preserving the virtue of the home. By refusing to marry Valancourt when he has lost her esteem, she aggressively upholds a standard of moral purity and rational prudence that the novel endorses and from which Valancourt lapses. Despite the novel's final assertion that "the bowers of La Vallée became, once more, the retreat of goodness, wisdom and domestic blessedness," to the reader the marriage of Emily and Valancourt may seem to rest on less secure foundations; having fallen once, Valancourt may all too easily fall again into violent passion and criminal excess.

Radcliffe again depicts the vulnerability of the Edenic home to the "snake" of patriarchal power in *The Italian*, where the "father" (Schedoni) is a priest as well as the murderer of his brother, the rapist of his brother's wife, and the man who encourages and almost carries out the desire of the Marchioness di Vivaldi to murder her future daughter-in-law. Ellena Rosalba is saved from both incest and death at the hands of her villainous uncle only because, at the last moment, Schedoni mistakenly concludes that he is her biological father and has more to gain from her marriage to Vivaldi than from her murder. Here, Radcliffe drives home her argument that the greatest evil women must fear arises *within* the sanctified family—both the patriarchal family and those institutions, such as the Catholic church, that purport to protect it. By locating masculine tyranny in the Roman Catholic Inquisition and the celibate priesthood, Radcliffe (like such other devout Christian women writers as Susan Ferrier, Elizabeth Hamilton, Jane West, Hannah More, and even Mary Wollstonecraft) leaves open the possibility that an enlightened, Protestant, married, and thereby domesticated clergy might come to recognize and espouse the values of feminine Romanticism.

In opposition to Edmund Burke and Salvator Rosa, Radcliffe constructs an alternative, entirely positive representation of the sublime. Burke had insisted that the psychological experience of the sublime originates in fear for one's life, aroused by the instinct of self-preservation in the face of the overwhelming power of nature, manifested by huge cliffs, raging rivers, or violent storms; as one's fear recedes, one emotionally progresses from astonishment to awe to a grateful and pleasurable acknowledgment of the power of the divine. But Ann Radcliffe, following the more positive vision of the sublime found in the writings of Immanuel Kant and anticipating the poetry of Coleridge and Wordsworth, suggests that one can reach a consciousness of the power and glory of divine creation without fear and trembling. Significantly, her heroines respond to the magnificence of Alpine scenery with pleasure rather than fear. For Emily St. Aubert and her father, the majestic Pyrenees "soften, while they elevate, the heart, and fill it with the certainty of a present God."

Radcliffe's work diverges from later poetic treatments of the sublime—in which the male Romantic poets appropriate and speak for "the mighty mind" of Nature—by imbuing the experience of the sublime with a recognition of the separateness of the perceiving self from nature. She thus insists upon a subjectivity constructed in relation to an other that cannot be possessed or absorbed into a transcendental ego. For Radcliffe, the experience of the sublime in nature is one that is beyond language, one that impresses the finite self with the presence of an infinite, never-fully-knowable other. At the same time, this confrontation with the divine elevates the perceiving self to a sense of her or his own integrity and worth as a unique product of divine creation. Rather than assuming Wordsworth's stance of the *spectator ab extra*, Radcliffe presents this heightened self-esteem as a means to a renewed appreciation of the equal value and dignity of other people. The feminine Romantic sublime is thus quintessentially democratic, as Emily St. Aubert, consoling her father upon his financial ruin, argues: "Poverty cannot . . . deaden our taste for the grand, and the beautiful, or deny us the means of indulging it; for the scenes of nature—those sublime spectacles, so infinitely superior to all artificial luxuries! are open for the enjoyment of the poor, as well as of the rich."

As it strengthens self-esteem, the feminine Romantic sublime produces a sympathy or love that connects the self with others. A shared enthusiasm for the grandeurs of Alpine scenery is what draws Emily and Valancourt together in love; the memory of those shared experiences unites them through their separate sufferings whenever they invoke their commitment to think of each other as the sun sets; and Emily's inability to forget those shared moments keeps alive her love for Valancourt even after she has prudently rejected an offer of marriage from her dishonored lover.

The feminine Romantic sublime both inspires and sustains love by giving each individual a sense of personal value and significance. It thus enables the women who experience it to achieve a mental escape from the oppressions of a tyrannical social order. Imprisoned by Schedoni in the convent of San Stefano in the Italian Alps, Ellena climbs a turret to a balcony above her bedroom and immediately loses both "the consciousness of her prison" and her fear of her jailer:

Here, gazing upon the stupendous imagery around her, looking, as it were, beyond the awful veil which obscures the features of the Deity, and conceals Him from the eyes of his creatures, dwelling as with a present God in the midst of his sublime works, with a mind thus elevated, how insignificant would appear to her the transactions, and the sufferings of this world! How poor the boasted power of man, when the fall of a single cliff from these mountains would with ease destroy thousands of his race assembled on the plains below! . . . Thus man, the giant who now held her in captivity, would shrink to the diminutiveness of a fairy; and she would experience, that his utmost force was unable to chain her soul, or compel her to fear him, while he was destitute of virtue.

For Edmund Burke and Salvator Rosa, the contemplation of sublime nature roused an Oedipal anxiety caused by the overwhelming power of the father. For Kant and Wordsworth, the joy of the sublime experience depended upon the annihilation of otherness, upon the erasure of the female. In the novels of Radcliffe and other Romantic women writers, the contemplation of sublime nature produces, first, the recognition that the self is separated from the other. If that other is an oppressor, the sublime arouses a sense of personal exaltation and an awareness of one's virtue and worth. Thus it produces tranquillity, a mental freedom from the tyrannies of men and women, whom it reduces to impotence. If the other is beloved, then the experience of the sublime mediates a renewed connection between the lovers based on individual integrity, self-esteem, and mutual respect.

This second experience of the sublime—as the achievement of mutual love—is most fully rendered in *The Wild Irish Girl* (1806) by Sydney Owenson, Lady Morgan. A spirited defense of all things Irish against a host of British imperialist prejudices, this novel employs Burke's and Rosa's categories of the masculine sublime only to under-cut them. Morgan's English protagonist, Horatio M——, travels fear-fully among the desolate, rugged mountains of western Ireland, but instead of Rosa's life-threatening banditti and outlaws, he encounters first a group of women spinning, led in their Irish songs by an impro-visatrice who celebrates the harmony between their work and a female Nature; then a helpful English-speaking guide; and finally, on the high road, instead of a murdering highwayman, a destitute but dignified peasant who shares his meager home and food with a "manly courte-ousness" that puts Horatio to shame. Morgan here suggests that in Ire-land the confrontation with a sublime and feminine Nature inspires not fear and trembling but a life of dignity and natural grace lived in peace-ful harmony with one's fellow human beings, however difficult it may be to eke a living from the "rigid soil."

Horatio's journey is then interrupted by the music of an Eolian lyre, accompanied by "the voice of a *woman*." Thus Morgan introduces her heroine Glorvina, the wild Irish girl with whom Horatio is to fall pas-sionately in love. Morgan's subversion of the masculine sublime then takes a comic turn. Just before hearing the seductive song of Glorvina, Horatio had indulged a desire to conquer and possess the landscape upon which he gazed ("I raised my eyes to the Castle of Inismore, sighed, and almost wished I had been born the lord of these beautiful ruins, the prince of this isolated little territory, the adored chieftain of these affectionate and natural people"). Entranced by Glorvina's siren song, he eagerly climbs the ruined walls, only to lose his footing and fall precipitously into the castle yard. His fall is metaphoric: the male's desire to master both Nature and the female voice is humorously, if rather brutally, undercut. Morgan's narrator usurps the role of one of Rosa's male banditti, but he is clearly harmless.

The female may not be so harmless, however. With broken arm and leg and severely gashed forehead, Horatio, taken into the Castle, falls into a delirious slumber: "I dreamed that the Princess of Inismore approached my bed, drew aside the curtains, and raising her veil, dis-covered a face I had hitherto guessed at, than seen. Imagine my hor-ror—it was the face, the head, of a *Gorgon!*" Again, the terror of the Burkean sublime—here represented as a man's fear of female sexuality, power, and his own castration—is parodied: "I cast my eyes through a fracture in the old damask drapery of my bed, and beheld—not the hor-rid spectre of my recent dream—but the form of a cherub hovering near my pillow—it was the Lady Glorvina herself!"

For Morgan, the sublime is characteristically the way into a love founded not on the male psyche's narcissistic absorption of his female antithesis or soul mate—as in Shelley's "Epipsychidion" or Byron's *Manfred*—but on the recognition of both difference and compatibility. Recovering from his injuries, the welcome guest of Glorvina and of her father, the Prince of Inismore, Horatio is ever more attracted to Glorv-ina, and the attraction is mediated by Rosa's sublime landscapes.

We both arose at the same moment, and walked in silence towards the win-dow. Beyond the mass of ruins which spread in desolate confusion below, the ocean, calm and unruffled, expanded its awful waters almost to apparent infinitude; . . . the tall spectral figure of Father John, leaning on a broken col-umn, appeared the very impersonation of philosophy moralizing on the insta-bility of all human greatness.

What a sublime assemblage of images!

'How consonant,' thought I, gazing at Glorvina, 'to the tone of our present

346 Columbia History of the Btritish Novel

feelings!' Glorvina bowed her head affirmatively, as though my lips had given utterance to the reflection.

How, think you, I felt, on this involuntary acknowledgement of a mutual intelligence?

Where Rosa or Burke would have represented Father John solely as a memento mori, in Morgan's rewriting his spectral presence instead inspires two people to enter into an unspoken dialogue that finally produces a shared feeling not of fear but of love. For Morgan, the heightened awareness of the self produced by the sublime leads not to self-absorbed reflection but to communication with other selves, to a "mutual intelligence" between two independent, sensitive people. Morgan finally hails this "sympathy" or domesticated sublimity as the essence of "reason and humanity."

The most profound analysis of the damage done both to men and to women by a patriarchal domestic ideology that confines the domestic affections to the private sphere and constructs Nature as a female other to be possessed rather than respected occurs in the finest Gothic novel of the Romantic period, Mary Shelley's *Frankenstein, or The Modern Prometheus* (1816). The story of a scientist who creates out of dead bodies a monster more powerful than himself—a monster that destroys its maker—*Frankenstein* should also be seen as a story about what happens when a man tries to have a baby without a woman. After laboring for nine months ("winter, spring and summer passed away") to complete his experiment, whose aim is to discover the cause of "generation and life" and to bestow "animation upon life-less matter," Victor Frankenstein flees in horror from his newborn creature. Reflecting the pregnancy anxieties of the nineteen-year-old, already thrice pregnant Mary Godwin, Frankenstein here embodies the author's own fears that she might not be able to love her child, especially if it were in some way abnormal, that she might be capable of desiring the extinction of her own offspring, and that her child might kill her, as she had inadvertently killed her own mother, Mary Wollstonecraft, who died of a puerperal fever caused by her failure to expel the placenta. Shelley's novel then details what happens to a child abandoned at birth by its only parent: the creature seeks human companionship, but, repeatedly thwarted in his desire for a family, becomes vicious, burns the DeLacey cottage, and finally kills Frankenstein's brother, friend, bride, and the creator himself. The novel thereby argues that a battered, rejected child becomes a battering, abusive parent: the creature's first victim, after all, is a small boy whom he wishes to adopt.

Why does Victor Frankenstein abandon his child? Initially, because he is large and ugly, a creature whose countenance Victor immediately "reads" as evil, as the face of "a miserable monster." But as the creature pursues Victor into the Alps, declaring his need for a female companion and his right to be included among the human species, Victor at last acknowledges his parental responsibilities and agrees to construct a female creature as an Eve for his Adam. Halfway through this second creation, Victor stops, and "trembling with passion tore to pieces" the female body lying before him, feeling the next morning "as if I had mangled the living flesh of a human being." Victor's violent destruction of the female creature, a destruction that is represented almost as a rape, points to the hidden agenda of Victor's scientific project. Insisting that he has killed the female in order to protect mankind, Victor's explanation uncovers a deeper anxiety:

She might become ten thousand times more malignant than her mate, and delight, for its own sake, in murder and wretchedness. He had sworn to quit the neighborhood of man, and hide himself in deserts; but she had not; and she, who in all probability was to become a thinking and reasoning animal, might refuse to comply with a compact made before her creation. They might even hate each other; the creature who already lived loathed his own deformity, and might he not conceive a greater abhorrence for it when it came before his eyes in the female form? She also might turn with disgust from him to the superior beauty of man; she might quit him, and he be again alone, exasperated by the fresh provocation of being deserted by one of his own species.

Even if they were to leave Europe, and inhabit the deserts of the new world, yet one of the first results of those sympathies for which the daemon thirsted would be children, and a race of devils would be propagated upon the earth, who might make the very existence of the species of man a condition precarious and full of terror.

What Victor Frankenstein most fears is the existence of an *independent* female, one who might think for herself and have her own desires, one so large and angry that she could obtain her own sexual mate by force if necessary (even, potentially, by raping Victor), and above all, one with the reproductive power to create an entire new species.

Terrified of the power of female sexuality, Victor both tries to destroy it (by tearing apart the female creature and by abandoning his own bride to his creature on her wedding night) and to possess it, by penetrating the womb of Mother Nature and discovering the secrets of "her hiding places." Drawing on the most advanced scientific research of the early nineteenth century—the chemical experiments of Sir Humphrey Davy and the use by Luigi Galvani of electricity to animate dead bodies—Frankenstein undertakes the project of the entire scientific revolution, as Mary Shelley understood it: to usurp the powers of Mother Nature in order to increase the prestige and social control of (male) scientists and, finally, in the most terrifying potential consequence of Victor's ability to create a man without a mother, to eliminate the biological and hence the cultural need for women altogether.

However, in Shelley's novel, Victor Frankenstein does not realize his goal of becoming the worshiped creator of a new race of supermen, because Mother Nature fights back, cursing Frankenstein with both physical and mental diseases so severe that he dies of exhaustion at the age of twenty-five. Moreover, she pursues him with fire and electricity—the very "spark of life," that he has stolen from her—hurling lightning, thunder, and rains upon him as he carries on his experiments. These atmospheric effects are not merely the conventional accoutrements of the Gothic novel, but also the manifestations of Nature's elemental powers, furies that pursue Victor like Orestes to his hiding places. Nature further punishes Victor by making it impossible for him to engage in *normal* reproduction, first by eliminating the natural bond of Victor as mother with his child—which would have enabled him to empathize with his creature and thus to prevent the creation of a freak who frightens all who see him—and second by ensuring that Victor's unnatural creation will destroy his wife, his family, and finally himself. The penalty of violating Nature, in Shelley's novel, is death.

Implicit in *Frankenstein* is an ideal: Shelley's belief that civilization can only be forwarded by human beings who constantly exercise the domestic affections. As Frankenstein comes to recognize,

A human being in perfection ought always to preserve a calm and peaceful mind and never to allow passion or a transitory desire to disturb his tranquillity. I do not think that the pursuit of knowledge is an exception to this rule. If the study to which you apply yourself has a tendency to weaken your affections, and to destroy your taste for those simple pleasures in which no alloy can possibly mix, then that study is certainly unlawful, that is to say, not befitting the human mind. If this rule were always observed; if no man allowed any pursuit whatsoever to interfere with the tranquillity of his domestic affections, Greece had not been enslaved; Caesar would have spared his country; America would have been discovered more gradually; and the empires of Mexico and Peru had not been destroyed.

Shelley here draws the analogy between the personal and the political that underpins the feminine Romantic ideology: only when all human beings exercise an ethic of care both at home and in the public realm, using their capacity for empathy and love to mother *all* living things— including monsters—and living in cooperative harmony with nature can the human community improve morally, politically, and scientifically. Significantly, the only member of the Frankenstein family alive at the end of the novel is Ernest, the farmer. A society built on the model of the family-politic advocated by both Mary Wollstonecraft and Maria Edgeworth is the only one, according to Shelley, with the capacity to "read" the face of the unfamiliar not as monstrous but as lovable. Opposing her husband's Promethean, revolutionary politics and his celebration of the Romantic imagination, Mary Shelley insisted, following Erasmus Darwin's scientific theories of the gradual evolution of the fittest, that men and women must unite as equal partners in the reproduction and preservation of life, controlling the unfettered scientific imagination with a specifically maternal, nurturing love that can embrace freaks and subjugate the pursuit of knowledge to the maintenance of family tranquillity. The failure to do so creates monsters capable of destroying civilization itself: as Victor's creature proclaims, "You are my creator, but I am your master;—obey!"

Shelley's later "society" novels, *Mathilda* (1819), *Lodore* (1835), and *Falkner* (1837), continue to depict the damage done when the mother is absent, showing how a daughter who devotes her life to her father, or father figure, and engages in the incestuous emotional dependence that devotion entails, is denied the psychological capacity for gender equality, for personal growth, and, in the case of Mathilda, even for life itself. The nihilistic vision of *The Last Man* (1826) explores both the futility of the human imagination in the face of indifferent Nature, and the failure of the masculine ego to take what few steps might suffice to save the human species (the irresponsible Adrian finally drowns rather than impregnate Clara Verney). Throughout her fiction, Shelley sustains the ideal of an egalitarian family, which she acknowledges to be a fiction in her own experience, but which she nonetheless insists is the only salvation available to a society corrupted by the systems of hierarchy and oppression that prop up the patriarchal bourgeois family and the imperialist nation it produces.

Whether one looks at the didactic or the Gothic tradition of women's fiction in the Romantic period, one finds a shared political ideology: a "revolution in female manners" that insists that good government, both at home and in the public sphere, depends on the education and equality of women, on the benevolent parenting of all living beings, and on meeting the needs of all who require care. Such a program, for these Romantic women writers, necessarily involves an acknowledged respect for the rights of Mother Nature as well as for all those classes, races, and nationalities previously defined as "the other." For such writers as Maria Edgeworth, Mary Wollstonecraft, Jane Austen, and Amelia Opie, the fate of African slaves in the Americas was directly analogous to the fate of women living in England. Despite the legal decision of Lord Mansfield in 1772 that "the air of England was too pure for a slave to breathe in," their fiction reiterates Wollstonecraft's claim that the badly educated and legally disenfranchised wives and daughters of England were but "slaves." They calculatedly used their fiction to promote a political program of sexual and racial liberation, one founded on the triumph of the "domestic affections." Their program failed in the antifeminist and antiegalitarian backlash of Victorian England, perhaps because it was too closely identified with the bourgeois values of the professional middle classes to which these women novelists belonged. Nonetheless, the social vision promoted in the novels of these Romantic women writers offered a genuine political alternative to the patriarchal system ensconced in early nineteenth-century British law, and it contributed significantly to the social revolutions of the twentieth century.

Anne K. Mellor

Selected Bibliography

Armstrong, Nancy. *Desire and Domestic Fiction: A Political History of the Novel.* New York: Oxford University Press, 1987.

Davidoff, Leonore, and Catherine Hall. *Family Fortunes: Men and Women of the English Middle Class, 1780–1850.* London: Hutchinson; Chicago: University of Chicago Press, 1987.

Ellis, Kate Ferguson. *The Contested Castle: Gothic Novels and the Subversion of Domestic Ideology.* Urbana and Chicago: University of Illinois Press, 1989.

Gilbert, Sandra M., and Susan Gubar. *The Madwoman in the Attic*. New Haven and London: Yale University Press, 1979.

Jones, Ann H. *Ideas and Innovations—Best-Sellers of Jane Austen's Age*. New York: AMS Press, 1986.

Kelly, Gary. *English Fiction of the Romantic Period, 1789–1830*. London: Longman, 1989.

Kowaleski-Wallace, Elizabeth. *Their Father's Daughters: Hannah More, Maria Edgeworth, and Patriarchal Complicity*. New York and Oxford: Oxford University Press, 1991.

Mellor, Anne K. *Mary Shelley: Her Life, Her Fiction, Her Monsters*. New York: Methuen; London: Routledge, 1988.

Mellor, Anne K. *Romanticism and Gender*. New York and London: Routledge, Chapman and Hall, 1992.

Poovey, Mary. *The Proper Lady and the Woman Writer: Ideology as Style in the Works of Mary Wollstonecraft, Mary Shelley, and Jane Austen*. Chicago and London: University of Chicago Press, 1984.

"Speak what we think": The Brontës and Women Writers

We do not hesitate to say that the tone of mind and thought which has overthrown authority and violated every code human and divine abroad, and fostered Chartism and rebellion at home, is the same which has also written Jane Eyre.
Elizabeth Rigby, Quarterly Review, 1848

English novels have for a long time . . . held a very high reputation in the world . . . for a certain sanity, wholesomeness, and cleanness unknown to other literature of the same class. . . . [Now] a singular change has passed upon our light literature. . . . It has been brought into being by society, and it naturally reacts upon society. The change perhaps began at the time when Jane Eyre made what advanced critics call her "protest" against the conventionalities in which the world clothes itself.
Margaret Oliphant, Blackwood's, 1867

The drawbacks of being Jane Eyre are not far to seek. Always to be a governess and always to be in love is a serious limitation in a world which is full, after all, of people who are neither one nor the other. . . . [Charlotte Brontë] does not attempt to solve the problems of human life; she is even unaware that such problems exist; all her force, and it is the more tremendous for being constricted, goes into the assertion, "I love," "I hate," "I suffer."
Virginia Woolf, 1923

Jane Eyre . . . the feminist individualist heroine of British fiction . . . an allegory of the general epistemic violence of imperialism . . .
Gayatri Spivak, 1985

READINGS of *Jane Eyre* changed the direction of English fiction in the nineteenth century and have charted the ways of discussing fiction in the twentieth. Charlotte Brontë called her book "a mere domestic novel" lacking any "subject of public interest." Yet readers since its publication have been debating its politics, pronouncing on the extraordinary natures of its heroine and hero, and celebrating or questioning the political meaning of this "mere domestic" fiction. Whether *Jane Eyre* is a woman's *Pilgrim's Progress* or a pilgrim's progress of feminism, whether its "furious love-making was but a wild declaration of the 'Rights of Woman' in a new aspect" (Mrs. Oliphant) or the creation of a feminist myth, whether it exposes the angel in the house as a simpering construction of a male-dominated society or performs textual services for the very patriarchy it critiques, the novel stands as witness to the extraordinary and continuing ways a female writer working in the 1840s, amid revolutions in Europe and wretched poverty and Chartist protests in England, intervened in the lives of readers.

Charlotte Brontë's other novels have seemed simply to swell the progress of *Jane Eyre*, and the novels of her sisters to stand as curiosities—though in the case of *Wuthering Heights*, a curiosity of such genius that few texts outside of Shakespeare and the Bible can have provoked such vigorously different and compelling interpretations. Anne Brontë's novels are worth the reading; but, finally, they serve to represent what Charlotte Brontë challenged through the writing of *Jane Eyre*. Anne Brontë also presents women gazing at "the dark side of respectable human nature." But neither *Agnes Grey* nor *The Tenant of Wildfell Hall*, for all the harsh realism of the latter, escapes the kind of conventional fiction "with a purpose" that Charlotte Brontë chose to produce, if at all, in a very different register. There is nothing like *Wuthering Heights* in Charlotte Brontë or in nineteenth-century English fiction. At once Romantic poem and realistic novel, it refuses to be a Victorian novel even as it often sounds like one—and by its end resembles one. In charting the readings of Currer Bell/Charlotte Brontë in the nineteenth and twentieth centuries, I will consider, at the end of this essay, Emily Brontë and *Wuthering Heights* as commentary on the personal, political, and literary issues raised by Charlotte Brontë and her novels.

Charlotte Brontë and the Condition of English Middle-Class Women

Readers need only consider the ways ideas about women and domestic life were articulated in nineteenth-century England to experience how radical *Jane Eyre* appeared to Charlotte Brontë's contemporaries. Mrs. Sarah Ellis, in *The Daughters of England* (1843), wrote: "[Love] is woman's all—her wealth, her power, her very being. Man, let him love as he may, has ever an existence distinct from that of his affections. He has his worldly interests, his public character, his ambition, his competition with other men—but woman centres all in that one feeling, and 'In that *she* lives, or else *she* has no life.' "

The implications of this ideology for the novel were articulated frequently, especially after the publication of *Jane Eyre*, and are succinctly stated by E. S. Dallas in *The Gay Science* (1866). Declaring that "woman embodies our highest ideas of purity and refinement," Dallas offers two premises to define the work of women in fiction: (1) "Woman peculiarly represents the private life of the race. Her ascendancy in literature must mean the ascendancy of domestic ideas, and the assertion of the individual, not as a hero, but as a family man—not as a heroine, but as an angel in the house." (2) "The first object of the novelist is to get personages in whom we can be interested: the next is to put them in action. But when women are the chief characters, how are you to set them in motion? The life of women cannot well be described as a life of action. When women are thus put forward to lead the action of a plot, they must be urged into a false position. . . . This is what is called sensation. It is not wrong to make a sensation; but if the novelist depends for his sensation upon the action of a woman, the chances are that he will attain his end by unnatural means."

It is no accident that Dallas, like Oliphant, is writing about sensation fiction, that "criminaliziation" of women that earned so many readers for Mrs. Braddon and other writers beginning in the 1860s. Charlotte Brontë did "'protest' against the conventionalities in which the world clothes itself." She damned angels-in-the-house, and produced in the governess Jane Eyre a female protagonist who takes to the road imaginatively as a girl and then literally as a young woman, with her only goal "the real world . . . [and] real knowledge of life amidst its perils." Jane Eyre is plain and outspoken and ambitious, a person of admitted "volcanic vehemence." She sees no essential differences between men and women except in the ways society confines women:

Nobody knows how many rebellions besides political rebellions ferment in the masses of life which people earth. Women are supposed to be very calm generally: but women feel just as men feel; they need exercise for their faculties, and a field for their efforts as much as their brothers do; they suffer from too rigid a restraint, too absolute a stagnation, precisely as men would suffer. . . . It is thoughtless to condemn them, or laugh at them, if they seek to do more or learn more than custom has pronounced necessary for their sex.

Jane Eyre also has no hesitation in describing her feelings, whether of hatred or of love, to the reader and to those in front of her. She cannot "conform to nature," whether the definer of that nature be her Aunt Reed and Reverend Brocklehurst, or her "lovers" Rochester and St. John Rivers. To avoid hell, she tells Brocklehurst, she will "keep in good health, and not die." Of Rochester's desire to dress her as a lady-angel, she tells the reader: "I never can bear being dressed like a doll by Mr. Rochester, or sitting like a second Danae with the golden shower falling daily round me." She rejects Rivers's commands to do her duty of self-sacrifice and become his missionary wife: "If I were to marry you, you would kill me." His reply: "Your words are such as ought not to be used: violent, unfeminine, and untrue."

  In a nineteenth-century context, the words *are* unfeminine and violent because they are spoken by a woman. George Eliot at once admired *Jane Eyre* and wished that its "characters would talk a little less like the heroes and heroines of police reports." Others writers regretted the vogue of plain "heroine governesses" that was inspired by the popularity of Brontë's novel. Some readers, forgetting Byron and George Sand and their influence (including on Charlotte Brontë), saw in Rochester the origin of "women's men" in fiction by women, brutes from "the school of Currer Bell." These critics are not fools. Rochester does speak from a very different world (and bedroom) than Ivanhoe, and speaks to Jane with a familiarity about sex and mistresses astonishing to family readers. He enters the novel by falling off his horse as the heroine watches. Soon the two are discussing their lack of physical attractions. It is not long before his bed is afire, and Jane is throwing water over it to quench the "devouring" flames. The madwoman in the attic, whose laugh accompanied Jane's rebellious protest about the "custom" of confining women to sewing and calmness, soon appears (as if from a Gothic novel) as Rochester's wife, her "giant propensities" and "pygmy intellect" making her insane, "a wife at once intemperate and unchaste," and driving her husband to incarcerate her in England at Thornfield and to seek "renewal" in Europe. That renewal involves him with a European array of mistresses before he meets Jane Eyre. That he asks her to be his woman of the conduct books—purifying and redeeming him through her love—would offer Jane the woman's ideal role, except that his need demands of her both the dependence and the inferior status of a mistress, which she will not give: "*I* care for myself."

To Victorian readers of respectable fiction, Jane Eyre was like no other. Accustomed to seek "moral signification" (Bulwer Lytton) in their narratives, and to find the moral allegory amid a novel's incidents, they confronted in Jane Eyre "the strength of true feeling," or what Mrs. Oliphant called "the natural heart," one who does right but gives God too little credit for her own self-sustaining nature. Jane's *I* is the *I* of Napoleonic individualism, spoken out of moral strength and yet against all socially inscribed conventional *female* morality of the period. ("Conventionality is not morality," the preface to the second edition thundered.) Jane's voice frightened because it speaks against social order as readers knew it; speaks against the very gender roles women were ideally expected to want to perform. Early on, in the red-room to which the young Jane is exiled after her outbreak against the injustice of the Reeds, she sees herself, in the mirror, as "half imp, half fairy." Imp or fairy: these are the roles in which the novel's men imagine women, and condemn or desire them. These are the confinements which Jane refuses. Her "I am not an angel . . . I will be myself" is a common refrain, nowhere given more compelling, and beautiful, illustration than in the passage in chapter 24 where Rochester tells his ward Adele that he "is to take mademoiselle to the moon" and dress her in clouds. Adele's response: "She is far better as she is . . . besides, she would get tired of living with only you in the moon." Rochester's is the language of romance, as St. John Rivers's words are the language of religion. Neither thinks of Jane Eyre as she is, no more than does John Reed or Brocklehurst. They expect her to live in their scripts, to take a subordinate role in their lives. We ought to remember that the book's title, *Jane Eyre: An Autobiography*," is ostensibly written by a married woman ten years after her marriage, yet she does not call her history "Jane Rochester: An Autobiography."

No wonder her protests shocked readers. No angel in the house, or her author, could be innocent, or believe in the sanctity of love, and still speak with a man so easily, if censoriously, about sex and his mistresses, and about her own feelings. No woman should want to control her fate so desperately that she seeks out new "servitudes" in order to experience "realities" conceived in her imagination, realities having no apparent connection to the domestic. No unmarried woman in reality should say no to a minister's request for marriage and service to God and, listening to a voice in the wind, return to a man who may yet be married. "Reader, I married him." What is the moral here?

Though French critic Eugene Forçade (Brontë's favorite critic of her novels) found *Jane Eyre* "a drama in which society plays more or less the cruel and tyrannical role assigned to fate in the tragedies of antiquity," and praised Brontë for her refusal to "call down a fiery judgment" on that society, few English readers could see anything beyond the passions of Jane Eyre, and even fewer could find a moral in them. In her *Shirley* of 1849, Charlotte Brontë took the reviewers' objections to Jane Eyre and readers' expectations of a moral and inscribed them in the text. She produced a hungry-forties novel, in the manner of Mrs. Gaskell and Disraeli: a third-person narrator represents the hopelessness of men without jobs, the mercenary individualism of the middle-class factory owners, the paternalistic concerns that should mark the wealthy (here impersonated by Shirley, the ambiguously named title heroine), and the despair of middle-class women unable to work. Indeed, this last focus frames all other concerns and indicates the force of Forçade's suggestion that Brontë could have called her novel "*Shirley, or the condition of women in the English middle-class.*"

Set in the period of the Napoleonic wars, *Shirley* offers a panoramic picture of a nation and its individuals in the "throes of a sort of moral earthquake." There is no patriotism, little real fellow feeling, a "great gulf" between the classes, and a sense of hopelessness that recalls Thomas Carlyle's analysis in *Chartism* (1839) and *Past and Present* (1842). The ideology of work that Carlyle preached ("The latest Gospel in this world is, know thy work and do it") is repeated in *Shirley*, and given special meaning because it is not only the gospel of the workers, but of Caroline Helstone, the title character's middle-class friend who is also the central female figure in the novel. The meditations of Caroline on work and the discussions between her and Shirley are a gloss on Carlyean ideas, already implicit in *Jane Eyre*, that a person without work is a person in torment. For Caroline, work might not "make a human being happy," but "successful labour has its recompense; a vacant, weary, lonely, hopeless life has none." She finds no virtue "in abnegation of self," in a self-denial that leaves no room for liberating work but only for "undue humility" and "weak concession." In one of her meditations that, along with her conversations with Shirley, articulate the real interest and agenda of the novel, she says: "I believe single women should have more to do—better chances of interesting and profitable occupation than they possess now. And when I speak thus, I have no impression that I displease God by my words, that I am either impious or impatient, irreligious or sacrilegious." Yet the rigidity of the social world—its religion, its class system, its prohibitions against respectable women working, its conventions that demand that a "good woman" be "half doll, half angel"—forces on women a psychological deadening and an entrapment in the self.

This presentation of the imprisoned female self in a society convulsed by social problems that have no solution is finally resolved in a way that belies the very issues *Shirley* has raised. Brontë chose to divide her Jane Eyre figure into the meek Caroline Helstone and the lively Shirley Keeldar, who is wonderful in her spirited defenses of women and in her comments on any issue that catches her attention. But while Caroline and Shirley can speak forthrightly and strongly about the fate of women in a male-governed social order, they are trapped in a social code that demands that women find confirmation of their worth in home and family. Caroline's Bunyanesque question, "What was I created for?" which propelled the plot of *Jane Eyre*, is counterpointed by her "yearning to discover and know her mother" and by her pinings after Robert Moore and "the little parlour of [his] house [which] was her earthly paradise." Shirley's independence is compromised by her desire for a man to reverence. The two heroines marry the brothers Moore, one a factory owner who learns to heed Caroline's pleas that he give more paternal attention to his workers' humanity, the other a schoolmaster who needs to be more masterly in his treatment of Shirley. The book ends in lovers' vows.

Almost. The narrator recognizes the escape the plot provides from the tough social reality depicted in the novel, and recognizes implicitly that, while Jane Eyre defined her domestic role, Shirley and Caroline submit to theirs as if there were no choice. Nor was there in the 1840s, or before. Jane was orphaned, independent: "Who in the world cares for *you?*" She was finally granted a fortune, a real "independence," as a confirmation of her singular moral individuality. In *Shirley*, the female protagonists are inserted into a densely figured historical background. In that environment progress for women must be purely personal—toward marriage. These women, independent as are their ideas, cannot imagine a world outside of loving. The marriage plot simply cannot cohere to the novel's political discussions. While Brontë recognizes the ways this plot confines women to domesticity, she fears the revolutionary nature of the alliance she has constructed in her narrative between middle-class women and lower-class (male) workers who beg for work so that they may respect the social order.

Still, the narrator faces with severe scrutiny the issues that the marriages gloss over. Hers is a voice of 1849 damning any notion that readers will tolerate anything like the real in their fictions. She begins the novel by announcing to the reader that "romance" is not on the menu, but rather "something real, cool, and solid," and concludes by seeing the whole as a "story." She muses often about readers' desires that novels avoid harsh reality (and writes some of the reviewers' negative comments about *Jane Eyre* into the mouths of characters):

Whenever you present the actual, simple truth, it is, somehow, always denounced as a lie: . . . whereas the product of your own imagination, the mere figment, the sheer fiction, is adopted, petted, termed pretty, proper, sweetly natural: the little, spurious wretch gets all the comfits,—the honest, lawful bantling, all the cuffs. Such is the way of the world.

In her closing tableau of vanished fairies, she challenges readers to feel any satisfaction, even if the novel does end in lovers' vows. "The story is told. I think I now see the judicious reader putting on his spectacles to look for the moral. It would be an insult to his sagacity to offer directions. I only say, God speed him in the quest."

At the end she undercuts the romance she has just told by displacing the novel's green world and throwing the reader into the ashy landscape of the present. This narrator's voice makes *Shirley* one of the most illustrative of the social-problem novels of the 1840s because of the problems it encounters in representing political action. Brontë's narrator refuses to traffic in any modern celebrations of progress. That voice reminds the reader that Chartist disturbances *now* constantly disprove the idea that some lasting good has come out of past actions. More importantly, it asserts that the politics of Victorian storytelling and the politics of class conflict are not easily accommodated. Indeed, the narrator places "offstage" the workers' attack on Robert Moore's mill (it is narrated through the heroines' effort to hear what is going on), a scene which Mrs. Gaskell or George Eliot would have rendered directly. Indeed, as Deirdre David noted in *Fictions of Resolution*, Mrs. Gaskell in *North and South* intensifies the meaning of "the threat which an uneducated and undisciplined working class presents to middle-class culture" by placing women at the front of the threatened group. Love stories centering on the feelings of women allow little room for political exploration when women are not recognized as political agents.

In her *Villette* of 1853, the reader's need for the "pretty, proper, sweetly natural" that was noted in *Shirley* becomes one of the defining characteristics of the relation between the narrator and the reader. Lucy Snowe, whose reticences and aversions to self-exposure contrast the stalwart self-presentation of Jane Eyre, never trusts readers' "sunny imaginations." Where Jane Eyre defies readers not to assent to her every action, Lucy Snowe knows her readers will accept nothing painful or unromantic. Again and again she draws some "wild dreamland" calculated to please them, only to destroy it: "Cancel the whole of that, if you please, reader—or rather let it stand, and draw thence a moral—an alliterative, text-hand copy—'Day-dreams are the delusions of the demon.'" The voice's bitterness and distrust rule all, even to the last page, where Lucy interrupts the narrative of the storm pursuing her lover in order to allow the "quiet, kind heart" and "sunny imaginations" of readers to envision a "union and a happy succeeding life" for her and M. Paul. For Lucy Snowe, truth has a terrible beauty that readers will not accept.

In *Villette* Brontë at once rewrites her previous novels and jettisons many of the elements that had defined her work. The protagonist's exile from England to the allegorical Labassecour is necessary if she is to find any liberating work. This exile removes the social world suggested in *Jane Eyre* and represented in *Shirley*. The heroine is somberly alone; even her language and her religion allow her no communion with others. Gone also are the Gothic elements and melodramatic contrivances of *Jane Eyre* (except for some stage business with a nun and the reemergence of the Bretton family in Villette). The only thing that survives is the Puritan autobiographical form Brontë used for *Jane Eyre* (and *The Professor*, written in 1846 but not published until 1857, after Brontë's death), with its depiction of life as a stern pilgrimage and its allegorical treatment of experience. In *Villette* that form is chastened in ways closer to Bunyan than to *Jane Eyre*. Yet even Bunyan allows his Christian an origin, a family on which to turn his back and choose God's way, and a Faithful and Interpreter to help him find that way. Brontë's Lucy Snowe admits no origin and no guides; she begins her "life" in a fictional convention: a godmother's house that recalls "the sojourn of Christian and Hopeful beside a certain pleasant stream." *Villette*, as Barbara Hardy has noted, "is as much a Providence novel as *Jane Eyre*, but the Providential pattern is shown, and seen by the heroine, to lead towards loss." Forçade's comment is apt: "Currer Bell has a mixture of restrained passion and irony, a kind of virile power; the struggles she delights in are those in which the individual, alone and thrown entirely on his own resources, has only his own inner strength to rely upon . . . she preaches with Titanic pride the moral power of the human soul; her books contain vigour and originality, never tears; she interests, but she does not soften us; she is protestant to the last fibre of her being."

From the beginning, Brontë presents in Lucy Snowe a protagonist who calls herself a "mere looker on at life," "a personage in disguise" who does not "look the character" of a major player in a narrative and, as a result, does not expect her life to provide material for romantic stories. Indeed the interests that drive her—to secure work in order to live and not be morbidly self-enclosed—have no place in women-centered romance, even though the imagination may want to indulge "the life of thought" and escape "that of reality." From the time she looks as a young girl on the idealized Paulina Home and sees that the child must "necessarily live, move, and have her being in another," whether father or lover, Lucy knows that such a life cannot be hers. She is too alienated and unconnected, and too ambitious to be herself—whatever that is. And if, at times, she envies women's ability to be angels in the houses of men (and wants to "live" in a romance with Graham Bretton), she knows that such a life will not satisfy. She knows too that marriage and novels that close in lovers' vows are allied in a way that leaves no room for representing a woman who cares for herself as an independent human being. Thus she must be a spectator, a reader of others' romances, whether of Ginevra Fanshawe's flirtatious fooleries or Paulina Home's progress toward domestic bliss in marriage to Bretton: "It was so, for God saw that it was good."

Lucy Snowe must also be a debater with men about her "role." The word appears repeatedly; indeed, few novels since *Mansfield Park* and

Vanity Fair have used the language of the theater and of art so tellingly to describe a woman's behavior in a patriarchal world. With Graham
Bretton, the doctor who is the novel's romantic hero, Lucy realizes that
"He wanted always to give me a role not mine," "to expect of me the
part of officious soubrette in a love drama." She adds: "Nature and I
opposed him." Nature and she also oppose the directions, given repeatedly, of M. Paul Emmanuel, the anti-hero (though not quite in the
Rochester mold) whom Brontë's contemporaries found so fascinating.
This little man, hardly heroic in appearance or action, sees in Lucy from
their first meetings a character of passion and ambition who "must be
kept down." He demands that she perform in his play, and she discovers
"a keen relish for dramatic expression" to be part of her nature, a part
she determines to repress. He demands that she look not at a painting
of Cleopatra, "une personne dont je ne voudrais ni pour femme, ni pour
fille, ni pour soeur," but at "La vie d'une femme," a series of four paintings depicting women from girlhood to widowhood that Lucy labels
"bloodless, brainless nonentities." Lucy finds him "like Napoleon
Bonaparte" in his desire to rule: "He would have exiled fifty Madame
de Staels, if they had annoyed, offended, out-rivaled, or opposed him."
He warns Lucy about her "contraband appetite for unfeminine knowledge," and tells her that

a "woman of intellect" . . . was a thing for which there was neither place nor
use in creation, wanted neither as wife nor worker. . . . He believed in his soul
that lovely, placid, and passive feminine mediocrity was the only pillow on
which manly thought and sense could find rest for its aching temples.

Yet this man becomes her "Greatheart" because he finally accepts her
need to define herself through work and through an independence that
is marked by her differences from all women. She comes to see him as
a man of "inward sight" whose mind is her "library," "collyrium to the
spirit's eyes." In him she finds the possibility of love that does not
demand a woman's role-playing nor require a woman's silencing. The
moment of her acceptance occurs when she can use the word "home."

I was full of faults; he took them and me all home. For the moment of utmost
mutiny, he reserved the one deep spell of peace. These words caressed my
ear:—
    "Lucy, take my love. One day share my life. Be my dearest, first on earth."
    We walked back to the Rue Fossette by moonlight—such moonlight as fell
on Eden—shining through the shades of the Garden. . . . Once in their lives

some men and women go back to these first fresh days of our great Sire and Mother . . .

Yet this acceptance, like most of Lucy's narrative, is defined not in personal terms but in allusions, in archetypal or conventional scenes (like her origin chapter) that displace Lucy Snowe from her history and substitute the language of familiar storytelling.

That language's limitations and dangers are exposed, and Lucy's terrible independence from them is articulated, in the storm scene that concludes the novel. Her repetition of Christ's words to the waters, "Peace be still," calms no storm and brings no Paul back, but produces, simply, a halt in the narrative. Language has no power except to record its powerlessness. Lucy Snowe's "book of life" ends not in marriage but with an elderly woman telling the story of how, with a man's help, she became a schoolmaster. *Villette* is the triumph of Charlotte Brontë's life of writing, her determined break with the marriage plot of English fiction.

Women Reading and Rewriting Charlotte Brontë

At one point in *Shirley*, as the two women discuss Milton's Eve, Shirley declares, "We are alone: we may speak what we think." The great mark of Charlotte Brontë's novels, as all her contemporaries noted, was this "speaking what we think," as if only narrator and reader were in conversation and all conventionalities were for the moment forgotten, or at least forced aside (the frequent direct addresses to readers in her pages emphasizes Brontë's efforts to educate her "romantic readers"). Such forceful speaking was the characteristic that removed her work from what one reviewer called "the generic term 'novel'" because, as another proclaimed, "there is nothing but truth and nature about it . . . no high life glorified, caricatured, or libelled; nor low life elevated to an enviable state of bliss; neither have we vice made charming." Such a comment recalls the silver-fork and Newgate novels of the earlier nineteenth century, and perhaps alludes to Dickens's handling of poor orphans. Brontë's orphans are as homeless, physically and metaphysically, as Dickens's children, but they are tougher, their lives incomparably more difficult psychologically and their feelings expressed in language and actions that would be impossible for a Dickens or Scott or Thackeray woman (or man).

Tellingly, Brontë's influence on her contemporaries, especially on the sensation novelists like Mrs. Braddon and on George Eliot, derives from this same boldness of representation, particularly in the insistence that women are ambitious and desire some independence. Of course, the sensation novel, which made vice charming by making its perpetrator a woman ("the fair-haired demon of modern fiction" was Oliphant's label), replaced moral stringency and individuality with female-generated crime and made homes either the scene of the crimes or the polluted territory of the woman's plotting. With their un-Brontësque golden curls and simpering voices, the sensational women like Lady Audley want (economic) independence and know how much the appearance of womanly virtue is worth financially. Yet the sensation novelists criminalize the very desire for independence that Brontë celebrates. With sensation novels, we are not far from the stereotypes of romance novels, which, in their blatant vulgarizing of feeling, recall as they ignore the severe intensities of feeling in the Brontës. (Mrs. Braddon, comparing Brontë and George Eliot, called Brontë the "only genius the weaker sex can point to in literature.")

George Eliot's response to Charlotte Brontë was more complicated. She admired the self-sacrifice represented in *Jane Eyre* but not the language and the plot. She found *Villette* "almost preternatural in its power." Her women face many of the same issues as Jane Eyre and Brontë's other women: Maggie Tulliver in the Red Deeps recalls Jane in the red-room; Dorothea Brooke's long night of suffering in *Middlemarch* recalls Lucy Snowe's isolation in the long vacation. But these women experience their alienation in a detailed and coercive social world that never submits to the will of the heroine. Indeed, the "web" (of heredity and environment) that is so stabilizing a force in George Eliot's novels makes the operation of such a will impossible. Like Brontë, George Eliot also confronted problems in using the marriage plot, and did not solve them. The drowning of Maggie Tulliver in *The Mill on the Floss* has impressed few readers as a solution to the issues of a woman wanting a world of independent action outside of (or within) loving, nor has Dorothea Brooke's exile to London as the wife of a rising politician. Finally, the sense that a Brontë protagonist lives to say "I feel, therefore I am" (as Patricia Spacks suggested about Emily Brontë's Catherine Earnshaw) marks a very different fictional world from those inhabited by Maggie Tulliver and Dorothea Brooke. George Eliot's subscription to certain essential differences inscribed by gender do not allow her the determined boldness of Brontë's representations. Maggie Tulliver's desire to "learn for herself what wise men knew" grows out of her social period and class, and also out of George Eliot's conviction that a woman, because she has "a class of sensations and emotions—the maternal ones—which must remain unknown to man," introduces "a distinctively feminine condition into the wondrous chemistry of the affections and sentiments, which inevitably gives rise to distinctive forms and combinations" in art and literature.

The progress of *Jane Eyre* through the texts of novelists provides compelling witness to Brontë's power over her readers. From Mrs. Gaskell, Mrs. Braddon, and Mrs. Humphry Ward to Jean Rhys, Doris Lessing, and Jamaica Kincaid, from filmmakers to contemporary romance writers, Brontë's women and their passionate feelings are discussed, critiqued, plagiarized, rewritten. Even a male character in Mary Ward's *History of David Grieve* (1890) falls into "mental tumult" while "measuring himself with the world of *Shirley*." Jean Rhys's *Wide Sargasso Sea* (1966) offers a retelling of the madwoman's story from her own perspective and from Rochester's. Even though Mrs. Gaskell, in her biography, set out to portray a Charlotte Brontë who was the angel in the house, who never put writing before duty and service to others, the "Jane Eyre" side of the author triumphed. E. S. Dallas, reviewing Gaskell's biography, noted that Brontë's "power of analysis . . . was one of the principal causes that contributed to the popularity of *Jane Eyre*": "It was a new sensation to see that class of feelings which regulates the relation of the sexes mercilessly and minutely laid bare upon the woman's side, and by the hand of a woman." Rejecting the censures of Harriet Martineau and later of Virginia Woolf about the limitations of Charlotte Brontë's heroines (they live only for love, their author never noticing that women have other "heartfelt interests"), writers in the nineteenth and twentieth centuries have agreed with Dallas and seen in Brontë and her central protagonists the "blows of a passionate realism" (Mary Ward) remarkable because the angle of vision is so assertively a woman's and the voice is one so determined to speak to other women, to represent them as they feel. The power of these representations Adrienne Rich aptly summarized in 1973: "Other novels often ranked greater. . . . But *Jane Eyre* has for us now special force and survival value." The reason: *Jane Eyre* is a "tale" whose "world . . . is above all a 'vale of soul making,'" and when a novelist finds herself writing a tale, it is likely to be because she is moved by that vibration of experience which underlies the social and political, though it constantly feeds both of these."

The meanings of this experience to women, whether as experience itself or as the sign of a woman writer doing revolutionary work, mark Brontë's special place in the lives of twentieth-century readers and critics. Indeed, the reading of *Jane Eyre* by critics signals a pilgrim's progress of feminism, though the nature of that progress has increasingly been questioned and even doubted. Elaine Showalter's *A Literature of Their Own: British Women Writers from Brontë to Lessing* (1977) and Sandra Gilbert and Susan Gubar's *Madwoman in the Attic* (1979) explore the crucial place of Brontë in the work of women writers, and it is a place that Jane Austen and George Eliot cannot occupy. They may speak what they think, but that thinking is always rigorously tethered to the dense social world in which their women must live, never liberated by the "vale of soul making."

If those vibrations of experience that Rich celebrates were the focus of Brontë's contemporaries and the reasons her work became a defining point for later women writers, the social and political environment that fed these experiences has increasingly commanded the attention of twentieth-century critics. Discussions of the political implications of Brontë's novels have rendered problematic, and sometimes compromised, the central place *Jane Eyre* has occupied in women's studies. From being a central liberating text, the novel has come to be seen by some as supporting the very social and gender organizations against which its protests raged, and which shocked or exhilarated earlier readers. Readers have come more and more to see that Brontë, even as she depicts the problems of women's lives in environments that allow them no independence, is through her langauge and the forms of her fictions inextricably connected to, and often complicit with, the very modes of cultural production that operate in any male-dominated society.

I started with Sarah Ellis and E. S. Dallas to indicate the challenges confronting Brontë, and to articulate, through their voices, the doctrines of "separate spheres" that had such supervisory power over women as wives and writers in Victorian England. (Mrs. Gaskell's biography makes clear how sustained and controlling this power was.) We are now coming to see the novel as a central participant in cultural dialogues of the period of its writing, taking a role—albeit in a domestic setting—equal to that taken by a parliament or a monarch. As Mary Poovey has noted, women in Brontë's period were considered "critical to social stability":

If only women would remain in the home, men of all classes argued, work would be available to men who needed it and both the family wage and morality would be restored. The assumptions implicit in this argument are . . . that morality is bred and nurtured in the home as an effect of maternal instinct, and that if lower-class women were to emulate middle-class wives in their deference, thrift, and discipline, the homes of rich and poor alike would become what they ought to be—havens from the debilitating competition of the market. . . . [Women were] moral and not economic agents, antidotes to the evils of competition, not competitors themselves.

This ideology is based on the image of the home as a sanctified and purifying sphere presided over by a maternal, nurturing woman who is untouched by the larger social and economic world. Women, after all, said Sarah Ellis, have no existence "distinct from that of their affections"; they lack a man's world of ambition or competition with other men.

But Charlotte Brontë, in giving her women the ambition and the need to leave the home for work and in presenting them as unmarried governesses, challenged this very image of women as nurturers in the home. The governess was a middle-class, "redundant" woman, forced to work, like a man, in order to earn her living; yet she was not lower class like other servants in the house of her employment. Thus, as Poovey notes, she at once "epitomized the domestic ideal . . . and threatened to destroy it." Her work was that of a middle-class mother; her worker's position was that of a wage earner. For many readers she came to represent the dangers of women working, the "sexual susceptibility" and "social incongruity" of a figure crossing the boundaries of work and class and gender. (Chapter 17 of *Jane Eyre*, in which Blanche Ingram and other guests at Thornfield discuss governesses, perfectly illustrates this thesis, as do Victorian critics of the novel who deplored the influence such a woman might have in a home.)

What makes Jane Eyre so compelling as a cultural barometer of the 1840s, as Cora Kaplan has noted, are the ways her progress illuminates the instabilities of class and gender identities. Her "Who am I?" and her endless questions challenge the role definitions accepted by Victorian society, question the confinement of the angel in the house, and even threaten the foundation of England. Mrs. Ellis voiced, in *The Women of England* (1839), a widely held belief: "How intimate is the connection which exists between the *women* of England, and the *moral* character maintained by their country in the scale of nations." The people who fear Jane Eyre, whether Mrs. Reed, Brocklehurst, Rochester, St. John Rivers, or Brontë's Victorian critics, are people who live, or want to live, in the context of unquestioned boundaries of class and gender. There is little difference, finally, among Mrs. Reed's complaint that Jane is "unnatural," Rochester's need to call her "unearthly," and St. John's label "unfeminine." Each adjective seeks to place her, to confine her to roles that she rejects. Each seeks to make her an angel, docile and compliant to established authorities.

Jane's individualism does not allow these confinements. She will choose for herself because she cares for herself, physically and metaphysically. It is this individualism as it is represented in the novel that now raises the most profound, and often troubling, social and political questions. The major Victorian novels are plotted as providential progresses; they depict an individual's progress toward an identity if one is male, or toward marriage as a confirmation of feminine identity and domestic stability if one is female. (*Vanity Fair* and *The Woman in White*, each with its two focal female figures, parody this tradition, and indicate how powerful it is.) Jane's insistence that "women feel just as men feel" marks her individualism as "unfeminine," even masculine. (It is worth noting here that many Victorian readers stressed Brontë's "masculine" or "virile" strength as a writer.) Jane's connection of her discontent to the "silent revolt" of millions like her resonateed in 1848 with awful implications for gender boundaries and for social ones. The novel's first chapter, which Cora Kaplan calls Jane's "primal scene," does more than present the child in revolt. In forcing Jane to see that her orphanage is also a function of social and gender differences, it represents the power politics of a woman's life. We respond at once to Jane's challenging of John Reed when he damns her as a beggar. His desire to deny her *his* books, *his* window, and *his* mirror indicates how males as represented in Brontë are born into a world where not to control woman's imaginations and self-constructions— their places in the hierarchies of class and gender—is to be impotent, unnatural.

Yet as Jane notes when asked if she might live with "low, poor relations," she is "not heroic enough to purchase liberty at the price of caste." It matters, essentially, to be middle class. Though this statement may be that of the young girl, the mature narrator reports with embarrassment the same beliefs when St. John Rivers secures her, then nineteen, a position as a teacher:

I must not forget that these coarsely-clad little peasants are of flesh and blood as good as the scions of gentlest genealogy. . . . I felt—yes, idiot that I am—I felt degraded. I doubted I had taken a step which sank instead of raising me in the scale of social experience. I was weakly dismayed by the ignorance, the poverty, the coarseness of all I heard and saw round me. . . . I know [these feelings] to be wrong—that is a great step gained.

The change to the present tense here tells something about the class politics that place this *novel* in the social discourses of the 1840s and about how much this novel participates in those politics. Jane is not allied in her own mind, except in an abstract sense, with Carlyle's workless laborers. When she proclaims to Rochester that they are equal, she means it; and her later inheritance adds material confirmation to this asserted equality. When she strives to see her equality with poor female children, she cannot forget the class differences (which St. John Rivers emphasized when he offered her the position); and the inheritance allows her to escape contact with such poverty. Like Gaskell and George Eliot, Brontë cannot imagine a secure world outside of middle-class borders. Woman in Brontë remains "the protectress of middle-class ideals" (in Deirdre David's words about Mrs. Gaskell).

Finally, Jane's individualism, which *she* defines as her need for home and hearthfires and the love they promise, mandates her place in the middle-class family. (Jane's use of the hearthfire as a symbol of love and security is one of the novel's recurring metaphors). Class and economic isolation and a woman's desire for wider experience, insisted upon at the novel's beginning, disappear, replaced by courtship and romantic love and a domestic hearth. The marriages at the novel's end—Jane's and those of the Rivers sisters—bespeak the secured spaces for independent, intelligent women, away from the workaday world, that this novel celebrates. Yet what purchases this security, some readers have argued, is a legacy from an uncle in Madeira and the monies Rochester has earned in the West Indies—both places of colonialism, slavery, and economic imperialism. For Gayatri Spivak, Kaplan, and other readers, Jane's individualism and her marriage constitute an apologia for British imperialism, a politics that, through the feminization and domestication of masculine ambition and individualism, tries to cleanse colonialism of its complicity in racism and slavery. The sources of the comfort in the novel and the foundations of the private life are found in colonialism.

The madwoman, Bertha Mason, has become an especially powerful site of this argument. Where earlier feminist readers saw the madwoman as Jane's "dark double," "the ferocious secret self Jane has been trying to repress ever since her days at Gateshead" (Gilbert and Gubar) and the warning of what she might become if she loses her self-integrity and control, readers now see Bertha as a sign of the economic agenda of the British middle-class world that allows Jane to make her progress and her choices. Bertha Mason is a white Jamaican Creole whose existence, mad or not, has become a function of patriarchal colonizers; her humanity is obliterated by the bourgeois will to power and control—control of women and of society. For Spivak, "the active ideology of imperialism" propels Jane Eyre toward that "community of families" of which she and Rochester form the center at the novel's end. This community must exile Bertha in order to preserve its distinct Englishness and the hierarchical order that gives the nation meaning (and sends St. John Rivers to reproduce its ideas in India).

For other readers Bertha's larger meaning resides in comments from Rochester about her "giant propensities" and from Jane about the relation of law to madness: "I will hold to principles received by me when I was sane, and not mad—as I am now." Bertha becomes the image of desire ungoverned, of sexuality outside the domestic sphere and the law, terrorizing the order of the family and thus the nation. "Bertha must be killed off, narratively speaking," Kaplan has written, "so that a moral, Protestant femininity, licensed sexuality and a qualified, socialized feminism may survive." As Poovey notes, Rochester, in recounting his history to Jane after the aborted wedding, insists on

an absolute distinction between some kinds of women, who cannot be legitimate wives, and Jane, who can. This distinction is reinforced by both racism and nationalist prejudice: that Bertha is "West Indian" explains her madness, just as Celine's French birth "accounts for" her moral laxity. But Jane . . . sees . . . the likeness that Rochester denies: *any* woman who is not a wife is automatically like a governess in being dependent, like a fallen woman in being "kept."

Jane leaves Rochester to remain sane. She returns when she is independent, able to express her desires—for order, love, and home. Her comments while at Morton signal her control of desire:

Meantime, let me ask myself one question: Which is better?—To have surrendered to temptation; listened to passion; . . . to have been now living in

France, Mr. Rochester's mistress. . . . Whether it is better . . . to be a slave in a fool's paradise in Marseilles . . . or to be a village school mistress, free and honest, in a breezy mountain nook in the healthy heart of England?

The language of desire has subsumed the historical material that produced Charlotte Brontë and *Jane Eyre*. For Nancy Armstrong, who regards fiction "both as the document and as the agency of cultural history," the Brontës "had more to do with formulating universal forms of subjectivity than any other novelists . . . because they perfected tropes to distinguish fiction from historically bound writing. These tropes translated all kinds of political information into psychological terms." The monstrous woman, signifying in the 1840s the threat to gender distinctions that so exercised Victorians, becomes in Brontë's handling detached from "place, time, and material cause." The West Indies, a Jamaican Creole: both become figures of desire and its suppression. For Armstrong, the significance of both Charlotte and Emily Brontë as novelists of the 1840s is located in the processes by which "their language of the self [becomes] the basis for meaning." The political is the personal figured domestically. In the words of Adrienne Rich: "A thinking woman sleeps with monsters."

Even as these readings return Brontë's novels to the world that produced them, they also remind us of how crucial, even coercive, were the traditions of fiction Brontë inherited. Earlier I noted her use of the providential plot, with its figures of personification and allegory. Bunyan and an English tradition of moral writing stand behind her novels. What should be stressed is that this tradition mandated the progress toward order—achieved in heaven for Bunyan and in marriage and domestic harmony for those citizens of Victorian novels. Forçade noted in his review of *Shirley* that "English novels are set before marriage, French novels after. . . . We know that in England . . . the conventions endow young girls with an independence of character, of will and behaviour, which tends rather to be curtailed when they marry." Charlotte Brontë in her "plain Jane's progress" (Gilbert and Gubar) does not challenge this pattern, though she uses it with some irony. She insists that women who feel as men do must thus redefine and expand women's spheres of action even as they continue to patrol moral territories with a vigor equal to that traditionally exercised by males in the political world. But the territory remains moral and domestic (and, at Ferndean, very isolated); it does not move into the larger world that a young Jane had imagined living in.

The novel itself, as a gendered form, thus demands Rochester's weakening at the end. He must himself make a moral progress so as to be worthy of Jane, so as to know indeed what it means to be dependent—like a woman. But more importantly, he must submit to Jane's moral superiority (which, the novel insists, is her power), and that submission is figured in his crippling and blindness, in his loss of power. *Jane Eyre* emphasizes the centrality—and the power—of women as moral agents in the 1840s. Elizabeth Rigby in her review grudgingly noted that "Jane does right, and exerts great moral strength, but it is the strength of a mere heathen mind which is a law unto itself." Exactly. The novel's voice is that of a powerful woman observing, celebrating, and contesting *with independent strength of will* the moral laws and cultural ideologies that made women commanding angels in the house. The closing marriage is inevitable because it represents both Jane's reward and the safe establishment of female governance in the home; its satisfies Jane's need for independence and a culture's need to see women as redeemers. The man will be cleansed, renewed by a feminine spirit. The woman, powerfully independent (in her own perspective), will freely choose to be the renewing agent.

Shirley critiques the ease of this ending, the unstoppable individualism that gathers everything unto itself. The essential social conservatism of the novel's politics, centered on "the structure of paternalism as a model for class relations," should not blind us, as Rosemarie Bodenheimer argues, to Brontë's exposure of the fissures and contradictions within this politics. For Brontë, who recognizes how interconnected are "concepts of class and gender," "a dominant social order necessarily creates and conceals an underside of rebellion and a responding violence of suppression." Brontë's "social idea" produces her "social critique." The marriage plot that absorbs the heroines, who join the workers in voicing the damning criticism, becomes at once escape and admission: a convenience for Brontë, a way to provide closure without resolving the issues raised, and a calculated refusal to articulate any idea of social progress. The marriage plot, and the social order, may silence women's questions. They cannot obliterate the need for answer. There is no moral here.

Villette devotes the first of its three volumes to a woman's need to find work, the second to her desire to participate in conventional romance, and the last to her discovery of "home" in an exceptional romance. Yet the final page, after the courtship and anticipated marriage have promised the kind of closure *Jane Eyre* provided, reminds readers that such romance is demonic delusion. Lucy Snowe can work as a schoolmaster. Period. Readers' disappointment that there is no marriage, no fulfillment of desire, suggests how wed we are to this plot—and how much Brontë accomplished in saying no to it. *Villette* is so bleak, and so moving, because this "no" argues that "escape from a world of patriarchal domination" requires "severance of all social connection" (the words are Bodenheimer's about *Shirley*, but they suggest something of the reason why Brontë placed Lucy Snowe in a foreign country). Lucy's "book of life" is indeed her, and Charlotte Brontë's, "heretic narrative," a narrative where a woman does more than patrol the moral territories of home and nation.

Wuthering Heights and Victorian Storytelling

Wuthering Heights "is a fiend of a book, an incredible monster. . . . The action is laid in Hell,—only it seems places and people have English names there." Dante Gabriel Rossetti's comments of 1854 offer a succinct summary of the critical history of Emily Brontë's novels. For readers from Charlotte Brontë to the present, there is no certain way to read this novel, no certain meaning to any of its characters, no certain social implications except ones so obvious as to be meaningless. Its author, said Victorian critics, is "a Salvator Rosa with his pen," her characters are "savages ruder than those who lived before the days of Homer," her language is horribly "coarse," and the effect of reading her work is "inexpressibly painful." Charlotte Brontë agreed and disagreed. In a preface she wrote to an 1850 edition of the novel, she praised the descriptions of the natural world (not offered as background or "spectacle," but "as what [the author] lived in, and by"), worked to find among characters "spots where clouded daylight and the eclipsed sun still attest their existence," labeled Heathcliff "unredeemed," and—most importantly—said that Emily Brontë imitates no action: "He wrought from a rude chisel, and from no model but the vision of his meditations."

Charlotte Brontë's sense that Emily Brontë represented what she lived "in, and by," places her work in a metaphysical landscape that few Victorian novels, striving for moral signification and a realism of social and psychological representation, would seek. *Wuthering Heights* shows characters undergoing a "moral teething" amid acts of physical and verbal violence that resemble Shakespeare or Elizabethan revenge drama more than novels of the 1840s, yet it presents its characters and its story through the eyes of two narrators so unsympathetic to the goings-on that those actions seem even more "real," whatever that means. One narrator, the aptly named Lockwood, comes from the city to tour the country and look for prospects of nature; he leaves the area with a benediction that is one of the most splendid paragraphs ever to close a novel. Standing by three gravestones, he notes:

I lingered round them, under that benign sky; watched the moths fluttering among the heath and hare-bells; listened to the soft wind breathing through the grass; and wondered how any one could ever imagine unquiet slumbers for the sleepers in that quiet earth.

The passage shows what a travel writer Lockwood is. It also tells something about his tour of the emotional landscapes in the wild story he has heard. In his perfectly balanced clauses and harmonically sounded vowels, no wayward human energies disrupt the storyteller's power or the listener's satisfaction. Who would think that he had heard a story (in one reviewer's phrase) "through which devils dance and wolves howl"?

The other narrator belongs to Wuthering Heights by proximity of birth, but belongs even more to the world of Thrushcross Grange by sympathies of class and culture and by modes of storytelling. Nelly Dean is the central narrator, and a wonderful one because she is so observant, and so sure of what she thinks should happen to people. Yet in her desire for household order (she is, after all, a housekeeper), for social order, and for religious tranquillity she expresses Emily Brontë's "genius" (a word also used by Victorian reviewers) in figuring through action and character the issues of nineteenth-century life in ways neither Charlotte Brontë nor any of their contemporaries attempted or thought desirable. Nelly Dean makes possible our understanding of *Wuthering Heights* as a Victorian novel because in her narration we see the sources and formal moves of Victorian storytelling. Leo Bersani has said that Emily Brontë, in telling the love stories of two generations united by family ties and by the two women named Catherine, presents in the second story "a conventionalized replay" of the first. Until the death of the first Catherine, "the voices of Lockwood and of Nelly Dean have had to obey rhythms and tones with which they are deeply out of sympathy; indeed, they seem to be in the wrong novel, they are ludicrous vehicles for the story they tell. But gradually the story begins to obey them. . . . It's as if Emily Brontë were telling the same story twice, and eliminating its originality the second time."

Emily Brontë does tell the same story twice, and when its strangeness, its originality, is exiled from the novel, Nelly can go to live at Thrushcross Grange and Lockwood can write his balanced periods. He arrives at a "misanthropist's heaven," and misreads the nature of everyone he encounters. Yet he has a dream whose violence is so seemingly unmotivated as to alert the reader to the kind of metaphysical universe Brontë has created. Lockwood's dream, Catherine Earnshaw's desire as a child that her father bring her a whip as a gift from the city, Heathcliff's description of the chandelier at Thrushcross Grange ("a shower of glass-drops hanging in silver chains from the centre" of the room): none of this is expected, all is believed. Brontë always chooses the unexpected to make her representations. Nelly, the voice of the Grange (with all the reading of its library to provide sources for her storytelling), first hears about that world from Heathcliff, who is an urban orphan with neither Christian name nor known origin. We as readers first experience Catherine Earnshaw through her diary; she makes her entrance into the novel in her own words, before she enters in Lockwood's dream and then in Nelly's chronological narrative of the "cuckoo's" history. That diary—"Catherine Earnshaw, her book"—is produced in the margins of a Testament, but it shows no biblical or religious consciousness: "An awful Sunday . . . H. and I are going to rebel." Yet, as Margaret Homans has noted, this writing is produced not simply in rebellion against the Heights and its restrictions, some of which are biblically enforced. Rebellion is also against writing, and against the biblical tropes, household securities, sentimentalized nature, and domesticated culture that it constructs. Catherine wants the moors, wants escape from the inside world of the Heights and, later, from the Grange, wants a freedom beyond any of the conventions that collectively denominate the realistic territories of nineteenth-century fiction—and of domestic life.

Her dream of going to heaven emphasizes this need to exist outside of social and cultural conventions and the narratives that give them power. For her, some dreams "have stayed with me ever after, and changed my ideas . . . altered the colour of my mind." Thus, in the heaven of her dream: "I broke my heart with weeping to come back to earth;

and the angels were so angry that they flung me out, into the middle of the heath on the top of Wuthering Heights; where I woke sobbing for joy. That will do to explain my secret." Yet, having had this dream, and declared "I *am* Heathcliff," Catherine marries Edgar Linton and becomes "the lady of Thrushcross Grange, and the wife of a stranger: an exile, and outcast from what had been my world." No wonder she says, in a phrase indicating her self-consciousness and her elusiveness, "I cannot express it. . . ."

Expressing "it" has been, always, the problem readers have with *Wuthering Heights*. Nothing permits an easy or familiar response. In Heathcliff and Catherine, Brontë offers lovers who, in death scenes, curse and damn each other. In Edgar Linton, she presents a husband who locks himself among his books to escape his wife's insane need for Heathcliff—yet he goes to the Heights to bring her the golden crocuses he thinks she needs for life, as it were—and who refuses to have himself buried in Linton family vaults, choosing instead to be buried near Catherine, on *her* moors. In Heathcliff, Brontë presents a figure who describes the wonders and foolishness of a materially refined world only to become a conventional villain who conquers that world and then finds it useless because it lacks Catherine. In him she also presents a lover whose feelings, like Catherine's, lie outside the tropes of language: "The entire world is a collection of memoranda that she did exist, and that I have lost her!" Then Brontë offers a second Catherine and an Earnshaw heir who, through moderation of feelings and the powers of civilizing education, inherit the world—that is, inherit the Grange and the Heights. And they have language in abundance to describe their feelings. The point where the second Catherine contrasts her "most perfect idea of heaven's happiness" with Linton Heathcliff's tells us much about the ways of nineteenth-century fiction: "He wanted all to lie in an ecstasy of peace; I wanted all to sparkle, and dance in glorious jubilee." The power of language to create and control, and to propose as models, worlds of domestic order and serenity resides with those who inherit this earth, and in Nelly and Lockwood who tell their story.

But of course, all their language does not explain "it," does not tell us finally why *Wuthering Heights* has continued to command readers' attention and to attract some of the most compelling criticism written about any Victorian novel. From the moment when Elizabeth Rigby called Catherine and Heathcliff "the Jane and Rochester animals in their native state," and Charlotte Brontë wrote her illuminating if uneasy apologia for her sister's "strange production," readers have provided keys to interpretation that finally suggest more about their own critical and cultural alliances than any certainty about *Wuthering Heights*. Q. D. Leavis saw in the novel "a method of discussing what being a woman means, and a tragedy of being caught between socially incompatible cultures." This reading required a Catherine "hardening into a fatal immaturity" and a Heathcliff reduced to a story device "wheeled out" in order to articulate certain thematic emphases. It required a celebration of the second Catherine because of the moral education she acquires (and her mother refused), and it required affirmation of Nelly Dean's essential views of the story (even as it noted her limitations).

For other readers the trials of the first Catherine focus "what being a woman means" by exposing the deadening confinements of patriarchal culture (we should remember that Catherine dies in childbirth). Joseph Boone, discussing "love and the form of fiction," sees in Brontë's handling of the marriage plot an insistence on "the harrowing effects of wedlock on female identity." "In contrast to the traditional female bildungsroman, in which the heroine's acquisition of mature identity is confirmed by marriage, the trajectories of courtship and wedlock forming the narrative of the two Catherines become the means of raising profoundly disturbing questions about the social institution of marriage." Other readers treat Catherine as profoundly narcissistic, solipsistic, and destructive in her selfish determination to satisfy her desire for Heathcliff and her social need for Linton, and as profoundly amoral in her destruction of her marriage. Her "I *am* Heathcliff" serves at once as the grand statement of a passion not to be articulated through metaphor, and as the sign of an indifference to "human domesticity" profoundly frightening in its implications. Leo Bersani has noted that the identification of Catherine and Heathcliff with the moors "dramatizes the potential eeriness, the dehumanization, of a closeness to the land or to nature, a closeness usually spoken about in more sentimental terms as a richly humanizing influence." The result is "a kind of restless immortality": "Death is the most appropriate metaphor for that radical transference of the self to another which Emily Brontë dramatizes in Heathcliff and Catherine."

Heathcliff has for contemporary critics been the site of the novel's most searching investigations into issues of class and sexuality, and into the meaning of form in fiction. For Terry Eagleton, Heathcliff is "both metaphysical hero, spiritually marooned from all material concern in his obsessional love for Catherine, and a skillful exploiter who cannily expropriates the wealth of others." Armstrong notes that "Heathcliff can retain his role as the hero of the tale so long as he remains virtually powerless." He is the hero only in connection to his feeling for Catherine, only in the power of their need for each other. He becomes the conventional melodramatic villain when he secures power and begins to expropriate the Earnshaw property. For Armstrong, this change in Heathcliff marks the point where capitalism replaces "a brutal feudalism as the chief source of villainy," and where we experience the social implications of the move from the Heights to the Grange. The change also signals a reversal of Brontë's narrative procedures. "Out of the pieces of earlier fiction comes a new kind of narrative art where value no longer resides in the claims of the individual but rather in the reconstitution of the family."

Thus the narrative begins, as Bersani said, to obey Nelly Dean and Lockwood and their desires for domestic order. The clichéd golden-haired heroine, the second Catherine, brings language and book learning to the brutalized orphan Hareton Earnshaw. Their reward for recognizing and restoring domestic order: property, marriage, and a promised happy-ever-after. And Nelly Dean—to some readers the novel's villain, to others the complicit agent of patriarchy, to still others an example of the insidious work of class ideology—presides over the eradication of the first Catherine and the nuptial anticipations of the second. More importantly, the woman servant who loves the spatial and temporal world of Thrushcross Grange tells the story of the woman who longed to escape it ("What were the use of my creation if I were entirely contained here?") and who said, "I have only to do with the present." Nelly, who early on tried to remove Heathcliff from the Heights as an alien "it," sees in the deaths of Catherine and Heathcliff and in the marriage of the second Catherine providential signs of the soundness of her interpretation ("I believe the dead are at peace") and of her social alignment. Narrative, the providential plot, and middle-class domestic order are indeed inextricably connected. Nelly's belief in religion focuses on its serenity and on its promised justice for the "good." Her belief in Thrushcross Grange focuses on the ways it represents an ideal society that rewards those who are good and who serve it with a peaceful domestic life. There is indeed no "happier woman than myself in England" when Catherine Linton and Hareton Earnshaw marry. A sad tale is not best for Nelly's winter; a domestic love story is.

Yet Brontë does not leave the reader at ease with this Macaulay of

Thrushcross Grange. After all, it is she who says, when Heathcliff reenters the married Catherine's life: "Well, we *must* be for ourselves in the long run; the mild and generous are only more justly selfish than the domineering." It is this obvious ethic of "just" selfishness—of protecting what is ours from those who are not like us—that makes Nelly (and the novel) disturbing, and indicates the ways her narrative mirrors the cultural work of Victorian fiction. Charlotte Brontë may hate the selfish; her narratives punish the egoists. Yet they all exile from the territories of the heroine those who differ from her, whether by class or religion or perception of the heroine's independence. The work of creating fellow feeling does not allow for much dissent. Nor does the story of *Wuthering Heights* as Nelly Dean and Lockwood tell it.

Yet unlike its chief narrators, *Wuthering Heights* as a novel, Eagleton reminds us, "confronts the tragic truth that the passion and society it presents are not fundamentally reconcilable—that there remains at the deepest level an ineradicable contradiction between them which refuses to be unlocked, which obtrudes itself as the very stuff and secret of experience." For Bersani, the social and financial comfort of the Grange, "as Catherine finally sees, is also a bondage; it encloses her in the oppressive security of the family." This security is for Nelly Dean the liberating necessity of life, its preservation the justification of selfishness, its story the foundation of her narrative of exile and homecoming.

Emily Brontë does tell the same story twice. The second time she writes a Victorian novel. Charlotte Brontë saw this, saw the value and feared the meaning of Emily Brontë's "meditations." Charlotte Brontë does in *Villette* free her protagonist from the marriage plot and from the smothering society of England. Yet she accomplishes this freedom by exiling Lucy Snowe and allegorizing feeling, making a woman's desires the buried life of the text, not the substance of her working life or her communion. For Emily Brontë, communion and work are beside the point. They may offer characters, male or female, local habitations and a name. But they are simply knowable; they are not what one is. To Nelly Dean, that "cool spectator" in whom Charlotte Brontë found a "specimen of true benevolence and homely fidelity," Catherine and Heathcliff make "a strange and fearful picture," and ruin a good story. Yet the questions they repeatedly ask, because they escape the confinements of Victorian realism, haunt the history of the novel, urging us to remember how uneasy English fiction has been with what does not exist, domestically and politically, by the nation's hearths.

Charlotte Brontë asks for woman to have the power both to express her desire through choosing its domestic enclosure, and to patrol the moral territories that encircle it. Emily Brontë sets the limitation of this choice: "I cannot express it; but surely you and everybody have a notion that there is, or should be, an existence of yours beyond you. What were the use of my creation if I were entirely contained here?" Catherine and Heathcliff are indeed "the Jane and Rochester animals in their native state"—before they entered the patriarchal story of inclusion and exclusion, domestic love and social security, that the Victorian novel, and the second half of *Wuthering Heights*, had to tell.

Barry V. Qualls

Selected Bibliography

Armstrong, Nancy. *Desire and Domestic Fiction: A Political History of the Novel.* New York: Oxford University Press, 1987.

Bersani, Leo. *A Future for Astyanax: Character and Desire in the Novel.* New York: Columbia University Press, 1984.

Bodenheimer, Rosemarie. *The Politics of Story in Victorian Social Fiction.* Ithaca, N.Y.: Cornell University Press, 1988.

Boone, Joseph Allen. *Tradition Counter Tradition: Love and the Form of Fiction.* Chicago: University of Chicago Press, 1987.

David, Deirdre. *Intellectual Women and Victorian Patriarchy: Harriet Martineau, Elizabeth Barrett Browning, George Eliot.* Itahca, N.Y.: Cornell University Press, 1987.

Eagleton, Terry. *Myth of Power: A Marxist Study of the Brontës.* London: Macmillan, 1975.

Gilbert, Sandra M., and Susan Gubar. *The Madwoman in the Attic: The Woman Writer and the Nineteenth-Century Literary Imagination.* New Haven, Conn.: Yale University Press, 1979.

Hardy, Barbara. *Forms of Feeling in Victorian Fiction.* London: Peter Owen, 1985.

Kaplan, Cora. *Sea Changes: Culture and Feminism.* London: Verso, 1986.

Poovey, Mary. *Uneven Developments: The Ideological Work of Gender in Mid-Victorian England.* Chicago: University of Chicago Press, 1988.

Showalter, Elaine. *A Literature of Their Own: British Women Novelists from Brontë to Lessing.* Princeton, N.J.: Princeton University Press, 1977.

Spivak, Gayatri. "Three Women's Texts and a Critique of Imperialism." *Critical Inquiry* 12 (Autumn 1985): 243–61.

Dickens

No other English novelist has ever been as popular as Charles Dickens, and it is impossible to grasp Dickens's place in cultural history without appreciating the extraordinary dimensions of that popularity. Sales of his first novel, *The Pickwick Papers*, took off like a rocket, igniting a kind of national Pickwick mania. Merchants flooded London with all kinds of "Pickwickian" paraphernalia, and hacks turned out numerous pirated imitations, "sequels," and theatrical adaptations (seven of these were staged even before the serialized issues of the novel had all been published). Nothing like the Pickwick phenomenon had ever happened before, in England or anywhere else, and it thrust Dickens into a national limelight that blazed fiercely, without interruption, over the rest of his career. His third novel, *Nicholas Nickleby*, sold fifty thousand copies on the first day of publication alone; *The Old Curiosity Shop* sold over a hundred thousand installments a week; and his journal *All the Year Round* had a circulation at one point of three hundred thousand. These figures (which do not include plagiarisms and imitations) suggest a complete command of the national literary attention—nearly as extensive in America as it was in England. Crowds used to gather on the New York and Boston piers to buy his serials the instant they arrived from England, and while awaiting the climactic chapters of *The Old Curiosity Shop*, they shouted up to the sailors, "Is Little Nell dead?" What is particularly remarkable is that Dickens managed to sustain this feverish level of celebrity for nearly thirty-five years. During the last twelve years of his life, he conducted a series of electrifying public readings in England, Scotland, Ireland, America, and Paris (over four hundred of them, all to packed houses) that became a ritual of mass adulation, the culmination of a love affair with his public that Kathleen Tillotson and John Butt have called, not unkindly, "by far the most interesting love-affair of his life."

Towering monumentally over the landscape of nineteenth-century fiction—"the Shakespeare of the novel," he was titled by the Cambridge critics F. R. and Q. D. Leavis—Dickens acquired his stature through his unique ability to cut across the social boundaries of his readership. In 1916, writing his own account of Dickens's oeuvre, the literary historian George Saintsbury claimed that "it is probably safe to say (here making no exception at all and giving him no companions) that no author in our literary history has been both admired and enjoyed for such different reasons; by such different tastes and intellects; by whole classes of readers unlike each other." Certainly, no writer's work has appealed to so wide an audience while also enjoying the favor of serious criticism. Saintsbury concluded that there is a heterogeneous quality in Dickens's work that allows readers to overlook aspects of it that are not to their taste, and to cherish those that are. Dickens's achievement is the result not of "a Shakespearean universality," but of the "diversity of [his] appeal," a quality of "mixed genius . . . [that] requires a corresponding variety of analysis to understand itself, its causes and its manifestations." Even today, Dickens seems amenable to highly particularized schools of critical reading that are often in conflict with each other—which may be one reason why his central place in the literary canon has survived vicissitudes of recent criticism that have been far less kind to writers such as Thackeray, Trollope, or Meredith. Although critics sometimes rhapsodize about the universal humanist values Dickens is said to embody, his wonderfully broad acclaim depends on distinct intellectual, ideological, and aesthetic compounds that enable him to address the values of very different readerly constituencies at the same time as he suppresses whatever conflicts might arise between them. It may well be that the boldness of his work's heterogeneity, its capacious eclecticism, is what has inspired in many people the sense that Dickens *is* the Victorian period.

Following Saintsbury's suggestion to apply "a variety of analysis" to account for Dickens's "mixed" appeal, one could do worse than to begin with his populism, and with the fundamental ambiguities of class affiliation it actually entails. The biographical sources for Dickens's populism are well known, though they have sometimes been viewed simplistically as the key to his entire vision. Dickens's childhood was haunted by severe bouts with poverty—the most legendary of these occurring when his father, a clerk in the naval pay office, was incarcerated in the Marshalsea prison for debt, while twelve-year-old Charles was taken out of school and sent to work in a blacking warehouse (events that are fictionalized in *David Copperfield* and *Little Dorrit*). Because of his father's gregariousness, his childhood also included a convivial acquaintance with all and sundry from the lower-middle and working classes. This social apprenticeship surely did fuel Dickens's lifelong fellow feeling with the humble and the downtrodden, and it led to his constant appeals for sympathetic understanding of the poor, which he molded around New Testament pieties. His annual Christmas stories, a tradition begun in 1843 with "A Christmas Carol," express these Christian principles of forgiveness, generosity, and brotherly love most directly. While Dickens did not, as some have claimed, "invent" the modern rituals of Christmas, he did much to promote the emerging Victorian sense of Christmas as a great festival of social goodwill, and to identify himself with it. On the most superficial level, the novels feature an incessant conflict between good and evil, the latter associated primarily with the lack of feeling—and also the stupidity—that follow from refusals of human brotherhood. Coupling the virtues of charity to the power of moral intelligence, Dickens was able to articulate a populism that combined an exuberant faith in the best potentials of humankind with an acute and unflinching recognition of its worst.

There is much evidence that Dickens was acknowledged among the lower classes as a friend of the poor man. His pioneering methods of cheap serial publication had something to do with his access to a lower-class readership. His affirmative incorporation into the novels of lower-class culture, especially of popular entertainments—the circus, the pantomime, the Punch and Judy show—was an additional factor. Dickens always associates these popular entertainments with the communal values of spontaneity, selflessness, and fellow feeling. Their affinity with "traditional" as opposed to modern patterns of social relationship is conveyed through the strangely dated entertainment figures he often celebrates—the itinerant puppetmasters and strolling actors that are so prominent in the early novels. More important, though, the perception of Dickens as the champion of the poor derived from his active support for lower-class political causes. While not avowedly partisan, Dickens was a consistent spokesman for the "common man," and was particularly concerned with the damage public institutions did to the poor. *Oliver Twist*, for example, begins with an attack on the workhouse and the New Poor Law of 1834, and it ends with a general outburst of indignation that slums like the fictional Jacob's Island have been allowed to fester. Dickens's social crusading extended outside the bounds of fiction, for he had other political instruments at his disposal: he was a popular public speaker, a pamphleteer, the founder and editor of the liberal *Daily News*, and the editor (for twenty years) of a widely read weekly—first *Household Words*, and then its successor, *All the Year Round*. Altogether, he was an effective spokesman for various causes: the legalization of Sunday amusements (which were the primary refuge of the working class from a workweek of exhausting labor), factory reform, improved education, sanitation, administrative reform, and other campaigns primarily intended to meliorate lower-class conditions. In the novels, his reformist attacks were usually directed less at specific institutions than at unimaginative and unfeeling bureaucracy in general, but his more pointed fictional satires often bore fruit on both small and large scales. The tyrannical Mr. Fang from *Oliver Twist*, who was modeled on a notoriously brutish magistrate named Laing, resulted in the man's removal from office, for example. More significantly, the satires on philanthropy in *Bleak House* were instrumental in bringing about a more systematic organization of Victorian charities (even if this organization entailed new problems of its own).

Dickens's appeal to the lower orders also owes something to the "popular style" of his narrative persona, which adopts attitudes and postures familiar to readers from lower social strata. His prevailing facetiousness of tone, his comically exaggerated types, his uninhibited punning, his cheerful satire, his mixture of farce and seriousness, and, most of all, his deep-seated and unrelenting grudge against snobbishness of any kind—all express a persona looking upward at the social scale, knowingly and defiantly, yet with its good humor, self-confidence, and unembittered vitality preserved intact. With its air of precocious cleverness, Dickens's tone has the impudence and the broad ironies one might find in a street urchin. His attack on snobbishness is virulent enough to have given offense to quite a few middle-class readers—like Saintsbury, who faulted Dickens for having started "that curious topsy-turvyfied snobbishness—that 'cult of the *lower* classes'—which has become a more and more fashionable religion"; or like Q. D. Leavis, who dismissed Dickens's attempts to satirize his more refined characters as "the painful guesses of the uninformed and half-educated writing for the uninformed and half-educated."

Dickens's popular affinities certainly did lead to some unfortunate indulgences in lower-class prejudices and philistinism. In *Barnaby Rudge*, for example, Lord Gordon, who was responsible for the Gordon riots against Catholics of 1780, is portrayed leniently as a well-meaning incompetent (Dickens was fervently antipapist, as well as casually anti-Semitic). Dickens's easy populism also led to occasional offenses against good taste—as in his sketch of Miss Mowcher in *David Copperfield*, which was modeled on a poor female dwarf who recognized her fictional portrait and complained bitterly to Dickens. It is his seemingly unself-critical indulgence of popular attitudes (in addition, of course, to the narrative conventions he borrows from popular art) that has led to most of the disparagement Dickens has suffered. Trollope parodied him, in *The Warden*, as "Mr. Popular Sentiment," and F. R. Leavis initially excluded him from the "Great Tradition" because he was too much a "popular entertainer," and "not completely serious." Surprise at Dickens's own personal "vulgarity" also was not uncommon. Richard Henry Dana wrote: "You admire him, & there is a fascination about him which keeps your eyes on him, yet you cannot get over the impression that he is a low bred man. . . . Take the genius out of his face & there are a thousand young London shop-keepers . . . who look exactly like him." Edward Fitzgerald thought him a "Cockney Snob." Even his good friend John Forster never ceased to feel that Dickens's public readings were beneath the dignity of a literary man.

Yet while Dickens's style—both personal and narrational—seemed to represent the humble man to himself flatteringly, it also domesticated the underdog sensibility in ways that Dickens's middle-class readers found congenial. The innocence and the disarming joviality of Dickens's devilry, coupled with a Christian sentimentalism very much in tune with evangelical tastes, had a particular charm for middle-class readers. In characters like Sam Weller from *The Pickwick Papers*, the process of domestication was already apparent: Weller, a Victorian Sancho Panza, manages to sublimate the acuteness of the street philosopher into a kind of wise deference and loyalty toward his master, Mr. Pickwick, whose inoffensive aloofness marks him as the idealistic but democratic gentleman. This kind of appreciative distancing of popular life, which (to put it most cynically) allowed Dickens's "slumming" middle-class readers to sample harmlessly what they conceived to be the uninhibited energies of the lower orders, results in the large psychological gap Dickens created between his middle-class protagonists and the more colorful, unrepressed minor characters who surround (and support) them. In their very blandness, Dickens's protagonists embody the moral authority of middle-class seriousness, reserve, and self-control, which anchors and controls the lower-class carnival backdrop meant to animate their moral progress.

The ambivalence of Dickens's populism is wonderfully complex, and not reducible simply to middle-class patronage. It is important to recognize, however, that his populism owes much to the tremendous optimism about reform that was in vogue among the newly enfranchised middle classes in the 1830s, at the formative stages of his career. As Humphry House has pointed out, Dickens's career "coincided almost exactly with the rule of the Ten-Pound Householders"—that is, with the period between the Reform Bills of 1832 and 1867. As a young parliamentary stenographer, Dickens copied down the first Reform Bill debates in 1831, and for the next few years he covered numerous important political speeches as a journalist. His reformist attitudes might be taken as a sentimentalized version of 1830s middle-class radicalism—Fitzjames Stephen once referred to him as the "representative man" of the reform period. In this sense, Dickens's outspokenness about social justice was largely expressive of middle-class idealism, though in his case it was pitched in a more-than-usually empathetic key. As a reviewer for the *Economist* pointed out in response to his Christmas story "The Chimes": "One of the most remarkable circumstances of the day is the passion . . . which prevails to improve the condition of the working classes. . . . Under the influence of this passion, all the so-called *light* writers, who catch their inspiration from the prevailing events, have turned political philosophers, perhaps without knowing it. . . . Mr. Dickens shares this national feeling." What is most important about Dickens's middle-class representativeness is that the gloomy pessimism setting into his social vision in the early 1850s reflects the class disillusionment of the disappointed thirties reformers. In this pessimism, too, the later Dickens was representative of the class within which he had established himself, rather than simply the brooding, wizened popular sage that he is often taken to have been.

But Dickens's middle-class identifications actually run counter to his populism in serious if largely suppressed ways. Some features of his vision of the popular crowd, for example, served middle-class desires to repress class conflict by reimaging mass society in reassuring terms. Dickens's seminal conception of the diverse and heterogeneous English crowd—that is, his creative reservoir of character sketching that has led many to speak sentimentally of "the Dickens world"—represents the full flowering of a middle-class rhetorical strategy for defusing the political significance of mass society. This rhetorical tradition depends on a particular anthology of crowd imagery that can be found originally in the cheap popular journals of the 1820s—the *Penny Magazine*, the *Mirror of Literature, Amusement, and Instruction*, the *Hive*. These journals systematically portray the mob in terms of its friendly individualism, breaking up the frightening images of nebulous mass society that haunt late-eighteenth-century writing into a rich array of individuated types. It is because of this tradition of writing that Gissing could complain, with a nostalgia that was only partially accurate, that the late-nineteenth-century masses had become more homogeneous than they were in Dickens's day. Dickens's work, which adapts the earlier writers' crowd imagery to a much wider audience, carries out an individualizing approach to mass society in various ways: by using proper names that summarize a character's predictable tendencies, by depicting individuals as singularly purposive, and by creating a kind of social taxonomy for placing strange eccentrics in comprehensible niches. Dickens's comic background characters are all monads—obsessives who seem uninterested in intercourse with other selves—and one effect of this gallery of eccentric types is to make the social crowd seem comforting, even friendly, in its willingness to yield up the quaintly insular identities of its atomized members.

This strategy of representing the crowd as a menagerie of eccentric types provided mass readers with a sense of the colorful, baroque plenitude of collective life. It sublimated political conflicts into a kind of mythologized pantheon of wackiness. But for the middle-class reader, more inclined to identify with the observer, this approach to the crowd had slightly different effects. It produced the sense that a "human" rationale could be discovered by the patient observer in what appeared to be the dehumanized surfaces of mass society. The implicit tone of "the Dickens world" is that of a complacent middle-class utopianism, in which a certain benign voyeurism seems to transcend class conflict and to produce a sense of national togetherness. This tendency to decollectivize the identity of the working classes corresponded, among other things, to Dickens's antipathy to extending any kind of political power to the lower class as a body. In *Hard Times*, he came out very strongly against unionization, and the mob scenes from *Barnaby Rudge* and *A Tale of Two Cities* pander to Victorian fears about the consequences of lower-class resistance to oppression.

The "Englishness" that Dickens was celebrated for having captured in his diverse portrait gallery (a reviewer recommended *Sketches by Boz* to foreign audiences as the best of guidebooks) also flattered middle-class interests, and consolidated middle-class values as national ones. The "Englishness" that Dickens did so much to define is usually considered to include, for example, the sincerity and honesty that are the hallmarks of Victorian middle-class ethics. (Dickens's novels relentlessly satirize the deceitfulness attributed to upper-class political and business figures, from the scheming of Ralph Nickleby to the pasteboard mask of Merdle in *Little Dorrit*.) It also included the pride in intelligent debunking and in the rejection of cant that characterized middle-class democratic self-consciousness. Other middle-class virtues that are funneled into Dickens's sense of "Englishness" include moral courage, personal independence and individuality, and an outspokenness about social justice. Most important, "Englishness" includes a sense of industriousness, enterprise, and individualist energy—tempered, of course, by the kindness and charity that Victorian culture identified with middle-class women. In this respect alone, Dickensian "Englishness" provides a place for women within a set of characteristics that tends to enshrine the middle-class male as the national norm.

"Englishness" also had its nationalistic implications. Dickens often stigmatized non-English cultures as lacking in "English" virtues like industry, sincerity, and healthy diversity. Thus, in *American Notes* he writes that the American people are "all alike. . . . There is no diversity of character," and his descriptions of French, Italian, and American national psyches usually attribute to them large doses of deceitfulness or laziness or both. More disturbing, articles in *Household Words* often took a brutal attitude toward native peoples in the colonies, and Dickens's strong authoritarian responses to the Indian Mutiny of 1857 and the Jamaica Rebellion of 1865 betray an occasionally genocidal disposition. On the heels of the Indian Mutiny, he wrote to Angela Burdett-Coutts: "I should do my utmost to exterminate the Race upon whom the stain of the late cruelties rested . . . to blot it out of mankind and raze it off the face of the Earth." Despite his general chauvinism about the English, however, Dickens did support the antislavery movement, which was very strong in England during the early part of his career. One of the most severe indictments of Harold Skimpole in *Bleak House* is the cavalier attitude Skimpole takes toward American slaves, and *American Notes* includes a ringing diatribe against slavery.

But perhaps Dickens's most serious betrayal of populist sympathies is his deep commitment to an individualist ethos. The central plot of the novels is always the emergence of an orphaned hero or heroine out of privation into a recognizably middle-class circle of kindness and care. This standard Dickensian trajectory is launched with the rescue of Oliver Twist from Fagin's den of thieves and his restoration to his rightful middle-class identity. It continues in the rise of such characters as Kit Nubbles, Walter Gay, Esther Summerson, Little Dorrit, and Pip, however much their success stories are tempered by Dickens's moral cautions against ambition. While these transparent dramatizations of self-pity have often been attributed to Dickens's feelings of emotional abandonment during his blacking warehouse days, it seems more appropriate to place them as a symptomatic expression of Victorian middle-class individualism. J. Hillis Miller's now classic work has shown how Dickens's novels are fundamentally concerned with the development and strengthening of individual identity. If nothing else, the novels' consistent encouragement of readers to identify sympathetically with a "wronged" hero should qualify any tendencies to see Dickens solely as a novelist of brotherhood or of social guilt.

One formal consequence of Dickens's divided class loyalties is his novels' enigmatic use of doubles. His wholesomely enterprising heroes are always doubled by unscrupulously ambitious villains in ways that both acknowledge and obscure the clash of middle-class individualism with Christian pieties about brotherhood. These villainous doubles often desire the very same social goals—in some cases even the same woman—as does the hero (thus Uriah Heep envies David Copperfield his social favor, and sees himself as a rival for Agnes; Bradley Headstone in *Our Mutual Friend* competes with Wrayburn for Lizzie Hexam; and Orlick in *Great Expectations* aspires after Biddy, the woman who belatedly becomes an object of Pip's affections). They also conveniently carry out vengeance against characters who obstruct the ambitions of the hero (Orlick murders Pip's sister Mrs. Joe; Rigaud in *Little Dorrit* destroys Mrs. Clennam). Readers have disagreed about Dickens's intentions in this evidently self-conscious doubling—

whether it is the effect of Dickens's bad conscience about the built-in hypocrisy of class society; whether it acknowledges moral ambiguities the better to reject them out of hand by scapegoating "evil" characters; or whether it provides some means of formulating coherent moral distinctions between the aggressive individualist and the virtuously "self-made" man. In any case, the obscurity of this pattern of doubling seems to be one effect of Dickens's ambivalence about the conflicts between middle-class and populist thinking, and it is a striking case of his having made it possible for readers to discover their own disparate moral and ideological predilections in his work.

The same contradictions underwrite Dickens's exceptional scrupulosity about the nonmercenary motives of his lovers, a characteristic that introduces a significant new shade of moral purity into British fiction. In *Little Dorrit*, for example, Arthur Clennam will not marry Little Dorrit, even after they confess their long-standing love, simply because of the accident of her rise in fortune. It is only when her inheritance is lost that the wedding can take place. Throughout the novels, Dickens displays an anxiety to separate economic and romantic motives. In the work of Austen, Scott, Trollope, Gaskell, and many other British novelists, conjunctions of love and spectacular upward mobility are represented as possible and even highly desirable. But with rare exceptions, Dickens's endings uneasily subdue the prospect of financial or social blessings—even though such blessings in some form never fail to accompany romance. The goal of Dickens's characters becomes a modest domestic happiness and a self-sufficiency gained through personal effort. Dickens's discomfort with problems of self-interest and disinterest is reflected in many other ways, including his fascination with hypocritical characters like Pecksniff in *Martin Chuzzlewit* and Uriah Heep in *David Copperfield*, and his stiff-necked reaction to accusations in the American press that his own campaign for an international copyright law was hypocritically self-interested.

Another formal strategy that helps to suppress the moral conflicts of the novels is Dickens's use of subplots—both comic and sensational—that diffuse the apparent moral meaning of his central action. The central plot of *Great Expectations*, for instance, condemns the desire to vindicate one's social exclusion by creating respectable surrogates—a dark form of patronage dramatized by Magwitch's creation of Pip as a gentleman and by Miss Havisham's creation of Estella as femme fatale. But this condemnation is oddly reversed in Pip's peripheral act of personal redemption. To make up for his sins of ambition, Pip clandestinely arranges for Herbert Pocket to gain his dreamed-of place in a large commercial firm. The connection between Pip's generosity and his self-vindication is made so clearly that when Herbert joyfully announces his success to Pip, unaware that Pip is his secret benefactor, Pip cries "tears of triumph." This kind of thematic diffusion ultimately works to set the moral experience of the protagonist apart—as an apparently unrepeatable, nonformulaic instance of spiritual grace—even as it seems to articulate clear moral imperatives.

To some extent, Dickens's ideological vacillations are reflected in his fuzzy, often ambiguous ideas about politics. His political philosophy, vague as it may have been, revolved around his belief that government should make itself the servant of public opinion. Lawmakers, he argued in an 1870 speech, should obey "the spirit of their times" and act as "the mere servants of the people." These sentiments seek a middle ground between Victorian political theorists who advocated principles of governmental interference and those who advocated governmental restraint. Dickens and many others in the Victorian mainstream favored a political order that would feature limited but nevertheless strong governance, and his hybrid formulation relied on the notion that government could mold itself—much as he apparently did himself—as an organic expression of the common will. Alexander Welsh explains that Dickens saw "the action of public opinion [as] at once democratic and authoritarian: by some unspecified process the people must 'force' the government to 'coerce' themselves." In one form or another, this kind of faith in "public opinion" as a more effective motor of government than either the franchise or complete centralization was widely shared in Victorian culture—by writers as diverse as Spencer, Mill, Carlyle, Ruskin, and George Eliot. For Dickens, such faith underlay his vicious satires of political authority and especially his contempt for Parliament, which he saw as unresponsive to public opinion. But it also underlay his bitter hatred of mobs, his opposition to further extension of the franchise, and his belief in the strict punishment of criminals. It lies at the root of his disillusion with American democracy, his revulsion from what he saw as the excesses of unhierarchical American liberties. Most tellingly, it feeds his remarkable respect for the military and the police. Throughout the novels, Dickens imagines the executive branch of government as a direct expression of the "public" desire for order, and police work in particular is strictly separated from repressive or incompetent agencies of social power. Dickens consistently idealized police figures like Bucket in *Bleak House* or the Night-Inspector in *Our Mutual Friend*, in marked contrast with his attitudes toward all other public officials, and he tended to see in the police the possibility of an organic authoritarianism.

The most important, most undiluted aspect of the bourgeois Dickens, however, is his attitude toward home and hearth. Dickens did more to affirm the middle-class separation of public and private spheres than any other Victorian novelist. He was instrumental in the widespread Victorian celebration of domesticity, having almost single-handedly rehabilitated and adapted the domestic novel to Victorian values. As an obituarist wrote: "His sympathy with the affections of hearth and home knows no bounds, and it is within this sphere that I confess I know of no other writer—in poetry or prose, amongst ourselves or other nations—to compare with him." *Fraser's Magazine*, in accounting for his tremendous popularity, found it to result, "above all, because of his deep reverence for the household sanctities, his enthusiastic worship of the household gods." Only within the home could Dickens seem to imagine a thoroughly genuine social grouping. Equally important, only within the home could religious values be fully sustained. In its defensive posture toward the outside world, the Dickensian insular family might be seen as the product of individualism, rather than an antidote to it. Nevertheless, the family flourishes in Dickens's novels as the chief site of intimacy and emotional redemption. One result of this apotheosis of home and hearth was Dickens's introduction of childhood as a central subject in English fiction. But the more significant consequence is his contribution to the cult of the domestic angel.

In the twentieth century, perhaps no other aspect of Dickens's work has drawn as much criticism as his portrayal of women. While Dickens's female portraiture does have its champions, and while it is important in any case to recognize Dickens as a man of his day—a man who actually began to transform himself when talk of the "Woman Question" arose (Bella Wilfer in *Our Mutual Friend* looks forward to more assertive late-century heroines, and her "doll-house" marriage is presented with uncharacteristic irony)—nevertheless, it seems foolish to deny that Dickens's women were the most powerful Victorian expressions of the stereotypical "angel in the house." Without exception, his heroines are passively virtuous, devoid of sexuality, rapturously domestic, and infantilized. Even as children, Dickens's female characters have irrepressible maternal instincts—Jenny Wren, Lizzie Hexam, Charley Neckett, and other female children in Dickens seem to have been born to mother their siblings—and often their fathers as well. But the most pronounced trait of these domestic angels is their affinity for the home. Rose Maylie, in *Oliver Twist*, of whom we are told that "if ever angels be for God's good purposes enthroned in mortal forms, they may be, without impiety, supposed to abide in such as hers," was "made for Home, and fireside peace and happiness." So angelic are these heroines that they often seem to have a special power over death, offering up to the hero their ability to mediate between himself and spiritual transcendence. Agnes Wickfield, perhaps the most idealized of all Dickens's women, serves as such an unearthly mediatrix for David Copperfield, who ends his narration by exclaiming: "Oh Agnes, oh my soul, so may thy face be by me when I close my life indeed; so may I, when realities are melting from me like the shadows which I now dismiss, still find thee near me, pointing upward!" In some cases, heroines exert this power by presiding over the spiritual rebirth of male characters—as Florence Dombey does for her father, or as Lizzie Hexam does for Eugene Wrayburn in *Our Mutual Friend*.

When Dickens did create positive images of willful women, he usually relegated them to the lower class (Mrs. Bagnet in *Bleak House*, or Peggotty in *David Copperfield*) to complement his feminization of working-class men—an inversion of gender roles that helps normalize middle-class sexual standards. Dickens's oppressive idealization of women also included a tendency to differentiate severely between angelic women and female monsters. It does not take much for a woman to fall in Dickens, and the drop from angel to "female dragon" (the epithet applied to Sally Brass in *The Old Curiosity Shop*) is a sharp and irreversible one. This opposition of angel to monster also generated Dickens's typically Victorian fascination with and fear of prostitutes (reflected most of all, perhaps, in his frenzied staging of the murder of Nancy from *Oliver Twist* as the climactic scene for his public readings). Given that he was an inveterate "streetwalker" himself (his characteristic restlessness carried him off routinely on twenty-mile tramps, often in the solitude of night), and that the self-dramatized recklessness that troubled his own love life so strongly parallels the waywardness he condemned in women, Dickens's punitive attitudes toward fallen women can be seen as an attempt to expurgate guilt over his own deepest desires. Perhaps no novel reveals the diabolical nature Dickens projected into women so much as *A Tale of Two Cities*, in which Madame Defarge and other nameless female insurrectionists embody what Dickens saw as the bloodthirsty irrationality of the French revolution. But all the novels conceive the feminine as a volatile essence in need of strict control, and Dickens is unforgiving when it comes to women who act on their sexuality—the fates of Little Em'ly and Edith Dombey have often struck readers as cases in which Dickens is particularly harsh.

Nonmonstrous women who nevertheless fail to meet the angelic ideal often function as way stations for male desire: the pattern of male psychological development in the novels seems to be articulated through a progressive evolution in male romantic choices. Thus, David Copperfield's maturity leads him through a dangerous infatuation with the (falling) lower-class woman, Little Em'ly, and a mistaken passion for the inadequate housekeeper, Dora, before he finally settles on the angelic Agnes. Arthur Clennam's immature preferences for the spoiled Pet and the hysterical Flora can be understood as stages in his own psychological growth from the perspective of his later love for Little Dorrit. In this way, women temper the individualist desires of middle-class men only by being subsumed into male psychology.

Nevertheless, Dickens has left plenty of material for feminist readers to recuperate. Dickens's portraits of "neurotic" women—Esther Summerson, Miss Havisham, Bella Wilfer—are perceptive and evocative enough to provide sympathetic evidence of the effects of the Victorian gender system on women. They also sometimes show how certain women were able to transform the social possibilities available to them in empowering, if limited, ways. Moreover, the domestic virtues of his female characters correspond to the palpable kinds of cultural authority that middle-class Victorian women achieved. This authority extends beyond concrete vocational possibilities to what Nancy Armstrong has called an "exclusive authority over domestic life, the emotions, taste, and morality," that ultimately identified the feminine with cultural power itself. Dickens's respect for feminine authority in the realm of culture is reflected in his own response to criticism in the 1860s that his works had "masculinized" the novel by importing political polemics. The later novels maintain a much more sentimental relationship to political concerns than does the earlier work, and they contrast strikingly with *Household Words* in this respect. For similar reasons, Dickens sought to associate his novels with the more feminized literary category of "romance." As he puts it in the preface to *Bleak House*: "I have purposely dwelt upon the romantic side of familiar things."

In addition to the specific compounds of intellectual and ideological content that I have so far cataloged, Dickens's ability to cut across readerly constituencies was driven by his remarkably intuitive identification with general Victorian tastes. Though his pride in his close relationship with his readers was perhaps overweening—he liked to speak of "that particular relation (personally affectionate and like no other man's) which subsists between me and the public"—his interdependence with his audience's dominant interests and values was indeed extraordinary. It is important not to conflate this identification with a simple attempt to manipulate readers. Hippolyte Taine was not alone in his sense that Dickens's representativeness was a sincere one: "Public opinion is [his] private opinion; [he] does not submit to it as an external constraint, but feels it inwardly as an inner persuasion." Dickens's rapport with readers was certainly something he took pains never to endanger. His carefulness included, among other things, his scrupulosity about the sexual purity of his work. Though he mocked Podsnap in *Our Mutual Friend*—for whom the "question about everything was, would it bring a blush to the cheek of a young person?"—there was a dose of Podsnappian prudery in Dickens himself. His carefulness with his readers also included a willingness to gratify popular tastes by ending his novels happily—in the case of *Great Expectations*, he actually revised the original ending in the direction of greater optimism, on the advice of Bulwer Lytton. But these measures were for the most part heartfelt, and expressive of his uncanny affinity for the subjects and attitudes that touched his readers' nerves.

The channels for feedback from his readers were opened in at least two concrete ways. One was the public readings, which allowed him to keep his finger directly on his audience's pulse. The other was his method of serial publication. In *Pickwick*, Dickens revived a system of publishing in monthly numbers that had been practiced sporadically in the eighteenth century but had since fallen out of favor. Dickens's revival of serial publication was made effective by advances in printing technology, by the integration of advertising with fiction, and by the growth of a literate popular audience. After *Pickwick*'s success, all of his later novels were published first either in monthly numbers, in monthly periodicals, or in Dickens's own weeklies. One effect of this form of publication was to intertwine the twists and turns of his plots with the rhythms of his readers' lives over a period of eighteen months, which did much to promote a sense of "living with" his characters. Another was to give him time to sample his reader's responses and to revise his plans accordingly. Thus, when sales of *Martin Chuzzlewit* flagged, Martin was packed off to America to spice up the plot; and responses to Dickens's short-lived weekly, *Master Humphrey's Clock*, spurred him to use it as the vehicle to launch *The Old Curiosity Shop*. Ironically, these effects of intimacy were achieved by making the actual conditions of publication more factorylike, more pressured by deadlines, more susceptible to standardization, and more immediately commodifiable.

As a reformer, too, Dickens was always reactive, no matter how much he may have presented himself as a social maverick. He never took up a reform issue unlikely to capture popular consensus. As Humphry House put it: "Detached now from his time he may seem more original and adventurous than he was; for then he was only giving wider publicity in 'inimitable' form to a number of social facts and social abuses which had already been recognized if not explored before him. . . . [He] caught exactly the tone which clarified and reinforced the public's sense of right and wrong, and flattered its moral feelings." In this way, his works are an invaluable expression of Victorian ethical priorities.

These various kinds of responsiveness guaranteed that there would be a good many issues upon which Dickens's vision crossed social boundaries, and indeed had a unifying appeal. One of these is his special role as the chronicler of the Victorian city. No one knew London better, and Dickens's extraordinary powers of observation made him a writer who, as Walter Bagehot put it, "describes London like a special correspondent for posterity." Reflecting widely shared Victorian misgivings about the benefits of industrial progress, there is often an apocalyptic note in Dickens's description of urban life, a tendency to use images of urban decay as signs for general moral chaos. His metaphors for the urban landscape—fog, mud, dirt, pestilence—suggest a systematic, animated evil, as if the city's growth had taken on a destructive, all-consuming life of its own. At the same time, Dickens codified in specific terms many of the pressing problems of the Victorian city: the depopulation of the ancient urban core; overcrowding in slum areas; the destruction of open spaces; the problem of the fringe areas of London (described in *Our Mutual Friend* as a "suburban Sahara"); the sense of individual loss of control over conditions (even for wealthy individuals like the Merdles in *Little Dorrit*, urban environments are overwhelming). These images of the city fascinated Victorian readers and articulated their new consciousness of themselves as urban dwellers in a way previously unrealized by British fiction.

Dickens's representation of the city does waver somewhat in its moral shadings. The city is most often represented as a place from which to escape, and in novels like *Our Mutual Friend* it is explicitly represented as a prison. In *Great Expectations*, Pip's first exploration of London lands him in front of Newgate prison, and in *The Old Curiosity Shop* Nell tries to save her grandfather by fleeing London. In this sense, too, Dickens's celebration of hearth and home is the direct antithesis of city life. Wemmick's castle in *Great Expectations* is the most famous example of this antithesis, but it appears as well in numerous domestic sanctuaries—like the Nubbleses' in *The Old Curiosity Shop* or the Cratchits' in "A Christmas Carol." Still, Dickens's evident love of urban energies often sets up a tension between his pessimistic urban thematics and the enthusiastic quality of his attention to urban scenes, events, and characters. This love of London shows itself explicitly in only the most fleeting ways—in the wide-eyed wonder of innocents like Esther Summerson on first entering London, or in the exhilaration of urban mastery exemplified by Bucket and other police operatives.

Dickens also seems to have struck a complex but common chord in his transformation of religious ideas into a secularized vision. He often used religious allusions to reinforce notions of transcendence or liberation—as in the kind of pilgrim's progress undergone by Nell and her grandfather in *The Old Curiosity Shop*, or in the rhetoric of his sentimental deathbed scenes. Religious orthodoxies underlie persistent Dickensian themes, such as the deception of riches and the evils of selfishness. His ending marriages, too, should be understood not simply as a conventional endorsement of domestic complacency, but as images of transcendent bliss—which is why they always invoke metaphors of changelessness and the stoppage of time. Despite his vicious satires of evangelicalism—Chadband in *Bleak House* or Howler in *Dombey and Son*, Mrs. Clennam's Puritanism in *Little Dorrit*—the novels show a broad religious influence ranging from the inflections of private feeling to public attitudes toward reform. But here, too, the influence runs in distinctly multiple channels. Religious themes of universal brotherhood are often countered by Dickens's tendency to espouse a more hierarchical Puritan pattern of election and reprobation. While this pattern is common in English fiction, Dickens intensified it by widening the gap between those who are destined for salvation and those who are not. Moral character is presented as innate in the novels, never as a matter of family or environmental conditioning. There is no accounting for the difference between Little Dorrit and her siblings, for example, or between Tom and Louisa Gradgrind in *Hard Times*. One of the more absurd symptoms of this predetermination is Dickens's tendency to endow his good characters with upper-class speech patterns. Though all those around them speak working-class dialects, children like Pip, Lizzie Hexam, and Sissie Jupe speak in the Victorian equivalent of BBC English. The radical apartness of Dickens's virtuous characters, their special state of grace, lends a quasi-religious justification to Dickensian individualism. Ultimately, though, the religious presence in Dickens is elusive: it is an inescapable overtone, but one that is difficult, finally, to decode.

In more purely aesthetic terms, the motley nature of Dickens's literary influences gives some indication of the mixed pleasures of his writing. He was deeply indebted to popular novelists of the early nineteenth century, especially Pierce Egan and Theodore Hook. His education in the popular theater was extremely thorough (he claimed to have gone to the theater every night for two to three years running in the early 1830s), and he drew on popular melodramas for his stagy plots and his more conventionalized character types. But Dickens also drew on eighteenth-century "classics" he read in his childhood—on Smollett, Fielding, Goldsmith, and Defoe—as well as on Cervantes and Scott. His descriptive tendencies owe something to the essays of Leigh Hunt. He knew Shakespeare exceptionally well, and Shakespearean influences show up in many ways—in his use of thematically cross-fertilizing subplots, for instance, or in many of his plot paradigms (*King Lear* in *The Old Curiosity Shop* and *Dombey and Son*; *Hamlet* in *Great Expectations*).

One of the more idiosyncratic hallmarks of the Dickens aesthetic is his striking power of description. He is especially good at evoking moral atmosphere through his description of physical details—closely observed things often seem to grow sentient with specific moral tendencies. Other formal aspects of his work that have inspired admiration include the inexhaustible comic creativeness of the novels and their vigorous narrative drive. His inventive prose style, as well as his ear for dialogue, prompted F. R. Leavis to claim that there was "surely no greater master of English except Shakespeare." Yet Dickens's greatest strength as a novelist lies in his dexterity with character. His literary fame began with the publication of *Sketches by Boz*, a collection of journalistic pieces notable for their extraordinary range and perceptiveness of characterization. His first works are designed to showcase his genius for character sketching—*The Pickwick Papers* includes over 350 characters. It is not until *Oliver Twist* that these seminal skills with characterization and description are coupled with his enduring tendencies toward sentiment, melodrama, and social crusading.

Despite his skill at characterization, Dickens has been routinely disparaged as a psychologist. This long-standing critical disdain results, however, from a failure to appreciate the kind of psychological analysis Dickens offers—a failure that is just beginning to be rectified. If one thinks of psychology as the depiction of an organic, complexly textured, and unified personality, then obviously Dickens is no Henry James. By contrast, his depiction of particular characters is always reductive, and always also the product of a deliberate effort to distort and exaggerate. Dickens is often said to have seen people the way a child sees grownups, focusing on what seems peculiar, arbitrary, unintelligible, comic, or terrifying. What is crucial about Dickens's interest in psychology, however, is his perception of the performative nature of the psyche. Dickens demonstrates the ways in which interiority is always staged, never fully organic and "inward." He counters the antitheatrical prejudices of the Victorian age, and its exaltation of sincerity, by presenting psychic states as a series of disjunctive, performative, and socially conditioned roles.

Of all English novelists, Dickens was no doubt most closely tied to the stage. He acted in scores of private and amateur theatricals, in addition to his histrionic public readings, and he wrote a number of minor plays, in some of which he performed himself. While Dickens's strong interest in theater carries over in numerous ways to his fiction, none is as important as his conception of the psyche as a kind of theater. Dickens always conceives inwardness as inextricable from the ways it is consciously or unconsciously presented to others, and this sense of the self as a role—or as a series of roles—led to a much stronger interest in psychic mechanisms than in the individuals within which these mechanisms are discontinuously played out. To appreciate Dickensian psychology, one must look beyond individual characters to his distribution of psychological dynamics across a range of complicating psychic models. His use of doubles and of diffusive subplots, for instance, fragments psychological dynamics in various ways, as does his tendency to prolif-erate related character types and his strong interest in states of altered consciousness. While this decentering psychological approach lends itself to diverse kinds of insight, Dickens is especially perceptive, as one would expect, about such things as displacement and sublimation, or about personality diffusion. "I think there's a pain somewhere in the room," says one exemplary subject, Mrs. Gradgrind, "but I couldn't positively say that I have got it."

One of the clearest instances of Dickens's more refractive view of the psyche is his perspective on what Freud called the death wish. Dickens's speculations on the death wish are, in fact, among his most important contributions to nineteenth-century thinking about the nature of sub-jectivity. In general terms, Dickens idealizes a kind of desire so intense as to seek its fulfillment beyond the limits of the self, in an expenditure of energy that thrills at risking personal coherence or safety. His rap-tures about acting itself always convey this delight at surpassing indi-vidual boundaries: "Assumption has charms for me—I hardly know for how many wild reasons—so delightful, that I feel a loss of, oh! I can't say what exquisite foolery, when I lose a chance of being someone in voice, etc., not at all like myself." The novels' complex fascination with death revolves around Dickens's perception that a certain kind of human desire abhors all limits and prefers a liberation from the con-straints of identity congruous, ultimately, with death. When Anthony Chuzzlewit dies, we are told: "The principle of life, shut up within his withered frame, fought like a strong devil, mad to be released, and rent its ancient prison-house." In this sense, Dickens's protagonists' war on their own self-interest can be said to have a libidinal as well as a moral purpose. At the same time, however, Dickens recognized that human beings recoil from the extremity of their own desires for self-transcen-dence, and seek to retain the exhilaration of such desire in some more safely individualized form. Dickens's own temperament brings to the foreground this psychic division: the same man who wandered restless-ly around London, who delighted in acting out the murder of Nancy, and whose morbidity took a hundred bizarre forms ("Whenever I am at Paris, I am dragged by invisible forces into the Morgue," he wrote in *The Uncommercial Traveller*), is also the man who idealized marriage and domestic retirement. The novels often revolve systematically around metaphors of imprisonment and release, as a way to formulate this psychic dilemma thematically.

One solution—stageable only within Dickens's diffuse, theatrical conception of the psyche—is to present an illusory psychic synthesis by distributing death drives and life drives to different phases of his narratives. House's remarks on the murder of Nancy call attention to such narrative self-division: "How utterly remote are these scenes and this state of mind from the earnest moralities of the Preface! To understand the conjunction of such different moods and qualities in a single man is the beginning of serious criticism of Dickens." Another is to project a single character's conflicting psychic impulses outward across a series of parallel characters. Among the many implications of Dickens's use of doubles, for instance, is that they sometimes express the secret envy of the protagonist for the villain's psychological affinities with violence and death. Many of Dickens's uncannily reckless villains—Quilp in *The Old Curiosity Shop* is the most extreme example—make the death drive vicariously enjoyable. Still another solution is to conceive single actions that seem to perform both life and death drives at once, even if they fail for that very reason to produce readily imitable moral formulas for behavior. Sidney Carton's enigmatic martyrdom, at the end of *A Tale of Two Cities*, is represented as both a fulfillment of his long-standing self-destructive impulses, and a moral recovery of himself. Carton's ambiguous, problematic kind of heroism is modeled on a formula Dickens began with Mark Tapley in *Martin Chuzzlewit*—Mark obsessively and paradoxically seeks to gain glory for himself through adventurous forms of self-sacrifice. One of the most consistent and affirmative ways Dickens represents psychic "integration" is through characters whose heroic self-sacrifice or self-repression seems to embody irreconcilable attitudes toward human boundaries: impulses toward a purifying expenditure of self, and toward a conserving restraint of desire.

Dickens multiplies the psychological significance of death in yet other ways, which makes it difficult to contain Dickensian psychology even within a more expansive model of the death drive like this one. Dickens's devotion to death, in some cases, represents simply a transmogrified Christian conception of transcendence. Death is imagined as a kind of passage to heaven—or at least, to a better place than earth. A more metaphysical undercurrent, however, is the notion that a brush with death provides psychological contact with some kind of foundational reality. As J. Hillis Miller puts it, death in Dickens is represented as "the mysterious origin of life, and no life that ignores its origin can be other than empty and false." For this reason, perhaps, near-death experiences are often the prelude to spiritual rebirth in Dickens. Scrooge's self-reformation in "A Christmas Carol," is the most famous example of such rebirth, but in the later novels these kinds of experience are quite common, especially in *A Tale of Two Cities* and *Our Mutual Friend*. The notion of death as a passageway to truth is not a new idea, but it does have a particular function in Victorian literature generally—not only in Dickens, but also in Tennyson, Arnold, George Eliot, and others. The emphasis in these writers' work falls on mourning and rebirth as a communal ritual, one in which social bonds are strengthened through a shared secularization of moral faith. This communal ritualization of death is central to Dickens's deathbed scenes (and it was restaged outside his novels in the uncanny public spectacles of mourning his readers indulged in for Little Nell, for Paul Dombey, and for Jo in *Bleak House*).

Besides stretching psychological resolutions across the boundaries of individual psyches—into nonindividualized patterns of communal ritual, or into seemingly contradictory psychic performances—Dickens also refracted psychological states through subtle patterns of symbolic displacement. Thus, for example, the characteristically Victorian guilt over sexual desire that seems to haunt his own life (biographers note his contorted emotional involvement with his sister-in-law, Mary Hogarth, his tendency to carefully controlled, mock infatuations, and the mysterious affair with Ellen Ternan that broke up his marriage) is dissolved in the novels through purely symbolic sexual liberations. In *Bleak House*, Esther Summerson's progress away from her engagement to Jarndyce and toward her marriage to Woodcourt, for example, symbolically repeats the "sin" of her mother's adultery while eliding Esther's own sexual desires. David Copperfield's two marriages also enact fantasies of sexual expansion in a symbolically adjusted manner. In all these ways, the novels explore psychological conditions but are free of the restrictive conventions of ego psychology, anticipating the decentered psychological approaches of modernist art.

An unresolvable, refractive, but purely aesthetic tension in Dickens's work that has helped widen his appeal is its striking combination of realism and fantasy. Dickens's admirers have often valued very different aspects of his novels along this axis. His realism is so scrupulous that it has inspired legions of Dickensians to hunt down the originals of the various characters and settings in the novels. More important, it has made Dickens perhaps the most important literary reference point of the Victorian period for historians and sociologists. The partisans of the "unreal" Dickens, however, celebrate his propensity for exaggerations and distortions, which sometimes reach hallucinatory proportions. Among other things, his taste for the uncanny, the improbable, and the grotesque has led to powerful kinds of symbolism that are not available to narratives more bound by the everyday—thus, the fog in *Bleak House* or the spectral marshy images from *Great Expectations* often seem to blur realistic description with archetypal meaning. Perhaps no other novelist has been able to combine Dickens's strict faithfulness to detail with the fantastic unreality of his general atmosphere. Ultimately, Dickens seems to be neither a realist nor a fantasist, but a novelist preoccupied—as were many Victorian writers—with the tension between fact and invention. His plans for *Household Words* capture this double focus well: while the magazine is designed to tell of the "social wonders, good and evil" of "the stirring world around us," it should adopt "no mere utilitarian spirit, no iron binding of the mind to grim realities," but rather should "cherish the light of Fancy which is inherent in the human breast." This precarious tension between realistic mimesis and self-generating meaning is expressed thematically in the novels through persistent conflicts between his characters' abilities to "make themselves up"—the extreme potential for self-creation of the autonomous individual—and their restrictive embeddedness in social conditions. It is also embodied in the prevailing theme of "interpretive power": many Dickens characters are involved in a pursuit of the "truth" hidden beneath layers of mystery, or, conversely, in turning factual reality into their own verbal constructs. *Bleak House* is perhaps the best example of a work obsessed with the fictional status of the truth: everyone in the novel is involved in tracking down truths of one kind or another, and a great source of the novel's comic—as well as tragic—interest depends on revealing how the pursuit of truth often indulges various kinds of fantasy. In characters like Micawber or Mr. Dick in *David Copperfield*, the potential for language to obliterate reality is pathologized, while first-person narrators like David Copperfield, Pip, and Esther Summerson exploit this potential more creatively.

It is tempting to read Dickens's work (as I have largely done) as one long novel—partly because the plots seem to matter less than such things as his evocations of atmosphere and his handling of character. Still, it is important to note at least a few landmarks in his development as a novelist, for the outlines of his career help chart a number of cultural changes from the 1840s through the 1860s. In the later novels, for instance, there is a new sense of social restraint. The lower-middle-class figures of Dickens's youth, rooted more in the uninhibited license of the Regency than in Victorian behavioral norms, yield to a general sense of social conformity that makes eccentrics stand out. In the late novels, too, it is the middle class that carries itself in more self-important ways, and the lower class that is demonstrably less assured. London, opened up by the police and by the surveillance of observers like Dickens himself, seems less mysterious, less enchanting. The mid-Victorian reaction against sentimentality (which culminated later in Oscar Wilde's famous put-down of Dickens: "A man would have to have a heart of stone to read the death of Little Nell without laughing") is reflected in his own abandonment of deathbed scenes after *Bleak House*, and in his partial adoption of the new cult of the "stiff upper lip" in characters like Arthur Clennam, Pip, and John Harmon. As far as his own development as a novelist goes, it is with *Dombey and Son* that Dickens leaps forward in his handling of the social landscape. At this point in his career, he becomes less vague about the social identities and environments of his characters, and provides more in the way of particularized observations about social niches. *David Copperfield* is usually credited with being the first fully unified Dickens novel, using the central consciousness of David himself to anchor the novel's vision. With *Bleak House*, there is a more sober turn to social issues and more of a sense that social problems are intractably systemic, along with a more gloomy pessimism about the prospects for change. In *Our Mutual Friend* and *Edwin Drood*, Dickens tries to incorporate some of the more elaborate plotting learned from his friend, Wilkie Collins, though he has none of Collins's narrative dexterity.

While Dickens is most famous, of course, as a novelist, it is important to remember that he had another significant career as an editor. He maintained a vigorous, inflexible control over nearly all the details of his weekly magazines, monitoring and often rewriting the work of his many contributors. His involvement in these periodicals, over the course of twenty years, was unceasing, and he was able to use them as a strong platform from which to address social problems. His generosity as an editor helped launch the careers of a number of younger writers, including Elizabeth Gaskell, Wilkie Collins, and George Meredith. In many ways, Dickens was also a key figure in the professionalization of literature during the nineteenth century. He was extremely skillful at exploring new methods of printing and advertising, and he was a central figure in the campaign for copyright laws, both domestic and international. Most important, through the social and political stature of his work, he endowed the writer with a new kind of public visibility and dignity. His only work to represent the figure of the writer—*David Copperfield*—relies heavily on notions of writerly disinterest, and on the inspirational, nonworkmanlike conditions of writerly labor to help support this newly professionalized image. Mary Poovey has shown as well that it was by "individualizing" the figure of the writer that Dickens helped resolve an entrenched Victorian ambivalence about whether the writer was a genius or an entrepreneur—for Dickens, the professional writer as creative individualist is necessarily both at once.

It would be as difficult to map out Dickens's complex influences on later writers as it is to explain his extraordinarily wide popularity, and for much the same reasons. The traces of Dickens's direct literary influence extend in appropriately multiple ways, from Russian novelists like Gogol, Tolstoy, and Dostoevsky through Joyce and Kafka, and they include a significant impact on the modernist theater of Ibsen and Shaw. Perhaps the most succinct summary of his influence is the formula applied by an obituary in the *Daily News*, which pronounced him "the one writer everybody read and everybody liked." While the past century has certainly qualified and complicated that simple impression, giving us a more variegated palate for the complex elixir of values, interests, and ideologies that Dickens brewed, it has done nothing to change the sense that Dickens is one Victorian writer everyone thinks it important to know well.

John Kucich

Selected Bibliography

Collins, Philip. "Dickens and His Readers." In Gordon Marsden, ed., *Victorian Values: Perspectives and Personalities in Nineteenth-Century Society*, 43–58. New York: Longman, 1990.
Ford, George. *Dickens and His Readers*. New York: Norton, 1955.
Gillman, Susan K., and Robert L. Patten, "Dickens:Doubles::Twain:Twins." *Nineteenth-Century Fiction* 39 (1985): 441–58.
House, Humphry. *The Dickens World*. Oxford: Oxford University Press, 1941.

Langbauer, Laurie. "Streetwalkers and Homebodies: Dickens's Romantic Women." In *Women and Romance: The Consolations of Gender in the English Novel*, 127–87. Ithaca, N.Y.: Cornell University Press, 1990.

Litvak, Joseph. "Dickens and Sensationalism." In *Caught in the Act: Theatricality in the Nineteenth-Century English Novel*, 109–48. Berkeley: University of California Press, 1992.

Miller, D. A. "Discipline in Different Voices: Bureaucracy, Police, Family, and *Bleak House*." In *The Novel and the Police*, 58–106. Berkeley: University of California Press, 1988.

Miller, J. Hillis. *Charles Dickens: The World of His Novels*. Cambridge, Mass.: Harvard University Press, 1958.

Poovey, Mary. "The Man-of-Letters Hero: *David Copperfield* and the Professional Writer." In *Uneven Developments: The Ideological Work of Gender in Mid-Victorian England*, 89–125. Chicago: University of Chicago Press, 1984.

Welsh, Alexander. *The City of Dickens*. Oxford: Clarendon, 1971.

Wilson, Edmund. "Dickens: The Two Scrooges." In *The Wound and the Bow*, 1–104. New York: Oxford University Press, 1941.

Thackeray and the Ideology of the Gentleman

THE novels of William Makepeace Thackeray (1811–1863) typically feature a sudden loss of fortune, usually a bankruptcy brought about by the failure of a speculative enterprise, and they also exemplify a special interest in—even obsession with—the figure of the gentleman. These are not unrelated narrative motifs. In Thackeray, as in the larger social discourse in which his work participates, the construction of the modern English gentleman served in large part as a response to Britain's shift from a landed to a credit economy with its attendant uncertainties and fluctuations. Although the gentleman was defined and redefined in different ways throughout the course of the century, nineteenth-century discourse on the gentleman always positioned him as a counter to the anonymous and volatile power of money. At the same time, it harnessed for the gentleman that very power by broadening the category to include the new classes created by the explosion of the commercial sphere since the eighteenth century.

Nineteenth-century writers like Thackeray built on the notion of the gentleman developed in the eighteenth century, when the requirement of "gentle birth" and landed property was first placed in serious question. In periodicals like the *Tatler* and the *Spectator*, early essayists like Joseph Addison and Richard Steele, while not severing the link to land and to rank, loosened it considerably. They began to treat as autonomous the ethical component of the gentleman (the code of duty and disinterest), which was originally rooted in the ownership of property and which signaled a commitment to the general rather than particular good. Like their eighteenth-century predecessors, the Victorians privileged an ethical model of the gentleman, but theirs tended to generalize private rather than public virtues. In the complicated political and economic matrix of an industrial society, the whole question of public virtue (knowledge of the general good) had become much more problematic, and Victorian definitions generally displaced the issue by valorizing what could be called relational virtues. The Victorian gentleman, that is, was modest, true, simple, pure, kindly, and upright in his dealings with others. His social authority depended on the moral notion of personal conduct, rather than on the civic notion of independence that had sustained earlier models. "What is it to be a gentleman?" Thackeray asked in his lecture on George IV in 1855, having dismissed the monarch himself, in a resonant phrase, as "a great simulacrum." Thackeray's answer sums up an important strain of Victorian thought in giving prominence to conduct rather than condition, to virtue as verb rather than noun: "To have lofty aims, to lead a pure life, to keep your honour virgin; to have the esteem of your fellow-citizens, and the love of your fireside; to bear good fortune meekly; to suffer evil with constancy; and through evil or good to maintain truth always" (*The Four Georges*).

Such foregrounding of conduct achieved two important things for "the middling classes" in Victorian England: the notion of conduct allowed for easier entry into the category of gentleman, since conduct is amenable to emulation; and it positioned the gentleman as less a leader than an ideal *member* of society, thereby widening the normative category. This does not mean that actual gentlemen were not leaders or that socioeconomic status was unimportant to the category. Such was far from the case. But the conduct-based, domestic model of the gentleman placed a premium on what the German philosopher Hegel called "maintaining individuals," and hence on the disciplinary virtues appropriate to maintaining a highly stratified and fluid economy of industry and credit. The writing of Thackeray and other realist novelists was instrumental in propagating this disciplinary model at mid-century. At the same time it was also instrumental in exposing, if not always consciously, the degree to which the model itself was highly, and interestingly, unstable. The Victorian gentleman is very much a hybrid construction: in him social and moral values uneasily fuse; aristocratic and middle-class interests compromise with and contest each other; and competing forms of masculinity forge a difficult alliance.

Thackeray's persistent interest in the gentleman is part of his enduring fascination with the workings of social power and authority in the mobile, urban world that he knew. It is no accident that the modern meaning of "snob" derives from Thackeray, notably from the success of a satiric series he produced for *Punch* in 1846 and 1847, "The Snobs of England, by one of themselves," which was later published in book form as *The Book of Snobs* (1848). The word originally meant a person of the lower class, and it had a special link to Cambridge University (attended by Thackeray), whose members used it to designate anyone outside the university. Thackeray extended the term to refer to anyone who sought after the trappings of a higher class; that is, to those governed by notions of status. In Thackeray "snob" retains its tone of contempt for the outsider, but the contempt is now motivated less by low social status itself than by the ambition of the outsider to be an insider. It thus becomes a term peculiarly tied to the possibility of social mobility, for its special meaning depends on a world where there is sufficient movement between class layers for social ambition to take widespread root. To Thackeray such ambition is a kind of meanness, a form of vulgarity. His celebrated definition of a snob in chapter 2 of *The Book of Snobs* makes meanness central to the notion: "*He who meanly admires mean things is a Snob.*" This of course begs the question of what constitutes "mean things," but to a gentleman like Thackeray there would be little doubt that a money economy would be behind all meanness. Through his redefinition of snobbery, he forged for himself a powerful and influential instrument for the critique of a money society, with its social insecurities and easy reproduction of the signs of status and taste. And "snobbery" is all the more effective a weapon because it acts as a gatekeeper concept, policing the boundaries of class and value. To search out snobs, as Thackeray was always doing in one way or another, is not simply to mock meanmindedness but to keep the socially pushy outside the discourse of genuine distinction and status, expelling them as interlopers and vulgar intruders.

In his prefatory remarks to *The Book of Snobs*, Mr. Snob claims that he has "an eye for a Snob." The exhaustive taxonomy of types of snobs that follows certainly bears him out, and Mr. Snob's acute "eye" reflects the way in which Thackeray's own life engendered in him a particular sensitivity to matters of class and status. Born and educated a gentleman, Thackeray's status fell with the loss of his paternal inheritance in the collapse of Indian banks in 1833 when he was twenty-two years old.

He now had to earn a living. After an attempt to become an artist in Paris, he moved to London where he spent over a decade making his way in the precarious (and low-status) world of journalism. Writing under a host of comic pseudonyms he produced reviews, travel books, short novels, satiric sketches, parodies, and so forth. With the publication of *Vanity Fair* (1847–1848), the novel for which he remains best known, he achieved fame and regained status, moving into London society. Other successful novels followed, and Thackeray left behind forever the scrambling for assignments and fees of his journalist years.

Thackeray thus experienced in his own life a variety of social milieux, and he knew at first hand something of the volatility and unpredictability of a money economy. He was never quite in the mainstream of his class (his family's Anglo-Indian connection set him apart at the outset from the regular English gentleman), but he was never quite outside it either, even when living in the bohemian world of painters and journalists. Not surprisingly, the characteristic terrain of his fiction is that ambiguous border: the obscure territory between classes, especially what his contemporary W. C. Roscoe called the "debateable land between the aristocracy and the middle classes"; sites of transition like boardinghouses and hotels; or informal public spaces such as clubs or taverns. Charting such fluid terrain in narratives that are themselves fluid and shifting, Thackeray provided his contemporaries with memorable images of the shaping of their culture.

The metaphor of Vanity Fair, which organized his first major success, proved to be the most memorable of these, becoming a byword of the period, and infusing all of Thackeray's later novels as well. Thackeray appropriated the image itself from John Bunyan's famous religious allegory, *The Pilgrim's Progress* (1678), in which the pilgrims pass through a town called Vanity, where a fair selling all kinds of things (including persons) takes place all year round. Thackeray reaccentuated the image for his own secular purposes, exploiting it to make the key point that in modern commercial society, the "fair" is unbounded and all-encompassing. It is no longer located in a particular place (a marketplace) but is now a definitive condition (an abstract market). A consequence of the abstracting power of money and credit, the market not only translates everything into terms of exchange (Bunyan's point) but renders even those terms themselves precarious and temporary. With its plot shaped by a series of rises and falls, the narrative of *Vanity Fair* is permeated with a sense of instability.

The motif of bankruptcy is prominent in the novel both literally and as a metaphor (Becky's fall, for example, is called a "bankruptcy"), and its prominence is in part a response to the unprecedented volatility of the British economy in the first half of the nineteenth century. The 1820s experienced the first modern trade cycle and a huge bank failure, whose ripple effect entangled well-known firms and individuals, including the best-selling novelist Sir Walter Scott. Each decade from 1820 to 1850 witnessed liquidity crises, spectacular rises and crashes in business and banking, booms and depressions in trade and agriculture, and radical changes in industrial technology that led to painful unemployment, notably in the textile sector. As a result economic and political ferment was constantly waxing and waning, and the 1840s (the decade in which *Vanity Fair* was written) were especially turbulent. Among other things, the decade saw the rise of organized working-class political agitation with the Chartists; the Irish famine and a mass of Irish immigrants in its wake; violent increases and drops in the price of corn; and a rapid expansion of the railways that produced not only thousands of miles of track but also the speculative frenzy known as the "railway mania." Hundreds of different kinds of railway shares were in circulation in the 1840s, and the inevitable crash soon came. There was a serious bank crisis in 1847, and the decade produced spectacular individual failures as well. One of the most striking was that of the self-made "Railway King," George Hudson, and there was also the failure of the second Duke of Buckingham, whose estate went on the block in 1848 while *Vanity Fair* was in its serial run. Although Sir Robert Peel and his government made some attempt in the mid-1840s to curb through legislation what Peel termed "reckless speculation," speculative "bubbles" continued to form and burst. One of the distinguishing features of the failures of the 1830s and 1840s was that these involved many more small speculators; hence they affected a much wider social range of people than the failure of "bubbles" in earlier periods had tended to do. A minor moment in *Vanity Fair* nicely sums up this sense of the widespread ripples of apparently distant financial disasters. In chapter 56 the narrator refers to the failure of "the great Calcutta House of Fogle, Fake, and Cracksman." The bank failed for a million pounds, he reports, plunging "half the Indian public into misery and ruin." It turns out that the directors of the bank managed to enrich themselves, but the smaller investors lost everything. The narrator mentions one such smaller investor, Scape, a character who never appears but whose carpets Jos Sedley buys at the forced sale of his estate. Scape is left destitute at the age of sixty-five, for he, unlike the directors, has made sure that all the tradesmen have been "honourably paid." In this concern for payment of debts, Scape is also unlike the novel's heroine Becky Sharp. Becky routinely decamps without paying those she owes, leaving devastated lives in her wake.

In moments like these, *Vanity Fair* suggests something of the uncertainties and complex interdependencies of a money and credit economy. It also points to the way in which credit itself replaces tangible notions of property and exchange with intangible ones. Concrete and material notions like land and goods give way to abstract and immaterial ones like credit and sign and the circulation of information. Becky Sharp, supreme manipulator of signs, is quite at home in such an economy, and she herself functions as its main sign in the novel. Becky is the bearer of the new, as signaled from the very opening of the novel when she flings away Dr. Johnson's venerable eighteenth-century dictionary. Without roots or a sense of place, Becky is infinitely adaptable and extraordinarily resilient, as she repeatedly rises, falls, and then recoups to try again. Becky always knows that in her world things are less important as substances than as signs, and she consistently "reads" the world in this way. She (like her author) is keenly aware of the semiotic dimension of culture, and of all the central characters, she is also the most adept at handling money, the pure signifier. For Becky the world is less given than constructed; words and signs do not so much reflect as produce meaning and the world. The most important skills, therefore, are pragmatic ones that enable one to decipher and manipulate the signs that count: money, reputation, status, and so forth. To achieve such pragmatic skill, one needs a sense of how the structure of values in a society works, and Becky achieves this early. By the time she is left alone in Brussels amid rumours of a Napoleonic victory, she has a finely honed sense of the economic rules of supply and demand. When Jos Sedley comes to her in a panic, wanting to buy horses so that he can leave the city, Becky demands a high price: "Rebecca, measuring the value of the goods which she had for sale by Jos's eagerness to purchase, as well as by the scarcity of the article, put upon her horses a price so prodigious as to make even the civilian [Jos] draw back." Jos pays, of course, and in this way he gives Becky her start as a businesswoman dealing in what one might call the informal sectors of the economy, a career that culminates in her accumulation of a hoard of jewels and money from the cynical but indulgent rake, Lord Steyne.

With Steyne, as in all her dealings, Becky depends on a certain kind of credit. She consistently obtains goods and services and money by manufacturing an appropriate reputation. So it is entirely in keeping that when she and Rawdon live in Paris after Waterloo, they do so entirely on credit. Thackeray recounts the story of their sojourn there in chapter 36, aptly titled "How to Live Well on Nothing a Year." The chapter records some of Becky's most effective demonstrations of her skill in handling the abstract counters of credit, for the main source of the couple's income in Paris is the rumor of Rawdon's expectation of an immense legacy from his rich old aunt, Miss Crawley (who has in fact disinherited him). Rawdon's gambling receipts provide a minimum of ready money, but these receipts begin to dwindle, and Becky realizes that their capital will soon be "zero." They must seek their fortune back in England.

Unfortunately, there is the little matter of bills in Paris and debts in London. To elude the current bills, Becky mounts an elaborate charade of the "death" of the rich aunt, and she succeeds superbly, getting out of Paris with the unpaid landlord and landlady "smiling farewell" as she goes. Their smiles do not last long, and the landlord ends up cursing "the English nation" for "the rest of his natural life." Meanwhile, Becky goes to London where she persuades Rawdon's creditors to settle his debts for one-tenth of their value, a success in negotiation that prompts a lawyer involved in the deal to declare that "there was no professional man who could beat her." The stage is now set for the assault on English society mounted by Becky on the strength of her investment in Lord Steyne. When that investment fails, a host of other people also lose, as did the unpaid small businesses and working people left behind in Paris. This time the landlord pays an even higher price, for Raggles and his family face ruin. Raggles, former butler to Miss Crawley, has extended credit to Becky and Rawdon for four years, and on the day after her fall, he laments that he has bills coming due and no means to meet them: "He would be sold up and turned out of his shop and his house, because he had trusted to the Crawley family."

It is in this general context of dependence on and betrayal of trust in a credit economy that the moralized figure of the Thackerayan gentleman takes his place. Marked by his code of duty, honor, and honesty, the gentleman helps to induce stability into the system. He acts in a sense as an institution, representing an attempt to formally constitute two concepts traditionally set up as oppositions in political and moral thought: virtue and commerce. Through the gentlemanly code, writers like Thackeray attempted to bring virtue into commerce or, more precisely, to encourage the formation of virtues useful to a high-risk and volatile economy. The emphasis on honesty and purity and stoicism represents an attempt to counter the instabilities and uncertainties of the economy at the level of individual performance and response. It operates as a kind of social discipline, encouraging the formation of certain habits and types of behavior, much as the voluntary societies of tradesmen formed in the previous century often encouraged prudence and integrity by making character rather than class or occupation the basis of entry into the society. The code of gentlemanly conduct also acts as a form of reliable information in a system where information is crucial but uncertain. A money economy depends on information and more particularly on kept promises, and the promise of a gentleman (in theory) can be relied upon. A gentleman, then, is literally one who is worthy of credit, and gentlemanliness itself becomes a sign of creditworthiness. The difficulty, of course, is that there proves to be no distinctive, unequivocal sign of gentlemanliness. And the problem is compounded by the fact that the modern gentleman, detached both from the land and from any specific occupation, is a highly abstract construct. The abstract nature of the gentleman indeed provides a useful flexibility for countering the elusive abstractions of a credit economy. But how is one to know that one is dealing with a gentleman? Certain signs (manners, accent, family pedigree) can be readily copied or faked, and the inner "truth" that constitutes the ground of the gentleman does not yield itself up to ready representations. Hence there arises in a writer like Thackeray a virtual obsession with identifying the "true" gentleman.

Vanity Fair is his first full-scale attempt to do so (his earlier narratives offered only partial accounts), and in it two main methods dominate. First, Thackeray provides a historical context for his argument by dramatizing a shift in the notion of the gentleman within the aristocracy itself in the early decades of the nineteenth century. Second, he works didactically by constructing in William Dobbin a model of the exemplary modern gentleman. The Crawley men lie at the center of the historical argument, and in the shift from the old Sir Pitt to the new Sir Pitt Thackeray exemplifies a change in the mode of gentility practiced by the landed classes that signals their accommodation with the mercantile classes.

Old Sir Pitt Crawley, member of Parliament for the "rotten borough" of Queen's Crawley, is a gentleman by virtue of birth, and that for him is sufficient. Nor do his crude manners, brutal behavior, inferior education, and poverty affect his status. This "sordid and foul" man, the narrator reports, is regarded as "a dignitary of the land, and a pillar of the state." He has encumbered his estate under a huge load of debt, some of it inherited but much the result of either his frequent litigations or his disastrous financial speculations. He turns his domestic space into a space of rivalry, tyranny, and cruelty. Linked to primary drives and to the body, he is depicted under the negative sign of unreason. Sir Pitt can barely write, and his speech is earthy and direct; his emotions are fierce and elemental, and sexual motifs accompany him right up to his undignified death.

By contrast, his elder son, the younger Pitt, is cast in the rational motifs of restraint and prudence. Equally repellent in his own way—calculating, cold, and hypocritical—the younger Pitt reflects changes in the culture of his class since his father's youth. He writes a pamphlet on malt, illustrating the new authority of economic discourse in his day; he cultivates the new politics represented by Wilberforce and the fight against the slave trade; and his ostentatious religiosity points to the way in which the evangelical religious revival of the late eighteenth and early nineteenth century penetrated even the upper classes. By his behavior and interests, in short, Pitt testifies to a new seriousness and sobriety in hereditary gentlemen, including a new sense of financial responsibility. Upon coming into his paternal inheritance, he immediately clears the estate of debt, and he improves both the country estate and the town house.

Unlike his slovenly and inarticulate father, who was associated with the land and the outdoors, the younger Sir Pitt is linked to texts and to interior spaces like the study. And in all things, he is thoroughly respectable and conventional. His desk, for instance, is covered with precisely those texts appropriate to a serious parliamentarian and Tory gentleman of the new modern age: parliamentary blue books, drafts of legislative bills, political pamphlets, the *Quarterly Review*, the *Court Guide*, and sermons. The appropriateness extends to his very appearance: "fresh, neat, smugly shaved, with a waxy clean face . . . in a starched cravat and a grey flannel dressing-gown—a real old English gentleman, in a word—a model of neatness and every propriety." Smug and calculating, Pitt lacks the generous virtues that were central to Thackeray's concept of the gentleman, and on this point Pitt's disreputable younger brother provides an exemplary lesson.

Through Rawdon Crawley, Thackeray suggests that one may in fact acquire genuine virtue rather than simply its outward signs, as does the younger Pitt. At the beginning of the novel, Rawdon is defined as a typical aristocratic young "blood" of the Regency period. He belongs to the fashionable Life Guards, and he lives a fast life, accumulating debts and gambling, while he waits for the inheritance he expects from his aunt. He has fought three duels, and he is adept at boxing, rat hunting, and other sports that were "the fashion of the British aristocracy" at the time. Like his disreputable old father, Rawdon operates within the older mode of masculinity, based on body rather than mind, which stands in direct contrast to the newer disembodied and mental mode exemplified by his elder brother. As in his father's case, Rawdon is uncomfortable with language as either spoken or written sign. Where his elder brother is immersed in textuality, Rawdon can barely read or write or articulate. The will that he writes before leaving for the battle of Waterloo is written in "big schoolboy handwriting"; and later in the novel when he sends a challenge to Lord Steyne after his traumatic discovery of Becky's betrayal, he and his second, Captain Macmurdo, compose the letter of challenge "with great labour and a Johnson's Dictionary, which stood them in much stead." Not surprisingly, Rawdon is regularly routed by those who do possess skill in language, as do Becky herself and Wenham, the fluent politician sent by Lord Steyne to get his lordship out of the duel. Wenham spins a smooth lie; Rawdon knows he is lying, but he does not know how to discredit or disprove the story.

Rawdon's failure in language, however, points to a simplicity of character that is potentially, if not necessarily, virtuous. Uncomplicated characters often possess qualities necessary for the Thackerayan gentleman, and Rawdon demonstrates in his response to Waterloo a military sense of honor that could be put to use in civil and domestic society. Waterloo in effect marks the beginning of the slow, halting move that he makes in the course of the novel from the social category of gentleman-by-birth to the ethical category of gentleman-by-virtue. The catalyst in his reformation is domesticity: love for his wife, Becky, begins the process, but fatherhood accelerates and confirms it. Rawdon's love for his son is absolute and all the more moving for being so inarticulate. Through this love Rawdon discovers a motivation other than self-interest, and learns the important moral idea of consequences.

Appropriately, Rawdon's relationship to money plays a key role in signaling his change of status. He spends his early life gambling and fleecing the naive and the snobbish (like George Osborne) by entrapping them in games they cannot win. He leaves unpaid his debts to tradesmen and landlords, never worrying about the consequences to them. As for his own frequent arrests for debt, Rawdon regards these as being in the normal course of things, and simply looks for someone to bail him out. But after the shock of Becky's perfidy, Rawdon assumes a new relationship to others and to the world. Becky's hoard of money is a crucial signifier here. Where Becky's lies about and her secret hoarding of money confirm her mercenary nature, Rawdon's subsequent dispersal of the funds she had reserved for herself confirms his status as a genuine gentleman.

The key scene is the interview with Pitt on the morning after the confrontation with Becky. Rawdon's brother assumes that he has come to borrow money, and starts to put him off. Rawdon interrupts: "'It's not money, I want,' Rawdon broke in. 'I'm not come to you about myself.'" He has come in the first place to ask Pitt to look after his son, and in the second place to ask him to help him settle accounts. Rawdon has with him Becky's funds. He gives Pitt over six hundred pounds to pay back Briggs, the companion whose legacy Becky borrowed and never replaced, despite having obtained money from Lord Steyne for that express purpose. He gives another portion for his son's upkeep, holding back "a few pounds" for Becky herself "to get on with." As he hands over this money, Rawdon drops some banknotes, including a thousand-pound note recently given to Becky by Lord Steyne. This note, Rawdon tells Pitt, is not included. He has other plans for its dispersal, planning to wrap the bullet he will use to kill Steyne in the note as an act of "fine revenge." The aristocratic code of revenge and honor moves into foreground at this moment, and it does so favorably, setting Rawdon apart from the mean-minded modern Pitt, who characteristically "stooped" to pick up the fallen banknotes. In his handling of money in this scene, Rawdon reinvigorates for a moment the old aristocratic rank of gentleman, restoring to it the sense of moral value from which he had severed it at the outset of his career. But confirmation that he has indeed been reformed is provided only by his subsequent behav-

ior as governor of Coventry Island. From his post, Rawdon "punctual-
ly" remits money for his debts, and he "regularly" writes to young Rawdon. Newly disciplined but no bourgeois, Rawdon in this whole
sequence enacts the combination of virtues (including the old landed
virtues of disdain for money for its own sake, duty to dependents, and
sense of honor) that Thackeray identified with the complete gentleman.

But Rawdon is linked to an archaic system, and so he cannot serve
as exemplary modern figure. This role is played by William Dobbin,
son of a wealthy grocer, who begins with neither social status nor much
in the way of looks, being physically awkward and afflicted with a lisp.
The point is reinforced by the illustrations that Thackeray drew for the
early chapters, for they highlight the oddness of the young Dobbin's
appearance. Clearly he is not born a gentleman. But he goes to a decent
public school (where he endures ridicule for his lowly family connection), and he later enters the gentlemanly profession of soldier. Dobbin
joins a line regiment, socially a long way from the aristocratic Guards
of Rawdon Crawley, but his regiment does a good deal more soldiering,
serving in various colonies of the empire where Dobbin spends years in
worthy but not glorious service. He returns near the end of the book as
Major Dobbin, more assured and also, at least according to the illustrations, more conventionally attractive as well.

If his appearance has changed, however, his character has not. Dobbin's keynote is fidelity; loyalty is his primary virtue. He is faithful to
the vain and arrogant George Osborne, and even more so to Amelia
Sedley, who becomes George's adoring wife and then his even more
adoring widow. Dobbin loves Amelia from the first, but he refuses to
court her for himself, even when the feckless George loses interest in
her and their engagement is broken off. Indeed, it is Dobbin who, in a
difficult demonstration of his lack of "selfish calculation," arranges the
marriage of the two. He finds the negotiation "about as painful a task
as could be set to him, yet when he had a duty to perform, Captain
Dobbin was accustomed to go through it without many words or much
hesitation."

Words like *duty, honest,* and *faithful* accompany Dobbin throughout
the narrative, much of which he spends either on the periphery of
scenes or outside them altogether. Always Dobbin controls his own
desire, subordinates his will to that of others, and takes duty as his guide
in both the public and the private spheres. In this way he is taken out

of the matrix of self-interest and desire routinely linked to trade and commerce, purged of the "special" interest of business and attached to the "general" interest of the nation. When the narrator comes to offer a definition of a real gentleman late in the novel, he cites Dobbin as exemplary. Gentlemen, the narrator comments, are men whose "aims are generous, whose truth is constant, and not only constant in its kind but elevated in its degree; whose want of meanness makes them simple; who can look the world honestly in the face with an equal manly sympathy for the great and the small." How many such men does one know? the narrator asks. For him, "my friend the Major" tops the list, a list that, at this point at least, explicitly contains only the one name.

But if Dobbin is the exemplary Thackerayan gentleman, he also points to the problems inherent in that model, problems that will place an increasing strain on the novels following *Vanity Fair*. As Dobbin's extraordinary patience and self-subordination demonstrate, the gentleman is essentially defined by negation—by what he does not do or desire or will. He identifies himself as a gentleman not so much by what he does as by how he responds to what is being done, and he is distinguished by a stoicism that borders on passivity. The gentleman, that is, represents an ideal that is essentially regulatory rather than productive; hence his ethic of reserve and restraint, and his difficulties with action. Hence too the curious lassitude and failure of energy that typically threaten the Thackerayan gentleman. Self-controlled and placing himself outside desire, the gentleman is detached from the passion of primary emotions and from sexuality. The Vauxhall episode early in *Vanity Fair* provides a symptomatic moment. At the gate to the park, George Osborne asks Dobbin to "just look to the shawls and things, there's a good fellow" while the two couples wander off, leaving Dobbin to pay their entrance fee as well. During supper, as the couples engage in their very different courtships, Dobbin vainly tries to engage their attention. But he remains excluded from sexual—and communal—space: "Nobody took any notice of him."

The gentleman's ethic of restraint is essentially an ethic of distance. To prove his disinterestedness, the gentleman must first be detached from the impure motives that motivate ordinary persons; second, he must position himself outside or to the side of contentious events, so that his judgment is not clouded by prejudice or partisanship. Moreover, as the lean figure of Dobbin suggests, the nineteenth-century gentleman (at least in the Thackerayan mode) takes on something of an ascetic cast. He has to set himself outside the culture of getting and spending, to make sure that he clearly distinguishes himself from the vulgar at both ends of the socioeconomic scale: that is, both from those who conspicuously consume and those who conspicuously have nothing to consume. A figure like Dobbin, who has wealth enough, defines himself as a pure and free gentleman precisely by *choosing* to live austerely.

The ascetic point is made even more clearly—and poignantly—by a telling detail in Thackeray's longest novel, *The Newcomes* (1853–1855). This is a complicated narrative of several generations of a London banking family, and it offers Thackeray's most elaborate investigation of Victorian commerce and "respectability." The novel is dominated by Colonel Newcome, a quixotic old soldier (much beloved by Thackeray's first readers) who has returned to England after thirty-five years of service in the East India Company. Himself unfulfilled in love and long the widower of a wife he did not much care for, the colonel dotes on his only son, Clive. Ominously, Clive falls hopelessly in love with a cousin who is out of his social reach, threatening to repeat the paternal pattern of romantic frustration. The colonel, simple and straightforward and always a gentleman, distrusts the complicated world of finance and commerce, and he lives frugally, his own wants being modest. But in a misguided attempt to gain the money he thinks will help his son win the bride he desires, Colonel Newcome invests in a new Indian bank (and naively encourages others to invest as well). Huge dividends pour in, the colonel buys a splendid mansion in Tyburnia, Clive fails to win the woman he loves and marries (unhappily) to please his father. The inevitable crash soon comes. When the creditors go through the now-empty mansion, they come upon the colonel's room. In a house filled with lavish rooms and furnishings, they discover, the colonel himself maintained the spartan habits of an old soldier: he slept on an iron bedstead in a "bare room" at the very top of the house.

Most of Thackeray's gentlemen live in a "bare room," often literally but usually metaphorically, operating under the sign of austerity. But the austere space of gentlemanliness is not a vital space, and Thackeray's gentlemen tend to be marked by a lack of energy and a profound melancholy. Dobbin himself suffers a long weariness of spirit, and he gains Amelia only after he has ceased to desire her. The life of Colonel Newcome is essentially a long disappointment, stoically borne; in its final days, it sharpens into acute suffering as the colonel is harrowed by recriminations and his own gnawing guilt over the matter of the bank. Another colonel in another Thackeray novel, *The History of Henry Esmond, Esq., A Colonel in the Service of her Majesty Q. Anne, Written by Himself* (1852), is similarly distinguished by melancholy and weariness. Henry Esmond's story may be set in the previous century, but neither the turn to the past nor the adoption of first-person autobiographical narration releases Thackeray in this novel from his brooding over the dilemmas of gentlemen in his own day. For all that Henry Esmond is caught up in dramatic intrigues of eighteenth-century European war and politics (including a plan to restore the Stuarts that almost succeeds), he tells his own story in a curiously detached tone, often speaking of himself in the third person as if he were already dead. His life is a series of renunciations: he renounces the title that is his birthright (so as not to displace his cousin), the hereditary loyalty to his king (who has behaved without honor and so forfeited allegiance), and the passionate love for the worldly and willful Beatrix (who has persistently refused him). Like Dobbin, Esmond marries after desire is all but played out.

For Thackeray the gentleman has to be austere, independent, controlled, apart from his body. The difficulty is that this tends to position him also outside energy, sexuality, and action.

What, then, is a gentleman to do? The issue of action for the Thackerayan gentleman is a serious one, for he is detached not only from the energy of "nature" (the body, desire) but from that of modern commercial civilization as well—at least in terms of direct participation. Gentlemen may handle money with integrity, but they do not make it; nor do they engage in manufacture. For Thackeray the whole realm of money and finance is particularly dubious, as indicated by his persistent activation of the demeaning typology of race to characterize it: money-hungry Jews, untrustworthy Indians, flashy West Indians, and so on. The Bundelcund Bank in which Colonel Newcome naively invests, for example, is run by a shady character named Rummun Loll (denounced by the gentlemanly Fred Bayham as a "mahogany-coloured heathen humbug"). The bank turns out to be a huge swindle (Loll dies, appropriately enough, on the night he planned an elaborate "masquerade"), and the narrator records his outrage at the whole affair. The Bundelcund Bank, he then goes on to say, was but "one of many similar cheats" that have victimized people like the colonel, "the simple folks" who "pass years of long exile and gallant endurance in the service of our empire in India." Imperial "service" opposes the "cheat" of commerce, reinforcing the incompatibility of the two codes that was made apparent earlier when Colonel Newcome responded to a crisis in the shares of the bank by invoking the military analogy of desertion: the colonel claimed that "to desert" the bank "at the hour of peril" was "like applying for leave of absence on the eve of an action. He would not see that the question was not one of sentiment at all, but of chances and arithmetic."

Many of Thackeray's exemplary gentleman are (like Colonel Newcome) soldiers, a traditional profession for gentlemen. Through soldiering they not only are reattached to the world of action and energy but become a sign of the nation itself: gentlemen of England. Indeed, one outlet for the gentlemanly ethic was patriotic service, and later in the century the public schools were to turn out hundreds of young men who identified themselves with the nation, learned "to play the game," and filled the civilian and military posts of empire. Thackeray's military gentlemen have a less corporate (and sporting) identity, and they are rather less aggressive in their imperialism. Their activity as soldiers takes place on the periphery of the narratives, and the novels in general contain a strong antimilitary note. Thus *Vanity Fair* deliberately refuses the glamour of war and conquest, assailing the "Devil's code of honour" that produces "alternations of successful and unsuccessful murder" between nations; while *Henry Esmond* is scathing about the whitewashing of a "bloody and ruthless" campaign in Joseph Addison's well-known poem called *The Campaign*.

At the same time, physical courage and prowess are important in a gentleman, and the code of the soldier gives positive value both to exemplary types like Dobbin and Colonel Newcome and to flawed figures like Rawdon Crawley and the vain George Osborne. Moreover, through the code, gentlemen not only attest to their sense of duty to the nation but also confirm a certain masculinity. Of the behavior of the characters at Waterloo, for example, the narrator reports: "All our friends took their share and fought like men in the great field." But fighting "like a man" may not always be compatible with acting "like a gentleman," a discrepancy that underlines the way the category of gentleman encompasses competing forms of masculinity whose collision accounts for the kind of paralyzing impasse in which Thackeray's gentlemen so often find themselves.

Indeed the category of gentleman raises not just the question of action but the question of gender, for the masculinity of the gentleman lies in uneasy proximity to the femininity of the domestic woman, perhaps the central cultural icon of the period. The gentleman is modest, simple, honest, and pure; he is motivated by duty to family and nation; he takes care of the weak and vulnerable; and he endures the fortunes of life with stoicism. He sounds in fact very much like the domestic heroine of so much realist fiction, and the image of Dobbin carrying shawls while others party at Vauxhall underscores his affinity with the long-suffering women of the Victorian novel. In important ways the authority of the gentleman overlapped with feminine authority in the period, and this helps to account for the insistence on "manliness" in the discourse on gentlemen. Thackeray himself repeatedly invokes this resonantly Victorian quality as an adjunct to gentlemanliness, setting it up as the "natural" core of the gentleman (much as "womanliness" functioned as the "natural" core of femininity). Typically accompanied by adjectives like *open* and *frank* and *honest*, manliness operates outside the self-restraint and self-consciousness of gentlemanliness. It regains for the gentleman access to emotion ("manly tears"), expression, and the body. But most of all it anchors him to virility; manliness, that is, guarantees the masculinity of the gentleman.

The frequent tavern scenes in Thackeray assume their significance precisely in relation to this question of gender and the gentleman, for they provide sites outside the domestic space of femininity in which men (including gentlemen) can establish themselves as properly masculine subjects. If race marks one limit of gentlemanliness, gender marks another. In both cases, however, the gentleman, inhabiting as he does a blurred and nebulous category, must actively strive to maintain the boundaries of exclusion. The tavern (and, to a lesser extent, the club) comes into play here, for it allows for the clear demarcation of gender, even as it plays with demarcations of class. In the pubs men from different spheres of life regularly meet to sing and drink and eat, creating informal clubs with names like the "Cave of Harmony" or the "Haunt" or the "Back Kitchen." Such places begin to play their prominent role in Thackeray's second major novel, *The History of Pendennis* (1848– 1850), where they are part of the urban life of London bachelors and men of letters. The protagonist of the novel, Arthur Pendennis, is introduced to them by George Warrington, a déclassé gentleman, who takes him to the "Back Kitchen" where "men of all sorts and conditions" meet in amity. The list includes country tradesmen and farmers, apprentices, medical students, university bucks, young guardsmen, members of Parliament, and even peers from the House of Lords.

Temporarily suspending the rules of everyday life, such places define masculinity as sociability and freedom from the routine constraints of life, notably those of domesticity. Here men smoke and drink and joke. The narrator of *The Newcomes* (who is the very Pendennis introduced to the "Back Kitchen" in the earlier novel) recalls entering the "Haunt" in his youth and being greeted "with a roar of welcome from a crowd of men, almost invisible in the smoke." In "haunts" like this, he continues, sculptors, painters, men of letters, and others would pass "pleasant hours in rough kindly communion." Allowing for freer forms of language and behavior than more formal public places or the domestic space, Thackeray's taverns take on something of a carnivalesque air. They are intervals in time and space, marked by a relative earthiness and by the communal puncturing of pretension. A philosopher who tries to lecture the crowd at the "Haunt," for instance, is defeated by general banter, while an essayist who gives himself airs is "silenced by the unanimous pooh poohing of the assembly."

In their suspension of the vertical distinctions of rank, the taverns also recall the coffeehouses and clubs of the eighteenth century, which shaped what the German social theorist Jürgen Habermas calls the "classical public sphere." The phrase refers to the liberal, bourgeois sphere of discourse that formed in opposition to the power of the aristocracy and the state early in the eighteenth century. The classical public sphere consisted of a whole set of institutions (such as coffeehouses and journals) that allowed for the public exchange of ideas and offered (theoretically) a space where the ordinary hierarchies of social and political life were suspended in the interest of the free pursuit of rational discourse. The roots of the Thackerayan gentleman in fact lie in this classical public sphere, for they are to be found in the informal essays of Addison and Steele. Their essays in journals like the *Tatler* and the *Spectator* not only set in place the standard terms of the critique of the aristocratic gentleman in the eighteenth century but themselves played an important role in the formation of the liberal public sphere in England. Thackeray transforms the ideal rational space of the public sphere into the bohemian space of the tavern. This informal gathering place resists not so much the state as the domestic sphere; its members are drawn together less by reason than by gender; and its characteristic language is not the rationality of "discourse" but the sounds of song (including a perennial favorite, "The Old English Gentleman"). Thackeray's taverns, assertively places of the male body and of male speech, constitute the primary site of "manliness" in his novels, and define those within them as clearly masculine subjects.

In an important move, Thackeray associates this manliness with the world of letters. Indeed Thackeray's model of manliness is "the manly, the English Harry Fielding." This phrase concludes his lecture on the novelist in the series on *The English Humourists* (1851), and it sums up the image of hearty, rural "Englishness" and robust "manliness" that Thackeray has foregrounded in his portrait of his eighteenth-century predecessor. Appropriately, the "Back Kitchen" of *Pendennis* meets at the "Fielding's Head," and a chair supposed to have been Fielding's is used by "the president of the night's entertainment." It is George Warrington who introduces Arthur Pendennis to the "Back Kitchen," and the occasion is part of Warrington's more general initiation of the aimless young protagonist into the world of letters. Warrington is the younger son of Sir Miles Warrington, and like many gentlemen he is ostensibly engaged in law. But he earns his living by writing for the periodical press, a fact he keeps generally quiet, given the low status of such activity. Although the example of Sir Walter Scott (poet, novelist, essayist) early in the century had done much to open up the higher genres of the literary profession to gentlemen, the lowly image of Grub Street still stuck. Thackeray himself was never quite sure that a literary career was indeed entirely suitable for a gentleman. All the same, its links to learning and to language made it a potential area of operation; moreover, its dependence on print culture meant that it offered a more modern career than a profession like that of soldier. Through the world of letters Thackeray in effect experimented with ways of connecting the gentleman more definitively with modernity.

Warrington himself is very much a "manly" gentleman. His first words in the novel are "Is that the beer?" and he is introduced sitting at a table in worn clothes, "unshorn and smoking a pipe." "He was drinking beer like a coalheaver," the narrator comments, "and yet you couldn't but perceive that he was a gentleman." At Oxbridge he was known as "Stunning Warrington," famous for both hard living and hard reading, but he now lives an obscure life in the shabby chambers he shares with Pendennis. In contrast to the room of the dandy Pendennis ("rather coquettishly arranged"), Warrington's own bedroom is plain, containing a bed, a shower bath, and a pile of books of poetry and mathematics.

Warrington thus partakes in the austerity and asceticism that mark the Thackerayan gentleman, and he shares the characteristic exclusion from desire and sexuality. He is a quasi bachelor, having married a woman of the lower class from whom he has long been separated. In the course of the novel he falls in love with the heroine, Laura (future wife of Pendennis), but he is of course prohibited from pursuing her. Unlike the soldier Dobbin, however, the literary Warrington exhibits a transgressive edge. He deliberately flaunts gentlemanly decorum, establishing in the process his "manliness." Warrington's desk is stained with circles made by ale pots, he drinks with boxers and other low status types, and he endorses marketplaces over Mayfair. All in all, Warrington explicitly prefers the world of low-class pubs to the society of his own class, "whose manners annoyed him, and whose conversation bored him." There is a conscious "slumming" in all this that reinforces Warrington's own status as a gentleman, and Thackeray knows it. His narrator reports that even though Warrington never thought of himself as in any sense superior to "Jack and Tom," nevertheless, "the deference which they paid him might secretly please him." Warrington, that is, engages in a sophisticated game of class whereby one can engage in activities considered "lowly" precisely because there is no danger that one will be defined by them. Everyone knows Warrington is a gentleman, so that his crossing of class lines (an apparent erasure of social difference) in fact works to affirm the point of social difference. As with asceticism, this kind of transgressive behavior functions primarily as a sign of the gentleman's freedom rather than as social critique.

The case of Warrington points to the way in which the nineteenth-century discourse of the gentleman at once opened up the category and closed it. Gentlemanliness was severed from outward signs to become an intangible property, an essence that one intuitively perceives: no matter what Warrington does, "you couldn't but perceive that he was a gentleman." To make the category viable for the modern world and yet to retain the exclusiveness on which its authority depended, Victorian writers like Thackeray stratified the category itself, allowing entry into the lower strata of gentlemanliness (primarily through education) but reserving the upper strata (or inner "spirit"). This lies outside acquirement and is not open to definition; discourse can only gesture toward it. In a symptomatic moment early in *The Newcomes*, Colonel Newcome asks the young Clive what makes a gentleman: " 'I can't tell you what it is, or how it is,' the boy answered, 'only one can't help seeing the difference. It isn't rank and that; only somehow there are some men gentlemen and some not, and some women ladies and some not.'" If it isn't "rank and that," what is it? Gentlemanliness remains finally elusive: somehow some are, and some are not.

In that "somehow" the category becomes remystified. Indeed, it achieves a new level of mystification, for gentlemanliness is now an elusive but real quality of moral superiority rather than a relatively straightforward designation of social position. It becomes the ultimate insider notion, more exclusive than if birth or money or education were definitive grounds of entry. One may be of high birth and good education and still not be a "true" gentleman, though one's chances are certainly better than if one is of low birth and poor education. In the latter case, it is impossible to be a gentleman of any sort, "true" or not. Witness J. J. Ridley of *The Newcomes*. He is a gifted artist who achieves success; more important, he possesses the very qualities of character officially endorsed as gentlemanly (simplicity, honesty, modesty, kindness, and so forth). But J. J. Ridley is the son of a butler, and so he cannot be a gentleman.

In effect, the redefined category of the gentleman in the nineteenth century infused class with virtue, providing for distinction and difference a moral argument that was nevertheless finally elusive. Socially authoritative, the category had real effects but could not itself be located either in a material or in a discursive grid. Witness the contrast, for example, with the old category of the landed gentleman, which was rooted in an argument about the dependence of public virtue on private property. Like money, the modern gentleman was a form of intangible property. This, in turn, meant that the category was in constant contestation, and it produced a complicated discourse that remained prominent throughout the century.

The Victorian period saw an outpouring of commentary on the "true" gentleman, on "nature's gentleman," on "the English gentleman," and so forth. Writers and painters drew on models from chivalry, from militant and nonmilitant forms of Christianity, from Nordic sagas, from the lore of combat. Others, like Thackeray himself, worked out of the domesticated model adapted to modern civil society developed in the eighteenth century, countering what they saw as its emasculating force through vigorous notions like "manliness." The amount of discourse suggests the ambiguity and flexibility that made this so compelling a category for men of several classes and different class fractions,

as they engaged in the complex negotiation of social power and authority. The self-made prophet of self-help, Samuel Smiles, preached that a
poor man might be a "true gentleman" by virtue of his virtues; Cardinal
Newman saw in the gentleman a secular ethic of withdrawal that
undermined religious commitment; Charles Kingsley sought to harness
the powers of the male body to a socialist conscience in his notion of
"muscular Christianity"; and Thomas Carlyle urged "Captains of
Industry" to adopt a "Chivalry of Work." Thackeray's voice in all this is
often troubled—and troubling—but for his own generation he was very
much the novelist as gentleman. Indeed, writes John Cordy Jeaffreson
in *Novels and Novelists from Elizabeth to Victoria* (1858), Thackeray was
not only "the true gentleman of our generation," but the figure who
"made us once more 'a nation of gentlemen'."

Ina Ferris

Selected Bibliography

Carlisle, Janice. *The Sense of an Audience: Dickens, Thackeray, and George Eliot at Mid-
Century.* Athens: University of Georgia Press, 1981.

Colby, Robert A. *Thackeray's Canvass of Humanity: An Author and His Public.* Columbus: Ohio State University Press, 1979.

Gilmour, Robin. *The Idea of the Gentleman in the Victorian Novel.* London: Allen and
Unwin, 1981.

Girouard, Mark. *The Return to Camelot: Chivalry and the English Gentleman.* New
Haven, Conn.: Yale University Press, 1981.

Levine, George. *The Realistic Imagination: English Fiction from Frankenstein to Lady
Chatterley.* Chicago: University of Chicago Press, 1981.

Lund, Michael. *Reading Thackeray.* Detroit: Wayne State University Press, 1988.

McMaster, Juliet. *Thackeray: The Major Novels.* Toronto: University of Toronto Press,
1971.

Rawlins, Jack P. *Thackeray's Novels: A Fiction That Is True.* Berkeley: University of California Press, 1974.

Ray, Gordon N. *The Uses of Adversity 1811–1846.* New York: McGraw-Hill, 1955.

———*Thackeray: The Age of Wisdom 1847–1863.* New York: McGraw-Hill, 1958.

George Eliot and the Novel of Ideas

S O powerful is George Eliot's writing and presence in our retro-spect of the nineteenth-century British novel that she seems to guarantee a whole tradition: that of ideas realized in fiction. Yet if we imagine her absence, a remarkable remapping occurs. Who are the novelists of ideas then? Bulwer Lytton, George Meredith, Samuel Butler, perhaps Grant Allen: inventive writers all, but writers also whose intelligence often seems ill matched to the fictions they shape. In most of their works there is a sense of strain, of reach, of flouting. The human figures of such fictions appear intermittent; the insights work free of the plots. At their most successful, ideas brace the work and surpass in interest the characters, who function to represent and interlock them. All these other writers of novels of ideas dwell within a particular understanding of how the mind best works. They are bravura writers, driving often obsessionally across a gap experienced between ordinary life and the aspirant intellect. This is not to belittle them: with such writers the reader experiences vertiginous pleasures and revelations. These often have to do with the varying tempo at which insight is allowed. The exhilarating skid and pounce as Meredith deflects the expected climaxes in *Diana of the Crossways* (1885) or the ingenuity of Butler's inversions of taken-for-granted morality in *Erewhon* (1872) are matched by Grant Allen's quasi-anthropological fantasy about British self-aggrandizement, seen backward from a twenty-sixth-century vantage point, in *The British Barbarians* (1895).

In George Eliot's writing, however, there is little fantasy and little transcendence except as they are generated within everyday experience by individuals' needs that never can be quite gratified. George Eliot's novels have a passion for the commonplace—by which, her fiction leads us to understand, is meant not only the phatic repetitions but also the hidden ferment of others' daily life to which no one can have access, save through the form of fiction. That paradox asserts the value of, and simultaneously brings into question, mimesis. Eliot, more perhaps than any other nineteenth-century novelist, muses on the ironies of persuasion. The reader, silently reading, seems to share incommunicable secrets and to work upon those secrets with an analytical insight granted for the occasion. That process of analysis is fueled by reference to an extraordinary range of thought systems and philosophical positions. Yet it is tempered by a feeling for the manifest, for the awkward, even paltry daily circumstance whose determining strength is felt only when it is resisted.

Eliot's fiction does not pretend that people are all preoccupied with sequences of abstraction, but from the start of her career with *Scenes of Clerical Life* (1857), her writing marks the turns of phrase, the silences, the mind's images, through which in daily experience insights and resistances are performed. These descriptions she amplifies by a range of discursive effects that call on the reader's self-awareness and will not allow us to unloose ourselves from the ineptness of ordinary event, ordinary feeling. It is this insistence at once on the marred and the eager that gives her writing its charge. Abstract systems and intimate feelings are not kept in separate boxes in her writing: the effect of reading *Middlemarch* is (as she said of the banker Bulstrode's dread of disclosure) "distinct and inmost as the shiver and the ache of oncoming fever when we are discussing abstract pain."

All George Eliot's novels except *Daniel Deronda* are set back in time, allowing an overview to writer and first readers. Her first novel—or collection of novellas—*Scenes of Clerical Life* (1857) looks back a couple of generations into a time that is assumed to be less sophisticated than the reader's own. Many of the novels are very precisely placed at moments of manifest social change. *Adam Bede* (1859) opens in 1799 and closes with the decision of the Methodists not to allow women to preach any more; *The Mill on the Floss* (1860) looks back to the period of Eliot's own girlhood—and, she later told Emily Davies, "In *The Mill on the Floss*, everything is softened, as compared with real life. Her own experience she said was worse"; *Silas Marner* (1861) opens "in the days when the spinning wheel hummed busily in the farmhouses"; *Felix Holt*

(1866) and *Middlemarch* (1872) both center upon the period leading up to the first Reform Bill in 1832, which much extended the franchise. *Romola*'s (1863) first sentence dates the book precisely: "More than three centuries and a half ago, in the mid spring-time of 1492. . . ." Only *Daniel Deronda* (1876) is ranged more or less alongside writer and first reader, embroiled directly in their own current concerns and thus giving no easy interpretative advantage.

Most of the novels are, moreover, set in social circumstances purporting to be just below those of the assumed reader—or at least of their aspirant reading habits and fictional identifications:

Considering these things, we can hardly think Dinah and Seth beneath our sympathy, accustomed as we may be to weep over the loftier sorrows of heroines in satin boots and crinoline, and of heroes riding fiery horses, themselves ridden by yet more fiery passions.

Poor Seth! he was never on horseback in his life except once, when he was a little lad, and Mr. Jonathan Burge took him up behind, telling him to "hold on tight." (*Adam Bede*)

As readers we are subjected here to an exposure that forces us to dissociate from the factitious habits of the fictive reader and instead identify with Seth, whose memories we enter in that loop of reminiscence from his childhood and the direct utterance, "Hold on tight." But the *effort* of identification is felt; the reader is implicitly complimented on her or his success in crossing the social divide. The effect here is ostentatious, not subtle. In her later career Eliot shifts more sinuously between the reader's imputed activities and free indirect style, in which narration and inner experience are enacted at once and without clear bounds. So her works both distance and grip close the participant. The effect is not vacillation but an assessing intimacy, seeking always to avoid falsity of scale—though, in the early novels particularly, not always evading condescension.

George Eliot shared the developmental views of her intellectual contemporaries which likened cultural and racial process to the individual's growth to adulthood. She believed herself to have been the first to use the word *meliorism* (though the dictionary records earlier examples). But she also more and more brought the easy identification between "development" and "progress" into contention. In *Middlemarch* one of the overarching themes proves to be how *little* the first reader in 1870s society can claim superiority or point to secure advances over the 1830s described—despite all the ironic efforts of the narration. This double impulse within George Eliot's thinking—to assimilate ideas and to assay them—constantly extends the scope of her material and troubles her interpretative values.

George Eliot was a prodigious reader—and thinker with her reading, a rather different matter—but it is exactly the range and eclecticism of her intellectual life that makes it hard to descry any binding system or single progenitor beyond the fiction. Indeed, that is what distinguishes her as a novelist of ideas. The great span and simultaneity of her reading means that she moves among ideas as a medium of being, not a template for interpretation. Perhaps it is therefore not surprising that the insistence of her work is, increasingly, on variability, on multiple instances each differing from its like, and on interpenetrating systems.

Her notebooks reveal the persistent range of her reading from day to day; her novels have recourse not only to that reading, but to the ordering ideas that pull across each other as she seeks shapes for meaning. A couple of pages from one of her reading notebooks, in which she wrote down quotations that impressed her, gives the flavor of her responsiveness (the writers quoted there are Martial, Pliny, Scaliger, Sophocles' *Antigone*, Cicero, Ecclesiasticus, Philip Sidney, Theocritus, Richard Savage, Heine, and, by reference, Abul Kasim Firdusi, the tenth-century Persian epic poet). Elsewhere we find material on astronomy, military tactics, Gregorian chant, language theory, Celtic myth, the legal position of women and *mutterrecht*, long quotations from Comte, gambling superstitions, mathematics, Clerk Maxwell's theory of ring vortices, and material from other zones of learning. In the novels themselves all that passionate reading becomes latent, there to be raised to the surface at will, yet rarely alluded to directly, implicated in the lives of unheroic characters.

Impulses for reinterpretation came to the author herself from unexpected angles: she told her friend Mrs. Congreve, for example, that her first skeptical thoughts about religion had come from reading the novels of Walter Scott, long before she encountered the systematic questionings of German historical criticism and translated Strauss's demythologizing *Life of Jesus* (1846). Scott's influence is clear in the plotting of *Adam Bede*, which draws directly on *The Heart of Midlothian* (each novel places near its center the fate of a young woman accused of infanticide, succored by a sisterly presence, and saved at the last moment by a theatrical, eleventh-hour pardon.) The presence of Scott's experiments in conjuring the life of Scotland thirty or forty years before he writes is clear also in the intense feeling for regional life and for dialect in her early novels, *Scenes of Clerical Life*, *Adam Bede*, and *The Mill on the Floss*. But Scott does not seem an obvious source for the stirrings of religious skepticism.

It is not uncommon for beginning novelists to be affected by their predecessors in fiction, nor to find them driving on past the solutions of those predecessors to uncover new questions, as George Eliot already in some measure does in *Adam Bede*. What is uncommon is to find a novelist emerging from a mind already so compellingly engaged with work, past and present, in many languages (Greek, Latin, French, Italian, German, Hebrew, Spanish) and across so broad a range of fields, including philosophy, theology, history, anthropology, sociology, and the work of contemporary scientists such as Faraday and Lyell and, later, Kelvin and Maxwell. That the writer herself should have emerged from the provinces as Marian Evans and have become known first as a literary journalist, coediting the *Westminster Review*, and making her way in London in the 1850s at a time before higher education was open to women, meant that many of her male contemporaries were inclined to view her as a phenomenon that proved nothing about the capacities of women, so extraordinary was she. But the route by which she entered the literary world is never obliterated in George Eliot's creativity. All her learning is exercised in the novels within the social scale of unremarked people. Ruskin, writing after George Eliot's death, fulminated against *The Mill on the Floss* because her characters were living within the constraints of ordinary life, not distinguished by the outer marks of heroism:

There is not a single person in the book of the smallest importance to anybody in the world but themselves, or whose qualities deserved so much as a line of printer's type in their description. There is no girl alive, fairly clever, half educated, and unluckily related, whose life has not at least as much in it as Maggie's, to be described and to be pitied.

What Ruskin saw as disabling most recent critics see as Eliot's radical achievement: her characters are at once strongly individual and yet typical. She does not exempt them from the frayed circumstances of everyday life, nor does she (except in the case of Romola) offer anything like a glorious outcome. For a time this refusal to release at least her heroines into unclouded success caused disquiet among feminist critics of the 1970s, in a period when role models were much needed. Since then, however, the novels' tonic absence of sentimentality about what an individual can achieve within the constraints of a particular society has been seen as having its own value for feminist analysis.

The Mill on the Floss remains probably the most popular of Eliot's novels and the one most frequently written about, apart from the work generally agreed to be her masterpiece, *Middlemarch*. In recent years *Daniel Deronda* has prodigiously excited readers and has opened up to fresh analyses. It is worth dwelling first on *The Mill* since it realizes with extraordinary intensity so many of the questions that prevail throughout Eliot's creative life. It was the first book written "in her own person," that is, once it was known to her readers that "George Eliot" was a woman, and (potentially known, though not to all readers) that she was living in an irregular union with a married man, George Henry Lewes. That felt relation with the readers' knowledge may have its bearing on the swerve of the plot at the end of the book where Maggie turns away from Stephen, whom she desires, and back to her family and her duty. "The great problem of the shifting relation between passion and duty is clear to no man who is capable of apprehending it." The inexhaustible tussle is, it seems, all that wisdom can consist in; the impossibility of any decided settlement is George Eliot's form of tragedy.

In *The Mill on the Floss* George Eliot took seriously an already fashionable topic: the young woman who excels intellectually. The novel is preoccupied with education and with power. Eliot demonstrates what it feels like to *want* and shows also that the wants of girls may be for learning as passionately as for love. The two desires, the book suggests, are not different in kind: they exercise mind and body at once. Such passions, the commentary sardonically suggests, are debarred by "good society" but endured by other, less fortunate layers of society.

But good society, floating on gossamer wings of light irony, is of very expensive production; requiring nothing less than a wide and arduous national life condensed in unfragrant deafening factories, cramping itself in mines, sweating at furnaces, grinding, hammering, weaving under more or less oppression of carbonic acid—or else, spread over sheepwalks, and scattered in lonely houses and huts on the clayey or chalky corn-lands, where the rainy days look dreary. This wide national life is based entirely on emphasis—the emphasis of want.

Daringly, she measures Maggie's needs alongside material poverty and oppression and insists on them all as part of that "emphasis" in contrast to the well-to-do.

Auguste Comte's then immensely influential argument that cultural development follows the same pathway as the life of the single individual is here turned back upon itself. Maggie develops through the three phases of cultural history in her own short lifetime: from the animistic (when she makes her doll into a fetish that she sticks with pins) to adult civilization. But George Eliot also shows that there is no inevitable pathway for the individual. The ontogeny-phylogeny parallel is delusive. To foreground this difficulty George Eliot brings to bear (and to the test) another popular plot of the time: the bildungsroman, in which a young person—usually male—learns first to roam beyond the limits of his society and then to come to terms with its demands, accommodating his identity to what is possible for adult life lived on society's terms. Instead of exhibiting such creative accommodation, in *The Mill* Tom Tulliver is shown as beginning to seize up psychically at a very young age precisely because he never succeeds in questioning the assumptions his society loads him with: he must be aggressive, hardworking, rule-bound. He cannot stretch the limits of society as the bildungsroman suggests a young man may do. Maggie, on the other hand, undertakes that role, moves beyond social limits and is then obliged to sacrifice most of her self. Philip, disabled and intelligent, is aligned with Maggie. Both are incapacitated by their society's belief in their powerlessness. And, as Sally Shuttleworth points out in her edition of the novel, the feminizing of Philip prevents him from being considered as an acceptable sexual partner for Maggie, by the book as much as by its readers.

The subtle accretion of happening, response, and reaction in this novel raises also the question of what we dignify with the title of event. And with the name of analysis. For *The Mill* is a novel that, while energetically analytical, allows much to pass by in dialogue and in description. Philip remarks, "I think there are stores laid up in our human nature that our understandings can make no complete inventory of." Maggie eagerly agrees. The example they use is that of the effects of music that augments the individual's scope while it is heard: "Certain strains of music affect me so strangely—I can never hear them without their changing my whole attitude of mind for a time, and if the effect would last, I might be capable of heroisms."

The impression of discovery and potential, which is so strong in this book, is produced by the way analysis, conversation, and humor lie athwart each other, passing between characters and commentary. That preserves the text itself from the rancors of power and allows a play of comedy over topics that are, equally, allowed their full scope. An example of this is the child Maggie's running away to join the gypsies. It is worth dwelling on this since the episode broaches issues to which I shall return later in this essay.

The eight-year-old Maggie, on her self-liberating (and colonizing) trip, is artfully led to compare herself to Columbus. She offers to exchange knowledge for food with the young gypsy woman whose camp she has entered. In her fantasy she expects to become the gypsy queen and educate them ("Everything would be quite charming when she had taught the gypsies to use a wash-basin, and to feel an interest in books"). But she finds herself disoriented while she prates of geography, ignorant of "the world we live in," among actual people of another tribe, men, women, and children. She is at the mercy of a strong family who speak a tongue she cannot understand and live their lives in ways that frighten her. Her colonizing notions have all to be given up and she is only thankful to be taken home by them. The satire on racial notions of superiority is marked yet never underscored. The subject of "the wandering tribes," and their supposed inferiority to "settled" communities, was a subject aired across a range of Victorian writings, after Blumenbach's earlier racial taxonomies, through to the ethnologist James Prichard and to Mayhew's *London Labour and the London Poor*, which was appearing serially during the 1850s. It is intriguing to see Eliot's witty work with it here. The topic of the racial or cultural "other" became crucial to her late work.

Maggie has arrived among the gypsies as a result of a passionate quarrel with her brother, in which her "pink-and-white" cousin Lucy has become the sacrificial victim. Having been excluded spitefully by her brother from sight of the water-snake, Maggie pushes Lucy into "cow-trodden mud." "There were passions at war in Maggie at that moment to have made a tragedy, if tragedies were made by passion only." But, Eliot continues, using the Greek in her text (which I here translate into English), "a certain largeness" is lacking to the possible action: "The utmost Maggie could do, with a fierce thrust of her small brown arm, was to push poor little pink-and-white Lucy into the cow-trodden mud." The furious struggles for power in which so much of childhood is wasted, or spent, yield to Eliot both comedy and a sense that what actually takes place as *event* in human life depends largely on the register of action available. Maggie, with her "small Medusa face," experiences murder as desire. George Eliot is closer here to post-Freudian and particularly Kleinian emphasis on the paranoid Grand Guignol of babyhood and childhood than to the more usual view among her contemporaries that childhood was a period of some calm.

Throughout the book Eliot emphasizes that tragedy does not require rulers to enact it. In contrast to Thackeray's manner in *Vanity Fair* of giving a tug on the strings of his novel and drawing our attention to his presence as puppeteer, George Eliot elevates her characters against the odds by invoking comparisons with heroic fates. The first book of the novel ends: "Mr. Tulliver had a destiny as well as Oedipus, and in this case might plead, like Oedipus, that his deed was inflicted on him rather than committed by him." The effect here is yet not quite unlike that of Thackeray: by such invocations the reader's sense of scale is unsettled and the characters are pushed away in a manner that we might now like to think postmodern were it not so manifestly premodern.

Despite (or perhaps because of) the prodigious scope of her learning, a sense of the partial and even the captious haunts George Eliot throughout her creative life. It is there already long before she became a novelist in a letter of 1840 where she speaks of her own knowledge as

an assemblage of disjointed specimens of history, ancient and modern, scraps of poetry picked up from Shakespeare, Cowper, Wordsworth and Milton, newspaper topics, morsels of Addison and Bacon, Latin verbs, geometry, entomology and chemistry, reviews and metaphysics, all arrested and petrified and smothered by the fast thickening every day accession of actual events, relative anxieties, and household cares and vexations.

It would prove later that the everyday would be the mulch out of which grew fiction and learning. But the feeling for (and anxiety toward) "assemblage" persists—as does the pressure of the circumstantial.

George Eliot entered the world of learning at a different angle from her educated male contemporaries: for them it represented first of all a dutiful adherence to the expectations of their social group. For her it was an "active love," "an experience springing out of the deepest need." So there need be no gap between the passional and the intellectual in her writing. Instead there is a constant multiplying of subject positions. Shifting registers of speech within the sentence, though not so rebarbative as in Hardy, are characteristic of George Eliot's mode of exploration in her novels. Her description of how knowledge grows in "Notes on Form in Art" (1868), written while she was working on *Middle-*

march, articulates her own experience and at the same time gives an acute description of the taxonomy of that novel, where the characters are bunched together under titles such as "Three Love Problems" and "Waiting for Death," and then are more and more discriminatingly explored in their differences and in the subtle divergence of their lots one from the other.

And as knowledge continues to grow but its alternating processes of distinction and combination, seeing smaller and smaller unlikenesses and grouping or associating these under a common likeness, it arrives at the conception of wholes composed of parts more and more multiplied and highly differenced, yet more and more absolutely bound together by various conditions of common likeness or mutual dependence.

The processes of *Middlemarch*, in its nine-hundred-odd pages, tease out and disturb this compacted argument into the sufferings, denials, and interpenetrating social, political, and emotional lives of some— relatively few—inhabitants of the town of Middlemarch. The unwritten complexity of further lives surrounds and at times bears down on the "sample" she has chosen. And the figures in the work, living out their lives in the provinces, are connected not only with their peers and neighbors but with national and epistemological changes they know nothing about, or understand ill, or live in the midst of without perceiving their significance. The coming of the railway and the Reform Bill, evolutionary theory and thermodynamics, germ theory, mythography, the education of women and women's position, Greek tragedy, and life sciences: ordinary activities instantiate, but cannot sufficiently stand in for, all these systems of understanding and of social change. Ideas in the later work of George Eliot surpass, but can only find their actuality in, individual lives. Perhaps in the light of this it becomes less surprising that a central grand theme of her work is failure—a theme in which characters and composition are alike ensnared and fulfilled.

Scholars and critics have explored her response to influential contemporaries: in particular, Auguste Comte, Charles Darwin, Herbert Spencer, and her own life companion, the biographer, dramatist, psychologist, and experimental scientist G. H. Lewes. Each of those critical explorations has demonstrated how thoroughly George Eliot engaged with the implications of others' ideas and engrossed them in her own fiction. But she does not always take the most evident patterns from others' arguments: so, *Daniel Deronda* reassesses the idea of evo-lutionary diversification and origins in the light of Talmudic hermeu-tics, and *Middlemarch* can be read as a riposte to Frederic Harrison's urging her to write a positivistic novel.

Equally, George Eliot's reading among the Greek tragic dramatists produces a particular tragic inflection within her own fiction: as she cites Sophocles or Euripides in relation to run-of-the-mill lives she insists on the reach of emotion, the meagerness of outlet and expres-sion, possible to her figures. That is the particular style of modern tragedy as she perceives it: that the humdrum curtails what in ritualized literature had scope to declare itself completely.

But her work suggests that the contraction has to do with a commu-nal refusal to participate in others' experiences, not with any person's inability to feel her or his own extremity. The business of her art is to release the observer (the reader) from the stupidity of seeing only the sameness in things. The circumstantial becomes crucial to interpreta-tion. Yet the works indicate also how necessary to survival is the capac-ity to blot out, at least intermittently, others' needs. That capacity may lead to villainy, as for Tito in *Romola*, but the absence of any power of blocking may destroy, as it does Latimer in "The Lifted Veil" and threatens to do Deronda in *Daniel Deronda*. In a famous passage in *Middlemarch* the narrative aligns writer, reader, and society on a com-mon charge: "We do not expect people to be deeply moved by what is not unusual." The passage itself is engagingly direct and yet freighted with an extraordinary range of reading:

That element of tragedy which lies in the very fact of frequency, has not yet wrought itself into the coarse emotion of mankind; and perhaps our frames could hardly bear much of it. If we had a keen vision and feeling for all ordi-nary human life, it would be like hearing the grass grow and the squirrel's heart beat, and we should die of that roar which lies on the other side of silence. As it is, the quickest of us walk about well wadded with supidity.

Eliot's diverse reading lies latent for the reader to raise to the surface at will: Wordsworth, ("the grass I seemed to hear it growing"), T. H. Hux-ley, *The Arabian Nights*, all are allusively present—and pulling in differ-ent directions, so that the passage is forthright and yet flexible.

It may be revealing to pay attention to at least two of those allusions since the movement of the paragraph demonstrates the the degree to which ideas are implicated, rather than displayed, in Eliot's composition. In "The Physical Basis of Life," an essay published in the *Westminster Review* in February 1869, Huxley illustrated the limits of human senses thus:

> The wonderful noonday silence of a tropical forest is, after all, due only to the dullness of our hearing; and could our ears catch the murmur of those tiny Maelstroms, as they whirl in the innumerable myriads of living cells which constitute each tree, we should be stunned, as with the roar of a great city.

The "myriads of living cells" are here conceived as individuals straining within the organic form of the tree, the intensity of individuated life producing a silent hubbub that would buffet the ears. Huxley moves from the "dullness" of our hearing to a recognition that we would be equally dulled, "stunned," by access to the sounds beyond our senses, "the roar which lies on the other side of silence."

   The passage also includes a degree of allusion to Eliot's own early story "The Lifted Veil" (1859), in which insight produced macabre disillusionment. (And, of course, the Huxley passage may harbor a reminiscence of that story.) Eliot broke off from the writing of her most confessional novel, *The Mill on the Floss*, to write "The Lifted Veil." Latimer has the power of seeing into others' minds, but this proves a malign gift:

> The rational talk, the graceful attentions, the wittily-turned phrases, and the kindly deeds, which used to make the web of their characters, were seen as if thrust asunder by a microscopic vision, that showed all the intermediate frivolities, all the suppressed egoism, all the struggling chaos of puerilities, meanness, vague capricious memories, and indolent make-shift thoughts, from which human words and deeds emerge like leaflets covering a fermenting heap.

Here insight is destructive of human community and analysis proves to be a form of repudiation. Latimer's life is fatally encumbered and vitiated by his preternatural identifications. The writer's own dread of discovering—when all the magic of narrative has been expended—only the humdrum, or worse, behind outer appearances seems to haunt the tale.

   How scornful, then, is the final phrase of the *Middlemarch* passage? The emphasis on how the quickest of us walk "well wadded with stupidity" draws not only on Huxley ("the dullness of our hearing") but also on the story of the Princess Parizade in "The Two Sisters" in *The Arabian Nights*. Parizade undertakes a perilous journey after her two brothers fail because they were drawn aside by threatening voices:

"innumerable voices, bursting out as it seemed from under the earth. Of these, some ridiculed, some abused, and others threatened him . . . in voices calculated to inspire shame, anger, and dismay." Parizade stops her ears with cotton so that "all she perceived was one confused noise." She pursues her journey courageously and, undeflected, gains the talking bird, the golden water, and the singing tree, the signs of joy, sex, and learning. This tale became for the young George Eliot an emblem of her own hoped-for career, and a talisman between herself and her great friend Barbara Leigh Smith Bodichon. (The two women allude to the tale in their letters to each other.)

The *Middlemarch* passage quoted above, and so often taken to typify George Eliot's liberal humanism, never quite settles into a single view. The writing catches the conflict present in the need to sympathize, a need that Eliot's own writing so often urges: too great an openness to the sensory or emotional may blunt sensibility anew or sap the courage to pursue a chosen path amid the pressure of demands.

The longing to sympathize is matched by the need to ironize: and so it is in her own writing. The passage sets in motion both these perceptions, though its own inclination is toward empathy. The reading, and self-reading, at work in George Eliot's fiction allows for a multifariousness that is not chaotic, an openness that is not simplistic. And the ability to perceive general systems working within ordinary instances frees her from the grind of denotative realism. Yet it exacts a price: how to sustain complexity without collapsing into contradiction or inertia. Deirdre David suggests that "the conflicts in Eliot's texts are sometimes so disjunctive that they lead to a confrontation of equally autonomous ideologies whose only dissolution seems to be an implicit cancellation of ideology itself."

Ideas are generated out of everyday life—sometimes *forced* out of it— and shape it too. Indeed, the worst that can befall a thinking person in her fiction is to fail to make the crossover between the impassioned work of thinking and the impassioned work of living. One of George Eliot's most telling insights is the debilitating difficulty experienced by many of her most powerful characters in moving between professional and other aspects of life. So in *Middlemarch* Lydgate, in particular, fails to apply his intelligence to other aspects of life outside the scientific: that failure combines with his false expectations of what women should be expected to provide emotionally for men. Driven by debt to consider returning the wedding present he gave to his wife Rosamond, Lydgate's imagination at last begins to work on his marriage: "Having been roused to discern consequences which he had never been in the habit of tracing, he was preparing to act on this discernment with some of the rigour (by no means all) that he would have applied in pursuing experiment." In *Romola*, and again most pervasively in *Middlemarch*, that problem besets characters—most of them, revealingly, male. Though, for different reasons, a woman like Rosamond has scarcely any crossover capacity at all, so locked is she face to face with that projected self-image enjoined on her by society: the perfect lady. Intriguingly, in *My Literary Life*, Lynn Linton spoke of George Eliot herself, with a denied but present sexual double entendre, as "a made woman," a product of a glacial self-fashioning that withdrew the possibility of spontaneity.

A short letter to her longtime friend Sara Hennell in January 1862 shows the typical melding of diverse reading and experience that George Eliot herself enjoyed: she writes of Max Muller's "great and delightful book" *Lectures on the Science of Language*, of Trollope's *Orley Farm*, of Herbert Spencer's *First Principles* and of his hypochondria ("The very watching against disease is becoming a disease in itself"). And she ends the letter with a dashingly revealing remark that opens up more than it quite knows it contains: "I am going to be taken to a pantomime in the day-time, like a good child, for a Christmas treat, not having had my fair share of pantomime in the world."

The glow of childishness, the hedonism of one "who has not had her fair share of pantomime in the world," casts light on the exactingness of the novels and their ripple of humor. She finds her ease in unexpected places. It may seem that Dickens is more at home in pantomime and George Eliot in opera, yet within her novels we encounter a constantly renewing eagerness that expresses itself in a profusion of metaphors— those lateral encounters that slip past the guard of logic and illuminate alternative perceptions and desires.

Before ever she began to write fiction herself, Eliot brooded on the relations between feeling and language, and on the degree to which feeling is shaped, balked, enacted within the conditions of a particular society's linguistic terms. As she does so often, she uses an anatomical image to express the predicament and to emphasize the inescapability of a society's terms: "The sensory and motor nerves that run in the same sheath, are scarcely bound together by a more necessary and delicate union than that which binds men's affection, imagination, wit, and humour, with the subtle ramifications of historical language."

George Eliot started her career as a translator and literary journalist. In this period of her life she worked anonymously, following the grain of another's thought and silently noting the gaps and crevices within argument and feeling. Each of the books she translated challenged orthodoxies of religious belief. Doing without God is hard for the novelist who seeks a providential form. When, much later, in *Middlemarch*, Eliot eschews the largesse of Fielding, with his theistic overview of all the fortunes in his world, she yet demurringly includes "the range of relevancies called the universe" even as she professes herself unable to engage with them because she must focus her experimental instruments on a particular place and company. One reason that she can so confidently effect this double task of attention and inattention is because, as translator in her youth of Feuerbach and Spinoza, she had lived through and controlled a particular kind of humanistic argumentation. In the activity of translating German historical criticism in Strauss's *Life of Jesus* and humanistic philosophy in Feuerbach, and in her work on Spinoza, she learned the relations between empathy and precision. The activity of close translation necessitated teasing out the nuances of meaning and transposing them to another readership, a different culture.

If translation enforces immersion, it may also provoke resistance—and indeed Eliot wearied of Strauss's limitations. Similarly, the activity of reviewing across a wide range of current writing not only was immensely educative in giving her access to diverse views but provoked an emulous wish to do as well, to do differently, to utter all that was not contained in the works that she must study. Because this early phase of her career was performed anonymously it allowed for bravura exposition of philosophical ideas without her being undermined by the assumption on the part of her readers that this was an untrained woman writing. It allowed also a cavalier disregard of the niceties of sisterhood, so that she dispraised women's "silly novels" because, she held, such works undermined the seriousness of professional writing by women and battened on the condescension of readers willing to believe women empty-headed. And she had fun dispraising them.

She characterizes the heroine of a "*mind-and-millinery*" novel as "usually an heiress":

Her eyes and her wit are both dazzling; her nose and her morals are alike free from any tendency to irregularity; she has a superb contralto and a superb intellect; she is perfectly well-dressed and perfectly religious; she dances like a sylph, and reads the Bible in the original tongues.

By the time she comes to write her own last novel, *Daniel Deronda*, that aspirant self-image is part of Gwendolen's tragedy, leading her to assume that her dominion is secure and betraying her into the clutches of a man with a perverse liking for dominating the dominant. And Eliot's description in this same early essay of another self-righteous plot is hideously inverted in *Deronda*:

or it may be that the heroine is not an heiress—that rank and wealth are the only things in which she is deficient; but she infallibly gets into high society, she has the triumph of refusing many matches and securing the best, and she wears some family jewels or other as a sort of crown of righteousness at the end.

Gwendolen certainly gets into "high society." The "family jewels" that Gwendolen puts on become a sign of enslavement and a lurid crown of infamy, indicating to her own scorched sensibility her betrayal of Mrs. Glasher, Grandcourt's cast-off partner and the mother of his children, who should be wearing them as his wife.

In recent years the life transformations as well as the written achievements of Mary Ann Evans, Marian Evans, Marian Lewes, George Eliot—and her familiar names of Pollyann, Mutti, Madonna, too—have become a focus of critical attention. That a single writer preoccupied with organic communities should have so many named identities, that a woman intellectual should choose a male pseudonym, that a rebellious atheist should so often imagine the religious life, and that a woman who set herself outside society by living with a married man for many years should yet have resisted publicly identifying herself with feminist causes: all these seeming contradictions have been felt to be in need of explanation.

Feminist criticism of George Eliot's work and recent critiques of her life have produced much innovative thinking about her that has moved away from the assumption that hers are "classic realist" texts, content to mirror a society and instruct the reader how to interpret that society. Instead, the emphasis has been upon what her friend Edith Simcox called the "irreconcileable tendencies" of her work or what Nancy Miller in *Subject to Change* describes as her insistence on "the difficulty of curing plot of life, and life of certain plots," the dilemma of her heroines being, even when technically free, "bound . . . to another script."

In such discussions *Romola* emerges as a pivotal text. George Eliot's earlier novels were all set in the English countryside. The particularity of her descriptions of country customs, manners, work, houses, flora and fauna, and regional speech, had been (and remain) a major part of these novels' pleasurability.

Romola is usually taken to be George Eliot's least successful work of fiction, a novel massively imperfect, encumbered by its own learning and by the desire to communicate to the reader all the circumstances of Renaissance Florence. Yet it is also among her most innovative fictions. The temporal distance of the historical novel made it possible for her to engage more directly than she had previously dared with the hypocrisies of her own society. Here, for the first time, she engaged with the dissimulations and self-unknowings of married life and political or public life at once. For example, Tito's decision to sell the library entrusted to him by Romola's dead scholar father is strictly legal. Tito tells Romola: "The event is irrevocable, the library is sold, and you are my wife." As in Victorian England, so in Renaissance Florence, a married woman's property passes to her husband. George Eliot's friend Barbara Leigh Smith Bodichon organized resistance to this law, and George Eliot—a rare act for her—publicly signed and distributed sheets for the petition. Suzanne Graver quotes from John S. Wharton's *Laws Relating to the Women of England* (1853), which makes it clear that, as the law still went in mid-nineteenth-century England, more was assumed than the woman's loss of financial control at marriage: not only the property but the person of the wife was absorbed into the identity of the husband. Marriage was "coverture," meaning "that the husband and wife are treated at Common Law as one person indivisible, the personal and separate existence of the wife being legally considered as absorbed and consolidated in that of her husband." In *Romola* Eliot shows, in contrast, the agonized and adamant resistance of Romola to any identification with her husband once she recognizes the selfishness of his aims.

Romola shows a capitalist society in crisis, urged to transform itself by a recoil of religious idealism realized in Savanorola. The problem of aesthetic values caught into those of the market is embodied in Tito's beauty and his possession of jewels, which gives him access to power within such a culture. Both Savanorola and Tito come to grief; Romola finds salvation. In this novel George Eliot uses distance to explore dilemmas fundamental to her own society, but she does not indicate possible communal transformations. Instead a solution of a kind is reached by means of transfiguration: Romola rescues a child and his village and becomes a kind of madonna, freed from the exigencies of marriage and the dominance of men: father, confessor, brother, and husband all die.

Nevertheless, *Romola* was also the work in which George Eliot moved further into the implications of the demands of relationships: what does a child owe a parent—and is it the less if the relationship is one of fostering, not of blood? or is it more? The problem of the demands that relationships impose is worked at through the relationships of Romola and her brother, each to their father. The brother exactly elects a religious life that sets him at odds with his father's needs. Romola wearies, but remains. Tito comes from far away and abandons the search for the foster father who had nurtured him and who may now be a slave. In one laconic sentence George Eliot summarizes Tito's inability to respond to such demands: "He would have been equal to any sacrifice that was not unpleasant." The mild word "unpleasant" sardonically dramatizes the flaccidness of Tito's moral fiber. He gives himself up to the present, which his beauty and skill makes incandescent for others as well as for himself.

But that emphasis on the present cut free from the drag of the past proves to be a corrupting force. Tito is not obliged thoroughly to understand himself. He can skim and slide from one group to another, from one emotional impulse to the next. He feels no loss in losing the past. In this he is at an extreme distance from his scholar father, Baldassarre, who lives in "the vague aching of an unremembered past," his store of knowledge slipped away from him in aphasia and amnesia. As Baldassarre struggles with his turgid memory the question is posed: "Was it utterly and for ever gone from him, like the waters from an urn lost in the wide ocean? or was it still within him, imprisoned by some obstruction that might one day break asunder?" In the event, Baldassarre's memory returns only in the moment of revenge as he murders Tito, never in benign access to the learned treasures that had earlier stocked his imagination. These different forms of memory loss set Tito and Baldassarre apart, not alongside each other.

Scholarship, hedonism, capital, religious fervor, marriage: all are brought to crisis in this novel, and all are found wanting. George Eliot herself saw *Romola* as an experiment, a move away from the English countryside that her readers associated her with. In all her books she was writing *against* pastoralism, against the townsperson's simplification of rural life and the idealization of rustic feelings. She sought to avoid both the epic and the puppet, to set her readers alongside experiences that they believed themselves apart from. Her insistence is always on the complexity of each person's life, the passionate stamina of being human. But she was not interested solely in individuals. Rather, she brought to the fore the degree to which people know themselves as part of a social group and the degree to which society determines individuality. Perhaps that was one reason she was fascinated by the move from the Midlands to Italy. Yet, as her contemporary critics were not slow to point out, the Renaissance society that she conjured was, in its ethical dilemmas, not unlike mid-nineteenth-century Britain—even while the people spoke an awkward scholarly dialect derived from written records. Lewes urged her publisher and friend, Blackwood: "When you see her, mind your care is to discountenance the idea of a Romance being the product of an Encyclopaedia." Yet that fascinated immersion in a society she did *not* know, could not tap into through the long roots of family association, brought quite new areas of her own productivity within George Eliot's reach: "If one is to have freedom to write out of one's own varying unfolding self, and not to be a machine always grinding out the same material or spinning the same sort of web, one cannot always write for the same public," she wrote of *Romola*. The experience of writing *Romola* liberated the daring to write large-scale and complicated accounts of the social forces at work in a particular place and time (as in *Middlemarch*), or even across the sweep of Europe and of racial diversity (as in *Daniel Deronda*).

In her later novels—*Felix Holt, Middlemarch, Daniel Deronda*—issues of gender and of race are (in differing degrees) knotted together. In recent years critics have been able to demonstrate how far, in general, shared ideologies and assumptions underpin the relationship between fiction and first readers and shape the novel form. Victorian fiction writers were not, for example, always more astute than their fellows in pinpointing the Orientalism and colonialism active (or somnolent) in British society. George Eliot does not often comment directly on such issues within the early novels (though the gypsy episode in *The Mill* hints at some of the problems), but in her later work she more and more explores the position of the incomer and the racial other.

She recognizes that nationalism is not a matter only of sovereign boundaries. It may be as active in small enclosed communities. Indeed, *Silas Marner* is the first of her works where the plot is organized about an exile. Silas, the linen-weaver, is one of the scattered "emigrants from the town into the country," one of "certain pallid undersized men, who, by the side of the brawny country-folk, looked like the remnants of a disinherited race." Ironically, as well as being a "remnant of a disinherited race" Silas is also a harbinger of the industrial future, working at the mercy of the demands of his loom. In *Silas Marner* Silas is eventually assimilated into the country community. In her later work no such complete accord is possible—and even in *Silas Marner* she has recourse to the terms of dream and fairy tale to make the possibility seem authentic. Silas learns skills across gender. Lost gold becomes a child's golden curls, and Silas's maternal nurturing of the lost little girl Eppie proves to be his way into full life. But a very tight piece of plotting is necessary to sustain the delicate balance between dream, wish fulfillment, and hard-headed social commentary that distinguishes this short book.

The other medium of interpretation in *Silas Marner* is gossip, particularly the ritual repetition of founding stories within the village community. Mr. Macey, in particular, tells repeated stories about meaning, function, and intention, which George Eliot carefully avoids overinterpreting, as in the tale of the couple whom the clergyman marries with gender-crossing words: "'Wilt thou have this man to be thy wedded wife?' says he, and then he says, 'Wilt thou have this woman to be thy wedded husband?' says he." Here, above all, George Eliot represents the robust variety within a community by means of conversation; the speech rhythms as well as the actual dialect words insist on the inner coherence of the group.

It is the last occasion on which she represents an indigenous English community as *worth* assimilating to. Even the town of Middlemarch, though it provides material for a major novel, is surveyed skeptically. The town's own assurance that it is at the center, or middle, of the world is offset in a number of ways: by the book's concern with systems and ideas beyond the mediocre conversation of the town's settled inhabitants, by allusion to those capital cities London, Paris, and Rome— dwindled beside the linguistic and material bulk of Middlemarch in the foreground—and by the fact that many of those with whom the reader is concerned prove to be incomers (Casaubon, Lydgate, Bulstrode, Ladislaw, Dorothea, and Celia, to say nothing of Raffles and Rigg). Moreover, many of those incomers central to the reader's concerns leave the place again, by death, default, or social exclusion. The "coherence" of Middlemarch the town is a narrative sleight of hand: the various figures whom the reader perceives as intimately connected by the analogies and disanalogies between their lives scarcely know each other across the class barriers of the place. Some of them come also from irremediably far away.

Ladislaw in *Middlemarch* is described by gossip as "the grandson of a thieving Jew pawnbroker" and "an Italian with white mice" (his grandfather was "a Polish refugee who gave lessons for his bread"). In the communal mind of "that part of the world that lay within park palings"—that is, the English landed gentry—all "foreigners" are held to be about equally contemptible and hence interchangeable. That Will's parentage is partly of that world counts not at all in the estimation of their neighbors. When Dorothea marries Will Ladislaw she aligns herself with a world outside the general prejudices of her class. He becomes eventually a reforming member of Parliament, helping to change settled, self-contented England—how, we do not know.

By the time she wrote *Daniel Deronda* George Eliot's concern with the damaging effects of British supremacism had become a motive force of the novel: in particular, the novel explores the imaginative debility of the English and its effects on national life and intimate experience alike. Eliot's own friendship with Emanuel Deutsch, scholar of the Near East, and himself born the son of a rabbi in Silesia, opened up further ranges of insight and inquiry. Deutsch's 1867 article on "The Talmud" in the *Quarterly Review* had excited very widespread interest and had drawn into the awareness of many English people for the first time the parallels between diverse religions, including Judaism, Buddhism, and Christianity. George Eliot's imagination was fired by Deutsch's writing and by his friendship. Writing to Harriet Beecher Stowe ten years later, after the novel had been published, she observed: "Moreover, not only towards the Jews, but towards all oriental peoples with whom we English come in contact, a spirit of arrogance and contemptuous dictatorialness is observable which has become a national disgrace to us."

Her late works more and more directly explore this "national disgrace." Fedalma in *The Spanish Gypsy* and, above all, Daniel in *Daniel Deronda* suggest how even those brought up, like Fedalma and Daniel, in the privileged midst of a dominant society may, in the end, be driven to reassert their difference. Each of them discovers their identification with an ethnic group demeaned by their foster society: gypsy and Jew. Each discovers a lost parent.

This is not to say that George Eliot always explores these questions of ethnicity and Orientalism along lines the present-day reader might expect or favor. In *Felix Holt* the dead wife of Harold Transome, whom he married in Smyrna where he worked as a banker after a spell in the British Embassy in Constantinople, is presented as a mere slave, at home in the harem of his dominance. But part of the point of that representation is to suggest how Mrs. Transome, the English conservative lady, adamant, self-aware, dignified, and privileged, is equally enslaved, equally at the mercy of terrors and lost eroticism. She fears both the men in her life, her son Harold and her long-ago lover, Jermyn, still the lawyer for the estate.

The secret that she carries within her—that Harold is Jermyn's illegitimate son—is like an unending pregnancy that burdens and constrains her every act. She chafes for independence, but the book opens already with the end of her mastery. She is no longer to have command of the estate that she has efficiently maintained during Harold's long absence abroad. She is to become again a woman enclosed and useless, as surely as Harold's wife has been in her haremlike sensibility. The notion that it is only Eastern potentates who enslave women (a popular self-gratifying view among Victorian and later Englishmen) is here shrewdly undermined. Yet the very fixture of Mrs. Transome's plight means that George Eliot can pursue it only so far. Mrs. Transome then recedes into the background, forming an immanent warning for both the reader and Esther of the impasse that women who dread men are locked within.

Whereas Mrs. Transome and Harold are each incapable of change, Felix and Esther begin to educate each other. George Eliot's own interest in issues of colonialism and imperialism is illustrated by the fact that the day after she sent off the manuscript of "Felix Holt's Address to Working-Men" (the very gradualist rather than radical tailpiece she wrote a year after the novel) she spent eight hours in the gallery of the House of Commons listening to the debate on Abyssinia. The outcome of the policy then being pursued was the assertion of British imperialism in Africa. During the years between *Felix Holt* and *Daniel Deronda* Eliot's reading in anthropology, history, and sociology, and her concern with current issues, had prepared her for a more investigative treatment of British power relations within and beyond the borders of the island.

Questions of gender and questions of cultural and national supremacism converge in her writing, often with a turn of humor that taxes the reader unawares. *Felix Holt* was written during the period leading up to the 1867 Reform Act, and while writing it George Eliot went through "the Times of 1832-33 at the British Museum, to be sure of as many details as I could." As she was to do again with greater complexity in *Middlemarch*, George Eliot created a satirical superstructure to the novel, addressed to her contemporary readers, by matching the periods of the two major franchise laws alongside each other. It is worth remembering that George Eliot did not live or write in, or write for readers who lived in, what we would now consider a democracy.

Most of the characters in *Middlemarch* lack the vote, but they crowd in upon the reader's attention according to hierarchies other than the franchise, important though that is in the turn of the book's affairs. In *Middlemarch* the effect, as one reads, is of an extraordinary inclusiveness. Yet the novel is also defined by what is *not* in Middlemarch the town, or, indeed, in *Middlemarch* the work. The urban poor, religious fervor, family meals, death of loved people: none of these are present in this capacious novel. Those who die before the book's ending (Casaubon and Featherstone) are much regretted only by themselves. Their attempts to impose their wills after death are thwarted by the action of the book. Instead, the effect of abundance and of fine discriminations is produced by the subtlety with which the diverse experiences of the characters shift, check, and illuminate each other. They do not run parallel; no likeness is complete, no distance absolute. Casaubon and Lydgate both seek origins and each is asking the wrong question, but the nature of the answers they seek is diverse: Casaubon's a repetitious collapsing together of things only superficially alike, Lydgate's a fructifying search for what initiates difference in the structures of the body. The clergyman Farebrother is the amateur taxonomist, Lydgate the professional experimenter—yet Farebrother can analyze and participate in others' feelings as Lydgate can never do. Dorothea is trapped by her status as a lady; Rosamond aspires to that status and is trapped equally by that aspiration. Dorothea works out for herself the rudiments of political economy; her laissez-faire uncle Mr. Brooke knows the terms but ignores the practice, letting his estate and tenants suffer from his parsimony even while he accepts the liberal Will Ladislaw as his political agent. Will, the outsider, eventually becomes an active member of Parliament, working to better the social system. Not only are the characters compared to each other but the book compares itself with epic and with spiritual journey, reaches toward them, and eschews them in the interest of a purely human level of analysis (no gods, no God, just people). Ironies are activated by these multiple (and multiplied) comparisons. Yet at the same time the reader is invited to participate intimately in the experience of one after another of the characters.

That intimacy is produced to a considerable degree by language of the body. People are, in George Eliot's words, "incarnate history." One of the worst things that can happen to a human person is the disjunction between theory and replenishing life, a fate she describes with extraordinary imagistic intensity as Dorothea weighs the burden that the dead Casaubon has placed upon her: to continue his ill-conceived work, preparing materials, "sorting them as food for a theory which was already withered in the birth like an elfin child." Here the images of food and stillbirth are locked painfully against each other, theory become a withered changeling. Dorothea refuses her dead husband's injunction and redeems her own youth.

Far more than has been acknowledged by much twentieth-century criticism, the body becomes the nexus of meaning in George Eliot's discourse. Many of her contemporaries, sharing the same discursive register, responded to the physicality of her writing. Some even felt an indelicacy in her intimate description, particularly the impropriety of a woman representing "the bodily feelings of the other sex" (and, perhaps here, the alarm at finding men the "other sex.")

But physical passion in George Eliot's novels is most often realized in loss, not presence. Her women, in particular, know the intensity of their love as they renounce it. The moment of sacrifice rather than of rapture is the typical form of awakening in her works. Repression itself becomes a form of desire. This is particularly striking in *The Mill on the Floss* where Maggie's ardent nature declares itself after childhood by a series of turnings away from fulfillment. Her yearning toward self-sacrifice, which is quizzically presented in the descriptions of her adolescent religious pietism, seems to be endorsed by the book's own later activity, which drives her first toward and then away from her passionate love for Stephen Guest. In *Middlemarch* Dorothea arrives at the moment of renunciation (though, in this book, mutual love is at last allowed its sway and Dorothea's willingness for martyrdom is surpassed in the coming together of herself and Will at last).

George Eliot's own contemporaries were much fascinated by her body, and particularly by the imputed cross-gender characteristics of her countenance. Henry James's account of George Eliot's appearance on his first encounter with her seems imbued with his earlier reading of her work. In a letter to his father, after an account of her physical plainness he swings theatrically to the other extreme:

A mingled sagacity and sweetness—a broad hint of a great underlying world of reserve, knowledge, pride, and power—a great feminine dignity and character in these massively plain features—a hundred conflicting shades of consciousness and simpleness—shyness and frankness—graciousness and remote indifference.—these are some of the more definite elements of her personality.

The emphasis on range and on swerves and secrecy, as well as on "plainness," form a critique of George Eliot's prose as much as of her body. The two are seen as somehow implicated in each other in James's description. (James arrived unexpectedly at a crisis moment during the fatal illness of Thornie, George Henry Lewes's son, so that the intensity and the reserve may have been a response to an awkward visit.)

Any account of the intellectual pressures in George Eliot's work must register the extent to which those pressures have become inseparable from the energies of daily life. It is not enough to speak of "background" or "context"; rather, ideas become condensed as event, person, commentary, dialogue. The uneasy accord among these various elements of the fiction is freighted with irreconcilable perceptions. That is to say, the ideas that George Eliot thinks with are there in the *relations* of the text, rather than always spelled out referentially. Indeed, ideas are implicit in the activity of the book's structure as well as in its language. One phenomenon that this produces is the multiplicity of systems that varying readers can draw out of a single passage, so that according to each one's own current preoccupation Darwin or Mill, or Anna Jameson, or Hans Andersen or Spencer can be brought to the surface (all these, and more, are active in the one-and-a-half-page prelude to *Middlemarch*).

Yet the text's vibration does not produce a deconstructive freedom for the reader. Not everything here lies level; some areas of the text continue to resist open interpretation. Precisely in that aspect of the text where Eliot seems most to register the presence of the reader, in those extranarrative swerves into second person plural (the "we" of her wooing voice directed toward us) are to be found the most determined areas of the fiction. The text will not budge, will not yield itself to counterinterpretation or unraveling here. A reader may refuse to cooperate, may resist the suggestion that inevitably we must recognize what is proposed to us as true of behavior beyond the fiction, true to each our own behavior. But to do so requires disengagement from the text. There is menace as well as sympathy in the predicament this creates for the refusing reader: it threatens to expose an ethical inadequacy in that very act of refusal, or to drive us into an extratextual realm whose existence it denies.

So the question of authority is renewed. Many critics have noted that Eliot tends to avoid scenes of confrontation in her work and that when in the early work, as in *Adam Bede*, they do occur, they tend to be highly stylized and masculine. Much later such scenes occur in a rather different temper: between Dorothea and Rosamond, between Gwendolen and Grandcourt's cast-off lover, the mother of his children, between Daniel and his long-lost mother who does not wish to become a nurturing mother again. In each of these cases at least one of the participants is deeply uneasy about the encounter. But in the actual writing of her novels Eliot persistently shifts register within a sentence, skirmishes with asides and ironies, mounts into metaphor. This is a far more flexible way of indicating conflict and demurring at certainties than imposing binary oppositions. In "Notes on Form in Art" Eliot commments, "Fundamentally, form is unlikeness." George Eliot's dialogue does not have the electrifying cogency of Jane Austen's, but the conversations articulate difference and leave room for the unsaid, as in Mrs. Poyser's conversation, or the talk between the sisters Dorothea and Celia or the children Maggie and Tom, or in the anguished tug of need between Gwendolen and Deronda. The multiplicity of positions brings authority into play so that the reader is often left uncertain as to the provenance of insights and opinions even while assenting to their (conflicting) claims.

The chancy, the circumstantial, the improbable coincidence—all are given key roles in Eliot's perceptions: Silas is driven out of his first community by the lot declaring him to have stolen funds, and the child Eppie toddles into his cottage while his consciousness is suspended in a fit; *Daniel Deronda* opens with Gwendolen in the gambling hall, losing at play, and ends with Deronda setting out for an unknown country (an as yet nonexistent country) to which he is bound by the hazard of his genetic inheritance. His is a chosen quest, but full of risk.

The multiplicity of systems at work and their convergence in each different center of human consciousness makes for chance in Eliot's work. She draws here on probability theory and on the then-current writing of the astronomer Richard Proctor, the logician John Venn, and the mathematician W. K. Clifford, which G. H. Lewes also used, emphasizing the unsoundness of prediction and induction. The reader, also, is alerted to an improbably high number of circumstances by the action of her fiction, and is made preternaturally aware. Above all, in her ordering of plot, George Eliot draws on her intense response to individuation. Each person is "incarnate history"—none alike. In the abstracted language of her "Notes on Form in Art," human beings set in historical conditions are examples of "the most varied group of relations bound together in a wholeness which again has the most varied relations with all other phenomena." Within the novels that perception may become a country town, St. Oggs or Middlemarch; it may equally become each one of the town's inhabitants. Coincidence in her novels is not simply a ruse of the novelist but a reminder of the multivalency of the world, visible when attention is fully aroused.

Gillian Beer

Selected Bibliography

Beer, Gillian. *Darwin's Plots: Darwin, George Eliot, and Nineteenth-Century Fiction.* London: Routledge, 1983..

Beer, Gillian. *George Eliot.* Brighton: Harvester; Indiana University Press, 1986.

Carroll, David, ed. *George Eliot: The Critical Heritage.* London: Routledge, 1971.

David, Deirdre. *Intellectual Women and Victorian Patriarchy: Harriet Martineau, Elizabeth Barrett Browning, George Eliot.* Ithaca, N.Y.: Cornell University Press, 1987.

Eliot, George. *Collected Poems*, ed. Lucien Jenkins. London: Skoob Books, 1989.

Graver, Suzanne. *George Eliot and Community: A Study in Social Theory and Fictional Form.* Berkeley: University of California Press, 1984.

Haight, Gordon, ed. *Selections from George Eliot's Letters.* New Haven and London: Yale University Press, 1985.

Miller, Nancy. *Subject to Change: Reading Feminist Writing.* New York: Columbia University Press, 1988.

Paxton, Nancy L. *George Eliot and Herbert Spencer: Feminism, Evolutionism, and the Reconstruction of Gender.* Princeton, N.J.: Princeton University Press, 1991.

Pinney, Thomas. *Essays of George Eliot.* London: Routledge, 1963.

Shuttleworth, Sally. *George Eliot and Nineteenth-Century Science: The Make-Believe of a Beginning.* Cambridge: Cambridge University Press, 1984.

Trollope

PEOPLE who know anything about Anthony Trollope (1815–1882) usually know that he got up early every morning and wrote thousands of words, and that by doing this he wrote many books. Some also know that he worked in the Post Office and "invented" the pillar box, or mailbox. Others, claiming a bit more knowledge, gleefully describe how he would finish a novel on one day and invariably begin another the next day; a further refinement has it that if he finished a novel halfway through his predawn writing stint he would immediately start on the next one. Some people explain how his *Autobiography*, published a year after his death, revealed these mechanical writing habits and destroyed his reputation; some maintain that these revelations ruined his reputation (at least with critics) for good; others argue he was under a cloud until the pioneering work of Trollope biographer and bibliographer Michael Sadleir in the 1920s. Others assert that the real Trollope revival came only during World War II, when nostalgia for the "tranquil world" of his novels brought solace to war-ravaged Britain; still others believe he has been resurrected only lately, through the TV serialization of the Palliser and Barchester novels, or by the in-progress publication, for the first time, of complete editions of his novels, in paper by Oxford University Press World's Classics, in hard cover by the Trollope Society (through whose lobby a commemorative stone to Trollope was laid in Poets' Corner Westminster Abbey in the spring of 1993). Such myths are good fun. None of them—other than the recent publishing ventures and admission to Poets' Corner—is more than half correct; some are simply wrong.

The easiest to sort out is his Post Office career. After a miserable boyhood and youth (the result chiefly of his father's poverty and his own shy temperament), and after seven years as an unhappy and ineffectual clerk at postal headquarters in London, Trollope got himself transferred to Ireland in 1841. There he quickly found himself, learned to like his work, made a start toward his long-deferred goal of writing novels, married, and gradually rose to the high rank of postal surveyor (roughly one-third from the top). In 1851, still technically only a surveyor's clerk but much valued for his energetic work, he was sent "on loan" to postal districts in the southwest of England for the purpose of extending the rural posts; at this time, while working in the Channel Islands, he introduced the pillar box. He was actually adapting the practice in use in nearby France. The first boxes were operating by November 1852 at St. Helier; by September 1853 the first box on the mainland was erected, at Carlisle; the first for Ireland were sent to Trollope in March 1855. Within a few years pillar boxes were installed throughout Great Britain, and public approval was almost universal. (Only an extreme conservative, like Trollope's own creation Miss Jemima Stanbury in *He Knew He Was Right*, could possibly object to the pillar boxes: "She had not the faintest belief that any letter put into one of them would ever reach its destination. She could not understand why people would not walk to the respectable post-office instead of chucking them into an iron stump,—as she called it,—out in the middle of the street with nobody to look after it.") Although introduction of the roadside pillar boxes was to be Trollope's most memorable innovation in the postal service, he himself was more proud of his work in extending the rural posts throughout much of Ireland and England. In late 1859 he transferred back to an English district. He was occasionally entrusted with special assignments to make postal arrangements and treaties—in Egypt, the West Indies, and the United States. In 1867, after thirty-three years, he retired early from the service, forgoing any pension. His face has never been on a postage stamp.

Trollope's writing habits were complex and various, as were, naturally, his attendant reputations during his lifetime and since. A discussion of these matters can provide helpful insights into a novelist whose work has never quite yielded up its mysteries in the way that, say, that of Dickens or Henry James apparently has. Trollope's peculiar appeal keeps eluding critics, who are far from consensus as to his merits, much less on some single key to his achievement. There is little agreement on which among his many novels represent him at his best.

Trollope wrote forty-seven novels, five volumes of collected short stories plus a handful of uncollected stories, four large travel books (on North America, the West Indies, Australia and New Zealand, and South Africa) and a slight book about Iceland, three biographies, a book on Caesar's *Commentaries*, four collections of "sketches" (hunting types, clergymen, travelers, tradesmen), an unpublished book of social criticism (*The New Zealander*), two unsuccessful, never-performed plays, and enough essays and reviews to fill three or four more volumes—some seventy books in all. (For a quick comparison, among Trollope's famous contemporaries Dickens wrote fifteen novels, Thackeray eight, George Eliot seven, Charlotte Brontë four.) What exactly do we know of that well-known energy and those famous or infamous working habits that enabled Trollope to pile up such astounding numbers?

The speed at which he wrote his books and the intervals he allowed between them are for the most part a matter of record. He got off to a late, slow start. He began his first novel, *The Macdermots of Ballycloran*, in 1843 and finished it in 1845; the book was not published until March 1847, when Trollope was just turning thirty-two. Between 1846 and 1847 (exact dates are uncertain until the mid-1850s) he wrote his second novel, *The Kellys and the O'Kellys*, and between 1848 and 1849 his third, *La Vendée*. His next novel, *The Warden*, a one-volume work and much shorter than the first three, which were traditional three-volume novels, was a long time in coming. His work extending the rural posts had kept him more than usually busy. Then, in May 1852, at Salisbury, "whilst wandering there on a midsummer evening round the purlieus of the cathedral" he conceived the story of *The Warden*, the first of the Barsetshire novels. But it was a full year later before he began writing the book, only to be interrupted by his recall to Ireland as acting surveyor; he did not finish the novel until October 1854. By early 1855 he had written some eighty-five pages of a sequel, *Barchester Towers*, but he broke off the novel to write what proved to be an unpublishable work of social criticism, *The New Zealander*. Having wasted a year and a half on that project, he resumed *Barchester Towers* in May 1856 and determined to increase his writing efficiency by two strategies. The first was the practice of writing while traveling. By now he moved about not so much on horseback or in horse-drawn coach but by railway: "Like others," Trollope recalled, "I used to read,—though Carlyle has since told me that a man when travelling should not read, but 'sit still and label his thoughts'. But if I intended to make a profitable business out of my writing, and, at the same time, do my best for the Post Office, I must turn these hours to more account than I could do even by reading." Trollope made up a writing tablet and soon found that he could compose as quickly in a railway carriage as at his desk. Years later he would have carpenters build writing desks in his cabins on ocean-crossing steamers.

The second system he adopted at this time was a working diary of his writing. In his commonplace book of the 1830s he had said that a young man ought to keep a careful account of every monetary transaction and that his own failure to do so had brought him near to "utter ruin." Since his move to Ireland in 1841 he had scrupulously recorded his daily travel expenditures for the Post Office, keeping track of every mile, every pound, shilling, and penny. Now past forty years of age, he adapted ledger-style columned record keeping for his writing, marking off the days in weekly sections, entering daily the number of pages written each session, and then noting the week's total. His "page" had approximately 250 words, and he set a goal of forty manuscript pages per week. He would have preferred to work seven days a week, but of course there were weeks when he could only manage a few days, and some weeks when illness or pressures of other work kept him from writing at all. He usually did the forty pages per week, though on a few occasions he pushed himself to more than a hundred pages in a week. The working diaries were an exercise in self-discipline. For whereas his postal work had its daily and weekly obligations—including frequent and lengthy written reports—his novel writing was under no compulsion, no deadline other than his own will, and the result had been what Trollope termed "spasmodic" efforts only. But henceforth he wrote under the pressure of these diaries, with the result that "if at any time I have slipped into idleness for a day or two the record of that idleness has been there, staring me in the face, and demanding of me increased labour, so that the deficiency might be supplied." A week without a sufficient number of pages was "a blister to my eye," Trollope wrote, and a month would have been "a sorrow to my heart." Lapses were indicated by entries such as "Sore throat," "Ill," Hunting," or "Alas." But such interruptions were to remain relatively few; by and large the working diaries recorded a steady outpouring of words that provided a deep source of satisfaction. The diary-regulated writing would lead to startling results: with *Barchester Towers*, which was written at a pace five times faster than that which generated *The Warden*, Trollope's celebrated productivity took hold, and for good.

Throughout the remaining years of the 1850s he produced *The Three Clerks*, *Doctor Thorne*, *The Bertrams*, a travel book on the West Indies, and a handful of short stories. The critics were already objecting to his writing so much; and Trollope was considering publishing a short novel about trade (*The Struggles of Brown, Jones, and Robinson*) anonymously. Publisher Edward Chapman, soon after accepting *The Bertrams*, declined the short novel: "I should not like to do it without your name & at the same time I feel convinced that it is better that your name should be withheld, for there is a strong impression abroad that you are writing too rapidly for your permanent fame." Chapman had doubtless just read Sir Henry Maine's article in the *Saturday Review*, which said that although *Doctor Thorne*, the latest proof of Trollope's "fecundity," was good news, it nonetheless caused uneasiness about the "rapid multiplication of his progeny." A few months later, the *National Review*, in an otherwise favorable overview of the four novels that began with *The Warden*, complained that the production of two three-volume novels within ten months did not allow an author time to "to give due polish and completion" to his work, and regretted that Trollope "should be guilty of the bad taste of counting quantity before quality." Of his next novel the *Spectator* said, "The fact is he writes too fast. An average six or eight months is too short a time for the gestation and production of a first-class novel." Trollope, though he paid close attention to reviews, dismissed these warnings. Writing years later in his *Autobiography* about beginning *The Bertrams* the day after finishing *Doctor Thorne*, he said, with some irony, that he had determined "to excel, if not in quality, at any rate in quantity." He considered himself a workman—he grew increasingly fond of comparing the writing of novels with the making of shoes—and was proud of never having "scamped" his work. "My novels," he continued, "whether good or bad, have been as good as I could make them. Had I taken three months of idleness between each they would have been no better." (In fact, as shall be seen, he frequently did allow months between novels.) But he did pay heed to the criticism of overproduction to the extent that he kept alive in the back of his mind the plan for anonymous publication (and in 1867 and 1868 he brought out two novels anonymously, *Nina Balatka* and *Linda Tressel*). He estimated that a sensible pace for him would be three novels every two years. Four times in *An Autobiography* he referred with undisguised amusement to an incident in 1857 when he was "scared from the august columns of Paternoster Row," that is, from the publishing house of Longmans, when one of the firm protested to him about some fertile writer (probably G. P. R. James) who had "spawned upon them (the publishers) three novels a year." Trollope's own output, he decided, would be confined to "half the fecundity of that terrible author of whom the publisher in Paternoster Row complained to me." As it turned out, he sometimes bettered this pace.

Trollope did not hit his full writing stride until he was transferred to the English postal district at the close of 1859. At this time he was commissioned to write the long, lead novel for the about-to-be-launched *Cornhill Magazine*, edited by Thackeray and published by George Smith. Both the novel, *Framley Parsonage*, and the magazine itself became huge hits, and Trollope, whose popularity had been steadily increasing since *The Warden* in 1855, was well on his way to becoming, as one reviewer said in 1862, "almost a national institution." It was in connection with the return to England and the writing of *Framley Parsonage* that Trollope explained, in *An Autobiography*, the practice of steady early rising: he had taken a house at Waltham Cross, twelve miles north of London, and he brought with him from Ireland his Irish groom, Barney, who had worked in his employ since the early 1840s. Now Barney was entrusted with the duty of calling Trollope at five o'clock every morning so that he could be at his desk by five-thirty. For this service, which included bringing a cup of coffee, Barney was paid an additional five pounds yearly. Trollope wrote that during all the Waltham Cross years, Barney was never late: "I do not know that I ought not to feel that I owe more to him than to any one else for the success I have had." He would spend the first half hour in reading the previous day's work, and then, with watch before him, he strove to write a page every fifteen minutes, or some ten pages—twenty-five hundred words—daily. A pace of ten pages per day would have produced in ten months three three-volume novels, the very number that had so exasperated the publisher in Paternoster Row. Beginning with *Framley Parsonage*, Trollope often averaged about six "volumes" a year—and by a volume he meant the roughly sixty to eighty thousand words that made up one of the volumes of the standard nineteenth-century three-volume novel. (Of his forty-seven novels, twenty-one were three-deckers, nine were longer, the equivalent of four or five volumes, like *Phineas Finn* and *The Way We Live Now*, and seventeen were shorter, in one or two volumes, like *Sir Harry Hotspur of Humblethwaite* and *Cousin Henry*.) His daily output over the years averaged under ten pages per sitting; and it was nowhere near constant, varying between lows of four pages and highs of sixteen. (The fastest burst of his writing career came in July 1864 when for fourteen days straight he composed fifteen pages daily of the two-volume *Miss Mackenzie*—he usually managed more pages per diem when writing short novels.) Only on extraordinary occasions did he write a novel nearly straight through without a break. Naturally, a short novel, and one written during a holiday, had a better chance for this distinction: *Lady Anna*, written entirely aboard ship en route to Australia in 1871, had but one day of interruption, for illness; *Dr. Wortle's School*, written while on holiday at a friend's rectory in 1879, had none at all. What kept the production below three long novels per year—in addition to interruptions from illness, hunting, extra postal work, unusually difficult travel, and the writing of magazine articles— was the time Trollope usually allowed between novels. These pauses were chiefly rest periods, though doubtless he occupied himself during apparently fallow stretches with occasional writing (not recorded in the diaries), proofreading, and much preparatory thinking about his fictional characters. The early novels, as we have seen, were separated by considerable gaps, even years. After *Barchester Towers*, the intervals varied crazily, ranging from more than three months down to three instances when Trollope completed a novel and began a new one the next day (never did he begin a new novel the very day he finished one). A rough average, for what it is worth, was about six weeks between books.

After retiring from the Post Office in 1867, when one might have expected his writing productivity to increase, he wrote somewhat less than while engaged in two professions. He maintained that three hours a day of writing—four on the right kind of holiday—was about all that one could do anyway, so retirement had little effect on his output. During the eight years prior to leaving the service he wrote fifteen novels (in forty-two "volumes"), one travel book, three collections of short stories, and enough journalism to fill a large-sized volume. During the following eight years he wrote thirteen novels (in forty "volumes"), one travel book, one collection of short stories, and less journalism. Thus the latter pace was slightly slower than that of the period before his retirement; and that of the last eight years of his life was in turn slightly slower than that preceding it.

Another important and in some sense more significant turn in Trollope's writing habits also stemmed from *Framley Parsonage*: this watershed novel turned him into a serial novelist. Of the thirty-seven novels published after *Framley Parsonage* only four were originally released in book form, and of these, two had been intended for serial publication that had gone awry, and another, published posthumously, would have been placed with a magazine had Trollope lived. Thus *Miss Mackenzie* (1865) was the only novel he wrote after *Framley Parsonage* that was not intended for serial publication. These serialized stories were written with an eye to division into installments; they appeared in many different configurations, sometimes improvised by the publisher, but generally under Trollope's control: monthly, in magazines or independent "parts" in six, eight, twelve, sixteen, or twenty installments; weekly, in magazines or "parts" in twelve, twenty-six, thirty-two, forty, or more installments.

There is no doubting Trollope's talent for proportioning his work to order. His "mechanical genius," as he laughingly called it, enabled him to write his novels to exactly prescribed limits—installments per novel, chapters per installment, pages per chapter, words per page. The most explicit account of this kind of accommodation is seen in his negotiations with George Smith for the publication of *The Last Chronicle of Barset*. In early January 1866 he wrote to Smith, proposing a long novel in twenty shilling parts; Smith answered that he was not sure about shilling-part serialization; he would prefer to pay three thousand pounds for the right to print any kind of part issue and a first book edition. Trollope agreed. Smith next said that he might like to run the story in thirty instead of the usual twenty numbers. Trollope responded with a letter that modestly revealed his virtuosity in treating the problem of lengths in serial fiction. If the story must be written for possible twenty- or thirty-installment publication, preparation must be made to accommodate the larger number of parts:

It would not be practicable to divide 20 numbers into 30 equal parts, unless the work be specially done with this intent. I commonly divide a number of 32 pages (such as the numbers of "Orley Farm") into 4 chapters each. If you wish the work to be so arranged as to run either to 20 or to 30 numbers, I must work each of the 20 numbers by 6 chapters, taking care that the chapters run so equally, two and two, as to make each four into one equal part or each 6 into one equal part. There will be some trouble in this, but having a mechanical mind I think I can do it. . . . You will understand that I wish to suit your views altogether; but that it is necessary that you should say—Write it in 20 parts or in 30 parts—or in parts to suit either number. And you will also understand that if your mind be made up either to 30 or to 20, you need not put my mechanical genius to work.

(Smith decided on twenty monthly parts; then, two days later, he changed his mind and was leaning toward weekly publication in thirty-two parts, this last being the form he eventually settled upon.)

Like all writers for serial publication Trollope believed that the installments of a serial novel were meant to encase sections of the story that would hang together and, as he explained, "entice" the reader to come back to the next number. A serial should have "at least an attempt at murder in every number," Trollope once told a publisher, though he himself could "never get beyond giving my people a fever or a broken leg." Moreover, serial publication, he said, "forces upon the author the conviction that he should not allow himself to be tedious in any single part." Trollope admitted his own work was "often" tedious, but insisted that the serial writer must feel that he "cannot afford to have too many pages skipped out of the few which are to meet the reader's eye at the same time. Who can imagine the first half of the first volume of *Waverley* coming out in shilling numbers?" These ideas, he explained, came to him while writing *Framley Parsonage*, which novel, in spite of its failings, had, he thought, at least "no long succession of dull pages." It can be argued that *Framley Parsonage* did more than give his popularity a tremendous boost and turn him permanently into a serial novelist; it would in the long run make him more careful in the balancing of plots and counterplots, and to this extent serial publication made him a better and slightly different novelist. During the serialization of this novel, Elizabeth Gaskell wrote to George Smith, "I wish Mr. Trollope would go on writing Framley Parsonage for ever." In some ways, he did just that.

An account of the apportioning of Trollope's writing into serialized segments, of early rising, of working diaries, and of writing while traveling on trains and ocean steamers leaves out what he would have described as the hardest and most important part of writing a novel—

his thinking about his characters, "living with" them, daydreaming about them. This practice went way back, having its origins in his unhappy school days at Winchester College where Trollope attended from his twelfth to fifteenth year. There he developed the habit of escaping from the discomforts, failures, and loneliness of his boarding school existence into an imaginary world. Even in earlier days, as a child, he had been often thrown upon himself. Other boys had not much played with him, and he had had to "form my plays within myself." Now, the practice became continuous, almost systematic:

Study was not my bent, and I could not please myself by being all idle. Thus it came to pass that I was always going about with some castle in the air firmly built within my mind. Nor were these efforts in architecture spasmodic, or subject to constant change from day to day. For weeks, for months, if I remember rightly, from year to year, I would carry on the same tale, binding myself down to certain laws, to certain proportions, and proprieties, and unities. Nothing impossible was ever introduced,—nor even anything which, from outward circumstances, would seem to be violently improbable. I myself was of course my own hero. Such is a necessity of castle-building. But I never became a king, or a duke,—much less when my height and personal appearance were fixed could I be an Antinous, or six feet high. I never was a learned man, nor even a philosopher. But I was a very clever person, and beautiful young women used to be fond of me. And I strove to be kind of heart, and open of hand, and noble in thought, despising mean things; and altogether I was a very much better fellow that I have ever succeeded in being since.

One can see here the seeds of his disposition as a novelist taking root. Certainly that was the way Trollope later interpreted his early habit of incessant "castle-building." When, at nineteen, he became a clerk in the London General Post Office, he kept up the practice. He had determined to become a writer and secretly confided this aspiration to his journal. In those pages he convinced himself that he had not the talent for poetry or drama, nor the erudition for history or biography: "But I thought it possible that I might write a novel."

Years went by, and he never made the attempt, all the while suffering his own private mental disgrace for not making the attempt. Still, Trollope continued the daydreaming that had begun at Winchester, carrying on a story in his mind for months and longer. It was an admittedly "dangerous mental practice," but one that taught him how "to maintain an interest in a fictitious story, to dwell on a work created by my own imagination, and to live in a world altogether outside the world of my material life." He later insisted that had it not been for this day-dreaming he would never have written a novel. It is worth noting of his subsequent writing career that when it came to the actual putting of pen to paper, the words seemed to come forth as though being dictated to a secretary. If a writer of fiction, Trollope said, has done his preparation, his thinking about his characters, he could work straight through for three hours, there being no need to "sit nibbling his pen, and gazing at the wall." A friend staying at a country house where Trollope was also a visitor related how Trollope came down to breakfast and said he had just "told himself" so many pages. And his manuscript pages were sent off to the printer as written—no second drafts, no fair copies, and usually no more than two or three words changed or crossed through on any page.

Late in life Trollope wrote a magazine article, "A Walk in a Wood," in which he dilated on how for him the most difficult part of creating a novel was not the actual writing, but the "thinking." By this, he explained, he did not mean thinking about the "entire plot" or overall story, since the larger incidents of his tales "are fabricated to fit my story as it goes on, and not my story to fit the incidents." (He mentions Lady Mason's confessing her forgery in *Orley Farm*, Lizzie Eustace's stealing her own diamonds in *The Eustace Diamonds*, and Mrs. Proudie's dying of a heart attack in *The Last Chronicle* as examples of large plot developments that had suddenly come upon him the midst of writing.) Rather, the hard work of thinking was expended on the "minute ramifications of tale-telling;—how this young lady should be made to behave herself toward that young gentleman;—how this mother or that father would be affected by the ill conduct or the good of a son or a daughter." Such thinking is best served by a peaceful atmosphere:

Bad noises, bad air, bad smells, bad light, an inconvenient attitude, ugly surroundings, little misfortunes that have lately been endured, little misfortunes that are soon to come, hunger and thirst, overeating and overdrinking, want of sleep or too much of it, a tight boot, a starched collar, are all inimical to thinking. . . . It is not the sorrows but the annoyances of life which impede. Were I told that the bank had broken in which my little all was kept for me I could sit down and write my love story . . . but to discover that I had given half a sovereign instead of sixpence to a cabman would render a great effort necessary before I could find the fitting words for a lover. These little lacerations of the spirit, not the deep wounds, make the difficulty. Of all the nuisances named, noises are the worst. . . . To think with a barrel organ within hearing is heroic. For myself, I own that a brass band altogether incapacitates me. No sooner does the first note of the opening burst reach my ear, than I start up, fling down my pen, and cast my thoughts disregarded into the abyss of some chaos that is always there ready to receive them.

Although he could do some thinking in a carriage and had even composed some "little plots" on horseback waiting at the covert side during a fox hunt, he much preferred to think about his characters while walking in a wood. It is best, he writes, to reject even the company of a dog, and to keep away from cottages, children, and other chance wanderers, "so much easier is it to speak than to think." Solitary woods were becoming rarer in England, but the "pure forests" of Switzerland and the Black Forest—late in life his favorite holiday places—were the perfect "hunting grounds" for thought.

The above article was written a decade after he retired from the Post Office, and one can see how in later years he was more productive in his novel writing while on holiday, but one wonders how he found time for his daydreaming during the many hectic years when he worked full time for the post office—which job, it should be said, he always regarded as his primary occupation.

An additional source of information about Trollope's writing habits can be discovered in a short autobiographical story, "The Panjandrum" (1870), which gives an account of how his daydreams fed his fiction. The story, set around 1840, tells of a hopeless scheme, a young man's attempt to found or be part of the founding group of a periodical. Six impoverished people determine to bring out a magazine that will be "the great future lever of the age." The narrator, plainly meant to represent Trollope himself, is chosen editor, in spite of his youth. At their meeting the projectors vote not to include novels, even though the editor had volunteered to try one. It later transpires that each of the group is entirely dissatisfied with all the others' contributions, including the editor's short story, and they break up, the plan of founding a magazine abandoned. However fictionalized, the story, as we are assured in *An Autobiography*, had been suggested by a struggle "in my own early days . . . over an abortive periodical which was intended to be the best thing ever done." The most interesting aspect of "The Panjandrum" is its detailed illustration of how Trollope's "castle-building" came to materialize on paper. It is not known whether he actually wrote a short story at this time; the account in "The Panjandrum" may simply reflect his later method. In the story, the young would-be writer, while walking in Regent's Park on a harsh, rainy day, sees a middle-aged servant woman leading a girl of ten or eleven with mud all over her stockings. As he passes them the girl says, "Oh, Anne, I do so wonder what he's like," and Anne tells her, "You'll see." The narrator begins thinking: who is it that the girl comes "tripping along through the rain and mud to see, and kiss, and love, and wonder at? And why hadn't she been taken in a cab? Would she be allowed to take off those dirty stockings before she was introduced to her new-found brother, or wrapped in the arms of her stranger father?" The aspiring novelist saw no more of the girl and servant, but "thought a great deal of the girl." "Gradually," we are told, "as the unforced imagination came to play upon the matter, a little picture fashioned itself in my mind." Walking the whole round of Regent's Park, he builds his castle in the air, a story called "The New Inmate": "The girl was my own sister,—a sister whom I had never seen till she was thus brought to me for protection and love; but she was older, just budding into womanhood." He furnishes a little white-curtained sitting room, provides her with books, a piano, a low sofa, and "all little feminine belongings." He sells his horse—"the horse of my imagination, the reader will understand, for I had never in truth possessed such an animal"—resigns from his club, and devotes himself to taking care of his sister. But she soon falls in love and is given in marriage to his friend Walker. The narrator, returning home out of the rain, cannot wait to take up his pen. For five days he works on the story. When not writing, while "walking, eating, or reading," he still thinks of the story. He dreams of it, weeps over it. The story becomes "a matter that admitted of no doubt"; the little girl with the muddy stockings is but a "blessed memory"; his newfound sister is "palpably" real:

All her sweetnesses were present to me, as though I had her there, in the little street turning out of Theobald's Road. To this moment I can distinguish the voice in which she spoke to me that little whispered word, when I asked her whether she cared for Walker. When one thinks of it, the reality of it all is appalling. What need is there of a sister or a friend in the flesh . . . when by a little exercise of the mind they may be there at your elbow, faultless?

When in *An Autobiography* Trollope describes himself as "living with his characters," as "weeping with them, laughing with them," when he says he ever lived much with the ghost of Mrs. Proudie after killing her off in *The Last Chronicle*, he is not speaking altogether figuratively. The fictional characters of his daydreams came to have an "appalling reality" for him.

He said of *Framley Parsonage*, for example, that in writing the book so quickly to order, he had not had much time to think about his characters, and by placing the novel in Barsetshire he was able "to fall back upon my old friends Mrs. Proudie and the Archdeacon." Moreover, Barsetshire itself was a "palpably real" place to him:

As I wrote it I became more closely acquainted than ever with the new shire which I had added to the English counties. I had it all in my mind,—its roads and railroads, its towns and parishes, its members of Parliament, and the different hunts which rode over it. I knew all the great lords and their castles, the squires and their parks, the rectors and their churches. This was the fourth novel of which I had placed the scene in Barsetshire, and as I wrote it I made a map of the dear county. Throughout these stories there has been no name given to a fictitious site which does not represent to me a spot of which I know all the accessories, as though I had lived and wandered there.

But his "personages" were always his first interest. He said of the Palliser novels that his main concern was the gradual growth of his characters with the passage of time. Plantagenet Palliser, Lady Glencora, and the Duke of Omnium, from earlier novels, along with newer characters from the first Phineas Finn novel, Finn himself, Lady Laura, Violet Effingham, and Madame Max Goesler kept "luring" him back: "So much of my inner life was passed in their company, that I was continually asking myself how this woman would act when this or that event had passed over her head, or how that man would carry himself when his youth had become manhood, or his manhood declined to old age." Of the "incidents" in the stories he claimed he knew practically nothing beforehand but devised them as he wrote. But by daydreaming, by living with his characters, he knew their personalities so thoroughly that the evil or good within them was as "clear to me as are the stars on a summer night."

As it turned out, his characters eventually came also to have, if not an appalling reality, at least an almost spooky presence for his readers. In a rather negative review of *Framley Parsonage*, the *Saturday Review*, while complaining that Trollope "is far less of a novelist than a good diner-out," had to admit that "It seems a kind of breach of hospitality to criticise *Framley Parsonage* at all. It has been an intimate of the drawing room—it has travelled with us in the train—it has lain on the breakfast-table. We feel as if we had met Lady Lufton at a country house, admired Lord Dumbello at a ball, and seen Mrs. Proudie at an episcopal evening party." When Trollope ended the Barsetshire novels with *The Last Chronicle*, R. H. Hutton, reviewing the book in the *Spectator*, faced the end of the series with only partially mock despair. "What am I to do without ever meeting Archdeacon Grantly?" Hutton quotes a friend as saying, "He was one of my best and most intimate friends. . . . It was bad enough to lose the Old Warden, Mr. Septimus Harding, but that was a natural death. . . . Mr. Trollope has no right to break old ties in this cruel and reckless way." Hutton professed "loneliness very oppressive" at the prospect of never again meeting Grantly, "the best known and most typical of his fellow-countrymen," and was indulging thoughts of leaving England for ever. The *London Review* expressed "gentle melancholy" at the leave-taking from Barsetshire, and, paraphrasing Trollope's words, said: "To us, as well as to him, Barset has long been a real county, and its city a real city; and the spires and towers have been before our eyes, and the voices of the people are known to our ears, and the pavements of the city ways are familiar to our footsteps." Mrs. Oliphant wrote in *Blackwood's Magazine*, "*We* did not ask that this chronicle should be the last. We were in no hurry to be done with our old friends. And there are certain things which he has done without consulting us against which we greatly demur. To kill Mrs. Proudie was murder, or manslaughter at the least."

When in 1874 *Phineas Redux*, the fourth of the six Palliser novels, brought that series once again before the reading public, one reviewer, having first noted that a rumor of Phineas's return had long been current, said: "Indeed, we all of us know those of Mr. Trollope's characters who appear and reappear in the main line of his social tradition, so much better than we know ninety-nine hundredths of our own friends, that if by any chance we can gather news of their future fortunes, however indirectly, from the one depository of the secret of their existence, there is none of us who would not avail himself of that opportunity far more eagerly than of any of the ordinary sources of social gossip." To his readers, Trollope's creations seemed almost more real than did their actual life counterparts; they were becoming nearly as real to some readers as they were to Trollope. Virginia Woolf was to say that we believe in Trollope's characters "as we do in the reality of our weekly bills," that we get from his novels "the same sort of refreshment and delight that we get from seeing something actually happen in the street below."

Trollope's critical reputation has long been a source of misinformation. Michael Sadleir's assertion in 1927 that Trollope's first novel, *The Macdermots of Ballycloran* was "stillborn" in 1847 and represented a "false dawn" runs contrary to fact. The book received at least thirteen reviews in England, almost all of them very positive. It is true that Trollope's first three novels did not sell, that only with *The Warden* and *Barchester Towers*, in 1855 and 1857, did he become popular. "The novel-reading world," he said, "did not go mad about *The Warden*; but I soon felt that it had not failed as the others had failed. . . . And I could discover that people around me knew that I had written a book." The reviewers liked especially the novel's "great cleverness." The *Leader* innocently said that *The Warden* "certainly promises well for the author's future, if he gives us more books." Two years later when *Barchester Towers* appeared, it met with almost unanimous praise from the critics, and again the label "clever" appeared everywhere. While the reviews were superb, Trollope himself could afford years later in *An Autobiography* to be more modest, saying only that *Barchester Towers*, like *The Warden*, "achieved no great reputation, but it was one of the novels which novel readers were called upon to read." It became, he went on, "one of those novels which do not die quite at once, which live and are read for perhaps a quarter of a century." In fact, *Barchester Towers* has come down to posterity as the quintessential Trollope novel; and as the title most available through the years, doubtless the most popular Trollope novel. With *Barchester Towers* he was well on his way to becoming what he had dreamed of years earlier, "something more than a clerk in the Post Office."

With *Framley Parsonage*, as has been seen, Trollope became a bestseller, destined to be dubbed the king of serial novelists during the 1860s. If Dickens and George Eliot remained preeminent, they produced during this decade three and four novels, respectively, while Trollope was coming before his public relentlessly, with some two novels a year, almost always to a good press. In 1865, for example, *Miss Mackenzie*, little known today, drew rave notices: the *London Review* called this tale, in which the central character is a spinster of thirty-five, neither witty nor very attractive, a "bold undertaking"; the *Reader* saluted it as a novel that "no one but Mr. Trollope would have had either the hardihood to undertake, or the ability to write so as to be readable"; the *Westminster Review*, calling Trollope "our most popular novelist," said he had never drawn a better female character; *The Times* wrote, "We know not any other living writer of fiction who would have been so bold as to undertake the dealing with such a subject." The *Saturday Review* said, "Nobody but Mr. Trollope would have dared to marry a heroine of some forty years to a widower of fifty with nine children." The high point in his critical career came with *The Last Chronicle of Barset* in 1867. Reviewers deemed it his best novel to date, a view summed up by Hutton (widely regarded as the shrewdest critic of the Victorian era): "Of its own kind," he wrote in the *Spectator*, "there has been no better novel ever written than the *Last Chronicle of Barset*."

A gradual falling off with the reviewers was to set in, most decidedly with *Lady Anna* (1874), and continuing through *The Way We Live Now* (1875), *The Prime Minister* (1876), *The American Senator* (1877), and *Is He Popenjoy?* (1878). Yet during the very last years of his life Trollope had at least six critical successes: *John Caldigate* (1879) received mostly good reviews; *Cousin Henry* (1879) did even better; *The Duke's Children* (1880) enjoyed great acclaim, a markedly different reception from that given four years earlier to the previous Palliser novel, *The Prime Minister*; *Dr. Wortle's School, Ayala's Angel* (both 1881), and *Mr. Scarborough's Family* (written in 1881, posthumous publication 1883) all had a fine press. It is hardly accurate to maintain, as many have done, that at the time of Trollope's death in December 1882 his critical reputation was in tatters.

Then, in October 1883, less than a year later, his *Autobiography* appeared. All its talk about the mechanical aspects of writing, its downplaying of "inspiration," its emphasis on monetary rewards for writers, its insistence on comparing the writing of novels to the making of shoes, led a few contemporaries and many subsequent critics to believe that *An Autobiography* demolished Trollope's already sinking reputation. This view was fostered by Michael Sadleir, who saw himself as Trollope's twentieth-century apologist. In his introduction to the 1923 World's Classics edition of *An Autobiography*, Sadleir wrote that the book "made its posthumous appearance, extinguished its author's good name for a quarter of a century, and vanished." In Sadleir's influential *Trollope: A Commentary* (1927) he elaborated, saying that with *An Autobiography* Trollope "from beyond the grave . . . flung in the face of fashionable criticism the aggressive horse-sense of his views on life and book-making"; this caused "malevolent hostility" and an overwhelming "tempest of reaction" against his work and ideas. But this scenario does not fit well with the facts.

For one thing, Trollope's working habits were scarcely a secret, as he had for years gone out of his way to talk about the very things thought to be the shocking "revelations" in the *Autobiography*. For that matter, reviewers had discussed them. The *Westminster Review*, for example, had said, "It is told of Mr. Trollope that he considers his own method of art to be purely mechanical, and that he has declared that he could teach easily any one to write as good books as his own in a short space of time." The *Saturday Review*, immediately after Trollope's death, but before the existence of *An Autobiography* was even heard of, said that only the "stupid critic" would think "that the steady regularity of Mr. Trollope's method of work is incompatible with genius." Furthermore, *An Autobiography* was universally acclaimed on its publication in 1883. In a laudatory two-part article, the *Times* combined enthusiasm for "this extremely frank autobiography" in which was found "more of the sensational than in any of his novels" with an appreciative survey of Trollope's writings. The revelation of his early miseries reminded the reviewer of those Dickens endured, a comparison made also by the *Daily Telegraph* and by many other reviews. The *Spectator* ran three positive reviews of *An Autobiography*. The *Saturday Review* admitted to the suspicion that "had Trollope been content to write a little less, he might have written a little better," but then drew back, saying, "It is possible that Trollope's system suited him best." The *Fortnightly Review* called *An Autobiography* a "most entertaining book," demonstrating the necessity of "ceaseless devotion of mind and unintermitting labour of body." The *Morning Post* commended its "entire unreserve" and thought it would encourage "despondent toilers" to persevere. The *Daily Telegraph* said the book was a "flood of light" thrown on the "inner life of Anthony Trollope . . . [which] will but serve to make his countrymen regard him with increased admiration and respect." Other favorable reviews appeared in the *Athenaeum*, the *Academy*, the *Christian World*, the *Edinburgh Review*, and *Blackwood's Magazine*. To say that *An Autobiography* killed Trollope's reputation is to disregard the record. (Among the few earlier critics to raise the issue of Trollope's talk about his writing habits as harmful to his reputation was George Gissing, who gave the question his own twist, saying that he *hoped* it were true that "the great big stupid public," was "really, somewhere in its secret economy, offended by that revelation of mechanical methods.")

Trollope, like other early Victorian novelists—and for that matter, like all novelists—did undergo a spell of disfavor after his death.

According to R. C. Terry, Trollope suffered some dozen years of neglect, leading up to the turn of the century; Sadleir, seeing himself as a "lonely pioneer for a writer with fairly dubious claims on posterity," considerably exaggerated Trollope's demise. Three early critics are especially important for the history of Trollope's "disappearance." George Saintsbury in 1895 held that Trollope's work was "of the day and the craftsman, not of eternity and art" and this augured "comparative oblivion" for him. (A quarter of a century later Saintsbury revised his judgment and placed Trollope just behind Austen, Scott, Dickens, and Thackeray.) In 1907 Herbert Paul pronounced that, although Trollope during his heyday was "more popular than any of his contemporaries," his books were now "dead." (Both the early Saintsbury and the Paul pieces, incidentally, are wistful, somewhat sad in their dismissal of Trollope; they praise the readability of something they then belittle— an old and long-lasting habit of critics of Trollope's fiction. As early as 1863 an anonymous reviewer of *Rachel Ray* wrote, "It may seem rather hard that critics should read Mr. Trollope's novels and enjoy them, and then abuse them for being what they are"; in 1865 the young Henry James, who twenty years later would do a complete about-face, began a review of *Miss Mackenzie,* "We have long entertained for Mr. Trollope a partiality of which we have yet been somewhat ashamed.") Lewis Melville, in 1906, wrote that Trollope suffered the "worst fate that can befall a writer: he has not been abused; he has not been ignored; and he is not disappearing; he has disappeared." Sadleir's version of the "disappearance" and critical disparagement of Trollope was based largely on Saintsbury, Paul, and Melville. It was surely not based on the American critic William Dean Howells, who during these years was saying that only Trollope could be bracketed with Jane Austen, that he was "undoubtedly one of he finest of artists," and that "the long line of his wise, just, sane novels" were on rereading "as delightful as ever."

Some subsequent high points for Trollope's critical reputation can be listed briefly here: the *Times Literary Supplement's* entire front page devoted to Trollope in September 1909; Sadleir's *Commentary* in 1927; David Cecil's Trollope chapter in his *Early Victorian Novelists* (1934); the work of Bradford Booth in the 1940s and 1950s, including the founding in 1946 of *The Trollopian* (subsequently renamed *Nineteenth-Century Fiction*); A. O. J. Cockshut's *Anthony Trollope: A Critical Study* (1955); and Robert Polhemus's *Changing World of Anthony Trollope* (1968). Thereupon has followed an outpouring of work on Trollope, some thirty full-length critical books, and, in the last five years, four major biographies (R. H. Super, Richard Mullen, N. John Hall, and Victoria Glendinning).

But there exists another and more important reputation, that with readers as opposed to that with critics. Readers Trollope has always had in great abundance. (Writers, too, for Trollope has ever been a writer's writer, from the early days when George Eliot wrote congratulating him on his mastery in organizing "thoroughly natural everyday incidents," calling this skill "among the subtleties of art which can hardly be appreciated except by those who have striven after the same result with conscious failure.") During Trollope's lifetime there was a close correlation between critical and readerly reputations, but since his death that has not been the case until recently. With the "common reader" Trollope's popularity has been and is extraordinary, and we know this not from the judgments and speculations of literary critics but from publishers' records. To take but the period of supposed greatest neglect, 1885 through 1915: a very incomplete tally for these thirty years shows that British publishers (including Ward Lock, Chapman & Hall, Chatto & Windus, Smith Elder, Longman, Macmillan, Bentley, John Lane, Blackie, Long, Bell, Dent, Oxford, Cassell, Collins, Routledge, Nelson, Bohn, Butterworth, Lever, Blackwood, and Sampson Low) issued more than 180 combined editions and reprintings of his books. American publishers (including Munro, Millar, Dodd Mead, Knight, Lupton, Lovell Coryell, Harpers, Page, Gebbie, Fowle, Century, DuMont, Dutton, Winston, Burt, and Lippincott) produced the even more impressive figure of almost 300 editions and reprintings. Even though the size of the printings is for the most part unknowable, the numbers are remarkable. It is clear that Trollope never suffered anything even remotely resembling total eclipse, even during years when his critical reputation was at its lowest. Today Trollope is more read than at any time since his own day. This fact is attested to by the great number of Trollope editions in print, a number that could soon reach the phenomenal total of 250, as Penguin Books follows Oxford University Press World's Classics in bringing out its own uniform paperback editions of all the novels, the short stories, and *An Autobiography*. And because very few of these books are produced for the lucrative classroom market—with its captive audiences—it may be said that more people choose to read Trollope than any other classic English author. The aforementioned recent outburst of critical attention simply means that Trollope criticism is catching up with the so-called ordinary reader, not to mention fellow novelists, in admiration for and loyalty to Trollope.

Meanwhile the "Trollope problem" persists in spite of admirable efforts by critics to explain him. It begins with the preliminary question of which Trollope books merit the most attention. The "chaos of criticism" articulated by Bradford Booth in 1958 still obtains: "Among Trollope's forty-seven novels there are only a handful that someone has not called his best." That critics and readers would disagree about the relative merits of books amid so large a number is only natural. But the degree of difference of opinion about Trollope's novels is singular. No one believes that *Barnaby Rudge* is Dickens's greatest work, or *Philip* Thackeray's, or *Romola* George Eliot's. But in Trollope's case, there are people who rate, say, *Is He Popenjoy?* as on a par with anything he ever wrote, while others dismiss it out of hand. Listing one's favorites among Trollope's many titles has long been a kind of unwinnable, endless game his readers play among themselves. It is true that from the first many people have given pride of place to the six novels of the Barchester series, with special favor going to *Barchester Towers* (often thought of as Trollope's *Pride and Prejudice* in wide appeal) and to *The Last Chronicle*—many people's choice, and Trollope's own, for his single best novel. Among other Barsetshire titles, Trollope's contemporaries set great store by *Doctor Thorne* and *Framley Parsonage*; later generations seem to give the edge to *The Small House at Allington*. Next in popularity, and for many twentieth-century readers an even more sustained and realized achievement, has been the six-novel Palliser series, admired largely as a collective portrait of Plantagenet Palliser and Lady Glencora; among these books, in Trollope's day *The Eustace Diamonds* may have been most popular; today the nod would perhaps go to the Phineas novels or *The Duke's Children*. Among the "independent" novels, *Orley Farm* stood out in Trollope's day, *The Way We Live Now* in ours. Other especially well-received works in Trollope's time were *The Three Clerks* and *Rachel Ray*; in the twentieth century, *Dr. Wortle's School* and *Ayala's Angel*. But strong claims are made for *He Knew He Was Right* and *Is He Popenjoy?* One would have thought that with the winnowing of time some agreement would be nearer, but such is hardly the case, owing chiefly to Trollope's startling evenness. The "essential Trollope" was present from beginning to end, a fact attested to by the high critical regard that has settled upon *The Macdermots of Ballycloran*, his very first novel, and upon *Mr. Scarborough's Family*, finished about a year before his death.

And, of course, the question of what constitutes the peculiar excellence of this "essential Trollope" is equally unanswerable. It probably lies in some elusive and complex mix—the proportions varying with each reader—of all those elements very different kinds of critics have praised in his works: the uncanny "realism" of his characters (this would have been Trollope's own explanation); his convincing dialogue; his believable plots; his talent for "dramatizing the undramatic"; his sympathy for all his characters; his "looking to circumstances" by a kind of foreshadowing of what today is called situation ethics; his "natural psychology"; his "photographic" fidelity in depicting social mores; the abiding comic vision; the pervasive presence of his narrator, whose worldly-wise yet kindly voice often makes even his less successful novels so readable; the plain, unobtrusive style, a style that doesn't call attention to itself but is nonetheless loaded with almost constant irony, an irony so quiet, nuanced, and subtle as frequently to go undetected. To fall back on this "little bit of each" approach may seem critically unadventurous. But at least it is sound. And it adds up, I think, to an endorsement of a dictum set forth by Gordon Ray, in one of the most useful essays on its subject: "Trollope was a great, truthful, varied artist, who wrote better than he or his contemporaries realized, and who left behind him more novels of lasting value that any other writer in English." That seems fair enough.

N. John Hall

Selected Bibliography

Booth, Bradford A. *Anthony Trollope: Aspects of His Life and Art*. Bloomington: Indiana University Press, 1958.
Cockshut, A. O. J. *Anthony Trollope: A Critical Study*. London: Collins, 1955.
Hall, N. John. *Trollope: A Biography*. Oxford: Clarendon, 1991.
Hall, N. John, ed. *The Trollope Critics*. London: Macmillan, 1981.
Halperin, John. *Trollope and Politics: A Study of the Pallisers and Others*. London: Macmillan, 1977.

Herbert, Christopher. *Trollope and Comic Pleasure.* Chicago: University of Chicago Press, 1987.

Kincaid, James R. *The Novels of Anthony Trollope.* Oxford: Clarendon, 1977.

Polhemus, Robert M. *The Changing World of Anthony Trollope.* Berkeley and Los Angeles: University of California Press, 1968.

Sadleir, Michael. *Trollope: A Commentary.* 1927. 3d ed. London: Oxford University Press, 1961.

Terry, R. C. *Anthony Trollope: The Artist in Hiding.* London: Macmillan, 1977.

Wilkie Collins and the Sensation Novel

The sensation of a moment often makes the thought of a life.
Wilkie Collins, Basil: A Story of Modern Life

THE critical history of sensation fiction reads remarkably like the plot of a typical sensation novel itself. Sometime around 1890, sensation novels mysteriously established themselves in the literary marketplace in England, where they met with astounding popularity and financial success. Like one of the scheming impersonators from their plots, however, the texts themselves were soon exposed by critics as frauds and condemned as unworthy even to bear the name "literature." About a decade later, just as mysteriously, sensation fiction essentially disappeared from the literary landscape, only to resurface toward the end of the century, this time disguised as another popular genre, the detective novel. It, too, was recognized and unmasked by scrupulous literary critics as an insignificant and possibly even dangerous form of escapism, unworthy of serious literary consideration but requiring severe moral opprobrium. When the techniques and conventions of popular art were appropriated by high modernist and postmodernist writers in the twentieth century, however, and even more recently, as the traditional standards of canon formation came under attack in the academy, literary critics once again exhumed the body of texts that made such a sensation in the 1860s, declaring them, almost melodramatically, to be authentic and valuable literary documents after all. If the sensation novel is considered as a legitimate example of "popular" culture, more significant for having been marginalized, its previous repudiation may be interpreted as revealing more about the serious threat it posed to the values of the dominant culture that rejected it than about its genuine literary merits. The "plot" of such a critical history, in fact, underscores how deeply the production and evaluation of literary texts may be entangled with the shifting circumstances of the historical situation in which they emerge, and, more specifically, how profoundly the critical reception of popular literary forms might reflect the very cultural stresses and contradictions that both call those forms into being and seek to obliterate them.

Histories of the novel have traditionally identified the origins of sensation fiction with the work of Charles Dickens's brilliant protégé, Wilkie Collins, if not with Dickens himself. But while he was the most distinguished among the writers of this most popular novelistic sub-genre in the nineteenth century, Collins did not invent the sensation novel. Dickens, his mentor and friend, did not invent it, nor did the other most famous and prolific practitioners of the form, Mary Elizabeth Braddon, Charles Reade, or Mrs. Henry Wood. The "sensation novel" was a genre invented in the 1860s by the same outraged literary critics and reviewers who condemned it. They coined the term and created the category to describe and contain a disreputable form of literature that they generally regarded as morally diseased, aesthetically bankrupt, and socially dangerous. Because of its treatment of scandalous domestic situations and its supposed appeal to physical and emotional sensations rather than to the higher rational faculties, the "sensation novel" became the exemplary case by which the corrupting influence of "low" art could be distinguished from the elevating effect of "high" art in mid-nineteenth-century England.

Despite its almost universal rejection by the literary establishment as morally and artistically nothing more than a scandal, the sensation novel was, however, commercially, nothing less than a sensation. Sensation novels made considerable fortunes for their writers, for the magazine publishers who initially presented them in installments to the public, for the book publishers who then produced them in bound volumes and often published pirated editions of them, for the producers who staged equally popular theatrical versions of the novels, and for the manufacturers of such products as soap and perfume commonly named after the protagonists and titles of the most sensational among them. The sensation novel was as much merchandise as it was art. But the widespread and intense controversy sensation fiction inspired suggested that it was merchandise of a very significant—perhaps even subversive—kind.

The prevailing critical consensus about the "sensation mania" of the 1860s was as paradoxical as it was ardent. While sensation fiction was commonly dismissed as "light" and insubstantial reading, it was also regarded as a virulent and dangerous phenomenon. The public's insatiable appetite for sensation fiction was thought to manifest a morbid and infectious social disease, a symptom of widespread cultural disorder, a nervous desire for excitement and "perversion" of the most undesirable and French variety. While sensation fiction elicited some of the most repressive of Victorian attitudes among critics, however, it also provoked important exchanges on the subject of literary realism during the period. Figures such as G. H. Lewes, George Eliot, Henry James, Anthony Trollope, and William Thackeray, among others, made some of their most sophisticated articulations and defenses of literary realism in the context of their generally negative reviews of sensation novels. What we now identify as the novel of high Victorian realism might well be said to have defined itself against the tenets of sensation fiction. In fact, the specter of sensation fiction so dominated the critical discourse of the 1860s that by the mid-1870s, Trollope would ironically suggest in his *Autobiography* that the sensation novel was responsible for giving rise to the realistic novel itself:

Among English novels of the present day, and among English novelists, a great division is made. There are sensational novels and anti-sensational, sensational novelists and anti-sensational, sensational readers and anti-sensational. The novelists who are considered to be anti-sensational are generally called realistic. I am realistic. My friend Wilkie Collins is generally supposed to be sensational.

Even that final line of defense fell, however, before the pervasive and corrupting influence of what the *Quarterly* dismissed as "mere trash or something worse." Trollope himself succumbed to writing a novel in the sensation mode with *The Eustace Diamonds* (1873), and in the Transome plot of *Felix Holt* (1866) even George Eliot, the acknowledged master of Victorian realism, was accused of being infected by what *Punch* called "the black, black ink" of sensation fiction.

If the sensation novel was an artificial invention of the conservative literary establishment of the 1860s, it also constituted a genuinely new and identifiable literary form—a form, however repudiated, that directly engaged the complex historical forces out of which it emerged. The commercial success of the genre is the first clue to that engagement.

The thematics of sensation fiction almost never concern trade or manufacturing or commerce. Rather, they are always deeply concerned with money and success, with the elaborate financial intrigues that surround the common preoccupations of the bourgeois family—inheritance, marriage, profession, and class status. Borrowing from the stock and trade of Victorian stage melodrama, the plots of sensation novels also invariably center around some menacing secret that threatens to expose the family's very identity as a humiliating lie and to destroy its financial and psychological security as well. That secret normally originates with an elaborate fraud that has taken place in the past, a secret plot in which class boundaries have been ruthlessly transgressed for profit: an illegitimate son passes himself off as a baronet and imprisons the true heir to his fortune in an asylum; a working-class woman murders her husband and changes her name to marry a gentleman; a servant-woman and her barren mistress exchange identities to provide the master with a child he wrongly believes to be his own. This fictional form that caused such a popular sensation among the middle class, in other words, worked directly on class anxiety and instability, symptomatic perhaps of a widespread nervousness at the very center of the culture's sense of itself. These plots offered up the disturbing possibility that the secret terms in which personal identities and intimate relations had been established within the culture and within the family were themselves fictions, acts of commerce, forms of trade, commodities to be bought and sold. While such novels may have reinforced superficially the conventional values of their readers by promising that every sin would come to light and that overweening class ambition would eventually end in disaster, the plots were on a more fundamental level deeply subversive of those same values. The secret they ultimately exposed was the essential commercialization of the family and of the individual subjects involved in its most intimate transactions.

The commerical interests of the period in which the sensation novel dominated the literary marketplace are the focus of a period of general European prosperity referred to by historian E. J. Hobsbawm as the "Age of Capital" (1848 to 1875), a period which in his analysis followed the "Age of Revolution" (1789 to 1848) and anticipated the "Age of Imperialism" (1875 to 1914). These are, of course, arbitrary dividing lines between interlocking historical movements, but they offer useful registration points for understanding a literary genre that dramatizes the ways the British economic revolution may be said to have swallowed up the failed European political revolutions and to have foreseen the eventual extension of British economic expansion into a worldwide empire. While sensation novels invariably deal harshly with the transgression of class lines—both upward and downward—they are not primarily concerned with preserving the integrity of traditional class boundaries. Rather, they are concerned with how those lines have been reconfigured as a form of social technology instead of as a mandate of natural inheritance. Written in the wake of the reform acts that were being debated in mid-century England to extend the franchise, these novels show how completely the restructuring of the social world had already been accomplished by the 1860s through economic means. They tell the story of the rise of a professional class of lawyers and physicians who established themselves as a powerful elite by taking control of the very terms upon which persons would be recognized and authenticated. In that story, the class warfare of 1848 has retreated from the street-corner barricades to be restaged inside the confines of the middle-class household.

These historical transformations are faintly detectable even in Margaret Oliphant's crucial early essay on "Sensation Novels," which appeared in *Blackwood's Edinburgh Magazine* in 1862. Mrs. Oliphant, who published a number of novels herself in the 1860s, defines the "entirely original position" Wilkie Collins's novels take up in the history of literature, claiming for them the status of "a new beginning in fiction." While Dickens, Bulwer Lytton, and even Nathaniel Hawthorne may be said to have written sensation novels earlier on, Collins charts a new path, which Oliphant sees as reflecting very specific historical circumstances. Unlike the more fantastic devices of his predecessors, she explains, Collins's sensational effects "are produced by common human acts, performed by recognizable human agents, whose motives are never inscrutable, and whose line of conduct is always more or less consistent." "A writer who boldly takes in hand the common mechanism of life," she goes on to say, "and by means of persons who might all be living in society for anything we can tell to the contrary, thrills us into wonder, terror, and breathless interest with positive personal shocks of surprise and excitement, has accomplished a far greater success than he who effects the same result through supernatural agencies, or by means of the fantastic creations of lawless genius or violent horrors of crime." This, Mrs. Oliphant claims, is the distinguishing feature of the new genre initiated by Wilkie Collins: it shocks and thrills us with the ordinary workings of ordinary life. This new kind of novel makes the disturbing discovery that the deepest mystery in the family is the "mechanism" that forms the family itself. As Henry James would put it three years later in an article on Mary Elizabeth Braddon, "to Mr. Collins belongs the credit of having introduced into fiction those most mysterious of mysteries, the mysteries which are at our own doors."

From the time the sensation novel was first identified as a distinct genre, literary historians have continued to treat it as a hybrid form, even a monstrous invention. It was a genre that attempted, with varying success, to blend the commonplace settings and characters from realistic and domestic fiction with the extremities of passion and plot from the Romantic and Gothic traditions. As is often the case with popular literature, this genre produces the effect of making the strange seem ordinary, much as the "higher" forms of art, in the analysis popularized by the Russian formalists, make the ordinary seem strange. But even Mrs. Oliphant's essay implicitly recognizes that the sensation novel was more than a purely literary experiment of this kind. It was also a direct response to the historical moment in which it arose, a moment she traces to the second Great Exhibition of 1862. That exhibition, she acknowledges, was but a pale imitation of the first grand spectacle of commerce and consumerism held at the Crystal Palace in 1851. While in 1851 the world was "lost in self-admiration," Mrs. Oliphant argued, "it is a changed world in which we are standing" in the England of 1862. To recover the thrill and spectacle of that earlier age, she says, America staged a bloody civil war to serve as "the grandest expedient for procuring a new sensation." In a somewhat less extreme reaction to these circumstances, England staged the sensation novel. There, she might have said had she explored the analogy further, the "mechanism" of ordinary life replaces the machinery of industry as a source of wonder and amazement, and the commodities of "common human agents" substitute for the spectacle of manufactured products once proudly exhibited in the hallways of the Crystal Palace. Thus the sensation novel is not, as it is generally regarded, a literature concerned primarily with the drama of thrilling events or with working out intricate plot lines. Rather, it is a literature that displays, during a time of cultural crisis, the social transformation of human agency into a commercial entity—into merchandise. In important ways, the sensation novel *was* the "Great Exhibition" of the 1860s. Considered in this light, it was also a serious and subversive art form. Sensation novels made visible and narratable the complex set of forces involved in a fundamental historical shift that reshaped English culture between 1848 and the end of the 1860s, and they traced the imprint of those forces on the nerves and bodies of ordinary characters and common readers alike.

Wilkie Collins's *Woman in White* (1859–1860) is the text most frequently regarded as inaugurating the genre of sensation fiction, and one of the novel's several narrators makes it a point to place its crucial events in the context of the Great Exhibition. "The year which I am now writing was the year of the famous Crystal Palace Exhibition in Hyde Park," says its middle-class hero, Walter Hartright. "Foreigners in unusually large numbers had arrived already, and were still arriving in England. Men were among us by hundreds whom the ceaseless distrustfulness of their governments had followed privately, by means of appointed agents, to our shores." It is not only the invasion of foreigners that is of concern here, but the invasion of suspicious foreign influences—specifically, the anarchistic impulses that fueled the revolutions of 1848 in Europe. That threat is vividly personified in the novel's larger-than-life villain, Count Fosco, who is ultimately exposed as a member of a secret anarchist organization based in Italy. The juxtaposition of the economic spectacle of the Crystal Palace with the political intrigues involving imported agents from the revolutionary movements of 1848 in this passage forms a striking image of the very historical transformation with which the sensation novel is centrally concerned. If the British industrial revolution succeeded where the European political revolutions failed, it did so not by replacing the dictatorship of the aristocracy with the dictatorship of the proletariat but by investing a new kind of authority in a new class of "professionals." The sensation novel tells the story of that political displacement. In a manner very different from that of the historical novel, the industrial novel, or the domestic novel that preceded it, the sensation novel dramatizes the realignment of political forces that redefined the means by which people understood their own identities in the society. This interpretation of the genre's significance may partially explain why a literature considered so negligible should also spark so much heated controversy in the culture, and why the life span of so popular an art form should be confined to a period slightly longer than a single decade.

Like most sensation novels, *The Woman in White* is first and foremost a novel preoccupied with mistaken identities and class status. Sir

Percival Glyde is not really the baronet he claims to be, since he was born a bastard and is therefore not the true heir to his title or his estate. Nor is Anne Catherick, whom he has falsely imprisoned in an asylum, really the servant-woman she seems to be. She is in fact Percival's presumed-dead wife, Lady Glyde, Laura Fairlie, who eerily resembles the real Anne and who, along with her body double, has been the object of a plot set in motion by Sir Percival that "involved nothing less than the complete transformation of two separate identities." Also true to type, the machinations of this plot consistently represent personal identity in the dual form of a commodity to be owned and a legal dispute to be resolved. "The one question to consider," the novel's male protagonist claims, "was whether I was justified or not in possessing myself the means of establishing Laura's identity at the cost of allowing the scoundrel who had robbed her of it to escape with impunity." Laura Fairlie's identity has been stolen from her by the fraudulent aristocrat Sir Percival Glyde in order to preserve the secret of his own illegal imposture and to maintain the inheritance he has also stolen by falsely marrying her. The economic and legal struggle over the "question" of personal identity is portrayed here, as it often is in such novels, in gendered terms—as a man's justified "possession" of some feminized property which has been unjustly "robbed" by another man. The intrigue of class identity and economic fortune at the center of the novel is complemented by an intrigue of sexual identity at its margins—in the person of the "masculine" Marian Holcombe and in the rather "feminine" Walter Hartright as well.

The "Preamble" to *The Woman in White* blends all of these concerns, identifying the text as the story of a man and a woman—a story, however, that will intentionally imitate the form of a legal brief. Because "the Law" is "the preengaged servant of the long purse," and therefore cannot be "depended upon to fathom every case of suspicion," the unnamed narrator proclaims at the outset of the text, this "story of what a Woman's patience can endure, and what a Man's resolution can achieve" will be told "as the story of an offense against the laws is told in Court." In the course of sorting through the series of confused identities that fill the ensuing narrative, the law is (as these passages show) repeatedly implicated with commercial interests. The identity of persons is shown to be inescapably determined by a combination of financial concerns and legal documentation. "With moderate assistance from the lubricating influences of oil or gold," the narrator asserts, "the events which fill these pages might have claimed their share of the public attention in a Court of justice."

The narrator who frames the text in these legal terms is, in fact, the novel's male protagonist, Walter Hartright. He also acts as the text's editor, assembling his narrative along with those of a number of others in such a way that the whole forms a pseudolegal deposition. Hartright designs the text to resemble a legal document, then, while he makes use of a number of genuine legal documents—birth certificates, baptismal accounts, marriage licenses, death certificates, medical records, and so on—to resolve the several "questions of identity" the story raises. Mr. Kyrle, one of the principal lawyers in the novel, also turns out to be one of the principal actors in this quest for documentary evidence, indispensable in Walter Hartright's attempt to solve the riddle of Laura Fairlie and Anne Catherick and that of Percival Glyde as well. "Questions of identity," the solicitor affirms, "where instances of personal resemblance are concerned, are, in themselves, the hardest of all questions to settle—the hardest, even when they are free from the complications which beset the case we are now discussing." As the undercover professional heroes of the novel, the solicitors Kyrle and Gilmore act to facilitate the settling of those questions by validating the documents that count as evidence of an authentic identity and declaring the truth of who persons really are. Like the physicians who maintain the asylum in which Laura and Anne are kept as prisoners, the lawyers frame the terms in which "questions of identity" can be asked and answered. Over the course of the novel, therefore, the romantic hero of the novel not only transforms himself from a drawing master into an illustrator for a newspaper, but he also transforms himself into an amateur attorney and private investigator in his quest to "establish" and "possess" the identity of the woman he loves. Hartright can only legally do so, however, once he first establishes her "as my Wife," a development which conveniently also enables his own son (with his own name) to become the heir of the contested patriarchal inheritance. In effect, the middle-class Hartright does legally and honestly what the villainous aristocratic poseurs, Sir Percival Glyde and Count Fosco, do surreptitiously and illegally: he assumes authority over and establishes the identity of his wife, making a considerable financial profit in the course of doing so.

In *The Woman in White*, the medical asylum and the law office are the centers of the immense power that is wielded over persons in the novel. Both places work to confine human subjects within a set of discourses and documents that determine their identities. As the editor and compiler of the text that makes up the novel, Hartright serves the interests of these two discursive fields. He constructs a text resembling a legal document to tell a story of the power of legal documents in resolving "questions of identity." He enlists the force of both legal and medical establishments in order to expose the truth long silenced within the walls of an asylum and to resolve "the hardest of all questions to settle": those questions involving authentic identity as they are linked to genuine class status. The bodies of the apparently working-class Anne and the gentlewoman Laura, which cannot otherwise be distinguished from one another, are identified solely on the basis of the legal and medical documents Hartright produces. He also takes the necessary "precautions" which "enabled the coroner and jury to settle the question of identity" of Percival Glyde as well. Ironically, however, in this novel that presents itself as an imitation of a juridical document, the fictionality of such authority is also suggested. When the already altered crucial record of Percival's birth is burned in the chapel in which his own body is also consumed, the same fire that destroyed his body destroyed the legal evidence that could confirm—or disprove—his fraud. The identity of his unrecognizable corpse can only be substantiated, therefore, by still another "document" found on the body—the watch upon which Percival's initials have been engraved. The "mechanism" of identification that carries authority in this text, it is implied here, is subject to and inscribed by the artificial machinery of time. What a man finally achieves in this novel, in fact, *is* what the woman must endure: the authority to establish an identity for herself—an activity that complements and perfects the intentions of the legal establishment it serves.

The plot of the typical sensation novel commonly follows this same pattern. It makes manifest the decline of the old gentry in the person of a fraudulent aristocrat (like the pretender Percival Glyde) or a weak and ineffectual one (like Laura's ailing uncle Frederick Fairlie). The plot registers the vacuum of power created by such figures and identifies the heirs to the vacated seats of their power and influence. The professional classes, represented by a set of stock characters in the sensation novel—the assiduous lawyer and the capable physician—establish themselves in (and by way of) these texts as the new aristocracy, the true elite. The lawyers are the ever-present advisors who interpret and manipulate the laws that establish the limits of personal freedom, negotiate between contending class interests, and define and legitimate the status of individuals. The doctors monitor the person's health, diagnosing and prescribing the proper care and management of body and mind, often making the crucial determination of whether the person in question is dead or alive, of sound mind and body or in need of confinement, capable of acting autonomously or in need of an executor to act on his or her behalf. These social agents come to replace any notion of natural political endowment or biological inheritance as the determining facts in a person's autonomous "identity," redefining the self as a legal construction and a medical case rather than a member of a social class or even of a family. In these novels, the authority of culture reasserts itself against nature at the moment when the idea of natural rights seemed to have established a new era for the liberation of persons that would lead to the collapse of patriarchy: sensation fiction shows patriarchy merely being reconfigured in the form of professionalism. While the illicit secrets and sensational effects of this kind of literature may provoke a thrill to the reader's pulse, bring a chill to the spine, or even capture the attention in an addictive way, they also register more impressively how much power certain legitimate cultural forces exercise over the bodies and minds of its readers every day.

Despite the widely recognized status of *The Woman in White* as the first great novel of its kind, most of Collins's earlier writing in the 1850s was also written in the sensation mode, and it just as clearly dramatizes the pattern of social transformation he developed with more sophistication in the 1860s. *The Dead Secret* (1857) is one of the most accomplished and provocative of these predecessors. Like *The Woman in White*, *The Dead Secret* solves a mystery of personal identity through the mediation and substantiation of legal and medical authority. It chronicles the discovery by Rosamond Treverton Frankland of the fact that she is not the daughter of the old wealthy family she had assumed herself to be, but was born secretly to one of her mother's servants, Sarah Leeson. Her father is not really Captain Treverton, "the eldest male representative of an old Cornish family," but a laborer who died in a mining accident before she was born. The novel begins with Mrs. Treverton on her deathbed writing a confession of these facts to her husband, or rather dictating the confession to her personal maid Sarah, the real mother of their child. The dying penitent forces Sarah to write down these facts and to agree not to remove the confession from the house or destroy it without first showing it to Captain Treverton. This document becomes the elusive dead secret of the novel's title, surreptitiously hidden away in the house, left undiscovered by the deceived daughter Rosamond (and by the reader) until near the end of the text, after Rosamond has been married to Leonard Frankland (her blind childhood sweetheart) and has given birth to a child of her own. The plotting of the narrative plays upon the reader's curiosity about the substance of this secret document, Rosamond's shocking discovery of her illegitimacy, and her response to the practical consequences of being disinherited as a result of it. The drama culminates in another sentimental deathbed scene just before Sarah Leeson dies, a scene in which Rosamond melodramatically accepts the menial servant as her real mother.

While on the surface this novel once again deals with the inevitable discovery of the secret sexual sin of the past as it crosses the shifting lines of class identity, the more profound achievement of the text is Collins's continued exploration of personal identity as a contested ground between apparent biological "facts" on the one hand and legal and medical expertise on the other. The underlying anxiety about class subversion is manifested less in the account of the cross-class dressing by Mrs. Treverton and Sarah Leeson when they exchange identities to perpetrate the fraud of Rosamond's birth than it is in the assertion of authority over both gentility and commoner alike by the legitimate and seemingly benign practices of the doctors and lawyers in the text. This appropriation of power once again signals the rise of these professionals as the culture's new ruling class, whose authority is rooted not in the force of tradition or birthright but in the power of professional discourse. The men of the old aristocracy remain literally and figuratively blind or dead in the novel, as their "true" status can only be constructed for them by the dictates of the proper legal and medical authorities to whom they repeatedly submit themselves. "It is impossible to proceed without seeking advice immediately," Rosamond's husband warns in characteristic fashion. "The lawyer who always managed Captain Treverton's affairs, and who now manages ours, is the proper person to direct us in instituting a search, and to assist us, if necessary, in making the restitution." This extension of patriarchal authority into the professions is even more urgently exercised upon the women in the novel, of course, for whom biological facts about maternity are established legally only with the "substantiated documentation" of the lawyers and the scientifically informed approval of the doctors who watch over them.

Here, maternity is as much a legal fiction as paternity. Both are literally only worth the paper they are written on.

The dramatization of this fundamental transition is perhaps the novel's most important accomplishment: the biological mother is replaced by the figure of the doctor and the patriarchal father is supplanted by the figure of the lawyer. The novel begins and ends with the death of a female parent, the first being the "false mother" of Rosamond Treverton and the last being her "true mother." But the determination of false and true depends entirely upon the discovery and legal confirmation of the deadly secret document that was dictated by the false mother to the true one, a text whose authority is then replaced by yet another document, which the lawyers declare that Sarah Leeson must endorse in order to authenticate herself as Rosamond's "true" mother. That authenticating document can only be signed with the permission and sanction of the doctor who oversees the care of Sarah's body and who takes complete responsibility for it. He dictates the terms upon which any interview and signing can take place, controlling who will conduct the interview and how and when it will occur. The doctor and the lawyer, in turn, reject the evidentiary value of another letter, which details the truth of Sarah Leeson's giving birth to Rosamond, because, it would seem, they had no hand in producing it. In a demonstration of professional control over the authenticity of self-assertion, that letter is first "critically dissected paragraph by paragraph" as if it were a diseased body under the doctor's surgical knife. It is then "carefully annotated by the doctor, for the purpose of extricating all the facts that it contained from the mass of unmeaning words," this time as if it were a legal deposition to be presented in court. The letter is subsequently submitted to the family solicitor, who "argued from his professional point of view against regarding the letter, taken by itself, as a genuine document," and against accepting it as "evidence" of Rosamond's "real parentage." Finally, the solicitor insists on the production of yet another "written declaration" which he will approve, and which will establish with certainty Rosamond's true identity. Together, the doctor and lawyer involve themselves in a textual reconception and rewriting of Rosamond's past that seems to supersede in importance the biological facts of her birth and the dead secret of her mother's "viva voce" confession, rendering the identity of her parents or her true class status relatively inconsequential by comparison.

In the prefaces to his later works, Collins would frequently argue that his interests as a novelist were not as deeply invested in the construction of plot as they were in the representation of character. His characterizations, however, have largely been dismissed by critics as superficial and conventionalized, while his plots have been praised as original, intricate, and compelling. But perhaps Collins's more significant contribution to the history of the novel is, true to his own claims, in the area of character—more specifically, in his replacement of the ideologically laden notion of Victorian moral "character" with the more socially determined conception of Victorian "identity." Indeed, as intricate as Collins's plots are in his best work, they remain the more highly conventionalized features of it. The plots invariably make use of the same set of materials: some secret from the past (the protagonist's illegitimacy, a lover's deception, a father's fraud) comes to light and reshapes the protagonist's place in the present in shocking ways, demanding a reconciliation with these distressing new circumstances and an acceptance of some new identity. But the agencies involved both in concealing the secret and in disclosing it are almost always some conspiracy of law and medicine. Those professions also act as the crucial authorities through whom a person can establish and sustain his or her new identity in society. Such authorities, then, essentially replace the notion of a free and natural-born "person" or an autonomous moral "character" with that of a legally constituted social "identity," something a person is neither born to nor in control of choosing. Identity, construed as a social invention in this way, is literally composed and executed by these professional figures and is subject to their monitoring and control. If the Great Exhibition of 1851 stood as a monument to the transformation of the 1848 spirit of class revolution into the spectacle of middle-class commerce and commodities, the sensation novel of the 1860s reads like an account of the transformation of archaic aristocratic privilege into a cult of modern professional expertise.

This very process of transformation is the basis of one of Collins's greatest sensation novels, *No Name* (1862–1863), which directly followed the publication of *The Woman in White*. Here, because of a legal technicality and a question about a dying man's medical condition, Andrew Vanstone's two daughters are declared illegitimate and are consequently disinherited, making them, literally, "Nobody's Children" under the law, legally entitled to bear "no name." It is this legal condition of being without an identity that is the essential condition in all these novels and the pretext upon which professional authority characteristically reasserts itself to rescue and reassign identity to the dispossessed figures within them. And yet, remarkably, in a world where no one seems to be who they claim to be, the lawyers and doctors are presented—in this novel as they almost invariably are throughout the entire genre—as straightforward and direct authorities whose testimony can be counted upon and whose unfailing energies strive to bring civil law together with "natural law." Nevertheless, they invariably institute a regime in which identity is conceived as a role imposed upon the subject by themselves, as representatives of the best interests of the culture.

As an actor himself and as a victim of repressive domestic laws, Collins may have perceived that in the culture in which he lived character was best understood as a role given to someone and scripted by another. Collins's long friendship and collaboration with Dickens began when Wilkie was cast as an actor in a Bulwer Lytton play produced by Dickens, and he always maintained a vital interest in the theatrical versions of his own novels. When Collins defended his treatment of character in the novels, he often appealed to the similarities he saw between the novel and the play, which two genres he regarded as "twin sisters in the family of Fiction." It is appropriate, therefore, that in *No Name* Vanstone's daughter Magdalen is not only the central body upon which the discourses of the law and medicine become focused and the sister who embraces and seeks to overcome her legal status as a nobody with no name, but she is also a very talented actress. Consistent with the conventions of the sensation novel, however, while her natural acting talent shows her capable of uncanny "appropriations" of others' "identities" in her elaborate effort to reclaim her own "natural" identity, Magdalen's attempt at autonomy fails while her more passive and conventional sister (who puts faith in her legal counsel's mediations on her behalf) succeeds in recovering the same inheritance the law had denied them both. Here, as in many sensation novels, the double identity is not just a hoax perpetrated by a person upon the world, it is also a confusion perpetrated by the world upon a person. These are plots in which a villain may be double-dealing, but where just as often the protagonist is also acting out two (or more) identities unawares, where "character" is being scripted by social forces from the outside rather than being generated from within.

The transformation of character from a natural inheritance into a legal construction takes place consistently not only in Wilkie Collins's novels but in the work of many of his counterparts in sensation fiction as well. In some of the most popular sensation novels of the 1860s a lawyer may even play the part of the heroic protagonist rather than simply a powerful background figure in the machinations of the plot as he does in *The Woman in White* or *The Dead Secret*. This is the case in Mrs. Henry Wood's immensely popular *East Lynne* (1861) and in Mary Elizabeth Braddon's *Lady Audley's Secret* (1861–1862) as well. In *East Lynne*, a successful young lawyer named Mr. Carlyle purchases the valuable old estate of East Lynne from the dissolute and bankrupt Earl of Mount Severn, William Vane. Carlyle marries the Earl's daughter, defeats another aristocratic scoundrel in a parliamentary election, and brings his opponent's double identity and his criminal past to light as well. In *Lady Audley's Secret*, another lawyer, this time the aimless gentleman Robert Audley, takes on the role of private investigator to look into the disappearance of the wife of his friend George Talboys, and then seeks to explain the subsequent mysterious vanishing of George Talboys himself. The lawyer eventually discovers that his own aunt, Lady Audley, who recently married his uncle, Sir Michael Audley, is the missing wife of his missing friend. She has, the young lawyer finds out, forsaken her husband (when he sought his fortune in the colonies), abandoned their child, created a new identity for herself as a governess, married Audley's uncle, and finally murdered her first husband to preserve the secret of her past and to defend her newfound wealth and status.

At the center of this plot of criminal discovery is, once more, the deeper plot of a woman's identity—that of Lady Audley—an identity over which, characteristically, a professional man takes charge. When Robert confronts his aunt with the results of his investigation and presents her with the evidence he has gathered, he threatens her with the power of a legal procedure that will unequivocally determine her identity for her: "I will gather together the witnesses who shall swear to your identity, and at peril of any shame to myself and those I love, I will bring upon you the just and awful punishment of your crime." When Lady Audley is forced to confess that crime, she also claims to suffer from insanity, a condition she claims to have inherited from her mother, who died in an asylum, herself a victim of the madness inherited in turn from *her* mother. When she does so, Lady Audley perceptively represents herself as an effect of these two professional discursive regimes. To deal with what the novel presents as the woman's situation in the world of professional male discourse, the lawyer in this text (naturally) enlists the services of a medical man: "I will appeal to the experience of this Dr. Mosgrave," he thought; "physicians and lawyers are the confessors of this prosaic nineteenth century. Surely he will be able to help me." These secular priests of professionalism diagnose and adjudicate her future as they have her past, consigning Lady Audley to an asylum, where, like her mother before her, she finally dies, out of sight. The combined authority of the law office and the asylum conspire once again to tell the woman's story for her, to expose her life as a dark "secret" and to contain her dangerous identity in a space (and a text) where she will no longer threaten the lives (and wealth) of men. This characteristic scene of the professionally extorted confession—medicalized and legalized as it is here—and the resultant confinement of the confessing subject for care may be seen as assisting in the construction of a social machinery for producing a very specialized kind of truth, a machinery which Michel Foucault has described in *The History of Sexuality* as fundamental to the emergence of bourgeois capitalist society in the nineteenth century.

The gendering of this pattern of professional male discipline and containment as it is imposed upon female subjects in these novels is an important part of that machinery, and it is elaborately responsive to the complicated sexual politics at work during the period in which the novels were written. Set not only in the general context of the Second Reform Act's extension of political representation in England but also against the more specific background of such developments as the passage in 1857 of the first of a chain of divorce acts called the Matrimonial Causes Acts, the introduction into Parliament of a women's suffrage bill for the first time in 1869, and the enactment into law of the Married Women's Property Acts in 1870 and 1882, sensation fiction has been read by modern feminist critics as part of a growing protest surrounding the larger issue of female political empowerment. Alternatively, the genre may also be seen as part of a rearguard defense by a realigned and newly professionalized patriarchy attempting to solidify its power against that protest. Indeed, the remarkable popularity and controversy the novels generated suggest that their appeal was due at once to the subversive notions they contained and to the ultimately conservative effects of their plots' conclusions. The double message these texts often signaled on such subjects implies that these alternative readings are more mutually reinforcing than they are contradictory, and that the novels forged in the popular arena another Victorian "compromise" between the reformist and repressive impulses within the culture.

From this perspective Mary Grice, the strange and beautiful woman at the center of Collins's *Hide and Seek* (1854), offers a key female figure for the entire genre. She springs from mysterious origins, and her secret past becomes the screen upon which the other characters in the novel project their fantasies. Perhaps her most suggestive attribute is that she is deaf and dumb, a situation she responds to by carrying a slate around with her for people literally to write their desires upon. Without a last name, without a history, without a voice to express herself, she is the blank slate of the novel, a field for the enterprises of a series of men to be realized within and inscribed upon. As an artist's model called "Madonna" by her admirers, she is the idealized female mystery to be solved, the secret that all men seek to know or seek to maintain as a secret, the body in question to be identified for those who are so fascinated by her. Finally, she becomes the key to the history of those men who are so intrigued by her, exposing them and their secret selves for who they really are as well. This demure and responsive "Madonna" also represents the companion figure to the aggressive and self-asserting "Magdalen" of the later *No Name*, where, as in many sensation novels, the two visions of Victorian femininity—the idealized virgin and the devious siren—will be placed side by side as alternative female types, one to be only mildly respected but rewarded and the other to be marveled over and yet chastened.

Despite the fact that strong and assertive women generally fared badly in sensation novels (or perhaps because of it), the prevailing assumption was that this was literature written for a largely female audience. Much of the contemporary criticism about the corrosive moral effects of sensation novels also expressed an anxiety about their influence over the young ladies who read them in such great numbers. But women were not only the most avid readers of these novels, they were among the most important writers of them as well. To the more than fifty novels written by Mrs. Wood alone and to the some eighty authored by Miss Braddon must be added those by less famous authors like Ouida, Florence Wilford, and Mrs. Grey. Across the considerable range of quality and seriousness such an impressive number of novels manifested, most of them can be aligned with either conservative or subversive forces in addressing the "woman question" of mid-nineteenth-century England. These texts may also be interpreted either as warnings about the dangers of breaking out of the conventional and compliant role that women were expected to play in the culture on the one hand, or, on the other, as models of resistance that critique the Victorian paradigm of the domesticated "angel in the house," exposing the "house" as nothing less than an asylum in disguise and revealing the "angel" to be an artificial ideal of patriarchal control imposed upon women with ideas. This latter reading affiliates sensation fiction with what feminist critics have identified as the "female Gothic" strain in the novel, the radical subgenre of Gothic fiction that dramatizes (as does a text like *Jane Eyre* or *Wuthering Heights*) a tale of domestic female victimization in which daughters seek out substitutes for a lost or dead mother figure.

But there were many male readers and writers of sensation novels as well, and in a number of the texts authored both by men and by women, the subject upon whom the forces of a professional elite are focused is a man. *Basil: A Story of Modern Life* (1852) is the first novel Collins wrote in the sensation mode, and in it the protagonist is the well-meaning son of an effete gentleman, deceived and betrayed by the middle-class family into which he has secretly married. The text is written in the voice of the son and finally submitted to the doctor who nursed him back to health after the mental breakdown he suffered at the end of the fateful year during which he discovered his wife's infidelity and the plot of extortion and revenge in which he had been entangled. Just as *The Woman in White* emulates a legal document, *Basil* takes the form of a medical file. Also like its more impressive successor, *Basil* offers itself as a confessional document subjecting its protagonist's identity to the critical gaze of professional eyes. Later, in *Armadale*, one of Collins's most effective novels of the 1860s, a medical asylum is used once again to confine a protagonist, this time the naive and well-intentioned heir Allan Armadale. The Sanatorium of the charlatan and criminal Dr. LeDoux is a medical establishment designed for the treatment of nervous diseases in women, but it becomes the scene of the imprisonment and attempted murder of Armadale (and of his double and namesake) by the devious plotter Lydia Gwilt, who has contrived the plan as part of her conspiracy of greed and revenge against the Armadale family. When her own plot to acquire the Armadale estate by manipulating medical and legal records is revealed, however, Lydia finally submits herself to the poison gas she had intended for the man she presumably married and tried to kill.

The pattern of exercising the power of professional expertise over the bodies of human subjects applies to men as well as to women in these novels. Considered together with the frequent confusion of gender roles in these plots, it forms a pattern that demands a more complex reading of the gender politics involved in these texts. What Collins and the other sensation novelists may be interpreted as doing here is extending the process of "feminizing" the middle-class Victorian subject, a process that critics like Nancy Armstrong have observed in the domestic novel of the 1840s and 1850s. While the domestic novel may have generated cultural authority for certain internalized, "feminine" attributes, the sensation novel elicits their disciplining from the outside. This genre not only authorized a professional discourse in deploying that disciplinary procedure, it helped to create the very clients that would sustain these professional classes and, by the end of the century, would bring into being a systematic science to diagnose and explain those clients. As both a scientific and a professional practice, psychoanalysis theorized and sought to treat as symptoms in its patients the very "symptoms" manifested in the plot of the typical sensation novel—the enduring and explosive forces of repressed secrets from the past—usually about sex—that become written upon the mind and body of the therapeutic subject, interrupt the "normal" development of adult sexual identity, and call for professional intervention and interpretation.

Remarkably, the accession to power of a professional class in these novels is consistently valorized and rarely critiqued in the novels themselves. In *Hard Cash*, Reade condemns the abuse of the asylum system just as in *The Law and the Lady* or *Man and Wife* Collins protests against the justice of certain laws governing marriage and divorce. But these reformist tendencies are confined in Collins to the later works, and are generally regarded now as departures from the sensation mode or as markers of a decline in literary quality. Even those later "purpose" novels do not register the kind of wholesale critique of the professional establishment we see in Dickens's *Bleak House*, however, a novel which in almost every way seems to anticipate the conventions of the sensation genre. There are memorable examples of satirical treatments of the legal or medical quack in the best of Collins's sensation novels—like the sinister Dr. LeDoux and his asylum for ladies in *Armadale*, or the self-serving and conniving legal clerk Bashwood in *No Name*, or the patent medicine salesman and professional impostor Mr. Wragge in *No Name*. But these are comic exceptions that prove the rule of general trustworthiness on the part of the large number of lawyers and medical men that figure so powerfully in these novels.

The most serious critique of such figures may be that presented by the anarchistic villain of *The Woman in White*, Count Fosco. Neither a doctor nor a lawyer himself, he nonetheless demonstrates and exposes the corruptive uses of both professional discourses. Fosco exploits his scientific knowledge in diagnosing the medical condition of Lady Glyde and Laura Fairlie, in administering drugs to them to control their behavior and memory, and in confining them in the medical asylum as he plots to exchange the two women's identities. Medicine is really the manipulation of the science of chemistry, he claims, and both essentially operate as systems of control: "Mind, they say, rules the world. But what rules the mind? The body (follow me closely here) lies at the mercy of the most omnipotent of all potentates—the Chemist." Fosco pronounces with equal cynicism on the law, describing it as nothing more, or less, than a powerful, discursive trick, as mere manipulative "clap-trap_: "The machinery it has set up for the detection of crime is miserably ineffective—and yet only invent a moral epigram, saying that it works well, and you blind everybody to its blunders for that moment." As an anarchist, however, passing himself off as an aristocrat committed to "defending the true aristocracy," Fosco finds his authority diminished by his association with an older political consciousness, that of the revolutionary period. In fact, it is the more sympathetic and responsible lawyers and physicians who express the reformed state of political affairs in these novels and are consistently granted the authority to speak the critical language of political reform. It is the solicitor Gilmore, in *The Woman in White*, who is accused by his partner of having radical views because of his unprejudiced commitment to justice for all regardless of station, just as the physician in *The Dead Secret* is the one who espouses the "republican" repudiation of aristocratic privilege. Their control over the discourses of power even entitles these professional figures to function as the voices of resistance and critique in the culture at the same time as they assume the very privilege and power they seem to condemn.

The elevation of professional figures of juridical control to a position of largely unchallenged authority in these novels responds to political anxieties present in England during the 1860s, when the prosperity of the 1850s and the attendant abatement of class conflict was threatened by economic recession and the possibly destabilizing effects of the Sec-

ond Reform Act. But as the growing importance of the medical professional in these novels attests, the sensation novel engages the force of
profound scientific as well as political and legal developments in the
culture. Henry James maintained that the works of Wilkie Collins
shouldn_t even be referred to as "sensation novels," but the complexity
of their design and content led him to conclude that Collins's novels
"are not so much works of art as works of science." Indeed, in the great
sequence of novels Collins published in the 1860s, beginning with *The
Woman in White* and extending through *No Name*, *Armadale*, and *The
Moonstone*, science becomes an increasingly powerful master discourse
in resolving the "questions of identity" at the heart of the plots. In *The
Moonstone*—regarded by many as Collins's greatest work, and, coincidentally, as the work in which he moved from writing in the sensation
mode to inventing the modern detective novel—the medical man Ezra
Jennings manages to succeed where even the detective Sergeant Cuff
and the legal advisor Mr. Bruff both fail. As the author of a controversial theoretical text on the functioning of the nervous system and as an
expert on the physiological basis of mental operations, Jennings proposes the "bold experiment" that reveals to the protagonist, Franklin
Blake, that he has committed a crime unconsciously, under the influence of certain drugs and as a result of certain physiological drives and
nervous impulses. In explaining to Blake the "physiological principle"
of how the body often controls the will, Jennings refers Blake to the
work of prominent Victorian scientists. The physician forces Blake to
admit that his body operated independently of his will in leading him
to commit a theft while asleep, and to confess at last, "I did it without
my own knowledge." Finally, in defense of his proposed course of action
to provide proof of this theory, Jennings establishes his authority when
he boldly proclaims, "Science sanctions my proposal."

Science is the sanctioning discourse in *The Moonstone*, superseding
even that of the law. What begins as the most political of Collins's novels (investigating the criminal implications of a plundering colonial policy in British India) ends by being the most scientific (shifting the focus
of the investigation from international politics to the precise physiological conditions that led to Blake's theft of the diamond). But this was
science with powerful political implications. Consistent with the claims
of an emerging Victorian science that adumbrated various materialist
theories of gender and personality, *The Moonstone* maintained that the
identity of the inner self and the final causes of behavior are ultimately

subject to physiological determinants rather than reflective of social and historical conditions. Victorian science would also maintain, similarly, that women were physiologically predisposed to the sort of "nervous hysteria" and "mania" we see manifested, diagnosed, and contained in *Lady Audley's Secret* and *The Woman in White*. Just as the controversial new theories of an emerging science called criminal anthropology were beginning to hypothesize a physiologically determined criminal type, the first full-length detective novel in English explains criminal behavior in pathological terms, as a biological rather than a sociological problem, calling for medical intervention rather than social reform. "Science" reveals this truth most explicitly to the protagonist in *The Moonstone* when Franklin Blake realizes, thanks to the "bold experiment" Jennings performs on Blake's body, that we must "become objects of inquiry to ourselves" and to the watchful eyes of science.

In her largely appreciative essay on *The Woman in White*, Mrs. Oliphant cautioned that the real danger of sensation fiction was not so much in what the genre was in itself, but in what it was likely to lead to: "What Mr. Wilkie Collins has done with delicate care and laborious reticence, his followers will attempt without any such discretion. We have already had specimens, as many as are desirable, of what the detective policeman can do for the enlivenment of literature: and it is into the hands of the literary Detective that this school of story-telling must inevitably fall at last." Mrs. Oliphant's prediction about the inevitable progression from sensation novel to detective fiction proved to be true. It was a progression, however, that Collins effected all by himself. The detective novel is, of course, the logical conclusion to a genre preoccupied with establishing the identity of a shadowy personality, with uncovering criminal activity, with explaining a secret from the past. But more importantly, the detective novel, with its validation of a professional hero who acquires the right to impose an identity on an unwilling suspect, fulfills the pattern of the professional appropriation of identity through the discourses of law and science, a pattern we have seen already sketched in some detail in the sensation novel. The "science of detection" as it was invented and implemented by the famous literary duo of Holmes and Watson two decades after *The Moonstone* appeared, is the fruit of that juridical-medical collaboration, and it also extends the process of "materializing" personal identity begun in the sensation school. As sensation novelists construed personal identity in terms of authenticating legal documents, the detective novelist translated identity into material evidence of the criminal's body—the incriminating footprint, the photograph, the strand of hair, the shape of the ear. Along with the numerous literary detectives that followed them, the private investigators, lawyers, and doctors of sensation fiction contributed to and popularized the production of an elaborate bureaucratic system of archives that could establish, monitor, and control personal identity by the use of official documents, which translated the body into the textual form of fingerprints, mug shots, physiological statistics, and medical histories.

This attention to rendering the secrets of the human body into a body of documentary evidence is not the only feature inherited by the detective novelist from the sensation novelist. *The Moonstone* is also a revealing transitional text between the two subgenres in its more explicit treatment of the problems of empire. To be sure, there had been colonial subplots in many of *The Moonstone*'s predecessors—Walter Hartright's adventures in South America in *The Woman in White*, Allan Armadale's birth and childhood in the West Indies in *Armadale*, George Talboys's fortune hunting in Australia in *Lady Audley's Secret*, and Andrew Vanstone's ill-fated military occupation of Quebec in *No Name*, to mention just a few. The secrets concealed within the private life of the family that so preoccupied these novels often could be traced back to some repressed trouble springing from colonial expansion, an issue that lurked in the background of the plot as a site where exotic and dangerous passions were cultivated. But in the object of the moonstone itself and in his direct treatment of the violent theft of the gem from India, Collins made the suppressed crime of imperial plunder at least symbolically central in *The Moonstone* rather than relegating it to the marginalized position it had occupied in his earlier sensation novels. In tales like "The Speckled Band," "The Boscombe Valley Mystery," "The Crooked Man," *The Sign of Four*, and many others, Arthur Conan Doyle would make the issue of imperial guilt and contamination a trademark of the British detective story at the turn of the century. The meeting and collaboration of Doctor Watson and Sherlock Holmes itself was only occasioned, after all, by Watson's return to England from Afghanistan where he had been wounded in the Afghan wars while serving as medical officer for the occupying British Army. When he lists the strongest areas of speciality in Holmes's considerable but selective knowledge, Watson should not have marveled that the master detective's knowledge of "sensation literature" was so "immense." In addition to heralding the extension of what Hobsbawm calls the "Age of Capital" into the worldwide markets of the "Age of Empire" for England and the other European powers as well, the literary development the Holmes phenomenon represents also suggests how the commercialization of the human subject, as it was documented in the sensation novel, was only a prelude to its more radical exploration and colonization, both at home and abroad. That process would not only be demonstrated quite effectively in the detective stories of Doyle, but also in the adventure stories written by figures like Rider Haggard, Rudyard Kipling, and Joseph Conrad.

But detective fiction is not the only reincarnation of the sensation novel that appeared in the latter years of the nineteenth century. The sensation around sensation fiction may have largely disappeared in the 1870s, due in part to broader cultural trends in the 1870s like the general return of consensus around the orthodoxies that had been under attack in the 1860s, and in part to more specific circumstances like the decline of Wilkie Collins's health and his move toward writing reformist fiction later in his life. However, many of the conventions of the sensation novel (and some of its controversy) were very vigorously sustained in a new form in the melodramatic naturalism of Thomas Hardy. Hardy's interest in the powerful role of physical drives and impulses in human behavior, in the inevitable and destructive exposure of the repressed secret of the past, and in the degree to which circumstances shape personal fates can be traced directly to the sensation novel. These emphases oppose the traditions of psychological and social realism as practiced by George Eliot, Henry James, and, to a lesser degree, Dickens and Trollope. The work of these novelists generally aimed at preserving the psychological and moral integrity of the character, necessarily diminishing the power of the forces that delimit subjectivity and determine moral choice. While there are certainly secrets and crimes in the plots of Eliot's novels, for example, such events are directed at moving the reader to contemplate the degree to which a character like Maggie Tulliver in *The Mill on the Floss* or Dorothea Brooke in *Middlemarch* has submitted herself to the drift of circumstances rather than acted responsibly and consciously. While Eliot is interested in the limiting "conditions" that constrain modern life, the real "mystery" to be investigated in her work is the moral question of how severely or with how much compassion we can judge Gwendolen Harleth's or Mr. Bulstrode's crimes—whether, indeed, they really, deliberately committed a crime or not.

For Hardy, as for the sensation novelists who preceded him, the focus is not upon the ethical complexities of rational choice or whether or not a crime has taken place, but upon the pressure of forces—biological, sociological, professional—that relentlessly push a person like Tess into an intolerable situation, or, like Jude, gradually just wear that person down. Florence Hardy's biography of her husband records a revealing entry in his diary for January 14, 1888, in which Hardy identifies the sensation novel as the model for his own interest in these forces: "A 'sensation novel' is possible in which the sensationalism is not casualty, but evolution," he says, "not physical but psychical [where] the effect upon the faculties is the important matter to be depicted." While Hardy unduly minimizes the psychological significance of the sensation novel here, he does recognize the genre's importance in emphasizing the "effect" exerted by events upon a character's body, just as his novels would emphasize the effect of circumstances upon a character's psyche. But unlike the novel of psychological realism, both the sensation novel and the naturalistic novel portray the human subject in more "modern" terms—as a problematic physical and psychical construction, as an "effect" composed by a complex of intersecting historical forces rather than as a rational, autonomous will imposing itself upon the world, however limited might be the opportunities that world offered.

The impact of those forces on the individual subject was not a mere abstraction in the sensation novel; it registered directly upon the lives of its authors as much as upon its characters. If the critical history of sensation fiction reads like the plot of a sensation novel, so do the life stories of the most eminent practitioners of the form. The secret scandals of their domestic circumstances often rival those of their most notorious characters in dramatizing the influence of institutional confinement, repressive legal and social conventions, and professional intervention into domestic matters. Miss Braddon bore five children out of wedlock while living illicitly with her publisher, whose first wife had died in the lunatic asylum where she had been confined. Dickens, separated from his wife and family, engaged in an infamous, protracted affair with the actress Ellen Ternan. Charles Reade lived on an intimate basis with his "housekeeper" for years, never marrying because he was committed to celibacy by the conditions of an Oxford fellowship. Wilkie Collins, appropriately, offers the most telling example of the scandalous, sensational life of these "other Victorians." The details of his personal affairs were diligently guarded secrets except to his most intimate friends. What is now clearly documented, however, is that Collins maintained two households, an arrangement that was made necessary by his extended liaison with Miss Caroline Graves (the original for the mysterious female figure of *The Woman in White*), a woman who eventually married someone else and who later resumed her affair with Collins after her marriage. Between the two phases of this liaison, Collins also took part in a relationship with another woman he never married, Martha Rudd, with whom he had two daughters and a son. In addition to the stresses of maintaining this double life, illness dramatically constrained Collins's later years, a period dominated by the dictates of his doctors and, as his later reformist work shows, by his own preoccupation with laws governing everything from divorce to vivisection in England. As Collins's physical ailments became increasingly debilitating, his addiction to opium also became more and more severe. After his astonishing success in the 1860s, the rapid decline of Collins's literary production in the subsequent decades has been variously attributed to some combination of gout (which crippled him with pain), Charles Reade (who encouraged him to write his less effective protest novels), and laudanum (which he consumed daily in quantities that would have killed most men).

These biographical details suggest that in creating a genre of sexual secrets, double identities, domestic intrigues, legal difficulties, and medical confinement, these prominent authors may have been playing out the mysteries of their own private lives as those lives collided with the repressive force of established social conventions. But more important, their considerable body of work also made plain the fact that those collisions were produced by urgent and historically specific conditions of mid-nineteenth-century England, conditions which carried profound implications for the identities people were able to assume—or that were being assumed for them—within the culture. As the Crystal Palace of 1851 perfectly symbolized the moment in the economic history of that culture when commodities had become established as objects of wonder, the sensation novel of the 1860s perfectly exhibited the human implications of that process. Both spectacles presented themselves as "great exhibitions" in which the values of the culture were displayed before it in a sensational form and sold back to it for its own consumption.

In 1859, the year that Wilkie Collins began writing *The Woman in White*, Karl Marx published *A Contribution to the Critique of Political Economy*, John Stuart Mill published *An Essay on Liberty*, and Charles

Darwin published *The Origin of Species*. Like Collins's novel, each of these texts mounts an elaborate investigation into the past that produces a radical reinterpretation of the present. Also like a sensation novel, each of them makes a claim about the nature of human identity and its relation to some wider context or determining set of fundamental forces. Marx's investigation of "material history" as a function of the economic conditions of production sees the individual as subject to a larger plot of class struggle: "It is not the consciousness of men that determines their being but, on the contrary, their social being that determines their consciousness." Mill's reconstruction of human history from a political perspective traces the evolution of governmental forms and the final emergence of modern democracy and liberal individualism. Directly engaging the problem of "how to make the fitting adjustment between individual independence and social control," Mill portrayed the full realization of individual autonomy as necessarily responsive to certain collective moral and political obligations, to the "debt" of liberty that exists between citizens. Darwin saw the entire human historical record as itself subject to a grander "natural history," which was governed by biological imperatives for species survival and the supporting "natural laws" of selection, struggle, and inheritance. Sensation novels may be seen as domesticating and integrating all these historical investigations—of social class, of political legislation, of biological inheritance—and the reconsiderations of personal destiny they required. These novels, consistently obsessed with some historical threat, repeatedly manifest an anxiety about some dangerous secret from the past, something volatile and destructive to the present that has been repressed and will certainly burst forth with violence into the present. By so doing, they narrate and resolve the very historical anxieties that were manifested in the emerging economic, political, and scientific theories with which this literature was contemporary. We might think of the invention of this immensely popular novelistic form as both symptom of and response to the array of radical new conceptions about the past that were coming into the consciousness of the culture at this critical moment, presenting their revolutionary implications and obligations in a form that incited as much pleasure as it did shock.

Ronald R. Thomas

Selected Bibliography

Armstrong, Nancy. *Desire and Domestic Fiction: A Political History of the Novel.* New York and Oxford: Oxford University Press, 1987.

Barickman, Richard, Susan MacDonald, and Myra Stark. *Corrupt Relations: Dickens, Thackeray, Trollope, Collins, and the Victorian Sexual System.* New York: Columbia University Press, 1982.

Boyle, Thomas. *Black Swine in the Sewers of Hempstead: Beneath the Surface of Victorian Sensationalism.* New York: Viking, 1989.

Brantlinger, Patrick. "What Is 'Sensational' about the Sensation Novel?" *Nineteenth-Century Fiction* 37 (June 1989): 1–28.

Cvetkovich, Ann. *Mixed Feelings: Feminism, Mass Culture, and Victorian Sensationalism.* New Brunswick, N.J.: Rutgers University Press, 1992.

Heller, Tamar. *Dead Secrets: Wilkie Collins and the Female Gothic.* New Haven, Conn.: Yale University Press, 1992.

Hughes, Winifred. *The Maniac in the Cellar: Sensation Novels of the 1860s.* Princeton, N.J.: Princeton University Press, 1980.

James, Henry. "Mary Elizabeth Braddon." *Nation,* November 9, 1865. Reprinted in Leon Edel, ed., *Henry James: Literary Criticism, Essays on Literature, American Writers, English Writers.* New York: Library of America, 1984: 741–46.

Loesberg, Jonathan. "The Ideology of Narrative Form in Sensation Fiction." *Representations* 13 (Winter 1986): 115–38.

Lonoff, Sue. *Wilkie Collins and His Victorian Readers.* New York: AMS Press, 1982.

Miller, D. A. *The Novel and the Police.* Berkeley: University of California Press, 1988.

Oliphant, Margaret. "Sensation Novels." *Blackwood's Edinburgh Magazine* 91 (May 1862): 564–84.

Rance, Nicholas. *Wilkie Collins and Other Sensation Novelists.* Rutherford, N.J.: Fairleigh Dickenson University Press, 1991.

Taylor, Jenny Bourne. *In the Secret Theatre of Home: Wilkie Collins, Sensation Narrative, and Nineteenth-Century Psychology.* London and New York: Routledge, 1988.

Disraeli, Gaskell, and the Condition of England

I N the 1840s, English legislators and political philosophers found themselves grappling with an unwelcome outcome of the economic growth of the previous century. These problems, which Thomas Carlyle captured with the phrase "the Condition of England," materialized in part because both the theory and the instruments of government developed in the eighteenth century proved inadequate to manage the tensions produced by rapid economic changes. In the most concrete terms, these tensions resulted from the intolerable pressures brought on by an increasingly densely congregated urban population, inadequate housing and sanitation, irregular employment, and government policies designed to manage rather than alleviate poverty. Conceptualized at a more abstract level, these tensions reflect the imperfect success with which the political philosophy of "liberalism" had thus far realized its paradoxical aim: to develop a form of government that could simultaneously allow individuals "free" expression of what seemed like idiosyncratic desires and unite those individuals into a single aggregate that was both amenable to rational oversight and capable of augmenting national prosperity.

In order to appreciate the characteristic features of the two closely related innovations in the British novel of the 1840s—the political novel and the social-problem novel—it is important to realize two things about this decade: first, that the deplorable living and working conditions of the laboring poor were startling revelations to much of the middle-class reading public; and second, that middle-class reformers were as divided about how best to comprehend social problems as about how to cure them. The question of which was more effective—a theoretical approach to the problems of poverty or imaginative engagement with one case at a time—had profound implications for the kind of writing granted social authority and for who was considered most knowledgeable about the poor. While all reformers wanted both to preserve individual liberty and to make the "population" productive, those who advocated theory thought that "experts"—statesmen, philosophers, and political economists—should address the problem analytically in official reports. Those who supported the case-by-case approach welcomed descriptive accounts by clergymen, journalists, and novelists as well.

The question of how best to comprehend the new urban landscape also made the issue of gender central to the treatment of poverty. Largely because of the eighteenth-century breakup of moral philosophy into political economy and aesthetics, ways of knowing were gendered in the early nineteenth century: the abstract reasoning of political economy was considered a masculine epistemology, while the aesthetic appreciation of concrete particulars was considered feminine. This did not mean that all imaginative literature was written by women, of course, or even that political economy was exclusively a male domain. It did mean that men who wrote poetry and novels struggled to acquire the dignity generally attributed to masculine pursuits—whether by asserting, as Percy Shelley did, that poets were the "unacknowledged legislators of the world" or by taking serious historical events as their subjects, as did Sir Walter Scott. It also meant that women who addressed political and economic subjects, like Mary Wollstonecraft and Harriet Martineau, had to contend with the charge that they were "masculine" or "unsexed" females.

When novelists entered the Condition-of-England debate in the 1840s, then, they were implicitly arguing that a feminized genre was more appropriate to the problems of the poor than were the abstractions of political economy. At the same time, however, when writers addressed social issues in fiction they were also claiming a more directly political role for the novel than feminized activities were generally granted. In this chapter I will examine some of the implications of gendered knowledge for the treatment of social problems and for the novel as a genre. Benjamin Disraeli's *Coningsby* (1844), which most identify as the first political novel, suggests how even novelistic knowledge could be represented as masculine if "politics" was sufficiently redefined. By contrast, Elizabeth Gaskell's *Mary Barton* (1847), which critics consider the first social-problem novel, argues for the feminization of knowing even in a world where the principles of political economy hold sway.

Before turning to these novels, I need to sketch in more detail some of the more theoretical approaches to the problems of the 1840s, for it was in relation to these formulations that novelists developed their ideas. Foremost among these masculine paradigms were the theories of political economists like Thomas Malthus and David Ricardo. Working from the basic economic "laws" that Adam Smith set out in 1776, political economists developed a "science" that, by the 1840s, was generally associated with two sets of conclusions. The first, which was invariably linked to Malthus's *Principles of Population* (1798), emphasized the incompatibility between some kinds of individual desire and the well-being of the nation. Because he thought that the population increased geometrically whereas food production could only grow in arithmetical increments, Malthus claimed that (the working class's) sexual self-control—what he called the "moral check"—was necessary to prevent widespread starvation, plague, or civil war. By contrast, political economists' second conclusion emphasized the essential compatibility between another kind of desire and national prosperity. This principle, which received its most scientific formulation in Ricardo's *Principles of Political Economy* (1817), maintained that the nation would necessarily prosper if individuals' desire for gain was left alone because the economy was providentially governed by its own, self-regulating laws. In the first decades of the century, these and other principles of political economy were made widely available to the middle class through the copious writings of J. R. McCulloch and to literate workers through Harriet Martineau's *Illustrations of Political Economy* (1832–1833).

A second important theoretical approach to the problems associated with poverty was offered by two of the most influential literary philosophers of the early nineteenth century, Samuel Taylor Coleridge and Thomas Carlyle. Both influenced by German idealism, both struggling to imagine a transcendental "idea" that could be realized in English society, Coleridge and Carlyle proposed slightly different versions of what Coleridge called "representativeness." For Coleridge, "representativeness" was best conveyed by what he called a "symbol." The symbol, he explained in *The Statesman's Manual* (1816) simultaneously partakes of an abstract idea and renders that idea intelligible by representing it in a specific image. This concept, when applied to social relations, laid the groundwork for Coleridge's theory of politics. In the political realm, Coleridge considered the constitution the most potent symbol, because it incarnates the "IDEA of the STATE." As he explained in *On the Constitution of Church and State* (1829), the "IDEA of the STATE" is also given concrete form in two institutions: the state, which represents people in the aggregate, and the church, which treats individuals as unique beings. The partnership of these two institutions therefore simultaneously gives every individual a (symbolic) role in the government by which he (and, even more indirectly, she) is represented and provides images by which social problems can be imaginatively transcended.

In "Signs of the Times" (1829), Carlyle offers his own theory about how to cure social ills. Like Coleridge's *Constitution*, "Signs of the Times" was written partly in response to debates about Catholic emancipation, which was enacted in 1829. Unlike Coleridge, however, Carlyle is primarily concerned with the challenge posed to individual spirituality by what he calls the "machinery" of parties and interest groups. In modern society, Carlyle complains, individual genius has been supplanted by institutionalized programs and spiritual values have been displaced by materialistic concerns. As a result, people increasingly act as if neither absolute truths nor moral imperatives exist. Carlyle proposes as a cure for such maladies a program of individual self-improvement that will both surpass and inspire national improvement, and whose institutional incarnations will embody the drive toward spiritual freedom now thwarted by the "Mechanical age." "Of this higher, heavenly freedom . . . all [man's] novel institutions, his faithful endeavours and loftiest attainments, are but the body, and more and more approximated emblem."

The diagnoses of Coleridge and Carlyle help explain how what I have called a "liberal" formulation could be adopted by theorists and statesmen across the political spectrum. These diagnoses also make explicit a tendency that all such theoretical approaches shared. Whether one thought that the solution to the problems associated with the Condition of England involved more government oversight, as the Whigs did, the conservation of traditional institutions like the church and the constitution, as Tories tended to do, or even complete parliamentary or economic reform, as did Chartists and Owenite socialists, almost everyone in the 1840s wanted to free individuals in order to realize national potential. At the same time that individual liberty was their concern, however, these theorists also tended to conceptualize the individual as an abstraction and to assume that this abstraction could be analyzed by generalizations because every person was animated by a single, universal desire (however that desire was defined). Indeed, the capacity for such abstraction was what typically characterized these theories as authoritative (and masculine) contributions to social analysis. By contrast, novelists who addressed social problems—even when they adopted the specific solutions generated by these theorists—rejected (or at least modified) the tendency toward abstraction that theorists displayed. When they plotted their solutions as stories of specific individuals, novelists disclosed a fact that theorists often overlooked: in a gendered society, individuals cannot be abstractions; even if their class position can be subordinated to the universal characteristics all "men" share, they—and their desires—are still socially differentiated by sex.

Coningsby

Coningsby, Benjamin Disraeli's eighth novel, is the first of what has come to be called the Young England trilogy, after the youth-worshiping politics Disraeli and his friends espoused. In 1870, Disraeli explained that his ambition in the early 1840s had been to explore what he held to be the primary issues of the day: "the derivation and character of political parties; the condition of the people which had been the consequence of them; the duties of the Church as a main remedial agency in our present state." While all of these topics are introduced in *Coningsby*, only the first receives extensive treatment. *Sybil, or The Two Nations* (1845) is devoted to the condition of the people, and *Tancred, or The New Crusade* (1847) takes up the historical role of the Jews in founding the Christian church. The three novels are alike, however, in arguing that the novelist can be an authoritative critic of social issues. *Coningsby* lays the groundwork for this claim. Its specific contribution entails eroticizing what contemporaries considered the most masculine of all activities so that it would be fit material for novelistic treatment, and politicizing the most feminized of all genres so that it would pass as an authoritative discourse. In order to effect this transformation, Disraeli subsumes erotics, politics, and the novel into a conceptual universe that is, for all intents and purposes, exclusively male.

Coningsby is primarily concerned not with specific solutions to the social problems of the day but with the process that Disraeli considered requisite to addressing these problems—the reconstitution of politics. This reform is accomplished primarily through a narrative of psychological maturation that gives politics both a story and an erotic cast. Like *Sybil*, then, as well as Gaskell's *North and South*, *Coningsby* shows how falling in love can perform political work. Unlike these other novels, however, the love in *Coningsby* is not exclusively heterosexual.

The main plot of *Coningsby* traces the transformation of Harry Coningsby from an inarticulate schoolboy into the self-possessed spokesman for Young England. At the beginning of the novel, which is set in May 1832, young Coningsby stands for the first time before his grandfather, the Marquess of Monmouth, the wealthiest noble in England. The boy hopes to win from the stern old man the patronage and affection that Monmouth denied to both of Coningsby's now-deceased parents. The decisive moment of Coningsby's maturation, which occurs some eight years later, also involves his grandfather. Eager to use Coningsby as a "brilliant tool" for advancing his own campaign for a dukedom, Monmouth commands Coningsby to stand as Tory candidate for Darlford against Monmouth's old enemy, the wealthy manufacturer Millbrook. Even though he knows it will enrage his grandfather, Coningsby refuses to obey Monmouth, both because he loves the mill owner's daughter and because the principles he has come to hold are not those of the Tory party. By resisting Monmouth, Coningsby avoids what Disraeli represents as the most dangerous snare for an ambitious youth—the "dazzling" allure of party intrigue. Instead of party, Coningsby trusts to himself: "If the principles of his philosophy were true, the great heart of the nation would respond to their expression," he decides. Thus the young "hero" comes to embody the formula Disraeli sets out early in the novel: "Great minds must trust to great truths and great talents for their rise, and nothing else."

The Carlylean celebrations of individual personality that punctuate *Coningsby* are complicated by Disraeli's equally powerful insistence that the "principles" that animate his hero are not of his own making. Indeed, Disraeli figures Coningsby's maturation as a series of

conversations rather than actions; in all but the last of these Coningsby is a silent vessel into which other men "pour" their ideas. As a
schoolboy at Eton, Coningsby listens to Oswald Millbrook expound
his father's theories; his first "adventure" after Eton is a chance meeting with the erudite Jew Sidonia, who lectures the boy on the "influence of individual character"; at the family seat of his friend Lord
Sydney, Coningsby learns the significance of ancient ceremonies and
manners from the Catholic Eustace Lyle; at Millbrook's home outside
of Manchester, Coningsby hears firsthand the manufacturer's
thoughts about class and merit; and from Sidonia again, first at Coningsby Castle, then in Paris, the youth learns that "national character"
and a strong monarchy more adequately represent the "people" than
can an elected House of Commons. At this level of the plot, there is
almost no conflict, not only because the significant "events" are conversations (or monologues), but also because Coningsby is so passive,
so unformed. At most, the young man admits to confusion or voices
criticism of the Whig party, but until he finally expounds the principles of Young England in Book 7, Coningsby's own ideas are presented as sketchily as is his appearance.

The peculiar amorphousness of young Coningsby does not undermine his heroic potential. Disraeli represents Coningsby's influence as
immediate, irresistible, and self-explanatory. At Eton, the boy attains
"over his intimates the ascendant power, which is the destiny of genius";
and when he finally stands for Darlford after Millbrook voluntarily
steps aside, Coningsby is received "as if he were a prophet" by supporters of every party. Coningsby's initial lack of character is, in fact, his primary qualification for inaugurating the reform that Disraeli envisions,
for by absorbing the ideas of various men, Coningsby is able to incarnate what Sidonia describes as "national character." "A character is an
assemblage of qualities," Sidonia explains; "the character of England
should be an assemblage of great qualities."

Just as Sybil unites the "two nations" by combining in herself the
aristocracy and the people, so Coningsby constitutes an "assemblage"
that reconciles the interests of a Whig mill owner, an apolitical
Catholic, and a Jewish financier. As an "assemblage," Coningsby most
clearly resembles not Parliament, whose deliberations have degenerated into gossip and self-serving intrigue, but the "free and intellectual
press," which Sidonia presents as above party and class and as capable
of restoring dignity even to the monarchy. "The representation of the

Press is far more complete than the representation of Parliament," Coningsby echoes two books later. "Let us propose . . . a free monarchy, established on the fundamental laws . . . ruling an educated people, represented by a free and intellectual press. Before such a royal authority, supported by such a national opinion, the sectional anomalies of our country would disappear."

If Disraeli considers the press so important and Parliament so ineffectual, it may seem strange that he brings Coningsby onto the public stage as a member of Parliament and offers as his only example of a journalist the despicable Rigby, author of "slashing" lampoons and would-be spoiler of Coningsby's success. Like the principles of Young England in general, however, Disraeli's image of the "free and intelligent" press as an "assemblage" of opinions is frankly idealized. Such idealization, in fact, serves as an explicit counter to what Disraeli and his companions considered the spiritually bankrupt and morally deadening tendencies of utilitarianism, political economy, and Whig party policies. In so doing, it also offers a reformed version of politics. For Disraeli, the ideal "politics" is noncontestatory, disinterested, and capable of subsuming opposing positions. It is, in other words, another version of what Coleridge called the symbol.

In one of the many narrative interpolations designed to educate the reader rather than Coningsby, Disraeli summarizes the dilemma that the politics of Young England were intended to address. The "Condition-of-England Question" has two facets, the narrator explains. The first attests to England's economic and military superiority; the second shows England's failure to manage the fruits of power. "There was no proportionate advance in our moral civilisation. In the hurry-skurry of money-making, men-making, and machine-making, we had altogether outgrown, not the spirit, but the organisation, of our institutions." The program of Young England was designed to rectify such problems without undermining England's prosperity. Specifically, the Tory Young Englanders wanted to improve the condition of the poor by restoring the aristocratic paternalism Disraeli associated with the age of chivalry. Government would be conducted by enlightened landowners; ritualized celebrations of the nation would reinvigorate the spirituality of the people; judiciously administered alms would restore the deference of the poor; and belief in the monarchy and the church would sustain everyone in hard times. With its idealized (and decidedly imprecise) agenda, Young England was developed as an alternative to the dismal science of political economy, which reduced the Condition of England issue to a "knife-and-fork question," and to the programs of political reform advanced by Chartists, radicals, and many Whigs.

At some points in *Coningsby*, Disraeli mocks the more "obsolete" ideas of Young England, as when he reduces Henry Sydney's lofty ideas to the absurd suggestion "that the people are to be fed by dancing round a May-pole." Nevertheless, like most other novelists who took up social issues, Disraeli clearly longed for a more spiritual, more imaginative alternative to political economy. Devising such an alternative and giving it psychological credibility are the principal functions of the conversations that make Coningsby what he comes to be. At one point in the novel, when Coningsby first visits Manchester, Disraeli even suggests that industrial machines will inspire the imagination, thereby not only reanimating but literally incorporating the people.

A machine is a slave that neither brings nor bears degradation; it is a being endowed with the greatest degree of energy, and acting under the greatest degree of excitement, yet free at the same time from all passion and emotion. . . . And why should one say that the machine does not live? . . . It moves with more regularity than a man. And has it not a voice? Does not the spindle sing like a merry girl at her work, and the steam-engine roar in joy chorus, like a strong artisan handling his lusty tools, and gaining a fair day's wages for a fair day's toil?

While Disraeli rapidly abandons the image of the happy machine, this figure does reveal two significant tendencies inherent in the Young Englanders' politics. First, the image of the happy machine converts the fact of an impoverished laboring class into a picture of singing workers, then displaces these imaginary workers (and the entire problem of unemployment) with the vision of an equally melodious automaton. Like the idea that the "peasantry" will be content with May Day celebrations instead of food, in other words, the image of the singing machine acknowledges class concerns but subordinates them to an idealized (non)solution. Second, the image of the happy machine alludes to but then completely effaces the problem of gender. In the idealized version of politics Disraeli develops in this novel, there is only one kind of subject. While this subject is theoretically representative—or even androgynous, like the machines making machines that so infatuate

Coningsby—we soon discover that this subject is actually gendered male.

The process by which gender gets written as masculine provides the narrative energy that is otherwise absent from *Coningsby*. If the primary plot of the novel is an additive account of the hero's transformation, which is indebted to the picaresque novel, then the two subplots that contain the novel's energizing conflicts are influenced by the Gothic novel and centrally concern gender. The more prominent of these subplots, which also reflects the influence of eighteenth-century inheritance plots, seems to be about women, since it focuses on Coningsby's mother and Millbrook's daughter Edith. Initially, Disraeli presents the boy's dim memories of his mother as "his only link to human society"; certainly, his thoughts of her constitute the character's only sign of psychological complexity. Disraeli first develops this complexity when Coningsby is inexplicably attracted to a portrait that hangs in Millbrook's house, then elaborates it when Coningsby falls in love with Edith Millbrook. Using Gothic conventions and language, Disraeli creates Coningsby's psychological depth by stressing the haunting association between Edith and this picture, which depicts Coningsby's mother. After Coningsby meets Edith in Paris, the narrator tells us, "a beautiful countenance that was alternately the face in the mysterious picture [i.e., his mother], and then that of Edith, haunted [Coningsby] under all circumstances." Presumably, no physical resemblance connects the two women, since the mystery of Coningsby's mother turns out to involve only the fact that Millbrook once loved her, not that she is Edith's mother too. In fact, what actually connects the two women and enables them to serve a single narrative function is that both point to the central role played by another secret relationship—that among three men.

Coningsby's attempts to realize his "secret joy" through marriage to Edith are baffled for much of the novel by this other secret. Although he does not know what it is, Coningsby knows that some secret passion must exist; "political opinion, or even party passion, could not satisfactorily account" for the "vindictive feud" that divides Monmouth and Millbrook. But while Coningsby is correct in suspecting a secret, he is incorrect in thinking that his mother is its real origin. When Coningsby makes his feelings about Edith clear, Millbrook reveals that he and Monmouth are actually bound to each other by hatred for Coningsby's father—the first because he stole Coningsby's mother from Millbrook, who was engaged to marry her; and the second for reasons that remain unclear. We learn only that "Lord Monmouth hated his younger son, who had married against his consent, a woman to whom the son was devoted." As a consequence of this hatred, Monmouth "hunted" the widow from his family, and, in retaliation for the sins of the father and son, Millbrook now persecutes Monmouth, first by purchasing an estate the old man coveted and then by winning the parliamentary seat Monmouth intended for his functionary Rigby.

The feud between the two men, along with their mutual, impassioned hatred for a third, therefore serves to convert Disraeli's idealized politics into the stuff of a novel by animating what passes for Coningsby's psychological complexity. This originary relationship among men makes another appearance in the novel, once more in connection with Coningsby but this time in the form of passionate love, not hate. Disraeli introduces this "frantic sensibility" in the guise of schoolboy friendship. "At school," the narrator explains,

friendship is a passion. It entrances the being; it tears the soul. All loves of after-life can never bring its rapture, or its wretchedness; no bliss so absorbing, no pangs of jealousy or despair so crushing and so keen! What tenderness and devotion; what illimitable confidence; infinite revelations of inmost thoughts; what ecstatic present and romantic future; what bitter estrangements and what melting reconciliations; what scenes of wild recrimination, agitating explanations, passionate correspondence; what insane sensitiveness, and what frantic sensibility; what earthquakes of the heart and whirlwinds of the soul are confined in that simple phrase, a schoolboy's friendship!

Predictably, the unformed Coningsby is not the bearer but the object of this "passionate admiration." When Coningsby saves his young admirer from drowning, Oswald Millbrook pours out his feelings to his hero in what can only be called a love letter. "I want . . . that we may be friends," the besotted Millbrook writes, "and that you will always know that there is nothing I will not do for you, and that I like you better than any fellow at Eton. . . . Not because you saved my life; though that is a great thing, but because before that I would have done anything for you."

It takes some time for Coningsby to replicate Oswald's outburst and even longer for Oswald to fulfill his promise. Along with the feud between their elders, however, this passionate homosocial attachment provides the motor of the romantic plot and the terms by which Disraeli idealizes politics. It is because Coningsby saved young Millbrook that he first visits the Millbrook home, where he sees the spellbinding portrait and Edith; it is because he loves Edith that he defies his grandfather; and it is because Oswald loves Coningsby that the former eventually persuades his father to relinquish his parliamentary seat. Even more important, it is because Coningsby returns Oswald's passionate affection that his grandfather disinherits him, which event first reduces Coningsby to the point that he needs Millbrook's patronage and then permits Oswald to fulfill his vow. Disraeli presents Coningsby's "impassioned" advances to Oswald as a metaphorical seduction, advanced by a man made desperate by the frustration of his heterosexual desires. After Mr. Millbrook reveals the secret of his feud with Monmouth, Coningsby "flings" himself into Oswald's arms and hurries his friend toward Coningsby Castle, which Oswald has been forbidden to enter. Despite Oswald's hesitation, a thunderstorm drives the young men toward shelter, just as another storm had kept Coningsby and Edith secluded in a cottage long past dinner the day before. "Hurried on by Coningsby," Oswald "could make no resistance." Once inside the castle, and professing himself "reckless as the tempest," Coningsby orders the servants away "and for a moment felt a degree of wild satisfaction in the company of the brother of Edith."

That Coningsby's "wild satisfaction" is transgressive is made clear both by the abrupt termination that Mr. Rigby's entrance brings to the midnight supper (and the chapter) and by Monmouth's irate response to Rigby's representation of "the younger Millbrook quite domiciled at the Castle." Disraeli is also careful to discredit such homosocial outbursts by other means. When Coningsby goes up to Cambridge, for example, he is represented as thinking with "disgust of the impending dissipation of an University, which could only be an exaggeration of their coarse frolics at school." Despite such explicit disclaimers, however, and despite the fact that their attachment to each other is sanctioned by the existence of Oswald's sister, Disraeli presents the relationships among the men as more vital, more long-lived, and more influential than anything else in the world. The sequence of formative conversations that constitutes the novel's primary plot, in fact, can be read as a series of repetitions of the protopolitical conversations that first "agitated [the schoolboys'] young hearts" and in which politics was so obviously simply the vehicle for other passions. The "keen relish" with which the boys read and discuss accounts of politics and the "excited intelligence" with which they worship their political heroes hint at the homoerotics with which Disraeli associates all interactions among men. This association returns in passing when we learn that male political canvassers wear dresses to round up voters, and with force when Coningsby is reunited with his friend at Oxford. Their "congress of friendship" unbroken, each man "poured forth his mind without stint," and the narrator blesses their union even as he describes the conversation in such a way as to suggest that one man—not two—is present. "Man is never so manly as when he feels deeply, acts boldly, and expresses himself with frankness and with fervour."

The homoerotics of manly conversation constitute Disraeli's version of a reformed politics. Because politics has been eroticized, it can be plotted in a novel; but because the erotic component of relationships has been purged of sexuality, the novel can be offered as an appropriate vehicle for political sentiment. At the conclusion of *Coningsby*, this transformation is graphically presented when the two charismatic boys-turned-men stand side by side at the head of their country, their infatuation with each other having been converted into an infatuation with England. "Men must have been at school together," the narrator approvingly notes, "to enjoy the real fun of meeting thus, and realising their boyish dreams. . . . Life was a pantomime; the wand was waved, and it seemed that the schoolfellows had of a sudden become elements of power, springs of the great machine."

The "great machine" of which Coningsby and Millbrook are the "springs" thus replaces the singing machines of Manchester. In the process, of course, women—both the "merry girl" whose voice echoed in the happy machine and Edith, who has finally become Coningsby's wife—simply disappear. Theoretically, they are represented by the men who animate the machine of national character; but since no woman has poured her ideas into Coningsby and since the psychological complexity apparently associated with women has been returned to its proper source, it is unclear how womanly influence will make itself felt or how women's interests will make themselves known. In *Sybil*, Disraeli does give a female character more prominence, but even there the titular character serves primarily as a source of inspiration for the man who reunites the classes in the style of Young England. When she is called on to act, Sybil becomes confused and lost; she fails to reach her father in time, and then she falls senseless in a faint. Disraeli's novels may use the Coleridgean idea of representativeness to join opposing classes in an

idealized compound, but in the process, they set aside another important opposition—the difference of sex.

Mary Barton

If Disraeli reads the condition-of-England question in the light of
history, Elizabeth Gaskell approaches it as a problem of epistemology. And if Disraeli counters the feminization of the novel by larding
his work with "manly conversations" and didactic asides, Gaskell uses
the gendered genre to foreground sexual difference as both social
symptom and cure. For Gaskell, the crisis of the "hungry forties"
should be addressed not by reforming politics or politicizing the
novel, but by taking full advantage of the imaginative engagement
associated with this genre and with women. This capacious mode of
knowledge will bridge the gulf between England's "two nations" by
feminizing both masters and workers—that is, by teaching them to
identify with each other, as women (and novelists) already do. For
Gaskell, then, the novel is uniquely qualified to promote this feminine epistemology, for fiction can breathe life into the abstractions of
political economy by taking the middle-class reader into the homes
and minds of the poor.

As we have seen, Disraeli's political novel suspends the (class and
political) differences among individuals by placing various interests side
by side within a single, representative figure. Approaching the condition-of-England question through imaginative engagement rather than
a political program, Gaskell presents the individual in a synecdochic
rather than symbolic relation to the whole. In *Mary Barton*, as in
Gaskell's other social-problem novels, it is possible to comprehend the
problems that afflict society or to test the theoretical conclusions of
political economy only by figuring these issues as individual case histories. Thus, for Gaskell, the story of the individual does not so much
contain the truth of society as a whole as it provides imaginative access
to the only form in which "society as a whole" makes sense. Presumably,
the identification by which the reader enters the story of the individual
can become the motor of social change, just as the mill owner Carson
is able to effect real improvements for his workers once he understands
the feelings of the men he employs.

Mary Barton has earned its critical reputation as a social-problem
novel at least in part because of Gaskell's detailed representations of the

deplorable conditions of working-class lives. Largely the story of three families—the Bartons; their working-class neighbors, the Wilsons; and the Carsons, who own the mill that (sometimes) employs the Manchester workers—*Mary Barton* graphically figures the details of poverty so as to transport the middle-class reader into places most would not see in a lifetime. Some of these places proclaim the triumph of human effort over obdurate materiality; such is the case with Alice Wilson's cellar, where "the floor was bricked, and scrupulously clean, although so damp that it seemed as if the last washing would never dry up." Others, however, suggest that filth is an inexorable fact of impoverished life. On an errand of mercy to a fellow worker, for example, John Barton and George Wilson descend into the cellar where the Davenports live and die.

You went down one step even from the foul area into the cellar in which a family of human beings lived. It was very dark inside. The window-panes many of them were broken and stuffed with rags, which was reason enough for the dusky light that pervaded the place even at mid-day. . . . On going into the cellar inhabited by Davenport, the smell was so foetid as almost to knock the two men down. Quickly recovering themselves, as those inured to such things do, they began to penetrate the thick darkness of the place, and to see three or four little children rolling on the damp, nay wet brick floor, through which the stagnant, filthy moisture of the street oozed up; the fireplace was empty and black; the wife sat on her husband's lair, and cried in the dark loneliness.

John Barton may be "inured to such things," but this description stresses that the narrator and the reader are not. The work of the novel is to make the contrast between the material conditions of such characters and those of the reader so vivid that men like Carson (and the reader), who have the power that money supposedly brings, will see this contrast as a mockery of the interests that Gaskell presents as common to all. At the conclusion of *Mary Barton*, Mr. Carson nurtures the "wish" that expresses Gaskell's polemical position:

that a perfect understanding, and complete confidence and love, might exist between masters and men; that the truth might be recognised that the interests of one were the interests of all, and, as such, required the consideration and deliberation of all; that hence it was most desirable to have educated workers, capable of judging, not mere machines of ignorant men; and to have them bound to their employers by the ties of respect and affection, not by mere money bargains alone; in short, to acknowledge the Spirit of Christ as the regulating law between both parties.

In order to emphasize the injustice of the material contrasts that separate rich from poor, Gaskell stresses what everyone shares: the desire for domestic well-being. So prominent is the domestic sphere in Gaskell's novel that every event, every topic of political controversy, every social and economic fact of life is filtered through the lens of domestic concerns. Gaskell's only references to the controversial issues of her day—the New Poor Law, for example, factory inspectors, and the high incidence of industrial accidents—present these facts as the material from which the poor must devise a "plan of living" their domestic lives. Similarly, the workers' presentation of the People's Charter to Parliament in 1839, which Disraeli converts into an extended dramatic episode in *Sybil*, occurs offstage in *Mary Barton*; Gaskell figures the impact of Parliament's rebuff not in political terms but as a blow to John Barton's dwindling optimism and therefore as a further erosion of the domestic stability he and his daughter so precariously maintain. Typical of the priority Gaskell assigns to domesticity is her treatment of England's most aggressive foray into international affairs, the economic expansionism we call imperialism. References to England's imperial exploits pepper the middle third of *Mary Barton*, for Will Wilson, Alice's godson, earns his living as a hand on a trading ship. We discover in passing that Will has been to Africa, Sierra Leone, China, Madeira, and both Americas. Gaskell construes Will's travels, however, strictly in terms of their potential impact on the home. His trips figure most prominently as absences for Alice, not as adventures or dangers for him, and the only exotica he brings back—a dried specimen of a flying fish and a tale about a mermaid—are immediately absorbed into domesticating contexts. The flying fish becomes part of Job Legh's naturalist collection, and the mermaid is first debunked and then supplanted by a real enchantress, as Job's granddaughter Margaret "enthralls" Will with her lovely singing.

Just as domestic concerns subsume foreign matters in *Mary Barton*, so the domestic story gradually absorbs the other plots that vie for attention. As Catherine Gallagher has argued, *Mary Barton* contains several competing plots, each of which is associated with a specific narrative mode. Among these are a farce, which is enacted by the mill owner's son Harry and by Sally Leadbitter, an apprentice at the milliner's; the sentimental romance associated with the young Mary and her fallen aunt Esther; and the tragedy of John Barton. For much of the novel, these narratives impede and threaten to disrupt the orderly progress of Mary's maturation and marriage to Jem Wilson. The farce and the sentimental romance dominate the first half of the novel. The cynical Harry Carson, who courts Mary partly for her beauty and partly for the fun of the chase, and the "plain" and "vulgar-minded" Sally Leadbitter first tempt, then try to coerce Mary into imitating a sentimental romance. Gaskell makes it clear that sentimental heroines exist only in literature; in the working-class world of Manchester, adopting the sentimental perspective can only lead to the catastrophe dramatized by Esther.

Esther is just one of the many "fallen women" to whom Gaskell gave sympathetic fictional treatment; others include the lost daughter of "Lizzie Leigh" (1850) and the heroine of *Ruth* (1853). In *Mary Barton*, the prostitute plays a more specifically didactic role than in Gaskell's other works. The younger sister of Mary's mother, Esther is so "puffed up" with her beauty that, shortly before the novel opens, she leaves her factory work to follow a handsome young soldier. After three years and the birth of a daughter, the soldier moves on, Esther's child falls ill, and, in order to feed the child, Esther takes to the streets. Her child long dead, Esther confides her history to Jem in hopes of saving Mary from a similar fate. For, despite the fact that Esther claims that her actions have separated her from decent women "as far asunder as heaven and hell," she repeatedly insists that Mary resembles her or that Mary resembles her daughter—just as John Barton thinks that Mary resembles both his wife and her sister. The narrator elaborates the possibility that women are somehow all alike later in the novel when Mary mistakes Esther for her mother, of whom she has just been dreaming. These suggestions form the sentimental paradigm that Mary must resist, for, in reducing every woman to an instance of the same, the sentimental romance obliterates all the discriminations that make domesticity possible: the differences among women that render a man's choice meaningful and valorize a woman's will; the judgment that protects marriage from temptations; the moral code that differentiates between marriage and the blissful life that Esther spent with her soldier.

John Barton's tragedy, which dominates the second half of the novel, poses an even greater danger to Mary's domestic story than does Esther's sentimental romance, for John's inability to tolerate what Gaskell presents as the bitter irony of life drives him to a savage imitation of the mill owner's insensitivity. Although Gaskell offers several explanations for John Barton's tragic fall, her descriptions repeatedly invoke the same image with which Esther tries to distinguish herself from other women—the image of the gulf. Initially, John Barton is tormented by the material "contrast" that grows starker as times get worse. At the conclusion of the novel, we learn that a moral version of this social contrast has tortured John ever since he learned to read and that trying to reconcile what the Bible says with what men do has produced a corresponding split within him: "I was tore in two sometimes," the dying Barton confesses, "between my sorrow for poor suffering folk, and my trying to love them as caused their sufferings." The psychological version of the social contrast is momentarily resolved when John Barton responds to Harry Carson's thoughtless caricature of the starving laborers by plotting the young man's death. This resolution, of course, is not the one Gaskell endorses: in murdering young Carson, Barton has replicated Carson's sin, for John reduces Harry to a figure as grotesque as those in the caricature—an "overbearing partner" in "an obnoxious firm." Killing Carson, in fact, not only widens the psychological gulf within John Barton but also imposes it upon his daughter. Once John has left home for parts unknown, Mary deals with her father's guilt by "separat[ing] him into two persons,—one, the father who had dandled her on his knee . . . ; the other, the assassin, the cause of all her trouble and woe."

Thus the "dark gulf" that haunts John Barton first as a fact about society, then as a psychological state, eventually deranges Mary. Indeed, it is this transfer of the ills of the social world into the woman's sphere by means of a male carrier that really imperils Mary's domestic narrative. Esther plays as critical a role in this process as she does in the sentimental romance, for despite her good intentions, her initial violation of domestic order has consigned her to a life on the streets of the masculine world. Now an uncomprehending watcher of the life she can no longer join, Esther inadvertently provokes the confrontation between Jem and Harry that leads to Jem's arrest. When she takes Mary the incriminating paper she finds at the murder scene,

Esther literally brings a bit of the street into the home; in so doing, she unintentionally renders Mary "the sole depository of the terrible secret" of John Barton's guilt. Desperate to save her lover without betraying her father, Mary is now thoroughly contaminated by the contradictions that mar the masculine world. Gaskell presents these contradictions as outbursts of psychological instability: Mary suffers mental confusion ("armies of thought . . . met and clashed in her brain"), paranoid projections of her fears ("the very house was haunted with memories and foreshadowings"), dissociation ("her very words seemed not her own"), and, finally, derangement and convulsions ("'Oh, Jem! Jem! you're saved; and I *am* mad—' and [Mary] was instantly seized with convulsions"). Even more telling, this hysteria spreads to the narrative itself: three times in the course of ten pages, the narrator breaks into the story to confess her own loss, her own guilt, her own longing for some contact with a spectral world. In the most startling of these outbursts, the narrator's parenthetical longing to sink herself in dreams seems nearly as "crazy" as the emotion that Mary fears will derange Mrs. Wilson.

Already [Mrs. Wilson's] senses had been severely stunned by the full explanation of what was required of her,—of what she had to prove against her son, her Jem, her only child,—which Mary could not doubt the officious Mrs. Heming had given; and what if in dreams (that land into which no sympathy nor love can penetrate with another, either to share its bliss or its agony,—that land whose scenes are unspeakable terrors, are hidden mysteries, are priceless treasures to one alone,—that land where alone I may see, while yet I tarry here, the sweet looks of my dear child),—what if, in the horrors of her dreams, her brain should go still more astray, and she should waken crazy with her visions, and the terrible reality that begot them?

Such interruptions differ both from the narrative asides in Disraeli's novels and from other narrative interpolations in this novel. Unlike the former, this digression does not present the author's position didactically; unlike the latter, it does not emphasize the contrast between the narrator and her subject matter but bespeaks an identification so powerful that the boundary between character and narrator threatens to dissolve. In so doing, the three digressions in chapters 24 and 25 signal that the feminized genre may be as susceptible to a hysterical breakdown as are the female characters of *Mary Barton*. In the narrative, the characters' derangements originate in contamination that has invaded the womanly world from outside: trying only to protect the home and tell home truths, Mrs. Wilson and Mary find themselves possessed of knowledge about men that will destroy their families; worse still, they find themselves subpoenaed to testify in court—that is, to make the most private knowledge public, to be themselves the violators of the domestic integrity that by rights they should defend.

I will return in a moment to the narrator's derangement. For now, it is important to see how Gaskell restores domestic order to what has become a hysterical narrative. More decisively than the economic crisis that threatens starvation, more persistently than the sentimental fate that Esther embodies, the woman's inability to remain immune to the contaminating mysteries of the masculine world imperils domestic stability and narrative coherence. All Mrs. Wilson knows is that Jem owns a gun, that it once belonged to his grandfather the gamekeeper, and that men sometimes "practice" (for what?) in the shooting gallery. Mary knows both more and less of this mysterious masculine universe. Going through her father's closet like a detective in search of clues, Mary discovers the other half of the incriminating paper, a woolen gun case, and some "little bullets or shot" ("I don't know which you would call them," the narrator hastily adds). John Barton's motives, by contrast, remain impenetrable to Mary (and, if her competing explanations are any indication, to the narrator): "His actions had become so wild and irregular of late, that she could not reason upon them."

Unable either to understand or to defend against the darkness that oozes into the home from this masculine sphere, Mary Barton's only recourse is to absorb its duplicity and, when forced, to substitute her womanly secret for the revelation the court solicits. Required to testify at Jem's trial, the reeling Mary holds "the tremendous secret [of her father's guilt] imprisoned within her" and releases instead "what woman usually whispers with blushes and tears, and many hesitations, to one ear alone," the secret of her love for Jem. While the narrator approves of Mary's confession, the fact that a woman must publicize this most intimate of all truths to hide a man's incomprehensible guilt attests to the damage that domesticity has suffered here. Mary's subsequent madness and convulsions constitute the woman's last defense against the disorder of the outside world. Only when John Barton voluntarily confesses and he and his other victim—Harry's father—find common comfort in the loss each has suffered can the domestic narrative resume. So great is the damage, however, that this narrative can only begin again in far-off Canada, which Gaskell depicts as "primeval"—that is, still unsullied by men.

While the narrator of *Mary Barton* repeatedly insists that the gulf between the classes can be bridged by knowledge, then, her narrative suggests that the gulf between the sexes will remain a gaping wound. In order to contain the ominous implications of this conclusion, Gaskell repeatedly seeks to absorb the masculine world into woman's sphere. She seeks to domesticate politics, for example, not only by subordinating narrative accounts of trade unionism and Chartist meetings to domestic events, but also by translating the political language of rights into a discourse about domestic needs. Thus we learn in passing that, with John Barton, "need was right," and, in the extended speech in which he rouses his companions to vengeance against the masters, Barton speaks of the needs of children, not the rights of men. "Our share we must and will have; we'll not be cheated. *We* want it for daily bread, for life itself; and not for our own lives neither . . . but for the lives of them little ones, who don't yet know what life is, and are afeared of death." In keeping with this domestication of politics, Gaskell provides a gallery of men who act as mothers: John Barton and George Wilson carry their babies at the novel's opening; as Ben Davenport sickens, the two men turn "rough, tender nurses" to his children and wife; Job Legh's long story of going to London tells how he learned to mother his granddaughter; Jem tends the stricken Mary with maternal solicitude; and, even in the depths of his despair, John Barton responds to a child crying for its mother.

Just as she domesticates politics, so Gaskell attempts to humanize political economy by casting its harsher equations as the feminized truisms of Christianity. In the process, value becomes a matter of quality, not quantity. Thus, in the concluding interview between mill owner and workers, Mr. Carson attempts to explain the iron law of market logic. "Two men live in a solitude," he declaims, "one produces loaves of bread, the other coats. . . . Now, would it not be hard if the bread-producer were forced to give bread for the coats, whether he wanted them or not, in order to furnish employment to the other: that is the simple form of the case; you've only got to multiply the numbers." Job Legh's response is clear: "God has given men feelings and passions which cannot be worked into the problem, because they are forever changing and uncertain," he counters. "Them that is strong in any of God's gifts is meant to help the weak,—be hanged to the facts!"

Despite advocating the feminized epistemology associated with the novel, Gaskell does not reject the principles of political economy. If anything, the narrator's concluding statement that "the interests of one were the interests of all" supports the economists' theories, just as her explanation that foreign competition justifies a temporary reduction of wages endorses the principle of laissez-faire. For the most part, however, Gaskell sidesteps the controversy surrounding political economy by avoiding disquisitions on theory of any kind. Rather than airing debates about the New Poor Law, free trade, or the wage fund, Gaskell presents the problem as one of communication and knowledge—as a conflict, that is, between the masculine refusal to know except in abstractions and the feminized imaginative embrace. Parliament rejects the People's Charter, the narrator suggests, because legislators did not want to know the conditions of the poor; the workmen in Manchester strike because the masters do not tell their employees about the foreign competition the mills face. If representatives for each side explained their interests in concrete terms, the narrator claims, mutual forbearance or even sympathy would result, as it does when Carson and Job Legh finally elaborate their positions for each other.

Despite these efforts to domesticate, so as to humanize, the masculine world of politics, theory, and work, however, Gaskell's narrator remains as aloof from its contaminating secrets as she clearly wishes her female characters could be. The narrator prefaces her summary presentation of the economic details her narrative requires with a distancing disclaimer ("I am not sure if I can explain myself in the technical terms of either masters or workmen"), and one of the two times she takes us into the world of work, she casts a Gothic mantle over the minutia of labor. In the foundry where Jem is employed, "a deep and lurid red glared over all. . . . The men, like demons, in their fire-and-soot colouring, stood swart around. . . . The heat was intense, and the red glare grew every instant more fierce." That the narrator's alienation from the masculine world of work is not simply a function of the infernal nature of smelting becomes clear from her casual denigration of less physical forms of employment. Thus the narrator dismisses medical men as compliant fools; lawyers as impatient, incompetent puppets; clerks as insensitive gossips; and policemen as "vulgar and uneducated" adventurers, who are little better than the criminals they stalk.

If Gaskell's narrative priorities suggest that the masculine world of politics and work must be cordoned off from the home, then does the overidentification that disrupts chapters 24 and 25 suggest that an equivalent darkness colors the domestic sphere? To what extent does the mental breakdown with which Gaskell afflicts Mary Barton implicate the imaginative identification that she explicitly recommends? If men could identify with each other as the narrator identifies with the women, what would happen to the psychological disengagement that political economists said was necessary for production, commerce, lawmaking, and justice? Could the domestic sphere really absorb all of these functions into itself, or is it rather protected—from women's own maddening excesses as well as from the inhumanity of men—by a strategic exclusion of that upon which its very existence depends?

Elizabeth Gaskell does not answer these questions in *Mary Barton*, and, although they return in many of her subsequent novels (particularly *Ruth* and *North and South*), she never so explicitly poses them as I have done here. For the most part, Gaskell treats class prejudice as the problem to be overcome and the "natural" attraction of one sex to the other as part of the solution to social strife. Presumably, the disorders that fester in separate spheres—the plots and politics and infernal sweat that men work up among themselves, the hysterical emotionalism that women together breed—remain unproblematic as long as marriage functions as the paradigm for proper social relations. The priority marriage must have—and the fragility of this solution—help explain why Esther plays such a crucial role in *Mary Barton*. The woman who lives out of wedlock must become a prostitute—the most contaminated and contaminating of all workers—because only her "fall" distinguishes moral domesticity from immoral domesticity. Moralizing domesticity, of course, goes hand in hand with defining the nondomestic world as immoral. Thus, the masculine realm that Disraeli elevated into a type of human intercourse becomes corrosive effluvia in *Mary Barton*. Source of so much distress but of domestic security as well, the manly world always threatens to seep into the home; every day, the woman pushes it back, just as she stanches the unspeakable current that flows beneath her cellar floor.

Given the assumptions that prevailed in England in the 1840s, it is not surprising that political philosophers and statesmen generally addressed the condition-of-England question in terms of human liberty and government oversight. For the vast majority of people who wrote about these problems—even for a woman like Harriet Martineau—the representative individual was a man and the self-evident priority was to set him free. Indeed, an individual man *could* be considered representative and capable of freedom because he stood for and supported others; according to the theory of virtual representation, the male "head of the household" represented the interests of his wife and children, just as he theoretically supported them by freely exchanging his labor for money. For the most part, social theorists simply set gender issues aside when they debated the Condition of England. Or, when they did discuss gender, it was to lament the chaos that industrialization had brought to the natural order: thus parliamentarians decried women working in factories; the Chartists railed against efforts to extend the franchise to women; and evangelicals and medical men lamented the number of women who walked the streets.

While novelists of the 1840s also addressed the condition-of-England question in terms of individual freedom and national prosperity, the conventions of their genre returned the issue of gender to the fore. This was true partly because only a feminized discourse such as the novel was assumed to be *necessarily* interested in sex. Just as men were considered representative humans and women were called "the sex," so the abstractions of masculinized political economy were considered "disinterested" knowledge while the imaginative forays of the feminized novel were assumed to reflect as well as dwell on the divisive "interests" of sex. Partly, the novel brings gender forward because plotting individual adventures in a direct commentary on a society where political, legal, and economic asymmetries were mapped onto sex was necessarily to imagine a gendered individual. Imagining "man" in the abstract or aggregate, political philosophers did not always think about gender—despite the fact that, as *Coningsby* illustrates so clearly, in a sexed society, even men together are gendered. What the novels of the 1840s tell us, then, is not how to rectify the Condition of England but how gender pervaded the social constitution of knowledge—and how, in so doing, gender was always part of the "truths" middle-class commentators discovered about the impoverished and themselves.

Mary Poovey

Selected Bibliography

Bodenheimer, Rosemarie. "Private Griefs and Public Acts in *Mary Barton*." *Dickens Studies Annual* 9 (1981): 195–216.

Brantlinger, Patrick. *The Spirit of Reform: British Literature and Politics, 1832–1867.* Cambridge, Mass.: Harvard University Press, 1977.

Braun, Thom. *Disraeli the Novelist.* London: Allen and Unwin, 1981.

Gallagher, Catherine. *The Industrial Reformation of English Fiction: Social Discourse and Narrative Form, 1832–1867.* Chicago: University of Chicago Press, 1985.

Yeazell, Ruth Bernard. "Why Political Novels Have Heroines: *Sybil*, *Mary Barton*, and *Felix Holt*." *Novel* 18 (1985): 126–44.

Shaping Hardy's Art: Vision, Class, and Sex

The cruelest man living could not sit at his feast, unless he sat blindfold.
Ruskin, Unto This Last

In a world where the blind only are cheerful we should all do well to put out our eyes.
Hardy, The Hand of Ethelberta

As the youthful schoolmaster gazed . . . he entered on rational considerations of what
a vast gulf lay between that lady and himself, what a troublesome world it was to
live in where such divisions could exist, and how painful was the evil when a man
of his unequal history was possessed of a keen susceptibility.
Hardy, "An Indiscretion in the Life of an Heiress"

THOMAS HARDY surely belongs among the greatest of Victorian storytellers. Early in his career, his *Under the Greenwood Tree* (1872) was, to his chagrin, taken to be the work of George Eliot. But Hardy's work is entirely distinct. In his rejection of the strategies of consolation that marked the work of his famous predecessors, his novels consistently imply a social and cosmic bleakness that has seemed to many readers almost absurd in its excess, and in its culmination in the suicide of the child, "Father Time," in *Jude the Obscure* (1894). Hardy's true greatness as a novelist, however, resides not in his cosmic or social philosophy but in the tensions and contradictions his novels generate as they register both an extraordinarily intense sensitivity to and pleasure in the physical world and life itself and a profound anxiety about the dangers of indulging that sensitivity. The old religious struggles for personal restraint and resistance to the world are replaced in Hardy, who no longer can believe in any world but the material, by a new aesthetic austerity. Self-control becomes for Hardy a condition for survival in a world he thought had no relation to human consciousness and sensibility.

I want to argue in what follows that the distinctive character of Hardy's fiction grows from the way his remarkable powers of sensuous responsiveness play off against the contingencies of society and biology. More specifically, I focus on the way his acute powers of observa-

tion, almost visionary in the intensity with which they register the phenomena of the natural world, complicate his attitudes toward the class
structures that govern society and the powerful sexual drives that govern human behavior. Hardy's visible world belies the human social
organizations and moral conventions that ostensibly contain it. It also
implies the pervasiveness of seeing: everything in Hardy's world is open
to observation—is, in all likelihood, being observed. There are no real
secrets in this world, only the desire to keep them.

Thus, for Hardy, the sexual desire that is implicit in the sensuous
intensity of vision is itself exposed to the observation of others. And
sexual desire is evidence of the fundamental animality of human nature:
the "ape and the tiger" that Tennyson wished dead. For Victorian writers, sexuality meant affiliation with the low rather than the high, and
particularly with the lower classes. To be a visionary of Hardy's sort is
not to be respectable. To love the visible world in all its sensuous particularity is to be self-evidently déclassé—either as artist, which allows
for a fairly complicated form of respectability in some cases, or as ple-
beian.

Hardy's vision forces him into dramatic self-contradiction. It reveals
to him the terrible injustice of class distinctions and the absurdity of
human conventions of respectability, but in his own life he struggled to
achieve respectability at all costs—usually through evasiveness and disguise (as when he wrote his autobiography under his wife Emma's
name). Vision also dramatizes the extraordinary seductiveness of sexuality and nature and at the same time their power to compromise and
elude him. It forces him and his characters into self-consciousness, and
his novels imply a constant alertness (never quite adequate to the
curiosity of the world) to the possibilities of shame and exposure. The
protagonists are damned by respectability *and* by resistance to it, for
convention is not merely outside them like a police force but inside
them like a conscience. In Hardy himself, the conscience produces not
guilt but shame. His characters are not guilty in their transgressions—
Tess Durbeyfield, for example, is a "pure woman," although she has
been raped and has become a murderer. But Hardy, in his evasiveness,
recognizes his own fear of the kinds of transgressions he allows Henchard in *The Mayor of Casterbridge* (1886), or Tess in *Tess of the
d'Urbervilles* (1891). His novels, in their evasiveness, reflect his shame
at that fear, his admiration of those uncompromising in their rejection
of the respectability that might protect them from their dooms.

Seeing too intensely, too intensely aware of the consequences of being seen, deeply sympathetic to the outcasts of society, desperate to avoid being himself cast out, passionately in love with the physical world, terrified of its indifference to his passion, Hardy writes novels whose power resides not in their implicit commentary on social or cosmic issues but in their ambivalent and culturally significant fusion of his great powers of vision with his deepest desires and anxieties about social success and sexual union.

Like the neurotic and often possessed John Ruskin, Hardy was, then, plagued with vision. The experience of the eye shapes Hardy's work, as it did Ruskin's. Their powers of vision invariably revealed to them much that they did not want to see, in particular their own complicity in the conventions and systems of social injustice and sexual desire that frightened and appalled them. With an architect's eye, Hardy saw history in objects; with a naturalist's eye, he saw how phenomena connect or conflict; with a novelist's eye, he read society in complexions, patterns of labor in postures, systems of hierarchy in costumes. And with the peculiar modern self-consciousness of the nineteenth century, he was constantly aware of the conditions that made observation possible. For Hardy as for Ruskin, deep uneasiness about the social position from which he was empowered to see provoked an even greater intensity of sight and sensitivity to the richness of the visible world and to its beauties, threats, deceptions, and injustices.

Thus, as I have been arguing, precise observation becomes inextricably linked to questions of class and of sexuality. (I want to emphasize sexuality over gender because the gender and class issues in Hardy seem to develop from the direct sexual energy that can be counted on, in almost every novel, to disrupt the narratives male protagonists write for themselves.) Class is a determiner of position for both observer and observed; sexual desire provokes intense observation and at the same time constantly threatens the stability of class. But differences in class and sexual energy led to radically different perspectives. For Ruskin, an evangelical child of commercial privilege, observation required not only the most accurate reporting but the most authoritative interpretation of the visible world. He developed an astonishingly powerful and beautiful voice, which—however muddled and uncertain Ruskin himself often became—pronounced upon the visible and hence upon the moral and the social with the authority and assuredness of a "graduate of Oxford," as he is described on the title page of the first volume of *Mod-*

ern Painters (1842). Hardy, whose Jude would gaze longingly toward the distant lights of "Christminster," avoided the prophetic forms of nonfiction and made his living writing novels, switching permanently to poetry only after a full, successful, and, from his point of view, thoroughly compromised career as novelist, rarely and evasively venturing into nonfiction. His prose often strains against the colloquial in what has been taken as his awkward and self-conscious attempt to prove he belonged among those graduates of Oxford who did not have to write for a living. Critically he has always paid the price for this. As Raymond Williams complains, traditional critics patronizingly identified Hardy as an "autodidact." And Hardy's excessive sensitivity to criticism suggests how vulnerable he was to precisely this kind of class-based judgment, how much he sought to disguise or overcome his social position, and how far he was compromised and shamed in his apparent condemnation of social hierarchies.

Though his early novels are full of caustic satire at the expense of the rich and the aristocratic, as a writer he differs most strikingly from Ruskin in his self-conscious evasiveness. For Ruskin, seeing is prophecy; writing is engagement with the real and persuasion to moral reform. For Hardy, seeing can indeed be prophetic, but it can also be delusive and it is always dangerous; and writing is a medium for lying and evasion as well as for representation. It is a salable commodity and constantly subject to misinterpretation and to unintended revelations. The difficulties of writing are allied to the complexities of seeing, for Hardy is as concerned with being seen as with seeing, and he is uncannily sensitive to the possibility that someone is watching. He is thus equally alert to the need for disguise and to the possibility that what one sees will be misunderstood, and particularly preoccupied with observation in unguarded moments. Seeing, like writing, both exposes and disguises, and unpredictably.

Self-consciousness and seeing are complexly interconnected, each visual event shaped in its significance by the degree to which observed and observer are alert to their conditions. Hardy's astonishing powers of natural description normally depend on the narrator's deep consciousness of the pervasiveness of watching and nature's relentless indifference to what the human sees. But his and his characters' observations of the human always risk the limitation of the observer's perspective, and the self-consciousness of the observed. Seeing does not necessarily empower, but it frequently wounds.

Self-consciousness in seeing is often imaged in Hardy by moments when the visual is framed quite literally, by windows. (Spying, an activity abundantly present in almost all of Hardy's novels, serves also to "frame" the visual.) Such framing can be taken as representative of Hardy's own writing, for while it provides an opening between two otherwise alien, distinct, and unself-consciously isolated worlds, it also implies incompleteness of connection. One can see through windows, even hear through them, but only rarely—although this too happens in Hardy's work—can one touch through them, only rarely can one directly affect or resist what appears in the frame. The world is not so much experienced through the frame as represented; the window gives access without necessitating engagement. Seeing, like writing, implies the absence (or distance) of what is seen or described. While windows seem to focus the visual world, and perhaps suggest a misleading relevance to the viewer, they often allow in more than the viewer wants and they cannot entirely contain the multiplicity and dangers of the material from which they ostensibly distance the viewer. The lives of Hardy's characters are as frequently disrupted by their own acts of observation as they are by being spied upon. In any case, like so much of Hardy's writing, the framed scene both represents and evades, makes vulnerable and protects, implies and circumvents, approaches contact and resists it. Hardy's writing is in many ways an elaborate strategy of containment and protection, usually about characters who struggle like their narrator to contain and protect themselves, but who, unlike Hardy's narrators, are not convinced of the futility of the effort. The persistent instances of framed vision, of spying, of almost naturalistic observation that parallel these strategies suggest that full protection is not possible. For vision is uncontrollable, like sexual energy; it is a vehicle of both suppression and desire, like writing itself.

The persistence of framed images of opening and containment tends to confirm J. Hillis Miller's shrewd argument that Hardy's "goal seems to have been to escape from the dangers of direct involvement in life and to imagine himself in a position where he could safely see life as it is without being seen and could report on that seeing." Hardy, says Miller, sought "to protect himself and to play the role of someone who would have unique access to the truth." Such ambitions largely determine both Hardy's strategies of representation and, very often, the subjects of his narratives.

But the revulsion from engagement is the other side of an intense ambition and sexual desire. Hardy's fictions flirt with the ideal, most peculiarly and schematically in *The Well-Beloved* (1892; 1897), where the protagonist pursues an ideal lover who is always, in the flesh, inaccessible, through three generations. The ideal is a persistent motif in Hardy, but his platonic and self-consciously childish fantasies (Jocelyn, the Shelleyan hero of *The Well-Beloved*, sees himself, as Hardy saw himself, as perpetually a child) are not only idealized but ironized. In *The Hand of Ethelberta* (1876), Christopher Julian, another artist-figure protagonist who is in love with Ethelberta, is described by his sister: "I should say you were a child in your impulses, and an old man in your reflections." The ideally named Knight of *A Pair of Blue Eyes* (1873) and Angel of *Tess of the d'Urbervilles* are responsible for the deaths of Elfride Swancourt and Tess herself. Idealists end up being murderers. Angel tells Tess (as Jocelyn was to feel about his lovers), that "the woman I have been loving is not you," but "another woman in your shape."

The quest for the ideal that characterizes so many of Hardy's plots (the inverse, of course, of their consistent patterns of frustration in which lovers never quite consummate their relationships) is an aspect of the intense sense of the time-bound character of the physical world that the prose so movingly (if sadly) celebrates. The frustration plot is a dramatization of Hardy's sense of the cost of passion, and this is not merely psychological and romantic, but social. Failures of physical love are consistent with narrative anticipation of loss and failure, a condition Father Time, in *Jude the Obscure*, almost laughably articulates: "I should like the flowers very much," he says, "if I didn't keep on thinking they'd be all withered in a few days." Even in the extremes of youthful passion Hardy's characters are beset with premonitions of fading flesh and dying romance. But the fear is a reflex of the desire. Hillis Miller insists that in Hardy's work there is always some barrier and distance between the lovers and that, like Jocelyn, Hardy seems to worship the goddess *in* the lover rather than the lover herself. Distance provokes desire (hence, for example, Jude's exhaustless passion for the elusive Sue), but proximity crushes it.

But it is not any old barrier that Hardy imagines. The phenomenological analysis of Hardy requires a social component, "social class." Hardy's obsession with detached and distanced observation is related to the distances established by class; the only access to a higher social position is through observation—as Jude observes Christminster, as Tess, undetected, observes Angel's comfortable clerical family, as the dying Giles Winterborne observes Grace. The centrality to Hardy of framed seeing is an aspect of his very drive to narrative itself, which seems to have depended from the first on the primary "barrier," class, the stability of which is always threatened by sexuality and ambition. "The Poor Man and the Lady" (1869?), Hardy's first (and lost) novel, is largely incorporated in "An Indiscretion in the Life of an Heiress," which hinges on a romance impeded by class difference. A remarkably large proportion of Hardy's novels play variations on the relation between romance and class. Even *Under the Greenwood Tree* (Fancy and the Vicar), intimates the theme, as does *Far from the Madding Crowd* (1874) (Bathsheba and Gabriel), *A Pair of Blue Eyes* (Elfride and Stephen), *Two on a Tower* (1882) (Lady Constantine and Swithin), *The Hand of Ethelberta* (which is entirely about Ethelberta's disguising her roots in the serving class), *A Laodicean* (1881) (Paula Powers—Colonel DeStancy-George Somerset), *The Woodlanders* (1887) (Giles Winterborne and Grace Melbury), *Tess of the d'Urbervilles* (Tess-Angel-Alec). Even where the obstacles to romance are not primarily class-related, as in *Return of the Native* (1877) and *Jude the Obscure*, class and romance are distinctly connected.

The power of sexuality to level class distinctions is a recurrent motif of the novels, and Hardy's Jude-like ambitions make him and his male protagonists susceptible to every Arabella. If the Avice of *The Well-Beloved* is endlessly elusive, Tess Durbeyfield is imagined with extraordinary sensuous particularity. The failures of touching in her novel are dramatized precisely as failures to honor Tess's physical nature, even by Tess herself. Here it is not a matter of a fantasy of the ideal (or "pure") woman in the woman but of the woman who in spite of herself insists on her humanity; idealization is the disaster. (In this respect, the narrative plays out precisely the tension that distinguishes Hardy's art more generally. That is to say, writing—the medium itself—both protects the narrator from the catastrophes of sexuality and insists on its irresistible attractiveness; it celebrates the physical and its indulgence and at the same time distances it from the narrator while leaving his creatures subject to its power.)

Sexual desire requires as antidote restraint from touching. But the difficulties of this are suggested, perhaps with unintentional comedy, by the figure of Colonel DeStancy in *A Laodicean*, who has sworn off women entirely but who is overwhelmed with desire once he observes the lovely but, for Hardy, characteristically elusive Paula Powers exercising in her gymnasium. For Hardy, writing and art are the protections against the inevitable cost of his own desires, the potential for absurdity or worse that he dramatizes in most of his novels. The patterns of frustration that so regularly constitute the motive force of Hardy's narratives combine a strong sense of sexual energy and a romantic fear of consummation. Few other novelists so ruthlessly deny consummation to pursuing lovers. While Cytherea Graye of *Desperate Remedies* (1871) is at last united with her lover, she is one of the rare ones in the Hardy canon. The novels depend on the pattern, sometimes almost symmetrical in its structuring, of pursuit and frustration, and they regularly refuse the expected climax in comic union that is characteristic of most earlier Victorian novels. The almost absurd pursuit across Europe of Paula Powers by George Somerset and Colonel DeStancy is only an obvious version of the characteristic Hardy frustration plot. Misunderstandings, misperceptions, and accidents of timing decisively deny lovers their opportunities for consummation.

The examples are everywhere. Elfride Swancourt in *A Pair of Blue Eyes* loses her first tepid love, Stephen Smith, is rejected, in the manner of Angel Clare, by Harry Knight, then marries a third party whom she doesn't love and dies before her two lovers can return to her. Christopher Julian, having pursued Ethelberta through the entire novel, fails by moments to stop her marriage to the degenerate Lord Mountclere; in *Two on a Tower*, Lady Constantine dies at the instant that Swithin St. Cleve, recovering from the shock of finding her looking so old, returns to fulfill his promise to marry her; in *The Trumpet Major* (1880), the more mature and faithful John Loveday ultimately loses his love, Anne Garland, to his unstable brother, Bob. In "An Indiscretion in the Life of an Heiress," Geraldine Allenville, after a novella full of diversions and denials, flees to her lover, Egbert Mayne, only to die just before their relationship can be consummated; Giles Winterborne watches over Grace Melbury and dies before she can return to him, precisely because of an obviously excessive sense of respectability and propriety. These kinds of frustrations climax in Hardy's novelistic career with the stories of Angel and Tess, Jude and Sue. Even when some minor consummations are allowed in the text, Hardy is begrudging, so that the marriage of the endlessly patient Diggory Venn to Thomasin Yeobright is withdrawn in a revealing footnote in which Hardy encourages the reader to "choose between two endings," of which the "more consistent conclusion" is governed by an "austere artistic code." Consummation not only entails a kind of postcoital lapse from passion and disintegration of desire; it also means the dangerous crossing of class boundaries, social impropriety (with attendant punishment), and the thwarting of professional and social ambition.

The transition from seeing (or writing) to engagement, which may well be provoked by seeing or writing, is usually the point of crisis and peripety in Hardy (which is one of the reasons that so many of his stories center on those rare moments when seeing gives way to touching: if frustration is agonizing, the consequences of consummation are catastrophic). The narrative compulsion to distance is a function of the intensity of desire imagined or dramatized in his work, and of the ambition that is a condition of the work itself; desire and ambition in this world are not quite respectable. Distance is the potential instrument of evasion and disguise. The novels express implicitly a continuing sympathetic imagination of recklessness and abandonment of constraint while at the same time dramatizing the way such abandonment inevitably entails catastrophe. Many of the novels develop as stories of the consequences of some single "lapse" into passion, ambition, or recklessness—Elfride's kiss of Stephen Smith in effect generates the plot of *A Pair of Blue Eyes*; Bathsheba's childish valentine to Boldwood leads to something like tragedy, as does her succumbing to the magnificently conscienceless sexuality of Sergeant Troy; *Two on a Tower* traces Lady Constantine's fall into passion for the young astronomer, Swithin, and the deadly consequences of that fall. Most notoriously, *The Mayor of Casterbridge* begins with Henchard's sale of his wife as he releases himself to his ambitions—"If I were a free man again I'd be worth a thousand pound before I'd done o't." Many of the novels explore the consequences of a protagonist's attempt to rise above his or her class—Stephen Smith, Swithin St. Cleve, George Somerset, Ethelberta, Clym Yeobright and Eustacia Vye, Grace Melbury, Jude. Their narratives tend to mix class ambition with sexual desire, social convention with "natural" force, in ways that often mean failure and death.

At the same time, they suggest ambition for power and recognition, fear of the consequences of such aspiration, refusal to impose on these patterns of frustration and disaster (or rare success) a George Eliot-like reading of the world as governed by moral Nemesis. Failure and defeat are not the consequences of the moral order of the universe but of the natural order itself and of the conflict between desire and the arbitrary restraints of social systems. The asymmetry between desire and social order suggests, as does so much else in Hardy, that the rules and language humans use to deal with the world are mere constructions. In such a world breaking the rules, abandoning constraint, is not evil; it is simply not respectable.

The other side of Hardy's evasiveness and caution, the desire to see without being seen, is the strong desire to touch and control and to be seen, but seen favorably. It may be the "Laodiceans" who survive in Hardy's world, but it is the Mayors—and even the Sergeant Troys—who win the narratives' deepest sympathy. In the long run, the "Laodiceans" are only a little less likely to suffer disaster than the Henchards: preoccupation with safety and invulnerability rarely means success, precisely because the world is not governed by moral Nemesis but by material laws that have no relation to human consciousness except that they may be perceived by it. Invulnerability becomes very problematic even at moments when the distance is maximal and is dramatized within the stories themselves in the events and perspectives of the characters.

The visual provides the detachment that allows Hardy to admire and even exacerbate his own sense of vulnerability, and at the same time to resist it. It is the formal expression of the intensity of Hardy's preoccupation with the humiliations of public exposure and the anxieties produced by his recognition of his complicity with forces and energies he rejects. It shapes his nervous sensitivity to questions of class, propriety, community judgment; it threatens always to reveal the sexuality hidden under layers of decorum and to express the dangerous desire that animates the social and the natural worlds. The sexuality to which Hardy was reluctantly but inescapably attracted through the simple physical presence of women always threatens to thwart social advancement, to make rational control impossible, to undermine respectability and power. More dangerously still, sexuality threatens to break down the strategies of defense by which protagonists seek to keep themselves, like Hardy's narrators, invulnerable. Hillis Miller notes that "all his life Hardy hated to be touched. To be touched is to be incarnated, to cease to be a spectator, and to be brought physically into the world of others, to become vulnerable to their energy and will. He wanted to remain invisible, untouchable, a disembodied presence able to see without being seen or felt."

The strong and persuasive readings of Hardy, particularly Miller's, account admirably for the formal features of his art, usually with attention to epistemological, phenomenological, or aesthetic concerns. J. B. Bullen keenly perceives the thematic and formal importance of seeing in Hardy, and connects it with aesthetic and pictorial traditions in ways that illuminate many of the novels. Talking of *Far from the Madding Crowd*, for example, he notes "how deeply the matrix of the story is penetrated by the moral implications of perception." Many of even the most pedestrian of Hardy's novels contain stunning moments of poetic vision that result from unexpected observations of people or events or natural phenomena unsuspectingly observed by acute, surprised, or wary eyes. In an extremely interesting discussion of Hardy's sense of the irrelevance of the material world to personal desire and feeling—an epistemological issue—Tom Paulin points to a Hardy sketch for his poem, "In a Eweleaze Near Weatherbury." The sketch superimposes a pair of spectacles on a drawing of the leaze, where the poet in his youth had danced with a lover. It is a striking, surreal image, evocative of Magritte both in the stark incompatibility of the human contrivance with the natural landscape and in the transparency of the spectacles, which allow the leaze to show through. Paulin sensibly emphasizes the "random and gratuitous" relationship between spectacles and landscape and the implicitly "anomalous relationship of man to the outer world which is the object of his knowledge." But the image is particularly striking in another way: it projects with a mad sort of simplicity the sense projected by so many of Hardy's novels, that everything in the world is under silent scrutiny. Nothing in the almost barren landscape of the leaze—material and unconscious as it is—escapes the narrator's or poet's eye, and nothing is aware that it is being observed.

The image has an almost paranoid quality, like the narratives themselves, and what might be discussed comfortably as an epistemological concern must be understood as a tensely emotional one: somebody is watching and ready to expose you. The function of poet and narrator is, precisely, to observe, and it is impossible to imagine the most profoundly nonhuman landscape that is not infected with the self-consciousness of an observer while at the same time remaining entirely indifferent to that consciousness. In the poem Hardy's sketch accompanies, the speaker, Jocelyn-like, feels himself to be precisely who he was when he danced many years before with his lover—"I remain what I was then." The longing for sexuality is there, but an irrepressible self-consciousness, intensely observant, detects the "little chisel / Of never-napping Time," which, when it thinks the poet sleeping, he feels "boring sly Within my bones."

A pair of spectacles is superimposed on all of Hardy's worlds. The world is watching and being watched, and the poems and novels strain to a condition of awareness that will protect against the watchers. In vain, of course. The self-conscious poet cannot stop, though he can detect the "boring." Seeing becomes a defense only in that it allows the observer to anticipate the worst, to know at the very height of passion that the passion is temporary. Being observant of an observant world means being alert to the catastrophes of unself-conscious lapsing into touch, the vengeance of a class-bound culture and a temporally bound sexuality.

In the rest of this chapter I want to look closely at two exemplary moments of vision in Hardy's work (since they link with many others in the other novels) to suggest how the psychological, phenomenological, and aesthetic qualities analyzed so brilliantly by critics like Bullen and Miller can be best understood in their relation to issues of class and sexuality. What shapes Hardy's art, his extraordinary loving and frightened perception of the visible world, his seeing, and his understanding of seeing, is largely the ambition and the associated shame and guilt and vulnerability that become the narrative centers of most of his novels.

It is possible to think of Hardy's novelistic career as framed by two window scenes that intimate the painful paradoxes of his visual imagination—the impossibility of engaging or affecting what is observed, its power to wound the perceiver, and its extraordinary mystery and beauty. The first of these, in *Desperate Remedies*, describes Cytherea Graye's almost surreal observation of her father's fall to his death; the last, in *Jude the Obscure*, records Jude's deathbed observation of the crowds in the Christminster Street and then, while he lies dead by the side of the window, the sounds of the cheers of the young men as "the doctors of the Theatre" confer "honorary degrees on the Duke of Hamptonshire and a lot more illustrious gents of that sort." The window is a constant resource for Hardy's storytelling, often opening up major new developments, providing the protagonists with access to important information, stimulating them to desire. It opens the world to inspection but at the same time marks a separation that the observer often spends much of the narrative trying to overcome. It might be taken as a metaphor for the characteristic Hardy method of narration, simultaneously engaging and distancing. The window, or some version of it that enhances or requires detached vision, is often the conduit through which energy and passion come to disrupt the lives of his protagonists. A complete list of "window" moments in Hardy would consume all the space available for this chapter. Here are some few examples: Colonel DeStancy in *A Laodicean* as he peers at Paula Powers during her gymnastics session; Angel Clare catching Tess unawares rising from sleep at a moment "when a woman's soul is more incarnate than at any other time," and spying the "red interior" of her yawning mouth; Anne at the beginning of *The Trumpet Major* as she watches the troops from whom her lover is likely to be chosen enter the town; the barber Percomb spying on Marty South in *The Woodlanders* preparing his rape of the lock, or Winterborne overseeing and protecting Grace and in effect killing himself; Swithin St. Cleve in *Two on a Tower* gazing at the heavens through his telescope and feeling the nauseating reflex of their vastness; Farfrae watching Henchard at the mayor's banquet and entering the mayor's life fatally through the window; Knight, in *A Pair of Blue Eyes*, staring into the fossils' eyes as his life hangs quite literally in the balance; the remarkable window scene in *Far from the Madding Crowd* at the harvest home banquet, in which Bathsheba and then Boldwood are inside the window at the same table at which Gabriel Oak sits without.

The scene in *Desperate Remedies* in which Cytherea Graye watches her father fall to his death is one of those breathtaking moments that give weight to even the thinnest and most compromised of Hardy's fictions. Its handling anticipates the themes and strategies that characterize Hardy's career-long search for a proper perspective, narrative orientation, and social position. The very awkwardness of its introduction (an awkwardness familiar even in Hardy's more mature fiction) signals a moment of central significance. Cytherea "unknowingly stood, as it were, upon the extreme posterior edge of a tract in her life, in which the real meaning of Taking Thought had never been known. It was the last hour of experience she ever enjoyed with a mind entirely free from a knowledge of that labyrinth into which she stepped immediately afterwards." Like so many of Hardy's characters to follow, Cytherea "unknowingly stood." The narrator is deeply interested in that condition of unknowing that precedes self-consciousness about seeing or being seen. But the fall from innocence here is a fall without the traditional moral implications of intention and complicity. While the scene registers literally the fall of her father to his death, it focuses more directly on the effects on Cytherea of what she accidentally sees, for which she is utterly unprepared. Cytherea falls, in that innocent moment of seeing, into knowledge, and, in particular, into knowledge of her own vulnerability to forces and observations over which she can have no control and for which she is not responsible. It is, assuredly, no accident that the fall is accompanied by a fall in social position, and henceforward it will be impossible for Cytherea ever to be unself-conscious about being observed or about her class status.

The sequence is written entirely from the outside so as to emphasize how things—and particularly Cytherea—appear. Just before the fall, the narrator pauses to talk about how Cytherea responds physically to emotion and thought: her eyes "possessed the affectionate and liquid sparkle of loyalty and good faith," they sparkle "during pleasant doubt." She gives an involuntary "minute start," and exerts "ecstatic pressure" on the listener's arm when she tells a secret. The details suggest an observer who always knows more than Cytherea means to tell about herself, and a Cytherea consistently unwary and innocent, hence vulnerable to the detective eye. The narrator observes Cytherea with a calculated minuteness and particularity altogether distinct from the nature of her own observations as she, unprepared, "glances" out the window from the theater of the local entertainment she is attending. The interest is in observing her observing, and the strategy not only emphasizes her vulnerability by specific reference to her unpreparedness, but it dramatizes that vulnerability by the narrative self-consciousness of its own minute watching.

Cytherea's distance from the scene she in turn watches (which becomes the real "local entertainment") leaves her powerless to do anything but observe. Vision gives her detective power but does not, as in the dominant scientific model of the moment, in any way empower her to affect what she sees; and what she sees is narrated in such a way as to parallel her own condition. Her father, an architect, is standing unselfconsciously on the scaffolding of a church spire with four workmen to whom he is giving directions. His focus is on their work and not on himself or his circumstances: "One idea above all others was conveyed to the mind of a person on the ground by their aspect, namely, concentration of purpose: that they were indifferent to—even unconscious of—the distracted world beneath them, and all that moved upon it. They never looked off the scaffolding." Here again is the dominant

Hardyesque motif. Like Cytherea and like most of Hardy's later protagonists, they are insufficiently aware of their own vulnerability and
the precariousness of their positions. Everyone in Hardy is either being
watched or in danger of it; as Cytherea is not conscious of the narrator's
detailed observation of her, her father and the workmen are unaware of
her watching them. In later Hardy, even those who are wary of being
observed end by being observed from an unexpected quarter. As the
opening window scene announces the dominant preoccupation of
Hardy with the perils of observation, so later in *Desperate Remedies*
there is an almost parodic parade of spiers who, in effect, demonstrate
the impossibility of going unobserved, of maintaining full concealment.
Each of the observers, except the professional, has a large stake in preserving a dishonorable secret that will sustain his or her position in society. Anne Seaway, rightly afraid for her life, observes the villainous and
beautiful Manston (who, accidentally observing himself in the mirror,
is precipitated into action). Carefully concealed from observation, she
follows him to a room where he has hidden the body of his true wife
whose place Anne is falsely taking; then Anne tries to flee, only to discover that there is another observer of Manston hiding there, a detective. She follows the as-yet-unidentified detective, who follows
Manston, who is bearing the body of his wife. Anne then discovers that
the man she is following is being followed by another woman (who, it
develops, is Cytherea Aldclyffe): "Intentness pervaded everything;
Night herself seemed to have become a watcher." The absurdity of the
scene does nothing to diminish the centrality of its images or the tensions it creates. Night in Hardy is indeed "a watcher." But so too is Day.
Everyone has something to hide; everyone will be exposed: Miss Aldclyffe is discovered; Manston's secret is revealed; the detective is himself caught and knocked out; Anne's participation in Manston's conspiracy is made clear to the detective. This mad and melodramatic
scene is, in the end, only an extension of that obsession with watching—that fear of exposure, that preoccupation with perspectives, that
almost desperate need to locate a position from which one might
observe unobserved and thus preserve one's respectability and status—
that is thematically initiated in the opening scene, in which Cytherea
watches her father fall, and that is repeated (sometimes in scenes almost
as absurd) throughout Hardy's later work.

In that scene, the ambiguous benefits of being an unobserved
observer are intimated because Cytherea is entirely unobserved by those

she watches (although she too quickly becomes an object of observation). Distance and impossibility of interference are registered by the way her father and the workmen appear to Cytherea: they seem "little larger than pigeons," and they make "their tiny movements with a soft, spirit-like silentness." At the moment when her father turns his attention to "a new stone they were lifting," Cytherea for the first time begins to register alarm: "'Why does he stand like that?' the young lady thought at length—up to that moment as listless and careless as one of the ancient Tarentines, who, on such an afternoon as this, watched from the Theatre the entry into their Harbour of a power that overturned the State." The expansion of the casual moment to mythic proportions—another characteristic move of Hardy's—heavily emphasizes the way observation will casually and surprisingly lead to a turn in one's own fortunes over which one has no power but the power of seeing it happen. While one cannot affect what one sees, what one sees can and almost invariably does affect the observer. The surprises inherent in observation increase the arbitrariness that is notoriously characteristic of Hardy's worlds, an arbitrariness that grows from the unintentional crossing of two or several lines of entirely independent action.

While Cytherea begins to be aware of her father's danger—"it is so dangerous to be absent-minded up there"—she can do no more than think it before her father "indecisively laid hold of one of the scaffold-poles, as if to test its strength, then let it go and stepped back. In stepping, his foot slipped. An instant of doubling forward and sideways, and he reeled off into the air, immediately disappearing downwards." All this is narrated from the distant vantage point of Cytherea and thus goes on in silence, with a casual ordinariness that magnifies the horror of the moment. And the prose diverts from what Cytherea cannot see—the actual death of her father—to her, as she rises in a "convulsive movement. Her lips parted, and she gasped for breath. She could utter no sound." Even the reaction of the audience in which she sits recapitulates the narrative strategies of the novelist and the sequence of the central event. "One by one the people about her, unconscious of what had happened, turned their heads, and inquiry and alarm became visible upon their faces at the sight of the poor child. A moment longer, and she fell to the floor." The audience too are observed observers, upon whom the seen event impinges incongruously with their circumstances.

The moment precipitates a crisis of class and shame, in effect revealing the social system upon which the heroine's life was unself-consciously built. *Desperate Remedies* establishes the pattern for Hardy's original sin that so many of his characters have to hide—the sin of class origins. Stephen Smith, Edward Springrove, Swithin St. Cleve, George Somerset, Christopher Julian, Michael Henchard, Giles Winterborne, Clym Yeobright, Jude Fawley—almost all of Hardy's male protagonists—live on the cusp of distinct classes and their fates are almost entirely bound up with their power to climb or their bad luck in falling, and, of course, with the community's understanding of their inherited and their achieved positions. The helpless Cytherea suddenly finds herself, as a consequence of the fall, in poverty, her father having failed in business and speculation. Parallel problems exist for many of Hardy's women, for example Grace Melbury, Ethelberta, and even Tess herself.

In *Desperate Remedies* Cytherea is in effect cast out of her community and her class by the fall of her father. Members of the community stare at her "with a stare unmitigated by any of the respect that had formerly softened it." *Desperate Remedies*, then, begins with the fear that dominates all of Hardy's books and most of his central characters: the fear of being an object of "staring," that is, of being shamed by losing social position and class status. That fear almost invariably is embodied through the "choral" figures in the community, who have traditionally been seen as one of the peculiar sources of Hardy's rural charm. What those characters say provides no mere echo of the choral function of various traditional literatures or touch of charming local color. They are formally and thematically essential to the narratives: they are the ubiquitous observers who satisfy the narrative compulsion to frame all actions through distanced observation, and even more fundamentally they are the bearers of the conventions of class and hierarchy so that it is their judgment that shapes the fate of the protagonists. To avoid the shame of being observed unawares by these people, and thus judged by them, Hardy's protagonists are driven to their often apparently mad attempts at evasion, those hopeless and frustrated and inevitably observed secret elopements, those disguises and evasions and pursuits that contribute so awkwardly at times to Hardyesque melodrama. These are the figures who shape the careers of characters like Henchard (whose fall is precipitated by the furmity woman's public exposure of him) and, in particular, of Hardy's heroines, who are of course especially vulnerable to judgments of the community—heroines like Elfride Swancourt, Lady Constantine Blount, and Sue Bridehead.

The power of community judgment, which almost certainly means also the power of class distinction, drives Hardy's characters to the same sort of neurasthenic sensitivity to the possibility of being shamed, of being caught acting with impropriety, that characterizes Hardy's own evasively led and publicly protected life. In *Desperate Remedies* the nature of that fear is made explicit almost from the start. Its importance to the whole canon of Hardy's writing could, of course, barely have been guessed when it appeared in this first novel. But it provides a clue to all the rest:

Now it is a noticeable fact that we do not much mind what men think of us, or what humiliating secret they discover of our means, parentage, or object, provided that each thinks and acts thereupon in isolation. It is the exchange of ideas about us that we dread most; and the possession by a hundred acquaintances, severally insulated, of the knowledge of our skeleton closet's whereabouts, is not so distressing to the nerves as a chat over it by a party of half-a-dozen—exclusive depositaries though these may be.

Hardy's is a culture of shame rather than of guilt. It is not so much the sin or the crime that disturbs as the possibility that two or more of the community may be talking about us without our knowledge, sharing knowledge of our wrongdoings. The threat is precisely the kind that Alexander Welsh discusses as "blackmail," the power of which is not in the secret but in the dissemination of it beyond the blackmailer. The distinction between shame and guilt is crucial for a writer like Hardy, who feels himself bound to "respectability" at the same time that he recognizes both its arbitrariness and its power to damage and restrict. But in Hardy's construction of a character like Tess shame and guilt become aspects of each other, and the imposition of social convention on the "natural," as Hardy understood it, constitutes one of the major crimes of Hardy's world. Without adequate knowledge, Tess internalizes the judgments of society, as they will be enacted by Angel later in the novel. Hardy's narrator, especially in earlier novels, disguises his recognition of the arbitrariness of the conventional and the respectable and thus guiltily participates in the judgment of figures like Tess. But Tess, on the narrator's explicit account, has not sinned and should not be guilty. In describing Tess after her encounter with Alex, the narrator contrasts her sense of guilt with her extraordinary and beautiful harmony with "the element she moved in." "Walking among the sleeping birds in the hedges, watching the skipping rabbits on a moonlit warren, or standing under a pheasant-laden bough, she looked upon herself as a figure of Guilt intruding into the haunts of innocence." Tess has absorbed her culture's assumptions and condemns herself, but in Hardy's world such guilt is mistaken. The true guilt belongs to those who are shamed by their acquiescence in arbitrary "shreds of convention."

It is Tess's innocence that leads her to guilt rather than shame. Hardy's characters often are not truly disturbed by the fact of their transgressions, while invariably they are almost overwhelmed by the possibility that their private indiscretions will become public matter. Hardy regularly invents grotesquely implausible plots that place his characters in technical jeopardy without ever compromising their innocence, but then has them act as though the technical transgression constitutes a deep moral violation. In *Desperate Remedies* Cytherea acts as though after marrying Manston she would be entirely compromised by any intimacy she might have with him even if she did not know at the time that he was already married to someone else. Lady Constantine behaves similarly in *Two on a Tower*, and Elfride Swancourt's kiss of Stephen Smith is sufficient to destroy her life. These extravagances in the early novels anticipate Tess's fate and Sue Bridehead's convincing and maddening modern neurosis of guilt in *Jude the Obscure*. In every case, the crime is not in the commission but in the power of social shame to create among the innocent destructive guilt. In all of these case, questions of sexuality, guilt, and shame are bound into questions of social hierarchy and respectability.

Hardy's revulsion from the arbitrariness of class hierarchy is built into almost every novel, as characters cross the boundaries (most strikingly in *The Hand of Ethelberta*) or are merely by virtue of bad luck dropped from the aristocracy to the agrarian poor, or by virtue of Hardyesque work and discipline (necessarily always with a trace of luck) are raised into the middle class. The reversals in their most extreme forms shape the narratives of several of Hardy's least successful novels, in which the overtness of the theme apparently damages his power to control it fully. In *A Laodicean*, for example, Paula Powers occupies the DeStancy mansion, bought by her rich industrialist father, and is almost corrupted by the attractions of the class she has dispossessed. Lady Constantine falls in love with Swithin St. Cleve, who is not only several years her junior but whose parents work menially on her estate. In *A Pair of Blue Eyes* Stephen Smith is first accepted as Elfride's lover because he is thought to be from good family and then rejected because his father is a "rural mechanic," although in fact he is wealthier than Elfride's father. But Hardy's revulsion in no way diminishes either his aspirations to join the system effectively or his shame at being no graduate of Oxford.

The guilt driving Hardy's novels is not the guilt of transgression, with which he shows himself to have enormous dramatic sympathy—in Henchard's overreaching, in Ethelberta's social deceits, in Jude's dreams of scholarly achievement. It is rather the guilt for feeling shame, for being, in spite of himself, bound by the very conventions and social discriminations, the very arbitrariness of class distinctions and hierarchies, that all of his best energies are driven to expose and denigrate. His very dissatisfaction with novel writing had much to do with the compromises forced upon him by conditions of the publisher's trade, by the fact, that is, that he had to write for money. As Harry Knight tells Elfride, "It requires a judicious omission of your real thoughts to make a novel popular." His sensitivity to observation is exacerbated by his fears not only that his real thoughts will be detected but that he has in fact deeply compromised himself. The complex publishing history of *Tess*, with its acquiescence in the bowdlerizations necessary for serial publication for money and its further revisions for the Wessex edition, suggest how thoroughly compromised Hardy was in the matter of making money and staying respectable. Hardy seems to have been both ashamed and guilty for being so.

Sexual energy, in particular, which almost all of the novels and their protagonists struggle to contain and disguise, is a danger here. It is dangerous because there is very little sign that the novels endorse the shame the protagonists, particularly the women, feel when this energy is aroused, crossing classes and disrupting the lives of everyone from Boldwood to Jude, from Bathsheba to Tess. Sex becomes a great leveler in that it guarantees exposure of the arbitrariness of class distinctions. But desire also leaves one vulnerable, forces one to take risks. The major figures in these novels are shamed by their desires, constrained therefore by the conventions, invariably caught out in their efforts at respectability and disguise, and driven to betrayals (often self-betrayals) as a consequence. Shame determines their actions at last. But the true crime is not desire; it is the unwillingness to honor it and the guilt for being unwilling—the guilt, for example, of Angel Clare.

Hardy's sympathies are, finally, with the intensities of sexual passion, with the recklessness and the excesses that his prose never allows one to forget for a moment and that his stories invariably punish with the forces of shame and convention. Just as Henchard's irrational energies both for restraint and for ambition mark him as doomed and irresistibly attractive as novelistic subject, so Tess's sexuality is honored by the text that kills her for it. Both move through their novels on the edge of advanced social standing; both, but particularly Tess, are trapped in the energies of sexuality. But for each, the primary narrative question is that of class. Ambition and sexuality threaten class hierarchies, so the migrant farm worker becomes mayor, the peasant girl marries a clergy-man's son. Their dignity is in the integrity of their "crimes," their power to stand against the forces that will condemn them, the deep internal struggles that are made all the more difficult by the intensity of their passions as they try to internalize the conventions that will destroy them. When Tess finally succumbs to her passion for Angel, the narra-tive comments:

In reality she was drifting into acquiescence. Every see-saw of her breath, every wave of her blood, every pulse singing in her ears, was a voice that joined with nature in revolt against her scrupulousness. Reckless, inconsiderate acceptance of him; to close with him at the altar, revealing nothing, and chancing discov-ery; to snatch ripe pleasure before the iron teeth of pain could have time to shut upon her; that was what love counselled; and in almost a terror of ecstasy Tess divined that, despite her many months of lonely self-chastisement, wrestlings, communings, schemes to lead a future of austere isolation, love's counsel would prevail.

Tess bears in her own consciousness the narrator's constant imagination of the consequences of passion, even in the midst of passion—Hardy's persistent awareness of the disparity between "natural" law and human conventions, the inevitability of doom to any "reckless" acquiescence in the "natural." It is not only Tess's desire that drives this narrative, it is the desire of the narrator who knows too much. Clearly, there is no "guilt" in Tess's ultimate acquiescence, but there is the inevitability of shame and of the imposition upon her of society's demand that there should be guilt. At the denouement, Hardy characteristically reestab-lishes the perspective of distance and disengagement at the point at which society imposes its violent punishment for guiltless violation of its rules of respectability. The moments of violence—the deaths of Alec and of Tess—are presented through strategies of visual distancing: the widening red spot on the ceiling observed by the landlady of the house at which Alec and Tess are staying; the remote prospect of the black flag that Angel and Liza-Lu observe from the top of the Great West Hill looking back at the town and the octagonal tower where Tess is executed. Such distancing here is particularly important because Angel and Liza-Lu represent another violation of the categories of class that proved so expensive to Tess.

Desperate Remedies, however extravagantly silly it may sometimes seem, anticipates much of Tess's story. The younger Cytherea succumbs, perhaps innocently, to Manston's approaches, as Tess does to Alec's; her false marriage to Manston can be taken to parallel Tess's false "marriage" to Alec; like Tess, Cytherea assumes that her false relation to Manston makes alliance with her true love, Edward Springrove, impossible, although there is no law, literal or figural, that bars the connection; and she keeps Springrove away even after it is clear that her marriage to Manston is invalid. While watching is a key element in the novel, the crucial fact about Cytherea is that, like Tess, she has fully internalized the social judgments, so that she herself does the watching. Interestingly, Hardy's first published novel tells that story twice, for Cytherea Aldclyffe, too, had been seduced by a false lover, and as a consequence left the man she truly loved, the younger Cytherea's father. Aldclyffe explains that she had done so because she *knew* that Mr. Graye, "had he known her secret . . . would have cast her out." Whether internally or externally, the judgment of the community is embedded in the revelations of observation, and these determine the directions of Hardy's narratives, which return obsessively to the questions of guilt, respectability, and class from the very beginning of his career.

They return again, yet further disenchanted, in *Jude the Obscure*, which completes my argument for the centrality of "seeing" in Hardy in part because it is so little concerned (for a Hardy novel) with seeing and in part because the window returns so significantly as a metaphor and a closing image. Yet distanced seeing initiates the narrative: Jude first sees the distant Christminster as a cluster of shining spots in the remote distance, then as "a halo or glow-fog." The imagination of Christminster, especially as the home of his former teacher, Phillotson, inspires Jude to dreams of learning and of the university life that goes with it. The dream of five thousand pounds a year (forty-five hundred for charity!) once again connects vision with questions of class.

While Jude's story is thus initiated in Hardyesque fashion, the novel is not preoccupied with watching and spying as is *Desperate Remedies*.

Nor does the narrator, with Hardy's usual gorgeous and moving concentration, focus on the visible world with a vital sense of the significance of apparently trivial details, like the insects caught in Tess's white gown; or the marks of social discrimination, as in *Far from the Madding Crowd*, where he notes the identifying signs of different agricultural laborers seeking employment: "Carters and wagoners were distinguished by having a piece of whip-cord twisted around their hats; thatchers wore a fragment of woven straw; shepherds held their sheep-crooks in their hands"; or the casual intersection of different forms of life, as in *A Pair of Blue Eyes*, in which Stephen spies on the unaware Elfride and Knight, and Mrs. Jethway watches them both. There, the striking light of a match

gave birth to dancing leaf-shadows, stem-shadows, lustrous streaks, dots, sparkles, and threads of silver sheen of all imaginable variety and transience. It awakened gnats, which flew towards it, revealed shiny gossamer threads, disturbed earthworms. Stephen gave but little attention to these phenomena, and less time.

Jude, it is true, learns to *resee* Christminster after his rejection, to understand that he is part of the city that is invisible and that

his destiny lay not with [the *ensemble* of the city's unrivalled panorama], but among the manual toilers in the shabby purlieu which he himself occupied, unrecognized as part of the city at all by its visitors and panegyrists, yet without whose denizens the hard readers could not read nor the high thinkers live.

Jude's narrative, pressing him irresistibly among the working class, turns him into an invisible man.

His novel moves, then, from distant seeing to touching, from an attempt to establish the position of unobserved observer to a frank confrontation with the consequences of physical engagement—from scholarship to the working class. Before the final window scenes, there are several other important ones, given over not to protected seeing, unobserved observing, or even to Cytherea's sort of vision of her father's death. Windows seem to exist in *Jude* not for the distancing protection they provide in many of the other novels, but as passages from vision to touch. In the scene of the trapped rabbit, both Jude and Sue, through different windows, hear the animal's scream. The sound and his own sensitivity to pain lead Jude to leave his room and to put the rabbit out of its agony. But they lead him also to Sue's window, where she, ready to respond in the same way and aware of Jude's sensibilities, is half expecting him. As they speak through the window, "she let go of the casement-stay and put her hand upon his, her moonlit face regarding him wistfully." Jude kisses her hand, and at the close of the interview, "in a moment of impulse," Sue "bent over the sill, and laid her face upon his hair, weeping, and then imprinting a scarcely perceptible little kiss upon the top of his head, withdrawing quickly so that he could not put his arms round her." The window, in the end, serves to protect from full sexual consummation, but the yielding to "impulse," a deadly act in Hardy's fiction, has already violated the strategies of distanced perception Hardy and his characters consistently use elsewhere.

Even more extravagantly, the window is the scene of Sue's fullest expression of her revulsion from touch. Instinctively, when Phillotson unself-consciously enters the bedroom where he and his first wife had slept but where Sue, refusing to be touched by Phillotson, now sleeps, Sue springs from the bed, "mounted upon the sill and leapt out." The impervious screen of the window is penetrated in *Jude*. The window, rather than a place of self-conscious observation, becomes a place of unself-conscious yielding to impulse. *Jude* risks violating distance and shattering the barriers of class and the conventions of sexual respectability. The consequence is, in a way, played out in Sue's last scene with Phillotson—perhaps the climax in Hardy's work of his exploration of the consequences of failing to maintain distance—when she begs him to let her cross the threshold to his room. Phillotson leads her through the doorway, "and lifting her bodily kissed her. A quick look of aversion passed over her face, but clenching her teeth she uttered no cry."

But the horror of public judgment, as it is discussed by the narrator of *Desperate Remedies*, remains powerful in the story, shaping Sue's curious career and Jude's as well. After their abortive attempt to marry, Jude and Sue find the grocer's boy no longer tips his hat to them, and they are encircled with "an oppressive atmosphere"; the communal rejection finally extends to Jude's work. Jude and Sue cannot escape observation—"I had no idea," says Jude, "that anybody was going to intrude into such a lonely place and see us," and they come to understand that they have lived in "a fool's paradise of supposed unrecognition." Here again, *Jude* brings to a climax the obsession of Hardy's novels with being observed: distraught at Father Time's suicide and the killing of her children, Sue hears "two persons in conversation somewhere without":

"'They are talking about us, no doubt!' moaned Sue. 'We are made a spectacle unto the world, and to angels, and to men!'" It is, ironically, this shamed assumption of being observed that leads her back to Phillotson and his repulsive but respectable touch.

Even the invisible are observed in Hardy's world, and even a novel deliberately withdrawn from the extraordinary if painful pleasures of Hardyesque observation of the natural world is built upon a recognition that everything is watched and judged. But the window that is central to the last moments of Hardy's career as novelist, as it is to Jude's last moments, is not the sort of medium of distanced observation that it would have been in earlier novels. This is no scene of a fall like Cytherea Graye's from innocence to knowledge. Rather, the scene begins with a fallen figure, almost without the powers of perception, who has never succeeded in rising above his class and whose sexual energies have been almost equally thwarted. Having lived in a fool's paradise of social invisibility, Jude, dying, becomes almost literally invisible—and blind. When he calls out for "a little water" in the room that Arabella has abandoned in answering the seductive call of the sounds of music and celebration that drift through the window, nobody can hear him. He is too ill to see out. In effect, while the narrator's eye ironically juxtaposes the inside and the outside, Jude is both blind and invisible. As Jude whispers the bleak verses from Job—"Let the day perish wherein I was born"—the voices from outside are counterpointed, cheering the Remembrance games with their "Hurrah." Jude's death is unwatched.

What enters Jude's consciousness through the window marks a final irony on a life that has failed to be respectable. While the ironies of this scene seem crudely to reinforce a bleak cosmic imagination of the darkness and irrelevance of human life, it is also a final narrative exploration of that strange complex of vision, class, and sex that I have been arguing is central to Hardy's entire narrative oeuvre. The scene, in which vision fails, can be taken as a critique of the very strategies of distanced, unobserved seeing that provoke Hardy's characters to shame and guilt in their quests both to protect themselves and to indulge their dangerous ambitions. Arabella survives by leaving the window and self-consciousness; Sue crosses the threshold to touching in a desiccated recuperation of propriety; Jude becomes invisible while the outside world retains its power to wound.

By foregoing his strategies of distanced and protected observation in *Jude the Obscure*, then, Hardy makes it clear why they are so important to him as a novelist. *Jude* is Hardy's most disturbing if perhaps not his most satisfying book for several reasons. First, it does not provide the consolations of the visible world that so extraordinarily enrich almost every one of his earlier novels, no matter how bleak their implications might be. It is difficult to find in *Jude* what Gillian Beer rightly finds in most of Hardy's work: "Alongside his doomed sense of weighted past and incipient conclusion, goes a sense of plenitude, an 'appetite for joy.'" Second, it foregoes the protection of distanced viewing. While the narrator's voice occasionally sagely and gloomily endorses a dark vision of modern civilization, most of such commentary is given to the characters themselves. There are few moments of visionary respite or protection as windows become permeable and touch replaces sight as the dominant, impelling narrative sense. Third, in *Jude* the fantasy of aspiration beyond the limits of the working class is entirely thwarted. Ironically, although one would imagine such thwarting is characteristic of all of Hardy's writing, his novels tend to reflect a vision of a mobile society in which, from one generation to the next, a Stephen Smith or a George Somerset or an Egbert Mayne might lift himself by professional and intellectual effort (and supreme alertness to observation) into the middle class. The comedy of *The Hand of Ethelberta* actually sustains Ethelberta's attempt to move into the aristocracy from a working-class family. In *Tess*, Liza-Lu does in fact end up with Angel Clare. But in Jude, the working class is invisible. Each figure is locked inside a conventional and repressive social system. And finally, sexuality, always dangerous in Hardy though always attractive, becomes thoroughly repulsive in the relation between Sue and Phillotson. Arabella's exuberant sexuality, perhaps the one instance of joyful touching in the book, insistently impedes the fragile and neurotic love of Sue and Jude and any possibility of Jude's advancement.

Finally, then, *Jude* rejects seeing as the narrative impulse of Hardy's writing. The daring of the novel's engagement with the modern and with his own career exposes Hardy to the sorts of critiques that, he imagines here, might well have thwarted his ambitions, his urgent need to remain unobserved and respectable. The visionary, the emphasis on seeing, diminishes as Hardy confronts the consequences of "touching" and engagement: *Jude* becomes a powerfully antivisionary narrative, and as such it can be taken as a fitting conclusion to Hardy's career as novelist.

George Levine

Selected Bibliography

Bayley, John. *An Essay on Hardy*. Cambridge: Cambridge University Press, 1978.

Boumelha, Penny. *Thomas Hardy and Women: Sexual Ideology and Narrative Form.* Madison: University of Wisconsin Press, 1985.

Bullen, J. B. *The Expressive Eye: Fiction and Perception in the Work of Thomas Hardy.* New York: Oxford University Press, 1986.

Garson, Marjorie. *Hardy's Fables of Integrity*. Oxford: Clarendon Press, 1991.

Goode, John. *Thomas Hardy: The Offensive Truth*. Oxford: Blackwell, 1988.

Lawrence, D. H. "Study of Thomas Hardy." In Edward D. MacDonald, ed., *Phoenix: The Posthumous Papers of D. H. Lawrence*. New York: Viking, 1936.

Miller, J. Hillis. *Thomas Hardy: Distance and Desire*. Cambridge, Mass.: Harvard University Press, 1970.

Millgate, Michael. *Thomas Hardy: A Biography*. New York: Random House, 1982.

Millgate, Michael, ed. *The Life and Work of Thomas Hardy*. Athens: University of Georgia Press, 1985.

Paulin, Tom. *Thomas Hardy: The Poetry of Perception*. Totowa, N.J.: Rowman and Littlefield, 1975.

The Nineteenth-Century Novel and Empire

WITH Balzac's *Human Comedy* in mind, Pedro Salinas has called the novel as such "the imperialistic genre." Perhaps the totalizing aspirations of all nineteenth-century European novels—including omniscient narration, empiricist description, individualistic assumptions about character, and other conventions of fictional realism—are forms of dominative and hence imperialistic representation. A contrary definition, however, would treat the novel as the undoing of totalizing, imperialistic aspirations. Echoing Mikhail Bakhtin, we might say that, far from being unified, coherent ideological constructions, novels are intrinsically pluralistic. Bakhtin's theory of heteroglossic discourse views the novel as generically subversive of the coherent, univocal structures of earlier literary genres. The novel tends to erode linguistic exclusiveness and therefore also the ideologies of linguistic and racial purity that underpin modern nationalisms and, hence, imperialisms. In contrast to the state-founding theme of the epic, the novel enters "into international and interlingual contacts and relationships."

It seems likely, however, that these two definitions of the novel are not mutually exclusive: the novel unifies as it pluralizes, or imperializes as it democratizes. But theoretical debates about the intrinsic ideological bearings of such a wide-ranging literary genre as the novel are likely to be inconclusive; as Bakhtin notes, "the experts have not managed to isolate a single definite, stable characteristic of the novel." Nevertheless, starting from the proposition that the British Empire is the outermost perimeter or context within which the expansive text of "English literature" has been written, *all* nineteenth-century British novels must in a general way be imperialistic, just as they are British. This is true whether or not specific novels deal explicitly with aspects of empire, and also whether or not those that do deal with empire are chauvinistic or critical in their treatment of imperialist ideology or specific instances of territorial conquest and control.

In relation to this broadly imperialist context, the history of nineteenth-century British fiction falls into three main periods. The first, that of literary and artistic Romanticism, extends from the French Revolution of 1789 down to the 1830s. The second, early and mid-Victorian phase runs from the 1840s through the decades of industrializing Britain's greatest international power and domestic prosperity (the 1850s and 1860s) to approximately 1880. And the third, late-Victorian and Edwardian phase continues into the twentieth century down to World War I. By 1800 several subgenres of fiction had evolved that were already important vehicles for imperialist ideology and, less frequently, for partial critiques of that ideology. These subgenres—travel-adventure stories, historical romances, "Eastern tales," war novels, and emigration novels among them—underwent various permutations through the three periods. After indicating how *all* nineteenth-century British fiction was affected by the imperial context, I will outline the main features of these more or less explicitly imperialistic subgenres.

The Imperial Context

Coupled with the earlier loss of the American colonies, the campaign against slavery helped give the Romantic period what has sometimes mistakenly been interpreted as an anti-imperialist tendency. Advocacy of free trade by the early political economists also seemed to downplay the colonies, if not to entail explicit advocacy of decolonization. Such an anti-imperialist tendency, it used to be held, extended through the early and mid-Victorian periods. Only in the third, late-Victorian phase did imperialism come to the fore as a factor in British politics and therefore also as a factor in British literature. But although Britain lost the American colonies in the 1770s and abolished slavery in 1833, it gained new colonies through its defeat of France. The antislavery campaign itself drew Britain deeper into Africa just as the consolidation and reform of the East India Company, from the time of the Warren Hastings trial through the Great Mutiny of 1857, secured British hegemony in India. Meanwhile, the pace of emigration to "the colonies of white settlement"—Canada, Australasia, South Africa—increased with Britain's domestic population explosion, while also increasing the economic, political, and scientific motivations for exploring and conquering the "blank spaces" still left on the global map.

In *The Expansion of England* (1883), Sir John Seeley could declare that "we seem, as it were, to have conquered and peopled half the world in a fit of absence of mind." Absent-mindedness, however, is very different from opposition to the expansion of empire. What emerged with the so-called New Imperialism of the late Victorian period was an often "jingoistic" self-consciousness about Britain's apparently manifest imperial destiny, aroused by the emergence of new and the resurgence of old imperial rivals (Germany and the United States come under the first heading, France and Russia under the second). To Seeley's absent-mindedness, an approximately accurate description of the first half or two-thirds of the century, Cecil Rhodes's late-Victorian expansionism offers an obvious counterpoint: Rhodes wanted "to paint the map of Africa British red," and he declared, "I would annex the planets if I could." Similar attitudes were often expressed in late-Victorian and Edwardian fiction, usually underwritten by social Darwinist racism, but sometimes also filtered through an ironic narrative perspective bordering on anti-imperialism, as in Joseph Conrad's *Heart of Darkness* (1899). But Conrad's Marlow himself declares that only in the "red" places on the map of Africa is any "real work" accomplished. With similar ambivalence, Harvey Rolfe in George Gissing's *Whirlpool* (1897) reacts to a friend's argument about "nigger-hunting" as the coming fashionable sport:

There's more than that to do in South Africa. . . . Who believes for a moment that England will remain satisfied with bits here and there? We have to swallow the whole, of course. We shall go on fighting and annexing until—until the decline and fall of the British Empire. . . . We shall fight like blazes in the twentieth century.

Even more than Rolfe, Gissing is appalled by what he treats as a sort of civilized cannibalism ("swallow[ing] the whole"), though he offers no alternative to it: constant warfare is the appalling name for the human condition, past, present, and future.

But constant "fighting and annexing" wasn't the only outcome of Britain's imperial aggrandizement. Besides the novel, new literatures sprang up because of Britain's overseas hegemony. In global terms, the most significant literary development throughout the century was the transplantation of the English language to North America, Australasia, South Africa, and India, and the emergence of new literatures—not "English literatures," of course, but literatures in English—around the world. "American literature" is the earliest, most spectacular instance of a new literature that arose from Britain's imperializing endeavors, but that also, through the American colonies' revolutionary self-assertion, developed in nationalistic opposition to Britain's imperial hegemony. Any account of the relationship between nineteenth-century British fiction and the British Empire would be incomplete without an emphasis on the imperial origins of national literatures also in Canada, Australia, New Zealand, South Africa, and India.

For the nineteenth-century British novel in general, the empire operates as an outer limit that stablizes and in some sense partially determines what happens at the center. The colonial "periphery" *always* appears marginally, though sometimes only as the faintest of traces, in the central, metropolitan texts of the century (see Perera's *Reaches of Empire*, 1991). Thus, Jane Austen's seemingly apolitical, domestic novels are just as imperial—though not overtly "imperialistic"—as Charles Kingsley's racist, militaristic, "bloodthirsty" (as Kingsley himself described it) historical novel *Westward Ho!* (1859). An obvious difference is that Austen, though writing in the midst of the Napoleonic era, saw no need to beat the tom-toms of patriotism, whereas Kingsley—dismayed by the muddle the British army was making of the Crimean War—felt compelled to write a swashbuckling, thoroughly chauvinistic romance. Concerned with the imperializing derring-do of the Elizabethan "sea dogs" who, along with the weather, defeated the Spanish Armada in 1588, *Westward Ho!* reads today like a Victorian *Rambo*.

In contrast, Austen etched her psychological portraits of quiet domestic life on a "little bit (two Inches wide) of Ivory," and her heroines never travel farther than London and Bath. Yet, though it is not described, Antigua is the place to which Sir Thomas Bertram travels in *Mansfield Park* (1813); the chief source of his family's prosperity is an Antiguan plantation where the labor is performed by slaves (about whose situation Austen says nothing at all). So, too, though episodes of war are not featured in *Persuasion* (1817), naval officers—Admiral Croft and Captain Wentworth—are central characters whose social standing is very much an issue for the other characters, and whose worldly travels and adventures during the Napoleonic era form a sharp contrast to Anne Elliot's quiet, submissive life. But for Austen, worldly adventures are not the exclusive prerogative of men: Admiral Croft's wife has been "a great traveller," who tells Mrs. Musgrove: "in the fifteen years of my marriage . . . I have crossed the Atlantic four times, and have been once to the East Indies, and back again . . . besides being in different places about home—Cork, and Lisbon, and Gibraltar." Despite writing to her niece Anna that "3 or 4 Families in a Country Village is the very thing to work on," Austen takes the empire for granted in all her novels, while also portraying it more or less explicitly, in *Mansfield Park* and *Persuasion*, as a source of adventure, wealth, and uncontroversial authority.

Throughout the nineteenth century, many other "domestic novels" follow the same pattern, according to which the quietest of lives in the seemingly most placid English towns or country estates turn out to have exotic connections to far-flung parts of the empire. A familiar example occurs in Dickens's *Great Expectations* (1869), where Pip's mysterious windfall turns out to come from the transported convict Magwitch, who while making his fortune in Australia dreams of making a gentleman back in England. Magwitch's vicarious ambition and his illegal return to England operate as a sort of "return of the repressed" from the colonies through most of the novel, forging the "gold and silver chains" that weigh Pip down with guilt. The pattern is reversed when Pip joins Herbert Pocket as assistant manager of "the Eastern Branch" of Clarriker and Co. in "the land of the Arabian Nights" (that is, Egypt).

Just as dramatic is the return of the repressed that occurs in Elizabeth Gaskell's *Cranford* (1853), in which Miss Matty's prodigal brother Peter reappears after years of military adventuring in India, both to rescue Matty from the genteel poverty into which she has fallen and to enliven the village society of spinsters and widows with colorful tales like that of his hunting expedition to the Himalayas, during which (so he tells Mrs. Jamieson) he "shot a cherubim." Peter's sometimes tall tales of imperial adventure are matched or overmatched not only by the tall tales of less honest Anglo-Indians in some of Thackeray's stories (particularly those of Jos Sedley in *Vanity Fair* [1848] and of the Major in "The Tremendous Adventures of Major Gahagan" [1838]) but also by the entire subgenre of the imperial/military adventure stories like

Westward Ho! that flourished throughout the century and which Gaskell gently mocks.

Romantic Imperialism

During the Romantic period, the fictional subgenres that are more or less explicitly imperialistic include the historical romance as practiced by Sir Walter Scott, the swashbuckling maritime novels written by Captain Frederick Marryat, Frederick Chamier, Edward Howard, and others, and novels in the tradition of the Eastern tale of Samuel Johnson's *Rasselas* (1759) and William Beckford's *Vathek* (1786). Scott also can be counted as one of the originators of a new regionalism in fiction, focused upon England's closest imperial frontiers in Scotland and Ireland, to which belong also Maria Edgeworth's *Castle Rackrent* (1800), Sydney Owenson's *Wild Irish Girl* (1806), and John Galt's *Annals of the Parish* (1821).

Like Romantic poetry and painting, Romantic fiction was responsive to the French Revolution, the Napoleonic Wars, and the Industrial Revolution. It was also occasionally responsive to the campaign against slavery, though with problematic results. The very title of Edgeworth's short story "The Grateful Negro" (1802) suggests what is problematic about most antislavery fiction—and, indeed, about most representations of racial and cultural difference throughout nineteenth-century British fiction, no matter how sympathetically inclined the writers are toward racial or cultural others. With unconscious irony, Edgeworth names her grateful negro "Caesar" and afflicts him with a bad case of Uncle Tomism: Caesar refuses to join the other slaves in their conspiracy against their West Indian masters, because his own master Mr. Edwards "treated his slaves with all possible humanity and kindness." Instead, Caesar informs on his best friend and the rebellion is repressed, though with so little violence that only Mr. Jefferies, whose harsh treatment of his slaves has been the main cause of rebellion, is the worse for wear.

Perhaps the most interesting abolitionist fiction was published after the 1833 triumph of the antislavery cause. Harriet Martineau's *Demerara*, from her "Illustrations of Political Economy" (1832–1834), is only slightly more realistic than Edgeworth's story, but at least Martineau recognizes that slavery does violence to human beings as well as to humane ideals. More noteworthy is Martineau's full-scale novel *The*

Hour and the Man (1841), which is an attempt to give a sympathetic rendering of Toussaint L'Ouverture and the Haitian revolution. But Martineau turns L'Ouverture into a too-perfect hero and fails to make any of her other characters lifelike, though not because she falls into the usual stereotypes of slaves or Africans: at least she treats L'Ouverture as on a par with any of the major figures of European history. On the other hand, most of the fiction of the Romantic period contains no hint of that greatest of liberal reform movements, the antislavery cause. There are abolitionist and, indeed, anti-imperialist sentiments in the Jacobin novels of the 1790s (see, for instance, the slave Fidel's tale of violent abuse in Robert Bage's *Man as He Is* [1792]), but such fiction largely disappeared after 1800, when the dominant ideological mode became anti-Jacobin, conservative, and increasingly imperialistic.

Scott's *Waverley* (1814) and *Ivanhoe* (1819) helped to establish the genre of the historical novel, which, though more often declaring its affiliation to Romanticism than to science and realism, nevertheless claimed to be omniscient, totalizing, and imperialist in its politics (like *Westward Ho!*). Scott's "historical romances" are usually versions of the state-building theme of epic, in that they tell about or at least adumbrate the unification first of England and later of England and Scotland: *Ivanhoe* proleptically affirms the gradual intermingling of Saxons and Normans; *Waverley* looks back to the Jacobite grand finale of 1745 but also foreshadows the absorption of the Highlands into the Lowlands, and of Scotland into England. Because the history of Scotland's incorporation into the United Kingdom was one of gradual conquest and domination by England, all of Scott's novels about the Jacobite cause are paradigmatically imperialistic, even while they mourn the passing of Scottish and especially Highland independence and traditions.

Scott inspired many imitators, and the historical novel flourished throughout the century. But with the exceptions of Thackeray's *Henry Esmond* (1852), Dickens's *Tale of Two Cities* (1859), George Eliot's *Romola* (1863), Thomas Hardy's *Trumpet Major* (1880), and a few others, almost all of this subgenre falls into two predictable categories: historical novels by conservative writers—Sir Arthur Conan Doyle's *White Company* (1891), for instance—mourn "the good old days" of "merry England" and aristocracy; those by liberal writers—Edward Bulwer-Lytton's *Harold, Last of the Saxons* (1848), for instance—look forward to the consolidation of the "liberties" of modern England. Both conservative and liberal historical novels tend to be ventures in "Whig history," or the interpretation of the past so that it patriotically validates the present.

Early nineteenth-century fiction about Ireland, even when it depicts Irish poverty and oppression, usually also validates England's imperial hegemony. This is true of Edgeworth's *Castle Rackrent* (1800) and *The Absentee* (1812), both of which deal with the hardships brought upon Irish peasants by irresponsible English landlords. As in "The Grateful Negro," Edgeworth in these two novels comes close to producing what might be called anti-imperialist stories; *Castle Rackrent* is, in Perera's words, "the first significant English novel to speak in the voice of the colonized." But the illiterate peasant Thady, who narrates Edgeworth's novella, is so thoroughgoing an Irish Uncle Tom that he defends his various irresponsible landlords on almost every occasion, while viewing his lawyer son Jason as a traitor for getting the better of his masters. "Faithful Thady" is thus an obvious example of one frequent stereotype in imperialist fiction, back to Robinson Crusoe's docile cannibal Friday and forward to Uncle Tom himself (in Harriet Beecher Stowe's powerfully influential antislavery best-seller, *Uncle Tom's Cabin* [1852]), through H. Rider Haggard's cooperative noble savage Umbopa (sidekick to Allan Quatermain in *King Solomon's Mines* and elsewhere), and on to the various Indian characters who engage in pro-British espionage in Kipling's *Kim*. Like "the grateful negro" or "faithful Thady," the good native (whether Irish, African, Indian, or whatever) always collaborates somehow, wittingly or unwittingly, in the subjugation of her or his fellow natives.

A different sort of imperialist stereotype is the non-British character whose weaknesses and misdemeanors demand British control. Fiction about Ireland is full of "Paddy" stereotypes even when the authors are Irish, as in William Carleton's *Traits and Stories of the Irish Peasantry* (1830, 1834), and most Eastern tales are even more obviously stereotypic. Thomas Hope's *Anastasius; or, Memoirs of a Greek* (1819) and James Morier's *The Adventures of Hajii Baba, of Ispahan* (1824) both feature stereotypic Orientals incapable of reason, sustained industry or work, honesty, or self-restraint and its European sexual corollary of "respect" for women (the lustful Oriental was also incapable of monogamy—hence, that endlessly titillating aspect of Oriental life as viewed through male British lenses, the harem). But as with *Rasselas*, the Eastern tales of Hope and Morier also hold up more or less self-conscious satiric mirrors to conservative, stuffy, irrational English society at home. Perhaps the most subtle way in which Morier's Hajji Baba mocks English values is through the very form of his storytelling: "The art of a story-teller is to make his tale interminable, and still to interest his audience," says Morier's narrator-protagonist, who is also, on many occasions, a self-convicted liar.

But isn't good storytelling a form of lying? Are aesthetically pleasing stories necessarily true or even realistic? Moreover, why should a good story come to an end? Why not meander endlessly, episodically? Why should the English regime of progress through industry (and imperial government) be the only way to organize stories, novels, life itself? Thus like Lord Byron in his Eastern narrative poems or like Rudyard Kipling in his picaresque adventure novel *Kim* at the end of the century, Morier offers, albeit implicitly, fictive alternatives to the very English values that both construct and deride the Orientalist stereotype that is Hajji Baba. A stereotype of the racial, sexual, or cultural "other" is always a misrecognized mirroring of the stereotyper (who invariably reduces otherness to some version of the same). The best Eastern tales of the century achieve partial recognition of this process; their writers at least vaguely realize that their stories are as much Western as Eastern—that is, that they are reflections of repressive values at home, though the name of the mirror is "abroad."

Early and Mid-Victorian Fiction

The first Australian novel, *Quintus Servinton, a Tale Founded upon Incidents of Real Occurrence* by Henry Savery, appeared in 1830; the first Indian novel written in English, Bankim Chandra Chatterjee's *Rajmohan's Wife*, appeared in 1864. The two dates span a period that historians used to describe as un-or even anti-imperialist, but during which territorial expansion and emigration to the colonies became standard themes in canonical British literature—the Micawbers' emigration to Australia in *David Copperfield* (1850), for example, or Mr. Rochester's and Bertha Mason's West Indian origins as well as St. John Rivers's mission to India in *Jane Eyre* (1848). India forms at least a background in several of Thackeray's novels; he was born in Calcutta, a fact that caused Henry James to wonder whether, in his "large and easy genius," there was "an echo of those masteries and dominations which sometimes straightened and sometimes broke the backs of so many of his ancestors and collaterals." Besides Jos Sedley's Oriental career in *Vanity Fair*, India is especially important in *The Newcomes* (1855), where Colonel Newcome, retired from service in the East, watches the family fortune vanish through the collapse of the Bundelcund Bank, due to the machinations of the Indian financier Rummun Loll—a "confounded old mahogany-coloured heathen humbug."

In the "hungry forties," with the rise of Chartism and especially after the great potato famine in Ireland of 1845 through 1847, emigration became more than just an easy escape or deus ex machina for characters in debt or in trouble in Britain. Moving beyond the stereotype of ignorant, drunken Paddy—the "stage Irishman" featured, for instance, in Samuel Lover's *Handy Andy* (1842)—Irish fiction achieved some tragic moments, especially in William Carleton's *Valentine McClutchy* (1845), *The Black Prophet* (1847), and *The Emigrants of Ahadarra* (1848). Though his earlier *Fardorougha, the Miser* (1837–1838) is more consistently realistic than the others, Carleton captures some of the desolation of his colonized country in, for example, chapter 17 of *The Black Prophet*, entitled "National Calamity":

Ireland, during the season . . . we are describing, might be compared to one vast lazar-house filled with famine, disease, and death. The very skies of heaven were hung with the black drapery of the grave. . . . Hearses, coffins, long funeral processions, and all the dark emblems of mortality were reflected, as it were, on the sky, from the terrible works of pestilence and famine which were going forward on the earth beneath it. . . .

Those who could left Ireland in droves, as the M'Mahon family is preparing to do in *The Emigrants of Ahadarra*. Absentee landlordism, the subletting of tenant farms into ever smaller and smaller plots of land, the overreliance on the potato as staple crop, and general all-around poverty, exploitation, ignorance, and villainy are factors that Carleton stresses as causing mass distress and mass emigration.

Novels about emigration, whether focused on Ireland or not, reached a peak in the 1850s. Three of the more prominent examples are Edward Bulwer-Lytton's *The Caxtons* (1850), on which Dickens may have drawn for the Australian ending of *David Copperfield*; Charles Reade's *It Is Never Too Late to Mend* (1856), with its Australian gold rush scenes and its aboriginal character Jacky; and Henry Kingsley's *Recollections of Geoffrey Hamlyn* (1859), featuring the emigration of Mary Thornton and most of the village of Drumston to Australia. In general, these and other English novelists in the 1850s and 1860s treat emigration as an attractive alternative for characters seeking to better their circumstances and perhaps, like several of Bulwer's characters, to return to England afterward. So Pisistratus Caxton goes fortune seeking in the Australian bush, where he has an exciting but idyllic time. Like other young English adventurers to the outback, or Canada, or Africa, or India in much imperialist fiction, "Sisty" gains "a health which an antediluvian might have envied, and . . . nerves so seasoned with horse-breaking, cattle-driving, fighting with wild blacks—chases from them and after them, for life and for death—that if any passion vex the breast of [Sisty or the other white] kings of the Bushland, fear at least is erased from the list." As contrasted to the bleak scenes of poverty and famine in Carleton's novels, Bulwer paints Australia as a wide-open space of Arcadian freedom and potential prosperity, empty except for a few subhuman savages. Even the social problems at home that might motivate emigration are not major ones; in Sisty's case they are not social at all, but merely the failed financial speculations of his Uncle Jack. The Australia portrayed by Bulwer is the British Empire as it was portrayed in much imperialist fiction throughout the century: realms of adventure and opportunity where England itself, if need be, could repair its fortunes.

In a very different manner, the Eastern tale also achieved an apotheosis of sorts in the early and mid-Victorian period, first through the publication of two quite dissimilar novels—Philip Meadows Taylor's *Confessions of a Thug* (1839) and Benjamin Disraeli's *Tancred, or The New Crusade* (1847)—and then through the dozens of hysterical, racist accounts of the Indian Mutiny of 1857, starting with Dickens's and Wilkie Collins's "The Perils of Certain English Prisoners" for the 1857 Christmas issue of *Household Words*. Dickens transposed the setting of the Mutiny from India to the "Mosquito Coast" of Central America, but his intention is unmistakable. As he wrote to Angela Burdett Coutts:

I wish I were Commander in Chief in India. The first thing I would do to strike that Oriental race with amazement . . . should be to proclaim to them . . . that I should do my utmost to exterminate the Race upon whom the stain of the late cruelties rested; and that I was . . . now proceeding, with merciful swiftness of execution, to blot it out of mankind and raze it off the face of the Earth.

A Tale of Two Cities (1859) may be a response to the Mutiny as well as to the French Revolution of 1789. Similarly, the sinister Indian background to Collins's *Moonstone* (1868), one of the best-known "sensation novels" of the 1860s, may reflect the fear and hatred aroused by the Mutiny (even though the Moonstone itself was first stolen from India), and so may the equally sinister Oriental motifs with which Dickens begins the unfinished *Mystery of Edwin Drood* (1870).

From George Lawrence's *Maurice Dering* (1864) and James Grant's *First Love and Last Love: A Tale of the Indian Mutiny* (1868) down to Henry Merriman's *Flotsam* (1892) and Flora Annie Steel's *On the Face of the Waters* (1897), the sentiments expressed by other English novelists writing directly about the Mutiny are seldom more temperate than Dickens's. Flora Annie Steel's novel is a partial exception, though a more striking one is Meadows Taylor's *Seeta* (1872), which offers both the best account of the motives for the Mutiny in any Victorian novel and also—another rarity—a highly sympathetic account of an interracial marriage between Seeta, the Indian heroine, and the English hero, Cyril Brandon. Taylor himself had married a Eurasian woman, and his long service as police superintendent for the Nizam of Hyderabad provided the experience that makes his *Confessions of a Thug* an even more significant achievement than *Seeta* or than any of his other novels about India.

Like Morier's *Hajii Baba*, all Eastern tales—indeed, perhaps all imperialistic novels—feature "natives" whose often amusing but always irrational, childlike behavior cries out for British rule. The most spectacular instance of a Victorian novel about such a character is *Confessions of a Thug*—an Eastern tale with a new, unhumorous twist, since it is also a stunning *roman policier*. Taylor has rightly been called the greatest Anglo-Indian novelist before Kipling, and in *Confessions* he produced one of the greatest crime novels of the nineteenth century— a sort of Orientalist version of Dostoevsky's *Crime and Punishment*—in which he put his own years of investigating Thuggee (a secret cult of professional robbers and murderers who worshipped Kali, Hindu goddess of destruction) to effective use. The narrative structure of Taylor's novel is paradigmatic of all imperialist fiction that purports to map the alien (and always supposedly irrational) mentality of the foreign other or "native." It is especially paradigmatic both because it is "panoptical" (in the sense Michel Foucault derives from Jeremy Bentham's plan for an ideal, all-seeing system of prison surveillance), and because Taylor is so obviously an interested, sympathetic observer of India and Indians. The novel takes the panoptical form of a silent British police "Sahib" listening to the horrific, interminable confession of Ameer Ali, who proudly rather than contritely narrates his initiation to the cult and his years as a practitioner of it, through dozens of robberies and murders. Like his unnamed Sahib, Taylor quite naturally assumes a dominative position: the imperialist writer, no matter how sympathetic or how unburdened by racism, is always in the position of the Sahib or of Colonel Creighton with his "ethnographic survey" in *Kim*, exploring the crime (so to speak) of being non-English or non-European.

Disraeli's very different *Tancred* was the last of his Young England trilogy, and like *Coningsby* and *Sybil* it features the political education of a young aristocrat bound for greatness. With the blessing of the wise Sidonia (the immensely wealthy, mysterious Jew who also mentors Coningsby), Tancred travels to Jerusalem and has a spectacular encounter with "the Angel of Arabia" on Mount Sinai. The angel tells him, among other things, that Europe is "the intellectual colony of Arabia" and that, if its faith is to be renewed, the revival will come through "Arabian principles." For "Arabia" (or peoples of Semitic origin including the Jews, because Disraeli like Sidonia believes that "all is race; there is no other truth") has been and will continue to be the source of the world's great religions, and therefore the source of civilization. Moreover, how have those religions, and therefore civilization, spread throughout the world? Disraeli's answer is that they have spread through the creation of empires. Tancred and his Syrian friend Fakredeen therefore hatch a world-conquering scheme, close to Disraeli's own designs for Britain's role in the Near East, India, and elsewhere. As Tancred informs the Queen of the Ansaray: "'We wish to conquer [the] world, with angels at our head'," though the novel peters out before that happens, ending anticlimactically when Tancred's doting parents come to Jerusalem.

Confessions and *Tancred* are both novels by men who participated directly in the government and, in Disraeli's case, expansion of the empire. The same can be said of Captain Marryat, who after Sir Walter Scott was the most influential shaper of the explicitly imperialist fiction of the century. Marryat's semiautobiographical, patriotic tales of youthful escapades and glorious combat in the Royal Navy during the Napoleonic Wars were highly popular from the 1830s on. Though not much read today, Marryat made a great impact on such later writers as Conrad and Graham Greene, and even Virginia Woolf wrote an appreciative essay about him ("The Captain's Death Bed"). Starting with

Frank Mildmay (1829) and running through *Newton Foster* (1832), *Peter Simple* (1834), *Mr. Midshipman Easy* (1836), and his *Robinson Crusoe*-like story for juvenile readers *Masterman Ready* (1842), Marryat offered picaresque tales about admirably brave boys or young men who (like himself) were delighted to quit home and shore for shipboard excitement and global adventuring. Most of Marryat's novels cannot be called historical, but they are reminiscences of past youth and bygone glories, and their celebrations of war, male camaraderie, and freedom from home spawned numerous imitations and offshoots through Captain Mayne Reid's *Rifle Rangers* (1850) and Robert Ballantyne's *Coral Island* (1858) down to G. A. Henty, Dr. Gordon Stables, W. H. G. Kingston, Robert Louis Stevenson, Sir Arthur Conan Doyle, and many others to World War I and beyond, written sometimes for adults but also for a burgeoning audience of juvenile readers.

From the 1870s to World War I

For this adolescent readership, increasingly important after the Education Act of 1870, new journals sprang up, featuring supposedly wholesome fare as an alternative to "penny dreadfuls" and other cheap literature. This was the explicit aim of *The Boy's Own Paper*, founded in 1879; its mainstay was the imperialist adventure story, and among its contributors were Ballantyne, Henty, Kingston, and Conan Doyle. From the 1860s forward, moreover, adventure fiction often drew its inspiration from the excitement generated by the exploration of central Africa and the search for the sources of the Nile. David Livingstone's *Missionary Travels* (1857) had been a best-seller, and an even greater publishing sensation was Henry Morton Stanley's *How I Found Livingstone* (1872). In between came Richard Burton's *Lake Regions of Central Africa* (1860), John Hanning Speke's *Discovery of the Sources of the Nile* (1864), and Samuel White Baker's *Albert N'Yanza* (1866). These great exploration narratives set the pattern for numerous African adventure stories, including Baker's own *Cast Up by the Sea* (1866) and Stanley's *My Kalulu: Prince, King, and Slave* (1889). The great Scottish explorer of Africa James Thomson also tried his hand at fiction with *Ulu: An African Romance* (1888), ostensibly for adults.

Imbued with social Darwinist ideas about race, both explorers' journals and the novels that imitated them reinforced the myth of Africa as the "dark continent," land of fetishism, slavery, and cannibalism. The stereotype was offered repeatedly in adventure stories for boys, like Ballantyne's *Gorilla Hunters* (1861), in which a white trader tells Peterkin:

... all the nigger tribes in Africa are sunk in gross and cruel superstitions. They have more fetishes, and greegrees, and amulets, and wooden gods, and charms, than they know what to do with, and have surrounded themselves with spiritual mysteries that neither themselves nor anybody else can understand.

"Superstitions," that is, that legitimize human sacrifice and cannibalism. In *Heart of Darkness*, Conrad does not challenge the stereotype, but instead challenges—through the powerful theme of Kurtz's "going native"—the assumption that European civilization is superior to African savagery.

Before Conrad, the most important English novelist to base much of his work on the myth of "the dark continent" was H. Rider Haggard, whose best-selling *King Solomon's Mines* (1885), *She* (1887), and *Allan Quatermain* (1887) follow the exploration paradigm into mysterious regions of savagery and "lost civilizations." One of Haggard's recurrent themes concerns a black African savagery in the present that has lost touch with an earlier, lighter-skinned civilization from Egypt or the Middle East. With Haggard time stalls, tries to march backward. In his daydream romances about Africa, including those about the rise and fall of the Zulu kingdom (*Nada the Lily* in 1892, for instance), he expresses racist, authoritarian attitudes toward adventure, masculinity, empire, and the "dark places" of the world that continue to influence popular culture. Films like the Indiana Jones series (and, of course, the recent cinema version of *King Solomon's Mines*) still express nostalgia for adventure, power, and the exotic that characterized late-nineteenth-century fiction about exploration and empire. If, as Chris Bongie writes in *Exotic Memories*, exoticism is "a discursive practice intent on recovering 'elsewhere' values 'lost' with the modernization of European society," Haggard's romances—and perhaps all imperialist fictions that follow the exploration-adventure paradigm—are always quests for an impossible, lost reality that ultimately assumes the frighteningly maternal, incestuous form that Haggard named "She" or "Ayesha." For Haggard, moreover, nostalgia about adventure and empire was part of his late-Victorian conservatism. More clearly than in most fiction of his era, in Haggard's work the voice of romance and empire was simultaneously, in Katz's words, "the voice of the moribund gentry." He seems today an archetypal reactionary whose stories consist of reactionary archetypes: myths of power, misogyny, magic, racial purity, and the mastery of both nature and the "darker races" by white male adventurers from England. His literary—or perhaps subliterary—energy derives largely from the directness and simplicity with which he renders these reactionary archetypes in narrative form.

Through gun power, fist power, and English pluck, Allan Quatermain and his white sidekicks, along with the faithful noble savage Umbopa, inevitably dominate the less noble savages whom they encounter. It goes without saying that they also dominate nature: the toll in the hunting episodes is just as horrific as in the battle scenes. Haggard had to defend himself against charges of bloodlust. Yet in his 1894 essay "'Elephant Smashing' and 'Lion Shooting,'" he mourns the disappearance of "the ancient mystery of Africa," and wonders where "the romance writers of future generations will find a safe and secret place, unknown to the pestilent accuracy of the geographer, in which to lay their plots?" Once all the wilderness is tamed, once the last stones crown the pyramids of the European empires, there will no longer be room for romance, adventure, freedom, nature. An interesting aspect of Haggard's writing is his apparent awareness of this tragic outcome, even while he advocates the completion and defense of what he clearly views as the ultimate imperial pyramid.

Olive Schreiner's *Story of an African Farm* (1883), which she published under the pseudonym Ralph Iron, offers an interesting contrast to Haggard's romances. Schreiner's account of the frustrated personal relations of two English girls, Em and Lyndall, growing up under the tyranny of their Boer stepmother Tant' Sannie, is both wistful and yet stiflingly realistic, as is her parallel account of the equally lonely, frustrated Waldo (son of Tant' Sannie's farm supervisor Otto). Schreiner's domestic realism, emanating from one of the distant reaches of the empire, offers no escapist or exoticist adventures to still farther, different places, as do Haggard's imperialist romances or the hundreds of boys' adventure novels that poured from British presses between Captain Marryat's era and World War I. After Lyndall has gone away for several years to school, she returns with strongly feminist ideas, but her romantic entanglement with Gregory Rose (who had been engaged to Em) leads to her pregnancy, the death of her baby, and her own death. Em and Gregory are (not exactly happily) reunited; Waldo, dreaming of Lyndall, whom he has loved all along, remains on the farm, lonelier than ever, presumably until his death.

Although Schreiner does not say much about whites' treatment of blacks, her portrayal of the psychic toll taken by the cruelty and oppressiveness of life on her South African farm approximates a critique of imperialism, expressed most directly in Lyndall's feminism, that becomes explicit in *Trooper Peter Halket of Mashonaland* (1897), her allegorical indictment of Cecil Rhodes's violent expansionism. Indeed, though Haggard and the writers of adventure fiction give the final third of the century a jingoistic tone, there is also an increasing note of skepticism or criticism, registered also in Robert Louis Stevenson's realistic stories about squalor and treachery in the South Seas, *The Beach of Falesá* (1893) and *The Ebb-Tide* (1894), which can be read as versions of *Heart of Darkness* transposed to Polynesia. Both novellas offer versions of the theme of "going native," and both are as dubious about the impact of Western civilization on non-Western societies as anything Conrad wrote.

Very different forms of social criticism are registered in Samuel Butler's *Erewhon* (1872) and in the greatest of nineteenth-century Australian novels, Marcus Clarke's *For the Term of His Natural Life* (1872). Based on Butler's five years as a sheep farmer in New Zealand, *Erewhon* offers a satiric, antipodal or upside-down utopia or dystopia (it is a little of each) that mocks, among other things, therapeutic approaches to crime and the false worship of machinery and technology. But if crime is treated as illness and illness as crime in *Erewhon*, that is certainly not the case in the Tasmanian convict settlements depicted in Clarke's great, grim masterpiece of melodramatic social realism.

Clarke's novel, which has been called an Australian *Les Misérables*, also offers an interesting contrast to that other great crime novel of the British Empire, *Confessions of a Thug*. In the story of unjustly convicted Rufus Dawes, most of the criminals are not larcenous, murderous Orientals or cannibalistic Africans, but larcenous, murderous, and indeed, in the most extreme instances, cannibalistic English and Irish prisoners. "All that the vilest and most bestial of human creatures could invent and practise, was in this unhappy country [Tasmania] invented and practised without restraint and without shame." Dawes's tormented life story can be read as a historical novel, but to most British versions of that genre, which celebrate the epic glories of discovery, conquest, and colonization—*Westward Ho!* again, for example—Clarke's novel offers a complete antithesis. Sylvia Vickers, the chief figure of innocence in the story besides Dawes himself, reverses Miranda's "brave new world" speech from Shakespeare's *Tempest* when she exclaims: "'Oh, how strangely must the world have been civilised, that this most lovely corner of it must needs be set apart as a place of banishment for the monsters that civilisation [has] brought forth and bred!'"

From the time of the Crimean War and the Indian Mutiny, even the most overtly patriotic, imperialistic novels often sound notes of warning or anxiety about the internal and external enemies of the empire. Beginning in the 1880s, fears of decadence, including the prospect of the decline and fall of the empire, were deliberately mocked by decadent movement writers (Oscar Wilde, Aubrey Beardsley, the early William Butler Yeats, and others). And to the frequent theme of "going native," as in *The Beach of Falesá* and *Heart of Darkness*, was added the equally distressing theme of *reverse* invasion and the possible conquest of England by its enemies, starting with Sir George Chesney's *Battle of Dorking* (1871) and running through William Le Queux's *Great War in England in 1897* (1897) and Bram Stoker's very different Gothic thriller *Dracula* (1897) down to World War I and beyond. H. G. Wells's "scientific romances" such as *The Time Machine* (1895), *The Island of Dr. Moreau* (1896), and *The War of the Worlds* (1897) provided fantasy variations on these imperial themes and anxieties, while the radioactive "quap" in Wells's *Tono-Bungay* (1909), dissolving en route to England, suggests the later, postcolonial theme of "the empire strikes back."

Before the 1880s, most writers of fiction about the British Empire took for granted that Britain was the vanguard nation, and that the British were God's or Nature's chosen instrument to bring the light of civilization, commerce, and Christianity to the "dark places" of the world. While the same chauvinism characterizes most fiction about adventures abroad and life in the colonies during and after that decade, a new anxiety and sometimes self-criticism also emerges, as in Gissing's *Whirlpool* or in Conrad's *Lord Jim* (1900). Jim's self-doubt about his courage and integrity seems an exact analogue to the mood of increasing uncertainty about Britain's place in the world and, indeed, about the meaning of its past imperial might and prosperity. A newspaper editor in Conan Doyle's *Lost World* (1911) says, "The big blank spaces in the map are all being filled in, and there's no room for romance anywhere." Once the "romance" of imperialist exploration and conquest is stripped away, the reality is just as Marlow describes it in *Heart of Darkness*: "The conquest of the earth, which mostly means the taking it away from those who have a different complexion or slightly flatter noses than ourselves, is not a pretty thing when you look into it too much."

Patrick Brantlinger

Selected Bibliography

Arac, Jonathan, and Harriet Ritvo, eds. *Macropolitics of Nineteenth-Century Literature: Nationalism, Exoticism, Imperialism.* Philadelphia: University of Pennsylvania Press, 1991.

Bakhtin, Mikhail. *The Dialogic Imagination: Four Essays.* Ed. Michael Holquist. Trans. Caryl Emerson and Michael Holquist. Austin: University of Texas Press, 1981.

Bhabha, Homi K., ed. *Nation and Narration.* London: Routledge, 1990.

Bongie, Chris. *Exotic Memories: Literature, Colonialism, and the Fin de Siècle.* Stanford: Stanford University Press, 1991.

Brantlinger, Patrick. *Rule of Darkness: British Literature and Imperialism, 1830–1914.* Ithaca, N.Y.: Cornell University Press, 1988.

Dabydeen, David, ed. *The Black Presence in English Literature.* Manchester: Manchester University Press, 1985.

Green, Martin. *Dreams of Adventure, Deeds of Empire.* New York: Basic Books, 1979.

Katz, Wendy. *Rider Haggard and the Fiction of Empire: A Critical Study of British Imperial Fiction.* Cambridge: Cambridge University Press, 1987.

Perera, Suvendrini. *Reaches of Empire: The English Novel from Edgeworth to Dickens.* New York: Columbia University Press, 1991.

Richards, Jeffrey, ed. *Imperialism and Juvenile Literature.* Manchester: Manchester University Press, 1989.

Said, Edward W. *Culture and Imperialism.* New York: Alfred A. Knopf, 1993.

Said, Edward W. *Orientalism.* New York: Vintage, 1979.

Suleri, Sara. *The Rhetoric of English India.* Chicago: University of Chicago Press, 1992.

Lewis Carroll and the Child in Victorian Fiction

What do you suppose is the use of a child without any meaning?
Lewis Carroll

L ewis Carroll's two books, *Alice's Adventures in Wonderland* (1865) and *Through the Looking-Glass and What Alice Found There* (1871), regarded when they were first published as amusing pieces in the developing subgenre of "children's books," turned out to be major works of nineteenth-century literature and part of the history of serious imaginative writing. Carroll's words and images created art so radical and variously appealing that it could, did, and does bring many kinds of readers to look with fresh wonder at the structure and meaning of experience. Charles Lutwidge Dodgson (1832–1898), the shy, eccentric bachelor, mathematician, logician, Oxford don, and cleric, made up tales for little girls, turned them into books by Lewis Carroll—his pen name—and, in doing so, astonishingly expanded the possibilities for art, fiction, and speculative thought. In creating the Alice texts, he became a master of what we might call a stream of unconsciousness that others could tap into and use. He points the way to both modernism and postmodernism, but he is also a writer who shows the fact and importance of the emergence in the nineteenth century of children as subjects in the enterprise of fiction—a key cultural fact that deserves recognition and attention.

Carroll's Alice is, after all, the most famous child in nineteenth-century prose. She de-centers, de-constructs, and de-familiarizes the Victorian universe. A telling passage in *Through the Looking-Glass*, when Alice first passes through the mirror and sees the chess-piece kings and queens come alive and appear as befuddled parents and incompetent self-managers, offers a symbol for Lewis Carroll's subject and method:

Alice looked on . . . as the King . . . began writing. A sudden thought struck her, and she took hold of the end of the pencil, which came some way over his shoulder, and began writing for him.

The poor King . . . at last . . . panted out "My dear! I really *must* get a thinner pencil. I can't manage this one a bit: it writes all manner of things that I don't intend—"

The child takes hold and writes what it wants, taking writing in new directions. That makes a good epigraph for Carroll's *Alice* fiction, and it can serve as a metaphor for the role of unconscious intention in all art. It points up the source of Charles Dodgson's imagination and also represents a process of high significance at work in nineteenth-century English literature. The royal road to the Freudian unconscious runs not only through dreamland, but through childhood.

Carroll's way is the way of regression. By befriending small girls, identifying with them, seeking to divert them, projecting himself back into childhood, and imagining stories explicitly for children, he managed to create two texts that have been, and are, as widely read, known, and quoted as any imaginative literature of the past two centuries. The Alice books do not directly address our serious, responsible, moral selves; Carroll turns his back on the adult world—the so-called real world. Nevertheless, this man who retreats into juvenility and dream states, reverts to play and nonsense, toys with language, avoids any overtly didactic or practical purpose, and escapes from society, history, and maturity into the fantasy of his own regressive mind, appears before us as a prophet of the twentieth-century romance with fantasy life and a father of the future in psychology, art, and literature.

Carroll represents his child in her dream visions, and he brings together in imagining her experience the literary convention of the dream, the mood and feeling of real dreams, and the full play of his fantasy—and he exploits their potential for comedy. Nobody before had done anything quite like that. In all that is comic, as in dreams and fantasy, there is something regressive that takes us back to the mental experience and the world of play that we first knew as children. Comedy, dreams, and fantasy all somehow involve *regression*, a word that may have frivolous, even pejorative connotations. But the regression in Lewis Carroll—comic or not—is the opening to progress.

Carroll's Alice implies and affirms the tie-in of fiction and the child to the processes of regression and the unconscious. Henry James, describing his girl-heroine Maisie in *What Maisie Knew* (1897), alludes neatly to the intimate relationship between the child and fiction, between child psychology and novelistic practice: "She was at the age for which all stories are true and all conceptions are stories." One point on which Lewis Carroll, the novel, and psychoanalysis agree is that no matter how we age, we keep this fiction-loving child somewhere, literally, in mind.

Regression means a going or coming back; it can be defined as a reverting to earlier behavior patterns, perceptions, and experiences so as to change or escape from undesirable situations and mental states. It is both radical and conservative: radical in rejecting the present and in juxtaposing material from both conscious and unconscious processes; conservative in holding on to time past. In Freudian dream psychology, regression means the translation of thoughts and emotions into visual images and forms of language when something in the mind resists or blocks their path to normal consciousness. It is a way of expressing and elaborating suppressed conflicts, memories, and daring psychic formations from infancy and childhood and letting them play on present realities. Regression can thus be a means of seeing life anew—of seeing it in *Wonderland*, for instance, as a falling into unknown territory beneath the surface of things, a mad tea party, and a farcical trial; or in *Through the Looking-Glass*, as an involuntary game, a series of dialogues with strange beings, an exercise in interpreting puzzling language, and a living out of preexistent linguistic formulas. The child's fantasy can be the generator of the adult's changing perception and world.

In *Finnegans Wake*, James Joyce, parodying the Holy Trinity, invents a Carrollian trinity that sums up the content and pattern of Carroll's creative regression: "Dodgfather, Dodgson & Coo." The words and syllables, in their order, suggest the Carrollian movement away from manly, rigid patriarchy, away from the fixed single self, and toward the child and its identity with some wondrous spirit of freedom and comic wordplay. That happy "Coo" can signify the *coup* by which the Holy Ghost, its symbol the gentle dove, and Carroll himself merge into the girl Alice; the company that makes up his metamorphosing plural selves; and the sound that, mocking sentimentality and pomposity, connotes skepticism and bespeaks the voice of the new turtle heard in the modern lands of the absurd and irrational. From out of his rabbit-hole and looking-glass world we can see coming not only such figures as Joyce, Freud, Oscar Wilde, Henry James, Virginia Woolf, Kafka, Proust, Artaud, Nabokov, Beckett, Waugh, Lacan, Borges, Bakhtin, and García Márquez, but also much of the character and mood of twentieth-century popular culture.

One of the main projects of the novel in the nineteenth and twentieth centuries has been to give expression to the child and a plot to childhood, and in this collective effort Lewis Carroll played a crucial part. Carroll and Alice give us a chance to see what the term "child" could mean in their Victorian society. The "child," of course, is not a static, given entity but a social construct that develops and changes in history. Focusing on Carroll and the Alice books can show why they have lasted and also how his child heroine relates to the children and childhoods represented by other important makers of fiction. That writers have made children subjects and objects of their work in the last two centuries has helped definitively to form people's thoughts and feelings about children. Our whole conception of childhood and children derives, in some degree, from the imaginative power of such writers as Rousseau, Wordsworth, Dickens, George Eliot, Freud, and, not least, Lewis Carroll.

Like Dante's Beatrice, Carroll's Alice is named after a real person. It was Alice Liddell, daughter of the Dean of Christ Church, who inspired the *Alice* books, and who, with her sisters, made the first audience for the stories from which the book grew. The comparison is not as far-fetched as it might appear, for Dodgson loved the girl Alice as surely as Dante loved the girl Beatrice; and he found, like many others of his era, a genuine faith in his sense of devotion to his idea of the child. The personal circumstances of Dodgson's life that led to *Alice in Wonderland* are well known and need only be mentioned briefly. He was the third child and eldest son in a large family of eleven children (seven sisters); his father was a patriarchal cleric, his mother a sweet, loving, child-burdened woman who died before Charles turned nineteen. Though he grew up a stammerer, he seems to have had a happy childhood at Daresbury and Croft, where his father was rector. He loved to care for, amuse, and entertain his siblings—his sisters especially—with stories, games, and nonsense. Though he respected his father's forceful personality and intellect and held him in awe, he identified emotionally with his mother. At school at Rugby, he seems to have been rather a misfit, but he did well in his studies and matriculated to Christ Church, Oxford. There he took a first in mathematics, won a scholarship, and eventually became a master and tutor in his subject. There also he lived out his life as a bachelor. Conventional, adult, genital sexuality and marriage were not for him; in fact, there is no evidence that he ever engaged in physical sex with anyone or wanted to. It was a sublimated libido that flowed compulsively, but with kindness and propriety, toward the figure of the child.

According to his biographer Derek Hudson, the psychological lesson of Dodgson's childhood above all others was that he could never, so long as he lived, be without the companionship of children, and by children he meant little girls. They were a necessity to him; "They are three-fourths of my life," he once said. In 1856 he befriended the Liddell children, offspring of the dean of his college, and fell in love with Alice just at the time when he took up photography (he became a leading amateur photographer and one of the century's outstanding photographers of children). On an afternoon boating excursion with the girls in 1862 he began diverting them with a tale of nonsense and wonder that he elaborated into *Alice's Adventures Under Ground* (a private book, which he illustrated, meant expressly as a gift for the "real" Alice) and, later, the two published Alice books. His art of fantasy is thus rooted in real occasions, aimed at particular people with their particular wants and needs, and created for very personal reasons. Many incidents in the history of his relationship with Alice and the other Liddells, such as getting caught and drenched in the rain on an outing, find their way into his texts. The genesis of Lewis Carroll's fiction is the wish to give pleasure to a child—to children—whom he adored and idealized, to make his specific audience happy, and to seduce its goodwill and affectionate regard for himself. His desire was to project himself into the life of a child, to bind that child to his imagination, to break down the social and psychological barriers between adult and child, and to re-create the child in his own fantasy life. Virginia Woolf wrote that "childhood was not dispersed in Dodgson as it usually is in adults, but remained in him entire, so he could do what no one else has ever been able to do—he could return to that world; he could re-create it."

As it happens, Carroll's desire and practice here—his intense subjectivity—signify a good deal about his originality and importance, and about fiction, literary transaction, and the emergence of the child in fiction. The child, according to Jacqueline Rose, in *The Case of Peter Pan*, *or The Impossibility of Children's Fiction*, appears in literature when the relationship between adult and child becomes a concern, a problem, a cultural issue. For many reasons—the rise of the middle classes, the subtle assaults on supernaturalism, the growing emphasis on the moral value of the family, the changing world's need to stress formal education, for example—that relationship, by the mid-nineteenth century, was much in question. With Carroll, however, we are talking of an adult's desire for the child—the desire, specifically, to serve the child, to make the child an icon and fetish, to use it to distance and dissolve threatening erotic energy, to introject the child into his psyche, and to live vicariously through the child. Freudians have had grand times analyzing the kinks in Charles Dodgson's personality, but the striking irony is that psychoanalysis and its theories that stress the determining significance of childhood experience and the importance of language, fantasy, dreams, jokes, and puns in showing the workings of the unconscious and the mind's reflective games, seem to flow right out of Carroll's wonderland.

In the Alice books Carroll can be seen working in the developing, often overlapping nineteenth-century traditions of children's literature and the child protagonist in fiction, but the immediacy of his original audience and the conflation of his central character, his hearers, himself, and the imaginative recreation of experiences he has shared with Alice Liddell and other little girls led him to break with convention. The purpose of most children's literature had been mainly didactic and moral: it was supposed to educate and lead children to adapt certain kinds of behavior, become better, grow up to be good people—for example, obedient Christians and productive citizens. And in the novels of Dickens, Charlotte Brontë, and George Eliot, children are generally portrayed either as agents who reflect on the moral condition and worth of the other characters and their world (*Oliver Twist* [1837], *Silas Marner* [1861]) or, most significantly, who show the development and logical relationship between a character's childhood and his or her later life and consciousness (*Great Expectations* [1861], *Jane Eyre* [1847])—"the continuity, the unity of human experience," as Peter Coveney puts it. Lewis Carroll's first intention would seem to have been to make his audience find *him* wonderful through his imaginative ingenuity and ability to delight, divert, and play seductively in language. What originally motivates the Alice tales, it seems, is a wish to break through to a new state, to go underground, to get through the usual conventional reflections to a new site of reflection behind the traditional moralizing mirrors of art—to move into the wonderland of the unconscious and the "other" where the beloved not-self somehow mirrors the self.

Carroll imagines such literary mirroring in the form of a picture—almost a photograph—in the memory of a child whom he has imagined. This becomes clear in a passage from *Through the Looking-Glass* describing the White Knight—a virtual self-portrait by the writer:

Of all the strange things that Alice saw in her journey . . . , this was one that she always remembered most clearly. Years afterward she could bring the whole scene back again, as if it had been only yesterday—the mild blue eyes and kindly smile of the knight—the setting sun gleaming through his hair, and shining on his armour in a blaze of light that quite dazzled her—the horse quietly moving about . . . —and the black shadows of the forest behind—all this she took in like a picture.

It is the invented Alice who validates and preserves Dodgson/Carroll's being and lets him make art out of the mirror stage, in which, according to Lacan, we take our image of ourselves early on from what we find another perceiving and desiring.

He particularized the audience for his fiction, writing both for a child—whom he was out to please, honor, and fascinate, not change, or use for moral propaganda, or show to be the parent of the adult the child would become—and for himself, a witty, repressed, curious intellectual with a brilliantly intuitive imagination and an obvious need to express safely the contents and fantasies of his complexly fissured mind. Because Charles Dodgson loved a real child, Lewis Carroll was moved to write fiction—a fiction that broke with realism, rejected a traditional marriage plot (staple of both the novel and the fairy tale), and mocked reality as "dull." The focus in Carroll is on the child itself, as in a portrait or photograph of a young girl, not on the state of childhood as a prelude to something else. His writing is for fun—the fun of Alice—but it also calls attention to a sense of life's alienation and to both the continuing presence and otherness of childhood for grown-ups.

Through the child, Carroll pushed the limits and conventions of fiction, expanded them, and made fantasy probing, speculative, radically comic, and intellectually rewarding. His libido drove him beyond memories and representations of realistic childhood experiences, such as

Dickens depicts, into the unconscious, where, for example, he finds and reflects through the mirror of his art an image of himself as a shy, joke-making insect—Victorian ancestor of Kafka's Gregor Samsa—fluttering helplessly about the flame of a little girl (see "Looking-Glass Insects," chapter 3, *Looking-Glass*). He moved from conscious social or practical purpose to comic subversion and new perspectives. Carroll pointed toward specialized and diverse audiences developing for fiction—for instance, children, nostalgic adults, teachers, child-rearers, academics, logicians, and intellectuals—and also toward the complicated and various motives that bring one to read and write fiction. (One motive that became important in the developing countercultural tradition in art would be to turn outsiders into insiders, giving them the last laugh.) The motives and circumstances behind the making of *Alice* let us see how the the reading public was fragmenting into special groups and also into what we might call a collection of myriad-minded, private reading selves.

The child as subject and the literary transaction were for Carroll ends, rather than means. Paradoxically, therefore, this outwardly orthodox, but odd, little-girl-struck author of what may have been the favorite children's book of the century helped to rid fiction of its heavy load of Victorian moral baggage and move it toward something like sovereign play in and for itself—pleasure for pleasure's sake and art for art's sake too. Thus, strangely enough, it previews both popular culture and modernism's high art of fiction with its exalted, romantic notions of "creative writing" and the writer. "Alice" was born out of the need to please some little girls and to turn the rational world upside down. A little child destined for the commercial stage, movies, cartoons, amusement-park rides, and TV—the whole money-making *Alice* industry whose history shows perfectly how the child has been commercialized in modern times—would lead the avant-garde.

The cult of the child flourished in Victorian times, and other authors, particularly Dickens, exploited to the last emotional pang the sympathy and identification that people had come to feel for children in print, especially orphans and lonely, misunderstood, victimized children. Of the major writers in the language, however, only Carroll and Mark Twain in *Tom Sawyer* and *Huckleberry Finn*, used the child *primarily* for comic purposes. Natural symbols of regeneration, children—in modern times normally much closer in years to birth than to death—live relatively free of the fear of time and give themselves to play, games, and the pursuit of pleasure. And if you write for them, you can give way to fantasy, say things that in another context might be construed as wild or blasphemous, and claim you're doing nothing but amusing children. But before you can fully realize the comic potential of the child, you have to rebel against the powerful idea that adult life is somehow superior to child life. You must must really admire, even envy, want to be, the child, and choose the child over the parent—even the parent in yourself and the parent that you are in your imagination. Lewis Carroll did. This laureate of growing up absurd knew that a part of the self resents having to grow up, and he insisted that maturity, whatever else it may be, is somehow a sham and a joke.

Such a writer and such a vision can succeed only when there is a deep, if repressed, skepticism about the authority—and authoritarianism—of the past, both individually and collectively. (cf. Günter Grass's Little Oskar in *The Tin Drum* in post-Nazi Germany.) The intensive questioning of authority and power that the Alice texts render could take place only when people, feeling themselves to be children of an incomprehensible or disappearing God, of the state, of a ridiculous universe, or of some other sort of unfathomable, but oppressive authority, and consciously or unconsciously resentful, were ready to defy and mock the omnipotence, mystery, wisdom, and reason of a rigid adult order—the internal and external ancien régime.

Philippe Aries, the pioneer historian of childhood, and his followers, critics, and revisers have tried to chronicle the processes by which childhood began to be recognized as something more than a period when, as Kimberley Reynolds puts it, "miniature adults were stuffed with food, information, and attitudes with which to become fully-developed adults"—when, in other words, children began to be perceived as different from adults. Whether this changing perception occurred in the early Renaissance, the seventeenth century, or, on a widespread scale in the early nineteenth century, by the late-Victorian period the child in art and literature reflected a concern for helping middle-class adults identify and resolve their problems by identifying with children. If we compare the nature of fiction through the Victorian era and the twentieth century with what it was at the beginning of the nineteenth century we see how a mushrooming emphasis on the child has changed things and led novelists to the rendering of children's points of view (Dickens, Proust, Joyce, D. H. Lawrence, Woolf), children as featured characters (George Eliot, Christina Stead, Thomas Mann), children as magnets for twisted, dangerous eroticisms (Joyce, Nabokov, Toni Morrison), children as lovely, innocent figures whose well-being is the touchstone of the good (Henry James), and children as a targeted audience (Robert Louis Stevenson, Oscar Wilde, J. M. Barrie, T. H. White). For the more privileged classes in the nineteenth century, home and family came to be idealized as sacred places. But, as Reynolds says in words that bear on Carroll, "The image of the child was simultaneously sentimental, escapist, the repository of all that was good and pure, and also the domain of covert desires and fantasies."

When Lewis Carroll began to write, there had been increasing public and private concern for more than a century about the condition of children. In the nineteenth century the state, mostly at the behest of the evangelical movement, had begun to take official notice and make some early efforts at regulating child labor, protecting child welfare, and mandating at least some schooling. Attitudes were changing. In the eighteenth century new interest and sentiment for children and new idealizations of family affection had appeared. Romanticization of childhood, though it had been slow to develop, went together with middle-class romanticization of women and motherhood. Historically, capitalism, the expansion of the empire, and the coming of industrialism had made a great many people richer and brought for the growing numbers of the privileged classes more leisure for their children and a longer period of childhood before beginning the work of the world. This led to growing emphasis on education and also on the aestheticizing of the child as people took pride in their progeny and wanted to show them off. The development of scientific method, rationalism, and new areas of knowledge challenged ideas of personal immortality and drove many to find hopes for a regenerative future in their children. Also, as time passed and the rudiments of modern medicine appeared, people saw greatly increased chances for infant survival; in many cases, that perception appears to have opened the floodgates for wholehearted sentimental feelings for children, who would no longer so often discourage their parents' by dying young.

Meanwhile, of course, print technology developed and literacy was spreading. It was necessary to teach children to read and to give them material suited to the education adults deemed proper for them, but some also thought that giving them things they might want to read for pleasure would develop their literacy skills. Later, in the Victorian era, came another technology highly significant in the history of the child as subject: the development of the camera, which made the personal fetishizing of the past and widespread preservation of familial images possible. Photography, as Lewis Carroll, like the later billion-dollar camera industrialists, knew so well, went hand in hand with the contemplation of children and childhood; the hugely popular loving, aesthetic contemplation of children in culture seems to be a relatively recent phenomenon—and one in which Carroll has surely had a hand.

In the nineteenth century, boarding schools proliferated, as did various other professional educational practices, and, Aries suggests, these were important in creating a separate sphere for children and a distinct juvenile literature because they increased the distance between the worlds of adult and child and cast doubt upon the suitability of shared reading material. Literature from the eighteenth century on, of course, was a growing enterprise that included a developing market for books aimed at children; and by the time Lewis Carroll started inventing stories for the Liddell girls, commercial as well as heuristic and religious motives were coming to figure more and more in the making of children's fiction. Publishers of children's books, then, though they were mainly interested in getting across theology, moral ideology, and pragmatic lessons that would make people more industrious, had nevertheless printed *The Arabian Nights' Entertainments* for children (1791), collections of Mother Goose tales or nursery rhymes (1744, 1780, 1810, 1842), fairy tales (1729, 1768, 1849), and, in the mid-nineteenth century, a number of boys' adventure stories relating to school, exploration, colonialism, and travel (e.g., Frederick Marryat's *Masterman Ready* [1841] and Thomas Hughes's *Tom Brown's Schooldays* [1856]). Such reading, among other things, inculcated a sense of wonder and a penchant for fantasy, nonsense, pleasure, adventure, and vicarious power. (Fiction for girls, as it slowly developed and differentiated itself in the nineteenth century, tended to stress their domestic and Christian duties and their chances of demonstrating the moral responsibility and moral superiority of their gender, and it allowed much less scope for fantastic adventures.) But before *Alice*, children's books, whether by Rousseau-influenced, neo-Enlightenment humanists like Thomas Day (*The History of Sandford and Merton* [1783]) and Maria Edgeworth (*Early Lessons* [1801]) or by God-fearing Calvinists like Hannah More and Mary Martha Sherwood (*The Fairchild Family* [1818–1847]), were under the restraining thumb of the moralists.

Moral controversy swirled about the developments of children's literature and fantasy modes. Historically, fairy tales seem to have been connected with the mythology of superstitions and magical cults—in other words, with outlawed religions. At first, fairy tales were condemned for lacking ethical purpose and religious seriousness, but then more flexible educators and guardians of orthodoxy found they could be expropriated and used to inculcate correct behavior in much the same way as traditional Christian dream visions had been used. By the time Carroll wrote the Alice books, nearly all children's stories pushed religion and ethics, and even fantasy was serving disciplinary ends. (Later in his life, in *Sylvie and Bruno* and *Sylvie and Bruno Continued* [1889 and 1893], Carroll—perhaps I should say Dodgson—would use it for the same ends, and spoil his genius.) *Wonderland* and *Through the Looking-Glass*, which he calls a "fairy-tale," mock this sort of thing and claim fantasy, miracle, dream techniques, and the child for comedy.

Fantasy as a literary genre was developed in the Victorian era most notably by Carroll, Thomas Hood, George MacDonald, Charles Kingsley, and William Morris. It grew out of the Romantic movement—specifically from such late eighteenth-century historical phenomena as intensified interest in childhood, the collecting and setting down of folk tales and verse, the revival of interest in beast fables, and the burgeoning market for children's stories. It seemed important to some that children's powers of fancy be developed—especially since the Romantics prized imagination—and that people should find ways to stay in touch with the playfulness of childhood. The cult of the exotic, the cultivation of the self's visionary powers, the fascination with irrational states of mind (including dream states), the felt need for new or rejuvenated myths and symbols to meet the breakdown of religious orthodoxy and the crises of faith, all helped to produce fantasy fiction and make it respectable. Victorian fantasy proclaims the continuing need for a renaissance of wonder (Carroll, at the end of *Wonderland*, calls the waking world "dull reality"—an astounding assertion if you think about it).

Before the Christian era, the classical male mind-set of the Greeks and Romans—in which children, being immature, were considered less human, less complex, and therefore less interesting than adults—had seemed relatively uncurious about the child as such. Christian dogma would change that indifference, though it would take a long time and involve much historical contention. Robert Pattison has shown how deeply a divided early Christian heritage has colored thoughts about children. On the one hand there was Augustine's expounding of the orthodox doctrine of Original Sin and the damnation of human offspring without Christian salvation, baptism, and intervention into the corrupt, selfish nature of children. On the other side, preparing the way to see the child as a religious symbol, were the scriptural "massacre of the innocents," the advent and representation of Christ as a miraculous babe, the words of Jesus, "Suffer little children . . . to come unto me for of such is the kingdom of heaven," and the influential Pelagian heresy arguing for a primary innocence in the child. Pattison says that Augustine, in his *Confessions*, brought confessional autobiography and Original Sin into the world together, and if this is so, he pioneered the psychological novel: "Augustine's doctrine laid the foundation for the child as literary image. He had connected childhood [including his own] and sin, made the infant an adult of sorts, and surrounded him with a fallen nature, which existed in that condition because of man's fallen will." That doctrine, which makes salvation of the child a precarious matter of the utmost religious urgency, became especially influential in the Reformation and helped lead, in the age of growing literacy, to the severely moralistic, often Calvinistic religious tracts, manuals, education literature, and monitory children's stories that proliferated especially in the first half of the nineteenth century and that were popular at least until World War I. More generally it has fostered the influential notion that the child's fate is crucial but the child's moral nature is, by itself, lost, or at least dangerously weak and in need of vigilant adult protection from the world's wickedness and its own innate propensities to do wrong.

In the social and intellectual upheaval of the last half of the eighteenth century, Jean-Jacques Rousseau, one of the most influential theorists of childhood, countered such ideas in *Emile* (1762), his treatise on proper education, and in his own famous *Confessions* (1781): A Pelagian, he sees the child as naturally good and ideology about Original Sin as pernicious, but he does support the Augustinian idea of childhood's importance. Education is vital—that is, education which leads the maturing human being to preserve in itself the goodness of the natural child and harmonize the excellence of nature with culture. The natural child, for Rousseau, is conceived as innocent of the contradictions and conflicts that disrupt a harmonious relationship with the world. Jacqueline Rose observes that for him sexuality—as culture had distorted it—and social inequality "were realities that the child could be used to circumvent" or remedy. His idea, which he expresses both theoretically and autobiographically, is that, as Rose puts it, "it is sexuality which most totally sabotages the child's correct use of language and its exact [proper, accurate] knowledge of the world."

Rousseau himself was deeply influenced by John Locke, whose rejection of innate ideas, stress on a blank-slate image of the child, and belief in empirical experience as the determiner of the child's being and the adult's fate have been of great moment in shaping the ways people imagine and educate children. Locke put forth the idea of the child's proper education through direct encounter with the real world in which the problematic nature of language and its imperfections did not figure. According to Rose, for many to this day who follow these philosophers, the child is set up as an uncontaminated, "pure point of origin in relation to language, sexuality, and the state." Thus, Carroll's comic focus in the Alice books on the problematics of language for children and adults alike (e.g., puns, the involuntary nature of language, its subjectivity, Humpty Dumpty's assertion that words mean whatever he wants them to, "the wood of no names") is one of his fiction's most original and important features. Rose notes that "literature for children first became an independent commercial venture in England in the mid-to late-eighteenth century, . . . when conceptualisation of childhood was dominated by . . . Locke and Rousseau," and one could say the same thing about the novel in general, whose advent as the dominant popular genre parallels the advent of the child as a popular subject of representation. For both these philosophers, however, as for the strict Christian believers, moral, social, and practical education, however defined, is the proper end of literature—not pleasure or any intrinsic interest. But they opened up childhood as a state of innocence, purity, and blankness, an enticing space for the projection of faith, hope, love, and desire. One key comparison to make between the child as a concept developed in the last two centuries and fiction is to see them both as sites where people could project themselves, could identify, could read what they wanted, could have hope of vicarious life for their own desires.

Adapting Rousseau's mode of introspection, his feeling for the goodness and the intensity of early life, and his sense of childhood's determining power, William Wordsworth gave nineteenth-century Britain its romantic image of the child: the child as "seer blessed," "father of the man," the "best philosopher," "trailing clouds of glory," a "darling of the pigmy size," the seed from which the poet's mind grows, and a little intimater of immortality. His visionary contemporary Blake also made children central, showing how the child could be featured as both religious symbol—image of innocence and holiness—and social symbol of a fallen, exploitive world (victim of industrial cruelty, poverty, disease, neglect). Following Augustine, Rousseau, and Wordsworth, the child becomes in fiction a figure leading to self-identity and self-knowledge, and following Blake, the child becomes a sacrificial social victim or an innocent little lamb of God, a natural stand-in for the mystical, holy Christ. "The purpose of the romantic image of the child," according to Peter Coveney, was "above all to establish a relation between childhood and adult consciousness," but it was also to serve, in a world increasingly skeptical of supernaturalism, as an image of faith. The Romantics, Coveney asserts, "were interested in growth and continuity, in tracing the organic development of the human consciousness, and also, in lowering psychic barriers between adult and child." In writing of the child, their interests were adult. Nevertheless, in finding certain superiorities in a child's being over an adult's, they opened the way to the cult of the child. And the fear of losing touch with childhood, so pronounced in Wordsworth, is one of the chief generating motives not only for Carroll's work but for much of the distinguished fiction of the last two centuries. The novel needed the subjectivity of the child in order to become a powerful mode of psychological exploration and suggestiveness.

It was Charles Dickens, more than any other writer, who made children crucial subjects of faith, erotics, and moral concern, and nothing he did as a novelist was more influential than choosing to represent children. To know and tell the stories of life, it was necessary to understand and imagine what happened to children—to Oliver Twist, Smike, Little Nell, Tiny Tim, Paul and Florence Dombey, David Copperfield, Esther Summerson, Jo the Sweep, Amy Dorrit, Pip, and the rest of his fiction's boys' and girls' chorus. Traumatized by experiences from his own childhood, he stamped the romantic image of the child upon the imagination of millions and taught people to feel and identify with abused, exploited children and with the psychology of early life. Two passages, one from *David Copperfield* (1850) and the other from the preface to *The Old Curiosity Shop* (1841), get at his vision of the child as a mirroring image of self-pity, imaginative vindication, and regenerative possibilities:

When my thoughts go back, now, to that slow agony of my youth, I wonder how much of the histories I invented for such people hangs like a mist of fancy over well-remembered facts! When I tread the old ground, I do not wonder that I seem to see and pity, going on before me, an innocent romantic boy, making his imaginative world out of such strange experiences and sordid things! (*David Copperfield*)

I had it always in my fancy to surround the lonely figure of the child [Little Nell] with grotesque and wild . . . companions, and to gather about her innocent face and pure intentions, associates . . . strange and uncongenial. (*The Old Curiosity Shop*)

Of this mass impulse to regression that Dickens tapped, expressed, and helped to form, Carroll made his fiction.

Dickens regards the child as both a center of innocence (Nell, Oliver, Florence) and as the crux of developing personal and cultural history (David, Pip). For the light it brings to the concept and figure of the child as moral savior, the revealing custom of feminizing and infantilizing the essence of virtue, and to Alice, *The Old Curiosity Shop* is especially relevant. People devoured the novel and its pathetic child-heroine Nell not for its literary merit or for simple diversion—no character in Dickens has been more severely criticized or raucously mocked—but for the sake of faith: the girl-child is presented as something good to believe in, a narrated icon. The power of Little Nell is the power of religious feeling. As I have shown in *Critical Reconstructions* (1993), she represents quite literally an assumption of the traditional religious power of the Virgin Mary and holy Christian sacrifice into the female child. The aura, effects, and influence of the girl-child as moral guide and redeemer show up not only in the popular sentiment of the age but in the work of such intellectual sophisticates as George Eliot with her little golden-haired Eppie in *Silas Marner* (1861), John Ruskin in his quasi-devotional writings about feminine purity and the sanctity of girlhood, Henry James in *What Maisie Knew*, and, naturally, Lewis Carroll. The child had traditionally been seen as the proper object for religious and educational instruction. Now, in *The Old Curiosity Shop*, she becomes popularly the subject, embodiment, and *teacher* of worthy and sacred values.

That "she," of course, matters: it is almost always a girl, not a boy, who stands for pure goodness (the sacrificial—and feminized—Paul

Dombey is the exception). Why? The boy in Dickens usually represents the struggling self; the girl is often the morally and spiritually perfect other, the ideal projection. The still-prevalent sexist Manicheism about children (see, for example, bad-boy Bart, good-girl Lisa in the animated hit TV show "The Simpsons"), famously summed up in the nursery rhymes "snips and snails and puppy dogs' tails; that's what little boys are made of," and "sugar and spice and everything nice; that's what little girls are made of," feeds *The Old Curiosity Shop* and Lewis Carroll too (for example, note, in *Wonderland*, chapter 6, the quick change from boy baby to pig and the lines, "Speak roughly to your little boy, / And beat him when he sneezes: / He only does it to annoy, / Because he knows it teases"). The rise of the novel, children's fiction, and the number of juvenile characters in literature did not create separate gender spheres, nor gender-specific social functions for males and females, but literature was a primary means of reflecting, transmitting, defining, and redefining important social images of gender. A boy in the time of the novel as dominant literary mode was supposed to grow up, find his manhood, become somebody, follow a vocation, make a living, achieve status, accomplish something, and, all in all, see and live life as a worldly process and profession of *becoming*, rather than just *being*. A girl was supposed to find love, which meant that she had to be, or at least *seem*, lovable and loving. A middle-or upper-class girl's fate, according to cultural ideology, would likely depend on being "attractive" and learning to please, serve, and ameliorate—to preserve and regenerate domestic harmonies and uphold spiritual and moral values. For the richer classes, the girl-child could be encouraged to behave modestly and nicely, dressed up and made pretty—aestheticized, idealized, and fetishized as a repository of civilized value. She was appreciated not for what she would become, but for the way she might appear to be: a breathing treasure, a pearl of great price, a lovely looking glass that would give people back pretty reflections in which they could find evidence of their noblest desires and their best selves. The expansion of wealth and of the middle classes meant that more and more families could aspire to have their own little Velazquez princesses.

In her cozy setting at the beginning of *Looking-Glass*, Alice typically represents the Victorian and modern wish to see the time of childhood as a bastion against the dangers and troubles of the grown-up world—a paradise at the beginning instead of the end of life. The Victorian girl-child could be posed and imagined as living proof that in a hard and changing world it was possible to maintain and nurture sweetness and natural purity. She made an ideal raison d'être for life's struggle and also symbolized an escape from it. Childhood became a kind of wildlife refuge for the fancy and wonder that might seem impractical in adult life. It is true that the privileged Victorians tended to make ornaments of their little girls (and often their little boys too), but to see what that means, we must understand that "ornament" had the radiant force behind it that the "ornament" of stained glass would have had at Chartres: visible evidence for faith.

Like Dickens, the great female novelists of mid-nineteenth-century England—Charlotte Brontë, Emily Brontë, and George Eliot—also render the subjectivity of the child, using it to explore the inseparable questions of gender and self-identity. They adopted and also rejected gendered stereotypes of children. *Jane Eyre* represents in Helen Burns (closely modeled on Charlotte's older sister, Maria, cruelly mistreated at school and dead at eleven) the same sort of martyrdom of an idealized, sacrificial girl-child as Dickens shows in Nell and Florence Dombey. Brontë, however, effectively dismisses Helen as a model for living girls to emulate, makes *Jane* the hero and first-person subject, and focuses on *her* childhood victimization and her progress from an abused girl to an assertive, vocationally competent, erotic, and successful adult. This governess manqué and creative genius doesn't sentimentalize children in her fiction, doesn't even seem particularly to like them, but renders childhood experience and trauma as crucial in forming character and fate.

Her sister Emily, in the early chapters of *Wuthering Heights* (1848), imagines in the childhoods of Cathy and Heathcliff the turbulent passion, polymorphous perversity, and determining effects of infantile sexuality that psychoanalysts, shocking propriety, would later claim to be natural—even normal. Like her sister, she breaks through conventional decorum, ridicules notions about little angels-in-the-house, and gets at the violence of childhood and its spawning of obsessions. But she does represent the second Cathy as the moral redeemer of the novel's world. George Eliot makes the girl-child of *Silas Marner* the figure that upholds civilization and leads to moral progress, but in *The Mill on the Floss* (1860) she addresses the issue of the gendered, sugar-and-spice stereotypes and the damage they can cause. Maggie Tulliver's long childhood is a depiction of how the girl is mother to the woman, but it is also a relentless narrative of steady, restrained, feminist anger and resentment about the horrors of abstracting girls and boys and making them conform to conventional, rigid gender roles.

As do the Alice books, the fiction of these novelists who seized upon childhood as a major subject revealingly renders tension between a passionate, sometimes sentimental will to identify with the child, together with a sense of the irrecoverability of childhood and alienation from the myth of the sanctified girl. The child who is seen as part and parent of the adult consciousness and point of view has already lost its being in the very act of that reflection. Edmond de Goncourt, using the documentary procedures of French realism and aiming exclusively at an adult audience, wrote the novel *Cherie* (1884), featuring a child protagonist, because he thought his role as novelist was to be "un historien des gens qui n'ont pas d'histoire": children before the novelists got at them, in other words, were people without history; but then, with the coming of novelistic retrospection, they tended to become part of the history of adults, rather than "people." The unself-conscious nature, special innocence, and uncurbed potential of the child are time-doomed, as Blake, singing of experience, knew. Moreover there is a serious psychological flaw in putting faith in the saintly child, because people, especially the introspective, remembering that they have been children, usually know somehow that—no matter how they want and try to deceive themselves—they were never pure, never angelic; an innocent child, in some dark recess of the psyche, is a falsehood and a moral reproach. Still, the Victorian writers of fiction, led by Dickens, moved people to identify with children, to take the child's part; and Carroll's subversion of the adult world—his identification of the self with a child rather than an adult—marks a revolution of sensibility and outlook.

Lewis Carroll actually loved and wanted to *be* the girl-child, the other, the not-self in a way that his distinguished older contemporaries in fiction did not. Dickens and George Eliot, writing of the child in *David Copperfield* and *The Mill on the Floss* respectively, seem to be working out the problem of *How did I come to be the person I am?* by answering imaginatively the question *What was my childhood like?* With Carroll, however, the questions seem to be about self-effacement and the suppression of the adult: How can I get away from a self-identity that seems ineffectual, irrelevant, bound for extinction, like the Dodgson Dodo in *Wonderland* or the autobiographical Gnat in *Looking-Glass?* How would it be possible not to be the person I am? How can I escape my sex? The answer: by sticking imaginatively close to the child

Alice. "No novelist," Harry Levin says of Carroll, "has identified more intimately with the point of view of his heroine." He moved beyond looking to the child for unworldly perfection, for a symbol of allegorical virtue, and for the analytic key to his own personality. In his Alice texts the child becomes the means to fantasy, to mental traveling, to play and comic liberation from the tyranny of adulthood with its pride, pretentiousness, and incessant moralizing.

Fantasy indicates the secularization of wonder, and Carroll, through the emergent child, is its prophet. Dreams for him sanction fantasy. Creating fantasy is, like dreaming, a way of internalizing miracles; but, of course, it is consciously done and historical. One reason he links dream vision and fantasy to childhood is that empirically, as psychology has since shown, the way people revisit their childhoods and the mental nurseries of their fantasy lives—and the way the child intrudes on the adult with its continuing presence—is often through dreams. Like dream work, fantasies, according to Freud and his followers, grow out of childhood experiences, words, and imaginings. They, too, are animated images of repressed hopes and stifled wishes set free.

Animation, the breath of life, motivates Carroll's comic dream and fantasy world: he animates fantastic images. Nursery rhymes, words, thoughts, poems, animals, chess pieces, and flowers all come alive, take visual shape, move and talk. As everything in a dream is part of the dreamer, so everything in wonderland and through the looking-glass is part of the fantasist's personality. Carroll animates new forms of life on every page. The cinematic movement of dreams in Carroll is the movement of animation. Tenniel's illustrations in the Alice books (Carroll's fussiness about them nearly drove the artist out of his mind) are as important to the text as those in any book I know. Repressed thought turns to visual images, and such images move and live in Carroll's fantasy of childhood. Try to think of Humpty Dumpty without benefit of the Carroll-Tenniel image and you can see the force of Carroll's animation. If you could combine his fantastic literary animation with his photographic interest, you would get "motion pictures"; and he is spiritual father, as sure as any technological innovator, to that revealing progeny of the twentieth century, animated cartoons. In these visions, whose main audience is supposedly children, horrendous falls, accidents, fights, murderous intentions, and carnivorous frenzies seem not only harmless but funny. Animation by definition excludes death, and these visual fantasies—classic examples of comic regression—present a world where infantile wishes predominate and mortality has no sway. It may be that one of greatest sources of pleasure in animation is that it seems to take us back to a time in childhood when we felt ourselves to be the center of life and made no distinction between the self and the other—when everything we knew was alive and personal, and we had no need to care about the alien. The animation of all, which we find in Carroll, the personalizing of objects, may express a craving to be all, to ingest all, and to eliminate boundaries—between people and things, between stories and life, between kinds of animal life, between differentiated physical drives and the different body parts signifying the oral, anal, and genital modes of sexuality, between mother and child.

In Carroll's hands fantasy becomes a comic mode to ponder and enjoy; it can purge contradictions and hard realities from the mind or at least turn them to play and jest. His comic fantasy depicts a world so outlandish that it never could be and therefore provides some relief from social pressures and moral responsibility; but his imagination very often gives us exactly the sort of silliness that goes on all the time in the real world. "We're all mad here," the Cheshire Cat insists; "Sentence first, verdict after," proclaims the King of Hearts; "I've believed as many as six impossible things before breakfast," says the White Queen to Alice, and "The rule is, jam tomorrow and jam yesterday—but never jam *to-day*": fantastic and funny lines, but also true to life.

The way to grow up and participate in experience in wonderland is to grow little, and the way to go forward in looking-glass land is to go backward—back to origins, early years, first principles, early pleasures, early fears, early desires—in order to see with fresh clarity what, through habit and personal and social repression, you have come to accept as the real and true and to find in a place of make-believe, in a world of fiction, that make-believe—fiction—*is* reality. The way to freedom and curious wonder is to recognize and comprehend the arbitrary, predetermined, and artificial structures of your life. The way to knowledge of culture and society is to explore your inner fantasy life. The way to honor intelligence is to know and laugh at its limitations. The way to celebrate creation is to play with its silly mysteries. The intention—conscious or not—that comes through in the Alice texts is, in effect, one meaning of humanity's comic capacity and literary capability: I will play with and make ridiculous fear, loneliness, smallness, ignorance, authority, chaos, nihilism, and death; I will transform, for a time, woe to joy.

Carroll offers a metaphorical, metonymical compendium of the obsessions and urgencies of the modern world of collective individualism, and the rhetoric of his fiction, persuading people that they can read and find reverberating significance in the child and her dream-life, makes him a major writer. The child, as psychology would show, just would not stay in a bracketed-off area, remote from serious adult life and history. Like the transmitters of myths, legends, sacred writings, and folklore, Lewis Carroll and such modern writers as Kafka and Beckett give people open-ended metaphors—word images that have the suggestive quality of their own dreams and eschew directly stated meanings. Carroll allows us to read our own stories, desires, fears, and to make fun of them. Through two very short and very funny books, Carroll shows us the frightful self-consciousness of modern times ("Who in the world am I? Ah, *that's* the great puzzle!"), the fantastic shapes of the inward journey (objects come alive; physical being becomes unstable; Alice never quite knows just where she is), the quest for innocence and withdrawal from a rude, jostling, intrusive society ("'No room! No room!'"; "At this the whole pack . . . came flying down upon her"). He conveys loneliness ("'Only it is so *very* lonely here!' Alice said . . . and, at the thought of her loneliness, two large tears came rolling down. . . . 'Oh, don't go on like that!' cried the poor Queen . . . : 'Consider what a great girl you are. Consider what a long way you've come today. Consider what o'clock it is. Consider anything, only don't cry!'"). He shows the frustration of intimacy ("She looked back, once or twice, half hoping that they would call after her: the last time she saw them, they were trying to put the Dormouse in the teapot.") and conveys the sense of living on the verge of hysteria ("His voice rose to a perfect scream"; "'I can't stand this any longer!'"). He gets at the feeling of existing in a dream or game whose form is constantly changing. He expresses a typical ambivalence toward authority, a rage for chaos (the witty and entertaining "mad tea-party" in *Wonderland* and *Looking-Glass's* wild "coronation" banquet) along with a desire to find and keep order and meaning without losing a sense of humor (the intricate chess-game structure of *Looking-Glass*). He imagines the relativity of being (sudden size changes in *Wonderland*), the problems of identity ("Who am I then? Tell me that first, and then, if I like being that person, I'll come up: if not, I'll stay down here till I'm somebody else"), and of split, diced personality (e.g., *Wonderland's* "This curious child was fond of pretending to be two people" and the Carrollian self-portraits in the Gnat, Humpty Dumpty, and the White Knight in *Looking-Glass*). He renders for us the fictional nature of reality as it is registered in the inevitably distorting mirrors of our perception ("Why, you're only a sort of thing in his dream!"). He shows us our necessarily equivocal fate as word-centered creatures who experience language both subjectively and objectively. (Alice's comment on the nonsense poem "The Jabberwocky," "Somehow it seems to fill my head with ideas— only I don't know exactly what they are!" describes his sense of language perfectly, provided that we stress "exactly" and keep in mind the bizarre, utilitarian richness of those "ideas.")

Carroll is important as a writer who makes fun of what Jacqueline Rose calls "the whole ethos of language as always reliable or true." As the child knows and shows, language is anything but a neutral, transparent medium that simply reflects an existing reality. Linguistic power creates a joyous surge of identity and also a knowledge of otherness, as Alice learns in *Looking-Glass* when she finds herself alienated from the faun once they pass out of the "wood of no names" and back into the realm of human language. Carroll stresses throughout both the delight and the farce of misunderstanding that are inherent in words and dialogue. The texts render what children feel about language as they struggle to master it: that it is slippery, confusing, hard, rule-ridden, and frustrating, but also creative, pleasurable, and full of play. Language proves our social being and determines our fate, but, as a child learns, it is also the means for defining and expressing our desires, our individuality, our confusions, our subjective freedom, and our bonds. We live by linguistic fictions. In Carroll, many of the characters act out verbal structures, for instance, Humpty Dumpty, the Tweedles, and even Alice, whose movements in *Looking-Glass* exactly conform to the predictive words of the Red Queen at the beginning.

Carroll helped to lead in making language a great subject for thought and comedy and literature, but for him it is nothing to be idealized. It can never be a precise communication system because it is inseparable from its users. From the first in *Through the Looking-Glass*, Carroll tells us that Alice moves in a dream world composed of words that exist independently of personal will. When the White King exclaims of his pencil, "It writes all manner of things that I don't intend," he is talking about the unmanageable nature of language, and he previews its role in the book, and in twentieth-century intellectual history. And when "Jabberwocky" appears to Alice, we know that we are in a fictional world of sense, absurdity, and wordplay all at once, like a child trying to fathom language.

'Twas brillig, and the slithy toves
Did gyre and gimble in the wabe:
All mimsy were the borogoves,
And the mome raths outgrabe.

The verse foreshadows the whole book. The extreme tensions in the poem—between the unconventional use of language (invented vocabulary) and the conventional (normal syntax, grammar, rhythm, and rhyme), between referential significance and self-contained nonsense—define and energize Carroll. "Jabberwocky" puts the focus on the very *fact* of language itself, whose very existence—as children see and feel—is just as marvelous, just as fantastic, as any of the meanings it conveys.

Even as the figure of the child in the last two centuries has called forth interpretation, assertions of authority, and projection, so has Carroll's fiction. Lewis Carroll's work is particularly susceptible to the regressive tendencies of critics and writers who find in it images, words, meanings, and emotions that liberate, clarify, articulate, and give play to their own ideas, longings, and obsessions. Alice defines her readers as their dreams and childhoods do.

Read what has been written about Carroll and you find a wonderland of interpretation. It has been argued, for example, that Queen Victoria wrote the Alice books, that Alice is a phallus, that she is an imperialist, that she is an existential heroine, a killjoy, a sex-tease, or a symbol for what every human being should try to be like in the face of an outrageous universe; it has been claimed that her pool of tears represents the amniotic fluid, that the Caucus race parodies Darwin, that it sports with Victorian theories about the Caucasian race, that the Alice books may contain a secret history of the Oxford movement, that they allegorize Jewish history, that the "Pig and Pepper" chapter is a description of toilet training, that the White Queen stands for John Henry Newman and the Tweedles for Bishop Berkeley; that these tales are dangerous for children, that they are literally nonsense and do not refer to the real world; that Carroll was a latent homosexual, an atheist, a schizophrenic, a pedophile, a faithful Christian, a fine man. Some of this criticism is brilliant, some is lunatic, some is both by turns, some is hilarious, much of it is fascinating and insightful, nearly all of it is entertaining, and most of it is offered with the dogmatic surety of Humpty Dumpty, who says, "I can explain all the poems that ever were invented—and a good many that haven't been invented just yet." My purpose here is not to patronize other commentators but to show that something in the nature of the writing itself—some vacuum of indeterminacy—sucks in a wide variety of reaction and engagement. Children are subject to authority, but Carroll puts authority in doubt and questions it. The Alice fiction deals with the crisis of authority in modern life, and readers are drawn to solve it. People project their wishes and beliefs and concerns onto these fictions as they lay them upon children. Like the parables of the Bible, like dreams, like depicted fantasies, Carroll stimulates a hermeneutics of subjective ingenuity and a multiplicity of views. These malleable texts resist closure of meaning; they remain open-ended and dialogical.

Of course, I am giving my own interpretation of Carroll, and obviously it stresses his use of a problematic dream-child in an antiauthoritarian, carnivalesque literary comedy and centers on the way that child opens up the play of language, the unconscious mind, and floating, contradictory desires. The world he creates is both referential and nonreferential, both like the world we live in and a different, fantasy world of nonsense. When the Mock Turtle tells Alice that in school he learned "Reeling and Writhing" and the different branches of arithmetic, "Ambition, Distraction, Uglification, and Derision," the text offers both an example of nonsensical, creative wordplay that breaks free of "reality" and a satire on what real children actually do learn in real schools. Through the child, Carroll gets across his sense of a fantastic, alternative world of being, a sense of rebellious knowledge of actuality, a sense of humor (i.e., putting life in a play-frame), and a sense of the importance and imprecision of language. The comic fantasy of chapters like "The Mock Turtle's Story," "A Mad Tea-Party," and "Tweedledum and Tweedledee" have the improvisation, the inventive drive, the Dionysian upswing of the best twentieth-century comic ensembles, such as the Marx Brothers and Monty Python's Flying Circus. This whirling dialogue of whimsy, wisecracks, puns, nonsense talk, and verse moves to overthrow the drabness of routine and predictability.

In "The Emperor's New Clothes," a child exposes the ruler's nakedness by cutting through lies and illusions to give people the perspective they need for seeing their own gullibility and the ruses of power. That's how Carroll works. He makes the child his protagonist, her dreams his narrative; and he pretends that children are his only audience so that he can rid himself and others of inhibitions and repressions. Through the

child, he strips away both personal and social conventions and prejudices (e.g., you must not think or talk disrespectfully of parents, royalty, or "sacred" things; life should make sense; we all speak the same language; personalities are coherent; poetry is elevated; a well-brought-up
little girl does not harbor murderous thoughts; the world of childhood
is simple); he holds them up to ridicule and sets loose possibilities for
imagining the unthinkable (e.g., original words and fantastic physical
beings, the pleasure of the obliteration of others, the animation of the
inanimate, the stupidity of mothers and fathers; the joys of madness).
In the reversed looking-glass of his art, Carroll uses Alice to show up
the silly childishness—in its pejorative sense—and the arbitrary limits
of the so-called adult world. He proves in the Alice books that even in
the most outwardly conventional and time-serving of adults there may
be a wild and brave child struggling to get out and mock the withering
realities that govern life. Such is the hope of this comedy of regression.

Carroll's way is to begin and frame his text with mawkish, sentimental descriptions of childhood. It is as if, in his introductory poems
and in the opening monologue of *Looking-Glass* featuring the girl-
child, he is trying to represent the most morally unobjectionable being
that he and his fellow Victorians could conceive of in order to smother
his psychic censor in a well of treacle. Watch a child alone at play with
its toys and dolls and after a while you may begin to hear and see these
figures taking on roles that dramatize aspects of the child's life. Different tones and voices arise, words come out that reveal thoughts and
visions neither you nor the child knew it possessed. Carroll's fiction is
like that. In *Looking-Glass*, after Alice babbles, "I wonder if the snow
loves the trees and fields that it kisses them so . . . and . . . says 'go to
sleep, darlings'" and Dr. Dodgson appears to lull himself to sleep, Mr.
Carroll suddenly bursts through the looking-glass and through the
double wall of superego and sentimentality: he quotes Alice saying,
"Nurse! Do let's pretend that I'm a hungry hyaena, and you're a bone!"
That explodes the pious little-girl image and releases manic, unpredictable energy into the text and a typically resonant complexity into
the character of Alice.

To show how significant the approach and the sudden move in portraying Alice here are and what is at stake with respect to both the fuller
rendering of children's psychology in fiction and the relationship of
Carroll and his heroine, I quote a passage from *What Maisie Knew*.
Henry James is imagining *his* girl-child—about the same age as Alice—

alone, confused in her feelings, and at odds with an awful adult world of arbitrary power and mysterious sexuality, and he begins to relate the subject of the child to fictional projections and transference: "The stiff dolls on the dusky shelves began to move their arms and legs; old forms and phases began to have a sense that frightened her. She had a new feeling, the feeling of danger; on which a new remedy rose to meet it, the idea of an inner self or, in other words, of concealment." The developing child in the history of the novel means an inner life and psychological conflict—the psychodrama of alienation, conscious and unconscious repressions, contradictory motives, and imaginative identifications. Edmund Wilson says that "the creatures that [Alice] meets the whole dream, *are* Alice's personality and her waking life," but, of course, they are Carroll's personality and life too.

Not surprisingly, the character and function of Alice have become bones of critical contention. I have put her by and large in a favorable light, but some in the late twentieth century, focusing on problems of race, class, and gender, judge her more negatively. She has been seen as a quintessential figure of Victorian ethnocentrism for her continual attempts to bring her own standards, customs, mores, and manners to bear on the beings and circumstances she meets in her wonderlands. Carroll does sometimes betray his own upper-class biases, and he does render Alice's privileged-class assurance, especially in her occasional bouts of snobbery and patronization in the early chapters of *Wonderland*. She can also be seen as an example of essentialist gender stereotyping that makes the Victorian girl into a litany of virtues (and Alice surely displays most of humanity's good qualities). Such views have merit and interest, but they miss the dream psychology and the plurality of being Carroll imagines for her and also, I think, the main historical point: this writer moved one of history's most notoriously marginalized groups of beings, children, to the center of existence.

He could identify with the otherness of childhood, and its diversity; and in narrating the progress of Alice on her journeys he could reveal, as Freud would do in his famous essay "A Child is Being Beaten," one of the momentous secrets of childhood—and life: the imaginative processes of transposed and projected violence. Of course, Carroll is, among other things, a colonialist of childhood. He imposes upon a child and children his own dream of childhood, his sense and definition of a child. But this dream is fluid, and he is also a liberator of childhood. The Alice tales end with the question of whose dream this is, and here

Carroll touches upon the imperialism of desire. The question suggests a sense of fiction's mediation between author, audience, and cultural context, and, fittingly in a book about a child, it opens up the subject of custody.

Henry James, writing in the preface to his prophetic novel *What Maisie Knew* about a child-custody battle, captures the feeling and the general conception that Carroll has for Alice and the child's role: ". . . the case being with Maisie to the end that she treats her friends to the rich little spectacle of objects embalmed in her wonder. She wonders, in other words, to the end." James goes on to discuss his own faith in the imaginary girl:

> Truly, I reflect, if the theme had had no other beauty it would still have had this rare and distinguished one of its so expressing the variety of the child's values. She is not only the extraordinary "ironic centre" I have already noted; she has the wonderful importance of shedding a light far beyond any reach of her comprehension. . . . I lose myself, truly, in appreciation of my theme on noting what she does by her "freshness" for appearances in themselves vulgar and empty enough. They become, as she deals with them, the stuff of . . . art; she has simply to wonder, as I say, about them, and they begin to have meanings, aspects, solidities, connexions—connexions with the "universal!"—that they could scarce have hoped for.

No words better indicate the far-ranging significance that Lewis Carroll's Alice and the emergence of wonder and respect for the child that she represents have had for modern fiction, history, and culture.

Robert M. Polhemus

Selected Bibliography

Aries, Philippe. *Centuries of Childhood.* Trans. Robert Baldrick. New York: Alfred A. Knopf, 1962.

Coveney, Peter. *The Image of Childhood.* Rev. ed. Baltimore: Penguin, 1967. Originally published as *Poor Monkey.* London, 1957.

Gray, Donald J., ed. *Lewis Carroll, Alice in Wonderland.* 2d ed. New York and London: Norton, 1992.

Darton, Harvey. *Children's Books in England: Five Centuries of Social Life.* 3d ed. Revised by Brian Alderson. Cambridge: Cambridge University Press, 1982.

Gardner, Martin, ed. *The Annotated Alice*. New York: Random House, 1990.

Hudson, Derek. *Lewis Carroll: An Illustrated Biography*. New York: Clarkson N. Potter, 1977.

Kincaid, James. *Child-Loving*. New York: Routledge, 1992.

Lennon, Florence Becker. *The Life of Lewis Carroll*. New York: Collier, 1962.

Pattison, Robert. *The Child Figure in English Literature*. Athens: University of Georgia Press, 1978.

Rackin, Donald. *Alice's Adventures in Wonderland and Through the Looking-Glass: Nonsense, Sense, and Meaning*. New York: Twayne, 1991.

Reynolds, Kimberley. *Girls Only?: Gender and Popular Children's Fiction in Britain, 1880–1910*. Philadelphia: Temple University Press, 1990.

Rose, Jacqueline. *The Case of Peter Pan, or The Impossibility of Children's Fiction*. London: Macmillan, 1984.

The Avoidance of Naturalism: Gissing, Moore, Grand, Bennett, and Others

B Y the end of 1895, Emily Morse Symonds had published, as George Paston, three mildly advanced novels which, if not outstandingly successful, had at least been reviewed favorably by Arnold Bennett, then literary editor of *Woman*. They met in January 1896 and immediately recognized each other as fellow professionals, exchanging "tips" and talking "shop" for hours on end. On December 23, 1896, he took her out to dinner and the theater. "Her book is going rather well, & she is half through her next (a tale of literary life) which she says will be her best."

The tale of literary life, *A Writer of Books* (1898) is indeed her best. Like the novel Bennett himself had completed in May 1896, *A Man from the North*, it is about a writer from the provinces arriving in London to make a name. Cosima Chudleigh, left to fend for herself when her father dies, wants to "get away from her present surroundings, begin a new existence, and lay the foundations of a career." The career, not marriage, will provide the new existence. Writing, in her view, involves research. She decides that she must witness an operation, as the "French realists" had done, in case any of her characters ends up on the operating table. She takes it for granted that the novelist should be a "scientific observer."

These assumptions reveal the continuing influence, in England in the 1890s, of French naturalism; that is, of the view that writers should not flinch from unpoetic subject matter and that they should treat whatever they write about with "scientific" exactitude and objectivity.

The assumptions, however, are Cosima Chudleigh's, not Symonds's. Cosima is eventually persuaded, by the man she loves, a critic of force and integrity, to abandon them and to develop instead the "personal flavour" that has always characterized English fiction.

French naturalism, resolutely unpoetic, exhaustively researched, was something English writers of any ambition measured themselves against. They could not ignore it. But unlike their American counterparts (Stephen Crane, Frank Norris, Theodore Dreiser) they did not, in the end, assimilate it. The story of that resistance, that avoidance, is, to some extent, the story of English fiction in the final decades of the nineteenth century.

In 1896, George Gissing reported that there was "no public for translated novels—except those of Zola." In England, Zola *was* naturalism. He had articulated the creed of objectivity in *Le roman expérimental* (1880). "We must operate with characters, passions, human and social data as the chemist and physicist work on inert bodies, as the physiologist works on living bodies." No subject matter was beyond him. He had "done" peasant life in *La terre*, the stock exchange in *L'Argent*, Bohemia in *L'Oeuvre*, heavy industry in *Germinal*, and so on. But it wasn't, finally, the methodology or the choice of subject matter that made Zola such a force. English writers have always found method, when proclaimed as such, fairly resistible. It was, rather, the view of existence written into, and encoded by, his narratives.

For the naturalist fiction that began to appear in France in the 1870s added a new pattern to the small stock of curves describing the shape lives take (or adapted an old one from Classical and Racinian tragedy): the plot of decline, of physical and moral exhaustion. Most nineteenth-century novels divided existence into a long rise stretching to the age of sixty, measured in social and moral terms, and a short (physical) decline. Naturalist fiction envisaged instead a rapid physical rise to the moment of reproduction in the twenties, then a long redundancy, a morbidity accelerated by the emergence of some innate physical and moral "flaw." Its narratives are shaped not by a process of moral and social adjustment but by the reiteration of genetic inheritance.

Zola's Rougon-Macquart novels (1871–1893) described the effects of heredity and environment on the members of a single family, tracing the passage of a genetic "flaw" down the legitimate line of the Rougons and the illegitimate line of the Macquarts. Henry James pointed out that the development of each section of the long chronicle was "*physio-logically* determined by previous combinations." In each generation, the inherited flaw topples an individual life into a downward spiral of disease, alcoholism, poverty, or madness. This downward spiral is the way in which naturalist novels, in Europe and America, spoke about individual and social development.

Physiological narratives fed an anxiety about social decline whose formal expression was the theory of "degeneration" that began to emerge, in the natural and medical sciences, during the second half of the nineteenth century. The age of "evolution," "progress," and "reform" developed an urgent interest in regression, atavism, and decline. Indeed, it was Darwin's theory of evolution by natural selection that, in Britain at any rate, provided a context. At first, the theory had seemed to suggest that evolution was inevitably progressive, slowly but surely transforming the simple into the complex, the primitive into the civilized. Increasingly, however, Darwin and his followers came to realize that evolution was not synonymous with progress. Environment operated in various ways to different effects, and the most adaptive inherited characteristics were not necessarily the "highest" or most "civilized" ones. Gradually, attention shifted to examples of regression. In *Degeneration: A Chapter in Darwinism* (1880), Darwin's disciple Edwin Ray Lankester pointed out that parasites, which necessarily postdate their host organisms, are nonetheless "*simpler* and *lower* in structure" than those organisms.

The implications for social theory seemed distressingly clear. Lankester himself talked of the decline of the "white races" into parasitism. Paradigms of regression created by the natural and medical sciences began to play an important part in the analysis of social change. Degeneration was seen as a self-reproducing pathological process: not the effect, but the cause of crime, poverty, disease (and experimental literature). Max Nordau's *Degeneration*, a lurid and influential treatise published in translation in 1895, proclaimed the end of civilization in biblical cadence. But his conviction that the European races were degenerating derived from medical science rather than from the Bible. Physicians, he said, had recognized in the behavior of the European elites a "confluence" of "degeneracy" and "hysteria." All the new tendencies in the arts could safely be regarded as "manifestations" of this confluence.

In 1910, Henry Adams pointed out that Europeans had become obsessed with "supposed social decrepitude," particularly in the cities.

"A great newspaper opens the discussion of a social reform by the axiom that 'there are unmistakeable signs of deterioration in the race.' The County Council of London publishes a yearly volume of elaborate statistics, only to prove, according to the London *Times*, that 'the great city of today,' of which Berlin is the most significant type, 'exhibits a constantly diminishing vitality.'" Evidence of diminishing vitality included not only the poor standard of health among army recruits, but also the falling birth rate, the decline of the rural population and the prevalence of alcoholism and nervous exhaustion. More or less any social "problem" could be attributed to it.

Naturalism's decline plot was the perfect match to the social narrative articulated by degeneration theory; too perfect a match, in fact, since it was itself regarded, by Nordau and others, as a symptom of degeneracy. British writers, then, were not simply competing with a new literary technique, a method and a choice of subject matter. Rather, they had to decide whether to exploit or moderate or deny an anxiety about social decline that was already a habit of mind among their readers.

Henry James, in Paris in 1884, told W. D. Howells that he respected Zola, despite his pessimism and his "handling of unclean things." It was the handling of unclean things that at first dictated the British response to Zola. Henry Vizetelly began to issue translations in the same year; he was tried for publishing obscene books in 1889, convicted, and sent to prison for three months. By that time, however, the other feature noted by James—the pessimism inscribed in naturalism's decline plots—had made its mark on the English novel.

Like Zola, George Gissing researched his subjects assiduously. His diary shows him going over "a die-sinker's place" in Clerkenwell, in preparation for *The Nether World* (1889), and getting some "useful ideas." Gissing was proud that Charles Booth had used his novels as a source of information about working-class life, and he returned the compliment by studying *Life and Labour of the People in London* (1892–1903) in the British Museum; he was both flattered and irritated to discover that the Reverend Arthur Osborne Jay's *Social Problem* (1893) had incorporated, without acknowledgment, a long passage from *The Nether World*. Like Zola, he tended to "do" a subject per novel: the literary marketplace in *New Grub Street* (1891), suburban life in *In the Year of Jubilee* (1894), and so on.

The subject he returned to most frequently during the 1880s, in *Workers in the Dawn* (1880), *The Unclassed* (1884), *Demos* (1886),

Thyrza (1887), and *The Nether World*, was urban deprivation. Gissing said that he wanted to capture "the very spirit of London working-class life," and he came closer to doing so than any other Victorian novelist except Margaret Harkness. Gissing's slums exist for us in their carefully differentiated sounds and smells, in the desires and anxieties that only an implacably earnest investigator would have troubled to disentangle from the received view of universal brutality and ignorance. He could always, and always meant to, tell the difference.

And yet the story told by these novels does not, in the end, differ all that much from the stories told by Zola and by degeneration theory. In *Workers in the Dawn* Arthur Golding, a would-be friend of the people, marries and attempts to reform a young prostitute, Carrie Mitchell. But his grammar lessons have no effect on a woman who is genetically programmed for a life of whoring and brandy drinking. When she leaves him for another man, he sadly pictures to himself the downward spiral of her future career: "how her passions, now set free from every restraint, would scourge her on from degradation to degradation, till she met her end in some abyss of unspeakable horror." Gissing's slums contain a residue of degenerates who so far exceed the norms of social classification that they can only be regarded as members of a different species. Clem Peckover, in *The Nether World*, is compared to a "savage," and to a "rank, evilly-fostered growth." "Civilisation could bring no charge against this young woman; it and she had no common criterion."

Gissing's methodical approach, and his degeneration plots, align him with Zola. But he never eradicated the personal flavor that was thought to distinguish English from French fiction. Carrie Mitchell was based on Nell Harrison, a young prostitute he himself had married and tried unsuccessfully to reform. Osmond Waymark, the hero of *The Unclassed*, recapitulates Gissing's own development from political radicalism through disillusionment to an increasingly bitter denunciation of universal vulgarity. Social commentary, in these novels, ebbs and flows according to the state of the author's investment in elite culture. Furthermore, "French" methods had always to contend with "English" moralism, with an inherited faith in the power of imaginative sympathy. The conclusion of *The Nether World*—a man and woman resolving to bring what comfort they can to those less resourceful than themselves—echoes the conclusions of Dickens's *Little Dorrit* (1857), Eliot's *Middlemarch* (1872), and, more distantly, Milton's *Paradise Lost*. Characteristically, however, Gissing does not allow his man and woman the comfort of each other; they go their own solitary ways.

In the early 1880s George Moore, the eldest son of a wealthy Liberal M.P. and stable owner, having failed to establish himself as an artist in Paris, took up naturalism. His first novel, *A Modern Lover* (1883), the story of a young artist, was, according to the *Spectator*, a frank homage to "Zola and his odious school." The initial situation of *A Mummer's Wife* (1885) reproduces, with equal frankness, the initial situation of Zola's *Thérèse Raquin* (1867), which Moore had thought of translating: sickly husband, neurotic wife, interfering mother-in-law, assertive lover, all penned in desolate rooms above a shop. Kate Ede elopes with an actor, Dick Lennox, and achieves some success on the stage. Now divorced and pregnant, she marries Lennox. But she has taken to drink, and her baby dies. Moore places her exactly on the curve of the degeneration plot. "She had met Dick in her seven-and-twentieth year, when the sap of her slowly-developing nature was rising to its highest point." After the climax of elopement, the taste of freedom, it's downhill all the way. The dissolute life of the traveling players wears her out. Abandoned by Lennox, she declines into alcoholism and prostitution, eventually dying a loathsome death. *A Mummer's Wife* is the nearest thing to French naturalism in English literature. It was duly banned by the circulating libraries.

In March 1887, Beatrice Potter shared a railway carriage with the historian and Liberal M.P. Sir George Trevelyan. "I begged him to go into a smoking carriage . . . for had I not in the pocket of my sealskin not only a volume of Zola, but my case of cigarettes! neither of which could I enjoy in his distinguished presence." The novel was *Au bonheur des dames*, in which Zola "did" department stores. Sir George eventually settled down with *The Princess Casamassima* (1887), James's stab at an unpoetic subject matter. Potter, who became, in partnership with Sidney Webb, the leading sociologist of her day, remained enthusiastic about Zola—as, indeed, did several writers with more consistently polemical intentions than Gissing or Moore.

Potter's cousin, Margaret Harkness (as John Law) published Zolaesque novels—*A City Girl* (1887), *Out of Work* (1888), *In Darkest London* (1889), *A Manchester Shirtmaker* (1890)—that earned the respect of Friedrich Engels. The influence of *Germinal* on mining novels like W. E. Tirebuck's *Miss Grace of All Souls'* (1895) or Joseph Keating's *Son of Judith* (1900) is evident enough. But working-class, or socialist, fiction never achieved the same prominence as two other genres shaped by polemical intent: slum fiction and New Woman fiction.

Slum fiction, pioneered in the 1880s by Gissing and Walter Besant, and developed in the 1890s by Rudyard Kipling, Arthur Morrison, Somerset Maugham and others, incorporated the decline plot wholesale but shifted the emphasis from heredity to environment. A number of stories—Gissing's *Demos*, Kipling's "The Record of Badalia Herodsfoot" (1890), Morrison's "Lizerunt" (1894), Maugham's *Liza of Lambeth* (1897)—concern women whose lives follow a similar pattern: courtship, and a glimpse of freedom, then marriage, marital violence, abandonment, and finally prostitution or death. These heroines are not degenerate. They are spirited women who have the vitality beaten out of them by an inhospitable environment and a series of brutal men. The contrast between female virtue and institutionalized violence allows for "English" pathos as well as "French" realism.

However, the remorseless downward spiral of the plot still carries the message that there is no escape, no possibility of transformation. In Morrison's *Child of the Jago* (1896), heredity combines with environment to corrupt the young hero. Morrison wanted to distinguish between a degenerate working class and one that is organically sound but damaged by its environment. The novel's reforming priest, Father Sturt, is based on the same Reverend Jay who had lifted a passage from *The Nether World*; Morrison later endorsed Jay's plan to establish penal settlements in isolated parts of the country where working-class degenerates could be confined for life and prevented from reproducing their "type."

Heredity was also a crucial concern in the New Woman novels that began to appear toward the end of the 1880s. Julia Frankau (writing as Frank Danby) out-Zolaed Zola in *A Babe in Bohemia* (1889). Lucilla Lewesham, a young girl brought up by her decadent father and his shrieking mistress, escapes moral contamination but not hereditary epilepsy. The book was savagely denounced in the press, and banned by the circulating libraries. Degeneration theory served Frankau's sensationalism admirably. Meeting her in 1911, Arnold Bennett found her "very chic"—and thoroughly ashamed of her novels. But even those New Woman novelists who had no reason to feel ashamed of their novels—George Egerton (i.e., Mary Chavelita Dunne), Emma Frances Brooke, Mona Caird, Ménie Muriel Dowie—had much to say about (male) degeneracy.

"Doctors-spiritual must face the horrors of the dissecting-room," Sarah Grand declared in the preface to *Ideala* (1888). Her heroine decides that the future of the race is a question of morality and health. "Perhaps I should . . . say a question of health and morality, since the latter is so dependent on the former." Both heroine and author deploy the biomedical categories of late nineteenth-century social psychology. Ideala believes that the British Empire, like the Roman, has decayed internally, and that the solution is not reform, but a program of physical and moral regeneration.

Grand's third novel, *The Heavenly Twins* (1894), was hugely successful and established her as one of the leading writers of the day. It has been claimed as a precursor of modernism, and does experiment with tone and point of view. But the experiments are largely confined to one of its three loosely connected case studies, the story of the "heavenly twins" Angelica and Diavolo. The other case studies can best be understood as versions of the naturalist degeneration plot. Edith Beale marries Sir Mosley Menteith, a syphilitic degenerate, gives birth to a child famously likened to a "speckled toad," and dies. The deformed child was a popular motif in naturalist fiction, incarnating degeneracy. Evadne Frayling marries one of Menteith's fellow officers. More worldly-wise than Edith, she recognizes his unsuitability at once, and declines to consummate the marriage. She remains unfulfilled, and cannot find a way to redeem her husband, whose habits are "the outcome of his nature."

Book 6 of *The Heavenly Twins* is narrated by Doctor Galbraith, a specialist in nervous disorders who examines and befriends Evadne. If Edith's story is a case study in degeneracy, Evadne's is a case study in that other modern disease, "hysteria." After her husband's death, Galbraith marries Evadne. But the outcome of his efforts to restore her to health remains uncertain. Paying a call in the neighborhood, Evadne encounters the "speckled toad" once again, and suffers a relapse. Degeneracy and hysteria may yet have the last word.

As, indeed, they threaten to do in the conservative polemic of contemporary popular fiction. Stevenson's Mr. Hyde gives "an impression of deformity without any namable malformation." In his concluding statment of the case, Dr. Jekyll speaks of the "bestial avidity" with which his monstrous double would relish the infliction of torture. Professor Moriarty, in Conan Doyle's Sherlock Holmes stories, has "hereditary tendencies of the most diabolical kind," a criminal "strain" in the blood.

According to Van Helsing, in Bram Stoker's *Dracula* (1897), the Count himself is a degenerate. "Lombroso and Nordau would so classify him." Dracula's invasion of England dramatizes anxieties that were the stock in trade of theorists like Nordau and Cesare Lombroso. He aims to pollute the entire English race, beginning with his natural allies, the parasites, outcasts, and madmen. Mary Shelley's Frankenstein had produced a monster by perverting Science and violating Nature; these fin-de-siècle monsters are the product of Nature, and can only be mastered by a combination of Science, faith, and bourgeois shrewdness.

Vizatelly's imprisonment seems to have taken the sting out of the moral objections to Zola. Thereafter, open hostility receded. In 1893, Zola was invited to London by the Institute of Journalists, and, much to Gissing's amusement, received by the Lord Mayor. Gissing noted that no prominent author had played any part in the welcome and that a testimonial dinner arranged by the Authors' Club was "in the hands of a lot of new and young men."

The young writer most likely to further the cause of naturalism in England was Hubert Crackanthorpe, who the year before had conducted a long and respectful interview with Zola, which he published in his experimental magazine, the *Albermarle*. He certainly made full use of the decline plot. In "A Conflict of Egoisms," in *Wreckage* (1893), degeneracy destroys a New Woman, the neglected wife of a novelist suffering from "brain exhaustion." Professionally mature but emotionally immature, she cannot cope with her husband's indifference, and retaliates by destroying the manuscript of his latest novel. He decides on suicide, but exhaustion gets him first; he drops dead as he is about to leap off a bridge. Crackanthorpe seems to have taken his own narratives a little too seriously. He drowned himself in the Seine in 1896.

Crackanthorpe, however, was an isolated enthusiast. Naturalism's more seasoned champions had long since ceased to champion. During the 1890s, Gissing concentrated on stories of intellectual life and middle-class rebellion. In 1891, Moore accused Zola of selling out. He now sailed under the flag not of Zola, but of Zola's erstwhile disciple, Huysmans—whose *A rebours* (1884) was a dandyish pastiche of naturalism—and of Wagner. From *Confessions of a Young Man* (1888) through to *Evelyn Innes* (1898) and *Sister Teresa* (1901), Moore's major concern was the pathology of faith and creativity.

And yet there is *Esther Waters* (1894), a peculiar hybrid of the "French" and "English" traditions. Esther is, in the French manner, the victim of forces beyond her control; but she has been equipped, in the English manner, with moral resilience. Moore's mixed feelings led him to anatomize working-class life by means of a decline plot, and yet at the same time to draw back from the apocalyptic determinism usually inscribed in such plots. William Latch's seduction and abandonment of Esther would not have been out of place in a novel by Mrs. Gaskell or George Eliot. When she subsequently returns, pregnant and impoverished, to her equally impoverished family and immediately quarrels with her drunken, brutal stepfather, it seems as though she has entered a different kind of novel altogether. Mr. Saunders, however, is, by a cunning displacement, merely her *step*father: the bloodlines through which contamination invariably flows in naturalist fiction have been cut.

In this novel, identities are made rather than inherited. Esther creates an identity by managing a business and bringing up her child. For every degenerate like Mr. Saunders, there is someone who has identified, and been identified by, a talent or an occupation. Lanky, narrow-chested Arthur Barfield, the son of Esther's first employer, comes into his own whenever he mounts a horse. In naturalist novels, people don't "come into" a new identity. In English novels, they do, but not, on the whole, by mounting a horse. Moore avoided both "French" determinism and the "English" conviction that the only paths to self-discovery are introspection and marriage.

In chapter 44, Esther, now a widow and once again destitute, returns to Woodview, the home of the Barfield family, which has itself been destroyed by gambling. The opening paragraph repeats word for word the opening paragraph of the first chapter, which describes Esther's arrival at the local station. In chapter 1, the first sentence of the second paragraph—"An oblong box painted reddish brown and tied with a rough rope lay on the seat beside her"—is full of anticipation; the person it refers to has not yet been identified, and we read on eagerly, seeking clues. In chapter 44, the sentence has been expanded. "An oblong box painted reddish brown lay on the seat beside a woman of seven or eight and thirty, stout and strongly built, short arms and hard-worked hands, dressed in dingy black skirt and a threadbare jacket too thin for the dampness of a November day." Now there is nothing left to anticipate: the older Esther is the sum of the experiences that have shaped her appearance. The narrative loop confirms the decline plot, returning her, roughened and diminished, to her starting point. But she is not defeated. Her decline cannot be attributed to the emergence of some moral or physical flaw. We are closer to the formal recapitulations of Henry James and James Joyce than to Zola's apocalypse.

Another writer who modified an earlier adherence to naturalism was Sarah Grand. *The Beth Book* (1897) reworks the Evadne story from *The Heavenly Twins*. Like Evadne, Beth Caldwell, cramped by lack of education and experience, marries a man, Dr. Dan Maclure, who turns out to be disreputable and corrupt. He has an affair with one of his patients, whom Beth regards as a "parasite." Both her husband and her most ardent admirer, a neurotic writer, are well embarked on decline: "The one was earning atrophy for himself, the other fatty degeneration."

But Beth, like Esther Waters, refuses to decline along with her menfolk. Nurtured by a community of intellectual women that includes the heroines of Grand's earlier novels, she discovers a talent for writing and public speaking. Grand cleverly alters the proportions of the decline plot by devoting more than half the novel to Beth's childhood and youth. The talents and pleasures Beth develops are grounded in those early experiences. The book's conclusion, however, a mystical reunion with a man she has fallen in love with, somewhat qualifies the carefully accumulated emphasis on independence, female community, and ordinariness.

Gissing, Moore, and Grand all seem half-persuaded by Zola's determinism, by the plausibility of genetic explanations. But in the end they refuse apocalypse; partly, I think, because apocalypse seemed like a foreign invention. Galbraith reappears to counsel Beth, and to offer some gruff literary advice. Her husband is predictably fond of French novels. Galbraith, like Quentin Mallory, thinks that French novels have destroyed the French nation. Grand supports him, in a footnote, with an account of the cowardly behavior of Frenchmen during a recent emergency. The revaluation of Englishness that was in progress at the time undoubtedly reinforced the determination of British writers to steer clear of naturalism. Gissing relied heavily on it in his most popular novel, the semiautobiographical *Private Papers of Henry Ryecroft* (1903). As for Moore, well, he learned to despise the English during the Boer War, and took up Irishness instead.

Gissing, Moore, and Grand fell back on English moralism. Other writers tried to sidestep the downward spiral of the decline plot without committing themselves to the counterbalance of moral absolutes. Oscar Wilde's *Picture of Dorian Gray* (1891), for example, makes dazzling play with the idea of degeneracy. Constantly collapsing the metaphoric into the literal, the metaphysical into the organic, it nonetheless refuses to come clean, to own up, to disavow appearances. For Wilde himself, however, the metaphor became distressingly literal. Max Nordau had classified him as a decadent and an egomaniac, claiming that his "personal eccentricities" were the "pathological aberration of a racial instinct." Wilde, at the end of his tether, complied with the metaphor. Submitting a plea for release from prison, he confessed to sexual madness and endorsed Nordau's classification of him as a degenerate.

Thomas Hardy came closer than Wilde, in his fiction if not in his life, to acknowledging that sin is a disease. In *Tess of the D'Urbervilles* (1891), Angel Clare characterizes Tess as the product of a degenerate family. He invokes against her the degeneration plot that the novel harbors all along, but which it has so far resisted through its emphasis on her singularity. Hardy can scarcely be said to endorse Angel's point of view. But one might argue that Angel's degeneration plot takes the novel over, carrying Tess through "relapse" to murder and beyond.

One review of *Jude the Obscure* (1896), headed "Hardy the Degenerate," claimed that the author had depicted a humanity "largely compounded of hoggishness and hysteria." Jude does seem cloudily aware of degeneration theory. Depressed by interminable quarrels with Arabella, he decides that the best way to express his "degraded position" is to get drunk. "Drinking was the regular, stereotyped resource of the despairing worthless." Jude will do what he thinks the hero of a naturalist novel would do. Appropriately enough, it is he who conveys the medical verdict on Father Time's massacre. Jude merely *quotes* degeneration theory. But he quotes it so convincingly that one cannot altogether avoid the suspicion that Hardy might have seen some truth in it. It would have suited his temperament. And *Jude the Obscure* does sometimes seem like a novel written by Angel Clare.

H. G. Wells took a more explicit interest in social and biological theory than Hardy or Wilde. *The Time Machine* (1895) explores the implications of the second law of thermodynamics, formulated in the 1850s, which envisages the gradual heat death of the universe. But its most gripping passages concern social rather than physical deterioration. When the time traveler reaches the year 802,701, he emerges into the middle of a crisis in the long-drawn-out feud between two degenerate species, the Eloi and the Morlocks (hysteria and hoggishness, again).

Wells told Huxley that he had tried to represent "degeneration follow-ing security." *The Time Machine* is a vision of social apocalypse framed within a vision of global entropy, and the rhetoric of apocalypse over-shadows the rhetoric of entropy.

Later writers distanced themselves less equivocally. In *The Secret Agent* (1907), it is the loutish anarchist Ossipon who characterizes Ste-vie and Winnie as degenerates. On the latter occasion, Conrad speaks contemptuously of Ossipon invoking Lombroso "as an Italian peasant recommends himself to his favourite saint." In Joyce's *Ulysses* (1922), it is Mr. Deasy, the bullying Anglo-Irish headmaster, who bends Stephen Dedalus's ear with a diatribe against the degeneracy of the Jews: "They are the signs of a nation's decay. Wherever they gather they eat up the nation's vital strength . . . Old England is dying." By that time, degen-eration theory no doubt seemed less compelling, if only through overuse.

Another response that requires some discussion, because it had pro-found consequences for the twentieth-century novel, was present in the philosophy of the New Woman writers in the early 1890s but not devel-oped into a new narrative form until somewhat later. Grant Allen, whose *Woman Who Did* (1895) was probably the most notorious of all the New Woman novels, preached a New Hedonism, a revision of sex-ual relationships that would eliminate "race degradation" and promote "race preservation." Women had either to separate themselves from men or to mate with those men who were still, despite everything, racially sound. Thus the heroine of Sarah Grand's "Eugenia" (1894), who is herself racially sound, rejects Lord Brinkhampton, a "neuropath" and degenerate, and proposes to the aptly named Saxon Wake. Wake is a "yeoman," but makes up racially for what he lacks socially. This will be the race-preserving, the eugenic—the Eugeniac—marriage. Such racially sound marriages should preferably be complemented, as Allen's language suggests and as the conclusion to *The Beth Book* makes clear, by a mystical union.

Mystical-eugenic unions were all very well, but they did presuppose an abundant supply of healthy, strong-willed young men and women. Narratives promoting race preservation had to balance the dream of a New Hedonism against the reality, as it was perceived, of social decrepi-tude. Whereas the New Woman novelists tended to pair different types of degeneracy—the hoggish and the hysterical, Morlock and Eloi—their successors tended to pair a couple seeking regeneration with a couple or couples doomed to degeneracy. This new pairing emerges tentatively in Gissing's *Odd Women* (1893) and *In the Year of Jubilee* (1894), then more strongly in Forster and Lawrence.

Forster's *Longest Journey* (1907) incorporates two separate plots, which just happen to coincide at a place called suburbia. In the first, sensitive Rickie Elliot's marriage to suburban Agnes Pembroke merely confirms the fatality of his physical disablement (hereditary lameness). Together, like a couple in a New Woman novel, they produce a horribly crippled daughter who soon dies. Thereafter Rickie "deteriorates." Rickie's race will die out, but his half brother, Stephen Wonham, the product of a more eugenic union with a staunch yeoman farmer, may yet flourish. Distanced genetically from Rickie, as Esther Waters is from her stepfather, Stephen belongs to a different bloodline, a different plot. The genetic distance is also a moral and emotional distance. Agnes Pembroke, who has already drained the life out of Rickie, regards Stephen as a monster. "He was illicit, abnormal, worse than a man diseased." Forster defends Stephen's abnormality against suburban convention, because he believes that it alone will preserve the race.

In Lawrence's *Women in Love* (1920), the degeneration plot and the regeneration plot seem about to fuse, as Ursula is paired momentarily with Gudrun, Birkin with Crich. But in the end they diverge as emphatically as the bloodlines, the histories, of Rickie Elliot and Stephen Wonham. Degeneration theory circumscribes the "barren tragedy" of Gerald's life. It surfaces in chapter 2, when the wedding party adjourns to Shortlands, and the talk turns to questions of race and nationality. Birkin has agreed with Gerald that "race is the essential element in nationality," and is caught "thinking about race or national death" when called upon to make a speech. Nobody else has mentioned race or national *death*. The thought disappears as Birkin rises to make his speech, but reappears in chapter 5. Birkin finds Gerald reading the *Daily Telegraph* at Nottingham Station. Gerald draws his attention to an essay arguing that "there must arise a man who will give new values to things, give us new truths, a new attitude to life, or else we shall be a crumbling nothingness in a few years, a country in ruin." Asked whether he thinks it's true, Birkin shrugs. His own analysis of national death, and his new gospel, are a good deal more radical than anything envisaged by the leader-writer of the *Daily Telegraph*, or indeed any other newspaper. But he cannot very well dispute the contention that the country is in ruin, and that a new attitude to life is required, since this is what he himself believes. Birkin's shrug is also the text's.

Gerald Crich will act out this analysis of race and national death. He is no degenerate. He does not suffer from some inherited flaw. But he is constantly placed, both as an individual and as the member of a class, by quotations from the discourse of race and national death. His great achievement has been to make the mines profitable, breaking with his father's mid-Victorian philosophy of paternalism and muddling-through, and promoting a new creed of organization and efficiency. One of the issues that separates father from son is the proper attitude toward the "whining, parasitic" poor. Thomas Crich feeds the suppli-cants; his wife and his son both want to turn them away. But the issue is framed in the son's terms rather than the father's, in the language of Lankester's Social Darwinism.

Gerald himself can be associated with early twentieth-century cam-paigns for "national efficiency": physical health; scientific and techno-logical training; military and naval preparedness; industrial moderniza-tion; a government of national unity. Gudrun imagines that she might inspire him to become the Napoleon or the Bismarck of modern Britain. "She would marry him, he would go into Parliament in the Conservative interest, he would clear up the great muddle of labour and industry." The application of business ethics and methods to public pol-icy was one of the causes promoted by the national efficiency move-ment. That would be Gerald's "new gospel," if he could only bring him-self to mean it.

That he cannot is due to his failure to form relationships. Gerald is not a degenerate destroyed by some inherited genetic flaw. He is a con-ditional degenerate—he often behaves *as if* he were drunk—who is corrupted by the degenerate environments he encounters. Degeneracy exists in the two bohemias—Halliday's and Loerke's—he inhabits briefly at the beginning and at the end of the novel. Halliday's circle is the kind that might easily have got itself denounced in Nordau's *Degen-eration*. Lawrence makes sure we get the point about Halliday: "His face was uplifted, degenerate, perhaps slightly disintegrate, and yet with a moving beauty of its own." While Birkin observes bohemia coolly, then passes on, Gerald lingers, intrigued, appalled, fascinated, drawn inexorably into moral, sexual, and physical conflict. He loses Minette to Halliday just as he will later lose Gudrun to Loerke.

Loerke, the "mud-child," the "very stuff of the underworld of life," is Lawrence's best shot at a degenerate. Extravagantly Jewish and homosexual, he fulfils to an almost parodic degree the requirements of stereotype. He is an evolutionary test case, a parasite, a creature developed at once beyond and below humanity, into pure destructiveness. Gudrun succumbs to Loerke; Gerald fights him and loses. Never himself a degenerate, Gerald, unlike Birkin, cannot create an alternative to degeneracy. His failure propels him, like Jude, into the final spiral of the degeneration plot. His desire for "finality" drives him on to a conclusion, but his "decay of strength" ensures that the conclusion will be death.

Gerald's story exemplifies the degeneration theory that glosses it so consistently. Rupert and Ursula's story, on the other hand, looks back to those tentative imaginings of mystical-eugenic union in Gissing and Grand, in George Egerton's "The Regeneration of Two" (1894), in Forster. Lawrence's parallel narratives are sometimes seen as part of a literary revolution, as distinctively modernist. But they might also be regarded as the solution, at once formal and ideological, to a problem first articulated thirty years before.

A passage in Arnold Bennett's journal for June 15, 1896, describes the aged male inmates of the Fulham Road workhouse. "Strange that the faces of most of them afford no vindication of the manner of their downfall to pauperdom! I looked in vain for general traces either of physical excess or of moral weakness." Well-read in French fiction, an admirer of novels like *A Mummer's Wife*, Bennett naturally looks for evidence of degeneracy in the undeserving poor. But he cannot find any. To his eyes, the faces reveal wear and tear, not monstrosity. Like his friend Emily Symonds, Bennett may have wondered whether he ought not to behave more like a naturalist. But temperament, and the relative eclipse of naturalism, dictated that his novels, beginning with *A Man from the North* (1898), should confine themselves to mundane wear and tear. Unlike Zola, or Gissing, or Moore, he did not attempt any "vindication" of biomedical theory.

By the end of the 1890s, the brief phase of the slum novel was effectively over. The East End of London was still a point of automatic reference in many novels, but the portrayal of working-class life became increasingly lighthearted. Symptomatic of the new mood was the instant success of William de Morgan's genial, old-fashioned romances. Dickens, not Zola, was the model. Addressing the Boz Club, William Pett Ridge claimed that Dickens had revealed the "romance" and the "cheerfulness" in the lives of "hard-up people." Some writers, he went on, described the poor as though they were "gibbering apes." But such "naturalism" was outmoded. "The reading public knows better; it knows that the Dickens view is the right view." Ridge, like Edwin Pugh and W. W. Jacobs, was proud to be considered a disciple of Dickens. His best-known working-class novel, *Mord Em'ly* (1898), is a sentimental, facetious tale about a slum girl whose vitality is nourished rather than impaired by London life.

At the same time, a new territory and a new class had become visible, as suburbia spread out from London and the major industrial centers and coastal resorts, boosted by railway expansion and the advent of the motorcar. Suburbia was as tribal as the slums, as tempting to the cultural anthropologist; more so, perhaps, since the new tribe was composed of avid novel-readers. The result was a flourishing genre of fiction which, taking its tone from Jerome's *Three Men in a Boat* (1889) and the Grossmiths' *Diary of a Nobody* (1892), celebrated or gently mocked suburban life-styles and values.

Critics of suburban life seized on its monotony. Ruskin put the objection pithily when he alluded to "those gloomy rows of formalised minuteness, alike without difference and without fellowship, as solitary as similar." Suburbia permitted neither difference nor community. It denied the vision fostered by Romanticism and embedded in nineteenth-century social theory, the vision of a society united by common human bonds but differentiated according to individual capacities and desires.

Suburban uniformity could be regarded as benevolent, according to the Dickens view, or petty and destructive, according to the Ruskin view. The real challenge was to see in the suburbs something other than uniformity. Bennett rose to the challenge—perhaps not in *A Man from the North*, which is written according to the Ruskin view, but certainly in *Clayhanger* (1910), *Hilda Lessways* (1911), and *The Card* (1911). There is nothing very startling about Bennett's point that suburbia exists in the eye of the beholder. But it is symptomatic of a new emphasis in English fiction that he should choose to write about suburbs rather than slums, and that he should discover in his chosen territory no more than the faintest trace of monstrosity.

Most unusually for a novelist, Bennett was interested in the way people remain in ignorance of themselves, and in the way such ignorance creates an identity. This interest required a new kind of plot. Many, if not most, plots—and certainly those favored by the great nineteenth-century English novelists—turn on moments of revelation, when the illusions nurtured by timidity, prejudice, or habit fall away, and a naked self confronts a naked world. These are the moments when identity is begun, renewed, or completed. French naturalism had added a different plot, in which the revelation is gradual, and of something already known but temporarily concealed: a moral or physical flaw, an organic "lesion." Both kinds of plot favor awareness. Illusions are there to be stripped away. There can be no self-discovery, no personal development, whether into enlightenment or into degeneracy, until they have been stripped away.

A curious episode in *The Old Wives' Tale* (1908) suggests that Bennett was never really very happy with either kind of plot. Grouchy, fallible, cautiously opportunistic, waveringly tyrannical Samuel Povey is summoned from his bed one night by his more expansive cousin, Daniel, and transferred, in effect, to another novel. Daniel begins by confessing that his wife is an alcoholic, and so tears to pieces in a moment "the veil of thirty years' weaving." Hinting at even darker horrors, he leads Samuel through his shop and into the house behind, where his son, one leg broken by a fall, and his wife, whom he has murdered in a fit of rage, lie sprawled. The "vile" Mrs. Povey isn't merely drunken, and dead—she is an emblem of degeneracy.

The experience transforms Samuel. He regards Daniel as a martyr, a man goaded beyond endurance. "Samuel, in his greying middle age, had inherited the eternal youth of the apostle." His new conviction makes him, for the first time in his life, a public figure. He launches a campaign to vindicate Daniel and secure his release. During the campaign, which fails, he contracts pneumonia and dies. His death provokes the narrator into a startling display of mawkishness.

Bennett finds himself caught between two traditions, French naturalism (Mrs. Povey's degeneracy) and English moralism (Samuel's transformation), neither of which suits him at all. The whole episode seems like a lengthy quotation from a second-rate novel by someone else. One moment only sounds like Bennett. On the night of the murder, halfway through an anguished debate with Samuel, Daniel meticulously empties the surplus of the corn he had used to throw at Samuel's bedroom window out of his jacket pocket into its receptacle. Bennett characterizes him, at this moment of crisis, through the part of his mind that doesn't yet realize what has happened. Crises are supposed to reveal, to set naked self against naked world. Bennett is more interested in the illusions that remain.

A new kind of plot was needed to demonstrate how such illusions—such nescience—might form a personality. Bennett's protagonists advance their hollowness into a world which, as they age, becomes ever more crowded, ever more impenetrable. They feel the changes in pressure within them, but the shell of their nescience never cracks, as it would in a "French" novel; nor is it ever filled up, with hard-earned wisdom, with love, as it would be in an "English" novel. The heroine of *Leonora* (1903), watching her husband die, realizes that she has been created not by love but by the "constant uninterrupted familiarity" of married life. It is an acknowledgment produced not by abrupt revelation but by illusions mutually adjusted over a long period of time.

The term Bennett found for lives not shaped by development or degeneration was "declension." A chapter in *Hilda Lessways* is entitled "Miss Gailey in Declension" and describes the deterioration of Hilda's dancing instructor. Declension involves a gradual loss of energy, will, presence, significance. But there is a gain to be had from the erosion of these qualities, which constantly demand that one live up to an ideal or self-image, or fashion oneself according to social convention. It is a gain of definiteness, of irreducible difference. I don't know whether Bennett had the grammatical sense of declension in mind. That sense is appropriate, because the declensions he portrays are not merely disablements, but variations in the form a person's life can take.

In the end, in Bennett's novels, loss and gain are hard to distinguish, as they are in many people's lives. Miss Gailey is a spinster, and his spinsters (Janet Orgreave, for example, in the Clayhanger series) remind us that an identity created by not willing, by not signifying, is at once, and inextricably, formation and deformation. Few people in Bennett's fiction escape declension. At the end of *Whom God Hath Joined* (1906), Laurence Ridware, who has just survived a punishing divorce, wonders whether he should propose to a much younger woman, Annunciata Fearns. But he simply doesn't have the energy. Edwin Clayhanger is motivated during his youth by a fierce hatred of Methodism. But by the time he is asked, in *These Twain* (1916), to serve as District Treasurer of the Additional Chapels Fund, he doesn't even have enough animosity left for a contemptuous refusal. His ambition goes the same way: "His life seemed to be a life of half-measures, a continual falling-short." Yet he is in his way fulfilled, even assertive.

Bennett regarded marriage as the test, and the fulfillment, of the identity that declension creates. Toward the end of *These Twain*, Hilda wants to move to the country, and she persists in her arguments even though she knows perfectly well that Edwin wants to stay in town. Edwin has to come to terms with the fact that his wife, in denying his clearly stated preference, is denying him.

If Hilda had not been unjust in the assertion of her own individuality, there could be no merit in yielding to her. To yield to a just claim was not meritorious, though to withstand it would be wicked. He was objecting to injustice as a child objects to rain on a holiday. Injustice was a tremendous actuality! It had to be faced and accepted. (He himself was unjust. At any rate he intellectually conceived that he must be unjust, though honestly he could remember no instance of injustice on his part.) To reconcile oneself to injustice was the master achievement.

To reconcile oneself to injustice is to acknowledge the irreducible difference of other people, an acknowledgment enforced not by revelation but by long familiarity. The passage brilliantly renders Edwin's habits of mind: the faint pomposity, the honesty that compels him *not* to confess to injustice and so claim the authenticity of sudden illumination. These habits are his difference from Hilda, and what she loves in him.

One final example will demonstrate the extent to which Bennett deviated from a degeneration plot, which was nonetheless very much in his mind. *The Old Wives' Tale* follows the destinies of the two Baines sisters: cautious, commonsensical Constance, who inherits her father's haberdashery store and marries the chief apprentice, Samuel Povey; and passionate, unsettled Sophia, who elopes to Paris with a commercial traveler, Gerald Scales. Bennett's treatment of sexual desire, which, traditionally, either reveals us to ourselves as we really are or destroys us, tested his faith in declension to the limit. Frank Harris expressed disappointment that there wasn't more of the "superb wild animal" about Sophia; Bennett thought him dismally sentimental.

Bennett undid the wild animal in Sophia by, so to speak, writing his declension plot *over* the degeneration plot of Zola's *Nana*, the story of the spectacular rise and fall of a courtesan. Sophia's Paris is Nana's Paris, Paris during the last celebrations before the calamity of 1870. The mob yelling "To Berlin! To Berlin!" while Nana dies horribly of smallpox is the mob Sophia encounters at the Place de la Concorde. Zola said that his novel described a pack of hounds after a bitch who is not even in heat. Sophia, the object of "inconvenient desires," walks unscathed amid the "frothing hounds" as though protected by a spell. Sophia, unlike Nana, does not sell herself to the men who pursue her. It is the courtesan Madame Foucault, resplendent when first encountered, but increasingly abject, and reduced finally to an "obscene wreck," who plays Nana's part. Heredity dooms Nana, the degenerate daughter of degenerate parents, but the Baines stock is sound.

Even so, desire has left its mark on that inheritance. One day Sophia, now the prosperous owner of the Pension Frensham, wakes up semi-paralyzed. Struggling to the foot of the bed, she examines herself in the wardrobe mirror and sees that the lower part of her face has been twisted out of shape. The doctor offers a swift diagnosis. "*Paralysie glosso-labiolaryngée* was the phrase he used." By the early 1890s, facial, and specifically glossolabial, paralysis had been recognized as one of the major symptoms of hysteria. Sophia realizes that the attack has been triggered by an encounter with a young man from Bursley, which destroys the barrier painstakingly erected between her two lives.

The second half of the nineteenth century has been described as the belle époque of hysteria, and Paris and Vienna, the classic fin-de-siècle capitals, as its native environment. In Paris, the master of ceremonies was Jean-Martin Charcot, who began to treat hysterics at the Salt-petrière in 1870. By observation, examination, and the use of hypnosis, he proved that their symptoms were genuine and genuinely disabling. Freud, who studied at the Saltpetrière from October 1885 to February 1886, credited Charcot with establishing the legitimacy of hysteria as a disorder. Charcot demonstrated that it afflicted men as well as women and was not simply related, as tradition had it, to the vagaries of the female reproductive system (the wandering womb). Even so, hysteria remained symbolically, if not medically, a female malady, and one associated with sexual disorders.

In an obituary written shortly after Charcot's death in 1893, Freud summed up his mentor's understanding of the etiology of hysteria: "Heredity was to be regarded as the sole cause." French psychiatrists, like their English counterparts, were wholehearted advocates of degeneration theory. Charcot's narratives of hysteria, with their genealogical trees full of interconnecting cases of alcoholism, epilepsy, criminality, and suicide, resemble the story line of Zola's Rougon-Macquart novels.

Freud argued, in a series of papers published in the 1890s and in *Studies on Hysteria* (1895), that Charcot and his followers had been "dazzled" by the apparently all-encompassing concept of heredity. In this, he added, they were responding to a pervasive belief in the degeneracy of Western societies. To reject heredity as a cause of mental illness, as Freud did, was to reject determinism; that is, a life story shaped by events not merely beyond the individual's control but beyond his or her experience.

Freud began to study cases of "acquired" rather than inherited hysteria, and to uncover a rather different story line. He decided that hysteria did not begin in the life of an ancestor, with an organic "lesion," but in the life of the patient, with a traumatic experience. During that experience, the patient was confronted with a feeling which she could not bring herself to acknowledge, and which she repressed, thus dividing her consciousness. This feeling, which could neither be acknowledged nor ignored, was then converted, after a period of latency, into hysterical symptoms.

Hysteria, then, began and ended within individual experience. Where women were concerned, Freud said, the "incompatible ideas" that produced trauma were likely to "arise chiefly on the soil of sexual experience or sensation." He gave two examples: a girl who blamed herself because, while nursing her sick father, she had thought about a young man; and a governess who had fallen in love with her employer. These two cases, written up in *Studies on Hysteria*, reveal the new story line: the origin in trauma, the latency period, the physical symptoms.

We might compare the first to the case of Sophia. Left alone in the house to watch her paralyzed father, Sophia spots Gerald and rushes down to speak to him. The encounter confirms her desire, her sexual awakening. When she goes back upstairs, she finds her father dead. Her body expresses the intensity of a guilt she can neither acknowledge nor ignore. "As she stood on the mat outside the bedroom door she tried to draw her mother and Constance and Mr. Povey by magnetic force out of the wakes into the house, and her muscles were contracted in this strange effort." Split between desire and remorse, she represses the latter and elopes with Gerald. But it is surely the remorse that returns, converted into facial paralysis. Sophia's hysteria begins in trauma and ends in physical symptoms. If Zola's narratives resemble Charcot's, then Bennett's resemble Freud's; and that is a measure of the lengths to which English fiction had gone, by the turn of the century, in its avoidance of naturalism.

David Trotter

Selected Bibliography

Baguley, David. *Naturalist Fiction*. Cambridge: Cambridge University Press, 1990.

Bjorhovde, Gerd. *Rebellious Structures: Women Writers and the Crisis of the Novel 1880–1900*. Oxford: Norwegian University Press, 1987.

Cave, Richard. *A Study of the Novels of George Moore*. Gerrards Cross: Colin Smythe, 1978.

Keating, Peter. *The Haunted Study: A Social History of the English Novel 1875–1914*. London: Secker and Warburg, 1989.

Klaus, H. Gustav, ed. *The Rise of Socialist Fiction 1880–1914*. Brighton: Harvester, 1987.

Pick, Daniel. *Faces of Degeneration*. Cambridge: Cambridge University Press, 1989.

Poole, Adrian. *Gissing in Context*. London: Macmillan, 1975.

Sutherland, John. *The Longman Companion to Victorian Fiction*. London: Longman, 1988.

Trotter, David. *The English Novel in History 1895–1920*. London: Routledge, 1993.

Rudyard Kipling to Salman Rushdie: Imperialism to Postcolonialism

IT is now more than half a century since Auden wrote that time had "pardoned Kipling and his views," pardoned him for "writing well," and yet each successive generation has felt itself the first to be able—finally—to come to terms with him. The New Critics, for example, seemed to believe that the end of the British Empire had made Kipling's "views" a dead issue. And in fact Indian independence did make it hard, at mid-century, to read the literature of imperialism with anything but a simplistic notion of progress in mind. The new day for which E. M. Forster's *A Passage to India* (1924) had longed had come to pass. The empire had been gotten rid of, and Kipling was therefore obsolete. If he were to be read at all, it would be for his "artistic merits" alone, though in practice that meant concentrating on what Edmund Wilson called "the Kipling that nobody read," the highly wrought late stories of English life, such as "The Gardener" or "The Wish House." Not coincidentally, these are in political terms among his least controversial tales. In contrast, the richly contextualized readings on which contemporary criticism relies allow for the engagement with politics that the New Criticism shunned, and so our attention has swung back toward the Indian fiction that established Kipling's fame. There the problem Kipling has always presented will always remain, even for those who believe that his early stories especially are more complex and ambivalent than his reputation as the Bard of Empire would make one expect. And yet it is precisely because of that problem—because the issues he raises have a renewed importance in a postcolonial world—that he now seems so central.

Kipling's work insists on the inseparability of imperial rule from military might, but he also reminds his readers, in his 1897 poem "Recessional," that trusting to "reeking tube and iron shard" alone will only ensure the British Empire's oblivion; that it is no substitute for the observance of some unspecified "Law." Written for Queen Victoria's Diamond Jubilee, the poem is quite rightly seen as his sternest warning against imperial excess. Yet those fears had been in his work from the start, most notably in his first great story, "The Man Who Would be King" (1888), a deceptively anxious parable of imperial conquest. Like most of Kipling's short fiction, the story carries an elaborate frame. One hot and stifling night, two former soldiers, Peachy Carnehan and Daniel Dravot, appear in the office of the unnamed narrator, a newspaperman, asking about a region called Kafiristan in the Hindu Kush. They have decided that "India isn't big enough for such as us." Administration has been so regularized that there is no longer any room for an initiative exercised on one's own behalf, and so "The country isn't half worked out . . . they that governs it won't let you touch it." They see Kafiristan as "A place where two strong men can Sar-a-whack"—an allusion to the private kingdom of Borneo's "White Rajah," James Brooke—a land they can seize for their own. The narrator obliges them with maps, surveys, the *Encyclopaedia Britannica*. But he warns that they'll be "cut into pieces" in the Afghan hills and that "no Englishman has been through" Kafiristan. That was a half-truth. An initial British foray into what is now called Nuristan had turned back after a few days in 1885, while the first ethnographic survey was done in 1889 and 1890; dates that effectively sandwich Kipling's tale. It was, however, known that the people were neither Hindus nor Muslims, and it was believed that, like many hill tribes, they claimed descent from Alexander the Great—in Carnehan's words, that "they think they're related to us English."

The story resumes two years later, on another baking night, when "what was left of a man" appears in the newspaper office, a "rag-wrapped, whining cripple" whom the narrator eventually recognizes as Peachy Carnehan. "Crowned kings we was," Peachy says, and tells his story, a cautionary tale of what happens when an empire is all that "Recessional" feared it might be. With twenty smuggled Martini rifles, the conquest of Kafiristan is easy. They pick out "twenty good men and shows them how to click off a rifle, and form fours, and advance in line," and are soon spoken of as gods, the sons of Alexander. But as a late-Victorian story of imperial conquest, "The Man Who Would be King" is also inevitably about the dynamics of the racial difference that underlies that conquest. The Kafiristanis, Peachy says, are "fair men . . . with yellow hair." And Dravot declares that "These men aren't niggers. They're English. . . . They're the lost tribes, or something like it, and they've grown to be English." Lost white tribes at the heart of the unknown figured heavily in the mythology of empire, for they marked the land as the white man's after all; in actual fact, the people of Kafiristan resemble those of North India. But in saying that the people have "grown" to be English, Dravot has in mind the way they take to military drill as much as their fair skin, thereby suggesting that "Englishness" may be an acquired characteristic, a matter of culture, not color.

That suggestion is underlined by one of their most "English" characteristics—the fact that they know the rudiments of Masonic ritual; what confirms Carnehan's and Dravot's new status as gods, in fact, is their superior mastery of the "Craft." Kipling himself had been initiated into a multiracial Lodge in Lahore, and Freemasonry stood for him as a prime example of the place he imagined in "The Ballad of East and West" where "two strong men stand face to face" in a way that cancels the difference between "East . . . West . . . Border . . . Breed . . . [and] Birth." Yet the Kafiristanis remain Asian, even if they are also Masons and Englishmen—"other," and yet not, in a way that begs the question of the basis of British rule. Does it depend on the superior discipline of British culture? But the story shows how culture can be acquired. On the color of their skin? Not in Kafiristan—which makes one think, whatever Kipling's intentions, that in India it might be. Or does it rest, perhaps, on those twenty Martini rifles?

But we cannot see Kafiristan in isolation from India. Kipling sets Carnehan and Dravot's eventual disaster against a frame tale of life in a stable British India, and yet their adventures in Kafiristan implicitly challenge that stability. If they are gods, one remembers that Indian servants in other stories call their masters "Heaven-born." In particular, Kafiristan serves as a trope for an issue Kipling could not squarely face—the Anglicization of India, T. B. Macaulay's plan to create, through education, "a class . . . Indian in blood and color, but English in opinions, in morals, and in intellect." Kipling's belief in both an essential India and an essential England made him—like most servants of the Raj—contemptuous

of such cultural hybrids. But "The Man Who Would be King" nevertheless suggests that a subject people might someday learn to use the master's tools against him—"form fours"—as indeed the Indian National
Congress would do with English liberalism and legal procedure.

The crisis for Carnehan and Dravot comes when their subjects realize they are indeed men, not gods. Dravot decides that he wants a wife.
But the woman he is offered bites his cheek, and the blood proves that
the two men are mortal. Dravot is killed outright; Carnehan is first crucified and then taken down so he can limp home and tell the story. Sexual desire across racial lines always ends unhappily in Kipling. For that
desire blurs the barrier between the races that the Raj insisted on maintaining: the juxtaposition of dark skin and light underlines the difference between them, while suggesting either that difference doesn't matter or that it is, indeed, a positive attraction. But there is a more complicated reason for the disaster. Kipling implies that the two men—and
Dravot especially—have broken "the Law." In the story that term refers
specifically to Masonic ritual; Peachy worries that they don't have the
authority to conduct the ceremonies they use to cement their power. Yet
the concept of "the Law" is crucial to Kipling's work as a whole. It figures in *The Jungle Books*, in *Kim*, and most famously in the fear
expressed in "Recessional" that, "drunk with sight of power," the English might become as one with the "lesser breeds without the Law"—
without a coherent code of conduct to which the self and its desires
remain firmly subordinate. In acting on his sexual desire Dravot breaks
the "Contrack" he and Carnehan have signed: "You and me will not,
while this matter is being settled, look at . . . any woman black, white
or brown, so as to get mixed up . . . harmful." But of course they have
broken another sort of Law as well.

What "redeems" the robbery of empire, says Conrad's Marlow in
Heart of Darkness (1902), is "the idea only"; another name, perhaps, for
"the Law." But Kipling's freebooters are without an "idea" to justify
their conquest; they have no goal beyond their own personal power and
wealth. "This business is our Fifty-Seven," Carnehan says when their
own mortality is discovered. It is an allusion to the Indian Army's revolt
in 1857, a warning of what the British might once again face if they for-
got the Law. And that parallel makes us ask if there is, in fact, any difference between the Raj and what these two men have done; makes us
ask if the "Law" is ever any more than what Marlow calls a "sentimental pretence." Perhaps we can hear it too as a warning about the temp-

tations of an African empire. In 1885 the Berlin Conference had divided the continent among the European powers. Leopold of Belgium was given the Congo as his private estate.

"We all came out from under Gogol's 'Overcoat,'" Dostoevsky said of the Russian writers of his generation. Much the same can be said of Kipling's importance for the literature of empire. He was not the first British fiction writer to deal with imperialism, or with India, and his work owes a great deal in particular to the tradition of the adventure novel, which for English writers has always had an imperial subtext. But before Kipling imperialism per se had largely been the province of the historian, not the novelist. None of his predecessors had placed either its administration, its ideology, or its subject peoples so explicitly at the center of their work. And all the vast literature of colonialism that followed, even or especially by those who wrote in reaction to him, is to be found somewhere on the Grand Trunk Road he built with the books from *Plain Tales from the Hills* (1885) to *Kim* (1901)—not only the work of major English successors like Forster or Paul Scott, or the Malaysian stories of a lesser figure like Somerset Maugham, but the Indian novel in English as well. What else is Salman Rushdie's catalog of the subcontinent's marvels in *Midnight's Children* (1981):

From Kerala, a boy who had the ability of stepping into mirrors and re-emerging through any reflective surface in the land . . . from Kashmir . . . a blue-eyed child of whose original sex I was never certain, since by immersing herself in water he (or she) could alter it as she (or he) pleased . . . at Budge-Budge outside Calcutta a sharp-tongued girl whose words already had the power of inflicting physical wounds . . . a boy who could eat metal and a girl whose fingers were so green that she could grow prize aubergines in the Thar desert . . .

What else but a fantastically stepped-up revision of Kim's entry into that great highway of Indian life?

. . . new people and new sights at every stride—castes he knew and castes that were altogether out of his experience . . . a troop of long-haired, strong-scented Sansis with baskets of lizards and other unclean food on their backs . . . an Akali, a wild-eyed, wild-haired Sikh devotee. . . . A little later a marriage procession would stride into the Grand Trunk with music and shoutings, and a smell of marigold and jasmine stronger even than the reek of the dust . . . [a] moneylender . . . native soldiers on leave, rejoicing to be rid of their breeches and puttees . . . [a] seller of Ganges water.

This chapter will chart what Sara Suleri has called "the rhetoric of English India" as it develops in the work of Kipling and his heirs. For Paul Scott India provided the mausoleum for "the last two great senses of public duty we [British] had as a people . . . the sense of duty that was part and parcel of having an empire"—the duty, once having taken possession of India, to govern it responsibly and well—"and the sense of duty so many of us felt that to get rid of it was the liberal human thing to do." In literary terms the first approximates to Kipling and the second to Forster. Yet the dichotomy between them no longer seems so clear. They disagree as to what ought to be done about imperialism, but the rhetoric through which each writer depicts India is many ways the same. Both, for example, see the Raj as outside history; both are subject to what the historian Francis Hutchins calls "the illusion of permanence" on which the Raj depended. Nevertheless, Scott's distinction between those "two great senses of public duty" remains a good one, and his own achievement in *The Raj Quartet* (1966–1975) lay in synthesizing the work of his predecessors to show how those duties came inevitably into conflict.

From Scott the rhetoric of English India leads to the work of the two major novelists of the Indian diaspora, Rushdie and the Trinidadian Hindu V. S. Naipaul; a brief comparison of their work will provide this chapter's conclusion. Other important novels have of course emerged from England's engagement with empire in other parts of the globe. One thinks especially of Jean Rhys's *Wide Sargasso Sea* (1966), and Timothy Mo's historical novel about the founding of Hong Kong, *An Insular Possession* (1986), not to mention the national literatures of Australia or Nigeria or South Africa. Yet nowhere was the *British* literary encounter with imperialism so complex, or of so sustained a quality, as in India, the oldest and most important of Britain's conquered territories; hence this chapter's emphasis. But the British novel of Africa is also important, and its terms differ in interesting ways from those in which the British saw India. Before turning to Naipaul and Rushdie, we will therefore pause to examine some of its major motifs.

What are some of the tropes on which the rhetoric of English India depends? Forster's Dr. Aziz thinks that the tourist's "pose of 'seeing' India . . . was only a form of ruling India." His words suggest a close relation between knowledge and power that anticipates the New Historicist assumption that they are secret sharers; that knowledge—literature—is often tainted by its association with power. But for Kipling there was nothing secret about it. He openly allied himself with power, and saw knowledge as its servant: his work was intended, at least in part, to inculcate the virtues he thought an imperial servant needed. More interesting, however, is the role of knowledge within his fiction itself. The Indian Survey Department in *Kim* uses its ethnographic and geographical records in the service of military intelligence. The police-man Strickland, who figures in half a dozen stories, believes he "should try to know as much about the natives as the natives themselves." He does so, crucially, by learning to pass for a native, knowing the other by becoming that other. His work is all the more efficient for it, yet in the end that "passing" merely underlines his Englishness, as it does in "Miss Youghal's Sais," where posing as an Indian servant allows him to stay close to the English girl he loves.

The famous ending of *A Passage to India* suggests another of this rhetoric's dominant figures—the half-kiss, the affectionate embrace of Fielding and Aziz, who know that despite their own wishes they can-not yet be friends. It is surely too easy to read this as a simple allegory for the frustration of homosexual desire. But homoeroticism also plays a significant role in Scott's work, in Ronald Merrick's pursuit of the Indian Englishman Hari Kumar; and one can argue its importance for Kipling too, in the relation between Kim and his lama, and in the inten-sity with which he depicts close friendships between men. Yet because that homoeroticism most often takes the form of a fascination with a racial other, it is inevitably linked, like Strickland's attempts to "pass for Hindu or Mohammedan, hide-dresser or priest," to the central trope of all colonial encounters: the attempt to find a language that will allow one to know and to describe the other, the alien, the strange.

And this is Kipling's subject even in what seem the slightest stories in his earliest books. The eponymous, mission-trained Lispeth in the first story of *Plain Tales from the Hills* falls in love with an Englishman, who of course abandons her and returns to England. Lispeth has seen maps and knows where England is, but because "she had no conception of the nature of the sea . . . no ideas of distance or steamboats, her notions were somewhat wild." And Kipling's English characters are in much the same position with regard to India. "The Phantom Rick-shaw" opens with the assertion that India's great virtue is its "Knowa-bility." But that knowability doesn't extend to the way his dead mis-tress's rickshaw follows Jack Pansay around Simla. India becomes mysterious, unknowable, uncontrollable, and so Kipling's characters constantly search for analogies between the subcontinent and the world elsewhere that they accept as normal. "Allowing for the difference between race and race, it's the story of Francesca da Rimini," says a policeman, contemplating the conclusion to a village adultery in "Through the Fire." Except the analogies never quite fit. There's always that allowance to make for "the difference between race and race," a difference such analogies both deny and yet affirm.

For these characters "home" is always elsewhere, never in India, where the heat and the isolation can so easily make a life go off the rails. But in Kipling's best tale he did find in India a home and a language in which to describe it, not as strange or as "other" but simply in terms of its variety and the endless interest that variety creates. That story is of course *Kim*, his only major novel. Kimball O'Hara is a soldier's orphan, born in India, "a poor white of the very poorest" whose tongue is more comfortable in Urdu than English, and whose nickname throughout the bazaars of Lahore is "Little Friend of All the World." He is nimble, and "burned black as any native"; he's often employed in executing the nighttime commissions of "sleek and shiny young men of fashion . . . the stealthy prowl through the dark gullies and lanes, the crawl up a waterpipe, the sights and sounds of the women's world." Yet though Kim has "known all evil since he could speak," he has remained untouched by it, for he plays "the game for its own sake" and not for hopes of reward. Kipling sets the boy between two men. The first is a Tibetan lama, come to India in search of a sacred river. Kim has never seen anyone like him, though he "thought he knew all castes," and so decides to accompany the lama to Benares as his *chela* or disciple; at first for the novelty, then because the lama seems so unworldly and helpless, and finally out of a deep affection. The second is the Afghan horse trader Mahbub Ali, who sometimes asks Kim "to follow a man for one whole day and report every soul with whom he talked." For Mahbub's stock-in-trade includes far more than horses. Kim doesn't know it yet, but he is also a government spy. When he learns that Kim plans to go to Benares, Mahbub asks Kim to carry a message along—a little message, for a British officer, about the pedigree of a horse; a message that will set an army in motion.

All that is in the first chapter, and for the rest of the novel Kim moves between the poles of behavior that the two men suggest. He delivers the message and wanders on with the lama, striding down the Grand Trunk

Road, exchanging insults with a rich widow, visiting an old soldier who is proud that he "stood fast to [his] salt" in 1857. He stumbles into the camp of his dead father's regiment, whose members send him to school, for as he tells the lama, the white men believe that "once a sahib always a sahib. . . . But remember, I can change swiftly." He decides to stay at school, however, after Mahbub Ali interests the government in him, and so he is brought up to play "the Great Game"—to use the skills he learned on the Lahore housetops in the service of the empire. Yet he never forgets his lama, and when he leaves school at last they meet again, to walk into the high hills, the Himalayas, the abode of the gods, where "each long perfect day rose behind Kim for a barrier to cut him off from his race and his mother-tongue." But the Raj follows him even there, and in the novel's climactic chapters Kim is ordered to help stop two map-drawing "emissaries of the dread Power of the North."

Early in the novel Kim appears before both Mahbub and the lama dressed in the clothes of a "Hindu urchin." Neither man recognizes him, and the issue of identity that shape-shifting raises is one of the book's central concerns. Kim's Englishness remains tenuous throughout, and indeed through him Kipling suggests that an Englishman who would be completely comfortable in India must not know England. Yet that very Englishness makes Kim at home throughout the subcontinent in a way that no Indian can be. His fascinated acceptance of all India paradoxically grows out of his detachment from it; because he doesn't belong to any one part of it, he can shuck one self for another, as if India were a show in which he has many roles to play. When the government's other spies have to play a role, they choose one that fits the type of person they already are; the Bengali Hurree Babu is always a Bengali, whose disguises are merely caricatures of himself. But Kim, who has no particular regional or religious or linguistic identity—all India is open to him.

One is tempted to say, in fact, that Kim can blend in everywhere precisely because, as an Englishman, he doesn't belong anywhere. He has no interest in being a sahib, but his ability to change his identity inevitably reminds us of the policeman Strickland. Kim may begin by "passing" for fun, but that ability is soon turned to the business of imperial control. For there is never any doubt that Kim will work on behalf of the government. At several points he pauses to ask "Who is Kim . . . What is Kim?" Those questions help resolve the tension between Mahbub's life of action and the lama's way of contemplation, but they also point to the split between India and England. Yet they carry none of the emotional charge that they will in later novels of colonial identity. The novel leaves Kim as a boy, and its readers have often wondered about him as a man—wondered if, as an adult in the growing struggle for independence, he would be forced to choose between the Raj and the people with whom he lives; if he would feel what Scott identified as the conflict between those two great duties. That, certainly, would make the boy's questions resonate. But Kim merely realizes that he is Kim; he may be able to shift identities, but the novel never raises the question of a political conflict between those identities.

For the India Kipling presents is essentially static. Kim's abilities may be predicated on his whiteness, but the novel as a whole remains deliberately abstracted from history. The events of 1857 are represented as a time out of legend. (Nowhere in his work, in fact, does Kipling treat them in any detail.) The enormous exacerbation of racial tension after 1857 plays no role in the novel. And though the book is nominally set in the 1880s, a time when in his newspaper articles Kipling often criticized the fledgling Indian National Congress, neither Congress nor the issues it addresses are even hinted at. The Raj may be threatened from without; within lie peace and harmony. For like all idylls, *Kim* depends on a rigorous exclusion. To open himself completely to India, to imagine it as home, Kipling had to exclude history. He fashioned in *Kim* an image of eternity that corresponds to the illusion of permanence surrounding British rule. And the images one remembers are, appropriately, those of an India that does not change: the mountains, the great road cutting across the Gangetic plain, the bewildering variety of people, laughter and the fellowship of the cookfire. It is a world without anguish, in which the main character remains uncorrupted by evil, prostitutes have a becoming modesty, and even Russian spies are not killed but merely led cunningly astray. That is the magic and the charm of *Kim*. It is also its limitation.

While many of Kipling's stories depict India as alien and mysterious, the emphasis of his work as a whole is on subduing the subcontinent to description, on making it "knowable," whether through Kim's lessons in map drawing or through the use of native informants in stories like "Tod's Amendment." But it is only the least sympathetic of Forster's characters in *A Passage to India* who find India knowable, who speak authoritatively about such things as "the educated native's latest dodge."

Forster's India is knowable only in its unknowability, for "How can the mind take hold of such a country?" To his character Mrs. Moore India seems like the undecipherable echo she hears in the Marabar Caves, answering "ou-boum" to all sounds whatsoever. Yet later, as she takes ship at Bombay, Mrs. Moore hears the landscape say something else. "So you thought an echo was India; you took the Marabar caves as final? . . . What have we in common with them . . . ?"

"Nothing embraces the whole of India," says Dr. Aziz, "nothing, nothing," for it is a place that cannot be fully described, fully known. Forster's India is, in Edward Said's words, "an Orient destined to bear its foreignness as a mark of its permanent estrangement from the West"—indeed, a place whose very essence lies in that estrangement. The schoolmaster Fielding has been given an open door into Indian life—Aziz shows him the picture of his dead wife, who had kept purdah when she was alive. But even Fielding can only stand on the threshold; and India remains a mystery. If to Aziz the British "pose of 'seeing India' . . . [is] only a form of ruling India," the novel as a whole suggests something else: see India, and realize all we don't understand about this alien land; see it, and realize that we have no business here.

Seeing India's otherness as a reason why Britain ought not to control it is indeed a step toward liberation; most servants of the Raj had confidently believed it justified their rule ("The Oriental is not capable of self-government"). Yet for readers after the end of empire, those positions—India as un/knowable—begin to seem the two sides of the same imperial coin. Each is an absolute, each an abstraction, and the novel finds no middle ground. As Aziz and Fielding cannot finally cross the gap that separates them, so too Forster himself has "not yet, not [here]" found a way to talk about cultural difference without turning it into "otherness."

That makes *A Passage to India* a more problematic text than its traditional reputation as the great anti-imperialist novel would suggest. "It's beginning at the wrong end, isn't it?" Fielding says to Aziz during a discussion of political reform. "I know, but institutions and governments don't." And Forster therefore insists on seeing British imperialism not in political terms but as a problem in individual human relations. The novel's scenario is perhaps too well known to require more than a brief account. Its central events grow from the Englishwoman Adela Quested's belief that Aziz has tried to rape her on a visit to the Marabar Caves. Forster lets his readers know that she is mistaken, but

Aziz is nonetheless committed for trial, and Fielding, the only Englishman to believe in his innocence, breaks with the British community. On the witness stand, however, Adela realizes she is wrong and recants, though what did in fact happen remains a mystery; and some critics have seen in that ambiguity a modernist's characterisic preference for the symbolic over the actual. Yet Adela's recantation also makes the trial much simpler. For it means that Forster doesn't have to pursue the political conflicts and complications her charge evokes, doesn't actually have to weigh the affront to Adela against the affront of British rule.

Aziz is set free, and the novel's last hundred pages dramatize the difficulties he and Fielding have in remaining friends, difficulties far greater than those usually faced by people from different cultures. For "Every human act in the East is tainted with officialism . . . [and] where there is officialism every human relation suffers." The tension in their friendship grows from the essential inequity between them that Britain's possession of India creates. Aziz cannot forget that in racial terms he is the ruled and Fielding the ruler, and he grows suspicious, for all the latter's willingness to break with the Raj. Finally they each retreat into their own people, the one into a nascent sense of Indian nationalism, the other into an English marriage. For as Aziz says at the end of the novel, India will have to drive the last Englishman into the sea before they can be friends once more. And indeed in the novel's closing image their whole world—"the horses . . . rocks . . . the temples, the tank, the jail, the palace, the birds . . . the sky"—weighs in against that friendship, so that imperialism comes to seem a force of nature, driving them apart, no matter how much they want to stay together.

Forster's ironic portrait of the Raj is a powerful one, and yet the novel's readers can easily draw the conclusion that its greatest evil lies in keeping these two men apart. Politics stand for Forster as an intrusion into private life. He has always been admired for the sane and skeptical humanity of his attack on the priggish and the closed-minded, and there is never any doubt about his opposition to imperialism as a system. Yet his account of British India increasingly seems a limited one. He began the novel after his first visit to the subcontinent in 1912 and 1913; it was interrupted by the Great War, and he resumed work on it after his second visit in 1921. In the intervening decade Indian nationalism coalesced around two events: Gandhi's emergence as a national leader, and the Amritsar Massacre of 1919, in which a British general ordered his troops to open fire on an unarmed crowd. Those developments made Forster resist the temptation to cast the book "as a little bridge of sympathy between East and West," and therefore shaped its dispiriting conclusion. But his India, like Kipling's, is essentially abstracted from history. His characters' manners remain those of the prewar years, and yet the novel's protracted composition led Forster to cut it free from contemporary reference. *A Passage to India* seems to float in time, unconnected to any sense of a continuously unfolding—indeed a rapidly changing—present, with its characters' lives unaffected by Amritsar, Congress, legislative reform, or the growth of communal tensions.

Because Forster's Raj seems incapable of change, it is in a sense as eternal as Kipling's; indeed one reads with the sense that neither of them could imagine it ending. The wit and playfulness of his narrative voice and the ease with which he unrolls his narrative are unmatched in the fiction of empire, and *A Passage to India* remains the canonical statement of liberal opposition to imperialism. Yet because Forster's empire remains frozen in time, that opposition emerges in emotional rather than political terms—as attitude, not action. It takes the form of an outraged fellow feeling and it has the peculiar effect of making imperialism seem more an English crisis than an Indian one. For like *Heart of Darkness*, Forster's novel is at its most acute in its analysis of what colonialism does to the colonizer. Aziz's trial aside, the greatest danger imperialism poses in *A Passage to India* is its power to make everyone, even its readers, into people like the butts of its satire, its collectors and magistrates and memsahibs. "I give any Englishman two years," says Aziz's cousin Hamidullah; after that, "they all become exactly the same," warped and bent by officialism. "When the white man turns tyrant," Orwell wrote, "it is his own freedom that he destroys. . . . He wears a mask, and his face grows to fit it." No novel of its period did more to show just how ghastly the empire-born mask of Britishness could be.

Forster's successors continued that analysis of what imperialism did to the English themselves. It is, for example, a major concern in Orwell's *Burmese Days* (1934), in many of Doris Lessing's superb African stories, and in J. G. Farrell's dissection of the twin myths of progress and empire in *The Siege of Krishnapur* (1973). It is also at issue in the richest narrative of English India, Scott's tetralogy about the end of British rule, *The Raj Quartet*. In its last volume, *A Division of the Spoils* (1975), the historian Guy Perron charts the ways in which

India has formed part of England's idea about herself and . . . been forced into
. . . being a reflection of that idea. Up to say 1900 the part India played in our
idea about ourselves was the part played by anything we possessed which we
believed it was right to possess. . . . Since 1900, certainly since 1918, the reverse
has obtained. The part played since then by India in the English idea of Englishness has been that of something we feel it does us no credit to have. Our
idea about ourselves will now not accommodate any idea about India except
the idea of returning it . . . in order to prove that we are English. . . . [But] India
itself, as itself . . . has played no part [in that idea] whatsoever.

Perron's acute analysis of the complex interrelations of England and
empire suggests the difficulty that even the Raj's greatest critics face in
writing about "India itself" rather than about the British in India. And
Scott has been attacked for doing just that, most notably by Salman
Rushdie, who sees in the *Quartet* a form of imaginative recolonization
in which Indians remain "bit players in their own history." Yet Rushdie
misses the degree to which passages like this one mount a critique of
that Orientalism; the *Quartet* has a self-consciousness about its own
representation of India that in many ways anticipates recent work in
cultural studies.

Moreover Scott shows the effect that the British inability to see
"India itself" has had on Indian history. In an essay called "After
Marabar" (1972) he argued that until mid-century not only India but
England had been locked in a "conflict between Turtonism and
Fieldingism." Turton is the District Collector in Forster's novel, the
schoolmaster's emblematic conservative counterpart, and their names
point to a confrontation between the status quo of class and country on
the one hand and reform on the other. It was, Scott wrote, the last time
one could feel an "absolute conviction about the right direction to take."
Yet in retrospect he believed that conviction had been simplistic. For
the Fieldings at home in England "Indian independence was something that would automatically happen" after winning the war against
"Turtonism in general." But it didn't. *The Raj Quartet* shows how the
inevitable conflict between "the two great senses of public duty" that
India presented made its independence into the site for "the death and
interment of liberal humanism," the place where that absolute conviction came up against the inadequacy of its own good intentions in the
form of the communal massacres and continuing legacies of the partition between India and Pakistan.

No plot summary of the *Quartet*'s two thousand pages could do justice to the complexity of its narrative procedures, its manifold layering of one character's point of view upon another's, its awareness of the fictiveness of historical interpretation, or its intricately Faulknerian sense of the way in which the past is never really past. What we must stress here is the way it provides the synthesis in the dialectic that Kipling and Forster began. Scott's predecessors abstracted their novels from history, but their own historical positions forced them to choose sides, to stand either firmly for or against imperialism, to emphasize just one of those two great duties. But writing after the end of empire, Scott can try to define what it meant, rather than simply document an attitude toward it. That allows the *Quartet*, more than any other English novel, to show how imperialism's illusion of permanence was both built and maintained. It also means that Scott can offer a compelling account of the imperial endgame, as his characters search for ways to pull out and yet maintain order, finding as they do that historical necessity develops out of the contingencies of the moment.

The central relation in the novel is that between Hari Kumar and the policeman Ronald Merrick. Brought to England as a baby and educated there in the hopes that he would return to India as a colonial administrator, Hari is one of Macaulay's brown-skinned Englishmen. But when his father's suicide leaves him broke and alone before he has finished his schooling, the only home Hari can find is with an aunt in the Indian city of Mayapore. And there he discovers that white people no longer notice him. Hari sees his own Englishness as a matter of class, of education, of a code of behavior that supersedes and is not bound by color. But it is easier for the white English to reject Hari than to face the challenge he presents. They can treat him as if he were English in England, but to hear his public school accent in India is to suspect that their own Englishness may be socially constructed and not essential. For few of them are honest enough to admit to the racism on which the Raj depends. They insist instead on the inseparability of culture and color: their own identities are intrinsic, but Hari's is acquired, for they see him not as English, but as someone trying to pass himself off as English.

Scott sets Hari against the policeman Merrick, who believes in the white man's right to rule, but without accepting the fictions through which the British attempt to "hide [their] prejudices and continue to live with them"—"Devotion. Sacrifice. Self-denial. . . . The whole impossible nonsensical dream" of the Raj's civilizing mission. The lower-middle-class Merrick knows he doesn't have the same "background" as the imperial servants with whom he lives. And he knows, therefore, that his privileges, and theirs too, depend not on those enabling fictions of duty and devotion but on race. He believes instead in what he calls "the situation"—a ritualized enactment of the contempt of the strong for the weak on which imperialism depends. For Merrick, as Hari recalls in describing an interrogation at the policeman's hands, the liberals "who pretended to admire Indian intellectuals" are as contemptuous of that "black reflection of their own white ideals" as the "upper-class reactionaries" are of the soldiers and servants whose much praised "bravery and loyalty" marks their inferior status. Merrick's "situation" gives the lie to any idea of "the Law" as an originating force of empire. It would be as damning as anything in Fanon if only he didn't use it as a way to justify his own brutality. But while Merrick himself connects that dark clarity about the nature of power to what he calls his "humble" origins, Scott suggests that it is more closely linked to the policeman's sexuality. During a part of his interrogation, Hari says, Merrick "had his hand between my legs." And Merrick finishes his questions by wiping blood across Hari's genitals.

Critical attention has recently turned toward the interrelation of gender and race, and in particular to the constantly shifting, firmly drawn and yet perpetually blurred lines of difference that characterize what Suleri describes as "the marked homoeroticism of the narratives of colonial encounter." Daphne Manners in the tetralogy's first volume, *The Jewel in the Crown* (1966), writes that the British have unsexed India, made it into a "nation of eunuchs." Merrick is a deeply closeted homosexual, as was Scott himself, and early in the novel's action he pursues Hari through a form of triangulated desire—by proposing to Daphne, whose interest in Hari he has noted. When she is raped he immediately has Hari arrested, and his actions are above all an expression of sexual contempt for a man who because he has been conquered is no longer a man. And yet that paradoxically makes him available as an object of desire, at one with an India whom the conqueror sees in feminine terms, a woman to be grasped in what Scott calls an "imperial embrace"—at once raped and told that she's loved.

To Sarah Layton in *The Day of the Scorpion* (1968) Merrick is the empire's "dark side. . . . You reveal something that is sad about us, as if out here we had built a mansion without doors and windows, with no way in and no way out. . . . And one day we shall lie exposed. . . ." Yet for Scott it is not homosexuality but rather its repression that figures as unnatural. Indeed the *Quartet* as a whole suggests the near impossibility of maintaining a healthily honest sexuality of any kind in a world where "the situation"—infinitely more powerful than Forster's "officialism"—has the power to blight all human relations. Merrick's actions with Hari go no further than that bloody smear of his hand. Late in the novel, however, he will start to dress in Pathan clothing, as if he were Kipling's Strickland, for a series of liasons with Indian boys. It is as if he can only step from the closet by first becoming the racial other; and it will lead to his death. The closet crumbles, until he lies "exposed," no longer sheltered in "that mansion without doors or windows" in which one tries both to hide the truth and to hide from it too; whether that truth be one of private desire or of the very foundations of British rule.

An image from *The Jewel in the Crown* sums up Scott's sense of the way those foundations have crumbled, "the sight of old Miss Crane sitting in the pouring rain by the roadside holding the hand of a dead Indian." She is a superintendent of mission schools and the dead man is one of her teachers. He has died because as they drove toward a line of rioters during the Quit India demonstrations of 1942, she couldn't bring herself to trust his instructions to speed up and crash through—couldn't accept that an Indian might know more about how to act in an emergency than she does. Instead she stops, trusting to the heaven's command of the Raj to see them safely home. She is spared, the teacher is not. He's beaten to death because he's with her, an Englishwoman; because the British can no longer protect those whom it is their self-appointed mission to protect. Miss Crane cannot protect her subordinate because her very presence makes him vulnerable in the first place. The imperial mission cancels itself out. Not only can the British no longer preserve the order they take as a justification for their rule; they are themselves responsible for its destruction.

If one of the central concerns of British fiction about India is suggested by the ambiguous title of Suleri's *Rhetoric of English India*, then the dominant issue in the British novel of Africa is that figured by Abdul JanMohamed's *Manichean Aesthetics*. Suleri charts the rhetoric that links English writing about India to Indians writing in English; she maps the border of identity crossed first by Kim and later by such cultural hybrids as Rushdie's Saladin Chamcha in *The Satanic Verses* (1988). Nothing like that happens in British fiction about Africa. Jan-

Mohamed's title points toward the firm separation of light from dark on which such fiction turns, the absolute opposition between Europe and Africa. Yet Africa does not figure simply as the other. Rather it is, as Christopher L. Miller has argued, the third term in the binary opposition of Europe and Asia—and hence a nullity. That discourse even takes the darkness of African skin as the absence of light, a sign that something is missing. The continent is not only dark, but empty as well, a blank space on which to inscribe a European meaning.

For colonialist writers Africa, far more than India, stands as a place onto which Western fears and desires can be projected. It is "primitive." Where India has ancient cities, in Africa one finds only natives wailing in the bush, so that in *Heart of Darkness* the continent becomes a metaphor for man's original state even as it also provides one for the darkness of the human heart. Going upriver is for Marlow a journey in two directions at once, both back and in. And Africa's emptiness has another consequence: it puts the whole continent up for grabs, as if it were all an enormous, unmapped Kafiristan. But Kipling's story remains nervous about imperial plunder. Its African counterpart does not. Published in 1885—the very year of the Berlin Conference—H. Rider Haggard's *King Solomon's Mines* suggests that Africa, being empty, is of course outside any "Law." Its treasures are there for the taking—for Africans, being Africans, cannot possibly have a legitimate claim to them. But unlike Dravot and Carnehan, Haggard's adventurers don't want a kingdom to rule. They merely want to take their loot back to England—and they succeed where Kipling's fail. Orwell wrote that Kipling never realized that the "box wallah," the merchant, calls the tune of empire; and the fiction of the Raj remained that of an administrative class. But in Africanist novels, from *King Solomon's Mines* down to Naipaul's *A Bend in the River* (1979), one is always aware of imperialism's original purpose, always aware of the continent as a place to make money.

Contemporary theories of discourse may make us doubt the possibility of ever coming to terms with anything "in itself"; nevertheless that was what Kipling and Forster tried to do with India. Such effort is rarely made in Africanist fiction. Evelyn Waugh's *Black Mischief* (1932) depends for its comedy on the mutual incomprehension of Europe and Africa. At the birth control gala, for example, the Africans see condoms as the "Emperor's juju," a fetish guaranteeing many children. Controlling births means making sure there are lots of them. But Waugh's dark continent is primarily intended to make a point about Europe; like the South American scenes in *A Handful of Dust* (1934), it throws the spotlight on "those other savages at home." There may be no meeting between the cultures, but still Waugh's Britain is not that different from Africa. His prose invites his readers to turn away in revulsion from the cannibals' "glistening backs heaving and shimmering" as they dance around the fire, but it also reminds them that one of those cannibals has come home to England. It too is one of what Conrad called the "dark places of the earth," and though that darkness may be obscured by its own light, it becomes visible enough when Europeans are placed against an African background.

Graham Greene's African novels use the continent in a similar way, taking it as the Manichean counterpart to the "sinless graceless chromium world" of Western modernity. The physically healthy protagonist of *A Burnt-Out Case* (1962), for example, comes to an African leper colony because Europe no longer offers the state of spiritual extremity he needs. As such Greene's Africa is indistinguishable from the other overheated landscapes in which he sets his work: Haiti, Vietnam, Mexico—the world collectively known as "Greeneland." Greene has protested against this way of seeing his work, arguing that each separate place has been "carefully and accurately described." But the documentary details make little difference. The mood of the fly-blown bungalows in which his characters live stays much the same, whatever the setting. *The Heart of the Matter* (1949) is one of Greene's richest books, but even there Africa merely provides the landscape against which to explore the protagonist's spiritual difficulties. The genre scenes through which he presents Henry Scobie's stark, bare life as a police officer in Sierra Leone are very fine, as such scenes always are in Greene's work: they depict his miserable marriage, his relations with the Syrian trader Yusef, the endless drinking, and the "flying ants scattering their wings over the table." And the author even manages to give a heroic quality to Scobie's stoic performance of a difficult job in a day when the grand rhetoric of empire has vanished. But Africa remains in the background, a land of heat and vultures that merely intensifies Greene's tale of Scobie's guilty Catholicism and eventual suicide.

Neither Greene nor Waugh makes a real effort to write about colonialism as a structure of consciousness; neither of them is greatly interested in Africa as Africa. Yet to note that is also to stress the way their books form part of the discourse Miller describes, in which the continent figures as but an "empty slate, written on by others." Joyce Cary does make the attempt, but his once greatly admired novels of colonial administration in Nigeria now serve primarily to remind us of the Manichean qualities of Africanist discourse. The best known of them, *Mister Johnson* (1939), is a portrait of a teenaged government clerk who uses his official status as a bargaining chip in negotiations, first for a bride and then for a loan. Johnson is charming, his high spirits are infectious, and he is also capable of sustained hard work. But he is, finally, a thief and a murderer, and Cary connects that disaster to his cultural displacement—to his fondness for gin and Western suits and his insistence that he is "an English gentleman . . . dat King of England is my king." The novel's other African characters see his behavior as ludicruous, even mad. Yet Cary manages to suggest that Johnson is in some ways typical: typical in his childlikeness, a function not of his youth but of his Africanness; typical too in his inability to seem anything but absurd in his fondness for English culture, a prototype of what Naipaul would later call a "mimic man." It is little wonder, then, that the first generation of Nigerian writers in English attacked Cary's work so strongly. The desire to show that Africa is *not* as Cary had seen it provided the motive force for Chinua Achebe's *No Longer at Ease* (1960); and Wole Soyinka's portraits of his parents' generation in *Ake* (1981) and *Isara* (1989) effectively challenge it as well.

Doris Lessing offers a richer body of work in her first novel, *The Grass is Singing* (1949), in her large volume of *African Stories* (1964) and the initial books of the Martha Quest series, and in parts of *The Golden Notebook* (1962). Another chapter in this volume deals with Lessing's work at length, and so her treatment here will be brief. Her subject, as Martin Green notes, is what happens "*after* the judgment on empire." That judgment led her for a time into the Communist Party, yet her concern lies not with the ideology of imperialism so much as with the daily grind of living in colonial society: a society of farmers and merchants and miners, of white people doing what would in England be ordinary jobs, and whose hallmark is not so much Forster's officialism as it is petty suburban prejudice. The long story "A Home for the Highland Cattle" provides a good example. Marina Giles comes to Rhodesia simply for the sake of a "proper house after all these years." She dislikes colonial society—reads the *New Statesman*, doesn't believe in the "colour bar." But that society's small frustrations wear her down, and she walks into the climate of suspicion it has created between servants and masters, who resent her for introducing "Fabian principles into a clear-cut situation." The reader's sympathies remain with Marina, yet Lessing also shows us that she knows nothing about the country in which she has chosen to live; and eventually Marina decides that she can't have seen what in fact she does see. She retreats into the self, trying not to share the prejudices of "white civilisation" but living in it anyway, "for the liberal, so vociferously disapproving in the first six months, is quite certain to turn his back on the whole affair before the end of a year."

Even those of Lessing's characters who work for the government are closer to Haggard's than they are to Kipling's, for they have come to Africa for the sake of a good job and a comfortable life, rather than out of any sense of mission. And such characters figure in the work of more recent novelists as well, as international experts or businessmen, or even the zoologists of William Boyd's *Brazzaville Beach* (1990). That emphasis on the colonial balance sheet makes the novelist's Africa a more polyglot world than the Raj, peopled by Belgians and Russians in *Heart of Darkness*, Middle Eastern shopkeepers in Waugh and Greene, more Belgians along with East Indian traders in Naipaul. Africanist novels, that is, tend to deal with "the international community," with small pockets of foreign nationals living in hot countries where they may have positions of privilege but do not necessarily rule. Perhaps for such characters the particular country or continent in which they live does not much matter: the unnamed African nation of *A Bend in the River* might as well be the Haiti of Greene's *Comedians* (1966) or the Costaguana of Conrad's *Nostromo* (1904). They are all dangerous, poor, and corrupt, and they all offer the chance to make a fortune. Such novels are not about the processes of imperial rule so much as about the general question of relations between north and south; though the economy they chart is now as often one of guilt as it is of capital. And indeed it is *Nostromo* as much as *Heart of Darkness* that lies behind most Africanist novels, and in particular behind the large body of recent fiction that Euro-American writers have set in a postcolonial Africa. For *Nostromo* is the great novel of economic imperialism: of the international interests whose investments must be protected, whether they are moral, political, or financial; and of what that protection costs. Africanist fiction is not on the whole as strong as the literature the British produced about the Raj. But because those investments did not vanish with independence, it is likely to provide a better model for the novels of a neocolonial age.

"The empires of our time were short-lived," Naipaul writes in *The Mimic Men* (1967), "but they have altered the world for ever; their passing away is their least significant feature." And Naipaul's own novels both chart that alteration and are themselves a product of it. The descendant of Hindus who came to Trinidad as indentured laborers, Naipaul has become over the last thirty-five years one of the most prominent figures in what was at first called "Commonwealth literature" and is now known as postcolonial literature. For one of the most important things those empires left behind were their languages, and the new literatures in English have been especially vital. The field is too large to survey here, though its importance is suggested by the Nobel Prizes awarded to the Nigerian Soyinka in 1986, the South African Nadine Gordimer in 1991, and the West Indian Derek Walcott in 1992. But this chapter would be incomplete if it did not deal, however briefly, with the way in which the novel has depicted the world after the formal end of colonialism, and in particular with the way in which, as Rushdie puts it, "the empire [now] writes back."

Naipaul's two Africanist novels, *In a Free State* (1971) and *A Bend in the River*, testify to what he describes as the great restlessness of our age, a restlessness whose mass migrations and cultural upheavals were created by imperialism, but which seems only to have increased as the empires themselves have receded. And that has been Rushdie's material as well. Few of their characters have received the sort of education that makes Scott's Hari Kumar into a "brown-skinned Englishman," though the term does have some reference to their own biographies. But both writers build their work around the issues such a character suggests, exploring the constantly shifting identities that imperialism has created, and the question of what it might mean, in the words of Kipling's Daniel Dravot, to "grow" to be English. Rushdie's Saladin Chamcha can even be seen as a postcolonial version of Kim: a professional mimic who can do a thousand English voices precisely because no one of them is authentically his own.

Both writers attended English universities, have settled and married in Britain, and have found their material in the experience of migrants and exiles. Both deal with characters whose lives, in Rushdie's words, have been "handcuffed to history," and thereby "transformed into grotesquery." Both are masters of a black and astringent comedy that grows from the confrontation of one culture with another: the way

Africa, India, and the West collide but do not cohere in *A Bend in the River*; or the meeting of the totalizing system of Islam with the pluralism of postcolonial society in *The Satanic Verses*. And both are enormously controversial, though Naipaul's attackers, who see his critique of the third world as a form of blaming the victim, have at least read him; most of the Muslims who condemn Rushdie for what they call the blasphemy of *The Satanic Verses* have not. They see the same phenomena—and yet present radically different visions of the possibilities for the self in a postcolonial world.

Novelists like the Nigerian Achebe or the Indian R. K. Narayan draw heavily on indigenous narrative traditions, oral storytelling in particular. Naipaul, in contrast, has always insisted on the impossibility of any tradition fully surviving the disruptions of imperialism. At their initiation, Brahmin boys are told to go to Benares and study; they take a few ritual steps on the way, and are then called back. But Ganesh Ramsumair in Naipaul's first novel, *The Mystic Masseur* (1957), keeps on walking. "Stop behaving stupid," his relatives tell him. "You think you really going to Benares? That is in India . . . and this is Trinidad." Naipaul plays the scene for laughter, but the point remains. His characters have the values of one world but must live in another, in a world of conflicting and interpenetrating cultures, and they can never quite get over it. For the disruptions of empire have created a sense of violation, of estrangement from one's origins, and a consequent longing for an idealized home that has made tragedy inevitable. The title figure of *A House for Mr. Biswas* (1961) may be rendered homeless by his financial dependence on his wife's family, but he also provides an emblem for all those to whom history has done the same thing.

Just as the white English in *The Jewel and the Crown* see Hari Kumar as someone pretending to be English, so most of Naipaul's characters stand as examples of what he calls a "mimic man." For in their "wounded civilization[s]" all terms of value and reference seem to come from outside, from the West. They mimic its manners—Ganesh Ramsumair eventually changes his name to G. Ramsey Muir—but they are not so much men who mimic as they are mimics of men, "pretend[ing] to be real." Jimmy Ahmed in *Guerrillas* (1975) preaches a form of black power (for all that he is half-Chinese) but feels powerful himself only when he attracts the attention of whites. He sees his success solely in terms of his acceptance in the metropolis; and the contempt with which he treats white people is an act of self-contempt as well. The narrator Salim in *A*

Bend in the River becomes so fascinated by the science he learns from popular magazines that he looks to the West as the exclusive source of knowledge and civilization, filled with a sense of how far he has to go to catch up. Neither man is whole, sufficient unto himself. They are instead dependent, at best "half-made," an imitation of what a man should be. So too the societies from which they come remain dependent on metropolitan values—or rather on the value the metropolis places on them, on their bauxite and sugar and trade.

For Salim the world has no place for "men who are nothing, who allow themselves to become nothing." But in a wounded civilization how can anyone make the self into something other than a mimic of a man? How does one move from dependency to development when the tools of the latter are so often the chains of the former? The colonial writer sees the library shelves of the metropolis as a sign of his own inconsequentiality. Yet he has no way to escape that sense of his own belatedness except by trying to fill a shelf of his own, embracing the very thing that oppresses him. And over the years Naipaul has filled that shelf. The early comic novels have given way to the bleak first-person narration of *The Mimic Men* or *A Bend in the River*; the number of travel books has increased—three on India alone—while the production of novels has slowed; the work has grown increasingly autobiographical, until in *The Enigma of Arrival* (1987) the line between fiction and memoir disappears. But always Naipaul has had the virtues of both continuity and surprise; however often he has revisited the same themes, the same places, his work has never stood still.

Rushdie's novels are as keenly attuned as Naipaul's to issues of cultural fracture, of worlds and histories and values in collision. Yet his work suggests not a tragic awareness but a ready acceptance of the fact that cultures are never inviolate. "Perhaps we are all," he writes, "black and brown and white, leaking into one another . . . *like flavours when you cook.*" Hence his gloriously ramshackle sentences, in which Bombay street slang flirts with Oxbridge English, a style in which, as in the poems of Baal in *The Satanic Verses*, "the demotic force[s] its way into lines of classical purity and images of love [are] constantly degraded by the intrusions of elements of farce." That style grows from Rushdie's attempt in *Midnight's Children* to use the English language as a way of imagining a form for India itself, "that 5000 year old country that has never before existed." But to do that he must first free English from its colonial past, remaking it into a new Indian language called Angrezi, the master's tongue appropriated for his own subversive purposes. Yet Angrezi's essential impurity contests not just the ideology of colonialism but that of India's "folkloristic straitjacket" as well. For Rushdie's refashioning of the language puts English at the heart of modern India's national identity in a way that challenges the nativist assumption that one can be perfectly non-Western. His style is an attempt to acknowledge India's heterogeneous history and complex heritage, to envision a structure in which all its multiple divisions of region and religion and language and caste can be contained. And his work as a whole stands as a model of what Mikhail Bakhtin calls the "dialogic" novel: a linguistic carnival, a polyphony of voices that turns all ideological certainties upside down, a quite literally heteroglot forum for an encounter not just between opposing characters but between different beliefs, languages, levels of discourse, and indeed whole cultures.

The Satanic Verses takes up such issues through its critique of the ideal of cultural purity, the "terrifying singularity" of Islam, in a way that enacts within the novel itself the very storm that has grown up around it. It recasts *Midnight's Children* in terms of the individual migrant whom Rushdie takes as the emblematic figure of our times. Migration makes the self indeterminate. For the migrant has chosen to translate one identity into another, and in doing so has set out "to make himself up." What Rushdie suggests is that such postcolonial selves should actively choose the hand that history has dealt them. If for Naipaul mimicry is a sign of cultural violation, for Rushdie a self-conscious mimicry becomes a way to shuttle between the hybrid selves of the postcolonial condition, to acknowledge that one lives in two worlds at once. And in that acceptance of discontinuity he sees not tragedy but liberation. It does not help the postcolonial man or woman surmount dependency so much as it denies its relevance, for without an ideal of cultural purity against which to measure the self, there can be no mimicry per se. Instead Rushdie posits a self that is rather like one of his own sentences, Indian and yet English too. And indeed he suggests that we all reject what Lawrence called "the old stable ego of the character" and learn instead to revel in its instability, even as we do in his style. The self becomes a pastiche, like the India Rushdie describes as "borrowing whatever clothes seemed to fit," a collage, a set of masks improvised for different occasions. It is the point at which the postcolonial and the postmodern coalesce.

Where Naipaul sees a cultural violation, Rushdie sees at least the possibility of freedom from an imprisoning authenticity. The pursuit of such an authenticity has led, in India, to the rise of linguistic and religious separatism on the one hand, and Hindu fundamentalism on the other. It has led, most famously, to the Ayatollah Khomeini's *fatwa* against *The Satanic Verses*, to demands for its author's death, and to Rushdie's continued life in hiding. And in England it has led to the nativism of the National Front, with its cries of "Wogs out!" Throughout this chapter we have seen the ways in which English writers drew, blurred, and insisted on the lines of racial difference that separated them from the subject peoples of their empire. Rushdie's work challenges those barriers, and in doing so helps construct an identity for a kind of man or woman that Kipling could not have imagined. Along with several other writers of his generation—Timothy Mo, Hanif Kureishi, Caryl Phillips—he shows the ways in which it is possible to be English and yet not white. And that is even one of Naipaul's themes in *The Enigma of Arrival*, an account of how he finally came to see himself at home in the chalk hills of Wiltshire.

"They have the power of description," a tiger-headed character in *The Satanic Verses* says of the white British society in which he lives, "and we succumb to the pictures they construct." For seeing India, or Africa, or the Caribbean is indeed a way of ruling them. One consequence of the end of the British Empire is that they have started to describe themselves.

Michael Gorra

Selected Bibliography

Appiah, Kwame Anthony. *In My Father's House: Africa in the Philosophy of Culture*. New York: Oxford University Press, 1992.

Cronin, Richard. *Imagining India*. New York: St. Martin's Press, 1989.

Green, Martin. *Dreams of Adventure, Deeds of Empire*. New York: Basic Books, 1979.

Green, Martin. *The English Novel in the Twentieth Century: The Doom of Empire*. London: Routledge and Kegan Paul, 1984.

Hutchins, Francis G. *The Illusion of Permanence: British Imperialism in India*. Princeton, N.J.: Princeton University Press, 1967.

JanMohamed, Abdul. *Manichean Aesthetics: The Politics of Literature in Colonial Africa.* Amherst: University of Massachusetts Press, 1983.

McClure, John A. *Kipling and Conrad: The Colonial Fiction.* Cambridge, Mass.: Harvard University Press, 1981.

Miller, Christopher L. *Blank Darkness: Africanist Discourse in French.* Chicago: University of Chicago Press, 1985.

Rubin, David. *After the Raj: British Novels of India Since 1947.* Hanover, N.H.: University Press of New England, 1986.

Said, Edward W. *Culture and Imperialism.* New York: Alfred A. Knopf, 1993.

Said, Edward W. *Orientalism.* New York: Pantheon, 1978.

Suleri, Sara. *The Rhetoric of English India.* Chicago: University of Chicago Press, 1992.

Bennett, Wells, and the Persistence of Realism

REALISM is not primarily a matter of confining a story to the realm of the possible or even the probable; rather, it involves a particular philosophical position. Realism assumes reality, that is, the existence of a phenomenal world separate from and knowable by consciousness. The struggle to recognize that separation and gather that knowledge is the chief theme of realist work. By the same token, the realist novel purports to sharpen a reader's perception of the real world exterior to it. Realist fiction tends toward comedy when the protagonist achieves the competence to distinguish reality from unreality—to choose the truly admirable mate, to disentangle the good from the pleasurable, to discard false gods for true. Realist fiction tends toward tragedy when the protagonist remains an incompetent judge, misled by romantic phantasms into some fatal misstep. Other factors complicate the identification of any single work as realist; one might argue, for instance, against identifying *Madame Bovary* as a "realist novel," despite its virulent antiromanticism, on the grounds that Flaubert's technique insistently draws attention away from the realities it exposes and toward the means of exposure. Every novel both makes meaningful reference to a world outside itself and is a self-contained, self-referential world of meaning. One may thus think of realism as an element more or less present in a work, rather than as a defining characteristic of it: whether or not one identifies a particular novel as realist will always depend on the context in which one makes the identification. Certainly, by comparison with the twentieth century, the nineteenth was a realist era. The modernist concentration on the phenomenal world as a production of language pushed the concerns of realist fiction to the margin, if not entirely off the page. Modernist novels undermine the very division between the "exterior" world and the "interior" consciousness on which realism is founded. They similarly deny the realist transference of interest from the fictive to the real world. James Joyce's *Ulysses*, for example, has a greatly diminished effect if read as a depiction of lives; it has little anecdotal power. Rather, the characters Joyce deploys are continually revealed to be fictional constructions that gloss other fictions.

The reputations of those Edwardian novelists perceived to be upholding the realist tradition consequently sank when the attitudes of modernism became predominant in academia. While the modernist tide has receded, the reputations of the chief Edwardian realists, Arnold Bennett and H. G. Wells, have only slightly recovered. Wells is known to most nonacademic readers as the ebullient founder of science fiction—he has even appeared as a fictionalized hero in this genre, pursuing Jack the Ripper down the ages in the film *Time After Time* (1980). Bennett, especially to American readers, is not known at all. Academics tend to identify Wells and Bennett as the opposition, whetstones against whom two better-regarded authors sharpened their theories— Henry James against Wells (but also Bennett) in a bitter controversy of the teens, Virginia Woolf against Bennett (but also Wells) in a less vitriolic dispute of the twenties. In both cases, the charge was abetting the persistence of realism. But to regard Wells and Bennett as collaborators in the same realist enterprise distorts both; indeed, they differ most profoundly in their relation to the realist tradition. Realism persisted in the works of both Bennett and Wells only in that each felt obliged to respond to it. But they wielded the conventions of realism to opposite effects. H. G. Wells reworked the form he had inherited in the hope of achieving a greater realism, of extending the range of unrealities he might expose. Arnold Bennett, on the other hand, used realist conventions in order to subvert them.

The coupling of Wells and Bennett as realists had less to do with the novels they wrote than with the image of the novelist they promulgated. The partly self-created public images of Wells and Bennett are worth examining in some detail. That the two most prominent serious novelists of the Edwardian period should be spoken of as one is not surprising; the names Wells and Bennett were frequently linked by the authors themselves. Wells sketches the dual portrait in his *Experiment in Autobiography* (1934):

We were both about of an age; to be exact he was six months younger than I; we were both hard workers, both pushing up by way of writing from lower middle-class surroundings, where we had little prospect of anything but a restricted salaried life, and we found we were pushing with quite surprising ease; we were learning much the same business, tackling much the same obstacles, encountering similar prejudices and antagonisms and facing similar social occasions. We both had a natural zest for life and we both came out of a good old English radical tradition. We were liberal, sceptical and republican.

Wells might have added that neither claimed to have set out to be an author of any sort, let alone a novelist. Nor was the slope of Parnassus as gently graded as Wells implied. Enoch Arnold Bennett, born on May 27, 1867, in Burslem, half-purposefully failed the bar in 1889, having no interest in becoming a lawyer. This intentional accident released him to London, where he became a law clerk for the firm of Brasseur and Oakley. To his delight and surprise, he fell in with artists. "It was soon afterwards," Bennett wrote in his anonymous autobiographical sketch, *The Truth about an Author* (1903), "that the artists whom I had twitted about their temperament accused me of sharing it with them to the full." Faced with such incontrovertible proof of his calling, Bennett surrendered his clerkship in 1893 to become assistant editor of the magazine *Woman*, the editorship of which he purchased in 1896 with money borrowed from his father. But his artist friends continued to twit Bennett until they had squeezed from him a "Yellow Book" short story ("A Letter Home," 1895) and then his first novel, *A Man from the North* (1898). Publication did not mean security, though Bennett achieved a steady enough income to resign his editorship of *Woman* in September 1900. He recalled in an *Evening Standard* review of Virginia Woolf's *A Room of One's Own* that "I have myself written long and formidable novels in bedrooms whose doors certainly had no locks, and in the full dreadful knowledge that I had not five hundred a year of my own—nor fifty." It was not until 1912 that Bennett struck literary oil, earning sixteen thousand pounds for the year, which he calculated to equal his combined income for all the years since his first paycheck in 1889.

Herbert George Wells, born September 21, 1866, in Bromley, took to literature even less purposefully than Bennett—not at the point of a dare, but of necessity. In the winter of 1893-94, a married teacher who had eloped with a student despite lacking the benefit of a divorce, Wells found himself unable to continue in his chosen profession due to tuberculosis. He took up the pen, he wrote in *Experiment in Autobiography*, because it was less taxing than the chalk: "Fate was pushing me to the writing desk in spite of myself. I decided that henceforth I must reckon class teaching in London as outside the range of my possibilities." After stunning early success—*The Time Machine* (1895) alone established a popular, if not quite a literary, reputation—Wells recovered from the controversies and setbacks of the early teens only with the commercial triumphs of *Mr. Britling Sees it Through* (1916) and *The Outline of History* (1920).

Whether Bennett or Wells might not have become novelists is, of course, impossible to determine, but it is significant that both of them willingly and publicly entertained that notion. In refusing the inevitability of authorship, each indirectly claimed a continuity between himself and the multitudes whom circumstances had not guided into literature. Bennett, especially, figured the artist as a sort of laborer, not the isolated antithesis of the salaried employee. He took particular criticism from F. R. Leavis for such contentions as "It is an essential part of the job of an artist to meet the demands of a market. He need not try to meet all of them, but he must meet some; because he must live, and if he has a family (as he should have) the family must live too." The calculated provocation in such pronouncements escaped Leavis; Bennett, after all, consistently boomed the work of such "highbrow" authors as James Joyce, E. M. Forster, Edith Sitwell, and D. H. Lawrence in his *Evening Standard* column. And Bennett was equally ready to blame readers for insufficient support, observing in his first column that "the population abuses its liberty not to read. Not enough new books are bought." Nevertheless, he and Wells both refused to figure the artist as a hothouse flower that required and deserved the special care of the mere workers who made bread. Bennett's jibe rests not only on the reasonable assumption that artists are not entitled to willfully condemn their spouses and children to everlasting penury, but also on an evolutionary vision of the social organism: if artists can interest no one in their work, perhaps they have become vestigial. Wells had mounted just such an argument concerning the decline of poetry in *The Outline of History*: "Developing more slowly and against the discouragement of the scholastic, academic and critical worlds, the form of prose fiction rose by degrees to equality with and then to a predominance over poetry. That was what people were really reading, that was what the times required."

Bennett, however, does not applaud these diminished expectations for literature; he instead goads artists into searching out where the audience for contemporary art lies. He had often declared, after all, that the British audience for serious art numbered only a few thousand, not enough to support anyone. The rest needed to be drawn in somehow; Bennett reflected in 1909's "The Novel Reading Public": "If you happen to be a literary artist . . . when you dine you eat the bread unwillingly furnished by the enemies of art and of progress! Still, there is a holy joy even in that." The same year, Wells's *Ann Veronica* appeared, with its contrast between the ineffectual poet, Manning, who clings resolutely to the circle of his own feelings, and the scientist-turned-playwright Capes (pronounced "Wells"), who makes his success by roiling the waters of a torpid public through the most public literary art. For Wells and Bennett, to practice a living art was to practice an art through which one might earn a living.

Both men recognized that success did not guarantee quality, nor quality ensure success. Both lamented public indifference to Conrad's work, both contributed anonymously to a fund established for the sustenance of D. H. Lawrence during the lean year of 1918. Certainly, though, Bennett and Wells realized their own ideal of the artist-worker, spinning out apparently endless skeins of words. Bennett even kept score, recording his word totals in his journal at the end of each year: 423,500 in 1908; 312,100 in 1909; 355,900 in 1910. These figures did not include the journal itself, which achieved more than a million words in the thirty-five years of its existence. Bennett credited such industry, not catering to popular tastes, for his relative wealth, arguing that "authors can only make a fair income if they have a great deal to say—like Shaw, Wells and me—and are incurably industrious, as we are. And they can only make it even then by not trying to make it. Shaw and Wells have always said: Be damned to popular taste. And I have given popular taste a miss for many years now."

Wells tallied more than a hundred books and pamphlets in his fifty-year career, including the only world history ever written by a novelist. Nor were books all that Wells and Bennett wrote; each understood the relation between keeping one's name before the public through journalism and attaining an audience for one's novels. They thus eventually earned far more than the daily bread in which Bennett had rejoiced early in 1909. Bennett perhaps spent more ostentatiously—he was particularly despised for his yachts, though he abandoned the sea when his daughter was born in 1926, not being nearly so rich as legend assumed. Wells, the practicing advocate of free love, generally found himself maintaining two households, yet left an estate about twice as large as Bennett's. Both paid heavily for their friendly rivalry of words and pounds in the contempt of the more fastidious generation of writers and critics who succeeded them. It was particularly difficult for these priests of culture to imagine that novelists with so prosaic a philosophy of their own art would work in any other but a strict realist mode. Such men of the world, the argument ran, could not possibly keep the taint of mundane interests from their work, could not avoid a superficial materialism. They could see only the most obvious realities. Besides, art was too hard for the big audiences Bennett and Wells had captured; ordinary readers want to believe they are reading stories of people, and grow impatient of any style that calls attention to the fact that they are reading fiction.

But in spite of their wealth of similarities—and their similarity of wealth—Wells and Bennett cannot be bracketed together as champions of realism. The crucial opposition in their attitudes toward their art reveals itself even in the modes by which each managed to write so prolifically. Arnold Bennett, his ideas organized in his mind on an afternoon or evening walk, devoted the same hours every morning for years to writing. He separated art and livelihood; while he wrote rapidly in any case, his journalism and lighter fiction had exceedingly shallow roots. He would allow the materials of his serious fiction to ripen for months or even years before reaping them in a novel. For instance, while he wrote *Riceyman Steps* in the incredible span of five months with virtually no revision, he had first conceived it two years earlier and had been collecting some of the incidents of which it was eventually composed as early as 1913 (ten years before its publication). While some of his voluminous other work has merit, Bennett lavished his best attentions on ten novels spaced quite evenly through his career: *A Man from the North* (1898), *Anna of the Five Towns* (1902), *The Old Wives' Tale* (1908), the Clayhanger trilogy (1910–1916), *The Pretty Lady* (1917), *Riceyman Steps* (1923), *Lord Raingo* (1926), and *Imperial Palace* (1930). He worked as diligently on several other works, but to less effect.

H. G. Wells, despite a similar fixity of hours, took a very different approach to his labors. He wrote in a creative fury, usually revising heavily in the afternoon what he had drafted the same morning. Wells wrote his way toward what he wanted to say, his eye fixed on the object of his writing, not on the writing itself. Bennett knew what he wanted to say; he wrote with his attention turned toward his own technique in writing it. Wells confessed fully attending to technique in only one of his forty-odd novels: *Tono-Bungay* (1909), though *Mr. Britling Sees It Through* (1916) and *Joan and Peter* (1918) also received unusual care. The rest he admitted to writing in the journalistic spirit, sufficient unto the work of the day with no pretensions to permanence. In disavowing the artfulness of ninety percent of his novels, however, Wells did not disavow their worth as much as it seems. Art and life remained resolutely separate for Wells, and he valued service to the latter over devotion to the former; he perceived the novel chiefly as a vehicle for the delivery of an idea, a means of transmission. Wells identified "art" with formula, understood the conventions of fictional presentation as barriers against the inclusion of real life. He was not a realist out of respect for a tradition, but as a function of his antitraditionalism. Bennett, however, perceived that the novelist's art was not separable from the novel's statement, that the mode of the novel was itself the transmission. H. G. Wells did not believe in the novel; Arnold Bennett believed in nothing else.

Tono-Bungay epitomizes Wells's work as perhaps no other single novel by a similarly productive novelist does. *Tono-Bungay* is ostensibly written by its main character, George Ponderevo, who feels his life is worth recording because he has chanced to observe at close quarters an unusually broad cross section of English society. Born to a life of service on a once-great country estate, Bladesover, he is fortunately exiled from his original station after besting a relative of the house's lady in a fistfight over his paramour, Beatrice Normandy, the sister of his opponent. After a brief, nightmare apprenticeship to a pietistic baker, George enters the house and employment of his Aunt Susan and Uncle Edward "Teddy" Ponderevo, a provincial chemist with bold ambitions if little sense. Although Teddy goes bust through ill-timed investments, losing George's small trust fund in the process, George is able to win sufficient scholarship money to attend university in London. He parts company with his insolvent uncle and beloved Aunt Susan for a time. But he eventually fixes himself to his uncle's star a second time, as he has no other way to earn a salary high enough to win the marital consent of Marion Ramboat, a middle-class woman who entirely lacks a taste for risk. Their marriage founders, but Teddy's new enterprise, a patent medicine called "Tono-Bungay," comes in spectacularly. At loose in the world of high finance, Teddy eventually overreaches himself. George attempts to retrieve the company's fortunes by liberating a large quantity of an extremely radioactive substance known as "quap" from an unnamed foreign power's African colony. He fails. In the meantime, Beatrice Normandy, his childhood love, has reentered George's life. This love, too, falters; Beatrice is already the mistress of a monied aristocrat. At the end of the novel Uncle Teddy dies, shattered by his financial fall, and Beatrice takes her final leave of George, abandoning him to contemplate the waste his life has been even as he embarks on a new career as a designer of warships. *Tono-Bungay* exceeds Wells's own hope to have written "a novel, as I imagined it, on Dickens-Thackeray lines," to have created a "social panorama in the vein of Balzac." This trio shared Wells's concern with seeing through to life, with engendering reactions to the society they represented rather than to the means of representation. Paradoxically, a certain laxity of construction—e.g., the Dickensian coincidence—bespeaks this intention: rough writing means the writing is not itself the point. Indeed, Dickens and Thackeray (though emphatically not Balzac) were precisely the novelists whom the contemporaries of Wells—Bennett prominent among them—abused as the artless inferiors of such continentals as Flaubert and Turgenev.

Wells did not merely follow his progenitors, however; he attempted to purge the novel's form of its lingering unrealisms. *Tono-Bungay* enacts that purgation, employing Dickensian characterization in order to critique it. Its population might have been recruited from the strongly marked "types" so numerous in Dickens (and in Balzac's *Comédie humaine*); every character but the narrator seems bounded by some identifying trait, some humor that endures all the onslaughts of experience. The names of such minor personages as Nicodemus Frapp and Lord Boom suggest the fixity of the human landscape one seems to encounter in *Tono-Bungay*. The method extends to major characters. Teddy Ponderevo expels breath with the same four-lettered "Zzzz" throughout the novel—he Zzzz's on his deathbed—and endlessly spouts the same barmy advice to his nephew. One can never forget the roundness of his belly, because the narrator continually reminds one of it. His wife, Susan, hitches the adjective "old" to every conceivable noun, and several inconceivable ones, thus establishing her indestructible wise insouciance. But Wells transforms the technique of the earlier realists in *Tono-Bungay*, in that the moral value of character does not depend on character itself. Character for Wells does not itself exist on a moral scale, as in Dickens or Balzac; rather, the interactions of each individuality with the extant social order produces a final mixed effect of good and ill. The social order, of course, impinges on Dickens's characters, but it does not permeate them. That is, character itself, forged though it may have been in particular social circumstances, has a moral dimension: Mr. Micawber is inherently good, Uriah Heep inherently bad. But in a startling revision of Dickens, Wells reveals Mr. Micawber and Uriah Heep to be the same man—Teddy Ponderevo, the bustling, energetic, good-hearted little Englishman, is also an embezzler, a fraud, and a forger. He is a megalomaniac because British capitalism channels his energies into self-aggrandizement. This energy is itself neutral: Teddy does not grow bad-intentioned with wealth. There are no conversions of character in *Tono-Bungay*, only changes of context.

In *Tono-Bungay*, Wells continually reconfigures Dickensian prototypes in order to suggest the inseparability of individual character from its social context. Like David Copperfield, George Ponderevo titles the chapters of his life story after what sound like mock-heroic steps toward self-possession: "How I became a London Student, and Went Astray," "Our Progress from Camden Town to Crest Hill." George's story, though, leads him not to a recognition of his essential self but to a recognition that his personal life is hopelessly enmeshed in the life of his times. The novel, indeed, modulates from the voice of Dickens to the voice of Conrad—a strategy thought by Mark Schorer, writing at a time when critics were hypnotized by the notion of organic unity, to be a disabling flaw. On the African expedition to recover his uncle's lost fortunes by the theft of the valuable radioactive substance known as "quap," George encounters the Conradian jungle, the moral idiocy of the physical universe—recognition of which can engender a concomitant decay in human morals, the illusion of a naturally authorized ethical code being lost. George, in fact, murders a man to keep him from reporting the illicit expedition's whereabouts. The action occurs thoughtlessly, in a moment, and alters George's subsequent behavior hardly at all. Inconsequential murder would violate the fundamental laws of the Dickensian universe—to Wells, an unreal universe he is determined to complicate. *Tono-Bungay* ends with a description of the Thames reminiscent of Conrad's in *Heart of Darkness*, in which Marlow reminds his listeners that London, too, "has been one of the dark places of the earth"—except that London's present, not its past, is now the emblem of meaninglessness and chaos: "The third [most modern] part of the panorama of London is beyond all law, order, and precedence, it is the seaport and the sea. . . . And amidst it all no plan appears, no intention, no comprehensive desire. That is the very key of it all." The novel has set the bright Dickensian vision of English "characters" in the frame of a world that forecloses the role of essential character in determining the moral status of a life.

In *Tono-Bungay*, Wells achieved his farthest-seeing analysis of the English social system that, for him, was the ultimate reality shaping English lives. The novel sets its spade into the long, hard roots of Edwardian England, tracing the stages of its growth, revealing it to be but the most recent moment in the nation's long life. Wells exposes the flimsy insecurity of his own age through a profusion of symbols, perhaps the most brilliant of which, as David Ludge has noted, are a series of architectural metaphors. George Ponderevo, much of an age with Wells himself, passes his infancy and boyhood as the son of a servant on the country estate of Bladesover. Bladesover, the House of England, is no Victorian construction, though Wells fills it with seriocomic Victorians; it was raised after the Glorious Revolution of 1688, and the sole intellectual proprietor in its history was an Enlightenment gentleman. The Glorious Revolution established the enduring English social dispensation; the novel frequently conflates the early eighteenth and early twentieth centuries. Even as the landed gentry die away, the aristocrats of wealth fill their places. The new sword will eventually outwear this old sheath, but the Bladesover model—a naturally privileged upper class in whose service the infinitely subdivided lower orders produce all the material goods of the world—still largely determines the modes of action available to individuals.

George relives the history of his nation in his own development, beginning as a blind adherent of Bladesover. His first education in other notions of society comes from Enlightenment texts. But the ideas in them have made no progress since the Enlightenment, have even lost ground. No one directs George to Swift and Paine; rather, he finds their works neglected in one of the estate's old dormers. When he is old enough, he attends "the sort of school the Bladesover system permitted." Just as the focus of English society has shifted in the past two hundred years from the country to London, so George is eventually drawn to the metropolis. And such a move is no move at all—George learns to recognize the enduring frame of Bladesover society behind the façades of London:

And I struck out a truth one day in Cromwell Road quite suddenly, as I looked over the Natural History Museum; "By Jove!" said I, "but this is the little assemblage of cases of stuffed birds and animals upon the Bladesover staircase grown enormous, and yonder as the corresponding thing to the Bladesover curios and porcelain is the Art Museum, and there in the observatories in Exhibition Road is old Sir Cuthbert's Gregorian telescope that I hunted out in the storeroom and put together."

When George contemplates a career of public service in scientific research, Uncle Teddy reminds him that modern science serves the new commercial Bladesover, not the public: "And who pays for that? . . . Enterprising business men! They fancy they'll have a bit of science going on, they want a handy Expert ever and again, and there you are!" For the rest of the novel, George watches his uncle recapitulate the fossilization of Bladesover, the replacement of its once-living aristocratic tissue with the new substance of money. In describing his rise, George notes that "in some of the old seventeenth and early eighteenth century prayerbooks at Bladesover there used to be illustrations with long scrolls coming out of the mouths of the wood-cut figures. I wish I could write all this last chapter on a scroll coming out of the head of my uncle."

The long national metamorphosis of which Teddy's career is a brief microcosm shows how inhabiting the Bladesover House has shaped the new money aristocracy. Sundered from the class in which they originated, they are soon weaned from any affection for the new. They join "in the plunder of the eighteenth century, buy rare old books, fine old pictures, good old furniture. Their first crude conception of dazzling suites of the newly perfect is replaced almost from the outset by a jackdaw dream of accumulating costly discrepant old things." Edward Ponderevo, who had longed to "make things happen," who had decried Lord Eastry's domination of provincial Wimblehurst—"*He* doesn't want anything more to happen. Why should he? Any change 'ud be a loss to him"—becomes an untitled equivalent of Lord Eastry, determined to do his "duty by the Parish," acclaiming the system that has worked the transformation: "It's staid and stable, and yet it has a place for new men. We come up and take our places." Indeed, no new social dispensation has arisen in England since the Anglican orthodoxy consolidated its grip in the eighteenth century. Even Teddy's fall reproduces an old pattern. George Ponderevo, describing his uncle's increasingly dubious financial maneuvers (such as refinancing his subsidiary companies by directing them to sell stock to each other), notes that "that was our method of equilibrium at the iridescent climax of the bubble." Perhaps the most famous stock manipulation in English history was the notorious South Sea Bubble scandal of 1711 to 1720, wherein a coterie of well-connected schemers (two of whom bore the uncannily appropriate names Blunt and Craggs) undertook to finance the national debt by speculation in essentially worthless stock. The bubble symbolizes the frailty of the social arrangement England has uncertainly ridden for the last two hundred years. George observes

that all this present commercial civilisation is no more than my poor uncle's career writ large, a swelling, thinning bubble of assurances; that its arithmetic is just as unsound, its dividends as ill-advised, its ultimate aim as vague and forgotten; that it all drifts on perhaps to some tremendous parallel to his individual disaster.

Wells extends the analysis before and beyond the Bladesover era via the last two houses Edward Ponderevo annexes. The penultimate Ponderevo mansion, Lady Grove, is also the oldest of the lot, its founders having fought in the First Crusade. Remote as it is, the period of Lady Grove's origin represents an awakening that sleeping Bladesover has forgotten. Wells wrote of the First Crusade in *The Outline of History*: "Here for the first time we discover Europe with an idea and a soul! . . . It is clear that we are dealing with something new that has come into the world, a new clear connection of the common interest with the consciousness of the common man." Even having long vanished, the period is less evanescent than Bladesover in its senile presence; on the house's earliest portraits, George finds "smiles of triumphant completion," while the Victorian decorations of the house seem "even more extinct . . . than the Crusades." But when Teddy attempts to go beyond Bladesover, to found his own house—"a Twentieth-Century House!"—Crest Hill, he fails utterly. The ultimate house of Ponderevo is, like the Europe of 1900, an incoherent accumulation of contradictory ideas, none themselves new. Its literal collapse prefigures the coming European smash.

Just as the new owners of England cannot build, so they cannot engender; George describes Crest Hill as "the empty instinctive building of a childless man." *Tono-Bungay* represents the most formidable union of Wells's political and sexual radicalisms, for it suggests that the modern capitalist version of Bladesover is powered by a diversion of sexual energies. Tono-Bungay, "The Secret of Vigour," becomes such a walloping success because of its whispered promise of forbidden sexual vitality. Indeed, the failure of sexual pleasure is the foundation of business; in the presence of Teddy, George's friend Bob Ewart explains the economics of desire: "What do we want? *You* know. *I* know. What we all want to be is something perpetually young and beautiful . . . pursuing coy half-willing nymphs through everlasting forests." "Damn clever fellow," Teddy praises Ewart after his departure. Ewart immortalizes his perception in a mock advertisement that, George writes, featured "my uncle, excessively and needlessly nude . . . engaged in feats of strength of a Gargantuan type before an audience of deboshed and shattered ladies." The motto of Tono-Bungay appears beneath the drawing.

Tono-Bungay is the false promise of sexual vigor in a world that denies the reality—denies it in order to sell the false promise. George's romantic life proves an apt emblem of Tono-Bungay's malign influence. He enters his uncle's employ in order to attain the three hundred pounds a year that Marion Ramboat demands before they wed. In effect, he must purchase sanction for the sexual union he desires—Bladesover extends property law to women. The marriage fails, however, because Marion cannot release the sexual instincts that it has always been in her best interests to repress—to yield too early would mean to lose the chance of marriage altogether, and so be hemmed in a sordid corner of life. The two can only meet on a presexual level: "There was a nonsensical sort of baby-talk I picked up . . . that became a mighty peacemaker." The enduring Victorian ideal of romantic love, with its willful indifference to physical facts, is thus depicted as a means for repressing socially inconvenient sexuality. A different sort of romance claims Teddy Ponderevo. In accordance with his Napoleonic conceit—he styles himself on that emperor—he briefly takes a mistress. His wife, Susan—who, the novel hints, really belongs with George, did convention allow such matches—puts a quick end to the affair. But the effect on Teddy is profound, nearly ruining his marriage. He cannot feel satisfied without the romantic illusion of careless love, the romantic elevation of the desires of the heroic self. Romance, whether in monetary or human commerce, receives a very bad press in *Tono-Bungay*.

The pain of frustrated sexuality colors every fiber of the novel. George Ponderevo's halting, disconnected narration is a long avoidance of his loss of Beatrice Normandy: "The pain I felt then I have felt a hundred times . . . that is what haunts this book, from end to end." Once George has told his central trauma, the novel ends, just as psychoanalysis would. But this failure of desire is hardly personal; it at once produces and is produced by the consciousness of the age. Wells ironically titles the chapter in which George relates the tale of his doomed love for Beatrice "Love among the Wreckage." Robert Browning's "Love among the Ruins," of course, contrasts love with the ruins of empire, concluding "love is best." In *Tono-Bungay*, there is no such contrast. The ruin of love preserves the sterile health of society; love is indeed among—in the sense of being part of—the wreckage. Beatrice is the daughter of a family with noble bloodlines but no wealth to support the old style of living. She attaches herself as mistress to a providing aristocrat, the only role such a system has reserved for her, work or a low marriage having been programmed out of her. Instead of leading her lover to paradise, she has herself been ruined by the Bladesover system.

This final failure drives George back once again into the service of a society that is sowing its own destruction. He returns first to his flying machines. The root of his Icarean endeavor to fly is the mingled desire to impress Beatrice and to forget his difficulties with her. George speaks figuratively of science as the perfect mistress, thus revealing the sexual displacement at the root of his infatuation with it. He experiences "contact with primary and elemental necessities" not through sexuality but through flight, which he describes in unmistakably sexual terms: "I set my teeth and groaned. It was a groan wrung out of me in spite of myself. My sensations of terror swooped to a climax." Flight means only escape, not spiritual elevation; George's one scientific triumph, a successful channel-crossing in his airship, occurs in a desperate attempt to spirit his uncle away from the authorities after his financial chicanery has been revealed. George concludes of his own tale: "I have called it *Tono-Bungay*, but I had far better have called it *Waste*. I have told of childless Marion, of my childless aunt, of Beatrice wasted and wasteful and futile." At the novel's end, George is engineering destroyers for the international market, apparently intent on speeding the passage of his era into oblivion. Frustrated love is death.

George Ponderevo's quest to retrieve quap from Mordet Island is on one level the logical international consequence of the national system. If all national production serves a few monarchs of commerce, then the products of all the world should serve the few monarchs among nations, especially England. Such an arrangement reduces the inhabitants of other lands to commercial obstacles; George declares "I meant to get that quap aboard if I had to kill some one to do it." And so he does. The African he shoots (in the back) has evidently already suffered a transition into the world of commerce: "He carried a musket, and a powder flask was stuck in his girdle." He is the mirror image and secret guilt of Blades-over; his corpse is disinterred from its grave twice, and it becomes confused for George with the nightmare vision of his uncle's face hovering dead-white over a garishly slit throat. But this adventure also implies that the universe, rather than being successively refined by evolutionary progress, might betray the same tendency to chaotic collapse as the European social order. The antithesis of Tono-Bungay, the reality to its vital lie, is the lethally radioactive quap. It parallels the real bankruptcy behind the Bladesover façade: "It is in matter exactly what the decay of our old culture is in society, a loss of traditions and distinctions and assured reactions." But quap is more than a symbol; it reveals the literal potential for dissolution in the physical universe, and for that very reason it cuts the pins from under any conceivable teleology. George entertains

a queer persistent fancy. Suppose indeed that is to be the final end of our planet; no splendid climax and finale, no towering accumulation of achievements but just—atomic decay! . . . If single human beings—if one single rickety infant—can be born as it were by accident and die futile, why not the whole race?

The idea that the social organism must evolve naturally toward justice and stability, cherished by such nineteenth-century thinkers as Herbert Spencer, is ironically reversed in *Tono-Bungay*, which denies progressive evolution as the universal principle of either humanity or matter. Wells the social realist and Wells the scientific romancer dovetail in *Tono-Bungay* as in no other novel.

Despite its indulgence in the most extreme apocalyptic prophecies, *Tono-Bungay* is in one sense an optimistic book. It assumes that illusions will vanish and that ultimate realities, however dire their consequences may be, will at last assert themselves. Teddy Ponderevo's empire must collapse if he cannot finally "show value"; that is, produce substantial assets to cover the rising debt of his false promises. Wells is true to the realist tradition in assuming a phenomenal world separate from and knowable by consciousness. For all the flamboyant, engaging improbability of its plot, *Tono-Bungay* is utterly realist in its continual, explicit correction of romantic illusions: the romance of commerce, the romance of the Napoleonic leader, the romance of romantic love. Even the mild experiment of displaying the influence of the narrator's consciousness on the tale he narrates does little to call into question the human capacity for distinguishing between illusion and reality. Wells, in fact, never creates more than one real consciousness—one real point of view—in a novel. Many of Wells's novels bear eponymous titles and practically all of them could. Wells never registers more than one guest at a time in his house of fiction; he is intent on examining Wells, on wrestling with his own real beliefs about the real world. As he cheerily blustered in a letter to Bennett, "I am a purblind laborious intelligence exploring that cell of Being called Wells." The fictionality of fiction held an ever-diminishing interest for him. "Who would read a novel," he asked rhetorically in 1934's *Experiment in Autobiography*, "if we were permitted to write biography—all out?" He goes on to speculate that prose fiction could not endure "against a literature of competent historical and contemporary studies."

Arnold Bennett, as Wells himself recognized, was an entirely different animal. The *Experiment in Autobiography* addresses the question of the "artistic temperament," to which Wells rather proudly lays no claim. After contrasting his own readily educated mind with the artistic resistance to education—where he sees sets of relations, authors like Conrad see things intensively as themselves—Wells considers the case of Bennett: "I would say that in my sense he was absolutely immune to education and that he did not need it. . . . The bright clear mosaic of impressions was continually being added to and all the pieces stayed in their places. He did not feel the need for a philosophy or for a faith or for anything to hold them together." Bennett is, in fact, a good deal like Bob Ewart of *Tono-Bungay*. The Ewart type is a commonplace in Wells's fiction, Wells having had just such a friend in youth, Sidney Bowkett. But Ewart, with his pipe, his Francophilia, his mistress, his detached vision of particulars, also owes something to the later friend. Indeed, George Ponderevo's description of Ewart's clear-sighted moral inertia sounds remarkably similar to Bennett's self-analysis in a letter he sent Wells in September 1905. George remarks:

It was only very slowly I came to gauge Ewart's real position in the scheme of things, to understand how deliberate and complete was this detachment of his from the moral condemnation and responsibilities that played so fine a part in his talk. He was essentially the nature of an artistic appreciator; he could find interest and beauty in endless aspects of things that I marked as evil, or at least as not negotiable.

Bennett had written to Wells:

I look down from a height on the show and contemplate a passion for justice much as I contemplate the other ingredients. Whereas you are simply a passion for justice incarnate. You aren't an artist, except insofar as you disdainfully make use of art for your reforming ends; you are simply a reformer. . . . Art, really, you hate. It means to you what "arty" means to me. . . . You will never see it, but in rejecting surface values you are wrong. As a fact they are just as important as other values. But reformers can't perceive this. They are capable of classing chefs, pianists and *trains de luxe* all together and saying: "Go to, I am a serious person."

Bennett's ideal was not an idle Epicurean aestheticism, however. His identification of himself as an artist gave him a position from which to subvert the very realist traditions that Wells sought to extend. In his debates with Wells, Bennett emphasized the necessary unreality of fiction. He responded to Wells's criticism of an "unrealistic" character in Bennett's *Sacred and Profane Love* by noting that any character is "an arrangement to suit the necessities of a convention; and here and there he bears a resemblance to a man." And Bennett's best novels are aggressively polyglossic, introducing several centers of consciousness that undermine each other's claims to authority. Bennett challenges the notion of a human reason adequate to disentangle reality from illusion, competent to recognize the unconscious motives that irremediably color perceptions.

No single novel apotheosizes Bennett's work, but *Riceyman Steps* (1923) was his most consciously mounted subversion of realist assumptions. By the time he wrote *Riceyman Steps*, he had long since abandoned any allegiance to realism; as early as January 1899 he had written in his journal, "The day of my enthusiasm for 'realism,' for 'naturalism,' has passed." Not that he proposed to range freely in the zodiac of his own wit; he continued in the same journal entry to declare his intention of "abiding by the envelope of facts." But the facts themselves were not the point; as Bennett had written in his journal a year earlier, "An artist must be interested primarily in presentment, not in the thing presented." *The Old Wives' Tale* (1908) is the fruition of Bennett's early emphasis on technique. Superficially the novel states only the obvious; everything declines and dies. But it discovers new meanings in the old theme by the highly articulated symmetries of its presentation. Set in the area of Bennett's birth, the six towns of England's potteries district, the novel depicts virtually the entire lives of Constance and Sophia Baines, the daughters of a shop owner in Bursley, "the mother of the Five Towns." It begins with the sisters on the threshhold of adulthood; it ends after Constance, the older, less rebellious and longer-lived, has died. Inspired by Maupassant's *Une Vie* (A woman's life, 1883), Bennett goes his master one better not only in doubling the depicted lives, but in using them as an extended metaphor for the life of the nation from the mid-1860s to the turn of the century. Where Maupassant's work is an intensive examination of individual psychology, Bennett's manipulates the congruities between personal and public life. It begins with the death of John Baines, the semiparalyzed father of Constance and Sophia Baines, who serves as a symbol of high Victorianism. Both Bursley and Constance, each in its way a "mother of the Five Towns," lose themselves when they lose their familiar points of reference. Bursley, at the end of the novel, is ripe to be swallowed up in a newly federated Five Towns (in real life, the six potteries towns were incorporated as Stoke-on-Trent). Constance contracts her final illness by walking, in raw weather, to cast her vote against Federation.

But Bennett extends the analysis by unexpected parallels between stay-at-home Constance and her rebellious sister Sophia. Both engage in simultaneous secret courtships in their youth. Sophia ultimately dies after an attack "determined by cold produced by rapid motion in an automobile." Like Constance, Sophia suffers the effects of rapid motion in a larger sense as well. As a young woman, she had eloped with Gerald Scales, who quickly proved a ne'er-do-well. Gerald eventually left Sophia, who finally recovered her fortunes by running a Parisian pension in as hard-handed a Five Towns manner as possible. She finally regained contact with her sister, sold the pension, and returned to the narrow, dark house she had fled. One day, the threatening news of Gerald's return comes. But when Sophia goes to meet him, she experiences "a genuine unforeseen shock, the most violent that she had ever had": Gerald's corpse, the shrunken body of a destitute old man, a man she had last seen in vigorous youth. On her automobile ride back to Bursley after viewing the body, Sophia suffers her fatal attack. The deaths of the two sisters are at once parallel and divergent. Both, of course, are victims of time, but while the rapidity of social movement undoes Constance, Sophia is staggered by generational succession. As Bennett's novel shows, and as Sophia partly recognizes, each generation relives the experience of its predecessors; there is no unique identity in the face of the universality of age and death. The novel is filled with casual references to ancestors and descendants who mimic the lives of the main characters; it quietly includes the generations of dogs who live and die within the lifetime of the sisters. The novel ultimately besieges the notion of essential identity from opposite directions: the world changes, and we are no longer who we thought, our points of orientation being gone; the world stays the same, and we are no longer who we thought, our lives replaying universal patterns.

But even *The Old Wives' Tale*, though to a lesser extent than *Anna of the Five Towns* (1902) or *Clayhanger* (1910), rests on the assumption that the world impinges on human consciousness more than the opposite, and that the dimensions of its influence may be judged by human reason. As do all the Five Towns novels, *The Old Wives' Tale* focuses on characters who have very little power, and who struggle with only partial success to organize their lives as they see fit, despite the restrictions of their familial, social, and physical environments. In all the Five Towns novels, particularly *Clayhanger*, the hope to reorganize society along more rational lines remains unrealized. When Bennett shifted the locale of his fiction to London, he began to focus on middle-aged men who have the power to implement their own visions of a rational life. The adequacy of that vision, and the objectivity of reason (particularly of the sort in which men have often asserted their superiority over women), are themselves called into question.

In 1917, Bennett decided that he had worked the Five Towns vein artistically dry and turned to London, devising what he called in a letter to André Gide "a new manner," which he first assayed in *The Pretty Lady* (1917) and perfected in *Riceyman Steps*. Never comfortable making claims for his own books, Bennett characterized *Riceyman Steps* to Gide as "réaliste," but then undercut the description by continuing that he was "almost succeeding" in his attempt "to invent a form to supersede Balzac's." Bennett had coveted the sociological method of *La comédie humaine* when he embarked on his series of Five Towns novels; now he sought a new balance between the comprehensible influences of social structures and the incomprehensible force of the unconscious. The First World War in particular broke Bennett of his earlier, Wellsian belief in the adequacy of conscious organization to revise the dangerous habits into which the industrial world had fallen. *Riceyman Steps* grew from the graveyard of the war. It grew, more particularly, from a yachting trip Bennett took in 1921, with the physician and anthropologist W. H. R. Rivers—Siegfried Sassoon's doctor—aboard for part of the cruise. Rivers, an early English disseminator of Freud's ideas, reported in his *Instinct and the Unconscious* (1921) that the war had hastened acceptance of Freudian ideas by the British medical community, shell shock demonstrating the operation of repression more convincingly than any prewar civilian neurosis had. He talked of Freud and war neurosis with Bennett, who later described that encounter as "the most truly educational experience I have ever had," noting particularly that Rivers had been "thrilling on the self-protective nature of shell-shock and kindred disorders." When the yacht docked at Southhampton, Bennett chanced upon a cluttered second-hand bookstore and conceived a story about two misers that would become *Riceyman Steps.*

George Moore described the plot of *Riceyman Steps*, which he greatly admired, as "A bookseller crosses the road to get married—that's all." Moore's description is not quite all, but it is much. The seller of rare and used books, a middle-aged denizen of Clerkenwell named Henry Earlforward, courts and marries Violet Arb, a widow who runs a confectioner's shop across the street from him. Before their marriage, they each employ a charwoman named Elsie Sprickett, who becomes their general maid once they have wed, Violet selling her business to move in with Henry. Elsie loves Joe, a neurasthenic veteran of the Great War, who is both the servant and patient of a panel doctor named Raste. Joe becomes wild one night, strikes Elsie, and departs for more than a year. The Earlforward marriage, happy at first, increasingly flickers into conflict over Henry's extreme parsimony. By the time Joe returns, feverish from a recurrence of his wartime malaria, both the Earlforwards are gravely ill. They die; Joe recovers. The bookshop's stock is sold; the shop itself is purchased by the same cheesemonger who had acquired Violet's premises. Elsie and Joe become maid and manservant to Dr. Raste.

The bookseller's shop is also a House of England, a shrunken, dusty Bladesover; old, valuable, unread books, "hopeless, resigned, martyrized," litter its floors; when a blind slips down, deepening the gloom, no attempt is made to raise it. The shop's inhabitants continually both recall and enact the social certainties of an earlier England. But the apocalypse has now come—"The truth is, we haven't been straight in here since 1914," Henry Earlforward declares to a customer early in the novel. The customer, Dr. Raste, represents one of the disorienting new conditions; an ex-soldier, he "had learnt manners above his original station in a strange place—Palestine, under Allenby." Earlforward conceives an immediate distaste for the doctor. He dislikes his "interfering" manner; in effect, he cannot stomach a man who represents in his own person the leveling changes the war has set in motion. Furthermore, Raste warns him of a possible extension of these disarrangements to his own establishment in the form of desertion by his charwoman, Elsie. Bennett had foreseen the war's acceleration of social change days after it began, marveling in his journal on August 10, 1914, that "the fear of revolution or serious social uproar after the War does not trouble anybody. Few even think of it." The brisk, efficient panel doctor invades the disorder of this essentially prewar house, yet himself acts as a symbol of postwar disorientations for the place's owner, to whom the shop is a scrupulously and delicately organized achievement.

Signs of apocalypse litter the novel, and yet they are apocalyptic chiefly from the conservative perspective of Henry and his wife Violet; or, rather, the undermining of their unchallenged perspective *is* the apocalypse. The postwar inflation and Bolshevism become for Henry evidence that England resembles ancient Rome on the verge of its collapse. But Henry spins this public apocalypse from his own need to maintain private control, using it to frighten his wife into obedience. He takes the opportunity of a newspaper report on a murder in a Clerkenwell communist club to inveigh against famine in the Volga region; the practice of severe economy seems the only means to achieve security in such a world of perils. In fact, he and his wife slowly starve themselves to death, hoarding gold against the imminent collapse of England. Henry's interpretations of public events are projections of his own mingled fears and desires for a personal apocalypse. On one hand, he craves the security of the known, the traditional, the past—a seller of antique books, he plans at the beginning of the novel to court Violet with tales of old Clerkenwell; he honeymoons with her among the lifeless figures of history at Madame Tussaud's; he approves her removal to London Hospital because it is the city's oldest. Henry's "grand passion" is not merely saving money; it is achieving predictability, paring down his life so as to avoid the accidents of desire. Through his miserliness, he withholds himself—to spend nothing is to do nothing, to risk nothing. And yet he unlocks his heart long enough to surrender himself to the unknown future, the unknown other, through marriage.

Henry Earlforward, in fact, is Arnold Bennett made up for a part. Though emphatically not a miser, Bennett, like Henry, considered himself "a great practical philosopher"; Bennett, like Henry, was "highly nervously organized," registering emotions as physical ailments; Bennett, like Henry, lived in a minutely organized fashion, even writing "pocket philosophies" with such titles as *The Human Machine* and *How to Live on Twenty-Four Hours a Day*; Bennett, like Henry, so offended his wife by his mild pertinacity that she branded him "an utterly selfish man." Through the figure of Henry, Bennett revises both himself and the realist assumptions of much prewar, premodernist fiction (including his own). In his notebook for *Riceyman Steps*, Bennett had written on a page headed "Henry": "Eternal delusion: he could manage." The war had taught Bennett to distrust the positivist assumptions that underlie even so pessimistic a novel as *Tono-Bungay*. Before the war, when Balzac was still his master, Bennett had created a miser in whom he embodied all the values he most despised: Ephraim Tellwright of *Anna of the Five Towns*, who represents paternalist authority, indifference to beauty, and the reign of unreasoning habit. Now he created a miser who embodied the traits he had always most valued: self-control, organization, reason. By so doing, he reenvisioned as a sort of neurosis the old progressive belief in the adequacy of reason to reorganize a manifestly ill-constructed society. Bennett thus bares the conservative root of the old progressivism. It refuses to acknowledge the irrational self, insisting on the vision of a reality separate from and knowable by consciousness, on the possibility of basing a just society on what the world itself, not desire, dictates. In *Riceyman Steps*, Bennett reinterprets the submission of desire to reason as self-protection. One submits to "impersonal" reason to avoid facing oneself, but nevertheless acts on desire; unconscious motives irremediably taint conscious reason. In particular, Bennett reads male reason as a means to impose dominion over women.

Riceyman Steps teems with unconscious communication, with the symbolic expression of unacknowledged motives. Late in the novel, Henry, apparently desperate to halt Elsie's gluttonous consumption of the minuscule portions of food he has already refused himself, asks Violet to help fool Elsie into believing he is dying. Elsie, he reasons, could not possibly scruple to steal food from a dying man. But the ruse is unconsciously directed elsewhere; Henry really is dying, as he unwittingly informs his wife through the medium of Elsie. Another instance of such communication occurs earlier, when Henry's wife pays to have his shop vacuum-cleaned as a wedding present, then recklessly continues to tidy up. Henry objects on the reasonable grounds that his business requires filth to convince customers that bargains lurk beneath the dust. But he also asks one of the workmen, referring to the vacuumed dirt, "Do you sell it? Do you get anything for it?" The question unveils a cluster of associated secrets. Even on his wedding night, Henry cannot resist the retention of waste, of money, of the self; soon, he will embark on a parallel string of rejections, disclaiming food, sex, the other. More and more as the novel continues, Henry perceives Violet as the enemy of his grand passion, acting in sinister concert with Elsie. Henry's rational, conscious organization is more and more clearly shown to be a device by which he unconsciously struggles to preserve the inviolability of his own perspective from the women of his house.

This post-Freudian image of the human mind calls for a literary perspectivism; that is, a recognition that no one angle of observation has absolute precedence over others. But Bennett's novel seems to employ an omniscient narrator who offers an authoritative perspective on events—in both senses of "authoritative." And Bennett wrote *Riceyman Steps* after he had reviewed *Ulysses*, beside which the polyglossia of *Riceyman Steps* seems very tame. In creating his own "form to supersede Balzac's," however, Bennett subverted the realist conventions from within, rather than fighting to escape the orbit of those conventions, as the modernists did. While the modernists assuredly developed many techniques that remained forever outside Bennett's scope, he developed a form that at once recognized the conventions of reading *as* conventions and retained the detailed portraiture of socioeconomic influences that such modernists as Joyce and Woolf sacrificed. Bennett accomplishes this feat by introducing an unreliable third-person narrator whose observations and analyses, though they seem to bear the weight of authorial judgment, undermine themselves in the course of the novel. Early in *Riceyman Steps*, the narrator describes the environs and populace of Riceyman Square as a

dingy and sordid neighborhood where existence was a dangerous and difficult adventure in almost frantic quest of food, drink and shelter . . . and where the immense majority of the population read nothing but sporting prognostications and results, and, on Sunday morning, accounts of bloody crimes and juicy sexual irregularities.

The relatively urbane Earlforwards seem "strangely, even fatally, out of place" in this neighborhood. But their story *is* a tale of "bloody crime and sexual irregularity." Violet complains of Henry's increasing sexual incapacity; he dies after a theft (of sixpence). They share the most squalid passions of the district they inhabit, if in sublimated form: Violet can, without a program, identify all but one of the notable murders in Madame Tussaud's Chamber of Horrors. Though it comes as a great surprise to the reader when, at the end of the novel, Henry and Violet themselves become the stuff that tabloids are made on, only the narrator's scrupulous identification with their point of view (and Elsie's) has prevented such a recognition. Such people as the Earlforwards never imagine their own lives as tabloid headlines.

The narrator does deploy the ambiguous "seems" in his early description of how the bookseller fits into Clerkenwell; it seems possible that an alert reader might distinguish reality from appearance in the world of the novel—or, rather, that the novel might constitute an education in such distinctions. But the more carefully one reads *Riceyman Steps*, the more clearly it reminds one of the indeterminacy of reading—that interpretation never depends solely on the object under interpretation, but on the angle of its relationship to the interpreter. Violet Arb enters the novel almost as an emblem of vivacity, as Henry's inverse. She continually, if affectionately, belittles his beloved Clerkenwell. But from another, more distant perspective, Violet is Henry's twin, not his opposite. When a new proprietor converts the nondescript confectioner's shop she had run into a wholesale cheese shop, Violet (like Henry) scoffs at its nightly "waste" of electricity, declaring that it must soon fail. The Earlforwards do no business there, it not being Violet's "sort of shop." But when Violet has entered London Hospital for her operation, Henry instructs Elsie to check on her condition by using the phone (he has none) at the cheese shop, Belrose's. The shop lives up to the pleasant associations of its name, exuding "a fine odour of cheese and humanity," making Violet and the dismal shop she had managed appear perfect representatives of the shabby Clerkenwell she had so often defined herself against. The Belrose perspective is no more real than Henry's, only different.

Such perspectivist ironies operate on every level of the novel. They invest the smallest details: on the honeymoon visit to Madame Tussaud's, Violet mistakes a wax figure for a human being, a human being for a wax figure. They determine the largest frame of its construction. The novel begins and ends from the perspective of a casual observer whose point of view is ultimately incommensurate with that of the characters, but that does not correct their perspectives. This observer sees Elsie at the end of the novel as "a dowdy, over-plump figure, whom nobody would have looked twice at. A simple, heavy face, common except for the eyes and the lips; with a harassed look; fatigued also." A scant few chapters earlier, Henry Earlforward, looking outward through the eyes of his illness at Elsie's triumphant health, dwelt upon: "Her youth, her reliability, her prettiness (he thought she was growing prettier every day—such dark eyes, such dark hair, such a curve of the lips), and her physical power and health!" Indeed, the novel hints that transfiguring sexual desire may contribute to Henry's image; "I'm only a stranger coming between you," Violet charges in one of her rages of honesty against her husband, noting that Elsie had been attached to Henry earlier than she. But none of these mirrors captures the one true image of Elsie because there is no such image to be captured.

The novel's plot reiterates the implications of its style. When Henry expires at the sight of an IOU for sixpence from Elsie, who has used his keys without his knowledge to abstract that amount from his safe, the prose seems merely an ossified remnant of Victorian melodrama: "There was no security at all in the world of perils. The foundations of faith had been destroyed. . . . His splendid fortitude, his superhuman courage to re-create his existence over the ruins of it and to defy fate, were broken down. Life was bigger, more cruel, more awful than he had imagined." The tone, however, mingles Henry's sensibility with the narrator's. Moreover, the theft represents the last step in the extinction of Henry's belief in the authority of his own judgment; the miser's death *is* the death of a faith. Elsie's act forces him to recognize a competing center of consciousness threatening his little patriarchy—the death of a realist faith has political implications as well. Elsie's relation with the Earlforwards reflects a number of sociological conditions. When the shop is vacuum-cleaned, Henry marvels to himself that it costs "the wages of a morning charwoman for over three months!" but he does not draw the obvious conclusion that charwomen are underpaid. Elsie, the underpaid servant who gradually asserts her power over him, is a cousin to Pieta Spinelly—who waitressed in the communist club where the murder that so horrified the Earlforwards occurred. At news of this relation, the Earlforwards feel that "communists seemed to have invaded the very house, and civilization itself was instantly threatened." Throughout the novel, Henry fears Elsie's defection, particularly when he is ill and she is strong; the emergence into a consciousness of power by the working class is the greatest fear of property holders.

At the same time, *Riceyman Steps* reiterates with brilliant compression the leading insight of Bennett's earlier *The Old Wives' Tale*: that the shifting of the reference points by which one lives cuts the ground from under one's own identity. In the later novel, however, no temporal change is necessary to unmake a life; recognition alone suffices. Henry's demise is the tale of just such an extinction. The phrase "he wanted to know where he was"—according to Dorothy Cheston Bennett, her husband's own formula—echoes through the novel. It occurs first on the honeymoon, marriage being the initial disorienting blow to Henry's version of reality, when Henry wields it to cut the trip short. But he eventually overcomes the temptation of love, and over a year later congratulates himself, after refusing Elsie a shilling to send a message to learn Violet's condition at London Hospital, on the grounds that "he alone had kept a true perspective, and he would act according to his true perspective." One threat dispatched, however, another arises. Twice Henry reflects of the newly assertive Elsie, who is feeding his invalid food to the malarial lover she has secretly sheltered in the house, that "he did not quite know where he was with her." Confirmation of his unknowing—his discovery of Elsie's theft—kills him. After Henry's death, after his stock has been auctioned, his shop sold to the effervescent Belrose, the phrase appears one last time, but now almost as a benediction. Elsie agrees to serve as Dr. Raste's table-maid, after first refusing the offer because she has decided she can best guard Joe by returning to charring; in the resultant confusion, "no one quite knew where he was." Insecurity, accepted, is life.

Arnold Bennett and H. G. Wells, the beginning of whose careers virtually coincide with the start of the new century, embody the literary conflict that would dominate it. The demand that art serve the cause of social reform or revolution has at times seemed undeniable in this century of unprecedented institutionalized brutality; at other times, the idea that art constitutes a cause in itself has won the day. Both Wells and Bennett felt this tension keenly. But while Wells restricted himself to one set of interests, Bennett attempted to reconcile the two demands. His work, still considerably less known than that of Wells, let alone such contemporaries with similar concerns as Conrad, E. M. Forster, and Ford Madox Ford, constitutes one of the century's most intriguing responses to its continuing riddles.

Robert Squillace

Selected Bibliography

Anderson, Linda R. *Bennett, Wells and Conrad: Narrative in Transition.* London: Macmillan, 1988.

Begonzi, Bernard, ed. *H. G. Wells: A Collection of Critical Essays.* Englewood Cliffs, N.J.: Prentice-Hall, 1976.

Bennett, Arnold, and Wells, H. G. *A Record of a Personal and a Literary Friendship.* Ed. Harris Wilson. Urbana: University of Illinois Press, 1960.

Drabble, Margaret. *Arnold Bennett.* New York: Alfred A. Knopf, 1974.

Hepburn, James. *The Art of Arnold Bennett.* Bloomington: Indiana University Press, 1963.

Huntington, John, ed. *Critical Essays on H. G. Wells.* Boston: G. K. Hall, 1991.

MacKenzie, Norman, and Jeanne MacKenzie. *H. G. Wells: A Biography.* New York: Simon and Schuster, 1973.

Pound, Reginald. *Arnold Bennett: A Biography.* New York: Harcourt, Brace, 1953.

Smith, David C. *H. G. Wells: Desperately Mortal.* New Haven, Conn.: Yale University Press, 1986.

Joseph Conrad

JOSEPH CONRAD is not only one of the greatest novelists who has written in English, but he is particularly important for understanding twentieth-century British culture. Although English was his third language, Conrad combined his unique personal background as a Polish émigré and as a seaman with the traditions of his adopted country to change permanently the English novel. He brought a new psychological and moral intensity to the English novel and its traditions of manners and morals. He recognized the role in human conduct of repressed desires, unconscious motives, and unacknowledged impulses. Because he wanted to dramatize how a writer comes to terms with words and meaning, he focused on the teller as much as the tale. Focusing on the problems of how we understand, communicate, and signify experience, he anticipated essential themes in the philosophy, linguistics, criticism, and literature of our era. He understood the potential of the novel for political and historical insights and thus enlarged the subject matter of the English novel. When he dramatized the dilemma of seeking meaning in an amoral universe, he addressed the central epistemological problem of the twentieth century. To achieve a more intense presentation of theme and a more thorough analysis of characters' moral behavior, he adopted innovative techniques, including nonlinear chronology and the meditative self-dramatizing narrator he called Marlow.

Lacking a father, a bachelor until he was thirty-eight, an exile from his native land who felt guilty for deserting not only his homeland but his father's political heritage, Conrad is particularly concerned with loneliness and isolation. Perhaps the passage from the German writer Novalis that serves as the epigraph to *Lord Jim* and is repeated in *A Personal Record* should serve as the epigraph to Conrad's whole career: "It is certain my conviction gains infinitely the moment another soul will believe in it." The desperate reaching out to an alter ego who might sympathetically respond to his frustrations—the pattern of his letters to Edward Garnett and R. B. Cunninghame-Graham—defines a central structural and thematic component of his work: a lonely soul—be it Marlow, Jim, the Captain in "The Secret Sharer," Razumov, Heyst, or Captain Anthony—reaches out for another who, he hopes, will recognize, understand, and authenticate him.

In the 1890 to 1930 period, the author's struggle with his subject becomes a major determinant of novel form. Thus, in the 1898 to 1900 Marlow tales—as in D. H. Lawrence's *The Rainbow* (1915), James Joyce's *Ulysses* (1922), and Virginia Woolf's *Mrs. Dalloway* (1925)—each author writes to define himself or herself. The writer does not strive for the rhetorical finish of earlier novels but, instead, like Rodin in such sculptures as *Balzac* (1895) invites the reader to perceive a relationship between the creator and the artistic work and to experience the dialogue between the creative process and the raw material. While the Victorian novelist believed that she had a coherent self and that her characters could achieve coherence, the modernist is conscious of disunity in her own life and the world in which she lives. The novelist becomes a divided self. He is both creator and seeker, the prophet who would convert others and the agonizing doubter who would convince himself while engaging in introspective self-examination. Even while the writer stands detached, creating characters, we experience his or her urgent effort to create a self. Thus the reader must maintain a double vision. He must apprehend the narrative and the process of creating that narrative. In such diverse works as the Marlow tales, *The Rainbow*, and *To the Lighthouse* (1927), the process of writing, of defining the subject, of evaluating character, of searching for truth, becomes part of the novel. Yet, as Woolf writes in "Mr. Bennett and Mrs. Brown" (1924), "where so much strength is spent on finding a way of telling the truth, the truth itself is bound to reach us in rather an exhausted and chaotic condition." "Finding a way"—the quest for values and for aesthetic form— becomes a major modernist subject.

Conrad believed that "another man's truth is a dismal lie to me." To understand why Conrad thinks each of us is locked into her or his own perceptions and that all values are ultimately illusions, perhaps we should examine Conrad's ironic image of the cosmos as created by an indifferent knitting machine—an image he proposed in an 1897 letter to his optimistic socialist friend Cunninghame-Graham:

There is a,—let us say,—a machine. It evolved itself (I am severely scientific) out of a chaos of scraps of iron and behold!—it knits. I am horrified at the horrible work and stand appalled. I feel it ought to embroider,—but it goes on knitting. You come and say: "This is all right: it's only a question of the right kind of oil. Let us use this,—for instance,—celestial oil and the machine shall embroider a most beautiful design in purple and gold." Will it? Alas, no! You cannot by any special lubrication make embroidery with a knitting machine. And the most withering thought is that the infamous thing has made itself: made itself without thought, without conscience, without foresight, without eyes, without heart. . . .

It knits us in and it knits us out. It has knitted time, space, pain, death, corruption, despair and all the illusions,—and nothing matters. I'll admit however that to look at the remorseless process is sometimes amusing.

Conrad uses this elaborate ironic trope to speak to the late-Victorian belief that the industrial revolution is part of an upwardly evolving teleology; this belief is really a kind of social Darwinism. According to Conrad, humankind would like to believe in a providentially ordered world vertically descending from a benevolent God—that is, to believe in an embroidered world. But we actually inhabit a temporally defined horizontal dimension within an amoral, indifferent universe—or what Conrad calls "the remorseless process."

Conrad dramatizes that humans always judge one another in terms of their own psychic and moral needs at the time that they are making judgments. But notwithstanding the fallibility of all judgments, we must strive to make objective judgments and to sustain values and ideals, even if we know that we will always fall short of them. Thus, when Conrad writes that all is illusion, he means that all we can do is make working arrangements with the cosmos, and that there are no absolute values derived from an external source. But he does not mean that all values are equal. Similarly, merely because we cannot discover an absolute, final, original reading, it does not follow that all readings are equal. Rather, as readers, even while acknowledging that our readings are a function of our limitations, we must strive to establish judgments and values within complex texts. By affirming the value of the search for meaning in the lives of his characters within his imagined world, Conrad is rhetorically enacting the value of this search in reading texts.

Beginnings

Conrad's first two novels, *Almayer's Folly* (1895) and *An Outcast of the Islands* (1896), reflect his state of mind and reveal his values. In these early novels, narrated by a conventional omniscient narrator, Conrad tests and refines themes and techniques that he will use in his subsequent fiction. In a way that will become characteristic of Conrad's early works, he uses fictional material from his own adventures as his source material. He not only draws upon his experience when he sailed as mate with the *Vidar* (1887–1888), but bases the title character of his first novel on a man he actually knew. While these two novels seem to be about remote events, they actually dramatize his central concerns.

Sambir, the setting for *Almayer's Folly* and *An Outcast of the Islands*, is the first of Conrad's distorted and intensified settings. Like the Congo in *Heart of Darkness* and Patusan in *Lord Jim*, Sambir becomes a metaphor for actions that occur there. It is also a projection of Conrad's state of mind as it appears in his letters of 1894 through 1896: exhaustion and ennui alternate with spasmodic energy. Conrad's narrator is in the process of creating a myth out of Sambir, but the process is never quite completed. Like Hardy's Egdon Heath, Sambir is an inchoate form that can be controlled neither by man's endeavors nor by his imagination. The demonic energy that seethes within the forests is a catalyst for the perverse sexuality of the novel's white people and their subsequent moral deterioration. With its "mud soft and black, hiding fever, rottenness, and evil under its level and glazed surface," Sambir refutes the romantic myth that beyond civilization lie idyllic cultures in a state of innocence. Sambir's river, the Pantai, is a prototype for the Congo; the atavistic influence it casts upon white men, drawing out long-repressed and atrophied libidinous energies, anticipates the Congo's effect on Kurtz. Sambir's primordial jungle comments on the illusion shared by Dain and Nina, as well as by Willems and Aissa, that passionate love can transform the world. Sambir's tropical setting seems to be dominated by the processes of death and destruction, and the jungle's uncontrollable fecundity expresses itself in devolution rather than evolution. The dominance of the Pantai and the forest implies that Conrad's cosmos is as indifferent to man's aspirations as the cosmos of his contemporary, Hardy, whose *Jude the Obscure* was also published in 1895.

Before he created Marlow, Conrad had difficulty controlling the personal turmoil that we see in his letters of the 1894 to 1896 period; he feels isolated in a meaningless universe; he is cynical about man's motives and purposes on this earth; he senses that he is an artistic failure; he doubts his ability to communicate even while expressing his desperate need to be understood. If his speaker's commentary is not always appropriate to the dramatic action that evokes it, it is because Conrad is using his speaker to explore his own bafflement in a universe he regards as amoral, indifferent, and at times hostile. In the first two novels, when Conrad uses the narrator as a surrogate for himself to place an episode in an intellectual and moral context, he is often testing and probing to discover what the episode means. Conrad subsequently learns to capitalize on his reluctance to be dogmatic; he dramatizes Marlow's process of moral discovery and shows how Marlow continually formulates, discards, and redefines his beliefs through experience. But because in 1894 and 1895 Conrad had difficulty embracing a consistent set of values, his narrator's commentary does not always move toward a consistent philosophic position, but rather may posit contradictory perspectives. Quite frequently, the omniscient voice of the first two novels, *Almayer's Folly* and *An Outcast of the Islands*, explores characters and action from the perspective of a man committed to family ties, the work ethic, sexual constraint, individual responsibility, and racial understanding. Yet these basic humanistic values are often at odds with the artistic tentativeness and moral confusion that derive from Conrad's uncertainty and anxiety. The unresolved tension between, on the one hand, Conrad's own personal concerns and, on the other, his attempt to objectify moral issues is revealed in conflicts between the values expressed by the narrator and the implications of his plot and setting.

Conrad's early artistic code, the original preface to *The Nigger of the Narcissus* (1897), is remarkable for its emphasis on creating a community of readers. Seen in the context of his own fear of loneliness and of not communicating, it reflects his decision that fiction will not only enable him to arrest the flux and turmoil within himself but also relieve him of his sense of isolation. Conrad defines art as "a single-minded attempt to render the highest kind of justice to the visible universe, by bringing to light the truth, manifold and one, underlying its every aspect." The artist's mission is to reveal the experience that unites all men and, in particular, to make the reader aware of the common humanity each shares with mankind. Conrad hopes for a community of responsive temperaments to verify the effectiveness of *his* creation; this hope may be behind the intensity of the famous but elusive assertion, "My task which I am trying to achieve is, by the power of the written word, to make you hear, to make you feel—it is, before all, to make you *see*."

Conrad's 1914 preface to the American edition makes clear that he meant the tale's focus to be on the crew's response to Wait: "In the book [Wait] is nothing; he is merely the centre of the ship's collective psychology and the pivot of the action." Sentimentalism is the peculiar form of egotism that preys upon the crew's response to Donkin's poverty at the outset and that causes the men to sacrifice their integrity in a desperate and pathetic effort to forestall Wait's inevitable death. Neither Wait nor Donkin has an identity independent of that conferred by the crew's sentimentalism; they flourish *because* the crew responds to them. Wait is in a parasitic relationship with the crew: "Each, going out, seemed to leave behind a little of his own vitality, surrender some of his own strength, renew the assurance of life—the indestructible thing!" Once the crew responds to Donkin with a "wave of sentimental pity," "the development of the destitute Donkin aroused interest." When he responds to Wait and Donkin against his better judgment, the sailor-speaker embodies Conrad's own fear of sentimentalism. After he had completed *The Nigger* but before it had begun to appear in the *New Review*, Conrad wrote "I feel horribly sentimental. . . . I want to rush into print whereby my sentimentalism, my incorrect attitude to life . . . shall be disclosed to the public gaze." Just as the eternal truths of Singleton and Allistoun triumph over the "temporary formulas" of Donkin and the crew's misguided sentimentalism, the fiction writer must eschew fashionable aesthetic philosophies: "Realism, Romanticism, Naturalism, even the unofficial Sentimentalism . . . all these gods must . . . abandon him . . . to the stammerings of his conscience and to the outspoken consciousness of the difficulties of his work," Conrad wrote in his 1897 preface. The speaker-crew member, and possibly Conrad too, wants to believe that the crew's experience with Wait represents a confrontation with death. If he were to lower the rhetorical ante, he would be left with his nominalistic adventure tale, which boldly reveals his own mediocre behavior. Sympathy with Wait almost causes the men, including the crew member, to refuse duty. Thus their catatonic fear of death, evoked by the presence of Wait, displaces the captain as master. Although the men detest Wait as a possible malingerer, they irrationally equate preserving him with forestalling their own deaths.

Conrad discovered that the voyage experiences of his sea career could free him from the debilitating restraints of shore life and be an ordering principle for his new career as a writer. Like the passing of a period in a man's life, a ship's docking is a kind of prolepsis of her final death. But when Conrad presents his narrative to his readers, the created world and the self embodied in that world achieve a kind of immortality.

The Marlow Tales

Conrad was concerned with the dilemma of transforming the "freedom" of living in a purposeless world from a condition into a value. And Marlow enabled him to examine this dilemma in "Youth" (1898), *Heart of Darkness* (1899), and *Lord Jim* (1900). Writing enabled Conrad to define his values and his character. He uses his narrators and dramatic personae to objectify his feelings and values. Marlow is a surrogate through whom Conrad works out his own epistemological problems, psychic turmoil, and moral confusion; his search for values echoes Conrad's. Thus he is a means by which Conrad orders his world. He is defining not only the form of the story but the relation between Conrad's past and present selves. The younger Marlow was explicitly committed to the same conventional values of the British Merchant Marine to which Conrad had devoted his early adulthood, but the mature Marlow has had experiences that have caused him to reevaluate completely his moral beliefs. That Marlow is a vessel for some of Conrad's doubts and anxieties and for defining the problems that made his own life difficult is clear not only from his 1890 Congo diary and the 1890 correspondence with Mme Poradowska, but even more so from the letters of the 1897 to 1899 period, selections from which have already been quoted.

The meaning of several other novels, most notably *The Nigger of the Narcissus* and *The Rescue* (1919), depends on understanding the way that Conrad's emotional life becomes embodied in the text. In *Nostromo* the suicidal despair of Decoud reflects a mood that Conrad had known many times in his novel-writing years. Even such an objective work as "The Secret Sharer" (1910) becomes more meaningful once we recognize that it has an autobiographical element. At the outset of his voyage, the captain not only relives emotions Conrad once felt during his first command but reflects the uncertainty and anxiety that Conrad experienced in the period when he wrote it.

"Youth," the first short story after *Tales of Unrest* (1898) was completed, addresses the dour view of European life presented in *Tales of Unrest*. Marlow is the heir of the white men of such early Conrad stories as "The Lagoon" (1896) and "Karain: A Memory" (1891)—those sensitive, if disillusioned, men who neither live passionately like the natives nor believe in any sustaining ideals. "Youth" is about Marlow's efforts to create a significant yesterday so that his life will not seem a meaningless concatenation of durational events. Marlow's narrative reflects his need to "arrest" time and preempt the future. Somewhere past the middle of his life, Marlow attempts to discover a symbolic meaning in the past voyage of the *Judea*. He wishes to believe that his first journey to the East was one of "those voyages that seem ordered for the illustration of life, that might stand for a symbol of existence." As Marlow recalls his great adventure, he discovers that, in spite of the voyage's failure, it not only contains great significance for him but enables him to recapture on occasion his feeling of youthful energy. Conrad takes a good-natured, ironical view of the supposedly mature Marlow's attempts to expose his own youthful illusions. While he purports to take an objective and detached view of a meaningful experience of his youth, the mature Marlow is revealed as a romantic sentimentalist. Conrad shows us that reality is partly subjective and that our illusions and oversimplifications are as real to us as so-called objective facts.

The primary subject of *Heart of Darkness* is Marlow, but the presence of Conrad is deeply engraved on every scene. Marlow's effort to come to terms with the Congo experience, and especially with Kurtz, is the crucial activity that engaged Conrad's imagination. Marlow's consciousness is the arena of the tale, and the interaction between his verbal behavior—his effort to find the appropriate words—and his memory is as much the action as his Congo journey. Both the epistemological quest for a context or perspective with which to interpret the experience and the semiological quest to discover the signs and symbols that make the experience intelligible are central to the tale.

For a contemporary reader, *Heart of Darkness* raises important questions because at first it seems to present women and blacks from a perspective that is reductive and even sexist and racist. We need to understand that the views expressed by Marlow are not Conrad's, and indeed are a dramatization of a perspective that Conrad uses ironically. Yet it is important to acknowledge that Conrad does not adequately separate himself from Marlow's view of women, a view that assumes that women are more sentimental, myopic, and domestic than their male peers. Marlow seems to believe that it is the male role to protect the women from the more searing truths and to help them live in their illusions. If we understand Marlow's patronizing attitude toward women as naive and simple, can we not use the text to show the difference between authorial and resistant readings—that is, between how texts are read when they are written and how they are read now? Does the lie to the Intended reveal Marlow's sexism? Is Conrad aware of Marlow's sexual stereotyping, even if he means the lie to the Intended to be a crucial moment of self-definition for Marlow? In a situation where opportunities for heterosexuality are limited, what does *Heart of Darkness* say about male bonding among the whites and about miscegenation? Are we offended that one of Kurtz's "abominable practices" is the taking of a savage mistress? If we can understand the agon as an enactment of how the natives' energy and instincts have been corrupted by materialistic, overly rational imperialists, we can see that the charge of racism is itself reductive.

It is useful to place *Heart of Darkness* in its cultural context. The story speaks to major turn-of-the-century concerns: the breakdown of moral certainty, the sense that each of us lives in a closed circle, and the consequent fear of solipsism. Conrad feared that each of us is locked in his or her own perceptions and despaired in his letters that even language will not help us reach out to others. Thus, the fear that "we live, as we dream—alone" is also an idea that recurs throughout the period of early modernism, a period in which humans felt, to quote the philosopher F. H. Bradley's *Appearance and Reality*, that "my experience is a closed circle; a circle closed from the outside. . . . In brief . . . the whole world for each is peculiar and private to that soul." That the frame narrator can retell to his audience the story shows that Marlow has communicated with someone and offers a partial antidote to the terrifying fear of isolation and silence that haunted Conrad. Conrad's narrative demonstrates how the Africans and Europeans share a common humanity: the

English too were once natives conquered by the Romans, and England too was once one of the dark places of the earth. Moreover, Europeans not only require laws and rules to restrain their atavistic impulses, but they become more monstrous than those they profess to civilize. Finally, terms like "savage" and "barbarian" are arbitrary designations by imperialists who in fact deserve these epithets more than the natives.

As an allegory of reading, *Heart of Darkness* resists easy simplifications and one-dimensional readings, resists attempts to explain in either/or terms. Even as *Heart of Darkness* remains a text that raises questions about the possibility of meaning, it suggests the plenitude of meaning. Just as Marlow gradually moves from seeing a drama of values to living a drama of characters, so as readers do we. Like him, we make the journey from spectator to participant. Are we not trying to make sense of Marlow as he is trying to make sense of Kurtz? And are we not also trying to make sense of the frame narrator who is trying to make sense of Marlow making sense of Kurtz? Does not the tale's emphasis on choosing a sign for our systems of meaning call attention to the arbitrary nature of choosing a framing sign and make us aware of the need for multiple perspectives? Do we not learn how one invests with value something not seen or known in preference to the ugly reality that confronts us? Is not Conrad's ironic parable about belief itself, including the Christian belief in whose name much of imperialism was carried on? Thus, in essence, the tale urges us toward a pluralistic perspective. Finally, one-dimensional readings bend to the need for a pluralistic reading that takes account of Marlow's disillusionment and his magnetic attraction to Kurtz as the nightmare of his choice. For Conrad has turned a story about a present journey to Africa into a journey through Europe's past, as well as into each human being's primitive psyche.

The Congo experience has plunged Marlow into doubt and confusion. Sitting "apart, indistinct, and silent" in his ascetic Buddha pose, Marlow is deliberately trying to separate himself from the cynicism and hypocrisy that he associates with Europeans. As in "Youth," while Marlow is telling the story he arrests the future, places his back against the present, and becomes part of the created world of his own imagination. The tale Marlow tells becomes not only a version of but an epistemological quest into "the culminating point of my experience." The experience proves recalcitrant to Marlow's efforts to understand it. Marlow's probing mind cannot impose an interpretation on Kurtz: "The thing was to know what he belonged to, how many powers of darkness claimed him for their own. That was the reflection that made you creepy all over. It was impossible—it was not good for one either—trying to imagine." Part of his hostility to his audience derives from his own frustrated desire to discover the language that will make his experience comprehensible to himself. Marlow's is the voice of a man desperately trying to create meaning; unlike Kurtz, who "could get himself to believe anything," Marlow has trouble convincing himself that there is the possibility of belief. Marlow's narration is a quest for the symbols and signs to explain the darkness that still haunts his imagination. Ernest Cassirer, in *The Logic of the Humanities*, provides a helpful gloss: "The possibility and necessity of . . . a 'breaking free' of the limitations of individuality emerges nowhere so clearly and indubitably as in the phenomenon of speech. The spoken *word* never originates in the mere sound or utterance. For a word is an intended meaning. It is construed within the organic whole of a 'communication,' and communication 'exists' only when the word passes from one person to another."

Marlow's experience in the Congo invalidated his belief that civilization equaled progress. While Kurtz, the man who seemed to embody all the accomplishments of civilization, reverted to savagery, the cannibals showed some semblance of the "restraint" that makes civilization possible. Kurtz was a poet, painter, musician, journalist, potential political leader, a "universal genius" of Europe, a man who "had come out equipped with moral ideas of some sort," and yet once he traveled to a place where the earliest beginnings of the world still survived, the wilderness awakened "brutal instincts" and "monstrous passions."

Marlow's journey from Europe to the Congo helped prepare him to sympathize with Kurtz. From the outset he was offended by the standards and perspectives of the European imperialists, and gradually he began to sympathize with the natives against the predatory colonialists. As an idle passenger on a boat taking him to the Congo, he caught glimpses of the inanity which he later encountered as an involved participant. Even then, he saw the fatuity of the "civilized" French man-of-war's shelling the bush: "Pop, would go one of the six-inch guns; a small flame would dart and vanish, a little white smoke would disappear, a tiny projectile would give a feeble screech—and nothing happened."

Soon, more than Marlow's Calvinistic belief in the redemptive powers of purposeful labor was offended. He viewed the company's outer station from an ironic standpoint, noticing the neglected machinery, lying like an animal's "carcass"; the "objectless blastings"; and the native workers, their rags resembling tails, chained together as if they were a team of mules. He mocked the folly of those who put out fires with buckets that have holes in the bottom and who considered diseased and starving men "enemies" and "criminals." His original epistemological stance, dependent not upon a naive, idealized conception of the trading company's commercial ventures but simply upon his belief that European civilization represents a tradition of humane values, was shaken. He began to realize that this version of civilization is not an "emissary of light" but an instance of exploitative imperialism at its worst. After arriving at the Central Station, Marlow's quest soon focused on discovering an alternative to the amoral pragmatism and cynicism illustrated by the manager and his uncle. The manager's only objection to Kurtz's abominations was that the results were unsatisfactory.

Conrad has Marlow describe his quest to meet Kurtz in romance terms to suggest ironically Marlow's kinship with folk and legendary heroes who also search for miracles and magicians to solve their problems and relieve their anxieties. Standing in the blood of his helmsman, Marlow could only think that Kurtz was dead, and that he would never be able to speak to Kurtz. It was as if he were frustrated in a journey to consult an oracle. After discovering that Kurtz had "taken a high seat among the devils of the land," he did not renounce his existential commitment to Kurtz as "the nightmare of my choice"; Kurtz still seemed preferable to the hypocrisy and malignity of the Europeans who have deprived language of its meaning, civilization of its ideals, and life of its purpose. Marlow, formerly a representative of European civilization, desperately identified with a man he knew to be ostracized by that civilization. Ironically, Marlow turned only to a different form of greed and egotism; Kurtz's atavistic impulses—modeled perhaps on the Belgian King Leopold's predatory imperialism—have a magnitude and purity that contrast with the pettiness and niggling greed of the imperialists.

We do not know how perceptive Marlow was when he met Kurtz, but Marlow *now* knows that Kurtz was without the restraint that even the helmsman and other cannibals had: "Mr. Kurtz lacked restraint in the gratification of his various lusts . . . there was something wanting in him—some small matter which, when the pressing need arose, could not be found under his magnificent eloquence." Earlier in his narration,

Marlow seems to be preparing to excuse Kurtz; he asserts that the "idea" behind an action can be redemptive for the committed individual. However, his narrative discredits this view that the ultimate test of an action is the sincerity of the concept that motivates it. Originally, Kurtz had "set up and [bowed] down before" a benevolent idea, but when the wilderness had "sealed his soul to its own by the inconceivable ceremonies of some devilish initiation," Kurtz's idea became its own solipsistic parody: "My Intended, my ivory, my station, my river, my—."

Marlow invests Kurtz with values that fulfill his own need to embody his threat of the jungle in one tangible creature. If Kurtz is considered the center of the "heart of darkness," the business of following Kurtz and winning the "struggle" enabled Marlow to believe that he had conquered a symbol of the atavistic, debilitating effects of the jungle. This belief is central to his interpretation of the journey's significance. For Marlow, capturing Kurtz after he escapes symbolizes a personal victory over darkness. Increasingly, Kurtz had been attracted to the jungle by the urge to go ashore for "a howl and a dance." Having given in to his primitive urges, he appropriately crawled away on all fours. Marlow recalls how he too was tempted by savage impulses and confused his heartbeat with the beat of the natives' drums. Uncharacteristically, he thought of giving Kurtz a "drubbing." He was "strangely cocksure of himself" and enjoyed stalking his prey. His assertion that "he left the track" indicates that he, too, was in danger now that he was alone in the jungle; he thought that he might never get back. But when Marlow confronted Kurtz, he recalls, "I seemed to come to my senses, I saw the danger in its right proportion." To Marlow, the confrontation represents coming to terms with the dark potential within himself against the background of primitive and unspeakable rites. But he did not surrender to the appeal of the wilderness precisely because he had internalized the restraints imposed by civilization.

That Kurtz achieved a "moral victory" may very well be a necessary illusion for Marlow. But did Kurtz pronounce a verdict on his reversion to primitivism and achieve the "supreme moment of complete knowledge"? Or is this what Marlow desperately wants to believe? Coming from a man who "could get himself to believe anything," how credible is Marlow's interpretation that "The horror! The horror!" was "an affirmation, a moral victory paid for by innumerable defeats, by abominable terrors, by abominable satisfactions"? When Kurtz had enigmatically muttered, "Live rightly, die, die . . . ," Marlow had wondered "Was he rehearsing some speech in his sleep, or was it a fragment of a phrase from some newspaper article?" Marlow had just remarked that Kurtz's voice "survived his strength to hide in the magnificent folds of eloquence the barren darkness of his heart." If Kurtz had kicked himself loose of the earth, how could he pronounce a verdict on his ignominious return to civilization or an exclamation elicited from a vision of his own imminent death? For the reader, Kurtz remains a symbol of how the human ego can expand infinitely to the point where it tries to will its own apotheosis.

Conrad takes issue with Victorian assumptions about univocal truth and a divinely ordered world. His use of Marlow's dramatized consciousness reflects his awareness that "we live as we dream—alone," and the concomitant awareness—seen in the development of cubism and Joyce's ventriloquy in *Ulysses*—that one perspective is not enough. One can see that Conrad, too, was freeing black and white from the traditional morphology of color, just as the fauvists and cubists were freeing traditional ideas of representation from the morphology of color; one can see that Conrad is also freeing his language from the morphology of representation—as in his use of adjectives for purely affective rather than descriptive reasons. Conrad's use of allegorized rather than nominalistic adjectives such as "subtle" and "unspeakable" invite the frame narrator and Conrad's readers to respond in terms of their own experiences and to validate in their responses that they, too, dream alone. Like Gauguin and Picasso, Conrad explores ancient voices and the presence of primitive cultures in modernist texts through the savage mistress and the other natives.

The process of reading *Lord Jim* involves the reader in the remorseless process of responding to different judgments of Jim's behavior. First, there is the judgment of the omniscient narrator, which precedes not only our meeting Marlow but our learning what happens on the *Patna*. Does the reader ever forget the original rigorous judgment established by the omniscient narrator in the first three chapters, a judgment that is based on adherence to absolute standards? Does not that judgment accompany the reader as he wends his way through Marlow's narrative of his own efforts to find some terms with which to understand Jim's terrible failure on the *Patna* when Jim, along with the rest of the white officers, abandons the native crew and passengers? And, of course, the reader must sort out the significance of Stein's oracular but hazy pronouncements. No sooner do we hear Marlow's judgment delivered in his long monologue after he has learned that Jim has succeeded on Patusan and, at least in Marlow's eyes, justified Marlow's confidence in him, than we are confronted with Marlow's final, inconclusive judgment after Jim has failed; this judgment is halfway between the rigorous one of the absolute narrator and the empathetic one that had informed Marlow's telling.

Prior to Marlow's first words in chapter 5, the omniscient narrator in the opening chapters judges Jim by fixed standards and shows him wanting. Without any ambiguity, Conrad uses this narrator to show us that Jim's jump from the *Patna* is a characteristic action rather than—as Jim would like to believe and as Marlow is at times tempted to accept—a gratuitous one that just happened to an unfortunate young man.

Lost in his fantasies of heroism, Jim fails to respond to an emergency on the training ship. Because Jim has not internalized the proper responses, when he is faced with an actual chance to take part in a rescue he becomes physically and morally paralyzed: "He stood still. It seemed to him he was whirled around." Jim's second failure occurs when, while serving as first mate, he loses his nerve. The omniscient narrator tells us that until then Jim had never been tested by "those events of the sea that show in the light of day the inner worth of a man, the edge of his temper, and the fibre of his stuff; that reveal the quality of his resistance and the secret truth of his pretences, not only to others, but also to himself."

Conrad's narrative coding continues to create a concatenation of episodes that judges Jim's moral dereliction and psychological incapacity. Each episode repeats the prior one's indictment, even while it adds another piece of evidence to the charge that Jim has not internalized the fixed moral standards of the merchant marine—the code stipulating honor, fidelity, courage, and a highly developed sense of responsibility—on which civilized life in the colonies depends. Thus Jim, after he recovers from his leg injury, throws in his lot with those who eschew the "home service" of the merchant marine for easier employment:

They loved short passages, good deck-chairs, large native crews, and the distinction of being white. . . . They talked everlastingly of turns of luck . . . and in all they said—in their actions, in their looks, in their persons—could be detected the soft spot, the place of decay, the determination to lounge safely through existence.

As in the above passage, it is characteristic of Conrad to introduce parallel phrases with recurring words; within a sentence these phrases often increase in intensity as they move to an explosive conclusion; thus in the first of these sentences, Conrad's appositional phrases move from the rather neutral descriptive phrases to the morally intense and scathing indictment (in the climactic phrase "the distinction of being white") of those who believe they are privileged on racial grounds. While Jim assumes that he will not be tarnished by the company of the kind of men who choose to work on boats like the *Patna*, the ironic narrator places Jim among these men with soft spots and places of decay. Conrad's adjectives here do not so much describe an internal condition as they participate in a structure of effects to give the reader a sense of Jim's moral flaw. We cannot visualize a soft spot or a place of decay any more than we can see an "*invisible* halt" (italics mine) in Jim's gait.

The fourth episode or vignette that inexorably illustrates that, contrary to Jim's contention, his jump was a characteristic rather than a gratuitous action is his behavior on board the *Patna*; as on the training ship his mind is wooed from his duty to the "human cargo" of pilgrims by fantasies of accomplishment: "His thoughts would be full of valorous deeds: he loved these dreams and the success of his imaginary achievements. They were the best part of his life, its secret truth, its hidden reality." That the words "achievement" and "secret" echo prior passages documenting his flawed nature shows how Jim is iterating his past, as he will throughout his life. Repeating the term "secret" underlines how Jim has separated himself from reality and has paradoxically created in his actions—as opposed to his dreams—a self that has no social role to play; Conrad thus gives the nuance of narcissism to Jim's self-indulgent fantasies. Living in the world of his fictions rather than in the world of actual duties and responsibilities, Jim is a hopelessly divided self unfit for his tasks.

Originally, Marlow wanted to judge Jim by absolute standards. Marlow would have liked to read Jim as if he, Marlow, were the omniscient narrator, and indeed for a brief moment Conrad teases us into thinking that we have been listening to Marlow—or at least an omniscient double of Marlow—all along. In the first moments of his monologue about Jim, Marlow aligns Jim with beetles, criminals, alloyed metal, and "to men with soft spots, with hard spots, with hidden plague spots" as if he were going to continue the narrator's indictment.

But the self-dramatizing Marlow soon reveals that he is vulnerable to those who, like Jim, claim extenuating circumstances, because Marlow does not sufficiently believe in himself to uphold absolute values. Marlow cannot, as Stein will advise, shut his eyes and see himself as a fine fellow, a saint. He must face the ambiguity of living in a relative world that lacks anterior concepts of order. Because of his own needs, he begins to read Jim as Jim would like him to. In Marlow's evolving sympathy with Jim as "one of us," in Marlow's taking up a position as Jim's apologist, in his gnawing and disturbing suspicion that he may not be able to claim a superior moral position because anyone might do what Jim did, Marlow begins to abandon the credo of the merchant marine and British imperialism and increasingly allows Jim to become a standard by which Marlow measures himself. But the omniscient narrator has taught us not to be a Jim-reader of Jim, and when Marlow becomes a Jim-reader of Jim, we back off from accepting Marlow's authority as a reader of himself. In Marlow's world, once he loses his beliefs in fixed standards, there are no sources or origins. The absence of sources and origins makes moral judgments difficult.

As Marlow becomes an apologist for Jim, the reader is expected to adopt a stance of judgment toward Marlow—is expected to see that Marlow, too, is a fallible human being who is different in degree but not in kind from Jim. On three occasions Conrad undercuts Marlow's pretensions to moral authority. First, during Jim's trial, Marlow offers Jim Brierly's plan to evade the trial and escape the rituals of civilized judgment; second, Marlow goes to Stein because he wishes to "dispose" of Jim, in part to avoid his bizarre fear of having Jim—in the role of a common vagrant—confront him in London; and, finally, during his visit to Patusan, Marlow loses control in his interview with Jewel for no reason other than his own need to assure himself that he is better than Jim at a time Marlow's ability to make moral distinctions is threatened: "I felt the sort of rage one feels during a hard tussle . . . 'You want to know [why the world does not want him]?' I asked in a fury. 'Yes!' she cried. 'Because he is not good enough,' I said brutally." Marlow's self-indulgent indiscretion—what purpose is served by telling Jewel that Jim is not good enough?—strikingly contrasts with the climax of *Heart of Darkness*. When an embittered and disillusioned Marlow returns to Europe, he is willing to lie to the Intended, although he hates a lie, and to let her think that Kurtz's last words were her name in order that she have the sustaining illusion of Kurtz's undying devotion.

While Marlow enacts the moment of irreconcilable impasse or *aporia* of modernism, Conrad, I am arguing, does not. For, as we have seen, Conrad's omniscient voice stands in judgment of Jim's behavior and of Marlow's understandable efforts as one of us—lonely, doubting humans in a confusing world that Conrad thought of as a "remorseless process"—to explain Jim's behavior. Conrad expects the reader to understand that Marlow's confidence in absolute values has been undermined by his own experience, and that readers must, like judges, sift through the data as objectively as possible, even while recognizing that, like Brierly and Marlow, we are all prone to skewed judgments based on our own needs. But while the novel tempts us to be a Jim-reader of Jim, or a Brierly-reader or a Stein-reader, and, even more urgently, to be a reader of Marlow—who at times is a Jim-reader, a Brierly-reader, and a Stein-reader—it finally insists on our being an omniscient reader and as unforgiving and unyielding in our judgments as the omniscient narrator.

Poignantly, by allowing Doramin to shoot him, Jim chooses the masculine world of physical action, represented by the pistol (recall how he had entered Patusan "with an unloaded revolver in his lap"), over the alternative, more feminine world of values represented by the talismanic friendship ring given to him by Stein—the ring that he gave to his messenger, "Tamb Itam, to give to Dain Waris as a sign that his messenger's words should be trusted." Just as his achievements in the native black world can never be as real to Jim as the failures in the white home world, feminine values—those of romantic love and personal ties—cannot be as real to him as the world of male heroism. Jim can love Jewel in his romance world of "knight and maiden," but not in the relative world of partial failures and relative successes By choosing to face the male pistol, Jim, in fact, ironically closes the eternal circle implied by the feminine ring.

The Political Novels

Conrad's novels about politics have been viewed both as nihilistic statements and as dramatizations of a political vision. While the subject of these novels—*Nostromo* (1904), *The Secret Agent* (1907), and *Under Western Eyes* (1911)—is often politics, their values are not political. The novels affirm the primacy of family, the sanctity of the individual, the value of love, and the importance of sympathy and understanding in human relations. His concern for the working class derives not from political theory but from his experience as a seaman and from his imaginative response to the miseries of others.

In the political novels Conrad is disillusioned with materialism and imagines that "industrialism and commercialism" may foster wars between democracies. Like Dostoevsky, Conrad disavows the "Crystal Palace," the Victorian symbol of science and progress. In a mechanistic, amoral world, Conrad understands the necessity for political and social organization. While he dissects flaws in various systems, states, and communities, he does not propose alternative programs. But he does insist on preserving the freedom of the individual to live his own life as long as he does not pose a physical threat to others.

The essay "Autocracy and War" (1905) helps us understand Conrad's political novels. The essay boils down to two central points. Above all, Conrad is opposed to autocracy. Secondly, he uncharacteristically affirms a belief in the evolution of both nations and mankind. In *Nostromo*, even when high-minded characters espouse ideals, political principles are thinly veiled disguises for the desire to control the enormous treasure of the San Tomé mine. Because of their own obsessions and moral weaknesses, the Goulds, Decoud, Antonia, Nostromo, and even the Viola family are engulfed by politics created by the insistent demands of materialism. *Nostromo* is the story of men who, while seeking to define their own lives in bold and heroic terms, become entrapped by the circumstances that they seek to control and the political activity in which they engage.

In *Nostromo*, the disrupted chronology, the rapidly shifting focus, and the ominous instability of the ending dramatize a world that has lost its moral center, a world in which, as Yeats put it in "The Second Coming," "the best lack all conviction, while the worst / Are full of passionate intensity." The form is a correlative to a narrative about a civilization that lacks a moral center. No matter what illusion or abstraction to which a character has committed himself—whether it be Viola's republicanism, Monygham's devotion, Gould's idealism, Nostromo's "good name"—each major character returns to a position in which he is alone, stripped of his public self, and exposed to the vicissitudes of an indifferent cosmos. At first, each major character is depicted as part of the social and political order of Sulaco; only then is he examined in his private facet and shown to be serving not the community but dimly understood psychic needs and unacknowledged obsessions.

Nostromo, the man garbed in silver trappings, is the offspring of the mine. Virtually anonymous, with only the vaguest claims to a personal past or national identity, he is metaphorically the spongy lump of silver metamorphosed into a fully grown adult. Nostromo is the child of materialism and imperialism; he is created by the needs of Mitchell and, later, by Gould, as a human instrument that can be depended upon to place the interests of those he serves before his own. That he belongs to the imperialists and their political interests is implied by the title that has been conferred upon him by those he serves: Nostromo, "our man." Such a name deprives him of a personal identity in the eyes of those he serves. When he flippantly promises the chief engineer that he will "take care" of Sir John "as if [he] were his father," he acknowledges the patrimony of materialism and concomitantly neglects his own need for human relationships.

Nostromo's relation to the cargadores and natives parallels Gould's position with the aristocrats. Both are motivated by intense vanity that is related to their need to compensate for a disrupted family. Both rely on taciturnity and detachment to maintain that position, and both are treated almost like royalty by obsequious followers because of the power they are perceived to hold. When Nostromo gradually drifts into bondage to the treasure, he becomes Gould's double. The terms on which he rebels only establish the dominance of the paternity of material interests. He wants to overthrow the flourishing regime he helped to establish. He supports a socialist party that seeks to undermine the authority figures whom he allowed to become his political fathers in place of Viola; he wants to assuage his guilt for betraying the trust of the people, specifically the cargadores, even though Sulaco's prosperity has clearly brought tangible benefits to the people. His rightful name, Fidanza, is an ironic suggestion of *fidanza*, the Italian word for confidence, the quality for which he is recognized by others but which in its most profound sense he lacks, and of the Latin root, *fidelitas*, or loyalty, the value he has implicitly renounced.

Gould's libidinous energies are engaged by the mine instead of by his relationship to his wife. The first silver that the mine produces is described in terms that suggest a demonic birth. In what might now be seen as an instance of Conrad's awareness of the commodification of women, Mrs. Gould is midwife to silver rather than mother to children.

Just as the uncorrupted waterfall becomes galvanized into a silver-fall, Gould's sexual substance becomes a stream of silver and his offspring a lump of silver. Mrs. Gould has sublimated her sexual needs and has tacitly permitted the production of the silver to become Gould's homage to her and to substitute for intercourse. The result is not only a childless marriage but her becoming a lonely, isolated, sexually frustrated woman. Potentially tender moments climax not with intimacy but with Gould's return to the mine at night. The spongy lump grows into a wall that divides her from her husband.

Decoud, the man who is alternately cynic and romantic, pragmatist and idealist; the man whose perceptive analysis of others often goes beyond the narrator's understanding; the man who uses the written word to rescue his identity is, like Marlow, a character from whom Conrad is at times barely able to distance himself. Decoud is Conrad's mirror, and the distance between Conrad's voice and his character dissolves when he narrates Decoud's complete inability to cope with his solitude. Decoud's final crisis approaches states of mind that Conrad experienced in the period from 1895 to 1898. Thus, in 1896 Conrad wrote to Edward Garnett:

I am paralyzed by doubt and have just enough sense to feel the agony but am powerless to invent a way out of it. . . . I knock about blindly in it till I am positively, physically sick—and then I give up saying—tomorrow! And tomorrow comes—and brings only the renewed and futile agony. I ask myself whether I am breaking up mentally. . . . Everything seems so abominably stupid. You see *the belief* is not in me—and without the belief—the brazen thick headed, thick skinned immovable belief nothing good can be done.

Decoud's suicide, nihilism, and self-hate objectify qualities that Conrad despised in himself.

Conrad's narrator undermines the heroic pretensions of his characters and disabuses the reader of the notion that materialism has its heroes. By using such legendary material as a quest for treasure and by including isolated acts of courage by those who are potential heroes, Conrad raises expectations of heroic behavior. But he deflates them as he gradually reveals the limitations and ineffectuality of his potential heroes: Gould, the king of Sulaco; Nostromo, the Adamic man; and Mrs. Gould, whose innocence and moral purity suggest the Madonna. The bathetic denouement of the romance plot which comprises the last three chapters is itself a comment on the possibility of reinvigorating the larger-than-life world of love and heroism embodied in romance or epic. Indeed, the heroic image that a man creates for himself—for example, Gould's image of himself as the bringer of justice and security, and Nostromo's image of himself as the man of incorruptible reputation—really has little to do with the basic interests of the community. Rather than heirs to a heroic tradition where men risked everything to save the community, these are men whose acts are corrupted by their motives.

The Secret Agent depends upon a tension between disintegration of content (Conrad's perception of turn-of-the-century London) and integration and cohesion of form (the language and the tightly unified narrative). Conrad creates a language that is moral, civilized, and rational, and a narrator with the intelligence and moral energy to suggest alternatives to the cynicism, amorality, and hypocrisy that dominate political relationships within London. Although the narrator, to whom the entire language of the book is assigned, at first seems isolated and detached from a world he abhors, he gradually reveals himself as a multidimensional figure whose concern and sympathy for those trapped within the cosmic chaos become part of the novel's values. The major character is the narrator; his action is to attack a world he despises. The satire in *The Secret Agent* depends upon the immense ironic distance between a civilized voice that justifiably conceives of itself as representing sanity, rationality, and morality, and the personae of London who are for the most part caught in a maelstrom of violence and irrationality beyond their control.

In *The Secret Agent*, Conrad takes issue with a common Edwardian view that time inevitably equals progress. Such writers as Butler and Shaw proposed the concept of an upwardly evolving life force. Conrad regarded as cant the political euphoria of the Fabians and his socialist friend, Cunninghame-Graham, and their sanguine conviction that a "benign" and "congenial" future awaits us once we locate and ameliorate the problems of civilization. Conrad's sense of history as a process inexorably indifferent to man's aspirations was shaped partly by his despair and indignation at the continuous suppression of Polish freedom. Thus, even the book's dedication to the utopian H. G. Wells has its ironic aspect. *The Secret Agent* proposes no solutions for the oppressive economic system or the negligent political system.

The narrator stresses that those who should protect society are as oblivious to the objective world outside themselves as those who would destroy it. Ethelred, the "great man" and "presence," is handicapped by poor vision; he expresses himself in a vigorous manner, but in his haughtiness refuses to concern himself with—has indeed a physical horror of—details. A not entirely unsympathetic caricature of an Edwardian progressive, Ethelred takes seriously his business as a reformer and lives as if time were measuring progress toward social goals. Whatever our present attitudes toward ecology, Conrad would have wished us to see that the energy devoted to the bill for the nationalization of fisheries was misspent and that Ethelred, with his obvious leadership capacities—his "powerful" touch and vigorous tone are stressed—is exhausting himself with trifles. (In three of his short stories of this period, we find that Conrad's fastidious and ineffectual counterparts are the Count and narrator of "Il Conde" and the narrators of "An Anarchist" and "The Informer.")

It may be that the fundamental importance of *Under Western Eyes*, the last of Conrad's major political novels, is its rejection of political commitment in favor of personal relationships and private commitments. The language teacher's retrospective narrative re-creates the process of coming to terms with the terrifying Dionysian world he has confronted. By the conclusion of part 1, we have learned enough about the fanaticism, mysticism, and irrationality of the Russians to begin to appreciate the intelligence and perspicacity with which the narrator has edited Razumov's record. In contrast to the revolutionary frenzy and the autocratic regime's fanaticism, the narrator's detachment and effort to discover the moral aspect of the tale become attractive.

Autocratic politics create a world in which personal lives are distorted by the political abstractions served by proponents and antagonists. Russia finally emerges as primitive and atavistic, a kind of European version of the Congo where possibilities exist that have all but been discarded by Western countries. On the other hand, Geneva is a civilization where the libidinous energies and the atavistic impulses may be squelched, but violence and anarchy are under control. It is very much to the point that the people who reside in Geneva, other than the revolutionaries, are engaged in shopkeeping, teaching, picnicking, walking; and that these quite ordinary activities can take place in Geneva, unlike Russia, without bombs and intimidation. Geneva may have its materialistic aspect, epitomized by the rather tasteless Chateau Borel that now stands abandoned by its absentee owners, but it makes possible the civilization of personal affections and the fulfillment of private aspirations that the autocratic and violent Russian world blunts. Conrad deliberately depicts Geneva as tediously geometric and rather claustrophobic. Razumov is contemptuous of its decorum; he regards the view of the lake as "the very perfection of mediocrity attained at last after centuries of toil and culture." The novel confirms the value of the mind's own interior space, of personal communication and private relationships; it rejects historical and geographical explanations that seek to place moral responsibility beyond the individual conscience. The humanity and perspicacity that the narrator brings to his reminiscence "contain" and undermine the Russian conception of a world of vast objective space.

The Later Fiction

We can divide Conrad's career after 1910 into three distinct phases. In the first, Conrad wanted to demonstrate that he was an English novelist, not a Slav writing in English, as some reviewers implied. The diffident, self-effacing narrator of *Under Western Eyes* owes something to this impulse. In a sense, *Under Western Eyes*, *Chance* (1912), and *Victory* (1915) are Conrad's English trilogy. Thus *Chance* and *Victory* focus explicitly on personal relationships and manners, and allude to contemporary issues in England. He had to prove to his audience and perhaps to himself that he had become an English writer. *Chance* and *Victory* represent Conrad's attempt to write English novels of manners and to explore the intricacies of personal relationships in the context of contemporary customs and values. He regarded *Victory* as a "strictly proper" work "meant for cultured people," and he thought that "The Secret Sharer" was English "in moral atmosphere, feeling and even in detail."

In the great 1910 story "The Secret Sharer," the captain-narrator, separated by a "distance of years" from the meeting with Leggatt, recounts a tale of initiation in which he successfully overcame debilitating emotional insecurity to command his ship. Like those of Eliot's Prufrock and Joyce's Gabriel Conroy, the integrity of the captain's personality is threatened by a disbelief in the authenticity of self. The significance of the events for the sensitive and intelligent captain is that he discovered within himself the ability to act decisively that he had lacked. As a younger man, the captain doubted himself, felt a "stranger" to the community to which he belonged, and wondered if he should "turn out faithful to that ideal conception of one's personality every man sets up for himself secretly." His concern *now* is to present the issues in terms of what Leggatt meant to him. Although he certainly knows that harboring an escaped murderer represents a threat to a maritime civilization and a violation of his own legal and moral commitment, his retelling ignores this.

The captain's interpretation of his experience dramatizes the process of his coming to terms with what Leggatt symbolizes. In reductive terms, Leggatt is a man of unrestrained id and underdeveloped superego. The captain, an example of hyperconscious modern man who fastidiously thinks of the consequence of every action to the point where he cannot *do* anything, is his opposite. Self-doubt and anxiety create an illogical identification with Leggatt as his "double." He risks his future to hide the man he regards his "other self." To avoid discovery, he begins to act desperately and instinctively without conscious examination of the consequences of each action. Leggatt's presence creates situations where the luxury of introspection is no longer possible. Symbolically, the captain completes himself. He finds within himself the potential to act instinctively and boldly that his "double" exemplifies. It can be said that his adult ego is created by appeasing the contradictory demands of the id and the superego. Despite the evidence that Leggatt murdered another man in a fit of passion, the captain holds to a belief in Leggatt's control and sanity and insists that the killing was an act of duty. But the reader does not forget that Leggatt committed a horribly immoral act *that he does not regret.*

In *Chance* and *Victory*, Conrad's subject matter is less his own life than the external world. The form and narrative technique stress his detachment and withdrawal. Even when he revives Marlow in *Chance*, that figure is no longer a surrogate who echoes his own anxieties and doubts. Although we certainly see important resemblances between Conrad and his characters Heyst and Captain Anthony, he is not primarily writing about fictional versions of himself.

Chance, the first novel after the three major political novels, sustains and intensifies the stress on private life and passionate love as the only alternatives to a world threatened by materialism, political ideology, and uncontrollable historical forces. In *Chance*, as in Conrad's earlier novels, each is lonely, isolated and separate, and requires the recognition of another as friend, lover, parent, child, or counsel to complete him. If there is an alternative in *Chance* to repression, isolation, and self-imprisonment, it is in the possibility of sympathy and understanding, and, most significantly, passionate love. Once one perceives the prominence of the prison metaphor within the texture of the novel, one realizes that Conrad's indictment of English life has the harshness and bitterness of *The Secret Agent*. *Chance* discovers a heart of darkness beneath the civilized exteriors of Edwardian London, just as *The Secret Agent* discovers it in the political machinations not only of anarchists and reactionaries but also of those charged with upholding the status quo. In *Chance*, the London of *The Secret Agent* still exists in all its shabby, ugly decadence; mankind is separated by individual dreams and illusions.

Although London is not the setting, *Victory* is the last of Conrad's novels that analyzes contemporary European culture. As we shall see, beginning with *The Shadow-Line* (1916), the subsequent novels beat a retreat from confronting the crisis of values that Conrad believed was undermining Western civilization. For Conrad, the crisis was epitomized by imperialism, capitalism, the decline of family and national ties, and the replacement of human relationships based upon personal ties with relationships based on economic consideration. *Victory* depicts an "age in which we are camped like bewildered travellers in a garish, unrestful hotel." Schomberg's hotel becomes a mnemonic device to recall that image, and Schomberg's malice, enervation, lust, and greed are the quintessence of that age. In a world dominated by various forms of materialistic adventurism—from the coal mine in the tropics to Zangiacomo's traveling band and Schomberg's parody of a hotel—Heyst's courtesy and delicacy stand as a vestige of an older tradition. But his manners and formality also serve as a barrier not only to reaching a complete understanding with Lena but also to contending with the forces of economic barbarism—Jones, Ricardo, and Schomberg. "Outward cordiality of manner" and "consummate politeness" become Heyst's refuge. *Victory* is about the decline in civility and morality not only in what Conrad had once called "an outpost of progress" but in Western civilization. Conrad perceived, as Thomas Mann had in *Death in Venice* (1912), that something had gone wrong with the amenities and proprieties that are the glue that holds civilization together.

In the period between 1912 and 1914, when Conrad wrote *Victory*, the stable, secure England in which Conrad had found a home was in danger of disintegration. Beset by political turmoil in the form of labor unrest, the women's movement, and the excesses and zeal of the Conservative opposition, which threatened to undermine parliamentary government, England must have seemed to him to be increasingly in danger of becoming like his native Poland. The ironically titled *Victory* is Conrad's response to an England torn by conflicting but powerful enclaves and suffering a loss of esteem in its own eyes as well as in those of other nations.

Heyst may represent Conrad's perception that a certain kind of man—polished, tolerant, polite, considerate of others, and of impeccable integrity and the highest personal standards—was becoming obsolete in England. For all his quirks, Heyst adheres to Edwardian propriety and decorum in all his actions with the single exception of his elopement. The negativism of Heyst's father may echo the anonymous 1905 pamphlet *The Decline and Fall of the British Empire*; in any case, it is an extreme rejection of the more optimistic of the social Darwinists. It may also be a criticism of *A Commentary* (1908) by Conrad's friend John Galsworthy. *Victory* is a novel that attacks imperialistic pretensions, decadent aristocracy, and business morality, only to give those forces the laurels of victory. The title *Victory* finally implies the triumph of materialism and greed over feelings and personal relationships. By using *business* interchangeably with *game*, Conrad emphasizes the effort of Edwardian culture to disguise in understatements its competitive and aggressive impulses.

The second phase of Conrad's later career derives more from a personal impulse. After *Chance* and *Victory*, he returns from contemporary issues to his own memories. *The Shadow-Line* and *The Arrow of Gold* (1919), like "The Secret Sharer" and "A Smile of Fortune" (1911), are expressive of Conrad's emotions and passions, but in these works, unlike the Marlow tales, Conrad re-creates emotions of the past more than he objectifies his present inner turmoil. As Conrad aged, he sought subjects in his personal and literary past, and his later fiction less frequently addresses his immediate personal problems or current public issues. *The Shadow-Line* and *The Arrow of Gold* reach back into his personal past, while *The Rescue* was completed primarily to settle his long-standing anxiety about a work that had been stalled for two decades. *The Rescue* returns to the romance world of Malay that provided the setting of his first two novels, *Almayer's Folly* and *An Outcast of the Islands*, as well as such early tales as "Karain" and "The Lagoon." It is a nostalgic look at his personal and literary past and provides something of an escape from Conrad's present anxieties and harsher memories.

Based on his command of the *Otago* in 1888, *The Shadow-Line* explores the difference between merely practicing skills and providing leadership to a community. Conrad had written in Richard Curle's copy of the novel, "This story had been in my mind for some years. Originally I used to think of it under the name of *First Command*. When I managed in the second year of war to concentrate my mind sufficiently to begin working I turned to this subject as the easiest. But in consequence of my changed mental attitude to it, it became *The Shadow-Line*." In contrast, the seemingly similar "Secret Sharer" emphasized the captain-narrator's personal psychological development rather than his ability to occupy a position in terms of standards established by maritime tradition. By fulfilling the moral requirements of a clearly defined position, the captain-narrator fulfills himself; he overcomes ennui, anxiety, and anomie and merges his psychological life with the demands of the external world. To oversimplify: *The Shadow-Line* affirms that hyperconsciousness is a moral rather than—as in "The Secret Sharer"— a psychological problem. The later work demonstrates how hyperconsciousness and its symptoms can be overcome by discovering the authentic self that exists beneath self-doubt and anxiety.

The last novel Conrad completed, *The Rover* (1923), was written with the idea of reaching that part of the mass of mankind which was literate. In important respects, it is a synopsis of a number of major themes in his previous work. Conrad spoke of *The Rover* in terms that suggest its special importance to him: "I have wanted for a long time to do a seaman's 'return' (before my own departure)." Peyrol's desire in his final voyage to merge his destiny with that of his nation may reflect Conrad's desire, as he approached death, to contribute meaningfully to Poland's destiny. His fantasy of a significant political act is embodied in Peyrol. If, like Nabokov's, Conrad's life was embodied in his imagination, he was never comfortable that he had turned his back on politics and the heritage of his father, whom he recalled as an idealistic patriot. The novel's title also refers to himself, the twice transplanted alien who finally found a home in England and no longer felt himself something of an outsider. Peyrol re-creates himself at fifty-eight when circumstances connive with his own weariness to deprive him of his past; he creates a new identity just as surely as a younger Conrad did when he left Poland to go to sea and, later, when he turned from the sea to a writing career. *The Rover* combines Conrad's fantasy of retreat with his lifelong fantasy of a heroic return home. (Neither his first visit to Poland in 1890 nor his second at the outbreak of the war quite fulfilled this fantasy.) *The Rover* associates Peyrol's return with Conrad's own romantic desire to return to his past. In *A Personal Record* (1912), writing of his first return to Poland, Conrad remarked that the faces "were as familiar to me as though I had known them from childhood, and my childhood were a matter of the day before yesterday."

In the final phase, he looks back in *The Rover* and the incomplete *Suspense* to the Napoleonic period and creates large historical canvases that recall the great political novels. While we do not know what he would have done in *Suspense*, his real concern in *The Rover* is coming to terms with his own approaching death. In that novel, the Napoleonic era provides the occasion for a moving lyrical novel about the possibility of facing death heroically. The principal character, an aging seaman and an outsider, is a fictional counterpart of Conrad.

Conrad's later works demonstrate the continuity of his career. Throughout his career his works are expressions of his quest for values and self-definition. Continuing the focus of the novels about politics (*Nostromo*, *The Secret Agent*, and *Under Western Eyes*), Conrad's later works are more concerned with family and personal relationships than are his prior works. Except for "The Secret Sharer" and *The Shadow-Line*, the later works are concerned with how and why people love one another. But they also address how historical and social forces limit and define the possibilities for love and action. Conrad never puts behind him the conviction that man is caught in a web of circumstances beyond his control. But he also believes in man's capacity to grow, to love, and to know himself. Conrad believes that, within an indifferent if not hostile universe, man's indomitable will enables him to survive despite setbacks and individual failures. Thus, he is not the nihilist and the prophet of darkness that he has been depicted as in much recent criticism.

Conrad's later work contains qualities that typify the work of many older artists: the revival of forms and themes of past artistic successes, references to earlier works, nostalgia for an earlier period of life, emphasis on turning points in life, and intermittent sensuality. But what is lacking in Conrad's later work is the creative rage of the older Yeats, the aging Monet's willingness to take a chance, the bold disregard for precedents of the Joyce who wrote *Finnegans Wake*, and the Olympian turning away from mere nominalistic details to focus on essential truths that characterize the later work of Matisse.

Daniel R. Schwarz

Selected Bibliography

Fleishman, Avrom. *Conrad's Politics: Community and Anarchy in the Fiction of Joseph Conrad*. Baltimore: Johns Hopkins University Press, 1967.

Fogel, Aaron. *Coercion to Speak: Conrad's Poetics of Dialogue*. Cambridge, Mass.: Harvard University Press, 1985.

Guerard, Albert J. *Conrad the Novelist*. Cambridge, Mass.: Harvard University Press, 1958.

Hay, Eloise Knapp. *The Political Novels of Joseph Conrad*. Chicago: University of Chicago Press, 1963.

Karl, Frederick. *Joseph Conrad: The Three Lives*. New York: Farrar, Straus, and Giroux, 1979.

Miller, J. Hillis. *Poets of Reality: Six Twentieth Century Writers*. Cambridge, Mass.: Belknap Press of Harvard University Press, 1965.

Moser, Thomas. *Joseph Conrad: Achievement and Decline*. Cambridge, Mass.: Harvard University Press, 1967.

Murfin, Ross, ed. *Heart of Darkness: A Case Study in Contemporary Criticism*. New York: St. Martin's Press, 1989.

Rosenfield, Claire. *Paradise of Snakes: An Archetypal Analysis of Conrad's Political Novels*. Chicago: University of Chicago Press, 1967.

Schwarz, Daniel R. *Conrad: "Almayer's Folly" through "Under Western Eyes."* London: Macmillan; Ithaca, N.Y.: Cornell University Press, 1980.

Schwarz, Daniel R. *Conrad: The Later Fiction*. London: Macmillan, 1966.

Watt, Ian. *Conrad in the Nineteenth Century*. Berkeley and Los Angeles: University of California Press, 1979.

D. H. Lawrence

FOR most of its history the British novel has been primarily a domestic melodrama about money and sex, and the modern novel is no exception. Nineteenth-century realism especially is an encyclopedia of entries on English class and gender anxieties, and on the links between them. There is, of course, another tradition of adventure and travel, rooted in the maritime imperialism of the British Isles. This tradition is also well represented by the modern novel, which often followed earlier travel-adventure narratives in providing a critical commentary on life at home. These three broad themes—money and class, sexuality and gender, and European civilization refracted against those alien to it—intersect with one another nowhere in British modernism more powerfully or disturbingly than in the novels of D. H. Lawrence. Lawrence displayed little of James Joyce's scrupulous concern for literary technique and the mot juste; he had no patience for the genteel humanism of E. M. Forster; and he was convinced that the inward-turning delineation of consciousness sought by Marcel Proust, Virginia Woolf, and fellow modernists was primarily a sign of Europe's death wish. But Lawrence's profoundly estranged vision, for all its obviousness, vulgarity, and narcissism, may represent the emotional and intellectual life of his time more immediately than does any other.

Lawrence was an individual at war with Western modernity itself—with its automation, industrialism, commercialism, militarism, imperialism, and dominion over nature (including the American taste for

indoor plumbing) as well as with its growing demand for social equality, democracy, and the rights of women. He cherished a "free proud singleness," yet yearned for a "permanent connection to others" (in Rupert
Birkin's words from *Women in Love*) that was organic and communitar-
ian. The conflicts began amid the particular details of his own existence, where he sought remedies for what he believed to be cosmic disorder. Lawrence's writing is a tangle of contradictions, almost all of
which have demonstrable roots in his family life. Yet these contradictions turn out to be inextricable from the larger cultural dilemmas of his
age. About his first novel, Lawrence told his friend Jessie Chambers, "I
think a man puts everything he is into a book—a real book." He rarely
belied the remark in practice. His fiction, "huge autobiography embroidered," in Richard Aldington's apt phrase, cannibalized the people and
events around him with a ruthlessness unmatched—even by Joyce or
Proust—in the twentieth century. But Lawrence also maintained the
conviction—it has been called both prophetic and Freudian—that in
his autobiographical analysis lay the cure for all of modernity's ills.

If Lawrence is a biographer's dream, however, he is a philosopher's
nightmare. For he adapts Nietzsche's view that rational thought,
despite its pretensions to disinterestedness, is nothing more than
unconscious memoir. In Lawrence, conscious memoir assumes the
character of metaphysics returned to its atavistic sources. He half invites
a reading of his fiction as one long rehearsal of psychological conflicts
he never succeeded in resolving. But in the first chapter of his *Studies in
Classic American Literature*, Lawrence stresses the opposition between
"two blankly opposing morals, the artist's and the tale's. Never trust the
artist. Trust the tale." His own mode of interpretion stands those
American classics on their heads. Lawrence translates Benjamin
Franklin's praise of utilitarian virtue as Franklin's way of justifying the
white man's eradication of the Indian; he rereads Melville's white
whale, not as a personal vision of good or evil but as the doomed image
of white America. The personal was for Lawrence as inseparable from
the philosophical and the political as it was from the novels themselves.

The obvious example of this imbrication of personal and public conflict is Lawrence's relationship to his parents. Lawrence was born in
1885, surrounded by the smoldering coal fields and shrinking pastures
of Nottinghamshire. He was the son of Arthur Lawrence, a barely literate coal miner who had given dancing lessons in his youth and Lydia
Beardsall, an acerbic mother with aspirations to gentility who worked

briefly and unsuccessfully as a student teacher before she married. Lawrence was deeply affected by the occasional violence of his father's anger, especially that aimed against his often bitter and disappointed mother. "I was born hating my father," he wrote to the Scottish poet Rachel Taylor just before his mother's death in December 1910; "as early as ever I can remember, I shivered with horror when he touched me." But he also saw his father, and miners in general, as exhibiting a natural nobility and a distinctly male sociality that were being suppressed by the forces of modernity—including willful, puritanical, and intellectually emancipated women.

Toward his mother, Lawrence recognized quite different affections and falsely assumed that she derived from a higher social class than had his father. "We have loved each other," he also wrote in the letter to Taylor, "almost with a husband and wife love, as well as filial and maternal." But while this maternal relationship was central to his happiness at home, Lawrence felt early on that it was also "terrible" and "abnormal." The maternal woman paradoxically became not only a welcome path to higher cultural status; she was equally the troubling source of modernity's reliance on intellection, calculation, homogeneity, and spirituality, and of its repression of instinctual spontaneity, uninhibited sexuality, and a natural community of unique individuals. By the time Lawrence wrote his essay "Education of the People" (1920), mothers had become the selfish instigators of modernity's debilitating self-consciousness. "Seize babies away from their mothers, with hard, fierce, terrible hands . . . mothers of England, spank your wistful babies . . . and make men of them." The essay ends with a call for a sharp distinction between the "productive" sphere of the modern bourgeoisie and modern women on one hand, and a "contestive" organic community of athletes and hand-to-hand soldiery akin to Plato's Republic on the other.

Lawrence's mother and father, figured as the passionate, naturally noble, but oppressed man and the spiritual, willful, and repressed woman, appear throughout Lawrence's novels. They are central to *The White Peacock* (1911), *Sons and Lovers* (1913), *The Rainbow* (1915), *The Lost Girl* (1920), *Aaron's Rod* (1922), *St. Mawr* (1925), *The Plumed Serpent* (1926), and *Lady Chatterley's Lover* (1928). Moreover, Lawrence tended to reproduce his parents' struggle in his own relationships, especially in an early and failed romance with Jessie Chambers and in his lasting, if stormy, marriage with Frieda Weekley. But there are two crucial variations that Lawrence's own experience introduced into the models he took from his parents.

First, Lawrence attained the cultural capital that his mother only vaguely symbolized. Indeed, he often portrayed himself as a fully formed intellectual at war with the intellect, a working-class artisan who had achieved cultural sophistication only to abandon the superfices of mind for the fundamentals of body and blood. Second, he could explore through his own experience a homosexual desire that went beyond the comradeship of the miners. Lawrence's sexual ambivalence, expressed with great force in the "Prologue" that he deleted from *Women in Love*, allows him to portray homoerotic desire—at times more overtly than at others—as itself a redemptive force. In episodes of *The White Peacock*, *Women in Love*, *Aaron's Rod*, *Kangaroo* (1923), and *The Plumed Serpent*, Lawrence documented the attraction of homosexual desire in only thinly veiled descriptions.

Lawrence met and eloped with Frieda von Richthofen Weekley, the wife of his French teacher at University College, Nottingham, in 1912. She would come to represent the great female principle in his thinking and his fiction. But she also appeared to be a refinement and synthesis of the qualities Lawrence attributed to his parents. Frieda possessed in actuality the cultured heritage that Lawrence had projected onto his mother; but she was at the same time spontaneous, physical, and sexually open, allowing him previously denied contact with the natural nobility supposedly hidden behind the crude behavior of his father. Lawrence's relationship with Frieda was in large part a struggle with a modern woman—she was sexually liberated and educated—who at times embodied the passionate sensuality Lawrence sought and at others proved to be an incomplete answer to his need for a community of individuals in "contestive" harmony. *The Trespasser* (1912), *Women in Love* (1920), *Mr. Noon* (part 1, 1934; complete, 1984), *Kangaroo*, even Lawrence's revision of Mollie Skinner's *Boy in the Bush* (1924), all rehearse this tension in one way or another.

Lawrence identified the intellectual, willful woman with the self-consciousness and automatism of modernity as a whole. He disliked the mentalism of psychoanalysis, and tried—in *Psychoanalysis and the Unconscious* (1921) and *Fantasia of the Unconscious* (1922)—to reinterpret some of its findings in terms of impulses arising from specific bodily regions. But he shared Freud's tendency to distinguish in women an active, clitoral orgasm of immature sexuality from a passive, vaginal, and mature response, and in the novels from *Women in Love* on linked the former to the calculating will plaguing modernity and the latter to organic nature. In *The Plumed Serpent*, it is a woman's (clitoral) control over orgasm that is problematic: Cipriano literally withdraws from Kate Leslie to prevent it, and she ends up all the more attached to him as a result. In *Lady Chatterley's Lover*, Mellors's marriage to the sensual but vulgar Bertha falls apart when her own too-clitoral, too-conscious sexuality overwhelms him: she refuses to achieve orgasm with him, preferring to wait until after his own. "She sort of got harder and harder to bring off," he tells Constance, "and she'd sort of tear at me down there, as if it was a beak tearing me." Rarely has the male fear of castration by a strong woman been depicted with such honesty, if not hysteria.

This dichotomy between the passive, vaginal woman and the active, clitoral one, however spurious it appears today, complemented Lawrence's sense that his homoerotic desire (like heterosexual sodomy) might promise not only an escape from women who demanded the same intellectual and political prerogatives as men, but salvation from modernity itself. Lawrence rejected the more expressive homosexuality he found in many around him, may have had only one homosexual encounter, and either deleted or destroyed (as is the case with the essay "Goats and Compasses") those of his writings that openly confronted his desire for men. The abhorrent nature of lesbianism emerges clearly in *The Rainbow* and "The Fox" (1922). But as with his response to the critics who saw only pornography in his treatment of heterosexual intercourse, Lawrence distinguished between two kinds of homosexuality. Violently repelled by the "corruption" and "deep inward dirt" of John Maynard Keynes and friends at Cambridge (a corruption that appears in the artist Loerke in *Women in Love*), he still yearned for a healthier, life-affirming, at times even puritanical homosexual "tenderness" (as in the same novel's Birkin.)

This vague quality of "tenderness"—the word was an earlier title for *Lady Chatterley's Lover*—would likewise differentiate two kinds of heterosexual sodomy. With Rupert and Ursula in *Women in Love* (chapter 29) or Mellors and Constance Chatterley in *Lady Chatterley's Lover* (chapter 16), sodomy represents the acme of their experience of one another. In the latter novel especially, sodomy at once transcends sensuality, tenderness, and love, "burning out the shames, the deepest, oldest shames, in the most secret places," though it depends on a completely submissive woman—"She had to be a passive consenting thing, like a slave, a physical slave. Yet the passion licked round her." But with Gerald and Gudrun in *Women in Love* (chapter 31), the same act forecasts their violent separation and Gerald's destruction, and follows Gerald's rejection of Rupert's affections. Like the later Freud, Lawrence accepted life and death instincts, and linked them to forms of sexuality. Whether or not one wishes to see Lawrence's use of heterosexual sodomy as a psychologically (and legally) censored mask for homosexuality, both heterosexual sodomy and homosexuality thus carry the risk of death for Lawrence even as, under the right circumstances, they promise liberating rebirth. Perhaps because of its untenability for him, homosexual love symbolized the possibility of social redemption in Lawrence's novels in ways that heterosexual love never could.

Though it is in one sense obvious that Lawrence never abandoned the project of sifting through his parents' marriage, it is also true that family life itself became a surrogate in his writings for powerful social conflicts. Biography is finally a seamless web of relations that extend from the home to the world. The tension between his mother and father, and between countless fictional couples derived from them, is also Lawrence's way of presenting class struggle in its grittiest form. There were major union strikes in 1893, 1912, and 1926. Conditions underground were hellish before the war, and death was routine. Throughout those prewar years, mine owners responded with a "peculiar mixture of paternalism and ruthlessness," in Jeffrey Meyers's apt phrase. The mental deliberateness and sexual impotence Lawrence associates with a hereditary or commercial elite were thus everywhere opposed by the damaged bodies and self-destructive resentment of the working class. Descriptions of mining villages, like those of Wiggiston in *The Rainbow*, are thus paradoxically haunted not only by Lawrence's deep resentment of modern capitalism but also by his animus toward the stunted miners themselves.

The only positive, heroic figures to arise from this impasse are those who through the force of some natural ability and insight struggle out of the working class, yet abandon labor's crass appeal for money. These figures recapture an organic contact with persons and things that remains merely an unconscious vestige in the modern laborer. Obviously, Lawrence is himself often the model for the type, which appears as Rupert Birkin in *Women in Love*, both Aaron Sisson and Rawdon Lilly in *Aaron's Rod*, Gilbert Noon in *Mr. Noon*, and Richard Lovatt

Somers in *Kangaroo*; as Don Ramon Carrasco and General Cipriano Viedma in *The Plumed Serpent*, figures now informed by Mexican politics and Lawrence's views of race consciousness; and, as if constituting the opening and closing statements of Lawrence's career, as the Pan-like gamekeepers Annable in *The White Peacock* and Oliver Mellors in *Lady Chatterley's Lover*.

The typology Lawrence derived from his parents would likewise embody modernity's struggle over gender and sexual identity. The militant drive for women's suffrage peaked in the years just preceding the war, the period of Lawrence's first literary efforts. (Women would not win the right to vote until 1918.) It was a time when otherwise respectable, bourgeois women smashed storefront windows and took up hunger strikes in prison. Though the resistance was largely an urban phenomenon, Lawrence registered its impact even in the rural isolation of his hometown, Eastwood. *Sons and Lovers* is primarily a bildungsroman about Paul Morel. Raised in a mining town, Paul suffers both from his father's brutality and his mother's dissatisfaction. When his older brother dies, Paul forms a powerful bond with his protective mother, one that threatens his father and makes any satisfying romantic relationship with his friend Miriam impossible. But Paul soon meets Clara Dawes, a divorced, liberated woman portrayed at first as a militant and bitter suffragist. Despite her strong suspicion of men and the memory of her drunken and abusive husband, she is attracted to the younger, intellectual Paul and finds a new sexual satisfaction with him.

While Lawrence's narration is clearly sympathetic to her position, the novel locates both the source of and the solution to her social discontent in her sexuality. By the end, Paul Morel has so arranged things that Clara, "ecstatic," winds up whispering to her ex-husband, "Take me back, take me back!" Paul begins to lose himself in the memory of his dead mother. But in the last lines, rather like Eugène de Rastignac at the end of Balzac's *Père Goriot*, he turns defiantly away from despair and back toward the "humming," sparkling town. The story of Clara, her husband, and Paul functions both as a wish-fulfilling resolution of the conflict between Lawrence's parents and as a recognition of his own inevitable exclusion. But it is also the means through which Lawrence encapsulated his understanding of the period's gender politics.

While the details vary, Lawrence returns numerous times to a scenario in which women's social discontent is linked to a failed erotic life with men. One must remember the link drawn at this time between women's emancipation and the repression of male sexuality. The slogan popularized by suffragist Christabel Pankhurst in 1913 was "Votes for Women and Purity for Men." Lawrence repeatedly attacked all that the slogan implied: in Lettie's tragic refusal of George in *The White Peacock*; in the contrast of Clara Dawes with Miriam Leivers in *Sons and Lovers*; in the disappointment of Anna and Will's marriage and in Ursula's destructive lesbian affair in *The Rainbow*; in Rupert's struggles with Hermione and Ursula and in Gudrun's fatal rejection of Gerald in *Women in Love*; in Alvina Houghton's sexual awakening at the hands of the brooding Italian, Ciccio, in *The Lost Girl*; in the Marchese's revitalizing affair with Aaron Sisson in *Aaron's Rod*; in the eventual submission of Kate Leslie to General Cipriano Viedma in *The Plumed Serpent*; in Lou Witt's sexual response to an untamable horse in *St. Mawr*; and, of course, in the erotic transformation of Connie Chatterley by Lawrence's most perfectly idealized image of himself, the gamekeeper Oliver Mellors in *Lady Chatterley's Lover*. The threat posed by modern woman is parried by the woman's renunciation of calculating intellect and by her sensual liberation through contact with a powerfully instinctual male—whether human, equine or, as in "The Fox," vulpine.

By the same token, male sexual response to women takes on dramatic significance. In essays like "A Study of Thomas Hardy" and "The Crown" (both completed in 1915) and in his two books on psychoanalysis, Lawrence outlines a male sexuality that depends for its success on spontaneous instinct, yet carries social significance of biblical proportions. Healthy sexuality in Lawrence, unlike that of many other male modernists, is finally not dependent on reproduction or fertility (though masturbation is still rejected) or on any organized, social function—but neither is it treated as if existing apart from these. Rather, sexuality forms a bodily religion all its own, one that is prerequisite to social change and well-being. And, as already noted, it is decidedly ambivalent in gender preference. There are strong indications, stated bluntly in the deleted prologue to *Women in Love*, that full satisfaction with a woman would always be impossible, and that only homosexual love, however threatening, might suffice. Nevertheless, it is from sexual fulfillment with a woman that Lawrence drew his most far-reaching hypotheses about the meaning of male sexuality.

Along with a never-used introduction to *Sons and Lovers*, the essays from 1915 outline Lawrence's attempted philosophical synthesis of sexual intercourse and Christian theology. "Down the road of the blood, further and further into the darkness, I come to the Almighty God Who was in the beginning, is now, and ever shall be," Lawrence wrote in "The Crown." "It is thus . . . that I come to the woman in desire. She is the doorway, she is the gate to the dark eternity of power, the creator's power." In the "Study of Thomas Hardy" (initially titled "Le Gai Savaire" [sic] after Nietzsche), Lawrence's literary revisionism is overwhelmed by his psychological and phenomenological reading of the Christian trinity.

The traditional formula from the Gospel of John—"And the word was made flesh"—is reversed, so that the flesh (now God the Father) appears to have been made word (Christ), with the eternal tension between them symbolized by the Holy Spirit. The Old (Jewish) Law of the Father is thus connected not only to the flesh, but to matriarchy and the dark body of the woman; and the New (Christian) Love of the Son is linked to the Word, self-awareness, light, and male individuation. Like Nietzsche's duality of Dionysus and Apollo, Father and Son are struggling opposites balanced, in a strange echo of Hegel and Carlyle, by Spirit. (The famous image of the lovers' star-equilibrium in chapter 23 of *Women in Love*, borrowed in all likelihood from Edward Carpenter, is one version of the Spirit's tense balancing act.) More important, it is now through the body of the woman that Lawrence believes he can make contact, as an individual, with the Power and the Law of the Father.

Such "pseudo-philosophy," as Lawrence himself called it, would be simply tiresome were it not for the light it sheds on one of Lawrence's major novels, *The Rainbow*, and on the mystical significance attached to nonrational physicality throughout his fiction. The novel traces three generations of male-female relationships from the mid-nineteenth century to the early twentieth. It opens, however, in the biblical cadences of an antediluvian era (the giant flood occurs later in the novel) filled with the autochthonous, near-incestuous Brangwen clan. The awkward but fulfilling marriage of the worldly Polish widow and expatriate Lydia Lensky to earthy Tom Brangwen is succeeded by the marriage of her daughter (by her first husband) Anna to Tom's nephew Will. But Anna's critical intellect is in conflict with the "dark emotional experience" that Will finds in their solitude and in the church, and their struggle is resolved only when Anna, "Victrix" at last, bears children. After the flood that kills patriarch Tom, her daughter Ursula's development occupies the latter half of the book.

Ursula reproduces her mother Anna and grandmother Lydia as she is courted in a near-mythic landscape. Like her mother, Ursula offers herself to the moon (and to her lover, Anton Skrebensky) in rites of sensual awakening and fertility: "Her body opened wide like a quivering anemone, a soft dilated invitation touched by the moon." Initial failure with Skrebensky is followed by a shame-inducing lesbian affair with the all-too-modern Winifred Inger—who winds up marrying Ursula's mechanical uncle, Tom, and settling in the equally mechanical town of Wiggiston. After disappointing attempts at schoolteaching and university, Ursula returns to Skrebensky. Though their passion explodes for a time, Ursula wants something beyond Skrebensky's power. The novel ends with one of Lawrence's most expressionistic scenes. Ursula, now pregnant by Skrebensky, is chased by a small group of horses galloping apocalyptically around her in a rain that "could not put out the hard, urgent, massive fire that was locked within these flanks, never, never"; she miscarries as a result of the encounter. But in the midst of the "dry, brittle, terrible corruption" spreading out from the coal town of Beldover, Ursula sees a rainbow promising a "new germination" and an end to modernity's horrors.

The sweep of generations in the novel loosely follows the progression of Father, Son, and (though only in the rainbow's promise) Holy Spirit outlined by Lawrence's metaphysics. The model also frames Lawrence's treatment of heterosexual love as an attempt to reestablish contact—through the body of the (symbolically maternal) woman—with a physical, nonverbal father who rejected his all-too-verbal son. Moreover, this "philosophy" also suggests the beginnings of Lawrence's later fictional meditations on power. In *Aaron's Rod, Kangaroo,* and *The Plumed Serpent* especially, legitimate social authority is rooted not in pragmatic or utilitarian human relations but in the flesh of the Father that reveals itself in wordless sexual power and ritual incantation.

Similarly, Lawrence's "philosophy" points to the underlying grounds of his racism. Jews, Celts, Italians, Indians, and Mexicans occupy highly ambivalent positions. They are all on the one hand closer to the primal sources embodied here by the Father (Lawrence believed that white skin was unnatural). Yet they are on the other constantly denigrated in the novels either for being oblivious to the force of their inheritance, as are the childlike Mexican peasants of *The Plumed Serpent*; dissolute perverters of the flesh in the name of machinery and calculation, like the Jewish homosexual Loerke in *Women in Love*; or sentimental egotists, like the Jewish, pseudofascist revolutionary Ben Cooley in *Kangaroo* (modeled after Lawrence's friend S. S. Koteliansky), who substitutes a personal, suffocating demand to be loved for the impersonal, unconscious racial power locked within him.

Finally, then, beyond both class and sexuality, the typology suggested by Lawrence's parents structures the relation of Europe to its ethnological opposites. Though there is no evidence that Lawrence read Ferdinand Tönnies's work on the distinction between community and society, he would have been acquainted with a similar distinction in Marxian thought from the Eastwood Fabian socialist William Hopkin. Lawrence's Luddism could be derived easily enough from his childhood experiences. But his social perspective also evolved from his reading of Blake, Carlyle, Ruskin, Whitman, and Nietzsche. His plans during the war for an ideal community, Rananim, recalled nineteenth-century utopianism dating back to Coleridge. He had a passing familiarity, through Frieda and her sister Else, with sociology derived from Weber, and a critical though unique appreciation of Freud's early work. Lawrence also had a fascination for anthropology and the study of myth; he had read Herbert Spencer's *Education*, E. B. Tyler's *Primitive Society*, at least parts of Sir James Frazer's *Golden Bough*, and Jane Harrison's *Ancient Art and Ritual*. As preparation for *The Plumed Serpent*, he consulted works of a more specific nature on Mexican culture, such as Zelia Nuttall's *Fundamental Principles of Old and New World Civilizations* and Lewis Spence's *Gods of Mexico*. And he was at least acquainted with the thought of Edward Carpenter, an important Midlands apologist for homosexuality, utopian socialism, and primitivism.

In all of this, however, it may be Tönnies's opposition of archaic community to modern society that is most useful in characterizing Lawrence's social perspective and his relationship to non-European culture. In *Gemeinschaft und Gesellschaft* (1887), Tönnies elaborates the distinction between rural and city life—one that begins in the West with Plato—in sharp detail. The original rural community is organized around the household economy, customary cooperation, and an art that is organically related to the life of the artist. The urban society that succeeds it, though with elements of community remaining, depends upon deliberative trade, calculation in business, and contractual agreement, industry based on the productive use of capital, and the self-evident validity of science. Though dispassionate in tone, Tönnies's writing reveals an unmistakable sympathy for the rural communities disappearing around him.

Moreover, Tönnies draws an important related distinction between two kinds of will. Natural will "is the psychological equivalent of the human body." It is inseparable from activity; inherited and organic in growth; sensuous and artistically creative; attributed to common people; and female in gender. Rational will, by contrast, "is the product of thinking itself" and possesses reality only with reference to the thinking subject. It is situated prior to activity for better control; conceptually dominated by an image of the future; tool-oriented and mechanical; attributed to the educated classes; and, finally, male in gender. Besides the obvious similarity between this perspective and Lawrence's, Tönnies remarks that since the male artist must have access to natural will, he may appear effeminate—as Lawrence knew he did—to others.

Tönnies's particular elaboration of this distinction is important for the modern period precisely because of its ambiguity. Though adapted to a large extent from earlier political economy and from Marx, his work nicely fits primitivist utopian models and was to be taken up by Nazism as well. It could be turned with equal zeal in egalitarian and authoritarian directions. Lawrence always demonstrated a sympathy for the workers and a hatred of the hereditary and commercial elite. Lord Chatterley, impotently bound to his mechanized wheelchair and to his lifeless, spiritualized writing, is Lawrence's most vicious portrait of that elite. But Lawrence had little regard for democracy in practice; his critique at times closely followed that of Plato's *Republic*. In general, he turned his longing for community in the authoritarian direction. Though briefly intrigued by Bertrand Russell and his democratic socialism—they planned both revolution and a lecture tour together—Lawrence insisted that only "a body of chosen patricians" and an elected, patriarchal "Dictator" could guide the community he envisioned.

The opposition of organic community to mechanical society, like that of natural to rational will, appears throughout Lawrence's work. It is central to his criticism of modern England and of modern Europe as well. In the first chapter of *Studies in Classic American Literature*, he writes: "Men are free when they belong to a living, organic, *believing* community, active in fulfilling some unfulfilled, perhaps unrealized purpose. . . . Men are freest when they are unconscious of freedom." His first sustained treatment of the theme is *The Rainbow*, but the distinction is also important to this novel's sequel, *Women in Love*, where the mechanical transformation of the mines initiated by Gerald Crich leads inexorably to Crich's icebound death in the Alps. Subsequent novels, based on Lawrence's travels, reinscribe the distinction in ethnographic terms. Italy, Australia, America, and Mexico each become a phase of his search for a new organic community.

Lawrence's life in England between 1912 and 1917, however interrupted by travel in Germany and Italy, made him feel increasingly persecuted by the government. In addition to his association with socialists in Eastwood, Lawrence had married a German woman of aristocratic background (her cousin, Manfred von Richthofen, was the "Red Baron," the most famous German pilot of the First World War). Lawrence was also a known pacifist; he openly opposed England's war effort and the nationalist jingoism surrounding it. On top of everything else, *Sons and Lovers* gained Lawrence a certain notoriety for its sexual explicitness. *The Rainbow* was suppressed by the government six weeks after publication in 1915. Lawrence and Frieda retreated to the coast of Cornwall, where they were harassed as possible spies by government officials. Lawrence also endured a number of medical examinations for military service (documented in the "Nightmare" chapter of *Kangaroo*) that, despite his chronic illness, granted him an ambiguous draft status. Believing that authorities were forcing him out of the country, he embarked on the extended periods of travel abroad that Catherine Carswell called his "savage pilgrimage."

Lawrence had once thought about writing a novel for every continent; he was convinced of the formative influence of geography on the consciousness of a people. "Every continent has its own spirit of place," he wrote in *Studies in Classic American Literature*. "Every people is polarized in some particular locality, which is home, the homeland." This sense of place is important to all of Lawrence's fiction, and often it is modernity's mechanical transformation of place that produces the emotional emptiness he diagnoses. In the novels written after he traveled to Italy, Ceylon, Australia, America, and Mexico, this sense of place acquires an ethnographic scope. Now, it is peasant life in Italy or the mythic heritage of the Aztecs in Mexico that holds the promise of renewed community and natural will.

Lawrence was generally disappointed by his travels. Rarely did a new place live up to, or alter, his expectations. *Kangaroo*, for example, ends with the inevitable turn away from human inadequacies toward the aboriginal flora, recalling similar gestures in *The White Peacock* or

Women in Love, which are set in Nottinghamshire. In Mexico, however, Lawrence went one step further. Out of a dizzying melange of Aztec creation myths, contemporary Mexican politics, the theosophy of Madame Blavatsky, and a Congregationalist hymnal, he produced a syncretic fantasy about the resurgence of natural will and organic community in a fraternal cult centered around the Aztec deity Quetzalcoatl. *The Plumed Serpent* is Lawrence's only fully realized picture of what the recreation of organic community in the modern world would entail, and it is significantly set far from Eastwood amid the phallic mysteries of an archaic brotherhood.

While the cult of Quetzalcoatl replaces the Christian cross of spiritual love with a drumming sensuality, Lawrence also finds in the stories of Quetzalcoatl (the Morning Star) and rival brother Huitzilopochtli (or Tezcatlipoca) another version of the irresolvable tension present in the Christian trinity. The Aztec belief in Quetzalcoatl's return to reestablish his reign on earth informs the story, which ends in ritual human sacrifice and Kate's decision to remain, in thrall, with Cipriano. It has often been claimed that Lawrence, to the relief of many readers, repudiated the hero worship and authoritarianism of *The Plumed Serpent* in a letter of 1928: "On the whole I agree . . . the leader-cum-follower relationship is a bore." But subsequent letters make it clear that he retained an allegiance to Quetzalcoatl and his high priests—"Yes, I am all for Lucifer, who is really the Morning Star"—to the end of his life.

Today the novels of D. H. Lawrence occupy a more tenuous position in the canon of English literature than they did a generation ago. But his work prompted sharply divided critical judgment from the beginning. *Sons and Lovers* made Lawrence's early reputation, but it is also his most conventionally realistic novel. Though many saw *The Rainbow*, *Women in Love*, and *Lady Chatterley's Lover* as important, even revolutionary books, the first was confiscated on publication for obscenity, the second found no publisher willing to take it for several years and suffered from the threat of libel, and the third was treated as pornography. Lawrence's antiwar, anti-English opinions certainly contributed to the ill will of the government and the fear of publishers, but many writers—from Ford Madox Ford to Ezra Pound—at one time or another agreed with the guardians of good taste about the outrageousness of his language and ideas.

The novels of the latter part of Lawrence's career received a generally poor response from the critics and the public, and his status declined somewhat in the 1930s with the rise of Nazism (as did Nietzsche's) and T. S. Eliot's attack in *After Strange Gods* (1934). But there was a renaissance of critical interest during the 1950s, led by F. R. Leavis, and Lawrence was newly annointed in the 1960s as a prophet of untrammeled sexuality and spontaneity. Kate Millett's treatment of Lawrence in *Sexual Politics* (1969) marked a turning point of sorts. Going beyond Simone de Beauvoir's earlier feminist appraisal, Millett's chapter on Lawrence was a denunciation all the more damaging for its precision and insight. After Millett, Lawrence's presentation of sexuality seemed more than ever like vulgar kitsch, his understanding of women undiluted chauvinist fantasy. In certain ways, Lawrence never recovered from the attack. But the question of his homosexuality has been more insightfully explored since Millett by Jeffrey Meyers and others, and a fair number of contemporary essays have addressed Lawrence's notions of language, identity, and race. The new, scholarly Cambridge edition of Lawrence's works is a significant contribution to the task of reappraisal.

Lawrence's novels have often been divided into three major phases—with *Lady Chatterley's Lover* as a sort of coda at the end. *The White Peacock*, *The Trespasser*, and *Sons and Lovers* all derive from Lawrence's early life in Eastwood; *The Rainbow* and *Women in Love*, begun as one novel called "The Sisters," from Lawrence's early life with Frieda and his rejection of England during the war; and the last group, including what has been called the "political" trilogy of *Aaron's Rod*, *Kangaroo*, and *The Plumed Serpent*, from his quest for a better life outside white, European civilization. This division further points up concomitant transformations in his literary technique. Lawrence responded to a wide range of literary influences, ranging from the Bible to Richard Wagner. From George Eliot came the idea of juxtaposing two couples and playing out the tensions between them, a structure used in *The White Peacock*, *Women in Love*, and *Kangaroo*; from James Fenimore Cooper came the melodramatic treatment of the Dark Savage versus the White Man (or White Woman) in *The Lost Girl*, *The Plumed Serpent*, and stories like "The Woman Who Rode Away." Leo Tolstoy's *Anna Karenina* was simply "the greatest novel in the world." But Thomas Hardy must be singled out for special emphasis.

Hardy too came from the English Midlands; his beloved pastoral Derbyshire was subject to as great a cultural, if not industrial, transformation as was Nottinghamshire in the late nineteenth century. Like Lawrence, Hardy was steeped in Christian scripture from his youth, yet came to believe in the need to recognize the older, more erotic, and more violent pagan gods repressed by Christ's message. (In *The Man Who Died* [1929], an anti-Christian allegory, Lawrence rewrites the life of Christ in response to this need. In *Apocalypse* [1931], Lawrence borrows from Nietzsche, Madame Blavatsky, and occultist Frederick Carter to reinterpret the Book of Revelation along similar lines. As in Sir James Frazer's *Golden Bough*, Judeo-Christian tradition now appears to be superimposed on an older mythic cosmology.) Lawrence and Hardy shared a decided hatred of modernity's hypocrisy and a profound love of nature. But Lawrence was satisfied neither with the finality of Hardy's tragic vision nor with his more conventional moralism.

Lawrence played down Hardy's documentary naturalism and emphasized the mythic forces just below the surface of his prose. The language of *The White Peacock* magnifies a personal sympathy with nature, in part because—unlike any of his succeeding ones—this first novel is written in the first person. Lawrence draws his narrator so transparently that the significance of the flora and fauna seems like a massive projection of the author himself. "I stood watching the shadowy fish slide through the gloom of the mill-pond," the novel opens. "They were grey, descendants of the silvery things that had darted away from the monks, in the young days when the valley was lusty. The whole place was gathered in the musing of old age." Yet Lawrence's representation of the valley of "Nethermere" is more than just bad aestheticism. It is a sustained attempt to give voice to the nonhuman world, to read the book of nature as if what were written there needed no human mind to give it meaning.

The White Peacock is about George Saxton, a passionate but uneducated farmer who is unable to consummate a relationship with the more cultured Lettie, sister of narrator Cyril Beardsall (who carries Lydia Lawrence's surname). George finds pleasure in Lettie's and Cyril's company, but winds up marrying the vulgar Meg, and slowly disintegrates in liquor and disease. Though formulaic, the novel is nonetheless striking for a carnivalesque episode recounting the welcome death of the narrator's estranged father. Moreover, it contains in muted form gestures that would later be expanded: immersion in nature to heal damaged sensation; homoerotic contact to heal a damaged sensuality; and the archetypal Lawrentian story of class and gender struggle in gamekeeper Annable's first marriage to the spiritual Lady Crystabel (the White Peacock of the title), which only produces, as the "woman's paper she subscribed to" puts it, "an unfortunate misalliance."

Like the Wagnerian *Liebestod* played out by the unhappily married Siegmund and his student Helena in *The Trespasser*, *The White Peacock* is methodical in its effect. Lawrence skirts the boundaries of the sensationalism associated with popular culture and ridiculed by high modernism. Indeed, Kate Millett decried the kitschy vulgarity of Lawrence's presentation of sexuality almost as much as his regressive sexual politics. Yet Lawrence quite consciously embraces here, for example, what John Ruskin had earlier criticized as the "pathetic fallacy," or unwarranted anthropomorphism. The opening line of part 2 of *The White Peacock*—"Winter lay a long time prostrate on the earth"—is in one sense simply immature writing. But equally inflated diction occurs throughout even his best work. Lawrence's is in fact an aesthetic of vulgarity—as *The Plumed Serpent*'s Western-style shoot-out and its lake of "flimsy, soft, sperm-like water. . . . the lymphatic milk of fishes" will illustrate.

Like his pseudophilosophy and his pseudopsychology, Lawrence's prose depends on extravagance, and it begins with his mode of composition. Lawrence rarely just edited his work in the conventional sense of the term—he rewrote things wholesale, sometimes as many as six or seven times. Precisely because neither the word nor the book was sacred by comparison to the flesh—an attitude contradicting certain Christian and modernist hermeneutics—language was always expendable. He wrote as if the only way to fill his words with authentic feeling was to bring them to a metaphorical and rhythmic intensity that risked sliding into the bathos of mass culture that he derided as well. Lawrence set himself the daunting task of verbalizing a sublime "struggle into conscious being" (as in the foreword to *Women in Love*) in a world that he believed had degraded being to mere verbal performance, and of doing so with tools—words—that increasingly appeared to be so much intellectual machinery. The frequent scenes of wordless physicality in Lawrence, like his interest in telepathic communication, testify clearly enough that language was itself the most intransigent barrier to the aims of his art. "It must happen beyond the sound of words," Rupert tells Ursula in *Women in Love*. On some level, Lawrence knew that his writing might only perpetuate the verbal consciousness he intended it to resist.

With the second phase of his work, *The Rainbow* and *Women in Love*, Lawrence abandoned both the romance and the realism of earlier efforts. In an oft-cited letter of June 5, 1914, to Edward Garnett, Lawrence answered some of his mentor's stylistic objections to an early version of *The Rainbow* called "The Wedding Ring." Lawrence makes qualified connections between his own aims and Marinetti's futurist explorations of what is "non-human" in humanity; he rejects the "moral scheme" into which realism's characters are still forced to fit—even the extraordinary heroes of Turgenev, Tolstoy, and Dostoevsky—as something "dull, old, dead. . . . You musn't look in my novel for the old stable ego of the character. There is another ego, according to whose action the individual is unrecognisable, and passes through, as it were, allotropic states which it needs a deeper sense than any we've been used to exercise, to discover are states of the same single radically-unchanged element." Though he would continue to rewrite his novel, these remarks point to significant departures.

First, rather than continuing to accommodate readers' objections that his characters seem indistinguishable from one another, Lawrence would simply reject expectations shaped by nineteenth-century realism. Though assuming superficially different profiles—different allotropes—each of his characters was in fact composed of the same substance, and it was the novel's new task to reveal that substance and the essential, nonsynchronous dualisms within it opposing blood and mind, male and female, law and love, stasis and motility. (This assault on the conventionally individualized ego is hardly unique to Lawrence, however; using a rather different vocabulary, Virginia Woolf would question nineteenth-century notions of character in similar ways.) The sometimes cloying repetitions of Lawrence's writing from this period—"the pulsing, frictional to-and-fro which works up to culmination" (from the foreword to *Women in Love*)—are an attempt to mimic the flows of nonhuman instinct rather than conscious intellect.

Second, the extravagance of his prose would no longer be reined in, as language still is in Hardy, by the need to make moral evaluations. The narrative could range beyond conventional notions of good and evil to conjure up the nonhuman element of human experience. Third, and increasingly in the novels from *Aaron's Rod* on, fiction would tend to be subordinated to predetermined typologies and pseudophilosophical imperatives—though Lawrence had claimed the reverse as his priority.

Women in Love, for most of Lawrence's critics, has been the novel that best carries out the first and second of the above aims while avoiding the worst pitfalls of the third. Ursula Brangwen, well past her ordeal with Anton Skrebensky in *The Rainbow,* is joined by her more cosmopolitan sister Gudrun, just back from art school in London, and they are soon paired with Rupert Birkin, inspector of schools, and Gerald Crich, heir to his father's mining company. There is now a modernist quality to the prose, though it remains unmistakably Lawrence's; it is more dramatic than descriptive, as the characters struggle with what Lawrence called "unborn needs and fulfilment." There is also a thinness to their "allotropic states," and an insistent similarity in the conflicts facing them. Lawrence suggests almost nothing of Ursula's and Gudrun's prior lives, and only as much about Gerald Crich as will enable the reader to identify him as Cain-like (he has accidentally killed his brother). The violent hatred between Rupert and Hermione is more or less incomprehensible on first reading, so little is revealed about its causes.

Moreover, the narrative is less a Stendhalian mirror traveling the road of life's superficial continuities than a series of attempts to penetrate the tired, mechanical allotropes of putatively realistic storytelling. Scene after scene is devoted to the same act of discovery, the same effort to plunge to the nonhuman depths of "underworld knowledge": Rupert's argument with Hermione over education in chapter 3, the play of the cats in chapter 8, the disastrous water party and failed rescue in chapter 14, the "rabbit-mad" violence in chapter 18, the homoerotic wrestling match in chapter 20, the confrontation with Loerke in chapter 30. Throughout, men and women try to find some heterosexual harmony, which means balance-in-separation for Rupert and "absolute surrender to love" for Ursula, even as the men turn repeatedly to one another to salve the pain of their enduring isolation and discontent.

There remains, to be sure, a large measure of subtly nuanced realism, both psychological and social. Lawrence's description of Thomas Crich's death, for example, rivals in its specificity of detail Tolstoy's psychological portrait in "The Death of Ivan Ilyich." And Lawrence still portrays the mining villages with particular attention to Nottinghamshire's industrialization, from the lockouts and the advent of automation to the political struggle and resentment. Even the bohemian community of English artists and intellectuals that Lawrence grew to hate is closely rendered. Middleton Murray, Katherine Mansfield,

Bertrand Russell, Lady Ottoline Morrell, all make their appearances in what is after all a biting roman à clef. There are vestiges of conventional plot development, with several parallel episodes in a loose pattern built around Rupert's partial restoration through Ursula and Gerald's failure with Gudrun, culminating in Gerald's snowbound suicide. But the narrative drive is in sustained tension—not unlike the star-equilibrium of Rupert and Ursula—with the recurrent attempts to find "the single radically-unchanged element" underlying it.

It is Gerald's desperate decision finally to lose his organic nature in industry that occupies the thematic and structural center of the book. "It was pure organic disintegration and pure mechanical organisation. This is the first and finest state of chaos." The coal is produced more efficiently than ever, the miners have been reduced to passivity, and even Gerald is no longer needed; he has at last succeeded in making himself superfluous. In fact, following his penchant for grand dualisms, Lawrence outlines two racially determined paths to destruction, to superflousness. Gerald's way is an uneasy mix of English industry, Teutonic myth, Wagnerian opera, and Nietzschean philosophy. As deus ex machina, he is simultaneously the Wotan who must perish in a Götterdämmerung and a Nietzschean Übermensch, all conscious will to power and automated domination of nature—"the finest state of chaos." Gerald embodies doomed, white European civilization, with no communal remedy in sight.

The alternative path to destruction—the "sun-destruction" and "burning death-abstraction" of the Sahara—in fact points to the potential for rebirth outside Europe that will find fictional equivalents a few years later. When Rupert first sees the "negro statues, wood-carvings from West Africa" in Halliday's London apartment, he admires their intense sensuality; "pure culture in sensation," he tells an uncomprehending Gerald, "really *ultimate* physical consciousness, mindless, utterly sensual." Rupert responds here to the "hundred centuries of development" standing behind the statue—a primal, non-Judeo-Christian era. But just as the vital race-consciousness of the Mexican-Indian peasants in *The Plumed Serpent* has nearly died out and must be revived by Ramon's cult of Quetzalcoatl, so Rupert believes that ethnographically the statue also points to racial decline. "It must have been thousands of years since her race died, mystically. . . . the goodness, the holiness, the desire for creation and happiness must have lapsed." What remains is the singular "knowledge in disintegration and dissolution, knowledge such as the beetles have." As in Lawrence's ideas about decadent forms of homosexuality, the Egyptian scarab he invokes implies excrement and death. The racial vitality that once lay behind the statues has been lost.

Rupert's third path, "the way of freedom," involves maintaining both a "proud singleness" in marriage with Ursula and a failed effort to achieve a *Blutbrüderschaft* with Gerald. But these are in many ways displacements of the lost communal blood-consciousness, vaguely imagined in *The Rainbow*, that would be given substance in Lawrence's research on Mexico. Lawrence wrote in the foreword to *Women in Love* that "the bitterness of the war may be taken for granted in the characters"; his work only grew more bitter in the years that followed. In almost all the novels that occur between *Women in Love* and *The Plumed Serpent*, the resentment that Lawrence had once tapped in the miners' villages of his youth is now turned in full force against the public. Sarcastic asides to the reader in *Aaron's Rod* and *The Lost Girl* openly mock the assumed audience's conventional tastes; *Mr. Noon* spitefully forces the "gentle reader" to swallow everything found offensive in earlier novels.

Yet the books of this period, especially *The Lost Girl* and *Aaron's Rod*, also add to the scope of Lawrence's fiction. The former concerns Alvina Houghton's decision to run off with a traveling band of theatrical players and her subsequent romance with the laconic but passionate Italian actor, Ciccio. The novel is more significant, however, for what the actors—an inter-European male clan organized around a matriarchal leader—perform. Adapting scenes from Cooper's "Leatherstocking" tales, the Europeans play savage American Indians, the invented Natcha-Kee-Tawara, both onstage and off. The fraternal clan of the actors—"one tribe, one nation"—both functions as a version of archaic community and prefigures the cult of Quetzalcoatl in *The Plumed Serpent*.

Aaron's Rod is usually considered the first of Lawrence's novels about power and the need for strong authority, themes further developed in *Kangaroo* and *The Plumed Serpent*. It is the story of miner's agent-cum-flautist Aaron Sisson and his abandonment of marriage and family for music, sexual adventure, and political conflict. In Italy, he falls under the spell of Rawdon Lilly, a pseudophilosopher of the phoenixlike nature of identity and power. "Your destiny comes from within, from your own self-form," Lilly says in the final chapter, called "Words." But that destiny may well require submission to a stronger man. "We've exhausted our love-urge, for the moment," Lilly concludes, in a historical vision similar to Nietzsche's and Yeats's. "We've got to accept the power motive, accept in a deep responsibility. . . . The will to power—but not in Nietzsche's sense. Not intellectual power. . . . But dark, living, fructifying power." Power here is in essence another form of the natural will that Lawrence located in instinct and spontaneous desire, expressed in terms of a new political authoritarianism.

Like *The Lost Girl*, *Aaron's Rod* points to the fully realized resurrection of organic community in *The Plumed Serpent*. Rawdon Lilly's ethnological speculations are of course those of Lawrence at this time, and their peculiarity is noteworthy.

There's a whole world besides this little gang of Europeans. Except, dear God, that they've exterminated all the peoples worth knowing. I can't do with folk who teem by the billion, like the Chinese and Japs and orientals altogether. Only vermin teem by the billion. Higher types breed slower. I would have loved the Aztecs and Red Indians. . . . They had living pride. . . . The American races—and the South Sea Islanders—the Marquesans, the Maori Blood. That was the true blood. . . . All the rest are craven—Europeans, Asiatics, Africans. . . . the mass-bullies, the individual Judases. (Chapter 9)

In contrasting Aaron to the wealthy, self-made Sir William Franks, Lawrence draws a distinction that also applies to the European and Aztec nations. "The one [Sir William] held life to be a storing-up of produce and a conservation of energy: the other [Aaron] held life to be a sheer spending of energy and a storing up of nothing but experience." As in Lawrence's contrasting views of Benjamin Franklin and rewriting, Aaron's belief in expenditure simultaneously counters the commercial utilitarianism of Europe while endorsing the "contestive" spending of energy that underlay Lawrence's view of organic community and of art. Lawrence may not have known the work of Franz Boas or Bronislaw Malinowski on potlatch and gift exchange, but *Aaron's Rod* elaborates an ethnology not very far from theirs.

At the conclusion of his wanderings, however, Lawrence revisits England in the setting of his last novel, *Lady Chatterley's Lover*. It is first a recapitulation of the story of passionate men, repressed women, and sexual salvation that can be found throughout Lawrence's work. But it is at the same time the last shift in Lawrence's style, one more attempt to transform the oft-heard charge of vulgarity into a literary virtue. For Lawrence's vulgarity appears finally as a way of remaining in touch with the vulgarity of his origins. It is deployed for precisely the reasons that Oliver Mellors uses his Midlands dialect in dealing with Constance Chatterley. Dialect is Mellors's chosen badge of honor, worn to indicate a proximity to earth, an identity that springs from organic community rather than mechanical society, and an ability to cross over—to trespass—the boundaries separating one class from another. Connie Chatterley's sister is convinced that Mellors is simply vulgar. But the keeper subtly mocks Hilda's priggishness in dialect she is too insensitive to appreciate. If Connie can learn to understand Mellors's tone correctly, the novel implies, readers can learn to understand Lawrence.

In effect, *Lady Chatterley's Lover* is only partially a hymn to erotic awakening and phallic consciousness; it is equally Lawrence's parable about modern literature. Clifford Chatterley, a true aristocrat, marries Constance Reid, of the "well-to-do intelligentsia"; she is the daughter of a pre-Raphaelite, Fabian socialist mother and a Royal Academy artist father. After a brief and tepid honeymoon, Clifford ships off to war in 1917 and returns soon after "more or less in bits," paralyzed from the hips down and impotent. Clifford recovers with a special appreciation for being alive, "but he had seen so much hurt that something inside him had perished, some of his feelings had gone. There was a blank of insentience." Clifford's unquenched ambitions are channeled, however, into writing "clever, spiteful, and yet . . . meaningless" stories. Indeed, this writing appears to suggest the elite literary modernism of Joyce and Proust that Lawrence had rejected. "The observation was extraordinary and peculiar. But there was no touch, no actual contact. And since the field of life is largely an artificially-lighted stage today, the stories were curiously true to modern life, to the modern psychology, that is." Like a tormented sublimation of his destroyed sexual response, Clifford's stories are everything Lawrence opposed in the literature of his time.

Later, Lord Chatterley abandons his writing in pursuit of something even more sterile. Like Gerald Crich before him, Clifford turns to the mines that his father had left him; urged on by the maternal Mrs. Bolton, he displays a childlike fascination with modern technology "as if really the devil himself had lent fiend's wits to the technical scientists of industry." In the wake of this Mephistophelian bargain with technology, Clifford sits "with a blank entranced expression on his face, like a person losing his mind," listening to the radio, "to the unspeakable thing." The trajectory of Clifford's slide to imbecility is hard to miss—from hereditary nobility to war, to impotence, to modern literature, to technical treatises "more interesting" than literature, and finally to that ultimate simulacrum of organic life, the "idiotically velveteen, genteel sort of voice" that bellows forth from the radio. In one stroke, Lawrence connects the desiccated pretensions of elite modernism with the infantile banalities of popular culture, effectively making them two sides to the same valueless coin and the same impotent man.

Against the artificial psychology of Clifford's stories and the simulated voice of his radio, Lawrence opposes Oliver Mellors. Mellors is the final Lawrentian trespasser—simultaneously gamekeeper and "poacher," in the words of Connie's half-admiring father. Like Lawrence, he is the son of a miner, self-educated yet finally disdainful of acquired culture. He leaves his wife to become a lieutenant in the overseas empire that both enraged Lawrence and fed his imagination. Yet Mellors chooses on return a social position lower than his father's, reaffirming with a vengeance his sense of place, nature, and instinct and renouncing material gain. He has effectively rejected women and society when Constance Chatterley enters his life. Mellors's reawakening of, and with, Lady Chatterley—who must learn all over again to be submissive after weaker lovers like Michaelis—is then also Lawrence's final attempt to reawaken the English to the "vast importance of the novel. It can inform and lead into new places the flow of our sympathetic consciousness, and it can lead our sympathy away in recoil from things gone dead." Even as "one England blots out another" in continuing modernization, Lawrence affirms his faith in the restorative potential of the genre, "properly handled."

Connie winds up pregnant in the fall, though Clifford is unwilling to grant her a divorce, while Mellors must avoid her for six months while his own divorce is settled. Reunion and new life will come in the spring. The concluding statement, a letter to Connie, belongs to Mellors. It is in part a social critique, reflecting on the dire fate of the deadened workers—"there's a bad time coming!"—and on their inability to look past immediate commercial interests to an artisanal, "pagan" community. But it is also a song of reconciliation with this enforced separation—"I love chastity now, because it is the peace that comes of fucking"—and of hope for even more "brilliant" sexual pleasure to come.

At the end of his last significant novel, facing his own physical destruction by tuberculosis, in all likelihood impotent, sterile, and afraid of death, Lawrence voices once again the conviction that had animated his life's work. The "little forked flame between me and you," writes Mellors—"my Pentecost"—remains the natural, bodily fire beyond conscious will, unextinguished by modernity's winds. But the "unnamed god" shielding that flame is not quite as prodigious as before. Mellors's abstinence seems almost a relief, a Schopenhauerian escape from the incessant pull of the blood; and the flame that remains is less the igniting spark of a new communal life than a votive candle threatened—as were Lawrence's own writings—by endless storm. Following a long string of English Romantics before him, Lawrence finally eases his public alienation through the idealized and poignantly deferred hope of private affection; like the lovers on Keats's urn, Mellors and Connie are at last suspended in a desire frozen in time. It is Mellors's unidealized parting shot—a comic, vulgar invocation of his drooping phallus—that makes Lawrence, if nothing else, more honest than the tradition that preceded him.

Vincent P. Pecora

Selected Bibliography

Daleski, H. M. *The Forked Flame: A Study of D. H. Lawrence*. London: Faber and Faber, 1965.

Holderness, Graham. *D. H. Lawrence: History, Ideology, and Fiction*. Atlantic Highlands, N.J.: Humanities Press, 1982.

Hough, Graham. *The Dark Sun: A Study of D. H. Lawrence*. London: Duckworth, 1956.

Kermode, Frank. *Lawrence*. London: Fontana, 1973.

Leavis, F. R. *D. H. Lawrence: Novelist*. New York: Simon and Schuster, 1955.

Meyers, Jeffrey. *D. H. Lawrence: A Biography*. New York: Alfred A. Knopf, 1990.

Millett, Kate. *Sexual Politics*. Garden City, N.Y.: Doubleday, 1969.

Nixon, Cornelia. *Lawrence's Leadership Politics and the Turn Against Women*. Berkeley: University of California Press, 1986.

Simpson, Hilary. *D. H. Lawrence and Feminism*. London: Croom Helm, 1982.

Spilka, Mark. *The Love Ethic of D. H. Lawrence*. Bloomington: Indiana University Press, 1955.

Isherwood, Huxley, and the Thirties

Perhaps the first issue to be resolved when dealing with any aspect of the 1930s is to determine when they actually occurred. History tends not to proceed in neatly defined decades, and despite the chronologically unambiguous beginning and end points asserted by the term, it is worth examining whether the thirties happily fit into the ten-year envelope reserved for them.

As it happens, Hitler cooperated with chronology to fashion the end of the thirties by launching the invasion of Poland on the morning of September 1, 1939. Two days later Britain declared war on Germany, and suddenly the anxieties that had pervaded the thirties—the specter of war abroad, the poverty and unemployment at home, a decaying social structure and the lack of perceived connection with a nourishing past—transformed themselves into a nation's preparation for its struggle for survival. Mobilization announced the beginning of a new era.

While the outbreak of World War II clearly demarcates the end of the period, it is not clear that anything particularly noteworthy occurred on January 1, 1930, to initiate it. Indeed, although assigning a distinct character to the thirties, as opposed to the twenties, has its justification, it also makes sense to see both decades as constituting a single large period standing between the end of one war and the start of another. The frenetic partying and brittle cynicism that we associate with the twenties' attempt to numb the horror of the First World War's bloody slaughter grow naturally into the thirties' despairing recognition that it is all about to happen again. Although the tone of the two decades is admittedly different, it is important to realize the extent to which the apprehensions of the one have their roots in the forced gaiety of the other.

The single text that perhaps most powerfully exemplifies the connection between the two decades is Evelyn Waugh's *Vile Bodies*, published in 1930. Spinning wildly out of control (a central event in the novel is in fact a chaotic car race) as they make their way from party to party, Waugh's Bright Young Things work full time to anesthetize themselves to the absence of meaning in their lives. They lack stable identities and access to their own feelings as well as to traditional sources of belief or pleasure of any kind. As one character quips after spending a night with the man she ostensibly loves: "All this fuss about sleeping together. For physical pleasure I'd sooner go to my dentist any day." Waugh's merciless—and wildly funny—depiction of these lost, isolated souls of the twenties concludes with a broken car stuck in the mud in the middle of "the biggest battlefield in the history of the world" while a catastrophic war rages around it. The prescient ending brings together into one stunning image the two strains of feeling which E. M. Forster thought distinguished the decades: "The twenties react after a war and recede from it, the thirties are apprehensive of a war and are carried towards it."

In suggesting the way in which the thirties can usefully be thought of as beginning in the twenties, with the response to the devastation of the war, I do not wish to diminish the thirties' special flavor. More than a simple chronological label encompassing a specific ten-year span, the term has acquired the force of a cultural metaphor, so that mention of "the thirties" evokes a distinct set of social, moral, political, and literary values inevitably associated with the period. Socially (and morally) those values have to do with a serious engagement with issues of injustice and inequality around the world, with a concern for the well-being of the underclasses, with a need, in short, for individuals to move beyond the constraints of their own selves in order to make empathetic contact with others. Politically, of course, the values are those of the left. While very few of the writers of the thirties were actual communists, their overriding sympathies tended to be with them, particularly in the face of the fascist threat posed by Hitler and Mussolini. The Spanish civil war, which broke out in 1936, provided a clear opportunity for choice, and very few could resist supporting the Republican cause. The complicated political tensions and interest groups that developed within the Loyalist side eventually muddied the clarity considerably, but for most of the period the oppression of fascist tyranny (though it had its proponents) was easy to oppose. In a poll taken in 1937 by the magazine *Left Review*, for example, 127 authors out of the 149 queried listed themselves as sympathetic to the Republic, with only five declaring their allegiance to Franco. Even allowing for the magazine's own interest in compiling such data (not all the responses were published), the results are impressive. It is worth noting in this regard that both "leftish" (1934) and "leftward" (1936) added themselves to the English vocabulary during this period.

The literary sensibility implicit in the metaphor of the thirties follows naturally upon the social and political. The closest we come to a manifesto of that sensibility (though it is really more signpost than manifesto) are the prefaces of two important anthologies of contemporary writing edited by Michael Roberts: a volume of poetry, *New Signatures*, published in 1932; and *New Country* (1933), containing both poetry and prose. (It is significant that poetry preceded the appearance of prose in these collections for it is primarily the poets—and their critics—who provided the decade's literary definition of itself. The thirties, in fact, may well be the last period in English literature in which poetry was taken at all seriously.)

In *New Signatures*, which features the work of W. H. Auden, C. Day Lewis, and Stephen Spender, the three canonical poets of the period, Roberts calls for a new, comprehensible poetry of direct language that can appeal to the "every day experience of normal human beings." Part of the job of the poet now is to find solutions to human problems, to "root out ugliness and evil," so that he must not only "be abreast of his own times," he must be understood by those for whom he writes: a leader, he "must not be out of sight of his followers." Constituting a "clear reaction against esoteric poetry," *New Signatures* rejects the obscurity and self-indulgence of T. S. Eliot's *Waste Land* in favor of a poetry that will struggle to reassert human values, not from a position of privileged distance, but in "solidarity with others."

In *New Country*, Roberts extends the social analysis of *New Signatures* in explicitly political ways. Having grown up in the shadow of the First World War (he was born in 1902), Roberts notes that his generation is once again facing an unsettled Europe in which "all that we see is threatened." The cause is the social system that exploits and tyrannizes the masses. The solution is not "a new moral code" but "a social system which will bring people into contact with those . . . who can advise and help them." The current class system must be abolished, Roberts argues, an accomplishment that can only be brought about by revolutionary efforts. Such activity is particularly important for the novelist. Since he writes about people, he faces a crucial choice: He can "either write in a way which shows the fatuity and hopelessness" of the doomed white-collar class, or he can focus instead on the working class, where he will discover "the clearest symbols of those passions and activities he values, for they will be less confused and muddled by the intricacies of a crumbling system." And with that commitment, a new prose will develop, freed from the murk and doubt of the past, a prose intelligible to the working class, which will in turn help "make the revolutionary movement articulate."

Although Roberts's revolutionary fervor was not blithely shared by many of the writers of his generation, his sense of the social obligations of the poet and novelist became an essential part of the decade's literary sense of itself. It also provided the impetus for an ongoing dialogue within individual writers over the extent to which the claims of art can be reconciled with the commitment to social action. While answers varied—with Spender, for example, despite his early political allegiance to communism, arguing that the artist must not compromise his vision and language in the interests of any cause—few writers were unaffected by the seriousness of the problem. As Spender points out in *The Creative Element*, if communism did not give writers a positive belief, it at least instilled in them a bad conscience. As long as we recognize that a decade's intellectual and literary complexity can never be reduced to any simplistic set of attitudes, then the concerns enunciated by Roberts in his two prefaces are useful in clarifying some of the meanings associated with the thirties as cultural metaphor.

A perusal of the novelists writing in the thirties makes clear how no generalization can hope to embrace the complexity and variety of the decade's prose fiction. Although demonstrably not an age of experiment, for example, the thirties nevertheless include two of the century's outstanding modernist works: Joyce's *Finnegans Wake* (1939) and Virginia Woolf's *The Waves* (1931). Arguably the most significant and demanding novels produced in this decade, both, in different ways, seek to extend the linguistic and formal possibilities of fiction. Neither, however, reflects in a significant way any of the characteristic concerns of the period, and it would make little sense, on the basis of these works, to think of Woolf or Joyce as "belonging" to the thirties. (Others of Woolf's books, such as *The Years* and particularly the nonfictional *Three Guineas*, most assuredly do belong.)

A third prodigiously modernist effort, which remains almost entirely unread today, is Wyndham Lewis's *Apes of God* (1930). A poet, painter, critic, and novelist, Lewis, who was at odds with most forms of modernism, including the work of Joyce and Woolf, founded the vorticist movement in painting before World War I, edited *Blast*, the movement's futurist magazine, and excoriated all forms of cultural and literary softness. His admiration for hard, precise images in poetry and painting led him also to find hard, intractable political leaders like Hitler appealing, in whose praise he wrote a small book in 1931. *Apes* is a scathing satire on the mendacity and hollowness of the British literary scene, especially Bloomsbury and the Sitwell family. Clotted, peopled with grotesques of all kinds, it is both excessive and extraordinary, a monument to Lewis's larger-than-life idiosyncracy.

While Woolf and Joyce, as well as Lewis, represent the high point of radical experimentation with form in the period, they were not the only ones to explore new methods. Two lesser-known writers—Dorothy Richardson and Ivy Compton-Burnett—also attempted, less successfully, to devise new forms for their work. Relentlessly pursuing the inner life of her protagonist, Marian, through her ten-volume *Pilgrimage* begun in 1915, Richardson demonstrates that the stream-of-consciousness technique in itself guarantees neither freshness nor insight. The new possibilities of the narrative method bog down in a wealth of undifferentiated impressions and thoughts. Marian's subjective reality is finally not interesting enough to sustain the reader.

Richardson's implacable interiority contrasts with Compton-Burnett's programmatically external approach to her fiction. In novels like *Men and Wives* (1931) and *More Women Than Men* (1933), consisting almost entirely of dialogue, she reveals the cruelty and violence lurking behind decorous late-Victorian family façades. The genteel, stylized nature of the dialogue provides an effective vehicle for her melodramatic plots, abounding in murder and suicide, which convey an unabashedly grim view of human nature.

Her exposure of what lies beneath British domestic surfaces has its overseas counterpart in novels demonstrating some of the social and moral difficulties of Britain's empire. Having served in the Indian Imperial Police for five years in Burma, George Orwell grew to hate imperialism, as he says, "with a bitterness which I probably cannot make clear." A product of that hatred, *Burmese Days* (1934) charts the psychological and moral costs incurred by an indefensible system that finally cause James Flory to blow his brains out. Orwell was one of the period's most engaged political writers. His detestation of fascism led him to join the fight against Franco in Spain, where he was seriously wounded. His experiences in Spain with the complex politics of the left nourished his anticommunism, and his two best-known books, *Animal Farm* (1945) and *1984* (1949), express his passionate opposition to totalitarian regimes of any kind.

J. Cary

Although not nearly as critical of British imperialism as Orwell, Joyce Cary recognized, during his six years as a civil administrator in Africa, the tensions and cultural contradictions it generated. The crowded landscape of his first three novels, *Aissa Saved* (1932), *An American Visitor* (1933), and *The African Witch* (1936), explore the consequences, for African and Englishman alike, of Britain's colonial presence. The most successful of his African novels, however, is *Mister Johnson* (1939), the story of the irrepressible African clerk whose uncomprehending enthusiasm for all things British leads inescapably to his death. Johnson's marvelous energy and spontaneity confer upon him an innocence that is unsullied even by the fact that he commits murder. As the creative shaper of his own life, he is the first of Cary's great artist-heroes, whose most brilliant embodiment is the painter Gulley Jimson, narrator of Cary's best book, *The Horse's Mouth* (1944).

Greene

Graham Greene is a major writer of the century who succeeds, through his relatively little-known minor works of the thirties, in catching the period's anxieties, its forebodings about the advent of another war, better than anybody else. Thrillers like *Stambul Train* (1932) and *A Gun for Sale* (1936), which he deprecatingly cast as "entertainments," are in fact well crafted, tautly written novels whose crisply noted descriptive details take on the force of metaphor. The shabby, sordid London in *A Gun for Sale* and *It's a Battlefield* (1934) moves beyond naturalistic observation to constitute the moral and psychological atmosphere for a generation trapped, isolated, scared. Characters in these early novels live in a world essentially devoid of meaning and go about their business without knowing what they are doing. The Assistant Commissioner investigating a murder in *It's a Battlefield*, for example, has no more understanding of what the issues really are than does

Raven in *A Gun for Sale*, who commits a murder for profit without any idea of why he was told to do so.

The brooding sense of evil permeating the early novels continues in *Brighton Rock* (1938), Greene's best-known work of the thirties, but here achieves a particular human focus in Pinkie, the unregenerate teenage killer. Ruthless and without compassion, the Catholic Pinkie is ultimately brought to justice by the efforts of Ida Arnold, the blowsy sensualist who knows the difference between right and wrong. In the conflict between the tormented ascetic (Pinkie is sexually a mess after having as a child regularly witnessed his parents copulating on Saturday nights—one of the novel's few false notes) and the innocent nonbeliever, Greene, a practicing Catholic, treats those great themes of the nature of evil, of sin and redemption, which he goes on to explore in his later fiction.

Greene was fascinated with the way popular forms (hence his attraction to the thriller—including *Brighton Rock*) could express the only true "subject-matter for art, life as it is and life as it ought to be." Part of that fascination led him to a lifelong interest in film, an interest shared, among others, by Waugh, Huxley, and Isherwood. In Greene's case, the influence of film on his fiction is evident in his use of realistic but highly charged detail, quick narrative cuts, and spare, telling dialogue. His thirties universe of doubt, distrust, and betrayal is masterfully fashioned out of these techniques.

Good novelists of the thirties, of course, are numerous. In paying attention to some I think prominent and interesting, I don't mean to slight the host of accomplished others—writers like William Plomer, Rose Macaulay, Anthony Powell, Rosamond Lehmann, Jean Rhys, Elizabeth Bowen, John Cowper Powys, Rex Warner, and Ralph Bates, to name a few—whose work is also of value. The extent of worthwhile fiction in the thirties simply exceeds the capacity of this discussion to deal with all of it.

Aldous Huxley and Christopher Isherwood were two very different kinds of writers and human beings whose lives, fundamentally studies in contrasts, at the same time share some curious parallels. Grandson on his father's side of the great Victorian biologist and intellectual T. H. Huxley, and related on his mother's side to Matthew Arnold, Huxley was born into one of the families—the Darwins, Wedgwoods, Macaulays, Arnolds, and Trevelyans are the others—who made up the ruling class of Britain's intellectual aristocracy. The history of nineteenth-century scientific, social, and educational thought was shaped by their influence. Along with impeccable genes, Huxley also inherited, as his friend Gerald Heard said, a substantial "weight of intellectual authority and a momentum of moral obligations." Isherwood's family, on the other hand, while respectably upper middle class and properly affluent, had no significant cultural legacy to leave to Christopher: his father was a soldier.

Huxley loved his mother deeply. Her death from cancer when he was fourteen was a tremendous blow to him. The death of Isherwood's father in the war when Christopher was only eleven was debilitating in different ways. It not only deprived him of a father, it left him to struggle with the mythic legacy of father-as-war-hero, a burden that took an immense toll on his own quest for a viable, stable identity. Equally important, it put him entirely in the hands of a mother whom he grew rapidly to loathe as manipulative and self-serving. The figure of the Evil Mother, as Cyril Connolly terms her, appears in Isherwood's first two novels as the embodiment of everything that must be resisted by the protagonists. Part of Isherwood's lifelong rebellion against the forces of convention and hypocrisy stems from his perception of the need to escape his mother's entrapment.

Huxleys were expected not only to succeed academically but to contribute something important to the world in one way or another. Aldous took those assumptions with him to Eton and then to Oxford, where he earned a First in English as well as the prestigious Stanhope Historical Essay Prize. Isherwood went to Cambridge where the necessity of frustrating his mother's expectations that he would become a don required him to fail. After deliberately not studying for the tripos examination at the end of his second year, he assured his failure by answering the questions with a mixture of gentle mockery, mediocre verse made up on the spot, and satire. Needless to say, he succeeded in convincing college authorities that he should not be there. Called back to Cambridge at the end of term, after he had left for London, he was permitted to remove his name from the college books to avoid the embarrassment of expulsion.

Such were the disparate origins of two writers who came to represent both the post- and prewar sensibilities of their generation. Given the differences, it is interesting to note some of the similarities in their careers: while traveling abroad both wrote the books that captured Britain's between-the-wars disillusionment and anxiety; both left

Britain permanently in the thirties and settled in California (where they became friends and even collaborated on some projects); both engaged in profitable stints of film writing in Hollywood; and both moved through an absence of religious commitment to find, while in California, some nourishing belief in mysticism and Eastern religion.

Despite Huxley's enormous popularity, particularly among students and the young intellectuals of his generation, no lasting consensus has developed about his status as a novelist, or even about whether he should be considered a novelist at all. Sir Isaiah Berlin saw him as one of the culture heroes of his time, helping to sweep away the intellectual and moral cobwebs of the past. Critic Jocelyn Brooks insisted, in 1963, that "no one under fifty can quite realize how exciting Huxley seemed to us who were schoolboys or undergraduates in the twenties." Novelist Angus Wilson is even more specific: "*Antic Hay* was all that I had devoutly hoped for . . . Aldous Huxley was the god of my adolescence." At the same time critics have often dismissed him as an essayist in novelist's clothing, as an essentially nonserious writer who somehow caught the nonserious spirit of the era. In his influential survey of the British novel, written in 1955, Walter Allen omitted him entirely from his chapter "1914 and After." Although critics recently have paid more attention to him, the dilemma still remains.

Huxley himself addressed part of the difficulty in understanding what he was doing through an entry in the notebooks of Philip Quarles, Huxley's novelist-surrogate in *Point Counter Point*:

Novel of ideas. The character of each personage must be implied, as far as possible, in the ideas of which he is a mouthpiece. In so far as theories are rationalizations of sentiments, instincts, dispositions of soul, this is feasible. The chief defect of the novel of ideas is that you must write about people who have ideas to express—which excludes all but about .01 per cent of the human race. Hence the real, the congenital novelists don't write such books. But then I never pretended to be a congenital novelist.

Quarles's commitment to the novel of ideas was Huxley's own and immediately suggests the difference between his practice and that of the "real" novelists. Huxley felt he had no particular gift for storytelling or plotting or character development—qualities traditionally associated with the art of the novel. Nor had he any reverence for them. "There aren't any divinely laid down canons of the novel," he wrote. "All you need is to be interesting."

In his search to be interesting, Huxley eschewed the tightly wrought, highly conscious formal structures of, say, Henry James or Conrad or Virginia Woolf. He needed something looser and more capacious: "My own aim is to arrive, technically, at a perfect fusion of the novel and the essay, a novel in which one can put all one's ideas, a novel like a hold-all." For one steeped in the knowledge of English fiction, as Huxley was, formal inspiration for the hold-all novel was instantly at hand in the work of Thomas Love Peacock, whose novels such as *Headlong Hall* (1816), *Nightmare Abbey* (1818), and *Crotchet Castle* (1831) bring various eccentric characters to a country house where they reveal themselves through polite conversation. Essentially a static form, the country house novel frees the novelist from having to worry about plot, or the before and after of the characters' existence. It was perfect for Huxley's purposes, and *Crome Yellow* (1921), Huxley's first novel (which he explicitly called "Peacockian") descends directly from it.

The advantages of a ready-made form that permitted his characters to do what they do best—talk—and required little else were not lost on Huxley. Even as he finished his first Peacockian effort, he was seized by an idea for a second, "a gigantic one in an Italian scene." The vision persisted through the interruption of *Antic Hay*, and in 1925 his next conversational "hold-all" novel, *Those Barren Leaves*, appeared. If the setting is different—in place of the Wimbushes at Crome we now have Mrs. Aldwinkle in Vezza—the structure is roughly the same: an assortment of idiosyncratic types congregate to discuss ideas, revealing in the process features of their own peculiarity that Huxley found symptomatic of the age.

Although it strains the definition somewhat because of its violence and the fact that its grotesque climax occurs elsewhere, the California estate of Mr. Stoyte in *After Many a Summer* (1939) is nevertheless recognizably a third instance of Huxley's adaptation of the Peacock model. Of all three it must be said that while the form is thoroughly useful, given Huxley's artistic intentions, it is neither resonant nor particularly interesting in its own right. It provides Huxley the vehicle he needs for his thought, nothing more.

Point Counter Point (1928) constitutes Huxley's most ambitious formal effort. Meditating, as the title suggests, on what he calls the "musicalization of fiction," Quarles wonders whether it is possible to devise a fictional form that can approximate the modulations of key and mood available to musical compositions: "All you need is a sufficiency of char-

acters and parallel plots. . . . You alternate the themes. . . . A novelist modulates by reduplicating situations and characters. He shows several people falling in love, or dying, or praying in different ways—dissimilars solving the same problem." If the musical analogy does not quite work, it does point to the considerable formal differences between *Point Counter Point* and the Peacock novels. In place of static conversation we have a vast number of people generating patterns of meaning as they jostle against each other throughout London. Talk still abounds, but the range of characters and the interaction between them distinguishes the novel in important ways from the others.

As seriously as he took the attempt to find proper forms to embody his novels of ideas (and this discussion shouldn't be left without mentioning the disaster of *Eyeless in Gaza*, whose self-consciously mixed-up chronology adds little but confusion), what finally matters are the ideas themselves. Testimony from those who fell under his sway emphasizes the enormous appeal of his sophisticated intelligence and immense learning. Widely considered to know everything, he was at home in art, history, music, philosophy, and psychology, as well as English, European, and Classical literature. What H. G. Wells could do in digesting and popularizing science, Huxley could do for it all—including science, as the prescient and credible *Brave New World* demonstrates.

For a generation that saw all of its certainties and securities blown away by the war, a scintillating, critical intellect was itself a stable point, a guarantee that the individual could still fashion its own order from the surrounding chaos. What Huxley's intellect went on to offer was not so much solutions as a diagnosis that confirmed his readers' understanding of the age's moral pathology. All his novels of the twenties and thirties, from *Crome Yellow* to *After Many a Summer*, exhibit the overwhelming sense of futility and meaninglessness that was the war's legacy. Although the tone is sometimes gentler (as in *Crome Yellow* and *Those Barren Leaves*) than at other times (*Antic Hay* and *Point Counter Point*), the satiric focus on the human consequences of the hollowness of the old pieties and the absence of any sustaining belief remains constant. The only reassurance Huxley provided the age was his honesty in confronting its failures.

Foremost among those failures is the impossibility of nourishing human contact. Huxley is the connoisseur of the failed relationship. Of all the myriad love relationships portrayed in Huxley's fiction of the twenties and thirties, with the single exception of that of the exemplary

if slightly implausible Rampions in *Point Counter Point*, there is not a single one that is not marked by betrayal, dislike, indifference, or even cruelty. Whether it is Denis's inability to win Anne's love in *Crome Yellow* or Shearwater's disregard of Rosie in *Antic Hay*, or Mrs. Aldwinkle's pathetic efforts to attract Chelifer in *Those Barren Leaves* or the multitude of *Point Counter Point's* infidelities, or the savage's violent rejection of Lenina's advances in *Brave New World*, people are brought together in Huxley's fiction only to illustrate how removed they are from each other. Denis's observation that "Parallel straight lines . . . meet only at eternity. . . . Did one ever establish contact with anyone? We are all parallel straight lines" defines the emotional climate not just of Huxley's first novel but of his entire fictional world.

"Passion is sanity," writes mild-mannered E. M. Forster, but in Huxley's world sexual passion is treated almost exclusively as a source of perverse satisfaction and an opportunity for exploitation. Coleman more or less rapes Rosie in *Antic Hay*; the vicious Spandrell in *Point Counter Point* gets his real pleasure not simply from seducing women but from convincing them afterward to hate themselves for finding any enjoyment in the act; Virginia Maunciple gives herself coldly to the repulsive Mr. Stoyte ("Uncle Jo"; he calls her "baby") in order to continue to enjoy the benefits of his California mansion. Sexuality and degradation invariably go together in Huxley, adding a curious dimension to the notion of the emancipated intellectual who helped liberate an age from stuffiness and cant of all kinds. Not very far beneath the surface of Huxley lurks a genuine distaste for the human body and its appetites that comes out in various ways in his work.

The values of friendship don't fare much better in Huxley's novels than do those of romantic love. Friends traduce each other with the same frequency as do lovers. Anthony Beavis, in *Eyeless in Gaza*, causes the suicide of his best friend, Brian Foxe, by capriciously allowing the woman Brian loves to fall in love with him. It is not just Philip Quarles who is "a tourist in the realm of feeling," but all of the isolated souls who stumble through Huxley's landscape.

Huxley's success as a novelist ultimately rests in the wit and skill with which he presents to his audience an image of their own cultural and moral disorientation. As he wrote to his father, who intensely disliked the grimness of *Antic Hay*, it "is a book written by a member of what I may call the war-generation for others of his kind; and . . . is intended to reflect—fantastically, of course, but none the less faithfully—the life and opinions of an age which has seen the violent disruption of almost all the standards, conventions and values current in the previous epoch."

But there is another strain in Huxley beyond that of the satiric chronicler of an age, and this is the writer interested in exploring solutions to the dilemma of those trapped within it. From *Those Barren Leaves* on, each of Huxley's novels posits some set of values or model of behavior that is designed, however tentatively, to hold out the possibility for personal and social regeneration. In the first of these Calamy, the inveterate seducer of women, decides that real freedom is to be found not in the endless round of sensual indulgences but in the effort to apprehend the reality that underlies the surface of things. It requires the renunciation of the world of appearances so that he can encounter the "universe" within him, which can only be approached "by way of introspection and patient, uninterrupted thought." Retreating to a simple cottage in the mountains, as the novel ends, Calamy prepares for his solitary journey.

In the midst of all the disastrous relationships of *Point Counter Point* stand the healthy, glowing Rampions, embodying the very doctrine of proportion that Mark Rampion, a version of D. H. Lawrence, expounds at length. Rampion calls for people to live with "their whole being." Barbarism, the opposite of civilization, involves being lopsided, and one can be a barbarian of the intellect as well as the body: "To be a perfect animal and a perfect human—that was the ideal." If no one else in the novel can approach that ideal, it nevertheless serves to define the condition of the failed, incomplete people Rampion sees around him.

As *Brave New World* is not so much a reflection of the present age as it is a projection into the future of trends already observable, the pattern we are discussing here is not altogether relevant. But we should recognize that the savage does represent an alternative set of values to the biologically manipulated hierarchy of the future. The savage's ideals of personal freedom are certainly preferable to what he finds, but he nevertheless is tainted by the lunacy of his own past. As Huxley later stated, offering the savage two choices, "an insane life in Utopia, or the life of a primitive in an Indian village," was a serious defect in the book.

Eyeless in Gaza is interesting in that its therapeutic gospel is delivered both through a preacher and a disciple. An admirer of F. M. Alexander, whose ideas on diet, movement, and body posture interested Huxley immensely, the enigmatic Dr. Miller stresses that a negative body can only breed negative thinking. Once the body has rid itself of the poisons of too much protein and milk, only then can the individual begin to appreciate the unity of all life and the degree to which each person is part of the larger order. Following Miller's instructions, Anthony Beavis, the novel's protagonist, changes his diet and in the process understands the need to go beyond the division and separation characterizing this world to a perception of unity that transcends individual identity.

For Beavis, this effort requires meditation, exercise, cultivating "the difficult art of loving people," and most particularly, working hard for a pacifist organization. Arguing that violent means cannot achieve a peaceful end, Huxley became an ardent pacifist in the thirties as he sought ways to contain fascism without relying on armed force. He was an active member of the Peace Pledge Union, writing a controversial pamphlet supporting its position, "What Are You Going to Do About It?" which was heavily criticized. Beavis's involvement with pacifism is thus not a trivial affiliation but an important index of his moral growth, permitting him the mystical vision of oneness that concludes the novel.

The most radical prophet of all is Mr. Propter, whose doctrine of salvation constitutes the moral and philosophic center of *After Many a Summer*. For Propter, "actual good is outside time." Anything having to do with time and self must be rejected. The goal is liberation—"from personality, liberation from time and craving, liberation into union with God." All human endeavor, beyond the disinterested quest for truth, is futile. Pete Boone, for example, who prides himself on having fought against fascism in the Spanish civil war, is frustrated by Propter's unwillingness to endorse the nobility of his cause. Propter, of course, sees all the solemn, time-bound ideals like self-sacrifice and social justice as fetters to keep people tied to the world of personality. As such, fascism and opposition to fascism come to the same thing.

Each successive attempt of Huxley's to locate some positive alternative to things as they are negates the previous one. Calamy's lopsided impulse for isolated contemplation is undercut as an ideal by the Rampions' commitment to the wholesome, integrated life, which is in turn repudiated by Miller's insistence that true freedom and fulfillment can be achieved only by struggling through division to understand the unity of all things, a vision that endorses Beavis's pacifist efforts. And Propter goes several steps further, rejecting all human endeavor entirely except as it is engaged in the disinterested quest for truth.

In every instance the elaboration of these ideals involves ponderous disquisitions which, important as they are to Huxley's aspirations for the novels, are aesthetically disastrous. D. H. Lawrence, for example, found *Point Counter Point*'s Mark Rampion, the character based on him (and unquestionably the most plausible of all the prophets in Huxley's fiction), "the most boring character in the book—a gas bag." Huxley is at his best in documenting absurdity and excoriating folly. His forays into the positive are decidedly less successful. Not only are they tedious, straining the already slightly suspect form of his novel of ideas, they are not particularly compelling as solutions. Certainly the useful social applications of Propter's philosophy seem elusive at best, and while the Rampions are firmly rooted in time, it is not clear how they managed to achieve their exemplary wholeness in a society that does not encourage it, or how others might go about it either.

It is also worth noticing that however inadequate they might be, those who presume to have the answers and embody the ideals are exclusively male. (Mrs. Rampion is not really an exception as she is more a dimension of her husband's wholeness than an advocate in her own right of Rampion's philosophy.) Women do not fare well in Huxley's work. Weak, addled, coldly indifferent, or victimized by men, they are never permitted to ascend to the higher wisdom Huxley accords his male prophets.

Happily, Huxley's flirtation with the higher wisdom, whose mystical forms he explored in much nonfictional work in the forties and fifties, never quite managed to subdue the exuberance of his portrayal of an age's sickness. Long after we have forgotten some of the lamentable philosophic posturings, memorable images of desperation and pathos remain: Shearwater in *Antic Hay*, dreaming of freedom as he frantically drives his stationary bicycle to nowhere in a heat-controlled room, his sweat rolling into a receptacle for analysis; Burlap and Beatrice, concluding *Point Counter Point* by pretending to be two children as they gaily splash each other in the bathtub; the foul, gibbering Fifth Earl of Goniston, 201 years old, reduced to the level of fetal ape as he demonstrates the glories of eternal life at the end of *After Many a Summer*. Although Somerset Maugham charged him with "deficient sympathy with human beings," and D. H. Lawrence hated his negativity, Huxley was read precisely because he succeeded in revealing, as Lawrence also confirmed, "the truth, perhaps the last truth, about you and your generation, with really fine courage." Unpleasant as that truth was, it was still necessary that it be shown.

Christopher Isherwood also sought to reveal truths about his generation, though the truths he pursued were always more complexly involved with efforts to understand himself than were Huxley's. Huxley the satirist, observing the spectacle of human futility, gives way to Isherwood the ironist, reflecting on the elusiveness and vagaries of the self even as it attempts to impose order on the world around it. Isherwood's fascination with the problem of how a writer deals with his own identity remains a central concern throughout his career, so that neat distinctions between fiction and autobiography lose their edge in his work. Even the biographical study of his family which he builds around the publication of letters and excerpts from his mother's diary in *Kathleen and Frank* is finally shaped into an occasion for Isherwood to examine how he came to be what he is.

Although Isherwood knew early on that he wanted to be a writer, he had to make himself one through a deliberate act of rebellion. The immediate objects of the rebellion were his mother and all the suffocating aspirations for respectability he felt she harbored for him. Failing his Cambridge tripos, as I said earlier, dealt effectively with the specific professional option his mother was advocating, that of becoming a university don. But in rejecting his mother's plans for him he was doing more than simply refusing a particular vocation; he was opting out of an entire structure of conventional expectations and proper role playing that he had come to associate with her. Isherwood could conceive of his freedom only in opposition to the majority culture sanctified by Kathleen.

Discussing, in *Christopher and His Kind* (1976), the homosexuality that was such a critical part of his life, Isherwood wonders, not altogether facetiously, to what degree his sexual preference represents an act of willful resistance to the pressures of social conformity: "Girls are what the state and the church and the law and the press and the medical profession endorse, and command me to desire. My mother endorses them, too. She is silently brutishly willing me to get married and breed grandchildren for her. Her will is the will of Nearly Everybody, and in their will is my death." Even if his nature were the same as those of the heterosexual majority, he concludes, it would still be necessary to fight them: "If boys didn't exist, I should have to invent them."

Much of this early, formative anger is channeled into his first novel, *All the Conspirators* (1928), which he began when he was twenty-one. In a new foreword to the book, written in 1958 (the decade of the Angry Young Men in British fiction), Isherwood defines the concerns of the

Angry Young Man of my generation [who] was angry with the Family and its official representatives; he called them hypocrites, he challenged the truth of what they taught. He declared that a Freudian revolution had taken place of which they were trying to remain unaware. He accused them of reactionary dullness, snobbery, complacency, apathy. While they mouthed their platitudes, he exclaimed, we were all drifting toward mental disease, sex crime, alcoholism, suicide.

Such is the emotional climate of the novel in which Philip Lindsay struggles to break free from the clutches of his mother and the deadly office job she has decreed for him. While Isherwood's sympathies in this intergenerational conflict are unambiguous—the author, Isherwood writes in the preface, "makes not the smallest pretence of impartiality. His battle-cry is 'My Generation—right or wrong'"—at the same time he achieves enough ironic distance from Philip to understand his moral failures. The book, in a sense, is a portrait of the neurasthenic as a young man. Infantilized by his mother, he flees real resolution by taking refuge in sickness. The rheumatic fever that he manages to incur—a fittingly childish disease—guarantees that he will have to be looked after for a long time. While Mrs. Lindsay's need to keep him dependent on her is clear, Isherwood avoids any temptation toward self-indulgence on behalf of the innocent hero. Isherwood's resentment at the selfish manipulations of the older generation notwithstanding, he understands the extent to which Philip shares culpability in permitting himself to be reduced to a passive invalid.

All the Conspirators is very much a first novel of a young writer, filled with self-consciously modernist techniques and solemn literary echoes. Quick narrative shifts, bits of stream of consciousness, dialogue between speakers whose identity is at first uncertain—all testify to Isherwood's having read his Joyce and Woolf. He even challenges the reader, in his preface, to try to understand who is speaking in the first few pages of the book's last chapter. More important than these primarily technical devices he adapted for his own purposes is the overall influence on his tone and point of view of E. M. Forster, a writer he admired and a man he went on to love deeply as a friend.

In *Lions and Shadows*, his fictionalized autobiography covering the period up to his departure for Berlin in 1929, Isherwood describes the revelation about the art of novel writing experienced by his friend Chalmers (actually the writer Edward Upward):

Forster's the only one who understands what the modern novel ought to be. . . . Our frightful mistake was that we believed in tragedy: the point is, tragedy's quite impossible nowadays. . . . We ought to aim at being essentially comic writers. . . . The whole of Forster's technique is based on the tea-table: instead of trying to screw all his scenes up to the highest possible pitch, he tones them down until they sound like mothers'-meeting gossip. . . . It's the completely new kind of accentuation—like a person talking a different language.

Chalmers's discovery was Isherwood's as well, and Forster's tea-tabling understatement provides Isherwood, from the very start of his writing career, with his characteristic way of rendering the world. Helping him to understand his limitations, Forster also directed him to his strengths. "I was a cartoonist," he writes insightfully in *Lions and Shadows* about his range and dramatic power, "not a painter in oils."

In *The Memorial* (1932), his next book, Isherwood moves from the metaphorical war between old and young of *All the Conspirators* to a consideration of the extent to which an entire society—young as well as old—has been destroyed by the actual armed conflict of the First World War. Isherwood never wavered from his early notion of the novel: "It was to be about war: not the War itself, but the effect of the idea of 'War' on my generation. It was to give expression, at last, to my own 'War' complex. . . ."

The embodiment of that complex is Eric Vernon, a form both of Philip Lindsay and of Isherwood, who bears with him Isherwood's own burden of having to live with the myth of the hero-father who died in the war, as well as the shame of never having had the opportunity to fight in it himself. Eric represents a character type to whom Isherwood, as a young writer—and for transparently personal reasons—was especially interested: "the neurotic hero," as he calls him in *Lions and Shadows*, "The Truly Weak Man." Unable directly to confront himself or the demands of his mother, Eric eventually manages to elude Lily's control over him by finding refuge in the greater authority of Catholicism. He delights in the new peace his decision has brought him, but Isherwood clearly sees it as an abnegation of personal freedom that is no solution at all.

Although Eric's effort to escape from Lily repeats the pattern of mother-son opposition of *All the Conspirators*, the novel sees failure and frustration everywhere, both within and across generational groupings. If the old cannot understand the young, they cannot understand each other, either. Death and decay brood over the novel, in which the comfort of the once-vital Victorian past, as symbolized by John Vernon, has now become a doddering burden, with his "silver moustache and slobbery mouth like a baby's . . . smiling with pleasure and amusement at his own helplessness and weight."

The novel's final scene captures the full sense of the futility of living in a world in which people cannot make significant contact with each other, in which language serves as a source of misunderstanding rather than connection. Margaret writes a fatuously sentimental letter to Edward, bravely acknowledging his homosexuality, claiming how close she feels to him, and assuring him that their total sexual incompatibility will become less and less important as time passes. Edward reads the letter in Berlin to his newest—but clearly by no means his last—young homosexual pickup, who understands neither Edward nor English. Isherwood gives the last words of the novel to the uncomprehending Franz, whose simplistic piety concludes the book on a painfully ironic note: "'You know,' said Franz, very serious and evidently repeating something he had heard said by his elders: 'that War . . . it ought never to have happened.'"

To reveal the disarray and lack of focus of a society to which war did indeed happen, Isherwood devised a form that would itself undercut the possibility of achieving any easy, stable view of things. Rather than a continuous narrative moving linearly across the years (1920 to 1929) covered by the novel, Isherwood chops up the narrative into four distinct "snapshots," and then presents them out of chronological order: 1928 is followed by 1920, 1925, and finally 1929. Though Isherwood argues in *Lions and Shadows* that in this "epic disguised as a drawing room comedy" it is more interesting to "start in the middle and go backwards, then forwards again," such a structure also has the effect of making us uncertain about our judgments, about where we stand in this confusing world. The reader has to work hard to put together the fragmented narration and, in the process, experiences some of the difficulty of the denizens of Isherwood's bleak world who grope their way through it without light or love or direction.

Even as he worked on *The Memorial* in Berlin (it was finally published in 1932), Isherwood was gathering material for a large novel whose title he projected as "The Lost." If "the lost" could also be said aptly to characterize the condition of the characters in his first two novels, the phrase had particular significance for Isherwood now as he looked about him in the political and moral cauldron that was Berlin in the early thirties. He attributed three separate meanings to the title: those who were blindly being led into the horrific Nazi future; those who were already designated, like the Jews, to be Hitler's victims; and those who, less tragically, were treated as social outcasts, like Sally Bowles, Otto Nowak, and Mr. Norris, among others. In addition, Isherwood notes in his diary that all his chief characters are linked by the fact that "each one of them is conscious of the mental, economic, and ideological bankruptcy of the world in which they live."

The idea for a single novel called "The Lost" became too tangled ever to materialize. Instead, Isherwood funneled the "mob of characters" he had already created in two different directions: Arthur Norris into a novel bearing his own name (the original English title, *Mr. Norris Changes Trains*, was transformed for American audiences into *The Last of Mr. Norris*), and the rest into *Goodbye to Berlin*. Although the single volume in which both have been published in the United States under the title *Berlin Stories* tends to obscure the fact that they are two distinct works, both are faithful to Isherwood's original vision, in that they document the lives of the lost. Berlin, not unlike Graham Greene's London, is both a physical city and a metaphorical presence, defining a world in which people no longer have the power to control their own destinies: "The whole city lay under an epidemic of discreet, infectious fear. I could feel it, like influenza, in my bones," comments the narrator of *The Last of Mr. Norris*. Political and social disintegration are simply the public forms of the private emptiness and fear that beset all the characters: the two blend seamlessly with each other. Permeating both novels, in John Lehmann's memorable phrase, is "the noise of history," announcing, to those prepared to hear it, the approaching cacophony of Germany's moral insanity. Above all, both seek to render the texture and oddity of the life Isherwood encountered in Berlin, "to present the bizarre as if it were humdrum and to show events which are generally regarded as extraordinary forming the daily routine of somebody's life."

Isherwood chose Norris for his first subject, he tells us, because "of all of his Berlin characters, Norris was the most bizarre." As we follow him through his endless string of duplicities, evasions, and betrayals, as we observe him with his cosmetics and wig and learn about his sexual pleasures, we have no difficulty understanding Isherwood's estimate of him. But more than simply a bizarre character in his own right, Norris is at the same time emblematic of the moral vacuum in which all the characters are living. Without any discernible conscience or principle, prepared to change trains and allegiances (hence the appropriateness of the original title) whenever necessary to ensure his survival, Norris in his own charming style is no less evil than the Nazis. Or than Schmidt, his unpleasant servant who functions as a kind of coarse and brutal double of Norris and with whom, at the end of the novel, he is "doomed to walk the earth together."

Norris is a compelling fictional character, and the novel works simply as a portrait of a subtly perverse creature making his way in a complicated, corrupt time. But the story of Norris is told not by an omniscient, third-person narrator but by William Bradshaw, a fact that deepens and enriches the novel considerably. For as the book progresses we realize that the focus is not on Norris alone but on what Bradshaw makes of Norris on the one hand, and what Isherwood makes of Bradshaw on the other. The fertile ambiguities begin with the name of the young English narrator. Isherwood's full name was Christopher William Bradshaw Isherwood, and in granting his narrator what he calls "his two superfluous middle names" Isherwood points to a relationship while simultaneously distancing himself from it. One of the important ways in which Bradshaw differs from Isherwood is in his lacking any perceptible sexual dimension. Although he was initially attracted to Berlin because, as he says in *Christopher and His Kind*, "Berlin meant Boys," Isherwood could not permit Bradshaw a homosexual life for two reasons: the social scandal it might cause his family at home and the aesthetic disturbance it would generate within the novel. If the narrator were to become odd and interesting because of his homosexual "fantasies, preferences, and prejudices," he might upstage the centrality of Norris, thereby blurring the emphasis Isherwood sought.

Isherwood, then, maintains an ambivalent connection to Bradshaw, best defined by Isherwood's own assertion that he "both acknowledged and disowned his kinship with the Narrator." A similar ambivalence exists between Bradshaw and Norris. From the very first page, when he meets Norris in the train, Bradshaw tries to fathom who Norris is. As evidence gradually piles up about Norris's corruption (provided, of course, by Bradshaw himself), Bradshaw remains strikingly unwilling to see him with any moral clarity. Despite warnings from Helen and others about Norris, Bradshaw endlessly slides away from making any responsible judgment, choosing always to accept Norris's own disingenuous explanations for his behavior. In his refusal to hold Norris to any serious accounting, his preference for the comfort of avoiding consequences—"At that moment, had he demanded it, I'd have sworn that two and two makes five"—Bradshaw gradually reveals himself to be as morally culpable as Norris himself. By the end of the novel, Isherwood has succeeded in implicating not only Bradshaw in Norris's corruption, but, insofar as we have permitted Bradshaw to shape our responses to Norris, ourselves as well. To what precise extent Bradshaw represents some critical view Isherwood came to have of his own moral stance during his time in Berlin it is impossible to say. What we can say with certainty is that Isherwood's use of Bradshaw as a character adds a moral resonance and a complexity to the novel that would be lacking if Bradshaw were only—or simply—the narrator of the tale.

Isherwood divided his novels into two categories: "constructed novels," in which he included *The Last of Mr. Norris* (along with *All the Conspirators* and *The Memorial*) and "dynamic portraits"—books "whose interest depends on the gradual revealing of a character, rather than on action, crisis, and confrontation"—where he places, among others, *Goodbye to Berlin*. If the distinction is not altogether useful in explaining the differences between the two Berlin novels, it does at least point to the emphasis on character, or better, characters, to be found in *Goodbye to Berlin*. The novel consists of four separate portraits or groups of portraits, framed by two lengthy excerpts from the narrator's diary, one from the fall of 1930, the other from the winter of 1932–33. Although the episodes are sufficiently self-contained to permit them to have been published separately, together they constitute not a set of fragments but an effectively organized whole, connected by tone, chronology, and assorted internal sets of parallels and contrasts. The individual portraits of Sally Bowles, the Nowaks, the Landauers, and others finally blend into a convincing portrait of an entire culture that is rapidly disintegrating. In this way the discontinuous form, far from undermining the novel's coherence, contributes significantly to it.

The presence of the first-person narrator, of course, telling the stories of the people he meets even as he himself experiences the decaying world in which they are all immersed, is the most potent unifying force in the novel. The person who observes it all is another Isherwood surrogate, this time bearing not the evasive name of "William Bradshaw" but the straightforward "Christopher Isherwood."

Goodbye to Berlin is the first novel—*Prater Violet* and *Down There on a Visit* were to follow—in which the narrator is called Christopher Isherwood. It is important not to make the mistake of many readers in thinking that Christopher the narrator is synonymous with Christopher the author. In each instance the Christopher-narrator is a free-standing character, treated by Christopher the author as such, rather than a purely autobiographical voice. The complicated relationship between them suggests the extent to which Isherwood remained fascinated by the shifting, elusive selves that exist in a single person's lifetime and the challenges those different selves pose to the writer in trying both to understand and then to represent them in works of fiction and autobiography. In different ways, all of Isherwood's work is an extended journey into the self.

The confusion surrounding the relationship between author and narrator in *Goodbye to Berlin* is compounded by the narrator's comment at the start of the book, "I am a camera." Made famous by John van Druten's stage adaptation of the novel (whose title it became), the statement has been taken as a description of author Isherwood's method of composition, rather than as a self-defining stance the narrator has assumed. Actively transforming the real-life models he met in Berlin into affecting fictional characters, Isherwood chooses to present them through the passive camera-eye of the narrator.

In doing so, he not only achieves the feeling of an unmediated, immediate grasp of the life going on around "Herr Issyvoo," as Fraülein Schroeder memorably calls him, but he also establishes the nature of the relationship between the narrator and what he observes. As he captures the different varieties and postures of the lost he encounters in Berlin (and on Ruegen Island), the narrator remains essentially cut off from the subjects of his snapshots, conscious largely of his own isolation and helplessness. Teaching students who are indifferent to what he offers, recording rather than participating in relationships, he lives without passion on the periphery of things, unable to make contact with life. Although cameras are not ordinarily defined by the pictures they take, in this case the lost whom he "photographs" for us speak to his own spiritual condition as well.

Goodbye to Berlin charts both the progressive slide into moral chaos of an entire culture, and the emotional and spiritual aridity of the man who witnesses it. Christopher's failures to connect in some lasting way with what he experiences is demonstrated on the novel's last page. "I catch sight of my face in the mirror," he observes, following a thought that at that very moment the Nazis might be torturing someone he knows, "and am shocked to see that I am smiling. You can't help smiling in such beautiful weather."

Narrator and author both left Berlin in 1933, when Isherwood started a six-year odyssey through various European countries. During this time, in addition to publishing *The Last of Mr. Norris*, he collaborated with W. H. Auden on their two poetic plays, *The Dog Beneath the Skin* and *The Ascent of F6*. Isherwood's wanderings finally came to an end in 1939, not with a return home but with the discovery of a new home in California. His postwar fiction, less acclaimed than his previous work, continued his explorations into the self, heavily influenced by his new studies in Vedanta and its belief that everyone possesses an unchanging, immortal self that is at one with the universe. These religious convictions significantly change the nature of his later fiction, with his earlier uncertainty now replaced by a confident set of spiritual values. In the words of Alan Wilde, Isherwood's most thoughtful critic, "If the prewar novels seek above all to *discover* value, the postwar books attempt rather to demonstrate the *consequences* of belief." Novels like *Prater Violet*, *Down There on a Visit*, *A Single Man*, and *A Meeting by the River* are separated by more than a continent from *The Berlin Stories*.

Even before Isherwood had published his first novel he was being hailed, as Stephen Spender learned from Auden, as "the Novelist of the Future." Cyril Connolly called him "a hope of English fiction," and Somerset Maugham announced that he "holds the future of the English novel in his hands." Despite all his marvelous gifts, however—his intelligence, the purity and naturalness of his prose, his subtly modulated ironies—it is fair to say that Isherwood never quite achieved the distinction projected for him. At this time, at least, it appears that the only works of his that will really endure are *The Berlin Stories*, and even these, successful as they are, seem too slight an accomplishment for a major talent. For John Lehmann, Isherwood's good friend, "*Mr. Norris Changes Trains* and the stories of *Goodbye to Berlin* seemed to me far too inadequate an *oeuvre* for someone who had been tipped, for every kind of good reason, as the most promising novelist of his generation." But if we relieve him of the burden of unfair expectations, we find a novelist whose clear view of the moral and political chaos of the thirties and its effect on personal life and private values plays a major role in helping define the period for us.

Michael Rosenthal

Selected Bibliography

Annan, Noel. *Our Age*. New York: Random House, 1990.

Connolly, Cyril. *Enemies of Promise*. New York: Moss/Persea Books, 1964.

Cunningham, Valentine. *British Writers of the Thirties*. New York: Oxford University Press, 1989.

Fraser, G. S. *The Modern Writer and His World*. London: Penguin, 1964.

Graves, Robert, and Alan Hodge. *The Long Weekend*. New York: Norton, 1963.

Green, Martin. *Children of the Sun*. New York: Basic Books, 1976.

Hynes, Samuel. *The Auden Generation*. New York: Viking, 1972.

Mowatt, C. L. *Britain between the Wars, 1918–1940*. Boston: Beacon, 1971.

Spender, Stephen. *World within World*. London: Hamish Hamilton, 1951.

Symons, Julian. *The Thirties*. London: Faber and Faber, 1960.

James Joyce

J AMES JOYCE is associated with modern narrative in the way Einstein is with modern physics or Freud with modern psychology. Though he is indisputably a giant of twentieth-century fiction, Joyce's status has little to do with the actual amount of his published writing. Compared to his nineteenth-century predecessors—Charles Dickens, Anthony Trollope, Henry James—or even his contemporary ones—Arnold Bennett, D. H. Lawrence, Joseph Conrad—Joyce's canon seems almost meager. His works consist of one collection of short stories, *Dubliners* (1914), two small collections of poems, several essays and newspaper articles, one play, *Exiles* (1918), an unfinished autobiographical novel, *Stephen Hero*, a finished one, *Portrait of the Artist as a Young Man* (1916), a modern comic epic, *Ulysses* (1922), and a formidable experiment in polyglot fiction, *Finnegans Wake* (1939).

If volume alone is not the reason for Joyce's premier position among modern novelists, what is? To answer this question is to begin where Joyce and his best recent critics begin: with the exuberant, revolutionary nature of his narrative language. For many years it was thought that Joyce's primary innovation was the development of stream of consciousness, a technique by which narrative penetrates the interior thoughts of characters and introduces experiences to fiction that had steadfastly been kept out: the mind's uncensored, disjunctive musings on taboo motives and bodily impulses, on associational reflexes, on errors, slips, inadvertencies. For Joyce, language is the artist's way into the deeper consciousness of the individual and the race.

But stream of consciousness is older than Joyce's first readers realized. As far back as Victor Hugo in the mid-nineteenth century, novelists had a notion of interior narration. Hugo writes in *Les Misérables:*

> It is certain that we talk to ourselves; there is no thinking person who has not done so. It may indeed be said that the *word* is never a more splendid mystery than when it travels in a man's mind from thought to conscience and back again to thought. . . . We say and exclaim within ourselves without breaking silence, in a tumult wherein everything speaks except our mouth. The realities of the soul are none the less real for being invisible and impalpable.

Of course, Joyce himself recognized that he was not the first writer to release the energies of interior narration in fiction. Rather, he located his true powers as a writer in the original and evocative units of language that composed the concentrated narrative phrases, sentences, and paragraphs—stream of consciousness or otherwise—in his books. No writer before him placed such priority on the structure, texture, sound, and shape of words on the page, whether to transport fiction to realms where it had never coursed before or to represent the full voicing of the era's many ideolects: sexual, musical, political.

Joyce thrived on the means available to the artist for sounding out language, for turning and twisting words into a pattern that connects or brings disparate phenomena together, from discrete sounds to the way words form in the mind, from the idioms of Victoriana to the excrescences of gutter slang, from the lyric phrase to the cloacal fart in the Sirens episode of *Ulysses* that serves as a commentary on local Irish politics: "Kraaaaaa . . . Pprrpffrrppffff." It is not enough for Leopold Bloom to point out the folds in a Dubliner's fat neck in the Aelous episode; the text of *Ulysses* has to offer fat folds: "Fat folds of neck, fat, neck, fat, neck." The plasticity of language is, of course, part of the fiction's great comic strength. Late in the day of *Ulysses*, Bloom finds himself embarrassedly making an excuse to an acquaintance about being in Dublin's red light district: "I was just making my way home. . . ." The excuse is so phony a horse pulling a nearby carriage reacts appropriately with a hearty laugh while whinnying into the very heart of Joyce's homing epic: "Hohohohohohoh! Hohohohome!"

As often occurs in Joyce's fiction, the working of a character's mind serves as a commentary on the nature of language as a creative property in and of itself. Here is Leopold Bloom in the Lestrygonian episode musing on his wife's wit. The process described is not altogether different from the process employed throughout *Ulysses* and for most all of *Finnegans Wake*.

She used to say Ben Dollard had a base barreltone voice. He has legs like barrels and you'd think he was singing into a barrel. Now, isn't that wit. They used to call him big Ben. Not half as witty as calling him base barreltone. Appetite like an albatross. Get outside of a baron of beef. Powerful man he was at stowing away number one Bass. Barrel of Bass. See? It all works out.

The goal of narrative language for Joyce is to make all the observations of life work out as part of the fabric of the modernist text. He identifies one of his techniques for doing so in *Finnegans Wake* at the same time he creates a word for it: "langwedge." Narrative language not only conveys meaning but mimics it. Leopold Bloom in the Lotuseaters episode of *Ulysses* notices that the last letter is worn off the legend in the crown of his hat. The text reveals what Bloom sees: "Plasto's high grade ha." The intrepid reader can take it a step further; the sentence, like the whole of the mock epic *Ulysses*, provides a high-grade laugh.

The breaking up and reformation of the very syllables that produce Joyce's words exemplify a tendency that had been there all along in his fiction from the very carefully selected keywords—paralysis, gnomon, simony—of his first story in *Dubliners*, to the young artist's fascination with the sound of the word "suck" in *Portrait of the Artist as a Young Man*, to the description of a widow's unkempt hair in the Sirens episode of *Ulysses*—wavyavyeavyheavyeavyevyevyhair un comb:'d." Joyce commodifies language, turns it into a value package where meaning derives from many sources—the accumulation of sounds, puns, metamorphic words, the arrangement of sentences and phrases. Early in *Finnegans Wake* we are simply told that "every word will be bound over to carry three score and ten toptypsical readings."

The means by which words participate in the formation of action and ideas has absorbed the attention of Joyce's finest critics in recent years. Of most interest is the way Joyce includes a variety of styles and voices in his fiction, making language reveal all the sounds a civilization makes, beginning with the nuances of character idioms and dialects. To experience Joyce's fiction is to see Ireland verbally or, better yet, to hear it visually. In the Hades episode of *Ulysses*, Leopold Bloom hears the sound before the word, and the Joycean text gives us the image of the brogue: "Oot: a dullgarbed old man from the curbstone tendered his wares, his mouth opening: oot. ——Four bootlaces for a penny." In the

Aeolus episode, Bloom casually articulates a principle that forms the basis of what Joyce accomplishes in narrative. In reference to the whir of the printing press in the newspaper offices for which he works as an advertising canvasser, Bloom says, "Almost human . . . doing its level best to speak." Everything in Joyce's life—remembered or projected—can be made manifest if he can construct the means to make it speak.

Hugh Kenner describes a variation on interior narration that he calls the "Uncle Charles Principle" (derived from a character in *Portrait of the Artist*), whereby Joyce melds his own style into the psyche of all those voices—individual and cultural—represented in his fiction, "an interference phenomenon between 'his' language and language not his, sometimes other characters', sometimes the author's." In the following example from the first chapter of *Ulysses*, the narrator's voice imitates the inner voice of Stephen Dedalus until Dedalus's inner voice actually takes over itself at the phrase "White breast." Joyce's narration works by a careful mimesis, a mimicry almost, marking distinctions that are not altogether easy to note:

Woodshadows floated silently by through the morning peace from the stairhead seaward where he gazed. Inshore and farther out the mirror of water whitened, spurned by lightshod hurrying feet. White breast of the dim sea. The twining stresses, two by two. A hand plucking the harpstrings, merging their twining chords. Wavewhite wedded words shimmering on the dim tide.

The subtle transference in the passage from a narrator's language to interior character monologue is characteristic of Joyce's fiction and bears comparison with the recently revived and scrutinized theories of the Russian critic Mikhail Bakhtin, whose analysis of the novel as a form—"another's speech in another's language"—generally describes a politics of fiction in which narrative offers a speaking platform to those who are rarely heard at all. What Bakhtin calls the heteroglossia of fiction is as well represented by the infinitely variable and various narrative styles of James Joyce as by any writer who ever set pen to paper.

Discovering, executing, and refining an array of narrative languages for all his characters and all his Irish settings is for Joyce akin to the formulation of artistic consciousness. He used the words he so carefully crafted in *Dubliners*, *Portrait*, *Ulysses*, and *Finnegans Wake* as a mirror of the substantiating intellect, as an emblem for the sustained and satisfied artist hero—the key idea behind his adaptation of Homer's

Odyssey in *Ulysses*—and as a way of reimagining a world that, after his departure from Ireland in 1904 at the age of twenty-two, existed predominantly in the pages of his books.

In his notes for his play, *Exiles*, Joyce comments, "A nation exacts a penance from those who dared to leave her payable on their return." Joyce pays the exile's greatest debt without ever returning—he re-creates the place from which he departs by the ingenuity of his word-driven imagination—what he called, in a wonderful pairing of artistic exile and artistic consciousness early in *Finnegans Wake*, his Irish "landescape." To be away from one's native land, and yet longing for its feel, its texture, its local life, leads, as another exile, Vladimir Nabokov, puts it, to the creation of "unreal estate." Joyce's language makes Ireland all over again. A telling instance occurs early in his *Portrait of the Artist* when the young narrator recalls the time he confused the "wild rose blossoms" from the popular Irish song with his own toddler version, "the green wothe botheth." The narrator wonders under what conditions somewhere in the world a person might create his own Irish symbol, a "green rose." The words on the page that frame the question provide the answer: the text produces the "green rose" as the young artist imagines it and the reader reads it.

Joyce's first efforts were short stories about those Dubliners he observed and listened to all his life. He had an early agenda derived partly from the personal animus he harbored against the inhibiting and stifling nature of modern Ireland. After Joyce completed his *Dubliners* collection in 1904 and sent the manuscript to Ireland for publication, an Irish printer destroyed the plates for fear of legal suits. Joyce wrote in a broadside what he often voiced about the Irish: "This lovely land that always sent / Her writers and artists to banishment / And in a spirit of Irish fun / Betrayed her own leaders one by one."

Each of the stories in *Dubliners* is written in a style Joyce described as "scrupulously mean," though he had a larger design in mind that would open up his land's spaces to the more encompassing territory of his vengeful imagination. He begins the first story of the volume, "The Sisters," with a reference to a dying priest, "There was no hope for him this time," and the phrase calls to mind the famous inscription on the gate to the underworld that initiates an earlier Western epic, Dante's *Divine Comedy*: "Abandon every hope, you who enter." That the city shield of Dublin represents two sisters framing the city's motto makes the title of the opening story an invitation to the reader to enter into

Joyce's version of Dublin as a dying city of Christendom, the dear dirty "Dustbin" of *Finnegans Wake*.

Joyce's Dubliners suffer strikingly similar Irish fates—the social, religious, and political atrophy that shrinks the human soul; the intense struggle and rivalry within families; the loss or bartering of vocations. Joyce recognized the Irish as a nation of self-betrayers, haunted by that particularly paralyzing element in the political culture that made life so difficult and dispiriting: the myth of legendary Irish political failure that immobilizes real national spirit and confidence in the face of British imperial domination. He had a thorough distrust of the sentimental lethargy of the popular imagination and of the blowhard nationalism that masks the bankrupt politics represented, say, in the *Dubliners* story "Ivy Day in the Committee Room." He scorned the intolerant biases of the Gaelic League, represented by Miss Ivors in "The Dead," and he feared the unpleasantness and futility of the radical Irish exiles beyond Irish borders, the "wild geese," who are little better than Irish drunks at home besotted by the product of the great national brewing industry, what Joyce called by the time of *Finnegans Wake*, the "wild guineese."

Joyce thought of *Dubliners* as a "chapter in the moral history of my nation," and his stories register something of his political soul, insofar as his politics originate from an inner core of respect and concern for those not so easily empowered, nationally or within the core of religious and familial life. His best vision in *Dubliners*, whatever the actual lot of the Irish, centers on what is often missing in Ireland: freedom from material domination and release from oppressive homegrown conventions. Joyce's sensibility is close to that of Leopold Bloom in the Cyclops episode of *Ulysses*—practical and humane: "Force, hatred, history, all that. That's not life for men and women, insult and hatred. And everybody knows that it's the very opposite of that is really life."

Dubliners is organized, as Joyce himself wrote, under four aspects: childhood, adolescence, maturity, and public life. Its longest and most sustained excursus on the Irish spirit comes with the final story, "The Dead," an appropriate title for the underworld motif present from the opening of "The Sisters." "The Dead" is an immensely skilled conversational tone poem in which the disappointing strains of present desires clash with the enchanting grief of past memories. There is in this story—a novella almost—a vibrancy and energy of Irish talk and an essentially humane display of Irish spirit. The world of the dead in

Dubliners, like Dante's Florentine one, is filled with the embers of local passions.

The husband of the story, Gabriel Conroy, confronts the remembered image of a bygone rival, his wife's long-dead admirer from many years before. Joyce contrives the pathos of the story so that Gabriel's blundering insensitivity to the deeply emotional reaction of his wife, Gretta, does not entirely cancel the legitimacy of his love for her. The renowned ending of the story, like so much else in Joyce, especially the fading strains of *Ulysses* and *Finnegans Wake*, is complex but strangely affirming. The word *yes* makes its way into the deep freeze of Ireland in a surge of emotion that crystallizes the world for the artist's vision of it: "Yes, the newspapers were right: snow was general all over Ireland. . . . His soul swooned slowly as he heard the snow falling faintly through the universe and faintly falling, like the descent of their last end, upon all the living and the dead."

It took ten years for *Dubliners* to see the light of day, from its inception in 1904 to its publication in 1914. In the interim Joyce scrapped his first narrative effort, an overtly autobiographical novel, *Stephen Hero*, and worked it into his equally autobiographical but far more inventive *Portrait of the Artist as a Young Man*. In part, *Portrait* presents the great influences of Joyce's formative years in the late 1890s, the one embodied in realist European drama, primarily that of Henrik Ibsen, and the other in the fin-de-siècle symbolist movement in France. Joyce's goal throughout his career was to combine these movements, to convey the voices and sounds of realistic civic surroundings in the powerful and resonant figure or symbol he called the epiphany. The epiphany is a manifest, discernible narrative moment where impressions become symbolically charged and meaningful.

Only an attuned and powerful artistic consciousness can perceive and arrange sequences of epiphanies within a complete narrative action, and Joyce's autobiographical fiction—in *Portrait* and through to *Ulysses* and *Finnegans Wake*—reflects the means by which writers struggle to form such a consciousness. Joyce was one of two prominent novelists of the twentieth century to make the progress of a career as a realist/symbolist writer a focal point of his fiction. The other was Marcel Proust. For both writers, young men are the subjects of books whose action, in part, consists of training them—as artists—to write something like the books they are in. In one of those phrases from *Ulysses* that aids the reader trying to grasp Joyce's methods, the narrative describes "a sort of retrospective arrangement" by which the present casts light back on the past. Progressive and retrospective arrangements provide a double texture, and part of the interest, say, in Stephen Dedalus as artist is the way he once was the portrait that Joyce would have him draw. This notion is implicit in the two ways of reading the title, a portrait of an artist when he was a young man or a portrait of an artist by a young man.

Joyce is well aware that his portraits, whatever their provenance, are of artists who have not accomplished very much at the time he writes of them. Indeed, the failures and trials of the artist are among the sorrier and funnier spectacles of life, and he is quick to include that part of the artist's story in his fiction as well. Much of *Ulysses* deals with the agonies of the same Dedalus who was so enthralled at his aesthetic prospects in *Portrait*. The same is true of *Finnegans Wake*. Nowhere does Joyce make more fun of the artist than in the portrait of Shem the Penman, where the exilic Irish artist is everything from a sham to a shame, the *Wake*'s "poor trait of the artless." As much as Joyce venerates the artist he also recognizes the selfishness and perversity of his being. "Shun the Punman," is the advice given in the *Wake*, and it is not altogether clear whether Joyce is describing or recommending the reaction by others to his surrogate self.

But the artist has to begin somewhere, and Joyce begins him at the beginning. *Portrait of the Artist* opens with the narrative formula, "Once upon a time." Joyce the innovator soon cancels the cliché with a supplement, "and a very good time it was there was a moocow coming down along the road and this moocow that was coming down along the road met a nicens little boy named baby tuckoo. . . ." Baby talk is the first portrait of the artist as a young man, though in the larger vein of the narrative—its mythic backdrop—the first sentence calls up the dilemma of Stephen's namesake, the Greek artist Daedalus, outsmarting the moocow or Minotaur in the Cretan labyrinth. Here, however, the putative speaking voice is that of Stephen Dedalus's real father, Simon Dedalus.

From the very beginning of the novel the key question for the young Irish artist is who possesses his narrative voice. The rest of the action of *Portrait* focuses on all the claimants—family, church, friends, educators, revolutionaries. Stephen's task by the end of the narrative is to replace the voices that had rivaled and usurped his own from childhood. Joyce concludes *Portrait* with a series of diary entries in which the young artist, in first person, invokes an even older father, the mythical Daedalus, to aid him in telling what he had formerly heard. If the novel is read retrospectively, the very first voice taken over in print—the first sentence we now have of the physical book *Portrait*—is the voice of the father rendered by the son. When Stephen invokes the mythic Daedalus in the last sentence of *Portrait* and asks for help from the old artificer—"Old father, old artificer, stand me now and ever in good stead"—he is asking for the linguistic power that would transform his real father's voice into an artistic resource. In life that voice was the child's memory; in book form it is the beginning of the artist's own portrait, his "once upon a time."

By *Ulysses*, Joyce makes it clear that the artist needs more than a voice; he needs a body. One key difference between *Portrait* and *Ulysses* is the degree to which the latter refocuses the artistic process away from intellect and onto the actual things people touch or onto the things that touch them. Joyce explores the crucial notion that he enters in his own notesheets for *Ulysses*: "The imagination has a body to it." "My book," Joyce told Frank Budgen of *Ulysses*, "is among other things the epic of the human body." Joyce took great care to make it so, developing as part of his style a method of narration where each chapter would correspond stylistically to a different body organ or body process. "How's the body?" McCoy asks Leopold Bloom in the Lotuseaters episode, and the answer to that question is what each character confronts before the action is done.

Joyce's willingness to make his story a body's day—its desires, its movements, its functions, its satisfactions—is among the most modernist of the narrative techniques in *Ulysses*. One of the inserted newspaper headlines in the Aeolus episode could well stand for the entire enterprise of *Ulysses*: "HOW A GREAT DAILY ORGAN IS TURNED OUT," and one of the great questions of the day turns on the same issue: whether Leopold Bloom or Blazes Boylan is the best man to "organize" (metaphorically and suggestively) the life of Molly Bloom and the resources, as she imagines them, of her body.

The story of the human body for Joyce is also the story of the artist's incorporation, that is of the artist's making his total experience the story of the race and all its extensions in time and space. Stephen Dedalus began the process by inscribing his name in the flyleaf of his geography book in *Portrait*, and then imagining how he might extend to the far reaches of the universe. In *Finnegans Wake*, Shem the Penman sums up his own career in the same way, as

the first till last alshemist wrote over every square inch of the only foolscap available, his own body, till by its corrosive sublimation one continuous present tense integument slowly unfolded all marry voising moodmoulded cyclewheeling history (thereby, he said, reflecting from his own individual person life unlivable, transaccidentated through the slow fires of consciousness into a dividual chaos, perilous, potent, common to allflesh, human only, mortal).

Shem's words track the course first set by the untested artist at the end of *Portrait*, who hopes to encounter "for the millionth time the reality of experience and to forge in the smithy of my soul the uncreated conscience of my race."

Part of Stephen's difficulty, however, is that he is listed in Joyce's detailed schematic notesheets for *Ulysses* as "having no body." To have "no body" for Joyce is not only to lack substance but to lack insight into the tangible resources of life, including a key notion in Joyce's fiction, the need for sexual sustenance. In the kind of aesthetic progress Joyce imagines, the artist first needs a muse in order to image a body, a muse represented in *Ulysses* by the substance, desire, and warmth of the feminine. And then, in a turnaround, the artist's muse becomes his subject, just as Joyce felt he could begin writing in earnest about something substantial only after his first and life-altering encounter with his future wife, Nora Barnacle, on June 16, 1904. That date becomes the day on which Joyce sets *Ulysses*. In the last chapter of *Ulysses*, Molly Bloom, meandering in her interior monologue all over her life and loves, thinks poignantly, "I wish somebody would write me a loveletter." Insofar as Joyce derives Molly's nature and language from Nora, somebody has.

As for Stephen Dedalus in *Ulysses*, he seems resistant to all the sustaining resources of the body. He rarely washes it, feeds it, or satisfies it. He is not even sure he possesses the same self day after day ("Molecules all change"). He does not, at present, want to be touched. Of course, in the Circe episode Bloom mishears Stephen's mumbling of Yeats's poem, "Who Goes with Fergus," and mistakenly provides what Dedalus still needs: "Ferguson, I think I caught. A girl. Some girl. Best thing could happen him."

Earlier in the day, Joyce asks the question about feminine sustenance for Stephen in light of Dedalus's own question to himself about the sexual component of Shakespeare's poems and plays and about his own ascendant sexual star—"Who will woo you? . . . Where's your configuration?" This is a question that had lingered from *Portrait of the Artist* when Stephen thought of himself, "But him no woman's eyes had wooed." Without a muse, a subject, a woman, and an inspiration, there is no writing. In the Wandering Rocks episode of *Ulysses*, Stephen imagines the advice books on the rack in the middle of the city, and centers on the one most appropriate for him: "How to soften chapped hands. Recipe for white wine vinegar. How to win a woman's love. For me this."

It is a matter of considerable importance to *Ulysses* that Joyce designates "Penelope" (that is, Molly Bloom) in his schematic notesheets as muse for the first part of *Ulysses* (Stephen's chapters) even though she only appears in the last. Molly Bloom herself makes the connection implicit in *Ulysses* when she says of poets, "they all write about some woman." Bloom, who fully appreciates woman's "splendour, when visible: her attraction, when invisible," had in his way already offered his wife to Stephen as a gift (more symbolic than actual) by showing him her alluring photograph and suggesting that Stephen provide Molly Italian lessons. Molly comprehends the gesture when she comments on Bloom's showing the photo: "I wonder he didn't make him a present of it altogether and me too after all." This makes a special kind of coincidental sense when the reader remembers that Stephen had earlier transformed his own initials into a hoped-for muse in the Library chapter: "S.D: sua donna."

For the fledgling artist—even if the context of the day has not fully settled in his mind—the feminine style and substance of the Penelope episode is a potential resource, the body of material upon which to begin. In art the beginning cannot be conceived until the end is imagined. "Done. Begin!" is the way Joyce phrases it in the Sirens episode. Stephen must at some point register a sense of how the intellect and the body serve each other in life and in art in order to benefit from the inspiration of his muse, who comes at him "rere" first. The same muse is very much present in *Finnegans Wake*: "Who in his heart doubts either that the facts of feminine clotheiring are there all the time or that the feminine fiction, stranger than the facts, is there also at the same time, only a little to the rere?"

Joyce continues the motif in *Finnegans Wake*, also recognizing the human comedy involved. The artist's muse is very personal, so the writer appeals for one in a newspaper "personal." The advertisement serves as another portrait of the artist in his pursuit of a feminine muse for the express purpose of helping the exiled writer represent city life in Dublin, Joyce's sustaining focus from 1904.

[Jymes wishes to hear from wearers of abandoned female costumes, gratefully received, wadmel jumper, rather full pair of culottes and onthergarmenteries, to start city life together. His jymes is out of job, would sit and write. He has lately commited one of the then commandments but she will now assist. Superior built, domestic, regular layer. Also got the boot. He appreciates it. Copies. ABORTISEMENT.]

Joyce has substituted his own name for that of Dedalus and Shem, but for any artist it is axiomatic that he or she must draw from the personal experiences that life offers, many of them intimate and some of them perverse. Issy in the *Wake* actually asks her father-writer ("ye auchtor"), "Did you really never in all our cantalang lives speak clothse to a girl's before?" Speaking clothes and speaking close to a girl are something of the same thing in Joyce's sexual aesthetics. Indeed, such proximities to the feminine characterize Leopold Bloom in *Ulysses* to a greater extent than any other Joyce creation. When Frank Budgen suggested to Joyce that Christ was the West's greatest all-round man, Joyce protested that the Savior was a bachelor and never lived with a woman. That was enough to count him out.

Joyce crafts for Bloom as his modern hero in *Ulysses* what he praised in Henrik Ibsen as an artist, "an eminently virile man [with] a curious admixture of woman in his nature." This, of course, is what Stephen Dedalus imagined as well for Shakespeare. In *Finnegans Wake*, Joyce constructs what amounts to an artistic manifesto around the feminine fiction, calling it a "mamafesta." All the energy and festiveness of his work is represented by the mamafesta, the testimony of his muse. This is something that Joyce understood deeply—the rhythms of the feminine voice and the role of the feminine in human nature were essential to him for the full range of life's experiences and adventures.

Such views do not necessarily make Joyce an ardent feminist. He did not take positions on feminist issues of his era; rather, he explored the feminine to increase the range of resources for the artist. Joyce was of the generation of Sigmund Freud and Krafft-Ebing, who felt less constraint than many of today's feminist critics would warrant in imagining the feminine from a male perspective. For Joyce the feminine is part of the story of the body, of human sexuality, of the bonds between man and woman, parent and child, of the natural processes of life itself and of the processes of life that art imitates. That is why he minted for his fiction virtually every word, expression, motion made by his wife, Nora Barnacle, and displayed them in his key women characters, Gretta Conroy in "The Dead," Molly Bloom in *Ulysses*, and Anna Livia Plurabelle in *Finnegans Wake*. It was almost as if Nora Barnacle offered Joyce his body language.

If Joyce's intent is to represent in fiction the full, rounded, masculine/feminine lives of his characters, why does he so artfully (and some would say artificially) design *Ulysses* to include elaborate parallels to the plot and events of the Homeric *Odyssey*? Though there are exceptions—the story "A Painful Case" in *Dubliners* or *Portrait of the Artist*—Joyce's works do not usually gain their epic dimension by the depiction of actions that evolve over long periods of time. Most of Joyce's narratives extend no more than a day and a night. In fact, *Ulysses* has been called, with a certain aptness, a day in the life of a Victorian novel. Considered solely in terms of its Irish subjects and locale, Joyce's work is consistent with the realist agenda of nineteenth-century fiction where characters of some distinction—smarter, dumber, unluckier, more fortunate—undergo experiences that, to a greater or lesser degree, affect their lives.

But Joyce clearly has something more in mind for his modern mock epics. He sees everyone living over and again in the same kind of universal plot, a story of separation, betrayal, return and satisfaction. In *Finnegans Wake*, the hero absorbs the role of the storyteller, "a broadcaster with local wicker jargon." The "broad cast" is what T. S. Eliot, in a famous description of Joyce's techniques, calls the "mythical method," the means by which Joyce adapted the legends and plots of the past into the idiosyncratic expressions of his own time and place. Behind the mythical method is the modernist notion of a special kind of imaginative coherence for contemporary randomness, an effort to collect from far and wide but always to localize in a series of styles and ideolects that reflect, in Joyce's own phrase, "the exaltations and degradations" of his culture.

When Leopold Bloom's name is listed among the mourners at Paddy Dignam's funeral during the day of *Ulysses* the afternoon newspaper drops the *l*. Only an explosion is left: "Boom." That is something of the general effect of Joyce's fiction; he distributes characters to other worlds and other dimensions. It is at the moment when Joyce's characters are dispersed into otherness—the moment when they impersonate the idea of character ("If we were all suddenly somebody else," says Bloom in the Hades episode of *Ulysses*)—that the idea of the Joycean parallel comes to the fore. Parallels for Joyce are indications of the repeating impulses of literary and personal history. They reveal something central about Joyce's modernist agenda: the drives, compulsions, movements, desires that constitute specific human actions are, in fact, encoded in recognizable patterns that transcend their local, contemporary expression to become a "fadograph of a yestern scene," *Finnegans Wake*'s new realism, a fading photograph of the western past juxtaposed against an evening and a night in a Dublin pub.

Joyce begins his important mythic parallels with the Irish Stephen Dedalus mirroring the original Greek Daedalus in *Portrait of the Artist*. He continues with that all-round modern Odysseus, Leopold Bloom, in *Ulysses*. By the time of *Finnegans Wake* parallels are the comic diet of the book. To initial, as Joyce does, the primary character in the narrative as HCE and then to make the initials an acronym for "Here Comes Everybody" is to give full voice to the inclusive principle that serves so much of his fiction. Joyce's repetition compulsion makes all stories "one thousand and one stories, all, told, of the same." More compactly in *Finnegans Wake*, all is "the seim anew"—that is, the "same," the connective "seam," the imitative "seem," and the "seme" or seed that generates the many from the one. That same story is essentially the family romance and all of its filiations: separation from and return to the family bed, sibling and generational rivalry, marital and extramarital desire, the pleasures, pains, and intimate secrets of parenthood and spousehood.

In *Ulysses* the family romance is by design Odyssean. Joyce exuberantly weaves thousands of parallels to the *Odyssey* into the fabric of the text, but Stephen Dedalus invokes the Odyssean parallel with much greater economy when he thinks about the plot of Shakespeare's life in terms of the Homeric pattern of wandering and homecoming: "There can be no reconciliation, Stephen said, if there has not been a sundering." The same notion occurs again to Stephen in a completely impersonal sense embodied in the musical octave in the Circe episode of *Ulysses*: "The fundamental and the dominant are separated by the greatest possible interval [which is] the greatest possible ellipse. Consistent with. The ultimate return. The octave." Even the clichés of the day in *Ulysses* pick up the Homeric epic parallel. Leopold Bloom remarks offhandedly in Nausicaa, "Longest way round is the shortest way home."

There is something inherently comic and parodic in the readaptation of Homeric literary structures—what Ezra Pound called Joyce's "poached epic"—for modern times. Joyce is fully aware that it is preposterous to displace a classic Mediterranean epic into the confines of the local Dublin itinerary of *Ulysses*, just as it is preposterous to conjure all the oft-told stories of civilization in the "worldstage's practical jokepiece" that is *Finnegans Wake*. But his impulses are encyclopedic and comic. His representational worlds contain multitudes. It is in this light that the Homeric parallels in *Ulysses* might be enjoyed as well as discerned.

The force of the parallel is based on the comedy of juxtaposition. In the Lotuseaters episode of *Ulysses*, Leopold Bloom stands on a street corner in Dublin and tries to view a woman's finely turned ankle as she boards a tram while a friend, M'Coy, inadvertently blocks his view of the woman's body. As M'Coy blabs on about the death of a mutual friend, Paddy Dignam, Bloom cuts into the palaver with the simple sigh: "Another gone." His sympathies are with Dignam; his disappointment is over the lost glimpse of a bare ankle. But to absorb the full wit of the scene is to recognize that Joyce recapitulates the moment in the parallel Lotus-eaters adventure of the *Odyssey* when Odysseus just gets a view of the desired Greek coastal landfall before being blown back out to sea.

As is often the case in *Ulysses*, the text itself offers the best explanations of the various narrative techniques Joyce employs in it, and the art of paralleling is no exception. During the Aeolus episode, Professor MacHugh listens to Stephen Dedalus construct a fable about Irish home life that invokes the story of the promised land of Moses and the Jews: "I see . . . we gave him that idea," the professor says after noticing that Dedalus has composed his fable out of the scraps of conversation he has just heard among local Dublin newspapermen musing about incidents in biblical and Roman history. It is the nature of a people's sense of themselves to find analogues for present action in the past. What Professor MacHugh "sees" is an instance of two cultures overlapped—Irish and Jewish. Joyce does the same for the Greek epic characters who appear in *Ulysses* as Irish.

Sundering, wandering, and return provide the overriding structure of Joyce's parallels, but there are Joycean plot initiators that are also universal. In almost all his fiction, the moment of sundering is necessitated by the acts of betrayal perpetrated by rivals. Rivalry is at the very core of Joycean narrative action. He cannot imagine the conduct of literature or life without it. Family members, fellow countrymen, rival artists were all marked by Joyce as obstacles to his own success, and he chose to represent in his fiction the stories of rivalry that mark the race. Among the many titles for the discovered document that turns up as an analogue for the whole of *Finnegans Wake* is *"A Dear Man and his Conspirators and how they all Tried to Fall him."* Odysseus might say the same of the action in the *Odyssey*, and, in Stephen Dedalus's theory worked out in the library episode of *Ulysses*, Shakespeare surely thought the same. Plots for Joyce stem from the inability to parcel out desire among rivals. Someone has—or someone else thinks that someone has—what another wants. As Joyce puts it in the *Wake*, still thinking of the analysis of Shakespeare's life and art, the *mine* and *thine* of life are always at issue, rivaled and doubled: "what is main and why tis twain, how one once meet melts in tother wants . . . all the rivals to allsea, shakeagain."

Rivals are rivulets born of the same source but moving in various directions. The nature of narrative action is to set devices in motion that portray the desire to retrieve what was lost to or taken by a rival, the *Wake*'s "polar anthisishis," where possessiveness is buried in opposition. There are rivals everywhere in Joyce, most powerfully described in Stephen's set piece on Shakespeare and most powerfully imaged in the twins Shem and Shaun from *Finnegans Wake*. The twins in the *Wake* are stand-ins for all the antitheses and rivalries in Joyce's work, between time and space, brains and brawn, even technological sight and sound: "Television kills telephony in brother's broil."

The literary action of taking back from those whose goal is to dispossess is not only at the heart of the *Odyssey* but at the heart of the career of the artist. To displace the more traditional rivaled hero with the rivaled artist is one of Joyce's major contributions to modernism. The artist is perpetually under attack in Joyce's vision, a combination of real and perceived abuse that cries for artistic revenge—"Hast thou found me, O mine enemy," Stephen Dedalus says to rival Buck Mulligan shortly after fronting his other Irish poetic brethren in the library who have excluded him from a planned reading: "See this. Remember." Stephen's earlier formula for the artist's life from *Portrait*—"silence, exile, and cunning"—was also part of his almost paranoid response to the Irish home front. His program is the opposite of the palaver, paralysis, and sentimentality of Irish life. *Finnegans Wake* picks up Stephen's message in one of the many a.k.a.'s for its central figure, HCE: "Hush, Caution, Echoland," a sort of revolutionary code in which "Echoland" is the sound and image of the artist's imaginative articulation from a state of exile. The struggle to regain control over rivals by artistic revenge becomes one of the goals of Stephen's and Joyce's modern odyssey.

In his own mind, Joyce takes over as the betrayed and exiled "Home-role poet," described in *Finnegans Wake*, a hero and writer who plays Homer's role and is played, in turn, by the characters he creates. One of the important things Joyce understands about Odysseus for his own *Ulysses* is that he is a special kind of hero, one who gains his revenge in part by the powers of his verbal imagination. Odysseus is as much a model for the voice of the epic as for the action in it. King Priam of Troy altered the heroic perspective from appearance to language when describing Odysseus in the *Iliad*, admitting that he was not much to look at: "Yes, you would call him a sullen man, and a fool likewise. / But when he let the great voice go from his chest, and the words came / drifting down like the winter snows, then no other mortal / man beside could stand up against Odysseus" (Book 3). Here is a Homeric portrait of the artist. Linguistic power is political power (Joyce's Irish "home-role" or home rule) so crucial for the writer who lives by mocking all the mockers in his own land.

In *Ulysses* the artistic rivalry plot centers on Stephen and Mulligan in a section of the narrative Joyce labeled the Telemachia: "He fears the lancet of my art as I fear that of his," says Stephen of Mulligan very early in the day. In the larger scope of the action involving Stephen during the day, Dedalus is betrayed and abandoned by supposed friends who turn out be be dedicated rivals. He ends up at the home of Leopold Bloom, but he is still leery when he leaves the Blooms' flat in the early morning hours of the next day.

A rivalry plot even more central to *Ulysses* occurs between Leopold Bloom and Blazes Boylan, Molly Bloom's afternoon lover on June 16, 1904. Readers must come to grips with the implicit contest between Bloom and Boylan because it controls the psyche of the book. In the *Odyssey*, the faithful Penelope fends off Odysseus's many rivals; in *Ulysses*, Molly admits Bloom's single nemesis into her bed. Odysseus slays his wife's suitors; Bloom does nothing. But in a more important sense, he transcends his rival by sheer strength of character, a revenge more amenable to Joyce, a pacifist by nature. Much can be said and thought concerning the immense range of narrative themes and techniques registered in *Ulysses*, but the final question is the most important: how does Leopold Bloom manage to return to his own bed satisfied at the end of the day?

Bloom's actions in regard to Molly reflect much of Joyce's own sense, in his long relationship with Nora Barnacle, that a challenge to complacency heightens desire. This is his great subject. Joyce suggested to Frank Budgen that at one very important level Bloom engineers his wife's relation with Blazes Boylan so that he can, at least imaginatively, energize his own dulled sexual energies. He is, in Joyce's words, the *mari complaisant*. The same theme echoes in Joyce's life. As Nora Barnacle told Budgen: "Jim wants me to go with other men so that he will have something to write about." Bloom, of course, represses his wife's affair in *Ulysses*; he prefers to think of Boylan as totally self-motivated. But readers of the day's action have centered attention in the last decade on actions in *Ulysses* that are not clearly revealed in the minute-by-minute chronicle of the day, on things left out rather than put in. Among the things left out is Bloom's far greater knowledge of the impending events of the day than the narrative has him let on.

The reader can gain better access to Bloom's motives by paying close attention to what he tells us only elliptically. For example, Bloom knows exactly when Boylan plans to arrive at his home, around four in the afternoon (though Boylan shows up late), and when Molly plans for him to leave, around six in the early evening. But Bloom is playing a delicate hand. He plans to stay out well beyond the time he knows Boylan will be gone, primarily to give himself and Molly time to contemplate the range of reactions to the day's events.

"Who's getting it up?" is the question that haunts Bloom during the day in reference to Molly's impending singing tour arranged by Boylan. The real direction of the question is obvious, but the answer is less clear. Bloom's description for the tour obliquely expresses his best hopes for Molly's adulterous liaison during the Lotuseaters episode: "Part shares and part profits." Perhaps Bloom even actively or by collusive hints conspired with Boylan in the way he seems to conspire with Stephen Dedalus in regard to Molly when he shows the young man his wife's photograph. After all, one of the sources for Bloom's first name is Leopold von Sacher-Masoch, who specialized, among other things, in contracting with his wife to find additional lovers to stimulate their relationship.

One strange character late in the day at the cabman's shelter actually hints at something mentioned by no one else in the narrative, either because he made it up or because it is one of the day's deeper secrets. In a conversation with Stephen Dedalus about the mysterious Bloom lingering in the background, the reprobate Corley says: "Who's that with you? I saw him a few times in the Bleeding Horse in Camden street with Boylan, the billsticker." This remark occurs in an episode where everyone is spinning out yarns, and, as is the case for other Dubliners, Corley may associate Bloom with Boylan merely because of general gossip about Molly. On the other hand, Bloom may not reveal everything to the reader about his actions and his motives.

Only in the Circe episode, where the mental lives of the characters are trashed by the dramatic narration that exposes them, does the text reveal what may be on Bloom's mind all along: in "five public conveniences he wrote pencilled messages offering his nuptial partner to all strongmembered males." For the most part, Bloom feels the need to be mentally careful about his thoughts of Molly's plans with Boylan partly because he wants to control what he, Bloom, hopes to get out of that meeting—something very private and subtle. Rage, unbridled jealousy, and humiliation are not on his emotional menu.

On several occasions during the day of *Ulysses* Bloom counts it his extraordinary ill fortune that the man who is about to cuckold him crosses his path. Again, there are two ways to look at this: either Bloom is just unlucky or Boylan's presence is a hint that Bloom has, in a way, arranged for him. To think about the action of the novel this way changes a number of things. Bloom at the level of the day's events has done what Shakespeare and Joyce have done at the level of the literary work's execution. They all have created adultery plots from rivalry plots to stimulate the hero to action or self-assertion. As Stephen puts it of Shakespeare's trials with Anne Hathaway, "*Et exaltabuntur cornua iusti*" (and the horns of the just shall be exalted). The best face to put upon it is that Bloom seeks from Molly's afternoon tryst a stimulus for his marriage because he recognizes that Molly's sexual stimulation is key to his own. One of Joyce's notesheet entries for the novel puts it starkly in reference to Boylan and a possible lover for Bloom, one Josie Breen: "LB couldn't adulter so gets BB to do it . . . Cdn't he go & fuck Mrs. Breen?"

What makes this reading of *Ulysses* compelling is that it centers the rivalry-adultery plot where Joyce sensed it belonged, with the "warring of heartshaker with housebreaker," as *Finnegans Wake* puts it. Joyce developed similar notions much more stridently for his one play, *Exiles*, written during a break from his intense work on *Ulysses*. The play works out of themes of sexual jealousy and sexual giving almost as a lend-lease program. Joyce prepared speculative notes for the play that are applicable to the adultery plot of *Ulysses*: "Bertha, to understand the chastity of her nature, must first lose it in adultery." In the play, Richard tells his young son that the only way to truly possess something is to give it away, because "it is yours for ever when you have given it. It will be yours always." Possessive jealousy in *Exiles* turns "into an erotic impulse," more a release than a trauma. As Joyce writes of the action, Richard "seems to feel the thrill of adultery vicariously and to possess a bound woman Bertha through the organ of his friend." In the play, Richard says outright, "I longed to be betrayed by you and by her—in the dark, in the night—secretly, meanly, craftily. By you, my best friend, and by her. I longed for that passionately and ignobly, to be dishonored for ever in love and in lust."

The physical act spoken about in *Exiles* is performed in *Ulysses*. Bloom hints at it in his comment to Stephen about Parnell at the cabman's shelter that adultery is "a case for the two parties themselves unless it ensued that the legitimate husband happened to be a party to it." Molly, too, senses that the Boylan rendezvous is not strictly her own affair, describing Bloom as "trying to make a whore of me," and understanding that "hed never have the courage with a married woman thats why he wants me and Boylan. . . ." Molly's adultery releases what is more important to Bloom than the act itself, a flood of memories on her part that makes Molly in a way inviolable and renewable. Bloom had earlier considered the results of the day's actions and even pondered the possibility of another child in Sirens: "Too late now. Or if not? If not? If still?" The reconnection to Bloom is one way to read the famous series of affirmations at the end of *Ulysses* that seem to draw Bloom all the way from Molly's first lover on Gibraltar to his own marriage proposal on Howth Head: "And I thought as well him as another and then I asked him with my eyes to ask again yes and then he asked me would I yes to say yes my mountain flower and first I put my arms around him yes and drew him down to me so he could feel my breasts all perfume yes and his heart was going like mad and yes I said yes I will Yes."

Ulysses ends in the marriage bed. Given the amount of Joyce's fiction that actually takes place in bed, from the conclusion of the short story "The Dead" to the end of *Ulysses* and to much of *Finnegans Wake*, it is revealing that his portmanteau word for the units of language, the alphabet, is "allaphbed." Allaphbed talk reveals all the permutations of the family romance, all the rivalries between generations, all the secrets of the most intimate habits of the race, the greatest and most perverse pleasures, the traumas, trials, and, ultimately, the tremendous satisfactions of human and marital love. Everything worth thinking about and living for is expressed by Joyce in "the lingo gasped between the kicksheets." Bed is life and death.

The relation between the linguistic unit and the bed as the source and symbol of bourgeois desire is played out to the full in *Finnegans Wake*. Joyce's last narrative, which he finished in 1939 two years before his death, is not an easy book, though serious readers would be mistaken to assume that it is altogether different from *Ulysses*. In *Finnegans Wake* Joyce puts the horizontal plot of the *Odyssey*—wandering and return—on a vertical axis—rise and fall. Because it is the story of so many stories, the title removes the expected possessive apostrophe from "Finnegans." Tim Finnegan in the Irish ballad falls off a ladder and dies, only to revive to participate in the "funagain" everybody seems to be having at his wake, the "grand funferall" of human history.

Finnegans Wake is the Irish Book of the Dead, or, more aptly, a riotous version of Henrik Ibsen's *When We Dead Awaken*. The narrative makes good on the offhand remark Bloom drops in the Hades episode of *Ulysses*: "The Irishman's house is his coffin," and Joyce takes special delight in the power of the artist to give voice to the quick and the dead in writing up the multivarious activity at the symbolic wake of *Finnegans Wake*: "Suppotes a Ventriloquorst Merries a Corpse." In the biblical Genesis, which serves as one of the many models for the narrative action of *Finnegans Wake*, a man and woman, Adam and Eve of the first human homestead, make a terrible mistake and experience mortality for their fall. In *Finnegans Wake*, first principals die a billion deaths but always rise again to celebrate the error-ridden romance of humanity's lives and loves. The unwary reader of fiction might demand from *Finnegans Wake* an explanation of how characters behave and what they should expect from the normal contingencies that affect a life. But Joyce's narrative explains very little; rather it invites everyone to join its events, to celebrate its readings. The *Wake* centers in Dublin every imaginary or real human foible that Joyce can possibly remember having taken place—"This is Dyoublong,"—and buries the question to which the answer is an inevitable yes, "Do you belong?"

There is no single satisfactory key or reading that suffices to explain all of *Finnegans Wake*, despite the efforts by critics to provide one. There are instead extremes of interpretation that set the boundaries within which Joyce operates. The literalist interpretation holds that every detail in Joyce's book is a description of the circumstances of one evening in the lives of a Dublin publican and his household, a wife, twin sons, a young daughter, and a maid and a handyman of sorts. The family-run pub is in Chapelizod, with living quarters upstairs and drinking quarters beneath. Alternately there is a reading of the book that works against the idea of any novelized or literalized events contained in it by claiming that the narrative has the structure of a night vision. It is not a dream so much as a giant phantasmagoric compilation in words and phrases of all the myths and neuroses engendered in and from a father's guilt-ridden human mind, or, in Wakean language, a "reconnoitring through his semisubconscious the seriousness of what he might have done had he really polished off his terrible intentions."

To choose insistently either the literalist or phantasmagoric reading of *Finnegans Wake* profits little. The pleasure in the *Wake* is to savor the scraps of local detail and then to imagine the most ingenious superimpositions upon those details by the manipulating, layering, or arranging of letters within words. Much is made in the *Wake* of an actual letter that seems to have been dug up from a dump heap near Phoenix Park in Dublin, a letter that includes or becomes the substance of the book. The letter is at once a document and a single "letter," an ornate illuminated design, put together with other letters in thousands of combinations, "riot of blots and blurs and bars and balls and hoops and wriggles," that opens up the world of possibilities for narrative. Playing on an ancient name for letter (rune) and the fall of the *Wake* (ruin), Joyce writes: "But the world, mind, is, was and will be writing its own wrunes for ever."

With the events of an evening and night in the life of the Earwicker family as his warp and woof, Joyce weaves the story of the family from Genesis, the Oedipal encounter of the weakened father and the empowered son ("Finn again's weak"), the romance of Tristan and Isolde, the geographical disposition of the city of Dublin between Howth

Head and the river Liffey, the military history of Western Europe, the story of Humpty Dumpty, and the wheels within wheels that contribute to the universal fable of all history for all time. The book ranges from a portrait of the "fall" as gossip to an allegory of the fall as gospel, from a rendition of history as chronicle to a presentation of life as a series of images on the latest invented plaything of the twentieth century, television.

The best way to approach this Joycean farrago is to read with a very open mind, eye, and ear. The look of the text demands that the eye see whatever words are buried in the disposition of letters on the page and that the ear hear homonyms and echoes. Limitation misses the point of *Finnegans Wake*. The book is really Joyce's fullest epiphany. Everything in it means something and something more. The narrative is a constant challenge for the reader, a challenge more or less satisfied as one reads more or less of the book. By offering so many possibilities for reading, Joyce builds a provisional story into the text at almost every point. A reader can go in a number of directions with almost any sentence or paragraph. What might seem impenetrable about Joyce's prose is in another sense reader friendly. Interpretation is only limited by a failure of ingenuity or endurance, a "mutton leg's getting musclebound from being too pulled."

Finnegans Wake may well seem an outrage at the expense of a reader's indulgence, but Joyce had been heading in that direction ever since he recorded his fascination with the look and sound of words in *Portrait of the Artist*. And in *Ulysses* he had already experimented with material that would find so welcome a home in the *Wake*. In the Circe episode the hallucinated figure of Shakespeare appears and utters a phrase that really belongs in *Finnegans Wake*: "Iagogo! How my Oldfellow chokit his Thursdaymornun. Iagogogo!" The name Iago is Italian for James, so Shakespeare seems to address Joyce while explaining how his alter ego, Othello, chokes Desdemona. (Alternatively, "Iagogogo" is the sound of an Irish drunk throwing up on Thursday morning.) The various readings make sense within the wider context of the betrayal/adultery plots to which Joyce alludes in *Ulysses*, but what really matters is the notion of impacted reading that takes place in the Joycean phrase, a reading that is occasionally necessary in *Ulysses* and always necessary in *Finnegans Wake*.

Take as another instance the reference in the Ithaca episode of *Ulysses* to Leopold Bloom as a kind of archetypal wanderer, "Darkinbad the Brightdayler." All of literature's sustaining, revivifying impulses are contained in that collection of syllables, the dark in bed soon-to-be-rising sun. Joyce keeps recycling his plots into his renewable language, just as *Finnegans Wake* takes over from the day-night world of *Ulysses* and produces a night-day world, circling round in space as well as time when the last sentence of the book, and its last plaintive words about the flow of the Liffey into old father ocean, "a long the," trails into the opening sentence, "riverrun, past Eve and Adam's." Or there is another way to look at it. For a writer as obsessed with language as James Joyce, it is an understated tribute that "the" is the last creative word he ever wrote. The reader, who has worked so hard to comprehend Joyce's language, now gets the chance to supply whatever word he or she deems appropriate for sustaining Joyce's narrative experiment.

Michael Seidel

Selected Bibliography

Beckett, Samuel, et al. *Our Exagmination Round His Factification for Incamination of "Work in Progress"* Paris: Shakespeare and Co., 1929. Reprint 1974.

Ellmann, Richard. *James Joyce: New and Revised.* New York: Viking, 1982.

Gifford, Don, with Robert J. Seidman. *Notes for Joyce: An Annotation of James Joyce's Ulysses.* Rev. ed. Berkeley and Los Angeles: University of California Press, 1988.

Hart, Clive, and David Hayman. *Joyce's Ulysses: Critical Essays.* Berkeley and Los Angeles: University of California Press, 1974.

Herr, Cheryl. *Joyce's Anatomy of Culture.* Urbana and Chicago: University of Illinois Press, 1986.

Kenner, Hugh. *Joyce's Voices.* Berkeley and Los Angeles: University of California Press, 1978.

Maddox, Brenda. *Nora.* Boston: Houghton Mifflin, 1988.

Scott, Bonnie Kime. *Joyce and Feminism.* Bloomington: Indiana University Press, 1984.

Staley, Thomas. *An Annotated Critical Bibliography of James Joyce.* New York: St. Martin's Press, 1989.

Virginia Woolf

V IRGINIA WOOLF adopted two very different novelistic perspectives in the course of her career, and alternated irregularly
between them. In literary circles, she is most famous for the
experimental, lyrical style of the novels she produced in midcareer—
Jacob's Room (1922), *Mrs. Dalloway* (1925), *To the Lighthouse* (1927),
and *The Waves* (1931). The focus on external events in these works is
tightly controlled; instead of chronicling action and achievement,
Woolf trains her narrative attention on more evanescent shapes of
thought and feeling as they are distributed among a seemingly random
group of people. The second kind of novel Woolf produced seems, at
the outset, more conventional. In these novels—*The Voyage Out* (1915),
Night and Day (1917), *Orlando* (1928), and *The Years* (1937), for example—she tells a story; she draws her characters with sharp definition,
inviting us to see them from the outside, from the familiar novelistic
perspective of impossibly privileged observer. Interestingly, though, the
two kinds of novels are designed to address similar issues, if from opposite angles: Woolf's characteristic chord is her often-subtle insistence
on the falseness of "normalcy"; the unnatural restrictiveness of habit,
both social and verbal; and the slow asphyxiation of imaginative freedom in the closed room of a dominant, prescriptive tradition, whether
that tradition be propagated through family, school, or nation.

The presence of clear-cut plot and character, then, almost always
signals the reader to look critically at the social script that has limited
the characters being presented (or, in the case of *Orlando*, to appreciate
Orlando's Houdini-like ability to escape—through magicomical trans-

formations of time and gender—the stories in which he/she finds herself defined). Woolf's more traditional novels, although too imaginatively sympathetic to be satire, nevertheless work to expose the invisible "plot" of the past against the present, of convention against the free exercise of imagination and sensation. For example, what makes a novel like *The Voyage Out* quietly subversive is the unraveling of the usual marriage plot; Rachel and Terence are sharply suspicious of the institution of marriage that they have agreed to enter, to the point that they are described as most united when Rachel proposes that they break it off. When they receive congratulations on their engagement, Rachel dismisses the language of social correctness as "sheer nonsense" in contrast with that of "novels and plays and histories." And in place of the consummation of marriage that we expect to find at the end of the novel, we are presented instead with Rachel's sickness and death. Although the methods are those of realism, the novel's displacement of expectation—a "happy" marriage—by what actually happens—fatal illness—suggests a reading of marriage as a kind of death for intelligent but sheltered women.

Woolf is famous for her eloquently argued protests against the different and unequal ways that men and women were (and are) educated and socialized. Her essays are more unsettling for being powerfully reasoned, yet remarkably unscarred by bitterness (see especially *A Room of One's Own* and *Three Guineas*). These feminist essays are the natural counterpart to her more realistic, storied novels, as is nowhere more apparent than in an early draft of the 1880 section of *The Years* (edited and published by Mitchell A. Leaska as *The Pargiters*). Woolf originally envisioned *The Years* as an essay-novel, in which each chapter is introduced and followed by a sympathetic but uncompromising analysis of social impositions on the characters. *The Years* therefore began as a hybrid of literature and criticism, and as such it serves to illustrate the elsewhere implicit interdependence of Woolf's more plotted novels and her feminist writing: the plot that circumscribes and defines character, Woolf suggests, is never written by the author, but by the combined determinants of class, gender, and the historical moment. It is only the pressure of society on individuals that creates representative "types" such as the Pargiter family, but even when such types have been cast, their suppressed uniqueness throws a shadow.

Society deforms the individual by forming her, by dictating a shape and a narrative for her life and her thoughts, as is shown through the character of Kitty Malone in *The Pargiters* and *The Years*. Kitty, as the daughter of the master of St. Katharine's of Oxford, is someone whose yearnings after female companionship and the life of a farmer are never realized, subordinated to her hostess duties of pouring out tea for undergraduates, and later to her duties as the wife of a lord. Woolf's most revolutionary stroke in her portrayal of Kitty is neither to criticize nor to endorse Kitty's silent, occasionally fretful acquiescence to her "education." Woolf argues that women are taught to give "restful sympathy" to men, told that the "art of pleasing . . . consists in entire self-effacement," and denied free expression of their doubts or questions. The restrictions that "educate" women in the art of pleasing others also direct them to repress their own sexual and emotional passions as shameful. It is because women are socially controlled through shame that scorn or criticism of them is not a useful response, or conducive to social change.

If Woolf declines to shame women for assuming the roles designed for them, she is equally resistant to idealizing their sacrifice; for, as she stresses in *A Room of One's Own*, idealization and contempt are analogous ways of denying—and thereby stifling—the complexity of the real. In a speech she gave before the London Society for Women's Service in 1931, Woolf famously describes her determination to kill domestic ideals of womanhood—such as "the angel in the house"—in simple self-defense: "I turned upon that Angel and caught her by the throat. I did my best to kill her . . . [for] she would have killed me. . . . That woman—but she was not a woman she was an Angel—has more blood on her hands than all the murderers who have ever been hanged."

Woolf never loses her acute awareness that Angel and Bitch are caricatures, and she is determined to resist such reductiveness in her own writing. When she turns to her attention to men, therefore, she tries to imagine them as they see themselves, without surrendering her independence of judgment. Her alert but sympathetic identification leads her to argue that men, like women, are defended against passion, but their defense works differently, bringing them compensations for combating their desire that are not available to women.

The scene that best illustrates Woolf's theory that men produce culture as a defense against passion is one in which Edward Pargiter, in his rooms at Oxford, turns from a fitful reading of *Antigone* to a brief feeling of passion for Kitty. The sequence of events is carefully recorded: he drinks a glass of excellent port; reads the scene between Antigone and

Ismene; begins to feel sexual desire. Edward experiences his desire as degrading and resolves almost immediately to fight it, which he does by turning to a chorus in *Antigone* in which the two sisters have no part. His mind triumphs, and he transforms his vision of Antigone and Ismene into "an *ideal of womanhood* [italics mine] which moved Edward not to desire them, but to desire to produce something, to be something which their spirit, the spirit of all that was holy, & pure, & lovely and at the same time. Just & magnificent & serene & high . . . would bless & sanction & reward." He puts *Antigone* away and begins a highly derivative poem to Kitty as "Persephone" (he has recently discovered that Persephone is her middle name). He writes until he is overcome with disgust at his own imitativeness, then he shreds the paper and throws it away. (The version of this scene in *The Years* is much abbreviated.)

In her analysis of this scene, Woolf contends that young men are much more familiar with their feelings than young women; and that young men have learned from other males that love is dangerous, along with the best method of exorcising it. She points out that Edward is successful in producing "a different and less disturbing emotion—a generalized idealisation of sex," which also generates self-approval for having "conquered" his original feelings. She argues that "when the writer idealises his subject he almost always sentimentalises himself"; his love for her, born of ignorance, is inevitably narcissistic. Finally, Woolf highlights the peculiarity of Edward's feeling for Kitty, its difference from his feeling for his male friends, by pointing out that it is imaginary (he hardly knew Kitty). As telling as Woolf's arguments are, even more powerful are the things she does *not* say: that although Edward would become an expert on *Antigone* (in *The Years*, he gives a copy of his translation of it to his cousin Sara Pargiter), he seems completely unaware of the ironic appropriateness of such "expertise." Antigone, whom he admires as "fierce and daring," is punished for these qualities by being buried alive at the end of the play, and it is precisely the practice of burying women alive that Woolf herself seeks to expose. The subtle evocation of women's buried lives is reinforced by Edward's allusion to Kitty as Persephone, whose marriage to Pluto, god of Hades, condemns her to spend half of every year in hell. What Edward cannot see is that he, too, wants to kill the girl he professes to admire, first by idealizing her, and then by marrying—and effectively burying—her.

Woolf's essays in *The Pargiters* invite us to contrast two pictures: a picture of young men joining the "great fellowship . . . of men together," a fellowship promoted by five hundred years of male boarding schools; and an image of girls, isolated from the company of both sexes and kept in ignorance of culture. Both are programmed to repress their sexual feelings, but men learn to do so in a way that produces culture and self-approval, whereas women do so in silence, isolation, and shame. The heroes of the book are not the Edward Pargiters, men who understand the intricacies of ancient Greek grammar with little comprehension of the contemporary resonance of Antigone's tragedy, but men like Sam Brook and Dr. Joseph Wright, who, out of a profound respect for their mothers, formulate a "revolutionary" conception of marriage that demands no burial. Woolf quotes from Joseph Wright's proposal to Elizabeth Mary Lea:

There will never be a "lord and master" in our home. . . . I should lead a most unhappy, and I will say, a most miserable life . . . if you could, under any possible circumstances, ever become a mere Hausfrau. . . . It is my greatest ambition that you shall *live*, not merely exist; and live too in a way that not many women have lived before, if unlimited devotion and self-sacrifice on my part can do anything towards attaining that end. . . .

Women who must repress their own feelings in service to the feelings of others, whose sexual and intellectual responses are curbed by shame and ignorance, are circumscribed yet again by the code of silence. Shrouded in secrecy, sexual fear mutates into furtive guilt, as Woolf demonstrates through an abortive adventure of Rose Pargiter's when she is ten years old. Rose wants to go to Lamley's toy store one evening to buy a fleet of ducks and swans for her bath. She gets permission to go, on condition that she not go alone; however, neither Bobby (Martin in *The Years*) nor Nurse will go with her, so she decides to go alone. She pretends to be making an adventurous night ride through hostile territory, when a man suddenly emerges from under the gas lamp near the pillar box. She pretends to shoot him, but his face is so horrible it shatters her illusion. On the way back, the man is still there, illuminated, leaning against the pillar box as if he were ill, and no one else is in sight. "As she ran past him, he gibbered some nonsense at her, sucking his lips in and out; & began to undo his clothes. . . ." Later that night she is awakened by nightmares that he is in her room, but she cannot relieve her terror by telling anyone, partly out of guilt (she had disobeyed) and partly out of shame: "It was horrid, nasty, what she had seen. . . . He had undressed."

In the third essay of *The Pargiters* Woolf severely indicts society for its secretiveness about what she calls "street love, common love." Denial of the realities of abuse is ineffective as a protection against it; as Woolf points out, "children of Rose's age are frequently assaulted, and sometimes far more brutally than she was." Woolf suggests that Rose feels guilty when she sees the man because his face, working with outlawed desire, reflects similarly outlawed feelings in herself that she fears; her fear of herself coalesces with her fear of the man, and her inability to distinguish clearly between the two creates a clandestine and distorted bond between herself and the abuser. Woolf traces the root of the problem to "the instinct to turn away and hide the true nature of the experience, either because it is too complex to explain or because of the sense of guilt that seems to adhere to it," criticizing novelists, biographers, and autobiographers for having refused to treat the subject more openly. Woolf goes on to show how Rose's hidden shame and fear poison her subsequent relationships with men.

In the final version of *The Years* (1937), Woolf is much less explicit about the implications of what happens to members of the Pargiter family. As the years wheel by, Woolf brings the reader into the family at intervals, ending when most of the children are in their seventies. Major historical events take place in the distant background: the deaths of Charles Stuart Parnell and Edward VII, the rise of Nazi Germany. The First World War is the only event to erupt briefly into the foreground, during a bombing raid on London. Parents, husbands die in the intervals between chapters, without seriously disabling the established structure of family life.

What then is *The Years* about? This family novel, meandering unevenly over fifty-odd years, seems radically discontinuous with *The Waves* (1931), which preceded it. And in one sense, the discontinuity is real: in *The Waves*, we know only the voices of the characters, their innermost thoughts and desires, whereas in *The Years* we see the characters primarily from the outside. Our lengthy immersion in the characters' lives is designed to enlist our tolerance, even sympathy. It isn't until we reach the "present day" that the novel unmasks its more radical purpose: to criticize not individuals but what Martin earlier called the "abominable system" of family life, in which a group of different people are made to live, "boxed up together, telling lies." Indicted along with family life are the more superficial conventions of social inter-course, the construction of identity as fixed and knowable rather than mysterious and fluid, and the novelistic habit of categorizing people. At the family party that concludes the book, North Pargiter wonders, "What do [politicians] mean by Justice and Liberty? . . . Something's wrong, he thought; there's a gap, a dislocation, between the word and the reality. If they want to reform the world, he thought, why not begin there, at the centre, with themselves?"

The Years suggests throughout that if political and social reform is to be more than mere rhetoric, it must include a restructuring of the fam-ily, the self, and artistic representations of the self. As North wanders through the party, over which the magnified self-interest and grotesque homogenization of the Third Reich distantly broods, North contem-plates "the contamination of family life":

This [family life] is the conspiracy, he said to himself; this is the steam roller that smooths, obliterates; rounds into identity; rolls into balls. He listened. . . . *my* boy—*my* girl . . . they were saying. But they're not interested in other peo-ple's children, he observed. Only in their own; their own property; their own flesh and blood, which they would protect with the unsheathed claws of the primeval swamp. . . . How then can we be civilised, he asked himself?

The characters in *The Years* continue to look for traces of life beneath the tangle of roles dictated by habit and tradition. North Pargiter, straight from a farm in Africa, sees society as a jungle in which he is "provided only with broken sentences, single words, with which to break through the briarbush of human bodies, human wills and voices, that bent over him, blinding him." Still, he believes that underneath the forms imposed on humanity, there is the "sweet nut," "the fruit, the fountain that's in all of us." That fountain, bubbling up beneath overgrown institutions of family, society, and language, evokes the Dionysian energy and alienated potential of the unconscious. In a conversation with Nicholas after an air raid, Eleanor asks, "How can we improve ourselves . . . live more . . . live more naturally . . . better?" and Nicholas answers,

"It is only a question . . . of learning. The soul. . . . It wishes to expand; to adventure; to form—new combinations? . . . Whereas now,"—he drew himself together; put his feet together; he looked like an old lady who is afraid of mice—"this is how we live, screwed up into one hard little, tight little—knot? . . . Each is his own little cubicle; each with his own cross or holy books; each with his fire, his wife . . ."

Peggy, too, wants a less predictable, imaginable way of life; in a bitter moment she lashes out at her brother in the fear that his life will be yet another compromise softened by token compensations: " 'You'll write one little book, and then another little book,' she said viciously, 'instead of living . . . living differently, differently.' "

The problem, of course, is how to support the desire of those accustomed to the security of social roles to "live differently," to expand and form new and more vital combinations. That the old system of decorum is moribund, enervating, powerless to promote real knowledge or intimacy, is beyond question. North thinks with disgust of the discomfort caused by "this half knowing people, this half being known, this feeling of the eye on the flesh, like a fly crawling." A little later the same evening he extends his critique of social intercourse to narrative convention when he watches Sara leave the room without looking in the mirror.

From which we deduce the fact, he said to himself, as if he were writing a novel, that Miss Sara Pargiter has never attracted the love of men. Or had she? He did not know. These little snapshot pictures of people left much to be desired, these little surface pictures that one made, like a fly crawling over a face, and feeling, here's the nose, here's the brow.

After years of writing experimental novels in which she had avoided using "little snapshot pictures" that promote the illusion of knowledge, Woolf returned to this technique in *The Years* to underscore its falseness, its inadequacy. *The Years* ends on what might seem to be an impossibly hopeful note, with the dawn sky wearing "an air of extraordinary beauty, simplicity and peace," in tribute to people like Eleanor, who even after seventy years of service to others, has somehow preserved the "keen sensation" of life. The dawn is full of optimism that the human race, still in its infancy, might grow to maturity. This optimism, never very robust, would not last long after 1937; it was shortly to be displaced by the despair of *Between the Acts*, the outbreak of World War II, and Woolf's own suicide in 1941.

If Woolf's last two novels were shadowed by the imminence of World War II, the possibility of a Nazi occupation of Britain, and the extermination of difference, the experimental novels published from 1922 to 1932 were haunted by the memory of World War I, which fueled an early and accelerating determination to live and record experience "differently." Woolf had sustained devastating private losses—of parents and siblings—before the war, but the war so amplified the sense of random loss that in 1925 Woolf suggested her work be categorized as something other than novels—"elegy?" she proposed. Intellectually, Woolf expressed contempt for war as the violent extension of the homosocial bond formed in all-male schools (see *Three Guineas*). In her manuscript notes for a 1931 speech (reprinted as the appendix to *The Pargiters*), Woolf calls war "a stupid and violent and hateful and idiotic and trifling and ignoble and mean display." In her novels, Jacob Flanders, Septimus Warren Smith, and Andrew Ramsay are all destroyed, in different ways, by World War I. Woolf tends to represent the war only in terms of its effects; most famously, in the "Time Passes" section of *To the Lighthouse*, she treats the war as absence and decay. During the war years, she trains her narrative attention on an empty house on the Isle of Skye as it is shrouded in darkness and battered by the forces of nature. Similarly, in *Jacob's Room* the war is figured only by a few vague rumors, until it is abruptly epitomized on the very last page as the listlessness of an empty room, absently strewn with invitations and letters as if its owner might someday return.

The innovation of a book about Jacob's room is that Jacob himself remains elusive, undefined, or else unnaturally reified. What magnetizes the narrative is not so much a protagonist as a vacancy, an inscrutable sign, a monument, which Jacob is long before his death. Insofar as he can be said to become anything, Jacob becomes a Greek statue of a hero, growing ever more "statuesque, noble and eyeless," an inert monument to "the oppression of eternity." Seen another way, Jacob is nothing, a tin soldier "driven by an unseizable force," blindly taking orders from "men as smoothly sculptured as the impassive policeman at Ludgate Circus."

Vacillating between the heroically statuesque and the meaningless, between solidity and ephemerality, Jacob signifies the unknowable privacy around which life collects. For the reader, too, he is a cipher; as the narrator explains, "It is no use trying to sum people up. One must follow hints, not exactly what is said, nor yet entirely what is done." Reading people is an arduous, not a casual activity, and the narrator reminds us that most people we encounter are closed books, like strangers in an omnibus: "Each had his past shut in him like the leaves of a book known to him by heart; and his friends could only read the title, James Spalding, or Charles Budgeon, and the passengers going the opposite way could read nothing at all—save 'a man with a red moustache.' " Similarly, what we are allowed to see of Jacob is simply his shell, his immediate environment, touched by his past, activities, and tastes: his room. "What do we seek through millions of pages? Still hopefully turning the pages—oh, here is Jacob's room."

Jacob's Room is a hopeless book, full of the "sorrow . . . brewed by the earth itself." Its tone is edged with an irony uncharacteristic of Woolf's later works; it mocks the travesty of what passes for communication, intimacy, and knowledge of others, with a submerged anger, a frustrated expectation that subsequently disappears. We come to know very little of Jacob—his outlines, but not his feelings: we learn that he collected butterflies, that he was not his mother's favorite, that he went to Cambridge, that he took a six-day yacht trip with Timmy Durrant in which his Shakespeare was knocked overboard and sank. We know that he is awkward and beautiful, that he disapproves of bowdlerizing Wycherley and has said so in a rejected essay on the Ethics of Indecency. We see him with prostitutes and with Clara, the "virgin chained to a rock" whom he most honors. We stumble upon Jacob, in what the narrator dryly calls his "innocence," wanting an equal relationship, a "comradeship," between a man and a woman, "all spirited on her side, protective on his, yet equal on both, for women, thought Jacob, are just the same as men," and we witness his disappointment, his "violent reversion to male society," when he discovers that one woman's lovely face—Florinda's—is "horribly brainless." We see him idealize painters in Paris and fall in love with a married woman amid the dazzling ruins of Greece.

Despite the truth of such bits and pieces of Jacob's life, however, "there remains over something which can never be conveyed to a second person save by Jacob himself. Moreover, part of this is not Jacob but . . . the room; the market carts; the hour; the very moment of history." The narrator is agonized by the miscarriage of so many efforts aimed at "reaching, touching, penetrating the individual heart," but is nevertheless firm in the judgment that "all people are . . . lonely," that we never know anything but shadows:

It seems then that men and women are equally at fault. It seems that a profound, impartial, and absolutely just opinion of our fellow creatures is utterly unknown. Either we are men, or we are women. Either we are cold, or we are sentimental. Either we are young, or growing old. In any case life is but a procession of shadows, and God knows why it is that we embrace them so eagerly, and see them depart with such anguish, being shadows.

Woolf's conviction that oversimplification, spiced with idealization or contempt, is "the manner of our seeing" and "the condition of our love" is reflected also in the fragmented, disjointed style of the narrative in *Jacob's Room*. The style repeatedly obstructs our desire to shape Jacob's past and his personality into coherence; it parades characters through the foreground who have only the most coincidental and transitory relevance; it scatters our attention in a multitude of directions and interferes with our attempts to eavesdrop on Jacob's conversations or peer voyeuristically into his private rooms. As the narrator wryly comments, "the march that the mind keeps beneath the windows of others is queer enough." The narrative balks this readiness to intrude, to appropriate the unknowable, by removing us from the stage of action, depriving us of the context for an occasion, and estranging us from Jacob's perspective. When Jacob quarrels with Bonamy in an inn, we hear only unreliable remnants of the argument from Mrs. Papworth in the scullery, who even has his name wrong; she calls him "Sanders" instead of Flanders.

Mrs. Papworth is here a representation of the reader; her misunderstandings and prejudices caricature our own. Like Mrs. Papworth, we stand outside the "room" of another person; we can catch only phrases—some distorted—which we lightly invest with our own meanings. The narrator parodies our prudishness as well as our ignorance, as when Jacob takes Florinda into his bedroom and shuts the door. The narrative stays behind, fantastically, absurdly fixated on a sealed blue envelope from Jacob's mother that becomes her representative. She is depicted first as broken-hearted, then as outraged at the woman, and finally as revolted by "the obscene thing" behind the door. The narrator ridicules such prudery in a woman who has had three children, advising her (and through her the high-toned reader) that it would be "better, perhaps, [to] burst in and face it than sit in the antechamber listening to the little creak."

The tone of *Jacob's Room* ranges from gloom to parody, from sympathy to ridicule, and the narrative perspective, like the tone, also refuses to remain stable. The focus is continually displaced from the center (Jacob himself) to the periphery, the implication being that Jacob both is and is not to be found in the world around him. The narrator accuses us of looking for a "perfect globe," a whole, self-enclosed entity, whereas she sees life as a hum, as air "tremulous with breathing" and "elastic with filaments." Besides, as the narrator remarks when Jacob is nineteen, "Nobody sees any one as he is. . . . They see a whole—they see all sorts of things—they see themselves. . . ." At the end of the novel, Woolf leaves the reader not with a knowledge of Jacob but with a sharp realization of having missed him, he who pressed poppies between the pages of his Greek dictionary and is now, his name suggests, in Flanders field.

In Woolf's next novel, *Mrs. Dalloway* (1925), she again presents her characters as intertwined even with people they pass in the street, but the protagonists themselves are more alive to the shifting boundaries of identity. If Jacob's uniqueness is hard to discern beneath the cast of masculine confidence that makes his "heroism" unexpectedly ordinary, if Jacob's death is oddly continuous with his life as a living statue, *Mrs. Dalloway* takes as its touchstone not death, but life: Clarissa's party and Septimus's suicide are converging ways of expressing and defending a precious and vital balance between connection and isolation. Jacob's shape is overdetermined by his beauty, his education, his class, and his gender; only at brief moments do suggestions of originality assert themselves, such as in his outrage against censorship or his desire for an equal partnership between the sexes. Clarissa is also to some extent shaped by her class and sex, but Woolf draws our attention to the part of her sensibility that eludes labels, that revels in the abundant sensuality of the moment, enriched by traces of the past.

Mrs. Dalloway at first appears, like *Jacob's Room*, to be magnetized by a single figure—Clarissa Dalloway. Partway through the novel, however, it becomes apparent that Clarissa has a male double, Septimus Warren Smith, a World War I veteran—now a clerk—thirty years younger than she. This unlikely counterpart to an aging society woman is both opposite and identical to her: Septimus, too, sharply registers the intensity of life, which to him, after the shock of combat and the death of his commanding officer, is both terrifying and sublime. Even in his madness he recoils against the horror of killing ("men must not cut down trees"), and lashes out against the lie of civilized life ("the world itself is without meaning"). Septimus, in agonized skepticism, sees himself as a scapegoat, sacrificed for a social construct devoid of truth, along with the "many millions of young men called Smith" that London has swallowed before him, but he is also a visionary, muttering to himself, "Communication is health; communication is happiness." How meaningful communication—as opposed to propaganda—operates is the informing question of this book.

For unlike *Jacob's Room*, *Mrs. Dalloway* does not despair of communication; it simply redefines it as indirect, and only partially subject to individual control. Communication in *Mrs. Dalloway* is closely akin to coincidence; it is the process of bringing two unrelated things into brief proximity and then releasing them. This brush with the unknown, lit up by brief sparks of recognition, is one piece of a huge, indifferent pattern made up of many such pieces; the individual can never control the pattern, but can only participate in it or artistically replicate it by cultivating a receptiveness to the unknown undulled by habit. Alternatively, the individual can, like Septimus, dedicate himself to a passive resistance against the authoritarian forces that violate the privacy of the individual.

When Woolf discusses coercive forms of authority, disguised as duty to the empire, to God, to one's family or even a loved one, her narrative, sharpened by anger, slips into caricature. The royal motorcar with drawn blinds that speaks with a "pistol shot"; the envious Miss Kilman in her green mackintosh with a prayer book; Sir William Bradshaw and Dr. Holmes, who preach proportion in the name of health; and finally Love that demands change, accommodation, surrender in deceptively sugared tones—all are treated as "obscurely evil, . . . capable of some indescribable outrage—forcing your soul, that was it" (Clarissa's words describing Bradshaw). Woolf depicts compulsory patriotism, piety, health, and romanticism as all under the sway of two "goddesses," Proportion and her more formidable sister, Conversion, who narcissistically demand conformity. Conversion is said to conceal herself "under some plausible disguise; some venerable name; love, duty, self sacrifice," but her "lust is to override opposition, to stamp indelibly in the sanctuaries of others the image of herself." It is this hypocritical exercise of power behind a mask of concern that pushes Septimus to his reluctant suicide, his Pyrrhic attempt to preserve "a thing . . . that mattered."

Similarly, Clarissa defended herself against the invasiveness of love by refusing to marry Peter Walsh; "with Peter everything had to be shared; everything gone into," whereas she and Richard give each other "a little licence, a little independence." Clarissa is firm in her belief that "there is a dignity in people; a solitude; even between husband and wife a gulf; and that one must respect." Peter's signature, as a potentially invasive man, is the pocket knife he often toys with, whereas the love of women is different, contained: when Sally Seton kisses Clarissa, Clarissa likens it to a wrapped gift. "And she felt that she had been given a present, wrapped up, and told just to keep it, not to look at it—a diamond, something infinitely precious, wrapped up, which, as they walked . . . she uncovered, or the radiance burnt through."

Having been given this "diamond," this love, by Sally Seton years ago, Clarissa herself has become a diamond, a multifaceted radiance that she can artistically assemble to produce both "terror" and "ecstasy." Implicit in the image of the diamond is the privilege of class and wealth, and a certain cold hardness, but the diamond also figures Clarissa's ability to assemble multiple facets into a dazzling unity; she is herself a kind of party, made up of many parts. Her radiance comes not from youthful beauty or apparel, but from her refusal to sort and label, to say of others or herself, "I am this, I am that." Clarissa intuitively declines to force others into categories they may not fit, with a social politeness underwritten and authorized by the agonized isolation of the double who differs so markedly from her in class and gender.

What draws Clarissa and Septimus unexpectedly close, despite the fact that they have never seen each other, is their joint respect for individual privacy coupled with a joy in communication. For Septimus, a mad poet-prophet, written words best exemplify the balance between the interconnecting, sensual beauty of language and its elusive, potentially deceptive meaning. So tears run down Septimus's face at the exquisite beauty of smoke words he cannot decipher; he declares himself a prophet of beauty—"beauty, that was the truth now"—and at the same time asserts that "the world itself is without meaning," that "the message hidden in the beauty of words . . . is loathing, hatred, despair." For Clarissa the double valence of privacy and contact is expressed through her parties. Richard and Peter both criticize her parties, suggesting she gives them out of snobbishness, but she claims that "both were quite wrong. What she liked was simply life. 'That's what I do it for,' she said, speaking aloud, to life. . . . They're an offering." The narrator probes, "What did it mean to her, this thing she called life?" And she explains that she brings people together fortuitously, without obligation or pressure, metonymically expressing their continuity with one another:

Oh, it was very queer. Here was So-and-so in South Kensington; some one up in Bayswater, and somebody else, say, in Mayfair. And she felt quite continuously a sense of their existence; and she felt what a waste; and she felt what a pity; and she felt if only they could be brought together; so she did it. And it was an offering; to combine, to create; but to whom?

Although social decorum is not invasive, neither is it inherently vitalizing. Instead, vitality is generated and expressed through improvisation, experimentation, a variation or revision of inherited forms. Peter Walsh replenishes his excitement with life when, shaking off habit, he impulsively follows a woman in a fever of heightened perception and invention: "it was half made up, as he knew very well; invented, this escapade with the girl; made up, as one makes up the better part of life, he thought—making oneself up; making her up; creating an exquisite amusement, and something more." The "something more" that Peter produces is life. Peter never speaks to the woman; he recognizes the ephemerality of his construction, and when it ends he lets it go. What makes Peter's pursuit of the unknown woman different from Holmes's pursuit of Septimus (and from Peter's own earlier suit to Clarissa) is simply this willingness to let go—of the moment and of the woman, whose path he hasn't tried to change at all.

In order to fashion a book that balances the familiar with the unexpected, one that prompts its readers to gather grains of information that might, belatedly, flower into serendipitous meaning, Woolf narrows her temporal focus and prefers the principle of association and juxtaposition to the logic of cause and effect. Like Joyce's *Ulysses*, *Mrs. Dalloway* takes place on a single June day, in 1923 instead of 1904. Unlike *Ulysses*, however, in *Mrs. Dalloway* the narrator never peels away from the story in gleeful parodies, setting up independent exchanges with the reader; instead, the narrator passes from character to character, from place to place, gathering the pollen of feeling and sensation from many sources, leaving the reader, "like a bee with honey, laden with the moment." The method of shifting the narrative focus from character to character is compatible with Peter's view that a respect for privacy, for the unknowable, makes life (or books) like "an unknown garden, full of turns and corners, surprising, yes; really it took one's breath away, these moments." It is also a way of instantiating one of Clarissa's theories of identity, designed to explain "the feeling they had of dissatisfaction; not knowing people, not being known," the dissatisfaction so apparent in *Jacob's Room* and *The Years*. Clarissa's idea is that the boundaries of individual, autonomous existence are illusory; the individual is randomly distributed across a moment and a place, and might even survive unseen. While sitting on a bus going up Shaftesbury Avenue, Clarissa thinks that

she felt herself everywhere; not "here, here, here"; and she tapped the back of the seat; but everywhere. She waved her hand, going up Shaftesbury Avenue. She was all that. So that to know her, or any one, one must seek out the people who completed them; even the places. Odd affinities she had with people she had never spoken to, some woman in the street, some man behind a counter—even trees, or barns.

The organization of the novel proceeds along a "spider's thread of attachment" that almost invisibly interweaves people and things. After different bystanders have puzzled over the skywriting, the narrative skips—with apparent randomness—from the Smiths to Maisie Johnson to Mrs. Dempster. A closer examination shows that the narrative sews these women together to show how each is implicit in the others; each represents a different stage of married life for women. Lucrezia Smith, who married and left her home in Italy when she was nineteen, is feeling homesick and isolated when Maisie Johnson asks the Smiths for directions to Regent's Park tube station, and suddenly the perspective shifts to Maisie. Maisie, unmarried and fresh from Edinburgh, recoils from the couple's strangeness, and is seized by a spasm of homesickness that echoes Rezia's. She is nineteen, the age Rezia was when she left home to marry Septimus. Watching Maisie, though, is Mrs. Dempster, an older version of her who deplores Maisie's hopeful ignorance: "That girl . . . don't know a thing yet. . . . Get married, she thought, and then you'll know." She finds herself wanting to warn Maisie and receive from her a kiss of pity for the hardness of married life: "What hadn't she given to it? Roses; figure; her feet too. . . . But, she implored, pity. Pity, for the loss of roses."

Threads of similarity, perceived only by those attuned to the artistry of chance (and the chance of artistry), lead the reader through a series of glancing encounters between people. The beauty of such encounters, which both reveal and deny affinity, is epitomized by the old lady that Clarissa can sometimes see through her window. "Somehow one respected that—that old woman looking out of the window, quite unconscious that she was being watched. There was something solemn in it—but love and religion would destroy that, whatever it was, the privacy of the soul." That lady represents for Clarissa the miracle, the mystery of life: "And the supreme mystery . . . was simply this: here was one room; there another. Did religion solve that, or love?" Later, at the party, when Clarissa hears of the young man's suicide, she parts the curtains of an empty room and looks out: "How surprising!—in the room opposite the old lady stared straight at her! . . . She was going to bed, in the room opposite. It was fascinating to watch her, moving about, that old lady, crossing the room, coming to the window. Could she see her?"

The image of the woman looking straight at Clarissa as Clarissa watches her—neither sure that the other sees her—preserves a balance between recognition and the unknown, and it frees Clarissa to feel not one but two contradictory responses to Septimus's death. Previously, she felt only desolation for the waste, but now she feels exhilaration at his defiance as well, a reprieve from fear, and she feels "somehow very like . . . the young man who had killed himself. She felt glad that he had done it; thrown it away. . . . He made her feel the beauty; made her feel the fun." And she prepares to reassemble, to rejoin her other reflection, the party she has made.

In *Mrs. Dalloway*, by limiting time to the chronological march of a single day, Woolf was able to explore a delicate network of spatial interconnections, woven by circumstance across London. In *To the Lighthouse* (1927), she takes the opposite approach: space is the anchored term, and time—for ten years in the middle of the novel—floats free. The setting of the novel is the Ramsays' house in the Hebrides (based on Woolf's parents' seaside house in Cornwall) and the narrative lens is trained on that house in all three sections of the novel. The first section takes place on a single September evening, the third section on a September morning ten years later. The middle section, "Time Passes," skims through a decade unified only by the house's emptiness, as it falls to near ruin during World War I.

To the Lighthouse also differs from *Mrs. Dalloway* in the way it defines its unifying center. In *Mrs. Dalloway*, the center is held by character—Clarissa, shadowed by Septimus; in *To the Lighthouse* the center is both architectural and human, impersonal and autobiographical: on the one hand, it is the house, reflected and reinterpreted as the lighthouse, and on the other it is Mr. and Mrs. Ramsay, based on Woolf's own parents, who in turn represent the union—both magical and violent—of so many other extremes that polarize the novel: light and shadow; the boar's skull and the shawl that covers it; isolation and relationship; thought and feeling; logic and beauty; shipwreck and safety.

The lighthouse and the Ramsays represent what Lily tries to express in her painting: "that razor edge of balance between two opposite forces." Whereas in *Mrs. Dalloway* it is the man who kills himself, in *To the Lighthouse* it is the woman; but hers is not a defiant death. The manner of her death, like Septimus's, is gendered: like many wives and mothers, she slowly, prodigally, gives her life to others: "Giving, giving, giving, she had died." In contrast, Mr. Ramsay, with comic intensity, imaginatively assumes a range of male roles from the heroic to the absurd: he plays a soldier riding to slaughter in blind obedience to a wrong order (echoing Tennyson's "Charge of the Light Brigade"); the responsible leader of a doomed polar expedition; and a shipwrecked castaway who drowns in magnificent isolation (following Cowper's "The Castaway"). His odd "compound of severity and humour" is described as "strangely . . . venerable and laughable at one and the same time." Absorbed in ruin, he is nevertheless "happier, more hopeful on the whole" than his wife, "Less exposed to human worries."

With their eight children and six guests, the Ramsays' joint creation is the house they fill with life; their reflection is the lighthouse. Woolf's focus on the house grows logically out of her attention to the room in earlier novels: in *Jacob's Room*, the room is an emblem of Jacob's immediate environment, the only part of him that can be known with certainty; in *Mrs. Dalloway*, Clarissa's filled drawing room becomes an emblem of Clarissa herself, and Septimus's separation from his body is figured as a self-propelled push from the window of his room. In *To the Lighthouse*, the narrative lens widens to include many rooms as Woolf's attention turns from the structure of individual identity to the architecture of the family (her own) and the corridors of the past. Mr. and Mrs. Ramsay are fictionalized portraits of Woolf's own parents, Leslie and Julia Stephen, who had both been dead for over twenty years. Woolf's challenge in writing the book parallels Lily's in painting the Ramsays: "Such were some of the parts, but how to bring them together?"

Woolf assembles the parts with a double focus on the horror and power of family relationships, both marital and parental. She uses the two houses, the Ramsays' summer house and the lighthouse, to represent such relationships from opposite perspectives, one beautiful and distant, one ordinary and close. As Lily thinks near the end of the novel, "so much depends . . . upon distance; whether people are near us or far from us, for her feeling for Mr. Ramsay changed as he sailed further and further across the bay." The long-delayed trip to the lighthouse reverses the customary perspective: James and Cam see up close what they formerly saw only from a distance. Until they were sixteen and seventeen, James and Cam had been unable to see their parents realistically; they were only ideal objects of love and hate, respectively. When they finally close the distance between themselves and the "silvery, misty-looking tower with a yellow eye," when they see the fabled lighthouse at close range, with its whitewashed rocks, its stark tower, and its windows, James realizes that the lighthouse is not one but both things, the near and the far, the ordinary and the symbolic. He achieves the fragile balance that Lily is able to capture, simultaneously, in her painting: "One wanted . . . to be on a level with ordinary experience, to feel simply that's a chair, that's a table, and yet at the same time, It's a miracle, it's an ecstasy."

The parallel between summer house and lighthouse is subtly established in the novel's first section. The guests and children return in the gathering twilight to the Ramsays' house for a celebratory dinner of boeuf en daube, and the house fills with lights: "The house was all lit up, . . . and [Paul Rayley] said to himself, childishly, as he walked up the drive, Lights, lights, lights, and repeated in a dazed way, Lights, lights, lights." The house has become, literally, a light house, filled with life and promise. But at the beginning of "Time Passes," "one by one the lamps were all extinguished" and "a downpouring of immense darkness began." The darkened house is stroked only by the rhythmical, blind eye of the lighthouse; the lighthouse, with its connotations of beauty, ruin, and distance, has supplanted its more familiar double.

The Ramsays, too, change with distance. Seen close up, Mr. and Mrs. Ramsay are both, in different ways, domineering: Mr. Ramsay slices through James's feelings with his uncompromising insistence on truth; he demands sympathy from his wife; he is tyrannical to his children. Mrs. Ramsay is equally willful and commanding, largely in her insistence that women must marry; she engineers the ill-fated engagement of Paul Rayley and Minta Doyle and would like for Lily to marry William Bankes. Marriage and family life are similarly grotesque when magnified by close contact: marriage is figured as loss (when Minta agrees to marry Paul, she simultaneously loses something valuable, represented by the loss of her brooch), and family life is a "horror" that makes privacy impossible. Regarded closely, human relations are painfully inadequate: "The most perfect was flawed" and "the worst . . . were between men and women." Men are sharply intrusive and women weak; both are driven by unconscious vanity, although the vanity takes opposite forms of egotism and self-sacrifice. Most horrifyingly, Victorian marriage stipulates that each partner be radically incomplete, so that balance is only achieved through a relation of mutual dependence that the younger people abhor.

As James thinks, however, "nothing [is] simply one thing," and Woolf's hardest challenge, like Lily's, is to represent the beauty of a relationship she would never want to emulate. Again like Lily, Woolf can only do this from a distance (both spatial and temporal), by depicting the Ramsays' compound identity in its austere, most private form as the lighthouse. As an image both phallic and vatic, a beacon of safety and beauty, it captures in symbolic form the mystery and utility of the Ramsays' model of marriage. The narrative underscores Mr. Ramsay's similarity to the lighthouse when it stresses his intensity of mind, his lonely vigilance, his blind determination:

It was his fate . . . to come out thus on a spit of land which the sea is slowly eating away, and there to stand, like a desolate sea-bird, alone. It was his power, his gift, suddenly to shed all superfluities, . . . to stand on his little ledge facing the dark of human ignorance. . . . He kept even in that desolation a vigilance which spared no phantom and luxuriated in no vision.

Mrs. Ramsay compares him to "a stake driven into the bed of a channel" that takes upon itself the duty of "marking the channel out there in the floods alone." In the third section, Cam reluctantly recognizes her father's resemblance to the monumental lighthouse, with its repeated, even mechanical, transmissions of warning against death and disaster.

The sublime beauty of Mrs. Ramsay is best expressed not by the tower or the rock but by the stroke of light alternating with the triangular wedge of darkness between strokes. She describes the experience of solitude as a sensation of shrinking, "with a sense of solemnity, to being oneself, a wedge-shaped core of darkness, something invisible to others." What Mrs. Ramsay believes to be invisible to others is apparent to Lily, since since it is as a triangular shadow that Lily paints Mrs. Ramsay. Mrs. Ramsay also identifies herself with the lighthouse beam—the third stroke: watching the strokes

in this mood always at this hour one could not help attaching oneself to one thing especially of the things one saw, and this thing, the long steady stroke, was her stroke. . . . She became the thing she looked at—that light. For example. . . . She looked up over her knitting and met the third stroke and it seemed to her like her own eyes meeting her own eyes, searching as she alone could search into her mind and her heart, purifying out of existence that lie, any lie. She praised heself in praising that light, without vanity, for she was stern, she was searching, she was beautiful like that light.

The light represents her as a stare, and also a star; it expresses "the sternness at the heart of her beauty," a distant luminosity (the German word for "star" is *stern*). She thinks of the steady light as pitiless and remorseless, "so much her, yet so little her"; yet it has brought her exquisite happiness, "stroking with its silver fingers some sealed vessel in her brain whose bursting would flood her with delight," till she exclaims, "It is enough!"

When the expedition to the lighthouse is finally completed, both the Ramsays and Lily experience the rhythmic alternation between near and far, light and shadow, ideal and real, simultaneously. When she draws a line down the center of her painting, completing it, Lily both connects and separates Mr. and Mrs. Ramsay at the same time as she links them to and severs them from herself. With some anger and much love, she is able to see the Victorian past, shattered by the war, as both crippling and entrancing, and she is finally able to put its beauty and tyranny, with her painting, away.

To the Lighthouse relies primarily on metaphors of art and architecture to illustrate and contain the past; the past is a house and a picture, a blurred image to be recalled and exorcised. Woolf's next serious experimental novel, *The Waves* (1931), focuses not on the past but on the present, and relies not on images but on voices. Furthermore, her analysis of identity is even more fragmented: instead of isolating two protagonists who reflect and complete each other, she features six characters who collectively make up and disrupt a compound identity. As one might expect from the use of voice and soliloquy, the arts that Woolf draws upon and critically reshapes are those of drama and especially narrative. For it is in *The Waves* that she launches her most sustained attack against stories.

If the novel is defined as an interweaving of stories, then *The Waves* is not a novel. In the second draft of *The Waves*, Woolf wrote, "The author would be glad if the following pages were read not as a novel." (In her diary entry of February 19, 1928, she wrote: "I doubt that I shall ever write another novel after O. I shall invent a new name for them.") The alternating voices that make up *The Waves* not only fail to constitute a story; they deny the very presuppositions upon which stories are built—that our experience of life is logical, consecutive; that characters are autonomous, unique, and therefore susceptible of characterization; that the best language is a full, rounded encapsulation of life. Instead, the "characters" in *The Waves* are not fully separate, either from one another, from parts of the landscape they have inhabited, or from odd moments in history. Each voice is both a fragment and a microcosmic composite of its world, seen in a momentary light, from a particular perspective, in a transitory mood.

Although the six main characters seem to take turns speaking, their monologues are far from realistic; they say things that aren't typically verbalized, especially in the first person. When Jinny wins a game, she says, "I must throw myself on the ground and pant. I am out of breath with running, with triumph." Woolf has attributed the "speech" of the body, its triumphant panting, to Jinny's consciousness; at other moments, it is the unconscious that speaks through the six characters, or the seasons, or the dead. By giving voice to all kinds of normally silent influences, Woolf underscores the "lie" of "common" language; here, the characters' representations of experience ring significantly false, not because they *are* false, but because we are not accustomed to think in the present moment, or to register consciously in language the range of feelings and connections that the voices of *The Waves* repeatedly articulate. The voices of the book say too much, which in turn exposes "realistic" representation as radically oversimplified. (As Rhoda asks, "What is the thing that lies beneath the semblance of the thing?"). Woolf suggests that what we need to replace the story, with its artificial, thin line of logically connected, consecutive events, is a way of registering the moment's overload, its abundance, its waste, as well as a new, more dynamically multiple conception of being and a more halting, imperfect language.

The Waves unfolds in nine parts, each of which is introduced by a brief description of a single scene of waves breaking against a shore. On the beach is a spike of sea-holly, the ribs of an eaten-out boat, a rusty cartwheel, a white bone, and a black boot without laces half mired in sand; a white house and garden with bird-laden trees stand nearby. The book begins in spring, just before dawn breaks over the waves, and it ends with waves of autumn darkness engulfing houses, hills, trees, streets, and girls. The waves are sometimes erotic—a girl's jeweled waves of hair as she lifts a lamp from a green mattress—sometimes hostile: turbaned black warriors throwing javelins at the sand. But their most important function is rhythmic and symbolic; they represent the contradictory unity of physical nature that continues only through rhythmic ruptures, like those of day, the seasons, and human life.

The structure of *The Waves* falls into two unequal parts: sections one through eight, after the initial description of the waves that begins each section, are all composed of monologues or brief dialogues in the present tense; everything is "current." The focus of individual sections varies, but the general movement is chronological, from childhood to school, college, and the departure and death of a mutual friend, Percival, whose fall from a horse in India marks the progressive erosion of the friends' youth. The second part of the book is the last section, entirely narrated by Bernard, who begins the "story" of their lives all over again, telling it more conventionally in the narrative past tense to an unknown interlocutor with whom he is having dinner. For readers who were disoriented by the immediacy and apparent disconnectedness of the book's first part, Bernard's monologue will come as a relief, but along with belated clarity he delivers a warning: he is the storyteller, but the stories he tells aren't true. The one new piece of information we get in Bernard's section—that Rhoda has committed suicide—is dropped almost in passing; it comes as a shock, but lacks the immediacy, the vividness with which Rhoda herself describes her yearning to jump off a precipice in Spain. Described from the outside, in retrospect, things are not the same; narrative needs, instead, the immediacy and personal utterances of drama without its deceptively tight, distanced, consecutive structure.

The characters in *The Waves* have an agonized awareness of the radical incompleteness of individuals, an incompleteness enclosed in separate, isolated bodies that can sometimes briefly be assembled. As Bernard, when trying to recount his life, explains, "it is not one life that I look back upon; I am not one person; I am many people; I do not altogether know who I am—Jinny, Susan, Neville, Rhoda, or Louis: or how to distinguish my life from theirs." At moments when the six come together, as at the dinner with Percival or later at Hampton Court, they can see "for a moment laid out among us the body of the complete human being whom we have failed to be, but at the same time, cannot forget" at the same time that they feel "the huge blackness of what is outside us, of what we are not." The six friends themselves come to resemble waves that rise together and break apart in a succession of current moments, flowing and ebbing with time. Their lives "stream away, down the unlighted avenue, past the strip of time, unidentified," yet at other moments they are represented not as water, but as people whom the flood of time will drown: "How can we do battle against this flood; what has permanence?" Woolf periodically dissolves her characters not only into one another, but also into the atomic chaos of the physical world where only the energies of life and death are constant.

The characters relate to one another with a changing calculus of resemblance. Jinny is a flame, living in and through the body, unattached to any one person; she does not dream. Rhoda, in contrast, feels that she has no body, and no face; she is purely a dreamer. Her element is water; for her all moments are violent, separate—her fear is that nothing persists. Society breaks her into pieces; she hates the details of individual life and yearns after geometrical abstractions and images of statues with no features. She longs for "alcoves of silence where we can shelter under the wing of beauty from truth." Susan opposes Rhoda in her solidity and hardness; the only fragility she admits is that of her children, represented as eggshells held between her knees. Hers is the realm of nature; she thinks sometimes, "I am not a woman, but the light that falls on this gate, on this ground. I am the seasons . . . ; the mud, the mist, the dawn." What differentiates Susan from Jinny's more erotic physicality is her rootedness, her fertility, her attachment to one person and one place. "Debased and hide-bound by the bestial and beautiful passion of maternity," she sees life as "a dwelling place made from time immemorial after an hereditary pattern."

Susan's single-minded attachment is differently reflected in Neville, who always seeks out "one person, always one person to sit beside." Neville—sharp, impatient, scholarly—is a changing person driven by an unchanging desire for Percival (who loved Susan) and an awareness of the "unchanging obstacle" of death. He has a passion for order that to some extent resembles Louis's. Like Louis, Neville feels alien—Louis because of his Australian accent and his commercial father, Neville because of his homosexuality. Louis is angry, resistant, anxious to "amalgamate discrepancies"; acutely conscious of exclusion and oppression, he once smashed a closed door with his naked fist, and he always hears the chained beast stamping. Like Rhoda, he feels young and vulnerable, but like Bernard he finds imaginative freedom in alternative selves. Bernard lives in the people he sees, but Louis, when he puts off "this unenviable body" in the darkness, lives multiply in history: "I am then Virgil's companion, and Plato's"; "I find relics of myself in the sand that women made thousands of years ago."

Woolf's compound portrait of the author is a blend of Rhoda and Bernard, who, like Clarissa and Septimus in *Mrs. Dalloway*, are both counterparts and opposites. Like Rhoda, Bernard has no self, but whereas she is lacerated by social contact, he cannot bear solitude; he needs the stimulus of other people for his stories. Whereas Rhoda hates detail, pursuing ideal form, Bernard proclaims, "I require the concrete in everything." Bernard is always making stories, creating consecutive series of events, but Rhoda's fear is that one moment does *not* lead to another. Rhoda desires to elude representation, Bernard to extend it indefinitely. As a storyteller, a phrasemaker, he lies, but he also tells us that he lies, cueing us to do what he does when he's alone: to take upon ourselves the mystery of things. As he rounds his perfect phrases, he rejects their fluency, confessing a longing "for some little language such as lovers use, broken words, inarticulate words, like the shuffling of feet on the pavement." When he tries to find a phrase for the moon, or love, or death, he repeats: "I need a little language . . . , words of one syllable such as children speak when they come into the room and find their mother sewing and pick up some scrap of bright wool, a feather, or a shred of chintz. I need a howl; a cry." Once, when he saw "through the thick leaves of habit," he realized that life was "imperfect, an unfinished phrase."

Life, as Woolf presents it, is a flow without end ("If there are no stories, what end can there be, or what beginning?"). To express the flow, Woolf sometimes uses images of waves and sometimes flowers: a lily (for Percival), a red carnation (for the six who sit around the dinner table with Percival), a rose (for Rhoda, whose name comes from the Greek word for rose). In those three flowers are the three major emphases of *The Waves*—death, the flesh (*carnation* is related to *carnationem*, meaning "fleshliness" or "corpulence"), and a transcendence that may be simply another word for death. All of these characters battle with boredom, with habit: "Was there no sword, nothing with which to batter down these walls, this protection, this begetting of children and living behind curtains, and becoming daily more involved and committed, with books and pictures?" And in this battle, this effort to see a fin (which is also a *fin*, or end) break the waste of waters, Louis burns his life out; Rhoda flies past to the desert; Neville chooses one out of millions; Susan loves and hates the heat of the sun; Jinny becomes an honest animal; and Bernard fights death.

Bernard thinks, "Life is not susceptible perhaps to the treatment we give it when we try to tell it." In *The Waves*, Woolf tries to give life a different treatment—more immediate, less consecutive, more alive to the shifting identities and differences between people and things, more respectful of feeling, incompleteness, imperfection. To read this kind of flow, to see these changing shapes, which do not round themselves into a story but more closely resemble a poem, Bernard advises us to multiply our perspectives (like Lily in *To the Lighthouse*, who says, "One wanted fifty pairs of eyes to see with"). He describes a more active and flexible method of reading the poem of life, which is also *The Waves*:

Certainly, one cannot read this poem without effort. The page is often corrupt and mud-stained, and torn and stuck together with faded leaves, with scraps of verbena or geranium. To read this poem one must have myriad eyes. . . . One must put aside antipathies and jealousies and not interrupt. One must have patience and infinite care and let the light sound . . . unfold too. Nothing is to be rejected in fear or horror. The poet who has written this page . . . has withdrawn. . . . Much is sheer nonsense. One must be sceptical, but throw caution to the winds and when the door opens accept absolutely. Also sometimes weep; also cut away ruthlessly . . . hard accretions of all sorts. And so . . . let down one's net deeper and deeper and gently draw in and bring to the surface what he said and she said and make poetry.

Woolf's final novels cope successively with the weight of the past, its drag on narrative, plot, and character. After *The Waves* was completed in 1931, Woolf again exhumed the past in *The Years*, treating it in the more conventional terms of the historical novel. In her last novel, *Between the Acts* (1941), she evokes the past yet again, through a village pageant that represents history as perfectly congruous with the hopeless present and a violent future. The pageant takes place on a June Sunday in 1939, with the events in Europe rumbling in the background: Germany had invaded Czechoslovakia in March of that year and in May had signed a full military alliance with Italy. The League of Nations, designed to prevent another world war, was dissolving, and in only three months Great Britain would declare war on Germany. Woolf, however, decides not to put war at the forefront of history; in the pageant, Miss LaTrobe doesn't even mention the British army, to the consternation of some members of the audience. Instead, her emphasis is on what falls *between* the actions, as well as on what falls between the acts of Miss LaTrobe's pageant of English history: as in *To the Lighthouse*, Woolf's attention falls on "the marriage plot." Here, however,

Woolf implicitly links global aggressiveness with violence against, neglect of, and lust for women; both the public and private spheres reel back into the beast. Barriers "which should divide Man the Master from the Brute were dissolved."

Between the Acts is perhaps the most despairing of Woolf's books, completed shortly before her own suicide. It begins with a discussion about a cesspool, and it ends with a reversion to primeval darkness in which "the house had lost its shelter," and in which Isa and Giles will fight and embrace, "as the dog fox fights with the vixen, in the heart of darkness, in the fields of night." The accumulated burden of the past weighs heavy; the present isn't enough, because of "the future, disturbing our present." "The future shadowed their present . . . ; a criss-cross of lines making no pattern." As William Dodge tells Isa, with "the doom of sudden death hanging over us . . . there's no retreating or advancing."

During the pageant, members of the audience mention dictators and Jewish refugees. Twelve aeroplanes fly overhead during the last scene. Giles, the "sulky hero," chafes with suppressed anger over the guns bristling in Europe and the band of men recently shot and imprisoned. He responds to the threat with a need to act, through violence or lust. He bloodies his shoes by stamping on a snake choking with a toad in its mouth, and finds relief in the action. Part of Mrs. Manresa's appeal for him is that she, too, as a "wild child of nature," makes him feel "less of an audience, more of an actor."

In sharp contrast to Giles, his wife Isa responds to a different, smaller "war." Whereas he reads about the shooting of sixteen men across the gulf in the newspaper, she reads about soldiers who drag a woman up to a "barrack room where she was thrown upon a bed. Then one of the troopers removed part of her clothing, and she screamed and hit him about the face." The echoes of this article follow her throughout the day. She is haunted by the desperation of domesticity: "She loathed the domestic, the possessive; the maternal." Her relations with her husband are strained; he adheres to a double standard, arguing that his infidelity makes no difference but hers does. Like Mr. Ramsay, he demands his wife's admiration, but unlike Mrs. Ramsay, Isa resists him. Isa, however, pays a price for her silent resistance; she wanders about, poisoned by the arrows of ambivalence—love and hate—for her husband, and yearning for death. She comes to resemble the silent lady (not an ancestor) pictured in the dining room, as well as the lady who was said to have drowned herself for love in the lily pond. The poems she quotes are clearly suicidal—Keats's "Ode to a Nightingale" and a melodic wish "that the waters should cover me . . . of the wishing well." Her fatal thoughts about marriage are further exposed in a rhyme about time that she composes to the rhythm of "tinker, tailor, soldier, sailor": "This year, last year, next year, never."

As in *The Waves*, in *Between the Acts* Woolf represents the author through two different characters, Isa and Miss LaTrobe. Isa writes "abortive" poetry she hides from her husband, and Miss LaTrobe writes village pageants to be staged and forgotten. It is not surprising, then, that her representation of history, like Isa's reading of the news, stresses the tyranny of love: her scenes are all about betrothals or abandonments. In the Elizabethan period, the prince is reunited with his beloved, and Isa repeats ambiguously, "It was enough. Enough. Enough." During the Age of Reason Flavinda elopes with Valentine, but Lady Harpy Harraden is left with no one, having been demoted from Aurora Borealis to a tar barrel. The Victorian Age centers around a proposal of marriage followed by a sentimental rendition of "Home Sweet Home." Mrs. Lynn Jones muses, "Was there . . . something . . . 'unhygienic' about the home? Like a bit of meat gone sour, with whiskers, as the servants called it? Or why had it perished?" Miss LaTrobe ("Whatshername"), the lesbian outcast, has presented a revisionary view of history, but the audience, although vaguely unsettled, has only partly understood the implied critique.

The link between Giles's suppressed anger and Isa's lyrical despair, like the link between the pageant and the impending war—LaTrobe's representation of the past and shadowy omens of a violent future—is the British Empire itself. As Budge the publican proclaims, dressed as a Victorian policeman, emblem of British authority: *"I take under my protection and direction the purity and security of all Her Majesty's minions; in all parts of her dominions; insist that they obey the laws of God and Man."* He describes the empire's interference in Ireland or Peru, adding, *"But mark you, our rule don't end there. It's a Christian country, our Empire; under the White Queen Victoria. Over thought and religion; drink; dress; manners; marriage too, I wield my truncheon. . . . That's the price of Empire; that's the white man's burden."*

Both Giles and Isa feel the "intolerable burden" of sitting passively, doing nothing, forced to watch the unchanging parade of domestic history. Giles feels as if he were "manacled to a rock" and "forced passively to behold indescribable horror." Later, Giles, William, and Isa all silently confess their unhappiness: "They were all caught and caged; prisoners; watching a spectacle." The repetition of history, like the repetition of flat fields, is "senseless, hideous, stupefying." LaTrobe's effort to make her audience see reaches its climax when she has the actors flash mirrors at the audience in her staging of the present time, and a voice from a megaphone amplifies the call for a more realistic consideration of ourselves. The voice tells us not to presume there's *"innocency in childhood,"* or *"faith in love,"* or *"virtue in those that have grown white hairs. Consider the gun slayers, bomb droppers here or there. They do openly what we do slyly. . . . O we're all the same."*

The history we admire, Woolf suggests, is all plot, and it's all the same. Isa asks herself, "Did the plot matter? . . . The plot was only there to beget emotion. There were only two emotions: love; and hate. There was no need to puzzle out the plot." Later, as night falls, her impatience with the sameness and divisiveness of love and hate returns as she thinks of her husband, " 'whom I love and hate.' Love and hate—how they tore her asunder! Surely it was time someone invented a new plot, or that the author came out from the bushes." So ends the present, with its bellows of dumb yearning, and its shower of tears. Isa, like Woolf herself, murmurs, "O that our human pain could here have ending!" and again, taking care not to move her lips, "O that my life could here have ending." To end the former was out of Woolf's power.

Vicki Mahaffey

Selected Bibliography

Abel, Elizabeth. *Virginia Woolf and the Fictions of Psychoanalysis.* Chicago: University of Chicago Press, 1989.

Bell, Quentin. *Virginia Woolf: A Biography.* New York: Harcourt Brace Jovanovich, 1972.

Bowlby, Rachel. *Virginia Woolf: Feminist Destinations.* New York: Blackwell, 1988.

DeSalvo, Louise. *Virginia Woolf: The Impact of Childhood Sexual Abuse on Her Life and Work.* Boston: Beacon, 1989.

Ferrar, Daniel. *Virginia Woolf and the Madness of Language.* Trans. Geoffrey Bennington and Rachel Bowlby. London: Routledge, 1990.

Gordon, Lyndall. *Virginia Woolf: A Writer's Life.* New York: Norton, 1984.

Marcus, Jane. *Virginia Woolf and the Languages of Patriarchy*. Bloomington: Indiana University Press, 1987.

Woolf, Virginia. *The Diary of Virginia Woolf*. Ed. Anne Oliver Bell, assisted by Andrew McNeillie. 5 vols. New York: Harcourt Brace Jovanovich, 1976–1984.

Woolf, Virginia. *The Waves: The Two Holograph Drafts*. Transcribed and edited by J. W. Graham. London: Hogarth, 1976.

Zwerdling, Alex. *Virginia Woolf and the Real World*. Berkeley: University of California Press, 1986.

Forster, Ford, and the New Novel of Manners

I T is a commonplace that the novel is a historical document, the product of its era, and this is nowhere truer than with the novel of manners. Registering the impact of society on the individual, this genre functions as both a record and a critique, represented by a long line of authors from Samuel Richardson to Anita Brookner. Any progression in the politics of the form is less clear, since some novelists of manners support the old decorum while others decry it as constrictive. To further complicate the issue, the revolts of one generation tend to become the conventions of the next. The most acute novelists of manners are inside the social framework to the point where they can render its tiniest nuances, yet also outside convention and therefore able to achieve sufficient perspective.

These authors often do not fit neatly into literary movements, as inheritors of one group and predecessors to another. E. M. Forster and Ford Madox Ford belong here, Edwardian in sympathy but modernist in their tendencies. Their peculiar centrality is a result of their situation on the fringe of a variety of movements, and though this placement has tended at times to marginalize their achievements, they have left an indelible mark on the British novel. Forster's brand of social irony, mixing muddle and grace, has become a literary hallmark, while Ford's impressionism, subordinating facts to the overall feel of the narrative, has been admired by writers from Ezra Pound to Graham Greene.

The cultural views of these two authors are an odd mixture stemming from their placement in time. The Edwardian era was an intermediate stage, an odd mingling of conservatism under Edward VII and slowly building reforms. Forster is often associated with the Blooms-bury Group but counts as an observer as much as a participator. Ford associated more with Pound & Co. but considered himself an overseer rather than an exact contemporary. As Forster wrote, "I belong to the fag-end of Victorian liberalism," and Ford, like his protagonist Christopher Tietjens, considered himself the last Tory in England. The resultant novels are forward-looking yet nostalgic, advocating social and political changes while yearning for an earlier, more abundant age. They are, in several senses of the term, transitional works.

At Cambridge during the 1890s, Forster was lured by the democracy of ideas while confronting the social reality of divisions based on class, money, and sex. Under the guiding spirit of G. E. Moore and others, secular ethics filled the gap left by a decaying moralism. The Cam-bridge group called the Apostles sought to elevate the secular, private soul in place of waning religion, in a move similar to American tran-scendentalism. In fact, like his protagonist Rickie Elliot in *The Longest Journey*, Forster in his early stories displays a fascination with a spiritu-al immanence that borders on pantheism. In the company of such fig-ures as E. M. Trevelyan, Goldsworthy Lowes Dickinson, and Bertrand Russell, Forster developed a liberal humanist philosophy that was to color all his works. The term itself shows a push-pull contrariety inso-far as *liberal* advocates a group program while *humanist* emphasizes the importance of the individual. Yet Forster's clear, essayistic style is even-handed, Hegelian in its active consideration of causes, proceeding toward some *Aufhebung* above mere manners and morals. His thesis anticipates that of Freud in *Civilization and Its Discontents*, in which individuals give up psychic freedom for the material benefits of society.

Forster's first published novel, *Where Angels Fear to Tread*, came out in 1905, four years after the end of the Victorian era and one year before the liberals took power in Parliament. In the tradition of the novel of manners, it is concerned with social structure and the restrictions of propriety. But it is also a paean to friendship and the improvement of the soul, and for a novel of manners it begins unpropitiously with a breach of etiquette and possibly of good sense. Lilia Herriton, a young widow, takes leave of her husband's protective family to travel to Italy and cannot help laughing at the assemblage that waves good-bye. Her trip to Italy itself is deemed ill advised by most of the group, who consider it neglect of her role as a widow and mother. (Forster's sexual politics are suffragist—for all sexualities.) In Monteriano, Lilia falls under the same romantic spell that once charmed Philip Herriton, her brother-in-law. The difference is that she falls in love with a young Italian named Gino and, in the kind of narrative truncation typical of early Forster, soon marries, gives birth, and dies.

The remainder of the novel focuses on Philip and his attempts to wrest control from Gino, first to dissuade Lilia from marriage (Philip is too late), later to rescue the baby from the father (Philip is misguided). In fact, as Forster wrote to Trevelyan, the novel is about "the improvement of Philip," with the public sphere yielding to the inner life, the conventional to the unpredictable, and the intellect to an aesthetic and emotional appreciation of truth in beauty. Victorians would label this kind of movement hedonistic. At the end of the novel, the baby dies as a result of Philip's sister Harriet's clumsy maneuvers. The consolation is that, through the ennobled suffering of the father, Philip and Lilia's original chaperone Miss Abbott learns to love Gino.

The novel is not romantic in the raw sentimental sense, and certainly not stuffy in a Victorian way. Of Lilia's house in Monteriano, Forster notes: "It was impossible to praise it as beautiful, but it was also impossible to damn it as quaint." Here is Forster's balanced aesthetic perception, determinedly fair-minded, yet gently puncturing pretension. In many ways his views resemble those of Jane Austen, balanced between the strictures of eighteenth-century neoclassicism and the freer rein of Romanticism. Forster, at a similar periphery between Victorianism and modernism, responds with a similar irony—irony in its most complex sense, the capability of holding two opposed views simultaneously.

Social breaches (and hoped-for connections) are the materials of Forster's fiction. Marriage versus love, and male versus female are just two of the dialectical oppositions pursued by both the characters and Forster as general commentator. His figures chafe under restrictive sexual roles, and his own homosexuality placed him at the edge of a social divide that he was forever trying to bridge. The title of the novel, taken from Pope's "Fools rush in where angels fear to tread," suggests a dichotomy between the foolish and the enlightened that merges only near the end. Only those willing to risk a loss of dignity can ever perceive the wholeness of existence.

Forster's way with character is through a sort of complex synecdoche, putting forth certain characters as representative types, yet retaining some individuality of character to rescue them from flatness. He does the same with place, summing up the theatre in Monteriano: "There is something majestic about the bad taste of Italy." England and Italy, represented by Sawston and Monteriano, also come across as two poles of life, dull respectability versus irresponsible romanticism, but there is a crossover in Philip, even if he cannot yet see the effect in himself. As Forster comments somewhat Austentatiously: "For our vanity is such that we hold our own characters immutable, and we are slow to acknowledge that they have changed, even for the better." By the end of the novel, Philip is able to say, "Gino is not ashamed of inconsistency. It is one of the many things I like him for." Miss Abbott concurs, and the two become friends. A gentle echo of Emerson's "A foolish consistency is the hobgoblin of little minds" runs throughout the work.

In *The Longest Journey*, published two years later, Forster expanded upon his humanist dialectic. Though at times a bit strained and didactic, the novel is Forster's most autobiographical and shows what Cambridge can and cannot do for a man. Hegel, Berkeley, Emerson, Samuel Butler, and Edward Carpenter are all influences on the mind of the protagonist Rickie Elliot. The rest is a matter of heredity (what Rickie brings to Cambridge) and experience (what he encounters when he leaves). The structure may be described as a novel of manners rescued by rudeness, with the height of learning at the start and the apogee of experience at the end.

Through Rickie, Forster strikes out against the social conventions that dictate a monogamy of the spirit. The novel's title is from Shelley's "Epipsychidion," in which "the longest journey" represents one's life when one is attached to only one other soul, and the rest are condemned to oblivion. The dedication, "*Fratribus*," is meant in an almost Lawrentian sense, a wished-for community of kindred male souls, with a homoerotic wistfulness that escapes authorial repression in only a few of Forster's short stories and *Maurice*. In a larger context, the hope is for a sympathetic society of the kind envisioned in Galsworthy's 1910 novel *Fraternity*, with a new spirituality to fill the religious void.

The Longest Journey opens with a group of Cambridge undergraduates debating a Berkeleyan uncertainty, à la G. E. Moore: whether objects have any independent existence outside those who observe them. Significantly, Rickie, though a member of the group, does not speak. He is not the clever type, and in any event he prefers to look out the window at reality. As he thinks after a talk with his philosophical friend Ansell, "They dealt with so much and they had experienced so little." Ansell's picture of the world is similar to what he draws repeatedly on paper: a series of circles inscribed within squares within circles ad infinitum, somewhat like the designs of Conrad's blessed idiot Stevie Verloc in *The Secret Agent* (published the same year). The difference is that Stevie's scrawls are a hopeless tangle of concentric circles, whereas Ansell's geometry is Hegelian, the sort of balance after which Forster strives and which Rickie tries to put into practice.

Yet experience is not the romantic proving ground of an earlier generation; rather, it continually reinforces the outsider status of Rickie, with his club foot, his sexual inadequacy, and his merely average mind. The hereditary conditions of Rickie's life are reminiscent of Ernest Pontifex in Butler's *Way of All Flesh* (a copy of which Forster inserts in *A Room with a View*). Given a morality divorced from the old religious concerns, Rickie must nonetheless make satisfactory sense of his society, and perhaps achieve some spiritual plane in a secular age. The problem with religion is that it pays insufficient attention to friendship, and scants love in favor of Love. As Forster remarks in a neat inversion: "Will it really profit us if we save our souls and lose the whole world?"

The opposite tendency is equally dangerous, in light of the modernist tendency of things to fragment and divide. Divisions are evident from the start: the emotional against the overly intellectual, the physical against the spiritual, and the sacred against the profane. The flat characters in Forster's pantheon represent half of a duality, as with Gerald Dawes, who is all body and no soul, or Herbert Pembroke, who never allows his emotions to carry him anywhere. Rickie and his half brother, Stephen Wonham, together present a study in the effects of heredity versus environment. Rickie remains mannerly, weak, and repressed, while Stephen is described as "a man dowered with coarse kindliness and rustic strength, a kind of cynical ploughboy." Like Gino in *Where Angels Fear to Tread*, Stephen is a type of naïf whom Forster shows at different angles in other novels: the yeoman farmers in *Howards End* who produced Leonard Bast, or the Italian cab driver seated with his lover in *A Room with a View*. Like Lawrence's Brangwens, they are rooted to the earth, hence the importance of landscape as character in all of Forster's fiction. The novel of manners postulates that the individual is a product of society, but Forster also notes, in a Hardyesque sense, that people are part of the land.

And so Rickie travels to Cadover to meet his aunt Emily Failing, but the grandeur of Salisbury and the Cadbury Rings mocks him. Society has hemmed him in; his marriage to Agnes Pembroke is loveless and a block to his continuing friendship with Ansell. He continues to write his pantheistic short stories but is unable to live any of them. The figures of Pan and Hermes referred to throughout the novel emphasize the subtle misrule Forster offers as an antidote. The essays of Rickie's late uncle Anthony Eustace Failing, based loosely on those of Edward Carpenter, suggest the social root of the problem: "Very notable was his distinction between coarseness and vulgarity (coarseness, revealing something; vulgarity, concealing something)." For Forster the revisionist in manners, true propriety is not a withholding, and for all his dichotomies Forster, like Hegel, aims toward a transcendent synthesis. In a splice of modernism and mannerism, Forster pursues the numinous found in the casual and the quotidian. His character Mr. Failing allies nonsense and beauty, and adds, "Attain the practical through the impractical. There is no other road."

Rickie himself eventually works out some of these connections on his own, despite his teaching post at a boys' school in Sawston that is a paradigm of all that is stunted and cut off, an updated, sex-changed version of Charlotte Brontë's Lowood. As Forster approvingly notes of Rickie, "He valued emotion—not for itself, but because it is the only final path to intimacy." Perhaps for this reason Rickie tries to save Stephen's life, though he dies of the attempt and feels, at the last, that his life has been a failure. But Forster is more optimistic: Rickie's stories are finally published posthumously to some success, and Stephen Wonham has a daughter to carry on their mother's name. Posterity is the property of the dead, but salvation may be bequeathed to the next generation.

Though published in 1908, *A Room with a View* was begun in 1903, thus antedating Forster's other novels. In it, Forster uses his favorite trick of exposing English manners by taking his characters abroad. Like Lilia Herriton and her chaperone Caroline Abbott in *Where Angels Fear to Tread*, Lucy Honeychurch is touring Italy with her caretaking relative Charlotte Bartlett, staying in one pension after another, along with a predictable guest list of elderly women, vacationing clergymen, and fellow travelers. Herein is a perfect proving ground for the flat characters that Forster describes in his *Aspects of the Novel*: if they are truly flat and conventional, they will not respond to the foreign environment but will act the same as at home. The progress of the novel traces Lucy's rounding-out through a Forsterian spiritual awakening: an awareness of what real affection is and a discarding of pretentious cant. It is about views and what obstructs them; it is *Pride and Prejudice* with a transcendental twist.

If the social grouping at the Pension Bertolini is a microcosm of British culture—the elderly Misses Alans, the Reverend Arthur Beebe, the "clever" novelist Miss Lavish—George Emerson and his father represent the force of the unconventional, with a lack of gentility made up for in a sincerity that verges on bluntness. Like Mr. Failing in *The Longest Journey*, Mr. Emerson and his pronouncements cut to the heart of things. When Lucy complains that their rooms have no view, for example, Mr. Emerson and his son simply offer to switch with them, an offer at first refused because it seems so unmannerly. But moving into George's room is the first symbolic step in adopting his views, signified in part by "an enormous note of interrogation" pinned above the washstand. Like George, Lucy will come to question the society in which she moves. Her character note is: "I do so always hope that people will be nice." George's statement is, "I shall want to live," but the two credos, with a little modification, are not so far apart as they seem.

The love interest in the novel, as in most of Forster, is divided into the artificial and the all-embracing. Cecil Vyse, who rates a brief reference in *Howards End*, is that novel-of-manners specialty, the Wrong Man. The extra spin Forster puts on his character is that Cecil is sensitive and aesthetic, despising the dull conventionality of Windy Corner, Lucy's home in Surrey. As Forster describes him, "he resembled those fastidious saints who guard the portals of a French cathedral." In a dig at the overly aesthetic Ruskin, continued in *Howards End*, Forster deprecates Cecil for his Gothic coldness, Forster himself opting for a livelier Hellenism. But he also accuses Cecil of "a certain devil whom the modern world knows as self-consciousness," a necessary precondition for awareness but in the end destroying spontaneity.

In contrast, George Emerson is all that Cecil is not: open, considerate if ill-considered at times, and above all impulsive in a way that Cecil can never be. Soon after Lucy returns from Italy, the Emersons move into a vacant house in Windy Corner, and Lucy is stirred to rethink her position vis-à-vis the two. In Forster's fiction, the actions of characters represent the working out of values, and so at times he is almost peremptory with them, remarking of Lucy: "She loved Cecil; George made her nervous; will the reader explain to her that the phrases should have been reversed?" Forster's well-known muddle is at work here, conflating social norms with personal aims, confusing apparent comfort with desire.

Like Philip Herriton, Lucy has had her view enlarged by Italy. But she is also blocked by the respectable Charlotte, who lives a repressed life and stands "brown against the view" when George kisses Lucy. Back in England, Lucy associates Cecil with a room and no view at all. George, on the other hand, is associated with a view of trees and sky, and the subtle pantheistic misrule that Forster advocates in *The Longest Journey*. It is best represented here in a nude male swimming scene that combines elements of a Hellenic celebration of the body with a rueful recognition of its transiency. More enduring, as Mr. Emerson points out, is truth. Combined with love, it achieves a mystical power, what Forster calls "the holiness of direct desire." It is with this feeling that Lucy breaks from propriety to go off with George.

For Forster, freedom exists on many emotional levels. In general, he preaches friendship and understanding rather than fiery passion. As George insists, liking one person is an extra reason for liking another. Moreover, even the most seemingly fixed characters have unsuspected depths, which is why it is possible for Philip Herriton to make friends with Miss Abbott at the end, or for George and Lucy to discover a core of decency in Charlotte, who enabled their marriage by causing Mr. Emerson to persuade Lucy. George divides the world into two classes: "those who forget views and those who remember them." The new couple has so clearly remembered the view from Italy that they return to the same spot for their honeymoon. In having his characters escape social constraints by departing, however, Forster evades a basic question: whether one can enjoy life whole and unfettered in contemporary England.

Howards End (1910) is an attempt to answer this question, as well as to address a series of related issues. The schisms of British society in the novel make up a whole catalog: aesthetics versus business, prose versus passion, inner life versus outer life, male versus female, body versus soul, city versus country, class versus class, past versus present, life versus death, and so on. Given these rifts, Forster's epigraph, "Only connect . . . ," seems almost wishful thinking. As Trilling remarked fifty years ago, the novel can be summed up as a question: Who shall inherit England?

Forster engages the problem humanistically, using the aesthetic Schlegels and the businesslike Wilcoxes to work out the difficulties. His dialectic is not entirely balanced—nothing can mask his greater appreciation for the cultured souls of this world—but he attempts a merge rather than a battle. And, no matter which side he is dealing with, he is never merely dismissive. When Helen Schlegel, who places all her faith in the spirituality of culture, parts company with her sister Margaret over Margaret's decision to marry Mr. Wilcox, Forster objects. Neither side, he insists, has a monopoly on the truth; nor is the Schlegels' Aunt Juley even right in asserting a middle ground: "No, the truth, being alive, was not halfway between anything. It was only to be found by continuous excursions into either realm, and though proportion is the final secret, to espouse it at the outset is to ensure sterility." Once again, the engine that Forster uses to cut through the divisions of British culture is a species of Hegelian dialectic, but transferred from the realm of philosophy to society.

The Schlegels are the highbrow representatives of culture, with a mixed German-English parentage. They keep up with the arts and social issues: they attend concerts of Beethoven in Queen's Hall; they participate in discussion groups about socialism. If they have a fault, it is that they are often impractical. Helen, for example, is convinced of the superiority of the inner life to the exclusion of hard facts, while Tibby retreats to the shelter of books. Only Margaret, a close persona for Forster himself, is aware enough to realize that Britain owes a lot to what F. R. Leavis contemptuously referred to as the "short-haired executive type." Henry Wilcox, whom she eventually marries, has grit, even if he also embodies double standards for class, race, and gender.

The Wilcoxes, for their part, are insensitive and hypocritical in their treatment of people. Their values are bigness and wealth, exactly the imperial directives that the Schlegels' father hoped to escape by leaving Germany. When Helen falls briefly in love with the youngest Wilcox son Paul, she finds herself in a world of telegrams and anger, a wall of newspapers behind which she can find little of real substance. The Wilcoxes display a civil contempt for those classes below them, they patronize women, and they pursue the fortunes of the empire with the zeal of jingoists.

This gulf between the Schlegels and the Wilcoxes is carved out by many of the social schisms that Forster bemoans. The goal, as he continually reminds the reader through a line from the Matthew Arnold sonnet "To a Friend," is to see life steadily and see it whole. Henry Wilcox, with his motto of "Concentrate," goes at life with steady intensity, while Margaret Schlegel can perceive the wholeness of life and the connections across the gulf, but usually cannot summon up the force of Henry's drive. As Margaret thinks: "Only connect the prose and the passion, and both will be exalted, and human love will be seen at its height. Live in fragments no longer." But she has little success with her new husband, who simply does not notice what she does.

Forster complicates the social dialectic by including a figure at the periphery of respectability, Leonard Bast. An otherwise anonymous clerk, Leonard pursues culture in the hopes of improving himself, while living a squalid existence in a stuffy flat with his fiancée Jacky. His attempts to read Ruskin's *Stones of Venice* are as laudable as they are poignant, since he lacks the cushion of money that allows one to forget about material comforts in favor of culture. He is, in fact, an emerging type of the era, the countrymen's sons described by Ford Madox Ford in *The Soul of London*. By synecdoche, Leonard is the growing class of urban laborers filling up London, some of whom Forster himself taught at the Working Men's College. Eventually, Leonard becomes the victim in the war between the Wilcoxes and the Schlegels and dies, ironically, beneath a shower of books.

Though Forster in his earlier novels used Italy as a liberating contrast to the repression of England, here he brings in Germany as a more complex counterpoint. The Germans in *Howards End* are both more brutishly determined and more aesthetically attuned than the British— and both sides have empires that seem destined to clash. In light of the date, 1910, Forster's novel sounds a real alarm, though far milder than in the war-scare literature of the period. It is worth noting that Forster, despite his stance against restraint, always remains mannerly, never raising his voice in his prose. He argues clearly, sensitively, and intelligently, hoping for the best.

Nonetheless, above the dialectic is a numinous force, found in Ruth Wilcox and her home, Howards End. Though she intrigues Margaret, she does not fit in well with Margaret's luncheon set, the Delightful People, a forerunner of the Bloomsbury Group. When Mrs. Wilcox dies and leaves her house, Howards End, to Margaret, her family chooses to disregard her will. Yet her presence broods over the novel. Forster uses most of his characters as arguments through representational synecdoche, but the grace associated with Mrs. Wilcox is connected by a topos, making her literally a grounded figure, with a memorial wych elm rooted in the earth by her home. When Margaret visits Howards End, the uncanny, in Freud a combination of the strange and the familiar, takes hold of her. The land and its spiritual wholeness, Forster suggests, are her roots, more important than any social phenomenon. Miss Avery, a farm woman at Howards End who seems more an immanent presence than another stock figure, is in a sense a solution to the fragmentation of modernism, a return to the pastoral tradition that comes about when Mr. Wilcox's world collapses around him.

The end is somewhat forced, perhaps because Forster is reaching for the kind of visionary closures achieved in the novels of D. H. Lawrence and Virginia Woolf, while the rest of the novel is so firmly established by the logic of character and circumstance. Through a union with Leonard Bast, Helen has a baby, and the assemblage at Howards End therefore represents a mix of upper and lower classes, business and artistic interests, urban and yeoman types, the old and the hope for the future. At the same time, Forster is too honest to ignore the "red rust" of growing cosmopolitanism: it is perceptible even from the fields of the countryside. As Helen notes grimly, "Life's going to be melted down, all over the world." The old social order wavers between rebirth and apocalypse.

These darker intimations cast a longer shadow in *A Passage to India*, published in 1924 after a long blockage and, for all intents and purposes, Forster's last novel. The Great War does not enter into it, a conscious decision on Forster's part to deal with the era he knew best, along with its ills. Here, the imperialist theme developed in *Howards End* becomes the overarching frame of the work, expanding the novel of manners into a novel of cross-cultural relations. Yet, as in the style of another practitioner in this area, Graham Greene, Forster's pervasive irony undercuts the very generalities built on the particulars he observes.

A Passage to India starts out as a picturesque novel, with a travelogue commentary on Chandrapore not unlike the Baedeker descriptions in Forster's Italian novels. For Forster, as always, character inheres in landscape, and both the geography and personality of India are divorced from the Western world. The Indian doctor Aziz and the British headmaster Fielding are the two principal characters, acting out the question argued by the Indians at the start of the novel: whether it is possi-

ble to be friends with an Englishman. The two cultures have pronounced differences, paralleling the *Howards End* distinction between
business-minded and aesthetic types. Aziz claims that money is nothing; Fielding repeats the adage "A penny saved is a penny earned." The
British are ruthlessly efficient or at least act that way; the Indians are
more spiritual, or at least they pretend to be above mere time. As Aziz's
uncle Hamidullah more accurately notes: "We can't keep engagements,
we can't catch trains." These contarieties make for the celebrated
Forsterian muddle, where different manners make for unintended
slights.

Forster, who spent more time in India than in Germany and Italy
combined, speaks comprehendingly of the animosities felt by both parties, but the Anglo-Indians come across mostly as bullies and prigs,
while the Indians are mostly put upon. A novel of manners is, after all,
generally a novel of types, partly so that the social statements are applicable to whole classes, but also because social restrictions tend to restrain
character. In fact, these restrictions derive not just from the difference
in societies but also from the imposition of one culture on another. The
colonial mentality encouraged by imperialism is deadly to the tolerance
that Forster holds as one of the cardinal modern virtues.

The plot proceeds by a series of meetings, which serve as points of
either synthesis or disjunction. The British magistrate Ronnie Heaslop
and his betrothed, Adela Quested, form the love interest, though Adela
eventually breaks off the relationship when she realizes what his character is really like—or how imperialism has ruined it. Ronnie stands at
the end of a long line of Forsterian bullies, here exposed against the
background of India. His mother Mrs. Moore, on the other hand, has
the same kind of mystical presence that Mrs. Wilcox has in *Howards
End*, and when she and Aziz meet in the mosque, they feel a rapport
that cannot be put into words. Similarly, when Aziz whacks a polo ball
back and forth with a British subaltern, he feels a companionship that
is real, if transitory.

Far more often, however, the two groups fail to connect. The Collector Turton's bridge party, supposedly an attempt to bridge the two cultures, is a failure. Fielding's get-together is not markedly better, though
he is certainly more tolerant than the established Anglo-Indians. His
growing friendship with Aziz is most satisfying in moments rather than
over time, as if the social fabric can be pierced in small spots, briefly and
unexpectedly, before inalterable convention reweaves the flaw. Even

within the same culture, as Forster also shows in his earlier novels, the barriers to understanding are formidable. In India, for example, caste, gender, and religion all frustrate cooperation within the society. Perhaps for this reason Aziz's attempts at a poem includes the idea "The song of the future must transcend creed," though the poem never gets written, and the only effect it has is to push him toward nationalism.

In no previous novel are Forster's ironies so defeating. When Aziz rips off his collar stud to lend to Fielding, who is missing his, the Anglo-Indians comment crassly on Aziz's untidy appearance. After Aziz rhetorically invites Adela and Mrs. Moore on an outing, they discommode him by accepting his invitation, though neither side particularly wants to go. Aziz's generosity is paid for with a wrongful accusation of molesting Adela in the Marabar Caves, and when the subaltern who played polo with Aziz hears of this, he wishes that more Indians were like his anonymous polo partner. Words do not imply what they mean, events are distorted by faulty recall, and appearances become reality with frightening speed.

If Forster has a claim to modernism, it is in his complex character dialectic and his inversions of the conventional. But the systemic irony in *A Passage to India*, undercutting all attempts at rational discourse, is a step beyond, into the depths of postmodernism. The same techniques hold, but the faith underlying them is gone. The most harrowing symbol of this altered view is the Marabar Caves, which mock all attempts at understanding with their nihilistic echo: "Hope, politeness, the blowing of a nose, the squeak of a boot, all produce 'boum.' Even the striking of a match starts a little worm coiling, which is too small to complete a circle but is eternally watchful." The onomatopoeia of an explosion levels all to zero without the wholeness of an *O*. The reference to the little worm evokes an image of the serpent Orborus with its tail in its mouth, the symbol of eternity, but diminished and without the completion of the circle.

Forster was often upset by the effects of modernism, from an unwholesome technological progress to schisms of creed and conscience. But the modernists' arguments for a reordering of society appealed to Forster in part, even if he wished to invert some of the underlying philsophy. The lesson of the Marabar Caves is of another order entirely. As the echo seems to murmur to Mrs. Moore: "Everything exists, nothing has value." It addles Mrs. Moore and makes Adela hallucinate. Historically, it is a precursor to European nihilism.

In the end, order is restored, but to little avail. Adela recants her rape story in the courtroom, but Aziz still feels humiliated, transferring his animosity from one British woman to Western imperialism in general. When Aziz and Fielding meet again, no real reconciliation is possible. The numinous force embodied in the late Mrs. Moore comes across as only a feeble echo in her simple-minded second son Ralph. And though Aziz and Fielding attempt to be friends again, something frustrates the effort: the temples, the palace, the birds, the earth itself "said in their hundred voices, 'No, not yet,' and the sky said, 'No, not there.' " The disunities are simply—or complexly—too great for liberal humanism to bridge. Hope may lie in the future or beyond this earth altogether.

Forster's last novel is really his second-to-last, *Maurice* (1971), whose composition and publication dates are separated by a distance of almost sixty years. The explicitly homosexual references are one reason Forster chose to suppress it in his lifetime, though the existence of the novel was an open secret after his final revisions in 1960. Another reason for the delay may have been his doubts about the quality of the work. The very barriers that made Forster such an acute social critic also prevented him from depicting anything but a sublimated homoerotic love in his other novels. When he describes what his friend Edward Carpenter called the tribe of Uranus, he loses some of his double-edged vision, perceiving only social forces of repression. The hero, Maurice Hall, is an erotic outlaw, and as Lasker Jones, one of the doctors he consults, tells him, "England has always been disinclined to accept human behavior."

Yet Forster never loses hold of his complex vision of love, an individual bond worth more to him than any social link. As Maurice tells the gamekeeper Alec (a figure who anticipates Lawrence's Mellors by two years), he dreams of a lifelong friend. The affection that so easily springs up between Alec and Maurice cuts across the bounds of class, convention, and character. Perhaps Forster's only misstep is in depicting such an idealized love as possible. Still, if this seems a betrayal of the Forsterian urge to get at the truth, it stems from the same throwback pastoral that concludes *Howards End*. As he writes in his "Terminal Note": "A happy ending was imperative"—and the plot suffers from this predetermination. Alec and Maurice presumably fade into a sylvan glade, the same woods in which Rickie Elliot located Pan and his satyrs.

As Forster noted in 1960, the novel seems dated not just because of the old references but also because "it belongs to an England where it was still possible to get lost." The last paragraph in the "Terminal Note" acknowledges ruefully that the public's ignorance and terror of homosexuality has merely been replaced by openness and contempt. This last Forsterian qualification, this keen sum-up of the ways of society, is as perceptive as it is sad.

To move from Forster to Ford is not as great a shift as it might seem. Both authors were consummate observers of their society, with the same sensitivity for scenting hypocrisy disguised as manners. Raised as a Hueffer with the Rossettis as cousins, Ford Madox Ford had to be either precocious or a failure. He was eighteen when his first book came out, a fairy tale called *The Brown Owl*, and in fact many of his novels retain a certain fairy-tale aspect. Even when his characters are trapped in modern society, there is a sense that a repeal may be possible, if only in the private dispensations of the mind.

From his early collaboration with Conrad (*The Inheritors*, *Romance*), he learned the modernist technique of combining impressionism and symbolism: the exact particulars of a scene merged with a looser, shadowy resonance. In Ford, the details are crucial not because they aspire to factual accuracy but because of what they suggest. Like Forster, he became an elder dean to the modernists, a movement that rarely respected its elders. He had, for want of a better term, true literary acumen, even if, also like Forster, he occasionally preached better than he practiced.

Ford's thirty-two novels are too various to group under one rubric and too uneven in quality to merit full discussion. The best that can be said of his first novel, *The Shifting of the Fire*, is Conrad's pronouncement: "delightfully young." Ford's first salient effort is *The Fifth Queen*, a trilogy of historical novels about Henry VIII's fifth wife Katharine Howard and the labyrinthine intrigue surrounding the court. As Roland Barthes observes in *S/Z*, the historical novel is a bricolage, the difficulty being to get the exact size of history within the fictional structure. Ford accomplishes this feat through social nuance and detail, creating a sixteenth-century novel of manners by seemingly reconstructing the entire context. The arcane vocabulary and immersion in period details rival the accomplishments of T. H. White.

The story of *The Fifth Queen* belongs to Katharine Howard, a forerunner of the controversial polymath Valentine Wannop in *Parade's End*. Her future husband represents the triumph of the Renaissance over the medieval, though his Lord Privy Seal Thomas Cromwell conspires for a return to the old order. The forces of evil and good are themselves somewhat confused, with characters such as the pedagogue Nicholas Udall and the spy Throckmorton as Dickensian figures of expediency. When Katharine makes a classical allusion to the Lacedaemions, Henry admonishes: "those were the days of a black and white world; now we are all grey or piebald." In the end, the king sends Katharine to her death, but he cannot be certain of her infidelity.

Ford himself keenly felt the changing of the old order. The Edwardian era, with its uncertain status of tradition and change, often resulted in what Forster termed muddle. The coming of modernism also signaled a new renaissance with the classical directives of Pound and T. S. Eliot, but somehow the odor of sanctity had departed. The modernists used memory to synthesize bits of past and present; Ford, whose recall was prodigious, invoked entire eras. In *Ladies Whose Bright Eyes*, a transhistorical romance, the publisher Sorrell accidentally returns to the fourteenth century in the kind of scenario made famous by Mark Twain. But whereas Twain's Connecticut Yankee brings the miracles of progress, Sorrell becomes more and more enamored of the old ways. It is an anti-Wellsian message akin to Forster's: our best hope for a future lies in our deep past. Unfortunately, Ford does not give Sorrell sufficient weight of character to make his views compelling. Ford's other attempts at historical novels, such as the earlier *"Half Moon"* or the later *A Little Less than Gods*, were unsuccessful for more or less the same reason: lack of psychological complexity.

Like Forster, Ford for a time was an author of unfulfilled potential. Only at age forty did he sit down to write what John Rodker once termed "the finest French novel in the English language." *The Good Soldier*, published in 1915, is a work of astonishing complexity, derived from Ford's impressions of prewar international society. It is a novel of manners and manors, told in such detail that it is hard to reconcile with the epistemological uncertainty underneath. Subtitled *A Tale of Passion*, it manages to reveal everything and nothing about a four- or five- or six-cornered affair of the heart.

The American protagonist John Dowell is ruefully articulate about his marriage to Florence and their almost coincidental relationship with the British Ashburnhams. As he says at the start: "My wife and I knew Captain and Mrs. Ashburnham as well as it was possible to know anybody, and yet, in another sense, we knew nothing at all about them. This is, I believe, a state of affairs only possible with English people." This aspect of the English tallies with Forster's estimate in *Abinger Harvest*: "well-developed bodies, fairly developed minds, and undeveloped hearts." Edward Ashburnham is an upper-class landowner, his wife Leonora a respectable Irish Catholic. Yet as the plot develops—or rather follows the convolutions of Dowell's recall—one learns that Ashburnham has had a series of affairs, that Florence had a few secrets of her own, and that Leonora has had the battle of her life keeping her marriage and the estate from falling apart. Dowell himself seems bloodless, though he talks of emotion, and calmly recollective, though his memory plays tricks on him. He is an unreliable narrator in a story with no other signposts to guide one, save the disjunctive irony of teller versus tale.

The connecting metaphor of the novel is the heart: Ashburnham has a weak heart and also wears his heart on his sleeve, Florence supposedly suffers from a bad heart but really acts in bad faith, while Leonora and Dowell both act "the sedulous strained nurse" to their spouses. A few of Ashburnham's women also have weak hearts: not just a physical debility, but an inability to control the passion just below the surface. The social fabric is such that it supports such lives while exposing nothing, and there is a great deal to be exposed. Ashburnham is the perfect British gentleman, lord of the manor with a military background and a history of sexual liaisons. Florence is of proper New England stock, but she has pursued an affair with a seedy type named Jimmy that she is at great pains to suppress. Dowell and Florence are part of the American expatriate set detailed by Henry James, and in fact the psychological intrigues set up are quite Jamesian.

But Ford is describing a less stable world than James's. As Dowell recalls the episodes and characters, he continually amends and revises. Ashburnham is a good sort, then an embarrassment to his name; Florence is a poor dear invalid, then a cunning manipulator of everyone around her. The metaphor of the heart turns out to be a symbol for unknown depths, and Dowell's continual response is a narratorial shrug. As he confesses early on:

I don't know. And there is nothing to guide us. And if everything is so nebulous about a matter so elementary as the morals of sex, what is there to guide us in the more subtle morality of all other personal contacts, associations, and activities? Or are we meant to act on impulse alone? It is all a darkness.

The tone is Conradian but without Marlow's illuminating intelligence. Often termed the quintessential modernist novel, *The Good Soldier* is in this respect almost postmodern in its assumptions about reality. Words, the great faith of the modernists, lead only further into the abyss.

The novel nonetheless has a social dimension to place it. Its original title, "The Saddest Story," refers in a larger sense to the slow decline of British culture. When Dowell decries the lack of permanance and stability, he is talking about the breakup of their foursome, but the whole of society is indicted. As in *Howards End*, the scale is miniature, the implications major, as in Dowell's recalling a metaphor "that the death of a mouse from cancer is the whole sack of Rome by the Goths." Cancer attacks from within, and in Ford's society most of the characters are infected with the modern-day equivalent of acedia: ennui. Boredom is a kind of withdrawal as much as it is a reaction to external events: here is the lack of engagement of the upper classes, coinciding with the straitjacket of social restraint. In its focus on the empty conventions of the upper classes, *The Good Soldier* anticipates the novels of Henry Green.

In a sense, the era itself is poisoned. Throughout the novel, the date August 4 recurs as a motif: it is the day of Dowell and Florence's marriage, as well as the day of both Leonora's maid Maisie Maidan's and Florence's death. August 4th also dates the onset of British involvement in the Great War (and by a curious coincidence, the Franco-Prussian War, as well). As Paul Fussell has shown, the Great War changed the thinking of a whole generation from idealism to cynicism, requiring a new language to record the movements of a society that sacrificed so much for so little. Or, as Philip Larkin writes in "MCMXIV": "Never such innocence again." *The Good Soldier*'s title is laced with irony.

Just as modernism existed in the decade following 1910, however, signs of social unrest in Britain predate the war. Labor reform, mass education, suffragism, and other movements all challenged what Samuel Hynes has called "the Edwardian garden party." The upper classes, confronting a changing world they little understood, either lolled or languished. Edward Ashburnham is one of Ford's familiar types, better suited to an earlier era. Anxious to do the right thing, he is torn between the inclinations of his heart and the confusing modern social mores that both condemn and condone his romantic actions. Unable to bear up under the strain, he finally tells Dowell, "I must have a little rest, you know," shortly before he commits suicide. Leonora soon remarries. Nancy Rutherford, Ashburnham's ward and last love, suffers a mental collapse, and the uncertain Dowell, now convinced he is in love with Nancy, tends her in the same way he did Florence. But the strain of keeping up appearances may be too much for him, as well. As he remarks in an unconscious echo of Ashburnham, "I am very tired of it all." The mood evokes earlier novels of manners like Richardson's *Clarissa*, where the only escape from imprisoning convention is death.

Ford expands upon the fate of social atavism in the tetralogy *Parade's End*. Written over a span of five years, *Some Do Not . . .* (1924), *No More Parades* (1925), *A Man Could Stand Up* (1926), and *The Last Post* (1928) sum up how British society altered irrevocably during the Great War. In a sense, *Parade's End* is another of Ford's historical narratives, but it is written with the regret of someone whose world has become history. In his opening rendition of "a perfectly appointed railway carriage," Ford depicts the old order: fine leather, ornate seat patterns, and a ride, thinks the protagonist Christopher Tietjens, smooth as British gilt-edged securities. But in a telling physical detail, Ford also presents the old order's obliviousness: "the mirrors beneath the new luggage racks immaculate as if they had reflected very little." Tietjens and his Tory society will be punished for their lack of forethought, even as they are praised for standing against debased modern values.

The story of Christopher Tietjens is more a movement than a plot, told as achronologically as *The Good Soldier*, though it slips in and out of many characters' minds. Yoked to his scheming, adulterous wife Sylvia, Tietjens bears his situation with a stoic fortitude that she and others find infuriating. Despite Sylvia's intrigues, his increasingly politicized job at the Imperial Department of Statistics, and the social affairs of the day, Tietjens preserves his eighteenth-century outlook, his Tory politics, and his encyclopedic mind. Like Edward Ashburnham, Tietjens quotes Swinburne, apt for the occasion but dead for the new era.

Novels of manners often have set pieces, representative of a certain social order or class, and Ford's breakfast scene at the Duchemins' ranks with Woolf's party at the Dalloways' or Forster's Marabar Caves expedition. The expansiveness of the setting and the distinguished list of generals, clergymen, and politicians attending are all the more poignant because they will soon be swept away in wartime. The propriety is emphasized by those who refuse to subscribe to it: the writer Mrs. Wannop, for example, whom Tietjens's father has supported for years and who Tietjens declares has written the only novel worth reading since the eighteenth century. Her daughter Valentine is a classicist of the highest order, who has nonetheless worked as a scullery maid to maintain financial independence. As an active women's suffragist, she represents the best of progressivism without the moral decay of the politicians.

Both physically and socially, Tietjens bulks large and awkward. In a Woolfian passage, Mrs. Duchemin thinks: "He was the male, threatening, clumsily odious and external!" But one of the consistent ironies in the plot is that Tietjens, so blunt and forthright, is misunderstood by everyone. Old General ffoliot thinks him a cad for deserting his wife, when the fault is Sylvia's. The rumors about Tietjens spread to the point where he loses his job and place in society. The scurrilous stories follow him even into the trenches, where he is reassigned despite his excellent performance because General Campion is sympathetic to Sylvia. These incidents illustrate the peculiar (and modernist) construction of social reality, where mere words have the repercussions of facts. At the same time, Ford's stream-of-consciousness technique emphasizes the undercurrents beneath the surface.

Tietjens remains steadfast in moral and intellectual outlook, holding off from sleeping with Valentine just before he goes off to war because, as the title of the second novel puts it, "Some do not—," and both he and Valentine are the type who practice restraint. Admittedly, at times this restraint reaches absurd proportions: when Tietjens's friend Macmaster hears that Sylvia has gone off with another man, Macmaster simply registers, "Ah!" Tietjens's brother and father wrongly think the worst of Tietjens, an impression Tietjens does nothing to correct, though it drives his father to suicide (the same shamed act of Ford's protagonist George Heinemann in *The Marsden Case*, written just before the tetralogy). As Ford writes in his poem "On Heaven":

> But one is English,
> Though one be never so much of a ghost;
> And if most of your life have been spent in the craze to relinquish
> What you want most,
> You will go on relinquishing,
> You will go on vanquishing
> Human longings, even
> In Heaven.

This is deadly accurate social commentary disguised as poetry. In fact, the trait Fussell terms British phlegm is on show throughout

Ford's works. At its best, it is a type of valor of which discretion is the better part; at its worst, it is repression, leading to noncommunication and extreme suffering.

The war explodes much of this social repression, mixing the classes in the trenches, mingling pity with fear and mangled limbs. Ford, who spent time at the front and suffered the shell shock he gives his protagonist, perfectly captures the surreal horror of the experience. He also precisely marks the end of an era: *"There will be no more parades,"* thinks Tietjens as he talks with General Campion, who has seen duty in India. "No more Hope, no more Glory." With the waning of imperialism comes the end of grandeur. Postwar England will offer a smaller, emptier existence, shown by the tiny, barren London flat he and Valentine move into after the war. An element of the absurd also marks this jumbled society, symbolized by the lunatic fringe of Tietjens's war comrades who crowd into Tietjens's flat.

Yet Tietjens manages to hold onto some vestige of the past, entering the antiques market with an American partner. Flouting social convention by living with Valentine and getting her pregnant, he renounces his Yorkshire heritage and refuses all help from his family. Only when his brother Mark, the embodiment of conservative England, becomes ill, does Tietjens return to Groby, the ancestral estate. Suffering from a seizure that has rendered him immobile, Mark in his condition sums up an entire era. As in *The Good Soldier*, paralysis is England's social disease. The new amoral, bored generation also cannot act, except to destroy tradition. When Sylvia persuades the new American tenant to chop down Groby Great Tree, the tallest cedar in England, she both emasculates the Tietjens men and destroys a great source of history. The wych elm in *Howards End* is a similar symbol, though Forster optimistically lets it stand. In any event, the two authors' hope for a new society is the same: Helen's baby in the fields, Valentine's "tiny brain that worked deep within her womb." Just before Mark dies at his "last post," he recalls a nursery song and so bequeaths the past to Valentine.

As Arthur Mizener notes, Ford's last novels, such as *Henry for Hugh* and *The Rash Act*, tend to emphasize technique at the expense of substance. They have the kind of clever reversals and plot devices that P. G. Wodehouse dealt in, but without the same lightness of touch. And just as Wodehouse tended to evoke a bygone era of England, Ford, like his fellow Edwardian Forster, found himself increasingly out of date. Faced with becoming an anachronism, Forster never completed another

novel; Ford, with a greater need for money and perhaps ego gratification, continued to write novels somewhat perfunctorily. His is an
uneven but distinguished record.

Some seventy years after Forster's and Ford's prime, society has
changed inalterably, and books such as *A Man Could Stand Up* serve not
just as drama but as historical commentary. The belated publication of
Forster's *Maurice* delivered an intact slice of Edwardiana. But these
works have not become curious period pieces, as have the novels of lesser writers, such as E. F. Benson or Ronald Firbank. These novels of
manners transcend the genre by dealing in universal truths and in the
end rejecting even these generalities for unsparing verities of character.
As Forster says of Beethoven in *Howards End*, one can trust him
because he bravely combines the splendor and the grimness of life and
this is equally true of both Forster and Ford.

The belated their stance remains ambivalent, urging change while defending
against desecration. Perhaps this is why, as Hynes shrewdly observes,
the Edwardian era was an age of reformers, not reforms. Still, if the historical character note of most Edwardians is nostalgia, these two manage to avoid sentimentality. One turns to both authors, in short, for
their powers of discrimination.

David Galef

Selected Bibliography

Bowers, Bege K., and Barbara Brothers, eds. *Reading and Writing Women's Lives: A
    Study of the Novel of Manners*. Ann Arbor: University of Michigan Research Press,
    1990.

Cassell, Richard A. *Ford Madox Ford: A Study of His Novels*. Baltimore: Johns Hopkins
    University Press, 1961.

Furbank, P. N. *E. M. Forster: A Life*. New York: Harcourt Brace Jovanovich, 1971.

Herz, Judith Scherer, and Robert K. Martin, eds. *E. M. Forster: Centenary Revalua-
    tions*. Toronto: University of Toronto Press, 1982.

Hynes, Samuel. *The Edwardian Turn of Mind*. Princeton, N.J.: Princeton University
    Press, 1968.

Mizener, Arthur. *The Saddest Story: A Biography of Ford Madox Ford*. New York: Car-
    roll and Graf, 1971.

Snitow, Ann Barr. *Ford Madox Ford and the Voice of Uncertainty.* Baton Rouge: Louisiana State University Press, 1984.

Stang, Sondra J., ed. *The Presence of Ford Madox Ford.* Philadelphia: University of Pennsylvania Press, 1981.

Stone, Wilfred. *The Cave and the Mountain: A Study of E. M. Forster.* Stanford: Stanford University Press, 1966.

Trilling, Lionel. *E. M. Forster.* Norfolk, Conn.: New Directions, 1943.

Samuel Beckett's Postmodern Fictions

S AMUEL BECKETT shares with Jorge Luis Borges the distinction of inaugurating in literature what has come to be called postmodernism. The term is still the subject of heated debate. It clearly refers to that which succeeds modernism, itself an international movement that broke with nineteenth-century forms of realism. But the impetus of modernism has continued to the present day, so that postmodernism coexists with that which it claims to displace. The phenomenon of postmodernism, then, cannot be explained in purely temporal terms. As the French philosopher Jean-François Lyotard has suggested, it represents a radical epistemological break with our understanding of what the human sciences have to offer. What characterizes the postmodern in Lyotard's eyes is the abandonment of those grand narratives that began with the Enlightenment, such as the liberation of humanity or the unification of all knowledge. The unstable, heterogeneous, and dispersed social reality of the postmodern cannot be contained within any totalizing theory. Without such metanarratives, Lyotard argues, each work of art, "working without rules in order to formulate the rules of what *will have been done*," becomes a unique event describing its own process of coming into being.

This is what Beckett's fictions do. Each one starts out anew, inventing its rules as it goes along. Its subject is itself, the narrating voice creating a world out of language. Before, between, and after the jabber of words that constitute the fiction is silence. How to express silence through sound? Beckett is preoccupied with this dilemma from the beginning of his career. Unlike pigment and musical notes, words signify beyond any writer's control. "Is there any reason," Beckett asked a friend in 1937, "why that terrible arbitrary materiality of the word's surface should not be permitted to dissolve . . . ?" As an avant-garde writer Beckett has fretted from the start of his career over the inescapable signification that accompanies the words he wants to use abstractly. In a world deprived of meaning, how can the linguistic artist express this meaninglessness with words that necessarily convey meaning? How can he produce what he called a "literature of the unword?" Throughout his long writing life Beckett conducted a war on words that led him to startling innovations in form and language. He went on experimenting to the end, never content with the increasingly minimal, pared-down fictions that characterize the second half of his writing life. Nothing satisfied him for long. Words, the enemy, continued to signify beyond every defeat he inflicted on them. His fictions are the progressive record of his fight to subdue language so that the silence of the real might make its presence felt. The fact that the later fictions resurrect themselves on the corpses of those that preceded them is the reason for the chronological consideration of his work in this chapter.

Silence features large in his earliest fiction, "Assumption" (a short story, 1929), *Dream of Fair to Middling Women* (a novel written in 1932, published 1983), *More Pricks than Kicks* (a novel, or ten connected short stories, 1934), and "A Case in a Thousand" (a short story, 1934). In "Assumption" the male protagonist is locked in a self-imposed silence. After he has met a woman who seduces him, a lifetime's suppressed scream escapes from him that sweeps her aside and leads to his death, "fused with the cosmic discord." Here in miniature is described the fate awaiting Belacqua, the antihero of "Dream" and *More Pricks*. Like his namesake in Dante's *Purgatorio*, Belacqua aspires to stasis and silence. Inevitably this makes him unlikable (he is constantly escaping social obligations) and uninteresting in conventional novelistic terms. As in "Assumption," sexuality is closely linked to death, figurative and literal. Sexual love means exile from the self. It is also likely to result in that unforgivable crime—bringing another unfortunate human being into this purgatorial life. So Beckett from the start offers us an antihero in an antinovel that scorns the conventions of romance.

In fact the Belacqua narratives implicitly reject the conventions of the entire genre of prose fiction. In his construction of fictional character Beckett explicitly renounces the appeal to "milieux, race, family, structure, temperament, past and present. . . ." He refuses to offer motive, for instance, when Belacqua decides to commit suicide: "The simplest course . . . is to call that deed ex nihilo and have done." Revealingly he offers the suggestion that, in acting so capriciously throughout the book, Belacqua may "be likened to the laws of nature." So much for claims to psychological realism by modernists such as Virginia Woolf and D. H. Lawrence. Beckett plays just as fast and loose with the plot. Pages are devoted to Belacqua's preparations of a lunchtime sandwich. But all "major" events are thrown away as asides. On the eve of her marriage to Belacqua, Lucy on horseback is run over by a "drunken lord" in a Daimler. Her horse dies instantly. "Lucy however was not so fortunate, being crippled for life and her beauty dreadfully marred." This arbitrary accident in turn becomes the key to the couple's happiness by removing her from the sexual arena. Three pages later the next section begins peremptorily: "Belacqua was so happy married to the crippled Lucy that he tended to be sorry for himself when she died, which she did on the eve of the second anniversary of her terrible accident." Beckett reverses the traditional understanding of what is and is not important within the event structure of a novel. Belacqua's death at the operating table is another pure accident that is dismissed in two sentences: "By Christ! he did die! They had clean forgotten to auscultate him!"

Throughout both Belacqua narratives the narrator plays an obtrusive, metafictional role. He comments on his own and others' fictional structures. "The only unity in this story," he interjects, "is, please God, an involuntary unity." He reminds us (also in "Dream") of the fictional status of his invented characters: "There is no real Belacqua, it is to be hoped not indeed, there is no such person." He shares with his readers his authorial manipulations of character and event, saying of Belacqua, "What shall we make him do now, what would be the correct thing for him to think for us?" At the same time Beckett plays tricks on his readers by showing his narrator to be unreliable, inconsistent, and deceitful. By the end of *More Pricks* the reader is left with no firm vantage point, no center from which to order the material of the book. Had the publisher allowed the final episode ("Echo's Bones") to appear with the others this narrative confusion would have been compounded by the postmortem appearance of Belacqua, who in one section obliges a local lord by spending the night with the lord's wife so as to leave him with an heir. Beckett's habitual association of sexuality with mortality here reaches bizarre proportions.

The language Beckett employs in these early fictions could be described as Irish baroque. Dialogue is mannered and consists largely of non sequiturs. Descriptive passages are characterized by a display of artifice and verbal ingenuity that is often divorced from fictional function. Beckett attempts to subvert the representational nature of words by the use of figurative language. In addition he relies heavily on literary allusion to foreground the opaque nature of his text. Both titles of the Belacqua narratives make bathetic allusion to literary classics, as does the name of the protagonist. Whole episodes form loose parodies of scenes from earlier writers' fictions. "Wet Night," for instance, is a poor imitation of a Proustian party scene. At times the narrative sinks under the weight of excessive allusion. At the same time Beckett uses intertextuality to remind the reader of the intrusion of literature into life, of the command language has over human destiny. Unfortunately, language in *More Pricks* also appears to have the upper hand in Beckett's fight to subvert its semantic properties.

Murphy (1938) shows Beckett exercising more control over this Irish baroque style. The opening sentence suggests the new sense of economy that characterizes his prose style in this book: "The sun shone, having no alternative, on the nothing new." Packed into this sentence are a parody of Ecclesiastes 1:5, a subscription to fatalism, and a statement of a major theme in the book—the absence of real change in human life. Beckett is trying to break through the illusion of order, of correspondence between signifier and signified, that words produce. *Murphy* offers a vision of the Creation as a huge verbal joke. Its hero, Murphy, not only reverses all commonly accepted social conventions (preferring rest to work, contemplation to sexual love, the insane to the sane); he simultaneously inverts traditional uses of language. In the beginning was the pun," he intones. Beckett employs puns, paradox, allusion, repetition, inversion—all in an attempt to disrupt the predictable semantic effects of language. Much of the resulting dialogue is highly mannered, showing more interest in creating mutually negating patterns of words than in mimetically reproducing plausible verbal exchanges. Take Murphy's exchange with Celia, the heroine-prostitute:

"How can I care what you do?"
"I am what I do," said Celia.
"No," said Murphy. "You do what you are . . ."

Murphy comes closer than his fictional predecessor to Dante's Belacqua (about whom he fantasizes) by inducing physical stasis in order to be free to explore the world of the mind. An entire chapter describes his mind and his attempts to retreat to what he fondly imagines is its freedom from worldly involvement. "Murphy's mind pictured itself as a large hollow sphere, hermetically closed to the universe without." Here Beckett pictures for the first time the skullscape of consciousness that is to become the principal arena for his major work. Murphy in fact feels divided in Cartesian fashion between body and mind—the perfect inheritor of an Enlightenment project gone awry. His mind is divided into three zones, light, half-light, and dark, roughly corresponding to the conscious, semiconscious, and unconscious. He aspires to enter the dark, which is "nothing but commotion." "Here he was not free, but a mote in the dark of absolute freedom." Murphy's biggest error consists in thinking that he can choose or will himself to become such a mote. Freedom in this book means total indifference to one's circumstances. The only character who approximates to this condition is Endon (Greek for "within"), a mental patient. Murphy plays chess with him only to realize that Endon plays chess with nobody but himself. He does not even acknowledge the existence of his opponent. Gazing into Endon's eyes Murphy realizes that Endon fails to see him. All he can perceive is his own reflection in Endon's eyeballs. "Mr. Murphy is a speck in Mr. Endon's unseen." No communication between minds is possible.

If Murphy represents the mind in Descartes's dual metaphysic, a bunch of Irish characters in search of Murphy for various reasons represent the tyranny of the body. Rushing between Cork, Dublin, and London, they are incessantly in motion. One of them (Cooper) is unable to sit down until the end of the book. They all subscribe to a Newtonian world governed by the conservation of momentum. One—Neary (an anagram for "yearn")—spends his time longing for one woman only to transfer his affections to another as soon as he wins her. "I greatly fear," his companion Wylie tells him, "that the syndrome known as life is too diffuse to admit of palliation. For every symptom that is eased, another is made worse." All action is shown to be pointless. Celia, trying to decide whether to return to Murphy or abandon him for good, asks, "What difference . . . would it make now, whether she went up the stairs to Murphy or back down them into the mew?" The narrator answers, "The difference between her way of destroying them both, according to him, and his way, according to her." Once again Beckett uses self-negating clauses to undermine both the validity of action and the semantic logic of words.

Murphy is characterized by many of the features of what has since become a recognizable Beckettian world. Love is exile from reality. Birth is a form of death. Sanity is insanity. Activity is nonproductive. Philosophy is the consolation of the deluded. Linguistically Beckett achieves similar effects. Psychotic patients' padded cells are in Murphy's eyes Spenserian "indoor bowers of bliss." Our possession of a mind and a body is dismissed in the misquoted words of Marlow's Barabas as "infinite riches in a W.C." (What could be more like Marlow's "little room" than that?) Murphy refers to "the moment of his being strangled into a state of respiration." (One remembers Beckett saying to John Gruen after being awarded the Nobel Prize, "The major sin is the sin of being born.") Exiting from life is already a problem: Murphy was earlier a theological student who spent his time "pondering Christ's parthian shaft: *It is finished.*" Repeatedly Beckett turns quotations back on themselves, especially biblical ones. As Murphy puts it, "What but an imperfect sense of humor could have made such a mess of chaos." *Murphy* is Beckett's most accessible novel. It is also a clever parody of many of the characteristics of the genre he was using.

Watt, Beckett's last novel to be written in English, was begun in Paris in 1942, continued in Rousillon where Beckett was hiding from the Gestapo in 1942 and 1943, and finished in Dublin and Paris in 1945. It was not published until 1953, after *Waiting for Godot* and the first two of his celebrated trilogy of novels (*Molloy, Malone Dies, The Unnamable*) had appeared in print. Beckett has called *Watt* "unsatisfactory" while affirming that "it has its place in the series." That seems a fair assessment of this peculiarly difficult book, which contains quintessentially Beckettian motifs that nevertheless fail to find wholly satisfactory fictional embodiment. The novel is almost without overtly significant incident. Watt makes his way to Mr. Knott's house, becomes second and then first servant there, fails to ascertain anything definable about Knott, is replaced, leaves the house, and ends up in a "mansion" that closely resembles a mental asylum.

In fact Watt's journey is an inner journey of the mind, what Beckett describes in one of the poems printed in the addenda to the book as "the dim mind wayfaring" and "the dark mind stumbling / through barren lands." Watt sees his quest in the former terms; the narrator sees it in the latter terms. Watt is an inveterate rationalist who pursues Cartesian rules for orderly enquiry with such rigor that he repeatedly exposes the futile nature of the entire epistemological endeavor. What gave Descartes and the entire Enlightenment project its sense of optimism was the need to invoke God as a way of bridging the otherwise baffling barrier between mind (or self) and body (or matter). Watt, a representative modern skeptic and agnostic in search of the self, brings the Enlightenment project to a standstill by taking it more seriously and pursuing it more thoroughly than any of his fictional predecessors. Watt comes face to face with the *néant* of the postwar, postmodern world epitomized by Knott and his house. Watt's "What?" is negated by Knott's "Not." The conjunction of these two figures produces whatnot, an absence of metanarratives, especially those of the late seventeenth- and eighteenth-century rationalists. Where Descartes argued his way from thought to being and thence to God, Watt finds that the application of reason leaves him doubting his own existence as well as that of a divine being.

Both words and numbers fail Watt. Numbers fail because they are the invention of the fallible human brain. A footnote following an exhaustive account of the members of the Lynch family reads: "The figures given here are incorrect. The consequent calculations are therefore doubly erroneous." When rationalists try to apply the arithmetical neatness of numbers to the web of language, all hell is let loose. Knott negates Watt's cogito by remaining wordless. His nothingness can only be circumscribed by Watt's words, which prove to be self-canceling. Watt realizes that "the only way one can speak of nothing is to speak of it as though it were something, just as the only way one can speak of God is to speak of him as though he were a man." Both God and the real have no adequate place in the symbolic order of language. They can only be given shape in the form of fictions. Form is all that is left. Linguistic form. Fictional form. Words turn out to be delusory semantic succor for Watt who, with his faulty reasoning, "had turned, little by little, a disturbance into words, he had made a pillow of old words, for his head."

Many of Watt's rationalist attempts to exhaust all the possibilities of a subject are listed exhaustively (and exhaustingly) over pages and pages of the novel, trying the patience of most readers. The most distinctive characteristic of this novel is its disruptive use of form to suggest the formlessness of the real. The first and last of its four sections are located in the everyday world that surrounds Knott's house. In section one Watt finds his way to the house and replaces the upstairs servant by moving in downstairs, the downstairs servant moving upstairs. The middle two sections describe Watt's stay in first the downstairs and then the upstairs floors of Knott's house. In section four Watt leaves the house on the arrival of a new servant downstairs. He makes his way to the train station where he buys a ticket to the end of the line. After his disappearance the station officials agree that "life isn't such a bad old bugger." Watt is returned to the world of delusion.

But in section three we learn that Watt is telling his story to Sam, the narrator of the book, in an asylum that he has reached after buying his ticket to the end of the line. The beginning of section four reads: "As Watt told the beginning of his story, not first, but second, so not fourth, but third, now he told its end." The contorted word order of this sentence draws attention to the contorted way in which the chronological order of Watt's narration has been rearranged by Sam. Neither order is that of the *fabula* (or basic story line); both are versions of *syuzhet* (or plotted rearrangement of the story). In Sam's version of the story it is Watt's stay at Knott's house that is illusory, contained within the "realistic" outer sections; in Watt's telling it is the everyday world of sections one and four that are made to appear illusory, contained within the two sections describing Watt's stay at Knott's house. By this means Beckett avoids giving primacy to either the world of the mind or that of the body. This neat interchangeability is further complicated by the fact that the opening and closing pages of the novel cannot have been witnessed by Watt or told by him to Sam. Moreover, Watt's only direct speech appears in section three where he communicates with Sam by pronouncing words, then sentences, backward. So the entire fiction paradoxically uses Sam's words to describe a near-wordless protagonist whose use of words has been negated by the wordless Knott.

After *Watt* Beckett underwent a double revolution. On a short visit to Dublin in 1946 he had a blinding flash of insight in which he realized that the "dark side" of his personality should provide him with the true subject of his work. His new aim was to conduct an interior excavation of that darkness that he "had struggled to keep under." At about the same time he began writing in an acquired, alien language—French—to curb the remnants of what I have called his Irish Gothic. In French, he claimed, "it is easier to write without style." He proceeded to write a novel, *Mercier et Camier*, that he witheld from publication until 1970, partly because he drew on some of it for *Waiting for Godot*. The same year he wrote four *nouvelles* that anticipate in theme and form the trilogy of novels that was to establish his reputation in the field of fiction. They show Beckett turning to the interior monologue as the form best suited to his new desire for self-excavation. Each protagonist, like his successors in the trilogy, tells himself "this story that aspires to be the last."

In a spurt of creativity between 1947 and 1949 Beckett wrote *Molloy* (1951), *Malone Dies* (*Malone meurt*, 1953), and *The Unnamable* (*L'innommable*, 1953). Each novel has its own pseudocouple, avatars or stand-ins for Beckett, the narrating subject. *Molloy* is divided into the story of Molloy from the moment he set out on crutches and bicycle to find his mother to his arrival in her room where he sits in bed writing his story, and the story of Moran, who sets out in search of Molloy with his son and ends up writing a report of his failure to find him. *Malone Dies* describes Malone, in bed in a room similar to that of Molloy's mother, writing stories (while waiting to die) about one Saposcat (a combination of *homo sapiens* and *skatos*, Greek for excrement), who turns into Macmann (son of man—or of Malone, the evil one). *The Unnamable* offers the narrative of a disembodied voice that conjures up images of two postmortem "vice-existers," Mahood (manhood?), a trunk and head without limbs stuck in a jar, and Worm, an even more rudimentary creature with minimal human attributes. All three novels focus on a representative human consciousness trying to come to terms with its existence by telling itself stories featuring itself as hero of its own fictions.

Each of the three novels is an exercise in self-destruction. *Molloy* illustrates in particular the antichronological thrust of Beckett's project. Moran's apparent failure to track down Molloy is undercut by the way he is transformed in the course of his search from the confident agent and authoritarian father at the start of his narrative to an uncanny copy (down to the crutches) of Molloy, whose story preceded his. The reason in part is that Moran, like Molloy, is searching for his true self, whatever that might be. "And as for myself, that unfailing pastime, . . . there were moments when it did not seem so far from me, when I seemed to be drawing towards it. . . ." That self is what Beckett once called "the narrator narrated." Beckett uses his successive pairs of protagonists to try to stalk this self, to illuminate his darkness that constantly recedes before the light of his narrational pursuit. So the trilogy is equally about the predicament of representative man who tries to reach the core of his being by recounting his life to himself, and about the predicament of the modern artist bent on exploring the source of his imagination by telling stories to himself (and others) that alienate him from the "real" world. The predicament, as Beckett described it in his early critical work on Proust, is that to be a modern artist "is to fail, as no other dare fail, that failure is his world, and to shrink from it desertion." As the Unnamable reassures himself, "I am doing my best, and failing again."

Seen thematically, each successive novel appears to repeat the pattern established in its predecessor. In the structuralist terms of the French semiotician A. J. Greimas, Beckett seems to be presenting the same "immanent level" of narration, the same paradigmatic story, in all three novels. And yet there is an apparent progression from the two narrators' accounts of their increasingly impeded physical journeys in *Molloy*, to Malone's written account of the wanderings of fictional substitutes, to the Unnamable's wholly verbal meanderings where to "go on" means to go on voicing his mental search for an escape from his world of words. In each novel the narrator succeeds in scaling down his need—from wanting to reach his mother, to wanting to die, to wanting to stop speaking. As the recurrent narrative structure only emerges after the second and third novels have been read, Beckett is able to lure his readers into the same illusion suffered by his successive protagonists—that they are making progress. In Beckett's bleak view of human existence we delude ourselves into thinking that things are changing in order to avoid the harsh truth that life is fundamentaly repetitive. As Malone reminds himself, "The forms are many in which the unchanging seeks relief from its formlessness." Perception is subjective and fallible. "What I best see I see ill," says the Unnamable. Memory fails us, so that we cannot remember whether we have been through any particular experience before. Time is circular, space illusory. "I am being given," Malone writes, "if I may venture the expression, birth into death." As John Fletcher pointed out, *Malone Dies* illustrates Georges Bataille's observation that man is the only creature who spends his life mythologizing his death.

So all the narrators and their doubles are seeking for a place of final rest—their mother's room (or womb), physical death, an end to speech. Each successive narrator pursues a more reductive search of the self;

each fails. Why? Because the self belongs to the void of the real. The void or *néant* belongs to a realm of silence. But humans are condemned to the false linearity, rationality, and semantic properties of language. Put in Lacanian terms, each of us longs to return to the blissful ignorance of infancy when our experience was one of pure libido (or Obidil, as Moran calls it, whom he "longed to see face to face"). Instead we are condemned to a symbolic order in which language constitutes us as subjects split within ourselves. We are split between a conscious self whose lack condemns us to a lifetime of unfulfilled desire and an unconscious forever deferred along the signifying chain of language. We are also split between a desire for unity and a lack of concrete being. This is what Moran terms "being dispossessed of self." The Unnamable resorts to paradox to describe the paradoxical nature of human consciousness divided within itself: "Where I am there is no one but me, who am not."

The trilogy takes this predicament of ours and doggedly explores it until it has reduced the problem to one of pure language in *The Unnamable*. The voice in this third novel desperately looks for a way to reach silence, just as the narrator looks for a way finally to end his narration by telling the story of himself instead of that of "the ponderous chronicle of moribunds" that the trilogy has produced. His problem is bound up in the nature of language, especially in the unique nature of the first- and second-person pronouns. Beckett appears to have anticipated the formulations of the French structuralist linguist, Emile Benveniste. Benveniste argues that the pronouns *I* and *you*, unlike other signifiers, only produce signifieds in concrete discursive contexts. Unlike *tree*, say, *I* has no concrete meaning until it appears in a specific context. There it signifies somebody only for the duration of the discourse in which it appears. "So," Benveniste concludes, "it is literally true that the basis of subjectivity is in the exercise of language." This also means that in between two discursive moments subjectivity evaporates. When Malone loses his pencil for forty-eight hours, on recovering it he writes, "I have spent two unforgettable days of which nothing will ever be known. . . ." This is why all the narrators in the trilogy pant on to the end— because it is only by continuing to speak in the first person that they can hope to constitute themselves as subjects. As the Unnamable says, "the discourse must go on," because "I'm in words, made of words, others' words."

Why "*others'* words"? Because, as Benveniste explains, any discursive use of *I* entails two subjects, the speaking subject, or "referent," and the subject of speech, or "referee." He goes on to insist that these two *Is* can never be collapsed into one another. The spoken subject acts as a signifier. By identifying with this signifier the speaking subject hopes to define his or her subjectivity. In Beckett's trilogy the spoken subject is invariably one of the speaking subject's many "vice-existers," by means of which the narrator seeks to signify his own self. He would like to collapse this distinction, to be, as the Unnamable longs to be, "the teller and the told." Instead the narrator is carried helplessly along a chain of signifiers—his "troop of lunatics," never reaching the signified of himself. "When I think," says the Unnamable,

of the time I've wasted with these bran-dips, beginning with Murphy, who wasn't even the first, when I had me on the premises, within easy reach, tottering under my own skin and bones, real ones, rotting with solitude and neglect, till I doubted my own existence, and even still, today, I have no faith in it, none, so that I have to say, when I speak, Who speaks, and seek, and so on and similarly for all the other things that happen to me and for which someone must be found, for things that happen must have someone to happen to, someone must stop them.

Here within one breathless sentence Beckett wittily follows full circle the chain of signifiers from Murphy and before that were intended to lead to their signified—the narrating self—and that by the end of this deliberately contorted syntactical structure still hold the speaking subject at a distance from himself.

Beckett knows, then, that he is bound to fail at his excavatory task. His failure is itself a satiric thrust not just at the metanarratives of humanist metaphysics but at the pretensions of verbal fictions that see themselves as narrating fictions instead of concentrating on the fiction of narration. This latter Beckett does by poking fun at the tricks language plays on the narrator. Moran, for instance, begins his narration in an orderly manner, giving his name, introducing his report, and setting the scene with: "It is midnight. The rain is beating on the windows." But his attempt to be factual and businesslike gradually breaks down and turns into the paragraphless flow of verbiage that characterized Molloy's previous narrative. Moran ends his monologue by celebrating the fictionality of his narrative: "It was not midnight. It was not raining." Malone follows a similar reversal by setting out to tell four different stories and then to conduct an inventory of his possessions, neither of which projects he completes.

But it is the Unnamable who best illustrates the verbal and pronominal impasse that all these narrators reach by the end. The narrative use of language literally proves his undoing. Beckett has called "writing style" "that vanity," "a bowtie about a throat cancer." The Unnamable illustrates this dangerously delusive nature of language in his funny, desperate, and perplexed frontal assault on what the French philosopher and critic Gaston Bachelard called a "logosphere," a verbal fabric out of which he too is constructed as a subject. The Unnamable's mental confusion within what he calls the "wordy-gurdy" is mirrored by the syntactical impasses he gets himself into: "But my good will at certain moments is such, and my longing to have floundered however briefly, however feebly, in the great life torrent streaming from the earliest protozoa to the very latest humans, that I, no, parenthesis unfinished. I'll begin again." This manner of propelling sentences along by fits and starts has been described by Ludovic Janvier as "style with engine trouble." In particular Beckett plays fast and loose with pronouns. "To get me to be he, the anti-Mahood," he starts off one sentence. On another occasion he finds himself talking of "we," only to ask himself whom "we" refers to. Within a sentence he gives up: "no sense in bickering about pronouns and other parts of blather." Toward the end of the Unnamable's monologue his words come spewing out in a torrent of syntactically disjointed phrases that constantly circle round the narrator's central dilemma. Just as the narrator is caught in a pronominal limbo between referent and referee, so all the positives within the narration are speedily negated, ending with the now-famous last lines in which changing verbal tenses and pronouns reflect the Unnamable's continuing confusion: "You must go on, I can't go on, I'll go on."

After completing *The Unnamable*, Beckett felt that he had exhausted his vein of self-immersive narration. The fifties were the years in which Beckett established his reputation as a dramatist with *Waiting for Godot*, *Endgame*, and *Krapp's Last Tape*. In 1950 he did begin writing a series of linked short prose texts in French that he reluctantly released for publication in 1955 as *Textes pour rien* (*Texts for Nothing*, 1967). In 1956 he claimed that the trilogy brought him to the point where subsequently he felt he was repeating himself: "In the last book—L'Innommable—there's complete disintegration. . . . There's no way to go on." He adds that *Texts pour rien* "was an attempt to get out of the attitude of disintegration, but it failed." Apart from a need to be wary of Beckett's constant put-downs of his own work, failure, as he wrote, is in his view the modern artist's world. As the voice remarks in the first text, "nothing like breathing your last to put new life in you." *Texts for Nothing* certainly does not match the virtuoso performance of *The Unnamable*. Yet it points forward to Beckett's last full-length novel, *How It Is*, by looking to form for a way out of the dead end reached at the close of *The Unnamable*.

It has long been recognized that the title, *Textes pour rien*, alludes to the musical term *mesure pour rien*, meaning "a bar's rest." Pauses in music are as necessary a part of the score as the pauses Beckett incorporates in *Godot* or *How It Is*. In the case of *Texts*, each of the thirteen short texts brings the Unnamable's successor's unstoppable torrent of speech to a temporary rest. Each text offers an evening's worth of narration. All thirteen texts also take the musical form of variations on a theme already adumbrated in the trilogy (although even that is modified by the abandonment of any serious attempt to tell a story). The voice explains why it keeps "trying to vary"—"you never know, it's perhaps all a question of hitting on the right aggregate." Beckett called the thirteenth text a coda. Seen in their entirety, the *Texts* form a musical coda to the trilogy. In *Beckett and the Voice of Species* Eric Levy has shown how each text introduces a question and ends with "a provisional conclusion which does not so much answer the query as remove the possibility of its being properly asked." The theme is that of a disembodied voice that is constantly looking to assume a concrete existence in its desire for selfhood. The variations that Beckett plays on this theme include imaging this situation as that of a body face down remembering images of life in the light above; portraying his predicament as that of both judge and party, witness and advocate at his own trial; searching for a missing person—himself; looking for the way out (anticipating *The Lost Ones*); giving up; and finally returning to the main theme, the realization that "there is nothing but a voice murmuring a trace." Both individual texts and the composition as a whole reveal a circularity beneath an initial appearance of progression.

This formal strategy of countering the linearity of language and its semantic content with a circularity of structure and motifs is given brilliant expression in Beckett's last full-length novel (as it was called in the French, but not the English edition), *How It Is* (*Comment c'est*, 1961). Written in French in 1960, this work reflects Beckett's conviction at that time that the modern artist could no longer try to reduce the chaos of existence to the orderliness of artistic form in the manner of Joyce and other modernists. Instead Beckett was looking for a new form that "admits the chaos," while remaining separate from it. The chaos that incorporates our condition takes the haunting form of a figure living out his existence crawling across the mud dragging with him a sack of canned food. His voice tells of his tortured life in three phases corresponding to the three sections of the novel. In part one ("before Pim") he describes his slow progress and the images that come to him from the old "life in the light." Part two ("with Pim") describes his overtaking another crawler, Pim, whom he tortures into speech. In part three ("after Pim") Pim gets away and the figure is left crawling on waiting to be overtaken by another crawler who will torture him in turn.

Beckett is offering us a savage image of what he sees as the hell of life on earth. He makes a number of oblique references to Dante's *Inferno*. The entire situation is reminiscent of Canto 7 where the souls of the sullen lie immersed in the mud rehearsing their lives in gurgles. In what he calls this "outer hell" Dante's sign above hell's gate ("Abandon hope all ye who enter here") is echoed in Beckett's text with "abandoned here effect of hope." The "muckheap" or "sewer" through which his protagonist crawls is Beckett's fiercest visual representation of the reality of human existence, the postmodern hell that confines us each to his or her own consciousness. We are back in the confusion of a dispersed subjectivity. But this time it is not the voice trying to rejoin its authorial origin. Instead Beckett offers a voice that ventriloquially reiterates in unpunctuated brief bursts of speech whatever is said to it: "how it is I say it as I hear it natural order more or less bits and scraps in the mud my life murmur it to the mud." Here the subject of speech portrays himself as the victim of the speaking subject, who is simultaneously the author responsible for this fictional creation and the god made responsible by uncomprehending humankind for its miserable condition.

Seen in Bakhtinian terms, *How It Is* turns out to be a celebration of what the Russian literary theorist Mikhail Bakhtin termed dialogism, of the independence of fictional voices from their authorial origin. The author is made to make way for the voices that speak through him, for the polyphonic nature of language itself. In part one the narrating voice adopts a similar posture to that adopted by the voice of the Unnamable—one of victimization at the hands of the unseen author. The author (or Author) is pictured as one who "lives bent over me," aided by a "scribe sitting aloof" who records "an ancient voice in me not mine."

The voice is tortured into speech by this alien figure. But in part two we witness the tortured narrator turn torturer of Pim who has been brought to life by the narrating voice: "but for me he would never Pim we're talking of Pim never be but for me." His torture takes the appropriate form of forcing the victim into the act of speech. Toward the end of part two the voice recognizes that "Pim never was . . . only one voice my voice never any other." Every victim becomes torturer in Beckett's contemporary Erebus. Finally in part three the narrating voice throws off all pretense of being under godlike authorial control. Having demonstrated in the manner of Descartes and Malebranche the need for a god ("need of one not one of us an intelligence somewhere") to coordinate the movements of his innumerable crawlers in the mud, he immediately undercuts this yearning for order by exploding the very idea of a just god—or a controlling author: "but all this business of voices yes quaqua yes of other worlds yes of someone in another world yes whose kind of dream I am yes said to be yes . . . all balls." Actually there's "only me yes alone yes with my voice yes," a voice detached from its origin as we have become detached from our god, a voice that belongs to the babel of heteroglossia.

How It Is is an artistic tour de force in which Beckett's discovery of a form that would not conceal the chaos is matched by a radically pared-down use of language that results in a heightened mode of prose poetry. His use of a three-part structure, as in the trilogy, reflects the repetitive circularity of human life. What he has done, he informs us, is to "divide into three a single eternity for the sake of clarity." As he admits toward the end of the novel, his protagonist's life actually consists of four phases: crawling toward a victim, torturing him, crawling on, and being overtaken by a torturer. But, the voice concludes, "of the four three quarters of our total life only three lend themselves to communication." Why? Because victim and victimizer play identical if complementary roles. But also because he only needs to narrate enough to show the reader that the series can continue ad infinitum. Three parts also enable Beckett to include a central section in which conditions promise to improve: "happy time in its way part two." This is only to give formal expression to the way life repeatedly deludes us into thinking that things are getting better before returning us (in part three) to the primordial mud that is our reality.

Compared to the manic, breathless pace of the prose in *The Unnamable*, the brief phrases that make up the unpunctuated versets of differing lengths in *How It Is* have a more deliberate, rhythmic quality to them, successfully reproducing the mutterings of a voice that has to pause for breath at frequent intervals. Those blank spaces between the versets (which Beckett only adopted in place of continuous prose just before printing the first edition) act as a visual metaphor for the silence to which the voice aspires, and for the *néant* where language with its semantic pretensions has no place. The murmurings of the narrator are so many stains on the silence of the real. Beckett talks in the text of his use of "little blurts midget grammar." By omitting so many of the normal elements of a conventional sentence he is able to undercut some of the denotative aspects of language while foregrounding its connotative and figurative uses. In the original French version, in particular, he plays punningly on the similarity in sound between words like *bout* (end) and *boue* (mud), *Bom* and *bon* (good), and especially between *comment c'est* (how it is) and *commencez* (begin) with which the novel teasingly ends. The lack of punctuation, capital letters (except proper nouns), and certain parts of speech, the use of poetic inversion, and the proliferation of allusions to other texts also increase the potential for multiple readings of parts of the text and make especially heavy though rewarding demands on the reader, offering an extreme example of what the French literary theorist Roland Barthes calls a "writerly" text.

How It Is is Beckett's last novel-length work of fiction. After 1960 his fiction took the form of what he variously called "residua," "*capua mortua*" or "*têtes mortes*" (death's-heads), "*foirades*" (little farts, or fizzles), and "fiascos." All of these later texts (it would be a misnomer to call them short stories) cultivate an art of minimalism. What they lack in length they make up for in density. As Beckett told me, these pieces are residual "(1) Severally, even when that does not appear of which each is all that remains and (2) In relation to whole body of previous work." While a number of these residua refer back to situations explored in earlier novels, many of them evolve from abandoned larger (and occasionally smaller) works. There are eight very brief "Fizzles" that were written between the very late 1950s and 1975. There are also six more substantial texts: *All Strange Away* (written 1963–1964), *Imagination morte imaginez* (*Imagination Dead Imagine*, written 1965), "Enough" ("*Assez*," 1965), *Le Dépeupler* (*The Lost Ones*, 1965–1966, completed 1971), *Bing* (*Ping*, 1966) and *Sans* (*Lessness*, 1969). Five of these texts evolve out of one another. *Imagination Dead Imagine* is the distillment of *All Strange Away*. *The Lost Ones* employs a similar fluctuation of heat and light as that which characterized the world of *Imagination Dead Imagine*. *Bing*, Beckett informed me, "is a separate work written after and in reaction to *Le Dépeupleur* abandoned because of its complexity getting beyond control." *Lessness* was written in direct reaction to *Ping*, causing the walls of *Ping*'s "true refuge" to fall down in the opening paragraph. "Enough" is the only text to stand outside the series ("I don't know what came over me," Beckett wrote of it).

With the exception of "Enough" all these residua and the later "Fizzles" eschew the use of the first-person pronoun. With each new text Beckett aspires to greater impersonality, although the detachment his narrator cultivates is frequently undermined by an ironic tone of exaggeration. In *The Lost Ones* his little people all progress to stasis. In *Imagination Dead Imagine*, *Ping*, and *Lessness* his protagonists have stopped even crawling and come to their final resting place, only betraying their continuing life of the mind by their breath or by movements of the eyes. In *Imagination Dead Imagine* Beckett conjures up the image of a man and a woman lying back to back in a rotunda; in *The Lost Ones* he uncharacteristically imagines a Lilliputian people inhabiting a cylinder fifty meters in circumference from which they seek vainly to escape; in *Ping* he evokes a "bare white body" confined upright to a white, box-like room two yards high and one yard square; and in *Lessness* the same body stands amid the grey ("never was but grey") ruins of the fallen-down walls that surrounded it in *Ping*. All of these haunting images are the products of Beckett's imaginative attempt to produce a simulacrum of the reality of human existence. This is an inner landscape of the mind, a skullscape, given its most literal realization in the rotunda of *Imagination Dead Imagine*, which is subject to fluctuations of light and heat reminiscent of the day and night, summer and winter, consciousness and unconsciousness, life and death, to which we and our minds are subject.

One of the striking features of these shorter texts is their use of arithmetically or proportionally shaped form. The delusions of mathematics constituted one of Beckett's favorite satirical targets in the earlier novels such as *Watt* and *How It Is*. In these residua Beckett has incorporated the delusive allure of numbers (that had ultimately trapped the eighteenth-century rationalists) into their structure, by means of which he attempts to express the illusory nature of life in general. *Imagination Dead Imagine* meticulously constructs and measures with all the finesse of Euclidean geometry an image that refuses to remain stable—which is only to be expected of a product of the artist's consciousness. The tone of scientific detachment employed by the narrator soon exposes him to the reader's ridicule as his effort to remain objective while faced with the evanescent product of the artistic imagination, proves increasingly ridiculous: "Neither fat nor thin, big nor small, the bodies seem whole and in fairly good condition, to judge by the surfaces exposed to view." This narrating zoologist-turned-pathologist fails to perceive the failure inherent in his scientific approach. What causes the image ultimately to disappear is the obvious relativity of the observer who cannot bear to concentrate for too long on an image of suffering humanity. "Only murmur ah, no more, in this silence, and at the same instant for the eye of prey the infinitesimal shudder instantaneously suppressed." Whether "the eye of prey" refers to the eye of one of the figures or to that of the supposedly impersonal observer, the effect is the same—"no question now of ever finding again that white speck lost in whiteness."

The Lost Ones employs a similar technique for similar ends. We are guided through the complex rules of this pygmy population inhabiting a cylinder subject to the same fluctuations of light and heat as in the previous text by a professorial narrator whose pomposity exposes him to ridicule. His sentences usually start with phrases such as "To be noted . . ." or "It might safely be maintained . . ." and end with such remarks as "So much for a first aperçu of . . ." or ". . . if this notion is maintained." When applied to subjects like human sexuality the pose inherent in this lofty attitude becomes the object of Beckett's overt satire: "The mucous membrane itself is affected which would not greatly matter were it not for its hampering effect on the work of love. But even from this point of view no great harm is done so rare is erection in the cylinder. It does occur none the less followed by more or less happy penetration in the nearest tube."

Having searched exhaustively for the self in the earlier fiction, it is improbable that Beckett would allow a narrator who pontificates in this manner to remain unscathed. Sure enough, within the first section the narrator undercuts his own stance by revealing the theoretical impossibility of acquiring the knowledge he claims to be purveying: "Such harmony only he can relish whose long experience and detailed knowledge of the niches are such as to permit a perfect mental image of the entire system. But it is doubtful that such a one exists." The narrator's inherently logocentric position is exposed by his unwitting act of deconstruction. Beckett multiplies the permutations of his miniature world over fourteen sections, at which point he abandoned the work until five years later when he added a final section. This posits a theoretical "last state of the cylinder" in which the last searcher gives up the search and joins the other vanquished. The narrator dryly calls this "the unthinkable end"—which it has to be if only because the narrator has still not given up his own search, which takes the narrative form of attempting to explain the appearance of order that prevails in the cylinder.

In these first two texts the narrator has employed mathematical and pseudoscientific methods to attempt to give substance to the insubstantial fabric of the artistic imagination. In *Ping* and *Lessness* the narrator hides behind an impersonal voice that betrays no obvious personality traits. But the text is constructed and shaped by mathematical manipulation. It is no coincidence that these texts belong to the heyday of French structuralism. In both texts reiterative individual components acquire meaning principally through the context in which they appear. *Ping* consists of 1,030 words made up of 120 different words that recur in the form of 100 different phrases. Certain combinations of words such as "bare white body fixed" appear frequently. But whereas the first appearance of this phrase is followed by further descriptive information ("one yard legs joined"), in subsequent appearances the context robs it of its certitude (e.g., "white on white invisible"). Beckett further subverts the impression of exactitude by introducing at random intervals the word *ping*, which invariably disturbs the image just described, as in "bare white body fixed ping fixed elsewhere." The word *ping* operates as a random principle, undermining the sense of structuralization that the ordering of words and phrases suggests, signifying the presence of a disordering element within the mathematically created illusion of order.

Beckett refines this arithmetic conception of form yet further in *Lessness*. As in *Ping*, both the symmetry and chaos of human life are reflected in the way its 120 sentences are ordered on the page. Our longing for order is reflected in formal terms by the way each sentence in the first half of the text is repeated in the second half, and by the way the sixty sentences in each half divide into ten sentences, each set belonging to one of six groups of images. Simultaneously Beckett incorporates the random nature of infinity, endlessness, into his formal organization by employing random paragraph lengths, a random sequence of the six images, and the random reappearance of each sentence in the second half. Beckett summons what he has called a "syntax of weakness" to reinforce these structural ploys. For the most part he uses minimal syntax to link the remnants of full sentences. He reserves the use of full syntax for the description of images that belong to the old, delusive life in the light. The juxtaposition is intentionally startling, exposing as it does the artificiality of the poetic use of language that blinds us to the grey reality of endlessness: "Little body ash grey locked rigid heart beating face to endlessness. On him will rain again as in the blessed days of blue the passing cloud." The poetic word inversion, the intrusion of the definite article, paralleled by the eruption of color and nostalgia in the second sentence perform a similar function to the use of "ping" in signaling the futility of the attempt to comprehend mathematically the ultimately random nature of chaos.

After two decades during which Beckett's fictional and dramatic works had become progressively more minimalist, he surprised everyone with a renewed burst of creativity, publishing three short novella-length texts in the early 1980s. These three works of fiction written in his late seventies constitute a second trilogy. The first of these, *Company*, was written in English between 1977 and 1979, translated into French, and then published in English in 1980 after Beckett revised it in the light of the French text. *Ill Seen Ill Said* was first written in French as *Mal vu mal dit*. Both French and English editions were first published in 1981. *Worstward Ho* was first written in English and published in 1983. (Beckett's only subsequent significant short work of fiction was *Stirrings Still* (1989), written on request to help out his old American publisher financially.) These three powerful and highly concentrated texts are not abandoned longer works or works in progress. They pursue Beckett's lifelong fight with language to new and quite extraordinary lengths. Beckett wrote back in 1937, "As we cannot eliminate language all at once, we should at least leave nothing undone that might contribute to its falling into disrepute." It is as if he was inspired to take up this assault on the false security that language offers us with renewed energy in his old age. Whereas the first trilogy was more closely integrated, with the third book's references back to characters and events in the earlier two volumes, these three texts are connected by their progressive reduction of the components that constitute a normal sentence. In *Company* a "voice comes to one in the dark." In *Ill Seen* the voice is "ill said." By *Worstward Ho* the voice is "missaid." One only has to pay attention to the titles of these three texts to see the progressive deterioration that each describes.

In *Company* Beckett's principal concern is with the enigma of the first-person pronoun. Where he assailed the fictionality of the "I" in the earlier trilogy by employing it throughout, in *Company* he acknowledges the dependence of the "I" on designating a "you" and a "he" for its very meaning. On the one hand Beckett describes a "he" who lies on his back in the dark; on the other hand he creates a voice that addresses the "he" as "you" in the course of describing incidents in his past life. The subject is split between a third-person thinking and reflecting mind whose thoughts are directed at the reader and a second-person voice of memory that is directed at the one in the dark. Fifteen of the ninety paragraphs employ the second person to evoke autobiographical scenes that bear a close resemblance to incidents in Beckett's own past as they are recounted in Deirdre Bair's biography of him. It quickly becomes apparent that the memories the voice recalls have become distorted with time. Some of the most nostalgic memories of happiness are lit by an unreal and idealized "sunless cloudless brightness." Another memory emphasizes its distance from the memorized event: "You lie in the dark with closed eyes and see the scene. As you could not at the time."

The other contemplative voice in the third person quickly finds itself in its own epistemological quagmire. For a start it is blessed with "reason-ridden" imagination. Further, whose is this voice? Clearly there has to be a third voice that is responsible for the other two: "Deviser of the voice and of its hearer and of himself." This leaves him with a "devised deviser devising it all for company." The possibility of proliferating these pronominal voices is virtually infinite. The only way of limiting them is for the second- and third-person pronouns to unite in an impossible first-person "I" that "will utter again. Yes I remember. That was I. That was I then." But Beckett has already demonstrated in the first trilogy the inescapable division that splits the subject between speaking subject and subject of speech. Language is the villain because it lures us into thinking that its identical use of the pronoun "I" in both cases means that a unified ego exists somewhere. The only way out of the impasse is to end the fiction, immobilize the devised and the deviser, and then bring the "words to an end. With every inane word a little nearer to the last." The final paragraph returns the "you" to where "you always were. Alone." All the pronominal presences were fictive additions that gave linguistic credence to an ultimately undefinable, non-verbal subject.

Ill Seen Ill Said is a fictive construct the subject of which is the construction of fiction, a work of imagination in which imagination is seen constantly at work. This text takes the postmodern trait of self-referentiality to unprecedented lengths. To record the process of composition in the very act of composing that record is to go beyond the by now familiar intrusion of the writer into his or her narrative. Not content with commentary, Beckett allows the narrator's concern with his craft to usurp his concern with his story. The story is minimal. It concerns an old woman who moves about a house and visits a nearby tombstone. Susan Brienza suggests that the tombstone could stand in for the grave of traditional fiction, and that the "Farewell to farewell" of the final paragraph (of the work's sixty-one) reveals the entire text to be a wake for his previous fictional output. Certainly it is the telling of the story rather than the story itself that preoccupies the narrator from the opening paragraph. Near the beginning the narrative voice urges itself into movement with "On," and pursues the metaphor of motion with commands like "Quick then," "Careful," or "Gently gently." Toward the close of the piece it applies verbal brakes with exclamations like "Less," "Enough," "No more."

These commands represent the artistic imagination caught in the very act of creation. At times it appears a godlike faculty. It summons up whatever objects it requires. "The cabin," it will announce, or, "Meagre pastures . . ." But then questions arise. "How come a cabin in such a place? How came?" The correction of tense shows the imagination already mistaking past for present, fiction for actuality. As the narrative proceeds the features summoned earlier with such authority begin to impose their own limitations on the imaginative faculty: "A moor would have better met the case. . . . In any case too late." Nevertheless the imagination's needs ultimately take precedence over internal demands for narrative consistency. What is initially ill seen soon enough becomes ill said. Words subsume the image that appears and disappears in increasingly distorted form, "well on the way to inexistence." The answer is to fall back on the inner eye of the imagination: "Nothing for it but to close the eye for good and see her. Her and rest." This inner sight is a verbal construct that has to be finally said ill enough to be rid of it. Even then the imagination has one last trick to play in the closing paragraph by prolonging its activity "one moment more. . . . Know happiness." The ill seen scenario of the narrative has been "devoured" by the ill said activity of artistic creation that has always been a principal preoccupation in Beckett's work.

What we witness in the second trilogy is the gradual replacement of the diegesis of narration (the indirect rendering of speech) by the mimesis (or direct rendering) of the act of narration. The images that provide the subject of narration in these texts are most prolific in *Company*. In *Ill Seen Ill Said* a drastically reduced visual content makes spasmodic appearances. In *Worstward Ho* the minimal images of a woman, an old man and a child, and a skull are first conjured up and then persistently reduced to a trunk or a one-eyed stare, until finally they reach the ultimate state in minimalization, "Three pins. One pinhole." Simultaneously the act of narration has taken over as subject. In effect Beckett has deconstructed the traditional form of narrative by seizing on the conventionally marginalized process of narration and reinscribing plot and character within this new hierarchy. This is a particularly appropriate strategy for a postmodernist to take if one accepts the hypothesis that one way of defining postmodernism is that it deconstructs modernism. In the case of literature such an act of deconstruction cannot ignore the logocentric use to which narration puts language. "Words are a form of complacency," Beckett wrote. In *Worstward Ho* he launches his fiercest assault on the deceptive way in which language has been used to privilege the pervasiveness of meaning, order, linearity.

The absence of a named speaker in *Worstward Ho* naturally directs the reader's attention to the role of language in this text. Opening with a linguistic reference back to *Ill Seen Ill Said*, it establishes within the first paragraph a new pared-down syntax that is simultaneously demanding and rewarding: "On. Say on. Be said on. Somehow on. Till nohow on. Said nohow on." That last sentence is also the sentence with which the piece ends. It incorporates the paradoxical nature of Beckett's last major attempt to force language to express the inexpressible, nonlinguistic void. His object is to use language to negate its signifying properties, something that he knows is ultimately unattainable. But he can at least "fail better," rob words of their positive semantic value by creating neologisms that draw attention to their deceptive nature. "What words for what then? How almost they still ring." To take the ring out of them Beckett employs double and treble negatives: "Unlessenable least." "Nohow naught." "Unmoreable unlessable unworseable evermost almost void." Beckett turns words on them-selves, compelling them to acknowledge their inadequacy, using their negation to accommodate the presence of true formless being. Yet even the radical antilanguage he forges in this text cannot always prevent the old ring from seeping through: "Vasts apart. At bounds of boundless void." Beckett announced at the start of his writing career his program: "An assault on words in the name of beauty." His last major text takes this assault to its furthest point even as it produces the aesthetic effect in the name of which he conducted his lifelong verbal war on words.

Brian Finney

Selected Bibliography

Bair, Deirdre. *Samuel Beckett: A Biography*. New York and London: Harcourt Brace Jovanovich, 1978.

Bakhtin, Mikhail. *The Dialogic Imagination: Four Essays*. Ed. Michael Holquist. Trans. Caryl Emerson and Michael Holquist. Austin: University of Texas Press, 1981.

Brienza, Susan. *Samuel Beckett's New Worlds: Style in Metafiction*. Norman: University of Oklahoma Press, 1987.

Coe, Richard. *Beckett*. Edinburgh and London: Oliver and Boyd, 1964.

Finney, Brian. *Since How It Is: A Study of Samuel Beckett's Later Fiction*. London: Covent Garden, 1972.

Fletcher, John. *The Novels of Samuel Beckett*. 2d ed. London: Chatto and Windus, 1970.

Kenner, Hugh. *Samuel Beckett: A Critical Study*. 2d ed. Berkeley: University of California Press, 1968.

Knowlson, James, and John Pilling. *Frescoes of the Skull: The Later Prose and Drama of Samuel Beckett*. New York: Grove Press, 1980.

Lyotard, Jean-François. *The Postmodern Condition: A Report on Knowledge*. Trans. Geoff Bennington and Brian Massumi. Minneapolis: University of Minnesota Press, 1984.

Rabinovitz, Rubin. *The Development of Samuel Beckett's Fiction*. Urbana: University of Illinois Press, 1984.

Satire between the Wars: Evelyn Waugh and Others

The Bogus World

"Oh, dear," she said, "this really is all too bogus."
Vile Bodies

WITH his usual economy, Evelyn Waugh needed only one word to express British satire's dominant theme between the world wars. Bogus was his word and his preoccupation. In *Vile Bodies* (1930), for instance, the term becomes a nearly universal expression of scorn. A social climber is known as "the most bogus man"; a suitor muses about marriage, wondering whether or not it "ought to *go on*—for quite a long time. . . . Otherwise it's all rather bogus, isn't it?"; a Jesuit, seeking to explain the younger generation's dissipation, observes that "this word 'bogus' they all use" is "in some way historical," denoting, as it does, their "almost fatal hunger for permanence."

Not only does the word chime sourly through Waugh's second novel, its synonyms and analogues resonate with telling persistence in the works of his fellow novelists—Aldous Huxley, George Orwell, and Graham Greene, among others. Diverse as these writers unquestionably are, their works, especially their earlier works, are united in their attack on a world that seemed to them increasingly synthetic. The general disillusionment that followed the Great War left them preternaturally alert to sham in everything from inferior goods to personal relationships to political ideologies. They became satirists, giving the lie to every pretense of order and authority mounted by a discredited officialdom. They were always ready to mock the establishment that had led the previous generation into a spectacularly wasteful conflict and was now haplessly stumbling toward a second conflagration.

Waugh registers the mood perfectly in *Vile Bodies*. The opening pages introduce us to Walter Outrage, "last week's prime minister." Despite his name, Outrage is timorously ineffectual. Crossing the English Channel, he is so anxious about the threat of rough waters that he doses himself with chloral. Repairing to his cabin for a drugged nap, he dreams of Oriental women, "a world of little cooing voices, so caressing, so humble; . . . little golden bodies, so flexible, so firm, so surprising in the positions they assumed." In his waking state, however, it turns out that Outrage once again falls quite short of his name. He is just as panicked by his temptations as he is by bad weather. Having been unable to refrain from flirting with the wife of the Japanese ambassador, he dithers irresolutely, unable to push the moment to its crisis when the obliging woman accepts his invitation to a private dinner. As in personal affairs, so in foreign. When someone refers to the war that is coming, he is befuddled. Why hasn't he been informed, he angrily wonders, adding with lame bravado, "I'll be damned . . . if they shall have a war without consulting me. . . . What do they want a war for, anyway?" As captain of his state, Outrage is clearly bogus.

The bogus theme is a commonplace in the fiction of this period. In novel after novel, it reveals itself in the increasingly synthetic elements of everyday life, especially architecture. The stately homes that populate Waugh's narratives, for instance, usually turn out to be of spurious provenance. Typically, they date from the eighteenth century but have been remodeled in the nineteenth in a faux-Gothic style favored by Victorian sentimentalists. Even those houses that seem to have retained their architectural integrity are fatally compromised by their changed surroundings. One of the few authentic eighteenth-century homes to make an appearance in his fiction is described as just barely maintaining its "grace and dignity and other-worldliness" as the "last survivor of the noble town houses of London" now "become a mere 'picturesque bit' lurking in a ravine between concrete skyscrapers, its pillared façade, standing back from the street and obscured by railings and some wisps of foliage." In this portrait, the genuine past is being squeezed from the frame by quaint simulations and blocks of functional modern housing.

With the passing of traditional architecture, an ersatz culture arises amid the wreckage. In *Brideshead Revisited* (1946), Waugh's narrator Charles Ryder takes on the ambiguous task of painting ancestral homes on the eve of their demolition. In elegiac tones, he theorizes that people are "something much less than the buildings" they make and inhabit. They are "mere lodgers and short-term sub-lessees of small importance in the long, fruitful life of their homes." This conceit, however, becomes anything but reassuring when applied to twentieth-century living quarters. If architecture determines identity, it follows that the tenants of the bogus buildings that clutter the contemporary landscape will be something less than authentic. To populate these structures, Waugh accordingly created a gallery of two-dimensional characters who roughly divide into two groups: the well-meaning traditionalists who live in parodies of a Gothic past and the willful moderns who enjoy a streamlined life in anonymous flats. The first inhabit a nostalgic dream of the past as it never was; the second refuse to be incommoded by loyalty to a tradition they neither respect nor understand.

Bed-sitting rooms and their transient residents become something of a motif in Waugh's fiction. Appointed with chromium-plated walls and natural sheepskin rugs, they express Waugh's vision of modern society: a curious blend of technological efficiency and primitive willfulness. When Ryder is told that Anchorage House is being razed so that a developer can put up a building with "shops underneath and two-roomed flats above," he describes the project as "just another jungle moving in," regaining its hold on formerly civilized precincts. But this efficiency housing has its apologists, especially among those who stand to profit from it such as Mrs. Beaver, the fashionable interior decorator in *A Handful of Dust* (1934). She argues that these flats meet "a long-felt need." After all, she explains, modern people only want a place "to dress and telephone" between business and social engagements. In the twentieth century, architecture blithely discards any attempt to create a sense of home, much less to enshrine an earlier tradition.

In its extreme manifestation, modern architecture willfully strives to erase the past altogether, replacing ornate style with functional utility. Its logical goal is expressed by the avant-garde architect Otto Silenus in Waugh's first novel, *Decline and Fall*. "The problem of architecture . . . is the problem of all art—the elimination of the human element from the consideration of form. The only perfect building must be the factory, because that is built to house machines, not men. I do not think it is possible for domestic architecture to be beautiful." In the streamlined architecture of modernity, traditional human considerations become inconveniences, for, as Silenus gloomily concludes, "All ill comes from man. Man is never beautiful; he is never happy except when he becomes the channel for the distribution of mechanical forces."

Waugh, of course, was not the first of his generation to use architecture as the gauge of the bogus. His older contemporary Aldous Huxley employed a similar strategy in *Antic Hay* (1923), a work Waugh much admired and one that may have supplied him with the germ he needed to develop his own architectural motif.

In this narrative, an architect named Gumbril builds a scale model of an idealized London for no other purpose than to have it stand as a reproach to 250 years of unremitting urban mismanagement. He bases his work on the discarded plans of Christopher Wren, whose enlightened project for rebuilding the city after the Great Fire of London in 1666 was rejected. Gumbril's model graphically reveals the missed opportunity. "Wren offered them open spaces and broad streets," he explains, "he offered them sunlight and air and cleanliness; he offered them beauty, order and grandeur; he offered to build for the imagination and the ambitious spirit of man. . . . But they preferred to re-erect the old intricate squalor." Yet he can't blame them, not when twentieth-century London is making even worse mistakes, putting up "a jumble of huge, hideous buildings." Regent Street, "the one street that was really like a symphony by Mozart—how busily and gleefully they're pulling it down. . . . Order has turned into a disgusting chaos." Making the same association Ryder does twenty-three years later in *Brideshead*, he continues, "We need no barbarians from outside; they're on the premises, all the time." As Gumbril raves on about the spoliation of London, however, the narrator pulls back to reveal another view from his son's perspective. While his father gestures passionately over his model, his "hair [blowing] wispily loose and [falling] into his eyes . . . his spectacles [flashing], as though they were living eyes," Gumbril Junior sees him as "a passionate and gesticulating silhouette" like "one of those old shepherds who stand at the base of Piranesi's ruins demonstrating obscurely the prodigious grandeur and the abjection of the human race." What we see is a man too blinded by his obsession to be able to do anything practical about improving the conditions he so bitterly condemns. Gumbril Senior is a touching but absurd figure. Much like Waugh's decent, well-educated characters, he can identify the problem, but he is powerless to correct it. No match for the barbarous powers of disorder that surround him, he retreats to his studio to dream. His son, on the other hand, decides to engage the world on its own terms. His strategy, however, is patently ludicrous, literally so. A diffident, disillusioned, history teacher, he is convinced his educational efforts have been futile, if not misleading. ("I've been . . . encouraging boys of fifteen and sixteen to specialize in history, . . . making them read bad writers' generalizations about subjects on which only our ignorance allows us to generalize.") He decides to quit his post so that he can make money with an invention of his own design: pneumatic trousers lined with inflatable rubber so that the artificially upholstered wearer need never suffer contact with the obdurate world around him. "Civilization's substitute for steatopygism," as he explains. "A boon to those whose occupation is sedentary." And, it might be added, a perfect solution for his overly intellectual class who would just as soon not be reminded of the physical basis of their daily lives. His ungainly invention couldn't be further from the elegance of his father's model, yet there is this resemblance: both men use their creations to keep uncomfortable realities at bay.

Huxley's characters typically contrive to place a bogus barrier between themselves and reality. In *Point Counter Point* (1928), Philip Quarles hides behind the architecture of his intellectualism, counseling those who allow their feelings to be shaped by poetry and novels that art shouldn't be taken too seriously. He is fond of pointing out how often the aesthetic view misleads people into emotional excesses and humiliating confusions. As if to counterpoint this counsel, the novel opens and closes with inconvenient pregnancies within his own family, the results of romance-inspired adulteries conducted by his naive brother-in-law and witless father. Despite all his intellectual armature, Philip has no answers for these real-life melodramas.

Huxley's most widely read work, *Brave New World*, portrays London some six hundred years on as a city that features architecture of astonishing design made possible by nontraditional building materials. One structure, "a squat grey building" of "only thirty-four stories," is appointed in nickel and glass. An updated cathedral stands out against the night sky, "flood-lighted, its three hundred and twenty metres of white Carrara-surrogate gleam[ing] with a snowy incandescence." Here, against an improbable cityscape, the bogus has become a prescribed way of life. In the narrative's weird utopia, dehumanization has been embraced as a species of social planning. In laboratories run on assembly-line methods, human fetuses are created in vitro so that they can be biologically engineered to the physical and mental specifications of their allotted places in society. Once the resulting children leave the production line, they are intensively conditioned to love the economically determined roles they will play throughout their existence. Even after they have been set to their adult tasks, they still remain close to their laboratory origins. So thoroughly uprooted from the ordinary terms of human existence, their bodies and minds must be artificially supplied with the chemicals and hormones that otherwise would be produced by the stimulus of normal experience. Since all births take place outside the womb, women must maintain their physical and mental health by periodically taking the hormones that accompany pregnancy. Insulated from the natural shocks of life, everyone is supplied with a "Violent Passion Surrogate" to keep the adrenal glands functioning. These manufactured human beings have achieved the synthetic ideal. They live and die amid the geometric architecture of Huxley's satire, untouched by either original thought or personal emotion.

George Orwell also gauges society by its architecture. In what is arguably his best novel, *Coming Up for Air* (1939), his protagonist George Bowling, a forty-five-year-old insurance salesman, complains of the housing lower-middle-class peddlers like himself have to live in. These projects, made up of "little stucco boxes," are "just a prison with the cells all in a row; a line of semi-detached torture-chambers where the poor little five-to-ten-pound-a-weekers quake and shiver," each in fear of losing his "brick dolls' house." The irony, Bowling points out, is that the residents don't even own their homes. While many are under the illusion that they do, in fact these are lease-held units owned by a building society that nevertheless manages to charge the occupants twice their worth.

As if this weren't enough, Bowling continues, contemporary food is equally phony. Ersatz comestibles have become the standard since the Great War. Reading labels, he notes that one product is made with neutral fruit juices and wonders what kind of fruit grows on a neutral fruit tree. Stopping for lunch, he bites into a thing calling itself a frankfurter, filled with fish! . . . It gave me the feeling that I'd bitten into the modern world and discovered what it was really made of. That's the way we're going nowadays. Everything slick and streamlined, everything made out of something else. Celluloid, rubber, chromium-steel everywhere, arc-lamps blazing all night, glass roofs over your head, radios all playing the same tune, no vegetation left, everything cemented over, mock-turtles grazing under the neutral fruit trees. But when you come down to brass tacks and get your teeth into something solid, a sausage for instance, that's what you get. Rotten fish in a rubber skin. Bombs of filth bursting inside your mouth.

In an attempt to escape the bogus world of 1938, Bowling returns to Lower Binfield, the small farming village of his turn-of-the-century childhood only to discover that it too has been infected with the streamlining disease. The food in the shops is made with margarine, the beer with chemicals. Worse, there's an upscale housing development on a hill just outside the village, designed in a faux-Tudor style. The inhabitants are a group of environmentally minded middle-class hypocrites who prate of the virtues of unspoiled landscapes and smugly deplore the filthy working-class industrial cities that make their genteel comfort possible. Meanwhile, they've turned Bowling's childhood fishing pond into a dump filled with the refuse of their synthetic lives.

Ten years later, in the totalitarian society depicted in his novel *1984* (1949), Orwell imagined the ruling Party members working in "enormous pyramidal structure[s] of glittering white concrete, soaring up, terrace after terrace, three hundred meters into the air," against a background of an unreconstructed war-torn London. In the "low-ceilinged" basement cafeterias of their state offices, lower-level bureaucrats are served a diet of synthetic foods whose ingredients are as nauseating as anything Bowling had to endure and even more obscure. At one luncheon, they dine on a stew described as "a filthy liquid mess that had the appearance of vomit." It's made with "cubes of spongy pinkish stuff which was probably a preparation of meat." Whatever they are, these foods are sold under this society's universal brand name, Victory, a label that speaks of the Party's unremitting attempt to bring the real world to heel, stamping out whatever is natural and authentic and replacing it with ersatz goods. It is in its own small but critical way part of rulers' program to establish their complete political control. Synthetic gin, synthetic cigarettes, synthetic food—the poorer the quality, the better. It's a recipe for making synthetic people. It is part of the grand strategy to distance people from reality, to render them dissociated, befuddled, confused, and, consequently, malleable. If you can't be sure of what it is you're eating, how can you be sure of anything else? It's not such a long stretch from a diet consisting of odious synthetics to a politics founded on a menu of transparent falsehoods.

Many of the satiric moments in Graham Greene's novels revolve around a similar preoccupation with substitutes. This is especially true in what he chose to call his "entertainments," which today seem as likely to claim our attention as his more serious fiction.

Rather than in large architectural structures, Greene liked to house the bogus in smaller containers. In *It's a Battlefield* (1934), a communist organizer aptly named Mr. Surrogate retreats to the metal confines of a lavatory stall to escape an embarrassing encounter. It seems his upper-class origins make him feel uncomfortable in the presence of his less cooperative working-class comrades. Hiding in the stall, he tries to make his protracted stay seem natural by flushing the toilet at intervals. His name and his ruse do more to reveal his lack of integrity than any explanation ever could.

In the justly famous scene from *The Third Man* (1949), Greene houses his most charming villain in a Ferris wheel cabin. Surrounded by the cagelike architecture of the wheel's "iron struts" and "black girders," the naive Rollo Martins has a moral showdown with his old friend, the perversely genial Harry Lime. As they rise in their swaying cabin, the occupied city of Vienna spreads below them, revealing the bombing scars it sustained in the Second World War. The narrator notes that "the horizon slid away" and "the piers of the Reichsbrucke lifted above the houses." This eerily unnatural perspective provides a fit setting for Harry to justify his deadly enterprise as a trafficker in adulterated penicillin. At the apogee of their ride, the wheel pauses long enough for a parody of Christ's temptation on the mountain as Harry invites Rollo to join his profitable scheme. It only requires that Rollo think of the people they see on the ground below as statistics, much as modern governments do. But Rollo counters Harry's offer by asking him if he has seen any of his victims, those whom his useless penicillin has left to die or, worse, contract gangrene and meningitis. Unmoved, Harry responds against a backdrop described as a "toy landscape" with "the stain of the sunset [running] in streaks over the wrinkled papery sky beyond the black girders." "Victims?" he asks.

Don't be melodramatic, Rollo. Look down there. . . . Would you really feel any pity if one of those dots stopped moving—for ever? If I said you can have twenty thousand pounds for every dot that stops, would you really, old man, tell me to keep my money—without hesitation? Or would you calculate how many dots you could afford to spare? . . . In these days, old man, nobody thinks in terms of human beings. Governments don't, so why should we? They talk of the people and the proletariat, and I talk of the mugs. It's the same thing. They have their five-year plans and so have I.

In a toyland society, nothing is quite real, except, of course, oneself. It makes getting ahead at the expense of others so much easier. Here Greene is perfectly explicit about the connection between a dehumanized public policy and individual behavior. Harry's deadly trade flourishes because the occupying Allied forces have restricted the limited penicillin supply to their military hospitals. The civilians under their "protection" must either do without or turn to illegal channels.

If officials treat people so heartlessly, Harry reasons, why shouldn't he? Yet, in true Greeneian fashion, it is Harry's marketing of a bogus medicine that enables him to provide a genuine cure for his former friend. Rollo suffers from a case of culpable innocence. He is as morally childish as the western melodramas he writes for a living, in which good and evil are instantly distinguishable. In contrast to Rollo's fiction, however, Harry's unspeakable villainy veils itself with engaging humor and undeniable vitality. He always made things seem such fun, Rollo reflects. As his name implies, Harry Lime is that ultimate of bogus allures, a charming Lucifer. He's a dark angel, simulating his former radiance by means of the limelight of his contrived charisma. It is this difficult truth that Rollo must master before he can become morally mature.

The central plot element of *Our Man in Havana* (1959) is so thoroughly bogus it's not there at all. The story is constructed around a vacuum, literally and figuratively. The narrative begins when James Wormold, a financially strapped British vacuum cleaner merchant, is lured into espionage. He's recruited by the suave but incompetent Hawthorne to run a network of spies in Havana, where he manages a Phastkleaner shop. Initially, Wormold objects on the reasonable grounds that he has no contacts and nothing to report. But Hawthorne presses him to do what he can for the good of his home country, baiting his appeal to British patriotism with a hundred fifty dollars a month and another hundred fifty in expenses, "free of income tax, you know."

Realizing his new employers have a vested interest in believing the worst, Wormold soon begins to invent high-tech horrors to satisfy their grim suspicions. Using his own merchandise for models, he draws pictures of monstrously elaborate weapons of mass destruction and tells his employers that these are being built by unnamed forces in the Cuban mountains. Inspecting the drawings in London, the chief of intelligence remarks that the weapons are surprisingly similar to vacuum cleaners. "The ingenuity, the simplicity, the devilish imagination of the thing," he nearly rhapsodizes. He is more perceptive than he could possibly understand. Greene's point in this delightful send-up of the espionage game is that suspicion creates a fatal vacuum in the imagination, a vacuum that sucks into its self-created maelstrom all the fear, hatred, and destructiveness of which the human heart is capable. The worse our imaginings, the better. The intelligence chief gleefully concludes that the weapons in Wormold's drawings are "so big that the H-bomb will become a conventional weapon." Astonished by his superior's evident relish, his assistant asks if this is desirable. The chief witheringly responds, "Of course it's desirable. No one worries about conventional weapons."

Espionage, it turns out, prizes absurdity. It urgently seeks to pervert the natural on behalf of the unnatural. Hawthorne assures Wormold that his vacuum shop is an ideal cover. Its "natural air" will disguise the very unnatural deceptions of his new profession. When Hawthorne forces him into a clandestine meeting in a men's room, Wormold sarcastically asks if it might be good strategy to change trousers before leaving in order to confuse enemy spies. After considering this ploy for a judicious moment, Hawthorne concludes quite seriously that it wouldn't "look natural, old man." In this novel, the bogus does a dizzy dance with itself.

A Portrait of the Artist as a Curmudgeon

Many writers have been driven to satire by our century's peculiar excesses. But, in England, the decades between the wars belong to Waugh. They bear his signature as no other. He may not have been as intellectual or as well-read as Huxley. He may not have been as politically astute as Greene and Orwell. But looking back from our end of the century, he seems to have had perfect pitch for his age, both by temperament and by craft.

Temperamentally, Waugh suited an age that was more than usually divided between tradition and innovation. He was himself alternately repelled and fascinated by his troubled times. They seemed to reflect his own inner division. Although he advertised himself as a reactionary, he recognized, in his own words, that "the artist, however aloof he holds himself, is always and specially the creature of the Zeitgeist." Waugh was torn between his conservative and anarchic selves. He was, in short, at war with himself. One part of him mourned the passing of the last century's gentlemanly code of values: decency, industry, and fair play. Another part, however, exulted in the mad gad-about of life of Mayfair's Bright Young People: willful, headlong, and "careless of consequence."

If Waugh often behaved like a curmudgeon, it was because he seems to have wanted to hide how much he was attracted to modernity, hide it, perhaps, even from himself. This may be why the element of disguise plays such an enormous role in his fiction. Characters are forever putting on and taking off new identities as readily as they do the false beards that seem to proliferate through his early works. So pervasive is disguise that some characters give up all effort to distinguish one person from another. In *Vile Bodies* the celebrated hotelkeeper, Lottie Crump, solves the problem of personal identification by reducing everyone to nameless anonymity. Even the most illustrious of title and fortune are reduced to the common denominator of "Mr. What-d'-you-call-him" and "Lord Thingummy." In a dehumanized world, there's not much to be gained by distinguishing between one person and the next. As long as they pay their bills, they're all the same.

For his own personal disguise, Waugh assumed the role of country squire disgusted with all developments later than 1910, not to mention quite a few before. Writing of himself in the third person in his autobiographical novel, *The Ordeal of Gilbert Pinfold* (1957), he announced that his "strongest tastes were negative. He abhorred plastics, Picasso, sunbathing, and jazz—everything in fact that had happened in his own lifetime." His manner of living gave color to these words. At thirty-four, he made a display of turning his back on his age and joining the squirearchy of the West Country. In later life, he used his loss of hearing to dramatize his distance from all things modern. He went about with an oversized Victorian ear trumpet, flourishing it this way and that to demonstrate visually his inability to hear what the contemporary world had to say to him. Tilting the trumpet toward an after-dinner speaker one evening, he made a show of initial interest. But before the talk was a few minutes old, he began to unstrap the contraption from his head, disassembling it and placing the pieces on the table next to his plate. His deliberately conspicuous performance had the desired effect. The speaker was so thoroughly discomfited he sat down before half his allotted time was up.

But, for all his advertised disgust with contemporary developments, Waugh kept remarkably informed about them. Throughout his writing career we find him addressing modern art, functional architecture, photography, and film—"everything in fact that had happened in his own lifetime." At fourteen he wrote an essay defending cubism against the "deliberate misunderstanding of a prejudiced public." At Oxford he rode motorcycles, flew with a stunt pilot, co-starred with Elsa Lanchester in a film of his own devising. In 1929, we find him commuting to Paris by plane. During the war, he volunteered for commando service, reporting later that his parachute training was wonderfully exhilarating. For all his country-squire affectations, Waugh was very much a man of his time.

Waugh has been viewed by some as a sharper-tongued P. G. Wodehouse, a more substantial Ronald Firbank, or, to borrow Sean O'Faolain's formula, "a purely brainless genius, with a gift for satire." He has been written off as a minor novelist who created his own idiosyncratic world redolent of Edwardian nostalgia. Recent criticism, however, has uncovered another Waugh, one who in fact had more in common with modernists such as Wyndham Lewis and T. S. Eliot. Like them, he was keenly interested in the peculiarities of life in our century. While he was never comfortable in his age, it is impossible to imagine him in any other. This is nowhere more apparent than in his approach to his art.

Although Waugh seems to have encouraged the notion that he was a spontaneous writer working with nonchalant ease, he in fact shared with his modernist contemporaries a deliberate and painstaking commitment to his craft. Waugh's official biographer, Christopher Sykes, reports that he was proud of his hands, which were disproportionately large for a man of his frame. He regarded them as craftsman's hands, adding that like a craftsman he liked to tinker with his work. In *The Ordeal of Gilbert Pinfold*, he places himself among "the artists and craftsmen of the late eighteenth century, . . . notable for elegance and variety of contrivance." His work, early and late, supports these self-assessments.

Waugh began his career with all the deliberation one would expect from a self-conscious artist. His early essays reveal a writer thoroughly aware of his forerunners, especially the modernists of the previous generation. He put himself to school to his older contemporaries. Doing so, he developed a prose style and narrative strategy of extraordinary energy and poise.

Waugh didn't turn to the better-known modernists, however. He didn't care for Virginia Woolf's novels, and while he admired James Joyce's early work, he was put off by what he considered the exorbitant subjectivity of his later fiction. (He claimed that reading *Ulysses* one could detect the master modernist going mad sentence by sentence.) Waugh decided that most modernist fiction was marred by self-indulgence. He found its inwardness suffocatingly irrelevant to his concerns. So instead of Woolf or Joyce, he claimed the decidedly minor satirist Ronald Firbank and the cranky modernist Wyndham Lewis as his literary mentors.

In a 1929 essay, Waugh argued that Firbank had "solved the problem which most vexes the novelist of the present time." This problem was how to reproduce the modernist sense of social and personal dissolution without capitulating to it. Waugh admired Firbank's wit, calling it "structural." Its speed and objectivity reminded him of cinematic editing. "His compositions are built up, intricately and with a balanced alternation of the wildest extravagance and the most austere economy, with conversational nuances. They may be compared to cinema films in which the relation of caption and photograph is directly reversed; occasionally a brief, visual image flashes out to illumine and explain the flickering succession of spoken words." Firbank gave Waugh the tactics he needed to display a crazed world without succumbing to its chaos: accelerated cinematic editing delivered deadpan by a detached narrator. It was a style that enabled him to impart a surreal quality to his satire while remaining unflappably aloof from the fray it reported. In *Decline and Fall* (1928), his narrator coolly introduces Oxford's Bollinger Club, an organization that draws its members from a rich vein of European lunacy. In a bemused tone, he reports of their "pouring into Oxford" for their irregularly held annual dinner:

Epileptic royalty from their villas of exile; uncouth peers from crumbling country seats; smooth young men of uncertain tastes from embassies and legations; illiterate lairds from wet granite hovels in the Highlands; ambitious young barristers and Conservative candidates torn from the London season and the indelicate advances of debutantes; all that was most sonorous of name and title were there for the beano.

The disparity between lineage and language in this catalog of decadence speaks for itself. There cannot be many other sentences that join "sonorous" with "beano." But then Waugh adds the patented Firbank touch. At the last Bollinger dinner, his narrator reports with undisguised relish, "a fox had been brought in in a cage and stoned to death with champagne bottles. What an evening that had been!" What *kind* of evening we're never told. But there is no need for an explanation. The flickering image says quite enough about this parody of upper-class habits.

If Firbank suggested the structure and attitude, Wyndham Lewis supplied the rationale. In 1930 Waugh reviewed Lewis's *Satire and Fiction*, reporting that it was a work "no novelist and very few intelligent novel readers can afford to neglect." He was especially attracted to Lewis's discussion of "the method of the external approach . . . the wisdom of the eye." Lewis urged novelists to turn away from the interior psychologizing on which modernists such as Woolf and Joyce had embarked and to focus instead on the outward appearances. He argued that the pursuit of truth in the subjective was not only self-indulgent but, worse, uninteresting. To exalt the interior feelings above an intellectual engagement with history was to betray one's artistic duty. To suppose that truth lay in "the dark places of psychology," as Woolf had put it, was to be either criminally self-indulgent or culpably misled.

For Lewis the exploration of the subconscious did not uncover what was distinctive about a person. Instead, it revealed the undifferentiated substratum of emotions and impulses common to all. Fiction, he argued, should concern itself with how particular individuals succeed or fail to shape this universal material into a distinctive personality, revealed in deeds and appearances. Most people, he believed, rarely did much with it at all. The general run of humanity, he assumed, fall into predictably conventional patterns. As creatures of their time, they deserve nothing more or less than the satirist's unsparing gaze. To gain the effect he wanted, Lewis reversed Henri Bergson's formula for humor. Bergson had argued that humor derives from describing human beings as though they were mechanisms. In Lewis's novels, humor arises when the puppet mechanisms that stand for his characters try to behave as though they were human.

Lewis's presence can be felt in much of Waugh's early fiction. In *Decline and Fall*, Paul Pennyfeather is Waugh's first puppet character, a young man with as much substance as his name implies. As the narrator mockingly reports, he is no more than a narrative convenience. He "would never had made a hero, and the only interest about him arises from the unusual series of events of which his shadow was witness." He may have been a "solid figure of an intelligent, well-educated, well-conducted young man" in another age, but not in this unseemly one. Paul's classical Oxford education and civilized manners are no match for the barbarous twentieth century. With a Firbankian wink, the narrator explains that "the whole of this book is really an account of the mysterious disappearance of Paul Pennyfeather, so readers must not complain if the shadow which took his name does not amply fill the important part of hero for which he was originally cast." Paul begins a line of hapless protagonists to follow. Adam Fenwick-Symes, the "hero" of *Vile Bodies*, is so lacking in character that the narrator introduces him with throwaway carelessness: "There was nothing particularly remarkable about his appearance. He looked exactly as young men like him do look." Adam warrants no further physical description anywhere in the narrative. When we first meet him, he is returning from Paris. He had gone abroad to write his autobiography, a presumptuous project for someone so personally indistinct and still in his twenties. Arriving in England, he passes through customs where an alert inspector spots his manuscript and his copy of Dante's *Purgatorio*. No slouch, the inspector informs Adam that he "knows dirt when I sees it, or I shouldn't be where I am today." A moment later, with all the force of British authority behind him, this moral guardian strips Adam of his personal and cultural past—his autobiography and his Dante—leaving him to drift aimlessly through London society, a featureless nonentity, submitting to a series of improvised roles—hack author, gossip columnist, vacuum salesman, impromptu pimp, and, finally, a soldier lost in the uncharted landscape of "the biggest battlefield in the history of the world." In this, Waugh's most experimental novel, his characters have no past, no future, no interior lives; their presence registers as little more than a hapless flickering against "an unusual series of events."

With the exception of his openly apologetic works involving his commitment to Roman Catholicism—*Brideshead Revisited, Helena*, and parts of the *Sword of Honour* trilogy—Waugh liked to devise paper-thin characters running amok in apparently aimless plots. These two-dimensional figures tend to fall into the two classes mentioned before: one traditional, the other modern. There are the well-meaning but dull citizens and the anarchic but engaging rogues. They often seem to belong different species. Captain Grimes and Paul Pennyfeather of *Decline and Fall*, for instance, work and socialize together but seem to belong to mutually exclusive moral universes. Grimes is the incorrigible rascal who flouts morals and manners so cheerfully that no one would seriously want to bring him to account. He may be a bisexual bigamist who leaves schoolmastering in Wales for pimping in South America, but these faults cannot be seriously held against a man who so genially confesses, "I can stand most sorts of misfortune, old boy, but I can't stand repression." Grimes goes his way "careless of consequence," slipping society's restraining nets with an ease that is as astonishing as it is comical. He is an untamable life force, disruptive of good manners, but quite beyond moral censure. Paul, on the other hand, lives his life as a divinity student with exemplary moderation (he smokes three ounces of tobacco a week and drinks a pint and a half of beer a day), keeps up with current affairs (he attends meetings at the League of Nations Union where he finds discussions of Polish plebiscites fascinating), and takes an interest in his nation's cultural past (he reads nightly installments of *The Forsyte Saga*). For his troubles he is sent down from Oxford, imprisoned for crimes he didn't commit, and, finally, forced to assume a false identity to escape his legal complications. There is no justice in Waugh's world, and that, of course, is the point. In Waugh's vision, modern society is bereft of any moral consensus and, as a consequence, human beings have been reduced to bogus shadows of themselves.

It is in *A Handful of Dust*, considered by many critics to be his best work, that Waugh makes his most trenchant criticisms of this bogus world. Tony Last is a variation on Waugh's standard protagonist: decent, educated, and almost criminally passive. As his name implies, Tony is the last of his line. Although he doesn't know it, he's the doomed gentleman in an age of crass opportunists. This ignorance defends him at first. Unlike others "all over England," he doesn't awaken each morning "queasy and despondent." Instead, a typical waking hour finds him in bed "happily planning the renovation of his ceiling." This ceiling, however, gives Tony away. It's another product of nineteenth-century nostalgia: a sham Tudor ceiling made to look coffered by means of molded slats. The house he prizes, we discover, was built in the eighteenth century and then given a spurious Gothic façade in 1864 amid the Victorian enthusiasm for things medieval. It's a fake and, however unwittingly, so is Tony Last.

Tony has the show of tradition and the style of the aristocrat, but concerning his origins he has little understanding and less curiosity. He seems to take them for granted. He performs the outward duties of the Christian gentleman, but he does so with no better motive than a genteel and sentimental nostalgia. He attends chapel on Sundays, sitting in his family's pew furnished with its own fireplace. Under the guise of tending his fire, Tony's grandfather had once rattled the hearth's grating with his poker whenever he disapproved of something in the parson's sermon; Tony, however, no longer troubles himself to keep a fire going, much less to raise theological objections. He sits uncomplainingly through the senile Reverend Tendril's sermons. These are homilies that have not been revised since he wrote them while serving with Queen Victoria's imperial army in India. His Christmas sermon is a particular favorite with his congregation. As they sit shivering in their pews, he commiserates with them, but he mistakes the nature of their discomfort. "How difficult it is for us . . . to realize that this is indeed Christmas," he ruefully observes. "Instead of the glowing log fire and windows tight shuttered against the drifting snow, we have only the harsh glare of the alien sun. . . . Instead of the placid ox and ass of Bethlehem . . . we have for companions the ravening tiger and the exotic camel, the furtive jackal and the ponderous elephant." The joke speaks for itself, but it also has further meaning. Tendril may be senile, but his sermons have an unwitting application. Tony Last is under the alien sun of the twentieth century, and the beasts of modernity are ravening all round him. His wife has taken up with the London fast set and has embarked on a pointless affair in the city while plotting to modernize Tony's beloved estate in the country. But Tony is too innocent to recognize her treachery. He is one of Waugh's decent, well-meaning bores, too complacent to maintain his guard against the barbarians at his gate. As one of Waugh's favorite metaphors would have it, he has "deserted his post" and, given the opportunity, "the jungle [is] creeping back to its old strongholds."

The sham of Tony's life is thoroughly exposed by Mrs. Rattery, his friend's current mistress. Before she arrives at his ancestral home, Tony had imagined her as "chorus girl, in silk shorts and brassiere, popping out an immense beribboned Easter Egg with a cry of 'Whoopee, boys.'" Instead she descends on Tony's estate in her own plane, emerging from the cockpit "tall and erect, almost austere in helmet and overalls," her greetings "deft and impersonal." Far from being the wanton of Tony's imaginings, Mrs. Rattery turns out to be one of Waugh's supremely modern women. She lives in the world without visible antecedents, "totally denationalized, rich without property or possessions, . . . changing her hotel on an average, once every three weeks," periodically "liable to bouts of morphine." Rootless and bored, she is the ultimate twentieth-century transient.

Like Margot Metroland in *Decline and Fall*, Julia Stitch in *Scoop*, and Virginia Crouchback in *The Sword of Honor*, Mrs. Rattery is one of Waugh's goddesses of modernity; her spirit presides over *A Handful of Dust* in much the same way these others reign in their respective narratives. She is what George Orwell called streamlined, a person who has dispatched the nostalgic accessories of the past and abandoned the needless bother of an interior life as if they were so much excess baggage. Asked her opinion of the Last estate, she replies that she never notices houses one way or the other. Houses, ancestral houses at least, establish a link from one generation to the next, but Mrs. Rattery simply does not value the continuity they represent. She is supremely indifferent to the conventional concerns people have for their past and future. Mrs. Rattery's existence is radically present tense. As such she is ideally suited for survival in the contemporary urban scene. Waugh gives her what seems to be his grudging admiration. She displays undeniable integrity. Having accepted the terms of modernity, she acts on them without shame or apology.

Mrs. Rattery's appearance in the novel is brief but pivotal. She brings the modern world to Hetton and with it the death of Tony's Victorian dream. During her visit, his son dies and his marriage unravels. It's not that she is responsible for these events or that she dislikes Tony. In fact, she is the only one who bothers to offer him any comfort during his ordeal. But in the design of the novel, her presence simply explodes Tony's self-indulgent idyll.

Like Waugh's other innocents, Tony must suffer for his dereliction. He meets his punishment in Brazil. Having belatedly awakened to his wife's betrayal, he embarks on a mad quest to find a lost civilization in the Amazonian jungles. Instead, he discovers that the modern savagery at home is only mirrored by the primitive savagery abroad. Succumbing to fever in the tropic clime, Tony wanders deliriously into the compound of a half-breed illiterate named Mr. Todd who has an unlikely passion for Dickens. He's so obsessed with Victorian sentiment that he makes a practice of having Dickens read to him aloud whenever he can get his hands on someone able to read. Soon Tony becomes his captive, reading and rereading the complete works while Mr. Todd ruminates on their significance. "Do you believe in God?" he asks one day. Tony replies, "I suppose so; I've never really thought about it much." Mr. Todd's rejoinder is withering: "Dickens did."

In Waugh's view, Tony, the would-be Victorian gentleman, has missed the point of his cultural allegiance altogether. He has supported tradition for tradition's sake, taking it as an end rather than a means. But tradition's real purpose, Waugh suggests, should be to provide structures through which the individual can become aware of the transcendental principle behind all traditions. Tony's dedication is shallow and, ultimately, sterile. He had thought his life would form a link in the continuous development of a purposeful future. Instead, he loses his heir and his estate. There is nothing to bequeath. Doomed to the Sisyphean task of reading the entire works of Dickens over and over again to his Brazilian captor, Tony meets his appropriate fate. He had affected the forms of the Victorian gentleman without troubling himself to examine the assumptions upon which these forms were based. His punishment is to be lifted out of history altogether and spend his last days steeped in what Waugh thought to be a sentimental fantasy of nineteenth-century life recorded in the melodramatic pages of Dickens's novels. It is a grotesque but fitting nightmare.

The lesson Tony learns too late in *A Handful of Dust* is the same one Charles Ryder in *Brideshead Revisited* and Guy Crouchback in *Sword of Honour* must master: the tradition they value so highly is not theirs by right of class, education, sentiment, or talent. While such distinctions may enable one to appreciate the tradition more deeply and to contribute to it more fully, these considerations must be secondary to its real mission, which in Waugh's view was to make God's word manifest in the world. No matter how genuine its provenance, when any aspect of this tradition is not serving this purpose, it becomes as bogus as any of the quaint Gothic makeovers or Bauhaus atrocities he ridicules elsewhere. This aspect of Waugh's intention is often misunderstood. He paints such charming portraits of country houses and their upper-class inhabitants that more than a few commentators have gone astray. In the case of *Brideshead*, Waugh even had to sustain the charge of perverting his religious devotion by fusing it with a romantic idealization of the aristocracy. In fact, he meant something quite different.

At the end of *Brideshead Revisited*, Ryder finally overcomes his abiding snobbery when he is forced to realize that his romance with the aristocratic Flyte family and their Roman Catholic culture is but a stage in a much more important journey, one with a decidedly Dantesque echo. He is seduced into accepting God step by step, first being drawn to his imperfect creatures: the charming Sebastian, then his sister Julia, and finally the Brideshead estate itself. Each in turn works a spell on him until he finds himself enamored of the principle upon which their lives, their home, and their tradition rest. But this is not enough. There is another step to be taken and it can only be gained through loss.

The novel opens and closes with Ryder once again at the Brideshead estate many years after his original involvement with its residents. He has been posted there unexpectedly in his capacity as an army officer during the Second World War. While nostalgic, his return is not an entirely happy experience. It was here that his engagement to Julia, the estate's heir, foundered irreparably. His feelings are further complicated by its present condition. The house has been transformed from a seat of aristocratic tradition into a military barracks. All has changed. As in the sixteenth century when the forces of the Reformation besieged it, history has once again violated the chaste Brideshead. Soldiers swagger through the halls and courts, cursing casually and throwing their spent cigarettes negligently into the fountain. But then Ryder notices that the light outside the chapel still burns and quite a few of the men attend services there. Brideshead has provided these men with a retreat from the horrors of war, and in doing so the house continues to serve its real purpose. It doesn't belong to the Flytes, much less to Ryder. It belongs to all who can read its message. Ryder finally understands: if tradition doesn't provide such occasions, it has no justification.

In *Unconditional Surrender* (1961), the last volume in the *Sword of Honour* trilogy, Guy Crouchback learns that even noble aspirations can turn bogus. To become the gentleman he has always longed to be, he must abandon his notions of chivalric heroism and noblesse oblige. As he entered the Second World War, he saw himself as a knight marching against the "huge and hateful . . . Modern Age in Arms" as it revealed itself in the Warsaw Pact between Hitler and Stalin. But in Yugoslavia he confronts the unromantic truth in the plight of Mme Kanyi.

Mme Kanyi, a Jewish refugee displaced by war and trying to save her people from the Yugoslavian Partisans, wonders how so many could have thought the conflict would lead to any good. Like Orwell's George Bowling, she has no interest in assigning blame. Everyone is guilty.

Is there any place that is free from evil? It is too simple to say that only the Nazis wanted war. These communists wanted it too. It was the only way in which they could come to power. Many of my people wanted it, to be revenged on the Germans, to hasten the creation of the national state. It seems to me there was a will to war, a death wish, everywhere.

Then she asks if there were people in England who had also seen the war as a means to achieve their personal ends. Guy, who had hoped to redeem his sterile life in virtuous combat, blurts out, "God forgive me, . . . I was one of them." Even the best of intentions can prove false, as Guy discovers tragically once again after this conversation. When he tries his best to save Mme Kanyi, he not only fails, he unwittingly provides cause for their execution. The Partisans have observed his meetings with her and use them as evidence to prosecute her.

Guy is not the knight-errant he envisioned himself to be at the war's beginning. There is, however, something for him to do. However inglorious in the world's eyes, it is "the chance of doing a single small act to redeem the times." Upon returning to England, he takes in his deceased wife's illegitimate child as his own. The novel's ending makes clear that this genuine act of charity redeems Guy from his bogus notions about what it takes to be a gentleman.

The Solid Sum of Two Plus Two

Satire is the genre of the plainspoken. It's taken up by people who are viscerally opposed to mystagogy and ready to attack it where and whenever it raises its hydra-headed complexities. It's not surprising, then, that satirists as politically diverse as Waugh and Orwell would have been repelled by contemporary gnosticisms, especially fascism and communism. In their assessment, such systems were nothing more than elaborate intellectual excuses for brutally acquiring power over others.

They both urged resistance to the dehumanizing designs of all modern political systems. The power of plain speech and objective truth were their chosen defenses.

Orwell's last novel, *1984*, and Waugh's tenth, *Helena*, couldn't be further apart in subject matter and tone, yet they have a common purpose. Orwell's is a grim parable of present tendencies projected into the near future; Waugh's, a spritely reworking of a Catholic legend dating from the fourth century. Both novels, however, are equally committed to exposing the destructive effects of modern thought, especially when it expresses itself as a ruthless solipsism capable of liquefying objective truth in the solvent of expedience, whether personal or political. This is why the protagonists of both novels undertake desperate struggles to establish standards of objectivity. Both Winston Smith and Helena seek some principle that can guarantee the knowability of external reality. In the absence of such certitude, those in power will inevitably package the truth to fit their own designs.

In *1984*, Orwell pushes this tendency to its limits and, doing so, reveals the consequences of believing in nothing. To paraphrase G. K. Chesterton, the danger of losing one's faith in a knowable world outside the self is not that one will believe in nothing but rather that one is liable to believe in anything. In Orwell's totalitarian state, this is precisely what is required of the citizenry. They are expected to pass the test of indiscriminate faith. They must believe in what they know to be false. Not just pretend, but believe it unreservedly. This is an exercise in mental gymnastics called doublethink. One is supposed to give unhesitating assent to official pronouncements that are self-evidently false. Although the Party leaders can and do rewrite history to conform to their changing policies, this alone does not satisfy them. They want to demonstrate conclusively to their citizens that they have the power to make anyone believe anything. The ceaseless broadcasts, pouring forth from ubiquitous telescreens, announce transparent lies. Absurdly optimistic predictions of economic improvement are routinely contradicted a few weeks later without comment. People are called upon to applaud a brutal victory over a heinous enemy who a few days before had been portrayed as an irreproachable ally.

This is not just the political expedience of keeping up with changing events. The Party actually uses these reversals as occasions to deliberately strain the credulity of even its most submissively loyal members. Winston is particularly shocked the evening the Party calls upon the

people to switch loyalties in midsentence. During a particularly feverish rally, they are led suddenly and inexplicably to chant execrations on
a nation they had been cheering as an ally only a moment before. At the
same time, their former enemy is instantly transformed into their most
trusted ally. The government that can get its people to doublethink perfectly, to give full-hearted assent to what they know to be incontestably
false, has in effect destroyed the grounds of intellectual and moral resistance in advance. Such a state of epistemological incoherence deprives
the individual of the fulcrum of objective truth. There is nothing on
which to exert the lever of personal conviction.

When the dissident Winston Smith is apprehended, he is put
through sustained brainwashing designed to make him "perfect." Part
of the process requires that he deny fundamental mathematics.
O'Brien, Winston's torturer cum father confessor, proposes that two
plus two equal five, but he is not satisfied when Winston acquiesces to
this absurdity. He demands that Winston *believe* the sum is five. In fact,
he must even transcend the report of his senses. When O'Brien holds
up four fingers, he demands that Winston at once see that there are four
and believe there are five and simultaneously know that he is exercising
the process of doublethink. "Only the disciplined mind can see reality,
Winston," O'Brien explains.

You believe that reality is something objective, external, existing in its own
right. . . . But I tell you, Winston, that reality is not external. Reality exists in
the human mind, and nowhere else. Not in the individual mind, which can
make mistakes, and in any case soon perishes; only in the mind of the Party,
which is collective and immortal. Whatever the Party holds to be truth *is* truth.
It is impossible to see reality except by looking through the eyes of the Party.

With impeccable logic, O'Brien demonstrates the political advantages
of believing in nothing: it renders one capable of believing in anything—anything, that is, that the Party decides will be true for the
moment.

When Winston protests that this is nonsense, that the Party can't
control the laws of nature, can't stop aging and disease, can't know the
minds of others, O'Brien calmly demurs. He points out reasonably that
whatever happens outside the mind is unknowable and whatever happens within is fully controllable. "We make the laws of nature," he
boasts. "Reality is inside the skull. . . . There is nothing that we could
not do. Invisibility, levitation—anything. I could float off this floor like

a soap bubble if I wished to." Without an objective standard to appeal to, Winston flails about to regain his intellectual footing. "The belief that nothing exists outside your own mind—surely there must be some way of demonstrating that it was false?" When he desperately insists that "there is something in the universe—I don't know, some spirit, some principle—that you will never overcome," O'Brien asks the question Mr. Todd had asked of Tony Last: "Do you believe in God?" Winston doesn't. "Then what is it, this principle that will defeat us?" O'Brien demands. "I don't know," Winston replies, appealing vaguely to "the spirit of Man." The novel's bleak ending does not make this seem an effective appeal.

It is typical of Orwell's integrity that he did not make things easy for himself in his inverted utopia. Elsewhere he had argued that belief in absolutes, whether God or political ideology, diminishes the individual human being. Yet here he displays the individual's vulnerability in a world stripped of any fixed coordinates external to the mind. In such a world, power, not impartial inquiry, must always be the final arbiter of truth.

Unlike Orwell, Waugh did believe in absolutes. After reading *1984*, he wrote to Orwell to say how much he admired his novel but added that he couldn't agree with its metaphysics. One can see why, especially in his novel *Helena*. Here he openly marshals the tenets of his faith to defeat the argument that reality is a purely mental affair. While his theology may only persuade the already convinced, it nevertheless allowed him to examine one of the critical problems of modern thought: How does one refute O'Brien's solipsistic logic without appealing to an absolute?

For Waugh there was but one way out of this impasse. As he had written in 1946, human nature could only achieve "its determining character" in the recognition "of being God's creature with a defined purpose." Only in light of this purpose, he believed, could the mind hope to address reality confidently and effectively. This is the burden of *Helena*.

Waugh liked to say that *Helena* was his best novel. Very few have agreed with this estimate. Unlike his other fiction, with the partial exception of *Brideshead Revisited*, it is frankly a work of apologetics. Yet it has its own charm as a historical romance, amusingly written in a modern vernacular, and it has special value for anyone interested in Waugh because it so clearly reveals the premises upon which his other novels rest.

The narrative retells the story of St. Helena, mother of Constantine and alleged finder of the True Cross. In Waugh's version of the legend, Helena's first promptings toward Christianity are much the same as his. Like him, she is drawn to its straightforward rational arguments and its insistence on its simple historical origins. She finds this a refreshing contrast to the exotic mystery cults of her day with their subtle metaphysics and ingenious exegesis of ancient myths.

Helena is constitutionally unreceptive to intellectuals who delight in speculation for its own sake. Marcias, the eunuch slave who was once her tutor, is such a thinker. A professional Gnostic, he gives lectures on the mystery religions. Helena attends one of his talks on the significance of the fertility goddess Astarte. At his recital's conclusion, she demands to know "when and where did all this happen?" Marcias informs her that her question is childish. "These things are beyond time and space." But the plainspoken Helena is not so easily put off. "It's all bosh," she concludes, using her favorite term of dismissal.

Marcias is portrayed as an irresponsible intellectual—a clever, talented man, obviously sophisticated and well-read, but without convictions. At bottom, he cares little for the consequences of his teachings except as they help or hinder his career. When things become at all difficult, he simply retreats into his mind, "sailing free and wide in the void he made his chilly home." He is as sterile intellectually as he is physically.

This is why Helena turns her back on him. Later, once her interest in Christianity has been aroused, she decides the best way to consolidate her faith and that of others will be to locate Christ's cross. She is convinced there can be no better proof of the incarnation than the historical artifact, the "solid chunk of wood" on which Christ was crucified. She will have nothing to do with Marcias's mysticism.

We meet variations of Marcias's type throughout Waugh's fiction—for instance, Mr. Samgrass in *Brideshead Revisited*. An Oxford don, Samgrass enjoys an encyclopedic grasp of history and culture, but he is, for all his intellectual attainments, essentially shallow. We're told that although

not a man of religious habit, . . . he knew more than most Catholics about their Church; he had friends in the Vatican and could talk at length of policy and appointments, . . . what recent theological hypothesis was suspect, and how this or that Jesuit or Dominican had skated on thin ice or sailed near the wind in his Lenten discourses; he had everything except the Faith.

Samgrass, or Sammy, as he is called by condescending acquaintances, is a little man who makes his way in the world by toadying to the whims of his aristocratic patrons. Despite his erudition, he is no more than a soulless flunky, at best an object of scorn, at worst an interfering nuisance.

Mr. Prendergast in *Decline and Fall* is a more pathetic version of the type. He is a parson who suffers "Doubts." He accepts an assignment as a prison chaplain because the post does not require that he hold any particular beliefs at all.

These figures and others like them have an identifiable source in Waugh's life. Looking back in 1949, he tells us of the theologian who "inadvertently made [him] an atheist" in his early youth. This happened the day he informed his public school class that none of the Bible's books were written by their supposed authors and then invited his students "to speculate in the manner of the fourth century on the nature of Christ." Once this worthy had "removed the inherited axioms" of his faith, Waugh reports that he found himself quite unable "to follow him in the higher flights of logic by which he reconciled his own scepticism with his position as a clergyman."

Waugh was always troubled by such sophistication. "If its own mind is not made up," he reasoned, religion, however erudite, "can hardly hope to withstand disorder from outside." When the mind retreats into itself, it either loses the strength to confront reality or, alternatively, it willfully constructs a private, self-centered reality. It was better, he reasoned, "to be narrow-minded than to have no mind, to hold limited and rigid principles than to have none at all."

Waugh portrayed both his decent agnostics and his unprincipled intellectuals as wholly unready to stand up to the barbarism that, in his view, was always clamoring at the gates of civilization. When a fanatic inmate decides Reverend Prendergast doesn't believe in Christ, he takes a saw and decapitates the hapless clergyman. This gruesome episode stands as a metaphor of one of Waugh's central themes: modern man rendered impotent by doubt, his intellect uselessly detached from reality.

As his Helena recoiled from the mystery cults of her time, so Waugh was repelled by what he took to be the subtle evasions of modern thought. Either there was a truth to be found or there was none at all. Either the human mind could discern a purpose to existence or life was meaningless. For Waugh there was no middle ground. From his conversion in 1930, the choice for him was always "between Christianity and Chaos." (This, of course, was true on intellectual grounds, not behavioral; Waugh readily acknowledged that his actions aligned with his ideals only intermittently. His personal incivility is legendary. He was a man capable of reducing sincere admirers to confusion and even tears for no better reason than personal pique. When asked how one who professed to be a Catholic could behave so horribly, he responded that were he not Catholic he would hardly be human at all.)

In telling the tale of Helena's discovery of the True Cross, Waugh was testifying to his conviction that we are meant to discover our purpose not in sophisticated metaphysics or otherworldly mysticism but in the ordinary world of the senses. In short, he believed that physical reality was sacramental. When Helena undertakes her mission, she has no interest in theological speculation. Nor does she care for the subtle distinctions of Christian dogmas such as the hypostatic union. Her search is not inward, but entirely outward. Her vindication is to be achieved not by retreating from but rather by engaging with the ordinary world. She is convinced that once she finds the "solid chunk of wood" on which Christ was crucified, she will have also reached a crucial intersection of time and eternity. This plain, homely artifact will prove that the external world is knowable and responds to our longing for meaning and certainty. If she is right, Waugh suggests, then our minds' representations, from the most pedestrian to the most sophisticated, even when misshapen or mistaken, can never be wholly futile. They arise from our interaction with the meaningful and knowable reality that surrounds us. As such, our perceptions and thoughts always carry with them revelatory potential. Waugh was convinced that viewed correctly—that is, through the eyes of faith—daily experience does nothing less than inform us, however imperfectly, of our purpose as created beings.

Helena's mission, then, speaks of Waugh's belief that in the beginning was the Word and the Word was made flesh, which is to say, in the argot of current literary criticism, that the original sign and its referent were one and the same. It followed for Waugh that, however uncertainly and fleetingly, language must have the power to put us in touch with the real presence of reality's eternal being, no matter how confusing our day-to-day experiences. Truth was to be located neither in the mind nor in experience but rather at their fruitful intersection. In his opinion, this homely position was enough to explode the lures of solipsism, ideology, or any other gnosticism.

It hardly need be said that many do not find Waugh's religious convictions congenial, including many of his own church. But this makes his current return to popularity all the more intriguing. Whatever one thinks of his answers, the questions he raises in *Helena* speak to our current anxieties. What can we know with certainty? How can we achieve a moral consensus without an appeal to absolute principles? Are we, as some recent neo-Kantian philosophical schools suggest, trapped in the web of our own semiology, forever uncertain about the nature of external reality? And, if so, are there any sound reasons to refrain from scrapping traditional concepts and refashioning human nature to meet political exigencies?

One doesn't have to subscribe to Waugh's theology to appreciate the urgency of his argument, not when so many find it so difficult to distinguish between the genuine and the bogus in human affairs.

George McCartney

Selected Bibliography

Blayac, Alain, ed. *Evelyn Waugh: New Directions*. London: Macmillan, 1992.

Carens, James F. *The Satiric Art of Evelyn Waugh*. Seattle: University of Washington Press, 1966.

Carpenter, Humphrey. *The Brideshead Generation: Evelyn Waugh and His Friends*. Boston: Houghton Mifflin, 1990.

Gorra, Michael. *The English Novel at Mid-Century*. New York: St. Martin's Press, 1990.

Heath, Jeffrey. *The Picturesque Prison: Evelyn Waugh and His Writing*. Montreal: McGill-Queens University Press, 1982.

Kenner, Hugh. *The Pound Era*. Berkeley: University of California Press, 1971.

Kernan, Alvin B. *The Plot of Satire*. New Haven, Conn.: Yale University Press, 1965.

Lodge, David. *Evelyn Waugh*. New York: Columbia University Press, 1971.

Lodge, David. *The Modes of Modern Writing*. Ithaca, N.Y.: Cornell University Press, 1977.

McCartney, George. *Confused Roaring: Evelyn Waugh and the Modernist Tradition*. Bloomington: Indiana University Press, 1987.

Pryce-Jones, David, ed. *Evelyn Waugh and His World*. Boston: Little, Brown, 1973.

The Reaction against Modernism: Amis, Snow, Wilson

D URING the 1950s—around the time that the *nouveau roman* was beginning to emerge in France and the postmodernist novel in America—many English novelists were moving in a different direction, turning back to traditional modes of fiction writing. Rejecting the experimental techniques of James Joyce, Virginia Woolf, and other modernists, the new generation of writers looked mainly to nineteenth-century authors for inspiration. Not all of the English novelists of that period were part of antimodernist movement; Lawrence Durrell, Nigel Dennis, William Golding, and Iris Murdoch are some notable exceptions. But many others, including C. P. Snow, Kingsley Amis, Angus Wilson, Doris Lessing, William Cooper, John Wain, Alan Sillitoe, John Braine, Pamela Hansford Johnson, David Storey, Honor Tracy, and Keith Waterhouse, rejected experimental writing and made a conscious effort to return to an earlier style.

By the early 1950s an element of hostility toward experimental writing was emerging in English literary circles. The following comment on the state of contemporary fiction by an anonymous reviewer in the *Times Literary Supplement* is typical: "Enough—some would say more than enough—has been achieved in the way of experiment." For some critics, James Joyce was the chief villain of the piece. Thus J. B. Priestley deplored "the fact, set down by Mr. Levin, Joyce's American enthusiast, that this disreputable author is today required reading in college courses. . . . (Anybody impressed by that can never have entered an American college)." Priestly was persuaded that Joyce had been overestimated as a writer. "Two questions still remain. Did he write like a great novelist? Does the intelligent reading public genuinely accept him as a great novelist? And the answer to both is *No.*"

Priestley's remarks appeared in the London *Sunday Times,* whose editor, Leonard Russell, held similar views about modernist writing. C. P. Snow described how, at the Savile Club in 1948, Russell listened sympathetically as he attacked "the Virginia Woolf novel of sensitivity and plotted its overthrow." Soon afterward, Russell offered Snow a position as a reviewer for the *Sunday Times.* Snow accepted, and between 1949 and 1953 he wrote well over a hundred reviews for that publication as well for the *New Statesman,* the *Spectator,* and other weeklies.

Other novelists of this period were also active as reviewers. Kingsley Amis, a poet and critic as well as a novelist, began reviewing books for the *Spectator* in 1953; he subsequently published some hundred pieces there. Around the same time, Angus Wilson was publishing articles and reviews in *Encounter,* the *Listener,* the *New Statesman,* the *Observer,* the *Spectator,* and other English journals. Snow, Amis, and Wilson thus became prominent both as advocates and as practitioners of an antimodernist aesthetic. As Wilson said in 1964,

A novelist like Snow and, to some extent, I myself, Amis, and others, have felt since [World War II] that the traditional novel still has much to offer. Man's relation to society was not given its place in novels like those of Virginia Woolf—a weakness of Woolf. The weakness of Virginia Woolf is not any kind of stated social belief, but the unstated social acceptance of the society in which she lived; in a way, it was her *strength,* because it allowed her to forget about society and examine the personality as a kind of metaphysical unit. English society was changing very greatly in 1945, and it has been changing really very much ever since then. . . . These changes led us to revive, in some degree, the traditional forms, I think.

Wilson contributed actively to the revival of interest in traditional fiction. He published studies of Dickens, Trollope, and Kipling, as well as articles and reviews in which he dealt sympathetically with Victorian writers. Snow began writing fiction before the Second World War, but his major output came afterward. He also completed critical studies of the authors he admired: a book on Trollope and another, *The Realists,* on eight nineteenth-century novelists. Amis similarly expressed his antipathy toward modernist writing in his reviews and critical essays and, like Wilson, published a book on Kipling.

Echoing through the writings of these and other English novelists of the 1950s is the complaint that modernist fiction had so baffled the public that readers were giving up on novel reading. As Pamela Hansford Johnson (who later would marry C. P. Snow) said in 1949,

In the nineteenth century [the ordinary reader] was happy. Dickens wrote for him; and Trollope, and Thackeray, and George Eliot. . . . But today he is seriously worried. Reading some of the weekend literary columns, he finds himself urged to admire some work which, when he buys or borrows it, he finds arid, unenjoyable, and not infrequently incomprehensible. He turns back from book to review. He thinks, "Is this man crazy or am I?" He has been taught to respect the critic. If the lesson is well-learned he may start to lose faith in himself. If he preserves his independence he then takes refuge, more often than not, in the detective story.

William Cooper, a friend of C. P. Snow's, felt that it was necessary to attack the experimental novel in order to find an audience for his own kind of fiction:

During the last years of the war a literary comrade-in-arms and I, not prepared to wait for Time's ever-rolling stream to bear Experimental Writing away, made our own private plans to run it out of town as soon as we picked up our pens again—if you look at the work of the next generation of English novelists to come up after us, you'll observe that we didn't entirely lack success in our efforts. . . . We meant to write a different kind of novel from that of the thirties and we saw that the thirties novel, the Experimental Novel, had got to be brushed out of the way before we could get a proper hearing.

It was Cooper's view that there was a strain of intellectual decadence in modernist writing:

The impulse behind much Experimental Writing is an attack from the inside on intellect in general, made by intellectuals so decadent that they no longer mind if intellect persists—in fact some of them sound as if they would be happier if it didn't. . . . In any part of intellectual society the decadent are at the present moment of history immediately identifiable: they are plugging a theory that everybody really knows *won't work*.

What exactly this "attack from the inside on intellect in general" was Cooper did not explain; nor did he indicate why, if the experimental writers were "plugging a theory that . . . *won't work*," he was so intent on attacking it.

John Wain, another author whose fiction first appeared in the 1950s, assured his readers that "the experimental novel died with Joyce." After *Ulysses*, there was little experimental novel writing that was "serious, or motivated by anything more than faddishness or the irritable search for new gimmicks." Wain included in this category even the novels of Samuel Beckett.

Persuaded that the time for experimentation was over, the antimodernist authors chose to model their own fiction on more traditional forms. For Doris Lessing, this meant returning to the style of the nineteenth-century realistic novelists:

> For me the highest point of literature was the novel of the nineteenth century, the work of Tolstoy, Stendhal, Dostoyevsky, Balzac, Turgenev, Chekhov; the work of the great realists. . . . I hold the view that the realist novel, the realist story, is the highest form of prose writing; higher than and out of the reach of any comparison with expressionism, impressionism, symbolism, naturalism, or any other ism.

While similar views were held by many other novelists of this period, I have chosen to focus on Amis, Snow, and Wilson because they were prolific both as critics and as novelists. The three are linked by some other similarities: they attended Oxford or Cambridge, for a time were engaged in university teaching, and eventually were knighted. (Snow, some years after receiving his knighthood, was made a life peer as Baron Snow).

Amis, Snow, and Wilson also had in common a strain of antielitism that influenced their aesthetic outlooks. To them, modernism seemed arcane, highbrow, antidemocratic—the relict style of a superannuated establishment. One of the set pieces in Amis's novels is a satirical turn directed at the posturing of pompous culturati. Wilson similarly expressed opposition to elitist pretensions; in a 1950 talk broadcast by the BBC he attacked Virginia Woolf because her "sort of elitist middle-class sensibility or at any rate that of her imitators had been one of the deepest complacencies that had brought England near to destruction." To Snow, modernism epitomized a return to aristocratic values that presented an impediment to the evolution of the new British meritocracy. All three authors, then, found in modernism—an apparently progressive literary movement—a strong element of social conservatism; often, this belief gave impetus to their attacks on it.

Kingsley Amis

In 1954, in the *Spectator*, Kingsley Amis announced his desire to ban from literature "all use of allegory, symbol, or other mystification capable of inducing a sober blurb-writer or reviewer to invoke the name of Kafka." Discussing Vladimir Nabokov's *Lolita*, Amis complained about the profusion of stylistic attributes such as "pun, allusion, neologism, alliteration, *cynghanedd*, apostrophe, parenthesis, rhetorical question, French, Latin, 'anent,' 'perchance,' 'would fain,' 'for the nonce.' " *Lolita*, according to Amis, was "bad as a work of art . . . and morally bad." Reviewing Nabokov's *Pnin*, Amis was no less hostile: "That this limp, tasteless salad of Joyce, Chaplin, Mary McCarthy, and of course Nabokov (who should know better) has had delighted noises made over it by Edmund Wilson, Randall Jarrell, and Graham Greene is a mystery of dimensions."

Amis's objections to Nabokov held for other authors whose prose showed signs of similar attributes:

Style, a personal style, a distinguished style, usually turns out in idiosyncratic noise level in the writing, with wow from imagery, syntax, and diction: Donne, Pater, Woolf. There is, however, a good deal of nostalgia for style nowadays among people of oldster age-group or literary training; it shows in snorting accusations of gracelessness levelled against some younger novelists and merges into the hankering for "experiment" that still dies hard.

In another article Amis went into detail about his aversion to experimental writing:

The idea about experiment being the life-blood of the English novel is one that dies hard. "Experiment," in this context, boils down pretty regularly to "obtruded oddity," whether in construction—multiple viewpoints and such— or in style; it is not felt that adventurousness in subject matter or attitude or tone really counts. Shift from one scene to the next in midsentence, cut down on verbs or definite articles, and you are putting yourself right up in the forefront, at any rate in the eyes of those who were reared on Joyce and Virginia Woolf and take a jaundiced view of more recent developments.

In mentioning "recent developments" Amis indicates that for him the age of modernism is past, and anything on the contemporary scene that resembles it should therefore be jettisoned. He does not, however, apply the same dismissive criterion to other writing from earlier eras. Amis considers himself a follower in the tradition of the English novelists of the eighteenth century, and has discussed his affinity for the fiction of Henry Fielding.

Amis has in a number of respects been influenced by Fielding. In Amis's first novel, *Lucky Jim* (1954), he gives a droll description of the progress of Jim Dixon, a young university lecturer exercised by the pretentious atmosphere of an English red-brick university. Poking fun at highbrow posturing becomes the instrument of Amis's satire, and in its blend of sharp observation, amusing predicaments, and lighthearted banter, *Lucky Jim* recalls *Tom Jones*.

Some of Amis's other novels similarly follow in the eighteenth-century tradition. *That Uncertain Feeling* (1955) resembles Fielding's *Joseph Andrews* as well as the works of Samuel Richardson, the writer Fielding was parodying in that novel. Updating the familiar fictional contest between virtue and ambition, Amis presents a hero who discovers that the price of a promotion is submission to the advances of the wife of a town councilman. Similarly, the central figure in Amis's novel *Take a Girl Like You* (1960) has a good deal in common with another eighteenth-century heroine, Samuel Richardson's Clarissa. Both of Amis's novels make for amusing reading, if not as amusing as *Joseph Andrews* or, for that matter, *Lucky Jim*.

Amis's subsequent writing seldom lived up to the promise of *Lucky Jim*. There, readers share in the author's delight as Jim Dixon hurls the proper measure of vitriol toward a deserving target. In Amis's later works the vitriol is at times poured by the barrelful, and the target seems to be anything that comes into range. Often, Amis's moral viewpoint becomes indistinct when he ridicules characters who represent antithetical sides of an issue. For example, in *Take a Girl Like You*, Amis derides the heroine for trying to preserve her virginity, as well as her antagonist for trying to rid her of it. Similarly, in *One Fat Englishman* (1963), Amis mocks the shortcomings of American culture as well as those of his hero, a snob who mocks the shortcomings of American culture.

There is a similar problem in *Jake's Thing* (1978), the story of an Oxford don whose declining sexual drive leads him to seek help from a number of inept—even goofy—mental health specialists. Amis's animosity is directed not only against incompetent therapists or even therapists in general, but also toward his own protagonist and assorted other characters. In *Stanley and the Women* (1984), Amis tells about the mental breakdown of the protagonist's son and in the process introduces still another deranged psychiatrist. But the dotty therapist is by now a stereotyped figure, and the satire again begins to turn sour. Too often, Amis's splenetic curmudgeons emerge as little more than mouthpieces for their author's irascible complaints.

Even so, after a shift of gears, Amis can surprise readers with a deft observation. In most of his novels he is at least in places shrewd and witty, a trait that can go far toward rehabilitating an otherwise dull chapter. (An example is the following description of a restaurant in *Jake's Thing*: "The food wasn't much good and they were rather nasty to you, but then it cost quite a lot.") Like the satirists he admires, Amis is in his best form with an appropriate target, exposing the rot as he shears away layers of encrusted hypocrisy.

Similar strengths and weaknesses can be found in many of Amis's novels. In some—particularly his earliest—he presents a satiric view of contemporary sexual issues and explores moral questions that are related to them; examples include *I Want It Now* (1968); *Girl, 20* (1971); and *Difficulties with Girls* (1988), where he returns to some of the characters he introduced in *Take a Girl Like You*. Some of Amis's other novels such as *Ending Up* (1973) and *The Old Devils* (1981) deal with more somber questions: problems of aging, alcoholism, illness, and impending death.

In other books Amis moves away from social issues to make use of popular genres. *Colonel Sun* (written under a pen name in 1968) is a respectful imitation of a James Bond thriller; *The Anti-Death League* (1966) is a spy novel; *The Riverside Villas Murder* (1973) and *The Crime of the Century* (1989) are mysteries; *The Alteration* (1976) and *Russian Hide and Seek* (1980) are science-fiction novels; and *The Green Man* (1970) is a ghost story. A similar interest in popular forms can be found in Amis's criticism. He published a study of science fiction, *New Maps of Hell* (1960), and in collaboration with Robert Conquest, edited *Spectrum: A Science Fiction Anthology* (1961). Amis also completed a book on Ian Fleming's novels, *The James Bond Dossier* (1965).

This interest in popular forms is a central element in Amis's writing; he wants even his serious novels to retain a broad appeal. In *I Like It Here* (1958), when Amis's hero visits the grave of Henry Fielding, he muses on Fielding's undiminished popularity: "Perhaps it was worth dying in your forties if two hundred years later you were the only non-contemporary novelist who could be read with unaffected and whole-hearted interest, the only one who never had to be apologized for or excused on the grounds of changing taste." That Fielding is "the only non-contemporary novelist" who can still be read with interest is disputable; but the comment reveals the populist sentiments that figure in Amis's view of modernism, in particular his feeling that it carries an air of snobbish exclusiveness. Thus he once complained that British culture seemed to him as if it were "the property of some exclusive club."

For Amis, the works of the modernists foster cultural posturing: the doyens of culture promote them until paying homage to the enshrined modernist aesthetic becomes the price of admission into a cultural elite. The cycle is accelerated by literary scholars who, responding more to one another's pronouncements than to their own artistic sensibilities, force sanctioned works onto the impressionable young. "Most scholars," Amis assures us, "are men of foggy aesthetic sense, the ideal audience for their own propaganda." Surveying this slough of intellectual self-deception, Amis takes it on himself to champion the ordinary reader, the main victim of the poseurs. Under this populist banner Amis has attacked, along with the modernists, such canonical icons as *Beowulf*, *The Faerie Queene*, and *Paradise Lost*.

Like many of the 1950s novelists, Amis praises those writers who maintain rapport with ordinary readers—those who, if they consider themselves serious writers, are also entertaining. In this context Amis speaks approvingly of such twentieth-century novelists as H. G. Wells, Evelyn Waugh, Aldous Huxley, Christopher Isherwood, Ivy Compton-Burnett, and Anthony Powell. Among American writers Amis praises Louis Auchincloss, Jerome Weidmann, John Cheever, Peter DeVries, and Mary McCarthy. On the other hand, Amis dismisses Hemingway and Faulkner; English readers, he feels, tend to find them "alien, strongly and essentially non-European."

Amis is surely justified in arguing that for art, affectation precludes the development of affection. And he may also be right that some members of an elite—critics, academics, upholders of a Bloomsbury establishment—did in fact try to turn the works of the modernists into shrine objects. But lost in his attacks is a judicious examination of the intrinsic worth of modernist writing. Amis invokes the names of Woolf and Joyce in jeremiads on their detrimental effects on culture, but he avoids discussing their works. He seems unaware that Joyce himself was a critic of social intolerance and cultural posturing. Nor does Amis ever consider whether Woolf's feminism might be as legitimate an expression of democratic principles as his own antielitist satires.

Even worse, Amis at times reveals something less than a whole-hearted allegiance to the same democratic principles. His characters continually vent their biases, often sounding very elitist indeed when they sound off against Americans, West Indians, Jews, foreigners, blind people, and women—particularly, and persistently, women. In *Jake's Thing*, a novel that gained notoriety for its expressions of misogyny, Amis tries to restore balance by ridiculing his hero, who accommodatingly labels himself a male chauvinist pig. But this attempt to have it both ways—to fire away at women while taking the occasional potshot at a woman-hater—only muddies the waters. As in some of his other novels, Amis's irresolute moral point of view transforms directed satire into pointless invective. Readers lose sympathy for Amis's characters, and even for Amis himself, when he seems to relish nothing so much as a testy crudeness in flaunting his characters' bigotry.

A similar characteristic undermines Amis's attacks on modernism: a sense that prejudice has too easily overcome objectivity, that long-held opinions blind him to the value—to the greatness—of the best modernist writers. Amis lacks nothing in intelligence, but his criticism is undermined by a streak of inflexibility. Having once expressed a view—no matter how outrageous—Amis finds it hard to backpedal: my biases, right or wrong. Having years ago decided to jettison the modernists, Amis gives little sign of considering whether his dismissals were hasty. It also seems imprudent for Amis to lavish praise on writers of modest accomplishments when Woolf, Joyce, Faulkner, Kafka, and Nabokov are dismissed.

Amis urges his contemporaries to dispense with style in their writing, but blithely ignores significant aesthetic questions such as whether it is indeed possible to write without style. It might seem that Amis is being hyperbolic, that in attacking modernist extravagance he is only advocating a plain style. But plain can lead to drab, and drabness takes its toll on Amis's novels as well as on those of his contemporaries. In his broad condemnation of modernism Amis precludes the use of innovative methods for himself as well as for any novelists who take his message seriously.

Amis's aesthetic led him to repudiate untried, venturesome, and innovative elements, to define anything arcane or unfamiliar as extravagant. Rejecting the modernists, Amis adopted an aesthetic xenophobia that restricted him to sedate, conventional practices; as a result his novels are often limited. It is in his satiric attacks that one finds a real sense of freedom, adventure, and playfulness; this, perhaps, is why Amis has sometimes been tempted to carry them too far.

C. P. Snow

As a reviewer, C. P. Snow often praised the younger writers of his generation for rejecting experimental writing. In a piece for the *New York Times Book Review* published in 1955, he included Kingsley Amis in this group:

There are a dozen or more promising novelists in England—Doris Lessing, William Cooper, Emyr Humphreys, Francis King, Kingsley Amis, J. D. Scott, Brigid Brophy, John Wyllie are some of the best. Not one of these, in his practice, shows any interest in the sensibility novel or the *avant garde* of ten or twenty years ago. Several of them have explicitly and roughly savaged it. None of them wants to shrink away from society; their attitude to their art is much tougher than their immediate predecessors; some of them are going to be heard of.

Like Amis, Snow at times wrote mysteries; in fact, his career as a novelist began with a detective novel, *Death Under Sail* (1932). In this book Snow's hero remarks on the "extraordinary prudery of the Irish Catholic," and holds it "responsible equally for the censorship in Boston (Mass.), gang warfare in America, [and] Mr. James Joyce. . . ." Elsewhere in *Death Under Sail* Snow includes a complaint about Joyce's "onanistic reveries." Forty-six years later—two years before his death in 1980—Snow told an interviewer that he had read the Bloomsbury writers—Woolf, Strachey, and Forster—but had found them "very foreign to my temperament, as they still are: nerves too near the surface; hearts too cold; and too lacking in real introspective candor."

Is Joyce's writing little more than the by-product of a repressed culture? Snow often complained about sexually explicit writing (as in his comment about Joyce's "onanistic reveries")—is it really Joyce who is the prudish one? And again: can Woolf and Forster really be considered "cold-hearted" or "lacking in real introspective candor"? Snow's dismissals often seem to be ill-considered or biased.

In different places Snow expressed a number of objections to modernist fiction: that it was unreadable; that it alienated ordinary readers; that it was causing the death of the novel; that it provided unsuitable models for younger writers; that it was hostile to science; that it was politically reactionary; that it was mindless; that it was arcane; that it was old-fashioned; that it was not truly experimental; and that it was too much like abstract painting. Some of these charges can be found in a *New York Times Book Review* essay he published in 1955:

The coroners of literature gathered hopefully around. The novels which were receiving the serious attention were the mindless and unreadable novels of sensibility. The coroners said that the novel was dead. The gap between this specialized art and any reading public was getting wider and wider. Plenty of novels, some good, some bad were reaching the reading public; but they were not the novels literary persons were writing about. Many intelligent readers were just plain baffled. They did not have the patience to follow the course of this esthetic war; but when asked to venerate—or above all, read—wodges of moment-by-moment sensation, they passively went on strike.

If modernist writing was on the verge of killing off the novel, how would this aesthetic homicide be accomplished? If large numbers of readers, reacting to Woolf's or Joyce's or Forster's novels, "passively went on strike," Snow gives no proof beyond anecdotal evidence. And if some modernist novels are challenging, there seems to be little evidence that "intelligent readers" en masse have been repelled by modernist writing generally—by such works as *Mrs. Dalloway* or *A Passage to India* or *A Portrait of the Artist as a Young Man*. Once again, Snow's charges cannot stand up to very much scrutiny.

Another of Snow's allegations had to do with the modernists' political views. Like Amis and Wilson, Snow was nettled by the middle-class conservatism of the Bloomsbury Group, but his allegations often went further than theirs. Writing in the *Times Literary Supplement*, Snow attacked the modernists for their reactionary politics:

This syndrome is seen at its most complete in writers like T. E. Hulme, Joyce, or Pound. It has been visible in a considerable sector of advanced literature all through the first half of the century. It is a social and psychological phenomenon of some interest, and I hope to deal with it a little more fully some time, in particular to explore the connection which seems to be close, though not in individual practitioners inevitable, between this sector of advanced literature and extreme social reaction—not conservatism, but extreme social reaction. This is a connection which is now clear, though, through a curious deficiency in social insight, we were slow to see it.

Whatever one might say about Hulme or Pound, Joyce—Snow's real target—was no social reactionary; nor does Snow ever submit evidence that he was. Snow's approach is based on guilt by association: if Hulme and Pound were both reactionaries and modernists, Joyce must also have been both. Interestingly, Snow has little to say about Hulme or Pound in his literary discussions; their names mainly come up in discussions of the modernists' political views.

Snow presents a similar argument in *The Two Cultures and the Scientific Revolution* (1959). Here he describes how an acquaintance complained to him that "most of the famous twentieth century writers" were reactionary. "Yeats, Pound, Wyndham Lewis, nine out of ten of those who have dominated literary sensibility in our time—weren't they not only politically silly, but politically wicked? Didn't the influence of all they represent bring Auschwitz that much nearer?"

Can it truly be argued that "nine out of ten of those who have dominated literary sensibility in our time . . . most of the famous twentieth century writers" contributed enough to Nazi ideology to "bring Auschwitz that much nearer"? Snow somehow manages to forget that Joyce and Woolf—the novelists whose names recur in his literary attacks—were neither pro-Nazi nor anti-Semitic. Could Snow have been unaware that Joyce was, if anything, philo-Semitic, or that Woolf married a Jew? Here again Snow is imprecise in representing that which he instinctively dislikes.

The central idea in Snow's attack on the modernists is that the work of an anti-Semite or reactionary must ipso facto be condemned. But when he finds it convenient, Snow can relinquish this principle. In *The Two Cultures and a Second Look* (1963) he says of Dostoevsky, "he was virulently anti-Semitic. . . . He was in fact the supreme reactionary." On the same page, however, he expresses an undiminished admiration for Dostoevsky: "Dostoevsky is to this day one of the novelists I most admire . . . besides Tolstoy there seem to me only two or three others who can live in the same light." Somehow Dostoevsky is admired even if he is a social reactionary, while Joyce is dismissed as a social reactionary even if he is not.

Dostoevsky and Tolstoy are among Snow's favorite authors. Writing in the *Review of English Literature* he said that he considered them—along with Proust, Balzac, and Dickens—the five best novelists of all time. In his 1978 critical study *The Realists*, Snow included chapters on these writers as well as Stendhal, Henry James, and the nineteenth-century Spanish novelist Benito Pérez Galdós. Trollope, George Eliot, and Wells are among the other English novelists Snow admired. In general Snow praises those nineteenth-century novelists who give realistic portrayals of contemporary social issues: elements that are no less important in Snow's own novels.

One of the reasons Snow is so opposed to modernist writing is its emphasis on individuals, particularly on socially alienated individuals. For him, "the novel only breathes freely when it has its roots in society." In *A Portrait of the Artist as a Young Man*, Joyce's Stephen Dedalus takes a distinctly contrary view: art that is primarily driven by social or moral concerns becomes too much like propaganda; and Joyce tried to keep his own writing from being subverted by social or political influences.

This provides another explanation for Snow's antagonism toward Joyce. Snow, an establishment figure, exemplified the very converse of the alienated individual; he believed in working from within the system. With the end of Churchill's dominance came a period when the Labour Party introduced reforms that would put talent ahead of heredity in determining social and political advancement. Snow—a scientist, science writer, academic, novelist, critic, and government administrator—was himself a good example of the kind of talented person who could rise in such an environment, and he was often invited to do government work. In the late 1930s he served on a committee whose mission was to recruit scientists for the British war effort; he subsequently became director of technical personnel for the British Ministry of Labor. After World War II he was put in charge of scientific personnel for the English Electric Company; later, he joined its board of directors. From 1945 to 1960, he served in the government as civil service commissioner; in 1964 he became parliamentary secretary for the Ministry of Technology.

Snow referred to those who were achieving positions of leadership in postwar Britain as "the new men" (women were apparently not perceived as a part of the meritocracy). Researchers, administrators, academics, civil servants, members of the professions: the best would rise to the top regardless of origins. In a transformed society those who had inherited titles, wealth, or influence would be replaced by the new men, who would in turn take on the task of building a better society. This combination of privilege and responsibility was an integral part of the credo of the new men, and was also at the root of Snow's literary outlook: for him, it seemed unthinkable that artistic considerations should take precedence over one's obligation to society. Hence any literature that seemed to be promoting social alienation had to be rejected.

Snow's Strangers and Brothers series has as a central theme a chronicling of the development of the new meritocracy. Lewis Eliot, the central figure in the series, is, as Snow himself was, one of the new men (indeed, Snow used the phrase for the title of a novel in the series). Snow's social realism is well suited to its subject; together with his celebration of the rise of the new class, it makes his fiction somewhat similar to that of the Marxist social realists.

Like the Marxist writers, Snow held that artists must put social concerns ahead of aesthetic considerations. Related to this art-versus-society question is a congruent issue, that of the place of morality in art. For many of the critics who were Snow's contemporaries—F. R. Leavis is perhaps the best-known example—the greatest novels were those with a strong ethical element. Such works were deemed superior to any that focused on aesthetic concerns; thus the decadence of fin-de-siècle art was attributed to a divestiture of moral concern brought on by an overly aesthetic approach. Leavis himself was not very receptive to modernist writing, and Joyce was pointedly omitted from his list of those who had maintained the great tradition in novel writing.

If Snow had harbored hopes that this apparent consonance of views would win him Leavis's admiration, he was very much mistaken. Leavis saw Snow as a member of a resented Oxbridge-London literary establishment; and in a 1961 farewell speech at Downing College, Cambridge, he launched a notably caustic attack on Snow. Snow, Leavis told his audience, "can't be said to know what a novel is. The nonentity is apparent on every page of his fictions. . . . I am trying to remember where I heard it (can I have dreamed it?) that they are composed for him by an electronic brain called Charlie, into which the instructions are fed in the form of the chapter headings." Even if Snow's writing is often uninspired, such invective can hardly be justified. (Interestingly, another of Leavis's immoderate attacks was directed at Amis: he once raised the fantastic charge that Amis was a pornographer.) Another reason for Leavis's sharpness was Snow's "two cultures" argument; in describing an apparent rift between scientists and humanists, Snow sided with the scientists. Leavis, of course, would have numbered himself among the humanists being chided about their ignorance of scientific matters.

Snow often wrote sympathetically about science, in his fiction as well as in his essays. In 1933 he published (anonymously) *New Lives for Old*, a work that provides a Wellsian glimpse of life in a more technologically advanced society. In Snow's first successful novel, *The Search* (1934), the central figure is a scientist who, like Snow himself, eventually decides to give up his scientific career.

In 1940 Snow published *Strangers and Brothers*, the first book in the eleven-novel Strangers and Brothers series (in order to avoid confusion Snow later changed this novel's name to *George Passant*). Told in the first person, the Strangers and Brothers novels deal with the observations and experiences of Lewis Eliot, a lawyer, academic, and government committee member; the action follows his progress from youth to old age. Snow's characters are often men of power and influence; many hold prestigious university affiliations or important government posts. The series is both a roman-fleuve and a roman à clef, and in interviews with the critic John Halperin, Snow took the trouble to identify many of the living counterparts to his characters. In the same way, Lewis Eliot is very much like C. P. Snow, a similarity which the author himself has acknowledged.

While Lewis Eliot is the narrator of the Strangers and Brothers novels, the characters at center stage in most of these works are his friends and acquaintances. The eponymous hero of the 1940 novel *George Passant* is an idealistic lawyer and teacher of law whose passion is helping young people; Passant befriends Lewis Eliot and a number of his friends, some of whom will reappear in Snow's later novels. *George Passant* ends with a trial: Eliot's his old benefactor has been accused of fraud, and Eliot—now a practicing lawyer—serves on Passant's defense team.

The Light and the Dark (1946) is set in Cambridge before and during World War II. Its protagonist, Roy Calvert, is a young Orientalist; and the drama in the novel evolves out of its descriptions of academic politics. Calvert is brilliant, witty, and dashing, but suffers from depression; eventually, realizing that he will never escape from his mental illness, he volunteers for dangerous war duty and dies in action.

Academic politics is no less important in *The Masters* (1951), whose action hinges on the election of a new master for a Cambridge college. Snow is good at describing small-group politics, and in this work he has found his subject. Snow's shrewd insights as the candidates vie for support make this his most interesting book. In another novel, *The Affair* (1960), Snow describes the furor over a Cambridge college's decision to dismiss a fellow. Once again Snow deals with academic politics; but the theme, by now a familiar one for his readers, is handled less successfully than in the earlier works.

In *The New Men* (1954) Snow returns to the world of science, describing events surrounding the development of the atomic bomb; the protagonist is Lewis Eliot's brother Martin, a physicist. In *Corridors of Power* (1964) political issues are examined on a higher level than in the other novels: that of affairs of state. However, *Corridors of Power* lacks the immediacy and persuasiveness of Snow's earlier fiction, perhaps in part because his work as a civil servant never quite brought him into the realm he depicts, that of the highest echelons of government.

Other works in Snow's Strangers and Brothers series, like those of the writers Snow admired, center on some important or interesting facet of contemporary society. In *The Conscience of the Rich* (1964) Snow describes a wealthy Jewish family; and in *The Sleep of Reason* (1968) he deals with student uprisings and depicts events that resemble the famous Moors Murders trial that had taken place a few years before.

Time of Hope (1949) and *Homecomings* (1956) deal mainly with events in Lewis Eliot's life. The first tells about Eliot's student years and the second about his marriage to the unstable Sheila—a marriage that ends with her suicide. *Last Things* (1970), the concluding book of the Strangers and Brothers series, returns to Eliot, who has remarried; the novel also serves as a denouement for the entire series, filling in details about the characters who had earlier appeared in it.

After the publication of *Last Things*, Snow completed three more novels. *The Malcontents* (1972) centers on the relationships of parents and children, and is in part based on Snow's own experiences as a father. *In Their Wisdom* (1974) tells of a serious eye operation like the one experienced by Snow himself and also described in *The Sleep of Reason* and *Last Things*. Snow's final novel, *A Coat of Varnish* (1978) is, like his first, a detective mystery.

As a novelist Snow adheres to the realistic principles of the nineteenth-century writers and avoids symbolism, allegory, and stylistic idiosyncrasies. Even so, the realism in Snow's novels sometimes breaks down. Lewis Eliot, like many first-person narrators, is continually enlisted as a confessor; he is made party to so many secrets that the reader's credulity is strained. Moreover, the characters in Snow's novels continually express their respect and admiration for Eliot; because he is so much like his author one begins to lose faith in the objectivity of the narrative, and another component of the nineteenth-century realistic aesthetic is undermined.

Snow's writing can be lackluster; the situations he describes are often predictable and recounted with little charm or humor. For all his democratic protestations, he sometimes seems snobbish, ready to titillate readers with a glimpse into the lives of the wealthy or powerful. At its best, however, his writing is engaging. Snow describes a period of change marked by technological discoveries, the rise of the welfare state, educational reforms, and altered class structures. He captures the mood of this era, and in doing so provides an understanding of the modus vivendi of the new British elite.

Angus Wilson

Like Amis and Snow, Angus Wilson was active as a critic, and his literary preferences can to some degree be defined by the subjects of his studies: *Émile Zola: An Introductory Study of His Novels* (1952), *The World of Charles Dickens* (1970), and *The Strange Ride of Rudyard Kipling* (1977). In various essays Wilson indicated that Richardson, Jane Austen, Thackeray, Trollope, George Eliot, Dostoevsky, Stendhal, Proust, and Dickens were among the writers who had most influenced him. Again like Amis and Snow, Wilson became central in the movement to revive interest in nineteenth-century fiction. As he explained in 1957, "I've deliberately tried to get back to the Dickens tradition." A few years later Wilson described his general approach to writing fiction: "My own novels are essentially traditional in form and my preoccupation is strongly—too strongly for some critics—a social and moral one."

For Wilson, as for other writers of the period, an emphasis on social concerns was linked to a rejection of experimental fiction. As he said in the *London Magazine* in 1954,

Most of the English novelists (perhaps all) who have arrived since the war have reflected the predominant, politically detached, social concerns of the community. This has led to a revival of traditional, nineteenth-century forms. It has told against experiments in technique and against exploration of personal sensitivity. I belong to this reaction myself and I believe that it has been a valuable one that has revitalized and restored the novel form.

Wilson was particularly in tune with the reaction against the Bloomsbury Group that was gaining momentum in the 1950s. Like some of the other writers of that period, he attacked Virginia Woolf as much for her social attitudes as for her writing style:

The first and most obvious limitation in Virginia Woolf's novels lies in her failure to extend her sympathies outside a narrow class range. . . . Unfortunately, she is not content to leave the subject of class outside her range—apart from the gallant old servants and the intimate flashes of understanding with shop assistants that are part of the armory of charm with which Mrs. Ramsay or Clarissa Dalloway or Elinor Pargiter surround themselves—aspects of the patronage which is revealed in a more deadly form in their dealings with their families and friends—apart from these Virginia Woolf is constantly feeling the need to face more tragic aspects of social inequality.

It is worth noting that in the same essay Wilson was careful to acknowledge that Joyce's works were free of the class animus that characterized Woolf's: "It is surely because of Joyce's real faith in the intellect that he was able to allow full scope to his contact with humanity and to distil from Leopold and Molly Bloom the essence of the tragedy of modern life, from which Virginia Woolf had always to protect herself." Wilson's argument, in contrast to those of Amis and Snow, is never overstated; moreover, it demonstrates that he has a good deal of familiarity with the works of Woolf and Joyce.

A number of years later Wilson developed a new appreciation for Woolf. As he said in a letter to me in 1967, "I feel that I underestimated Virginia Woolf as a writer. . . . Though her influence in England is spent, she is an important figure for the novel generally." In another letter Wilson had more to say on this subject:

Perhaps the most striking change has been my conviction that the class sympathies I disliked in Virginia Woolf are superficial and unimportant. I have learned to estimate *Mrs. Dalloway*, *The Waves*, and *Between the Acts* as among the finest novels in the twentieth century, although, perhaps, by their superb achievement barring that particular poetic road to later English novelists. As for Joyce, my admiration has increased as I have come to appreciate the plays and novels of Beckett.

A similar change marked Wilson's development as a novelist. His earliest short stories and novels were written in a realistic style that reflected the influence of the nineteenth-century writers he admired. The stories he published in two early collections, *The Wrong Set* (1949) and *Those Darling Dodos* (1951), are typically social satire flavored by the influence of Dickens, Trollope, Austen, and later writers like Huxley, Waugh, and Ivy Compton-Burnett. Here Wilson mainly examined the tensions that arise from class differences—a topic also favored by the writers who influenced him.

In Wilson's first novel, *Hemlock and After* (1952), the protagonist is Bernard Sands, a writer engaged in establishing a retreat for artists and poets. Sands is decent, kind, intelligent, but also vulnerable: he is a homosexual living in pre–Wolfenden Commission England, a time when homosexual activity was was punishable by law. A foil to Sands is Vera Curry, a ruthless antagonist who seems almost Dickensian in the way she personifies evil.

Dickensian characters proliferate in Wilson's next novel, *Anglo-Saxon Attitudes* (1956; the title is from Lewis Carroll). Drawing on his experience as a librarian and administrator at the British Museum, Wilson describes a scholarly scandal loosely based on the Piltdown Man hoax. His panoramic book is concerned with social and moral questions; drawing on a large cast of characters Wilson offers a far-ranging picture of contemporary English society. Deliberate in his employment of nineteenth-century techniques, Wilson is one of the few novelists whose work gains in vitality and color because of its return to a traditional style. *Anglo-Saxon Attitudes* is one of Wilson's finest books and also one of the best British novels of the 1950s.

The Middle Age of Mrs. Eliot (1959), narrower in scope than its pre-decessor, is about a widow, Meg Eliot, and the readjustment she undergoes after her husband's death. Here Wilson's writing shows (appropriately enough) the influence of George Eliot; there are also borrowings from Jane Austen, Trollope, and Henry James. Providing readers with a clue to his novel's origins, Wilson includes a list of his heroine's favorite books: *Emma*, *The Mill on the Floss*, *The Small House at Allington*, *The Portrait of a Lady*.

The Old Men at the Zoo (1961) marks another of the shifts in approach that attest to Wilson's inventiveness. Armageddon—the third world war—has come and gone; surprisingly, it has caused little destruction. The main problem in postwar England is hunger, and this leads the protagonist, another of Wilson's essentially decent figures, to a moral dilemma. A naturalist who studies badgers, he comes to prefer them even to humans; but now, if he is to survive, he must trap them and eat their flesh. Evident here is Wilson's larger concern: the way war leads to dehumanization.

Late Call (1961) is set in one of England's New Towns—the towns built to house a population displaced by World War II bombing and urban development. Wilson's middle-aged heroine is driven to learn about her childhood, and this provides Wilson with a means for contrasting her New Town environment with the English communities of an earlier time. Like some other writers of the period, Wilson uses a New Town setting as a vehicle for depicting the disillusionment that came in the wake of the Labour government's welfare-state policies: first a glittering promise of a suburban utopia and then the insipid fulfillment—a community deficient in the attractions of city and country life alike.

In the 1960s, around the time that Wilson began to describe his growing appreciation for the modernist writers, he himself adopted some experimental techniques in his fiction. *No Laughing Matter* (1967), a family saga partly based on Wilson's own life, has as its backdrop a panorama of some fifty years of English social life. Its style is more adventurous than that of Wilson's earlier novels: he makes use of inner monologues, symbolism, and allegory, and even parodies such writers as Beckett. As Wilson told me in 1967, "I think that my position has been greatly modified, even strongly changed by my own development as a novelist—my feeling that the traditional form was inhibiting me from saying all that I wanted to say. To some extent I tried to move out of it in *The Old Men at the Zoo*, and I do more so in my new novel."

These experimental devices add an interesting texture to Wilson's novel, and many critics saw them as another indication of Wilson's inventiveness and imaginative breadth. In some quarters, however, he was dismissed with the kind of attack that was commonplace in the 1950s: his perceived failures as a writer were attributed to his use of experimental methods.

Wilson has from time to time written travel pieces, and the same interest is reflected in *As If by Magic* (1973), a novel that ranges over a broad geographical area. The central figure in the book is one of Wilson's decent humanists, a geneticist who develops new strains of rice and travels to different countries visiting plant-breeding installations where the rice is being tested. Also explored in this novel is the theme of the separation of the generations as exemplified in the protagonist's relationship with his university-student goddaughter.

Setting the World on Fire (1980) represents still another shift in subject matter: here Wilson concerns himself with the world of the English upper classes. Wilson's protagonists—two brothers—receive elite educations, have ample opportunities to develop their talents, and enjoy the privileges of wealth. As foils, Wilson presents a group of terrorists, the enemies of the world represented by his protagonists.

In sum, a number of traits recur in most of Wilson's works: a precision in conveying details, a willingness to explore new directions, and a moral outlook informed by generous humanistic principles. These qualities help to explain why Wilson's response to the antimodernist movement was finally so different from Snow's or Amis's. Reluctant to repeat himself, Wilson was open to trying new techniques and willing to reconsider his earlier rejection of experimental writing. When he did attack Woolf, his remarks were characterized by fairness and an intelligent understanding of her work. One of the best novelists of his generation, Wilson has also proved himself a knowledgeable and perceptive critic.

Conclusion

In the early 1950s the English literary world was dominated not by the modernist writers but by the critics, reviewers, and academics who were their apologists. Enthusiastic about experimental writing, these critics seemed to the next generation of writers too authoritarian, too dismissive of nineteenth-century writing, and too ready to use the modernists in promoting their own elitist views.

The 1950s writers rebelled. Their views became dominant, and eventually they replaced the previous generation of critics. Traditionalism was no longer unfashionable, and the social novel displaced the novel of alienation. But in their revolutionary zeal many members of the new generation of writers adopted the tactics of the old. Too often, their goal was not merely to open the way for one style of writing but also to close it to others. Thus, in destroying one establishment, the 1950s writers created another; and its parochialism was no less repressive. The reputations of writers like Joyce and Woolf were finally not very much damaged by the antimodernist movement. But at the time the message for unpublished novelists was unmistakable: climb onto the antimodernist bandwagon or be left behind.

Angus Wilson was one of the first to describe how a new dogmatism was springing up in place of the old. "Orthodoxy of the social novel," he wrote in 1954, "would be as deplorable as the orthodoxy of Bloomsbury. I should be happy to see more than Mr. William Golding swimming against the tide with success."

It is with good cause that Wilson mentioned Golding: the latter was one of the novelists being attacked at that time. *Lord of the Flies*, Golding's first novel (and for many readers his best), was published in 1954; the reviews ranged from lukewarm to very hostile. In particular, Golding was scolded for the deviations from realism introduced by the allegorical aspects of his novel. It was not until a number of years had passed and *Lord of the Flies* appeared in paperback that the book found a sympathetic audience.

The novels of Lawrence Durrell were given an equally hostile reception. Here again it is worth quoting Wilson, who notes a connection between the insularity of Durrell's critics and the vehemence of their attacks:

Since France, and with her most of Western Europe, has persisted in experimental novel writing, all this tends to increase the division between English literary culture and European, to encourage a a self-satisfied insular attitude which reaches occasional peaks in the clownishness in Kingsley Amis' attacks on "abroad." It was to be seen very clearly when Lawrence Durrell's quartet appeared. On the whole the work received a fierce handling from English critics. In many ways it deserved it. Mr. Durrell's aims are magnificent, but his execution was often slipshod and pretentious, and the language floridly vulgar.

Yet too often the implication of English critics was that Durrell's novel had failed because it was experimental and therefore out-of-date; what is more, there was a distinct implication that this was bound to happen when a chap becomes an expatriate, lives abroad, and cuts himself off from the main stream of his country's development. This sort of criticism is too illiberal, mistaken and bad. It is the dangerous result of a too-rigid swing of the pendulum.

Some observers have argued that this kind of literary xenophobia ended with the 1950s. But if the insularity Wilson deplored became less common in the next decade, it had not disappeared. For example, B. S. Johnson, a young English writer who published a number of experimental novels in the 1960s, was left bitter by the experience. In the introduction to his *Aren't You Rather Young to Be Writing Your Memoirs* (1973), he complained about the refusal of English readers to come to terms with writers like Joyce and Beckett, and about the persistent hostility to anything that came close to avant-garde writing.

A year later, in a radio discussion, Kingsley Amis's son Martin (himself a novelist of some repute) discussed his father's rejection of experimental writing. "I have always thought it remarkable," said the younger Amis, "that someone who is as linguistically aware as my father should never have sought to experiment in prose at all, or to have seen any virtue whatever in slightly experimental prose." This remains a central question: why the advocacy of one style should so insistently demand the rejection of another.

I hope it is clear that I am not attacking traditionalism in fiction, or saying that the 1950s novelists should have followed a modernist style: *Anglo-Saxon Attitudes* is an example of the memorable fiction that can be produced when a writer returns to a traditional style. Rather, my point is that art produced in an atmosphere of repression and conformity can become dull, weak, tame, colorless; and that this in fact often occurred in the English fiction of the 1950s.

Rubin Rabinovitz

Selected Bibliography

Acheson, James, ed. *The British and Irish Novel since 1960*. New York: St. Martin's Press, 1991.

Bergonzi, Bernard. *The Situation of the Novel*. London: Macmillan, 1970.

Biles, Jack, ed. *British Novelists since 1900*. New York: AMS Press, 1987.

Bradbury, Malcolm, ed. *The Novel Today: Contemporary Writers on Modern Fiction*. Glasgow: Fontana, 1977.

Bradbury, Malcolm, and David Palmer, eds. *The Contemporary English Novel*. London: Arnold, 1979.

Burgess, Anthony. *The Novel Now: A Student's Guide to Contemporary Fiction*. London: Faber, 1971.

Ford, Boris, ed. *The New Pelican Guide to English Literature*. Vol. 8, *The Present*. Harmondsworth, Eng.: Penguin, 1983.

Gardner, Averil. *Angus Wilson*. Boston: Twayne, 1985.

Gardner, Philip. *Kingsley Amis*. Boston: Twayne, 1981.

Halio, Jay, ed. *Critical Essays on Angus Wilson*. Boston: G. K. Hall, 1985.

Halperin, John. *C. P. Snow: An Oral Biography*. New York: St. Martin's Press, 1983.

Stevenson, Randall. *The British Novel since the Thirties*. Athens: University of Georgia Press, 1986.

Sleeping with the Enemy: Doris Lessing in the Century of Destruction

There's something I have to reach. I have to tell people. People don't know it but it is as if they are living in a poisoned air. They are not awake. They've been knocked on the head, long ago, and they don't know that is why they are living like zombies and killing each other.
Briefing for a Descent into Hell

The reason, as we all know, why readers yearn to "believe" cosmologies and tidy systems of thought is that we live in dreadful and marvellous times where the certainties of yesterday dissolve as we live.
The Sirian Experiments

WHEN Doris Lessing immigrated to London from Rhodesia at the end of the decade that opened with World War II and closed with the Iron Curtain coming down, her host nation had strong and cohesive opinions about its culture. A challenge to the distinction between high and low culture had yet to be successfully mounted, and high culture remained largely the preserve of white men born in England, educated at Oxford or Cambridge, and working in or publishing out of London. In that London of the fifties, Lessing recalls in a recent sketch published in *The Real Thing* (1992), "there were no foreigners, only English, pinko-grey as Shaw said, always *chez nous*, for the Empire had not imploded, the world had not invaded, and while every family had at least one relative abroad administering colonies or dominions, or being soldiers, that was abroad, it was there, not here, the colonies had not come home to roost." Some inroads had, of course, been made, particularly by novelists, into this very narrow terrain. James Joyce was acknowledged to be a contributor to British culture in spite of his Irish origins, Virginia Woolf had been admitted in spite of her sex, and D. H. Lawrence was knocking at the door in spite of his humble beginnings. But no person of color, no voice from the colonized of the third world, had yet penetrated the canon, and the culture the British revered as representative of themselves and as the best in the world, the culture that it had been the mission of the empire to carry to the four corners of the world, remained in the hands of an elite group of native-born white men, whose virtues and rightful sway it subtly but relentlessly asserted.

Marginal on every count but race to this construction of British culture, Doris Lessing has never been a friend or comfort to the cultural authorities and establishments of her nation, which is perhaps why her work continues to suffer relative neglect in her own country. Bringing to bear a colonial eye on Britain's imperial and racist ambitions, a socialist eye on its capitalist underpinnings, a feminist eye on its sexist presumptions, and a populist eye on its elitist rankings of form, genre, and readership, Lessing has never offered the British the image of themselves they like to see. In *The Sirian Experiments*, for example, Lessing presents her compatriots with Tafta, a kind of essence of the British technocrat:

He glistened with health, was rather fleshy, and he emanated a calm, self-satisfied conceit. His garb was that now worn everywhere over the planet, as if it had been ordered by a dictator—but these animals have never been able to relinquish uniforms. He wore blue very tight trousers of a thick material which emphasized his sexuality, and a tight singlet.

He was resting one buttock on the edge of a table, swung one leg, and smiled easily and confidently down at his audience.

Surveying British culture from the outside or underside, Lessing repeatedly draws the attention of her countrymen to their image in the eyes of those who do not share their presumption of rightful ascendancy.

One of many things Lessing has been unwilling to let the British forget about themselves is how often they have been at war in this century. Lessing is, oddly, one of the few British novelists of the generation that spans nearly all of Britain's wars in this century to fix her eyes on the history of human violence in our time. The century of destruction to which the title of this chapter refers is the name Lessing gives in *Shikasta* to the earth's present century, a century she describes in that novel as one of continual warfare, ecological devastation, raging epidemics, and ever-mounting arsenals of lethal weaponry. Born in 1919 of a World War I amputee and his nurse, Lessing recognized early that hers was a generation steeped in war. In an interview with Roy Newquist that first appeared in *Counterpoint* in 1964 and again in *A Small Personal Voice* in 1975, Lessing defined the people she was writing about in Children of Violence, a series of novels she had already been working on for close to fifteen years, as people like myself, people my age who are born out of wars and who have lived through them, the framework of lives in conflict. I think the title explains what I essentially want to say. I want to explain what it is like to be a human being in a century when you open your eyes on war and on human beings disliking other human beings. I was brought up in Central Africa, which means that I was a member of the white minority pitted against a black majority that was abominably treated and still is. . . . It was all grossly unfair, and it's only part of a larger picture of inequity.

One-third of us—one third of humanity, that is—is inadequately housed and fed. Consciously or unconsciously we keep two-thirds of mankind improperly housed and fed. That is what the series of novels is about—this whole pattern of discrimination and tyranny and violence.

Lessing delineates here the patterns of violence—racial, sexual, cultural, and economic—that have continued to preoccupy her throughout her long and prolific career.

As a child, Lessing opened her eyes every day on the wreckage of World War I. Rhodesia was one of several remote and contested British colonies that drew a steady stream of veterans fleeing not just poverty and unemployment in postwar England but also the jingoism and cultural chauvinism that had dispatched them so jauntily to kill and die in the trenches. Lessing's first thoughts about war and its effects on the men and women who live through it were inspired by the evidence of human damage she saw all around her and, most graphically, at home. In the early, rather elegiac recollections of her father that appear in *A Small Personal Voice*, Lessing suggests that his spirit, like his leg, was amputated in the war to end all wars.

The boy who was beaten at school, who went too much to church, who carried the fear of poverty all his life, but who nevertheless was filled with the memories of country pleasures; the young bank clerk who worked such long hours for so little money, but who danced, sang, played, flirted—this naturally vigorous, sensuous being was killed in 1914, 1915, 1916. I think the best of my father died in that war, his spirit was crippled by it.

The love of life that survived public school education, religious intolerance, and economic exploitation could not survive World War I.

In the much later memoir of her parents that appeared in *Granta* in 1985, Lessing returns to the mutilated bodies of her father and his Rhodesian neighbors in a somewhat different key:

These nice people had one thing in common I didn't see then. They were survivors of World War I. The men had artificial arms or legs or eye-patches.

They would discuss the whereabouts of various bits of shrapnel that were for-ever travelling about their bodies out of sight, but sometimes emerging from healthy tissue to tinkle into a shaving mug or onto a plate. . . . There was a man with a steel plate which kept his brains in, and another rumoured to have a steel plate holding in his bowels. They talked about the war, both men and women—the war, the war, the war—and we children escaped from it into the bush.

When Lessing evokes these mutilated bodies for a third time in *Shikas-ta*, the macabre note of the *Granta* piece has deepened into an irony that overwhelms the elegiac cast of the original recollection. We no longer see through the eyes of a daughter wistfully reminiscing about her father whose spirit, like his body, was irreparably crippled by World War I. The bullet-studded and metal-plated bodies of the white farm-ers are now observed "from below" by the race they have overpowered and exploited, and their scarred and maimed bodies are read as signs not of their victimization but of the inexplicability of their conviction of superiority:

There was a fight this afternoon among two young men of different tribes. Its cause was frustration.

The white farmer had then lectured the two on their warlike spirit, their primitive ways. It was backward and primitive to fight, he had said. The white people were here to save the unfortunately backward blacks from this belliger-ence, by their civilised and civilising example.

The older man was sitting upright, the firelight moving on his face, which was showing relish and enjoyment. He was entertaining them: his family has been the traditional storytellers of his subtribe. The younger men, listening, were laughing.

The older man was surveying the white culture from below, the sharp slave's-eye view.

He was enumerating the white farms and the white men who owned them.

This was about five years after the end of World War I, which had been presented to these black people as one fought to preserve the decencies of civil-isation. There were half a dozen farmers in the area who had fought on the other side in that war, who also presented their part in it as a defence of the fundamental decencies.

"On the farm across the ridge, the man with one arm . . ."

"Yes, yes, that is so, he has only one arm."

"And on the farm across the river, the man with one leg . . ."

"Yes, only one leg, one leg."

"And on the road into the station, the man who has a metal plate to hold his intestines in."

"Yes, what a thing, that a man must keep in his intestines with a piece of iron."

"And on the farm where they are mining for gold, the man who has a metal piece in his skull."

"Ah, ah, a terrible thing, so many of them, and all wounded."

"And on the farm . . ."

Special benefits had been offered to ex-soldiers who would emigrate and take over this land. And so it was that to the eyes of the black people, the white people were an army of cripples. Like an army of locusts, who, after a few hours on the ground, show themselves legless, wingless, dozens of them, unable to take off again, when the main armies leave. Locusts, eating everything, covering everything, swarming everywhere. . . .

And again and again during that evening, these people dissolved into fits of laughter, putting together the white cripples of the area, the solemn lecture by the crippled farmer, and the picture of their two healthy young men, fighting briefly in the dust. They laughed and they laughed, staggering with laughter, rolling with laughter, howling with laughter.

In this series of takes and retakes of Lessing's memorials to her soldier-father, the wounded World War I veteran is portrayed from radically different points of view, and both the author and the reader undergo violent shifts of emotion and judgment as they awaken to ways of seeing this figure they had not known existed. The goal of the process is not to substitute the eyes of the black man for those of the white man or of the white woman, but to focus the reader's attention on this figure of the good soldier and to raise questions about why it is we call him civilized and civilizing, while we label the healthy young men fighting with their hands briefly in the dust barbaric.

The "sharp slave's-eye view" that surveys British culture from below forms a counterpart in *Shikasta* to the equally sharp, intergalactic point of view that surveys British culture from immeasurably above. When read as a whole, Lessing's fiction reveals itself to be a system of visions and revisions, of dissolves and retakes, of sightings from different angles, of returns to the familiar after forays into the ever more disconcertingly alien and remote. The Martha Quest of the early volumes of *Children of Violence*—a young woman who reflects, more or less faithfully, the life, loves, and opinions of her author—dissolves into the multiple selves of Anna Wulf in *The Golden Notebook*, and the narrative itself begins to draw attention to its seams, to its existence as a product of its author's choices and strategies. Linda Coldridge, first sighted as the madwoman in the basement of her husband's house in *The Four-*

Gated City, returns in *Shikasta* as a Canopean. Ben, the genetic throw-back of *The Fifth Child*, is a contemporary descendant of the Lombi, encountered in *The Sirian Experiments* as a product of intergalactic genetic engineering. The long cold dying that is done by an ordinary old woman in *The Diary of a Good Neighbor*, and by an entire planet in *The Making of the Representative for Planet 8*, is also done, Lessing writes in her afterword to that novel, by a personal friend of hers and by the Scott antarctic expedition. In *Shikasta*, a history of the earth's near future is recorded simultaneously by people living it and by beings for whom it will be a very slim volume in a very large library. Falling in love opens gateways in the mind of an unexceptional middle-aged woman in *If the Old Could . . .*, gateways between the sexes in *The Golden Notebook*, and gateways between realms in *The Marriages Between Zones Three, Four, and Five*. These multiple levels of awareness and enactment produce not cacophony or dissonance but the narrative equivalent of a chord or contrapuntal harmony.

The liberation of consciousness from the tyranny of self, the capacity to entertain multiple points of view—"to be in the world but not of it," as Lessing likes to quote from the Sufis—is both the central project of Lessing's fiction and her solution to the discrimination and violence she has never been able to shut her eyes on. If not the last, at least the most thorough and indefatigable of the romantics, Lessing ultimately acknowledges no limits to the imagination and uses fiction, which she likes to compare to science, as her instrument of exploration of all areas of consciousness presumed to be closed to us (the consciousness of animals, for example, or of extraterrestrials, or of the enemy, or of the opposite sex, or even simply of each other). In fiction, Lessing becomes other people, undergoes experiences not available to her, inhabits other species, other times, other spaces.

Though she refuses to acquiesce to any circumscription of her imagination, Lessing does repeatedly remind her readers that she works in fiction, not in history or science. "Why is it," she asks in her preface to *The Sirian Experiments*,

that writers, who by definition operate by the use of their imaginations, are given so little credit for it? We "make things up." This is our trade.

I remember, before I myself attempted this genre of space fiction, reading an agreeable tale about a species of highly intelligent giraffes who travelled by spaceship from their solar system to ours, to ask if our sun was behaving cruelly to us, as theirs had recently taken to doing to them. I remember saying to myself: Well, at least the writer of this tale is not likely to get industrious letters asking what it is like to be a giraffe in a spaceship.

Though accused as often of dogmatism as of bad writing, Lessing harps on her increasing predilection for speculation, her waning capacity for conviction. "Once upon a time," she writes in the same preface, "when I was young, I believed things easily, both religious and political; now I believe less and less. But I wonder about more." One thing Lessing wonders about is why we grant our scientists the most fabulous fictions, while we pin our novelists to the facts. "What *of course* I would like to be writing," she goes on to muse, "is the story of the Red and White Dwarves and their Remembering Mirror, their space rocket (powered by anti-gravity), their attendant entities Hadron, Gluon, Pion, Lepton, and Muon, and the Charmed Quarks and the Colored Quarks. But we can't all be physicists." Lessing hints here that she missed her calling, but she yearns less for physics than for the license we grant our scientists to chart the unknown.

Though the territory Lessing has recently claimed is not "as is" but "as if," she knows well enough how products of the imagination get harnessed to the wheels of the powers that be. Anna Wulf, Lessing's alter ego in *The Golden Notebook*, is acutely aware of her first novel as a commodity in a capitalist economy. The black notebook opens with "scattered musical symbols, treble signs that shifted into the $ sign and back again," and in that notebook Anna keeps a running account of the material that inspired her first novel (the color bar in Rhodesia), the profits she has made from it, and the uses to which the publishing, film, and television industries wish to put it. Anna is so appalled at the gutting of her novel for profit that she can't publish another. In the red notebook, Anna displays the same clear grasp of the uses to which communist ideology wishes to put her fiction; she finds them equally unnerving. The writer's block with which Anna struggles throughout *The Golden Notebook* is, in part, a response to the block so painstakingly erected between writer and reader by a publishing industry dedicated not to literature but to profit or propaganda. In her preface to *The Golden Notebook*, Lessing says that the last thing she wants to do is refuse to support women, but feminists and antifeminists alike have mutilated her novel by using it as a weapon in the sex war. When Lessing publicly admitted to the Jane Somers hoax—to publishing *The Diary of a Good Neighbor* in 1983 and *If the Old Could . . .* in 1984 under a pseudonym—she said she wanted to show young writers that publishers and reviewers respond not to the work but to the name of the author on it. In her afterword to *The Making of the Representative for Planet 8*, Lessing emphasizes the volatility of all events and artifacts in history, a recognition that leads the archaeologist Frederick Larson in *Briefing for a Descent into Hell* to lose his faith in his profession. Visiting a dig in Wiltshire, Frederick witnesses a colleague assert authoritatively to a group of students that a recently excavated trench was the foundation for a stone building. A student pipes up that he has seen a similar trench in Africa function as the foundation for a wooden building on stilts. When the same colleague gives Frederick a tour of the site later that day, he announces in the same authoritative tone that "this is the foundation of a wood and not a stone building." What shakes Frederick's belief in his discipline to the roots at this moment is the sheer accident ("if there had been no student back from a jaunt to Africa . . .") that has constructed this "emphatic pronouncement of archeology." "What lies behind facts like these," Lessing asks,

that so recently one could not have said Scott was not perfect without earning at least sorrowful disapproval; that a year after the Gang of Four were perfect, they were villains; that in the fifties in the United States a nothingman called McCarthy was able to intimidate and terrorise sane and sensible people, but that in the sixties young people summoned before similar committees simply laughed?

One thing that lies behind facts like these is that a writer cannot control how her fictions will be used, but Lessing does not regard this as an adequate reason to stop producing them, since we cannot become—we cannot even recognize—what we have not first imagined.

Lessing's refusal to let consciousness sleep, or even rest, is something many of her critics find unbearable in her, but it has made her a very long-distance thinker. In *Canopus in Argos*, Lessing's series for what she calls in *The Fifth Child* "the barbarous eighties," she claims as her proper sphere all time and all space. She claims this territory not metaphorically or microcosmically, as her nineteenth-century counterpart George Eliot did, but directly and descriptively. *Canopus in Argos* offers selections from the Canopean archives, historical records kept on a planet in a distant galaxy that document the experience of planets and galaxies over stretches of time and space barely comprehensible to the human mind. A "home epic," George Eliot half-modestly called *Mid-*

dlemarch, a novel that shrinks the epic to women's sphere; "space fiction," Lessing brazenly calls *Canopus in Argos*, a series of novels that explodes our understanding of both home and epic by placing them in the context of "a realm where the petty fates of planets, let alone individuals, are only aspects of cosmic evolution."

Canopus, a name Lessing traces to *The Lights of Canopus*, an ancient Persian translation of the *Bidpai* tales designed to teach young princes how to rule, denotes simultaneously an intergalactic system, the most highly developed culture of that system, and any individual member of that culture. The consciousness of Canopus is not bounded by time, space, or personal identity (and certainly not by sex, class, race, nationality, religion, etc.), and it places all events on our own and on other planets in the context of the universe. This galactic point of view did not come easily or suddenly to Doris Lessing. First she had to work her way through all the more familiar perspectives women have taken in fiction. The first four volumes of Children of Violence (published between 1952 and 1965) fit comfortably in the genre most commonly associated with women novelists, the semiautobiographical, confessional bildungsroman. What is remarkable about them is how free of confession they are. Like *Canopus in Argos*, they read like history, but the history is the readily recognizable one of a young person growing up in a mappable place and a datable time, told by an author who has grown up looking over this young person's shoulder.

After the second volume of Children of Violence, however, Lessing had begun to find this way of seeing suffocating. *The Golden Notebook* (1962) records her struggle to to break free from the woman looking over her shoulder, from her habit of seeing herself and her world through her own eyes. The struggle is an urgent one, as though Lessing indeed is unable to breathe. Constructing a frame or skeleton novel, which she ironically calls *Free Women* and which she describes in her introduction to *The Golden Notebook* as "a conventional short novel . . . which could stand by itself," Lessing proceeds to shatter this familiar specimen of realistic fiction by hinting at fictions she might have told but didn't and by pouring in between the chapters of *Free Women* all the material that the conventions of the novel require her to omit. *The Golden Notebook* records Lessing's struggle with her medium, with the way of seeing the novel, as an inherited literary form, imposed on her.

Her instrument of expression, however, was only part of Lessing's problem. Though the novel encouraged her to see in the ways the form had made familiar, she herself, as though by instinct, was clinging to the personal point of view, to the conviction that she was the only truth she could know. Virginia Woolf's Lily Briscoe fights hard in *To the Lighthouse* to say, "But this is what I see, this is what I see." That battle Lessing won almost with ease; now she wanted to see the way others see. To break free from the gaze of her own eyes, Lessing chose to explore ways of seeing conventionally called insane. She began to pay urgent attention to people who claimed they were merely conduits for voices not their own, and to people who claimed they had lived or were living lives not their own. The breaking down of personality Lessing achieved through madness and mental telepathy at the conclusion of *The Golden Notebook* and throughout *The Four-Gated City* and *Briefing for a Descent into Hell* brought her back finally to history, but to a history made literary this time not by a personal point of view but by a multiplication of points of view that renders the historical, the documentary, the objective, and the personal equally fictive, and by the projection of history into unknowable regions of time and space. In *Memoirs of a Survivor*, Lessing so subtly interweaves present fact with future possibility that we slip into the future without knowing precisely when we have crossed the line. In *Shikasta*, Lessing's extended sense of history reaches to earth's unrecorded past as well as to its unrecordable future.

Lessing's assault on conventional constructions of the self as continuous, integral, and placed in time and space, derives its energy and its urgency not from her adherence to postmodernist assertions about the elusiveness of identity and truth, but from her growing moral conviction that the egoism of Western civilization will be the death of us all. "There's something I have to reach. I have to tell people," moans poor Charlie in *Briefing for a Descent into Hell*, and these two sentences summarize the ethical imperatives that have driven Lessing to write. The first fictional name she gave herself was Quest. Her devotion to writing (and she has been an extraordinarily productive writer who has published in a wide range of forms and venues) arises not out of a desire to entertain or make money or win prizes or even achieve aesthetic perfection. Writing is, for Lessing, an instrument of illumination. An urgent seeking and questioning permeate her early novels and continue to impel the protagonists of her later books. Martha Quest seeks the four-gated city, Charles Watkins needs to find "Them," the narrator of *Memoirs of a Survivor* has to get through the wall, Ambien II desires to enter the consciousness of Canopus, Al*Ith is compelled to seek admission into Zone Two. While exploration and a quest for enlightenment structure the narratives of both her early and her recent novels, the *Canopus in Argos* series stages a new relation between Lessing and this narrative. While once she had something she had to reach, now she has something she has to tell. The five volumes of *Canopus in Argos* purport to be textbooks, teaching manuals, how-to guides for those who wish to enlighten others, as well as vehicles for self-enlightenment. The quester has turned teacher, and the narrative is impelled not by exploration but by instruction.

Lessing's later fiction self-consciously stages for the reader the process of awakening that she herself, through the medium of her earlier fiction, discovered, explored, and mapped. *The Summer Before the Dark*, *Canopus in Argos*, and *The Diaries of Jane Somers* are carefully plotted routes to enlightenment—to a more accurate understanding of what it means to be human and to a vicarious experience of what it might feel like to be *we*, instead of *I*. "Sleeping with the enemy" in the title of this essay signals a crucial adventure along this route, the transgression of the categorical imperative that demands that an individual, a group, a sex, a race, a culture, or a nation know itself and recognize itself only by excluding the other. Repeatedly in Lessing's later fiction, a man or a woman or the representative of a particular culture, realm, planet, or galaxy, moves from a position of enmity—an attitude of superiority and hostility to the other—to a recognition of a larger pattern in which the relation between the two is symbiotic rather than antagonistic.

This process of coming to recognize oneself in the enemy and of awakening to a larger context or pattern in which the bellicosity of a particular species or culture is an aberration in a benign necessity, a temporary dissonance in a cosmic harmony, is staged over and over again in Lessing's fiction. Her first and most fatalistic novel, *The Grass Is Singing* (1950), is about the failure of this process, a failure embodied historically in the color bar in South Africa. The doom announced on the first page of the novel is embedded in the concept of apartheid itself, in the iron curtain it draws between white and nonwhite races. Mary Turner's recognition of the common humanity of a black man is a catalyst not for her enlightenment but for her murder, and Lessing herself refuses to enter imaginatively into the consciousness of her black male character. While Moses is intensely physically present in the novel, the reader is denied even the briefest glimpse of events from his point of view.

The triumph of the color bar in *The Grass Is Singing*, its effectiveness in constraining the imagination and maintaining hostility between the races, generates in Lessing a passion for transgression. *The Golden Notebook* forces its heroine, Anna Wulf, to gradually recognize herself in a creature she initially constructs as male, subhuman, and purely other:

I slept and I dreamed the dream. This time there was no disguise anywhere. I was the malicious male-female dwarf figure, the principle of joy-in-destruction; and Saul was my counterpart, male-female, my brother and my sister, and we were dancing in some open place, under enormous white buildings, which were filled with hideous, menacing, black machinery which held destruction. But in the dream, he and I, or she and I, were friendly, we were not hostile, we were together in spiteful malice.

The lines between male and female, joy and terror, self and antiself disintegrate here, and the dream signals Anna's entrance into the world of the inner golden notebook where, as Lessing writes in her preface to the novel, "things have come together, the divisions have broken down, there is formlessness with the end of fragmentation—the triumph of the second theme, which is that of unity."

What Anna does as dream work with the dwarf-figure, she accomplishes in waking life with Saul Green. In the terrifying but ultimately fruitful struggle between this woman and man that both concludes and generates *The Golden Notebook*, Anna and Saul relentlessly construct and deconstruct one another, entering each other's personalities and emotions, forcing each other through all the most painful and humiliating scenarios of the battle between the sexes, oscillating between hostilities so intense they can only be described in the language of armed combat and sympathies so profound they can only be depicted as convergences of the self with the other. Both Anna and Saul are brought to the brink of self-annihilation by the assault on the cage of selfhood they wage for and against one another, an assault Anna compares to the global wars seething incessantly around them. The "I, I, I, I, I" Anna and Saul hurl at one another like bullets from a machine gun are "part of the logic of war," and the couple's construction of one another as enemies "reflects the real movement of the world towards dark, hardening power." Yet they rescue one another finally through the teamwork that allows each to give the other the first line of the novel in which the breakdown or the crack-up of the self is experienced as a precursor to the discovery of an imaginative realm where "joy [is] never anything but the song of substance under pressure forced into new forms and shapes." As Anna watches a character she has created suddenly take on a new largess of personality, she muses to herself that "quite possibly these marvellous, generous things we walk side by side with in our imaginations could come in existence, simply because we need them, because we imagine them." In *The Marriages Between Zones Three, Four, and Five*, a similar marriage of enemies is achieved between the solipsistic and hostile cultures of Zones Three and Four through the intercourse of their representatives, Al*Ith and Ben Ata. This marriage erodes the boundaries between the two zones, and, as Saul gives Anna the line she needs to begin her novel, so Al*Ith receives from the hitherto inaccessible Zone Five the words she needs to enter the hitherto unimaginable Zone Two.

Nowhere does Lessing enact this process of recognition and awakening on a grander scale, however, than in *The Sirian Experiments*, where she tells the tale of how Ambien II, one of five supreme rulers of the Sirian Empire, comes to identify herself with her intergalactic empire's archrival and enemy, Canopus. Representing Ambien II's efforts to explain herself to her four Sirian colleagues who have placed her in "corrective exile" for treason, the novel is, of all Lessing's books, the one most explicitly about instruction, about how to learn and how not to. Ambien II's account of the process that led her to an awareness of the true nature of Canopus includes a detailed analysis of what led her astray and of what might explain her long and profound misreading of Canopean motives and methods. The account also details Ambien II's discovery that she has been under the deliberate tutelage of Canopus—that her Canopean mentor, Klorathy, has devised for her precisely the sentimental education she needs to become Canopean herself and to nudge her entire empire in that direction.

Ambien II is a peculiar creature, reflective perhaps of Lessing in her sixties, who described herself in an interview as "unmarriageable, by now," reflective certainly of a kind of woman we don't encounter often in Western fiction. As Ambien II explains early on in the novel, her childbearing years are far behind her, and though she sustains a close and trusting relation with Ambien I, the father of her two children, sex is no longer of much interest to either one of them. Being Sirian, Ambien has a long, long time to live past her childbearing years, and she has already inhabited for thousands and thousands of years a female body that is subject to neither reproduction nor overwhelming desire.

Though certain men in the novel—Tafta, for example, who represents the purely self-serving planet of Shammat, or Nasar, when Ambien II encounters him in Koshi as Canopus "gone wrong"—call her "a dry bone of a woman" and deride her for being such a "desiccated bureaucrat of a Sirian" instead of the silky, beguiling, dewy peach of a woman Adalantaland's Elyle is, the novel itself steadily undermines the potency of gender distinctions. Ambien II has outlived her female body and graduated to one more suitable and instrumental to her current purposes; Ambien I appears to have done the same with his male body; and the two have come to embody what is signaled in their names, a postgendered condition.

Though sexual desire in Ambien II rarely speaks above a whisper, she does want a special, intimate, warmly personal relation with her Canopean mentor, and this significantly impedes her progress. Prior to her first meeting with him on earth, Ambien II admits to a hope that Klorathy will take the place of a boon-companion recently struck by a meteorite. When she encounters him again shortly after the earth has toppled over on its axis and only partially righted itself, she is dismayed at his coldness and at his pedantic insistence that "events," not "catastrophe," is the proper term for the devastation of the planet: "I was thinking that a being able to view the devastation of a whole planet with such accurate detachment was not likely to be warmly responsive to a close personal relationship: at the time, that my own personal concerns were being intruded by me did not strike me as shameful, though it does now." Klorathy suggests that if she wants to understand his "accurate detachment," she should stay on with him for awhile. "You want me to stay?" Ambien II replies. Though Klorathy says again that he thinks she should stay, he does not say, I *want* you to stay, and so Ambien II immediately leaves with Ambien I, her familiar with whom she shares an easy emotional and intellectual intimacy. Ambien II's sensual and personal inclinations interfere with her ability to be with Klorathy during their next encounter on Planet 11, as well. The light and atmosphere of this planet are repellent to Ambien II, and she is physically nauseated by the frail, pale, air-eating, insectlike creatures that inhabit it. "I have never been able to overcome," Ambien II acknowledges, "an instinctive abhorrence for creatures dissimilar to my own species." When Klorathy explains to her that these are among the most highly evolved of the beings under Canopean care, Ambien's senses are too affronted to allow her to remain long enough to discover why.

While Ambien II's body—its senses, its sexuality, its gender, its instinctive investment in the pleasant, the personal, and the familiar—slows her progress toward Canopus, her mind erects far more effective barriers. Canopus is, after all, the old enemy of Sirius. It hasn't been so very long since they were at war with one another, and the peace between them has not yet achieved an end to hostility. Ambien II approaches Canopus with two powerful and oddly contradictory misconceptions. She assumes Canopus is her enemy and she assumes Canopus is her mirror image. Since suspicion dictates all of Sirius's interactions with Canopus, leading Sirians to lie to Canopean officials and spy on Canopean territories as a matter of course, Ambien II presumes that suspicion is also the fountainhead of Canopus's relations with Sirius. Since exploitation and greed dictate Sirius's relations with her colonies and subject peoples, Ambien II assumes these are the motives that guide Canopus's colonial policies. This habit of regarding Canopus as never more, and usually less, than the equal of Sirius leads Ambien II and her compatriots into consistent misreadings and misjudgments of Canopean undertakings. As Ambien II acknowledges in retrospect,

they have never had anything to learn from us. But we have consistently interpreted their attitude as one of dissimulation, believing them to be pretending indifference, out of pride, while secretly ferreting out any information they could, even sending spies into our territories and making use of our work without acknowledgement.

Language fails to bridge the gap between the two empires for a similar reason. Sirius persists in assuming that Canopus means what Sirius means by such words as harmony, good fellowship, and cooperation. Sirius confidently uses such words to describe its relations with the Lombis, for example, whom the Sirians have kidnapped from their home planet, dressed up in painfully cumbersome space suits to farm an otherwise uninhabitable planet, and then dumped on yet a third planet to be the subjects of an experiment to see if the evolution of a species can be prevented. And when Canopus uses the word "symbiotic" to describe the relation between a group of its colonists and the indigenous apes, Sirians interpret the word to mean "the superior immigrants being set free for higher tasks by using the apes as servants." The debate that has raged among Lessing's readers and critics about her use of the colonial metaphor throughout the *Canopus in Argos* series may have its origins in a similar linguistic dilemma. Debased by the history of its implementation, colonialism—for us as for the Sirians—has come to be synonymous with exploitation and to signify the only possible relation of dominant to subject races or species. The result, as the witness from Rhodesia points out at the trial that concludes *Shikasta*, the first volume of the series, has been the abandonment of the colonized. To reacquaint our imaginations with the possibility of a responsible and benign tutelage of dependent races and species, Lessing attempts to infuse the concept of colonialism with new ethical imperatives, to revive our faith in a language of care and cooperation; but many of her readers persist in assuming she means what they mean by colonial service.

Only when Ambien II begins to suspect at last that Canopus means what it says and that Canopus is not similar and, at best, equal to Sirius, but unfathomably other and better, is she ready to learn. Her program of instruction is a novelistic one, consisting of an immersion in a series of illustrative instances. To her immense frustration, Ambien II's questions are never directly answered. Rather, she is provided with experiences that enact the answers, if she has the eyes to see and the ears to hear. "You have to know it," Klorathy tells Ambien II. "You are a stubborn one, Sirius. You are not one of those who can be told a thing, and absorb it." Dispatched by her mentor to the cities of Grakconkranpatl and Lelanos, Ambien II comes to know first her own greatest weakness. Reminiscent—in their stark contrast between the heavy, the uniform, and the murderous and the light, the various, and the harmonious—of Ben Ata's masculine Zone Four and Al*Ith's feminine Zone Three as well as of the Aztec and Mayan cultures, these cities are the site of Ambien's II's temptation and fall. As Ambien II witnesses the overthrow of Lelanos by Grakconkranpatl, she is so racked by sorrow and nostalgia for the civil harmonies of the once-lovely city, for the beauties of its rule, that she succumbs to the temptation to rule Lelanos herself:

I was . . . full of grief on behalf of Lelanos, the deprived—the deprived of *me*, and my expert and benevolent guidance. But as I waited there on my little platform among the snowy and bluish cubes and spheres, the deep blue of the . . . sky enclosing the lovely scene, I looked down on little people far below, and it was as if I held them in my protection; as if I was promising them an eternal safety and well-being.

Ambien II's desire to serve and protect, to infuse the colonial situation with moral dignity and generosity, is too perilously close to its murderous underside, that presumption of superiority that quickly succumbs to self-aggrandizement and delusions of omnipotence.

Klorathy drives home the dangers of Ambien II's excessive self-regard by forcing her to witness the Lelannian experiments. Having absorbed its ancient enemy, Lelanos now rules with a systematic brutality and inhumanity unknown even to the dark and savage priests of Grakconkranpatl. At a central research center in Lelanos, Ambien II discovers the Lelannians testing the local tribesmen's capacities for endurance and perseverance by throwing them into a very large and slick-sided tank of water and timing how long they swim before they drown. A second experiment slowly heats the tank of water and records at what temperature each of the tribesmen succumbs. A third seeks to perfect the art of organ and limb transplantation by grafting the breasts of females to their backs, or the sexual organs of males to their faces. The Lelannians are able to conduct such experiments with a clear conscience because of their unshakable conviction of their own superiority to all other species: "Their faces showed always the self-esteem that was their curse, the mark of their incapacity. The ground of their nature was this conviction of superiority, of innate worth over other species."

When Klorathy asks Ambien II what she thinks they should do about this deplorable species, she retorts, "I would call in our fleet of Flame Makers and destroy these squalid little animals." Her state of mind is reminiscent of the one that drives Kurtz, in Conrad's *Heart of Darkness*, to scrawl, "Exterminate all the brutes," across his tract on the civilizing mission of the white man in Africa. She simply can't understand why Canopus continues to waste its time on such an inferior species. "Sirius," Klorathy gently replies, "very often a great deal of time, effort, and resources are spent on 'inferior' species. Everything is relative, you know!" The inferior species to which Klorathy is referring is, of course, Ambien II's own, but she does not "choose to 'hear' this. Not at that time."

When Ambien II finally does choose to hear, when she absorbs the nature of the evil that attracts her and understands that subject species are to be nurtured, not used, and that she herself must act toward the populations under her control as Canopus has acted toward her, she is ready to learn the Canopean technique of containing destruction and altering history by "occupying a mind for a brief and exact purpose." Her first trial comes when she is dispatched to save the skills and knowledge of the intricate and affluent culture of the Arabian Queen

Shaz'vin from total annihilation at the hands of ravaging Mongol horsemen. Ambien II briefly enters the mind of the queen and guides her to make the decisions that preserve not her realm but the memory of it. Under Ambien II's tutelage, the queen rescues enough citizens with the skills and knowledge of their destroyed culture to pass it down to both their own descendants and those of the savage horsemen. Ambien's experience of inhabiting the mind of the queen is precisely analogous to the Sufi concept, mentioned earlier in this essay, of being in the world but not of it:

> I did not lose my Sirian perspectives, the Sirian scope of time and space. But I was inside, too, this civilisations's view of itself as all there was of the known world—for on its edges were, to the north, the threatening horsemen, to the northwest, very far away, dark forests full of barbarians whom these people scarcely accounted as human at all, believing them not much more than beasts—and from their point of view, accurately—. . . . The world as understood by this great and powerful Queen was, though it stretched from one end of the main landmass to the other, circumscribed indeed, and the stars that roofed it were understood only—and to a limited extent—by their influences on their movements . . . on *our* movements . . . an odd, a startling, a disturbing, clash of focusses and perspectives encompassed me; and as for the historical aspect, this queen knew the story of her own civilisation and some legends, mostly inaccurate, of a "distant" past, which to me, and my mind, was virtually contemporary with her.

This odd, startling, disturbing clash of temporal and spatial perspectives, of the passionately personal with the accurately detached, of the circumscribed with the infinite, is both the achievement of the *Canopus in Argos* series as a whole and Klorathy's very specific formula for saving the earth in the century of destruction from a white race whose creed will be, "If it is there, it belongs to us. If I want it I must have it. If what I see is different from myself then it must be punished or wiped out. Anything that is not me, is primitive and bad."

Having slept with the enemy in the ways that matter to her and to the universe, Ambien II is ready to take his place, to become herself a Klorathy to the other four members of the Sirian Five, for whom she will write her "history of the heart," *The Sirian Experiments*. The loving tutelary relationship embodied in Ambien II's candid confessions to her colleagues, in the infinite patience and long-range planning of Klorathy's guidance of his benighted pupil, in the giant's careful mentorship of creatures both smaller and immeasurably less intelligent than themselves in *Shikasta*, in Al*Ith's reluctant but nonetheless resourceful and compassionate amatory instruction of Ben Ata in *The Marriages Between Zones Three, Four, and Five*, in George Sherban's futile but devoted efforts to enlighten his sister Rachel in *Shikasta*—this relationship is the substance of Lessing's late fiction. It compels the content of her narratives, informs her relationship with her readers, and reflects her most passionate moral and imaginative commitments.

While Lessing's most recent fiction is instructive rather than about instruction, its impulse is still to shake us awake, to alert us to the extreme fragility of civilization in our time. Returning from the heady reaches of outer space to the kind of place most of us call home, Lessing shatters our faith in these safe havens we create to keep our hearts in. In *The Fifth Child*, for example, Harriet and David Lovatt spin round themselves the happy household and extended family they believe will keep the violence and disintegration of their society and its institutions at bay. But the center of their charmed circle cannot hold, and the lovely loving family is destroyed from within by the conception and birth of the alien child, Ben, whom the family can neither accommodate nor expel. By the end of the novel, the idea of home has been turned inside out. The pretty family is broken and gone, and home now belongs to Ben and his gang. The spacious Victorian mansion that was to be a haven from violence has become a breeding ground for it. Home is similarly invaded in *The Good Terrorist* by squatters, transients, and terrorists, and the happy homemaker, the tidy housekeeper, the busy and resourceful little woman, becomes herself, by the end of the novel, a devotee of violence, not as a means but as an end in itself. "I do have a sense, and I've never not had it, of how easily things can vanish," Lessing acknowledged in an interview about *The Fifth Child* with Mervyn Rothstein in the *New York Times*.

It's a sense of disaster. I know where it comes from—my upbringing. That damn First World War, which rode my entire childhood, because my father was so damaged by it. This damn war rammed down my throat day and night, and then World War II coming, which they talked about all the time. You know, you can never get out from under this kind of upbringing, the continual obsession with this. And after all, it's true. These wars did arise, and destroyed a beautiful household, with all the loving children.

Doris Lessing is many different things to her readers, most of whom, sooner or later, feel forsaken or betrayed by her. Though dogged by accusations of being too dogmatic and polemical, Lessing has never pleased any political party, theory, or faction for very long. Though acclaimed for her realism, the mirror Lessing holds up to human nature and human achievement is brutally frank and never flattering. But neither political unorthodoxy nor candor quite accounts for the response she gets each time her fiction takes a new turn. Her readers and reviewers are rarely astonished and delighted at the startling new prospects she offers; rather they sound a note of resentment or indignation, as though she has let them down or done them a personal injury. Their response is less, I think, to the content of Lessing's vision than it is to the kind of relation she establishes with her readers. She is their Klorathy, their Canopus, their mentor and guide to moral probity and the prefigurative powers of the imagination. While she does full justice to her readers' intelligence, never pretending that the future they face is anything less than terrifying, she also convinces them that their efforts at rescue and reform are necessary and useful. Her readers feel for her an attachment and devotion that Lessing both appreciates and deplores. The problem with her readers, Lessing complained after the publication of the first volume of *Canopus in Argos* is that they want her to keep doing the same thing, to keep being the writer they know and love. To her earliest fans, she was a left-wing writer about Africa, a stalwart critic of capitalism and the color bar, and a brilliant conduit to the exotic. To these readers, *The Golden Notebook* was an enigma or a disappointment, and *The Four-Gated City*, the kiss of death. But these novels brought her new and equally passionate readers. Ex-communists recognized in them their own struggles and disillusionments. The fledgling antinuclear and environmental movements discerned in them the work of a powerful ally. Political and social historians found in them an extraordinarily acute and sophisticated rendering of the cultural climate of Europe during the early years of the Cold War. Postmodernist literary critics celebrated the deconstruction of modernist aesthetics and the disintegration of the narrative of commitment. Members of the reviving feminist movement greeted them, along with *The Summer Before the Dark,* as bibles of women's liberation. All these readers were uneasy, however, about the futurist ending of *The Four-Gated City* and about its legitimization of madness and extrasensory perception, an uneasiness that turned to dismay with the publication of *Briefing for a Descent into Hell* and *Memoirs of a Survivor.* Though these novels discouraged her political and academic following, they were warmly welcomed by the psychoanalytic community. Laingians saw in them a validation of their contention that the only sane members of a mad society are those whom that society calls insane, Jungians discovered in them a gold mine of archetypes, and devotees of psychic phenomena took them as an affirmation of the untapped resources of the human mind. These novels also began to attract the mystics and sci-fi fans and devotees of the scathing political satires of Jonathan Swift, who would crow over *Canopus in Argos* and lead some of the more conventional newspapers and journals to headline their reviews of the series "The Spacing Out of Doris Lessing" or "Lessing Slips Her Moorings in Space." Though the readers who celebrated Lessing as the great political realist of our time were thoroughly disenchanted by her forays into Sufism, Swiftianism, and outer space, they have recently been won back by the more familiar landscapes of *The Diaries of Jane Somers*, *The Fifth Child*, and *The Good Terrorist*. Lessing's unpredictability has undoubtedly cost her the loyalty of some of her readers and has probably cost her the Nobel Prize, but it is also precisely what makes her such a canny illuminator of these "dreadful and marvellous times where the certainties of yesterday dissolve as we live."

Lynne Hanley

Selected Bibliography

Draine, Betsy. *Substance Under Pressure: Artistic Coherence and Evolving Form in the Novels of Doris Lessing*. Madison: University of Wisconsin Press, 1983.
Modern Fiction Studies 26 (Spring 1980). Special issue on Doris Lessing.
Pratt, Annis, and L. S. Dembo, eds. *Doris Lessing: Critical Studies*. Madison: University of Wisconsin Press, 1974.
Rubenstein, Roberta. *The Novelistic Vision of Doris Lessing: Breaking the Forms of Consciousness*. Urbana: University of Illinois Press, 1979.
Sprague, Claire. *Rereading Doris Lessing: Narrative Patterns of Doubling and Repetition*. Chapel Hill: University of North Carolina Press, 1987.
Sprague, Claire, ed. *In Pursuit of Doris Lessing: Nine Nations Reading*. New York: St. Martin's Press, 1990.
Taylor, Jenny, ed. *Notebooks/Memoirs/Archives: Reading and Rereading Doris Lessing*. Boston: Routledge and Kegan Paul, 1982.
The Doris Lessing Newsletter.

Drabble to Carter: Fiction by Women, 1962–1992

Visit to Jane Austen's house. . . . I put my hand down on Jane's desk and bring it up covered with dust.
Barbara Pym, journal entry, August 11, 1967

Oh indeed! We knew we only sold the simulacra.
"Fevvers," winged heroine of Angela Carter's Nights at the Circus

THE contemporary novelists discussed in this chapter—Margaret Drabble, Barbara Pym (three later works), Anita Brookner, A. S. Byatt, Fay Weldon, Penelope Lively, and Angela Carter—are by no means a homogenous group. Thirty years of personal history as well as widely varying reactions to intercurrent discourses such as feminism and postmodernism (which are discussed below) have made major differences among them—in some cases, differences between their own earlier and later work. Yet most of this chapter will focus on traits in common. A collective, synoptic approach is appropriate if only as a corrective to the atmosphere of competition in which each has always worked—ranked and set against each other as competitors for popular success, for publishers' limited marketing resources, and for the literary prizes that in Britain confer, if not canonization, at least a conditional (though frequently controversial) beatification on contemporary novels. Three of these writers have received Britain's most publicized literary award, the Booker Prize: Antonia Susan Byatt for *Possession* in 1990, Penelope Lively for *Moon Tiger* in 1987, and Anita Brookner for *Hotel du Lac* in 1984. (In 1984 Lively was also named on the shortlist of six finalists for her *According to Mark.*) Fay Weldon has been short-listed for the prize (for *Praxis*, in 1979), and in 1983 she was the first (and is still the only) woman chosen to chair the panel of judges. Angela Carter served with Weldon on the judges' panel in 1983, but none of Carter's novels was ever short-listed for the Booker Prize. No novel by Margaret Drabble has appeared on the Booker shortlist, nor did the three novels published by Barbara Pym after the establishment of the Booker Prize in 1969 receive this recognition; although in 1977 the chair of the judges' panel, Philip Larkin (a great admirer of Pym's fiction), managed to introduce *Quartet in Autumn* among the dozen works that received serious discussion.

End of a Dying Tradition?

These data about the Booker Prize are not provided to classify the novelists by prestige and rank, but to illustrate a paradox: if the Booker shortlist is used as the barometer of status, the three writers most celebrated in the United States (Drabble, Pym, and Carter) have received least recognition in Britain. The probable reason for this, and a trait central to all these novelists (whether recognized or snubbed by the Booker committees) is the strongly "English" flavor of their best novels—their shared willingness to focus on continuing, revising, or enlarging (rather than breaking with) specifically English literary traditions.

Even the least insular of these seven writers, Angela Carter, who died in February 1992, situated her last and best novels—*Wise Children* (1991) and *Nights at the Circus* (1984)—largely in London, and in the past. While strongly committed to revising traditional notions of female sexuality in such nonfiction as *The Sadeian Woman* (1979), Carter's fiction over the thirty years of her career became increasingly genial, ebullient, tender, allusive. All reviewers recognized the revisiting of Shakespeare (especially his early comedies) in her final novel, *Wise Children*. Carter herself (who early in her career had declared a preference for Racine) told the London *Sunday Times* in 1991 that she had always seen herself as a character in Shakespeare, but had increasingly identified with his comic creations: "All these years, I've been fighting the Falstaff in my soul. All these years, I've had this deep conviction that I was the Prince of Denmark when, really and truly, I was Juliet's Nurse."

An emphasis on continuities in English culture is even clearer among the others. Barbara Pym's habitual allusions to canonical English poets and novelists (particularly to Jane Austen) are often misread as merely nostalgic, a misconception that subsequent discussion of Pym's three late novels will challenge. Fay Weldon, like Pym, has long been associated with notably "English" projects: she achieved her earliest fame as the scriptwriter for several episodes of "Upstairs, Downstairs" and wrote the teleplay for the BBC's serialization of Austen's *Pride and Prejudice* in 1983. In *Letters to Alice: On First Reading Jane Austen* (1985) even Weldon's title stands as an affirmation of English cultural continuities, from Austen to Lewis Carroll's curious girl-child to Virginia Woolf's classic essay on first reading *David Copperfield*. In *Alice*, Weldon presents an aunt's defense of novel reading to a niece who has turned to punk rock. The "Englishness" of *The Life and Loves of a She-Devil* (the controversial novel on which this chapter's discussion of Weldon will focus) is more veiled: Weldon has told interviewers that the novel was set in suburban Australia. Yet a specific setting is not disclosed within the novel itself, and the world of this text looks much the way Margaret Thatcher's Britain would probably look to Jane Austen: a place of increasing material comforts but decreasing emotional contact: "Eden Grove is a friendly place. My neighbors and I give dinner parties. . . . We discuss things, rather than ideas; we exchange information, not theories. . . . It is a good life. [My husband] tells me so. He comes home less often, so does not say so as often as he did."

A. S. Byatt's *Possession* stresses a continuum of English settings (and literary achievement) extending from the past into the present. Set partly in the nineteenth century, Byatt's novel is, among other things—as Diane Johnson recognized in the *New York Review of Books*—"an affirmation of the Victorian novel." Anita Brookner, the only child of Jewish emigrants from Poland, was seven when her sensitive father guided her through the works of Dickens, hoping that this quintessentially English writer would help his daughter to master the strange new culture into which the family had been transplanted. While Brookner has protested in interviews that she still feels like an estranged outsider in England, she nonetheless situates most of her fiction—*Family and Friends*, 1985; *Latecomers*, 1989; *Brief Lives*, 1990—in London during World War II and the immediate postwar period. Penelope Lively's *Moon Tiger* (1987), too, which declares itself as a "history of the world," nonetheless concerns itself mainly with wartime Egypt (where Lively spent her childhood) and pre-and postwar England. Margaret Drabble (like Barbara Pym) chooses contemporary rather than historical English settings. Yet in the last thirty years, Drabble has turned increasingly from her early novels of veiled autobiography—fictional accounts of marriage, motherhood, divorce—to a remarkable chronicling of the shifting political and economic fortunes of England itself: its recession of the 1970s in *The Ice Age* (1977), for instance; and its retreat from the welfare state during the 1980s in *The Radiant Way* (1987) and its sequels, *A Natural Curiosity* (1989) and *The Gates of Ivory* (1992).

The frequent allusion to specifically "English" experience (literary and historical) in the novels of these writers is appreciated by anglophilic American readers but has been in recent years increasingly out of fashion in Britain itself. Increasingly since the establishment of the Booker Prize in 1969, the judges (newly appointed each year) have chosen fiction written from multicultural or postcolonial perspectives—including Booker Prize novels by Salman Rushdie (1981), Kazuo Ishiguro (1989), Keri Hulme (1985), Peter Carey (1988), and Ben Okri (1991). Writers from the Celtic cultures within Britain and Eire (Glasgow's James Kelman, for instance, short-listed in 1989), have also been receiving long-delayed recognition. In contrast to these new voices, so often intent on dramatizing a break with tradition, the seven writers discussed in this chapter emphasize their ties to canonical fiction and specifically English subject matter, and may have seemed to the Prize committees by contrast rather tame. As mentioned, Carter is not a true exception to this rule, though her writings on sexuality (and such protofictional projects as her bawdy feminist revisions of fairy tales) at least made it clear that an interest in allusion to canonical literature is not necessarily an indication of reactionary values. Others among these seven have actively contributed to a perception of their work as conservative. Margaret Drabble, goaded in 1967 by an interviewer marveling at her love of realism (she has written a book on Arnold Bennett), declared roundly: "I'd rather be at the end of a tradition which I admire than at the beginning of a tradition which I deplore."

In the years that each won the Booker Prize, *Possession, Moon Tiger*, and *Hotel du Lac* were all perceived as conservative choices. A factor in the success of these three novels was probably that all marked a change of emphasis, a new direction. Anita Brookner was an art historian who had produced highly regarded studies of Watteau, Greuze, and David before beginning her career as a novelist in 1981; and *Hotel du Lac*, the least chilly of Brookner's early narratives (the heroine's surname "Hope" is finally apposite, not ironic) remains her most ingratiating novel. Penelope Lively was until her first appearance on the Booker shortlist best known as a writer of historical/folkloric fiction for young adults: *Moon Tiger* took her constant theme—the haunting persistence of the past—to a more powerful level than earlier novels. A. S. Byatt's *Posses-*

sion, too, was her breakthrough novel, less dryly academic than earlier fiction almost overwhelmed by the influence of Iris Murdoch. (Byatt, a former lecturer in English, published the first book-length critical study of Murdoch in 1965.) At the time she was named to the Booker shortlist, Fay Weldon was best known, as mentioned, as a playwright, scriptwriter, and cultural gadfly, not as a novelist.

By contrast, Drabble, Pym, and Carter—the three of highest reputation in the United States—demonstrated between 1962 and 1992 a steady commitment to quality fiction writing: all have loyal followings of readers who tend to see their separate novels in the context of their careers as a whole. Drabble's first novel, *A Summer Bird-Cage*, was published in 1962 when she was twenty-four; Angela Carter's *Shadow Dance* in 1965 when she was twenty-five. Pym (delayed by World War II) was thirty-seven when she published *Some Tame Gazelle* in 1950; it was begun in 1935, when she was twenty-two. Again, without denigrating those who have been recognized by the Booker Prize committees, it may be observed that the traits that the prize favors—the big book, the breakthrough book, the novel-of-the-year rather than the lifetime achievement—have subtly disadvantaged all these seven writers, especially the three most exclusively committed to the possibly dying tradition of novel writing. Steadily productive novelists working veins of subject matter that they have gradually made their own (a description that covers all these writers) have in recent years been taken somewhat for granted in Britain.

Daughters of Austerity

One final point of preliminary background should help to focus subsequent discussion of these writers' novels: the related matters of their age and their shared preoccupation with the English past, literary and historical. This interest has, as mentioned, often been misread as insular and nostalgic—except in the case of Angela Carter, even reactionary. Yet true nostalgia requires some experience of the halcyon days revisited; and except for Barbara Pym (born in 1913 and a generation older than the rest when she began to publish) these novelists all were infants or children during World War II. They were born in 1928 (Brookner), 1933 (Weldon and Lively), 1936 (Byatt), 1939 (Drabble), and 1940 (Carter). Except for Pym (who served in Italy as a Wren during the war), all experienced severe disruptions early in life. Angela Carter was born in Eastbourne several months after her mother had been evacuated from South London because of the blitz; the family was separated from her father, a journalist who stayed in London. Later in the war, Carter was evacuated again, to a mining village in South Yorkshire. Antonia Drabble Byatt and Margaret Drabble, who are sisters, were separated when Antonia was evacuated from Sheffield to Pontefract in Yorkshire. Weldon, born in Worcestershire, emigrated to New Zealand early in childhood but following her parents' divorce returned to England with her mother, grandmother, and sister: the disruption of her parents' marriage, not the war itself, displaced Weldon. Lively, born in Cairo, spent her childhood near an active theater of combat. Brookner, although herself born in London, was, as mentioned, the only child of Jewish émigrés; she grew up keenly aware of her family's marginal status as displaced persons: "We were aliens. Jews. Tribal. . . . I loved my parents painfully, but they were hopeless as guides."

Given this shared background of early estrangement and disruption (common to people of their generation, and certainly also to Pym's) it is not surprising that these writers, daughters of wartime and its consequent austerity, have found it difficult to get out of England in their most deeply felt work. These writers share no jingoist certainty that "there will always be an England." They grew up with images of ruin and destruction, and came of age as novelists (Pym included) in the two decades during which England undertook to redesign itself through radical reforms: the welfare state, the comprehensive education movement. Theirs is the generation that rebuilt London and redesigned English society. It is natural that they remain interested in—committed to—the place.

Mass Culture, High Culture

The middle ground between popular success and critical acclaim that all the novelists discussed in this chapter to some degree have occupied may explain two frequent targets of their irony: mass culture on the one hand and high culture on the other. Critical resistance to popular forms of narrative is implied, for instance, by several major characters (Edith Hope in Brookner's *Hotel du Lac*; Mary Fisher in Weldon's *Life and Loves of a She-Devil*) who are writers of best-selling romance novels but cannot achieve an equivalent romantic triumph in their private lives; or by such characters as Bill Potter, the Leavis-like academic in Byatt's

Virgin in the Garden (1978) who in a comic rage burns his daughter's treasured cache of Georgette Heyer Regency romances. In Lively's *Moon Tiger* (1987), Claudia Hampton (herself a best-selling historian) nonetheless feels scorn for the former lover who has made a fortune producing historical documentaries for the mass audience of television: "By the time we have reduced everything to entertainment we shall find that it was no joke after all." Drabble has also created characters (Charles Headland, for instance, in *The Radiant Way* [1987]) who shape public opinion through television documentaries—popular entertainments no more innocent than romances, for documentaries also manipulate the mass audience primarily (though more covertly) through appeals to the emotions. Pym's references to mass culture are typically bemused and dry: in *A Few Green Leaves* (1980), Emma Howick notes the proximity of an automobile graveyard to the Anglican burying ground and reflects, "Was there not something significant and appropriate about this particular kind of graveyard being opposite the church—a kind of mingling of two religious faiths, the ancient and the modern? 'A Note on the Significance of the Abandoned Motor-Car in a West Oxfordshire Village' might pin it down, she thought."

While Angela Carter's fiction abounds in friendly references to popular forms of entertainment—the variety and specialty acts featured in vaudeville, the peep show, pantomime, the music hall, the striptease, the wild-West show, the sideshow, the séance, the circus—she is not herself providing such easily categorized performances: like other contemporary women novelists, Carter links popular culture to seductive yet fraudulent representation. In *Nights At The Circus* (1984), flying heroine Sophia Fevvers may well be a fake; in Carter's darker satire *The Infernal Desire Machines of Dr. Hoffman* (1972), sadistic and fantastic plot lines have been foisted on the world by a mad scientist who, like a novelist, is empowered to simulate "reality," defined as a theatre of the cruel in which lifelike characters serve only to flesh out and enact, under Hoffman's sadistic gaze, their own enslaving desires.

If marking varying degrees of distance from mass culture's facile promise of mindless pleasure, these novelists show an even greater distrust of high culture and high seriousness. Sensitive or bookish characters fail in these novels when they choose the emotional isolation engendered by vicarious living only in the literary or historical past: lost in their dreams, such characters fail to seize their own day. Byatt's Roland Michell in *Possession* (1990), for instance, researches a Victorian poet (tellingly named "Ash") in dusty regions of the British Library: his desk at home is dominated by a large framed photograph of the poet's death mask. In Byatt's comic climax, Roland (now, like his epic namesake, completely mad) joins a band of frenzied academics who—dignity and restraint cast aside—dig up Ash's grave. Anita Brookner's shy, expectant protagonist in *Lewis Percy* (1989) is likewise an academic who has great difficulty living his own life: Lewis labors over an ambitious thesis on nineteenth-century fiction ("The Hero as Archetype") while a habitual inertia causes hope to wither around and within him. In *A Few Green Leaves* (1980), the last novel published by Pym before her death, the rector's sister Daphne Dagnall turns even more decidedly from the here and now, pining for a primitive Greek culture glimpsed during her brief holidays in the Cyclades. Yet Daphne, who would love to be metamorphosed like her mythical namesake, can change little about her life. Comically doomed to central heating rather than the harsh sunlight of eternal summer in Greece, Daphne escapes Oxfordshire—but only as far as "a delightful wooded common" in suburban Birmingham.

If contemporary women writers in Britain commonly set themselves at varying distances both from mass culture and from the kind of high seriousness that estranges people from the here and now, they share an equal ambivalence toward the cultural avant-garde. All write almost aggressively accessible fiction, and several (notably Penelope Lively and Angela Carter) have written with great success for children. All these writers (in *Possession*, even Byatt) reject modernism's privileging of innovations in technique and purity of form. They can seem almost defiantly "un-new," openly reusing plots and characters from their own earlier work—or even (in an implied commentary on the arbitrary nature of plot-building) stealing plots from earlier canonical fiction. What must be an intimidating literary heritage—two centuries of superlative British writing by and about women—combines with this shared rejection of high modernism (and its emphasis on new forms) to encourage the ironic replaying of traditional plots among these writers, and their frequent reincarnation of classic characters (or reassignment of classic names).

Recapitulation of characters from the literary canon may be seen, for instance, in Barbara Pym's naming against type in *The Sweet Dove Died* (1978): Pym's point in calling her central character Miss Eyre is apparently to stress how little her character has in common with Charlotte

Brontë's heroine: Pym's Miss Eyre is a cold-hearted, aging beauty, a model of perfect grooming and a collector of Victorian objects. Her rival for the affections of an attractive younger man is Miss Sharpe, a slovenly, earnest young writer who stands as an equally false echo of Thackeray and *Vanity Fair*.

Angela Carter likewise specializes in ironic contact with the literary canon, although the literary monuments she parodies or appropriates are outside as well as within the insular British canon. In her most allusive novel, *The Infernal Desire Machines of Dr. Hoffman*, Carter juxtaposes plot lines and characters not only from E. T. A. Hoffman but also Voltaire (*Candide*), Poe, Borges, de Sade, Swift (voyage 4 of *Gulliver's Travels*) and American science-fiction writer Philip K. Dick. Carter is something of a special case in her conspicuous hospitality to vernacular, popular style; her characters are often Cockney castaways speaking the demotic English of the music hall. Yet one of Carter's lessons is that appearances can be deceiving. The colloquial can simultaneously be the "literary," as when Dora in *Wise Children* cries "What larks" and raises the ghost of Joe Gargery in Dickens's *Great Expectations*. Carter's fiction achieves its energy through such superimpositions and juxtapositions. Her central characters are half-breeds (the narrator of *Dr. Hoffman*), freaks or frauds (Fevvers in *Nights at the Circus*), bastards (Dora Chance of *Wise Children*): literal embodiments of the clashing cultures and values (high and low, "civilized" and "primitive," idealized and carnal) Carter seeks to dramatize and in her last two novels (*Nights at the Circus* and *Wise Children*) even to reconcile.

Postmodernism and the "Playgiarized" Classic

The strong shared element of parodic allusion in plot, characterization, and style shows the influence of the post-1960 movement in aesthetics known as postmodernism, for what Raymond Federman has termed "playgiarism" is a hallmark of postmodern style. Whether in architecture or in fiction, a chief characteristic of the postmodern is its eclecticism, its rejection of the austerities of high modernism with its emphasis on functionalism of form. Rejection of modernism is seen in these writers' hybridized texts: their forms are the collage (the alternations of viewpoint and time frame in Lively's *Moon Tiger*), the pastiche (the extensive selection of neo-Victorian poems and fairy tales incorporated into Byatt's *Possession*), the burlesque (the caricatures of male mid-life crisis and feminist consciousness-raising in Weldon's *Life and Loves of a She-Devil*), the parody (the retelling of Austen's *Emma* in Pym's *A Few Green Leaves*). A rejection of high modernism may also been seen among these writers when apparently realistic fictions remain pointedly uneventful (as in Brookner's *Brief Lives* [1990])—so that form serves no apparent function—or when an eventful narrative is left deliberately unresolved (as in Drabble's *Ice Age* [1977], which concludes with its likable protagonist, Anthony Keating, indefinitely confined to an Eastern European prison camp).

In *Postmodernism*, a work generally critical of the claims of postmodern aesthetics, Fredric Jameson nonetheless notes that indeterminate plot lines and a patchwork of allusions to past traditions (popular and "high") in postmodern art do not proceed from simple nostalgia but rather from "resistance" to the earlier material appropriated: "What was the delectation with a fantasy past now turns out to look more like the construction of a Utopian future." Seen in this light of "resistance," Pym's often-noted revisitings of Jane Austen (seen by most critics as possessing—as Jean Baudrillard has said dismissively of Borges—only the "discreet charm of second-order simulacra") appear in a more transgressive light, as a stealing of Austen's fire. Emma Howick, heroine of Pym's *Few Green Leaves*, for instance, has not only been named by her mother in the absurd hope that "some of the qualities possessed by the heroine of [Austen's *Emma*] might be perpetuated"—as if one's reading somehow mutated one's genes—but also, as Jane Nardin writes in her Twayne guide to Pym, is comically "doomed to relive a modernized version of the earlier story . . . the tale of a young woman who thinks she loves the socially suitable candidate for her affection [selfish Frank Churchill in Austen; selfish Graham Pettifer in Pym] but who finally discovers that she really loves an older man whose virtue is his strongest attraction."

Yet a motive of dissimulation—common among these writers—suggests the satiric intention behind this blatant simulation of Austen's plot by Pym. Dragged into the unheroic present, Austen's comic masterpiece can only mock its own monumentality: the genial old plot drapes loosely around these reduced modern characters. Pym's updated George Knightley, for instance, is Tom Dagnall, a clergyman who features in the thoughts of several cultured characters solely as "poor Tom." Though his story is no tragedy on the scale of Edgar's in *King Lear*, Pym's "poor Tom" does suffer the effects of being usurped by the fraudulent—a bastardized English culture if not a bastard brother. For in 1980, Tom Dagnall is an anachronism, an intelligent and well-meaning rector whose traditional duties have been subsumed by social workers, National Health Service physicians, the providers of council housing, and even American-style discount shopping centers. (None but the shabby-genteel shop at Tom's jumble sales: in 1980 the poor can afford new clothing made from hideous synthetic fabrics). Only when the eccentric Miss Lickerish dies does Tom Dagnall feel the satisfaction of being needed by his community; but it is a sad business to be needed chiefly as a speaker of words over the dead. From these depressing circumstances, Tom (like his sister Daphne and so many characters in these novels) escapes into the distant past in his quest to uncover the ruins of a "D.M.V." (deserted medieval village); with an absurdity he is aware of, he nonetheless sees himself as a reincarnation of the antiquary Anthony à Wood (d. 1695).

If Austen's Mr. Knightley—principal landholder near Highbury village and a person of commanding presence and rectitude besides—is the center of all authority in *Emma*, then "poor Tom" Dagnall is the center of no authority at all. What is postmodern about *A Few Green Leaves* is Pym's draining of power from Austen's classic—especially from Austen's hero. (This is not to mention Pym's surgical removal of any heroic glamour from the auras of Shakespeare and Anthony à Wood.) Ihab Hassan has identified such subversions of canonical works as "de-canonization," one of his eleven hallmarks of postmodern style: "[De-canonization] applies to all . . . conventions of authority . . . a massive 'delegitimization' of master-codes, a desuetude of the master-narratives. . . . Derision and revision are versions of subversion" (*Exploring Postmodernism*). In *A Few Green Leaves*, the marble mausoleum of the defunct family of de Tankerville, in need of constant upkeep yet the only handsome monument in a churchyard now cluttered with cheap headstones and plastic flowers, is Pym's bittersweet image of the cultured past (gorgeous but inert) and the rather decadent invitation it extends to the vulgar present: the inviting "idea of chilly marble on a hot summer day."

Dissimulating Portraits: Womens' Plots

Beyond gender, British nationality, their shared portion of historical time, and their common tendency to view both popular and "high" culture (past and present) with postmodern irony, these writers between the publication of Margaret Drabble's first novel (*A Summer Bird-Cage*, 1962) and Angela Carter's last (*Wise Children*, 1991) have been engaged primarily in experiments in characterization, creating their novels around exemplary viewpoints rather than experiments in form. These are portrait artists, though they work in a diversity of media and styles: the miniature or cameo (Brookner's *Lewis Percy*, 1989), the stylized group portrait (Pym's *Quartet in Autumn*, 1977), the caricature (Weldon's *Life and Loves of a She-Devil*, 1983), the surreal (Carter's *Infernal Desire Machines of Dr. Hoffman*, 1972), the neo-real (Drabble's *Ice Age*, 1977). Byatt's two best novels have experimented with the double-exposed portrait: in *The Virgin in the Garden* (1978), the boast of young Elizabeth I—"I shall not bleed"—is dramatized in more than one sense by a group of young people rehearsing a play about the first Elizabeth during England's celebration of Elizabeth II's coronation in June of 1953. In *Possession* (1990), the erotic secrets of two Victorian poets are literally unearthed by twentieth-century counterparts: Byatt's nineteenth- and twentieth-century couples mirror each other, for both are drawn into sexual intimacy by shared literary passions. Penelope Lively, too, double-exposes past on present: in *City of the Mind* (1992) the protagonist, Matthew Halland, is haunted by the history of the London buildings he must renovate or raze in order to complete his own designs, just as he must somehow redesign himself to manage his grief over the breakdown of his marriage.

Many of these novels are primarily portraits of women (Carter's *Wise Children*; Brookner's *Hotel du Lac*). Recently, there has been a tendency to expand, using group portrayals (Brookner's *Latecomers* [1988], about two Holocaust survivors) or a global canvas (Drabble's *The Gates of Ivory* [1992], in which the English playwright Stephen Cox—also a character in *The Radiant Way* and *A Natural Curiosity*—vanishes in Pol Pot's Cambodia). Yet this shift to a wider canvas has occurred without a sacrifice of the idiosyncratic voice. In *Moon Tiger* (1987), Lively's narrator Claudia Hampton is writing (as she dies in a hospital bed) a "history of the world, yes. And in the process, my own. . . . I shall . . . flesh it out." Brookner, an expert in the emblematic portraits of Watteau, Greuze, and David, is another clear example of the portrait artist, interested in the novel primarily as a vehicle of character study, as is Pym. (Once asked what novel she would bring to a desert island, Pym chose not the expected Austen novel but Henry James's *Golden Bowl*.)

Byatt, whose early fiction has an academic tendency to telegraph its message, thematizes this concern by opening *The Virgin in the Garden* with a scene set in the National Portrait Gallery in 1968; the disillusioned poet Alexander Wedderburn "consider[s] those words, once powerful, now defunct, national and portrait. They were both to do with identity: the identity of a culture (place, language, history), the identity of an individual human being as an object for mimetic representation." Likewise, the work of these seven novelists is a gallery of contemporary "national portraits." All have been intent on defining a central figure or group so powerfully that, as in a good portrait, the social and aesthetic values behind the posing of the group (the artist's, the subject's, the culture's) also are implicitly examined. Some portrait artists flatter; others are plainly or cruelly accurate or grotesquely distorting. The same spectrum between sentiment and satire is seen in these novels: most of these writers, in fact, exhibit a curious facility for portrayals that blend the satiric with the palliative and sentimental.

In "Emphasis Added," Nancy K. Miller has argued that a preoccupation with ironic portraiture is characteristic of fiction by women and is often accompanied by a lack of interest in dramatically "satisfying" or architectural plotting: this feminist reading of women's writing parallels a postmodern reading (which interprets the lack of interest in architectural plotting as a resistance to high modernism and its emphasis on form as function). Indeed, reviewers have sometimes judged these novels harshly because of digressive plotting or resistance to dramatic closure. In a *New Yorker* review, John Updike in 1976 complained of Margaret Drabble that "she does not encompass her material; rather she seems half lost within it—mystified by her characters, ruminative where she should be expository, expository where she should be dramatic, shamelessly dependent upon coincidence, lackadaisical about locating her themes, and capable, for long stretches, of blocking in episodes devoid of dynamic relevance to what one takes to be the action." Such criticisms could never be applied to the minimalist and tightly constructed novels of Pym or Brookner, but they have been criticized for the relentless uneventfulness of their fiction—another way to refuse Updike's expectation of "dynamic relevance" and "action."

While Weldon and Carter have produced narratives crammed with glorious incident (*Life and Loves of a She-Devil; Wise Children*), they have done so in mockery of that expectation of a shapely plot that causes Updike's exasperation with Drabble: in both those novels the plots are driven by a continuous stream of bizarre coincidence. Weldon's novel is based on a series of apparent coincidences (the seemingly unrelated mishaps that combine to destroy the husband who has rejected the "she-devil," Ruth Patchett). Yet it is Ruth herself—not Nemesis—who is grimly crafting this vindictive plot and meting out poetic justice. This updated Ruth's sad heart "patches" its wounds by rejecting the Biblical Ruth's traditional role as the virtuous and obedient matron. Weldon's Ruth instead abandons her two small children when she loses her husband (who leaves her for another woman). Transformed by her rage at his abandonment into a "ruthless" she-devil, Ruth acquires enormous wealth, manipulates dozens of characters, and makes a new body for herself through years of plastic surgery—and all to torment and humble her faithless husband, a clownish figure appropriately named Bobbo. As with Carter's "conspiracy" at the center of *The Infernal Desire Machines of Dr. Hoffman*, this is plotting with a vengeance, and that is the point. Authors are puppeteers; their plots are arbitrary. Carter's *Wise Children*, too, emphasizes the arbitrary nature of plotting through repeated introduction of wild conjunctions. Carter's heroine is appropriately named Dora Chance; with her twin sister Nora she shares a stage identity as one-half of "The Lucky Chances." All sexual coupling has its comically coincidental aspects (as Fielding and Sterne were among the first novelists to point out). Yet it is more than usually by lucky chance that Dora and Nora enter the world. For they have been told that they are the consequence of a particularly improbable conjunction—the casual rape of a shy chambermaid in a seedy Brixton boarding house by a great Shakespearian actor. (An early sketch for this plot centered on fortuitous insemination is provided by Carter's story "The Kitchen Child," first published in 1979 and later in *Black Venus*, 1985).

Plot among these writers, then, may be overdetermined; it also may simply be *withheld*: too much happens, or nothing. The autobiography of Fay Dodworth Langdon, the first-person narrator in Brookner's *Brief Lives* (1990), is one example of the latter. Fay lives emotionally in her own distant past, when she was a radio singer ("Arcady, Arcady was my song"); she even cherishes warm memories of the deadeningly quiet Sundays of her childhood, spent in a drab quarter of London: "we would be reading, the simple honest stories Mother brought home from the Boots Lending Library and which for us were a source of endless pleasure, an integral part of Sunday, with nothing harsh or disturbing to tell us, and always a happy ending." Fay is a character trapped in a nearly eventless plot that never reveals itself to her, though readers soon see a pattern: everyone Fay "loves" dies and deserts her. Yet with the exception of her adored father, who died late in her childhood, Fay seems incapable of acknowledging her emotional ties to other people—including her mother and her husband—until long after they have died and left her alone. So love itself has been manifest to Fay only in its most painful form: grief, acute and chronic. This novel is a case study, a portrait of the sorrow that is Fay's only powerful characteristic. Attempting to read Fay as a heroine can lead only to the conclusion of an angry reader of *Brief Lives* who wrote the *Sunday Times* objecting to its favorable review of the novel: "Am I the only reader for whom the heroines of Ms Anita Brookner's novels are not pathetic waifs but cold-blooded, egocentric, manipulative bitches?"

In any event, the loneliness Fay complains of in her old age—which she attributes to the fading of her beauty—is shown to be the result of an unacknowledged contradiction in her nature. She thinks she yearns for conventional relationships, and yet to her fastidious taste, every relationship she does enter is flawed and insufficient. Following the sudden death of a man with whom she has for some time been conducting a clandestine affair, Fay assesses her mood with her usual horrifying calm: "It was not Charlie that I missed, but rather the person for whom Charlie had been a substitute, whoever that was." She can take no pleasure even in the everyday chores of the "ordinary" life she says she aspires to:

I dread the weekends. I dread the pretense that drives me to the shops on a Saturday morning, and the shame of buying a solitary chop. . . . I dread the calm of Saturday afternoons, punctuated only by the distant roar from the football terraces. Something stops me from going out, as if I might be in danger of missing a visitor, though no one ever comes. I sit by the window, my hands in my lap, looking out and waiting. . . . I watch the light fade with a sort of anguish, an anguish which is not entirely temporal. I perceive the symbolism of the end of the day.

Fay's story (unlike the unsophisticated fiction of her childhood) has not been simple or honest, and there is no hope of a happy ending. In *Brief Lives*, the sparseness of events focuses attention entirely on the transient moods of a self-deluding narrator.

For these writers, technique often lies—as with Brookner's use of Fay to center *Brief Lives*—in a form-fitting of the plot to a central individual consciousness. If that character (the subject of the portrait) should finally die (as Claudia Hampton does in the conclusion of Lively's *Moon Tiger*), a strong sense of closure may be provided. More often, however, these novels end oddly, awkwardly—as though there is something forced or painful about the novelists' separation from their characters. Conclusions may feature an explosion of gaudy improbabilities and last-minute revelations—as in Carter's *Wise Children*—or simply fade to black: three friends watch a sunset in Drabble's *Radiant Way*.

As Nancy Miller notes (her context is the fiction of George Eliot and Mme de Lafayette): "To build a narrative around a character whose behavior is deliberately idiopathic . . . is not merely to create a puzzling fiction but to fly in the face of a certain ideology (of the text and its context). . . . If we were to uncover a feminine 'tradition'—diachronic recurrences—of such ungrammaticalities, would we have the basis for a poetics of women's fiction?" Contemporary British novels by women, with their common emphasis on "idiopathic" narrative viewpoint and their eccentric ironies and indeterminacies (Miller's "ungrammaticalities") do bear out Miller's point that "the peculiar shape of a heroine's destiny in novels by women, the implausible twists of plot in these novels, is a form of insistence about the relation of women to writing: a comment on the stakes of difference."

None of these writers engages wholeheartedly in the dramatic simulation Updike expected of Drabble in 1976. The simulated subjects within their frames quite often, as in Fay's softly enunciated despair throughout *Brief Lives*, suggest a dissimulating author whose intelligence is not at one but rather at war with the self-deluding goals of her own characters. Anita Brookner is the force keeping Fay Langdon (the surname is almost an anagram for England, a homophone for London) from the simpler story Fay herself would have preferred to enact. *The Infernal Desire Machines of Dr. Hoffman*, Carter's most insistently metafictional novel, also finally stands as a critique of traditional closure. For Carter's novel simply runs down (in an appropriately mechanical way), and her narrator—like Brookner's Fay—turns a disappointed face outward to the readers he presumes are likewise disappointed: "If you feel a certain sense of anticlimax, how do you think I felt?"

"Gender and the Autonomous Text": The Solitary Woman

Many of these dissimulating portraits are of women, and many raise questions traditional in British fiction centered on female experience and education. What can a woman become? What should she become? Such questions have been central to novelists (predominantly though not exclusively female) from Frances Burney and Jane Austen through the Brontës, George Eliot, and Virginia Woolf; their implied answers are embodied in the characters (almost always young women) they designate as central, and in the plots that frustrate or fulfill their human potential. Can a woman be heroic entirely within the domestic sphere and the traditional roles of daughter, sister, lover, wife, mother? (Austen's Emma Woodhouse answers yes; Flaubert's Emma Bovary answers no.) Can a bright, sensitive woman deprived of an education make up for the deficiency by marrying a mentor? (For Burney's Evelina Anville, a comic yes; for Eliot's Dorothea Brooke, a tragic no.) Are the traits conducive to social popularity—beauty, cleverness, a respected profession, good bloodlines, wealth by inheritance or marriage—necessary to a credible heroine? (Woolf's Clarissa Dalloway offers a qualified assent; Eliot's Mary Garth a scornful negative.) On these issues, there is no break between these contemporary women writers and British fictional tradition—no need for a break, perhaps, because the tradition itself is not oppressively unitary or monolithic: it has already supported numerous conflicting and powerful voices.

In the answer to one traditional question about women, however, there is some oppressive uniformity in earlier British fiction by and about women, and some resistance from contemporary women novelists. Can self-sufficiency, singleness, be seen as heroic (or at least fictionally interesting) in a person; more particularly, in a woman? "Women must marry," Mrs. Ramsay repeatedly says in part 1 of *To the Lighthouse*. Her certainty is framed by Woolf and received by Lily Briscoe with considerable irony, but although Lily is a great improvement on earlier renditions of the English spinster, it is Mrs. Ramsay herself, the Madonna dry Lily has so much difficulty capturing on canvas, who centers Woolf's novel as she finally centers Lily's painting. To be a heroine—i.e., to stand as a good example of a life—a woman character must, in British fictional tradition, aspire toward an extended life, changing and being changed by other people. Even Charlotte Brontë's Jane Eyre, who is small, plain, poor, and passionate—an embodied rejection of the more facile conventions for novel-heroines—hates her orphaned singleness, yearning for her lost family as she yearns for her absent soul mate. For all her intensity as a narrator, Jane as a heroine is actually (as is characteristic of the English tradition) a compromise figure situated between the feral passion of the unmanageable lunatic Bertha Mason Rochester and the chilly self-possession of the compulsively regulated spinster Eliza Reed. Even the Brontës, who broke so many rules, exhibit—in their obsessive emphasis on exogamy—the essential gregariousness of the British tradition, which until quite recently has not much interested itself (as North American, Latin American, and European fiction traditionally have) in the singular, the antisocial, the hermetic.

Despite their prevailing emphasis on correspondences between their narratives and those of the classic English tradition, these contemporary women novelists have interested themselves in reexamination of earlier models of "singularity." All these novelists share what amounts to a refusal to prescribe sociability. Drabble explores the singular woman character as early as her first novel, *A Summer Bird-Cage* (1962), in the enigmatic person of the narrator's bohemian friend Simone, "nationless, sexless, hopelessly eclectic, hopelessly unrooted." A Simone-like figure in later novels is Esther Breuer, the sexually and socially unclassifiable art historian of *The Radiant Way* and its sequels. Yet Drabble's free spirits are peripheral characters. Simone's participation in *A Summer Bird-Cage* is limited to the postcards she sends the heroine from Italy. And Esther, one of the three school friends who center Drabble's trilogy, was dispatched to Italy in the second novel. Esther is, in fact, the least interesting of the three friends, probably as a direct result of symbolizing the woman outside norms. Defined in terms of what she does not do—marry, have a child, hold a steady job— Esther is one of nature's free-lancers, anxious even over the minimal commitment and nurture required by the potted palm a lover has given her. Over the years, she obtrudes her neurotic concern over the health of this ever-sickly plant into every discussion her friends initiate about the state of their (equally fragile) marriages.

Solitary characters such as Esther Breuer, in refusing to be changed by other characters, tend to retard the action. Fay Weldon solves this difficulty in *Life and Loves of a She-Devil* by chronicling the vendetta of a sociopath: Ruth may be profoundly antisocial, but she is eager to interact with people in order to secure her goal of vengeance. Byatt's plot in *Possession*, too, becomes absorbing despite a cast of introverts (it is not promising to learn in early chapters that both of Byatt's shy modern protagonists cherish fantasies of resting in the pristine white cots of their early childhood). Byatt's four lonely literary people, past and present, are slowly drawn together by a festive plot, moved along less by actions than by the characters' growing insight into the pseudo-Victorian poetry, letters, and fairy tales inserted into the narrative that they are studying. Byatt's two modern scholars are Roland Michell, an unemployed graduate student unhappy in a relationship he has outgrown; and Maud Bailey, a feminist scholar recovering from an affair fecklessly embarked upon during a conference on "Gender and the Autonomous Text." Maud and Roland find each other, if only briefly, while researching an even more unlikely erotic conjunction between the two Victorians they study. Randolph Henry Ash, Roland's Browningesque poet, is discovered to have been trapped in a marriage never consummated; seeking solace, Ash had (as Maud and Roland gradually discover, searching letters and texts for clues) briefly loved the fey, difficult Christabel LaMotte, a figure reminiscent both of Christina Rossetti and Emily Dickinson. As her twentieth-century descendant Lord Bailey scoffs: "[Christabel] didn't *do* anything. Just lived up there in the east wing and poured out all this stuff about fairies. It wasn't a *life.*" Christabel LaMotte, before the discoveries of Roland and Maud, was thought to have loved only once—the artist Blanche Glover, who mysteriously drowned herself. But Maud's and Roland's researches reread Christabel as a tortured early feminist: she bore Ash's daughter but then surrendered her to a conventional married sister. Ultimately, Maud discovers that she herself, director of Women's Studies at Lincoln University, is a descendant of the child of LaMotte and Ash, and so is herself the creation of the relationship she has been reconstructing. A novel of correspondences—letters, analogies, patterns—rather than of direct actions, *Possession* nonetheless provides a full and genial narrative that takes its characters out of isolation and defeat.

Pym and Brookner also place their solitary characters in the center of narrative, but the festive resolution offered by Byatt in *Possession* is usually denied. Pym's badly dressed heroines—thirtyish Emma Howick in *A Few Green Leaves* is introduced to readers as "rather the type that the women's magazines used to make a feature of 'improving' "—are dreamily detached from social expectations that (in the words of Byatt's Lord Bailey) they will "*do*" something. In chapter 12 Emma's mother thinks about her daughter and "poor Tom" Dagnall as she drifts asleep ("perhaps the thought of Tom had induced drowsiness"); she hopes Emma and Tom will become romantically involved. The following paragraph explores Emma's own thoughts as she too falls asleep thinking of Tom: her train of thought, however, is comically unpromising: "He was an essentially good person. . . . But to get down to practical details or brass tacks, could Tom *really* help her if she asked him? Would he, for instance, be capable of cleaning her top windows, which was what she really needed?" Gently comic in structure (with frequent imagery of death and loss adding a darker undertone), *A Few Green Leaves* concludes rather happily, with mild Emma's having become sufficiently aware of Tom to encourage his tentative efforts to attach her: "She could . . . she was beginning to realize, embark on a love affair which need not necessarily be an unhappy one." In Pym's bleaker novel *The Sweet Dove Died* (1978), however, there is no such final transformation of the well-meaning solitary woman: a kindly but embittered divorced woman ("poor Liz") lives for her Siamese cats, and an aging sentimentalist, Meg, remains devoted to Colin, an indifferent young man. These loving characters are merely absurd; and the selfish woman who centers the novel, Leonora Eyre, ends as she began, pursuing a cultivation of perfect form that protects her from her friends' absurdity and yet estranges her from any human warmth.

At first, Claudia Hampton in Lively's *Moon Tiger* seems, like Leonora Eyre, coldly egocentric for all her courage in facing a painful death ("God is an unprincipled bastard, wouldn't you agree?"). Claudia has always made her own rules, from engaging in a long incestuous affair with her brother to bearing a child out of wedlock during the 1940s. Lively, however, gradually reveals a sympathetic motive for Claudia's harshly autocratic independence, which has poisoned her relationship with her subdued and resentful daughter. On assignment to Cairo as a news correspondent during World War II, Claudia had briefly but deeply loved a soldier who was killed; soon afterward she had miscarried their child. Claudia then hardened; and that uncompromisingly hard voice dominates her narrative—until a luminous conclusion.

Another stubbornly idiopathic, intractable—unmarriageable—character seen finally in a kindlier light is Marcia Ivory in Pym's *Quartet in Autumn*. Miss Ivory lives alone following the death of her mother, the evidently more traumatic death of her cat Snowy, and her mandatory retirement from a dull office job in central London. Recent radical surgery for breast cancer (which will be unsuccessful in arresting the disease) confirms Marcia as an emblem, by turns comic and poignant, of human loss. As she solemnly informs a Remembrance Day collector: "I, too, have had *something removed.*" Given Marcia's recent losses, it makes a kind of mad sense when, declining into senility, she spends her days sorting a huge collection of plastic bags and counting the empty milk bottles stored in her garden shed. There is anger implicit in Pym's portrayal of this fierce yet forlorn solitude, in which Marcia numbly accumulates empty receptacles, hoarding cans of food she will never survive to be nourished by. Pym shows that Marcia's isolation is only half-chosen; it is also imposed by neighbors and co-workers who find her frightening and difficult: she avoids other people in part because she resents the hypocrisy of their occasional strained overtures. Pym's social satire is not directed at Marcia herself; perhaps it is aimed at Jonathan Cape and the other British publishers who branded her work as unpublishable for sixteen years, rejecting successive drafts of *Quartet in Autumn* and *The Sweet Dove Died* between 1961 and 1977. For *Quartet in Autumn* opens with an uncharacteristically direct and defensive statement of theme: "The position of an unmarried, unattached, ageing woman is of no interest whatever to the writer of modern fiction." Pym's novel will be different, however, for it is Marcia (not her saner and more presentable co-worker Letty) who posthumously becomes the novel's heroine (if heroism is power to change things) when she unexpectedly wills her mother's house to Norman, among the "quartet" of four office workers the one whose life will be most improved by this gesture. For Norman—an unpopular man only slightly less odd than Marcia herself—lives in a rented room, doesn't drive, and has never had anything of his own.

In Brookner's *Hotel du Lac*, Edith Hope, a writer of high-end romance novels, is also solitary until the conclusion of her novel, when—like Pym's Norman—she receives a gift, though it is only the gift of insight. Unlike Brookner's Fay Langdon, Edith Hope finally does not seem lonely—merely alone, and by choice. Edith refuses two conventionally suitable marriages in the course of her novel, choosing, in fact, "hope"—her passionate affair with a married man who has told her he has no intention of divorcing his wife—over safety, over everything. During the twelve-hour period in which she is engaged to her second suitor, Edith writes, "One does not receive proposals of marriage every day in this enlightened world, although curiously enough I have had two this year. I seem to have accepted them both. The lure of domestic peace was obviously too great for one of my timorous nature to resist. But I shall settle down now. I shall have to, for I doubt if I have anything more to look forward to." As Brookner sees her heroine outside of marriage—outside the reproductive, social, and what was once considered the natural order—marriage would represent a failure of Edith's integrity, a concession to her own timidity and fear of aging. Helped by the revelation that the man who has just proposed marriage to her has spent the night with another woman, Edith is able to go back to passion, knowing that it is her choice, however problematic. Her story concludes with a telegram she sends from her Swiss hotel to her "unsuitable" lover: wryly Edith changes her first message ("Coming home")—"not entirely accurate"—to "Returning." So Brookner writes a reverse bildungsroman: her heroine forgets the disillusioned values she has learned and returns to what she always knew about herself: "The tears that had fallen from her fine light eyes seemed to have sharpened her vision."

The Tortoise and the Hare: Women and Competition

A final general point of similarity among these writers is that all have shared an emphasis on women's relationships with each other; and all have considered—reaching a variety of conclusions—the proposition that women are necessarily competitors. In *Hotel du Lac*, Brookner's heroine describes the attraction of the romance novels that she writes: to Edith, the chief appeal is that they lie about women and competition:

What is the most potent myth of all? . . . The tortoise and the hare. . . . People love this one, especially women. Now you will notice . . . that in my books it is the mouselike unassuming girl who gets the hero, while the scornful temptress with whom he has had a stormy affair retreats baffled from the fray, never to return. The tortoise wins every time. This is a lie, of course. . . . Aesop was writing for the tortoise market.

Barbara Pym, whose cool intelligence is warmed by faith (God, and occasionally even the novelist, will provide a suitable inheritance for the meek), also writes for "the tortoise market," though in two novels she provides a dark variation on Aesop. In novels that share similar plots, *A*

Glass of Blessings (1958) and *The Sweet Dove Died* (1978), Pym denies victory to the hare without awarding it to the tortoise. For the central "hares" (Wilmet Forsyth and Leonora Eyre, respectively) are not allowed to retain their power over the elusive younger man that each pursues: in both novels, a male rival finally defeats their fantasies. Pym's two plots involving attractive gay men act sardonically to exclude all female players—tortoises or hares—entirely from the race.

Beyond such individual variations on the theme of female competition, there has also been a historical shift in recent years, a change strongly evident in the differences between the narrators of the earliest and latest of the novels under consideration: Drabble's *Summer Bird-Cage* (1962) and Carter's *Wise Children* (1991). Sarah Bennett, narrator of Drabble's novel, is, like other novel characters, a creature of her times, which happen to have preceded the feminist movement and its consciousness-raising. Sarah is, in fact, generally unawakened, latent. She shares more than a surname with Austen's heroine Elizabeth Bennet in *Pride and Prejudice*. Sarah Bennett wryly—and without Elizabeth Bennet's sisterly compassion—observes the romantic difficulties of her more beautiful older sister Louise. (Louise suggests George Eliot's Dorothea Brooke as well: she marries a much older man, a novelist who sees her as a lovely possession; like Dorothea in *Middlemarch*, Louise is courted before and after her marriage—and visited during a miserable European honeymoon—by an attractive suitor much younger than her husband.) Drabble updates the nineteenth-century allusions—Sarah has just completed a brilliant undergraduate career at Oxford and is working at the BBC. Yet she has never seriously considered the career for which she is most suited, academics, because she fears it will make her somehow less attractive: "You can't be a sexy don. It's all right for men . . . but for women it's a mistake." Sarah's sister Louise has erred by seeking a financially advantageous yet emotionally barren marriage, an error Sarah is fully capable of seeing. She is less aware of her own folly in placing her young life in limbo as she awaits the return of her fiancé, Francis, from an extended period of study in the United States. Like Austen's Elizabeth Bennet, Drabble's Sarah Bennett is comically blinded by pride in her superior intellect; like her, Sarah is far too articulate to be either naturally charitable or universally popular. Unlike Austen's heroine, however, Sarah Bennett displays a smug consciousness of her own superiority—taking frequent solace in thoughts of her youth, intelligence, and beauty. Thinking of the legs of her dowdy cousin Daphne ("muscular and shapeless round the ankles and covered in hair and bluish pimples"), Sarah thinks complacently: "It must be so frightful to have to put things on in order to look better, instead of to strip things off." Sarah's narcissistic flaw is the making of the novel, as her portrayal allows for satiric dissection of the by turns placid and nervous contemplation of their own "giftedness" and entitlement that preoccupy both Sarah and Louise.

Contempt for cousin Daphne (who seems modeled after Kingsley Amis's Margaret Peel in *Lucky Jim*, a novel Sarah praises in her own narrative) is one of the few passions the sisters share. Daphne inspires their only intimate discussion in the novel, when Louise warns Sarah against her:

"One can scarcely think of people like [Daphne] . . . as human beings. She's like a different species. . . . She reminds me of those tame shabby animals in zoos . . . so docile and herbivorous that they don't even bother to put them behind bars. . . . Herbivores. Sadly smelling, depressed animals."

"And you feel you're a carnivore?"

"Well, if that is the definition of a Daphne, yes, I do. And you too. We're the predatory type, don't you think? The flesh eaters? I'd rather eat than be eaten. If Daphne weren't another species I would have to feel sorry for her, but as it is . . ."

"As it is," I said, "You devour her unashamed."

"Oh, I don't deliberately devour . . ."

"But one does feed off them."

"If you mean that my way of life—our way of life—exists through the existence of theirs . . . well, yes, I suppose one does. It's a minority way, isn't it, Sal? Money, theatres, books . . ."

"And we can't live without the herbivores?"

"How could we? We live by our reflection in their eyes."

Drabble is no longer fond of her first novel, though it is among her best. The sketch of woman-to-woman hostilities before the feminist movement is discomfortingly sharp, which is as satire should be. (While Drabble seems rather invested in the types of privilege she simultaneously appears to be satirizing, this is true of many other satires—Thackeray's *Vanity Fair*, for one.) Nonetheless, Sarah Bennett does seem a product of now-defunct certainties—particularly in her assumption that ambitious women fall into two groups, necessarily opposed: attractive "flesh-eating" predators or repellent, tame "herbivores." In later fiction such as *The Radiant Way* and its sequels, *A Nat-*

ural Curiosity and *The Gates of Ivory*, Drabble has changed her focus: in those novels three women friends, closely attending to each other's welfare, center the fiction. Yet differences among women continue to interest Drabble, who is possessed by (in the words of her recent title) a devouring "natural curiosity" about her characters and their motives. Simply, those differences are no longer seen as necessarily invidious.

If Drabble herself has moved away from Sarah Bennett's viewpoint, Sarah's antithesis is to be found in Dora Chance, Carter's narrator in *Wise Children* (1991). Dora's surname reminds us that she navigates by chance, lacking normal advantages (let alone the rich entitlement—money, Oxford, unlimited nurture—that makes Sarah and Louise feel so guilty). Dora, a chorus girl of illegitimate and mysterious birth, may be descended from a famous family of Shakespearean actors, but she has been raised in a seedy quarter of Brixton by a retired prostitute with a heart of gold. While Drabble's Sarah Bennett rejects any serious thoughts of a career as she awaits the return of her lover, Dora Chance has worked professionally since childhood, when she and her twin sister Nora (sisters are soul mates here, not rivals) shared billing in "Babes in the Wood," a holiday pantomime. Unlike Sarah—who has it all, including youth, beauty, and brains—Dora Chance is blowsy, past her years of beauty (though she would deny being past her prime). Conspicuously underprivileged, Dora and her sister received their only higher education (in a subplot lifted from Dickens's *Little Dorrit*) from a down-on-her-luck dance teacher. Dora has also, she makes clear, had a splendid life. Fearless as ever in old age, she and Nora conclude the narrative by adopting twins on their seventy-fifth birthday.

The traditional women's roles, theatrical and social, have eluded them: they have never married or borne children or even "played Cordelia"—loved and suffered as acknowledged daughters: they spend their lives attempting to discover whether Sir Melchior Hazard, "the greatest Lear of his day," is their biological father. Yet Dora and Nora have thrived under surrogate care and on the margins. Unintellectual, overpainted, Rabelaisian, Dora is frank in narrating the sexual adventures that have enlivened her life. Yet no experience has ever threatened her closest bond, which is—and here Carter provides a narcissistic touch—with her own image, her identical twin. If sisterhood is competition in Drabble's first novel ("She taught me to want to outdo her," complains Sarah of Louise), it is a mirror of self-esteem in Carter's last: to love a sister (a woman like oneself) is finally to love oneself. Carter's final plot twist provides a concluding image that reconciles gender differences as well, when the old twins accept the role of foster mothers to two new infant Hazards. Fished casually out of the pockets of hundred-year-old Peregrine Hazard (Melchior's twin and Dora's uncle [father?]), the infant mixed-race twins (miraculous offspring of Gareth, a young Hazard supposedly celibate) are not identical but fraternal, "boy and girl, a new thing in our family."

The spirit of reconciliation so pronounced in Carter's final novel marks an affirmative point of departure for this discussion of women novelists between 1962 and 1992. To summarize and conclude, all these writers have emphasized their links to the literary past and specifically to the English literary canon; and all have examined the heroic capacities of solitary characters. All have assessed the contemporary state of the war between men and women, as well as the present state of the war "down among the women" themselves, to steal a phrase from Weldon's early novel. All have suffered somewhat among reviewers and other canon-makers because they are generally agnostics on dogmas central to high modernism, especially any emphasis on innovations in technique and form. They have all focused instead on the portrayal of characters—not invariably or immediately likable characters—around whom some kind of plot gradually coalesces. Among these writers, Weldon, Carter, and Drabble have been notable for incorporating into their fiction, from their earliest novels, a clear recognition of the radical changes brought about since the 1970s by the emerging discourses of feminism. And yet it would be wrong to see any of these writers solely in terms of a commitment to social change, for even those committed to change are also eager to show what remains usable in tradition. Possibly because their own early lives were dominated by images of a world in ruins and an imperative to rebuild, social change is typically seen as a matter of improvement or renovation rather than a radical razing or demolition: this is true even of Angela Carter, who rewrote fairy tales instead of repudiating them. Though among these writers only Weldon and Carter are outright comediennes, all are playful in the sense that their allusive styles exhibit considerable intellectual play. And yet, like the predecessor they so often invoke (says Carter's Dora, parodying a primer, "A. [is for] for Austen, Jane"), all instruct by pleasing. Their often dissimulating portraits encourage a reader's moral engagement, an assessment of the choices and values represented by the subject. In a review of *The Radiant Way*, Margaret Atwood quoted a prediction of the *New York Times* that Margaret Drabble will be "the novelist we will turn to a hundred years from now to find out how things were." The same prediction might well hold true for all these seven writers and the painstaking "national portraits" they have drawn from the elusive materials of daily life among men and women of the late twentieth century.

Carol McGuirk

Selected Bibliography

Bloom, Harold, ed. *Twentieth Century British Literature*. Chelsea House Library of Literary Criticism. 6 vols. New York: Chelsea, 1985.

Robinson, Sally. *Engendering the Self: Representation in Contemporary Women's Fiction*. SUNY Series in Feminist Criticism and Theory. Albany: State University Press of New York, 1991.

Rushdie, Salman. "Angela Carter, 1940–92: A Very Good Wizard." *New York Times Book Review*, March 8, 1992, p. 5.

Sadler, Lynn Veach. *Anita Brookner*. Boston: Twayne, 1990.

Sadler, Lynn Veach. *Margaret Drabble*. Boston: Twayne, 1986.

Salwak, Dale. *The Life and Work of Barbara Pym*. Iowa City: University of Iowa Press, 1987.

Schlueter, Paul, and June Schlueter. *An Encyclopedia of British Women Writers*. New York: Garland, 1988.

Schmidt, Ricarda. "The Journey of the Subject in Angela Carter's Fiction." *Textual Practice* 3, no. 1 (Spring 1989): 56–75.

Schumann, Kuno. "English Culture and the Contemporary Novel." In *Anglistentag 1981*. Frankfurt am Main: Lang, 1983.

Todd, Janet, ed. *Dictionary of British Women Writers*. London: Routledge, 1989.

The Contemporary Novel

Kneel then and pray. The blade flashes a smile.
This your new life. This murder is yours.
James Fenton, "A Staffordshire Murderer"

THEY have made an appalling mistake, in glee, in anguish, in innocence or heartlessness; convinced perhaps that there was no mistake, but only liberation or a form of fidelity. Years later, when the disasters have spoken, when murder or madness or suicide or incest or the withering of love has declared itself, the survivors face their half-focused regrets, reaching no conclusion. This story, in various versions, recurs so often in recent British fiction that it begins to look like a major contemporary myth: forgive us, for we know not what we have done. Yet the helplessness *in* this story intersects with a curious, extreme control *of* the story, whose language and narrative techniques offer fastidious and elegant evocations of the most desperate messes. The more desperate the mess, it seems, the more elegant the writing. A style from a despair, perhaps. Or a style from something less terminal and traditional than despair: disarray, uncertainty, a flight from guilt; something between ignorance and knowledge, too knowing for the one and too hapless for the other.

Two teenagers in Ian McEwan's *Cement Garden*, 1978, are said to look at each other "knowingly, knowing nothing." Children and memories of childhood figure prominently in this fiction, but the children are often torturers or apparent aliens, vivid refutations of the legend of original innocence. Yet there is something vulnerable, even (almost) innocent about these children, and much in these novels that seems morbid or clinical in tone is simply wary, scared. Knowingness is not knowledge, and the children are an image, perhaps, of a felt relation to an overreported, underexperienced reality. We've seen it all before, they can't pull the wool over our eyes. But we've seen it mainly on television, and we can't really tell wool from information. The narrator of Julian Barnes's *Flaubert's Parrot* (1984), speaks of "our own wry, unfoolable age," but we are not as wry or as smart as we think. The attempted wryness is mere mask. We can't be fooled because we take no risks; because we suspect everything, turn our very doubt into armor, our bewilderment into poise.

This stylish disarray is not the only story in recent British fiction, and it is not necessarily the most important one. There are also stories of less dandyish disaffections and less private-seeming preoccupations; stories of gender, of empire and independence, of AIDS, of the end of the world. But the story of the bewildering crime or calamity is the one that appears most frequently and affords the best introduction to what I take to be a new, or at least substantially altered, structure of literary form and feeling.

The new writing is more brittle, less easygoing, but also more experimental and less provincial, than its immediate (or even fairly remote) ancestors; than the work of Iris Murdoch and Anthony Powell, say, whose casual and capacious English styles assert rather than deny the mind's ability to cope with the word's surprises; or of William Golding, whose stark fables interrogate but do not abandon a severe theology. The older writers who seem closest to the new sensibility are Anthony Burgess, John Fowles, and Muriel Spark: Burgess because he has always, in the wake of his master, Joyce, made language the unruly hero of his novels, Fowles because he is not afraid of the unleashed intellect, whatever excesses it may commit, and Spark because the black brilliance of her macabre comedies matches the violence and enormity so common in later fiction. The hacked corpse of her *Territorial Rights* (1979) travels, so to speak, all the way to McEwan's *The Innocent* (1990), and travels in company. There are bodies everywhere in recent fiction, and not only in detective novels. At the same time, detective novels, with the work of P. D. James and others, have become more reflective, harder to tell from fiction outside the genre; and Michael Dibdin's thrillers *Ratking* (1988), *Vendetta* (1990), and *Cabal* (1992), like the novels of Graham Swift and Kazuo Ishiguro, to be discussed a little later, place us in a world where a mystery's solution is called for but is finally the least of our problems. The frightening question is what to do with the truth when it surfaces; what it means, who can be trusted with it.

Gothic Innocence

It is impossible, of course, to date shifts in sensibility with any accuracy; hard enough to argue that a bundle of novels, however impressive, represents any such thing. I would suggest though that the early work of Beryl Bainbridge (*Harriet Said, Sweet William* [1975]) and Ian McEwan (*The Cement Garden, The Comfort of Strangers* [1981]) represents a convenient marker, and that McEwan's continuing work (*A Child in Time* [1987], *The Innocent, Black Dogs* [1992]) is a useful guide. A publisher's reader, turning down Bainbridge's first novel, said, "What repulsive little creatures you have made the two central characters." Repulsive is not the right word, and it was certainly a mistake to refuse that elegant and troubling book. But the two girls in *Harriet Said* do ruin any comfortable ideas we may have about sheltered youth, as they taunt an old man and finally kill his wife.

McEwan's *Cement Garden* begins: "I did not kill my father but I sometimes felt I had helped him on his way." If the narrator had killed his father, he would still be talking in this offhand fashion, as indeed he does when he tells us that he and his sisters have buried their dead mother in cement in order to keep the authorities from finding out that they are orphans, and that incest seems to him the natural expression of a beleaguered affection. And earlier, when he describes his newly dead mother:

The room was full of sunlight. Mother lay propped up by pillows, her hands under the sheet. She could have been about to doze off, for her eyes were not open and staring like dead people's in films, nor were they completely closed. . . . Mother's feet appeared, they stuck out from underneath the blanket, bluish-white with a space between each toe.

The close observation, the reference to films, the lack of expressed surprise or distress—all signal a character more frightened than he wishes to seem, but we know this only because we recognize that horror has its reticences as well as its extravagances; because we have made the boy's strangeness our own. Both Bainbridge and McEwan suggest to us how normal the abnormal can feel once we are caught up in it. They invite us to think the unthinkable, or if we can't think it, to live it imaginatively, as if it were no longer alien to us, or as if there were no more aliens.

For McEwan, the innocent is never entirely innocent; it always has a real but murky relation to whatever crime hangs in the memory. But an innocence remains nevertheless, a bewilderment no simply guilty person would feel. Even McEwan's adults are children, sometimes cripplingly so, as in *A Child in Time*, where a politician commits suicide because he cannot bring his residual childhood into line with his frantic public life; where a father cannot mourn his lost daughter without recreating his parents' marriage and the moment of his own conception.

McEwan deals in the gothic in a rather special sense—in what we might call the gothic of everyday life. In a Hitchcock film, for instance, innocence says, It looks as though I did it, but I didn't. In McEwan it says, I may have done it, but you have to hear the whole story, or, I did it, but only because I was ambushed by some stranger hiding in my personality. "He was innocent," one of McEwan's characters thinks, "but it would take some explaining."

By gothic I mean that moment in a fiction when all the emotions go underground, when what has seemed like a logical if perhaps violent plot turns to outright nightmare, driven by forces that no one will name. The corpse, for instance, already a practical problem in material reality, takes up residence in the mind; the monster doubles in size, the aggrieved woman becomes a shrieking harpy. McEwan's great gift is for getting his characters onto this level of experience by the most casual-seeming means: they step into the gothic the way other people step onto buses, and the sheer ordinariness of their arrival in terror takes the breath away.

"They knew one another much as they knew themselves, and their intimacy, rather like too many suitcases, was a matter of perpetual concern." McEwan's writing is patient, inventive, intelligent, attentive to detail. The tone is always steady, underplayed, even (especially) when it deals with repellent material. The books are also funny, in a macabre way, particularly *The Innocent*, where quite ghastly bits of behavior keep stumbling across the structure of farce, as if farce were in the end the natural form of horror; horror's home.

"*Tout comprendre, c'est tout condamner,*" Adam Mars-Jones says in *Lantern Lecture* (1981), inverting a famous phrase. The third section of this subtle book is based on the historical case of Donald Neilson, also known as the Black Panther, who in the early 1970s killed three postmasters and left a kidnapped girl to die in a drainage complex. Mars-Jones's interest is in the odd and disastrous collusion between Neilson's craziness and the police's incompetence.

There is a frightening image of chance here. Nothing goes as anyone plans; people die because the killer is scared of his victims, the girl dies because the intended ransom trail cannot be followed. Neilson, as Mars-Jones imagines him, doesn't mean to kill anyone, and keeps seeing the deaths he causes as mere snags in his grand scheme, accidents for which he cannot be held accountable. The irony of the book is complicated, since its language puts us in Neilson's place without putting us into his mind. He can have thought what the prose has him think, but not, plausibly, with the wit and lucidity Mars-Jones lends him—that is the work of fiction. The interest of Neilson's trial, in this view, is not the establishment of the guilt or innocence of the accused but the discovery of whether he can "hold on to his idea of himself under cross-examination." He does, but we don't, and the result is to spread some sort of innocence, however qualified or reprehensible, all over the place, to continue the dark but candid world of McEwan's butchers and buriers, and Bainbridge's murderous young girls. We come to invert the inversion of the aphorism about understanding; that is, we put it back on its feet. To understand everything *is* to forgive everything—or it would be if we understood everything, or anywhere near it. As it is, our impulse to forgiveness is just a name for our bafflement. We have lost our villains in the same way as we have lost our feeling for abnormality. There is a principle of tolerance here, of course, but there is also, more urgently, a sense of helplessness, as if we had mislaid the concept of justice somewhere and could not go back for it. "All these cruelties," a character thinks in Swift's *Shuttlecock* (1981), "were no more than a way of making remorse possible."

The Body of Crime

"I find it very difficult," Auden said of detective stories, "to read one that is not set in rural England." Rural England, for Auden and a whole generation of crime writers and crime readers, was an emblem of innocence. The corpse on the carpet stains and complicates this innocence, but the detective clears up the mess: "Innocence is restored," in Auden's words, "and the law retires forever." The object is not justice but the disappearance of the need for justice. We gather in the library, and are content to identify the culprit—as if there were only one kind of guilt, and none of it were ours.

What is missing here is any sense of monstrosity in the solution as well as in the crime, and this is precisely what recent British fiction provides. Even the dreamlike Edwardian village is now a version of what Auden calls the Great Wrong Place, its echoes of old pieties a mockery of the very idea of a settled or certain peace. P. D. James's *Devices and Desires* (1989), which we can take as emblematic of recent developments in detective fiction, is set in darkest East Anglia, and borrows its title from the Anglican prayer book: "We have erred and strayed from thy ways like lost sheep, we have followed the devices and desires of our own hearts." A psychopath called the Whistler is on the loose, killing young (and then not-so-young) women. But is he a psychopath, and is there only one of him? Or her? Suspects include several scientists at a nearby nuclear power station, a retired schoolmistress, a writer of cookery books, a protester against the use of nuclear energy, a secretary who has secretly joined an international terrorist organization, and Adam Dalgliesh, James's poet-detective, who has just inherited an old mill in the area and is awkwardly close to several of these people. The book ends in a brilliant train of misdeductions and evasions, and an explicit contrast with detective fiction of the old school, where "problems could be solved, evil overcome, justice vindicated, and death itself only a mystery which would be solved in the final chapter." This book itself of course finally belongs to this old school, and does solve its central mystery, but it also shows with unusual clarity what the school is up to.

Dalgliesh, reflecting on his detective work, is also, necessarily, reflecting on the sort of fiction he is in:

Perhaps this was part of the attraction of his job, that the process of detection dignified the individual death . . . mirroring in its excessive interest in clues and motives man's perennial fascination with the mystery of his mortality, providing too, a comforting illusion of a moral universe in which innocence could be avenged, right vindicated, order restored. But nothing was restored, certainly not life, and the only justice vindicated was the uncertain justice of men.

"Excessive interest" hints at a reservation about the whole business, as do "comforting illusion" and "nothing was restored." The passage as a whole confirms Auden's diagnosis of the genre, but denies his conclusion about it. This not mere escape. Or, an escape that so thoroughly knows it is an escape becomes a form of realism, and asks to be judged like any other form of activity.

The individual death is important, though, dignified or not. The most urgent argument in the book is that death is not, as the genre so often suggests, "only a mystery." A policeman calls a rotting female corpse a thing, and is severely rebuked by Dalgliesh: "Sergeant, the word is 'body.' Or, if you prefer, there's 'cadaver,' 'corpse,' 'victim,' even 'deceased.' . . . What you are looking at was a woman. She was not a thing when she was alive and she is not a thing now." This is a little preacherly, but the question, I take it, is not about words only. It is about our feelings on the subject of endings, the abrupt crossing from life into death, the sudden absence of human identity. This is no longer the excuse for a story of detection, it is what stalks detection itself, the story behind the stories.

The End of History

A strand of rope, a child on a swing, a hanging body: these images, in Kazuo Ishiguro's *Pale View of Hills* (1982), haunt the mind of a Japanese woman thinking back over her life in Nagasaki after the war. She is in England now; her lively, modern, half-English daughter has left home, and her Japanese daughter, from her first marriage, has recently committed suicide in Manchester. The implicit question in this wonderfully delicate novel is one of connection: what is the link, if there is a link, between the girl's early life in Japan and her early death in England; and more largely, between this time and that, between suicide here and the bomb-blasted landscape there. The narrator remembers the months of her pregnancy, after the Nagasaki bomb, during the Korean War; recalls, indeed almost becomes, a woman she knew, involved with a foreigner, neglecting her child for her lover and her pride. Both women are then figuratively associated with a child-murderer on the loose, as if to be a mother, in that time and that place, is to be a murderer—or even worse, perhaps, to have failed to be a murderer, to have willfully prolonged life in a blighted world. The dominant image of the novel, which we watch through a little girl's eyes, or more precisely through the eyes of a mother watching her daughter watch, is of a woman drowning her child in war-ruined Tokyo, and the most tempting interpretation of the later suicide is as a painful imitation of this act, the delayed completion of an infanticide:

There was a canal . . . and the woman was kneeling there, up to her elbows in water. A young woman, very thin. I knew something was wrong as soon as I saw her. You see . . . she turned round and smiled at Mariko [the speaker's five-year-old daughter]. . . . At first I thought the woman was blind, she had that kind of look, her eyes didn't actually seem to see anything. Well, she brought her arms out of the canal and showed us what she'd been holding under the water. It was a baby. I took hold of Mariko then and we came out of the alley.

Ishiguro himself was born in Nagasaki in 1954, but moved to England in 1960 and has lived there since. He is thus, like Timothy Mo and Salman Rushdie, an English writer of cross-cultural allegiances, rather than a foreign writer who resides in Britain, and his Japan, although impeccably researched and limpidly evoked, is always part metaphor. This state of affairs remains (mildly) masked in Ishiguro's second novel, *An Artist of the Floating World* (1986), which explores the bewildered complicity of a generation of Japanese in the war aims of their prewar ruling class; but becomes very clear in his next book, *The Remains of the Day* (1989), where an English butler, looking back on his life, sees that what he thought of as dignity was a ghastly sacrifice of everything human in himself, a ruin that mistook itself for a monument. His story is paralleled by that of the aristocrat he served, a kindly but stupid man who thought well of Hitler out of sheer muddled naïveté. What interests Ishiguro is not the condemnation or forgiveness of these figures but the size and nature of their error. "Japan" and "England" become forms of historical delusion, moral locations where old virtues turn quietly into implacable vices.

"We're cutting back on history," a headmaster says in Swift's *Waterland* (1983), and later, more violently, "We're cutting back History. . . . History will merge with General Studies." The headmaster doesn't intend any irony, or general commentary on his age, but the reader can hardly miss the point. The present time of the narrative is 1979; between then and the date of the novel's publication falls the shadow of the Falklands War, and of the revival of a tub-thumping patriotism, served by that war perhaps rather than brought on by it. A sentimentalized "history" (Agincourt, Dunkirk, the heart-warming Victorian family) became the home of everything the present was thought to lack, and yet in the novel history is sacrificed for the sake of the economy, cuts made for efficiency. This is not quite what happened in British education, although the cuts were real enough; but it is what happened in British culture at large. Against this tangled trend, this loss of history at a time when "history" is applauded, novelists asserted not that they knew what history was but that they knew what it meant to lose track of it. This is the historical inflection of the story about the uncomprehended crime. "The past is a receding shore-line," Barnes writes in *Flaubert's Parrot*, it is what the mind cannot grasp and cannot do without. But it is also, Ishiguro and Swift suggest, what grasps us, what we cannot evade.

Heraclitus was wrong, Swift's narrator says in *Waterland*. "We are always stepping into the same river." Tom Crick, an about-to-be-sacked history teacher, abandons the French Revolution for stories about his childhood and his ancestors, impelled by the fact that his wife has gone quietly crazy and stolen a baby from outside a supermarket, claiming the child has come to her from God. The children realize that their teacher isn't giving them the history they are supposed to learn, but they also realize that history is everywhere. Crick's narrative (partly told to the children, we assume, and partly imagined by him as being told to them, a long internal monologue) embraces murder, madness, incest and abortion, two World Wars, a history of brewing, an essay on the procreative processes of eels ("natural history"), and many dark and allegorical thoughts about earth and water, floods and reclaimed land ("For consider the equivocal operation of silt," "For what is water, children, . . . but a liquid form of nothing?").

Swift's earlier and later work (*The Sweetshop Owner* [1980], *Out of this World* [1988], *Ever After* [1992]) is full of people who know only cruel and crooked paths to love, but in *Waterland* more than anywhere else, these intricate relations become historically entangled and irrevocable, a cage of consequences. Crick seems at first to want to understand the past, but we soon realize that he chiefly wants to tame it, tire it out. "I don't care what you call it—explaining, evading the facts, making up meanings, taking a larger view, putting things into perspective, dodging the here and now, education, history, fairy-tales—it helps to eliminate fear." This is the function of history for Crick, "History itself, the Grand Narrative, the filler of vacuums, the dispeller of fears of the dark," and the only alternative to this compulsion would be an untenable belief in the ubiquity of accident. "Now why can't everything happen by accident? No history. No guilt, no blame. Just accidents." But as Crick knows and says, the consoling verdict of "Accidental Death" is merely the way history talks when it doesn't know any better. Crick has become not the enemy of the recent British confusion about history and "history" but its intelligent yet helpless embodiment. History, as we learn and he doesn't, *is* guilt and blame, and a chief source rather than a dispeller of fears of the dark.

There are great and brilliantly evoked fears in the world of Julian Barnes's novels: night terrors, blockages of feeling, agonies of self-consciousness. The characters hunt emotions, like the boys in *Metroland* (1980), and then panic at what they find. They hide in ordinariness, like the narrator of *Flaubert's Parrot*, as if a wary banality could protect us from pain. What they fear most is their own judgment, which could always be wrong, and worse still, might be right.

One chapter in *A History of the World in 10 1/2 Chapters* (1989), pictures a permissive heaven that is everything you want, and open to everyone. The mildly hedonistic narrator, fond of eating, shopping, having sex, and meeting famous people, decides he also needs to be judged. "It's what we all want, isn't it? I wanted, oh, some kind of summing up, I wanted my life looked at." His wish is granted, and a "nice old gent" in a nice old building reviews the whole case history and comes up with a considered verdict. He says, "You're OK." And when the narrator seems to expect a little more, the old gent repeats, "No, really, you're OK." This is not the judgment (or the heaven) we can really want, but it may well be the one we deserve, the one most persistently implied in our earthly behavior. Barnes's book suspends us between this horrible laxity and the cruelly selective salvation of the Ark, which occupies another chapter.

When you think of the Flood whose side are you on? Is there a relation between an ark and a raft, say, the corpse-littered planking that appears in Géricault's *Raft of the Medusa*, reproduced as a centerfold in Barnes's book? History tells us that these people were saved, but the painting doesn't, and Barnes's most eloquent pages concern this terrible doubt of art. Is that golden glow a sunrise or a sunset; is the tiny ship on the horizon coming or going? Worse, is it perhaps a sunrise but not for these people? A raft could then be defined: a failed ark. And then why do the survivors in this painting look so healthy? Who are these muscled folks, where are the withered and bedraggled castaways we have a right to expect? Even the corpses look like athletes. Barnes's answer is that Géricault wants to take us "beyond mere pity and indignation" into a realm where even the mightiest of human efforts are not necessarily vain but are always unanswered—or answered only by pitifully inadequate gestures.

There is no formal response to the painting's main surge, just as there is no response to most human feelings. Not merely hope, but any burdensome yearning: ambition, hatred, love (especially love)—how rarely do our emotions meet the object they seem to deserve? How hopelessly we signal; how dark the sky; how big the waves.

A lively, much-loved, unfaithful woman commits suicide, leaving her doctor-husband to mourn in the cramped but loyal way that is all his nature affords. This is the plot of *Mme Bovary* and also of *Flaubert's Parrot*, a witty and graceful work that is part novel, part stealthy literary criticism—just as *A History of the World in 10 1/2 Chapters* is part fiction, part memoir, and part art history. "It was the fault of destiny," Charles Bovary says at the end of his story, unwittingly assuming a sort of grandeur through the very hollowness of the phrase. Barnes's English protagonist says: "I loved her; we were happy; I miss her. She didn't love me; we were unhappy; I miss her. There is a limited choice of prayers on offer; gabble the syllables." Charles Bovary, however, had not read the novel he was in, and Geoffrey Braithwaite has. He is a devotee of Flaubert, a visitor of shrines and statues. He is moved by the sight of the tumbler Flaubert took his last drink from, of the handkerchief with which he last mopped his brow. For the writing of "Un coeur simple," where a parrot merges with the Holy Ghost in the mind of a dazed and dying servant-woman, Flaubert borrowed a stuffed parrot from the local museum. Where is it now? Well, two places in and near Rouen claim to have it, and there are still other dusty candidates. Does it matter, since surely the real parrot is in the text? No, only the textual parrot is in the text, and Braithwaite takes the elusive identity of the historical parrot as a model for many larger questions, including all the questions he cannot directly face concerning his dead wife. "How do we seize the past? . . . Why should it play our game? . . . What knowledge is useful, what knowledge true?"

Was the stuffed parrot (whichever parrot) a symbol of Flaubert's voice, as Braithwaite likes to think, a silenced squawker, a travesty of what a writer does? Parrots, as Flaubert knew, are prone to epilepsy. Braithwaite writes notes on the animals in Flaubert's letters and novels; gives us what he imagines is Louise Colet's version of her stopping-and-starting romance with the novelist; answers what he (wrongly) takes to be "the case against Flaubert"; gives the reader an examination; lampoons many fetishes of contemporary fiction. Barnes hides discreetly behind Braithwaite like a parrot vanishing into a description, giving his book an elusive air that neatly mimes its subject. How delicate or how serious is Barnes's mockery of the good doctor? How tender is the writer's pity for his character's flat and intractable grief? What is sure is that the writing is unfailingly sharp and often very funny. "She was, it seems, a bit fast; though speed, of course, is always exaggerated by those standing still."

The world didn't end at Nagasaki (or in the fens of *Waterland*, or with the Ark, or at Rouen), but it could have, and what Maggie Gee austerely calls "the final violence" is the subject and the resolution of her brilliant novel *The Burning Book* (1983). The work recounts the terminal life and times of the Ship family, a sort of cartoon assembly of dippy, strangled Englishness, the text interspersed with quotations about Hiroshima and armaments. Gee's pathos stems from the fact that even her cartoons feel pain and can die, stranded as many people must be in this particular nightmare, "in a novel too late to be bought." The deaths of the family, and of countless others, are followed by three black pages, an intimation of burning and mourning; but those pages in turn are followed by a chapter "against ending": "Always beginning again, beginning against ending." Against the one ending feared above all, of course, but also against other unacceptable endings, against the very assumption that beginning again is always possible, as if a novel could never be too late.

Midnight's Fictions

"London is full of short stories walking round hand in hand," the narrator says in Martin Amis's *Money* (1984). And not just London. The 1980s witnessed an astonishing rebirth of storytelling in British fiction. The stories might be desolate, or even insane, but there were plenty of them, and they were full of emotional or intellectual energy, untapped for generations while novelists attended to more serious matters. "Oh dear, yes," Forster had said, "the novel tells a story"—a regrettable necessity rather than any sort of challenge. What vanishes in recent British writing is the note of polite regret, to be replaced by a slightly febrile excitement: everyone has a story, always has had, what are we waiting for.

This shift cannot be attributed to a single writer, but if it could that writer would be Salman Rushdie, whose *Midnight's Children* (1980) effected a massive, garrulous liberation in British fiction—the tall tales of *Waterland*, for instance, are scarcely imaginable without it. Rushdie himself declared his debt to Günter Grass ("he opened doors in my mind"), and wrote appreciatively of García Márquez, and has predictably been labeled a magic realist. The debts are real enough, but the label is misleading. Fiction for Rushdie, in *Midnight's Children* as in *Shame* (1983) and *The Satanic Verses* (1988), is a means of interrogating the real rather than celebrating its variety.

The central fable of the early novel, a telepathic generation of 1,001 children born in the first hour of India's independence in 1947, which is also the first hour of the partition of India and Pakistan, is a metaphor for missed possibilities rather than found marvels. They are the India that might have been, the promise that difficult midnight was unable to keep. This is what the narrator calls "the fantastic heart" of his story:

Reality can have a metaphorical content; that does not make it less real. A thousand and one children were born; there were a thousand and one possibilities which had never been present in one place at one time before; and there were a thousand and one dead ends. Midnight's children can be made to represent many things . . .

And again: "Who am I? Who were we? We were are shall be the gods you never had." That, despairing as it may seem, is the optimistic reading, and at other times Rushdie's generally cheery narrator has darker thoughts: "Midnight has many children; the offspring of Independence were not all human. Violence, corruption, poverty, generals, chaos, greed . . . I had to go into exile to learn that the children of midnight were more varied than I—even I—had dreamed."

India itself is imaginary for Rushdie, "a country which would never exist except by the efforts of a phenomenal collective will—except in a dream we all agreed to dream." But then the imaginary is not opposed to the real, it is a large part of it. Agreed dreams are just what countries are, India is exemplary but not exceptional, and Rushdie's later work, addressing the dictatorship in an imaginary nation that much resembles Pakistan, and the crazed redrawings of the world in which fundamentalisms of all kind indulge, continues to mingle fiction and history, or rather to confront those two forms of narrative with each other, revealing the (rather tawdry) novels that pass for historical fact, and the deep historicity of what seem to be wild imaginings.

The terrible fate of *The Satanic Verses*, banned in India and many other countries, burned by Muslims in Bradford, England, announces the even worse fate of its author, sentenced to death by an outraged Iranian government, and at the time of this writing still living in hiding, with round-the-clock police protection. Such a situation confirms Rushdie's own darkest intuitions. In this sprawling and bustling novel, which takes us from Bombay to South London, from Argentina to Everest, a group of monsters, humans half-turned into tigers, demons, snakes, wolves, water buffalo, meet up in a hospital, and offer a simple explanation of their monstrosity. "They describe us," the monsters say. They: the others, the white, the normal, the officers of a homogenized culture. We might add: the tyrants, the bigots, all who care more for their own mythologies than for the discernible reality of others. "That's all. They have the power of description, and we succumb to the pictures they construct." We succumb. There is passivity here and Rushdie is implicitly arguing against it, but there is also a precise evocation of how description works when it becomes effective currency, or the only currency; how difficult it is to escape even the most fantastic and unlikely identity once it is firmly ascribed to you. And once someone has a stake in the ascription.

Rushdie's fiction tells a story, but it also tells the story's story; the narrator narrates his narrating. It could not be otherwise in a world so saturated with stories, and yet Martin Amis manages to go Rushdie one better. His *Money* is subtitled "A Suicide Note," and the idea, it seems, is that our narrator, the boisterous, violent, drunken, unlovable John Self, will be dead by the time we get to the end of the text. "You can never tell, though, with suicide notes, can you?" Amis writes in a preface, and sure enough John Self seems to survive, a beneficiary of life's kindness to bastards. But then within his rambling, pushy, often very funny tale, a tribute to Amis's ability to find an English that is not mid-Atlantic but transatlantic, an amazing mixture of American slang and British snot, there is this writer, a fellow called . . . Martin Amis. Does he survive along with Self? What would Self have made of Flaubert's parrot?

Money is probably the strongest of all Amis's very clever novels, because the sheer nastiness of the central character fuels a seemingly inexhaustible wit. John Self on the tennis court, John Self trying (in vain) to rape his girlfriend, John Self exploring pornography, John Self throwing up in various choice locations—these are all set pieces that argue a kind of dark love for the horrors of the contemporary world, as if its very tackiness made it a candidate for affection. And the prose has fine, fulsome metaphors: "I am still a high-risk zone. I am still inner city."

My head is a city, and various pains have now taken up residence in various parts of my face. A gum-and-bone ache has launched a cooperative on my upper west side. Across the park, neuralgia has rented a duplex in my fashionable east seventies. Downtown, my chin throbs with lofts of jaw-loss. As for my brain, my hundreds, it's Harlem up there, expanding in the summer fires.

There are cities and cities, though. Glasgow is described in Alasdair Gray's *Lanark* (1981) as "the sort of industrial city where most people live nowadays but nobody imagines living." It would be hard to imagine. The gloom and drabness of Gray's Glasgow is paralleled only by that of the same city seen by his grimly amused compatriot James Kelman. Both Glasgows make Amis's sleazy London and New York seem perfectly pastoral places by comparison. Yet, gloomy as the scene is, it provokes some of the most stylish and imaginative writing to have appeared in Britain recently. Gray and Kelman, like Rushdie and Amis, are writers for whom literature exists; they don't hide their reading as a previous generation was wont to do. Indeed they flaunt their allusions with a carelessness that is the reverse of the pretention British writers have always so feared. "To be alone and without gods is death says Hölderlin," we read in Kelman's *Disaffection* (1989), "but Hölderlin was wrong and is a poor bastard. . . . Fuck Hölderlin he's deid and buried." *Lanark* has a long mock note of its own "plagiarisms," running from Anon and Borges to Xenophon and Zoroaster. *Hamlet* is an influence, we learn, because it is a play "in which heavy-handed paternalism forces a weak-minded youth into dread of existence, hallucinations and crime." The story of *Lanark*, no less.

Apart from their Glasgow and their wit and their literary resources Gray and Kelman are quite different; Gray an experimentalist, juggling time and tones, starting his book at a late stage of his story, placing his prologue in the middle, Kelman a sort of dour, demotic Kafka, dryly observing the follies of terminally bewildered people. Patrick Doyle, in *A Disaffection*, is a Latin teacher in a bleak school, worrying a little about his age, and Kelman's language catches Patrick's complicated awareness of his own comic status, the self-mockery amid the gloom: "He did not wish to dwell continually on the passing years. Here he was turning thirty years of age. Thirty years of age is regarded as a landmark, a watershed, a stage of departure. At that age Jesus Christ entered the teaching profession and Joseph K worked out his guilt."

Fiction in these novels is not an alternative to history, it is a reading of history's failures, a mode of irony. From Rushdie's teeming India through Amis's hustling England and America to Gray and Kelman's northern dampnesses, the imagination asks us to think about what is missing from these worlds, what strange losses have occurred of what ought to be human. In a lighter though not less brilliant vein the early novels of Peter Ackroyd (and indeed Ackroyd's biographies of Eliot and

Dickens) explore a similar question through travels to the past, whether in the impeccable Wildean pastiche of *The Last Testament of Oscar Wilde* (1983), the historical crime-world of *Hawksmoor* (1985), or the intricate literary fakeries of *Chatterton* (1987). It's not that the past is another country, as L. P. Hartley memorably said in *The Go-Between*. The past is *our* country, scarcely disguised; the angled mirror of our diffuse and distressed present.

The Sexual Circus

Angela Carter is mistress of a complicated and quirky register of tones and voices—as if a disrespect for stylistic decorum was itself a style and a liberation. Her fiction and her prose are full of re-angled fables and fairy tales, and more broadly, all her work resists the subservience of fiction to gloomy fact. Her most substantial and rewarding novel, *Nights at the Circus* (1984), although set in the last months of the nineteenth century, refuses all allegiance to what Carter mockingly calls "authentic history." It charts another, livelier but no less human, narrative, a story of hubris, imagination, and desire. Yet what is most disconcerting about the book, perhaps, is not its lovingly assembled collection of freaks or its capacious plot, always ready to welcome a stray tale to its ample bosom, but its very odd diction. "Lor' love you, sir," it opens in stage cockney, introducing us to Fevvers, the famous winged lady trapeze artist, toast of Europe, friend of Toulouse-Lautrec, a woman who has "deformed the dreams" of an entire generation in Vienna. She is a sort of Zuleika Dobson of the music halls, a large, coarse, kindly person, constantly downing eel pies and bacon sandwiches and champagne, but she does also fly.

What made her remarkable as an *aerialiste* . . . was the speed—or rather the lack of it—with which she performed even the climactic triple somersault. . . . The music went much faster than she did; she dawdled. Indeed, she did defy the laws of projectiles, because a projectile cannot *mooch* along its trajectory.

Are her wings real or fake, fact or fiction? Fevvers laughs at the very idea of the question. She was brought up in an East End brothel run by a one-eyed Madame whimsically known as Nelson; puts in a spell at the dreaded Madame Schreck's museum of women monsters; escapes from the clutches of a wealthy necromancer who is intent on having her as a human sacrifice; signs up with a circus touring Russia, where she runs into bandits, shamans, revolutionaries. "Nobility of spirit hand in hand with absence of analysis," she thinks, "that's what's always buggered up the working class." She doesn't always speak like an extra from *My Fair Lady*. "Like any young girl," she says early in her tale, "I was much possessed with the marvellous blooming of my until then reticent and undemanding flesh." And later: "The clock was, you might say, the sign, or signifier of Ma Nelson's little private realm." You might say: we are clearly in a zone of parody here, but parody of what? "This is some kind of heretical possibly Manichean version of neo-Platonic Rosicrucianism, thinks I to myself." The parody, I suggest, attacks all dialects, high or low, that think they are better than others; and furthermore, attacks the very idea of a single narrative voice, even when it comes from one person. More subtly, the parody subverts notions of taste and writerly control.

The books ends in glee, that of Fevvers and everyone else in her world: "The spiralling tornado of Fevvers' laughter began to twist and shudder across the entire globe, as if in a spontaneous response to the giant comedy that endlessly unfolded beneath it, until everything that lived and breathed, everywhere, was laughing." Fevvers has understood the joke of life, and also the freedom that lives in jokes, including the freedom from taking her own symbolism too seriously. She is the New Woman, as Ma Nelson says, "the pure child of the century that just now is waiting in the wings, the New Age in which no woman will be bound down to the ground." It's hard to be sure whether "waiting in the wings" is a gag about flight or just one metaphor stepping on the toes of another. The conflation of being bound and bowing down is similarly ambiguous. But then this uncertainty is the secret of Carter's later prose, and this is how Fevvers talks, a sort of Mrs. Malaprop who has read Kate Millett: "And once the old world has turned on its axle so that the new dawn can dawn, then, ah, then! all the women will have wings, the same as I." Fevvers is a revision, an inversion of the myth of Leda and the Swan, prominently mentioned in the text. The knockabout prose, the intellectual burlesque, help us to see that urgent causes can work through cliché and come out the other side.

And the same causes can work around clichés as well as through them. What Carter does in this novel with tigers, to take one instance among many, says a great deal about what she thinks is possible and desirable for women and men. The tigers in the circus wonder, every time they go into their act, why they are so pleased to do as they are told: "For just one unprotected minute, they pondered the mystery of their obedience and were astonished by it." In a later, haunting image, tigers disappear into mirrors when the circus train crashes: broken tigers into broken glass. "On one fragment of mirror, a paw with the claws out; on another, a snarl. When I picked up a section of flank, the glass burned my fingers." Later still, a group of tigers, entranced by music, lie on the roof of a house in the middle of the Siberian nowhere, "stretched across the tiles like abandoned greatcoats." It would be easy to maul these scenes with interpretation; hard to miss their magical air of violence not tamed but transposed, their hint of Blakean innocence, and their less peaceful suggestion that even mirrored creatures can snarl and burn.

The nervous, passionate young lesbians of Jeanette Winterson's fiction seem to take us a long way from the motherly, heterosexual Fevvers, and of course they do. But Winterson's writing is not all that far from Carter's, or indeed from that of many of her British contemporaries. There is a continuing sharpness and intelligence in the voice, an appetite for swift, throwaway jokes, even as the ground of the story keeps changing. "A complicated narrative structure disguised as a simple one," Winterson says of her first novel, *Oranges Are Not the Only Fruit* (1985); "it employs a very large vocabulary and a beguilingly straight-forward syntax." A good example of the effect would be the following sentence, describing the state of affairs in a rigidly religious home after young Jeanette ("Is Oranges an autobiographical novel? No not at all and yes of course") has been found in bed with a girl: "The days lingered on in a kind of numbness, me in ecclesiastical quarantine, them in a state of fear and anticipation." The book has chapters named after books of the Old Testament, and opens with epigraphs from Mrs. Beeton (about the scum that forms on marmalade if you don't skim the top) and Nell Gwynn (who said, apparently, "Oranges are not the only fruit"). A central story is told by Jeanette's mother ("She had never heard of mixed feelings. There were friends and there were enemies"), who when young thought she was in love because she experienced a sensation she had never known before: "a fizzing and a buzzing and a certain giddiness." It turned out to be caused by a stomach ulcer, and the mother's moral is plain: "So just you take care, what you think is the heart might well be another organ."

It might be several other organs, and if there is an appealing simplification of life in the thought that oranges *are* the only fruit (another dictum of Jeanette's mother's), there is a genuine liberation in the knowledge that they are not. It is the liberation Jeanette finds as she fights her way free of religion and home, into an understanding of her past and her present and her sexuality; into the knowledge, as she briskly puts it, that "not all dark places need light." "I have to remember that," she adds; the missionary impulse dies hard.

When we say the world is small we mean it isn't much of a world; more of a village or a club, lacking the profusion and unpredictability that worlds are supposed to have. The world Alan Hollinghurst evokes in *The Swimming Pool Library* (1988) is not small. Almost anything can happen in it;, it has many inhabitants and plenty of new recruits. But it is cruelly, brilliantly specialized, haunted by repetitions, by a relentless sense of what its narrator might call déjà eu. William Beckwith is gay in both senses, queer and pleasure-seeking, and his promiscuity is nothing short of heroic. At one point he remembers his "sex-obsessed" younger days, but he thinks of it all the time now. "I was determined to have him," he says of a lad in a Stepney churchyard; "I must have him," of an Arab boy in Hyde Park. He doesn't have either, as it turns out, but these are rare misses. Beckwith is terribly conscious of his mostly overwhelming appeal, and a friend suggests his last words are likely to be "How do I look?" Beckwith cruises clubs, hotels, Soho cinemas, parks, swimming pools; falls in love with teenagers, gets roughed up, toys with the idea of writing the biography of a lord whose life he happens to have saved. The year of the narrative is 1983, and Beckwith remembers it as "the last summer of its kind there was ever to be." "I was riding high on sex and self-esteem," he continues, "it was my time, my *belle epoque*—but all the while with a faint flicker of calamity, like flames around a photograph, something seen out of the corner of the eye."

This is to say that the novel is a memorial to the randy, reckless world AIDS has depopulated. Beckwith recalls this world fondly, but also with an astringent and undeceived precision. Hollinghurst's gamble, which comes off magnificently, is to get us to feel the charm of this disreputable and self-absorbed young man; to like him without approving of him. It's hard not to appreciate a person who can so breezily bend Yeats to his irreverent purpose and speak of "the young up one another's arse," an entirely new view of why one might want or not want to leave for Byzantium. It is true too that a more respectable homosexual culture is evoked through the names of Forster and Britten, and with the beautifully described appearance of the aged Peter Pears at a performance of *Billy Budd*.

But then we need to remember that AIDS is *not* mentioned in the book, because AIDS had not arrived in the consciousness of the summer it recounts. The disease casts a horrific shadow, but only a shadow, and there are dooms that *have* arrived in the novel's pages and are its commanding subjects. The beautiful Beckwith knows he is not like the old blokes in the loo in the park, but also knows he may not always be so different: "I felt a faint revulsion—not disapproval, but a fear of one day being like that." Ronald Firbank becomes a mannered patron saint of the book, and is glimpsed in a film taken shortly before his death, "a bona fide queen," coughing, laughing, enjoying an "impromptu kind of triumph." The triumph is real but also pathetic, because it is pure style and parody, bereft of all the hectic physical attractions Beckwith lives by and cannot think of living without. Can this be all that liberation means? Looking for a boyfriend who has disappeared, Beckwith is beaten up by a group of skinheads, and understands (none too soon, we may feel) the ridiculous physical (and other) risks he has long been taking. "It was actually happening. It was actually happening to me." And he grasps for the first time the "vulnerability of the old, unfortified by good luck or inexperience." It's not that Beckwith suddenly turns virtuous, or that the book becomes uplifting; only that Beckwith glimpses the precariousness of his glory, and of glories like his. When the old lord sees Beckwith's face with its broken nose, he says, "Well, at least I saw it before they spoilt it"—as if the face were a house or a landscape or a painting.

For a gay writer seeking to treat the subject of AIDS, Adam Mars-Jones writes in his introduction to *Monopolies of Loss* (1992), there is "a particular political variant of denial."

At a time when media coverage tends to push the issues of AIDS and homosexuality closer and closer together, as if epidemic and orientation were synonymous, how can you justify writing fiction that brings this spurious couple together all over again? Surely the truly responsible thing to do now would be to write sexy nostalgic fiction set in the period before the epidemic, safeguarding if only in fantasy the endangered gains of gay liberation?

Mars-Jones answers himself, "Well no." I don't think he means that the truly irresponsible thing is to write novels like *The Swimming Pool Library*, only that the contemporary life of AIDS is also an important (and so far largely taboo) subject for fiction. "The novel seems the obvious form for so weighty an issue." "Weighty" is a fraught and bittersweet joke, given the physical manifestations of AIDS, and Mars-Jones has so far managed only short stories on this topic. In 1987, he and Edmund White published a volume called *The Darker Proof*, feeling it was possible that "the big issue and the little form had a paradoxical affinity." *Monopolies of Loss* includes Mars-Jones stories from that book and some new ones. I mention them here both for their scrupulous evocation of important questions and because I think the future of the British novel may come to depend more and more on its dialogue with shorter fiction.

What marks this book is its compassion and its range, its sense that AIDS, however fearsome, is not alone among human calamities. AIDS isolates a person, we learn in a story called "Slim," "only . . . from the young, the well, the real." Only. That's a lot of people to be isolated from, but it's not everyone. "All the time my Gran was ill we never once said *cancer*, but now cancer is a soft word I am hiding behind. . . . Cancer. What a relief. Cancer. Oh, that's all right." Of course it isn't all right. The new fear falsifies the old; a sign of how terrible the new fear is. In a later story a man who does not have AIDS commits suicide, and the homosexual community finds it hard to forgive or understand him. "It seemed to us that he'd just thrown away a body that any of our sick friends . . . would have jumped at. . . . We were angry. Didn't Victor know there was a war on?" He didn't; or if he did, his private, old-fashioned misery mattered to him more than the war, more than his own continued existence. "He had no loyalty to life. He felt no patriotism to the mortal country." The victims of AIDS are patriots by comparison; not just because they are losing life but because they know what the loss of life actually means. When Mars-Jones writes of succeeding infections "holding court" among a young man's "ruined defences," there is an eerie majesty in the metaphor that celebrates not the drama of the disease, but the tragic grandeur of the fading mortal country.

Michael Wood

Selected Bibliography

Anderson, Linda, ed. *Plotting Change*. London: Arnold, 1990.
Carter, Angela. *Nothing Sacred*. London: Virago, 1982.

Crawford, R., and T. Nairn, eds. *The Arts of Alasdair Gray*. Edinburgh: Edinburgh University Press, 1991.

Kirkpatrick, D. L., ed. *Contemporary Novelists*. 4th ed. London and Chicago: St. James Press, 1986.

Lee, Alison. *Realism and Power*. London: Routledge, 1990.

Massie, Alan. *The Novel Today*. London and New York: Longman, 1990.

McHale, Brian. *Postmodernist Fiction*. London: Methuen, 1987.

Rushdie, Salman. *Imaginary Homelands*. London: Penguin, 1990.

Biographies of British Novelists

Peter Ackroyd (1949–)
Novelist and critic, Ackroyd has been successful at combining these roles in his literary output. Along with his biographies of T. S. Eliot and Ezra Pound, he has made his reputation with novels like *The Great Fire of London* (1982), *The Last Days of Oscar Wilde* (1983), *Hawksmoor* (1985), and *Chatterton* (1987).

Kingsley Amis (1922–)
Amis was educated at St. John's College, Oxford, and went on to become a lecturer at University College, Swansea, in Wales, and then at Cambridge from 1949 to 1963. He began his career as a poet, publishing two volumes of verse, *Bright November* (1947) and *A Frame of Mind* (1953), but he achieved overnight fame with the success of *Lucky Jim* (1954), a satirical novel about a disaffected and subversive instructor at a provincial university. Primarily a comic moralist and satiric social observer of a modern England he finds repellent, Amis has been a prolific novelist whose work has encompassed a number of subgenres such as science fiction, murder mysteries, and fantasy. Among his novels are *That Uncertain Feeling* (1955), *I Like It Here* (1958), *Take a Girl Like You* (1960), *One Fat Englishman* (1963), *The Anti-Death League* (1966), *The Green Man* (1969), *The Alteration* (1976), and *The Old Devils*, which won the Booker Prize in 1986. Amis was knighted in 1990.

Penelope Aubin (1685–1731)
The daughter of a French émigré, Aubin was born in England. After a series of odes written in tribute to Queen Anne in 1707, she turned her attention to novels. In 1721 she began a period in which she turned out seven successful

novels in eight years, including *The Strange Adventures of the Count de Vinevil and His Family* (1721), *The Life of Madam de Beaumount, a French Lady* (1721), and *Count Albertus* (1728).

Jane Austen (1775–1817)
The sixth of seven children, Austen was encouraged to read and write by her father, the Reverend George Austen. Her letters tell us little about her intimate relationships, though she did have several suitors (none of whom she ever married). Instead, she spent her life among her close family, writing her novels at Chawton, Hampshire, in the family parlor. When she was just fourteen she wrote *Love and Friendship*, followed by *A History of England* at fifteen. A year later saw *A Collection of Letters* and, not long after, *Lesley Castle*. Her major novels were published, though not written, in the following order: *Sense and Sensibility* (1811), *Pride and Prejudice* (1813), *Mansfield Park* (1814), *Emma* (1816), and *Northanger Abbey* and *Persuasion* (posthumously, 1818). Austen advanced the development of the novel, combining social critique with an elegant, economical style.

Robert Bage (1720–1801)
Bage was a skilled philosopher, political activist, and novelist who managed to integrate his Quakerism with a commitment to Rousseauist political theory. His primitivist novels were praised by Scott. They are *Mount Henneth* (1781), *Barham Downs* (1784), *The Fair Syrian* (1787), *James Wallace* (1788), *Man as He Is* (1792), and his most accomplished work, *Hermsprong, or Man as He Is Not* (1796).

Jane Barker (1652–1727)
Born in Northamptonshire, Barker is notable for her depiction of the lives of educated, unmarried women in seventeenth-century England and for her persistent exploration of the separation of the public and private lives of women. After a period of exile in France, she returned to England in 1713 and began publishing her novels. Many of her poems and novels are essentially autobiographical, written in the persona of "Galesia." Her novels include *Exilius, or The Banish'd Roman* (1715), *Love Intrigues* (1713), *A Patch-Work Screen* (1723), and *The Lining of the Patch-Work Screen* (1726).

Samuel Beckett (1906–1989)
Raised as a Protestant in Dublin, Beckett was educated at Trinity College where he studied English, French, and Italian. He went to Paris to be an English language instructor at the École Normale Supérieure and soon after met James Joyce, who became his lifelong friend. His first published piece of fiction was a story, "Assumption" (1929). After returning to Ireland as a lecturer

at Trinity College, he began a five-year sojourn in Europe. Finally settling in Paris, Beckett published his volume of stories *More Pricks than Kicks* (1934), as well as two novels of note, *Murphy* (1938) and *Watt* (1953). He published a trilogy in French that is distinguished by its existential lyricism: *Molloy* (1951), *Malone meurt* (1951; Beckett's English translation, 1958), and *L'Innommable* (1953; English, 1960). His most famous work remains his play *Waiting for Godot* (1952), a masterpiece of the theater of the absurd. Beckett received the Nobel Prize in 1969.

William Beckford (1759–1844)
An immensely wealthy man who was the son of a Lord Mayor of London, Beckford was also a member of Parliament and an art collector of some renown. His major literary achievement was the Oriental novel *Vathek*, although his travel pieces *Dreams, Waking Thoughts, and Incidents* (1783) and *Recollections of an Excursion to the Monastries of Alcobaca and Batalha* (1835) are also well regarded.

Aphra Behn (1640–1689)
In 1663, Aphra Behn and her family traveled to the British colony of Surinam. She was briefly married to a merchant, after which she took as her lover John Hoyle, the son of the regicide Thomas Hoyle. In 1666, during the Dutch war, she became a spy in the service of Charles II in Antwerp and remained throughout her life a partisan of the Stuarts. Behn's literary career began in 1670 with a series of plays, of which the most popular was *The Rover* (in two parts, 1677–1681). In *The Lucky Chance* (1686) she satirizes marriage. She is best known, however, for *Oroonoko, or The History of the Royal Slave*, in which she hearkens back to her trip to Surinam. In its excoriation of the African slave trade and of Christian hypocrisy, it qualifies as one of the first English philosophical novels.

(Enoch) Arnold Bennett (1867–1931)
Upon arriving in London at the age of twenty-one, Bennett embarked on a career in writing. After some minor publishing successes, he became assistant editor and then editor of the magazine *Woman* in 1893. He spent ten years in Paris from 1902 to 1912, then returned to England for good. Bennett's reputation is owed mainly to his novels about the region of his childhood known fictively as the Five Towns, *Anna of the Five Towns* (1902) and *The Old Wives' Tale* (1908). He followed these successes with the Clayhanger series: *Clayhanger* (1910), *Hilda Lessways* (1911), *These Twain* (1916), and *The Roll Call* (1918). His other novels include: *The Grand Babylon Hotel* (1902), *The Card* (1911), *Mr. Prohack* (1922), and *Riceyman Steps* (1923).

Elizabeth Bowen (1899–1973)

Bowen was born in Dublin and spent most of her life on her family's estate in County Cork. She spent ten years in London with her husband, an experience that contributed to her facility with descriptions of urban and rural settings. Her best-known novels include *The Hotel* (1927), *The Last September* (1929), *The House in Paris* (1935), *The Death of the Heart* (1938), and *The Heat of the Day* (1949).

Malcolm Bradbury (1932–)

Bradbury, educated at Leicester, London, and Manchester, is a professor of literature and American studies. He has combined important critical work with a career as a satirical novelist. His best-known novels are *Eating People Is Wrong* (1959), *Stepping Westward* (1965), *The History of Man* (1975), and *Rates of Exchange* (1983).

Mary Elizabeth Braddon (1837–1915)

Braddon was educated privately and became an actress early in life. She was the mistress and eventually the wife of the publisher John Maxwell, with whom she had six children. Her most famous work, *Lady Audley's Secret* (1862), brought her great financial success and a reputation for glamorous and violent fiction. She went on to publish prolifically, including the novels *Aurora Floyd* (1863), *The Doctor's Wife* (1864), *Henry Dunbar* (1864), and *Ishmael* (1884).

Anne Brontë (1820–1849)

Heavily influenced by her Wesleyan Aunt Branwell, Anne Brontë remained deeply religious throughout her life. She was governess to the Ingham family at Blake Hall in 1839, and then to the Robinsons in York from 1841 to 1845. These experiences provided the material for her novel *Agnes Grey* (1847). Her second novel was *The Tenant of Wildfell Hall* (1848).

Charlotte Brontë (1816–1855)

Left to the care of her aunt at the age of five, Charlotte, like her sisters, had an imaginative and inquisitive childhood. Charlotte spent her fifteenth year at Miss Wooler's school at Roe Head, to which she returned as a teacher between 1835 and 1838. After two stints as a governess, in 1842 she went to Brussels with Emily to study languages. Her first publication was a collection of her own poetry as well as that of her sisters, entitled *Poems, by Currer, Ellis and Acton Bell* (1846). Charlotte's first novel, *The Professor*, was not published, but her next, *Jane Eyre* (1847), was well received. Another novel, *Shirley*, appeared in 1849. After the death of her aunt and two sisters, she formed a friendship with Elizabeth Gaskell, who later became her biographer. Brontë's other important works are *Villette* (1853) and the fragment "Emma" (1860).

Emily Brontë (1818–1848)
For a short time Emily Brontë was schooled at Cowan Bridge with her sister Charlotte, but most of her education was carried out at home. Emily was a governess at Law Hill, but only briefly. Afterward she went to Brussels with Charlotte to study languages. Most of her remaining years were spent at Haworth. In 1846, Emily's poems were published as a joint publication between her, Anne, and Charlotte, under the title, *Poems, by Currer, Ellis and Acton Bell*. Her best-known work, *Wuthering Heights*, was published in 1847.

Frances Brooke (1724–1789)
Brooke spent most of her life in London, though she spent a significant part of her early life in Quebec with her husband. Her popular and important *History of Lady Julia Mandeville* (1763) followed a period that saw her produce *The Old Maid* (1755–1756), *Letters from Juliet Lady Catesby* (1760), and various translations of Riccoboni. Her later works include the novels *The History of Emily Montague* (1769), *The Excursion* (1777), a tragedy, the *Siege of Sinope* (1781), and the musical play *Rosina* (1783).

Anita Brookner (1938–)
Born in London to German parents, Brookner was educated at King's College, University of London, and in Paris. She is currently a Fellow of New Hall, Cambridge, where she is a well-respected art historian specializing in eighteenth- and nineteenth-century French art. She is the author of six novels: *The Debut* (1981), *Providence* (1982), *Look at Me* (1983), *Hotel du Lac* (1984), *Family and Friends* (1985), and *A Misalliance* (1986).

Anthony Burgess (1917–)
Born and educated in Manchester, Burgess spent six years as an education officer in Malaya and Borneo with the colonial service. From this experience came the *Malayan Trilogy* (1972), consisting of the novels, *Time for a Tiger* (1956), *The Enemy in the Blanket* (1958), and *Beds in the East* (1959). His most famous work, *A Clockwork Orange* (1962), a harrowing story of fascism and youth culture, was made into the cult film classic by Stanley Kubrick in 1971. Other notable novels include *Inside Mr. Enderby* (1963), *Enderby Outside* (1968), *The Clockwork Testament* (1974), and *Earthly Powers* (1980).

Frances (Fanny) Burney, Mme d'Arblay (1752–1840)
Having grown up among the elite of London's literary society, Burney soon became an important figure in her own right. The publication of her first novel, *Evelina* (1778), brought her wide acclaim, and it was followed by *Cecilia* (1782). Soon after marrying the French refugee General d'Arblay, she published *Camilla* (1796). After Napoleon interned the couple, they remained in

France from 1802 to 1812. Her other works include *The Wanderer* (1814), the edited memoirs of her father (1832), an *Early Diary 1768–78*, and a later edition, *Diary and Letters . . . 1778–1840* (1842–1846).

A. S. Byatt (1936–)

Byatt was born in Sheffield and attended Newnham College, Cambridge. From *Shadow of a Sun* (1964) through *The Game* (1967), *The Virgin in the Garden* (1978), and *Possession* (1991), her novels are elaborate explorations of the intersection of art, history, and relationships.

Lewis Carroll (Charles Lutwidge Dodgson) (1832–1898)

Carroll came from an unusually literary and creative family that was fond of producing magazines filled with word games and puzzles. After graduating from Christ Church, Oxford, he became a lecturer there in mathematics in 1855. He is best known for his children's book *Alice's Adventures in Wonderland* (1865) and its sequel, *Through the Looking-Glass and What Alice Found There* (1871). His other works include *Phantasmagoria and Other Poems* (1869), *The Hunting of the Snark* (1876), and *Sylvie and Bruno* (1889; vol. 2, 1893).

Angela Carter (1940–1992)

Born in Sussex and educated at the University of Bristol, Carter spent much of her life in academia as a writer-in-residence. Her novels, particularly *Heroes and Villains* (1969) and *Nights at the Circus* (1984), are often cited as examples of magic realism in English.

Joyce Cary (1888–1957)

Born in Londonderry and educated at Clifton College, Oxford, Cary went on to study art in Edinburgh and Paris. After serving in the Balkan War, he fought with the Nigerian regiment in the Cameroons campaign. When he returned to England in 1920 he began his career as a writer. His most acclaimed works are his novelistic trilogies: *Herself Surprised* (1941), *To Be a Pilgrim* (1942), and *The Horse's Mouth* (1944); and *Prisoner of Grace* (1952), *Except the Lord* (1953), and *Not Honour More* (1955).

(William) Wilkie Collins (1824–1889)

Collins was the son of a landscape painter and was educated at several London private schools. His major formative experience came during a two-year tour of Italy taken with his family from 1836 to 1838. His first book was a biography of his father; it was followed by numerous pieces written for Dickens's periodicals as well as other journals. His first novel, *Antonina* (1850), is about the fall of Rome. Collins made his lasting reputation, however, within the genre of mystery and suspense novels. He is regarded as a pioneer of the form. *Basil* (1852) was his first such "novel of sensation," followed by *The Woman in White* (1860), *No Name* (1862), *Armadale* (1866), and *The Moonstone* (1868).

Joseph Conrad (Teodor Josef Konrad Korzeniowski) (1857–1924)

Born in the Ukraine of Polish parents, Conrad grew up in Poland and in Russia. He first went to sea in 1874 on a French ship and eventually became a Master in the English Merchant Marine service as well as a naturalized British subject. After twenty years at sea, he determined to become a writer in England. His first novel was *Almayer's Folly* (1895), which was followed by *An Outcast of the Islands* (1896), *The Nigger of the Narcissus* (1897), *Lord Jim* (1900), *Typhoon* (1902), *Heart of Darkness* (1902), *Nostromo* (1904), *The Secret Agent* (1907), *Under Western Eyes* (1911), *Chance* (1913), and *Victory* (1915). One of the greatest prose stylists in his adopted language, Conrad is a master of atmosphere and symbolism whose novels depict the cultural collisions peculiar to late-nineteenth-century European imperialism and the loneliness and anxiety of modern Western consciousness.

Daniel Defoe (1660–1731)

The London-born son of a butcher, Defoe spent his early life as a traveling hosiery merchant and as the owner of a brick and tile factory. His first book-length work, *An Essay on Projects* (1697), reveals an energetic and original mind, an inquiring, visionary intelligence that soon turned to political writing such as the enormously popular poem *The True-Born Englishman* (1701), and the satirical pamphlet *The Shortest Way with the Dissenters* (1702), for which he was briefly imprisoned and made to stand in the pillory. Financial difficulties led to several bankruptcies, and Defoe became a prolific professional author and secret political operative for successive Tory and Whig governments. From 1704 to 1713, he single-handedly produced *The Review*, a thrice-weekly political periodical, along with innumerable pamphlets and book-length works on politics, history, morality, and commerce. He is best known for the series of narratives he produced after the spectacular success of *Robinson Crusoe* (1719): among them *Moll Flanders* (1722), *A Journal of the Plague Year* (1722), and *Roxana* (1724).

Charles Dickens (1812–1870)

The son of a feckless government clerk, Dickens was born in Portsmouth but came when he was ten to live in London with his family. When his father was imprisoned for debt two years later, Dickens was forced to work in a blacking (shoe polish) warehouse. He later worked as an office boy and then a secretary, eventually finding work as a reporter covering debates in Parliament for the

Morning Chronicle and contributing to a variety of journals and magazines. Some of these were collected into his first published volume, *Sketches by Boz* (1836–1837), which was accompanied by the serial publication of the phenomenally successful *Pickwick Papers* (1836–1837). Other serialized works followed quickly: *Oliver Twist* (1837–1838), *Nicholas Nickleby* (1838–1839), *The Old Curiosity Shop* (1840), and *Barnaby Rudge* (1841). An 1842 trip to America produced *American Notes* (1842) and influenced the composition of *Martin Chuzzlewit* (1843–1844). His best-known works from later years include "A Christmas Carol" (1843), *David Copperfield* (1849–1850), *Bleak House* (1852–1853), *Hard Times* (1854), *Little Dorrit* (1855–1857), *A Tale of Two Cities* (1859), *Great Expectations* (1860–1861), *Our Mutual Friend* (1864–1865), and *Edwin Drood* (1870), left unfinished by his sudden death that year. Indefatigable and prolific, perhaps the most influential and best-known writer of his day, Dickens also produced voluminous journalism and edited several periodicals, in addition to reading from his works in public to great acclaim.

Benjamin Disraeli (1804–1881)
Prime Minister of England in 1868 and from 1874 to 1880, Disraeli was the son of a prominent literary man, Isaac Disraeli, and was educated at home, where he read widely in his father's library. A precocious author who published his first novel, *Vivian Grey* (1826–1827), when he was just twenty-two, Disraeli studied law briefly at Lincoln's Inn, published more novels and lived the life of a man-about-town in London. But he found his real career when he entered Parliament in 1837. His best-known work is the trilogy of political novels that Disraeli viewed as his most effective writing: *Coningsby* (1844), *Sybil* (1845), and *Tancred* (1847). Politics absorbed much of his time, and he did not publish another novel until 1872, *Lothair*.

Arthur Conan Doyle (1859–1930)
A doctor who was educated at Edinburgh, Doyle is best known for his archetypal eccentric detective, Sherlock Holmes. Doyle's first published piece was *A Study in Scarlet* (1887), and his first published collection was *The Adventures of Sherlock Holmes* (1892). Two other Holmes collections followed: *The Memoirs of Sherlock Holmes* (1894) and *The Hound of the Baskervilles* (1902). Besides the Holmes series, Doyle was the author of a number of other romances: *Micah Clarke* (1889), *The White Company* (1891), *The Exploits of Brigadier Gerard* (1896), *Rodney Stone* (1896), and *The Lost World* (1912).

Margaret Drabble (1939–)
Born in Sheffield, Drabble attended Cambridge and then went on to spend a year with the Royal Shakespeare Acting Company. Her first novel, *A Summer*

Bird-Cage, was published in 1963. Since then she has published prolifically, including novels, screen and television writing, and an award-winning biography of Arnold Bennett. *The Realms of Gold* (1975) and *The Ice Age* (1977) are regarded by most critics as her best novels.

Maria Edgeworth (1768–1849)

Edgeworth was schooled for a time in England, though the rest of her life was spent in Ireland. After first publishing the feminist treatise *Letters to Literary Ladies* in 1795, she went on to be a prolific writer of some note. She anticipated the historical novels of Scott with her *Castle Rackrent* (1800). Other novels depicting Irish life include *The Absentee* (1812) and *Ormond* (1817).

George Eliot (Mary Ann, later Marian, Evans) (1819–1880)

After an education that encouraged her to convert to Evangelicalism and then to a freethinking religious creed, Eliot's first publication was an anonymous translation of Strauss's *Life of Jesus* (1846). She became a contributor to the *Westminster Review* and moved to London in 1851. Eliot's growing fascination with the philosophy of Feuerbach led to her 1854 translation of his *Essence of Christianity*. Soon afterward she informally became the companion of G. H. Lewes, a union that lasted until he died. Her first major novel, *Adam Bede* (1859), was a popular and critical success. It was followed by *The Mill on the Floss* (1860) and *Silas Marner* (1861). *Romola* (1862–1863) and *Felix Holt, the Radical* (1866) were written after a period in Florence. Her last major novels, *Middlemarch* (1871–1872) and *Daniel Deronda* (1874–1876) gained her great renown. Her *Impressions of Theophrastus Such* (1879) appeared shortly before her death.

Henry Fielding (1707–1754)

Educated at Eton, Fielding settled in London as a young man and began a difficult but prolific period as a playwright. From 1729 to 1737 he wrote satirical plays, including *The Author's Farce* (1730), *Rape upon Rape* (1730), and his best-known drama, *Tom Thumb* (1730), a wild satire on the bloated tragedies that were all the rage. In 1734 Fielding married Charlotte Cradock, the woman who became the inspiration for the heroine in *Amelia* and for Sophia in *Tom Jones*. He became manager of the New Theatre in 1736, for which he wrote and produced the popular political satires *Pasquin* and *The Historical Register for 1736*, the latter of which earned the censorship of the Walpole government. The Lord Chamberlain's Licensing Act of 1737 brought the effective end of Fielding's theatrical pursuits. Fielding proceeded to read for the bar, but his ill health prevented him from successfully practicing. In 1741, he wrote a parody of Richardson's *Pamela*, entitled *An Apology for the Life of Mrs.*

Shamela Andrews. This was followed by three great novels: *The Adventures of Joseph Andrews and His Friend, Mr. Abraham Adams* (1742), *The History of Tom Jones, a Foundling* (1749), and *Amelia* (1751). A great part of his later life was spent as a judge for Westminster, crusading against corruption, public hanging, and organized crime. He died in Lisbon, Portugal, where he had gone for the benefit of his chronically poor health.

Sarah Fielding (1710–1768)

Fielding was Henry Fielding's sister. She grew up near London and spent much of her life there and, later, near Bath. A member of Samuel Richardson's circle, she published her most famous work, *The Adventures of David Simple*, in 1744. This work was followed by two other related volumes, *Familiar Letters Between the Principal Characters in David Simple* (1747) and *Volume the Last* (1753).

Ronald Firbank (1886–1926)

As an independently wealthy man, Firbank was able to travel widely and publish his own work. Known for his flamboyant homosexuality and his innovative literary and personal style, Firbank was educated at Trinity Hall, Cambridge, and began to publish shortly after graduation. Among his works are *Odette d'Antrevernes* (1916), *Vainglory* (1915), *Inclinations* (1916), *Caprice* (1917), *Valmouth* (1919), *Santal* (1921), and *The Flower Beneath the Foot* (1923). His first novel not published by himself was *Prancing Nigger* (1924), also known as *Sorrow in Sunlight*.

Ford Madox Ford (1873–1939)

Ford grew up steeped in the aesthetics of the Pre-Raphaelites and that influence stayed with him throughout his life. After Ford met Conrad in 1898, the two began to collaborate on a variety of projects, most notably the novels *The Inheritors* (1901) and *Romance* (1903). When the relationship died, Ford went on to his own rather influential literary career, producing over eighty books. His novels include the *Fifth Queen* trilogy (1907, 1907, 1908), *The Good Soldier* (1915), and *Parade's End* (1924–1928). Ford's major literary contributions seem to have been in his role as editor, first of the *English Review* and later the *Transatlantic Review* (1924), and as a critic who developed a theory of novelistic impressionism.

E. M. Forster (1879–1970)

After graduating from King's College, Cambridge, Forster traveled through Italy and Greece, and his first novel, *Where Angels Fear to Tread* (1905), has an Italian setting. Three more novels followed in quick succession: *The*

Longest Journey (1907), *A Room With a View* (1908), and perhaps his most important novel to that point, *Howard's End* (1910). Forster lived with his mother in Weybridge for many years until her death, although he served with the International Red Cross in Egypt during World War I and spent a year in India in 1912 and 1913. Out of that experience, he wrote what most readers regard as his greatest novel, *A Passage to India* (1924). Although he stopped writing novels after that, he continued to write shorter fiction, and his essays and literary criticism are a substantial and important body of work, notably *Aspects of the Novel* (1927) and *Two Cheers for Democracy* (1951). In 1946 Forster was made an honorary fellow of his old college at Cambridge, Kings, and he lived there until his death. *Maurice*, a novel written in 1913–14 and based on his own intensely private homosexual life, was published posthumously in 1971.

George Robert Gissing (1857–1903)

While a student at Owens College in Manchester, Gissing became infatuated with a young prostitute, and in his efforts to help her committed some thefts for which he was expelled and sent to prison. After working briefly as a journalist in the United States and experiencing great poverty and hardship, he returned to England and while sustaining himself as a clerk began to write novels. A small legacy enabled him to complete his first published novel, *Workers in the Dawn* (1880). For the next twenty years, Gissing published nearly a novel a year, achieving limited commercial success but earning the respect of fellow writers like Henry James and H. G. Wells. Reflecting his years of economic struggle, Gissing's novels such as *The Nether World* (1889) and *Born in Exile* (1892) evoke the oppressiveness of nineteenth-century urban life among the English working class. In novels such as *Thyrza* (1887) and *The Odd Women* (1893), Gissing explored the problems of women in the modern age, and his best-known work, *New Grub Street* (1891), dramatizes the plight of the writer in a world indifferent to his art.

William Godwin (1756–1836)

Godwin's beliefs proceeded on a course from Dissenting minister to atheist and philosopher of early anarchism. His radical view of reason prescribed the elimination of laws and government institutions. Husband of the famous feminist writer Mary Wollstonecraft, Godwin was also the father of the novelist Mary Shelley. In addition to his famous work *Enquiry Concerning Political Justice* (1793), Godwin was the author of many novels, among them *Caleb Williams* (1794), *St. Leon* (1799), *Fleetwood* (1805), *Mandeville* (1817), *Cloudesley* (1830), and *Deloraine* (1833).

William Golding (1911–1993)
Golding was born in Cornwall and was graduated from Brasenose College, Oxford. He has been an actor, theater producer, teacher, and aviator in the Royal Navy. His first novel, *Lord of the Flies* (1954), has proved popular and lasting. This was followed by *Pincher Martin* (1956), *The Brass Butterfly* (a play, 1958), *Free Fall* (1959), *The Spire* (1964), *The Pyramid* (1967), *The Scorpion God* (1971), *Darkness Visible* (1979), the winner of the Booker Prize *Rites of Passage* (1980), and *The Paper Men* (1984). Golding won the Nobel Prize in 1983.

Oliver Goldsmith (1730?–1774)
Goldsmith was reared in Lissoy and educated at Trinity College, Dublin. He continued his studies at Edinburgh and Leyden, and took an extended tour through France, Switzerland, and Italy. Arriving in London in 1756 with no money, Goldsmith struggled to make a living as a physician, usher, and hack writer. He became a well-known and influential contributor to a variety of periodicals, as well as a charter member of Dr. Johnson's literary club. Johnson was instrumental in getting *The Vicar of Wakefield* (1764) published when Goldsmith was destitute. Goldsmith's most famous poem was *The Deserted Village* (1770), and his comedy *She Stoops to Conquer* (1773) was an unmitigated success on stage.

Graham Greene (1904–1991)
Educated at Balliol College, Oxford, Greene began to write fiction while still at university. After his conversion to Roman Catholicism and a stint as a journalist at the *Times*, he began to write full time. His first really successful novel, *Stamboul Train* (1932), was followed by a great amount of writing—novels, short stories, travel books, children's stories, etc. Much of his writing is concerned with danger and risk-taking and with the mystery of Catholic divinity, and his novels amply reflect these themes. Among them are *Brighton Rock* (1938), *The Power and the Glory* (1940), *The Heart of the Matter* (1948), *The Quiet American* (1955), and *Our Man in Havana* (1958).

H. Rider Haggard (1856–1925)
After spending six years of his young adulthood in South Africa, Haggard went on to serve on official commissions dealing with agriculture, emigration, and forestry. Haggard is best known as the author of over thirty adventure novels, set in exotic places like Iceland, Turkey, Egypt, and Mexico. His most successful novels, *King Solomon's Mines* (1886) and *She* (1887), are set in Africa.

Thomas Hardy (1840–1928)
Born near Dorchester, the son of a stonemason, Hardy went to school until the age of sixteen, when he began an apprenticeship with an architect. When he was twenty-two he went to London to work, and upon returning to work in

Dorchester he began his first novel, *The Poor Man and the Lady*. During this period as an architect he produced his first published novels: *Desperate Remedies* (1871), *Under the Greenwood Tree* (1872), *A Pair of Blue Eyes* (1873), and *Far from the Madding Crowd* (1874). In the period between 1874 and 1895, Hardy was extremely productive, writing short stories, poems, and the following novels: *The Hand of Ethelberta* (1876), *The Return of the Native* (1878), *The Trumpet Major* (1880), *A Laodicean* (1881), *Two on a Tower* (1882), *The Mayor of Casterbridge* (1886), *The Woodlanders* (1887), *Wessex Tales* (1888), *Tess of the D'Urbervilles* (1891), *A Group of Noble Dames* (1891), *Life's Little Ironies* (1894), and *Jude the Obscure* (1896). Hardy gave up writing fiction late in life and devoted himself to poetry.

Mary Hays (1760–1843)

The daughter of Rational Dissenters, Hays was born in Southwark, London. Much of her education came through her correspondence with John Eccles, after whose death she began to write poetry and fiction. In the 1790s she began to find her voice as a feminist, keeping company with Mary Wollstonecraft and William Godwin. With the help of Godwin she published *Memoirs of Emma Courtney* (1796), which was followed by *A Victim of Prejudice* (1799). She was also the author of *Appeal to the Men of Great Britain in Behalf of the Women* (1798) and *Female Biography* (1803).

Eliza Haywood (1693?–1756)

Both an actress and a prolific writer of novels, Haywood in *Memoirs of a Certain Island Adjacent to the Kingdom of Utopia* (1725) imitated the scandal chronicles of Delariviere Manley, and achieved considerable fame with a steady stream of amatory fictions in the 1720s, notably *Love in Excess* (1720). In the wake of Richardson's and Fielding's success, she produced her most accomplished novels, *The History of Miss Betsy Thoughtless* (1751) and *The History of Jenny and Jemmy Jessamy* (1753).

James Hogg (1770–1835)

Known as the "Ettrick Shepherd," Hogg was born in Ettrick Forest and was indeed a shepherd. Sir Walter Scott discovered him after he read Hogg's poems. He made his reputation with the collection of poems *The Queen's Wake* (1813). His best-known prose works are *The Three Perils of Man* (1822), *The Private Memoirs and Confessions of a Justified Sinner* (1824), and *The Domestic Manners and Private Life of Sir Walter Scott* (1834).

Thomas Holcroft (1745–1809)

Holcroft went from stableboy to cobbler, to actor and finally to author. An atheist who was heavily influenced by Godwin's radical philosophy, Holcroft was nearly convicted of high treason in 1794. He was the author of several plays, among them *The Road to Ruin* (1792), and a number of novels, which include *Anna St. Ives* (1792) and *The Adventures of Hugh Trevor* (1794).

Aldous Huxley (1894–1963)
Though he was nearly blind, Huxley managed to take his degree from Balliol College, Oxford. He soon plunged into a life of writing and published three volumes of poetry by 1919. Huxley's satiric genius was displayed in numerous short stories and novels: *Limbo* (1920), *Crome Yellow* (1921), *Mortal Coils* (1922), *Antic Hay* (1923), *Those Barren Leaves* (1925), *Point Counter Point* (1928), *After Many A Summer* (1939), and *Island* (1962). His most enduring and popular work remains *Brave New World* (1932), while works such as *Eyeless in Gaza* (1936), *The Doors of Perception* (1954), and *Heaven and Hell* (1956) also contributed to his popularity.

Mrs. Elizabeth Inchbald (1753–1821)
Inchbald was a playwright, actress, and novelist. She was a close friend of William Godwin until his marriage to Mary Wollstonecraft. Inchbald's best-known pieces are the primitivist romances *A Simple Story* (1791), and *Nature and Art* (1796). Her plays include *Lovers' Vows* (1798)—which is famous for its enactment in Austen's *Mansfield Park*—and *I'll Tell You What* (1795).

Christopher Isherwood (1904–1986)
Isherwood was born in Cheshire and went to Cambridge, where he began writing. Two early novels, *All the Conspirators* (1928) and *The Memorial* (1932), were published just before and during a four-year period in Berlin. *Mr. Norris Changes Trains* (1935) and *Goodbye to Berlin* (1939) draw heavily on his life in prewar Germany. His post-Berlin novels were intended to be part of a long novel called "The Lost," which was never completed. His sketches were published under the title *New Writing*; one of them, "Sally Bowles," was eventually made into the movie *Cabaret*. After leaving Germany, Isherwood traveled with his lifelong friend W. H. Auden to China and then to America, where he eventually settled and became a citizen. His eccentric works are many: a collaboration with Auden, *The Ascent of F6*, the autobiographical *Lions and Shadows* (1938), the novels *Down There on a Visit* (1962) and *A Single Man* (1964), and an account of his life as a young homosexual, *Christopher and His Kind* (1976).

James Joyce (1882–1941)
Joyce was born in Dublin and attended Jesuit schools and University College, Dublin. Disgusted with Irish provincialism and Roman Catholic bigotry, he

left Ireland for Paris in 1902; except for two brief visits, he lived with his wife, Nora Barnacle, in Europe for the rest of his life, in Paris, Trieste, and Zurich. The publication of his collection of short fiction, *Dubliners* (1914), occasioned his last visit to Ireland, and his autobiographical novel, *A Portrait of the Artist as a Young Man* was published serially in the celebrated journal *The Egoist* in 1914 and 1915. Hampered by a severe case of glaucoma, Joyce survived in large part through the support of patrons like Harriet Shaw Weaver. Joyce published his greatest work, *Ulysses*, in Paris in 1922, and although banned in the United States as obscene it was immediately hailed by many as a modernist masterpiece that revolutionized the art of the novel. His last work, *Finnegans Wake* (1939), has drawn much critical attention, but its forbidding complexity has discouraged most readers.

Charles Kingsley (1819–1875)

Kingsley was educated at King's College, London, and at Magdalene College, Cambridge. In 1844 he became the rector of Eversley in Hampshire. His blank verse drama, *The Saint's Tragedy* (1848), was a characteristically political work, which led to his active participation in the movement for political and social reform. This commitment is also reflected in his novels of working-class life, *Yeast* (1850) and *Alton Locke* (1850). *Hypatia, or New Foes with Old Faces* (1853) deals with the Greek Neoplatonist who was put to death by Christians in A.D. 415. The Crimean War and his own patriotism inspired the novel *Westward Ho!* (1855). His other novels of note include *Two Years Ago* (1857), *Hereward the Wake* (1866), *Heroes* (1856), and *The Water-Babies* (1863).

Rudyard Kipling (1865 –1936)

Born in India, the son of a scholar and artist, Kipling was raised from the age of six in England by a foster family in Southsea, where he was lonely and unhappy. He was educated at the United Services College, a school for army officers' children, and returned to India when he was seventeen in 1882. There he began to work as a journalist and shortly after published *Plain Tales from the Hills* (1888), a book that made him overnight a literary celebrity. His short fiction and poems about military life in India such as those in *Barrack-Room Ballads* (1892) won him wide acclaim in England. From 1892 to 1896 he lived in Vermont with his American wife, and while there he wrote *The Jungle Book* (1894). Other popular children's books followed, such as *Just So Stories* (1902), *Puck of Pook's Hill* (1906), and *Rewards and Fairies* (1910). *Kim* (1901) is generally thought to be his masterpiece, marking him as one of the great chroniclers of British colonial expansion. In 1907, Kipling was the first British writer to receive the Nobel Prize.

D. H. Lawrence (1885–1930)

Lawrence was born into a family of five children in Nottinghamshire, the son of a schoolteacher and a miner. Amid often brutal poverty, Lawrence managed with the love and help of his mother to excel in school; he won a scholarship to attend high school until he was forced to find a job. After a period of working he resumed his education at Nottingham University College with the aim of earning a teaching certificate. It was at this point that he began writing, mostly poetry and short stories. His first novel, *The White Peacock* (1911), was followed by *The Trespasser* (1912) and then by his great autobiographical novel *Sons and Lovers* (1913). Having eloped with Frieda Weekley in 1912, Lawrence embarked on a turbulent marital life that included an enormous amount of travel to such places as Ceylon, Australia, the United States, and Mexico. *The Rainbow* (1915) marked the beginning of his persistent troubles with censorship, a problem that dogged the publication of *Women in Love* (1920) for five years and would later make *Lady Chatterley's Lover* (1928) notorious. His other novels of note include *The Lost Girl* (1920), *Aaron's Rod* (1922), *Kangaroo* (1923), and *The Plumed Serpent* (1926).

Sophia Lee (1750–1824)

Lee was a dramatist and novelist who ran a private school in Bath. She is best known for her play *The Chapter of Accidents* (1780) and her novels *The Recess* (1783–1785) and the autobiographical *Life of a Lover* (1804).

Charlotte Lennox (1720–1804)

Lennox was born in America, the daughter of New York's lieutenant governor. After arriving in England and failing to launch a career as an actress she began to write novels. Her works are nuanced exercises in the novel of sentiment. They include *Life of Harriot Stuart* (1750); *The Female Quixote* (1752), her most renowned work; and *Henrietta* (1758). She also published a volume of translations of Shakespeare's sources entitled *Shakespear Illustrated* (1753–1754), and a dramatic comedy, *The Sister* (1769).

Doris Lessing (1919–)

Born in Persia to British parents, Lessing moved with her family at the age of five to a farm in Southern Rhodesia. After dropping out of school at fifteen, she worked as a nursemaid, secretary, and telephone operator. When her first marriage ended she became active in leftist politics. In 1949, Lessing went to England with her youngest child and published her first novel, *The Grass Is Singing* (1950). Her great quintet of novels, Children of Violence, comprises the somewhat autobiographical life of one Martha Quest from her youth in Rhodesia to the year 2000: *Martha Quest* (1952), *A Proper Marriage* (1954), *A Ripple from the Storm* (1958), *Landlocked* (1965), and *The Four-Gated City*

(1969). Her most famous and perhaps most political novel is *The Golden Note-book* (1962), a work that has become a feminist classic. Her late novels include *Briefing for a Descent into Hell* (1971) and *Memoirs of a Survivor* (1975).

Matthew Gregory Lewis (1775–1818)
Best known for his Gothic novel *The Monk* (1796), Lewis was educated at Westminster and Christ Church, Oxford. He was also the author of a number of dramas that reflect the influence of German Romanticism and went on in turn to influence some of the early work of Sir Walter Scott.

David Lodge (1935–)
Lodge is known for both his novels and his criticism. A graduate of University College, London, he was appointed professor of modern English literature at the University of Birmingham in 1976. As a critic his contributions have been versatile as well as accessible. His novels are satirical and theoretically knowing. They include *The British Museum Is Falling Down* (1965), *Changing Places* (1975), *How Far Can You Go?* (1980), and *Small World* (1984).

Henry Mackenzie (1745–1831)
Besides being a lawyer and Comptroller of the Taxes for Scotland, MacKenzie was the author of an enormously important novel, *The Man of Feeling* (1771). He also published the novels *The Man of the World* (1773) and *Julia de Roubigné* (1777), and a play, *The Prince of Tunis* (1773). Mackenzie edited and contributed to two magazines, the *Mirror* and the *Lounger*, and headed the commission that investigated Macpherson's Ossianic poems.

Delariviere Manley (1663–1724)
Manley led a sensational private life in which she carried on a bigamous marriage with her cousin John Manley and was a mistress to the warden of the Fleet Prison, John Tilly. She is known for her novels *The New Atalantis* (1709), a satire on Whigs and public figures, and *The Adventures of Rivella* (1714), an autobiographical piece. Manley succeeded Jonathan Swift as editor of the *Examiner* in 1711.

Olivia Manning (1908–1980)
Manning was reared in Portsmouth and spent an important period of her adult life in Hungary, Greece, Egypt, and Jerusalem. This period provided the basis for her two great war trilogies: *The Balkan Trilogy* (*The Great Fortune*, 1960; *The Spoilt City*, 1962; *Friends and Heroes*, 1965) and *The Levant Trilogy* (*The Danger Tree*, 1977; *The Battle Lost and Won*, 1978; and *The Sum of Things*, 1980).

Captain Frederick Marryat (1792–1848)
Marryat was both writer and naval captain. His initial, semiautobiographical novel, *The Naval Officer: or Scenes and Adventures in the Life of Frank Mildmay* (1829) was well received. He resigned his commission in 1830 to pursue his literary career, during which he wrote fifteen novels. His best-known later novels are *Peter Simple* (1834), *Jacob Faithful* (1834), and *Mr. Midshipman Easy* (1836).

Charles Maturin (1782–1824)
A graduate of Trinity College, Dublin, Maturin was briefly a headmaster of a school. He is best known for his work in the Gothic novel, publishing *The Fatal Revenge* in 1807, *The Wild Irish Boy* in 1808, and *The Milesian Chief* in 1811. After some success in the theater, Maturin returned to novels and produced his most important work, *Melmoth the Wanderer* (1820).

W. Somerset Maugham (1874–1965)
Born in Paris, Maugham was sent to England shortly after being orphaned. After graduating from the King's School, Canterbury, he attended Heidelberg University and went on to study medicine a St. Thomas's Hospital in London. In 1897 he published his first novel, which was to mark the beginning of a long, prolific, and successful career in writing. After a series of well-received plays, Maugham published his most famous novel, *Of Human Bondage* (1915), followed by *The Moon and Sixpence* (1919), *Cakes and Ale* (1930), and *The Razor's Edge* (1944).

George Augustus Moore (1852–1933)
Moore is known for having brought many of the innovations of French realism into the domain of the English novel. His best-known work, *Esther Waters* (1894), is set among the Irish horse farms of his childhood. Moore's first novel, *A Modern Lover* (1883), caused much controversy due to its frank depiction of the life of the artistic demimonde. His other novels include *A Mummer's Wife* (1885), *Evelyn Innes* (1898), *Sister Teresa* (1901), *The Brook Kerith* (1916), and *Heloise and Abelard* (1921).

V. S. Naipaul (1932–)
Born in Trinidad into a Brahmin family, Naipaul was educated at Queens Royal College, Port of Spain, and went on a scholarship to University College, Oxford. After marrying an Englishwoman, he settled in London, became a literary journalist, and turned eventually to writing fiction with *The Mystic Masseur* (1957). Set in the Caribbean and based on his own early years in Trinidad, *A House for Mr. Biswas* (1961) established Naipaul's reputation as a novelist. His Booker Prize–winning novel *In a Free State* (1971) began a trend in his fiction and his reportage toward the uncompromising and pessimistic

portrayal of postcolonial culture and politics. Notable for exploring such issues are the novels *Guerrillas* (1975) and *A Bend in the River* (1979) and personal narratives such as *India: A Wounded Civilization* (1977), *A Congo Diary* (1980), *The Return of Eva Peron* (1980), and *Among the Believers* (1982).

George Orwell (Eric Arthur Blair) (1903–1950)
Born in Bengal, Orwell was brought to England and educated at St. Cyprian's and Eton. His experience with the Indian Imperial Police in Burma provided the material for his first novel, *Burmese Days* (1928). After resigning in disgust over the degradations of imperialism, he moved to Paris where he struggled to publish some of his early novels. A trip to northern England in 1936 inspired the impassioned documentary piece *The Road to Wigan Pier* (1937), and a stint with the Republican fighters in the Spanish civil war resulted in his enduring paean to antifascist struggle, *Homage to Catalonia* (1939). A fiercely independent democratic socialist, Orwell is perhaps best known for his satirical novels *Animal Farm* (1945) and *Nineteen Eighty-four* (1949).

Barbara Pym (1913–1980)
Educated at St. Hilda's College, Oxford, Pym worked at the International African Institute in London. Her novels are satirical and domestic tragedies; they include *Excellent Women* (1952), *Less than Angels* (1955), *A Glass of Blessings* (1958), and *Quartet in Autumn* (1977).

Ann Radcliffe (1764–1823)
The wife of William Radcliffe, who managed the *English Chronicle*, Radcliffe was the most successful author of Gothic fiction of her time. Among her best-known works are *The Romance of the Forest* (1791), *The Mysteries of Udolpho* (1794), and *The Italian* (1797).

Charles Reade (1814–1884)
Born in Oxfordshire, Reade went to Magdalen College, Oxford, in 1831. His relationship with Oxford was a long one and included many positions from fellow to a variety of administrative posts. After traveling outside England, Reade returned in 1842 and began to study for the bar. Not long after, he began studying medicine in Edinburgh. His literary ambitions took flight with his publication of a stage version of Smollett's *Peregrine Pickle* in 1851, after which he began a long career as a theater manager and dramatist. His play *Masks and Faces* was turned into a novel, *Peg Woffington* (1853). He went on to publish a number of novels that were seen as Dickensian in theme and style, and which brought him much acclaim from critics and the reading public: *Christie Johnstone* (1853), *It Is Never Too Late to Mend* (1856), *Foul Play* (1869), *The Autobiography of a Thief* (1858), *Jack of All Trades* (1858), *Love Me Little, Love Me*

Long (1859), *The Cloister and the Hearth* (1861), *Hard Cash* (1863), *Griffith Gaunt* (1866), and *Put Yourself in His Place* (1870).

Clara Reeve (1729–1807)
Born in Ipswich, Reeve published *The Champion of Virtue; a Gothic Story* in 1777. It was reprinted a year later as *The Old English Baron* and received much acclaim. The novel's indebtedness to Walpole's *Castle of Otranto* was the cause of a controversy between Reeve and Walpole. Reeve went on to write several other novels, as well as a critical piece entitled *The Progress of Romance* (1785).

Jean Rhys (1894–1979)
Born in Dominica in the West Indies, Rhys first came to England in 1907. After attending the Perse School and the Academy of Dramatic Art, she worked as a chorus girl, film extra, and cook. Living in Paris with her husband, she wrote a series of novels in the 1930s that depict the marginal existence of aging and attractive women who have to depend on men. Among her best-known works, which were rediscovered by feminist readers in the 1970s, are *Quartet* (1929), *After Leaving Mr. Mackenzie* (1931), *Good Morning, Midnight* (1938), and *Wide Sargasso Sea* (1966).

Samuel Richardson (1689–1761)
By his own account, Richardson had an early affinity for storytelling, and by age thirteen he was writing love letters for hire. Apprenticed to a printer, in 1721 he began his own printing business and in that same year he married Martha Wilde. By 1731 his wife and six children had all died, leaving him to suffer periodic nervous breakdowns in his later life. Richardson married Elizabeth Leake in 1733, and they had four daughters. His printing business reached its height of prosperity in 1742 when he obtained the post of Printer of Journals for the House of Commons. Richardson embarked upon a publishing project to produce a volume of model letters "on such subjects as might be of use to country readers who are unable to indite for themselves," and that volume seems to have provided the impetus for his epistolary novel *Pamela, or Virtue Rewarded* (1740), which was enormously successful. Richardson produced a sequel in 1741, and in 1747–48 published *Clarissa*, a much more elaborate and ambitious epistolary novel that was hailed by most readers as a masterpiece and made him the most famous English writer of his generation. In his last and least successful novel, *Sir Charles Grandison* (1753–1754), Richardson attempted to portray a virtuous hero.

Mary Robinson (1758–1800)
Robinson was an actress, playwright, poet, and novelist, and for a brief time was mistress to the prince of Wales, later George IV. She spent ten months in

debtor's prison with her husband, after which she began publishing poetry. During the 1780s she reached the height of her fame as an actress. In the 1790s she fell in with a circle of radical feminists, including Mary Wollstonecraft, Mary Hays, Charlotte Smith, and William Godwin. Godwin was instrumental in the writing of her most popular novel *Walsingham; or, The Pupil of Nature* (1797).

Salman Rushdie (1947–)
Born in Bombay, Rushdie attended school in Bombay, in England, and eventually at King's College, Cambridge. After working as an actor in experimental theater and as a copywriter, he published his first novel, *Grimus* (1975). A five-month trip to Pakistan and India prepared him to write the Booker Prize–winning *Midnight's Children* (1981). His novel *The Satanic Verses* (1988) created an intercultural controversy when the Ayatollah Khomeini deemed the novel sacrilegious and called for the death penalty against Rushdie. He is also the author of *Shame* (1983), *The Jaguar Smile* (1987), *Haroun and the Sea of Stories* (1990), and *Imaginary Homelands: Essays and Criticism* (1991).

Olive Schreiner (1855–1920)
The daughter of a missionary, Schreiner was born in Cape Colony. She moved to England in 1881 and became a governess, after already having published her most acclaimed book, *The Story of an African Farm* (1883), an early feminist novel. She published two other novels with feminist themes, *From Man to Man* (1927) and *Undine* (1929), as well as numerous articles on South African politics and a treatise, *Women and Labour* (1911).

Paul Scott (1920–1978)
Scott was born in London and went on to hold a commission in the Indian army during World War II. His favorite subject for exploration was the state of Anglo-Indian relations under the Raj, best exemplified in his famous Raj Quartet: *The Jewel in the Crown* (1966), *The Day of the Scorpion* (1968), *The Towers of Silence* (1971), and *A Division of Spoils* (1975). His last novel, *Staying On* (1977), elaborates upon the lives of two minor characters from the Quartet.

Sir Walter Scott (1771–1832)
Scott was born in College Wynd, Edinburgh, and was educated at Edinburgh University. After an apprenticeship with his father, he was called to the bar in 1792. He became a devotee of romantic Border tales and ballads, as well as romantic French, German, and Italian poetry. His earliest publications were translations of Bürger and Goethe. Scott married a Frenchwoman, Margaret Charlotte Charpentier, in 1797, and two years later was

appointed sheriff-depute of Selkirkshire. His passion for Border lore resulted in a three-volume collection entitled *Minstrelsy of the Scottish Border*
(1802–1803), and this was soon followed in 1805 by the poem *The Lay of the
Last Minstrel*. The period from 1808 to 1817 saw the publication of his best-
known poems: *Marmion*, *The Lady of the Lake*, *The Bridal of Triermain*, *The
Lord of the Isles*, and *Harold the Dauntless*. Scott found much more success as
a novelist and his work was prodigious. The better-known novels include
Waverley (1814), *Guy Mannering* (1815), *The Antiquary* (1816), *The Heart of
Midlothian* (1818), *The Bride of Lammermoor* (1819), *Ivanhoe* (1819), *Kenilworth* (1821), *Woodstock* (1826), *St. Valentine's Day, or The Fair Maid of Perth*
(1828), and *Castle Dangerous* (1831). Scott was also the author of important
works on literary history, folklore, and history. He is generally credited with
having pioneered the historical novel and with transforming the novel into a
romantic genre.

Mary Shelley (1797–1851)
The daughter of Mary Wollstonecraft and William Godwin, Shelley became
the wife of the Romantic poet Percy Bysshe Shelley in 1816. Her best-known
novels are the Gothic classics *Frankenstein, or The Modern Prometheus* (1818),
Valperga (1823), *The Last Man* (1826), and *Lodore* (1835).

Charlotte Smith (1748–1806)
Smith is best remembered for her novels, though she achieved success in a variety of genres. Her *Elegiac Sonnets* were published in 1784; her novels were all
published in the years between 1788 and 1793. The two most admired novels
were *Emmeline* (1788) and *The Old Manor House* (1793).

Tobias Smollett (1721–1771)
Born near Dunbarton in Scotland, Smollett attended Glasgow University.
Though trained as a surgeon, he never made an adequate living at it. After
joining the navy as a surgeon's mate, Smollett sailed to the West Indies where
he met his wife and observed corruption and mismanagement in the navy that
formed part of the subject of his very successful first novel, *The Adventures of
Roderick Random* (1746). Upon his return to London in 1744, he practiced
medicine and wrote fiction (notably *Peregrine Pickle* [1751] and *Ferdinand
Count Fathom* [1753]), eventually turning exclusively to literary work, becoming a translator, historian, and editor of the influential journal *The Critical
Review* in 1756. He traveled to France and Italy for his health, publishing a
record of his travels, *Travels through France and Italy* (1766). His masterpiece
is generally thought to be *The Expedition of Humphry Clinker* (1771), published
only months before his death.

C. P. Snow (1905–1980)

The son of a church organist, Snow was born and raised in Leicester. After working for several years as a research scientist at Cambridge, he went on to administrative posts at the university. His novels deal in some way either with the life of science or with the ascension of a lower-middle-class protagonist to fame and fortune. The major novels include *Death under Sail* (1932), *New Lives for Old* (1933), *The Search* (1934), *George Passant* (1940), *The Light and the Dark* (1947), *Time of Hope* (1949), *The Masters* (1951), *The New Men* (1954), *Homecomings* (1956), *The Conscience of the Rich* (1958), *The Affair* (1959), *Corridors of Power* (1963), *The Sleep of Reason* (1968), and *Last Things* (1970).

Laurence Sterne (1713–1768)

Sterne was raised in various military stations throughout Ireland and England. After attending Jesus College, Cambridge, he took holy orders and embarked on a career as a country pastor. When he angered ecclesiastical authorities with his *Political Romance*, Sterne left his parish and began work on *Tristram Shandy* (1759). Though controversial, the novel made him famous and he continued it with several more volumes in 1761, 1765, and 1767. Ill health sent him to France for a period, which provided much of the material for his *Sentimental Journey Through France and Italy* (1767). Sterne continues to receive intense critical attention for his highly experimental narratives, which are thought to anticipate much of what has come to be known as stream of consciousness.

Robert Louis Stevenson (1850–1894)

Stevenson was born in Edinburgh where he later attended university, studying first engineering and then law. Because he suffered from a chronic lung disease, Stevenson spent much of his life traveling in search of a more healthful climate. His first full-length novel, *Treasure Island*, was published in 1883. Having achieved a measure of success, Stevenson went on in the 1880s to publish a number of enduring works of adventure and romance: *The Strange Case of Dr. Jekyll and Mr. Hyde* (1886), *Kidnapped* (1886), and *The Master of Ballantrae* (1889). He died in Samoa while at work on an unfinished masterpiece, *Weir of Hermiston* (1896).

Graham Swift (1949–)

Swift was educated at Cambridge and York Universities. Beginning with his powerful and much-praised novel *Waterland* (1983), he has established himself as one of the most original younger novelists now at work in England. Among his other novels are *The Sweetshop Owner* (1985), *Shuttlecock* (1985), *Out of This World* (1988), and *Ever After* (1992).

Jonathan Swift (1667–1745)

An Anglo-Irishman by birth, Swift graduated from Trinity College, Dublin, and spent several years in the household of Sir William Temple, a retired English diplomat. After becoming an ordained minister in 1694, Swift vainly sought ecclesiastical preferment and composed during these years a satire in defense of his patron, Temple, *The Battle of the Books* (1697), which he published with his complex satire against what he called the "corruptions in religion and learning," *A Tale of a Tub* (1704). The author of numerous political pamphlets and poems during his long career, Swift began as a writer for the Whigs but became disenchanted with that party's sympathy for religious dissent from the Church of England and moved to the Tory side. Resident for long periods in London on ecclesiastical business, he became an intimate of Tory writers and politicians such as Pope, Gay, Arbuthnot, Prior, Harley, and Bolingbroke, who formed the famed Scriblerus Club. With the defeat of the Tories after the death of Queen Anne, Swift spent most of his time in Ireland, where he was Dean of St. Patrick's in Dublin and became a fierce advocate of Irish rights against English oppression. His greatest work, *Gulliver's Travels* (1726), is a general satire on human nature but is grounded in Swift's political passions in its attacks on the Hanoverian monarchy and the political establishment headed by Robert Walpole.

Philip Meadows Taylor (1808–1876)

Born in Liverpool, Taylor was a soldier in the Indian army and later became a correspondent for the *Times* from 1840 to 1853. His popular novel *Confessions of a Thug* (1839) was the product of investigative pieces he had written on Thuggee, a terrorist movement in India. His stories written after his return to England in 1860 include the historical pieces *Tara: A Mahratta Tale* (1843), *Ralph Darnell* (1865), and *Seeta* (1872).

William Makepeace Thackeray (1811–1863)

Born in India to an official of the East India Company, Thackeray was raised and educated in England from the age of six. After attending Trinity College, Cambridge, he went to France and Germany, and when he returned to London studied law briefly. After working as a journalist for a time, he studied art in Paris and continued to work as a journalist upon his return to England in 1837. A popular satirist in journals such as *Fraser's* and *Punch*, he began to publish his best-known novels serially in 1848 with *Vanity Fair*, followed by *Pendennis* (1848–1849), *Henry Esmond* (1852), and *The Newcomes* (1853–1855). A lecture tour to America in 1852 led to another novel published serially, *The Virginians* (1857–1859).

Anthony Trollope (1815–1882)

Though he attended both Harrow and Winchester, Trollope was not successful in school, and his father's business failures drove the family to move to Belgium. Trollope went on to become a clerk in the General Post Office in London in 1834 and was later transferred to Ireland in 1841. His duties in the postal service carried him on trips to Egypt, the United States, and the West Indies. His Post Office career did not stand in the way of his literary endeavors. His first publication was *The Macdermots of Ballycloran* (1847), but it was *The Warden* (1855), the first of the Barsetshire series, that finally won him acclaim. The rest of the series followed: *Barchester Towers* (1857), *Doctor Thorne* (1858), *Framley Parsonage* (1861), *The Small House at Allington* (1864), and *The Last Chronicle of Barset* (1867). His other great series was known as the "Political" or "Palliser" novels, beginning with *Can You Forgive Her?* (1864) and continuing with *Phineas Finn* (1869), *The Eustace Diamonds* (1873), *Phineas Redux* (1876), *The Prime Minister* (1876), and *The Duke's Children* (1880). Trollope is credited with establishing the novel series in English. He was extremely prolific, producing an astonishing number of novels, including *The Bertrams* (1859), *The Belton Estate* (1866), *He Knew He Was Right* (1869), *The Way We Live Now* (1875), *The American Senator* (1877), and *Mr. Scarborough's Family* (1883).

Horace Walpole (1717–1797)
The fourth earl of Orford, Walpole was educated at Eton and at King's College, Cambridge. He spent a period of his young adulthood traveling through Europe with his friend Thomas Gray, and then he was elected to Parliament from Callington, Castle Rising, and Lynn. After settling in the house known as Strawberry Hill and starting his own printing press, Walpole began to publish his own work as well as Gray's. His most notable works remain *A Catalogue of the Royal and Noble Authors of England* (1758), *Anecdotes of Painting in England* (1762), and *The Castle of Otranto* (1764).

Evelyn Waugh (1903–1966)
Waugh was educated at Hertford College, Oxford, and proceeded to work as an assistant schoolmaster until his first novel, *Decline and Fall* (1928), was published to wide acclaim. After a brief marriage, Waugh converted to Roman Catholicism in 1930. His early novels were successful works of satire: *Vile Bodies* (1930), *Black Mischief* (1932), *A Handful of Dust* (1934), and *Scoop* (1938). Waugh was also an accomplished travel writer who produced pieces on Africa (*Remote People*, 1931) and South America (*Ninety-two Days*, 1934). His later novels include the celebrated *Brideshead Revisited* (1945), *The Loved One* (1948), and *The Ordeal of Gilbert Pinfold* (1957), a hilarious self-parody.

Fay Weldon (1933–)
Born in Worcester, Weldon was educated at the University of St. Andrews and worked in advertising. After devoting herself to writing she began working in

theater and television, but it is for her novels that she is best known. Her novels mix the heady feminism of the 1970s with both comedy and tragedy. The novels include *The Fat Woman's Joke* (1967), *Down Among the Women* (1971), *Female Friends* (1975), *Praxis* (1978), and *Puffball* (1980).

H. G. Wells (1866–1946)

Apprenticed at fourteen to a draper in Bromley, Kent, Wells won a scholarship to study with T. H. Huxley and graduated from the University of London in 1888. A high school teacher of biology until 1893, Wells began a career as a prolific writer with novels that initiate the modern subgenre of science fiction: *The Time Machine* (1895), *The Wonderful Visit* (1895), *The Island of Dr. Moreau* (1896), *The Invisible Man* (1897), and *The War of the Worlds* (1898). Later he turned to realism and political and social issues, and these books of his middle period include *Kipps* (1905), *Tono-Bungay* (1909), *Ann Veronica* (1909), *The History of Mr. Polly* (1910), and *The New Machiavelli* (1911). In the last part of his life, Wells wrote novels advocating his ideas such as *The World of William Clissold* (1926), and these are generally considered inferior to his earlier work.

Dame Rebecca West (1892–1983)

Educated in Edinburgh, and for a brief time in London, West adopted her name at the age of nineteen from a character in an Ibsen play. Her ardent feminism was expressed in journals such as the *Freewoman*, the *New Freewoman*, and the *Clarion*. Her novels include *The Return of the Soldier* (1918), *The Judge* (1922), *The Strange Necessity* (1928), *Harriet Hume* (1929), *The Thinking Reed* (1936), *The Fountain Overflows* (1956), and *The Birds Fall Down* (1966). She also published widely on topics as diverse as Yugoslavia and the Nuremberg trials.

Angus Wilson (1913–1993)

Wilson was born in Durban, South Africa, and was educated at Merton College, Oxford. His nonliterary career included stints at the Foreign Office and as deputy superintendent of the Reading Room of the British Museum. His early writings were mostly short stories until he published *Hemlock and After* (1952). This was followed by a steady stream of witty and satirical works that sometimes edge into black humor: *Anglo-Saxon Attitudes* (1956), *The Middle Age of Mrs. Eliot* (1958), *The Old Men at the Zoo* (1961), *Late Call* (1964), *No Laughing Matter* (1967), *As If by Magic* (1973), and *Setting the World on Fire* (1980).

Mary Wollstonecraft (1759–1797)

One of Britain's greatest and earliest feminists, Wollstonecraft first made her name with *Thoughts on the Education of Daughters* (1787). After spending some time in Ireland, she returned to write reviews and translations for the publisher J. Johnson. During a period in which she moved among the circle of Godwin, Holcroft, and Fuseli, she published her greatest works: *A Vindication of the Rights of Men* (1790), a piece in reply to Burke; *A Vindication of the Rights of Woman* (1792), her most important; and a novel, *Mary* (1788). She had a daughter in Paris by the American writer Gilbert Imlay, but later married Godwin, with whom she had Mary Shelley.

Virginia Woolf (1882–1941)

The daughter of the English essayist and historian Sir Leslie Stephen, Virginia Stephen was educated at home and read widely in her father's huge library. After she married the critic Leonard Woolf in 1912, they moved to the London district called Bloomsbury, and their home became a center for the artists, thinkers, and writers who have come to be called the Bloomsbury Group. She and Leonard founded the Hogarth Press in 1917. Woolf's first novel, *The Voyage Out* (1915), was relatively conventional, but the works that followed such as *Night and Day* (1919) and *Jacob's Room* (1922) featured an innovative lyricism and complex narrative structure. With the publication of *Mrs. Dalloway* (1925), *To the Lighthouse* (1927), and *The Waves* (1931), Woolf perfected her radical departures from the traditional English novel and established herself as one of the central figures of the modernist movement. In spite of serious psychological problems that had led to mental breakdowns in 1895 and 1915, Woolf wrote many essays and book reviews, as well as more conventional, lighter novels such as *Orlando* (1928) and *The Years* (1937). Among her most important critical volumes are the classics of modern feminism *A Room of One's Own* (1929) and *Three Guineas* (1938). Shortly after finishing her final novel, *Between the Acts* (1941), Woolf committed suicide.

Notes on Contributors

Gillian Beer is Professor of Literature and Narrative at Cambridge University and a Fellow of Girton College, Cambridge. Her publications include *Darwin's Plots*, *George Eliot*, and *Arguing with the Past*.

John Bender is Professor of English and Comparative Literature at Stanford University. He is the author most recently of *Imagining the Penitentiary: Fiction and the Architecture of Mind in Eighteenth-Century England*, which was awarded the Gottschalk Prize by the American Society for Eighteenth-Century Studies in 1987.

Toni O'Shaughnessy Bowers teaches eighteenth-century literature and women's studies at the University of Pennsylvania. She has published essays on eighteenth-century subjects and is currently completing the manuscript of her book entitled "Making Motherhood: British Literature and Middle-Class Maternal Ideals, 1680–1760."

Patrick Brantlinger is Professor of English and chair of the department at Indiana University. His most recent books are *Rule of Darkness: British Literature and Imperialism 1830–1914* and *Crusoe's Footprints: Cultural Studies in Britain and America*.

Jill Campbell teaches English at Yale University. She is the author of *Natural Masquerades: Gender and Identity in Fielding's Plays and Novels*, and she is currently writing a book on Pope, Lord Hervey, Lady Mary Wortley Montagu, and the construction of gender in eighteenth-century England.

Deirdre David is Professor of English and chair of the department at Temple University. The author of *Fictions of Resolution in Three Victo-*

rian Novels and *Intellectual Women and Victorian Patriarchy*, she is now completing a study entitled "'Grilled Alive in Calcutta': Women, Empire, and Victorian Writing."

Ina Ferris is Professor of English at the University of Ottawa, Canada. Among her publications are *The Achievement of Literary Authority: Gender, History and the Waverley Novels* and *William Makepeace Thackeray*. She is currently working on a study of the national tale in the early Romantic period.

Brian Finney is adjunct Professor at the University of Southern California. Among his publications are *Since How It Is: A Study of Samuel Beckett's Later Fiction, Christopher Isherwood: A Critical Biography*, and *The Inner I: British Literary Autobiography of the Twentieth Century*. He is currently at work on a book about the current generation of British postmodernist novelists.

David Galef is Assistant Professor of English at the University of Mississippi. Specializing in British modernism, he has published *The Supporting Cast: A Study of Flat and Minor Characters* and essays on Conrad, Joyce, Woolf, T. S. Eliot, and many others.

Michael Gorra is Associate Professor of English at Smith College. He is the author of *The English Novel at Mid-Century* and is completing a book on imperialism and the novel in the twentieth century.

George E. Haggerty is Associate Professor of English at the University of California, Riverside. He is the author of *Gothic Fiction/Gothic Form* and a wide range of essays on the eighteenth-century English novel. He is also the coeditor, with Bonnie Zimmerman, of *Professions of Desire: Lesbian and Gay Studies in Literature*. He is completing a book entitled *Forms of Resistance: The Female Novel of the Later Eighteenth Century*.

N. John Hall is Distinguished Professor of English at Bronx Community College and the Graduate School, City University of New York. Among his publications are *The Letters of Anthony Trollope* and *Trollope: A Biography*. He is currently writing a book on Max Beerbohm.

Lynne Hanley is Professor of Literature and Writing at Hampshire College. She is the author of *Writing War: Fiction, Gender and Memory*, and is currently writing a book entitled "The Other Wars" on the representation of modern warfare in novels and memoirs by women of color and women of "enemy" nations.

Richard Kroll is Associate Professor of English at the University of California, Irvine. He is the author of *The Material Word: Literate Cul-*

ture in the Restoration and Early Eighteenth Century. He has published essays on Restoration drama and Hobbes, Davenant, Dryden, and Locke, and he is currently at work on two anthologies of critical essays on intellectual and literary history, and a study of eighteenth-century notions of dissent.

John Kucich is Professor of English at the University of Michigan. He is the author of *Excess and Restraint in the Novels of Charles Dickens* and *Repression in Victorian Fiction*. He is currently writing a book about the relationship between ethics and politics in Victorian fiction.

George Levine is Kenneth Burke Professor of English and Director of the Center for the Critical Analysis of Contemporary Culture at Rutgers University. His most recent books are *The Realistic Imagination*, *Darwin and the Novelists*, and the volume of essays he has edited, *Realism and Representation*. He is currently working on a study of scientific objectivity, particularly in the nineteenth century, in its relation to literature and narrative.

Vicki Mahaffey is Associate Professor of English at the University of Pennsylvania. She is the author of *Reauthorizing Joyce* and numerous articles on modern literature. A Guggenheim Fellow in 1993–94, she is finishing a book entitled "The Fraying of the Plot: The Sub/Version of Representation in Modern Literature."

George McCartney teaches at St. John's University. His articles have appeared in various magazines and journals and his study of Evelyn Waugh, *Confused Roaring*, is published by Indiana University Press.

Carol McGuirk is Professor of English at Florida Atlantic University. Her research interests range from eighteenth-century poetry to contemporary fiction and cultural studies. Recent publications include an essay on William Gibson's cyberpunk novels of the 1980s for *Fiction 2000: Cyberpunk and the Future of Narrative* and an annotated edition of the poems of Robert Burns published by Penguin.

Anne K. Mellor is Professor of English and Women's Studies at the University of California at Los Angeles. Her most recent book is *Mary Shelley: Her Life, Her Fiction, Her Monsters*. She has edited *Romanticism and Feminism* and *The Other Mary Shelley: Beyond Frankenstein*.

Vincent P. Pecora is Associate Professor of English at the University of California, Los Angeles. Among his publications is *Self and Form in Modern Narrative*. He is currently writing a book on ethnology, modernism, and modern literary theory.

Robert M. Polhemus is Howard H. and Jessie T. Watkins Professor of English at Stanford University. He is the author of *Comic Faith: The Great Tradition from Austen to Joyce*, *The Changing World of Anthony Trollope*, and *Erotic Faith: Being in Love from Jane Austen to D.H. Lawrence*. He is currently at work on a book on faith in the child and child abuse in literature and contemporary life.

Mary Poovey is Professor of English at The Johns Hopkins University. Among her publications are *The Proper Lady and the Woman Writer* and *Uneven Developments*. She is currently writing a book on the development of statistical thinking in the eighteenth and early nineteenth centuries.

Barry V. Qualls is Professor and Chair of English at Rutgers University. Among his publications are *The Secular Pilgrims of Victorian Fiction: The Novel as Book of Life* and articles on the Bible and literature. He is currently at work on a study of English readings of the Bible and Bunyan in the nineteenth century.

Rubin Rabinovitz is Professor of English at the University of Colorado, Boulder. Among his publications are *The Reaction Against Experiment in the English Novel*, *Iris Murdoch*, *The Development of Samuel Beckett's Fiction*, *Innovation in Samuel Beckett's Fiction*, a book on computer word processing, and many essays on modern literature.

John Richetti is Leonard Sugarman Professor of English and chair of the department at the University of Pennsylvania. He is the coeditor of the Cambridge University Press Series in Eighteenth-Century Literature and Thought. Among his publications are *Popular Fiction Before Richardson: Narrative Patterns 1700–1739*, *Defoe's Narratives*, and *Philosophical Writing: Locke, Berkeley, Hume*. He is currently at work on a history of the eighteenth-century British novel and its relationship to social change.

Michael Rosenthal is Professor of English and Comparative Literature at Columbia University. In addition to numerous essays and reviews on twentieth-century British literature, he is the author of *Virginia Woolf* and *The Character Factory: Baden Powell's Boy Scouts and the Imperatives of Empire*. He is currently writing a biography of Nicholas Murray Butler.

G. S. Rousseau is Professor of English and Eighteenth-Century Studies at the University of California, Los Angeles. Among his recent publications is a trilogy of books, *Enlightenment Crossings*, *Perilous Enlightenment*, and *Enlightenment Borders: Pre- and Post-Modern Discourses*. Together with Sander Gilman, Roy Porter, and Elaine Showalter, he most recently published *Hysteria Beyond Freud*.

Daniel R. Schwarz is Professor of English at Cornell University. Among his publications are *Conrad: "Almayer's Folly" to "Under Western Eyes," Conrad: The Later Fiction, The Transformation of the English Novel, 1890–1930,* and *The Case for a Humanist Poetics.* In 1992–93 he held the Visiting Citizen's Chair of English at the University of Hawaii.

Michael Seidel is Professor of English and chairman of the department at Columbia University. He is the author of books on James Joyce, on Daniel Defoe, on narrative theory, and on satire. He also writes on baseball history, including books on Joe DiMaggio and Ted Williams.

Patricia Meyer Spacks is Edgar F. Shannon Professor and chair of the department of English at the University of Virginia. Among her publications is *Desire and Truth: Functions of Plot in Eighteenth-Century English Novels.* She is currently completing a book on boredom.

Robert Squillace is currently Assistant Professor of English at Wittenberg University. He has published an essay on Hardy's *Return of the Native* and is coediting with Edward Mendelson a new edition of Arnold Bennett's *Riceyman Steps.* He is now completing a study of Bennett's fiction.

G. A. Starr is Professor of English at the University of California, Berkeley. Among his publications are *Defoe and Spiritual Autobiography* and *Defoe and Casuistry.* His current research is on sentimental literature and on world's fairs.

John Allen Stevenson is Associate Professor of English at the University of Colorado, Boulder. He has written on both the eighteenth- and nineteenth-century British novel and is currently working on the political origins of the Gothic novel.

Kristina Straub is Associate Professor of Literary and Cultural Studies at Carnegie Mellon University. She has published a book on Frances Burney, *Divided Fictions: Fanny Burney and Feminine Strategy,* and a book on eighteenth-century actors, *Sexual Suspects.* She has coedited with Julia Epstein *Body Guards: The Cultural Politics of Gender Ambiguity* and is currently working on a study of identity in eighteenth-century narratives of sexual transgression.

Ronald R. Thomas is Associate Professor of English at Trinity College in Hartford, Connecticut. Among his publications are *Dreams of Authority: Freud and the Fictions of the Unconscious* and a number of articles on the novel, including essays on Dickens, Stevenson, and Beckett. He is currently working on a book entitled "Private Eyes and Public

Enemies: The Science and Politics of Identity in American and British Detective Fiction."

James Thompson is Professor of English at the University of North Carolina at Chapel Hill. His most recent book is *Between Self and World: The Novels of Jane Austen*, and he is currently completing a study of the origins of the novel and political economy.

David Trotter is Quain Professor of English Language and Literature at University College, London. Among his publications are *The Making of the Reader: Language and Subjectivity in Modern American, English and Irish Poetry*, *Circulation: Defoe, Dickens and the Economies of the Novel*, and *The English Novel in History 1895–1920*.

James Grantham Turner is Professor of English at the University of California, Berkeley. In addition to editing *Politics, Poetics and Hermeneutics in Milton's Prose* and *Sexuality and Gender in Early Modern Europe: Institutions, Texts, Images*, he has written *The Politics of Landscape: Rural Scenery and Society in English Poetry, 1630–1660* and *One Flesh: Paradisal Marriage and Sexual Relations in the Age of Milton*.

William Warner is Professor of English and Comparative Literature at the State University of New York, Buffalo. Among his publications are *Reading Clarissa* and *Chance and the Text of Experience*. He is currently working on a study of the early British novel entitled *The Elevation of the Novel in Britain*.

Judith Wilt is Professor of English at Boston College. She is the author of *Ghosts of the Gothic: Austen, Eliot, and Lawrence*, *Secret Leaves: The Novels of Walter Scott*, and *Abortion, Choice, and Contemporary Fiction: The Armageddon of the Maternal Instinct*.

Michael Wood is Professor of English Literature at the University of Exeter. Among his publications are *Stendhal*, *America in the Movies*, *García Márquez: One Hundred Years of Solitude*, and numerous essays on fiction and film. He has recently completed a study of Nabokov, and is currently working on a biography of Marcel Proust.

Index

Abandonment, 45, 86, 346–47

Abolition. *See* Antislavery movement

Academy (periodical), 473

Achebe, Chinua, 653; *No Longer at Ease,* 650

Ackroyd, Peter, 980–81; *Chatterton,* 981, 989; *The Great Fire of London,* 989; *Hawksmoor,* 981, 989; *The Last Days of Oscar Wilde,* 989; *The Last Testament of Oscar Wilde,* 981

Act of Settlement, 108

Adams, Henry, 610–11

Addison, Joseph, 20, 407, 424; *The Campaign,* 422

Adolescence, 181–82

Adorno, Theodor, 295

Adultery, 65, 784

Adulthood, 195, 257, 604

Adventure, xvi–xvii, 2, 47, 149

Adventure stories, 20, 503, 1000; imperial/military, 564–65, 573

Africa, 991; imperialism in, 561–62, 634–35, 647–52, 745; as setting, 47, 575–76, 994, 1000; stereotypes of, 573–75

Agency: political, 67–69

AIDS, 985–86

Albermarle (magazine), 616

Aldington, Richard, 716

Alexander, F. M., 752

Allen, Grant: *The British Barbarians,* 429; *Woman Who Did,* 620

Allen, Walter, 20, 478

All the Year Round (journal), 381

Altick, Richard: *The English Common Reader,* 327

Amatory fiction, 50, 70–71; agency expressed in, 67–69; culture and, 63–64; function of, 62–63; Harlequin romances as, 59–60; plots of, 51–52; sexuality in, 52–59; vows in, 65–67; women and men in, 60–62

America. *See* North America

American Revolution, 266, 267, 330, 484, 561

Amis, Kingsley, 895, 896, 898, 908; *The Alteration,* 901, 989; *The Anti-Death League,* 901, 989; *Bright November,* 989; *Colonel Sam,* 901; *The Crime of the Century,* 901; *Difficulties with Girls,* 901; *Ending Up,* 901; on experimental writing and modernism, 899–903, 916–17; Fielding's influ-

Amis, Kingsley (continued)
    ence on, 900–902; *A Frame of Mind,*
    989; *Girl, 20,* 901; *The Green Man,*
    901, 989; *I Like It Here,* 901, 989; *I
    Want It Now,* 901; *The James Bond
    Dossier,* 901; *Jake's Thing,* 900–1, 901,
    903; *Lucky Jim,* 900, 962, 989; *New
    Maps of Hell,* 901; *The Old Devils,*
    901, 989; *One Fat Englishman,* 900,
    989; *The Riverside Villas Murder,* 901;
    Russian Hide and Seek, 901; satire of,
    903–4; *Spectrum,* 901; *Stanley and the
    Women,* 900–901; *Take a Girl Like
    You,* 900–1, 901, 989; *That Uncertain
    Feeling,* 900, 989
Amis, Martin, 916–17, 980; *Money,* 977,
    979–80
Amritsar Massacre, 642–43
Andersen, Hans Christian, 453
Androgyny, 254–55
Angels, 393; in the house, 354, 392, 497,
    791
Angry Young Men, 755–56
Animation, 598–99
Anne, Queen of England, 20, 989
Anonymity: Scott's use of, 305–7; Trol-
    lope's use of, 460–61
Anthropology, 501, 725
Antielitism, 898, 902
Anti-heros, 843–44
Anti-imperialism, 562, 567
Antinovels, 1, 6–7, 843
Antipamela, 85
Anti-Semitism, 906
Antislavery movement, 389, 415, 561,
    565–66
Apartheid, 928–29
Apostles, 820
*Arabian Nights' Entertainments for Chil-
    dren, The,* 589
Architecture: as bogus, 868–73, 883, 885–
    86; in Gothic novels, 220, 233–34

Aries, Philippe, 587
Aristocracy, 88, 181, 333; intellectual,
    746–47; Richardson's portrayals of,
    83–84, 90
Aristotle, 273
Arithmetic. *See* Mathematics
Armstrong, Nancy, 58, 371, 378, 394,
    498
Arnold, Matthew, 402, 746; "To a
    Friend," 827–28
Arouet, François-Marie. *See* Voltaire
Artaud, Antonin, 582
Assimilation, 448–49
Athenaeum (periodical), 473
Atwood, Margaret, 964–65
Aubin, Penelope, 13, 139, 989; *Charlotta
    Du Pont,* 202; *Count Albertus,* 990;
    *The Life of Madam de Beaumount, a
    French Lady,* 990; *The Strange Adven-
    tures of the Count de Vinevil and His
    Family,* 990
Auchincloss, Louis, 902
Auden, W. H., 631, 742, 1002; *The
    Ascent of F6,* 763; on detective stories,
    970–71; *The Dog Beneath the Skin,*
    763
Augustine: *Confessions,* 591
Austen, Cassandra, 175
Austen, George, 990
Austen, Jane, xv, 20, 79, 128, 148,
    199–200, 328, 331–32, 336, 350,
    366, 390, 474, 821, 911–12, 955; *A
    Collection of Letters,* 990; critiques of,
    296–98; *Emma,* 275–76, 283–85,
    289, 296–97, 913, 948–49, 990; *A
    History of England,* 990; Imperial
    influences in, 563–64; *Lady Susan,*
    275; *Lesley Castle,* 990; literary influ-
    ence of, 275–77; *Love and Friendship,*
    990; *Mansfield Park,* 275, 290–93,
    362, 563–64, 990, 1002; narrative
    style of, 277–94; *Northanger Abbey,*

xix–xx, 275, 277–83, 284, 287, 990; *Persuasion,* 275, 288–90, 563–64, 990; *Pride and Prejudice,* 275–76, 285–88, 290, 825, 941, 961, 990; *Sanditon,* 275; *Sense and Sensibility,* 190, 275, 291, 339, 990; *The Watsons,* 275

Australasia, 562–63

Australia, 563, 568–70, 636, 727

Authority, 218, 267–68, 311, 394, 409, 801; in Eliot's work, 453–54; in Lawrence's work, 735–36; novelistic, 294–95, 297; skepticism of, 587, 603

Author of Waverley, 305. *See* Scott, Walter

Autobiography, 20; in novels, 148, 203–5, 360–61, 716, 755–57, 761–63, 771–73, 990, 1003–4, 1006; spiritual, 24, 26–27, 35, 88

Aztecs, 727–28

Bachelard, Gaston, 854

Bacon, Francis, 9–10

Bage, Robert: *Barham Downs,* 990; *The Fair Syrian,* 990; *Hermsprong,* 249–50, 255–57, 260, 267–68, 271–73, 990; *James Wallace,* 990; *Man as He Is,* 255, 566, 990; *Mount Henneth,* 990; narrative structure of, 272–73; on political issues, 267–68

Bagehot, Walter, 396

Banbridge, Beryl: *Harriet Said, Sweet William,* 968

Bair, Deirdre, 863

Baker, Ernest: *History of the English Novel,* 20–21

Baker, Samuel White: *Albert N'Yanza,* 573; *Cast Up by the Sea,* 573

Bakhtin, Mikhail M., xii–xiii, 103–5, 329, 560, 582, 655, 768; on dialogism, 856–57

Ballantyne, Robert: *Coral Island,* 573; *The Gorilla Hunters,* 574

Ballaster, Ros, 70

Balzac, Honoré de, xv, 21, 666, 906; *Human Comedy,* 560, 665, 676; *Père Goriot,* 721

Bank of England, 108

Bankruptcy, 407, 411

Barbauld, Laetitia, 17

Barker, Jane, 13, 88, 218; autobiographical writing of, 203–5, 990; *Bosvil and Galesia,* 203–5, 210; *Exilius,* 990; *Love Intrigues,* 990; *The Lining of the Patch-Work Screen,* 990; *A Patch-Work Screen for the Ladies,* 203–4, 990

Barnacle, Nora, 1003

Barnes, Julian: on fear, 974–75; *Flaubert's Parrot,* 967, 973–76; on history, 973–76; *A History of the World In 10' Chapters,* 975–76; *Metroland,* 975

Barrie, J. M., 588

Barthes, Roland, 275, 858; *S/Z,* 833

Bataille, Georges, 851

Bates, Ralph, 746

Bathurst, Allen Bathurst, 1st Earl, 168–69

Baudrillard, Jean, 948

Bayly, Charles: *Practice of Pietie,* 39

Beardsley, Aubrey, 577

Beckett, Samuel, 582, 600, 898, 912; *All Strange Away,* 858–59; "Assumption," 743, 990; "A Case in a Thousand," 843; character construction by, 843–44, 850–51; *Company,* 862–63, 865; *Dreams of Fair to Middling Women,* 843–44; *Endgame,* 854; "Enough" ("Assez"), 858; French used by, 849–50; *How It Is (Comment c'est),* 855–59; *Ill Seen Ill Said (Mal'vu mal dit),* 862, 864–65; *Imagination Dead Imagine (Imagination morte imaginez),* 858–60; *Krapp's Last Tape,* 854; use of language by, 552–58,

Beckett, Samuel (continued)
842–43, 845–47, 862–66; *Lessness
(Sans)*, 858–59, 861; *The Lost Ones
(Le Dépeupleur)*, 855, 858–61; *Malone
Dies (Malone meurt)*, 847, 850–52,
991; mathematics, use by, 859–62;
Mercier et Camier, 850; and modernism, 855–56; *Molloy*, 847, 850–51,
991; *More Pricks than Kicks*, 843–45,
991; *Murphy*, 845–47, 991; narrative
structure used by, 847–49; *Ping
(Bing)*, 858–59, 861; residua of,
858–62; *Stirrings Still*, 862; *Textes
pour rien (Texts for Nothing)*, 854–55;
The Unnamable (L'innommable), 847,
850, 852–55, 857, 991; *Waiting for
Godot*, 847, 850, 854–55, 991; *Watt*,
847–49, 859, 991; *Worstword Ho*,
862, 865–66

Beauties of Sterne, The, 166

Beckford, William: *Azemia*, 257–58;
*Dreams, Waking Thoughts, and Inci-
dents*, 991; *Modern Novel Writing*,
257–58; *Recollections of an Excursion
to the Monastries of Alcobaca and
Batalha*, 991; *Vathek*, 232–34, 239,
565, 991

Behavior: and character, 295–96; gender
and, 254–55, 261–63; men's, 255–57

Behn, Aphra, 1, 6–7, 12, 15, 51, 62, 71,
214; criticism of, 13, 18; *The Dumb
Virgin*, 53, 61; *The Fair Jilt*, 52,
56–57; gender reversal in, 56–57;
History of the Nun, 65–67; *Love-Letters Between a Nobleman and His Sister*, 52, 65, 88; *The Lucky Chance*,
991; *The Nun*, 60; *Oroonoko*, 14, 991;
The Rover, 991; sexual themes in,
52–53, 56; *The Unfortunate Bride*, 58;
writing structure of, 24–25

Benevolence, 338; and social action, 249,
257

Bennett, Dorothy Cheston, 683

Bennett, (Enoch) Arnold, 614, 684, 765,
942, 997; *Anna of the Five Towns*,
663, 676, 679, 991; *The Card*, 624,
991; *Clayhanger*, 624, 676, 991; Clayhanger trilogy, 663, 991; as critic,
661–62, 673; Five Towns novels,
676–77; *The Grand Babylon Hotel*,
991; *Hilda Lessways*, 624, 626, 991;
Imperial Palace, 663; *Leonora*, 626;
Lord Raingo, 663; *A Man from the
North*, 608, 623–24, 660, 663; *Mr.
Proback*, 991; narrative style of,
674–83; naturalism and moralism in
works of, 625–26; *The Old Wives'
Tale*, 625–27, 663, 675–76, 683, 991;
The Pretty Lady, 663, 676; as realist,
659–60, 663; *Riceyman Steps*, 663,
674, 677–83, 991; *The Roll Call*, 991;
Sacred and Profane Love, 674; on sub-
urban life, 624–25; success of,
662–63; *These Twain*, 626–27, 991;
The Truth about an Author, 660;
Whom God Hath Joined, 626

Benveniste, Emile, 852–53

Beowulf, 902

Bergson, Henri, 880

Berlin, Isaiah, 748

Berlin: as setting, 758–61, 1002

Berlin Conference, 635, 648

Bersani, Leo, 374, 378

Besant, Walter, 614

Beyle, Marie-Henri. *See* Stendhal

Bible, 31–32, 39

Bidpai tales, 926

Bigamy, 65, 67–68

Bildungsroman, xiii, 195–96, 377; and
sentimental novels, 181–82, 189–91,
196

Bishop, Elizabeth: "Crusoe in England,"
23

Black Panther, 969

Blacks, 693

Blackwood's Edinburgh Magazine, 470, 473, 483

Blair, Eric Arthur. *See* Orwell, George

Blake, William, 593, 725

Blavatsky, Madame, 730

Blessington, Lady: *The Governess,* 339

Bloom, Leopold, 912

Bloom, Molly, 912

Bloomsbury Group, 820, 905, 911–12, 915–16

Blumenbach, Johann Friedrich, 436

Bodichon, Barbara Leigh Smith, 441, 445

Bogusness: as theme, 868–76, 882–83, 885–87

Bongie, Chris: *Exotic Memories,* 574

Booker Prize, 939–40, 942, 989, 1000, 1006, 1009

Boone, Joseph, 377

Booth, Bradford, 474, 476

Booth, Charles: *Life and Labour of the People of London,* 611

Booth, Wayne: *The Rhetoric of Fiction,* 296–97

Borges, Jorge Luis, 582, 842, 947, 948

Boswell, James, 161

Bowen, Elizabeth, 746; *The Death of the Heart,* 992; *The Heat of the Day,* 992; *The Hotel,* 992; *The House in Paris,* 992; *The Last September,* 992

Bow Street Runners, 109–10

Boyd, William: *Brazzaville Beach,* 651

Boy's Own Paper, The, 573

Bradbury, Malcolm: *Eating People Is Wrong,* 992; *The History of Man,* 992; *Rates of Exchange,* 992; *Stepping Westward,* 992

Braddon, Mary Elizabeth, 354, 363–65, 480, 484, 496, 504; *Aurora Floyd,* 992; *The Doctor's Wife,* 992; *Henry Dunbar,* 992; *Ishmael,* 992; *Lady Audley's Secret,* 494–95, 501–2, 992

Bradley, F. H.: *Appearance and Reality,* 693

Bradshaigh, Lady, 94–95, 99, 175

Braine, John, 895

Brazil, 884–85

Brontë, Anne: *Agnes Gray,* 353, 992; *Poems, by Currer, Ellis and Acton Bell,* 992–93; *The Tenant of Wildfell Hall,* 353, 992

Brontë, Charlotte, 230, 380, 458, 824; and Emily Brontë, 373–74, 376–77, 379; characters developed by, 354–59, 361–63; children in works of, 584, 596; "Emma," 992; influence of, 363–67; *Jane Eyre,* 352–59, 361, 364–73, 497, 568, 584, 596, 946–47, 955–56, 992; narrative style of, 360–61; *Poems, by Currer, Ellis and Acton Bell,* 992–93; politics of, 359–60; *The Professor,* 360, 992; *Shirley,* 357–60, 363, 365, 371–73; on social issues, 367–71; *Villette,* 360–64, 372–73, 379, 992; on women's roles, 371–73, 955–56

Brontë, Emily, 371, 955–56; children in works of, 596; on class and sexuality, 377–79; criticism of, 376–79; on moral issues, 373–74; narrative style of, 374–76; *Poems, by Currer, Ellis and Acton Bell,* 992–93; *Wuthering Heights,* 353, 373–80, 497, 596, 993

Brooke, Emma Frances, 614; *The Excursion,* 993; *The History of Emily Montague,* 993; *History of Lady Julia Mandeville,* 993; *Letters from Juliet Lady Catesby,* 993; *The Old Maid,* 993; *Rosina,* 993; *The Siege of Sinope,* 993

Brooke, Henry, *Fool of Quality,* 185

Brookner, Anita, 943; *Brief Lives,* 941, 952–54; *The Debut,* 993; *Family and Friends,* 941, 993; *Hotel du Lac,* 939,

Brookner, Anita (continued)
942, 944, 950, 959–60, 993; *Latecom-
ers*, 941, 950; *Lewis Percy*, 946, 950;
Look at Me, 993; *A Misalliance*, 993;
narrative style of, 944, 950, 952–54;
Providence, 993; on women, 959–60
Brooks, Jocelyn, 748
Brophy, Brigid, 904
Brothels. *See* Prostitutes, prostitution
Browning, Robert: "Love among the
Ruins," 671
Brunton, Mary, 328, 331; *Self-Control*,
339
Buckingham and Chandos, Richard, 2d
duke of, 411
Bulwer-Lytton, Edward, 356, 429, 483,
493; *The Caxtons*, 569–70; *Harold,
Last of the Saxons*, 566
Bunyan, John, 20, 361, 371; *Pilgrim's
Progress*, xvii–xviii, 4, 24, 27–28, 410
Burckhardt, Sigurd, 177
Burdett-Coutts, Angela, 388
Burgess, Anthony, 967; *Beds in the East*,
993; *A Clockwork Orange*, 993; *The
Clockwork Treatment*, 993; *Earthly
Powers*, 993; *Enderby Outside*, 993;
The Enemy in the Blanket, 993; *Inside
Mr. Enderby*, 993; *Malayan Trilogy*,
993; *Time for a Tiger*, 993
Burke, Edmund, 214, 248, 333; *Philo-
sophical Enquiry into the Origin of Our
Ideas of the Sublime and the Beautiful*,
227; on the sublime, 340, 342,
344–46
Burlesque, 947–48
Burma, 744, 745
Burney, Charles, 212
Burney, Frances (Fanny) (Mme
d'Arblay), 145, 199, 219, 276, 303;
Camilla, 208–10, 213, 216, 993;
Cecilia, 206–7, 212–16, 252, 993;
Diary and Letters . . . (1778–1840),

994; *Early Diary 1768–78*, 994;
Evelina, 196–97, 205, 208–9, 213,
215, 252, 332, 993; as heroine,
200–201; marriage of, 207–8; as
novel writer, 199–200, 205–6, 217;
The Wanderer, 206–11, 213–14, 216,
339, 994; "The Witlings," 212; on
women's lives, 206–15, 955; as writer,
215–16
Burton, Richard: *The Arabian Nights*,
439–41; *Lake Regions of Central
Africa*, 573
Butler, Samuel, 706; *Erewhon*, 429, 576;
Hudibras, 63; *Way of All Flesh*, 823
Butler, Marilyn, 297–98
Butt, John, 382
Byatt, Antonia Susan (A. S. Byatt):
character development by, 944–46;
The Game, 994; narrative style of,
947, 950; *Possession*, 939, 941–43,
945–47, 950, 957, 994; *Shadow of a
Sun*, 994; *The Virgin in the Garden*,
945, 950–51, 994; on women,
956–57
Byrne, Clara Dacre, 339
Byron, George Gordon Byron, 6th
Baron, 301, 355, 568; *Manfred*, 345

Cabaret, 1002
Caird, Mona, 614
California, 748
Calvinism, 185, 591, 695–96
Cambridge University, 409, 820
Canada, 562–63
Cannibalism, 47, 239
Capitalism, 108, 115, 209–10, 217, 328,
330, 378
Carey, Peter, 942
Carleton, William, 570; *The Black
Prophet*, 569; *The Emigrants of
Ahadarra*, 569; *Fardorougha, the
Miser*, 569; *Traits and Stories of the*

Irish Peasantry, 567; *Valentine McClutchy*, 569

Carlyle, Thomas, 391, 418, 508, 510, 513, 725; *Chartism*, 357; *Past and Present*, 357; "Signs of the Times," 511

Carpenter, Edward, 723, 725, 824, 832

Carroll, Lewis (Charles Lutwidge Dodgson), 589, 913, 941; *Alice's Adventures in Wonderland*, 579, 581, 586, 590, 595, 597, 600, 994; *Alice's Adventures Under Ground*, 583; children in works of, 582, 584–87, 594, 603–6; criticism of, 602–3; dream- life used by, 600–601; fantasy used by, 583, 598–99; gender images used by, 595–96; *The Hunting of the Snark*, 994; identification with children by, 597–98; "The Jabberwocky," 601–2; use of language by, 592, 601–2; *Phantasmagoria and Other Poems*, 994; regression used by, 580–81; *Sylvie and Bruno*, 590, 994; *Sylvie and Bruno Continued*, 590; *Through the Looking-Glass and What Alice Found There*, 579–81, 585, 586, 590, 595–97, 600–602, 604, 994. *See also* Dodgson, Charles Lutwidge

Carter, Angela, 939, 942–44; *Black Venus*, 952; *Heroes and Villains*, 994; *The Infernal Desire Machines of Dr. Hoffman*, 945, 947, 950–52, 954; "The Kitchen Child," 952; on mass culture, 945; narrative style of, 946, 950, 951–52, 981–83; *Nights at the Circus*, 940, 945, 947, 981–83, 994; *The Sadeian Woman*, 940; *Shadow Dance*, 943; *Wise Children*, 940, 947, 950, 961, 963–64; on women, 961, 963–64

Carter, Frederick, 730

Carter, Margaret L., 244

Cary, Joyce: *The African Witch*, 745; *Aissa Saved*, 745; *An American Visitor*, 745; *Except the Lord*, 994; *Herself Surprised*, 994; *The Horse's Mouth*, 745, 994; *Mister Johnson*, 650, 745; *Not Honour More*, 994; *Prisoner of Grace*, 994; *To Be a Pilgrim*, 994

Cash, Arthur, 157

Cassirer, Ernest: *The Logic of the Humanities*, 695

Castle, Terry, 97

Castles: in Gothic novels, 220, 223, 225–27

Catholicism, 45, 79, 267, 273, 342, 385; in Scott's novels, 317, 321; Waugh's views on, 882, 886, 892–94

Cavaliers, 122, 124

Cecil, David: *Early Victorian Novelists*, 474

Celts, 315, 724

Censorship, 176–77, 1004

Cervantes, Miguel de, 19, 133; *Don Quixote*, 6, 127, 131; *Exemplary Novels*, 51

Ceylon, 727

Chambers, Jesse, 716–17

Chamier, Frederick, 565

Chaplin, Charles, 899

Chapman, Edward, 460

Charcot, Jean-Martin, 628

Charity, 257, 339, 383

Charles I, King of England, 40

Charles II, King of England, 13, 34, 313

Charlie, Bonnie Prince. *See* Stuart, Charles Edward

Chartism, 353, 357, 359, 411, 569

Chateaubriand, François-Auguste-René, Vicomte de: *Atala*, 184

Chatterjee, Bankim Chandra: *Rajmohan's Wife*, 568

Cheever, John, 902

Chesney, George: *Battle of Dorking*, 577

Chesterton, G. K., 888

Childhood, 583, 596, 604; in Carroll's works, 585–86, 605–6; in literature, 587–88

Children, 59, 106, 170, 601; abandonment of, 45, 86, 346–47; in Dickens's works, 392–93; historical considerations of, 590–93; in literature, 587–88, 593–98; as theme, 136, 140, 579–81, 583–86, 603–4, 966–67; in Victorian society, 582, 586–89, 604–5; violence and, 919–20

Children's books, 579, 584, 587–89, 1003

Chivalry, 145, 310

Christianity, 316, 512, 591, 694, 728; heroes and, 123–124; and paganism, 320, 730; and sexuality, 722–23; as theme, 45, 131, 891–93

Christian World (periodical), 473

Churchill, Winston, 907

Cibber, Colley, 94

Cities: Dickens on, 396–97; Isherwood on, 759–61; Joyce on, 769–70, 776; social degeneration of, 610–11; as theme, 144, 149, 152, 979–80. *See also* Urban life; *individual cities by name*

Civil war: English, 39–40; Spanish, 741–42, 745, 753

Clarke, Arthur, 302

Clarke, Marcus: *For the Term of His Natural Life*, 576–77

Class, 15, 79, 86, 155, 331, 410, 483, 588, 737, 743, 828, 839, 915; and Dickens's popularity, 382–83; distance and, 538–39; and gender, 730–31; gentlemen and, 426–28; and identity, 485–86; issues of, 82–85, 207, 377–78, 389–90, 535–36, 549, 715, 913; politics of, 321–24, 360, 367–69; professional, 488–91; and sexuality, 539–41, 544–45, 551–54.

See also Middle class; Poverty; Working class

Class struggle, 720

Cleland, John: *Memoirs of a Woman of Pleasure*, 85, 139

Clergy, 156, 238–39, 342. *See also* Priests and priesthood

Clifford, W. K., 454

Cockshut, A. O. J.: *Anthony Trollope*, 474

Cohn, Dorrit: *Transparent Minds*, 293

Cold War, 937

Coleridge, Samuel Taylor, 17, 73, 175–76, 342; *On the Constitution of Church and State*, 511; *The Statesman's Manual*, 510–11

Collins, William, 330

Collins, (William) Wilkie, 404, 480, 503; *Antonina*, 994; *Armadale*, 497–98, 500, 502, 995; *Basil*, 479, 497, 995; *The Dead Secret*, 489–91, 494, 499; *Hide and Seek*, 496; on identity and class, 485–89, 492–94, 500; *The Law and the Lady*, 498; life of, 504–5; *Man and Wife*, 498; *The Moonstone*, 500–502, 571, 995; mystery used by, 489–90; *No Name*, 492–93, 496, 498, 500, 502, 995; "The Perils of Certain English Prisoners," 570; as sensation novelist, 483–84, 995; *The Woman in White*, 485–89, 494, 497, 499–502, 505, 995

Colonialism, 369, 447, 450, 561–62, 649–50; childhood and, 605–6; education and, 652–53; Lessing on, 932–34

Color bar, 928–29

Comedy, 76, 87, 124, 127, 141, 179, 212, 300, 387, 558, 586, 592, 658; fantasy and, 598–99, 603; in imperial novels, 648–49; Joyce's, 775–76, 778, 785–86; Restoration, 88–91

Comic novels, xiii, 12

Commerce: as theme, 45–46

Communism, 743

Community: and society, 725–28, 736

Competition: among women, 960–65

Compton-Burnett, Ivy, 902, 912; *Men and Wives*, 744; *More Women Than Men*, 744

Comte, Auguste, 435, 438

Condition-of-England, 508; debate over, 509–12, 521, 531

Congo, 635, 694–95

Congreve, Richard, 9, 21, 90

Congreve, Mrs., 432

Connolly, Cyril, 747

Conquest, Robert, 901

Conrad, Joseph (Teodor Josef Konrad Korzeniowski), 503, 572, 649, 662, 749, 765; *Almayer's Folly*, 688–89, 711, 995; *The Arrow of Gold*, 711; artistic code of, 689–91; "Autocracy and War," 703; *Chance*, 708–10, 995; on cultural context, 693–98; emotional life of, 691–92; *Heart of Darkness*, 562, 574, 577, 634–35, 648, 651, 667, 688, 691–98, 701, 934, 995; on imperialism, 634–35; *The Inheritors*, 833, 998; on judgment, 698–702; "Karain," 692; "The Lagoon," 692; life of, 685–86; *Lord Jim*, 577, 686, 688, 691, 698–702, 995; Marlow tales, 691–702; *The Nigger of the Narcissus*, 689–91, 995; *Nostromo*, 651, 691–92, 702–6, 713, 995; *An Outcast of the Islands*, 688–89, 711, 995; *A Personal Record*, 686; political novels by, 702–8; psychological themes of, 685, 712; *The Rescue*, 691, 711; *Romance*, 833, 998; *The Rover*, 712–13; search for meaning by, 687–88; *The Secret Agent*, 620, 702, 706–7, 710, 713, 823, 995; "The Secret Sharer," 686, 692, 708–9, 711–12; sentimentalism of, 690–91; settings used by, 688–89; *The Shadow-Line*, 710–12; "A Smile of Fortune," 711; *Suspense*, 713; *Tales of Unrest*, 692; *Typhoon*, 995; *Under Western Eyes*, 702, 707–8, 713, 995; *Victory*, 708–11, 995; *Vidar*, 688; "Youth," 691–92

Consumption, 108, 210

Cooper, James Fenimore, 729; "Leatherstocking" tales, 735

Cooper, William, 895, 897, 904

Cornhill Magazine, 461

Corruption, 88, 145

Costes de la Calprenède, Gauthier de, 51

Counterpoint (periodical), 919

Counter-public sphere, 331–32

Court Secret, The, 131

Courtship-comedy, 76

Coutts, Angela Burdett, 570

Coveney, Peter, 584, 593

Coventry, Francis, 4, 7, 15, 17; "An Essay on the New Species of Writing Founded by Mr. Fielding," 1–2, 8

Cowper, William, 330

Crackanthorpe, Hubert: *Albermarle*, 616; *Wreckage*, 616

Crane, Stephen, 609

Crime: and detective novels, 501–2; in Fielding's works, 114–15; heredity and, 615–16; innocence and, 968–69; in sensation novels, 494–95; as theme, 24, 33, 494–95, 503, 970–72

Crisp, Samuel, 212, 215

Critical Review, The, 1010

Criticism: literary, 1–2; of modernists, 895–96; of novels, 3–5, 7–9

Cromwell, Thomas, 834

Crusades: in Scott's novels, 315–19

Crystal Palace Exhibition, 484–85

Culture, xiii–xiv, xv, xx, 13, 15–16, 19, 28, 63, 144, 222, 303, 320, 388, 394, 435, 718, 827, 945, 1007; British, xix, 918–19, 940–42; challenges to, 221–23; changes in British, 107–8, 123–24, 403–4; in Conrad's works, 693–98; and imperialism, 653–56, 995; Indian, 830–31; literary, 108–9; morality and, 762–63; novels' role in, 3–4, 17; and passion, 791–92; postmodernism and, 949–50; progress of, 431–32; sensation novels and, 479–80, 495–96; and sexuality, 591–92; subversion of, 239–40

Cunningham-Graham, R. B., 686–87, 706

Dacre, Charlotte: *Zafloya*, 234–35
Daily News, 384
Daily Telegraph, 473
Dallas, E. S., 365–66; *The Gay Science*, 354
Dana, Richard Henry, 385
Danby, Frank. *See* Frankau, Julia
Dante Alighieri: *Inferno*, 856
D'Arblay, Alexandre, 207–8
D'Arblay, Frances Burney, Mme. *See* Burney, Frances
Darnel, Aurelia, 144
Darwin, Charles, 438, 453; on natural selection, 610; *The Origin of Species*, 506
Darwin, Erasmus, 349
Davidoff, Leonore: *Family Fortunes*, 330
Davies, Emily, 430
Davy, Humphrey, 348
Davy, Mary: *Reform'd Coquet*, 332
Day, Thomas: *The History of Sandford and Merton*, 589
Day, William Patrick, 244
Day Lewis, C., 742
Death, 189, 310, 671, 790, 847, 971–72; in Beckett's works, 851–52; in *Clarissa*,

78–79; in Dickens's works, 400–402, 404; in Joyce's works, 785–86; sexuality and, 720, 843–844; as theme, 93, 770–71, 977
Decline and Fall of the British Empire, The, 711
Defoe, Daniel, 20, 50, 128, 132, 329; *Captain Singleton*, 23, 29–30, 33, 35–39, 47, 398; character development by, 40–48, 202; *Colonel Jack*, 23, 26, 29, 33, 36–38, 41–42, 45–46, 48; *An Essay on Projects*, 995; *An Essay upon Literature*, 36; forensics in, 33–34; history in work of, 26–27, 36–40; identity as theme in, 42–44; irony in, 33–35; *A Journal of the Plague Year*, 23, 31–34, 36, 42, 45, 47–48, 995; on meaning of experiences, 30–32; *Memoirs of a Cavalier*, 23, 28, 36, 39–40; *Moll Flanders*, 23–24, 26, 28–29, 32–33, 35–37, 40–46, 995; *The Review*, 995; *Robinson Crusoe*, xvi–xviii, 23–24, 26, 28–29, 31–36, 39–46, 567, 995; *Roxana*, 23–24, 26, 29–30, 33, 36, 40–41, 43–47, 202, 995; *Serious Reflections [on] Robinson Crusoe*, 26–27, 34; *The Shortest Way with Dissenters*, 995; structural style of, 24–25; *The True-Born Englishman*, 995; wealth as theme in, 29–30
Degeneracy, degeneration theory: of cities, 610–11; as theme, 612–16, 619–23, 625, 627–28
Dehumanization: war and, 913–14
Democracy: Liberal, 302
Demon-lovers, 228, 230
Dennis, Nigel, 895
Descartes, René, 846, 848, 857
Detective novels, 501–3, 970
Determinism, 106–7
Deutsch, Emmanuel: "The Talmud," 449

DeVries, Peter, 902

Dialects, 104, 737

Dialogism, xiii, 329, 856–57

Diaries: working, 459–60

Dibdin, Michael: *Cabal,* 967; *Ratking,* 967; *Vendetta,* 967

Dickens, Charles, xiii, xv, xvii–xviii, 21, 128, 143, 190, 363, 458, 504, 582, 665–66, 765, 896–97, 906, 911–13, 941, 981, 995; *All the Year Round,* 381, 384; *American Notes,* 388–89, 996; *Barnaby Rudge,* 385, 388, 476, 996; *Bleak House,* 384, 389, 392–93, 395, 397, 402–4, 498, 996; celebrity of, 381–82; children in works of, 582, 584, 587, 593–97; "The Chimes," 386; "A Christmas Carol," 190, 383, 397, 402, 996; class issues in works of, 389–90; on city life, 396–97; and Wilkie Collins, 480, 483, 493; cultural changes in, 403–4; *Daily News,* 384; *David Copperfield,* 383, 385, 389–90, 393–94, 402–5, 568–69, 593–94, 597, 666, 941, 996; *Dombey and Son,* 397–98, 404, 595–96; as editor, 404–5; female characters of, 392–94; *Great Expectations,* 389–91, 395, 397–98, 403, 564, 584, 947, 996; *Hard Times,* 388, 398, 996; *Household Words,* 384, 388, 403; *Little Dorrit,* 383, 388–90, 394, 397–98, 612, 963, 996; *Martin Chuzzlewit,* 390, 396, 400–401, 996; *Master Humphrey's Clock,* 396; moral issues in, 390–91; *The Mystery of Edwin Drood,* 404, 571, 996; nationalism of, 388–89; *Nicholas Nickleby,* 381, 388, 996; *The Old Curiosity Shop,* 381, 393, 396–98, 401, 593–96, 996; *Oliver Twist,* 384, 389, 393, 399–401, 996; *Our Mutual Friend,* 389, 392–393, 395–97, 402, 404, 996; "The Perils of Certain English Prisoners," 570; *The Pickwick Papers,* 381, 385, 395, 399, 996; on politics, 391–92; populism of, 383–88; psychology in works of, 399–402; realism of, 402–3, 503; religious themes in, 397–98; serial publication of, 395–96; *Sketches by Boz,* 388, 399, 623–24, 996; *A Tale of Two Cities,* 388, 394, 401–2, 566, 570, 996; *The Uncommercial Traveller,* 400

Dickinson, Emily, 957

Dickinson, Goldsworthy Lowes, 820

Diderot, Denis, 73–74, 97–98

Discourse: indirect, 289–90, 293–94; novelistic authority and, 294–95

Disraeli, Benjamin: *Coningsby,* 509–10, 512–20, 996; on gender issues, 516–18, 531; on homosocial issues, 518–20; *Lothair,* 996; on politics, 513–16; *Sybil,* 512, 520–21, 523, 996; *Tancred,* 512, 570, 572, 996; *Vivian Grey,* 996; Young England trilogy, 512

Dodgson, Charles Lutwidge, 584; life of, 582–83. *See also* Carroll, Lewis

Domestic life, xvi–xvii, 112, 335; in Austen's works, 276–80; in Brontës' works, 354, 359, 380; in Dickens's works, 392–93; non-erotic, 337–39; patriarchal, 346–49; spheres in, 331–32, 340; Victorian, 392–93, 497; women's role in, 366–67, 371–72, 525–26

Dostoevsky, Fyodor Mikhaylovich, xv, 703, 732, 906, 911; *Crime and Punishment,* 571

Doubling, 389–90

Dowie, Ménie Muriel, 614

Doyle, Arthur Conan, 503, 615, 573; *The Adventures of Sherlock Holmes,* 996; "The Boscombe Valley Mystery," 502; "The Crooked Man," 502;

Doyle, Arthur Conan (continued)
  The Exploits of Brigadier Gerard, 996;
  The Hound of the Baskervilles, 996;
  The Lost World, 577, 996; *The Memoirs of Sherlock Holmes,* 996; *Micah Clarke,* 996; *Rodney Stone,* 996; *The Sign of Four,* 502; "The Speckled Band," 502; *A Study in Scarlet,* 996; *The White Company,* 566, 996
Drabble, Margaret, 939–40, 943–45, 951; *The Gates of Ivory,* 942, 950, 963; *The Ice Age,* 942, 950, 997; *A Natural Curiosity,* 942, 950, 962–63; *The Radiant Way,* 942, 945, 950, 954, 956, 962, 964–65; *The Realms of Gold,* 997; settings used by, 941–42; *A Summer Bird-Cage,* 943, 950, 956, 961–62, 997; on women, 956, 961–65
Dreams, 581, 598, 600–601, 603
Dreiser, Theodore, 609
Dryden, John, 128; *Absalom and Achitophel,* 25
Dublin: as setting, 769–70, 776, 779
Dunlop, John, 7, 14, 17; *History of Fiction,* 5, 9–13; novel as multinational in, 19–20
Dunne, Mary Chavelita. *See* Egerton, George
Durrell, Lawrence, 895, 916

Eagleton, Terry, 83, 377–79
East India Company, 561
Echelin, Lady, 5; on *Clarissa,* 95–96
Economy, xviii, 63, 108, 340, 407; English, 128–29, 508; political, 44, 509–10, 516, 529; and sensation novel, 482–83, 499–500; Thackeray on, 411–14, 421; women and, 369–70
Edgeworth, Maria, 303, 328, 331, 349–50; *The Absentee,* 333, 567, 997;

Belinda, 332–34; *Castle Rackrent,* 565, 567, 997; *Early Lessons,* 589; on equality, 333–34; "The Grateful Negro," 565; *Letters for Literary Ladies,* 336–37, 997; on love, 336–37; *Ormond,* 997
Edgeworth, Richard Lovell, 337
Edinburgh Review, 305, 473
Education, 155, 333, 434, 717, 791; of children, 588, 591–92; of colonials, 652–53; female, 224, 339; in history, 973–74; process of, 189–91; as theme, 136, 264
Education Act of 1870, 573
Edward VII, King of England, 784, 820
Edwardian era, 659, 706, 819–20, 834, 839–40; imperialism and, 561, 573–78
Egan, Pierce, 398
Egerton, George (Mary Chavelita Dunne), 614; "The Regeneration of Two," 623
Egoist, The (journal), 1003
Egypt, 941
Eliot, George (Marian Evans), xv, xviii, 21, 81, 230, 277, 355, 360, 366, 369, 391, 402, 458, 475, 481, 533, 897, 906, 911, 954–55, 980; *Adam Bede,* 430, 432, 454, 997; authority of, 453–54; Brontë's impact on, 363–65; character development by, 441–42, 451–52; children in works of, 582, 584, 587, 594, 596; cross-gender characteristics of, 452–53; *Daniel Deronda,* 430–31, 434, 439, 444, 447, 449–50, 454, 997; everyday experiences in, 429–30; *Felix Holt, the Radical,* 430–31, 447, 450–51, 997; "Felix Holt's Address to the Working-Men," 450; on gender and supremacism, 450–51; on heroines, 443–44; on heroism *vs.* ordinary life, 433–34;

on history, 454–55; ideas used by, 438–40; *Impressions of Theophrastus Such,* 997; on knowledge, 437–38; "The Lifted Veil," 439–40; *Middlemarch,* 364, 430–32, 434, 437–43, 447–49, 451–55, 503, 612, 925–26, 961, 997; *The Mill on the Floss,* 364–65, 430, 433–37, 440, 447, 452, 503, 596–97, 913, 997; "Notes on Form in Art," 437–38, 454–55; on power and society, 434–36; on race, 436–37, 447–50; reinterpretation by, 432–33; *Romola,* 431, 439, 442, 444–47, 476, 566, 997; on rural life, 446–47; *Scenes of Clerical Life,* 430, 433; *Silas Marner,* 430, 447–48, 584, 594, 596, 997; on social change, 430–31; *The Spanish Gypsy,* 449

Eliot, T. S., 708, 777, 834, 878, 989; *After Strange Gods,* 729; *Waste Land,* 742

Elitism, 902

Ellis, Kate Ferguson, 231

Ellis, Sarah, 366; *The Daughters of England,* 354; *The Women of England,* 367–68

Emblems: narrators as, 41–42

Emigration, 569–70

Emotions, 91, 271; in Austen's works, 280–82, 284–87, 291–92; in Conrad's work, 691–92; expression of, 259–60; gender and, 791–93; in Gothic novels, 227, 969; in Inchbald's work, 260–64; women's, 259, 793–94

Encounter (periodical), 896

Energy, 259–60, 262

Engels, Friedrich, 613

England, 314, 333; as setting, 306, 940–42

English Review, 998

Enlightenment, 74, 298, 301, 667, 846, 848

Environment: role of, 609–10, 614

Epics, xii, 9, 306; Fielding's use of, 115–16, 119; mock, 777–79; as model, 112–13

Epstein, Julia, 210, 215–16

Equality: gender, 251, 254–55, 331, 333–34, 339

Eroticism, 13, 75, 512, 520, 588, 637; in Richardson's works, 94, 99–100; women's suffrage and, 721–22

Espionage, 876. *See also* Spying

Essex, Robert Devereux, 2d earl of, 226

Ethics, 820, 908; gentlemanly, 407–8, 419–20

Ethnicity, 449–50. *See also* Race

Eugenics, 620

Evans, Marian (Mary Ann). *See* Eliot, George

Evening Standard, 661

Evil Mother, 747

Examiner (journal), 1005

Exoticism, 574

Experiences: meanings of, 30–31

Experimental writing, 897–98; Amis on, 899–900, 916–17. *See also* Modernism and modernists

Fairie Queen, The, 902

Fairfax, Thomas, 40, 45–46

"Fair Triumvirate," 51

Fairy tales, 590

Family, 45, 152, 222, 328, 331, 333, 346, 349, 367, 392, 482; in Gothic novels, 222, 231; in Joyce's works, 778–79, 786–87; in Lawrence's works, 717–18, 720; primacy of, 330, 703, 713; in Richardson's novels, 74, 97–98, 100; in Smollett's novels, 139, 147; Sterne's, 155–56; in Woolf's novels, 794–96, 807–8

Famine: Irish potato, 411

Fantasy, 220, 237, 583, 590; Carroll's
    use of, 598–99, 602–3
Farce: by Fielding, 103–4; in Gaskell's
    works, 523–24
Farrell, J. G.: *The Siege of Krishnapur*,
    643
Fascism, 745, 753
Faulkner, William, 902–3
Fear, 974–75
Federman, Raymond, 947
Feelings. *See* Emotions
Felski, Rita, 331
Females. *See* Women
Femininity, 195, 202, 254, 318, 370;
    definitions of, 209, 250; and sexuali-
    ty, 776–77
Feminism, 22, 251, 302, 333, 498, 509,
    902, 939; in Brontës' writings, 353,
    370; of *Jane Eyre*, 352–53; and social
    issues, 525–26, 529; and women nov-
    elists, 217–18, 964, 1001, 1005,
    1009, 1014
Feminist criticism, xvi, 18, 217–18, 231,
    444; of Burney, 199, 219; of Gothic
    novels, 225–26, 231; of Sterne,
    176–77
Fenton, James: *A Staffordshire Murder*,
    966
Ferrier, Susan, 328, 331–32, 342; *Mar-
    riage*, 334–36
Feuerbach, Paul Johann Anselm von
    Ritter, 443; *Essence*, 997
Fiction: creating, 11–12; criticism of,
    3–5; definition of, 9–10; history of,
    10–11. *See also by type*
Fielding, Charlotte Cradock, 997
Fielding, Henry, xiii, xvii–xviii, 4, 9, 12,
    20, 50, 132, 138, 152, 157–58, 214,
    277, 329, 398, 901–2; *The Adventures
    of Joseph Andrews and His Friend, Mr.
    Abraham Adams*, 7–8, 77, 84–86,
    105–7, 111–12, 119–21, 138, 202,
900; *Amelia*, 107, 113–14, 123–25,
    296, 308, 425, 997–98; *An Apology for
    the Life of Mrs. Shamela Andrews*, 77,
    84–86, 110–11, 118–19, 124, 998;
    The Author's Farce, 103–7, 997; char-
    acter development by, 116–17,
    122–23, 165–66, 189, 276; civil activ-
    ities of, 109–10; critiques of, 1, 8,
    17–18, 443; on culture change,
    123–24; discourse by, 103–5; epics
    and, 115–16; on female heroism,
    124–25; on historical determinism,
    106–7; *The Historical Register for
    1736*, 997; *The History of Tom Jones, a
    Foundling*, 2, 7–8, 105–7, 111,
    121–23, 137–38, 157, 161, 166, 201,
    303, 900, 997–98; on identity, 105–6;
    Jonathan Wild, 114–18; literary histo-
    ry by, 102–3; narrative technique of,
    24, 110–15, 119–20, 137; novel
    acceptability, 5–7; *Pasquin*, 997; plays
    by, 103–4, 997; political writings of,
    118–19, 121–22; *Rape upon Rape*,
    997; replacement fictions by, 3,
    14–15; and Richardson, 73, 84–85,
    95, 112–13; as satirist, 84–85, 128,
    264; *Tom Thumb*, 124, 997; and Wal-
    pole, 107, 109
Fielding, Sarah, 94, 139; *The Adventures
    of David Simple*, 185, 192, 194, 998;
    *Familiar Letters Between the Principle
    Characters in David Simple*, 998;
    Remarks on Clarissa, 95; *Volume the
    Last*, 998
Finances, 482; and identity, 486–87
Firbank, Ronald, 878–80, 985; *Caprice*,
    998; *The Flower Beneath the Foot*,
    998; *Inclinations*, 998; *Odette
    d'Antrevernes*, 998; *Prancing Nigger*,
    998; *Santal*, 998; *Sorrow in Sunlight*,
    998; *Vainglory*, 998; *Valmouth*, 998
Fitzgerald, Edward, 385

Flaubert, Gustave, xv, 21, 160, 665; *Madame Bovary*, 658, 955, 976

Fleming, Ian, 901

Fletcher, John, 851

Fools: wise, 183

Forçade, Eugene, 357, 371

Ford, Ford Madox, 728, 819; *The Brown Owl*, 833; *The Fifth Queen*, 833–34, 998; *The Good Soldier*, 834–37, 839, 998; *Half Moon*, 834; *Henry for Hugh*, 839; historical novels by, 833–34; *The Inheritors*, 833, 998; *Ladies Whose Bright Eyes*, 834; *The Last Post*, 837; *A Little Less than Gods*, 834; *A Man Could Stand Up*, 837, 840; *The Marsden Case*, 838; narrative style of, 833–40; *No More Parades*, 837; *Parade's End*, 833, 837–38, 998; *The Rash Act*, 839; *Romance*, 833, 998; *The Shifting of the Fire*, 833; social commentary by, 838–39; *Some Do Not . . .* , 837

Forensics, 33–34

Fornightly Review, 473

Forster, E. M., 623, 635, 661, 715, 741, 751, 819, 904; *Aspects of the Novel*, 824–25, 999; character development by, 824–26, 828–29; *Howards End*, 823, 25–30, 832, 839–40, 999; on imperialism, 636–37, 640–43; on India, 829–32; and Isherwood, 756–57; on landscape, 823–24; *The Longest Journey*, 621, 820, 822–23, 825–826, 999; *Maurice*, 822, 832–33, 840, 999; narrative style of, 820–33; *A Passage to India*, 631, 636–37, 640–43, 829–32, 905, 999; *A Room with a View*, 823–26, 999; *Two Cheers for Democracy*, 999; *Where Angels Fear to Tread*, 820–21, 823, 998

Forster, John, 385

Forsyte Saga, The, 882

Foucault, Michel, 5, 221, 237, 294–95, 304, 571; *The History of Sexuality*, 495

Fowles, John, 967

France, 85, 247, 306, 561; naturalist fiction in, 609–10; romances from, 1–2, 51

Franco, Francisco, 742, 745

Frankau, Julia: *A Babe in Bohemia*, 614

Fraser's Magazine, 392, 1012

Frazer, James: *The Golden Bough*, 725, 430

Freedom(s), 316, 752–53, 820, 826

Freewoman (journal), 1014

Free trade, 561

Frei, Hans, 35

French Revolution, 210, 247, 251, 294, 297–98, 394, 561, 565

Freud, Sigmund, 222, 240–41, 400, 582, 776; *Civilization and Its Discontents*, 820; *Studies on Hysteria*, 628–29

Frow, John, 7

Fukuyama, Francis, 307; *The End of History and the Last Man*, 302–3

Gallagher, Catherine, 523

Galsworthy, John: *A Commentary*, 711; *Fraternity*, 822

Galt, John: *Annals of the Parish*, 565

Galvani, Luigi, 348

Gandhi, 642

García Márquez, Gabriel, 582, 977

Gardiner, Marguerite, 328

Garnett, Edward, 686, 705, 732

Gaskell, Elizabeth, 360, 365–66, 369, 390, 404, 464, 992; *Cranford*, 564; farce used by, 523–24; "Lizzie Leigh," 524; *Mary Barton*, 510, 521–30; *North and South*, 360, 530; *Ruth*, 524, 530; on social issues, 521–23, 528–30

Gay, John, 108; *The Beggar's Opera,* 115

Gee, Maggie: *The Burning Book,* 977

Gender, 16, 194–95, 290, 333, 423, 450, 605; behavior and, 254–57, 261–63; and class, 535, 730–31; criticism and, 216–17; Eliot's views of, 452–53; emotions and, 791–93; equality of, 331, 339–40; identity and, 120–21, 218, 596, 721; ideology of, 200, 215, 329–30; issues of, xvi, 15, 201, 207, 250–53, 715, 955; literary criticism and, 303–4; and novel writing, 307–8; Orientalism and, 316–19; politics and, 509–10, 516–17, 531; of professionals, 494–96; reversal of, 56–57; roles of, 367–68; social images of, 595–96

Gentlemen, 155, 667; ethics of, 407–8; images of, 122–23; Thackery's treatment of, 409, 413–27; Victorian, 427–28

Gentry, 83, 88

Geography, 36–37

George II, King of England, 146

George IV, King of England, 317, 408, 1008

Géricault, Théodore: *Raft of the Medusa,* 975

Gibbon, Edward: *Decline and Fall of the Roman Empire,* 315

Gide, André, 676

Gilbert, Sandra M., 231; *Madwoman in the Attic,* 366

Gissing, George Robert, 473, 623; *Born in Exile,* 999; *Demos,* 611, 614; *The Nether World,* 611–13, 999; *New Grub Street,* 611, 999; *The Odd Women,* 621, 999; *The Private Papers of Henry Ryecroft,* 618; *Thyrza,* 612, 999; *The Unclassed,* 611–12; *Whirlpool,* 562, 577; *Workers in the Dawn,* 611–12, 999; on working

class, 611–12, 614; *In the Year of Jubilee,* 611, 621; on Zola, 609, 616, 618

Glendenning, Victoria, 475

Glorious Revolution, 64–65, 67, 108, 121, 667

Godwin, Mary Wollstonecraft. *See* Wollstonecraft, Mary

Godwin, William, 12, 248, 294, 331, 967, 1001–2, 1009, 1015; *Caleb Williams,* 241–42, 249, 255, 260, 268–72, 274, 330, 999; *Cloudesley,* 999; *Deloraine,* 999; *Enquiry Concerning Political Justice,* 999; *Fleetwood,* 999; *Mandeville,* 999; plot construction by, 271–74; on political issues, 268–71; *St. Leon,* 999

Goethe, Johann Wolfgang von, 154; *Werther,* 337–38

Golding, William, 895; *The Brass Butterfly,* 1000; *Darkness Visible,* 1000; *Free Fall,* 1000; *Lord of the Flies,* 916, 1000; *The Paper Men,* 1000; *Pincher Martin,* 1000; *The Pyramid,* 1000; *Rites of Passage,* 1000; *The Scorpion God,* 1000; *The Spire,* 1000

Goldsmith, Oliver, 398; *The Deserted Village,* 1000; *She Stoops to Conquer,* 1000; *Vicar of Wakefield,* 185, 1000

Goncourt, Edmond de: *Cherie,* 597

Gordimer, Nadine, 652

Gordon, Lord George, 385

Gothic novels, 220, 497, 969, 1006–7; criticism of, 225–26, 244–45; cultural values and, 221–23; history in, 319–20; horror in, 242–43; Irish, 849–50; paranoia in, 243–44; perversity in, 232–40; and sentimental fiction, 224–25; sexuality in, 241–42

Government: role of, 511–12, 515–16, 531

Grand, Sarah, 623; *The Beth Book,* 618, 620; "Eugenia," 620; *The Heavenly Twins,* 615, 618; *Ideala,* 615

Grant, James, *First Love and Last Love,* 571

Grass, Günter, 977; *The Tin Drum,* 587

Graver, Suzanne, 445

Graves, Caroline, 505

Graves, Richard, *The Spiritual Quixote,* 145

Gray, Alasdair, *Lanark,* 980

Gray, Thomas, 330, 1013

Great Britain, 306. *See also* England; Ireland; Scotland

Great Exhibition of 1862, 484–85

Great Mutiny of 1857, 388, 562, 570

Great Unknown, 305. *See also* Scott, Walter

Great Wrong Place, 971

Green, Martin, 650

Greene, Graham, 572, 819, 829, 867, 899; *Brighton Rock,* 746, 1000; *A Burnt- Out Case,* 649; *Comedians,* 651; *A Gun for Sale,* 745–46; *The Heart of the Matter,* 649, 1000; *It's a Battlefield,* 745–46, 874–75; *Our Man in Havana,* 875–76, 1000; *The Power and the Glory,* 1000; *The Quiet American,* 1000; satire by, 874–76; *Stambul Train,* 745, 1000

Greimas, A. J., 851

Grey, Mrs., 496

Grossmith, George: *Diary of a Nobody,* 624

Gruen, John, 847

Gubar, Susan, 231; *Madwoman in the Attic,* 366

Guilt, 550–51, 793–94

Gypsies, 317, 436–37, 447, 449

Habermas, Jürgen, 424

Haggard, H. Rider, 503; *Allan Quartermain,* 574; "'Elephant Smashing' and 'Lion Shooting'," 575; *King Solomon's Mines,* 567, 574, 648, 1000; *Nada the Lily,* 574; romance and empire in, 574–75; *She,* 574, 1000

Haiti, 566, 651

Hall, Catherine: *Family Fortunes,* 330

Hamilton, Elizabeth, 328, 342

Hanoverians, 313, 317

Hanway, Mary Ann: *Ellinor,* 254–55, 258, 264, 272

Hardwicke, Earl, 146

Hardy, Barbara, 361

Hardy, Emma, 534

Hardy, Florence, 504

Hardy, Thomas, 437, 503–4, 1000; on class and sexuality, 534, 535–36, 538–44, 549–54; on containment and protection, 537–38; *Desperate Remedies,* 540, 544–51, 554, 556–57, 1001; *Far from the Madding Crowd,* 539, 543, 1001; *A Group of Noble Dames,* 1001; *The Hand of Ethelberta,* 533, 538–39, 551, 558, 1001; "An Indiscretion in the Life of an Heiress," 533, 539; *Jude the Obscure,* 533, 538–39, 544, 551, 554-58, 619, 689, 1001; *A Laodicean,* 539–40, 542, 545, 551, 1001; and D. H. Lawrence, 729–30; *Life's Little Ironies,* 1001; *The Mayor of Casterbridge,* 534, 541, 1001; on moral order, 541–42, 619; *A Pair of Blue Eyes,* 538–41, 545, 551–52, 555, 1001; "The Poor Man and the Lady," 539, 1001; *The Return of the Native,* 539, 1001; self-consciousness of, 536–37; *Tess of the d'Urbervilles,* 534, 538–39, 552–54, 558, 619, 1001; *The Trumpet Major,* 540–41, 545, 566, 1001; *Two on a Tower,* 539–41, 545, 551, 1001;

Hardy, Thomas (continued)
   Under the Greenwood Tree, 533, 539, 545, 555, 1001; on vision, 544–49, 554–58; *The Well-Beloved,* 538–39; *Wessex Tales,* 1001; *The Woodlanders,* 539, 545, 1001
Harkness, Margaret, 612; *A City Girl,* 613; *In Darkest London,* 613; *A Manchester Shirtmaker,* 613; *Out of Work,* 613
Harrison, Frederic, 439
Harrison, Jane: *Ancient Art and Ritual,* 725
Hartley, L. P.: *The Go-Between,* 981
Hassan, Ihab: *Exploring Postmodernism,* 949
Hastings, Warren, 561–62
Hawthorne, Nathaniel, 483
Hays, Mary, 218, 331, 372, 1009; *Appeal to the Men of Great Britain on Behalf of the Women,* 1001; *Female Biography,* 1001; *Memoirs of Emma Courtney,* 248, 255, 259–60, 272, 1001; *A Victim of Prejudice,* 339, 1001
Haywood, Eliza, 1, 6–7, 15, 62, 71, 131, 139, 214; *Anti-Pamela,* 85; *British Recluse,* 60–61; criticism of, 13, 18, 218; *Force of Nature,* 60; on love, 51–52; *The History of Jenny and Jemmy Jessamy,* 1001; *History of Miss Betsey Thoughtless,* 218, 332, 1001; *Love in Excess,* 14, 54–55, 58, 60–61, 68–69, 1001; *Memoirs of a Certain Island Adjacent to the Kingdom of Utopia,* 1001; *The Perplex'd Dutchess,* 53; *Reflections on the Various Effects of Love,* 51; structure of writing of, 24–25
Hazlitt, William, 17, 214
Heard, Gerald, 747
Hedonism, 620–21
Hegel, Georg Wilhelm Friedrich, 301–2, 408

Hemingway, Ernest, 902
Hennell, Sara, 442
Henry IV, King of England, 311
Henry V, King of England, 311
Henty, G. A., 573
Herbert, Frank, 302
Heredity, 629; crime and, 615–16; role of, 609–10, 614–15
Henry VIII, 833
Heroes, 228, 249, 254, 732; ideology of, 255–57; ineffective, 705–6; modernism, 780–81; in Scott's novels, 308–10, 321; sentimental, 183–84, 186–89, 195
Heroines, 62, 260, 955; androgyny in, 254–55; comedic, 89–90; Eliot on, 443–44; gender issues and, 251–52; Gothic, 225–28, 232; and love, 201–7; in Richardson's novels, 74, 81; Romantic, 332–33; sentimental, 181, 193–96; as victims, 249–50
Heroism, 131, 514, 699; epic, 115–16; female, 113, 124–25; in Fielding's novels, 122–23; masculine, xvi, 79, 112; *vs.* ordinary life, 433–34
Heteroglossia, xii, 104, 329, 768
Hiroshima, 977
Historical novels, 320, 339, 814; Ford's, 833–34; role of, 566–67; Scott's, 308–19, 566, 1010
Histories, 1, 6, 145, 247
Historiography, 304
History, xviii–xix, 8–9, 116, 506, 509, 819; in Defoe's work, 26–40; and economy, 482–83; in Fielding's work, 102–3, 105–7, 121, 125; individuals and, 454–55; literary, 10–12, 15, 17–18, 20–22; in Scott's novels, 308–21; social, 112–13; as theme, 973–76, 980–81; of thought, 746–47; Wells on, 661–62. *See also* Universal History
Hitler, Adolf, 740–41

Hive (journal), 387

Hobbes, Thomas, 165; *Leviathan,* 44

Hobsbawm, E. J., 482, 503

Hoffman, E. T. A., 947

Hogarth, William: 127; "The Rake's Progress," 136

Hogg, James: *The Domestic Manners and Private Life of Sir Walter Scott,* 1001; *The Private Memoirs and Confessions of a Justified Sinner,* 239, 243–44, 1001; *The Queen's Wake,* 1001; *The Three Perils of Man,* 1001

Holcroft, Thomas, 1001; *The Adventures of Hugh Trevor,* 1002; *Anna St. Ives,* 249–54, 260, 262, 271–72; *The Road to Ruin,* 1002

Hollinghurst, Alan: *The Swimming Pool Library,* 984–85

Holy Trinity, 581

Home, 139. *See also* Domestic life

Homer, 8; *Iliad,* 781; *Odyssey,* 768, 777–82, 785

Homespun, Prudentia. *See* West, Jane

Homoeroticism, 637, 646, 719

Homophobia, 240–41

Homosexuality, 623, 647, 725, 913; attraction of, 718–19; in Disraeli's works, 518–20; Forster on, 832–33, 999; in Gothic novels, 239–41, 244; in Hollinghurst's novels, 984–86; in Isherwood's novels, 755, 760, 1002; Lawrence and, 720, 724, 729

Hong Kong, 636

Hood, Thomas, 590

Hook, Andrew, 303

Hook, Theodore, 398

Hope, Thomas: *Anastasius,* 567–68

Hopkin, William, 725

Horror, 242–43

House, Humphrey, 386, 396

Household Words (journal), 384, 388, 403, 570

Howard, Edward, 565

Howard, Katherine, 833–34

Howells, William Dean, 474, 611

Hudson, Derek, 583

Hudson, George, 411

Hughes, Thomas: *Tom Brown's Schooldays,* 589

Hugo, Victor: *Les Misérables,* 766

Huitzilopochtli (Tezcatlipoca), 728

Hulme, Keri, 942

Hulme, T. E., 184, 905–6

Humanism, 441, 822, 832

Hume, David: *Treatise on Human Nature,* 187

Humor, 328; in Eliot's work, 450–51; sentimentalism and, 183–84; sexual, 176–77

Humphreys, Emyr, 904

Hunter, J. Paul, 20, 217

Hutchins, Francis, 636

Hutton, R. H., 470

Huxley, Aldous, 867, 876, 902, 912; *After Many a Summer,* 749–50, 753–54, 1002; *Antic Hay,* 748–49, 751–52, 754, 870–71, 1002; on architecture, 870–72; *Brave New World,* 750–52, 871–72, 1002; *Crome Yellow,* 749–51, 1002; *The Doors of Perception,* 1002; *Eyeless in Gaza,* 750–53, 1002; family of, 746–47; *Heaven and Hell,* 1002; *Island,* 1002; life of, 747–48; *Limbo,* 1002; *Mortal Coils,* 1002; narrative style of, 749–54; *Point Counter Point,* 748–52, 754, 871, 1002; *Those Barren Leaves,* 749–52, 1002

Huxley, T. H., 439, 746, 1014; "The Physical Basis of Life," 440

Huysmans, Joris–Karl, *Arebours,* 616

Hysteria, 628–29

Ibsen, Henrik: *When We Dead Awaken,* 785

Idealism, 127, 510

Ideas, 429; Eliot's use of, 438–40

Identity, 21, 107, 149, 362, 389, 444, 482, 655, 712, 721, 928; architecture and, 869–70; children and, 593, 597; class, 82–83, 737; of Defoe's characters, 44–45; in Dickens's works, 389–90; female, 200, 377; gender, 120–21, 218, 367–68, 596; human, 107, 506; imperialism and, 639–40, 645; making, 617–18; mistaken, 485–87; personal, xv, 105, 111–12; power and, 487–89; private, 43–44; professional, 490–93; role of, 105–6; in Scott's works, 311–12; social, 42–43; women's, 208–15, 494–95; working-class, 387–88

Ideology, 248, 250, 274, 328, 378; domestic, 335, 346–49, 367; gender, 200, 215, 329–30; of heroes, 255–56; Romantic, 333, 339

Illness, 148, 629, 756

Imlay, Gilbert, 210, 1015

Immigrants: Irish, 411

Imperialism, 349, 450, 523, 560–61, 606, 631, 839, 1009; in Africa, 647–52; in Conrad's works, 694–96, 995; criticism of, 330–31; culture and, 652–56, 918–19; and detective novels, 502–3; in India, 636–47; Kipling's views on, 632–35; marriage and, 369–70; 1930s, 744–45; in novels, 563–67; romance of, 577–78; Romantic, 565–68; Victorian, 568–73; Victorian- Edwardian, 573–77; Waverley Novels and, 314–15

Imprisonment, 144–46, 400

Incest, 52, 340; in Gothic novels, 220, 222–23, 226, 230, 235–36, 242

Inchbald, Elizabeth: *I'll Tell You What,* 1002; *Lovers' Vows,* 1002; narrative structure used by, 273–74; *Nature and Art,* 1002; *A Simple Story,* 249, 260–64, 267, 270, 273, 1002; use of emotions by, 260–64

Independence: female, 358–59, 370

India, 563, 883, 978; culture in, 653–55; English, 562, 633–34, 636–47; as setting, 568–71, 829–32, 980, 1012

Indian Mutiny. *See* Great Mutiny of 1857

Indian National Congress, 634, 640

Individualism, xiv–xv, 23, 185, 271, 294, 389, 600, 703; Dickens on, 389–90, 392, 394, 398; female, 364, 368, 369; in sentimental novels, 191–92

Industrial Revolution, 565

Injustice, 259–60

Innocence, 968–69

Inquisition, 237, 342

Intimacy, 75, 92

Intrigue, 6, 14, 16, 50, 136

Ireland, 155, 333; famine in, 411, 569; imperialism in, 565, 567; Joyce and, 769–70

Irony, 127, 170, 183, 430, 682, 821; Conrad's use of, 693–94; Defoe's use of, 28, 33–35; Eliot's use of, 451–52; Smollett's use of, 140–41

Isherwood, Christopher William Bradshaw, 746, 902; *All the Conspirators,* 755–57, 761, 1002; *The Ascent of F6,* 763, 1002; autobiography in novels of, 755–57, 761–63; *Berlin Stories,* 759, 763; *Christopher and His Kind,* 755, 760, 1002; on city life, 759–61; *The Dog Beneath the Skin,* 763; *Down There on a Visit,* 761, 763, 1002; *Goodbye to Berlin,* 761–63, 1002; *Kathleen and Frank,* 755; *The Last of Mr. Norris (Mr. Norris Changes Trains),* 759–61, 763, 1002; life of, 747–48; *Lions and Shadows,* 756–58,

1002; "The Lost," 758–59, 1002; *A Meeting by the River,* 763; *The Memorial,* 757–59, 761, 1002; *New Writing,* 1002; *Prater Violet,* 761, 763; *A Single Man,* 763, 1002; on society, 757–58

Ishiguro, Kazuo, 942, 967; *An Artist of the Floating World,* 973; *Pale View of Hills,* 972–73l; *The Remains of the Day,* 973

Islam, xiv, 302, 316, 320

Italy, 51, 727, 820–21, 999

Jacobites and Jacobitism, 64, 67, 121–22, 310, 313, 566

Jacobs, W. W.: *Mord Em'ly,* 624

Jamaica Rebellion, 388

James, G. P. R., 461

James, Henry, xv, 21, 41, 128, 147, 481, 503, 568, 618, 659, 749, 765, 835, 906, 913, 999; children in works of, 582, 588, 594, 604–5, 606; on Eliot, 452–53; *The Golden Bowl,* 950; *The Portrait of a Lady,* 913; *The Princess Casamassima,* 613; on sensation novels, 484, 500; *What Maisie Knew,* 581, 594, 604–6; on Zola, 609–11

James, P. D., 967; *Devices and Desires,* 971–72

Jameson, Anna, 453

Jameson, Fredric, 295; *Postmodernism,* 948

James II, King of England, 34, 64–65, 67

Jane Austen Society, 275

JanMohamed, Abdul: *Manichean Aesthetics,* 647–48

Janvier, Ludovic, 854

Japan, 144, 972–73

Jarrell, Randall, 899

Jay, Arthur Osborne, 614; *Social Problem,* 611

Jeaffreson, John Cordy: *Novels and Novelists from Elizabeth to Victoria,* 428

Jerome, Jerome K.: *Three Men in a Boat,* 624

Jews, 449, 512, 623, 910, 944; in Lawrence's novels, 724–25; in Scott's novels, 315–18

Johnson, B. S.: *Aren't You Rather Young to Be Writing Your Memoirs,* 916

Johnson, Barbara, 231

Johnson, Diane, 941

Johnson, Pamela Hansford, 895, 897

Johnson, Samuel, 7–8, 17, 73, 111; *London,* 133; *Rambler No. 4,* 1, 2; *Rasselas,* 35, 565, 567; on Richardson, 94, 158; on Sterne, 159, 161–63

Jones, Ann H.: *Ideas and Innovations,* 327

Journalism, 20, 131–32, 410, 443

Journals: symbolism of, 77–78

Joyce, James, xix, 618, 661, 708, 715, 744, 898, 912, 915, 918, 1002; Amis on, 899, 902–3; autobiography in works of, 771–72, 1003; children in works of, 587, 588; "The Dead," 770–71, 777; *Dubliners,* 765, 767–71, 777, 1003; *Exiles,* 765, 769, 784; *Finnegans Wake,* 581–82, 743, 765, 767–68, 770–72, 774–78, 780–81, 784–88, 1003; "Ivy Day in the Committee Room," 770; use of language by, 765–69; narrative style of, 772–88; opposition to, 895–96; "A Painful Case," 777; *Portrait of the Artist as a Young Man,* 765, 767–68, 771–74, 777–78, 780–81, 787, 905, 907, 1003; "The Sisters," 770; Snow on, 904–8; *Stephen Hero,* 765, 771; *Ulysses,* 620, 659, 680, 686, 698, 765–79, 781–85, 787–88, 803, 879, 1003

Justice, 268
Juvenal: Third Satire of, 133

Kafka, Franz, 582, 600, 899, 903
Kahane, Claire, 228; "The Gothic Mirror," 225–26
Kant, Immanuel, 342, 344
Kaplan, Cora, 367–70
Keating, Joseph: *Son of Judith,* 613
Kelman, James, 942, 980; *A Disaffection,* 980
Kettle, Arnold: *Introduction to the English Novel,* 20
Keynes, John Maynard, 719
Kincaid, Jamaica, 365
King, Francis, 904
Kingsley, Charles, 428, 590; *Alton Locke,* 1003; *Hereward the Wake,* 1003; *Heroes,* 1003; *Hypatia,* 1003; *Recollections of Geoffrey Hamlyn,* 569; *The Saint's Tragedy,* 1003; *Two Years Ago,* 1003; *The Water–Babies,* 1003; *Westward Ho!,* 563, 566, 1003; *Yeast,* 1003
Kingston, W. H. G., 573
Kipling, Rudyard, 503, 648, 896; *Barrack-Room Ballads,* 1003; "The Gardener," 631; *The Jungle Books,* 634, 1003; *Just So Stories,* 1003; *Kim,* 567–68, 572, 634–35, 637–40, 1003; "The Man Who Would Be King," 632–34; "The Phantom Rickshaw," 637–38; *Plain Tales from the Hills,* 635, 637, 1003; *Puck of Pook's Hill,* 1003; "Recessional," 632, 634; "The Record of Badalia Herodsfoot," 614; *Rewards and Fairies,* 1003; "Through the Fire," 638; views on empire of, 631–40; "The Wish House," 631
Knowledge, 17, 593; growth of, 437–38; history as, 26, 38–39; topographical, 36–37

Korzeniowski, Teodor Josef Konrad. *See* Conrad, Joseph
Kubrick, Stanley, 993
Kureishi, Hanif, 656

Labour Party, 907
Lacan, Jacques, 222, 241, 582
Laclos, Pierre-Ambrose-François Choderlos de, 93; *Les liaisons dangereuses,* 73
Lafayette, Mme de, 954: *Princesse de Clèves,* 6
Lanchester, Elsa, 878
Landscape, 340; importance of, 823–24
Language, 104, 442; Beckett's use of, 842–43, 845–47, 849–50, 852–58, 862–66; Carroll's use of, 592, 601–2, 603; Indian, 654–55; Joyce's use of, 765–69; Lawrence's use of, 731–33, 736–38; literary use of, 27, 117–19
Lankester, Edwin Ray, 610
Larkin, Philip, 940
Laurentini, Madame, 228
Law: in sensation novels, 488–94, 498
Law, John. *See* Harkness, Margaret
Lawrence, Arthur, 716–17
Lawrence, D. H., xi–xiii, 185, 587, 655, 661–62, 752, 754, 765, 829, 844, 918; *Aaron's Rod,* 717–18, 720, 722, 724, 729, 732, 735–36, 1004; *Apocalypse,* 730; *Boy in the Bush,* 718; *Classic American Literature,* 716; on community and society, 725–27; "The Crown," 722–23; degeneration plots of, 621–23; "Education of the People," 717; family of, 716–18; *Fantasia of the Unconscious,* 718; "The Fox," 719, 722; "Goats and Compasses," 719; *Kangaroo,* 718, 720–21, 724–25, 727, 729, 735, 1004; *Lady Chatterley's Lover,* 717, 719–22, 728–29, 736–39, 1004; literary influences on, 729–30;

Lawrence, D. H. (continued)
The Lost Girl, 717, 722, 729, 735–36, 1004; *The Man Who Died,* 730; narrative techniques of, 730–39; *Mr. Noon,* 718, 720; *The Plumed Serpent,* 717–19, 721–22, 724–25, 728–29, 731, 734–36, 1004; *Psychoanalysis and the Unconscious,* 718; racism of, 724–25; *The Rainbow,* 686, 717, 719–20, 722–24, 726–29, 732–33, 735, 1004; religious mysticism in, 723–24; *St. Mawr,* 717, 722; on sexuality, 722–23, 737–39; "The Sisters," 729; on social discontent, 720–22; *Sons and Lovers,* 717, 721–22, 727–29, 1004; *Studies in Classic American Literature,* 726–27; "A Study of Thomas Hardy," 722–23; travels of, 727–28; *The Trespasser,* 718, 729, 731, 1004; "The Wedding Ring," 732; and Western modernity, 715–16; *The White Peacock,* 717–18, 721–22, 727, 729–31, 1004; "The Woman Who Rode Away," 729; on women, 718–20; *Women in Love,* 621–23, 716, 718–20, 722–24, 726–29, 731–35, 1004

Lawrence, Frieda von Richthofen Weekley, 717–18, 725, 727, 1004
Lawrence, George: *Maurice Dering,* 571
Lawrence, Lydia Beardsall, 716–17
Leaska, Mitchell A., 790
Leavis, F. R., 11, 277, 661, 728, 827, 908; on Dickens, 382, 385, 398; *The Great Tradition,* 174–75
Leavis, Q. D., 377, 382, 384–85
LeBrun, Annie, 244
Lediard, Thomas: *The German Spy,* 131
Lee, Harriet, 329
Lee, Sophia: *The Chapter of Accidents,* 1004; *Life of a Lover,* 1004; *The Recess,* 226–27, 1004

Left Review, 742
Lehmann, John, 759, 763
Lehmann, Rosamond, 746
Leicester, Robert Dudley, earl of, 226
Lennox, Charlotte, 139, 145; *Female Quixote,* 203
Le Noir, Elizabeth, 328; *Clara de Montfier,* 336
Leopold, 635, 696
Le Queux, William: *Great War in England in 1897,* 577
Le Sage, Alain-René: *Gil Blas,* 131
Lesbianism, 333, 719, 724
Lessing, Doris, 365, 643, 895, 898, 904; on Africa, 650–51; *African Stories,* 650; *Briefing for a Descent into Hell,* 918, 925, 927, 937, 1005; on British culture, 918–19; *Canopus in Argos,* 925–26, 928, 932–35, 937–38; character development by, 929–32; Children of Violence series, 650, 919–20, 922, 926–27, 1004; colonial metaphor used by, 932–34; criticism of, 936–37; *The Diaries of Jane Somers,* 928, 938; *The Diary of a Good Neighbor,* 923–24; *The Fifth Child,* 923, 925–26, 936, 938; *The Four-Gated City,* 922–23, 927, 937, 1004–5; *Free Women,* 926; *The Golden Notebook,* 650, 922, 923–24, 926–27, 929–30, 937, 1005; *The Good Terrorist,* 936, 938; *Granta,* 920; *The Grass Is Singing,* 650, 928–29, 1004; "A Home for the Highland Cattle," 650–51; *If the Old Could . . . ,* 923–24; *Landlocked,* 1004; *The Making of the Representative for Planet 8,* 923, 925; *The Marriages Between Zones Three, Four, and Five,* 923, 930, 936; *Martha Quest,* 650, 1004; *Memoirs of a Survivor,* 927–28, 937, 1005; narrative style of, 922–29; *A Proper Mar-*

Lessing, Doris (continued)
  riage, 1004; *Ripple from the Storm,*
  1004; *Shikatsa,* 919, 921–23, 933,
  936; *The Sirian Experiments,* 918–19,
  923–24, 930–32, 935–36; *A Small*
  Personal Voice, 919–20; on social
  issues, 937–38; *The Summer Before*
  Dark, 928; on war, 919–22
L'Estrange, Roger: *Five Letters from a*
  Nun to a Cavalier, 51
Letters, 75, 77, 88–89, 118, 147
Levin, Harry, 597–98
Lévi-Strauss, Claude, 236
Levy, Eric: *Beckett and the Voice of Species,*
  855
Lévy, Maurice: *Le roman "gothique"*
  anglais, 223
Lewes, George Henry, 434, 438,
  453–54, 481, 997
Lewes, Marian. *See* Eliot, George
Lewes, Thornie, 453
Lewis, Matthew Gregory, 320: *The*
  Monk, 235–37, 239, 1005
Lewis, Wyndham, 878–79, 881, 906;
  Apes of the Gods, 744; *Satire and Fic-*
  tion, 880
Liberty, 512, 531, 566
Licensing Act, 997–98
Liddell, Alice, 582–84
Lights of Canopus, The, 926
Lillo: *London Merchant,* 74
Linton, Lynn: *My Literary Life,* 442
Listener (periodical), 896
Literacy, 37–38, 47
Literature, 21, 119; imperialism and,
  562–63; professionalization of, 404–5
Lively, Penelope, 944; *According to Mark,*
  939; *City of the Mind,* 950; *The Moon*
  Tiger, 939, 941–42, 945, 947, 950,
  958; narrative style of, 945–47, 950
Livingstone, David: *Missionary Travels,*
  573

Locke, John, 27, 41, 165, 173, 592;
  Essay Concerning Human Understand-
  ing, 44, 170–72; *Principia,* 172; *Two*
  Treatises of Government, 44
Lodge, David: *The British Museum Is*
  Falling Down, 1005; *Changing Places,*
  1005; *How Far Can You Go?,* 1005;
  Small World, 1005
London, 46, 132, 828, 944; Dickens on,
  396–97; police in, 109–10; as setting,
  136, 149, 623, 624, 745, 870–72
London Magazine, 911
London Review, 470–71
Lounger (magazine), 1005
L'Ouverture, Toussaint, 566
Love, 92, 191, 390, 671, 724, 847; in
  amatory fiction, 51–52, 57, 60–61;
  erotic, 336–37; failed relationships in,
  750–51; heroines and, 201–7; illicit
  heterosexual, 238–39; learning about,
  190–91; *vs.* passion, 338–39; roman-
  tic, 133–34; sublime of, 344–46; as
  theme, 51–52, 60, 81–82, 136; and
  women's identities, 208, 210–11; in
  Wuthering Heights, 376–77
Lovell, Terry, 216–17
Lover, Samuel: *Handy Andy,* 569
Lower class: political causes of, 383–85,
  388. *See also* Working class
Lukács, Georg, xiii, 298; *The Historical*
  Novel, 305; *The Theory of the Novel,*
  xi–xii, 295
Luria, Gina, 254
Lyotard, Jean-François, 842

Macaulay, Rose, 746
Macaulay, T. B., 301, 633
McCarthy, Mary, 899, 902
McCulloch, J. R., 510
MacDonald, George, 590
McEwan, Ian: *Black Dogs,* 968; *Cement*
  Garden, 966–69; *A Child in Time,*

968–69; *The Comfort of Strangers,* 968; *The Innocent,* 967–69

Mackenzie, Henry, 182, 329; *Julia de Roubigné,* 1005; *The Man of Feeling,* 183, 186–90, 194, 257, 1005; *The Man of the World,* 1005; *The Prince of Tunis,* 1005

McKeon, Michael, 9, 20, 58, 203, 217

Magic: in Scott's novels, 316, 320, 322–25

Maine, Henry, 460

Malaysia, 635, 711

Malebranche, Nicolas de, 857

Males. *See* Men

Malthus, Thomas: *Principles of Population,* 510

Manley, Delariviere, 1, 6–7, 15, 51, 53, 60, 71, 1001; *The Adventures of Rivella,* 1005; on bigamy, 67–68; criticism of, 13, 18, 218; *New Atalantis,* 14, 54–55, 58, 61–63, 65, 1005; on novel reading, 62–63; sexuality in, 54, 58; structure of writing of, 24–25

Manley, John, 1005

Manliness, 257. *See also* Gentlemanliness; Masculinity

Mann, Horace, 163

Mann, Thomas, 587; *Death in Venice,* 710

Manners, 819; Ford's novels on, 833–40; Forster's novels on, 820–33

Mansfield Katherine, 733

Mansfield, William Murray, 1st earl of, 350

Manning, Olivia: *The Balkan Trilogy,* 1005; *The Battle Lost and Won,* 1005; *The Danger Tree,* 1005; *Friends and Heroes,* 1005; *The Great Fortune,* 1005; *The Levant Trilogy,* 1005; *The Spoilt City,* 1005; *The Sum of Things,* 1005

Marana, Giovanni Paolo: *The Turkish Spy,* 131

Maritime novels, 565

Marivaux, Pierre Carlet de Chamblain de, 19

Marriage, xvi, 53, 59, 65, 96, 144, 149, 214, 290, 332, 342, 359, 495, 627, 790, 801–2, 991; in Brontë's works, 369–72; degeneracy and, 620–21; egalitarian, 333, 335–36, 339; and fate, 249–50; and literary career, 205–8; as loss, 807–8, 814–16; love in, 92, 206–7; role of, 196, 201–2, 209; Romantic, 334–35; and social place, 76, 125; as threat, 188–89

Married Women's Property Acts, 495

Marryat, Frederick, 565, 572; *Frank Mildmay,* 573, 1006; *Jacob Faithful,* 1006; *Masterman Ready,* 573, 589; *Mr. Midshipman Easy,* 573, 1006; *Newton Foster,* 573; *Peter Simple,* 573, 1006

Mars-Jones, Adam: *The Darker Proof,* 986; *Lantern Lecture,* 969–70; *Monopolies of Loss,* 985–86

Martineau, Harriet, 365, 509; *Demerara,* 565–66; *The Hour and the Man,* 565–66; *Illustrations of Political Economy,* 510, 565

Marx, Karl: *A Contribution to the Critique of Political Economy,* 505–6

Marxism, 22, 908

Mary II, Queen of England, 64

Mary, Queen of Scots, 226

Masculinity, 195, 216, 231, 255, 303–4, 338, 345, 368; critiques of, 218, 330, 332; definitions of, 250–51; of gentlemen, 408, 422–24; of novel, 513, 517; of politics, 509–10

Masks, masking, 105–6

Massé, Michelle, 232

Materialism, 84, 703, 709

Maternity. *See* Mothers and motherhood

Mathematics: in Beckett's works, 859–62

Matrimonial Causes Act, 495

Maturin, Charles Robert: *The Fatal Revenge*, 1006; *Melmoth the Wanderer*, 237–40; *The Milesian Chief*, 1006; *The Wild Irish Boy*, 1006

Maugham, W. Somerset, 635, 754; *Cakes and Ale*, 1006; *Of Human Bondage*, 1006; *Liza of Lambeth*, 614; *The Moon and Sixpence*, 1006; *Razor's Edge*, 1006

Maupassant, Guy de, *Une vie*, 675

Maxwell, John, 992

Mayhew, Thomas: *London Labour and the London Poor*, 436

Mayoux, Jean-Jacques, 174

Medicine: in sensation novels, 488–92, 497–98

Melville, Lewis, 474

Men, xv, 112, 195, 224, 394; behavior of, 255–57; in Brontë's works, 361–62; emotions of, 250–51, 791–93; eroticism of, 721–22; married, 51–52; nature of, 60–61; as novel writers, xvi, 217, 304; oppression by, 177–78; passion and, 791–92; in Richardson's novels, 74, 78–81; sexual desire of, 54–55; trust of, 211–12

Meredith, George, 316, 382, 404; *Diana of the Crossways*, 429

Meritocracy, 907–8

Merriman, Henry: *Flotsam*, 571

Messenger, Ann, 67

Methodism, 150

Mexicans, 724

Mexico, 727–28, 735

Meyers, Jeffrey, 720, 729

Middle class, xviii, 74, 152, 200, 328, 368, 370, 482, 498, 588, 646; and Dickens, 385–89, 404; social reform by, 508–9; values of, 83, 221–23, 334, 369

Military, 112, 632; and gentlemanliness, 416, 418, 420–22

Mill, John Stuart, 391, 453; *An Essay on Liberty*, 506

Miller, Christopher L., 648–49

Miller, J. Hillis, 389, 401, 537–38, 542–43

Miller, Nancy, 954; "Emphasis Added," 951; *Subject to Change*, 444

Millett, Kate, 731; *Sexual Politics*, 729

Millgate, Jane, 306

Milton, John: *Paradise Lost*, 4, 119, 167, 612, 902

Mind: operation of, 170–72

Mining and miners, 720, 727

Mirror (magazine), 1005

Mirroring: literary, 585

Mirror of Literature, Amusement, and Instruction (journal), 387

Mo, Timothy, 656, 973; *An Insular Possession*, 636

Modern age, xi–xii, xiv

Modernism and modernists, xix, 154, 579, 615, 659, 702, 819, 834; Beckett and, 855–56; criticism of, 897–900, 902–7; in Forster's work, 821, 829, 831; Joyce and, 780–81; Lawrence and, 715–17; 1930s, 743–44; rejection of, 947–48; Waugh and, 879, 884

Moers, Ellen, 244

Monastic life, 238–39

Money, 45–46

Montagu, Mary Wortley, 73, 94

Moore, George Edward (G. E.), 820, 822

Moore, George Augustus, 677; *The Brook Kerith*, 1006; *Confessions of a Young Man*, 616; *Esther Waters*, 616–18; *Evelyn Innes*, 616, 1006; *Heloise and Abelard*, 1006; *A Modern Lover*, 613, 1006; *A Mummer's Wife*, 613, 1006; *Sister Teresa*, 616, 1006

Moors Murders, 910

Moral character, morality, xx–xxi, 13, 188, 257, 356, 383, 534, 685, 716, 901; children's books and, 589–90; culture and, 762–63; in Defoe's works, 29, 35–36; in Dickens's works, 390–91, 398, 401; and natural order, 541–42; in Richardson's writing, 73, 79, 81, 87, 97–98, 247–48; in *Tristram Shandy*, 175–76; women and, 330, 371–72; in *Wuthering Heights*, 373–74

Moral devices: narrators as, 41–42

Moralism, 618–19, 625–26, 730, 820

More, Hannah, 251, 336, 342; *Coelebs in Search of a Wife*, 332; *The Fairchild Family*, 589

Morgan, Lady. *See* Owenson, Sydney

Morgan, William de, 623

Morier, James: *The Adventures of Hajji Baba, of Ispahan*, 567–68, 571

Morrell, Lady Ottoline, 734

Morris, William, 590

Morrison, Arthur: *Child of the Jago*, 614; "Lizerunt," 614

Morrison, Toni, 588

Mother Goose tales, 589

Mother Nature, 348

Mothers and motherhood, 347, 497, 588; in Gothic novels, 225–28, 235; in Isherwood's works, 747, 755–56; role of, 348–49. *See also* Maternity

Motion picture(s), 746, 748, 878

Mullen, Richard, 475

Muller, Max: *Lectures on the Science of Language*, 442

Murder, 910, 968–70; in Dickens's works, 393, 401; in Gothic novels, 235–36, 239–40; as vehicle, 744–46

Murdoch, Iris, 895, 943, 967

Murray, Hugh: *The Morality of Fiction*, 188, 192–93

Murray, Middleton, 733

Mussolini, Benito, 741

Mystery, mysteries, 489–90, 503, 903, 967, 995–96

Mythology, 725, 728

Nabokov, Vladimir, 582, 587, 903; *Lolita*, 899; *Pnin*, 899

Nagasaki, Japan, 972–73

Naipaul, V. S., 636, 650; *Among the Believers*, 1007; *A Bend in the River*, 648, 651–54, 1007; *A Congo Diary*, 1007; *The Enigma of Arrival*, 654, 656; *In a Free State*, 652, 1006; *Guerrillas*, 653, 1007; *A House for Mr. Biswas*, 653, 1006; *India*, 1007; *The Mimic Men*, 652, 654; *The Mystic Masseur*, 653, 1006; *The Return of Eva Peron*, 1007

Napier, Elizabeth, 244–45

Napoleonic Wars, 294, 357, 565

Narayan, R. K., 653

Narrators: as moral devices, 41–42

Nationalism: Eliot on, 447–48; English, 388–89; Indian, 642–43, 831; of novel, 19–21

National Review, 460

Naturalism, 503, 623, 629, 730; decline in, 610–11; French, 608–10, 616–17, 625–26; modification of, 617–18

Naturalist fiction, 609–10

Nature, 130, 151, 348, 616; and moral order, 541–42; sublime in, 343–44

Nazism, 726, 729, 794, 906; cultural morality and, 762–63

Neilson, Donald, 969–70

Newcastle, Thomas Pelham-Holles, duke of, 146

New Critics, 631

New Freewoman (journal), 1014

New Hedonism, 620–21

New Imperialism, 562

Newman, John Henry (Cardinal New-
    man), 428
New Poor Law, 384, 523
Newquist, Roy, 919
New Statesman (periodical), 896
New Towns, 914
New Woman fiction: themes in, 614–16,
    620–23
New World, 150
New Yorker, 951
New York Review of Books, 941
New York Times Book Review, 904–5
New Zealand, 563, 576, 944
Nietzsche, Friedrich Wilhelm, 302, 725,
    730
Nigeria, 636, 650
Nihilism, 831
Nineteenth-Century Fiction (periodical),
    474
Nobel Prizes, 652, 991, 1000, 1003
Nordau, Max, 611, 619; *Degeneration*,
    610
Normans, 315
Norris, Frank, 609
North America, 563, 727
Novak, Maximillian, 34
Novalis (Friedrich von Hardenberg), 686
Novellas, 1, 6, 51
Novel reading, 2–3, 5, 62–63, 327
Novels, 20; apologies for, xix–xx; cultural
    force of, 3–4; as dialogical, xii–xiii;
    rampant production of, 4–5; serious
    novels, 12; typology of, 12–13. *See
    also by individual type*
Nuns, 60, 65
Nursery rhymes, 589
Nuttall, Zelia: *Fundamental Principles of
    Old and New World Civilizations*, 725

Oaths, 63–64
Observer (periodical), 896
Oedipus complex, 222, 237

O'Faolain, Sean, 878
"Office of Intelligence: Or, Universal
    Register of Persons and Things,
    The," 109
Okri, Ben, 942
Oliphant, Margaret, 352, 470, 501;
    "Sensation Novels," 483–84
Opie, Amelia, 328, 350; *Adeline Mow-
    bray*, 331; "The Father and the
    Daughter," 339
Orientalism, 146–47, 644; in Eliot's
    novels, 449–50; in Scott's novels,
    303, 314–19
Orientals: stereotyping of, 567–68,
    572–73
Original Sin, 591
Orwell, George (Eric Arthur Blair), 867,
    876; *Animal Farm*, 745, 1007; on
    bogusness, 872–74; *Burmese Days*,
    643, 745, 1007; *Coming Up for Air*,
    872–73; *Homage to Catalonia*, 1007;
    on imperialism, 643, 744–45; *1984*,
    745, 873–74, 888–90, 1007; *The
    Road to Wigan Pier*, 1007
Ouida, 496
Owenson, Sydney (Lady Morgan), 328;
    on sublime love, 344–46; *The Wild
    Irish Girl*, 344–46, 565
Oxford University Press World's Clas-
    sics, 456, 475

Pacifism, 727, 753
Paganism, 320–21, 730
Paine, Thomas, 248
Pamela Censured (Anonymous), 85,
    93–94
Pankhurst, Christabel, 722
Paranoia, 241, 243–44
Parliament, 247–48
Parnell, Charles Stuart, 794
Parodies, 174, 385, 1013; of Richardson's
    work, 84–86, 110–11, 118–19, 998

Parry, James: *True Anti-Pamela,* 85

Party writers, 20

Passion, 339, 394, 751, 791; consequences of, 552–54; excess, 337–38; and reason, 252–54, 259

Paston, George. *See* Symonds, Emily Morse

Patriarchy, 328, 333, 340, 350, 378, 380; domestic, 346–49; and identity, 311–12, 362; opposition to, 331–32; as theme, 46–47, 94, 97; violence of, 232, 342

Patronage, 34, 108, 128, 158, 386, 390

Pattison, Robert, 590–91

Paul, Herbert, 474

Paulin, Tom: "In an Eweleaze Near Weatherbury," 543

Peacock, Thomas Love: *Crotchet Castle,* 749; *Headlong Hall,* 749; *Nightmare Abbey,* 749

Pelham, Henry, 121

Penguin Books, 475

Penny Magazine, 387

People's Charter to Parliament, 523

Perera, Suvendrini, *Reaches of Empire,* 563

Pérez Galdós, Benito, 906

Peri Bathous, 169

Perkins, David, 17

Persecution, 269–70

Perversity: in Gothic novel, 232–40

Phallocentrism, 177, 229

Phelps, William Lyon: *Advance of the English Novel,* 20

Philips, Katherine: "Orinda," 204

Phillips, Caryl, 656

Philosophy, 716, 847

Picaresque fiction, 132–34, 137–39

Plantagenets, 313

"Playgiarism": and postmodernism, 947–49

Plays, 132, 398, 763, 993, 1000, 1002, 1007; by Beckett, 847, 850, 854, 991;

by Henry Fielding, 103–4, 124, 997; by Joyce, 765, 769

Plomer, William, 746

Poe, Edgar Alan, 947

Poetry, 307, 632, 661–62, 742, 989, 1001; satirical, 128, 132; sublime in, 342–43

Police: establishment of, 109–10

Political novels, 508–10

Politics, xviii, 15, 27, 121, 145, 247–48, 302, 353, 520, 909, 996, 1003, 1007, 1009; of AIDS, 985–86; in Bage's work, 267–68, 990; British, xix, 149–50, 1012; in Brontë's work, 359–60; of class, 321–24, 367–69, 383–84; in Conrad's work, 702–9, 713; in Dickens's work, 391–92; feminist, 217–18; gender and, 509–10; in Godwin's work, 268–71, 999; government role and, 511–12; in historical novels, 319, 322; Indian, 642–43; liberal, 511–12; and lower class, 383–85, 388; of modernists, 905–6; in narratives, 46–47; 1930s, 741–42; patriarchal, 331–32, 349; and poverty, 510–11; in Roberts's work, 742–43; Romantic writers and, 330–32, 350; satire and, 115, 146; in sensation novels, 499–500; sexuality of, 495–96; in Charlotte Smith's work, 265–67, 330–31; in Smollett's work, 264–65; and social issues, 512–13; and social reform, 508–9

Polyglossia, xii, 680. *See also* Heteroglossia

Polynesia, 576

Pope, Alexander, 108, 148, 168–69; *Dunciad,* 25, 146; *Rape of the Lock,* 202–3; satires by, 127–28

Populism: Dickens's, 383–88

Pornography, 54, 86, 93, 719

Porter, Anna Maria, 328

Porter, Jane, 328; *Thaddeus of Warsaw,* 339

Portuguese Letters, 51

Postal service, 457, 1013

Postmodernism, 579, 937, 939; Beckett and, 842–66; "playgiarism" and, 947–49

Potter, Beatrice, 613

Pound, Ezra, 728, 779, 819, 834, 905–6, 989

Pound & Co., 820

Poverty, 268, 434, 508–9, 567; Dickens's concerns with, 383–84; and politics, 510–11; as theme, 24, 522–23

Powell, Anthony, 746, 902, 967

Power, xv, 91, 105, 108–9, 221, 409, 605; and identity, 487–89; in Lawrence's work, 735–36; in novel reading, 2–3; of professionals, 497–500; in society, 434–36; subversive, 58–59; of women, 53, 495

Powys, John Cowper, 746

Prévost d'Exiles, Antoine-François: *Manon Lescaut,* 88

Prichard, James, 436

Priestly, J. B., 895–96

Priests and priesthood, 56, 155–56, 342. *See also* Clergy

Primitivism, 189, 725

Proctor, Richard, 454

Professionals: gendering of, 494–96; power of, 497–500; social identity of, 488–89, 490–91, 492–93

Property, 408, 445

Prostitutes and prostitution, 52, 85, 188, 393; in Gaskell's works, 524, 530; and seduction, 77–78

Protestantism, 45, 189, 342, 370, 591

Proust, Marcel, 582, 587, 715, 771, 906, 911

Psychoanalysis, 718, 938

Psychology, 73, 248, 250, 296, 308, 581, 716, 835; of children, 604–5; in Conrad's work, 685, 712; in Dickens's writing, 399–402. *See also* Universal Psychology

Public sphere: gentlemen and, 424–25

Pugh, Edwin, 624

Punch, 481, 1012

Punter, David, 244

Puppet shows, 103, 105–6, 138

Puritanism, 24, 184–85, 397

Pygmalion, 98

Pym, Barbara, 939, 941, 943; character development by, 946–47; *Excellent Women,* 1007; *A Few Green Leaves,* 945–46, 948–49, 957–58; *A Glass of Blessings,* 960–61, 1007; *Less Than Angels,* 1007; narrative style of, 948–50; *Quartet in Autumn,* 940, 950, 958–59, 1007; on science and technology, 945; *Some Tame Gazelle,* 943; *The Sweet Dove Died,* 946–47, 958–59, 961; on women, 957–61

Quakers, 43, 990

Quetzalcoatl, 728, 734

Quixotism: English, 144–45

Race: degeneracy and, 331, 334, 610–11, 620, 622–23, 634; Dickens on, 385, 388; Eliot on, 436–37, 447–48; Lessing on, 928–29; Scott's treatment of, 303, 315–19; and sexuality, 688–89; social Darwinism and, 573–74. *See also* Orientalism

Race-consciousness: Lawrence on, 721, 734–35

Racism, 562, 693; and imperialism, 563, 645; Lawrence's, 724–25

Radcliffe, Ann, 12, 224–25, 320, 328, 331, 339; as Gothic novelist, 227–30; *The Italian,* 340, 342, 1007; on mas-

Radcliffe, Ann (continued)
culinity, 332; *The Mysteries of Udolpho,* 227–28, 340–44, 1007; *The Romance of the Forest,* 228–30, 1007; use of sublime by, 340–45
Radcliffe, Mary–Ann: *Manfroné, or, The One–Handed Monk,* 230–32
Radcliffe, William, 1007
Radway, Janice, 59
Railways, 411, 438, 459
Raj, British, 633–47, 1009
Raleigh, Walter: *The English Novel,* 20
Rape, 253; in amatory fiction, 54, 57; in Richardson's novels, 79, 91, 93, 96–97; and sex, 61, 67, 69
Ray, Gordon, 477
Reade, Charles, 480, 504–5; *The Autobiography of a Thief,* 1007; *Christie Johnstone,* 1007; *The Cloister and the Hearth,* 1008; *Foul Play,* 1007; *Griffith Gaunt,* 1008; *Hard Cash,* 498, 1008; *It Is Never Too Late to Mend,* 569, 1007; *Jack of All Trades,* 1007; *Love Me Little, Love Me Long,* 1007–8; *Masks and Faces,* 1007; *Peg Woffington,* 1007; *Put Yourself in His Place,* 1008
Reader (journal), 471
Realism, xvii–xviii, 50, 129, 165, 216, 224, 294, 319, 503, 658–59, 663, 715, 906–7, 911; demand for, 131–32; in Dickens's work, 402–3; formal, 21, 28; Lawrence's use of, 732–34; magic, 977, 994; novelistic, xv, 21–22; psychological, 504, 844; Richardson's use of, 93–94, 276; Smollett's use of, 135–37, 143–45; Victorian, 379, 481; in Wells's work, 664–74
Realist/symbolist writing, 771–72
Reason: and passion, 252–54, 259
Reeve, Clara, 4–5, 12, 21, 175, 320; *The Champion of Virtue,* 224, 1008; novel

as multinational in, 19–20; *The Old English Barn,* 224, 1008; *Old Manor House,* 249–50; *The Progress of Romance,* 1–3, 7–9, 11, 14–17, 1008
Reform: social, 83–84, 384–85, 508–9, 1003
Reform Acts, 386, 431, 438, 450, 495
Reformation, 591
Regeneration: as plot, 620–23
Regression, 580–81
Reid, Mayne: *Rifle Rangers,* 573
Relationships: between the sexes, 194, 807–8; failed, 750–51
Religion, xiv, 45, 173, 415, 445, 449, 728, 730, 820; children in, 591, 593–94; Dickens on, 385, 397–98; and sentimental novels, 184–85; and sexuality, 722–24; skepticism of, 432–33, 443; as theme, 79, 150, 983–84
Repression: political, 247–48
Research, 608, 725
Restoration, 13–14, 25, 34, 64, 185; comedy of, 88–91
Review, The (journal), 995
Review of English Literature (periodical), 906
Rhodes, Cecil, 562, 576
Rhodesia, 650, 920–21
Rhys, Jean, 746; *After Leaving Mr. Mackenzie,* 1008; *Good Morning, Midnight,* 1008; *Quartet,* 1008; *Wide Sargasso Sea,* 365, 636, 1008
Ricardo, David: *Principles of Political Economy,* 510
Rich, Adrienne, 371
Richard Coeur de Leon, 316
Richardson, Dorothy: *Pilgrimage,* 744
Richardson, Elizabeth Leake, 1008
Richardson, Mary Wilde, 1008
Richardson, Samuel, 1, 9, 12, 20, 24, 50, 132, 152, 157–58, 163–64, 201, 277,

Richardson, Samuel (continued)
329, 911; character development by,
xviii, 88–93, 258, 260, 296, 307;
Clarissa, 2, 6–7, 73–74, 77–80, 83,
87–100, 152, 165, 201–2, 248,
252–53, 260, 837, 900, 1008; *Collection of the Moral and Instructive Sentiments, Maxims, Cautions, and Reflexions, Contained in the Histories of Pamela, Clarissa, and Sir Charles Grandison*, 87; criticism of, 8, 17–18,
73–74, 93–96; eroticism, 99–100;
Familiar Letters, 75, 98; and Fielding,
112–13; life of, 74–75; on morality,
97–98, 247–48; narrative structure of,
81–82; novel acceptability, 5–7;
Pamela, 2, 7, 75–77, 81–87, 89, 93,
110–13, 118–20, 202, 248, 252, 260,
998, 1008; parodies of, 84–86,
110–11, 119–20, 258; realism in,
93–94, 276; replacement fiction by, 3,
14–15; seduction by, 98–99; *Sir Charles Grandison*, 79–81, 83, 94, 96,
99–100, 175, 185, 202, 300, 1008; on
social issues, 82–84, 87–88, 112–13,
202; use of rape by, 96–97; *The Young Man's Pocket Companion*, 74, 88
Richard II, King of England, 311
Richthofen, Else von, 725
Ridge, William Pett, 623–24
Rigby, Elizabeth, 352, 372, 376
Roberts, Michael: *New Country*, 742–43;
New Signatures, 742; on politics,
742–43
Robinson, Mary, 1008; *Walsingham*,
249, 251, 254, 264, 269–70, 272,
1009
Roche, Regina Maria: *The Children of the Abbey*, 339–40
Rodker, John, 834
Rogers, Richard: *Seven Treatises Leading and Guiding to True Happiness*, 39

Rogue tales, 127
Romance(s), 1, 6, 12, 51, 59, 88, 212,
524, 890, 996, 1010; in Brontë's
work, 359, 373; criticism of, 1–2, 15;
and empire, 574–75, 577–78; in
Gothic novels, 220, 224, 226–27;
Harlequin, 59–60; history of, 8–9;
Richardson's, 79–81; Smollett's, 131,
133–34, 144; women and, 202–3; of
working class, 623–24
Romanticism, 184, 297–98, 339, 624,
1005; children and, 592–93; gender
ideology and, 329–30, 333–34,
348–49; imperialism and, 561,
565–68; love and, 336–37; marriage
and, 334–36; passion and, 337–38;
politics and, 330–32, 350; reformed
heroines and, 332–33; sublime in,
342–44; women writers and, 328–29
Rosa, Salvator, 340, 342, 344, 346
Roscoe, W. C., 410
Rose, Jacqueline, 591–92; *The Case of Peter Pan*, 583–84
Rossetti, Christina, 957
Rossetti, Dante Gabriel, 373
Rousseau, Jean-Jacques, 19, 192, 990; on
children, 582, 591–92; *Confessions*,
591; *émile*, 591; *La nouvelle Héloise*,
337
Rowe, Elizabeth, 13, 88
Royalty, 311–13
Rudd, Martha, 505
Rupert, Prince, 40
Rural life, 446–47
Rushdie, Salman, 636, 644, 942, 973; on
colonialism, 652–53; *Grimus*, 1009;
Haroun and the Sea of Stories, 1009;
Imaginary Homelands, 1009; *The Jaguar Smile*, 1009; *Midnight's Children*, 635, 654–55, 977–78, 1009; *The Satanic Verses*, 647, 653–56, 977–79;
Shame, 1009

Ruskin, John, 391, 433, 725; *Modern Painters*, 535–36; *Stones of Venice*, 828; on suburban life, 624; *Unto This Last*, 533

Russell, Bertrand, 726, 734, 820

Russell, Leonard, 896

Sade, Marquis de (Donatien-Alphonse-François, Comte de Sade), 947; on *Clarissa*, 73, 98–99, 100

Sadleir, Michael, 456, 471; *Trollope: A Commentary*, 472, 474

Sadomasochism, 220

Said, Edward, xiv; *Orientalism*, 314–15

Saint-Pierre, Bernardin de: *Paul and Virginia*, 193–94 Saintsbury, George, 20, 382, 474

Salinas, Pedro, 560

Sand, George, 355

Saracens, 316, 318–19

Sartre, Jean-Paul, 295

Satire, 63, 112, 127, 203, 213, 436, 451, 536, 568, 867–68, 945, 962, 991, 1005; Amis's, 900–903; Fielding's, 107–8, 114–16, 118–20, 264; Greene's, 874–76; Huxley's, 870–72, 1002; Orwell's, 872–74, 887–90; political, 115, 391; Pym's, 948–49, 1007; role of, 128–31; and sentimentalism, 183–84; Smollett's, 133–35, 137–39, 141–42, 145–50; Sterne's, 154, 165, 168–70, 173–74, 177–78; Swift's, 130, 1012; Thackeray's, 409, 1012; Waugh's, 867–70, 876–87, 890–94, 1013; Wilson's, 912–13

Saturday Review: on Trollope, 460, 469–70, 472–73

Savery, Henry: *Quintus Servinton, a Tale Founded upon Incidents of Real Occurrence*, 568

Saxons, 315

Scandal, 504–5

School life, 136, 140

Schreber, Dr., 240–41

Schreiner, Olive: *From Man to Man*, 1009; *The Story of an African Farm*, 575–76, 1009; *Trooper Peter Halket of Mashonaland*, 576; *Undine*, 1009; *Women and Labour*, 1009

Science, 20, 616, 703, 945; in sensation novels, 499–501; Snow on, 908–10, 1011

Science fiction, 302, 901; Lessing and, 923–24, 938; Wells and, 659, 1014

Scotland, 121, 127, 137, 565–66; Walter Scott and, 312–14

Scott, J. D., 904

Scott, Margaret Charlotte Charpentier, 1009

Scott, Paul, 635; *The Day of the Scorpion*, 646–47, 1009; *A Division of the Spoils*, 643–44, 1009; homoeroticism in novels of, 637, 646; *The Jewel in the Crown*, 646, 653, 1009; *The Raj Quartet*, 636–37, 643–47, 1009; *The Towers of Silence*, 1009; *Staying On*, 1009; views on empire of, 643–47

Scott, Sarah: *Millennium Hall*, 192

Scott, Walter, xviii, 17, 20, 127, 276, 300, 328, 339, 425, 990, 1001, 1005, 1009; *The Abbot*, 306, 411; *Anne of Geierstein*, 306; anonymity of, 305–7; *The Antiquary*, 305–6; *The Betrothed*, 307; *The Black Dwarf*, 306; *The Bridal of Triermain*, 305, 1010; *The Bride of Lammermoor*, 306, 312, 322, 324; *Castle Dangerous*, 1010; on class politics, 321–24, 390; *Count Robert of Paris*, 307; *The Fair Maid of Perth*, 306; *The Fortunes of Nigel*, 306; *Guy Mannering*, 305; *Harold the Dauntless*, 1010; *The Heart of Midlothian*, 306, 432; history in works of, 308–10, 509; on imperialism, 314–15, 565;

Scott, Walter (continued)
  influence of, 432–33; *Ivanhoe*, 306,
  312, 315–17, 322, 566; *Kenilworth*,
  306; *The Lady of the Lake*, 305, 1010;
  The Lay of the Last Minstrel, 305,
  307, 1010; *A Legend of Montrose*,
  306; life of, 304–5; *The Lord of the
  Isles*, 1010; on magic and witchcraft,
  322–25; *Marmion*, 1010; *The Minstrelsy of the Scottish Border*, 305,
  1010; *The Monastery*, 306; *Old Mortality*, 306, 308, 321; Orientalism in
  works of, 315–19; patriarchy as
  theme of, 311–12; *Peveril of the Peak*,
  306; *The Pirate*, 306; *Quentin Durward*, 306; race consciousness of,
  317–19; *Redgauntlet*, 306, 316; *Rob
  Roy*, 306, 311; *Rokeby*, 305; *St.
  Ronan's Well*, 306; *St. Valentine's
  Day*, 1010; and Scotland, 312–14;
  Siege of Malta, 307; supernatural tales
  in, 320–21; *Tales of My Landlord*,
  306; *Tales of the Crusaders*, 306–7;
  The Talisman, 307, 315–16, 318–20;
  and Universal History, 302–4, 308,
  312–14; *Waverley*, 305, 309–12, 315,
  317, 324, 566, 1010; Waverley Nov-
  els, 301, 303–5, 308–15, 321–25;
  Woodstock, 306
Scriblerus Club, 108, 112
Scriblerus Secundus, 108
Scudéry, Madeleine de, 51, 88
Sea stories, 127
Second Reform Act, 495, 500
Sedgwick, Eve Kosofsky, 239, 244;
  Between Men, 240–41
Seduction, 88, 93; in amatory fiction,
  68–69; and prostitution, 77–78; as
  theme, 51–52, 54–55, 68–69, 91–92
Seeing. *See* Vision
Seeley, John: *The Expansion of England*,
  562

Self-consciousness, 717, 974–75; in
  dreams, 600–601; in seeing, 536–37,
  545; and sexuality, 543–44
Self-doubt, 708–9
Selfhood, 151–52
Self-reflection, 37–38
Sensation novels, 479–81, 506, 995; as
  art form, 484–85; authors of, 504–5;
  Brontë's impact on writers of,
  363–64; imperialism in, 502–3; science in, 498–502; thematics of,
  482–95; women and, 495–98
Sensibility, 682; excess, 337–38; gender
  and, 250–52; role of, 165–66, 193; in
  society, 80–81; in Sterne's novels,
  184–85; in *Tristram Shandy*, 166–68;
  in Wollstonecraft's novels, 258–59,
  265
Sentiment: role of, 192–93
Sentimentalism, 182, 187, 189, 191,
  197; in Conrad's work, 690–91;
  humor and, 183–84; role of, 192–94
Sentimental novels, 181–82, 249; character changes in, 189–90; education
  and, 190–91; gender roles in, 195–97;
  and Gothic novels, 224–25; heroes
  in, 186–88; individualism in, 191–92;
  origins of, 183–84; religion and,
  184–85
Serial publication, 144, 552, 1003, 1012;
  of Dickens's works, 395–96, 996; of
  Trollope's work, 456, 463–65
Services: information, 109, 115
Seven Years' War, 149
Sévigné, Mme de, 88–89
Sex and sexuality, 6, 46, 75, 85, 89, 91,
  149, 175, 188, 221, 233, 235, 239,
  241, 261, 426, 510, 534, 543–44,
  620, 681, 751, 792, 901, 940; in amatory fiction, 52–59; children and,
  591–92, 605; and class, 535, 539,
  542, 544–45, 551–54; and death,

843–44; female, 225–26, 345, 347–48, 357, 394; femininity and, 776–77; in Joyce's work, 782–85; Lawrence's views of, 729, 731, 737–39; in Lessing's works, 931–32; male, 377–78, 722; and race, 688–89; and rape, 61, 67, 69; and religion, 722–24; in Scott's novels, 646–47; Sterne's views on, 176–77; subversion and, 58–59, 92, 237; in Wells's novels, 670–71; women's, 202, 204–7, 218, 718–20, 793

Sexual aggression, 220–23, 253

Sexual desire, 634, 931; in amatory fiction, 54–55, 61; in Gothic novels, 234–35, 239; in Hardy's works, 534, 538–41; love and, 61, 339; surveillance and, 241–42

Sexual relationships: in amatory fiction, 53, 67–68

Shakespeare, William, 303, 398; *Antony and Cleopatra,* 312; *As You Like It,* 312; *Hamlet,* 398; *Henry IV,* 311; *King Lear,* 398, 948–49; *Macbeth,* 312, 322; *The Tempest,* 577; *Troilus and Cressida,* 312

Shame, 550–51

Shaw, George Bernard, 706

Shelley, Mary, 302, 331, 340, 999, 1015; domestic ideology of, 346–49; "Epipsychidion," 345, 822; *Falkner,* 349; *Frankenstein, or, The Modern Prometheus,* 231, 239, 242–43, 328, 346–49, 616, 1010; *The Last Man,* 349, 1010; *Lodore,* 349, 1010; *Mathilda,* 349; *Valperga,* 1010

Shelley, Percy Bysshe, 509, 1010

Sheridan, Richard Brinsley, 12

Sherwood, Mary Martha: *The Fairchild Family,* 589

Showalter, Elaine: *A Literature of Their Own,* 366

Sidney, Philip: *Arcadia,* 75

Silence: Beckett's use of, 843–44

Sillitoe, Alan, 895

Simcox, Edith, 444

Sin. *See* Original Sin

Sitwell, Edith, 661

Skinner, Molly: *Boy in the Bush,* 718

Slavery, 318, 350, 450, 991. *See also* Antislavery movement

Slum fiction, 614, 623

Smiles, Samuel, 428

Smith, Adam, 510

Smith, Charlotte, 1009; *Desmond,* 265, 336; *Elegiac Sonnets,* 1010; *Emmeline, the Orphan of the Castle,* 224, 265, 1010; *Ethelinde,* 224; *The Old Manor House,* 224, 265–67, 272, 330–31, 1010; politics in, 265–67, 330–31; sentimentalism of, 224–25; social issues in, 330–31

Smith, George, 461, 463–64

Smith, Patricia Juliana, 333

Smollett, Tobias George, xiii, xvii, 1, 8, 12, 20, 183, 398; *The Adventures of an Atom,* 144, 146–47; *The Expedition of Humphry Clinker,* 144, 147–52, 1010; *The Adventures of Roderick Random,* 129, 131, 133–37, 141–42, 1010; *Advice,* 132; career of, 132–33; *Ferdinand Count Fathom,* 141–44, 1010; narrative structure of, 137–39, 142–45; *Peregrine Pickle,* 133, 137–43, 1007, 1010; picaresque fiction of, 132–33; realism of, 135–37; *The Regicide,* 132, 136; *Reproof,* 132; satire of, 135, 141–42, 146–49; *Sir Launcelot Greaves,* 144–45; society depicted by, 140–41, 264; themes of, 139–40, 149–52; *Travels through France and Italy,* 144, 146, 170, 1010; worldview of, 127–28

Snobs, 409

Snow, C. P., 895–98, 911; *The Affair,* 909, 1011; *A Coat of Varnish,* 910; *The Conscience of the Rich,* 910, 1011; *Corridors of Power,* 910, 1011; *Death Under Sail,* 904, 1011; *George Passant,* 909, 1011; *Homecomings,* 910, 1011; *In Their Wisdom,* 910; *Last Things,* 910, 1011; *The Light and the Dark,* 909, 1011; *The Malcontents,* 910; *The Masters,* 909, 1011; and meritocracy, 907–8; on modernism, 904–7; *New Lives for Old,* 908–9, 1011; *The New Men,* 910, 1011; *The Search,* 909, 1011; *The Sleep of Reason,* 910, 1011; *Strangers and Brothers,* 909; Strangers and Brothers series, 908; themes used by, 908–10; *Time of Hope,* 910, 1011; *The Two Cultures and a Second Look,* 906; *The Two Cultures and the Scientific Revolution,* 906

Social action, 248–49

Social change: in Eliot's works, 430–31

Social Darwinism, 562, 473, 622, 687, 711

Social hierarchy, 193–94. *See also* Class

Socialism, 614, 725–27, 908

Social issues, 901; in *Mary Barton,* 521–23; in *Pamela,* 76–77; politics and, 512–13; women's, 330–31

Social order, 59, 128; changing, 333–34, 829, 834, 839. *See also* Class

Social organization, 534, 703

Social-problem novels, 508

Social theory, 610–11

Society, xviii–xix, xx–xxi, 21, 27, 52, 76, 139, 217, 279, 296, 408, 447, 624, 820, 839, 944; in Berlin, 759–61; Brontë's depictions of, 359–60; changes in, 112–13, 742–43; and community, 725–27; depictions of, 264–65, 357; individual and, 790–91, 823–24; 1930s, 744–46, 752–53;

power in, 434–36; progress of, 431–32; protection of, 706–7; responsibility to, 247, 253; restructuring, 907–8; schisms in, 827–28; sensibility in, 80–81; Smollett on, 140–41; Wells's views on, 667–68; women in, 62–63, 354–55, 366–67, 370–73; World War I and, 757–59

Sociology, 725

Sodomy, 136, 719–20

Somers, Jane, 924–25. *See also* Lessing, Doris

South Africa, 562–63, 575–76, 636, 928–29, 1009

South Sea Bubble, 128, 130, 669

South Seas, 576

Sovereignty: political, 34–35

Soyinka, Wole, 652; *Ake,* 650; *Isara,* 650

Spain: civil war in, 741–42

Spark, Muriel: *Territorial Rights,* 967

Spectator (periodical), 407, 424, 460, 470, 896, 899

Speech, xii, 104, 398. *See also* Language

Speke, John Hanning: *Discovery of the Sources of the Nile,* 573

Spence, Lewis: *Gods of Mexico,* 725

Spencer, Herbert, 391, 438, 453; *Education,* 725; *First Principles,* 442

Spencer, Jane, 201, 205, 216, 332; *Rise of the Woman Novelist: From Aphra Behn to Jane Austen,* 218

Spender, Stephen, 742; *The Creative Element,* 743

Spinoza, Baruch, 443

Spivak, Gayatri, 352, 369

Spying: as theme, 36, 537, 545, 554

Spy novels, 131, 901

Stables, Gordon, 573

Stanley, Henry Morton: *How I Found Livingstone,* 573; *My Kalulu,* 573

Stapledon, Olaf, 302

Staves, Susan, 64

Stead, Christina, 587

Steel, Flora Annie: *On the Face of the Waters*, 571

Steele, Richard, 20, 407, 424

Stendhal (Marie-Henri Beyle), xv, 906, 911

Stephen, Fitzjames, 386

Stephen, Leslie, 1015

Stereotypes, 143; of Africa, 573–75; Dickens's use of, 392–93; gender, 195–96, 605; Romantic imperial, 567–68; satire and, 900–901; Victorian imperial, 569, 571–72

Sterne, Laurence, xiii, 20, 128, 179, 182, 258, 308, 329; celebrity of, 157–59, 161; criticism of, 174–77; and Johnson, 161–62; life of, 155–56; *The Life and Opinions of Tristram Shandy, Gentleman*, 146, 151–52, 154–57, 159, 162–78, 1011; on Locke, 170–72; narrative structure of, 172–73; narrative style of, 159–61, 163–65; *Political Romance*, 1011; as satirist, 168–70, 173–74, 177–78; *A Sentimental Journey Through France and Italy*, 158, 162, 166, 170, 184–85, 191–94, 1011; *Sermons of Mr. Yorick*, 159; use of sensibility by, 166–68

Stevenson, Robert Louis, 573, 588; *The Beach of Falesá*, 576–77; *The Ebb-Tide*, 576; *Kidnapped*, 1011; *The Master of Ballantrae*, 1011; *The Strange Case of Dr. Jekyll and Mr. Hyde*, 615; *Treasure Island*, 1011; *Weir of Hermiston*, 1011

Stoker, Bram: *Dracula*, 577, 616

Storey, David, 895

Stowe, Harriet Beecher: *Uncle Tom's Cabin*, 567

Strachey, Lytton, 904

Strauss, David Friedrich: *Life of Jesus*, 432, 443, 997

Stuart, Charles Edward (Bonnie Prince Charlie), 121, 123

Stuarts, 34, 121, 123, 313, 317

Sublime: of love, 344–46; of nature, 343–44; terror of, 340–44

Suburban life, 624–25

Subversion, 237, 239–40

Suffrage: women's, 721–22

Suicide, 1015; as theme, 815–16; as vehicle, 75, 210–13, 744, 844, 976

Suleri, Sara, 636; *Rhetoric of English India*, 647

Summers, Montagu, 52–53

Sunday Times, 896

Super, R. H., 475

Supernatural agency, 220, 320–21

Supremacism: British, 449, 450–51

Surr, Thomas, 328

Surveillance: and sexual desire, 241–42

Swift, Graham, 967; *Ever After*, 974, 1011; *Out of This World*, 974, 1011; *Shuttlecock*, 970; *The Sweetshop Owner*, 974, 1011; *Waterland*, 973–74, 977, 1011

Swift, Jonathan, 108, 144, 168–69, 1005; *The Battle of the Books*, 1012; *Gulliver's Travels*, 41, 130–31, 135, 146, 151, 947, 1012; satire of, 127–28, 1012; *A Tale of a Tub*, 25, 129, 145, 169, 1012

Switzerland, 306

Sykes, Christopher, 878

Symbolism, 77, 106, 839, 995; of children, 592–93, 594–96

Symonds, Emily Morse: *A Writer of Books*, 608–9

Sympathy, 165–66

Taine, Hippolyte, 9, 11, 19, 395

Tatler (periodical), 407, 424

Taylor, Philip Meadows: *Confessions of a Thug*, 570–72, 576; *Ralph Darnell*, 1012; *Seeta*, 571, 1012; *Tara*, 1012

Taylor, Rachel, 717

Templeton, Laurence, 306. *See also* Scott, Walter

Tenniel, John, 598

Tennyson, Alfred Lord, 402

Ten-Pound Householders, 386

Ternan, Ellen, 504

Terror, 227, 229, 247

Terry, R. C., 474

Thackeray, William Makepeace, xviii, 143, 382, 458, 481, 568, 665, 897, 911; *The Book of Snobs,* 409–10; on economy, 411–14; *The English Humourists,* 425; *The Four Georges,* 408; on gentlemen, 407–8, 414–27; *The History of Henry Esmond, Esq.,* 316–17, 421–2, 566, 1012; *The History of Pendennis,* 423–24, 1012; life of, 409–10; *The Newcomes,* 420–22, 424, 426–27, 569, 1012; *Philip,* 476; "The Tremendous Adventures of Major Gahagan," 564; *Vanity Fair,* 362, 368, 410–20, 422, 437, 564, 569, 947, 962, 1012; *The Virginians,* 1012

Thieves, 114–15

Thomson, James: *Ulu,* 573

Thought, 192; history of, 746–47

Thrillers, 745, 967

Tillotson, Kathleen, 382

Times, The: on Trollope, 471–72

Times Literary Supplement, 474, 895

Tirebuck, W. E.: *Miss Grace of All Souls',* 613

Todd, Janet, 51

Tolstoy, Leo, xv, 732, 906; *Anna Karenina,* 729; "The Death of Ivan Ilyich," 733

Tönnies, Ferdinand: *Gemeinschaft und Gesellschaft,* 725–26

Topography, 36–37

Tories, 322, 1012

Tracy, Honor, 895

Transatlantic Review, 998

Transparency: authority from, 294–95, 297

Travel: Lawrence's, 727–28; as theme, 146, 523; writers on, 20, 144, 146, 170, 914, 991, 1010–11

Trevelyan, E. M., 820

Trevelyan, George, 613

Trollope, Anthony, xvii, 143, 382, 390, 503, 765, 896, 897, 906, 911–12, 1012; *The American Senator,* 472, 1013; *An Autobiography,* 456, 460–61, 467–68, 471–73, 475, 481; *Ayala's Angel,* 472, 476; *Barchester Towers,* 458, 460, 462, 471, 476, 1013; Barsetshire novels, 456, 458, 1013; *The Belton Estate,* 1013; *The Bertrams,* 460, 1013; *Can You Forgive Her?,* 1013; character development by, 468–70; criticism of, 473–77; *Cousin Henry,* 462, 472; *Doctor Thorne,* 460, 476, 1013; *Dr. Wortle's School,* 462, 472, 476; *The Duke's Children,* 472, 476, 1013; *The Eustace Diamonds,* 466, 476, 481, 1013; *Felix Holt,* 481; *Framley Parsonage,* 461, 463, 469–71, 476, 1013; *He Knew He Was Right,* 457, 476, 1013; *Is He Popenjoy?,* 472, 476; *John Caldigate,* 472; *The Kellys and the O'Kellys,* 458; *Lady Anna,* 462, 472; *The Last Chronicle of Barset,* 463, 466–67, 470, 472, 476, 1013; *Linda Tressel,* 461; *The Macdermots of Ballycloran,* 458, 471, 477, 1013; *Miss Mackenzie,* 462–63, 471, 474; *Mr. Scarborough's Family,* 472, 477, 1013; "The New Inmate," 468; *The New Zealander,* 458; *Nina Balatka,* 461; *Orley Farm,* 442, 466, 476; "The Panjandrum," 467–68; Palliser novels, 456, 469,

Trollope, Anthony (continued)
472, 476, 1013; *Phineas Finn,* 462,
1013; *Phineas Redux,* 470, 1013; popularity of, 471–72, 475–76; *The Prime
Minister,* 472, 1013; *Rachel Ray,* 474,
476; serial publication of works of,
463–65; *Sir Harry Hotspur of Humblethwaite,* 462; *The Small House at
Allington,* 476, 913, 1013; *The Struggles of Brown, Jones, and Robinson,*
460; *The Three Clerks,* 460, 476; *La
Vendée,* 458; "A Walk in a Wood,"
466; *The Warden,* 385, 460–61, 471,
1013; *The Way We Live Now,* 462,
472, 476, 1013; working habits of,
457–63, 465–68, 473
Trollope Society, 456
Trollopian, The (periodical), 474
Truth, 686–87, 698, 753, 927
Turgenev, Ivan Sergeyevich, 665, 732
Twain, Mark, 182; *A Connecticut Yankee
in King Arthur's Court,* 834; *Huckle-
berry Finn,* 586; *Tom Sawyer,* 586
Tyler, E. B.: *Primitive Society,* 725
Tyranny, 267–68, 342

Universal History, 301; in Scott's novels,
302–4, 307–8, 312–13, 317–25
Universal Liberal History of Western
Culture, 301–2
Universal Psychology, 307–8, 310–12,
317, 322
Updike, John, 951
Upper class, 915
Upward, Edward, 756
Urban life, 129, 150, 509, 612, 828;
Dickens on, 396–97; as theme, 613,
999
Utopianism, 725, 726

Values, 151, 194, 302, 342, 568; in Conrad's novels, 702–3, 710–11, 713; in

Forster's novels, 825–26; middle
class, 83, 221–23, 334; 1930s,
741–42; social, 85–86
Victimization, 240, 249–50; of women,
52, 57, 212, 223, 225–26, 231–32,
265–66, 497
Victoria, Queen of England, 632
Victorian era, 368, 402, 481, 492,
497–98, 590, 690, 744, 777, 821,
883; children in, 582, 586–89,
595–96, 604–5; Dickens and, 382,
388, 392–93, 395; gentlemen of, 408,
427–28; imperialism in, 561–62,
568–73; politics of, 359–60, 391–92;
scandal in, 504–5; storytelling in,
373–80
Villains, 187, 401
Violence, 134, 196, 213, 744, 814, 969,
977; children and, 919–20; distancing
and, 553–54; and gender equality,
339–40; sexual, 61, 69, 97, 232
Virtue(s), 112–13, 120, 195
Vision: in Hardy's works, 544–58; and
self-consciousness, 536–37
Vizetelly, Henry, 611, 616
Voice(s), 13; multiple, xii, 117–18, 123;
in *Tristram Shandy,* 160–61
Voltaire (François-Marie Arouet de
Voltaire), 73; *Candide,* 947
Vows: broken, 65–67

Wagner, Richard, 616
Wain, John, 895, 898
Waiting: as theme, 212–13
Walcott, Derek, 652
Wallace, William: *The Scottish Chiefs,*
339
Walpole, Horace, 12, 163, 320; *Anecdotes
of Painting in England,* 1013; *The
Castle of Otranto,* 220–23, 225, 232,
1008, 1013; *A Catalogue of the Royal
and Noble Authors of England,* 1013

Walpole, Robert, 12, 107–9, 115, 121, 130, 169, 222, 997, 1012

War, 136; dehumanization and, 913–14; Lessing on, 919–21

Warburton, William, Bishop of Gloucester, 158, 175

Ward, Mrs. Humphrey, 365

Ward, Mary: *History of David Grieve*, 365

Warner, Rex, 746

Warton, John S.: *Laws Relating to the Women of England*, 445

Waterhouse, Keith, 895

Watt, Ian, 9, 28, 165, 217; on Austen, 276–77, 294, 296; on Defoe, 34, 41; *Rise of the Novel*, 20–21, 23–24, 216, 276

Waugh, Evelyn, 582, 746, 902, 912; *Black Mischief*, 648–49, 1013; *Brideshead Revisited*, 869, 882, 885–86, 890–92, 1013; on Catholicism, 892–94; characters developed by, 891–92; as curmudgeon, 876–78; *Decline and Fall*, 869–70, 878–79, 881–82, 884, 892, 1013; *A Handful of Dust*, 649, 869, 882–85, 1013; *Helena*, 888, 890–91, 893; *The Loved One*, 1013; narrative styles of, 881–87, 890–91; *Ninety-two Days*, 1013; *The Ordeal of Gilbert Pinfold*, 877–79, 1013; *Remote People*, 1013; satire of, 867–70; *Scoop*, 884, 1013; *Sword of Honour*, 882, 884–86; *Unconditional Surrender*, 886–87; *Vile Bodies*, 741, 867–69, 881, 1013; on writing styles, 878–81

Wealth, 2, 29–30, 38–39

Weaver, Harriet Shaw, 1003

Weber, Max, 725

Weidmann, Jerome, 902

Weldon, Fay, 943, 1013–14; *Down Among the Women*, 1014; on English culture, 940–41; *The Fat Woman's Joke*, 1014; *Female Friends*, 1014; *Letters to Alice*, 941; *Praxis*, 939; *The Life and Loves of a She-Devil*, 941, 944, 948, 950–52, 956; narrative style of, 944, 947–48, 950–52; *Praxis*, 1014; *Puffball*, 1014; "Upstairs, Downstairs," 941; on women, 956, 964

Wells, Herbert George (H. G.), 302, 684, 706, 750, 902, 906, 999; *Ann Veronica*, 662, 1014; degeneracy theory in works of, 619–20; *Experiment in Autobiography*, 660–61, 673; *The History of Mr. Polly*, 1014; *The Invisible Man*, 1014; *The Island of Dr. Moreau*, 577, 1014; *Joan and Peter*, 664; *Kipps*, 1014; *Mr. Britling Sees It Through*, 661, 664; *The New Machiavelli*, 1014; *The Outline of History*, 661–62, 669; as realist, 659, 664–74; success of, 662–63; *The Time Machine*, 577, 619–20, 661, 1014; *Tono-Bungay*, 577, 664–74, 679, 1014; *The War of the Worlds*, 577, 1014; *The Wonderful Visit*, 1014; *The World of William Clissold*, 1014

Welsh, Alexander, 308, 310, 391

West, Jane, 328, 342; *The Advantages of Education*, 339

Westminster Review, 433, 471, 473

West, Rebecca: *The Birds Fall Down*, 1014; *The Fountain Overflows*, 1014; *Harriet Hume*, 1014 *The Judge*, 1014; *The Return of the Soldier*, 1014; *The Strange Necessity*, 1014; *The Thinking Reed*, 1014

Whigs, 109, 122, 169–70, 1012

White, Edmund: *The Darker Proof*, 986

White, Hayden, 304

White, T. H., 588

Whitman, Walt, 725

Whores. *See* Prostitutes and prostitution

Wilde, Alan, 763

Wilde, Oscar, 404, 577, 582, 587; *The Picture of Dorian Gray,* 618–19

Wilford, Florence, 496

William III (William of Orange), King of England, 64

Williams, Helen Maria, 331–32; *Julia,* 337–39

Williams, Raymond, 216, 536

Williamson, Henry, 63

Wilson, Angus, 748, 895–98; *Anglo-Saxon Attitudes,* 913, 917, 1014; *As If By Magic,* 914, 1014; on Bloomsbury Group, 911–12; *Émile Zola,* 911; *Hemlock and After,* 913, 1014; *Late Call,* 914, 1014; *The Middle Age of Mrs. Eliot,* 913, 1014; narrative styles of, 912–15; *No Laughing Matter,* 914, 1014; *The Old Men at the Zoo,* 913–14, 1014; *Setting the World on Fire,* 1014; on social novel, 915–16; *The Strange Ride of Rudyard Kipling,* 911; themes of, 913–15; *Those Darling Dodos,* 912; *The World of Charles Dickens,* 911; *The Wrong Set,* 912

Wilson, Edmund, 605, 631, 899

Winterston, Jeanette: *Oranges Are Not the Only Fruit,* 983–84

Wissenfarth, Joseph, 244

Witches and witchcraft, 317, 322–24

Wodehouse, P. G., 878

Wolfenden Commission, 913

Wolff, Cynthia Griffin, 228

Wollstonecraft, Mary, 17, 210, 218, 264, 294, 332, 337, 342, 346, 349–50, 999, 1001, 1009–10; *Maria, or The Wrongs of Woman,* 248, 255, 258–60, 265, 331; *Mary,* 252, 1015; sensibility in works of, 258–59; *Thoughts on the Education of Daughters,* 1014; *A Vindication of the Rights of Men,* 1015; *Vindication of the Rights of Woman,*

251, 258, 331, 334, 336, 1015; *The Wrongs of Woman, see above: Maria, or the Wrongs of Woman*

Woman (magazine), 660, 991

Woman in White, The, 368

Women, 59, 74, 112–13, 195, 434, 614, 693, 790, 815, 950, 999; in Brontë's works, 363–65, 372–73; competition among, 960–65; in Dickens's works, 392–94; emotions of, 250, 259, 791–93; equality of, 254–55, 339–40; in Gaskell's works, 525–27; as Gothic novel writers, 224–32; identities of, 208–15, 494–95; Lawrence's views of, 718–20; and magic, 322–23; nature of, 60–61; novel reading by, 2–3, 62–63; as novel writers, xvi, 199–201, 203–7, 215–18, 327–29; role of, 178, 371–73; romance and, 202–3; and sensation novels, 496–98, 501; sexuality of, 54–59, 176–77, 202, 205, 218, 721–23; social agendas of, 330–31; in society, 354–55, 366–67; solitary, 955–60; victimization of, 52, 223, 225, 231–32, 265–66

Wood, Anthony à, 949

Wood, Mrs. Henry, 480, 496; *East Lynne,* 494

Woolf, Leonard, 1015

Woolf, Virginia Stephen, xix, 199, 352, 365, 470, 582, 587, 659, 715, 732, 749, 829, 844, 898, 915, 918, 941; Amis on, 902–3; *Between the Acts,* 796, 814–17, 912, 1015; "The Captain's Death Bed," 572; character development by, 796–817; on family life, 794–96, 807–8; *Jacob's Room,* 789, 797–801, 806, 1015; "Mr. Bennett and Mrs. Brown," 686; *Mrs. Dalloway,* 686, 789, 800–806, 813, 905, 912, 955, 1015; *Night and Day,* 789, 1015; *Orlando,* 789–90, 1015;

Woolf, Virginia Stephen (continued)
The Pargiters, 790–91, 793–94, 797,
912; perspectives in work of,
789–90; rejection of, 895–96; *A
Room of One's Own,* 660, 790–91,
1015; Snow on, 904, 906; on society
and individual, 790–92; *Three
Guineas,* 744, 790, 797, 1015; *To the
Lighthouse,* 686, 789, 797, 805–9,
814, 927, 955, 1015; *The Voyage
Out,* 789–90, 1015; *The Waves,* 743,
789, 794, 810–14, 912, 1015; Wilson on, 911–12; on women, 793–94,
814, 955; *The Years,* 744, 789–96,
803, 814, 1015
Wordsworth, William, 342–44, 439; on
children, 582, 592–93
Work, James, 172
Work: women's, 206, 209–10
Working class, 411, 510, 521–22, 718,
726, 999; identity of, 387–88;

611–12; political causes, 383–84; as
theme, 613–14, 617, 623–24
World War I, 561, 642, 794; impacts of,
xi–xii, 677, 740, 757–61, 796, 839,
867–68, 920–22; as theme, 797–98
World War II, 740–41, 796–97, 847,
943–44; as setting, 875, 886–87, 941
Wren, Christopher, 870
Wyllie, John, 904

Yeats, William Butler, 577
Young, Edward: *Conjectures on Original
Composition,* 87

Zola, Émile, 611, 616; *L'Argent,* 609; *Au
bonheur des dames,* 613; *Germinal,*
609, 613; influence of, 612–15, 618;
Nana, 627–28; *L'Oeuvre,* 609; *La
roman expérimental,* 609; Rougon-
Macquart novels, 609–10, 628; *La
terre,* 609; *Thérèse Raquin,* 613